THE ANNOTATED®
Shakespeare

THE ANNOTATED®
Shakespeare

VOLUME II

The Histories, Sonnets and Other Poems

Edited, with Introductions, Notes, and Bibliography by

A. L. ROWSE

Clarkson N. Potter, Inc./Publishers New York
DISTRIBUTED BY CROWN PUBLISHERS, INC.

Annotated, illustrated and designed by
Octavian Books Limited
Copyright © 1978 Orbis Publishing Limited

Published simultaneously in Great Britain by
Orbis Publishing Limited, 20–22 Bedfordbury,
London WC2

Printed in the U.S.A.

Library of Congress Cataloging in Publication Data
Shakespeare, William, 1546–1616.
    The annotated Shakespeare
    Bibliography: p.
    CONTENTS: v. 1. Comedies.—v. 2. Histories.—
v. 3. Tragedies and romances.
    I. Rowse, Alfred Leslie 1903–   II. Title.
PR2754.R67   822.3′3   78-12271
ISBN 0-517-535092   ISBN 0-517-53576 (v. 2.)

Annotation and introduction text composed by
SX Composing Ltd., Rayleigh, Essex

The Shakespeare text used in this edition is that of the
Globe Edition (edited by William George Clark and
William Aldis Wright), Macmillan, 1900
10   9   8   7   6   5   4   3

CONTENTS

SHAKESPEARE'S HISTORIES Introduction 6

THE FIRST PART OF KING HENRY VI (1590) Introduction 12
Play 18

THE SECOND PART OF KING HENRY VI (1590) Introduction 72
Play 78

THE THIRD PART OF KING HENRY VI (1591) Introduction 140
Play 146

KING RICHARD III (1592) Introduction 208
Play 214

KING RICHARD II (1595) Introduction 288
Play 295

KING JOHN (1596) Introduction 348
Play 354

THE FIRST PART OF KING HENRY IV (1597) Introduction 404
Play 410

THE SECOND PART OF KING HENRY IV (1598) Introduction 466
Play 472

KING HENRY V (1599) Introduction 534
Play 540

KING HENRY VIII (1613) Introduction 600
Play 606

SHAKESPEARE'S POEMS Introduction 669
A Lover's Complaint (1591) Introduction 670
Poem 672
Venus and Adonis (1593) Introduction 680
Poem 684
The Rape of Lucrece (1594) Introduction 708
Poem 712
THE SONNETS (1592–1594/5) Introduction 748
Poems 752
The Phoenix and the Turtle (1601) Introduction 792
Poem 794

Bibliography 796

Acknowledgements and Index 798

Shakespeare's Histories

THE ESSENCE OF THE RENAISSANCE EXPERIENCE was a heightened self-consciousness, a self-awareness: one can see it in painting in the new, unexampled development of portraiture. In England its fullest expression is to be seen in literature with William Shakespeare. The full flowering of the Renaissance impulse was rather late in reaching Britain, impeded as it was by the absorption of the Reformation experience. From the 1580s onwards these twin impulses fused in the national self-consciousness and bounding self-confidence generated by the struggle with Spain – a small half-island country against the world-empire of Philip II's Spain and Portugal combined.

It was not simply rejoicing over the defeat of the Spanish Armada, as literary folk are apt to think; there were three Armadas which met with disaster, in 1588, 1596 and 1597,

Opposite: *Frontispiece to Histories volume of J.O. Halliwell's edition of Shakespeare's works, 1853*

Below: *Defeat of Spanish Armada. Engraving by Cornelius Vroom (1566–1619)*

and the mood of boastful self-confidence (cf. Drake) – or the natural inspiration of patriotism – antedated these events. In the early 1580's the struggle with Spain, the madrigals, great literature (with Sidney and Spenser), and the Elizabethan drama all begin together.[1]

The dramatists of the English chronicle-plays found appealing subjects in England's past, but no-one to more purpose than the rather late-comer on the scene, the actor, who was a junior to the university wits. He was thus able to profit immensely from the work of the best of them – those whom in time he would come to rival as artistic equals, Sidney and Spenser, Lyly and Marlowe.

The actor – who was also a poet and a quick reading man – had two chief store-houses of information open to him: Edward Hall's *The Union of the two noble and illustrious families York and Lancaster* and Holinshed's *Chronicles of England, Scotland and Ireland*. (Raphael Holinshed was a fellow Warwickshire man, but various others contributed largely to the big book.) The second and much fuller edition of Holinshed came out in 1587, the year before the first Armada, just at the right time for the actor, commencing author, to make the utmost use of it. Various editions of Hall had come out long before, in the 1540's and 1550's, and Hall exerted a formative influence in shaping up and giving meaning to the muddled and murderous events of the 15th century, as Holinshed, a pedestrian chronicler of them, never could.

For Hall had a dominant theme. The conflict regarding the succession to the throne, which went back to the deposition of Richard II in 1399 and Bolingbroke's assumption of the crown as Henry IV, had ultimately let loose dissension and civil war, with all its horrors, which was settled only by the union of the Lancastrian heir with the Yorkist heiress, Henry VII and his wife Elizabeth. Beside the horrors there were all the dramas, political and personal. The whole 15th century provided a marvellous store-house – and we must remember how new and exciting all this was, apart from verbal memory and folk-tradition. For history was not taught at school; all education was based on the classics. So that the images and comparisons that spring naturally to Shakespeare's mind, apart from nature, are classical; he follows his historians faithfully, even in their mistakes, shaping them up, shortening, cutting naturally for his dramatic purposes.

What stands out with his history plays against the numerous ordinary chronicle-plays is that he sees the pattern, the significance of events – in that like Hall, not Holinshed. From the very beginning with the *Henry VI* trilogy he is concerned with the phenomena of social disorder, the awful consequences of the breakdown of authority, a hopeless king like Henry VI or an unreliable one like Richard II, the dire necessity of order and obedience, of competence in the ruler, obedience in the subject.

How different Shakespeare was in this respect from the other dramatists! He is more like Sidney and Spenser. Where did he get his extraordinary social concern from, his political understanding, his involvement with the problems of kingship he kept worrying at? Philip Sidney was a member of the governing class; Spenser was recruited to it. Shakespeare developed a thoroughly governing-class attitude to these questions (with its corollary in his view of the people). After all, he regarded himself always as a gentleman, which he was through his mother, an Arden; even his father was an alderman, eventually bailiff, i.e. mayor, of Stratford. As an observant boy of six or seven he would have seen the disturbance set off by the Northern Rebellion of 1569–70,[2] the recruits raised and sent north, armed from the town's armoury.

Moreover Shakespeare was a family man, grafted into society and undertaking his responsibilities – unlike the inhabitants of literary Bohemia, Robert Greene, living with a whore, sister of a hanged thief, or unmarried Kyd and Marlowe, the latter as unorthodox about religion as he was about sex. These people displayed no sense of social

1. Cf. my *The Elizabethan Renaissance*, vol II, *The Cultural Achievement*.

2. Of the Catholic Earls of Northumberland and Westmorland against the Elizabethan Protestant Settlement.

Far left: *Title page of Holinshed's* Chronicles, *1587, the major source for Shakespeare's history plays*

Left: *Sir Philip Sidney (1554–86) poet, critic, courtier and soldier whose works influenced Shakespeare's early poems and plays*

Below left: *Edmund Spenser (c.1552–99) author of the allegorical epic romance,* The Faerie Queene

responsibility and not much political understanding in their work. Shakespeare did to an extent so remarkable that it has come to be fully appreciated only in our own politically disturbed time.

His life fell between two distracted periods: the Wars of the Roses (his grandfather might well have been at Bosworth, as Elizabeth I's was), and the Civil War, during which his daughter entertained Charles I's poor Queen at New Place. Shakespeare knew too well how thin is the crust of civilisation, how easy for society to break down, to fall into what dark waters beneath. And, a kindly man, who hated cruelty, he knew that social breakdown brought only all the more suffering with it. We in our time have the bitterest reasons for appreciating that, in all the wars and revolutions since the breakdown of European civilisation in 1914.

This overriding theme, with all its consequences, recurs and is demonstrated in play after play, not only the English histories but in the Roman histories, the tragedies and tragi-comedies. For Shakespeare's histories are more like his own tragedies and comedies than they are like other people's histories, let alone the ordinary shapeless chronicle-plays. Indeed, it is a tragi-comedy, *Troilus and Cressida*, that most explicitly expresses his views on the necessity of hierarchical order according to social function. Ulysses' famous speech on Degree practically versifies the Homily on Obedience,[1] which Elizabethans had regularly brought home to them in church.

'Every degree of people, in their vocation, calling and office, hath appointed to them their duty and order. Some are in high degree, some are in low; some

1. From the Elizabethan Book of Homilies ordered to be read in church.

9

kings and princes, some inferiors and subjects, priests and laymen, masters and servants, fathers and children, husbands and wives, rich and poor – and every one have need of other, so that in all things is to be lauded and praised the goodly order of God, without the which no house, no city, no commonwealth can continue and endure. Take away Kings, princes, rulers, magistrates, judges and such states of God's order, no man shall ride or go by the highway unrobbed, no man shall sleep in his own house or bed unkilled, no man shall keep his wife, children and possessions in quietness.'

Hardly any of the chronicle plays saw into the meaning of events, they merely narrated them: and in fact, in spite of their popularity, Shakespeare owed very little to them. He owed much more to Hall, with whose message of national unity and social integration he agreed, and on this basis made his own mixture, never failing to draw the moral, as a good historian should.

The chronicle-plays were, however, inspired by patriotism and here Shakespeare agreed with them. There was every reason why he should: the little country was up-and-coming – 'they are people such that mend upon the world'. It was an obvious source of inspiration to all writers and artists to be alive and working at such a time – their work shows it.

Politics and history are two sides of the same coin, and Shakespeare was historically minded, again exceptionally – more so than any other dramatist. Ten of his plays deal with English history, four with Roman, one with Scottish, two with the pre-history of Britain – *King Lear* and *Cymbeline* – which to Elizabethans enjoyed a similar status to that of history proper. But Shakespeare's love of the past, and its rich layers of lore, is liable to appear anywhere – in Mercutio's long evocation of it, that crops up unexpectedly like something left over from *A Midsummer Night's Dream*, which is largely created out of this material.

> O, then I see Queen Mab hath been with you.
> She is the fairies' midwife, and she comes
> In shape no bigger than an agate stone
> On the forefinger of an alderman . . .

(Did his father, the alderman, wear such a ring?) Along with the fairy-tale lore comes contemporary social life, as with Bottom and his fellows, or just as the citizens' life of Windsor goes in harness with the legend of Herne's haunted Oak.

> Sometimes she gallops o'er a courtier's nose,
> And then dreams he of smelling out a suit;
> And sometime comes she with a tithe-pig's tail,
> Tickling a parson's nose as a'lies asleep,
> Then dreams he of another benefice.

He was not interested in the future, as secondary artists are – Shaw, for example (even he was better inspired with *St. Joan*) – for the past is inspirational and inspires poetry, the future polemics and propaganda.

What made him so absorbed by the problems of kingship – not only the sad stories of the deaths of kings, which lent themselves obviously to pomp and circumstance on the stage? The old tradition that he took 'kingly parts' may offer a clue, for the mimetic faculty of an actor would lead him into the inwardness of the part. John Davies of

Hereford saw the point:

> Had'st thou not played some kingly parts in sport,
> Thou hadst been a companion for a king,
> And been a king among the meaner sort.

Did he think of himself as a king? Or, in modern jargon, did he identify? There was no reason why he should not. He was immensely ambitious: as has been pointed out, to challenge all three *genres* of drama at the very beginning of his writing and about the same time – history with *Henry VI*, tragedy with *Titus Andronicus*, comedy with *The Comedy of Errors*. Robert Greene was quite right in spotting that euphoric self-confidence of the actor. And, after all, wasn't he a king in his profession?

From the first, then, we notice variety, a Protean variety, even within the one category of English history plays. An elastic potentiality is suggested, even in work that is raw and crude; the immeasurable capability of development we learn only later. We shall observe with each play what makes it different from the others. Even within the first trilogy, the Second Part of *Henry VI* is more diverse than the First; the Third differs again in being more of a revenge-play. *Richard III* is a grand historical melodrama. *Richard II* is totally different: the most formal and ceremonial, the most lyrical and poetic, of the history-plays. *King John* is a reversion to chronicle-play; the two parts of *Henry IV*, a superb fusion of history with comedy. *Henry V*, with its prominent Chorus, is epical; *Henry VIII* something of a stately pageant with ceremonial shows.

From the first the ability to plot a play went along with the forward thinking out of the intellectual theme. These capacities rarely go together. Anthony Munday, for example, was highly regarded as a 'plotter', but the rest of him was pedestrian. Shakespeare was a planner in all senses of the word: in his art, as in his life, he brought it off.

In his earlier English history plays he is close in attitude to Daniel's *Civil Wars*, the one contemporary who approaches Shakespeare in historic concern and with a similar political outlook. Shakespeare owed something to this book, though we need not suppose him incapable of thinking up for himself a comparable epic of England's past in the form of drama. For, where Daniel was a sympathetic, reflective mind, the actor-dramatist was all for action, with far greater power. And, later on, we find Daniel learning from Shakespeare.

More remarkably, and yet not unexpectedly, we find Marlowe, from whom Shakespeare gained much, learning from the actor turned dramatist. Marlowe's last and most mature play, *Edward II*, was indebted to *Henry VI* for its wider spread of characterisation, its portrayal of a non-hero in place of the Marlovian concentration upon a Tamburlaine. Indeed, so much attention is paid to uncovering 'sources' for Shakespeare – often with irrelevant pedantry, when Shakespeare could have picked up the ideas anywhere or possibly have thought of them for himself – that we are apt to overlook his influence upon others or their response in competition with him. It was a highly competitive age: hence its achievement. Marlowe's *Edward II* and the admirable *Woodstock* play are indebted to Shakespeare; the Chamberlain's Company's success with *Henry IV* led immediately to the Admiral's commissioning *Sir John Oldcastle* from Munday, Drayton and Hathaway.

Everything shows Shakespeare's essential independence of mind, for all that he providently used everything that came to hand. His greatest debt, however, was to the time in which he lived. France and Italy had no chronicle plays to build on. The Elizabethans had every reason to be proud of their country and of themselves: the age itself inspired them, bore them up and carried them upwards.

King Henry VI

1590

Henry VI in his youth. Engraving from Old England, Vol I, 1854

THIS IS ALMOST CERTAINLY SHAKESPEARE'S FIRST PLAY. The combination of dramatic effectiveness with the forward planning of a whole trilogy announced the arrival of a new playwright of power and promise, as also the self-confidence Robert Greene had observed in the actor. These plays were immensely successful in the Elizabethan age, and made the actor's name as a dramatist. They have again proved their actability and appeal to audiences in our time, with a certain amount of judicious cutting – for the abounding author simply flowed over.

In the interval these plays have been disconsidered, misconceived and subjected to every kind of absurdity from critics and commentators, even eminent ones like Coleridge. He, however, was hardly a model of common sense. The inspired sense of Dr. Johnson saw that 'in the production of genius there will be inequality' – particularly in its early productions, we may add; that 'the diction, the versification, and the figures are Shakespeare's' – overwhelmingly obvious today with our greater knowledge of Elizabethan usage. It was also apparent to Johnson, coming to the Second Part of the trilogy, that 'this play begins where the former ends, and continues the series of transactions, of which it presupposes the First Part already known. There is sufficient proof that the Second and Third Parts were not written without dependence on the First.' But, of course. In spite of that mighty sign-post we have had a welter of conjecture and commentary, superfluously confusing the reader, as again with regard to the Sonnets.

A further difficulty arose from the fact that memorial reconstructions of the Second and Third Parts were issued as quartos in 1594 and 1595, while the full text of the trilogy, published many years later in the First Folio, 1623, was unsatisfactory. In a way this was understandable, for the printers had complicated materials to work from and added their own mistakes. The very inconsistencies point to the author, for one cannot always remember what one has written; and Shakespeare had never had time to tidy up and revise his earliest work. Why should he? – the play was the thing; it had had resounding success, and it had launched him.

The Background. As always we must keep in mind the two-fold background – that of the stage, dramatic and literary, and that in the events of the time.

The immense patriotic excitement generated by the struggle with Spain, the mood of national self-confidence, pride and self-glorification – again natural enough in a youthful, emerging people – at the triumph over the Spanish Armada in 1588 expressed itself in a surge of self-consciousness and interest in the nation's past. The expanded edition of Holinshed's *Chronicles*, of 1587, provided keen purveyors of popular entertainment with a storehouse of subjects for dramatisation. A common stock came into existence of subjects, themes and reactions to them, as also of diction and images, largely from the classical education then general. People naturally borrowed from each other, especially those working in proximity as Marlowe and Shakespeare were, in this exciting, kaleidoscopic, confused time.

The dominant influence observable again and again in *Henry VI* is Marlowe's. He had patented this grandiloquent poetic diction, in splendid blank verse, in *Tamburlaine*. The actor copied it – indeed he may have had it in his head from acting in it; though already he had his own grandiloquence, which reverberated in the theatre and which Elizabethans relished. One notices already in this early play his characteristic words – his fondness for words ending in 'ive', submissive, intermissive; for words like presage, peruse, periapt. Where Marlowe's blank verse is more splendid to date, Shakespeare has much more rhyme – he is a natural poet, with obvious capacity for development, perhaps greater potentiality, for there is more variety and diversity. A couple of scenes in this play are almost wholly in rhymed couplets; these also conclude each scene, and very often a single speech. (This must have had its punctuating, if not detonating, effect.)

Marlowe was the senior, the initiator, the leader; but the influence was not all one way. Before he died, so lamentably, he copied from *Henry VI* and wrote his *Edward II*. A purely literary influence, observable in phrases, is Spenser, whose *Faerie Queene* came out this year, 1590. Ubiquitous is the influence of school education in the classics and of Bible and Prayer Book from constant early attendance at church. A number of classical references are traceable to Cooper's *Thesaurus*, the Latin dictionary which Vicar Bretchgirdle had bequeathed for the use of the scholars at Stratford Grammar School – he had christened William in 1564. Other references, to Froissart, for example, show the quick reading man, adept at picking up tips from everywhere – as an actor would be. Anyhow, the years before 1590 would have left time for reading.

Theme. Though there are touches from Holinshed, the dominant theme in shaping the *Henry VI* plays came from Edward Hall's book, *The Union of the two noble and illustrious families York and Lancaster*, of which there had been several editions in the 1540's. This book elaborated the message of the Tudor dynasty – the ending of the uncivil strife of the Wars of the Roses in Henry VII's union with Elizabeth, heiress of the house of York. The conflict between these two houses, unleashed by the incapacity and imbecility of poor Henry VI, led to the discord and breakdown of social order, which is foreshadowed in this play, being a secondary theme in it and the primary subject of its successors, including *Richard III*. It all went back to the revolution of 1399 and Bolingbroke's ejection of Richard II from the throne; from this exfoliated another quartet of historical plays. One sees what a prodigious, powerful planner the actor-dramatist was to become.

In the First Part the main theme is that of the war against France, the conflict unleashed by Charles VI's (Henry VI's grandfather) imbecility, and Henry V's astonishing, Napoleonic conquest. Fighting the French was a traditional activity in England, ever since the Norman Conquest (and in spite of the fact that the dynasty was French – even Henry VII was more French than English). The subject immensely appealed to the simple souls of the Elizabethans, to anti-French feeling, the boastful pride in themselves of a young people, the gallant memories of the Hundred Years War, such heroes as 'fighting Talbot, the Terror of the French.'

Talbot is the popular hero of this play (typically he gave his name to a hunting dog) – and apparently was played by an actor the more appealing for being undersized; 'gallant little fellow', one can hear them saying. Thomas Nashe, himself one of this early group, familiar with Marlowe and Shakespeare, testified to the play's appeal. 'How it would have joyed brave Talbot (the terror of the French) to think that he should triumph again on the stage, and have his bones new embalmed with the tears of ten thousand spectators at least – at several times – who imagine they behold him fresh bleeding.'

The villain of the piece, if we may so call a Saint, is Joan of Arc: she is rendered as the 15th century soldiers who fought in France thought of her – as a witch and a strumpet. (After all, had she not been condemned as such by the Church? – when she was probably only a chaste, repressed Lesbian.) The tyro of a dramatist gave the groundlings what they expected, though there is no reason to suppose that he knew any better. Except that, when she speaks for herself, the dramatist's sympathy cannot help breaking in:

Talbot, Earl of Shrewsbury presenting a book to Margaret of Anjou and Henry VI. Engraving from a manuscript c.1445

14

Virtuous and holy, chosen from above,
By inspiration of celestial grace,
To work exceeding miracles on earth.
I never had to do with wicked spirits . . .
A virgin from her tender infancy,
Chaste and immaculate in very thought,
Whose maiden blood, thus rigorously effused,
Will cry for vengeance at the gates of heaven.

Hers is the Shakespearean humanity, thus early expressed, which was true to his nature and paid such dividends later in the sense of dramatic justice. We may also notice the reiteration of *v*s, conscious or unconscious, that bespeak the poet naturally inspired.

Already the characters are more individualised, the scenes more varied, than in Marlowe. The rivalry between Humphrey, Duke of Gloucester, and Cardinal Beaufort is sketched, which will have formidable development in the next play. Suffolk's character is already headed forward, for he is portrayed as falling in love with Margaret of Anjou, whose marriage to Henry VI he negotiated, with such fatal consequences. The age of the young King presents a difficulty: a child at the beginning, he has to be ready for marriage at the end. However, that presented no difficulty to Elizabethans, who did not look for probability in their plays but strong scenes.

Scenes. Of these we have plenty. Perhaps the best remembered today is the plucking of white and red roses in the Temple Garden, for which there is no historical warrant, but from which in the play the rival parties take their emblems: Yorkist white, Lancastrian red. The simple spectacle must have provided something different in the elementary equipment of the early Shakespearean theatre. The gallery above the stage served for walls, battlements, etc. to scale; we know that Hell reverberated below the stage. In this play a chair is brought in two or three times, to carry a sick or dying character. There were ceremonies, several funeral processions and dead marches, a coronation, drums and trumpets, much marching to and fro, fighting of groups or individuals, the confrontation of colours – Gloucester's blue-coats against Winchester's tawny-coats.

We are in the early Elizabethan theatre, crude and rhetorical, but spectacular and effective. We must remember the redoubled impact upon spectators, when there were no act- or scene-divisions, and – with the stage partly surrounded, partly occupied by spectators – the audience felt themselves part of the action, as we know from contemporary evidence. It is thus absurd to condemn these early plays as 'episodic' – for, of course, they consist of episodes: strong scenes were what was wanted. What is more remarkable is that there should have been such effective over-all planning, the feat of reducing so many years, indeed decades, of history to some dramatic form. Every opportunity is taken by the practising dramatist to help the illusion of unity: this is the function of forward-looking prophecies, backward-looking curses, dreams and omens. They all help to knit things together, so that in the end each play has the dramatic unity of rise-climax-fall.

Personal. Not many flecks of Shakespeare's own time occur in this play dealing with events a century and a half before, but there are some. After the defeat of the Armada there was a good deal of doubt and dispute as to the right policy to pursue. This is reflected in –

The Swan Theatre where Shakespeare and his company played in 1596–97. This sketch c.1596 by Johannes de Witt is the only contemporary illustration of the interior of an Elizabethan theatre

One would have lingering wars with little cost;
Another would fly swift but wanteth wings;
A third thinks, without expense at all,
By guileful fair words peace may be obtained.

(The Queen preferred the third course.)

The Tower was still the country's chief arsenal and storehouse, as when Gloucester says,

> I'll to the Tower with all the haste I can
> To view th'artillery and munition.

The French King hails Joan of Arc as another

> Helen, the mother of great Constantine.

The Gild Chapel at Stratford had a wall-painting of this legend; it had fallen to John Shakespeare as burgess to whitewash the painted Doom there (he is most unlikely to have been a Catholic).

In Gloucester's berating the Cardinal, who was bishop of Winchester – the mutual insults must have delighted the simple audience – he does not fail to rake up the Stews on the South Bank, which were on episcopal property:

> Thou that giv'st whores indulgences to sin . . .
> Winchester goose!

This was a venereal swelling in the groin, Elizabethan rather than medieval.

We note that Sir William Lucy, of the family out at Charlecote, was given a good part. Shakespeare himself is audible in his grand words, impressive to an audience:

> In dumb significants proclaim your thoughts;

or 'with sudden and extemporal speech'; eyes wax dim, 'as drawing to their exigent', etc. Suffolk, speaking of Margaret of Anjou, says:

> She's beautiful, and therefore to be wooed;
> She is a woman, therefore to be won.

These words are improved on in *Venus and Adonis*, and something very close appears in Marlowe's *Hero and Leander*. Perhaps they were a commonplace of the time.

Text. The only text of the *First Part of King Henry VI* is that of the Folio, but its unsatisfactory state means that it requires careful editing. Until quite recently there has been much confusion and superfluous conjecture as to composite authorship. We now know that there is no need for this. The best editions of all three plays, by Dr. Andrew S. Cairncross, (The Arden Shakespeare), clear up the confusions. Characteristically he retains the reading 'Falstaff' from the Folio where most editors have instated 'Fastolf' from the Chronicles. It does not seem to have occurred to anybody that, in spite of the spelling, Falstaff would have been the common pronunciation of Fastolf.

Similarly for a superfluous annotation, under a misapprehension, take the line:

> Our isle be made a nourish of salt tears.

One editor comments: 'Elizabethan form of "nurse". Three ideas seem to be presented: (a) the men will all be killed, only the women left; (b) the women will nurse their babes at their weeping eyes; (c) England (i.e. the women) will be one "nourish", feeding her offspring (at her weeping eyes) on salt tears (instead of milk).' Ludicrous as well as superfluous: 'nourish' is a simple misprint for the common Elizabethan word 'marish', i.e. marsh.

17

THE FIRST PART OF
KING HENRY THE SIXTH.

DRAMATIS PERSONÆ.

KING HENRY the Sixth.
DUKE OF GLOUCESTER, uncle to the King, and Protector.
DUKE OF BEDFORD, uncle to the King, and Regent of France.
THOMAS BEAUFORT, Duke of Exeter, great-uncle to the King.
HENRY BEAUFORT, great-uncle to the King, Bishop of Winchester, and afterwards Cardinal.
JOHN BEAUFORT, Earl, afterwards Duke, of Somerset.
RICHARD PLANTAGENET, son of Richard late Earl of Cambridge, afterwards Duke of York.
EARL OF WARWICK.
EARL OF SALISBURY.
EARL OF SUFFOLK.
LORD TALBOT, afterwards Earl of Shrewsbury.
JOHN TALBOT, his son.
EDMUND MORTIMER, Earl of March.
SIR JOHN FASTOLFE.
SIR WILLIAM LUCY.
SIR WILLIAM GLANSDALE.
SIR THOMAS GARGRAVE.
Mayor of London.
WOODVILE, Lieutenant of the Tower.
VERNON, of the White-Rose or York faction.

BASSET, of the Red-Rose or Lancaster faction.
A Lawyer. Mortimer's Keepers.

CHARLES, Dauphin, and afterwards King, of France.
REIGNIER, Duke of Anjou, and titular King of Naples.
DUKE OF BURGUNDY.
DUKE OF ALENÇON.
BASTARD OF ORLEANS.
Governor of Paris.
Master-Gunner of Orleans, and his Son.
General of the French forces in Bourdeaux.
A French Sergeant. A Porter.
An old Shepherd, father to Joan la Pucelle.

MARGARET, daughter to Reignier, afterwards married to King Henry.
COUNTESS OF AUVERGNE.
JOAN LA PUCELLE, commonly called Joan of Arc.

Lords, Warders of the Tower, Heralds, Officers, Soldiers, Messengers, and Attendants.

Fiends appearing to La Pucelle.

SCENE: *Partly in England, and partly in France.*

● *A bullet beside a text line indicates an annotation in the opposite column*

ACT I.

SCENE I. *Westminster Abbey.*

Dead March. Enter the Funeral of KING HENRY the Fifth, *attended on by the* DUKE OF BEDFORD, *Regent of France; the* DUKE OF GLOUCESTER, *Protector; the* DUKE OF EXETER, *the* EARL OF WARWICK, *the* BISHOP OF WINCHESTER, Heralds, *&c.*

● *Bed.* Hung be the heavens with black, yield day to night!
Comets, importing change of times and states,
● Brandish your crystal tresses in the sky,
And with them scourge the bad revolting stars
That have consented unto Henry's death!
King Henry the Fifth, too famous to live long!
England ne'er lost a king of so much worth.

1 *Hung . . . black.* It was a convention of the Elizabethan theatre to drape the stage in black for tragedies.

3 *crystal.* Bright.

Opposite: Joan of Arc. Painting by Jean Auguste Dominique Ingres (1780–1867)

Richard Beauchamp, Earl of Warwick, shown holding in his left arm the child-king Henry VI, and in his right one of the many churches he endowed. From a contemporary manuscript

---

16 *lift*. Lifted.

17 *mourn . . . blood*. Fight the French.

37 *protector*. i.e. in charge of the kingdom during the minority of the sovereign.

Glou. England ne'er had a king until his time.
Virtue he had, deserving to command:
His brandish'd sword did blind men with his
    beams: 10
His arms spread wider than a dragon's wings;
His sparkling eyes, replete with wrathful fire,
More dazzled and drove back his enemies
Than mid-day sun fierce bent against their faces
What should I say? his deeds exceed all speech:
● He ne'er lift up his hand but conquered.
● *Exe.* We mourn in black: why mourn we not
    in blood?
Henry is dead and never shall revive:
Upon a wooden coffin we attend,
And death's dishonourable victory   20
We with our stately presence glorify,
Like captives bound to a triumphant car.
What! shall we curse the planets of mishap
That plotted thus our glory's overthrow?
Or shall we think the subtle-witted French
Conjurers and sorcerers, that afraid of him
By magic verses have contrived his end?
    Win. He was a king bless'd of the King of
    kings.
Unto the French the dreadful judgement-day
So dreadful will not be as was his sight.   30
The battles of the Lord of hosts he fought:
The church's prayers made him so prosperous.
    Glou. The church! where is it? Had not
    churchmen pray'd,
His thread of life had not so soon decay'd:
None do you like but an effeminate prince,
Whom, like a school-boy, you may over-awe.
● *Win.* Gloucester, whate'er we like, thou art
    protector
And lookest to command the prince and realm.

Thy wife is proud; she holdeth thee in awe,
More than God or religious churchmen may.   40
   Glou.   Name not religion, for thou lovest the
     flesh,
And ne'er throughout the year to church thou go'st
Except it be to pray against thy foes.
   ● *Bed.*   Cease, cease these jars and rest your
     minds in peace:
Let's to the altar: heralds, wait on us:
Instead of gold, we'll offer up our arms;
Since arms avail not now that Henry's dead.
Posterity, await for wretched years,
When at their mothers' moist eyes babes shall
     suck,
● Our isle be made a nourish of salt tears,   50
And none but women left to wail the dead.
Henry the Fifth, thy ghost I invocate:
Prosper this realm, keep it from civil broils,
Combat with adverse planets in the heavens!
A far more glorious star thy soul will make
● Than Julius Cæsar or bright ——

      Enter a Messenger.

   Mess.   My honourable lords, health to you all!
Sad tidings bring I to you out of France,
Of loss, of slaughter and discomfiture:
Guienne, Champagne, Rheims, Orleans,   60
Paris, Guysors, Poiƈtiers, are all quite lost.
   ● *Bed.*   What say'st thou, man, before dead
     Henry's corse?
Speak softly, or the loss of those great towns
● Will make him burst his lead and rise from death.
   Glou.   Is Paris lost? is Rouen yielded up?
If Henry were recall'd to life again,
These news would cause him once more yield
     the ghost.
   Exe.   How were they lost? what treachery
     was used?
   Mess.   No treachery; but want of men and
     money.
Amongst the soldiers this is muttered,   70
That here you maintain several faƈtions,
And whilst a field should be dispatch'd and fought,
You are disputing of your generals:
One would have lingering wars with little cost;
Another would fly swift, but wanteth wings;
A third thinks, without expense at all,
By guileful fair words peace may be obtain'd.
Awake, awake, English nobility!
Let not sloth dim your honours new-begot:
● Cropp'd are the flower-de-luces in your arms;   80
Of England's coat one half is cut away.
   Exe.   Were our tears wanting to this funeral,
These tidings would call forth their flowing tides.
   Bed.   Me they concern; Regent I am of
     France.
Give me my steeled coat. I'll fight for France.
Away with these disgraceful wailing robes!
Wounds will I lend the French instead of eyes,
● To weep their intermissive miseries.

   Enter to them another Messenger.

   Mess.   Lords, view these letters full of bad
     mischance.
France is revolted from the English quite,   90
Except some petty towns of no import:
The Dauphin Charles is crowned king in Rheims;
The Bastard of Orleans with him is join'd;
Reignier, Duke of Anjou, doth take his part;

44 *jars.* Quarrels.

50 *nourish.* A misprint of the Elizabethan word 'marish', meaning a marsh. See introduction.

56 *Caesar.* In Ovid's *Metamorphoses* the soul of the dead Caesar became a star in the heavens.

Duke of Bedford, uncle to the King and Regent of France, kneels before St George. Engraving from Bedford Missal, 1430

62 *corse.* Corpse.

64 *lead.* Lining of the wooden coffin.

80 *flower-de-luces.* The fleur-de-lis, or lily of France quartered with the English lions in the royal coat of arms.

88 *intermissive.* Temporarily interrupted.

116–117 *pikes...stakes...hedges.* Stakes fixed into the ground to protect archers from the charge of enemy cavalry.

126 *agazed.* Aghast, astounded.

132 *vaward.* Vanguard.

154 *Saint George's feast.* 23rd April.

The Duke of Alençon flieth to his side.
   Exe. The Dauphin crowned king! all fly to
   him!
O, whither shall we fly from this reproach?
   Glou. We will not fly, but to our enemies'
   throats.
Bedford, if thou be slack, I'll fight it out.
   Bed. Gloucester, why doubt'st thou of my for-
   wardness?   100
An army have I muster'd in my thoughts,
Wherewith already France is overrun.

        Enter another Messenger.
   Mess. My gracious lords, to add to your laments,
Wherewith you now bedew King Henry's hearse,
I must inform you of a dismal fight
Betwixt the stout Lord Talbot and the French.
   Win. What! wherein Talbot overcame? is't so?
   Mess. O, no; wherein Lord Talbot was o'er-
   thrown:
The circumstance I'll tell you more at large.
The tenth of August last this dreadful lord,   110
Retiring from the siege of Orleans,
Having full scarce six thousand in his troop,
By three and twenty thousand of the French
Was round encompassed and set upon.
No leisure had he to enrank his men;
• He wanted pikes to set before his archers;
Instead whereof sharp stakes pluck'd out of hedges
They pitched in the ground confusedly,
To keep the horsemen off from breaking in.
More than three hours the fight continued;   120
Where valiant Talbot above human thought
Enacted wonders with his sword and lance:
Hundreds he sent to hell, and none durst stand
   him;
Here, there, and every where, enraged he flew:
The French exclaim'd, the devil was in arms;
• All the whole army stood agazed on him:
His soldiers spying his undaunted spirit
A Talbot! a Talbot! cried out amain
And rush'd into the bowels of the battle.
Here had the conquest fully been seal'd up,   130
If Sir John Fastolfe had not play'd the coward:
• He, being in the vaward, placed behind
With purpose to relieve and follow them,
Cowardly fled, not having struck one stroke.
Hence grew the general wreck and massacre;
Enclosed were they with their enemies:
A base Walloon, to win the Dauphin's grace,
Thrust Talbot with a spear into the back,
Whom all France with their chief assembled
   strength
Durst not presume to look once in the face.   140
   Bed. Is Talbot slain? then I will slay myself,
For living idly here in pomp and ease,
Whilst such a worthy leader, wanting aid,
Unto his dastard foemen is betray'd.
   Mess. O no, he lives; but is took prisoner,
And Lord Scales with him and Lord Hungerford:
Most of the rest slaughter'd or took likewise.
   Bed. His ransom there is none but I shall pay:
I'll hale the Dauphin headlong from his throne:
His crown shall be the ransom of my friend;   150
Four of their lords I'll change for one of ours.
Farewell, my masters; to my task will I;
Bonfires in France forthwith I am to make,
• To keep our great Saint George's feast withal:
Ten thousand soldiers with me I will take,

Whose bloody deeds shall make all Europe quake.
   Mess. So you had need; for Orleans is besieged;
The English army is grown weak and faint:
The Earl of Salisbury craveth supply,
And hardly keeps his men from mutiny,   160
Since they, so few, watch such a multitude.
   Exe. Remember, lords, your oaths to Henry
     sworn,
Either to quell the Dauphin utterly,
Or bring him in obedience to your yoke.
   Bed. I do remember it; and here take my
     leave,
To go about my preparation.   [*Exit.*
   Glou. I'll to the Tower with all the haste I can,
To view the artillery and munition;
And then I will proclaim young Henry king.
                      [*Exit.*
   Exe. To Eltham will I, where the young king is,
Being ordain'd his special governor,   171
And for his safety there I'll best devise. [*Exit.*
   Win. Each hath his place and function to
     attend:
I am left out; for me nothing remains.
● But long I will not be Jack out of office:
The king from Eltham I intend to steal
● And sit at chiefest stern of public weal. [*Exeunt.*

SCENE II. *France. Before Orleans.*

Sound a flourish. Enter CHARLES, ALENÇON,
   and REIGNIER, *marching with drum and
   Soldiers.*

●   *Char.* Mars his true moving, even as in the
     heavens
So in the earth, to this day is not known:
Late did he shine upon the English side;
Now we are victors; upon us he smiles.
What towns of any moment but we have?
At pleasure here we lie near Orleans;
Otherwhiles the famish'd English, like pale ghosts,
Faintly besiege us one hour in a month.
●   *Alen.* They want their porridge and their fat
     bull-beeves:
Either they must be dieted like mules   10
And have their provender tied to their mouths
Or piteous they will look, like drowned mice.
   Reig. Let's raise the siege: why live we idly
     here?
Talbot is taken, whom we wont to fear:
Remaineth none but mad-brain'd Salisbury;
And he may well in fretting spend his gall,
Nor men nor money hath he to make war.
   Char. Sound, sound alarum! we will rush on
     them.
Now for the honour of the forlorn French!
Him I forgive my death that killeth me   20
When he sees me go back one foot or fly. [*Exeunt.*

*Here alarum; they are beaten back by the
   English with great loss. Re-enter* CHARLES,
   ALENÇON, *and* REIGNIER.

   Char. Who ever saw the like? what men
     have I!
Dogs! cowards! dastards! I would ne'er have
     fled,
But that they left me 'midst my enemies.
   Reig. Salisbury is a desperate homicide;
He fighteth as one weary of his life.
The other lords, like lions wanting food,

Hall of Eltham Palace, one of Elizabeth I's royal
residences; by the latter half of the 17th century it was
uninhabitable. Engraving from *Old England*, 1854

175 *Jack out of office.* A person without employment;
the Bishop is playing upon the slightly derogatory term
'Jack-in-office', meaning a self-important functionary.

177 *sit . . . weal.* Be at the helm of the ship of state.

1 *Mars his.* Mars's.

9 *want.* Lack. *bull-beeves.* Beef was supposed to give
courage.

23

29 *Froissart.* French chronicler (1338–1410).

Froissart reading. Engraving from *Old England*, 1854

30 *Olivers and Rowlands.* Two famous knights of Charlemagne about whom there were many legends.

41 *gimmors.* Gimmals. Interlocking rings or joints in machinery for transmitting motion e.g. clockwork.

48 *cheer appall'd.* Face grown pale.

71 *She . . . dash.* She has made a bold beginning.

Joan of Arc greets the Dauphin at Chinon, 1428. Illustration from a contemporary German tapestry

Do rush upon us as their hungry prey.

   Alen. Froissart, a countryman of ours, records,
England all Olivers and Rowlands bred   30
During the time Edward the Third did reign.
More truly now may this be verified;
For none but Samsons and Goliases
It sendeth forth to skirmish.   One to ten!
Lean raw-boned rascals! who would e'er suppose
They had such courage and audacity?
   Char. Let's leave this town; for they are hare-
     brain'd slaves,
And hunger will enforce them to be more eager:
Of old I know them; rather with their teeth   39
The walls they'll tear down than forsake the siege.
   Reig. I think, by some odd gimmors or device
Their arms are set like clocks, still to strike on;
Else ne'er could they hold out so as they do.
By my consent, we'll even let them alone.
   Alen.   Be it so.

     Enter the BASTARD *of Orleans.*

   Bast. Where's the Prince Dauphin? I have
     news for him.
   Char. Bastard of Orleans, thrice welcome
     to us.
   Bast. Methinks your looks are sad, your cheer
     appall'd:
Hath the late overthrow wrought this offence?
Be not dismay'd, for succour is at hand: 50
A holy maid hither with me I bring,
Which by a vision sent to her from heaven
Ordained is to raise this tedious siege
And drive the English forth the bounds of France.
The spirit of deep prophecy she hath,
Exceeding the nine sibyls of old Rome:
What's past and what's to come she can descry.
Speak, shall I call her in?   Believe my words,
For they are certain and unfallible.
   Char.   Go, call her in. [*Exit Bastard.*] But
     first, to try her skill,   60
Reignier, stand thou as Dauphin in my place;
Question her proudly; let thy looks be stern:
By this means shall we sound what skill she hath.

   Re-enter the BASTARD *of Orleans, with* JOAN
     LA PUCELLE.

   Reig.   Fair maid, is't thou wilt do these won-
     drous feats?
   Puc.   Reignier, is't thou that thinkest to be-
     guile me?
Where is the Dauphin? Come, come from behind;
I know thee well, though never seen before.
Be not amazed, there's nothing hid from me:
In private will I talk with thee apart.   69
Stand back, you lords, and give us leave awhile.
   Reig. She takes upon her bravely at first dash.
   Puc. Dauphin, I am by birth a shepherd's
     daughter,
My wit untrain'd in any kind of art.
Heaven and our Lady gracious hath it pleased
To shine on my contemptible estate:
Lo, whilst I waited on my tender lambs,
And to sun's parching heat display'd my cheeks,
God's mother deigned to appear to me
And in a vision full of majesty
Will'd me to leave my base vocation   80
And free my country from calamity:
Her aid she promised and assured success:
In complete glory she reveal'd herself;

And, whereas I was black and swart before,
With those clear rays which she infused on me
That beauty am I bless'd with which you see.
Ask me what question thou canst possible,
And I will answer unpremeditated:
My courage try by combat, if thou darest,
And thou shalt find that I exceed my sex.   90
Resolve on this, thou shalt be fortunate,
If thou receive me for thy warlike mate.
   Char. Thou hast astonish'd me with thy high
     terms:
Only this proof I'll of thy valour make,
In single combat thou shalt buckle with me,
And if thou vanquishest, thy words are true;
Otherwise I renounce all confidence.
   Puc. I am prepared: here is my keen-edged
     sword,
Deck'd with five flower-de-luces on each side;
The which at Touraine, in Saint Katharine's
    churchyard,   100
Out of a great deal of old iron I chose forth.
   Char. Then come, o' God's name; I fear no
    woman.
   Puc. And while I live, I'll ne'er fly from a
   man.
     [*Here they fight, and Joan La Pucelle
                      overcomes.*
   Char. Stay, stay thy hands! thou art an
   Amazon
● And fightest with the sword of Deborah.
   Puc. Christ's mother helps me, else I were
    too weak.
   Char. Whoe'er helps thee, 'tis thou that must
    help me:
Impatiently I burn with thy desire;
My heart and hands thou hast at once subdued.
Excellent Pucelle, if thy name be so,   110
● Let me thy servant and not sovereign be:
'Tis the French Dauphin sueth to thee thus.
   Puc. I must not yield to any rites of love,
For my profession's sacred from above:
When I have chased all thy foes from hence,
Then will I think upon a recompense.
   Char. Meantime look gracious on thy pros-
    trate thrall.
   Reig. My lord, methinks, is very long in talk.
●   *Alen.* Doubtless he shrives this woman to her
    smock;
Else ne'er could he so long protract his speech.
   Reig. Shall we disturb him, since he keeps
    no mean?   121
   Alen. He may mean more than we poor men
    do know:
These women are shrewd tempters with their
    tongues.
   Reig. My lord, where are you? what devise
    you on?
Shall we give over Orleans, or no?
   Puc. Why, no, I say, distrustful recreants!
Fight till the last gasp; I will be your guard.
   Char. What she says I'll confirm: we'll fight
    it out.
   Puc. Assign'd am I to be the English scourge.
This night the siege assuredly I'll raise: 130
● Expect Saint Martin's summer, halcyon days,
Since I have entered into these wars.
Glory is like a circle in the water,
Which never ceaseth to enlarge itself
Till by broad spreading it disperse to nought.

105 *Deborah.* Prophetess who delivered Israel from the oppression of the Canaanites (Judges iv and v).

111 *servant.* Lover.

Portrait of the English actress, Mary Kingsley, as Joan of Arc by Gilbert A. Pownall, 1914

---

119 *shrives . . . smock.* Hears her confession while she is wearing only an undergarment.

131 *Saint Martin's summer.* Summer weather which occurs in late autumn: Feast of St. Martin, 11th November.

139 *Which Caesar . . . once.* Plutarch narrates that once when Julius Caesar was upon a particularly dangerous voyage, the master of the ship wished to turn back. Caesar told him not to be afraid because he had 'Caesar and his fortune with thee'.

142 *Helen.* Mother of the Roman Emperor Constantine who was inspired by a vision to look for the true cross.

Vision of St Helena. Painting by Paolo Veronese (b.*c*.1528–1588)

143 *Saint Philip's daughters.* Four virgins who had the gift of prophecy (Acts, xxi. 9).

2 *conveyance.* Trickery, double-dealing.

With Henry's death the English circle ends;
Dispersed are the glories it included.
Now am I like that proud insulting ship
● Which Cæsar and his fortune bare at once.
   Char. Was Mahomet inspired with a dove?
Thou with an eagle art inspired then.   141
● Helen, the mother of great Constantine,
● Nor yet Saint Philip's daughters, were like thee.
Bright star of Venus, fall'n down on the earth,
How may I reverently worship thee enough?
   Alen. Leave off delays, and let us raise the
      siege.
   Reig. Woman, do what thou canst to save our
      honours;
Drive them from Orleans and be immortalized.
   Char. Presently we'll try: come, let's away
      about it:
No prophet will I trust, if she prove false.   150
                        [*Exeunt.*

SCENE III. *London. Before the Tower.*

Enter the DUKE OF GLOUCESTER, *with his*
     Serving-men *in blue coats.*

   Glou. I am come to survey the Tower this
      day:
● Since Henry's death, I fear, there is conveyance.
Where be these warders, that they wait not
     here?
Open the gates; 'tis Gloucester that calls.
   First Warder. [*Within*] Who's there that
      knocks so imperiously?
   First Serv. It is the noble Duke of Glou-
      cester.
   Second Warder. [*Within*] Whoe'er he be,
      you may not be let in.
   First Serv. Villains, answer you so the lord
      protector?
   First Warder. [*Within*] The Lord protect
      him! so we answer him:
We do no otherwise than we are will'd.   10
   Glou. Who willed you? or whose will stands
      but mine?
There's none protector of the realm but I.
Break up the gates, I'll be your warrantize:
Shall I be flouted thus by dunghill grooms?
   [*Gloucester's men rush at the Tower Gates, and*
        Woodvile the Lieutenant speaks within.
   Woodv. What noise is this? what traitors have
      we here?
   Glou. Lieutenant, is it you whose voice I hear?
Open the gates; here's Gloucester that would
     enter.
   Woodv. Have patience, noble duke; I may
      not open;
The Cardinal of Winchester forbids:
From him I have express commandment   20
That thou nor none of thine shall be let in.
   Glou. Faint-hearted Woodvile, prizest him
     'fore me?
Arrogant Winchester, that haughty prelate,
Whom Henry, our late sovereign, ne'er could
     brook?
Thou art no friend to God or to the king:
Open the gates, or I'll shut thee out shortly.
   Serving-men. Open the gates unto the lord
      protector,
Or we'll burst them open, if that you come not
     quickly.

Enter to the Protector at the Tower Gates WIN-CHESTER *and his men in tawny coats.*

   Win. How now, ambitious Humphry! what means this?

● *Glou.* Peel'd priest, dost thou command me to be shut out?   30

● *Win.* I do, thou most usurping proditor,
And not protector, of the king or realm.

   Glou. Stand back, thou manifest conspirator,
Thou that contrivedst to murder our dead lord;

● Thou that givest whores indulgences to sin:

● I'll canvass thee in thy broad cardinal's hat,
If thou proceed in this thy insolence.

   Win. Nay, stand thou back; I will not budge a foot:

● This be Damascus, be thou cursed Cain,
To slay thy brother Abel, if thou wilt.   40

   Glou. I will not slay thee, but I'll drive thee back:
Thy scarlet robes as a child's bearing-cloth
I'll use to carry thee out of this place.

● *Win.* Do what thou darest; I beard thee to thy face.

   Glou. What! am I dared and bearded to my face?
Draw, men, for all this privileged place;

● Blue coats to tawny coats. Priest, beware your beard;
I mean to tug it and to cuff you soundly:
Under my feet I stamp thy cardinal's hat:
In spite of pope or dignities of church,   50
Here by the cheeks I'll drag thee up and down.

   Win. Gloucester, thou wilt answer this before the pope.

● *Glou.* Winchester goose, I cry, a rope! a rope!
Now beat them hence; why do you let them stay?
Thee I'll chase hence, thou wolf in sheep's array.
Out, tawny coats! out, scarlet hypocrite!

Here Gloucester's men beat out the Cardinal's men, and enter in the hurly-burly the Mayor of London *and his* Officers.

   May. Fie, lords! that you, being supreme magistrates,

● Thus contumeliously should break the peace!

   Glou. Peace, mayor! thou know'st little of my wrongs:
Here's Beaufort, that regards nor God nor king,

● Hath here distrain'd the Tower to his use.   61

   Win. Here's Gloucester, a foe to citizens,
One that still motions war and never peace,
O'ercharging your free purses with large fines,
That seeks to overthrow religion,
Because he is protector of the realm,
And would have armour here out of the Tower,
To crown himself king and suppress the prince.

   Glou. I will not answer thee with words, but blows.   [*Here they skirmish again.*

   May. Nought rests for me in this tumultuous strife   70
But to make open proclamation:
Come, officer; as loud as e'er thou canst,
Cry.

   Off. All manner of men assembled here in arms this day against God's peace and the king's, we charge and command you, in his highness' name, to repair to your several dwelling-places;

30 *Peel'd.* Bald, tonsured.

31 *proditor.* Traitor (also with a pun on 'protector').

35 *Thou . . . sin.* The Southwark stews were public brothels upon the land of the Bishop of Winchester. The sign on one house was a 'Cardinal's Hat'.

Winchester House in Southwark, the official residence of the Bishop of Winchester, is indicated by the number 20 on the bottom of this detail from a map of 1593

36 *canvass.* Toss as in a canvas sheet.

39 *Damascus.* According to tradition Cain killed Abel in the place where Damascus was founded.

44 *beard.* Defy.

47 *Blue coats to tawny coats.* Gloucester's men wore blue coats and Winchester's tawny.

53 *Winchester goose.* Contemporary slang for one symptom of venereal disease, a swelling in the groin.

58 *contumeliously.* Contemptuously, insolently.

61 *distrain'd.* Seized.

Lord Mayor and Sheriffs of the City of London, 1586

---

84 *call for clubs.* Call out the apprentices of the city upon the occasion of a riot.

90 *stomachs.* i.e. angry tempers.

8 *espials.* Spies.

15 *piece of ordnance.* Cannon.

and not to wear, handle, or use any sword, weapon, or dagger, henceforward, upon pain of death.

Glou. Cardinal, I'll be no breaker of the law:
But we shall meet, and break our minds at large.

Win. Gloucester, we will meet; to thy cost, be sure:
Thy heart-blood I will have for this day's work.

May. I'll call for clubs, if you will not away.
This cardinal's more haughty than the devil.

Glou. Mayor, farewell: thou dost but what thou mayst.

Win. Abominable Gloucester, guard thy head;
For I intend to have it ere long.

[*Exeunt, severally, Gloucester and Winchester with their Serving-men.*

May. See the coast clear'd, and then we will depart.
Good God, these nobles should such stomachs bear!   90
I myself fight not once in forty year.   [*Exeunt.*

SCENE IV. *Orleans.*

Enter, on the walls, a Master Gunner *and his* Boy.

M. Gun. Sirrah, thou know'st how Orleans is besieged,
And how the English have the suburbs won.

Boy. Father, I know; and oft have shot at them,
Howe'er unfortunate I miss'd my aim.

M. Gun. But now thou shalt not. Be thou ruled by me:
Chief master-gunner am I of this town;
Something I must do to procure me grace.
The prince's espials have informed me
How the English, in the suburbs close intrench'd,
Wont through a secret grate of iron bars   10
In yonder tower to overpeer the city
And thence discover how with most advantage
They may vex us with shot or with assault.
To intercept this inconvenience,
A piece of ordnance 'gainst it I have placed;
And even these three days have I watch'd,
If I could see them.
Now do thou watch, for I can stay no longer.
If thou spy'st any, run and bring me word;
And thou shalt find me at the governor's. [*Exit.*

Boy. Father, I warrant you; take you no care;
I'll never trouble you, if I may spy them. [*Exit.*

Enter, on the turrets, the LORDS SALISBURY *and*
TALBOT, SIR WILLIAM GLANSDALE, SIR
THOMAS GARGRAVE, *and others.*

Sal. Talbot, my life, my joy, again return'd!
How wert thou handled being prisoner?
Or by what means got'st thou to be released?
Discourse, I prithee, on this turret's top.

Tal. The Duke of Bedford had a prisoner
Call'd the brave Lord Ponton de Santrailles;
For him was I exchanged and ransomed.
But with a baser man of arms by far   30
Once in contempt they would have barter'd me:
Which I disdaining scorn'd and craved death
Rather than I would be so vile-esteem'd.
In fine, redeem'd I was as I desired.
But, O! the treacherous Fastolfe wounds my heart,
Whom with my bare fists I would execute,
If I now had him brought into my power.

Sal. Yet tell'st thou not how thou wert entertain'd.

Tal. With scoffs and scorns and contumelious taunts.

In open market-place produced they me,   40
To be a public spectacle to all:
Here, said they, is the terror of the French,
The scarecrow that affrights our children so.
Then broke I from the officers that led me,
And with my nails digg'd stones out of the ground,
To hurl at the beholders of my shame:
My grisly countenance made others fly;
None durst come near for fear of sudden death.
In iron walls they deem'd me not secure;
So great fear of my name 'mongst them was spread
That they supposed I could rend bars of steel   51
● And spurn in pieces posts of adamant:
● Wherefore a guard of chosen shot I had
That walk'd about me every minute while;
And if I did but stir out of my bed,
Ready they were to shoot me to the heart.

Enter the Boy *with a linstock.*

Sal. I grieve to hear what torments you endured,
But we will be revenged sufficiently.
Now it is supper-time in Orleans:
Here, through this grate, I count each one   60
And view the Frenchmen how they fortify:
Let us look in; the sight will much delight thee.
Sir Thomas Gargrave, and Sir William Glansdale,
Let me have your express opinions
● Where is best place to make our battery next.

Gar. I think, at the north gate; for there stand lords.

Glan. And I, here, at the bulwark of the bridge.

Tal. For aught I see, this city must be famish'd,
Or with light skirmishes enfeebled.

[*Here they shoot. Salisbury and Gargrave fall.*

Sal. O Lord, have mercy on us, wretched sinners!   70

Gar. O Lord, have mercy on me, woful man!

Tal. What chance is this that suddenly hath cross'd us?
Speak, Salisbury; at least, if thou canst speak:
How farest thou, mirror of all martial men?
One of thy eyes and thy cheek's side struck off!
Accursed tower! accursed fatal hand
That hath contrived this woful tragedy!
In thirteen battles Salisbury o'ercame;
Henry the Fifth he first train'd to the wars;
Whilst any trump did sound, or drum struck up,
His sword did ne'er leave striking in the field.   81
Yet livest thou, Salisbury? though thy speech doth fail,
One eye thou hast, to look to heaven for grace:
The sun with one eye vieweth all the world.
Heaven, be thou gracious to none alive,
If Salisbury wants mercy at thy hands!
Bear hence his body; I will help to bury it.
Sir Thomas Gargrave, hast thou any life?
Speak unto Talbot; nay, look up to him.
Salisbury, cheer thy spirit with this comfort;   90
Thou shalt not die whiles—
He beckons with his hand and smiles on me,
As who should say 'When I am dead and gone,
Remember to avenge me on the French.'

Lord Talbot, later Earl of Shrewsbury. Engraving from *Old England*, 1584

---

52 *adamant.* A legendary stone of impenetrable hardness.

53 *shot.* Gunners.

SD *linstock.* Stock for holding the match to fire a gun.

65 *battery.* Assault.

107 *Pucelle or puzzel.* Virgin or harlot. *dolphin or dogfish.* A quibble on 'Dauphin', and the word 'dogfish' used as a term of abuse.

6 *Blood . . . thee.* The superstition that if you could get blood from a witch you would be freed from her power.

Talbot: 'My thoughts are whirled like a potter's wheel'. Engraving by F.W. Fairholt from a badge *c.*1600. From J.O. Halliwell's edition of Shakespeare's works, 1853–65

21 *Hannibal.* Hannibal's stratagem of tying blazing faggots to the horns of two thousand oxen which created such alarm amongst the Roman army that the Carthaginians were able to break through the Roman encirclement.

Plantagenet, I will; and like thee, Nero,
Play on the lute, beholding the towns burn:
Wretched shall France be only in my name.
[*Here an alarum, and it thunders and lightens.*
What stir is this? what tumult's in the heavens?
Whence cometh this alarum and the noise?

Enter a Messenger.

Mess. My lord, my lord, the French have gather'd head: 100
The Dauphin, with one Joan la Pucelle join'd,
A holy prophetess new risen up,
Is come with a great power to raise the siege.
[*Here Salisbury lifteth himself up and groans.*
Tal. Hear, hear how dying Salisbury doth groan!
It irks his heart he cannot be revenged.
Frenchmen, I'll be a Salisbury to you:
● Pucelle or puzzel, dolphin or dogfish,
Your hearts I'll stamp out with my horse's heels,
And make a quagmire of your mingled brains.
Convey me Salisbury into his tent,   110
And then we'll try what these dastard Frenchmen dare.   [*Alarum. Exeunt.*

SCENE V. *The same.*

Here an alarum again: and TALBOT *pursueth the* DAUPHIN, *and driveth him: then enter* JOAN LA PUCELLE, *driving Englishmen before her, and exit after them: then re-enter* TALBOT.

Tal. Where is my strength, my valour, and my force?
Our English troops retire, I cannot stay them;
A woman clad in armour chaseth them.

Re-enter LA PUCELLE.

Here, here she comes. I'll have a bout with thee;
Devil or devil's dam, I'll conjure thee:
● Blood will I draw on thee, thou art a witch,
And straightway give thy soul to him thou servest.
Puc. Come, come, 'tis only I that must disgrace thee.   [*Here they fight.*
Tal. Heavens, can you suffer hell so to prevail?   9
My breast I'll burst with straining of my courage
And from my shoulders crack my arms asunder,
But I will chastise this high-minded strumpet.
[*They fight again.*
Puc. Talbot, farewell; thy hour is not yet come:
I must go victual Orleans forthwith.
[*A short alarum: then enter the town with soldiers.*
O'ertake me, if thou canst; I scorn thy strength.
Go, go, cheer up thy hungry-starved men;
Help Salisbury to make his testament:
This day is ours, as many more shall be. [*Exit.*
Tal. My thoughts are whirled like a potter's wheel;
I know not where I am, nor what I do: 20
● A witch, by fear, not force, like Hannibal,
Drives back our troops and conquers as she lists:
So bees with smoke and doves with noisome stench
Are from their hives and houses driven away.
They call'd us for our fierceness English dogs;
Now, like to whelps, we crying run away.
[*A short alarum.*

Hark, countrymen! either renew the fight,
• Or tear the lions out of England's coat;
Renounce your soil, give sheep in lions' stead:
Sheep run not half so treacherous from the wolf,
Or horse or oxen from the leopard,   31
As you fly from your oft-subdued slaves.
     [*Alarum. Here another skirmish.*
It will not be: retire into your trenches:
You all consented unto Salisbury's death,
For none would strike a stroke in his revenge.
Pucelle is enter'd into Orleans,
In spite of us or aught that we could do.
O, would I were to die with Salisbury!
The shame hereof will make me hide my head.
   [*Exit Talbot. Alarum; retreat; flourish.*

SCENE VI. *The same.*

Enter, on the walls, LA PUCELLE, CHARLES,
REIGNIER, ALENÇON, *and Soldiers.*

 Puc. Advance our waving colours on the
  walls;
Rescued is Orleans from the English:
Thus Joan la Pucelle hath perform'd her word.
• *Char.* Divinest creature, Astræa's daughter,
How shall I honour thee for this success?
Thy promises are like Adonis' gardens
That one day bloom'd and fruitful were the next.
France, triumph in thy glorious prophetess!
Recover'd is the town of Orleans:
More blessed hap did ne'er befall our state.   10
 Reig. Why ring not out the bells aloud
  throughout the town?
Dauphin, command the citizens make bonfires
And feast and banquet in the open streets,
To celebrate the joy that God hath given us.
 Alen. All France will be replete with mirth
  and joy,
When they shall hear how we have play'd the
  men.
 Char. 'Tis Joan, not we, by whom the day
  is won;
For which I will divide my crown with her,
And all the priests and friars in my realm
Shall in procession sing her endless praise.   20
• A statelier pyramis to her I'll rear
Than Rhodope's or Memphis' ever was:
In memory of her when she is dead,
Her ashes, in an urn more precious
Than the rich-jewel'd coffer of Darius,
Transported shall be at high festivals
Before the kings and queens of France.
• No longer on Saint Denis will we cry,
But Joan la Pucelle shall be France's saint.
Come in, and let us banquet royally,   30
After this golden day of victory.
     [*Flourish. Exeunt.*

ACT II.

SCENE I. *Before Orleans.*

Enter a Sergeant *of a band, with two* Sentinels.

 Serg. Sirs, take your places and be vigilant:
If any noise or soldier you perceive
Near to the walls, by some apparent sign
• Let us have knowledge at the court of guard.
 First Sent. Sergeant, you shall. [*Exit Ser-
  geant.*] Thus are poor servitors,

28 *England's coat.* Coat of arms.

4 *Astræa's.* Astræa being the Goddess of Justice.

21—22 *pyramis . . . Memphis'.* According to legend, Rhodope, a celebrated Greek courtesan, married a king of Memphis and built the third pyramid.

28 *Saint Denis.* Patron saint of France.

Sophia Baddeley, 18th century actress, as La Pucelle, 1776

4 *court of guard.* Guardhouse.

A scaling ladder, used to scale the walls of a city.
Engraving from Robert Ward's *Animadversions of War,*
1639

SD *dead march.* i.e. for Salisbury's funeral.

11 *secure.* Careless, thinking themselves safe.

14 *quittance.* Repay.

41 *trow.* Think.

When others sleep upon their quiet beds,
Constrain'd to watch in darkness, rain and cold.

Enter TALBOT, BEDFORD, BURGUNDY, *and
forces, with scaling-ladders, their drums
beating a dead march.*

Tal. Lord Regent, and redoubted Burgundy,
By whose approach the regions of Artois,
Wallon and Picardy are friends to us,   10
● This happy night the Frenchmen are secure,
Having all day caroused and banqueted:
Embrace we then this opportunity
● As fitting best to quittance their deceit
Contrived by art and baleful sorcery.
    Bed. Coward of France! how much he wrongs
        his fame,
Despairing of his own arm's fortitude,
To join with witches and the help of hell!
    Bur. Traitors have never other company.
But what's that Pucelle whom they term so
    pure?   20
    Tal. A maid, they say.
    Bed.   A maid! and be so martial!
    Bur. Pray God she prove not masculine ere
        long,
If underneath the standard of the French
She carry armour as she hath begun.
    Tal. Well, let them practise and converse with
        spirits:
God is our fortress, in whose conquering name
Let us resolve to scale their flinty bulwarks.
    Bed. Ascend, brave Talbot; we will follow
        thee.
    Tal. Not all together: better far, I guess,
That we do make our entrance several ways;   30
That, if it chance the one of us do fail,
The other yet may rise against their force.
    Bed. Agreed: I'll to yond corner.
    Bur.   And I to this.
    Tal. And here will Talbot mount, or make
        his grave.
Now, Salisbury, for thee, and for the right
Of English Henry, shall this night appear
How much in duty I am bound to both.
    Sent. Arm! arm! the enemy doth make
        assault!   [*Cry: 'St George,' 'A Talbot.'*

*The French leap over the walls in their shirts.
Enter, several ways, the* BASTARD *of Orleans,*
ALENÇON, *and* REIGNIER, *half ready, and half
unready.*

    Alen. How now, my lords! what, all un-
        ready so?
    Bast. Unready! ay, and glad we 'scaped so
        well.   40
● *Reig.* 'Twas time, I trow, to wake and leave
        our beds,
Hearing alarums at our chamber-doors.
    Alen. Of all exploits since first I follow'd
        arms,
Ne'er heard I of a warlike enterprise
More venturous or desperate than this.
    Bast. I think this Talbot be a fiend of hell.
    Reig. If not of hell, the heavens, sure, favour
        him.
    Alen. Here cometh Charles: I marvel how
        he sped.
    Bast. Tut, holy Joan was his defensive guard.

Enter CHARLES *and* LA PUCELLE.

Char. Is this thy cunning, thou deceitful dame? 50
● Didst thou at first, to flatter us withal,
Make us partakers of a little gain,
That now our loss might be ten times so much?
 Puc. Wherefore is Charles impatient with his friend?
At all times will you have my power alike?
Sleeping or waking must I still prevail,
Or will you blame and lay the fault on me?
Improvident soldiers! had your watch been good,
This sudden mischief never could have fall'n.
 Char. Duke of Alençon, this was your default, 60
That, being captain of the watch to-night,
Did look no better to that weighty charge.
 Alen. Had all your quarters been as safely kept
As that whereof I had the government,
We had not been thus shamefully surprised.
 Bast. Mine was secure.
 Reig.   And so was mine, my lord.
 Char. And, for myself, most part of all this night,
Within her quarter and mine own precinct
I was employ'd in passing to and fro,
About relieving of the sentinels: 70
Then how or which way should they first break in?
 Puc. Question, my lords, no further of the case,
How or which way: 'tis sure they found some place
But weakly guarded, where the breach was made.
● And now there rests no other shift but this;
To gather our soldiers, scatter'd and dispersed,
● And lay new platforms to endamage them.

Alarum. Enter an English Soldier, *crying 'A Talbot! a Talbot!' They fly, leaving their clothes behind.*

 Sold. I'll be so bold to take what they have left.
The cry of Talbot serves me for a sword;
For I have loaden me with many spoils, 80
Using no other weapon but his name. [*Exit.*

SCENE II. *Orleans. Within the town.*

Enter TALBOT, BEDFORD, BURGUNDY, *a* Captain, *and others.*

 Bed. The day begins to break, and night is fled,
Whose pitchy mantle over-veil'd the earth.
Here sound retreat, and cease our hot pursuit.
                    [*Retreat sounded.*
 Tal. Bring forth the body of old Salisbury,
And here advance it in the market-place,
The middle centre of this cursed town.
Now have I paid my vow unto his soul;
For every drop of blood was drawn from him
There hath at least five Frenchmen died to-night.
And that hereafter ages may behold 10
What ruin happen'd in revenge of him,
Within their chiefest temple I'll erect
A tomb, wherein his corpse shall be interr'd:
Upon the which, that every one may read,
Shall be engraved the sack of Orleans,

51 *flatter.* Deceive.

75 *shift.* Device, stratagem.

77 *platforms.* Plots.

28 *trull*. Whore.

41 *lies*. Lives, dwells.

The Countess of Auvergne. Engraving from a painting by W.Q. Orchardson (1835–1910)

6 *Tomyris*. The Scythian Queen, Tomyris, in revenge for the death of her husband at the hands of the Persians, killed Cyrus the Great and put his severed head into a wine skin full of blood.

7 *rumour*. Reputation, renown.

The treacherous manner of his mournful **death**
And what a terror he had been to France.
But, lords, in all our bloody massacre,
I muse we met not with the Dauphin's grace,
His new-come champion, virtuous Joan of Arc,
Nor any of his false confederates.   21
   Bed.   'Tis thought, Lord Talbot, when the
    fight began,
Roused on the sudden from their drowsy beds,
They did amongst the troops of armed men
Leap o'er the walls for refuge in the field.
   Bur.   Myself, as far as I could well discern
For smoke and dusky vapours of the night,
• Am sure I scared the Dauphin and his trull,
When arm in arm they both came swiftly running,
Like to a pair of loving turtle-doves   30
That could not live asunder day or night.
After that things are set in order here,
We'll follow them with all the power we have.

         Enter a Messenger.

   Mess.   All hail, my lords!   Which of this
    princely train
Call ye the warlike Talbot, for his acts
So much applauded through the realm of France?
   Tal.   Here is the Talbot: who would speak
    with him?
   Mess.   The virtuous lady, Countess of Auvergne,
With modesty admiring thy renown,
By me entreats, great lord, thou wouldst vouch-
    safe   40
• To visit her poor castle where she lies,
That she may boast she hath beheld the man
Whose glory fills the world with loud report.
   Bur.   Is it even so?   Nay, then, I see our wars
Will turn unto a peaceful comic sport,
When ladies crave to be encounter'd with.
You may not, my lord, despise her gentle suit.
   Tal.   Ne'er trust me then; for when a world
    of men
Could not prevail with all their oratory,
Yet hath a woman's kindness over-ruled: 50
And therefore tell her I return great thanks,
And in submission will attend on her.
Will not your honours bear me company?
   Bed.   No, truly; it is more than manners will:
And I have heard it said, unbidden guests
Are often welcomest when they are gone.
   Tal.   Well then, alone, since there's no remedy,
I mean to prove this lady's courtesy.
Come hither, captain. [*Whispers.*] You per-
    ceive my mind?
   Capt.   I do, my lord, and mean accordingly.
                    [*Exeunt.* 60

SCENE III. *Auvergne. The* COUNTESS'S *castle.*

    Enter the COUNTESS *and her* Porter.

   Count.   Porter, remember what I gave in
    charge;
And when you have done so, bring the keys
    to me.
   Port.   Madam, I will.   [*Exit.*
   Count.   The plot is laid: if all things fall out
    right,
I shall as famous be by this exploit
• As Scythian Tomyris by Cyrus' death.
• Great is the rumour of this dreadful knight,
And his achievements of no less account:

Fain would mine eyes be witness with mine ears,
● To give their censure of these rare reports.   10

    Enter Messenger *and* TALBOT.

  Mess. Madam,
According as your ladyship desired,
By message craved, so is Lord Talbot come.
  Count. And he is welcome. What! is this
    the man?
  Mess. Madam, it is.
  Count.   Is this the scourge of France?
Is this the Talbot, so much fear'd abroad
That with his name the mothers still their babes?
I see report is fabulous and false:
I thought I should have seen some Hercules,
A second Hector, for his grim aspect,   20
And large proportion of his strong-knit limbs.
Alas, this is a child, a silly dwarf!
● It cannot be this weak and writhled shrimp
Should strike such terror to his enemies.
  Tal. Madam, I have been bold to trouble you;
But since your ladyship is not at leisure,
I'll sort some other time to visit you.
  Count. What means he now? Go ask him
    whither he goes.
  Mess. Stay, my Lord Talbot; for my lady
    craves
To know the cause of your abrupt departure.   30
  Tal. Marry, for that she's in a wrong belief,
I go to certify her Talbot's here.

    Re-enter Porter *with keys.*

  Count. If thou be he, then art thou prisoner.
  Tal. Prisoner! to whom?
  Count.   To me, blood-thirsty lord;
And for that cause I train'd thee to my house.
● Long time thy shadow hath been thrall to me,
For in my gallery thy picture hangs:
But now the substance shall endure the like,
And I will chain these legs and arms of thine,
That hast by tyranny these many years   40
Wasted our country, slain our citizens
And sent our sons and husbands captivate.
  Tal. Ha, ha, ha!
  Count. Laughest thou, wretch? thy mirth
    shall turn to moan.
● *Tal.* I laugh to see your ladyship so fond
To think that you have aught but Talbot's shadow
Whereon to practise your severity.
  Count. Why, art not thou the man?
  Tal.   I am indeed.
  Count. Then have I substance too.
  Tal. No, no, I am but shadow of myself: 50
You are deceived, my substance is not here;
For what you see is but the smallest part
And least proportion of humanity:
I tell you, madam, were the whole frame here,
● It is of such a spacious lofty pitch,
Your roof were not sufficient to contain 't.
● *Count.* This is a riddling merchant for the
    nonce;
He will be here, and yet he is not here:
How can these contrarieties agree?
  Tal. That will I show you presently.   60
    [*Winds his horn. Drums strike up: a*
      peal of ordnance. Enter Soldiers.
How say you, madam? are you now persuaded
That Talbot is but shadow of himself?

10 *censure.* Judgment, opinion.

23 *writhled.* Wrinkled.

36 *thrall.* In bondage.

45 *fond.* Foolish.

55 *pitch.* Height.

57 *riddling merchant.* Riddle-monger. *for the nonce.* For the time or occasion (a line-filler).

Talbot: 'How say you, madam? . . .' Talbot summons his soldiers. Engraving from a painting by John Opie (1761–1807)

68 *bruited*. Noised abroad, reported.

79 *cates*. Delicacies.

17 *quillets*. Legal subtleties, precise distinctions.

18 *no wiser than a daw*. i.e. a simpleton (proverb).

21 *purblind*. Partly blind.

26 *significants*. Signs.

Plantagenet: 'From off this brier pluck a white rose with me'. Engraving from a painting by Josiah Boydell

These are his substance, sinews, arms and
  strength,
With which he yoketh your rebellious necks,
Razeth your cities and subverts your towns
And in a moment makes them desolate.
  Count. Victorious Talbot! pardon my abuse:
● I find thou art no less than fame hath bruited
And more than may be gather'd by thy shape.
Let my presumption not provoke thy wrath; 70
For I am sorry that with reverence
I did not entertain thee as thou art.
  Tal. Be not dismay'd, fair lady; nor mis-
  construe
The mind of Talbot, as you did mistake
The outward composition of his body.
What you have done hath not offended me;
Nor other satisfaction do I crave,
But only, with your patience, that we may
● Taste of your wine and see what cates you have;
For soldiers' stomachs always serve them well. 80
  Count. With all my heart, and think me
  honoured
To feast so great a warrior in my house.
    [*Exeunt.*

SCENE IV. *London. The Temple-garden.*

Enter the EARLS OF SOMERSET, SUFFOLK, *and*
WARWICK; RICHARD PLANTAGENET, VER-
NON, *and another* Lawyer.

  Plan. Great lords and gentlemen, what means
  this silence?
Dare no man answer in a case of truth?
  Suf. Within the Temple-hall we were too loud;
The garden here is more convenient.
  Plan. Then say at once if I maintain'd the
  truth;
Or else was wrangling Somerset in the error?
  Suf. Faith, I have been a truant in the law,
And never yet could frame my will to it;
And therefore frame the law unto my will.
  Som. Judge you, my Lord of Warwick, then,
  between us. 10
  War. Between two hawks, which flies the
  higher pitch;
Between two dogs, which hath the deeper mouth;
Between two blades, which bears the better
  temper:
Between two horses, which doth bear him best;
Between two girls, which hath the merriest eye;
I have perhaps some shallow spirit of judgement;
● But in these nice sharp quillets of the law,
● Good faith, I am no wiser than a daw.
  Plan. Tut, tut, here is a mannerly forbearance:
The truth appears so naked on my side 20
● That any purblind eye may find it out.
  Som. And on my side it is so well apparell'd,
So clear, so shining and so evident
That it will glimmer through a blind man's eye.
  Plan. Since you are tongue-tied and so loath
  to speak,
● In dumb significants proclaim your thoughts:
Let him that is a true-born gentleman
And stands upon the honour of his birth,
If he suppose that I have pleaded truth,
From off this brier pluck a white rose with me. 30
  Som. Let him that is no coward nor no flat-
  terer,
But dare maintain the party of the truth,

Pluck a red rose from off this thorn with me.
- *War.* I love no colours, and without all colour
Of base insinuating flattery
I pluck this white rose with Plantagenet.
    Suf. I pluck this red rose with young Somerset
And say withal I think he held the right.
    Ver. Stay, lords and gentlemen, and pluck no more,
Till you conclude that he upon whose side   40
The fewest roses are cropp'd from the tree
Shall yield the other in the right opinion.
    Som. Good Master Vernon, it is well objected:
If I have fewest, I subscribe in silence.
    Plan.   And I.
    Ver.   Then for the truth and plainness of the case,
I pluck this pale and maiden blossom here,
Giving my verdict on the white rose side.
    Som. Prick not your finger as you pluck it off,
Lest bleeding you do paint the white rose red   50
And fall on my side so, against your will.
    Ver. If I, my lord, for my opinion bleed,
Opinion shall be surgeon to my hurt
And keep me on the side where still I am.
    Som. Well, well, come on: who else?
    Law. Unless my study and my books be false,
The argument you held was wrong in you;
                               [*To Somerset.*
In sign whereof I pluck a white rose too.
    Plan.   Now, Somerset, where is your argument?
    Som. Here in my scabbard, meditating that
Shall dye your white rose in a bloody red.   61
    Plan. Meantime your cheeks do counterfeit our roses;
For pale they look with fear, as witnessing
The truth on our side.
    Som.   No, Plantagenet,
'Tis not for fear but anger that thy cheeks
Blush for pure shame to counterfeit our roses,
And yet thy tongue will not confess thy error.
- *Plan.* Hath not thy rose a canker, Somerset?
    Som. Hath not thy rose a thorn, Plantagenet?
    Plan. Ay, sharp and piercing, to maintain his truth;   70
Whiles thy consuming canker eats his falsehood.
    Som.   Well, I'll find friends to wear my bleeding roses,
That shall maintain what I have said is true,
Where false Plantagenet dare not be seen.
    Plan. Now, by this maiden blossom in my hand,
I scorn thee and thy fashion, peevish boy.
    Suf. Turn not thy scorns this way, Plantagenet.
- *Plan.* Proud Pole, I will, and scorn both him and thee.
    Suf. I'll turn my part thereof into thy throat.
    Som. Away, away, good William de la Pole!
We grace the yeoman by conversing with him.   81
    War. Now, by God's will, thou wrong'st him, Somerset;
His grandfather was Lionel Duke of Clarence,
Third son to the third Edward King of England:
- Spring crestless yeomen from so deep a root?
- *Plan.* He bears him on the place's privilege,
Or durst not, for his craven heart, say thus.
    Som. By him that made me, I'll maintain my words

34 *colours.* Equivocal usage: 'tints or hues' and 'pretences'.

68 *canker.* Maggot, worm in the bud.

78 *Pole.* De la Pole, Suffolk's family name.

The Temple Garden scene. Engraving from a painting by John Pettie (1839–93)

85 *crestless yeoman.* i.e. ignoble, not having a coat of arms.

86 *bears . . . privilege.* Takes advantage of the fact that the Temple being founded as a religious house was a sanctuary. The Temple was 'privileged' twice-over as it was a law-court.

92 *attainted*. His blood inherited the 'taint' of treason from his father.

96 *attached, not attainted*. Arrested but not convicted of treason by bill of attainder.

100 *partaker*. Supporter.

108 *cognizance*. Badge. *blood-drinking*. Bloodthirsty.

115 *braved*. Insulted.

5 *pursuivants*. Herald's attendants.

6 *Nestor-like*. Nestor being the Greek king in Homer's *Iliad* who lived three life-times.

9 *exigent*. Conclusion.

On any plot of ground in Christendom.
Was not thy father, Richard Earl of Cambridge,
For treason executed in our late king's days?　91
● And, by his treason, stand'st not thou attainted,
Corrupted, and exempt from ancient gentry?
His trespass yet lives guilty in thy blood;
And, till thou be restored, thou art a yeoman.
● *Plan.* My father was attached, not attainted,
Condemn'd to die for treason, but no traitor;
And that I'll prove on better men than Somerset,
Were growing time once ripen'd to my will.
● For your partaker Pole and you yourself,　100
I'll note you in my book of memory,
To scourge you for this apprehension:
Look to it well and say you are well warn'd.
　　Som. Ah, thou shalt find us ready for thee
　　　　still;
And know us by these colours for thy foes,
For these my friends in spite of thee shall wear.
　　Plan. And, by my soul, this pale and angry
　　　　rose,
● As cognizance of my blood-drinking hate,
Will I for ever and my faction wear,
Until it wither with me to my grave　110
Or flourish to the height of my degree.
　　Suf. Go forward and be choked with thy am-
　　　　bition!
And so farewell until I meet thee next.　[*Exit.*
　　Som. Have with thee, Pole. Farewell, am-
　　　　bitious Richard.　　　　　　　[*Exit.*
● *Plan.* How I am braved and must perforce
　　　　endure it!
　　War. This blot that they object against your
　　　　house
Shall be wiped out in the next parliament
Call'd for the truce of Winchester and Gloucester;
And if thou be not then created York,
I will not live to be accounted Warwick.　120
Meantime, in signal of my love to thee,
Against proud Somerset and William Pole,
Will I upon thy party wear this rose:
And here I prophesy: this brawl to-day,
Grown to this faction in the Temple-garden,
Shall send between the red rose and the white
A thousand souls to death and deadly night.
　　Plan. Good Master Vernon, I am bound to
　　　　you,
That you on my behalf would pluck a flower.
　　Ver. In your behalf still will I wear the same.
　　Law. And so will I.　　　　　　　131
　　Plan. Thanks, gentle sir.
Come, let us four to dinner: I dare say
This quarrel will drink blood another day.
　　　　　　　　　　　　　　　[*Exeunt.*

SCENE V.　*The Tower of London.*

Enter MORTIMER, *brought in a chair, and*
Gaolers.

　　Mor. Kind keepers of my weak decaying age,
Let dying Mortimer here rest himself.
Even like a man new haled from the rack,
So fare my limbs with long imprisonment;
● And these grey locks, the pursuivants of death,
● Nestor-like aged in an age of care,
Argue the end of Edmund Mortimer.
These eyes, like lamps whose wasting oil is spent,
● Wax dim, as drawing to their exigent;
Weak shoulders, overborne with burthening grief,

And pithless arms, like to a wither'd vine   11
That droops his sapless branches to the ground:
Yet are these feet, whose strengthless stay is
    numb,
Unable to support this lump of clay,
Swift-winged with desire to get a grave,
As witting I no other comfort have.
But tell me, keeper, will my nephew come?
    First Gaol. Richard Plantagenet, my lord,
    will come:
We sent unto the Temple, unto his chamber;
And answer was return'd that he will come.   20
    Mor. Enough: my soul shall then be satisfied.
Poor gentleman! his wrong doth equal mine.
● Since Henry Monmouth first began to reign,
Before whose glory I was great in arms,
● This loathsome sequestration have I had:
And even since then hath Richard been obscured,
Deprived of honour and inheritance.
But now the arbitrator of despairs,
Just death, kind umpire of men's miseries,
● With sweet enlargement doth dismiss me hence:
I would his troubles likewise were expired,   31
That so he might recover what was lost.

    Enter RICHARD PLANTAGENET.

    First Gaol. My lord, your loving nephew now
    is come.
    Mor. Richard Plantagenet, my friend, is he
    come?
    Plan. Ay, noble uncle, thus ignobly used,
Your nephew, late despised Richard, comes.
    Mor. Direct mine arms I may embrace his
    neck,
And in his bosom spend my latter gasp:
O, tell me when my lips do touch his cheeks,
That I may kindly give one fainting kiss.   40
And now declare, sweet stem from York's great
    stock,
Why didst thou say, of late thou wert despised?
    Plan. First, lean thine aged back against mine
    arm;
And, in that ease, I'll tell thee my disease.
This day, in argument upon a case,
Some words there grew 'twixt Somerset and me;
Among which terms he used his lavish tongue
And did upbraid me with my father's death:
Which obloquy set bars before my tongue,
Else with the like I had requited him.   50
Therefore, good uncle, for my father's sake,
In honour of a true Plantagenet
And for alliance sake, declare the cause
My father, Earl of Cambridge, lost his head.
    Mor. That cause, fair nephew, that imprison'd
    me
And hath detain'd me all my flowering youth
Within a loathsome dungeon, there to pine,
Was cursed instrument of his decease.
    Plan. Discover more at large what cause that
    was,
For I am ignorant and cannot guess.   60
    Mor. I will, if that my fading breath permit
And death approach not ere my tale be done.
Henry the Fourth, grandfather to this king,
Deposed his nephew Richard, Edward's son,
The first-begotten and the lawful heir
Of Edward king, the third of that descent:
During whose reign the Percies of the north,

23 *Henry Monmouth.* Henry V, born at Monmouth.

25 *sequestration.* Seclusion, imprisonment.

30 *enlargement.* Release.

Richard Plantagenet with Mortimer in the Tower.
Engraving from Bell's edition of *Shakespeare,* 1773–4

88 *weening.* Thinking.

89 *have . . . diadem.* Have me crowned king.

105 *cloy'd.* Bored.

Death of Mortimer. Engraving from a painting by James Northcote (1746–1831)

122 *dusky.* Gloomy.

Finding his usurpation most unjust,
Endeavour'd my advancement to the throne:
The reason moved these warlike lords to this   70
Was, for that—young King Richard thus removed,
Leaving no heir begotten of his body—
I was the next by birth and parentage;
For by my mother I derived am
From Lionel Duke of Clarence, the third son
To King Edward the Third; whereas he
From John of Gaunt doth bring his pedigree,
Being but fourth of that heroic line.
But mark: as in this haughty great attempt
They laboured to plant the rightful heir,   80
I lost my liberty and they their lives.
Long after this, when Henry the Fifth,
Succeeding his father Bolingbroke, did reign,
Thy father, Earl of Cambridge, then derived
From famous Edmund Langley, Duke of York,
Marrying my sister that thy mother was,
Again in pity of my hard distress
● Levied an army, weening to redeem
● And have install'd me in the diadem:
But, as the rest, so fell that noble earl   90
And was beheaded.   Thus the Mortimers,
In whom the title rested, were suppress'd.
    Plan.   Of which, my lord, your honour is the last.
    Mor. True; and thou seest that I no issue have
And that my fainting words do warrant death:
Thou art my heir; the rest I wish thee gather:
But yet be wary in thy studious care.
    Plan.   Thy grave admonishments prevail with me:
But yet, methinks, my father's execution
Was nothing less than bloody tyranny.   100
    Mor.   With silence, nephew, be thou politic:
Strong-fixed is the house of Lancaster
And like a mountain, not to be removed.
But now thy uncle is removing hence;
● As princes do their courts, when they are cloy'd
With long continuance in a settled place.
    Plan.   O, uncle, would some part of my young years
Might but redeem the passage of your age!
    Mor.   Thou dost then wrong me, as that slaughterer doth   109
Which giveth many wounds when one will kill.
Mourn not, except thou sorrow for my good;
Only give order for my funeral:
And so farewell, and fair be all thy hopes
And prosperous be thy life in peace and war! [*Dies.*
    Plan.   And peace, no war, befall thy parting soul!
In prison hast thou spent a pilgrimage
And like a hermit overpass'd thy days.
Well, I will lock his counsel in my breast;
And what I do imagine let that rest.
Keepers, convey him hence, and I myself   120
Will see his burial better than his life.
        [*Exeunt Gaolers, bearing out the body
                of Mortimer.*
● Here dies the dusky torch of Mortimer,
Choked with ambition of the meaner sort:
And for those wrongs, those bitter injuries,
Which Somerset hath offer'd to my house,
I doubt not but with honour to redress;
And therefore haste I to the parliament,
Either to be restored to my blood,
Or make my ill the advantage of my good. [*Exit.*

ACT III.

SCENE I. *London. The Parliament-house.*

Flourish. Enter KING, EXETER, GLOUCESTER, WARWICK, SOMERSET, *and* SUFFOLK; *the* BISHOP OF WINCHESTER, RICHARD PLANTAGENET, *and others.* GLOUCESTER *offers to put up a bill;* WINCHESTER *snatches it, and tears it.*

Win. Comest thou with deep premeditated lines,
With written pamphlets studiously devised,
Humphrey of Gloucester? If thou canst accuse,
Or aught intend'st to lay unto my charge,
Do it without invention, suddenly;
As I with sudden and extemporal speech
Purpose to answer what thou canst object.
　Glou. Presumptuous priest! this place commands my patience,
Or thou shouldst find thou hast dishonour'd me.
Think not, although in writing I preferr'd　10
The manner of thy vile outrageous crimes,
That therefore I have forged, or am not able
● Verbatim to rehearse the method of my pen:
No, prelate; such is thy audacious wickedness,
● Thy lewd, pestiferous and dissentious pranks,
As very infants prattle of thy pride.
Thou art a most pernicious usurer,
Froward by nature, enemy to peace;
Lascivious, wanton, more than well beseems
A man of thy profession and degree;　20
And for thy treachery, what's more manifest?
In that thou laid'st a trap to take my life,
As well at London bridge as at the Tower.
Beside, I fear me, if thy thoughts were sifted,
The king, thy sovereign, is not quite exempt
From envious malice of thy swelling heart.
　Win. Gloucester, I do defy thee. Lords, vouchsafe
To give me hearing what I shall reply.
If I were covetous, ambitious or perverse,
As he will have me, how am I so poor?　30
Or how haps it I seek not to advance
Or raise myself, but keep my wonted calling?
And for dissension, who preferreth peace
More than I do?—except I be provoked.
No, my good lords, it is not that offends;
It is not that that hath incensed the duke:
It is, because no one should sway but he;
No one but he should be about the king;
And that engenders thunder in his breast
And makes him roar these accusations forth.　40
But he shall know I am as good—
　Glou.　　　　　　　As good!
● Thou bastard of my grandfather!
　Win. Ay, lordly sir; for what are you, I pray,
● But one imperious in another's throne?
　Glou. Am I not protector, saucy priest?
　Win. And am not I a prelate of the church?
　Glou. Yes, as an outlaw in a castle keeps
And useth it to patronage his theft.
　Win. Unreverent Gloster!
　Glou.　　　　　　Thou art reverent
Touching thy spiritual function, not thy life.　50
　Win. Rome shall remedy this.
　War.　　　　　Roam thither, then.
　Som. My lord, it were your duty to forbear.
　War. Ay, see the bishop be not overborne.
　Som. Methinks my lord should be religious

Winchester: 'Comest thou with deep premeditated lines . . .' Gloucester (Edgar Wreford), Henry VI (Jack May) and Winchester (Alfred Burke), Old Vic, 1955

SD *Bill.* A petition in Parliament; in this case a bill of indictment against Winchester.

13 *rehearse . . . pen.* Recount what I have written.

15 *lewd.* Wicked, depraved. *pestiferous.* Pernicious.

42 *bastard.* Winchester was an illegitimate son of John of Gaunt, Duke of Lancaster.

44 *imperious.* Ruling.

63 *verdict*. Decision at law. The reference is to Gloucester's claim to be restored to his father's lands and titles. *enter talk*. Come under discussion.

64 *have a fling*. Make a verbal assault.

66 *weal*. Common good.

99 *inkhorn mate*. Pedant, bookworm.

Notary carrying pen and ink-horn on his belt. Engraving by F.W. Fairholt from J.O. Halliwell's edition of Shakespeare's works, 1853–65

And know the office that belongs to such.
  War. Methinks his lordship should be humbler;
It fitteth not a prelate so to plead.
  Som. Yes, when his holy state is touch'd so near.
  War. State holy or unhallow'd, what of that?
Is not his grace protector to the king?   60
  Plan. [*Aside*] Plantagenet, I see, must hold his tongue,
Lest it be said 'Speak, sirrah, when you should;
• Must your bold verdict enter talk with lords?'
• Else would I have a fling at Winchester.
  King. Uncles of Gloucester and of Winchester,
• The special watchmen of our English weal,
I would prevail, if prayers might prevail,
To join your hearts in love and amity.
O, what a scandal is it to our crown,
That two such noble peers as ye should jar!   70
Believe me, lords, my tender years can tell
Civil dissension is a viperous worm
That gnaws the bowels of the commonwealth.
  [*A noise within*, 'Down with the tawny-coats!'
What tumult's this?
  War.   An uproar, I dare warrant,
Begun through malice of the bishop's men.
                   [*A noise again*, 'Stones! stones!'

Enter Mayor.

  May. O, my good lords, and virtuous Henry,
Pity the city of London, pity us!
The bishop and the Duke of Gloucester's men,
Forbidden late to carry any weapon,
Have fill'd their pockets full of pebble stones 80
And banding themselves in contrary parts
Do pelt so fast at one another's pate
That many have their giddy brains knock'd out:
Our windows are broke down in every street
And we for fear compell'd to shut our shops.

Enter Serving-men, *in skirmish, with bloody pates.*

  King. We charge you, on allegiance to ourself,
To hold your slaughtering hands and keep the peace.
Pray, uncle Gloucester, mitigate this strife.
  First Serv. Nay, if we be forbidden stones,
we'll fall to it with our teeth.   90
  Sec. Serv. Do what ye dare, we are as resolute.   [*Skirmish again.*
  Glou. You of my household, leave this peevish broil
And set this unaccustom'd fight aside.
  Third Serv. My lord, we know your grace to be a man
Just and upright; and, for your royal birth,
Inferior to none but to his majesty:
And ere that we will suffer such a prince,
So kind a father of the commonweal,
• To be disgraced by an inkhorn mate,
We and our wives and children all will fight 100
And have our bodies slaughter'd by thy foes.
  First Serv. Ay, and the very parings of our nails
Shall pitch a field when we are dead.
                              [*Begin again.*
  Glou.   Stay, stay, I say!
And if you love me, as you say you do,
Let me persuade you to forbear awhile.
  King. O, how this discord doth afflict my soul!

Can you, my Lord of Winchester, behold
My sighs and tears and will not once relent?
Who should be pitiful, if you be not?
Or who should study to prefer a peace,   110
If holy churchmen take delight in broils?
   War. Yield, my lord protector; yield, Winchester,
Except you mean with obstinate repulse
To slay your sovereign and destroy the realm.
You see what mischief and what murder too
Hath been enacted through your enmity;
Then be at peace, except ye thirst for blood.
   Win. He shall submit, or I will never yield.
   Glou. Compassion on the king commands me stoop;
Or I would see his heart out, ere the priest   120
● Should ever get that privilege of me.
   War. Behold, my Lord of Winchester, the duke
Hath banish'd moody discontented fury,
As by his smoothed brows it doth appear:
Why look you still so stern and tragical?
   Glou. Here, Winchester, I offer thee my hand.
   King. Fie, uncle Beaufort! I have heard you preach
That malice was a great and grievous sin;
And will not you maintain the thing you teach,
But prove a chief offender in the same?   130
● *War.* Sweet king! the bishop hath a kindly gird.
For shame, my lord of Winchester, relent!
What, shall a child instruct you what to do?
   Win. Well, Duke of Gloucester, I will yield to thee;
Love for thy love and hand for hand I give.
   Glou. [*Aside*] Ay, but, I fear me, with a hollow heart.—
See here, my friends and loving countrymen,
This token serveth for a flag of truce
Betwixt ourselves and all our followers:
So help me God, as I dissemble not!   140
   Win. [*Aside*] So help me God, as I intend it not!
   King. O loving uncle, kind Duke of Gloucester,
How joyful am I made by this contract!
Away, my masters! trouble us no more;
But join in friendship, as your lords have done.
   First Serv. Content: I'll to the surgeon's.
   Sec. Serv.   And so will I.
   Third Serv. And I will see what physic the tavern affords.
          [*Exeunt Serving-men, Mayor, &c.*
   War. Accept this scroll, most gracious sovereign,
Which in the right of Richard Plantagenet   150
We do exhibit to your majesty.
   Glou. Well urged, my Lord of Warwick: for, sweet prince,
An if your grace mark every circumstance,
You have great reason to do Richard right:
Especially for those occasions
At Eltham Place I told your majesty.
   King. And those occasions, uncle, were of force:
Therefore, my loving lords, our pleasure is
● That Richard be restored to his blood.
   War. Let Richard be restored to his blood;
So shall his father's wrongs be recompensed   161
   Win. As will the rest, so willeth Winchester
   King. If Richard will be true, not that alone

121 *privilege.* Advantage, i.e. that I should be the first to yield.

131 *kindly gird.* The king's rebuke is apposite as he is urging Winchester to practise the precepts of the religion he preaches.

Humphrey, Duke of Gloucester. Engraving from a 15th century painted window by F.W. Fairholt from J.O. Halliwell's edition of Shakespeare's works, 1853–65

159 *restored to his blood.* Have his lands and titles returned.

170 *reguerdon.* Recompense, reward.

183 *disanimates.* Discourages.

2 *policy.* Stratagem.

View of Rouen. Engraving from *Old England*, 1854

But all the whole inheritance I give
That doth belong unto the house of York,
From whence you spring by lineal descent.
   Plan. Thy humble servant vows obedience
And humble service till the point of death.
   King. Stoop then and set your knee against
    my foot;
And, in reguerdon of that duty done,   170
I gird thee with the valiant sword of York:
Rise, Richard, like a true Plantagenet,
And rise created princely Duke of York.
   Plan. And so thrive Richard as thy foes may
    fall!
And as my duty springs, so perish they
That grudge one thought against your majesty!
   All. Welcome, high prince, the mighty Duke
    of York!
   Som. [*Aside*] Perish, base prince, ignoble
    Duke of York!
   Glou. Now will it best avail your majesty
To cross the seas and to be crown'd in France:
The presence of a king engenders love   181
Amongst his subjects and his loyal friends,
As it disanimates his enemies.
   King. When Gloucester says the word, King
    Henry goes;
For friendly counsel cuts off many foes.
   Glou. Your ships already are in readiness.
   [*Sennet. Flourish. Exeunt all but Exeter.*
   Exe. Ay, we may march in England or in
    France,
Not seeing what is likely to ensue.
This late dissension grown betwixt the peers
Burns under feigned ashes of forged love   190
And will at last break out into a flame:
As fester'd members rot but by degree,
Till bones and flesh and sinews fall away,
So will this base and envious discord breed.
And now I fear that fatal prophecy
Which in the time of Henry named the Fifth
Was in the mouth of every sucking babe;
That Henry born at Monmouth should win all
And Henry born at Windsor lose all:
Which is so plain that Exeter doth wish   200
His days may finish ere that hapless time. [*Exit.*

      SCENE II. *France. Before Rouen.*

Enter LA PUCELLE *disguised, with four* Soldiers
with sacks upon their backs.

   Puc. These are the city gates, the gates of
    Rouen,
Through which our policy must make a breach:
Take heed, be wary how you place your words;
Talk like the vulgar sort of market men
That come to gather money for their corn.
If we have entrance, as I hope we shall,
And that we find the slothful watch but weak,
I'll by a sign give notice to our friends,
That Charles the Dauphin may encounter them.
   First Sol. Our sacks shall be a mean to sack
    the city,   10
And we be lords and rulers over Rouen;
Therefore we'll knock.   [*Knocks.*
   Watch. [*Within*] Qui est là?
   Puc. Paysans, pauvres gens de France;
Poor market folks that come to sell their corn.
   Watch. Enter, go in; the market bell is rung.

Puc. Now, Rouen, I'll shake thy bulwarks to
the ground.   [*Exeunt.*

Enter CHARLES, *the* BASTARD *of Orleans,*
ALENÇON, REIGNIER, *and forces.*

Char. Saint Denis bless this happy stratagem!
And once again we'll sleep secure in Rouen.
  • *Bast.* Here enter'd Pucelle and her practisants;
Now she is there, how will she specify   21
Where is the best and safest passage in?
    Reign. By thrusting out a torch from yonder
tower;
Which, once discern'd, shows that her meaning is,
No way to that, for weakness, which she enter'd.

Enter LA PUCELLE *on the top, thrusting out a
torch burning.*

    Puc. Behold, this is the happy wedding torch
That joineth Rouen unto her countrymen,
But burning fatal to the Talbotites!   [*Exit.*
    Bast. See, noble Charles, the beacon of our
friend;
The burning torch in yonder turret stands.   30
    Char. Now shine it like a comet of revenge,
A prophet to the fall of all our foes!
    Reign. Defer no time, delays have dangerous
ends:
  • Enter, and cry 'The Dauphin!' presently,
And then do execution on the watch.
        [*Alarum. Exeunt.*

An alarum. Enter TALBOT *in an excursion.*

    Tal. France, thou shalt rue this treason with
thy tears,
If Talbot but survive thy treachery.
Pucelle, that witch, that damned sorceress,
Hath wrought this hellish mischief unawares,
That hardly we escaped the pride of France.   40
        [*Exit.*

An alarum: excursions. BEDFORD, *brought in
sick in a chair. Enter* TALBOT *and* BURGUN-
DY *without: within* LA PUCELLE, CHARLES,
BASTARD, ALENÇON, *and* REIGNIER, *on the
walls.*

    Puc. Good morrow, gallants! want ye corn
for bread?
I think the Duke of Burgundy will fast
Before he'll buy again at such a rate:
  • 'Twas full of darnel; do you like the taste?
    Bur. Scoff on, vile fiend and shameless court-
ezan!
I trust ere long to choke thee with thine own
And make thee curse the harvest of that corn.
    Char. Your grace may starve perhaps before
that time.
    Bed. O, let no words, but deeds, revenge this
treason!
    Puc. What will you do, good grey-beard?
break a lance,   50
And run a tilt at death within a chair?
  • *Tal.* Foul fiend of France, and hag of all
despite,
Encompass'd with thy lustful paramours!
Becomes it thee to taunt his valiant age
And twit with cowardice a man half dead?
Damsel, I'll have a bout with you again,
Or else let Talbot perish with this shame.

Pucelle: 'Behold, this is the happy wedding torch'.
Engraving by Kenny Meadows from Barry Cornwall's
Works of Shakespeare, 1846

20 *practisants.* Plotters.

34 *presently.* Immediately.

44 *darnel.* Weeds.

52 *hag of all despite.* Malicious witch.

64 *Hecate*. Goddess of witchcraft.

Hecate, three-fold goddess of the moon, the underworld and witchcraft. From a 19th century engraving

83 *Cœur-de-lion's*. King Richard the Lion-Heart's.

89 *crazy*. Feeble, broken down.

95 *Pendragon*. Uther Pendragon, the father of King Arthur.

Puc. Are ye so hot, sir? yet, Pucelle, hold thy peace;
If Talbot do but thunder, rain will follow.
  [*The English whisper together in council.*
God speed the parliament! who shall be the speaker? 60
  Tal. Dare ye come forth and meet us in the field?
  Puc. Belike your lordship takes us then for fools,
To try if that our own be ours or no.
  Tal. I speak not to that railing Hecate,
But unto thee, Alençon, and the rest;
Will ye, like soldiers, come and fight it out?
  Alen. Signior, no.
  Tal. Signior, hang! base muleters of France!
Like peasant foot-boys do they keep the walls
And dare not take up arms like gentlemen. 70
  Puc. Away, captains! let's get us from the walls;
For Talbot means no goodness by his looks.
God be wi' you, my lord! we came but to tell you
That we are here.   [*Exeunt from the walls.*
  Tal. And there will we be too, ere it be long,
Or else reproach be Talbot's greatest fame!
Vow, Burgundy, by honour of thy house,
Prick'd on by public wrongs sustain'd in France,
Either to get the town again or die:
And I, as sure as English Henry lives 80
And as his father here was conqueror,
As sure as in this late-betrayed town
Great Cœur-de-lion's heart was buried,
So sure I swear to get the town or die.
  Bur. My vows are equal partners with thy vows.
  Tal. But, ere we go, regard this dying prince,
The valiant Duke of Bedford. Come, my lord,
We will bestow you in some better place,
Fitter for sickness and for crazy age.
  Bed. Lord Talbot, do not so dishonour me:
Here will I sit before the walls of Rouen 91
And will be partner of your weal or woe.
  Bur. Courageous Bedford, let us now persuade you.
  Bed. Not to be gone from hence; for once I read
That stout Pendragon in his litter sick
Came to the field and vanquished his foes:
Methinks I should revive the soldiers' hearts,
Because I ever found them as myself.
  Tal. Undaunted spirit in a dying breast!
Then be it so: heavens keep old Bedford safe!
And now no more ado, brave Burgundy, 101
But gather we our forces out of hand
And set upon our boasting enemy.
  [*Exeunt all but Bedford and Attendants.*

An alarum: excursions. Enter SIR JOHN FASTOLFE *and a* Captain.

  Cap. Whither away, Sir John Fastolfe, in such haste?
  Fast. Whither away! to save myself by flight:
We are like to have the overthrow again.
  Cap. What! will you fly, and leave Lord Talbot?
  Fast.   Ay,
All the Talbots in the world, to save my life.
  [*Exit.*

Cap. Cowardly knight! ill fortune follow
thee! [*Exit.*

Retreat: excursions. LA PUCELLE, ALENÇON,
and CHARLES *fly.*

Bed. Now, quiet soul, depart when heaven
please, 110
For I have seen our enemies' overthrow.
What is the trust or strength of foolish man?
They that of late were daring with their scoffs
Are glad and fain by flight to save themselves.
[*Bedford dies, and is carried in by two in
his chair.*

An alarum. Re-enter TALBOT, BURGUNDY,
and the rest.

Tal. Lost, and recover'd in a day again!
This is a double honour, Burgundy:
Yet heavens have glory for this victory!
Bur. Warlike and martial Talbot, Burgundy
Enshrines thee in his heart and there erects
Thy noble deeds as valour's monuments. 120
Tal. Thanks, gentle duke. But where is
Pucelle now?
● I think her old familiar is asleep:
● Now where's the Bastard's braves, and Charles
his gleeks?
● What, all amort? Rouen hangs her head for
grief
That such a valiant company are fled.
Now will we take some order in the town,
Placing therein some expert officers,
And then depart to Paris to the king,
For there young Henry with his nobles lie.
Bur. What wills Lord Talbot pleaseth Bur-
gundy. 130
Tal. But yet, before we go, let's not forget
The noble Duke of Bedford late deceased,
● But see his exequies fulfill'd in Rouen:
● A braver soldier never couched lance,
A gentler heart did never sway in court;
But kings and mightiest potentates must die,
For that's the end of human misery. [*Exeunt.*

SCENE III. *The plains near Rouen.*

Enter CHARLES, *the* BASTARD *of Orleans,*
ALENÇON, LA PUCELLE, *and forces.*

Puc. Dismay not, princes, at this accident,
Nor grieve that Rouen is so recovered:
Care is no cure, but rather corrosive,
For things that are not to be remedied.
Let frantic Talbot triumph for a while
And like a peacock sweep along his tail;
We'll pull his plumes and take away his train,
If Dauphin and the rest will be but ruled.
Char. We have been guided by thee hitherto
● And of thy cunning had no diffidence: 10
One sudden foil shall never breed distrust.
Bast. Search out thy wit for secret policies,
And we will make thee famous through the world.
Alen. We'll set thy statue in some holy place,
And have thee reverenced like a blessed saint:
Employ thee then, sweet virgin, for our good.
Puc. Then thus it must be; this doth Joan
devise:
By fair persuasions mix'd with sugar'd words
We will entice the Duke of Burgundy
To leave the Talbot and to follow us. 20

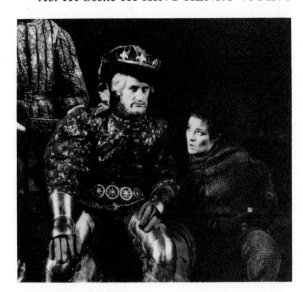

Charles (Charles Kay) and Joan (Janet Suzman), Royal
Shakespeare Co, 1964

122 *familiar.* A witch's assistant spirit.

123 *braves.* Bravado, taunts. *gleeks.* Gibes.

124 *amort.* Dispirited. dejected.

133 *exequies.* Funeral rites.

134 *couched lance.* i.e. the point being lowered ready for
an attack.

10 *diffidence.* Lack of confidence.

21 *sweeting.* Sweetheart.

24 *extirped.* Extirpated, rooted out.

    Char. Ay, marry, sweeting, if we could do that,
France were no place for Henry's warriors;
Nor should that nation boast it so with us,
But be extirped from our provinces.
    Alen. For ever should they be expulsed from France
And not have title of an earldom here.
    Puc. Your honours shall perceive how I will work
To bring this matter to the wished end.
                      [*Drum sounds afar off.*
Hark! by the sound of drum you may perceive
Their powers are marching unto Paris-ward.   30

Here sound an English march. Enter, and pass over at a distance, TALBOT *and his forces.*

There goes the Talbot, with his colours spread,
And all the troops of English after him.

French march. Enter the DUKE OF BURGUNDY *and forces.*

Now in the rearward comes the duke and his:
Fortune in favour makes him lag behind.
Summon a parley; we will talk with him.
                  [*Trumpets sound a parley.*
    Char. A parley with the Duke of Burgundy!
    Bur. Who craves a parley with the Burgundy?
    Puc. The princely Charles of France, thy countryman.
    Bur. What say'st thou, Charles? for I am marching hence.
    Char. Speak, Pucelle, and enchant him with thy words.   40
    Puc. Brave Burgundy, undoubted hope of France!
Stay, let thy humble handmaid speak to thee.
    Bur. Speak on; but be not over-tedious.
    Puc. Look on thy country, look on fertile France,
And see the cities and the towns defaced
By wasting ruin of the cruel foe.
As looks the mother on her lowly babe
When death doth close his tender dying eyes,
See, see the pining malady of France;   49
Behold the wounds, the most unnatural wounds,
Which thou thyself hast given her woful breast.
O, turn thy edged sword another way;
Strike those that hurt, and hurt not those that help.
One drop of blood drawn from thy country's bosom
Should grieve thee more than streams of foreign gore:
Return thee therefore with a flood of tears,
And wash away thy country's stained spots.
    Bur. Either she hath bewitch'd me with her words,
Or nature makes me suddenly relent.
    Puc. Besides, all French and France exclaims on thee,   60
Doubting thy birth and lawful progeny.
Who join'st thou with but with a lordly nation
That will not trust thee but for profit's sake?
When Talbot hath set footing once in France
And fashion'd thee that instrument of ill,
Who then but English Henry will be lord
And thou be thrust out like a fugitive?

Call we to mind, and mark but this for proof,
Was not the Duke of Orleans thy foe?
And was he not in England prisoner? 70
But when they heard he was thine enemy,
They set him free without his ransom paid,
In spite of Burgundy and all his friends.
See, then, thou fight'st against thy countrymen
And join'st with them will be thy slaughter-men.
Come, come, return; return, thou wandering
  lord
Charles and the rest will take thee in their arms.
  Bur. I am vanquished; these haughty words
    of hers
Have batter'd me like roaring cannon-shot,
And made me almost yield upon my knees. 80
Forgive me, country, and sweet countrymen,
And, lords, accept this hearty kind embrace:
My forces and my power of men are yours:
So farewell, Talbot; I'll no longer trust thee.
  Puc. [*Aside*] Done like a Frenchman: turn,
    and turn again!
  Char. Welcome, brave duke! thy friendship
    makes us fresh.
  Bast. And doth beget new courage in our
    breasts.
  Alen. Pucelle hath bravely play'd her part in
    this,
And doth deserve a coronet of gold.
  Char. Now let us on, my lords, and join our
    powers, 90
● And seek how we may prejudice the foe.
                                        [*Exeunt.*

SCENE IV. *Paris. The palace.*

Enter the KING, GLOUCESTER, BISHOP OF WIN-
CHESTER, YORK, SUFFOLK, SOMERSET, WAR-
WICK, EXETER: VERNON, BASSET, *and others.*
To them with his Soldiers, TALBOT.

  Tal. My gracious prince, and honourable
    peers,
Hearing of your arrival in this realm,
I have awhile given truce unto my wars,
To do my duty to my sovereign:
In sign whereof, this arm, that hath reclaim'd
To your obedience fifty fortresses,
Twelve cities and seven walled towns of strength,
Beside five hundred prisoners of esteem,
Lets fall his sword before your highness' feet,
And with submissive loyalty of heart 10
Ascribes the glory of his conquest got
First to my God and next unto your grace.
                                        [*Kneels.*
  King. Is this the Lord Talbot, uncle Glou-
    cester,
That hath so long been resident in France?
  Glou. Yes, if it please your majesty, my
    liege.
  King. Welcome, brave captain and victorious
    lord!
When I was young, as yet I am not old,
I do remember how my father said
A stouter champion never handled sword.
Long since we were resolved of your truth, 20
Your faithful service and your toil in war;
Yet never have you tasted our reward,
● Or been reguerdon'd with so much as thanks,
Because till now we never saw your face:
Therefore, stand up; and, for these good deserts,

View of Paris. From John Speed's *A Prospect of the Most
Famous Parts of the World,* 1631

91 *prejudice.* Injure.

23 *reguerdon'd.* Rewarded.

Talbot, Earl of Shrewsbury, receives a sword from the King. Engraving from a contemporary manuscript

38 *law of arms.* Fighting in the king's palace was a punishable offence.

44 *miscreant.* Wretch.

15 *craven's leg.* Coward's leg.

We here create you Earl of Shrewsbury;
And in our coronation take your place.
    [*Sennet. Flourish. Exeunt all but Vernon*
                        and Basset.
    Ver. Now, sir, to you, that were so hot at
    sea,
Disgracing of these colours that I wear
In honour of my noble Lord of York: 30
Darest thou maintain the former words thou
    spakest?
    Bas. Yes, sir; as well as you dare patronage
The envious barking of your saucy tongue
Against my lord the Duke of Somerset.
    Ver. Sirrah, thy lord I honour as he is.
    Bas. Why, what is he? as good a man as
    York.
    Ver. Hark ye; not so: in witness, take ye
    that.   [*Strikes him.*
    Bas. Villain, thou know'st the law of arms is
    such
That whoso draws a sword, 'tis present death,
Or else this blow should broach thy dearest
    blood.   40
But I'll unto his majesty, and crave
I may have liberty to venge this wrong;
When thou shalt see I'll meet thee to thy cost.
    Ver. Well, miscreant, I'll be there as soon
    as you;
And, after, meet you sooner than you would.
                        [*Exeunt.*

ACT IV.

SCENE I. *Paris. A hall of state.*

Enter the KING, GLOUCESTER, BISHOP OF WIN-
CHESTER, YORK, SUFFOLK, SOMERSET, WAR-
WICK, TALBOT, EXETER, *the* Governor of
Paris, *and others.*

    Glou. Lord bishop, set the crown upon his
    head.
    Win. God save King Henry, of that name
    the sixth!
    Glou. Now, governor of Paris, take your oath,
That you elect no other king but him;
Esteem none friends but such as are his friends,
And none your foes but such as shall pretend
Malicious practices against his state:
This shall ye do, so help you righteous God!

Enter SIR JOHN FASTOLFE.

    Fast. My gracious sovereign, as I rode from
    Calais,
To haste unto your coronation,   10
A letter was deliver'd to my hands,
Writ to your grace from the Duke of Burgundy.
    Tal. Shame to the Duke of Burgundy and
    thee!
I vow'd, base knight, when I did meet thee next,
To tear the garter from thy craven's leg,
                    [*Plucking it off.*
Which I have done, because unworthily
Thou wast installed in that high degree.
Pardon me, princely Henry, and the rest:
This dastard, at the battle of Patay,
When but in all I was six thousand strong   20
And that the French were almost ten to one,
Before we met or that a stroke was given,
Like to a trusty squire did run away:

In which assault we lost twelve hundred men;
Myself and divers gentlemen beside
Were there surprised and taken prisoners.
Then judge, great lords, if I have done amiss;
Or whether that such cowards ought to wear
This ornament of knighthood, yea or no.
    Glou. To say the truth, this fact was infamous
And ill beseeming any common man,   31
Much more a knight, a captain and a leader.
    Tal. When first this order was ordain'd, my lords,
Knights of the garter were of noble birth,
Valiant and virtuous, full of haughty courage,
Such as were grown to credit by the wars;
Not fearing death, nor shrinking for distress,
But always resolute in most extremes.
He then that is not furnish'd in this sort
Doth but usurp the sacred name of knight,   40
Profaning this most honourable order,
And should, if I were worthy to be judge,
● Be quite degraded, like a hedge-born swain
That doth presume to boast of gentle blood:
    King. Stain to thy countrymen, thou hear'st thy doom!
Be packing, therefore, thou that wast a knight:
Henceforth we banish thee, on pain of death.
                       [*Exit Fastolfe.*
And now, my lord protector, view the letter
Sent from our uncle Duke of Burgundy.
    Glou. What means his grace, that he hath changed his style?   50
No more but, plain and bluntly, 'To the king!'
Hath he forgot he is his sovereign?
Or doth this churlish superscription
Pretend some alteration in good will?
What's here? [*Reads*] 'I have, upon especial cause,
Moved with compassion of my country's wreck,
Together with the pitiful complaints
Of such as your oppression feeds upon,
Forsaken your pernicious faction
And join'd with Charles, the rightful King of France.'   60
O monstrous treachery! can this be so,
That in alliance, amity and oaths,
There should be found such false dissembling guile?
    King. What! doth my uncle Burgundy revolt?
    Glou. He doth, my lord, and is become your foe.
    King. Is that the worst this letter doth contain?
    Glou. It is the worst, and all, my lord, he writes.
    King. Why, then, Lord Talbot there shall talk with him
And give him chastisement for this abuse.
How say you, my lord? are you not content?   70
●   *Tal.* Content, my liege! yes, but that I am prevented,
I should have begg'd I might have been employ'd.
    King. Then gather strength and march unto him straight:
Let him perceive how ill we brook his treason
And what offence it is to flout his friends.
    Tal. I go, my lord, in heart desiring still
You may behold confusion of your foes. [*Exit.*

43 *hedge-born swain.* Base-born peasant.

Gloucester reads the news of Burgundy's defection to the French. Engraving by Kenny Meadows from Barry Cornwall's *Works of Shakspere*, 1846

71 *prevented.* Anticipated.

78 *Grant me the combat.* i.e. permission to fight a duel.

92 *sanguine colour.* Blood-red.

94 *repugn.* Oppose, deny.

98 *confutation.* Refutation.

102 *forged quaint conceit.* Artful phraseology.

103 *set a gloss . . . intent.* Give a glittering surface to deceive.

107 *Bewray'd.* Betrayed.

113 *emulations.* Rivalries.

120 *pledge.* Challenge.

Enter VERNON *and* BASSET.

●   *Ver.* Grant me the combat, gracious sovereign.
   Bas.   And me, my lord, grant me the combat too.
   York.   This is my servant: hear him, noble prince.   80
   Som.   And this is mine: sweet Henry, favour him.
   King.   Be patient, lords; and give them leave to speak.
Say, gentlemen, what makes you thus exclaim?
And wherefore crave you combat? or with whom?
   Ver.   With him, my lord; for he hath done me wrong.
   Bas.   And I with him; for he hath done me wrong.
   King.   What is that wrong whereof you both complain?
First let me know, and then I'll answer you.
   Bas.   Crossing the sea from England into France,
This fellow here, with envious carping tongue,
Upbraided me about the rose I wear;   91
● Saying, the sanguine colour of the leaves
Did represent my master's blushing cheeks,
● When stubbornly he did repugn the truth
About a certain question in the law
Argued betwixt the Duke of York and him;
With other vile and ignominious terms:
● In confutation of which rude reproach
And in defence of my lord's worthiness,
I crave the benefit of law of arms.   100
   Ver.   And that is my petition, noble lord:
● For though he seem with forged quaint conceit
● To set a gloss upon his bold intent,
Yet know, my lord, I was provoked by him;
And he first took exceptions at this badge,
Pronouncing that the paleness of this flower
● Bewray'd the faintness of my master's heart.
   York.   Will not this malice, Somerset, be left?
   Som.   Your private grudge, my Lord of York, will out,
Though ne'er so cunningly you smother it.   110
   King.   Good Lord, what madness rules in brainsick men,
When for so slight and frivolous a cause
● Such factious emulations shall arise!
Good cousins both, of York and Somerset,
Quiet yourselves, I pray, and be at peace.
   York.   Let this dissension first be tried by fight,
And then your highness shall command a peace.
   Som.   The quarrel toucheth none but us alone;
Betwixt ourselves let us decide it then.   119
●   *York.*   There is my pledge; accept it, Somerset.
   Ver.   Nay, let it rest where it began at first.
   Bas.   Confirm it so, mine honourable lord.
   Glou.   Confirm it so! Confounded be your strife!
And perish ye, with your audacious prate!
Presumptuous vassals, are you not ashamed
With this immodest clamorous outrage
To trouble and disturb the king and us?
And you, my lords, methinks you do not well
To bear with their perverse objections;
Much less to take occasion from their mouths   130
To raise a mutiny betwixt yourselves:
Let me persuade you take a better course.

Exe. It grieves his highness: good my lords,
be friends.
King.   Come hither, you that would be
combatants:
Henceforth I charge you, as you love our favour,
Quite to forget this quarrel and the cause.
And you, my lords, remember where we are;
In France, amongst a fickle wavering nation:
If they perceive dissension in our looks
And that within ourselves we disagree,   140
● How will their grudging stomachs be provoked
To wilful disobedience, and rebel!
Beside, what infamy will there arise,
When foreign princes shall be certified
That for a toy, a thing of no regard,
King Henry's peers and chief nobility
Destroy'd themselves, and lost the realm of
France!
O, think upon the conquest of my father,
My tender years, and let us not forego
That for a trifle that was bought with blood! 150
Let me be umpire in this doubtful strife.
I see no reason, if I wear this rose,
                    [*Putting on a red rose.*
That any one should therefore be suspicious
I more incline to Somerset than York:
Both are my kinsmen, and I love them both:
As well they may upbraid me with my crown,
Because, forsooth, the king of Scots is crown'd.
But your discretions better can persuade
Than I am able to instruct or teach:
And therefore, as we hither came in peace,   160
So let us still continue peace and love.
Cousin of York, we institute your grace
To be our regent in these parts of France:
And, good my Lord of Somerset, unite
Your troops of horsemen with his bands of foot:
And, like true subjects, sons of your progenitors,
Go cheerfully together and digest
Your angry choler on your enemies.
Ourself, my lord protector and the rest
After some respite will return to Calais;   170
From thence to England; where I hope ere long
To be presented, by your victories,
With Charles, Alençon and that traitorous rout.
          [*Flourish. Exeunt all but York, Warwick,
                              Exeter and Vernon.*
War. My Lord of York, I promise you, the
king
Prettily, methought, did play the orator.
York. And so he did; but yet I like it not,
In that he wears the badge of Somerset.
War. Tush, that was but his fancy, blame
him not;
I dare presume, sweet prince, he thought no
harm.
York. An if I wist he did,—but let it rest; 180
Other affairs must now be managed.
                    [*Exeunt all but Exeter.*
Exe. Well didst thou, Richard, to suppress
thy voice;
For, had the passions of thy heart burst out,
I fear we should have seen decipher'd there
More rancorous spite, more furious raging broils,
Than yet can be imagined or supposed.
But howsoe'er, no simple man that sees
This jarring discord of nobility,
This shouldering of each other in the court,
This factious bandying of their favourites,   190

141 *grudging stomachs.* Rebellious dispositions.

Henry VI. Engraving from *Old England*, 1854

An army storms a city's walls. Woodcut from Holinshed's *Chronicles*, 1577

---

11 *quartering*. Dividing the body into quarters.

15 *owl of death*. In Ovid, the owl is a messenger of death.

26 *apparent spoil*. Obvious annihilation.

28 *ta'en the sacrament*. i.e. taken a solemn vow at Holy Communion.

29 *rive*. Fire.

45 *park'd . . . pale*. A comparison (lines 45–54) of Talbot's force, trapped by the French, to deer at bay in a pale (i.e. fenced-in area).

49 *rascal-like*. Like the poorest deer of the herd.

But that it doth presage some ill event.
'Tis much when sceptres are in children's hands;
But more when envy breeds unkind division;
There comes the ruin, there begins confusion.
                                                    [*Exit.*

SCENE II. *Before Bourdeaux.*

Enter TALBOT, *with trump and drum.*

Tal.   Go to the gates of Bourdeaux, trumpeter;
Summon their general unto the wall.

Trumpet sounds.   Enter General *and others, aloft.*

English John Talbot, captains, calls you forth,
Servant in arms to Harry King of England;
And thus he would: Open your city gates;
Be humble to us; call my sovereign yours,
And do him homage as obedient subjects;
And I'll withdraw me and my bloody power:
But, if you frown upon this proffer'd peace,
You tempt the fury of my three attendants,   10
● Lean famine, quartering steel, and climbing fire;
Who in a moment even with the earth
Shall lay your stately and air-braving towers,
If you forsake the offer of their love.
● *Gen.*   Thou ominous and fearful owl of death,
Our nation's terror and their bloody scourge!
The period of thy tyranny approacheth.
On us thou canst not enter but by death;
For, I protest, we are well fortified
And strong enough to issue out and fight: 20
If thou retire, the Dauphin, well appointed,
Stands with the snares of war to tangle thee:
On either hand thee there are squadrons pitch'd,
To wall thee from the liberty of flight;
And no way canst thou turn thee for redress,
● But death doth front thee with apparent spoil
And pale destruction meets thee in the face.
● Ten thousand French have ta'en the sacrament
● To rive their dangerous artillery
Upon no Christian soul but English Talbot.   30
Lo, there thou stand'st, a breathing valiant man,
Of an invincible unconquer'd spirit!
This is the latest glory of thy praise
That I, thy enemy, due thee withal;
For ere the glass, that now begins to run,
Finish the process of his sandy hour,
These eyes, that see thee now well coloured,
Shall see thee wither'd, bloody, pale and dead.
                                                    [*Drum afar off.*
Hark! hark! the Dauphin's drum, a warning bell,
Sings heavy music to thy timorous soul;   40
And mine shall ring thy dire departure out.
                                                    [*Exeunt General, &c.*
Tal.   He fables not; I hear the enemy:
Out, some light horsemen, and peruse their wings.
O, negligent and heedless discipline!
● How are we park'd and bounded in a pale,
A little herd of England's timorous deer,
Mazed with a yelping kennel of French curs!
If we be English deer, be then in blood;
● Not rascal-like, to fall down with a pinch,
But rather, moody-mad and desperate stags,   50
Turn on the bloody hounds with heads of steel
And make the cowards stand aloof at bay:
Sell every man his life as dear as mine,
And they shall find dear deer of us, my friends.

God and Saint George, Talbot and England's
  right,
Prosper our colours in this dangerous fight!
                                    [*Exeunt.*

SCENE III. *Plains in Gascony.*

Enter a Messenger *that meets* YORK. *Enter*
YORK *with trumpet and many* Soldiers.

York. Are not the speedy scouts return'd
  again,
That dogg'd the mighty army of the Dauphin?
  Mess. They are return'd, my lord, and give it
  out
That he is march'd to Bourdeaux with his power,
To fight with Talbot: as he march'd along,
By your espials were discovered
Two mightier troops than that the Dauphin led,
Which join'd with him and made their march for
  Bourdeaux.
  York. A plague upon that villain Somerset,
That thus delays my promised supply   10
Of horsemen, that were levied for this siege!
Renowned Talbot doth expect my aid,
• And I am lowted by a traitor villain
And cannot help the noble chevalier:
God comfort him in this necessity!
If he miscarry, farewell wars in France.

Enter SIR WILLIAM LUCY.

  Lucy. Thou princely leader of our English
  strength,
Never so needful on the earth of France,
Spur to the rescue of the noble Talbot,
Who now is girdled with a waist of iron   20
And hemm'd about with grim destruction:
To Bourdeaux, warlike duke! to Bourdeaux,
  York!
Else, farewell Talbot, France, and England's
  honour.
  York. O God, that Somerset, who in proud
  heart
• Doth stop my cornets, were in Talbot's place!
So should we save a valiant gentleman
By forfeiting a traitor and a coward.
Mad ire and wrathful fury makes me weep,
That thus we die, while remiss traitors sleep.
  Lucy. O, send some succour to the distress'd
  lord!   30
  York. He dies, we lose; I break my warlike
  word;
We mourn, France smiles; we lose, they daily
  get;
All 'long of this vile traitor Somerset.
  Lucy. Then God take mercy on brave Tal-
  bot's soul;
And on his son young John, who two hours since
I met in travel toward his warlike father!
This seven years did not Talbot see his son;
And now they meet where both their lives are
  done.
  York. Alas, what joy shall noble Talbot have
To bid his young son welcome to his grave?   40
Away! vexation almost stops my breath,
That sunder'd friends greet in the hour of death.
Lucy, farewell: no more my fortune can,
But curse the cause I cannot aid the man.
Maine, Blois, Poictiers, and Tours, are won away,

13 *lowted.* Mocked, made a fool of.

25 *cornets.* Cavalry officers.

55

Infantry on the march. Woodcut from Holinshed's *Chronicles*, 1577

---

4 *sally.* Sortie.

5 *buckled with.* Grappled with.

6 *sullied . . . honour.* Tarnished the splendour of his former reputation.

'Long all of Somerset and his delay.

                    [*Exit, with his soldiers.*

  Lucy. Thus, while the vulture of sedition
Feeds in the bosom of such great commanders,
Sleeping neglection doth betray to loss
The conquest of our scarce cold conqueror,   50
That ever living man of memory,
Henry the Fifth: whiles they each other cross,
Lives, honours, lands and all hurry to loss. [*Exit.*

    SCENE IV. *Other plains in Gascony.*

Enter SOMERSET, *with his army; a* Captain *of*
TALBOT'S *with him.*

  Som. It is too late; I cannot send them now:
This expedition was by York and Talbot
Too rashly plotted: all our general force
● Might with a sally of the very town
● Be buckled with: the over-daring Talbot
● Hath sullied all his gloss of former honour
By this unheedful, desperate, wild adventure:
York set him on to fight and die in shame,
That, Talbot dead, great York might bear the
    name.
  Cap. Here is Sir William Lucy, who with me
Set from our o'ermatch'd forces forth for aid.   11

    Enter SIR WILLIAM LUCY.

  Som. How now, Sir William! whither were
    you sent?
  Lucy. Whither, my lord? from bought and
    sold Lord Talbot;
Who, ring'd about with bold adversity,
Cries out for noble York and Somerset,
To beat assailing death from his weak legions:
And whiles the honourable captain there
Drops bloody sweat from his war-wearied limbs,
And, in advantage lingering, looks for rescue,
You, his false hopes, the trust of England's
    honour,   20
Keep off aloof with worthless emulation.
Let not your private discord keep away
The levied succours that should lend him aid,
While he, renowned noble gentleman,
Yields up his life unto a world of odds:
Orleans the Bastard, Charles, Burgundy,
Alençon, Reignier, compass him about,
And Talbot perisheth by your default.
  Som. York set him on; York should have sent
    him aid.
  Lucy. And York as fast upon your grace ex-
    claims;   30
Swearing that you withhold his levied host,
Collected for this expedition.
  Som. York lies; he might have sent and had
    the horse;
I owe him little duty, and less love;
And take foul scorn to fawn on him by sending.
  Lucy. The fraud of England, not the force of
    France,
Hath now entrapp'd the noble-minded Talbot:
Never to England shall he bear his life;
But dies, betray'd to fortune by your strife.
  Som. Come, go; I will dispatch the horsemen
    straight: 40
Within six hours they will be at his aid.
  Lucy. Too late comes rescue: he is ta'en or
    slain;
For fly he could not, if he would have fled;

And fly would Talbot never, though he might.
   Som. If he be dead, brave Talbot, then adieu!
   Lucy. His fame lives in the world, his shame
    in you.   [*Exeunt.*

SCENE V. *The English camp near Bourdeaux.*

Enter TALBOT *and* JOHN *his son.*

Tal. O young John Talbot! I did send for thee
To tutor thee in stratagems of war,
That Talbot's name might be in thee revived
When sapless age and weak unable limbs
Should bring thy father to his drooping chair.
But, O malignant and ill-boding stars!
Now thou art come unto a feast of death,
A terrible and unavoided danger:
Therefore, dear boy, mount on my swiftest horse;
And I'll direct thee how thou shalt escape   10
By sudden flight: come, dally not, be gone.
   John. Is my name Talbot? and am I your
    son?
And shall I fly? O, if you love my mother,
Dishonour not her honourable name,
To make a bastard and a slave of me!
The world will say, he is not Talbot's blood,
That basely fled when noble Talbot stood.
   Tal. Fly, to revenge my death, if I be slain.
   John. He that flies so will ne'er return again.
   Tal. If we both stay, we both are sure
    to die.   20
   John. Then let me stay; and, father, do
    you fly:
Your loss is great, so your regard should be;
My worth unknown, no loss is known in me.
Upon my death the French can little boast;
In yours they will, in you all hopes are lost.
Flight cannot stain the honour you have won;
But mine it will, that no exploit have done:
You fled for vantage, every one will swear;
But, if I bow, they'll say it was for fear.
There is no hope that ever I will stay,   30
If the first hour I shrink and run away.
Here on my knee I beg mortality,
Rather than life preserved with infamy.
   Tal. Shall all thy mother's hopes lie in one
    tomb?
   John. Ay, rather than I'll shame my mother's
    womb.
   Tal. Upon my blessing, I command thee go.
   John. To fight I will, but not to fly the foe.
   Tal. Part of thy father may be saved in thee.
   John. No part of him but will be shame
    in me.
   Tal. Thou never hadst renown, nor canst not
    lose it.   40
   John. Yes, your renowned name: shall flight
    abuse it?
   Tal. Thy father's charge shall clear thee
    from that stain.
   John. You cannot witness for me, being slain.
If death be so apparent, then both fly.
   Tal. And leave my followers here to fight
    and die?
My age was never tainted with such shame.
   John. And shall my youth be guilty of such
    blame?
No more can I be sever'd from your side,
Than can yourself yourself in twain divide:
Stay, go, do what you will, the like do I;   50

13 *Quicken'd . . .spleen.* i.e. my rage made me young again.

15 *Gallia.* France.

35 *mickle.* Much.

For live I will not, if my father die.
    Tal. Then here I take my leave of thee, fair son,
Born to eclipse thy life this afternoon.
Come, side by side together live and die;
And soul with soul from France to heaven fly.
                            [Exeunt.

Scene VI. *A field of battle.*

Alarum: excursions, wherein Talbot's Son *is hemmed about, and* Talbot *rescues him.*

    Tal. Saint George and victory! fight, soldiers, fight:
The regent hath with Talbot broke his word
And left us to the rage of France his sword.
Where is John Talbot? Pause, and take thy breath;
I gave thee life and rescued thee from death.
    John. O, twice my father, twice am I thy son!
The life thou gavest me first was lost and done,
Till with thy warlike sword, despite of fate,
To my determined time thou gavest new date.
    Tal. When from the Dauphin's crest thy sword struck fire,   10
It warm'd thy father's heart with proud desire
Of bold-faced victory. Then leaden age,
• Quicken'd with youthful spleen and warlike rage,
Beat down Alençon, Orleans, Burgundy,
• And from the pride of Gallia rescued thee.
The ireful bastard Orleans, that drew blood
From thee, my boy, and had the maidenhood
Of thy first fight, I soon encountered,
And interchanging blows I quickly shed
Some of his bastard blood; and in disgrace   20
Bespoke him thus; 'Contaminated, base
And misbegotten blood I spill of thine,
Mean and right poor, for that pure blood of mine
Which thou didst force from Talbot, my brave boy:'
Here, purposing the Bastard to destroy,
Came in strong rescue. Speak, thy father's care,
Art thou not weary, John? how dost thou fare?
Wilt thou yet leave the battle, boy, and fly,
Now thou art seal'd the son of chivalry?
Fly, to revenge my death when I am dead: 30
The help of one stands me in little stead.
O, too much folly is it, well I wot,
To hazard all our lives in one small boat!
If I to-day die not with Frenchmen's rage,
• To-morrow I shall die with mickle age:
By me they nothing gain an if I stay;
'Tis but the shortening of my life one day:
In thee thy mother dies, our household's name,
My death's revenge, thy youth, and England's fame:
All these and more we hazard by thy stay;   40
All these are saved if thou wilt fly away.
    John. The sword of Orleans hath not made me smart;
These words of yours draw life-blood from my heart:
On that advantage, bought with such a shame,
To save a paltry life and slay bright fame,
Before young Talbot from old Talbot fly,
The coward horse that bears me fall and die!
And like me to the peasant boys of France,

To be shame's scorn and subject of mischance!
Surely, by all the glory you have won, 50
An if I fly, I am not Talbot's son:
● Then talk no more of flight, it is no boot;
If son to Talbot, die at Talbot's foot.
● *Tal.* Then follow thou thy desperate sire of
  Crete,
Thou Icarus; thy life to me is sweet:
If thou wilt fight, fight by thy father's side;
And, commendable proved, let's die in pride.
[*Exeunt.*

SCENE VII. *Another part of the field.*

Alarum: excursions. Enter old TALBOT
led by a Servant.

Tal. Where is my other life? mine own is
  gone;
O, where's young Talbot? where is valiant John?
Triumphant death, smear'd with captivity,
Young Talbot's valour makes me smile at thee:
When he perceived me shrink and on my knee,
His bloody sword he brandish'd over me,
And, like a hungry lion, did commence
Rough deeds of rage and stern impatience;
But when my angry guardant stood alone,
● Tendering my ruin and assail'd of none, 10
Dizzy-eyed fury and great rage of heart
Suddenly made him from my side to start
Into the clustering battle of the French;
And in that sea of blood my boy did drench
His over-mounting spirit, and there died,
My Icarus, my blossom, in his pride.
Serv. O my dear lord, lo, where your son is
  borne!

Enter Soldiers, *with the body of young* TALBOT.

● *Tal.* Thou antic death, which laugh'st us here
  to scorn,
Anon, from thy insulting tyranny,
Coupled in bonds of perpetuity, 20
● Two Talbots, winged through the lither sky,
In thy despite shall 'scape mortality.
O thou, whose wounds become hard-favour'd
  death,
Speak to thy father ere thou yield thy breath!
Brave death by speaking, whether he will or no;
Imagine him a Frenchman and thy foe.
Poor boy! he smiles, methinks, as who should say,
Had death been French, then death had died
  to-day.
Come, come and lay him in his father's arms:
My spirit can no longer bear these harms. 30
Soldiers, adieu! I have what I would have,
Now my old arms are young John Talbot's grave.
[*Dies.*

Enter CHARLES, ALENÇON, BURGUNDY, BAS-
TARD, LA PUCELLE, *and forces.*

Char. Had York and Somerset brought rescue
  in,
We should have found a bloody day of this.
Bast. How the young whelp of Talbot's, raging-
  wood,
Did flesh his puny sword in Frenchmen's blood!
Puc. Once I encounter'd him, and thus I said:
'Thou maiden youth, be vanquish'd by a maid:'
But, with a proud majestical high scorn,
He answer'd thus: 'Young Talbot was not born

52 *boot.* Use.

54–55 *sire . . . Icarus.* Daedalus and his son Icarus sought to escape from King Minos of Crete by flying with wings of feathers and wax. Icarus soared too near the sun, his wings melted and he fell to his death.

10 *Tendering my ruin.* Taking care of me in my extremity.

18 *antic.* Grotesque.

21 *lither.* Yielding.

Talbot, dying, with the body of his son. Engraving by Kenny Meadows from Barry Cornwall's *Works of Shakspere,* 1846

41 *giglot.* Wanton.

Submission of Bordeaux to the French, 1453. Engraving from a late 15th century manuscript

---

60 *Alcides.* Hercules.

63 *Washford.* Wexford.

78 *Nemesis.* Goddess of retribution.

93 *phoenix.* Mythical Arabian bird that rose from the ashes of its own funeral pyre to live another life-cycle.

● To be the pillage of a giglot wench:'   **41**
So, rushing in the bowels of the French,
He left me proudly, as unworthy fight.
   Bur. Doubtless he would have made a noble knight:
See, where he lies inhearsed in the arms
Of the most bloody nurser of his harms!
   Bast. Hew them to pieces, hack their bones asunder,
Whose life was England's glory, Gallia's wonder.
   Char. O, no, forbear! for that which we have fled
During the life, let us not wrong it dead.   **50**

Enter SIR WILLIAM LUCY, *attended;* Herald *of the* French *preceding.*

   Lucy. Herald, conduct me to the Dauphin's tent,
To know who hath obtain'd the glory of the day.
   Char. On what submissive message art thou sent?
   Lucy. Submission, Dauphin! 'tis a mere French word:
We English warriors wot not what it means.
I come to know what prisoners thou hast ta'en
And to survey the bodies of the dead.
   Char. For prisoners ask'st thou? hell our prison is.
But tell me whom thou seek'st.
●   *Lucy.* But where's the great Alcides of the field,   **60**
Valiant Lord Talbot, Earl of Shrewsbury,
Created, for his rare success in arms,
● Great Earl of Washford, Waterford and Valence;
Lord Talbot of Goodrig and Urchinfield,
Lord Strange of Blackmere, Lord Verdun of Alton,
Lord Cromwell of Wingfield, Lord Furnival of Sheffield,
The thrice-victorious Lord of Falconbridge;
Knight of the noble order of Saint George,
Worthy Saint Michael and the Golden Fleece;
Great marshal to Henry the Sixth   **70**
Of all his wars within the realm of France?
   Puc. Here is a silly stately style indeed!
The Turk, that two and fifty kingdoms hath,
Writes not so tedious a style as this.
Him that thou magnifiest with all these titles
Stinking and fly-blown lies here at our feet.
   Lucy. Is Talbot slain, the Frenchmen's only scourge,
Your kingdom's terror and black Nemesis?
O, were mine eye-balls into bullets turn'd,
That I in rage might shoot them at your faces!   **80**
O, that I could but call these dead to life!
It were enough to fright the realm of France:
Were but his picture left amongst you here,
It would amaze the proudest of you all.
Give me their bodies, that I may bear them hence
And give them burial as beseems their worth.
   Puc. I think this upstart is old Talbot's ghost,
He speaks with such a proud commanding spirit.
For God's sake, let him have 'em; to keep them here,
They would but stink, and putrefy the air.   **90**
   Char. Go, take their bodies hence.
   Lucy. I'll bear them hence; but from their ashes shall be rear'd
● A phœnix that shall make all France afeard.

Char. So we be rid of them, do with 'em what
thou wilt.
And now to Paris, in this conquering vein:
All will be ours, now bloody Talbot's slain.
[*Exeunt.*

ACT V.

SCENE I. *London. The palace.*

Sennet. Enter KING, GLOUCESTER, *and* EXETER.

King. Have you perused the letters from the
pope,
The emperor and the Earl of Armagnac?
Glou. I have, my lord: and their intent is this:
They humbly sue unto your excellence
To have a godly peace concluded of
Between the realms of England and of France.
• *King.* How doth your grace affect their motion?
Glou. Well, my good lord; and as the only
means
To stop effusion of our Christian blood
And stablish quietness on every side.   10
King. Ay, marry, uncle; for I always thought
It was both impious and unnatural
• That such immanity and bloody strife
Should reign among professors of one faith.
Glou. Beside, my lord, the sooner to effect
And surer bind this knot of amity,
• The Earl of Armagnac, near knit to Charles,
A man of great authority in France,
Proffers his only daughter to your grace   19
In marriage, with a large and sumptuous dowry.
King. Marriage, uncle! alas, my years are
young!
And fitter is my study and my books
Than wanton dalliance with a paramour.
Yet call the ambassadors; and, as you please,
So let them have their answers every one:
I shall be well content with any choice
Tends to God's glory and my country's weal.

Enter WINCHESTER *in Cardinal's habit, a*
Legate *and two* Ambassadors.

Exe. What! is my Lord of Winchester install'd,
And call'd unto a cardinal's degree?
Then I perceive that will be verified   30
Henry the Fifth did sometime prophesy,
'If once he come to be a cardinal,
He'll make his cap co-equal with the crown.'
King. My lords ambassadors, your several suits
Have been consider'd and debated on.
Your purpose is both good and reasonable;
And therefore are we certainly resolved
To draw conditions of a friendly peace;
Which by my Lord of Winchester we mean
Shall be transported presently to France.   40
Glou. And for the proffer of my lord your
master,
I have inform'd his highness so at large
As liking of the lady's virtuous gifts,
Her beauty and the value of her dower,
He doth intend she shall be England's queen.
King. In argument and proof of which contract,
Bear her this jewel, pledge of my affection.
And so, my lord protector, see them guarded
And safely brought to Dover; where inshipp'd
Commit them to the fortune of the sea.   50
[*Exeunt all but Winchester and Legate.*

7 *affect their motion.* React to their advice.

13 *immanity.* Savagery.

17 *knit.* Closely related by blood.

Winchester in Cardinal's habit. Engraving from *Old
England*, 1854

54 *grave ornaments.* Regalia.

Before Angiers. From G. Braun and F. Hogenberg, *Civitates Orbis Terrarum,* 1572

2 *periapts.* Amulets or charms.

6 *monarch of the north.* The demon Amaymon.

10 *familiar spirits.* Witches' accomplices. *cull'd.* Gathered.

11 *powerful . . . earth.* Dwelling place of fiends.

Win. Stay, my lord legate: you shall first receive
The sum of money which I promised
Should be deliver'd to his holiness
● For clothing me in these grave ornaments.
   Leg. I will attend upon your lordship's leisure.
   Win. [*Aside*] Now Winchester will not submit, I trow,
Or be inferior to the proudest peer.
Humphrey of Gloucester, thou shalt well perceive
That, neither in birth or for authority,
The bishop will be overborne by thee: 60
I'll either make thee stoop and bend thy knee,
Or sack this country with a mutiny.   [*Exeunt.*

SCENE II. *France. Plains in Anjou.*

Enter CHARLES, BURGUNDY, ALENÇON, BASTARD, REIGNIER, LA PUCELLE, *and forces.*

   Char. These news, my lords, may cheer our drooping spirits:
'Tis said the stout Parisians do revolt
And turn again unto the warlike French.
   Alen. Then march to Paris, royal Charles of France,
And keep not back your powers in dalliance.
   Puc. Peace be amongst them, if they turn to us;
Else, ruin combat with their palaces!

Enter Scout.

   Scout. Success unto our valiant general,
And happiness to his accomplices!
   Char. What tidings send our scouts? I prithee, speak.   10
   Scout. The English army, that divided was
Into two parties, is now conjoin'd in one,
And means to give you battle presently.
   Char. Somewhat too sudden, sirs, the warning is:
But we will presently provide for them.
   Bur. I trust the ghost of Talbot is not there:
Now he is gone, my lord, you need not fear.
   Puc. Of all base passions, fear is most accursed.
Command the conquest, Charles, it shall be thine,
Let Henry fret and all the world repine.   20
   Char. Then on, my lords; and France be fortunate!   [*Exeunt.*

SCENE III. *Before Angiers.*

Alarum. Excursions. Enter LA PUCELLE.

   Puc. The regent conquers, and the Frenchmen fly.
● Now help, ye charming spells and periapts;
And ye choice spirits that admonish me
And give me signs of future accidents. [*Thunder.*
You speedy helpers, that are substitutes
● Under the lordly monarch of the north,
Appear and aid me in this enterprise.

Enter Fiends.

This speedy and quick appearance argues proof
Of your accustom'd diligence to me.
● Now, ye familiar spirits, that are cull'd   10
● Out of the powerful regions under earth,
Help me this once, that France may get the field.
       [*They walk, and speak not.*
O, hold me not with silence over-long!

Where I was wont to feed you with my blood,
I'll lop a member off and give it you
In earnest of a further benefit,
So you do condescend to help me now.
                    [*They hang their heads.*
No hope to have redress?   My body shall
Pay recompense, if you will grant my suit.
                    [*They shake their heads.*
Cannot my body nor blood-sacrifice   20
● Entreat you to your wonted furtherance?
Then take my soul, my body, soul and all,
Before that England give the French the foil.
                    [*They depart.*
See, they forsake me !   Now the time is come
● That France must vail her lofty-plumed crest
And let her head fall into England's lap.
My ancient incantations are too weak,
And hell too strong for me to buckle with :
Now, France, thy glory droopeth to the dust. [*Exit.*

Excursions.   Re-enter LA PUCELLE *fighting
hand to hand with* YORK : LA PUCELLE *is
taken.   The French fly.*

York.   Damsel of France, I think I have you
    fast :   30
Unchain your spirits now with spelling charms
And try if they can gain your liberty.
A goodly prize, fit for the devil's grace !
See, how the ugly witch doth bend her brows,
● As if with Circe she would change my shape !
    Puc.   Changed to a worser shape thou canst
        not be.
    York.   O, Charles the Dauphin is a proper man ;
No shape but his can please your dainty eye.
    Puc.   A plaguing mischief light on Charles and
        thee !
And may ye both be suddenly surprised   40
By bloody hands, in sleeping on your beds !
● *York.*   Fell banning hag, enchantress, hold
        thy tongue !
    Puc.   I prithee, give me leave to curse awhile.
    York.   Curse, miscreant, when thou comest to
        the stake.   [*Exeunt.*

Alarum.   Enter SUFFOLK, *with* MARGARET *in
his hand.*

    Suf.   Be what thou wilt, thou art my prisoner.
                            [*Gazes on her.*
O fairest beauty, do not fear nor fly !
For I will touch thee but with reverent hands ;
I kiss these fingers for eternal peace,
And lay them gently on thy tender side.
Who art thou? say, that I may honour thee.   50
    Mar.   Margaret my name, and daughter to a
        king,
The King of Naples, whosoe'er thou art.
    Suf.   An earl I am, and Suffolk am I call'd.
Be not offended, nature's miracle,
● Thou art allotted to be ta'en by me :
So doth the swan her downy cygnets save,
Keeping them prisoner underneath her wings.
Yet, if this servile usage once offend,
Go and be free again as Suffolk's friend.
                    [*She is going.*
O, stay !   I have no power to let her pass ;   60
My hand would free her, but my heart says no.
As plays the sun upon the glassy streams,

21 *wonted furtherance.* Accustomed assistance.

La Pucelle and the Fiends. Drawing by J.M. Wright
(1777–1866)

25 *vail.* Lower.

35 *Circe.* Enchantress in the *Odyssey* who turned men
into beasts.

42 *Fell banning hag.* Vile, cursing witch.

55 *allotted.* Fated.

63

63 *counterfeited.* Reflected.

80 *Fond.* Foolish.

81 *paramour.* Mistress.

83 *cooling card.* Card played by an opponent which shatters one's hopes.

101 *enthrall'd.* Captured.

109 *cry you mercy.* Beg your pardon. *Quid for Quo.* Fair exchange, tit for tat.

Margaret of Anjou (Helen Mirren) and Suffolk (Peter McEnery) Royal Shakespeare Co, 1977

● Twinkling another counterfeited beam,
So seems this gorgeous beauty to mine eyes.
Fain would I woo her, yet I dare not speak:
I 'll call for pen and ink, and write my mind.
Fie, de la Pole! disable not thyself;
Hast not a tongue? is she not here?
Wilt thou be daunted at a woman's sight?
Ay, beauty's princely majesty is such,   70
Confounds the tongue and makes the senses rough.
  Mar. Say, Earl of Suffolk—if thy name be so—
What ransom must I pay before I pass?
For I perceive I am thy prisoner.
  Suf. How canst thou tell she will deny thy
    suit,
Before thou make a trial of her love?
  Mar. Why speak'st thou not? what ransom
    must I pay?
  Suf. She's beautiful and therefore to be woo'd;
She is a woman, therefore to be won.
  Mar. Wilt thou accept of ransom? yea, or no.
●   *Suf.* Fond man, remember that thou hast a
    wife;   80
● Then how can Margaret be thy paramour?
  Mar. I were best to leave him, for he will not
    hear.
●   *Suf.* There all is marr'd; there lies a cooling
    card.
  Mar. He talks at random; sure, the man is
    mad.
  Suf. And yet a dispensation may be had.
  Mar. And yet I would that you would answer
    me.
  Suf. I 'll win this Lady Margaret. For whom?
Why, for my king: tush, that's a wooden thing!
  Mar. He talks of wood: it is some carpenter.
  Suf. Yet so my fancy may be satisfied,   91
And peace established between these realms.
But there remains a scruple in that too;
For though her father be the King of Naples,
Duke of Anjou and Maine, yet is he poor,
And our nobility will scorn the match.
  Mar. Hear ye, captain, are you not at leisure?
  Suf. It shall be so, disdain they ne'er so much:
Henry is youthful and will quickly yield.
Madam, I have a secret to reveal.   100
●   *Mar.* What though I be enthrall'd? he seems
    a knight,
And will not any way dishonour me.
  Suf. Lady, vouchsafe to listen what I say.
  Mar. Perhaps I shall be rescued by the French;
And then I need not crave his courtesy.
  Suf. Sweet madam, give me hearing in a
    cause—
  Mar. Tush, women have been captivate ere
    now.
  Suf. Lady, wherefore talk you so?
●   *Mar.* I cry you mercy, 'tis but Quid for Quo.
  Suf. Say, gentle princess, would you not sup-
    pose   110
Your bondage happy, to be made a queen?
  Mar. To be a queen in bondage is more vile
Than is a slave in base servility;
For princes should be free.
  Suf.   And so shall you,
If happy England's royal king be free.
  Mar. Why, what concerns his freedom unto me?
  Suf. I 'll undertake to make thee Henry's queen,
To put a golden sceptre in thy hand
And set a precious crown upon thy head,

If thou wilt condescend to be my—
   Mar.   What?   120
   Suf. His love.
   Mar. I am unworthy to be Henry's wife.
   Suf. No, gentle madam; I unworthy am
To woo so fair a dame to be his wife
And have no portion in the choice myself.
How say you, madam, are ye so content?
   Mar. An if my father please, I am content.
   Suf. Then call our captains and our colours
       forth.
And, madam, at your father's castle walls
We'll crave a parley, to confer with him.   130

A parley sounded. Enter REIGNIER *on the walls.*

See, Reignier, see, thy daughter prisoner!
   Reig. To whom?
   Suf.   To me.
   Reig.   Suffolk, what remedy?
I am a soldier and unapt to weep
Or to exclaim on fortune's fickleness.
   Suf. Yes, there is remedy enough, my lord:
Consent, and for thy honour give consent,
Thy daughter shall be wedded to my king;
Whom I with pain have woo'd and won thereto;
And this her easy-held imprisonment
Hath gain'd thy daughter princely liberty.   140
   Reig. Speaks Suffolk as he thinks?
   Suf.   Fair Margaret knows
● That Suffolk doth not flatter, face, or feign.
   Reig. Upon thy princely warrant, I descend
To give thee answer of thy just demand.
                    [Exit from the walls.
   Suf. And here I will expect thy coming.

Trumpets sound. Enter REIGNIER, *below.*

   Reig. Welcome, brave earl, into our terri-
      tories:
Command in Anjou what your honour pleases.
   Suf. Thanks, Reignier, happy for so sweet a
      child,
Fit to be made companion with a king:
What answer makes your grace unto my suit? 150
   Reig. Since thou dost deign to woo her little
      worth
To be the princely bride of such a lord;
Upon condition I may quietly
Enjoy mine own, the country Maine and Anjou,
Free from oppression or the stroke of war,
My daughter shall be Henry's, if he please.
   Suf. That is her ransom; I deliver her;
And those two counties I will undertake
Your grace shall well and quietly enjoy.
   Reig. And I again, in Henry's royal name,
As deputy unto that gracious king,   161
Give thee her hand, for sign of plighted faith.
   Suf. Reignier of France, I give thee kingly
      thanks,
● Because this is in traffic of a king.
   [Aside] And yet, methinks, I could be well con-
      tent
● To be mine own attorney in this case.
I'll over then to England with this news,
And make this marriage to be solemnized.
So farewell, Reignier: set this diamond safe
In golden palaces, as it becomes.   170
   Reig. I do embrace thee, as I would embrace

142 *face.* Dissemble, deceive.

164 *traffic.* Business.

166 *mine own attorney.* Act on my own behalf.

186 *peevish.* Trifling, silly.

188–189 *labyrinth ... Minotaurs.* The legendary maze of King Minos in Crete, where lived a monster, half bull, half man.

193 *Repeat their semblance.* Recall their image.

Joan of Arc in prison. Engraving from a painting by Paul Delaroche, 1825.

2 *kills ... heart.* Causes great sorrow.

7 *miser.* Wretch.

13 *first fruit ... bachelorship.* Born out of wedlock.

17 *obstacle.* Obstinate; used perhaps to give rustic flavour to the peasant's speech.

18 *collop.* Slice.

21 *avaunt.* Be gone.

The Christian prince, King Henry, were he here.
  Mar. Farewell, my lord: good wishes, praise and prayers
Shall Suffolk ever have of Margaret.   [*Going.*
  Suf. Farewell, sweet madam: but hark you, Margaret;
No princely commendations to my king?
  Mar. Such commendations as becomes a maid,
A virgin and his servant, say to him.
  Suf. Words sweetly placed and modestly directed.
But, madam, I must trouble you again;   180
No loving token to his majesty?
  Mar. Yes, my good lord, a pure unspotted heart,
Never yet taint with love, I send the king.
  Suf. And this withal.   [*Kisses her.*
  Mar. That for thyself: I will not so presume
• To send such peevish tokens to a king.
        [*Exeunt Reignier and Margaret.*
  Suf. O, wert thou for myself! But, Suffolk, stay;
• Thou mayst not wander in that labyrinth;
There Minotaurs and ugly treasons lurk.
Solicit Henry with her wondrous praise: 190
Bethink thee on her virtues that surmount,
And natural graces that extinguish art;
• Repeat their semblance often on the seas,
That, when thou comest to kneel at Henry's feet,
Thou mayst bereave him of his wits with wonder.
        [*Exit.*

SCENE IV.   *Camp of the* DUKE OF YORK *in Anjou.*

Enter YORK, WARWICK, *and others.*
  York. Bring forth that sorceress condemn'd to burn.

Enter LA PUCELLE, *guarded, and a* Shepherd.
•   *Shep.* Ah, Joan, this kills thy father's heart outright!
Have I sought every country far and near,
And, now it is my chance to find thee out,
Must I behold thy timeless cruel death?
Ah, Joan, sweet daughter Joan, I'll die with thee!
•   *Puc.* Decrepit miser! base ignoble wretch!
I am descended of a gentler blood:
Thou art no father nor no friend of mine.
  Shep. Out, out! My lords, an please you, 'tis not so;   10
I did beget her, all the parish knows:
Her mother liveth yet, can testify
• She was the first fruit of my bachelorship.
  War. Graceless! wilt thou deny thy parentage?
  York. This argues what her kind of life hath been,
Wicked and vile; and so her death concludes.
•   *Shep.* Fie, Joan, that thou wilt be so obstacle!
• God knows thou art a collop of my flesh;
And for thy sake have I shed many a tear:
Deny me not, I prithee, gentle Joan.   20
•   *Puc.* Peasant, avaunt! You have suborn'd this man,

Of purpose to obscure my noble birth.
    Shep. 'Tis true, I gave a noble to the priest
The morn that I was wedded to her mother.
Kneel down and take my blessing, good my girl.
Wilt thou not stoop? Now cursed be the time
Of thy nativity! I would the milk
Thy mother gave thee when thou suck'dst her
    breast,
● Had been a little ratsbane for thy sake!
Or else, when thou didst keep my lambs a-field,
I wish some ravenous wolf had eaten thee!   31
Dost thou deny thy father, cursed drab?
O, burn her, burn her! hanging is too good.
                    [*Exit.*
    York. Take her away; for she hath lived too
    long,
To fill the world with vicious qualities.
    Puc. First, let me tell you whom you have
    condemn'd:
Not me begotten of a shepherd swain,
But issued from the progeny of kings;
● Virtuous and holy; chosen from above,
By inspiration of celestial grace,   40
To work exceeding miracles on earth.
I never had to do with wicked spirits:
But you, that are polluted with your lusts,
Stain'd with the guiltless blood of innocents,
Corrupt and tainted with a thousand vices,
Because you want the grace that others have,
You judge it straight a thing impossible
To compass wonders but by help of devils.
No, misconceived! Joan of Arc hath been
A virgin from her tender infancy,   50
Chaste and immaculate in very thought;
● Whose maiden blood, thus rigorously effused,
Will cry for vengeance at the gates of heaven.
    York. Ay, ay: away with her to execution!
    War. And hark ye, sirs; because she is a
    maid,
● Spare for no faggots, let there be enow:
Place barrels of pitch upon the fatal stake,
That so her torture may be shortened.
    Puc. Will nothing turn your unrelenting
    hearts?
Then, Joan, discover thine infirmity,   60
That warranteth by law to be thy privilege.
I am with child, ye bloody homicides:
Murder not then the fruit within my womb,
Although ye hale me to a violent death.
    York. Now heaven forfend! the holy maid
    with child!
    War. The greatest miracle that e'er ye
    wrought:
● Is all your strict preciseness come to this?
●   *York*. She and the Dauphin have been jug-
    gling:
I did imagine what would be her refuge.
    War. Well, go to; we'll have no bastards
    live;   70
Especially since Charles must father it.
    Puc. You are deceived; my child is none of
    his:
It was Alençon that enjoy'd my love.
●   *York*. Alençon! that notorious Machiavel!
It dies, an if it had a thousand lives.
    Puc. O, give me leave, I have deluded you:
'Twas neither Charles nor yet the duke I named,
But Reignier, king of Naples, that prevail'd.
    War. A married man! that's most intolerable.

29 *ratsbane.* Rat poison.

39–40 *Virtuous . . . grace.* Parallel with the Virgin Mary.

52 *rigorously effused.* Cruelly shed.

56 *enow.* Enough.

67 *preciseness.* Strict morality.

68 *juggling.* Euphemism for sexual intercourse.

74 *Machiavel.* Unscrupulous politician or statesman (after Machiavelli, author of *The Prince*).

Niccolò Machiavelli (1469–1527), Florentine statesman, political theorist and writer. Painting by Angelo Bronzino (1503–72)

87 *reflex.* Reflect.

124 *in regard.* Since.

125 *of.* Out of.

York. Why, here's a girl! I think she knows
　　not well,　　　　　　　　　　　　　　80
There were so many, whom she may accuse.
　War. It's sign she hath been liberal and free.
　York. And yet, forsooth, she is a virgin pure.
Strumpet, thy words condemn thy brat and thee:
Use no entreaty, for it is in vain.
　Puc. Then lead me hence; with whom I leave
　　my curse:
● May never glorious sun reflex his beams
Upon the country where you make abode;
But darkness and the gloomy shade of death
Environ you, till mischief and despair　　90
Drive you to break your necks or hang your-
　　selves!　　　　　　　　　[*Exit, guarded.*
　York. Break thou in pieces and consume to
　　ashes,
Thou foul accursed minister of hell!

　　Enter CARDINAL BEAUFORT, Bishop of
　　　　Winchester, *attended.*

　Car. Lord regent, I do greet your excellence
With letters of commission from the king.
For know, my lords, the states of Christendom,
Moved with remorse of these outrageous broils,
Have earnestly implored a general peace
Betwixt our nation and the aspiring French;
And here at hand the Dauphin and his train　100
Approacheth, to confer about some matter.
　York. Is all our travail turn'd to this effect?
After the slaughter of so many peers,
So many captains, gentlemen and soldiers,
That in this quarrel have been overthrown
And sold their bodies for their country's benefit,
Shall we at last conclude effeminate peace?
Have we not lost most part of all the towns,
By treason, falsehood and by treachery,
Our great progenitors had conquered?　　110
O, Warwick, Warwick! I foresee with grief
The utter loss of all the realm of France.
　War. Be patient, York: if we conclude a
　　peace,
It shall be with such strict and severe covenants
As little shall the Frenchmen gain thereby.

　　Enter CHARLES, ALENÇON, Bastard, REIGNIER,
　　　　and others.

　Char. Since, lords of England, it is thus
　　agreed
That peaceful truce shall be proclaim'd in France,
We come to be informed by yourselves
What the conditions of that league must be.
　York. Speak, Winchester; for boiling choler
　　chokes　　　　　　　　　　　　120
The hollow passage of my poison'd voice,
By sight of these our baleful enemies.
　Car. Charles, and the rest, it is enacted thus:
● That, in regard King Henry gives consent,
● Of mere compassion and of lenity,
To ease your country of distressful war,
And suffer you to breathe in fruitful peace,
You shall become true liegemen to his crown:
And, Charles, upon condition thou wilt swear
To pay him tribute, and submit thyself,　　130
Thou shalt be placed as viceroy under him,
And still enjoy thy regal dignity.
　Alen. Must he be then as shadow of himself?

Adorn his temples with a coronet,
And yet, in substance and authority,
Retain but privilege of a private man?
This proffer is absurd and reasonless.
 Char. 'Tis known already that I am possess'd
With more than half the Gallian territories,
And therein reverenced for their lawful king: 140
Shall I, for lucre of the rest unvanquish'd,
● Detract so much from that prerogative,
As to be call'd but viceroy of the whole?
No, lord ambassador, I 'll rather keep
That which I have than, coveting for more,
Be cast from possibility of all.
 York. Insulting Charles! hast thou by secret
  means
Used intercession to obtain a league,
And, now the matter grows to compromise,
● Stand'st thou aloof upon comparison? 150
Either accept the title thou usurp'st,
● Of benefit proceeding from our king
● And not of any challenge of desert,
Or we will plague thee with incessant wars.
 Reig. My lord, you do not well in obstinacy
To cavil in the course of this contract:
If once it be neglected, ten to one
We shall not find like opportunity.
 Alen. To say the truth, it is your policy
To save your subjects from such massacre 160
And ruthless slaughters as are daily seen
By our proceeding in hostility;
And therefore take this compact of a truce,
Although you break it when your pleasure serves.
 War. How say'st thou, Charles? shall our
  condition stand?
 Char. It shall ;
Only reserved, you claim no interest
In any of our towns of garrison.
 York. Then swear allegiance to his majesty,
As thou art knight, never to disobey 170
Nor be rebellious to the crown of England,
Thou, nor thy nobles, to the crown of England.
So, now dismiss your army when ye please;
Hang up your ensigns, let your drums be still,
For here we entertain a solemn peace. [*Exeunt.*

Scene **V.** *London. The palace.*

Enter SUFFOLK *in conference with the* KING,
GLOUCESTER *and* EXETER.

 King. Your wondrous rare description, noble
  earl,
Of beauteous Margaret hath astonish'd me :
Her virtues graced with external gifts
Do breed love's settled passions in my heart :
And like as rigour of tempestuous gusts
Provokes the mightiest hulk against the tide,
So am I driven by breath of her renown
Either to suffer shipwreck or arrive
Where I may have fruition of her love.
 Suf. Tush, my good lord, this superficial tale
Is but a preface of her worthy praise ; 11
The chief perfections of that lovely dame,
Had I sufficient skill to utter them,
Would make a volume of enticing lines,
● Able to ravish any dull conceit:
And, which is more, she is not so divine,
So full-replete with choice of all delights,
But with as humble lowliness of mind

142 *Detract . . . prerogative.* i.e. takes away so much from the right of the sovereign.

150 *comparison.* i.e. of the status quo with our terms.

152 *Of benefit.* As a bounty.

153 *challenge of desert.* Any rightful claim of yours.

15 *conceit.* Thought.

25 *give . . . sin.* Condone sin.

27 *lady of esteem.* Daughter of the Earl of Armagnac.

31 *triumph.* Tournament.

32 *lists.* The palissades surrounding a tilting-yard.

56 *attorneyship.* Proxy.

57 *affects.* Loves.

81 *attaint.* Stained, marked.

She is content to be at your command;
Command, I mean, of virtuous chaste intents, 20
To love and honour Henry as her lord.
   King. And otherwise will Henry ne'er presume.
Therefore, my lord protector, give consent
That Margaret may be England's royal queen.
  ● *Glou.* So should I give consent to flatter sin.
You know, my lord, your highness is betroth'd
● Unto another lady of esteem:
How shall we then dispense with that contract,
And not deface your honour with reproach?
   Suf. As doth a ruler with unlawful oaths; 30
● Or one that, at a triumph having vow'd
● To try his strength, forsaketh yet the lists
By reason of his adversary's odds:
A poor earl's daughter is unequal odds,
And therefore may be broke without offence.
   Glou. Why, what, I pray, is Margaret more
     than that?
Her father is no better than an earl,
Although in glorious titles he excel.
   Suf. Yes, my lord, her father is a king,
The King of Naples and Jerusalem; 40
And of such great authority in France
As his alliance will confirm our peace
And keep the Frenchmen in allegiance.
   Glou. And so the Earl of Armagnac may do,
Because he is near kinsman unto Charles.
   Exe. Beside, his wealth doth warrant a liberal
     dower,
Where Reignier sooner will receive than give.
   Suf. A dower, my lords! disgrace not so your
     king,
That he should be so abject. base and poor,
To choose for wealth and not for perfect love. 50
Henry is able to enrich his queen
And not to seek a queen to make him rich:
So worthless peasants bargain for their wives,
As market-men for oxen, sheep, or horse.
Marriage is a matter of more worth
● Than to be dealt in by attorneyship;
● Not whom we will, but whom his grace affects,
Must be companion of his nuptial bed:
And therefore, lords, since he affects her most,
It most of all these reasons bindeth us, 60
In our opinions she should be preferr'd.
For what is wedlock forced but a hell,
An age of discord and continual strife?
Whereas the contrary bringeth bliss,
And is a pattern of celestial peace.
Whom should we match with Henry, being a king,
But Margaret, that is daughter to a king?
Her peerless feature, joined with her birth,
Approves her fit for none but for a king:
Her valiant courage and undaunted spirit, 70
More than in women commonly is seen,
Will answer our hope in issue of a king;
For Henry, son unto a conqueror,
Is likely to beget more conquerors,
If with a lady of so high resolve
As is fair Margaret he be link'd in love.
Then yield, my lords; and here conclude with me
That Margaret shall be queen, and none but she.
   King. Whether it be through force of your
     report,
My noble Lord of Suffolk, or for that 80
● My tender youth was never yet attaint
With any passion of inflaming love.

I cannot tell; but this I am assured,
I feel such sharp dissension in my breast,
Such fierce alarums both of hope and fear,
As I am sick with working of my thoughts.
Take, therefore, shipping; post, my lord, to
    France;
Agree to any covenants, and procure
That Lady Margaret do vouchsafe to come
To cross the seas to England and be crown'd 90
King Henry's faithful and anointed queen:
For your expenses and sufficient charge,
● Among the people gather up a tenth.
Be gone, I say; for, till you do return,
I rest perplexed with a thousand cares.
And you, good uncle, banish all offence:
● If you do censure me by what you were,
Not what you are, I know it will excuse
This sudden execution of my will.
And so, conduct me where, from company, 100
I may revolve and ruminate my grief.   [*Exit.*
    Glou. Ay, grief, I fear me, both at first and
      last.   [*Exeunt Gloucester and Exeter.*
    Suf. Thus Suffolk hath prevail'd; and thus
      he goes,
● As did the youthful Paris once to Greece,
With hope to find the like event in love,
But prosper better than the Trojan did.
Margaret shall now be queen, and rule the king;
But I will rule both her, the king and realm.
                       [*Exit.*

93 *tenth.* i.e. tax on personal property levied to meet expenses such as a royal marriage; from this practice the word 'royalty' is derived.

97 *censure.* Judge. *what you were.* Henry is making a veiled reference to an adulterous affair Gloucester had in order to gain the Duke's acquiescence in his marriage with Margaret.

104 *Paris . . . Greece.* Paris, son of the King of Troy, ran off with Helen, wife of the King of Sparta. The result was the ten years' siege of Troy.

Rape of Helen by Paris. Detail from a painting by follower of Fra Angelico (d. 1455)

King Henry VI

1590

Margaret of Anjou, wife of Henry VI. Engraving from Old England, Vol I, 1854

DR. JOHNSON considered the Second Part of the trilogy the best. Certainly it marks an improvement on the First in variety and character of action – the wide spread from the feuds and factions at Court around the King, the conjuring of the Duchess of Gloucester, her trial and penance, the killing of Suffolk at sea, the realistic lower-class scenes of Jack Cade's Rising, a portrayal of the common people which was to have a prodigious development all the way to *Julius Caesar* and on to *Coriolanus*. The characters are also more varied and developed. Henry VI reaches maturity as the kind, saintly man he was, more fit for a monk than a king. This provokes its reaction in his wife, the passionate Margaret of Anjou, whose nerves are on edge at her husband's impotence and weakness, while her love for Suffolk comes into the open. (The love between these two had its echo in that between Queen Isabella and Mortimer in *Edward II*, which Marlowe would shortly write.) The characters of spirited old Salisbury, the ambitious York aiming at the Crown, Suffolk with the arrogance that brought his fate upon him, the uncouth proletarian Cade – all stand out as individuals.

Style. The language also is in keeping. Henry VI's is notably Biblical as becomes him. For the first time Shakespeare gives expression to his attentive ear for lower-class speech – Cade's talk is the most memorable to us in the play. To Peter, the Armourer's man, is given the first malapropism of which Shakespeare was to make such use for jokes, with Bottom, Dogberry, Elbow and Mistress Quickly. Peter reports his master as saying that the King was an 'usurer', when he meant 'usurper'. The language of the play as a whole is also more varied, richer, stuffed with classical allusions, mainly from Ovid, not only the favourite *Metamorphoses* but also the *Tristia*. Everywhere is evidence of the actor's enormous verbal receptivity; it was not only that he picked up words and phrases everywhere, making the utmost use of Latin school tags to suggest more classical expertise than he had – though even a Cambridge man like Nashe could make simple howlers – but Shakespeare needed all this virtuosity to express his teeming mind. In these early plays we watch him flexing his muscles.

The puns are simple enough – history did not provide such opportunities as the banter of the comedies, but Shakespeare made the utmost of what he could:

> Unto the main! O father, Maine is lost!
> That Maine which by main force Warwick did win . . .
> Main chance, father, you meant, but I meant Maine,
> Which I will win from France or else be slain.

Less rhyme occurs in this play, but it punctuates speeches no less than scenes. The imagery is more notable, and everybody has been struck by the slaughter-house, butchering and butcher images that constantly occur when Shakespeare thought of the breakdown of social order, of faction-fighting and civil war. The subconscious associativeness of his mind is hardly less remarkable than his conscious intention, and is perhaps more intimately revealing of the man. The images cluster together like seaweed under the ocean; his subconscious worked for him almost as much as his conscious mind. Dreams are a constant element in all the plays.

An image sometimes has an obsessive visual power that suggests recollection:

> And as the butcher takes away the calf,
> And binds the wretch and beats it when it strains,
> Bearing it to the bloody slaughter-house . . .
> And as the dam runs lowing up and down,
> Looking the way her harmless young one went,
> And can do naught but wail her darling's loss . . .

This was a familiar enough spectacle in the vicinity of Smithfield (where Webster's father was a butcher), or in a country town like Stratford. John Aubrey has been much discounted for saying that Shakespeare's father was a butcher, when all the records show that he was a glover. But, of course, in a country town the handling of skins would have gone with butchering, in which the glover would lend a hand. Aubrey went on, 'and I have been told heretofore by some of the neighbours that, when he was a boy, he exercised his father's trade; but when he killed a calf he would do it in a high style, and make a speech.' It is in character.

For Shakespeare's grand style thus early we may take young Clifford's speech towards the end of the play, which foreshadows the Wars of the Roses that will be the theme and content of the next.

> O! let the vile world end,
> And the premised flames of the last day
> Knit earth and heaven together,
> Now let the general trumpet blow his blast,
> Particularities and petty sounds
> To cease!

And so on – the theme of revenge is developed in accordance with the rules of rhetoric, citations from the Bible and Ovid to round it out.

Theme. The main theme of this play is the fatal marriage of Henry VI to Margaret of Anjou. According to the Chronicles she came to him not only without dowry, but her father received Anjou and Maine, which were strategic keys to Normandy and led to its loss. (After all, the Plantagenets had come from Anjou, the English royal house was ultimately from the Norman Conquest.) The losses in France led to sharpening of internecine conflict in England; only a strong king could have imposed order, and Henry VI was not only a weak but a hopeless one. One cannot but have some sympathy with him, with all the nasty egos scuffling for place and power around him – no wonder he was sick of it all. In our day, when politicians and Trade Union bosses are so much more disinterested, we find the slanging matches going on around the King distasteful and positively boring – like debates in Parliament, our form of them. Elizabethans did not: they revelled in these declamatory amenities. Early Elizabethan theatre was very oratorical and given to stomping about the stage; we are grateful for the rapid development of a subtler and more natural dramaturgy, in which Shakespeare was to be the leader.

Occasionally passages, especially genealogies, are taken straight out of the Chronicles – prose rapidly versified, as with the argument about the renewal of the French war at the beginning of *Henry V*. We must remember that Elizabethans did not have the advantage that we have of being taught English history at school – it was all the more exciting and new to them; the one advantage they did have was that they were closer to the tradition – as with the youthful misrule of Prince Hal, for example.

Shakespeare makes no doubt, however, that the Wars of the Roses were ultimately due to the sin of Bolingbroke in usurping the throne of Richard II. The historian may well think that he blames Bolingbroke too harshly: for (a) Richard became impossible as king; (b) Bolingbroke was led on not only to claim his rights as Duke of Lancaster but the crown itself, as a matter of sheer self-preservation; (c) he was called to the job by the will of the country, so far as it could be expressed by Parliament and Church, and he made a far better king. Richard was the son of Edward III's eldest son, the Black Prince; Edward's second son died young. The third son, Lionel Duke of Clarence, had only a daughter – so the Yorkists derived their claim through the female line. John of Gaunt was the fourth son, but his son was the next heir *in the male line* after Richard. That weighed in the balance too; but it led Henry IV to make away with Richard: there was the crime. We watch its working out, its nemesis, in these plays as in a Greek tragedy.

Variety. We are grateful for a let-up from this sombre theme in the variety of episodes this play presents. We have the interesting scene of the Duchess of Gloucester calling up the spirits. One of these answers to the name of Asnath. There is no reason why this should not be Asmenoth, 'guider of the North', referred to in Greene's *Friar Bacon and Friar Bungay*, one of his more popular plays. And may not the episode be as responsible as anything for Greene's charge of plagiarism against the actor turned dramatist? True, Marlowe conjures up the spirits more effectively than anybody in *Doctor Faustus*, but Green's play is probably earlier than Marlowe's, and certainly than Shakespeare's.

The episodes of the Armourer, charged with accusing York of treason, provide some comic relief – his last appearance is a drunken scene, with his apprentices drinking to him, and of course a fight ensues. The scenes that appeal most today are the realistic ones of Jack Cade's Rising, in which we have Shakespeare's first depiction of the people – upon which subject he never changed, from play to play until the ultimate hardening of the lines in *Coriolanus*. It is interesting that the Elizabethan groundlings did not apparently resent the unfavourable picture he gives of them. Perhaps they recognised its truth, or the easy-going nature, not without sympathy, of the rendering; in any case, Elizabethan humbug was religious rather than political. (Does the subject populace in Communist countries resent the evident assumptions of their rulers as to their nature? Apparently not.)

Cade promises the people, almost as if it were a general election:

> There shall be in England seven half-penny loaves sold for a penny;
> the three-hooped pot shall have ten hoops . . . All the realm shall be in
> common . . . And when I am king, as king I will be –
All: God save your Majesty!
Cade: I thank you, good people – there shall be no money. All shall eat and
> drink on my score, and I will apparel them all in one livery, that they
> may agree like brothers . . .
Butcher: The first thing we do, let's kill all the lawyers.

At the next appearance of the mob, in Smithfield, Cade commands:

> Now go some and pull down the Savoy; others to the Inns of Court. Down with
> them all!

This must have been popular. In fact, it had been John of Gaunt's palace of the Savoy
that was wrecked in the Peasants' Revolt of 1381, with all its treasures, jewels, tapestries,
books and manuscripts. For Elizabethans did not expect the people to care for learning,
any more than a society run by Trade Union standards cares for culture. Cade charges
Lord Say (builder of beautiful Broughton Castle):

> Thou hast most traitorously corrupted the youth of the realm in erecting a
> grammar school. And whereas, before, our forefathers had no other books but
> the score and the tally, thou hast caused printing to be used . . .

This is the beginning of a comic speech, good-humoured enough for Shakespeare; all
the same, Cade does not fail to have Lord Say's and his son-in-law's heads struck off and
brought in upon two poles for contemplation.

The gravamen of Cade's speeches is:

> Henceforward all things shall be in common.

The 16th century was well aware of the phenomenon of Communism. The Peasants'
Revolt in Germany, of 1526, with the Anabaptist horrors at Münster, had sent a thrill
of trepidation throughout Europe, comparable to that aroused by the Bolshevik
Revolution of 1917 in Russia, with all that that bloody event portended for the whole
world.

Shakespeare is but at the beginning of expounding through the lessons of history –
for to the Elizabethans history was a moral and didactic study – his conviction that the
breakdown of authority and social order leads only to more and worse cruelties and
suffering than before. It is not likely that this man, who understood human nature
better than anyone, was wrong – the experience of our deplorable century has proved
how much more right he was than the exceptionally liberal and civilised 19th century.
We shall see the consequences of the breakdown in 15th century England in the next
play.

The Elizabethan Age. Ireland was, as always, unfortunately topical. In the prolonged
conflict with Spain the Elizabethans could not allow the neighbouring island to be
conquered. Hence the increasing tempo of the struggle there. A post arrives:

THE
First part of the Con=
tention betwixt the two famous Houſes of Yorke
and Lancaſter, with the death of the good
Duke Humphrey:

And the baniſhment and death of the Duke of
Suffolke, and the Tragicall end of the proud Cardinall
of *VVincheſter*, vvith the notable Rebellion
of *Iacke Cade*:

*And the Duke of Yorkes firſt claime vnto the
Crowne.*

LONDON
Printed by Thomas Creed, for Thomas Millington,
and are to be ſold at his ſhop vnder Saint Peters
Church in Cornwall.
1594.

> To signify that rebels there are up,
> And put the Englishmen unto the sword.
> Send succours, lords, and stop the rage betime,
> Before the wound do grow uncurable.

We hear of the 'uncivil kerns of Ireland': this is what the Elizabethans thought them, not having the advantage of our anthropological knowledge to explain a primitive pre-medieval society: 'uncivil' meant not reduced to civility. The 'gallowglass' we hear of are the warrior following of the Celtic tribal chieftains who kept Northern Ireland and the Hebrides in constant turmoil during Elizabeth's reign.

Places referred to are familiar. York summons his armed following to St. George's Field: this was one of the chief training grounds for the musters at the time, on Bankside between Southwark and Lambeth. Bedlam was on the way out of the City through Bishopsgate to the theatres in Shoreditch; Robert Greene was to be buried there in 1592.

Personal. The countryman addicted to out-of-doors sports reveals himself again in very knowledgable talk about hawking.

> Believe me, lords, for flying at the brook –

this was the regular term for hawking by the waterside, evidently for waterbirds, duck and mallard.

> I saw not better sport these seven years' day;
> Yet, by your leave, the wind was very high,
> And, ten to one, old Joan had not gone out –

i.e. the old bird had not flown. Capering

> upright like a wild morisco,
> Shaking the bloody darts as he his bells,

takes us back to the Cotswolds, where morris-dancing never died out, and whence its general revival this century came. And what are we to think of the reference,

> . . . like rich hangings in a homely house?

Rich hangings in a great house were no rarity; but Wilmcote, his mother's home, was exceptional for the large number of hangings in a farmhouse.

Text. There are two texts of this play: that of the Quarto published in 1594 under the title, *The First Part of the Contention of York and Lancaster*, and that of the First Folio, which was based partly upon that and partly upon the Company's fuller transcript of the author's manuscript. This complicated process of transmission gave rise to doubtful readings and much discussion; printers added their mistakes. The confusion has now been largely cleared up and does not anyway detract from enjoyment of the play. For modern production it needs cutting, which is precisely what the Shakespearean actors did, as we see from the shorter Quarto version.

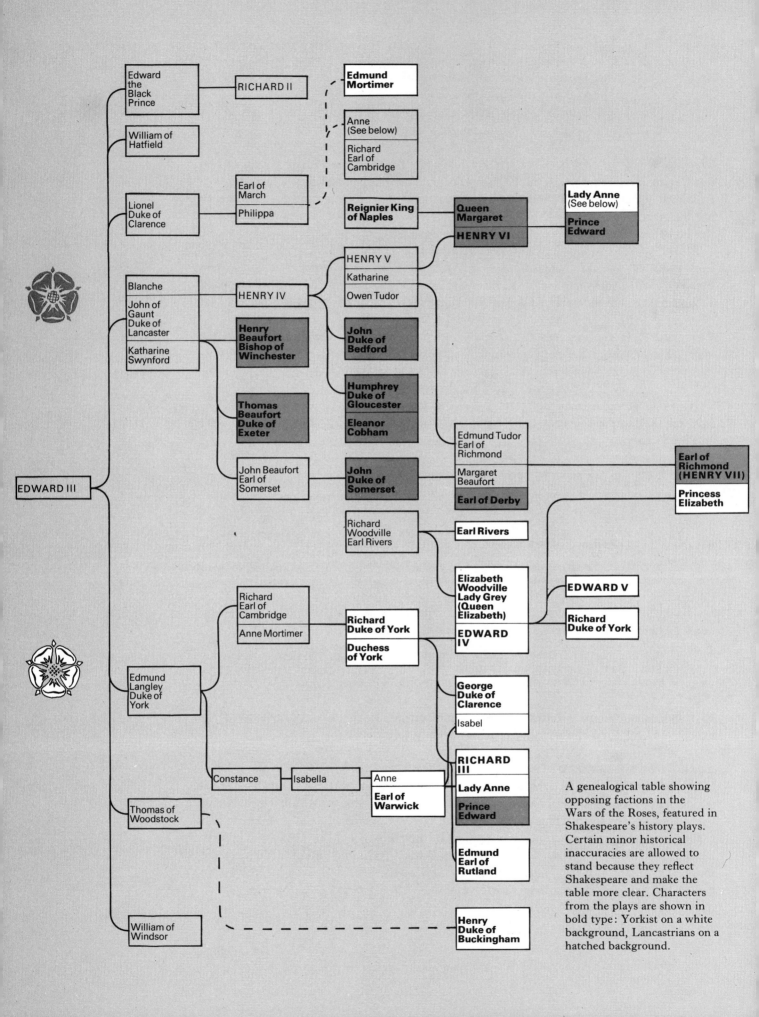

A genealogical table showing opposing factions in the Wars of the Roses, featured in Shakespeare's history plays. Certain minor historical inaccuracies are allowed to stand because they reflect Shakespeare and make the table more clear. Characters from the plays are shown in bold type: Yorkist on a white background, Lancastrians on a hatched background.

THE SECOND PART OF
KING HENRY VI.

DRAMATIS PERSONÆ.

KING HENRY the Sixth.
HUMPHREY, Duke of Gloucester, his uncle.
CARDINAL BEAUFORT, Bishop of Winchester, great-uncle to the King.
RICHARD PLANTAGENET, Duke of York.
EDWARD and RICHARD, his sons.
DUKE OF SOMERSET.
DUKE OF SUFFOLK.
DUKE OF BUCKINGHAM.
LORD CLIFFORD.
Young CLIFFORD, his son.
EARL OF SALISBURY.
EARL OF WARWICK.
LORD SCALES.
LORD SAY.
SIR HUMPHREY STAFFORD, and WILLIAM STAFFORD, his brother.
SIR JOHN STANLEY.
VAUX.
MATTHEW GOFFE.
A Sea-captain, Master, and Master's-Mate, and WALTER WHITMORE.
Two Gentlemen, prisoners with Suffolk.
JOHN HUME and JOHN SOUTHWELL, priests.

BOLINGBROKE, a conjurer.
THOMAS HORNER, an armourer.   PETER, his man.
Clerk of Chatham. Mayor of Saint Alban's.
SIMPCOX, an impostor.
ALEXANDER IDEN, a Kentish gentleman.
JACK CADE, a rebel.
GEORGE BEVIS, JOHN HOLLAND, DICK the butcher, SMITH the weaver, MICHAEL, &c., followers of Cade.
Two Murderers.

MARGARET, Queen to King Henry.
ELEANOR, Duchess of Gloucester.
MARGARET JOURDAIN, a witch.
Wife to Simpcox.

Lords, Ladies, and Attendants, Petitioners, Aldermen, a Herald, a Beadle, Sheriff, and Officers, Citizens, 'Prentices, Falconers, Guards, Soldiers, Messengers, &c.

A Spirit.

SCENE: *England.*

● *A bullet beside a text line indicates an annotation in the opposite column*

ACT I.

SCENE I. *London. The palace.*

Flourish of trumpets: then hautboys. Enter the KING, HUMPHREY, *Duke of* GLOUCESTER, SALISBURY, WARWICK, *and* CARDINAL BEAUFORT, *on the one side; the* QUEEN, SUFFOLK, YORK, SOMERSET, *and* BUCKINGHAM, *on the other.*

Suf. As by your high imperial majesty
I had in charge at my depart for France,
● As procurator to your excellence,
To marry Princess Margaret for your grace,
So, in the famous ancient city Tours,
● In presence of the Kings of France and Sicil,
The Dukes of Orleans, Calaber, Bretagne and Alençon,
Seven earls, twelve barons and twenty reverend bishops,
I have perform'd my task and was espoused: And humbly now upon my bended knee,   10
In sight of England and her lordly peers,
Deliver up my title in the queen
To your most gracious hands, that are the substance
Of that great shadow I did represent;
The happiest gift that ever marquess gave,
The fairest queen that ever king received.
King. Suffolk, arise. Welcome, Queen Margaret:

Marriage of Henry VI and Margaret of Anjou. Engraving from *Old England*, 1854

3 *procurator.* Agent, proxy.

6 *Sicil.* i.e. Sicily; Reignier, Queen Margaret's father.

Henry VI (Jack May) and Queen Margaret (Rosalind Boxall) with attendants, Old Vic Theatre, London, 1953

---

27 *beads*. i.e. prayer beads for the saying of the rosary.

28 *alder-liefest*. Most dear.

33 *y-clad*. Clad.

43 *Imprimis*. Firstly.

I can express no kinder sign of love
Than this kind kiss. O Lord, that lends me life,
Lend me a heart replete with thankfulness! 20
For thou hast given me in this beauteous face
A world of earthly blessings to my soul,
If sympathy of love unite our thoughts.
   Queen. Great King of England and my gracious lord,
The mutual conference that my mind hath had,
By day, by night, waking and in my dreams,
• In courtly company or at my beads,
• With you, mine alder-liefest sovereign,
Makes me the bolder to salute my king
With ruder terms, such as my wit affords 30
And over-joy of heart doth minister.
   King. Her sight did ravish ; but her grace in speech,
• Her words y-clad with wisdom's majesty, .
Makes me from wondering fall to weeping joys;
Such is the fulness of my heart's content.
Lords, with one cheerful voice welcome my love.
   All [*kneeling*]. Long live Queen Margaret, England's happiness !
   Queen. We thank you all. [*Flourish.*
   Suff. My lord protector, so it please your grace,
Here are the articles of contracted peace 40
Between our sovereign and the French king Charles,
For eighteen months concluded by consent.
•   *Glou.* [*Reads*] 'Imprimis, It is agreed between

the French king Charles, and William de la Pole, Marquess of Suffolk, ambassador for Henry King of England, that the said Henry shall espouse the Lady Margaret, daughter unto Reignier King of Naples, Sicilia and Jerusalem, and crown her Queen of England ere the thirtieth of May next ensuing. Item, that the duchy of Anjou and the county of Maine shall be released and delivered to the king her father'— *[Lets the paper fall.*

King. Uncle, how now!

Glou. Pardon me, gracious lord;
Some sudden qualm hath struck me at the heart
And dimm'd mine eyes, that I can read no
further.

● *King.* Uncle of Winchester, I pray, read on.

Car. [*Reads*] 'Item, It is further agreed between them, that the duchies of Anjou and Maine shall be released and delivered over to the king her father, and she sent over of the King of England's own proper cost and charges, without having any dowry.'

King. They please us well. Lord marquess,
kneel down:
We here create thee the first duke of Suffolk,
And gird thee with the sword. Cousin of York,
We here discharge your grace from being regent
I' the parts of France, till term of eighteen months
Be full expired. Thanks, uncle Winchester,
Gloucester, York, Buckingham, Somerset,
Salisbury, and Warwick; 70
We thank you all for this great favour done,
In entertainment to my princely queen.
Come, let us in, and with all speed provide
To see her coronation be perform'd.

[Exeunt King, Queen, and Suffolk.

Glou. Brave peers of England, pillars of the
state,
To you Duke Humphrey must unload his grief,
Your grief, the common grief of all the land.

● What! did my brother Henry spend his youth,
His valour, coin and people, in the wars?
Did he so often lodge in open field, 80
In winter's cold and summer's parching heat,

● To conquer France, his true inheritance?
And did my brother Bedford toil his wits,
To keep by policy what Henry got?
Have you yourselves, Somerset, Buckingham,
Brave York, Salisbury, and victorious Warwick,
Received deep scars in France and Normandy?
Or hath mine uncle Beaufort and myself,
With all the learned council of the realm,
Studied so long, sat in the council-house 90
Early and late, debating to and fro
How France and Frenchmen might be kept in
awe,
And had his highness in his infancy
Crowned in Paris in despite of foes?
And shall these labours and these honours die?
Shall Henry's conquest, Bedford's vigilance,
Your deeds of war and all our counsel die?
O peers of England, shameful is this league!
Fatal this marriage, cancelling your fame,
Blotting your names from books of memory, 100

● Razing the characters of your renown,
Defacing monuments of conquer'd France,
Undoing all, as all had never been!

Car. Nephew, what means this passionate
discourse,

● This peroration with such circumstance?

Anjou and Maine, the English territories given to Reignier, Margaret's father, as part of the marriage treaty. From John Speed's *A Prospect of the Most Famous Parts of the World*, 1631

56 *Uncle of Winchester.* i.e. great-uncle. Winchester was half brother to Henry IV, grandfather of Henry VI.

78 *brother Henry.* Henry V.

82 *true inheritance.* i.e. his historic claim through the female line.

101 *Razing the characters.* Erasing the inscriptions.

105 *peroration . . . circumstance.* i.e. rhetoric with such detail.

109 *rules the roast.* Takes the lead.

115 *Warwick.* The Earl of Warwick, the kingmaker.

133 *fifteenth.* Personal property tax.

Humphrey, Duke of Gloucester, uncle to the King and Protector of the Realm. Engraving from *Old England*, 1854

151 *next of blood.* As long as King Henry had no child of his own, Gloucester, as Henry's uncle, was next in line to the throne.

163 *flattering gloss.* Smooth, specious talk.

For France, 'tis ours; and we will keep it still.
   Glou. Ay, uncle, we will keep it, if we can;
But now it is impossible we should:
• Suffolk, the new-made duke that rules the roast,
Hath given the duchy of Anjou and Maine   110
Unto the poor King Reignier, whose large style
Agrees not with the leanness of his purse.
   Sal. Now, by the death of Him that died for all,
These counties were the keys of Normandy.
• But wherefore weeps Warwick, my valiant son?
   War. For grief that they are past recovery:
For, were there hope to conquer them again,
My sword should shed hot blood, mine eyes no tears.
Anjou and Maine! myself did win them both;
Those provinces these arms of mine did conquer:
And are the cities, that I got with wounds,   121
Deliver'd up again with peaceful words?
Mort Dieu!
   York. For Suffolk's duke, may he be suffocate,
That dims the honour of this warlike isle!
France should have torn and rent my very heart,
Before I would have yielded to this league.
I never read but England's kings have had
Large sums of gold and dowries with their wives;
And our King Henry gives away his own,   130
To match with her that brings no vantages.
   Glou. A proper jest, and never heard before,
• That Suffolk should demand a whole fifteenth
For costs and charges in transporting her!
She should have stay'd in France and starved in France,
Before—
   Car. My Lord of Gloucester, now ye grow too hot:
It was the pleasure of my lord the king.
   Glou. My Lord of Winchester, I know your mind;
'Tis not my speeches that you do mislike,   140
But 'tis my presence that doth trouble ye.
Rancour will out: proud prelate, in thy face
I see thy fury: if I longer stay,
We shall begin our ancient bickerings.
Lordings, farewell; and say, when I am gone,
I prophesied France will be lost ere long. [*Exit.*
   Car. So, there goes our protector in a rage.
'Tis known to you he is mine enemy,
Nay, more, an enemy unto you all,
And no great friend, I fear me, to the king.   150
• Consider, lords, he is the next of blood,
And heir apparent to the English crown:
Had Henry got an empire by his marriage,
And all the wealthy kingdoms of the west,
There's reason he should be displeased at it.
Look to it, lords; let not his smoothing words
Bewitch your hearts; be wise and circumspect.
What though the common people favour him,
Calling him 'Humphrey, the good Duke of Gloucester,'   159
Clapping their hands, and crying with loud voice,
'Jesu maintain your royal excellence!'
With 'God preserve the good Duke Humphrey!'
• I fear me, lords, for all this flattering gloss,
He will be found a dangerous protector.
   Buck. Why should he, then, protect our sovereign,
He being of age to govern of himself?

Cousin of Somerset, join you with me,
And all together, with the Duke of Suffolk,
- We'll quickly hoise Duke Humphrey from his
seat.
   Car. This weighty business will not brook
delay;   170
- I'll to the Duke of Suffolk presently.   [*Exit.*
   Som. Cousin of Buckingham, though Hum-
phrey's pride
And greatness of his place be grief to us,
Yet let us watch the haughty cardinal:
His insolence is more intolerable
Than all the princes in the land beside:
If Gloucester be displaced, he'll be protector.
   Buck. Or thou or I, Somerset, will be pro-
tector,
Despite Duke Humphrey or the cardinal.   179
         [*Exeunt Buckingham and Somerset.*
   Sal. Pride went before, ambition follows him.
While these do labour for their own preferment,
Behoves it us to labour for the realm.
I never saw but Humphrey Duke of Gloucester
Did bear him like a noble gentleman.
Oft have I seen the haughty cardinal,
More like a soldier than a man o' the church,
As stout and proud as he were lord of all,
Swear like a ruffian and demean himself
Unlike the ruler of a commonweal.
Warwick, my son, the comfort of my age,   190
- Thy deeds, thy plainness and thy housekeeping,
Hath won the greatest favour of the commons,
Excepting none but good Duke Humphrey:
- And, brother York, thy acts in Ireland,
In bringing them to civil discipline,
Thy late exploits done in the heart of France,
When thou wert regent for our sovereign,
Have made thee fear'd and honour'd of the people:
Join we together, for the public good,
In what we can, to bridle and suppress   200
The pride of Suffolk and the cardinal,
With Somerset's and Buckingham's ambition;
And, as we may, cherish Duke Humphrey's deeds,
While they do tend the profit of the land.
   War. So God help Warwick, as he loves the
land,
And common profit of his country!
   York. [*Aside*] And so says York, for he hath
greatest cause.
-   *Sal.* Then let's make haste away, and look
unto the main.
   War. Unto the main! O father, Maine is lost;
That Maine which by main force Warwick did win,
And would have kept so long as breath did last!
Main chance, father, you meant; but I meant
Maine,
Which I will win from France, or else be slain.
         [*Exeunt Warwick and Salisbury.*
   York. Anjou and Maine are given to the
French;
Paris is lost; the state of Normandy
- Stands on a tickle point, now they are gone:
Suffolk concluded on the articles,
The peers agreed, and Henry was well pleased
To change two dukedoms for a duke's fair daughter.
I cannot blame them all: what is't to them?   220
- 'Tis thine they give away, and not their own.
Pirates may make cheap pennyworths of their
pillage
And purchase friends and give to courtezans,

169 *hoise.* Hoist.

171 *presently.* Immediately.

191 *housekeeping.* Hospitality.

194 *brother.* Brother-in-law.

208–212 *main.* Word play on main: 1) the most
important stake (from a term in the dice game, hazard);
2) *Maine*, the lost French province; 3) *main force*,
superior might.

216 *Stands . . . point.* In a tottering position.

221 *thine.* i.e. York's (addressing himself).

225 *silly*. Unfortunate.

234–235 *fatal . . . Calydon.* Meleager, prince of Calydon, died when his mother burnt the wooden fire-brand which the Fates had decreed must be kept alight if he was to live.

240 *Nevils'*. i.e. Salisbury's and Warwick's.

244 *Lancaster*. Henry VI, Duke of Lancaster.

253 *fall'n at jars*. Lapsed into quarrelling.

254 *milk-white rose*. Emblem of the House of York.

2 *Ceres*. Goddess of agriculture.

18 *canker*. An ulcerous disease.

Still revelling like lords till all be gone:
- While as the silly owner of the goods
Weeps over them and wrings his hapless hands
And shakes his head and trembling stands aloof,
While all is shared and all is borne away,
Ready to starve and dare not touch his own:
So York must sit and fret and bite his tongue, 230
While his own lands are bargain'd for and sold.
Methinks the realms of England, France and Ireland
Bear that proportion to my flesh and blood
- As did the fatal brand Althæa burn'd
Unto the prince's heart of Calydon.
Anjou and Maine both given unto the French!
Cold news for me, for I had hope of France,
Even as I have of fertile England's soil.
A day will come when York shall claim his own:
- And therefore I will take the Nevils' parts   240
And make a show of love to proud Duke Humphrey,
And, when I spy advantage, claim the crown,
For that's the golden mark I seek to hit:
- Nor shall proud Lancaster usurp my right,
Nor hold the sceptre in his childish fist,
Nor wear the diadem upon his head,
Whose church-like humours fits not for a crown.
Then, York, be still awhile, till time do serve:
Watch thou and wake when others be asleep,
To pry into the secrets of the state;   250
Till Henry, surfeiting in joys of love,
With his new bride and England's dear-bought queen,
- And Humphrey with the peers be fall'n at jars:
- Then will I raise aloft the milk-white rose,
With whose sweet smell the air shall be perfumed;
And in my standard bear the arms of York,
To grapple with the house of Lancaster;
And, force perforce, I'll make him yield the crown,
Whose bookish rule hath pull'd fair England down.
[*Exit.*

SCENE II. *The* DUKE OF GLOUCESTER'S *house.*

Enter DUKE HUMPHREY *and his wife* ELEANOR.

Duch.   Why droops my lord, like over-ripen'd corn,
- Hanging the head at Ceres' plenteous load?
Why doth the great Duke Humphrey knit his brows,
As frowning at the favours of the world?
Why are thine eyes fix'd to the sullen earth,
Gazing on that which seems to dim thy sight?
What seest thou there? King Henry's diadem,
Enchased with all the honours of the world?
If so, gaze on, and grovel on thy face,
Until thy head be circled with the same.   10
Put forth thy hand, reach at the glorious gold.
What, is't too short? I'll lengthen it with mine;
And, having both together heaved it up,
We'll both together lift our heads to heaven,
And never more abase our sight so low
As to vouchsafe one glance unto the ground.
Glou.   O Nell, sweet Nell, if thou dost love thy lord,
- Banish the canker of ambitious thoughts.
And may that thought, when I imagine ill
Against my king and nephew, virtuous Henry,   20
Be my last breathing in this mortal world!

My troublous dream this night doth make me sad.
   Duch. What dream'd my lord? tell me, and
     I'll requite it
With sweet rehearsal of my morning's dream.
   Glou. Methought this staff, mine office-badge
     in court,
Was broke in twain; by whom I have forgot,
But, as I think, it was by the cardinal;
And on the pieces of the broken wand
Were placed the heads of Edmund Duke of
     Somerset,
And William de la Pole, first duke of Suffolk. 30
This was my dream: what it doth bode, God
     knows.
   Duch. Tut, this was nothing but an argument
That he that breaks a stick of Gloucester's grove
Shall lose his head for his presumption.
But list to me, my Humphrey, my sweet duke:
Methought I sat in seat of majesty
In the cathedral church of Westminster,
And in that chair where kings and queens are
     crown'd;
Where Henry and dame Margaret kneel'd to me
And on my head did set the diadem.   40
   Glou. Nay, Eleanor, then must I chide out-
     right:
Presumptuous dame, ill-nurtured Eleanor,
Art thou not second woman in the realm,
And the protector's wife, beloved of him?
Hast thou not worldly pleasure at command,
Above the reach or compass of thy thought?
● And wilt thou still be hammering treachery,
To tumble down thy husband and thyself
From top of honour to disgrace's feet?
Away from me, and let me hear no more!   50
   Duch. What, what, my lord! are you so choleric
With Eleanor, for telling but her dream?
Next time I'll keep my dreams unto myself,
● And not be check'd.
   Glou. Nay, be not angry; I am pleased again.

Enter Messenger.

   Mess. My lord protector, 'tis his highness'
     pleasure
You do prepare to ride unto Saint Alban's,
Where as the king and queen do mean to hawk.
   Glou. I go. Come, Nell, thou wilt ride with us?
   Duch. Yes, my good lord, I'll follow presently.
     [*Exeunt Gloucester and Messenger.*
Follow I must; I cannot go before,   61
While Gloucester bears this base and humble
     mind.
Were I a man, a duke, and next of blood,
I would remove these tedious stumbling-blocks
And smooth my way upon their headless necks;
And, being a woman, I will not be slack
To play my part in Fortune's pageant.
● Where are you there? Sir John! nay, fear not,
     man,
We are alone; here's none but thee and I.

Enter HUME.

   Hume. Jesus preserve your royal majesty! 70
●   *Duch.* What say'st thou? majesty! I am but
     grace.
   Hume. But, by the grace of God, and Hume's
     advice,
Your grace's title shall be multiplied.

Humphrey, Duke of Gloucester and Eleanor his wife, joining the confraternity of St Albans, 1431. Engraving from a contemporary manuscript

47 *hammering.* Hammering out, designing.

54 *check'd.* Rebuked, reprimanded.

68 *Sir John.* Old form of address for priests.

71 *grace.* Correct address for a duchess.

93 *coast*. Quarter, direction.

99 *buz*. Whisper.

100 *broker*. Agent.

106 *attainture*. Conviction, attainder.

107 *Sort . . . will*. Whatever happens.

3—4 *in the quill*. In writing.

Duch. What say'st thou, man? hast thou as yet conferr'd
With Margery Jourdain, the cunning witch,
With Roger Bolingbroke, the conjurer?
And will they undertake to do me good?
   Hume. This they have promised, to show your highness
A spirit raised from depth of under-ground,
That shall make answer to such questions   80
As by your grace shall be propounded him.
   Duch. It is enough; I'll think upon the questions:
When from Saint Alban's we do make return,
We'll see these things effected to the full.
Here, Hume, take this reward; make merry, man,
With thy confederates in this weighty cause.
                        [*Exit*.
   Hume. Hume must make merry with the duchess' gold;
Marry, and shall. But, how now, Sir John Hume!
Seal up your lips, and give no words but mum:
The business asketh silent secrecy.   90
Dame Eleanor gives gold to bring the witch:
Gold cannot come amiss, were she a devil.
●Yet have I gold flies from another coast;
I dare not say, from the rich cardinal
And from the great and new-made Duke of Suffolk,
Yet I do find it so; for, to be plain,
They, knowing Dame Eleanor's aspiring humour,
Have hired me to undermine the duchess
●And buz these conjurations in her brain.
●They say 'A crafty knave does need no broker;'
Yet am I Suffolk and the cardinal's broker.   101
Hume, if you take not heed, you shall go near
To call them both a pair of crafty knaves.
Well, so it stands; and thus, I fear, at last
Hume's knavery will be the duchess' wreck,
●And her attainture will be Humphrey's fall:
●Sort how it will, I shall have gold for all. [*Exit*.

SCENE III. *The palace.*

Enter three or four Petitioners, PETER, the Armourer's man, being one.

   First Petit. My masters, let's stand close: my lord protector will come this way by and by,
●and then we may deliver our supplications in the quill.
   Sec. Petit. Marry, the Lord protect him, for he's a good man! Jesu bless him!

Enter SUFFOLK and QUEEN.

   Peter. Here a' comes, methinks, and the queen with him. I'll be the first, sure.
   Sec. Petit. Come back, fool; this is the Duke of Suffolk, and not my lord protector.   10
   Suf. How now, fellow! wouldst any thing with me?
   First Petit. I pray, my lord, pardon me; I took ye for my lord protector.
   Queen. [*Reading*] 'To my Lord Protector!' Are your supplications to his lordship? Let me see them: what is thine?
   First Petit. Mine is, an't please your grace, against John Goodman, my lord cardinal's man, for keeping my house, and lands, and wife and all, from me.   21
   Suf. Thy wife too! that's some wrong, indeed. What's yours? What's here! [*Reads*] 'Against

● the Duke of Suffolk, for enclosing the commons
of Melford.' How now, sir knave!
Sec. Petit. Alas, sir, I am but a poor petitioner of our whole township.
Peter. [*Giving his petition*] Against my
master, Thomas Horner, for saying that the
Duke of York was rightful heir to the crown. 30
Queen. What say'st thou? did the Duke of
York say he was rightful heir to the crown?
Peter. That my master was? no, forsooth:
my master said that he was, and that the king
was an usurper.
Suf. Who is there? [*Enter Servant.*] Take
● this fellow in, and send for his master with a pur-
suivant presently: we'll hear more of your matter
before the king.   [*Exit Servant with Peter.*
Queen. And as for you, that love to be pro-
tected   40
Under the wings of our protector's grace,
Begin your suits anew, and sue to him.
                          Tears the supplications.
● Away, base cullions! Suffolk, let them go.
All. Come, let's be gone   [*Exeunt.*
Queen. My Lord of Suffolk, say, is this the guise,
Is this the fashion in the court of England?
Is this the government of Britain's isle,
And this the royalty of Albion's king?
What, shall King Henry be a pupil still
Under the surly Gloucester's governance?   50
Am I a queen in title and in style,
And must be made a subject to a duke?
I tell thee, Pole, when in the city Tours
● Thou ran'st a tilt in honour of my love
And stolest away the ladies' hearts of France,
I thought King Henry had resembled thee
In courage, courtship and proportion:
But all his mind is bent to holiness,
● To number Ave-Maries on his beads;
His champions are the prophets and apostles, 60
His weapons holy saws of sacred writ,
His study is his tilt-yard, and his loves
Are brazen images of canonized saints.
I would the college of the cardinals
Would choose him pope and carry him to Rome,
● And set the triple crown upon his head:
That were a state fit for his holiness.
Suf. Madam, be patient: as I was cause
Your highness came to England, so will I
In England work your grace's full content.   70
Queen. Beside the haughty protector, have we
        Beaufort
The imperious churchman, Somerset, Bucking-
        ham,
And grumbling York; and not the least of these
But can do more in England than the king.
Suf. And he of these that can do most of all
Cannot do more in England than the Nevils:
Salisbury and Warwick are no simple peers.
Queen. Not all these lords do vex me half so
        much
As that proud dame, the lord protector's wife.
She sweeps it through the court with troops of
        ladies,   80
More like an empress than Duke Humphrey's wife:
Strangers in court do take her for the queen:
She bears a duke's revenues on her back,
And in her heart she scorns our poverty:
Shall I not live to be avenged on her?
● Contemptuous base-born callet as she is,

24 *enclosing the commons.* Fencing off public land: a grievance of the poor.

37–38 *pursuivant.* Officer of the court.

43 *cullions.* Wretches, scum.

54 *tilt.* Tournament, mock fight on horseback.

59 *Ave-Maries.* Hail Marys, prayers to the Blessed Virgin.

66 *triple crown.* i.e. crown worn by the Pope.

86 *callet.* Trollop.

91 *limed a bush.* Set a trap.

SD *sennet.* Trumpet call.

120 *censure.* Opinion, judgement.

131 *rack'd.* Taxed extortionately.

She vaunted 'mongst her minions t'other day,
The very train of her worst wearing gown
Was better worth than all my father's lands, 89
Till Suffolk gave two dukedoms for his daughter.
  ● *Suf.* Madam, myself have limed a bush for her,
And placed a quire of such enticing birds,
That she will light to listen to the lays,
And never mount to trouble you again.
So, let her rest: and, madam, list to me;
For I am bold to counsel you in this.
Although we fancy not the cardinal,
Yet must we join with him and with the lords,
Till we have brought Duke Humphrey in disgrace.
As for the Duke of York, this late complaint 100
Will make but little for his benefit.
So, one by one, we'll weed them all at last,
And you yourself shall steer the happy helm.

Sound a sennet. Enter the KING, DUKE HUM-
PHREY of Gloucester, CARDINAL BEAUFORT,
BUCKINGHAM, YORK, SOMERSET, SALISBURY,
WARWICK, *and the* DUCHESS OF GLOUCESTER.

  King. For my part, noble lords, I care not
      which;
Or Somerset or York, all's one to me.
  York. If York have ill demean'd himself in
      France,
Then let him be denay'd the regentship.
  Som. If Somerset be unworthy of the place,
Let York be regent; I will yield to him.   109
  War. Whether your grace be worthy, yea or no,
Dispute not that: York is the worthier.
  Car. Ambitious Warwick, let thy betters speak.
  War. The cardinal's not my better in the field.
  Buck. All in this presence are thy betters,
      Warwick.
  War. Warwick may live to be the best of all.
  Sal. Peace, son! and show some reason,
      Buckingham,
Why Somerset should be preferr'd in this.
  Queen. Because the king, forsooth, will have
      it so.
  Glou. Madam, the king is old enough himself
  ● To give his censure: these are no women's matters.
  Queen. If he be old enough, what needs your
      grace   121
To be protector of his excellence?
  Glou. Madam, I am protector of the realm;
And, at his pleasure, will resign my place.
  Suf. Resign it then and leave thine insolence.
Since thou wert king—as who is king but thou?—
The commonwealth hath daily run to wreck;
The Dauphin hath prevail'd beyond the seas;
And all the peers and nobles of the realm
Have been as bondmen to thy sovereignty.   130
  ● *Car.* The commons hast thou rack'd; the
      clergy's bags
Are lank and lean with thy extortions.
  Som. Thy sumptuous buildings and thy wife's
      attire
Have cost a mass of public treasury.
  Buck. Thy cruelty in execution
Upon offenders hath exceeded law
And left thee to the mercy of the law.
  Queen. Thy sale of offices and towns in France,
If they were known, as the suspect is great,
Would make thee quickly hop without thy head.
      [*Exit Gloucester. The Queen drops her fan.*

Give me my fan: what, minion! can ye not? 141
    [*She gives the Duchess a box on the ear.*
I cry you mercy, madam; was it you?
   Duch. Was't I! yea, I it was, proud French-
    woman:
Could I come near your beauty with my nails,
● I'd set my ten commandments in your face.
   King. Sweet aunt, be quiet; 'twas against her
    will.
   Duch. Against her will! good king, look to't
    in time;
She'll hamper thee, and dandle thee like a baby:
● Though in this place most master wear no breeches,
She shall not strike Dame Eleanor unrevenged.
                   [*Exit.*
   Buck. Lord cardinal, I will follow Eleanor,
And listen after Humphrey, how he proceeds:
● She's tickled now; her fume needs no spurs,
She'll gallop far enough to her destruction. [*Exit.*

     Re-enter GLOUCESTER.

   Glou. Now, lords, my choler being over-blown
With walking once about the quadrangle,
I come to talk of commonwealth affairs.
As for your spiteful false objections,
Prove them, and I lie open to the law:
But God in mercy so deal with my soul, 160
As I in duty love my king and country!
But, to the matter that we have in hand:
I say, my sovereign, York is meetest man
To be your regent in the realm of France.
   Suf. Before we make election, give me leave
To show some reason, of no little force,
That York is most unmeet of any man.
   York. I'll tell thee, Suffolk, why I am
    unmeet:
First, for I cannot flatter thee in pride;
Next, if I be appointed for the place, 170
My Lord of Somerset will keep me here,
● Without discharge, money, or furniture,
Till France be won into the Dauphin's hands:
● Last time, I danced attendance on his will
Till Paris was besieged, famish'd, and lost.
   War. That can I witness; and a fouler fact
Did never traitor in the land commit.
   Suf. Peace, headstrong Warwick!
   War. Image of pride, why should I hold my
    peace?

    Enter HORNER, *the Armourer, and his
        man* PETER, *guarded.*

   Suf. Because here is a man accused of treason:
Pray God the Duke of York excuse himself! 181
   York. Doth any one accuse York for a
    traitor?
   King. What mean'st thou, Suffolk; tell me, what
    what are these?
   Suf. Please it your majesty, this is the man
That doth accuse his master of high treason:
His words were these: that Richard Duke of
    York
Was rightful heir unto the English crown
And that your majesty was an usurper.
   King. Say, man, were these thy words?
   Hor. An't shall please your majesty, I never
said nor thought any such matter: God is my
witness, I am falsely accused by the villain.
●   *Pet.* By these ten bones, my lords, he did

145 *ten commandments.* Slang for finger-nails.

149 *most . . . breeches.* Old proverb meaning the wife rules the house (wears the trousers).

Duchess: 'She shall not strike Dame Eleanor unrevenged'. Duchess of Gloucester (Margaret Courtney) and Queen Margaret (Barbara Jefford), Old Vic Theatre, London, 1957

153 *tickled.* Provoked. *fume.* Anger.

172 *furniture.* War equipment.

174 *Last time.* Probably referring to the siege of Bordeaux in Talbot's fatal campaign of 1453.

193 *ten bones.* Ten fingers.

196 *mechanical*. Manual labourer.

208 *doom*. Decision.

17 *gear*. Proceedings, business.

Bolingbroke: 'Patience, good lady . . .' Engraving from a painting by John Opie (1761–1801)

speak them to me in the garret one night, as we were scouring my Lord of York's armour.

   York. Base dunghill villain and mechanical, I'll have thy head for this thy traitor's speech. I do beseech your royal majesty, Let him have all the rigour of the law.   199

   Hor. Alas, my lord, hang me, if ever I spake the words. My accuser is my 'prentice; and when I did correct him for his fault the other day, he did vow upon his knees he would be even with me: I have good witness of this; therefore I beseech your majesty, do not cast away an honest man for a villain's accusation.

   King. Uncle, what shall we say to this in law?

   Glou. This doom, my lord, if I may judge: Let Somerset be regent o'er the French, Because in York this breeds suspicion: 210 And let these have a day appointed them For single combat in convenient place, For he hath witness of his servant's malice: This is the law, and this Duke Humphrey's doom.

   Som. I humbly thank your royal majesty.

   Hor. And I accept the combat willingly.

   Pet. Alas, my lord, I cannot fight; for God's sake, pity my case. The spite of man prevaileth against me. O Lord, have mercy upon me! I shall never be able to fight a blow. O Lord, my heart!   221

   Glou. Sirrah, or you must fight, or else be hang'd.

   King. Away with them to prison; and the day of combat shall be the last of the next month. Come, Somerset, we'll see thee sent away.   [*Flourish. Exeunt.*

SCENE IV. GLOUCESTER'S *garden*.

Enter MARGERY JOURDAIN, HUME, SOUTH-
WELL, *and* BOLINGBROKE.

   Hume. Come, my masters; the duchess, I tell you, expects performance of your promises.

   Boling. Master Hume, we are therefore provided: will her ladyship behold and hear our exorcisms?

   Hume. Ay, what else? fear you not her courage.

   Boling. I have heard her reported to be a woman of an invincible spirit: but it shall be convenient, Master Hume, that you be by her aloft, while we be busy below; and so, I pray you, go, in God's name, and leave us. [*Exit Hume.*] Mother Jourdain, be you prostrate and grovel on the earth; John Southwell, read you; and let us to our work.

Enter Duchess *aloft*, HUME *following*

   Duch. Well said, my masters; and welcome all. To this gear the sooner the better.

   Boling. Patience, good lady; wizards know their times:
Deep night, dark night, the silent of the night,
The time of night when Troy was set on fire; 20
The time when screech-owls cry and ban-dogs howl
And spirits walk and ghosts break up their graves,
That time best fits the work we have in hand.
Madam, sit you and fear not: whom we raise,

● We will make fast within a hallow'd verge.

> [*Here they do the ceremonies belonging,
> and make the circle; Bolingbroke or
> Southwell reads,* Conjuro te, &c. *It
> thunders and lightens terribly; then
> the Spirit riseth.*

Spir. Adsum.

M. Jourd. Asmath,
By the eternal God, whose name and power
Thou tremblest at, answer that I shall ask;
For, till thou speak, thou shalt not pass from
    hence.   30

    Spir. Ask what thou wilt. That I had said
    and done!

●   *Boling.* 'First of the king: what shall of him
    become?'   [*Reading out of a paper.*

    Spir. The duke yet lives that Henry shall
    depose;
But him outlive, and die a violent death.

> [*As the Spirit speaks, Southwell
> writes the answer.*

    Boling. 'What fates await the Duke of
    Suffolk?'

    Spir. By water shall he die, and take his end.

    Boling. 'What shall befall the Duke of
    Somerset?'

    Spir. Let him shun castles;
Safer shall he be upon the sandy plains
Than where castles mounted stand.   40
Have done, for more I hardly can endure.

    Boling. Descend to darkness and the burning
    lake!
False fiend, avoid!

> [*Thunder and lightning. Exit Spirit.*

Enter the Duke of York *and the* Duke of
Buckingham *with their* Guard *and break in.*

    York. Lay hands upon these traitors and
    their trash.
● Beldam, I think we watch'd you at an inch.
What, madam, are you there? the king and com-
    monweal
Are deeply indebted for this piece of pains:
My lord protector will, I doubt it not,
● See you well guerdon'd for these good deserts.

    Duch. Not half so bad as thine to England's
    king,   50
Injurious duke, that threatest where's no cause.

    Buck. True, madam, none at all: what call
    you this?
Away with them! let them be clapp'd up close,
And kept asunder. You, madam, shall with us.
Stafford, take her to thee.

> [*Exeunt above Duchess and Hume, guarded.*

We'll see your trinkets here all forthcoming.
All, away!

> [*Exeunt guard with Jourdain, Southwell, &c.*

    York. Lord Buckingham, methinks, you
    watch'd her well:
A pretty plot, well chosen to build upon!
Now, pray, my lord, let's see the devil's writ. 60
What have we here?   [*Reads.*
'The duke yet lives, that Henry shall depose;
But him outlive, and die a violent death.'
Why, this is just
● 'Aio te, Æacida, Romanos vincere posse.'
Well, to the rest:
'Tell me what fate awaits the Duke of Suffolk?
By water shall he die, and take his end.

---

25 *hallow'd verge.* Magic circle.

SD *Conjuro te.* I conjure you (beginning of an invocation).

32–41 The prophecies link together the various fatalities in the play – the deaths of Gloucester, Suffolk, Somerset.

45 *Beldam.* Hag.

49 *guerdon'd.* Rewarded (ironical).

65 *Aio te . . . posse.* The prophecy is ambiguous, like the famous warning given by the Pythian Apollo to King Pyrrhus on the eve of his going to war against Rome: 'I tell you, descendant of Aeacus, you the Romans can conquer'.

Hawking in medieval times. From Joseph Strutt's *Sports and Pastimes of the People of England*, 1810

1 *at the brook.* Hawking for waterfowl.

2 *seven years' day.* For the last seven years.

4 *Joan . . . out.* i.e. if the wind had not been so high she would have taken her flight at the game.

10 *protector's hawks.* Also alluding to the heraldic insignia of Gloucester: a falcon with a maiden's head.

22 *smooth'st.* Flatters.

24 *Tantæne . . . iræ?* Do heavenly minds nourish such great wrath (Virgil's *Aeneid*).

What shall betide the Duke of Somerset?
Let him shun castles;   70
Safer shall he be upon the sandy plains
Than where castles mounted stand.'
Come, come, my lords;
These oracles are hardly attain'd,
And hardly understood.
The king is now in progress towards Saint
    Alban's,
With him the husband of this lovely lady:
Thither go these news, as fast as horse can
    carry them:
A sorry breakfast for my lord protector.
    Buck. Your grace shall give me leave, my
    Lord of York,   80
To be the post, in hope of his reward.
    York. At your pleasure, my good lord. Who's
    within there, ho!

          Enter a Servingman.

Invite my Lords of Salisbury and Warwick
To sup with me to-morrow night. Away!
                    [*Exeunt.*

ACT II.

Scene I. *Saint Alban's.*

Enter the King, Queen, Gloucester, Cardinal, *and* Suffolk, *with* Falconers *halloing.*

- *Queen.* Believe me, lords, for flying at the
    brook,
- I saw not better sport these seven years' day:
Yet, by your leave, the wind was very high;
- And, ten to one, old Joan had not gone out.
    King. But what a point, my lord, your falcon
    made,
And what a pitch she flew above the rest!
To see how God in all his creatures works!
Yea, man and birds are fain of climbing high.
    Suf. No marvel, an it like your majesty,
- My lord protector's hawks do tower so well;   10
They know their master loves to be aloft
And bears his thoughts above his falcon's pitch.
    Glou. My lord, 'tis but a base ignoble mind
That mounts no higher than a bird can soar.
    Car. I thought as much; he would be above
    the clouds.
    Glou. Ay, my lord cardinal? how think you
    by that?
Were it not good your grace could fly to heaven?
    King. The treasury of everlasting joy.
    Car. Thy heaven is on earth; thine eyes and
    thoughts
Beat on a crown, the treasure of thy heart;   20
Pernicious protector, dangerous peer,
- That smooth'st it so with king and commonweal!
    Glou. What, cardinal, is your priesthood
    grown peremptory?
- Tantæne animis cœlestibus iræ?
Churchmen so hot? good uncle, hide such ma-
    lice;
With such holiness can you do it?
    Suf. No malice, sir; no more than well be-
    comes
So good a quarrel and so bad a peer.
    Glou. As who, my lord?
    Suf.   Why, as you, my lord,
An't like your lordly lord-protectorship.   30

Glou. Why, Suffolk, England knows thine insolence.

Queen. And thy ambition, Gloucester.

King. I prithee, peace, good queen,
And whet not on these furious peers;
For blessed are the peacemakers on earth.

Car. Let me be blessed for the peace I make,
Against this proud protector, with my sword!

Glou. [*Aside to Car.*] Faith, holy uncle, would 'twere come to that!

Car. [*Aside to Glou.*] Marry, when thou darest.

Glou. [*Aside to Car.*] Make up no factious numbers for the matter;   40
In thine own person answer thy abuse.

Car. [*Aside to Glou.*] Ay, where thou darest not peep: an if thou darest,
This evening, on the east side of the grove.

King. How now, my lords!

Car.   Believe me, cousin Gloucester,

• Had not your man put up the fowl so suddenly,
We had had more sport. [*Aside to Glou.*] Come with thy two-hand sword.

Glou. True, uncle.

Car. [*Aside to Glou.*] Are ye advised? the east side of the grove?

Glou. [*Aside to Car.*] Cardinal, I am with you.

King.   Why, how now, uncle Gloucester!

Glou. Talking of hawking; nothing else, my lord.   50
[*Aside to Car.*] Now, by God's mother, priest, I'll shave your crown for this,

• Or all my fence shall fail.

• *Car.* [*Aside to Glou.*] Medice, teipsum—
Protector, see to't well, protect yourself.

• *King.* The winds grow high; so do your stomachs, lords.
How irksome is this music to my heart!
When such strings jar, what hope of harmony?

• I pray, my lords, let me compound this strife.

Enter a Townsman *of Saint Alban's, crying* 'A miracle!'

Glou. What means this noise?
Fellow, what miracle dost thou proclaim?   60

Towns. A miracle! a miracle!

Suf. Come to the king and tell him what miracle.

Towns. Forsooth, a blind man at Saint Alban's shrine,
Within this half-hour, hath received his sight;
A man that ne'er saw in his life before.

King. Now, God be praised, that to believing souls
Gives light in darkness, comfort in despair!

Enter the Mayor *of Saint Alban's and his brethren, bearing* SIMPCOX, *between two in a chair,* SIMPCOX's Wife *following.*

Car. Here comes the townsmen on procession,
To present your highness with the man.

King. Great is his comfort in this earthly vale,   70

• Although by his sight his sin be multiplied.

Glou. Stand by, my masters: bring him near the king;
His highness' pleasure is to talk with him.

44 *put . . . fowl.* Raised the game.

Cardinal: ' . . . Come with thy two-hand sword'. From a German engraving, 1610

---

52 *fence.* Fencing skill.

53 *Medice, teipsum.* Physician, heal thyself.

55 *stomachs.* Tempers.

58 *compound this strife.* Settle this dispute.

71 *multiplied.* i.e. having another sense (sight) to lead him astray, he will sin more.

Abbey of St Albans, which contained the shrine to St Alban. Engraving from *Old England*, 1854

King. Good fellow, tell us here the circum-
stance,
That we for thee may glorify the Lord.
What, hast thou been long blind and now re-
stored?
Simp. Born blind, an't please your grace.
Wife. Ay, indeed, was he.
Suf. What woman is this?
Wife. His wife, an't like your worship. 80
Glou. Hadst thou been his mother, thou
couldst have better told.
King. Where wert thou born?
Simp. At Berwick in the north, an't like
your grace.
King. Poor soul, God's goodness hath been
great to thee:
Let never day nor night unhallow'd pass,
But still remember what the Lord hath done.
Queen. Tell me, good fellow, camest thou
here by chance,
Or of devotion, to this holy shrine?
Simp. God knows, of pure devotion; being
call'd
A hundred times and oftener, in my sleep, 90
By good Saint Alban; who said, 'Simpcox,
come,
Come, offer at my shrine, and I will help thee.'
Wife. Most true, forsooth; and many time
and oft
Myself have heard a voice to call him so.
Car. What, art thou lame?
Simp.   Ay, God Almighty help me!
Suf. How camest thou so?
Simp.   A fall off of a tree.
Wife. A plum-tree, master.
Glou.   How long hast thou been blind?
Simp. O, born so, master.
Glou.   What, and wouldst climb a tree?
Simp. But that in all my life, when I was a
youth.
Wife. Too true; and bought his climbing very
dear. 100
Glou. Mass, thou lovedst plums well, that
wouldst venture so.
Simp. Alas, good master, my wife desired
some damsons,
And made me climb, with danger of my life.
Glou. A subtle knave! but yet it shall not
serve.
Let me see thine eyes: wink now: now open
them:
In my opinion yet thou see'st not well.
Simp. Yes, master, clear as day, I thank God
and Saint Alban.
Glou. Say'st thou me so? What colour is this
cloak of?
Simp. Red, master; red as blood. 110
Glou. Why, that's well said. What colour is
my gown of?
Simp. Black, forsooth: coal-black as jet.
King. Why, then, thou know'st what colour
jet is of?
Suf. And yet, I think, jet did he never see.
Glou. But cloaks and gowns, before this day,
a many.
Wife. Never, before this day, in all his life.
Glou. Tell me, sirrah, what's my name?
Simp. Alas, master, I know not.
Glou. What's his name?

Simp. I know not. 120
Glou. Nor his?
Simp. No, indeed, master.
Glou. What's thine own name?
Simp. Saunder Simpcox, an if it please you, master.
Glou. Then, Saunder, sit there, the lyingest knave in Christendom. If thou hadst been born blind, thou mightst as well have known all our names as thus to name the several colours we do wear. Sight may distinguish of colours, but suddenly to nominate them all, it is impossible. My lords, Saint Alban here hath done a miracle; and would ye not think his cunning to be great, that could restore this cripple to his legs again?
Simp. O master, that you could!
Glou. My masters of Saint Alban's, have you not beadles in your town, and things called whips?
May. Yes, my lord, if it please your grace.
Glou. Then send for one presently.
May. Sirrah, go fetch the beadle hither straight. [*Exit an Attendant.* 141
Glou. Now fetch me a stool hither by and by. Now, sirrah, if you mean to save yourself from whipping, leap me over this stool and run away.
Simp. Alas, master, I am not able to stand alone:
You go about to torture me in vain.

Enter a Beadle *with whips.*

Glou. Well, sir, we must have you find your legs. Sirrah beadle, whip him till he leap over that same stool.
Bead. I will, my lord. Come on, sirrah; off with your doublet quickly. 151
Simp. Alas, master, what shall I do? I am not able to stand.
[*After the Beadle hath hit him once, he leaps over the stool and runs away; and they follow and cry, 'A miracle!'*
King. O God, seest Thou this, and bearest so long?
Queen. It made me laugh to see the villain run.
Glou. Follow the knave; and take this drab away.
Wife. Alas, sir, we did it for pure need.
Glou. Let them be whipped through every market-town, till they come to Berwick, from whence they came. 160
[*Exeunt Wife, Beadle, Mayor, &c.*
Car. Duke Humphrey has done a miracle to-day.
Suf. True; made the lame to leap and fly away.
Glou. But you have done more miracles than I;
You made in a day, my lord, whole towns to fly.

Enter BUCKINGHAM.

King. What tidings with our cousin Buckingham?
Buck. Such as my heart doth tremble to unfold.
A sort of naughty persons, lewdly bent,
Under the countenance and confederacy
Of Lady Eleanor, the protector's wife,
The ringleader and head of all this rout, 170

136 *beadles.* Parish officers.

Gloucester: ' . . . Sirrah beadle, whip him till he leap over that same stool'. Engraving by Kenny Meadows from Barry Cornwall's *Works of Shakspere*, 1846

156 *drab.* Slut.

167 *naughty.* Wicked.

170 *rout.* Rabble.

Edward III, through whose third son, Duke of Clarence, York claimed the right to the throne

---

173 *apprehended in the fact.* Caught in the act.

181 *keep your hour.* Keep your appointment for the duel.

188 *tainture . . . nest.* Corruption of your household.

196 *pitch . . . nobility.* Reference to the proverb 'he who touches pitch shall be defiled'.

3 *close.* Secluded.

Have practised dangerously against your state,
Dealing with witches and with conjurers:
Whom we have apprehended in the fact;
Raising up wicked spirits from under ground,
Demanding of King Henry's life and death,
And other of your highness' privy-council;
As more at large your grace shall understand.
    Car. [*Aside to Glou.*] And so, my lord protector, by this means
Your lady is forthcoming yet at London.
This news, I think, hath turn'd your weapon's edge: 180
'Tis like, my lord, you will not keep your hour.
    Glou. Ambitious churchman, leave to afflict my heart:
Sorrow and grief have vanquish'd all my powers;
And, vanquish'd as I am, I yield to thee,
Or to the meanest groom.
    King. O God, what mischiefs work the wicked ones,
Heaping confusion on their own heads thereby!
    Queen. Gloucester, see here the tainture of thy nest,
And look thyself be faultless, thou wert best.
    Glou. Madam, for myself, to heaven I do appeal, 190
How I have loved my king and commonweal:
And, for my wife, I know not how it stands;
Sorry I am to hear what I have heard:
Noble she is, but if she have forgot
Honour and virtue and conversed with such
As, like to pitch, defile nobility,
I banish her my bed and company
And give her as a prey to law and shame,
That hath dishonour'd Gloucester's honest name.
    King. Well, for this night we will repose us here: 200
To-morrow toward London back again,
To look into this business thoroughly
And call these foul offenders to their answers
And poise the cause in justice' equal scales,
Whose beam stands sure, whose rightful cause prevails.   [*Flourish. Exeunt.*

SCENE II. *London. The* DUKE OF YORK's *garden.*

Enter YORK, SALISBURY, *and* WARWICK.

    York. Now, my good Lords of Salisbury and Warwick,
Our simple supper ended, give me leave
In this close walk to satisfy myself,
In craving your opinion of my title,
Which is infallible, to England's crown.
    Sal. My lord, I long to hear it at full.
    War. Sweet York, begin: and if thy claim be good,
The Nevils are thy subjects to command.
    York. Then thus:
Edward the Third, my lords, had seven sons: 10
The first, Edward the Black Prince, Prince of Wales;
The second, William of Hatfield, and the third,
Lionel Duke of Clarence; next to whom
Was John of Gaunt, the Duke of Lancaster;
The fifth was Edmund Langley, Duke of York;
The sixth was Thomas of Woodstock, Duke of Gloucester;
William of Windsor was the seventh and last.

Edward the Black Prince died before his father
And left behind him Richard, his only son,
Who after Edward the Third's death reign'd as
    king;   20
Till Henry Bolingbroke, Duke of Lancaster,
The eldest son and heir of John of Gaunt,
Crown'd by the name of Henry the Fourth,
Seized on the realm, deposed the rightful king,
Sent his poor queen to France, from whence she
    came,
And him to Pomfret; where, as all you know,
Harmless Richard was murder'd traitorously.
    War. Father, the duke hath told the truth;
Thus got the house of Lancaster the crown.
    York. Which now they hold by force and not
    by right;   30
For Richard, the first son's heir, being dead,
The issue of the next son should have reign'd.
    Sal. But William of Hatfield died without an
    heir.
    York. The third son, Duke of Clarence, from
    whose line
I claim the crown, had issue, Philippe, a daughter,
Who married Edmund Mortimer, Earl of March:
Edmund had issue, Roger Earl of March;
Roger had issue, Edmund, Anne and Eleanor.
    Sal. This Edmund, in the reign of Boling-
    broke,
As I have read, laid claim unto the crown;   40
And, but for Owen Glendower, had been king,
Who kept him in captivity till he died.
But to the rest.
    York.   His eldest sister, Anne,
My mother, being heir unto the crown,
Married Richard Earl of Cambridge; who was
    son
To Edmund Langley, Edward the Third's fifth
    son.
By her I claim the kingdom: she was heir
To Roger Earl of March, who was the son
Of Edmund Mortimer, who married Philippe,
Sole daughter unto Lionel Duke of Clarence: 50
So, if the issue of the elder son
Succeed before the younger, I am king.
    War. What plain proceeding is more plain
    than this?
Henry doth claim the crown from John of Gaunt,
The fourth son; York claims it from the third.
Till Lionel's issue fails, his should not reign:
It fails not yet, but flourishes in thee
And in thy sons, fair slips of such a stock.
Then, father Salisbury, kneel we together;
And in this private plot be we the first   60
That shall salute our rightful sovereign
With honour of his birthright to the crown.
    Both. Long live our sovereign Richard, Eng-
    land's king!
    York. We thank you, lords. But I am not
    your king
Till I be crown'd and that my sword be stain'd
With heart-blood of the house of Lancaster;
And that's not suddenly to be perform'd,
But with advice and silent secrecy.
Do you as I do in these dangerous days:
Wink at the Duke of Suffolk's insolence,   70
At Beaufort's pride, at Somerset's ambition,
At Buckingham and all the crew of them,
Till they have snared the shepherd of the flock,
That virtuous prince, the good Duke Humphrey:

John of Gaunt, father of Henry Bolingbroke, Duke of
Lancaster (Henry IV). Engraving from *Old England*,
1854

---

36 *Edmund Mortimer.* Like the chronicles which he
followed, Shakespeare's account of the Mortimer
family tree is historically inaccurate. Edmund Mortimer,
3rd Earl of March and son-in-law of Lionel Duke of
Clarence, had two sons – Roger 4th Earl of March and
Sir Edmund. It was Sir Edmund who was captured by
Glendower and married his daughter (*1 Henry IV*). It
was another Edmund, Roger Mortimer's son Edmund,
5th Earl of March and nephew of the Glendower's son-
in-law, Sir Edmund, who was York's maternal uncle
and had been designated heir to the throne by Richard
II. These two Edmunds are also confused in *1 Henry IV*
and *1 Henry VI*.

53 *proceeding.* Pedigree.

58 *slips.* Cuttings.

31 *king his.* King's.

41 *bears . . . maim.* Suffers such bitter humiliation. *pulls.* Pluckings.

'Tis that they seek, and they in seeking that
Shall find their deaths, if York can prophesy.
 Sal. My lord, break we off; we know your
  mind at full.
 War. My heart assures me that the Earl of
  Warwick
Shall one day make the Duke of York a king.
 York. And, Nevil, this I do assure myself:
Richard shall live to make the Earl of Warwick
The greatest man in England but the king.
         [*Exeunt.*

    SCENE III. *A hall of justice.*

Sound trumpets. Enter the KING, *the* QUEEN,
GLOUCESTER, YORK, SUFFOLK, *and* SALIS-
BURY; *the* DUCHESS OF GLOUCESTER, MAR-
GERY JOURDAIN, SOUTHWELL, HUME, *and*
BOLINGBROKE, *under guard.*

 King. Stand forth, Dame Eleanor Cobham,
  Gloucester's wife:
In sight of God and us, your guilt is great:
Receive the sentence of the law for sins
Such as by God's book are adjudged to death.
You four, from hence to prison back again;
From thence unto the place of execution:
The witch in Smithfield shall be burn'd to ashes,
And you three shall be strangled on the gallows.
You, madam, for you are more nobly born,
Despoiled of your honour in your life,   10
Shall, after three days' open penance done,
Live in your country here in banishment,
With Sir John Stanley, in the Isle of Man.
 Duch. Welcome is banishment; welcome were
  my death.
 Glou. Eleanor, the law, thou see'st, hath
  judged thee:
I cannot justify whom the law condemns.
 [*Exeunt Duchess and other prisoners, guarded.*
Mine eyes are full of tears, my heart of grief.
Ah, Humphrey, this dishonour in thine age
Will bring thy head with sorrow to the ground!
I beseech your majesty, give me leave to go; 20
Sorrow would solace and mine age would ease.
 King. Stay, Humphrey Duke of Gloucester:
  ere thou go,
Give up thy staff: Henry will to himself
Protector be; and God shall be my hope,
My stay, my guide and lantern to my feet:
And go in peace, Humphrey, no less beloved
Than when thou wert protector to thy king.
 Queen. I see no reason why a king of years
Should be to be protected like a child.
God and King Henry govern England's realm. 30
 ● Give up your staff, sir, and the king his realm.
 Glou. My staff? here, noble Henry, is my
  staff:
As willingly do I the same resign
As e'er thy father Henry made it mine;
And even as willingly at thy feet I leave it
As others would ambitiously receive it.
Farewell, good king: when I am dead and gone,
May honourable peace attend thy throne! [*Exit.*
 Queen. Why, now is Henry king, and Mar-
  garet queen;
And Humphrey Duke of Gloucester scarce him-
  self,   40
 ● That bears so shrewd a maim; two pulls at once;
His lady banish'd, and a limb lopp'd off.

● This staff of honour raught, there let it stand
Where it best fits to be, in Henry's hand.
   Suf. Thus droops this lofty pine and hangs his
     sprays;
Thus Eleanor's pride dies in her youngest days.
   York. Lords, let him go. Please it your majesty,
This is the day appointed for the combat;
And ready are the appellant and defendant,
The armourer and his man, to enter the lists,   50
So please your highness to behold the fight.
   Queen. Ay, good my lord; for purposely there-
     fore
Left I the court, to see this quarrel tried.
   King. O' God's name, see the lists and all
     things fit:
Here let them end it; and God defend the right!
●   *York.* I never saw a fellow worse bested,
Or more afraid to fight, than is the appellant,
The servant of this armourer, my lords.

Enter at one door, HORNER, *the Armourer, and
his* Neighbours, *drinking to him so much that
he is drunk; and he enters with a drum before
him and his staff with a sand-bag fastened to
it; and at the other door* PETER, *his man,
with a drum and sand-bag, and* 'Prentices
drinking to him.

   First Neigh. Here, neighbour Horner, I drink
to you in a cup of sack: and fear not, neighbour,
you shall do well enough.   61
   Sec. Neigh. And here, neighbour, here's a cup
● of charneco.
   Third Neigh. And here's a pot of good double
beer, neighbour: drink, and fear not your man.
   Hor. Let it come, i' faith, and I'll pledge you
● all; and a fig for Peter!
   First 'Pren. Here, Peter, I drink to thee:
and be not afraid.
   Sec. 'Pren. Be merry, Peter, and fear not thy
master: fight for credit of the 'prentices.   71
   Peter. I thank you all: drink, and pray for
me, I pray you; for I think I have taken my last
draught in this world. Here, Robin, an if I die,
I give thee my apron: and, Will, thou shalt have
my hammer: and here, Tom, take all the money
that I have. O Lord bless me! I pray God! for
I am never able to deal with my master, he hath
learnt so much fence already.
   Sal. Come, leave your drinking, and fall to
blows. Sirrah, what's thy name?   81
   Peter. Peter, forsooth.
   Sal. Peter! what more?
   Peter. Thump.
   Sal. Thump! then see thou thump thy master
well.
   Hor. Masters, I am come hither, as it were,
upon my man's instigation, to prove him a knave
and myself an honest man: and touching the
Duke of York, I will take my death, I never
meant him any ill, nor the king, nor the queen:
and therefore, Peter, have at thee with a down-
right blow!
   York. Dispatch: this knave's tongue begins
to double.
Sound, trumpets, alarum to the combatants!
   [*Alarum. They fight, and Peter strikes
                him down.*
   Hor. Hold, Peter, hold! I confess, I confess
treason.   [*Dies.*

43 *raught.* Reached, obtained.

56 *worse bested.* In a worse situation.

63 *charneco.* Sweet white wine.

67 *a fig for Peter.* Term of derision.

99

8 *Uneath.* Hardly, scarcely.

31 *Mail'd up.* Wrapped up – a term in falconry.

33 *deep-fet.* Deep-fetched, heart-felt.

38 *Trow'st thou.* Do you think.

Duchess of Gloucester carrying a burning taper.
Engraving by Kenny Meadows from Barry Cornwall's
Works of Shakspere, 1846

York. Take away his weapon. Fellow, thank
God, and the good wine in thy master's way. 99
 Peter. O God, have I overcome mine enemy
in this presence? O Peter, thou hast prevailed
in right!
 King. Go, take hence that traitor from our
  sight;
For by his death we do perceive his guilt:
And God in justice hath reveal'd to us
The truth and innocence of this poor fellow,
Which he had thought to have murder'd wrong-
  fully.
Come, fellow, follow us for thy reward.
   [*Sound a flourish. Exeunt.*

SCENE IV. *A street.*

Enter GLOUCESTER *and his Servingmen, in
mourning cloaks.*

 Glou. Thus sometimes hath the brightest day
  a cloud;
And after summer evermore succeeds
Barren winter, with his wrathful nipping cold:
So cares and joys abound, as seasons fleet.
Sirs, what's o'clock?
 Serv.   Ten, my lord.
 Glou. Ten is the hour that was appointed me
To watch the coming of my punish'd duchess:
• Uneath may she endure the flinty streets,
To tread them with her tender-feeling feet.
Sweet Nell, ill can thy noble mind abrook   10
The abject people gazing on thy face,
With envious looks, laughing at thy shame,
That erst did follow thy proud chariot-wheels
When thou didst ride in triumph through the
  streets.
But, soft! I think she comes; and I'll prepare
My tear-stain'd eyes to see her miseries.

Enter the DUCHESS OF GLOUCESTER *in a white
sheet, and a taper burning in her hand; with*
SIR JOHN STANLEY, *the* Sheriff, *and* Officers.

 Serv. So please your grace, we'll take her
  from the sheriff.
 Glou. No, stir not, for your lives; let her
  pass by.
 Duch. Come you, my lord, to see my open
  shame?
Now thou dost penance too. Look how they gaze!
See how the giddy multitude do point,   21
And nod their heads, and throw their eyes on thee!
Ah, Gloucester, hide thee from their hateful looks,
And, in thy closet pent up, rue my shame,
And ban thine enemies, both mine and thine!
 Glou. Be patient, gentle Nel!; forget this grief.
 Duch. Ah, Gloucester, teach me to forget
  myself!
For whilst I think I am thy married wife
And thou a prince, protector of this land,
Methinks I should not thus be led along,   30
• Mail'd up in shame, with papers on my back,
And follow'd with a rabble that rejoice
• To see my tears and hear my deep-fet groans.
The ruthless flint doth cut my tender feet,
And when I start, the envious people laugh
And bid me be advised how I tread.
Ah, Humphrey, can I bear this shameful yoke?
• Trow'st thou that e'er I'll look upon the world,
Or count them happy that enjoy the sun?

No; dark shall be my light and night my day; 40
To think upon my pomp shall be my hell.
Sometime I'll say, I am Duke Humphrey's wife,
And he a prince and ruler of the land:
Yet so he ruled and such a prince he was
As he stood by whilst I, his forlorn duchess,
● Was made a wonder and a pointing-stock
To every idle rascal follower.
But be thou mild and blush not at my shame,
Nor stir at nothing till the axe of death
Hang over thee, as, sure, it shortly will; 50
For Suffolk, he that can do all in all
With her that hateth thee and hates us all,
And York and impious Beaufort, that false priest,
Have all limed bushes to betray thy wings,
And, fly thou how thou canst, they'll tangle thee:
But fear not thou, until thy foot be snared,
● Nor never seek prevention of thy foes.
   Glou. Ah, Nell, forbear! thou aimest all awry;
● I must offend before I be attainted;
And had I twenty times so many foes, 60
And each of them had twenty times their power,
All these could not procure me any scathe,
So long as I am loyal, true and crimeless.
Wouldst have me rescue thee from this reproach?
Why, yet thy scandal were not wiped away,
But I in danger for the breach of law.
Thy greatest help is quiet, gentle Nell:
I pray thee, sort thy heart to patience;
These few days' wonder will be quickly worn.

Enter a Herald.

   Her. I summon your grace to his majesty's
     parliament, 70
Holden at Bury the first of this next month.
   Glou. And my consent ne'er ask'd herein be-
     fore!
This is close dealing. Well, I will be there.
                  [*Exit Herald.*
My Nell, I take my leave: and, master sheriff,
Let not her penance exceed the king's commission.
   Sher. An't please your grace, here my com-
     mission stays,
And Sir John Stanley is appointed now
To take her with him to the Isle of Man.
   Glou. Must you, Sir John, protect my lady
     here?
   Stan. So am I given in charge, may't please
     your grace. 80
   Glou. Entreat her not the worse in that I pray
You use her well: the world may laugh again;
And I may live to do you kindness if
You do it her: and so, Sir John, farewell!
   Duch. What, gone, my lord, and bid me not
     farewell!
   Glou. Witness my tears, I cannot stay to speak.
         [*Exeunt Gloucester and Servingmen.*
   Duch. Art thou gone too? all comfort go with
     thee!
For none abides with me: my joy is death;
Death, at whose name I oft have been afear'd,
Because I wish'd this world's eternity. 90
Stanley, I prithee, go, and take me hence;
I care not whither, for I beg no favour,
Only convey me where thou art commanded.
   Stan. Why, madam, that is to the Isle of Man;
There to be used according to your state.
   Duch. That's bad enough, for I am but re-
     proach:

46 *pointing-stock.* Laughing stock.

57 *seek prevention.* i.e. to anticipate the machinations of your enemies.

59 *attainted.* Convicted of treason.

Isle of Man, to where Eleanor, Duchess of Gloucester, was banished. From John Speed's *Theatre of the Empire of Great Britaine*, 1611–12

107 *shifted*. Changed (with a pun on 'shift' or 'chemise').

King, Queen and Parliament in the Abbey at Bury St Edmunds. Engraving from *Old England*, 1854

18 *grin*. Show teeth.

19 *lion*. Heraldic emblem of England and the king.

36 *fond*. Foolish.

And shall I then be used reproachfully?
  Stan. Like to a duchess, and Duke Hum-
    phrey's lady;
According to that state you shall be used.   99
  Duch. Sheriff, farewell, and better than I fare,
Although thou hast been conduct of my shame.
  Sher. It is my office; and, madam, pardon me.
  Duch. Ay, ay, farewell; thy office is dis-
    charged.
Come, Stanley, shall we go?
  Stan. Madam, your penance done, throw off
    this sheet,
And go we to attire you for our journey.
  ● *Duch.* My shame will not be shifted with my
    sheet:
No, it will hang upon my richest robes
And show itself, attire me how I can.
Go, lead the way; I long to see my prison.   110
                [*Exeunt.*

ACT III.

SCENE I. *The Abbey at Bury St Edmund's.*

Sound a sennet. Enter the KING, *the* QUEEN,
CARDINAL BEAUFORT, SUFFOLK, YORK,
BUCKINGHAM, SALISBURY *and* WARWICK *to
the Parliament.*

  King. I muse my Lord of Gloucester is not
    come:
'Tis not his wont to be the hindmost man,
Whate'er occasion keeps him from us now.
  Queen. Can you not see? or will ye not ob-
    serve
The strangeness of his alter'd countenance?
With what a majesty he bears himself,
How insolent of late he is become,
How proud, how peremptory, and unlike him-
    self?
We know the time since he was mild and affable,
And if we did but glance a far-off look,   10
Immediately he was upon his knee,
That all the court admired him for submission:
But meet him now, and, be it in the morn,
When every one will give the time of day,
He knits his brow and shows an angry eye
And passeth by with stiff unbowed knee,
Disdaining duty that to us belongs.
● Small curs are not regarded when they grin;
● But great men tremble when the lion roars;
And Humphrey is no little man in England.   20
First note that he is near you in descent,
And should you fall, he is the next will mount.
Me seemeth then it is no policy,
Respecting what a rancorous mind he bears
And his advantage following your decease,
That he should come about your royal person
Or be admitted to your highness' council.
By flattery hath he won the commons' hearts,
And when he please to make commotion,
'Tis to be fear'd they all will follow him.   30
Now 'tis the spring, and weeds are shallow-
    rooted;
Suffer them now, and they'll o'ergrow the garden
And choke the herbs for want of husbandry.
The reverent care I bear unto my lord
Made me collect these dangers in the duke.
● If it be fond, call it a woman's fear;
  Which fear if better reasons can supplant,

I will subscribe and say I wrong'd the duke.
My Lord of Suffolk, Buckingham, and York,
Reprove my allegation, if you can;   40
Or else conclude my words effectual.
  Suf. Well hath your highness seen into this
    duke;
And, had I first been put to speak my mind,
I think I should have told your grace's tale.
The duchess by his subornation,
Upon my life, began her devilish practices:
Or, if he were not privy to those faults,
Yet, by reputing of his high descent,
As next the king he was successive heir,
And such high vaunts of his nobility,   50
Did instigate the bedlam brain-sick duchess
By wicked means to frame our sovereign's fall.
Smooth runs the water where the brook is deep;
And in his simple show he harbours treason.
The fox barks not when he would steal the lamb.
No, no, my sovereign; Gloucester is a man
Unsounded yet and full of deep deceit.
  Car. Did he not, contrary to form of law,
Devise strange deaths for small offences done?
  York. And did he not, in his protectorship, 60
Levy great sums of money through the realm
For soldiers' pay in France, and never sent it?
By means whereof the towns each day revolted.
  Buck. Tut, these are petty faults to faults
    unknown,
Which time will bring to light in smooth Duke
    Humphrey.
  King. My lords, at once: the care you have
    of us,
To mow down thorns that would annoy our foot,
Is worthy praise: but, shall I speak my con-
    science,
Our kinsman Gloucester is as innocent
From meaning treason to our royal person   70
As is the sucking lamb or harmless dove:
The duke is virtuous, mild and too well given
To dream on evil or to work my downfall
  Queen. Ah, what's more dangerous than this
    fond affiance!
Seems he a dove? his feathers are but borrow'd,
For he's disposed as the hateful raven:
Is he a lamb? his skin is surely lent him,
For he's inclined as is the ravenous wolf.
Who cannot steal a shape that means deceit?
Take heed, my lord; the welfare of us all   80
Hangs on the cutting short that fraudful man.

Enter SOMERSET.

  Som. All health unto my gracious sovereign!
  King. Welcome, Lord Somerset. What news
    from France?
  Som. That all your interest in those terri-
    tories
Is utterly bereft you; all is lost.
  King. Cold news, Lord Somerset: but God's
    will be done!
  York. [*Aside*] Cold news for me; for I had
    hope of France
As firmly as I hope for fertile England.
Thus are my blossoms blasted in the bud
And caterpillars eat my leaves away;   90
But I will remedy this gear ere long,
Or sell my title for a glorious grave.

38 *subscribe.* Testify in writing.

45 *subornation.* Inducement to commit crime.

51 *bedlam.* Deranged.

74 *fond affiance.* Foolish confidence.

79 *steal a shape.* Assume a disguise.

91 *gear.* Business.

Somerset (Oliver Ford-Davis) and Henry VI (Alan
Howard) Royal Shakespeare Co, 1977

112–113 *doit, groat.* Coins of small denomination.

130 *condign.* Severe.

147 *complot.* Conspiracy.

Enter GLOUCESTER.

Glou. All happiness unto my lord the king!
Pardon, my liege, that I have stay'd so long.
　　Suf. Nay, Gloucester, know that thou **art**
　　　come too soon,
Unless thou wert more loyal than thou art·
I do arrest thee of high treason here.
　　Glou. Well, Suffolk, thou shalt **not see me**
　　　blush
Nor change my countenance for **this** arrest:
A heart unspotted is not easily daunted.　　100
The purest spring is not so free from mud
As I am clear from treason to my sovereign:
Who can accuse me? wherein am I guilty?
　　York. 'Tis thought, my lord, that you took
　　　bribes of France,
And, being protector, stay'd the soldiers' pay;
By means whereof his highness hath lost France.
　　Glou. Is it but thought so? what **are** they
　　　that think it?
I never robb'd the soldiers of their **pay,**
Nor ever had one penny bribe from France.
So help me God, as I have watch'd the night, 110
Ay, night by night, in studying good **for** England,
● That doit that e'er I wrested from the king,
Or any groat I hoarded to my use,
Be brought against me at my trial-day!
No; many a pound of mine own proper **store,**
Because I would not tax the needy commons,
Have I dispursed to the garrisons,
And never ask'd for restitution.
　　Car. It serves you well, my lord, to say so
　　　much.
　　Glou. I say no more than truth, so help me
　　　God!　　120
　　York. In your protectorship you did devise
Strange tortures for offenders never heard of,
That England was defamed by tyranny.
　　Glou. Why, 'tis well known that, whiles **I was**
　　　protector,
Pity was all the fault that was in me:
For I should melt at an offender's tears,
And lowly words were ransom for their fault.
Unless it were a bloody murderer,
Or foul felonious thief that fleeced poor passengers,
● I never gave them condign punishment:　　130
Murder indeed, that bloody sin, I tortured
Above the felon or what trespass else.
　　Suf. My lord, these faults are easy, quickly
　　　answer'd:
But mightier crimes are laid unto your charge,
Whereof you cannot easily purge yourself.
I do arrest you in his highness' name;
And here commit you to my lord cardinal
To keep, until your further time of trial.
　　King. My lord of Gloucester, 'tis my special
　　　hope
That you will clear yourself from all suspect: 140
My conscience tells me you are innocent.
　　Glou. Ah, gracious lord, these days are dangerous:
Virtue is choked with foul ambition
And charity chased hence by rancour's hand;
Foul subornation is predominant
And equity exiled your highness' land.
● I know their complot is to have my life,

And if my death might make this island happy
And prove the period of their tyranny,
I would expend it with all willingness: 150
But mine is made the prologue to their play;
For thousands more, that yet suspect no peril,
Will not conclude their plotted tragedy.
Beaufort's red sparkling eyes blab his heart's malice,
And Suffolk's cloudy brow his stormy hate;
Sharp Buckingham unburthens with his tongue
The envious load that lies upon his heart;
And dogged York, that reaches at the moon,
Whose overweening arm I have pluck'd back,
● By false accuse doth level at my life: 160
And you, my sovereign lady, with the rest,
Causeless have laid disgraces on my head
And with your best endeavour have stirr'd up
● My liefest liege to be mine enemy:
Ay, all of you have laid your heads together—
● Myself had notice of your conventicles—
And all to make away my guiltless life.
I shall not want false witness to condemn me,
Nor store of treasons to augment my guilt;
The ancient proverb will be well effected: 170
'A staff is quickly found to beat a dog.'
   Car. My liege, his railing is intolerable:
If those that care to keep your royal person
From treason's secret knife and traitors' rage
Be thus upbraided, chid and rated at,
And the offender granted scope of speech,
'Twill make them cool in zeal unto your grace.
   Suf. Hath he not twit our sovereign lady here
● With ignominious words, though clerkly couch'd,
As if she had suborned some to swear   180
False allegations to o'erthrow his state?
   Queen. But I can give the loser leave to chide.
   Glou. Far truer spoke than meant: I lose, indeed;
Beshrew the winners, for they play'd me false!
And well such losers may have leave to speak.
   Buck. He'll wrest the sense and hold us here all day:
Lord cardinal, he is your prisoner.
   Car. Sirs, take away the duke, and guard him sure.
   Glou. Ah! thus King Henry throws away his crutch
Before his legs be firm to bear his body.   190
Thus is the shepherd beaten from thy side
● And wolves are gnarling who shall gnaw thee first.
Ah, that my fear were false! ah, that it were!
For, good King Henry, thy decay I fear.
                [*Exit, guarded.*
   King. My lords, what to your wisdoms seemeth best,
Do or undo, as if ourself were here.
   Queen. What, will your highness leave the parliament?
   King. Ay, Margaret; my heart is drown'd with grief,
Whose flood begins to flow within mine eyes,
My body round engirt with misery,   200
For what's more miserable than discontent?
Ah, uncle Humphrey! in thy face I see
The map of honour, truth and loyalty:
And yet, good Humphrey, is the hour to come
That e'er I proved thee false or fear'd thy faith.
What louring star now envies thy estate,

160 *accuse.* Accusation.

164 *liefest liege.* Most dear sovereign.

166 *conventicles.* Secret meetings.

179 *clerkly couch'd.* In a scholarly style.

192 *gnarling.* Snarling.

226 *mournful crocodile.* According to popular belief the crocodile lured its victims by a display of sobbing and crying.

Crocodile with victim. Illustration from a 12th century bestiary

---

236 *colour.* Pretext, justification.

240 *haply.* Perhaps.

244 *fain.* Willing.

259 *chaps.* Chops.

261 *quillets.* Legal subtleties.

265 *mates.* Checkmates.

That these great lords and Margaret our queen
Do seek subversion of thy harmless life?
Thou never didst them wrong nor no man wrong;
And as the butcher takes away the calf   210
And binds the wretch and beats it when it strays,
Bearing it to the bloody slaughter-house,
Even so remorseless have they borne him hence;
And as the dam runs lowing up and down,
Looking the way her harmless young one went,
And can do nought but wail her darling's loss,
Even so myself bewails good Gloucester's case
With sad unhelpful tears, and with dimm'd eyes
Look after him and cannot do him good,
So mighty are his vowed enemies.   220
His fortunes I will weep and 'twixt each groan
Say 'Who's a traitor? Gloucester he is none.'
　　[*Exeunt all but Queen, Cardinal Beaufort,
　　Suffolk, and York; Somerset remains apart.*
　　Queen.　Free lords, cold snow melts with the sun's hot beams.
Henry my lord is cold in great affairs,
Too full of foolish pity, and Gloucester's show
● Beguiles him as the mournful crocodile
With sorrow snares relenting passengers,
Or as the snake roll'd in a flowering bank,
With shining checker'd slough, doth sting a child
That for the beauty thinks it excellent.   230
Believe me, lords, were none more wise than I—
And yet herein I judge mine own wit good—
This Gloucester should be quickly rid the world,
To rid us from the fear we have of him.
　　Car.　That he should die is worthy policy;
● But yet we want a colour for his death:
'Tis meet he be condemn'd by course of law.
　　Suf.　But, in my mind, that were no policy:
The king will labour still to save his life,
● The commons haply rise, to save his life;   240
And yet we have but trivial argument,
More than mistrust, that shows him worthy death.
　　York.　So that, by this, you would not have him die.
● *Suf.*　Ah, York, no man alive so fain as I!
　　York.　'Tis York that hath more reason for his death.
But, my lord cardinal, and you, my Lord of Suffolk,
Say as you think, and speak it from your souls,
Were't not all one, an empty eagle were set
To guard the chicken from a hungry kite,
As place Duke Humphrey for the king's protector?   250
　　Queen.　So the poor chicken should be sure of death.
　　Suf.　Madam, 'tis true; and were't not madness, then,
To make the fox surveyor of the fold?
Who being accused a crafty murderer,
His guilt should be but idly posted over,
Because his purpose is not executed.
No; let him die, in that he is a fox,
By nature proved an enemy to the flock,
● Before his chaps be stain'd with crimson blood,
As Humphrey, proved by reasons, to my liege.
● And do not stand on quillets how to slay him: 261
Be it by gins, by snares, by subtlety,
Sleeping or waking, 'tis no matter how,
So he be dead; for that is good deceit
● Which mates him first that first intends deceit.

Queen. Thrice-noble Suffolk, 'tis resolutely
    spoke.
Suf. Not resolute, except so much were done;
For things are often spoke and seldom meant:
But that my heart accordeth with my tongue,
Seeing the deed is meritorious,   270
And to preserve my sovereign from his foe,
● Say but the word, and I will be his priest.
    Car. But I would have him dead, my Lord
        of Suffolk,
Ere you can take due orders for a priest:
● Say you consent and censure well the deed,
And I'll provide his executioner,
I tender so the safety of my liege.
    Suf. Here is my hand, the deed is worthy
        doing.
    Queen. And so say I.
    York. And I: and now we three have spoke
        it,   280
● It skills not greatly who impugns our doom.

Enter a Post.

● *Post.* Great lords, from Ireland am I come
        amain,
To signify that rebels there are up
And put the Englishmen unto the sword:
Send succours, lords, and stop the rage betime,
Before the wound do grow uncurable;
For, being green, there is great hope of help.
    Car. A breach that craves a quick expedient
        stop!
What counsel give you in this weighty cause?
    York. That Somerset be sent as regent thi-
        ther: 290
'Tis meet that lucky ruler be employ'd;
Witness the fortune he hath had in France.
    Som. If York, with all his far-fet policy,
Had been the regent there instead of me,
He never would have stay'd in France so long.
    York. No, not to lose it all, as thou hast done:
I rather would have lost my life betimes
Than bring a burthen of dishonour home
By staying there so long till all were lost.
Show me one scar character'd on thy skin: 300
Men's flesh preserved so whole do seldom win.
    Queen. Nay, then, this spark will prove a
        raging fire,
If wind and fuel be brought to feed it with:
No more, good York; sweet Somerset, be still:
Thy fortune, York, hadst thou been regent there,
Might happily have proved far worse than his.
    York. What, worse than nought? nay, then,
        a shame take all!
    Som. And, in the number, thee that wishest
        shame!
    Car. My Lord of York, try what your for-
        tune is.
● The uncivil kerns of Ireland are in arms   310
● And temper clay with blood of Englishmen:
To Ireland will you lead a band of men,
Collected choicely, from each county some,
And try your hap against the Irishmen?
    York. I will, my lord, so please his majesty.
    Suf. Why, our authority is his consent,
And what we do establish he confirms:
Then, noble York, take thou this task in hand.
    York. I am content: provide me soldiers, lords,
Whiles I take order for mine own affairs.   320

272 *priest.* i.e. adminster the last rites.

275 *censure.* Approve.

Suffolk: 'Here is my hand . . .' Beaufort (David Dodi-mead), Margaret (Barbara Jefford), York (Jack Gwillim) and Suffolk (Derek Godfrey), Old Vic Theatre, London, 1957

281 *skills . . . doom.* It does not matter much who opposes our decision.

SD POST. A messenger.

282 *amain.* Hastily, quickly.

310 *uncivil kerns.* Irish light-armed foot-soldiers.

311 *temper.* Soften.

332 *misdoubt.* Uncertainty, lack of confidence.

343 *starved.* Frozen.

354 *flaw.* Squall.

363 *porpentine.* Porcupine.

365 *Morisco.* Moorish or Morris dancer.

A Moorish dancer. Engraving copied from a German illustration of 1577

Suf. A charge, Lord York, that I will see perform'd.
But now return we to the false Duke Humphrey.
  Car. No more of him; for I will deal with him
That henceforth he shall trouble us no more.
And so break off; the day is almost spent:
Lord Suffolk, you and I must talk of that event.
  York. My Lord of Suffolk, within fourteen days
At Bristol I expect my soldiers;
For there I'll ship them all for Ireland.
  Suf. I'll see it truly done, my Lord of York.
                                        [*Exeunt all but York.*
  York. Now, York, or never, steel thy fearful thoughts,   331
● And change misdoubt to resolution:
Be that thou hopest to be, or what thou art
Resign to death; it is not worth the enjoying:
Let pale-faced fear keep with the mean-born man,
And find no harbour in a royal heart.
Faster than spring-time showers comes thought on thought,
And not a thought but thinks on dignity.
My brain more busy than the labouring spider
Weaves tedious snares to trap mine enemies.   340
Well, nobles, well, 'tis politicly done,
To send me packing with an host of men:
● I fear me you but warm the starved snake,
Who, cherish'd in your breasts, will sting your hearts.
'Twas men I lack'd and you will give them me
I take it kindly; yet be well assured
You put sharp weapons in a madman's hands.
Whiles I in Ireland nourish a mighty band,
I will stir up in England some black storm
Shall blow ten thousand souls to heaven or hell;
And this fell tempest shall not cease to rage   351
Until the golden circuit on my head,
Like to the glorious sun's transparent beams,
● Do calm the fury of this mad-bred flaw.
And, for a minister of my intent,
I have seduced a headstrong Kentishman,
John Cade of Ashford,
To make commotion, as full well he can,
Under the title of John Mortimer.
In Ireland have I seen this stubborn Cade   360
Oppose himself against a troop of kerns,
And fought so long, till that his thighs with darts
● Were almost like a sharp-quill'd porpentine;
And, in the end being rescued, I have seen
● Him caper upright like a wild Morisco,
Shaking the bloody darts as he his bells.
Full often, like a shag-hair'd crafty kern,
Hath he conversed with the enemy,
And undiscover'd come to me again
And given me notice of their villanies.   370
This devil here shall be my substitute;
For that John Mortimer, which now is dead,
In face, in gait, in speech, he doth resemble:
By this I shall perceive the commons' mind,
How they affect the house and claim of York.
Say he be taken, rack'd and tortured,
I know no pain they can inflict upon him
Will make him say I moved him to those arms.
Say that he thrive, as 'tis great like he will,
Why, then from Ireland come I with my strength
And reap the harvest which that rascal sow'd; 381
For Humphrey being dead, as he shall be,
And Henry put apart, the next for me.   [*Exit.*

SCENE II. *Bury St Edmund's. A room of state.*

Enter certain Murderers, *hastily.*

First Mur. Run to my Lord of Suffolk; let him know
We have dispatch'd the duke, as he commanded.

● *Sec. Mur.* O that it were to do! What have we done?
Didst ever hear a man so penitent?

Enter SUFFOLK.

First Mur. Here comes my lord.
Suf. Now, sirs, have you dispatch'd this thing?
First Mur. Ay, my good lord, he's dead.
Suf. Why, that's well said. Go, get you to my house;
I will reward you for this venturous deed.
The king and all the peers are here at hand. 10
Have you laid fair the bed? Is all things well,
According as I gave directions?
First Mur. 'Tis, my good lord.
Suf. Away! be gone. [*Exeunt Murderers.*

Sound trumpets. Enter the KING, *the* QUEEN, CARDINAL BEAUFORT, SOMERSET, *with Attendants.*

King. Go, call our uncle to our presence straight;
Say we intend to try his grace to-day,
If he be guilty, as 'tis published.

● *Suf.* I'll call him presently, my noble lord.
[*Exit.*

King. Lords, take your places; and, I pray you all,

● Proceed no straiter 'gainst our uncle Gloucester
Than from true evidence of good esteem 21
He be approved in practice culpable.
Queen. God forbid any malice should prevail,
That faultless may condemn a nobleman!
Pray God he may acquit him of suspicion!
King. I thank thee, Meg; these words content me much.

Re-enter SUFFOLK.

How now! why look'st thou pale? why tremblest thou?
Where is our uncle? what's the matter, Suffolk?
Suf. Dead in his bed, my lord; Gloucester is dead.
Queen. Marry, God forfend! 30
Car. God's secret judgement: I did dream to-night
The duke was dumb and could not speak a word.
[*The King swoons.*
Queen. How fares my lord? Help, lords! the king is dead.
Som. Rear up his body; wring him by the nose.
Queen. Run, go, help, help! O Henry, ope thine eyes!
Suf. He doth revive again: madam, be patient.
King. O heavenly God!
Queen. How fares my gracious lord?
Suf. Comfort, my sovereign! gracious Henry, comfort!
King. What, doth my Lord of Suffolk comfort me?

3 *O that . . . do!* Oh that the deed had not been done!

18 *presently.* Immediately.

20 *straiter.* Strictly, more severely.

52 *basilisk.* Mythical reptile thought to be able to kill by a mere breath or look.

A basilisk. Illustration from a 12th century bestiary

---

89 *he . . . caves.* Aeolus, the God of winds, kept them imprisoned in a cave.

97 *splitting rocks.* i.e. rocks that split ships.

Came he right now to sing a raven's note,　　40
Whose dismal tune bereft my vital powers;
And thinks he that the chirping of a wren,
By crying comfort from a hollow breast,
Can chase away the first-conceived sound?
Hide not thy poison with such sugar'd words;
Lay not thy hands on me; forbear, I say;
Their touch affrights me as a serpent's sting.
Thou baleful messenger, out of my sight!
Upon thy eye-balls murderous tyranny
Sits in grim majesty, to fright the world.　　50
Look not upon me, for thine eyes are wounding:
● Yet do not go away: come, basilisk,
And kill the innocent gazer with thy sight;
For in the shade of death I shall find joy;
In life but double death, now Gloucester's dead.
　　Queen. Why do you rate my Lord of Suffolk
　　　　thus?
Although the duke was enemy to him,
Yet he most Christian-like laments his death:
And for myself, foe as he was to me,
Might liquid tears or heart-offending groans　　60
Or blood-consuming sighs recall his life,
I would be blind with weeping, sick with groans,
Look pale as primrose with blood-drinking sighs,
And all to have the noble duke alive.
What know I how the world may deem of me?
For it is known we were but hollow friends:
It may be judged I made the duke away;
So shall my name with slander's tongue be
　　　　wounded,
And princes' courts be fill'd with my reproach.
This get I by his death: ay me, unhappy!　　70
To be a queen, and crown'd with infamy!
　　King. Ah, woe is me for Gloucester, wretched
　　　　man!
　　Queen. Be woe for me, more wretched than
　　　　he is.
What, dost thou turn away and hide thy face?
I am no loathsome leper; look on me.
What! art thou, like the adder, waxen deaf?
Be poisonous too and kill thy forlorn queen.
Is all thy comfort shut in Gloucester's tomb?
Why, then, dame Margaret was ne'er thy joy.
Erect his statua and worship it,　　80
And make my image but an alehouse sign.
Was I for this nigh wreck'd upon the sea
And twice by awkward wind from England's bank
Drove back again unto my native clime?
What boded this, but well forewarning wind
Did seem to say 'Seek not a scorpion's nest,
Nor set no footing on this unkind shore'?
What did I then, but cursed the gentle gusts
● And he that loosed them forth their brazen caves:
And bid them blow towards England's blessed
　　　　shore,　　90
Or turn our stern upon a dreadful rock?
Yet Æolus would not be a murderer,
But left that hateful office unto thee:
The pretty-vaulting sea refused to drown me,
Knowing that thou wouldst have me drown'd on
　　　　shore,
With tears as salt as sea, through thy unkindness:
● The splitting rocks cower'd in the sinking sands
And would not dash me with their ragged sides,
Because thy flinty heart, more hard than they,
Might in thy palace perish Margaret.　　100
As far as I could ken thy chalky cliffs,
When from thy shore the tempest beat us back,

I stood upon the hatches in the storm,
And when the dusky sky began to rob
My earnest-gaping sight of thy land's view,
I took a costly jewel from my neck,
A heart it was, bound in with diamonds,
And threw it towards thy land: the sea received it,
And so I wish'd thy body might my heart:
And even with this I lost fair England's view 110
And bid mine eyes be packing with my heart
And call'd them blind and dusky spectacles,
For losing ken of Albion's wished coast.
How often have I tempted Suffolk's tongue,
The agent of thy foul inconstancy,
● To sit and witch me, as Ascanius did
When he to madding Dido would unfold
His father's acts commenced in burning Troy!
Am I not witch'd like her? or thou not false like
  him?
Ay me, I can no more! die, Margaret!   120
For Henry weeps that thou dost live so long.

Noise within. Enter WARWICK, SALISBURY,
and many Commons.

War. It is reported, mighty sovereign,
That good Duke Humphrey traitorously is mur-
  der'd
By Suffolk and the Cardinal Beaufort's means.
The commons, like an angry hive of bees
That want their leader, scatter up and down
And care not who they sting in his revenge.
Myself have calm'd their spleenful mutiny,
Until they hear the order of his death.
  King. That he is dead, good WARWICK, 'tis
    too true;   130
But how he died God knows, not Henry:
Enter his chamber, view his breathless corpse,
And comment then upon his sudden death.
  War. That shall I do, my liege. Stay, Salis-
    bury,
With the rude multitude till I return. [*Exit.*
  King. O Thou that judgest all things, stay
    my thoughts,
My thoughts, that labour to persuade my soul
Some violent hands were laid on Humphrey's life!
If my suspect be false, forgive me, God,
For judgement only doth belong to thee.   140
Fain would I go to chafe his paly lips
With twenty thousand kisses and to drain
Upon his face an ocean of salt tears,
To tell my love unto his dumb deaf trunk
And with my fingers feel his hand unfeeling:
But all in vain are these mean obsequies;
And to survey his dead and earthy image,
What were it but to make my sorrow greater?

Re-enter WARWICK *and others, bearing* GLOU-
  CESTER'S *body on a bed.*

  War. Come hither, gracious sovereign, view
    this body.
  King. That is to see how deep my grave is
    made;   150
For with his soul fled all my worldly solace,
For seeing him I see my life in death.
  War. As surely as my soul intends to live
With that dread King that took our state upon him
To free us from his father's wrathful curse,
I do believe that violent hands were laid
Upon the life of this thrice-famed duke.

116–117 *Ascanius . . . Dido.* It was actually Cupid
disguised as Ascanius who bewitched Dido. *madding.*
Becoming mad with love.

J. Aickin, 18th century English actor, as Henry VI, 1776

161 *timely-parted ghost.* A person who has died of natural causes.

176 *lodged.* Levelled, beaten down.

187 *timeless.* Untimely.

191 *puttock's.* Kite's.

205 *arrogant controller.* Interfering critic or detractor.

Suf. A dreadful oath, sworn with a solemn tongue!
What instance gives Lord Warwick for his vow?
War. See how the blood is settled in his face.
• Oft have I seen a timely-parted ghost, 161
Of ashy semblance, meagre, pale and bloodless,
Being all descended to the labouring heart;
Who, in the conflict that it holds with death,
Attracts the same for aidance 'gainst the enemy;
Which with the heart there cools and ne'er returneth
To blush and beautify the cheek again.
But see, his face is black and full of blood,
His eye-balls further out than when he lived,
Staring full ghastly like a strangled man; 170
His hair uprear'd, his nostrils stretched with struggling;
His hands abroad display'd, as one that grasp'd
And tugg'd for life and was by strength subdued:
Look, on the sheets his hair, you see, is sticking;
His well-proportion'd beard made rough and rugged,
• Like to the summer's corn by tempest lodged.
It cannot be but he was murder'd here;
The least of all these signs were probable.
Suf. Why, Warwick, who should do the duke to death?
Myself and Beaufort had him in protection; 180
And we, I hope, sir, are no murderers.
War. But both of you were vow'd Duke Humphrey's foes,
And you, forsooth, had the good duke to keep:
'Tis like you would not feast him like a friend;
And 'tis well seen he found an enemy.
Queen. Then you, belike, suspect these noblemen
• As guilty of Duke Humphrey's timeless death.
War. Who finds the heifer dead and bleeding fresh
And sees fast by a butcher with an axe,
But will suspect 'twas he that made the slaughter?
• Who finds the partridge in the puttock's nest, 191
But may imagine how the bird was dead,
Although the kite soar with unbloodied beak?
Even so suspicious is this tragedy.
Queen. Are you the butcher, Suffolk? Where's your knife?
Is Beaufort term'd a kite? Where are his talons?
Suf. I wear no knife to slaughter sleeping men;
But here's a vengeful sword, rusted with ease,
That shall be scoured in his rancorous heart 199
That slanders me with murder's crimson badge.
Say, if thou darest, proud Lord of Warwickshire,
That I am faulty in Duke Humphrey's death.
[*Exeunt Cardinal, Somerset, and others.*
War. What dares not Warwick, if false Suffolk dare him?
Queen. He dares not calm his contumelious spirit
• Nor cease to be an arrogant controller,
Though Suffolk dare him twenty thousand times.
War. Madam, be still; with reverence may I say;
For every word you speak in his behalf
Is slander to your royal dignity.
Suf. Blunt-witted lord, ignoble in demeanour!
If ever lady wrong'd her lord so much, 211
Thy mother took into her blameful bed
Some stern untutor'd churl, and noble stock

Was graft with crab-tree slip; whose fruit thou art
And never of the Nevils' noble race.

● *War.* But that the guilt of murder bucklers
thee
And I should rob the deathsman of his fee,
Quitting thee thereby of ten thousand shames,
And that my sovereign's presence makes me mild,
I would, false murderous coward, on thy knee 220
Make thee beg pardon for thy passed speech
And say it was thy mother that thou meant'st,
That thou thyself wast born in bastardy;
And after all this fearful homage done,
Give thee thy hire and send thy soul to hell,
Pernicious blood-sucker of sleeping men!
Suf. Thou shalt be waking while I shed thy
blood,
If from this presence thou darest go with me.
War. Away even now, or I will drag thee
hence:
Unworthy though thou art, I'll cope with thee 230
And do some service to Duke Humphrey's
ghost. [*Exeunt Suffolk and Warwick.*
King. What stronger breastplate than a heart
untainted!
Thrice is he arm'd that hath his quarrel just,
And he but naked, though lock'd up in steel,
Whose conscience with injustice is corrupted.
[*A noise within.*
Queen. What noise is this?

Re-enter SUFFOLK *and* WARWICK, *with their
weapons drawn.*

King. Why, how now, lords! your wrathful
weapons drawn
Here in our presence! dare you be so bold?
Why, what tumultuous clamour have we here?
Suf. The traitorous Warwick with the men
of Bury 240
Set all upon me, mighty sovereign.
Sal. [*To the Commons, entering*] Sirs, stand
apart; the king shall know your mind.
Dread lord, the commons send you word by me,
Unless Lord Suffolk straight be done to death,
Or banished fair England's territories,
They will by violence tear him from your palace
And torture him with grievous lingering death.
They say, by him the good Duke Humphrey
died:
They say, in him they fear your highness' death;
And mere instinct of love and loyalty, 250
Free from a stubborn opposite intent,
As being thought to contradict your liking,
Makes them thus forward in his banishment.
They say, in care of your most royal person,
That if your highness should intend to sleep
And charge that no man should disturb your rest
In pain of your dislike or pain of death,
Yet, notwithstanding such a strait edict,
Were there a serpent seen, with forked tongue,
That slily glided towards your majesty, 260
It were but necessary you were waked,
Lest, being suffer'd in that harmful slumber,
● The mortal worm might make the sleep eternal;
And therefore do they cry, though you forbid,
That they will guard you, whether you will or no,
From such fell serpents as false Suffolk is,
With whose envenomed and fatal sting,
Your loving uncle, twenty times his worth,
They say, is shamefully bereft of life.

216 *bucklers.* Shields.

Sword and buckler in Elizabethan days. From Giacomo
di Grassi's *True Art of Defence,* 1594

263 *mortal worm.* Deadly snake.

271 *hinds*. Menials, yokels.

274 *quaint*. Clever.

285 *His majesty*. God.

310 *mandrake's groan*. The mandrake was a plant with a forked root like a man. It was supposed to groan if pulled out of the ground; its cry could kill the hearer.

Mandrake root in the form of a man. From a medieval woodcut

Commons. [*Within*] An answer from the king, my Lord of Salisbury! 270

● *Suf.* 'Tis like the commons, rude unpolish'd hinds,
Could send such message to their sovereign:
But you, my lord, were glad to be employ'd,
● To show how quaint an orator you are:
But all the honour Salisbury hath won
Is, that he was the lord ambassador
Sent from a sort of tinkers to the king.
Commons. [*Within*] An answer from the king, or we will all break in!
King. Go, Salisbury, and tell them all from me,
I thank them for their tender loving care; 280
And had I not been cited so by them,
Yet did I purpose as they do entreat;
For, sure, my thoughts do hourly prophesy
Mischance unto my state by Suffolk's means:
● And therefore, by His majesty I swear,
Whose far unworthy deputy I am,
He shall not breathe infection in this air
But three days longer, on the pain of death.
[*Exit Salisbury*.
Queen. O Henry, let me plead for gentle Suffolk!
King. Ungentle queen, to call him gentle Suffolk! 290
No more, I say: if thou dost plead for him,
Thou wilt but add increase unto my wrath.
Had I but said, I would have kept my word,
But when I swear, it is irrevocable.
If, after three days' space, thou here be'st found
On any ground that I am ruler of,
The world shall not be ransom for thy life.
Come, Warwick, come, good Warwick, go with me;
I have great matters to impart to thee.
[*Exeunt all but Queen and Suffolk*.
Queen. Mischance and sorrow go along with you! 300
Heart's discontent and sour affliction
Be playfellows to keep you company!
There's two of you; the devil make a third!
And threefold vengeance tend upon your steps!
Suf. Cease, gentle queen, these execrations
And let thy Suffolk take his heavy leave.
Queen. Fie, coward woman and soft-hearted wretch!
Hast thou not spirit to curse thine enemy?
Suf. A plague upon them! wherefore should I curse them?
● Would curses kill, as doth the mandrake's groan,
I would invent as bitter-searching terms, 311
As curst, as harsh and horrible to hear,
Deliver'd strongly through my fixed teeth,
With full as many signs of deadly hate,
As lean-faced Envy in her loathsome cave:
My tongue should stumble in mine earnest words;
Mine eyes should sparkle like the beaten flint;
Mine hair be fix'd on end, as one distract;
Ay, every joint should seem to curse and ban:
And even now my burthen'd heart would break,
Should I not curse them. Poison be their drink! 321
Gall, worse than gall, the daintiest that they taste!
Their sweetest shade a grove of cypress trees!
Their chiefest prospect murdering basilisks!
Their softest touch as smart as lizards' stings!

Their music frightful as the serpent's hiss,
And boding screech-owls make the concert full.
All the foul terrors in dark-seated hell—
    Queen. Enough, sweet Suffolk; thou torment'st thyself;
And these dread curses, like the sun 'gainst glass,
Or like an overcharged gun, recoil,   331
And turn the force of them upon thyself.
•   *Suf.* You bade me ban, and will you bid me leave?
Now, by the ground that I am banish'd from,
Well could I curse away a winter's night,
Though standing naked on a mountain top,
Where biting cold would never let grass grow,
And think it but a minute spent in sport.
    Queen. O, let me entreat thee cease. Give me thy hand,
That I may dew it with my mournful tears;   340
Nor let the rain of heaven wet this place,
To wash away my woful monuments.
O, could this kiss be printed in thy hand,
That thou mightst think upon these by the seal,
Through whom a thousand sighs are breathed for thee!
So, get thee gone, that I may know my grief;
'Tis but surmised whiles thou art standing by,
As one that surfeits thinking on a want.
I will repeal thee, or, be well assured,
Adventure to be banished myself: 350
And banished I am, if but from thee.
Go; speak not to me; even now be gone.
O, go not yet! Even thus two friends condemn'd
Embrace and kiss and take ten thousand leaves,
Loather a hundred times to part than die.
Yet now farewell; and farewell life with thee!
    Suf. Thus is poor Suffolk ten times banished;
Once by the king, and three times thrice by thee.
'Tis not the land I care for, wert thou thence;
A wilderness is populous enough,   360
So Suffolk had thy heavenly company:
For where thou art, there is the world itself,
With every several pleasure in the world,
And where thou art not, desolation.
I can no more: live thou to joy thy life;
Myself no joy in nought but that thou livest.

        Enter VAUX.

    Queen. Whither goes Vaux so fast? what news, I prithee?
    Vaux. To signify unto his majesty
That Cardinal Beaufort is at point of death;   370
For suddenly a grievous sickness took him,
That makes him gasp and stare and catch the air,
Blaspheming God and cursing men on earth.
Sometime he talks as if Duke Humphrey's ghost
Were by his side; sometime he calls the king
And whispers to his pillow as to him
The secrets of his overcharged soul:
And I am sent to tell his majesty
That even now he cries aloud for him.
    Queen. Go tell this heavy message to the king.
        [*Exit Vaux.*
Ay me! what is this world! what news are these!   380
• But wherefore grieve I at an hour's poor loss,
Omitting Suffolk's exile, my soul's treasure?
Why only, Suffolk, mourn I not for thee,

333 *ban.* Curse, with word play on 'ban' and 'banish'd'.

Queen: 'O, let me entreat thee cease.' Suffolk with Queen Margaret. Engraving from a painting by William Hamilton (1751–1801)

381 *an hour's poor loss.* The Cardinal was an old man and so had not much of life to lose.

399 *Elysium.* Abode of the blessed after death.

407 *Iris.* Messenger of Hera, Queen of the Gods.

Death of Cardinal Beaufort. Painting by Sir Joshua Reynolds (1723–1792)

And with the southern clouds contend in tears,
Theirs for the earth's increase, mine for my
　　sorrows?
Now get thee hence: the king, thou know'st, is
　　coming;
If thou be found by me, thou art but dead.
　　Suf. If I depart from thee, I cannot live;
And in thy sight to die, what were it else
But like a pleasant slumber in thy lap?　　390
Here could I breathe my soul into the air,
As mild and gentle as the cradle-babe
Dying with mother's dug between its lips:
Where, from thy sight, I should be raging mad
And cry out for thee to close up mine eyes,
To have thee with thy lips to stop my mouth;
So shouldst thou either turn my flying soul,
Or I should breathe it so into thy body,
● And then it lived in sweet Elysium.
To die by thee were but to die in jest;　　400
From thee to die were torture more than death:
O, let me stay, befall what may befall!
　　Queen. Away! though parting be a fretful
　　corrosive,
It is applied to a deathful wound.
To France, sweet Suffolk: let me hear from thee;
For wheresoe'er thou art in this world's globe,
● I'll have an Iris that shall find thee out.
　　Suf. I go.
　　Queen.　　And take my heart with thee.
　　Suf. A jewel, lock'd into the wofull'st cask
That ever did contain a thing of worth.　　410
Even as a splitted bark, so sunder we:
This way fall I to death.
　　Queen.　　　　This way for me.
　　　　　　　　　　[*Exeunt severally.*

SCENE III. *A bedchamber.*

Enter the KING, SALISBURY, WARWICK, *to the*
CARDINAL *in bed.*

　　King. How fares my lord? speak, Beaufort,
　　to thy sovereign.
　　Car. If thou be'st death, I'll give thee Eng-
　　land's treasure,
Enough to purchase such another island,
So thou wilt let me live, and feel no pain.
　　King. Ah, what a sign it is of evil life,
Where death's approach is seen so terrible!
　　War. Beaufort, it is thy sovereign speaks to
　　thee.
　　Car. Bring me unto my trial when you will.
Died he not in his bed? where should he die?
Can I make men live, whether they will or no? 10
O, torture me no more! I will confess.
Alive again? then show me where he is:
I'll give a thousand pound to look upon him.
He hath no eyes, the dust hath blinded them.
Comb down his hair; look, look! it stands up-
　　right,
Like lime-twigs set to catch my winged soul.
Give me some drink; and bid the apothecary
Bring the strong poison that I bought of him.
　　King. O thou eternal Mover of the heavens,
Look with a gentle eye upon this wretch!　　20
O, beat away the busy meddling fiend
That lays strong siege unto this wretch's soul
And from his bosom purge this black despair!
　　War. See, how the pangs of death do make
　　him grin!

Sal. Disturb him not; let him pass peaceably.
King. Peace to his soul, if God's good pleasure be!
Lord cardinal, if thou think'st on heaven's bliss,
Hold up thy hand, make signal of thy hope.
He dies, and makes no sign. O God, forgive him! 29
War. So bad a death argues a monstrous life.
King. Forbear to judge, for we are sinners all.
Close up his eyes and draw the curtain close;
And let us all to meditation. [*Exeunt.*

ACT IV.

SCENE I. *The coast of Kent.*

Alarum. Fight at sea. Ordnance goes off.
Enter a Captain, *a* Master, *a* Master's-Mate,
WALTER WHITMORE, *and others; with them*
SUFFOLK, *and others, prisoners.*

Cap. The gaudy, blabbing and remorseful day
Is crept into the bosom of the sea;
● And now loud-howling wolves arouse the jades
That drag the tragic melancholy night;
Who, with their drowsy, slow and flagging wings,
● Clip dead men's graves and from their misty jaws
Breathe foul contagious darkness in the air.
● Therefore bring forth the soldiers of our prize;
● For, whilst our pinnace anchors in the Downs,
Here shall they make their ransom on the sand, 10
Or with their blood stain this discolour'd shore.
Master, this prisoner freely give I thee;
And thou that art his mate, make boot of this;
The other, Walter Whitmore, is thy share.
First Gent. What is my ransom, master? let me know.
Mast. A thousand crowns, or else lay down your head.
Mate. And so much shall you give, or off goes yours.
Cap. What, think you much to pay two thousand crowns,
● And bear the name and port of gentlemen?
Cut both the villains' throats; for die you shall:
The lives of those which we have lost in fight 21
Be counterpoised with such a petty sum!
First Gent. I'll give it, sir; and therefore spare my life.
Sec. Gent. And so will I and write home for it straight.
● *Whit.* I lost mine eye in laying the prize aboard,
And therefore to revenge it, shalt thou die;
[*To Suf.*
And so should these, if I might have my will.
Cap. Be not so rash; take ransom, let him live.
● *Suf.* Look on my George; I am a gentleman:
Rate me at what thou wilt, thou shalt be paid. 30
Whit. And so am I; my name is Walter Whitmore.
How now! why start'st thou? what, doth death affright?
Suf. Thy name affrights me, in whose sound is death.
● A cunning man did calculate my birth
● And told me that by water I should die:
Yet let not this make thee be bloody-minded;
● Thy name is Gaultier, being rightly sounded.

Sea captain with Suffolk as his prisoner, on the sea coast near Dover. Engraving by Kenny Meadows from Barry Cornwall's *Works of Shakspere*, 1846

3 *jades.* Horses in poor condition.

6 *Clip.* i.e. 'embrace' and 'strike'

8 *soldiers . . . prize.* Soldiers we have captured.

9 *pinnace.* A small rowing or sailing vessel.

19 *port.* Style.

25 *laying the prize aboard.* Boarding the captured ship.

29 *George.* Badge of a Knight of the Garter, because it represented St George killing the dragon; the feast of the order was held on St George's Day (23rd April).

34 *cunning man.* Fortune teller.

35 *water.* The pun depends on the Elizabethan pronunciation of Walter with the 'l' silent. The 'cunning man' was actually the spirit in I. iv. 36, who prophesied, 'By water he shall die'.

37 *Gaultier.* Walter in French.

42 *arms.* Coat of arms.

50 *King Henry's blood.* Suffolk's false claim.

61 *voiding lobby.* Waiting room, ante-chamber.

70–71 *Pole . . . kennel.* Multiple punning on 'poll' (head), 'Pole' (Suffolk's family name – pronounced 'pool') and 'pool' (of water). *kennel.* Open drain.

80 *affy.* Affiance, betroth.

84 *Sylla.* Lucius Cornelius Sulla (138–78BC) authorised the first Roman proscriptions.

Whit. Gualtier or Walter, which it is, I care
    not:
Never yet did base dishonour blur our name,
But with our sword we wiped away the blot; 40
Therefore, when merchant-like I sell revenge,
● Broke be my sword, my arms torn and defaced,
And I proclaim'd a coward through the world!
   Suf. Stay, Whitmore; for thy prisoner is a
    prince,
The Duke of Suffolk, William de la Pole.
   Whit. The Duke of Suffolk muffled up in rags!
   Suf. Ay, but these rags are no part of the duke:
Jove sometime went disguised, and why not I?
   Cap. But Jove was never slain, as thou shalt be.
● *Suf.* Obscure and lowly swain, King Henry's
    blood,   50
The honourable blood of Lancaster,
Must not be shed by such a jaded groom.
Hast thou not kiss'd thy hand and held my stirrup?
Bare-headed plodded by my foot-cloth mule
And thought thee happy when I shook my head?
How often hast thou waited at my cup,
Fed from my trencher, kneel'd down at the board,
When I have feasted with Queen Margaret?
Remember it and let it make thee crest-fall'n,
Ay, and allay this thy abortive pride;   60
● How in our voiding lobby hast thou stood
And duly waited for my coming forth?
This hand of mine hath writ in thy behalf
And therefore shall it charm thy riotous tongue.
   Whit. Speak, captain, shall I stab the forlorn
    swain?
   Cap. First let my words stab him, as he hath
    me.
   Suf. Base slave, thy words are blunt and so
    art thou.
   Cap. Convey him hence and on our long-boat's
    side
Strike off his head.
   Suf.   Thou darest not, for thy own.
● *Cap.* Yes, Pole.
   Suf.   Pole!
   Cap.   Pool! Sir Pool! lord! 70
Ay, kennel, puddle, sink; whose filth and dirt
Troubles the silver spring where England drinks.
Now will I dam up this thy yawning mouth
For swallowing the treasure of the realm:
Thy lips that kiss'd the queen shall sweep the
    ground;
And thou that smiledst at good Duke Humphrey's
    death
Against the senseless winds shalt grin in vain,
Who in contempt shall hiss at thee again:
And wedded be thou to the hags of hell,
● For daring to affy a mighty lord   80
Unto the daughter of a worthless king,
Having neither subject, wealth, nor diadem.
By devilish policy art thou grown great
● And, like ambitious Sylla, overgorged
With gobbets of thy mother's bleeding heart.
By thee Anjou and Maine were sold to France,
The false revolting Normans thorough thee
Disdain to call us lord, and Picardy
Hath slain their governors, surprised our forts
And sent the ragged soldiers wounded home. 90
The princely Warwick, and the Nevils all,
Whose dreadful swords were never drawn in vain,
As hating thee, are rising up in arms:
And now the house of York, thrust from the crown

By shameful murder of a guiltless king
And lofty proud encroaching tyranny,
Burns with revenging fire; whose hopeful colours
● Advance our half-faced sun, striving to shine,
● Under the which is writ 'Invitis nubibus.'
The commons here in Kent are up in arms: 100
And, to conclude, reproach and beggary
Is crept into the palace of our king,
And all by thee. Away! convey him hence.
    Suf. O that I were a god, to shoot forth
        thunder
Upon these paltry, servile, abject drudges!
Small things make base men proud: this villain
    here,
Being captain of a pinnace, threatens more
Than Bargulus the strong Illyrian pirate.
Drones suck not eagles' blood but rob bee-hives:
It is impossible that I should die 110
By such a lowly vassal as thyself.
Thy words move rage and not remorse in me:
I go of message from the queen to France;
I charge thee waft me safely cross the Channel.
    Cap. Walter,—
    Whit. Come, Suffolk, I must waft thee to thy
        death.
●   *Suf.* Gelidus timor occupat artus, it is thee
    I fear.
    Whit. Thou shalt have cause to fear before
    I leave thee.
What, are ye daunted now? now will ye stoop?
    First Gent. My gracious lord, entreat him,
        speak him fair. 120
    Suf. Suffolk's imperial tongue is stern and
        rough,
Used to command, untaught to plead for favour.
Far be it we should honour such as these
With humble suit: no, rather let my head
Stoop to the block than these knees bow to any
Save to the God of heaven and to my king;
And sooner dance upon a bloody pole
Than stand uncover'd to the vulgar groom.
True nobility is exempt from fear:
More can I bear than you dare execute. 130
    Cap. Hale him away, and let him talk no more.
    Suf. Come, soldiers, show what cruelty ye
        can,
That this my death may never be forgot!
● Great men oft die by vile bezonians:
A Roman sworder and banditto slave
● Murder'd sweet Tully; Brutus' bastard hand
Stabb'd Julius Cæsar; savage islanders
● Pompey the Great; and Suffolk dies by pirates.
    [*Exeunt Whitmore and others with Suffolk.*
    Cap. And as for these whose ransom we have
        set,
It is our pleasure one of them depart: 140
Therefore come you with us and let him go.
    [*Exeunt all but the First Gentleman.*

Re-enter Whitmore *with* Suffolk's *body.*

    Whit. There let his head and lifeless body
        lie,
Until the queen his mistress bury it.   [*Exit.*
    First Gent. O barbarous and bloody spectacle!
His body will I bear unto the king:
If he revenge it not, yet will his friends;
So will the queen, that living held him dear.
    [*Exit with the body.*

98 *half-faced sun.* Heraldic device of Edward III and Richard II.

99 '*Invitis nubibus*'. In spite of clouds.

117 *Gelidus . . . artus.* Cold fear siezed my limbs.

134 *bezonians.* Beggars.

136 *Tully.* Marcus Tullius Cicero. *Brutus' bastard.* Brutus was incorrectly believed to be an illegitimate son of Julius Caesar.

138 *Pompey.* Defeated by Julius Caesar, Pompey fled to Egypt where he was murdered by his own ex-officers in the pay of Ptolemy.

24 *Wingham.* Village near Canterbury.

31 *Argo.* Ergo (therefore).

Sketch of Jack Cade by Inigo Jones (1573–1651) for a Court Masque

35 *cade.* Barrel of 500 herrings.

51 *furred pack.* Pack made of skin, with the hair outward. *bucks.* Dirty linen.

59 *valiant.* Insolent.

SCENE II. *Blackheath.*

Enter GEORGE BEVIS *and* JOHN HOLLAND.

Bevis. Come, and get thee a sword, though made of a lath : they have been up these two days.

Holl. They have the more need to sleep now, then.

Bevis. I tell thee, Jack Cade the clothier means to dress the commonwealth, and turn it, and set a new nap upon it.

Holl. So he had need, for 'tis threadbare. Well, I say it was never merry world in England since gentlemen came up. 10

Bevis. O miserable age ! virtue is not regarded in handicrafts-men.

Holl. The nobility think scorn to go in leather aprons.

Bevis. Nay, more, the king's council are no good workmen.

Holl. True ; and yet it is said, labour in thy vocation ; which is as much to say as, let the magistrates be labouring men ; and therefore should we be magistrates. 20

Bevis. Thou hast hit it ; for there's no better sign of a brave mind than a hard hand.

Holl. I see them ! I see them ! There's Best's son, the tanner of Wingham,—

Bevis. He shall have the skins of our enemies, to make dog's-leather of.

Holl. And Dick the Butcher,—

Bevis. Then is sin struck down like an ox, and iniquity's throat cut like a calf.

Holl. And Smith the weaver,— 30

Bevis. Argo, their thread of life is spun.

Holl. Come, come, let's fall in with them.

Drum. Enter CADE, DICK *Butcher,* SMITH *the Weaver, and a Sawyer, with infinite numbers.*

Cade. We John Cade, so termed of our supposed father,—

Dick. [*Aside*] Or rather, of stealing a cade of herrings.

Cade. For our enemies shall fall before us, inspired with the spirit of putting down kings and princes,—Command silence.

Dick. Silence ! 40

Cade. My father was a Mortimer,—

Dick. [*Aside*] He was an honest man, and a good bricklayer.

Cade. My mother a Plantagenet,—

Dick. [*Aside*] I knew her well ; she was a midwife.

Cade. My wife descended of the Lacies,—

Dick. [*Aside*] She was, indeed, a pedler's daughter, and sold many laces. 49

Smith. [*Aside*] But now of late, not able to travel with her furred pack, she washes bucks here at home.

Cade. Therefore am I of an honourable house.

Dick. [*Aside*] Ay, by my faith, the field is honourable ; and there was he born, under a hedge, for his father had never a house but the cage.

Cade. Valiant I am.

Smith. [*Aside*] A' must needs ; for beggary is valiant.

Cade. I am able to endure much. 60

Dick. [*Aside*] No question of that : for I have seen him whipped three market-days together.

Cade. I fear neither sword nor fire.

Smith. [*Aside*] He need not fear the sword; for his coat is of proof.

Dick. [*Aside*] But methinks he should stand in fear of fire, being burnt i' the hand for stealing of sheep.

Cade. Be brave, then; for your captain is brave, and vows reformation. There shall be in England seven halfpenny loaves sold for a penny: the three-hooped pot shall have ten hoops; and I will make it felony to drink small beer: all the realm shall be in common; and in Cheapside shall my palfry go to grass: and when I am king, as king I will be,—

All. God save your majesty!

Cade. I thank you, good people: there shall be no money; all shall eat and drink on my score; and I will apparel them all in one livery, that they may agree like brothers and worship me their lord.

Dick. The first thing we do, let's kill all the lawyers.

Cade. Nay, that I mean to do. Is not this a lamentable thing, that of the skin of an innocent lamb should be made parchment? that parchment, being scribbled o'er, should undo a man? Some say the bee stings: but I say, 'tis the bee's wax; for I did but seal once to a thing, and I was never mine own man since. How now! who's there? 91

Enter some, bringing forward the Clerk of Chatham.

Smith. The clerk of Chatham: he can write and read and cast accompt.

Cade. O monstrous!

Smith. We took him setting of boys' copies.

Cade. Here's a villain!

Smith. Has a book in his pocket with red letters in 't.

Cade. Nay, then, he is a conjurer.

Dick. Nay, he can make obligations, and write court-hand. 101

Cade. I am sorry for 't: the man is a proper man, of mine honour; unless I find him guilty, he shall not die. Come hither, sirrah, I must examine thee: what is thy name?

Clerk. Emmanuel.

Dick. They use to write it on the top of letters: 'twill go hard with you.

Cade. Let me alone. Dost thou use to write thy name? or hast thou a mark to thyself, like an honest plain-dealing man? 111

Clerk. Sir, I thank God, I have been so well brought up that I can write my name.

All. He hath confessed: away with him! he's a villain and a traitor.

Cade. Away with him, I say! hang him with his pen and ink-horn about his neck.

[*Exit one with the Clerk.*

Enter MICHAEL.

Mich. Where's our general?

Cade. Here I am, thou particular fellow. 119

Mich. Fly, fly, fly! Sir Humphrey Stafford and his brother are hard by, with the king's forces

Cade. Stand, villain, stand, or I'll fell thee down. He shall be encountered with a man as good as himself: he is but a knight, is a'?

65 *proof.* Tested.

74 *Cheapside.* Chief shopping street in old London.

75 *palfry.* Saddle horse.

106 *Emmanuel.* Letters were headed 'Emmanuel' – 'God be with you'.

Cade with the Clerk of Chatham. Engraving by Kenny Meadows from Barry Cornwall's *Works of Shakspere*, 1846

141 *shearman*. Worker who cut the nap from cloth.

166 *span-counter*. Game in which the aim was to throw a counter within the span of the first counter. *crowns*. Pun on 1) coinage; 2) kingdom; 3) 'the French disease'.

170 *Say*. Lord Treasurer.

172 *mained*. Maimed.

Mich. No.
Cade. To equal him, I will make myself a knight presently. [*Kneels*] Rise up Sir John Mortimer. [*Rises*] Now have at him!

Enter SIR HUMPHREY STAFFORD *and his* Brother, *with drum and soldiers.*

Staf. Rebellious hinds, the filth and scum of Kent,   130
Mark'd for the gallows, lay your weapons down;
Home to your cottages, forsake this groom:
The king is merciful, if you revolt.
Bro. But angry, wrathful, and inclined to blood,
If you go forward; therefore yield, or die.
Cade. As for these silken-coated slaves, I pass not:
It is to you, good people, that I speak,
Over whom, in time to come, I hope to reign;
For I am rightful heir unto the crown.
Staf. Villain, thy father was a plasterer; 140
And thou thyself a shearman, art thou not?
Cade. And Adam was a gardener.
Bro. And what of that?
Cade. Marry, this: Edmund Mortimer, Earl of March,
Married the Duke of Clarence' daughter, did he not?
Staf. Ay, sir.
Cade. By her he had two children at one birth.
Bro. That's false.
Cade. Ay, there's the question; but I say, 'tis true:
The elder of them, being put to nurse,   150
Was by a beggar-woman stolen away;
And, ignorant of his birth and parentage,
Became a bricklayer when he came to age:
His son am I; deny it, if you can.
Dick. Nay, 'tis too true; therefore he shall be king.
Smith. Sir, he made a chimney in my father's house, and the bricks are alive at this day to testify it; therefore deny it not.
Staf. And will you credit this base drudge's words,
That speaks he knows not what?   160
All. Ay, marry, will we; therefore get ye gone.
Bro. Jack Cade, the Duke of York hath taught you this.
Cade. [*Aside*] He lies, for I invented it myself.
Go to, sirrah, tell the king from me, that, for his father's sake, Henry the Fifth, in whose time boys went to span-counter for French crowns, I am content he shall reign; but I'll be protector over him.
Dick. And furthermore, we'll have the Lord Say's head for selling the dukedom of Maine. 170
Cade. And good reason; for thereby is England mained, and fain to go with a staff, but that my puissance holds it up. Fellow kings, I tell you that that Lord Say hath gelded the commonwealth, and made it an eunuch: and more than that, he can speak French; and therefore he is a traitor.
Staf. O gross and miserable ignorance!
Cade. Nay, answer, if you can: the Frenchmen are our enemies; go to, then, I ask but this:

can he that speaks with the tongue of an enemy
be a good counsellor, or no?

All. No, no; and therefore we'll have his
head.

Bro. Well, seeing gentle words will not prevail,
Assail them with the army of the king.

Staf. Herald, away; and throughout every
town
Proclaim them traitors that are up with Cade;
That those which fly before the battle ends
May, even in their wives' and children's sight,
Be hang'd up for example at their doors :   190
And you that be the king's friends, follow me.

[*Exeunt the two Staffords, and soldiers.*

Cade. And you that love the commons, follow
me.
Now show yourselves men; 'tis for liberty.
We will not leave one lord, one gentleman :
• Spare none but such as go in clouted shoon;
For they are thrifty honest men and such
As would, but that they dare not, take our parts.

Dick. They are all in order and march toward
us.

Cade. But then are we in order when we are
most out of order. Come, march forward.   200

[*Exeunt.*

Scene III. *Another part of Blackheath.*

Alarums to the fight, wherein both the STAF-
FORDS *are slain. Enter* CADE *and the rest.*

Cade. Where's Dick, the butcher of Ashford?

Dick. Here, sir.

Cade. They fell before thee like sheep and
oxen, and thou behavedst thyself as if thou hadst
been in thine own slaughter-house : therefore thus
• will I reward thee, the Lent shall be as long again
as it is; and thou shalt have a license to kill for
a hundred lacking one.

Dick. I desire no more.   10

Cade. And, to speak truth, thou deservest no
less. This monument of the victory will I bear
[*putting on Sir Humphrey's brigandine*]; and
the bodies shall be dragged at my horse heels till
I do come to London, where we will have the
mayor's sword borne before us.

Dick. If we mean to thrive and do good,
break open the gaols and let out the prisoners.

Cade. Fear not that, I warrant thee. Come,
let's march towards London.   [*Exeunt.* 20

Scene IV. *London. The palace.*

Enter the KING *with a supplication, and the*
QUEEN *with Suffolk's head, the* DUKE OF
BUCKINGHAM *and the* LORD SAY.

Queen. Oft have I heard that grief softens the
mind
And makes it fearful and degenerate;
Think therefore on revenge and cease to weep.
But who can cease to weep and look on this?
Here may his head lie on my throbbing breast:
But where's the body that I should embrace?

Buck. What answer makes your grace to the
rebels' supplication?

King. I'll send some holy bishop to entreat;
For God forbid so many simple souls   10

Map showing Blackheath. From John Speed's *Theatre
of the Empire of Great Britaine, 1611–12*

---

195 *clouted shoon.* Hobnail boots.

7–8 *Lent . . . kill.* Butchers were not permitted to
slaughter during Lent.

SD *brigandine.* A coat of mail.

39 *Killingworth*. Kenilworth castle in Warwickshire.

Engraving of Kenilworth Castle in 1620

Should perish by the sword! And I myself,
Rather than bloody war shall cut them short,
Will parley with Jack Cade their general:
But stay, I'll read it over once again.
   Queen. Ah, barbarous villains! hath this lovely
     face
Ruled, like a wandering planet, over me,
And could it not enforce them to relent,
That were unworthy to behold the same?
   King. Lord Say, Jack Cade hath sworn to
     have thy head.
   Say. Ay, but I hope your highness shall have
     his.   20
   King. How now, madam!
Still lamenting and mourning for Suffolk's death?
I fear me, love, if that I had been dead,
Thou wouldest not have mourn'd so much for me.
   Queen. No, my love, I should not mourn, but
     die for thee.

Enter a Messenger.

   King. How now! what news? why comest
     thou in such haste?
   Mess. The rebels are in Southwark; fly, my
     lord!
Jack Cade proclaims himself Lord Mortimer,
Descended from the Duke of Clarence' house,
And calls your grace usurper openly   30
And vows to crown himself in Westminster.
His army is a ragged multitude
Of hinds and peasants, rude and merciless:
Sir Humphrey Stafford and his brother's death
Hath given them heart and courage to proceed:
All scholars, lawyers, courtiers, gentlemen,
They call false caterpillars and intend their death.
   King. O graceless men! they know not what
     they do.
   Buck. My gracious lord, retire to Killing-
     worth,
Until a power be raised to put them down.   40
   Queen. Ah, were the Duke of Suffolk now
     alive,
These Kentish rebels would be soon appeased!
   King. Lord Say, the traitors hate thee;
Therefore away with us to Killingworth.
   Say. So might your grace's person be in
     danger.
The sight of me is odious in their eyes;
And therefore in this city will I stay
And live alone as secret as I may.

Enter another Messenger.

   Mess. Jack Cade hath gotten London bridge:
The citizens fly and forsake their houses: 50
The rascal people, thirsting after prey,
Join with the traitor, and they jointly swear
To spoil the city and your royal court.
   Buck. Then linger not, my lord; away, take
     horse.
   King. Come, Margaret; God, our hope, will
     succour us.
   Queen. My hope is gone, now Suffolk is de-
     ceased.
   King. Farewell, my lord: trust not the
     Kentish rebels.
   Buck. Trust nobody, for fear you be betray'd.
   Say. The trust I have is in mine innocence,
And therefore am I bold and resolute.   60
                     [*Exeunt.*

SCENE V. *London. The Tower.*

Enter LORD SCALES *upon the Tower, walking.*
Then enter two or three Citizens *below.*

Scales. How now! is Jack Cade slain?
First Cit. No, my lord, nor likely to be slain;
for they have won the bridge, killing all those
that withstand them: the lord mayor craves aid
of your honour from the Tower to defend the
city from the rebels.
Scales. Such aid as I can spare you shall
        command;
But I am troubled here with them myself;
The rebels have assay'd to win the Tower.
But get you to Smithfield and gather head,   10
And thither I will send you Matthew Goffe;
Fight for your king, your country and your lives;
And so, farewell, for I must hence again.
                           [Exeunt.

SCENE VI. *London. Cannon Street.*

Enter JACK CADE *and the rest, and strikes*
his staff on London-stone.

Cade. Now is Mortimer lord of this city. And
• here, sitting upon London-stone, I charge and
• command that, of the city's cost, the pissing-
conduit run nothing but claret wine this first
year of our reign. And now henceforward it
shall be treason for any that calls me other than
Lord Mortimer.

Enter a Soldier, *running.*

Sold. Jack Cade! Jack Cade!
Cade. Knock him down there. [*They kill him.*
Smith. If this fellow be wise, he'll never call
ye Jack Cade more: I think he hath a very fair
warning.
Dick. My lord, there's an army gathered
together in Smithfield.
Cade. Come, then, let's go fight with them:
but first, go and set London bridge on fire; and,
if you can, burn down the Tower too. Come,
let's away.   [*Exeunt.*

SCENE VII. *London. Smithfield.*

Alarums. MATTHEW GOFFE *is slain, and all*
the rest. Then enter JACK CADE, *with his*
company.

Cade. So, sirs: now go some and pull down
• the Savoy; others to the inns of court; down
with them all.
Dick. I have a suit unto your lordship.
Cade. Be it a lordship, thou shalt have it for
that word.
Dick. Only that the laws of England may
come out of your mouth.
Holl. [*Aside*] Mass, 'twill be sore law, then;
for he was thrust in the mouth with a spear, and
'tis not whole yet.   11
Smith. [*Aside*] Nay, John, it will be stinking
law; for his breath stinks with eating toasted
cheese.
Cade. I have thought upon it, it shall be so.
Away, burn all the records of the realm: my
mouth shall be the parliament of England.
Holl. [*Aside*] Then we are like to have
biting statutes, unless his teeth be pulled out.

Tower of London. Engraving from a print of 1597

2 *London-stone.* A Roman milestone in Cannon Street.

3—4 *pissing-conduit.* A small water fountain used by the
poor.

2 *Savoy.* London residence of the Duke of Lancaster.

The Savoy Palace, London residence of the Duke of
Lancaster. Engraving from *Old England,* 1854

24–25 *one . . . pound.* A joking exaggeration.

31 *Basimecu.* 'Baise mon cul' (kiss my backside).

34 *besom.* Broom.

38–39 *score . . . tally.* Tallies were two halves of a stick split and divided between the creditor and the debtor. Scores were notches on the tallies recording the transactions.

48–49 *could not read.* i.e. they couldn't read the 'neck verse' in Latin which would have enabled them to claim 'benefit of clergy'. This would entitle them to exemption from hanging by a secular court on the grounds that, as clerics, they could be tried only by an ecclesiastical court.

61 *bona . . . gens.* Good country, bad people.

Say: 'Hear me but speak . . .' Lord Say (Charles West) with Jack Cade (Harold Innocent), Dick the Butcher (Ronald Fraser) and Cade's followers, Old Vic, 1957

77 *book.* Learning. *preferr'd.* Recommended.

Cade. And henceforward all things shall be in common. 21

Enter a Messenger.

Mess. My lord, a prize, a prize! here's the Lord Say, which sold the towns in France; he that made us pay one and twenty fifteens, and one shilling to the pound, the last subsidy.

Enter GEORGE BEVIS, *with the* LORD SAY.

Cade. Well, he shall be beheaded for it ten times. Ah, thou say, thou serge, nay, thou buckram lord! now art thou within point-blank of our jurisdiction regal. What canst thou answer to my majesty for giving up of Normandy unto Mounsieur Basimecu, the dauphin of France? Be it known unto thee by these presence, even the presence of Lord Mortimer, that I am the besom that must sweep the court clean of such filth as thou art. Thou hast most traitorously corrupted the youth of the realm in erecting a grammar school: and whereas, before, our forefathers had no other books but the score and the tally, thou hast caused printing to be used, and, contrary to the king, his crown and dignity, thou hast built a paper-mill. It will be proved to thy face that thou hast men about thee that usually talk of a noun and a verb, and such abominable words as no Christian ear can endure to hear. Thou hast appointed justices of peace, to call poor men before them about matters they were not able to answer. Moreover, thou hast put them in prison; and because they could not read, thou hast hanged them; when, indeed, only for that cause they have been most worthy to live. Thou dost ride in a foot-cloth, dost thou not?

Say. What of that?

Cade. Marry, thou oughtest not to let thy horse wear a cloak, when honester men than thou go in their hose and doublets.

Dick. And work in their shirt too; as myself, for example, that am a butcher.

Say. You men of Kent,—

Dick. What say you of Kent? 60

Say. Nothing but this; 'tis 'bona terra, mala gens.'

Cade. Away with him, away with him! he speaks Latin.

Say. Hear me but speak, and bear me where you will.
Kent, in the Commentaries Cæsar writ,
Is term'd the civil'st place of all this isle:
Sweet is the country, because full of riches;
The people liberal, valiant, active, wealthy;
Which makes me hope you are not void of pity.
I sold not Maine, I lost not Normandy, 70
Yet, to recover them, would lose my life.
Justice with favour have I always done;
Prayers and tears have moved me, gifts could never.
When have I aught exacted at your hands,
But to maintain the king, the realm and you?
Large gifts have I bestow'd on learned clerks,
Because my book preferr'd me to the king,
And seeing ignorance is the curse of God,
Knowledge the wing wherewith we fly to heaven,
Unless you be possess'd with devilish spirits, 80
You cannot but forbear to murder me:

This tongue hath parley'd unto foreign kings
For your behoof,—
  Cade. Tut, when struck'st thou one blow in
the field?
    Say. Great men have reaching hands: oft
      have I struck
Those that I never saw and struck them dead.
  Geo. O monstrous coward! what, to come
behind folks?
    Say. These cheeks are pale for watching for
      your good.   90
  Cade. Give him a box o' the ear and that will
make 'em red again.
    Say. Long sitting to determine poor men's
      causes
Hath made me full of sickness and diseases.
  Cade. Ye shall have a hempen caudle then
and the help of hatchet.
  Dick. Why dost thou quiver, man?
  Say. The palsy, and not fear, provokes me.
  Cade. Nay, he nods at us, as who should say,
I'll be even with you: I'll see if his head will
stand steadier on a pole, or no. Take him away,
and behead him.
    Say. Tell me wherein have I offended most?
Have I affected wealth or honour? speak.
Are my chests fill'd up with extorted gold?
Is my apparel sumptuous to behold?
Whom have I injured, that ye seek my death?
These hands are free from guiltless blood-
      shedding,
This breast from harbouring foul deceitful
      thoughts.
O, let me live!   110
  Cade. [*Aside*] I feel remorse in myself with
his words; but I'll bridle it: he shall die, an
it be but for pleading so well for his life. Away
with him! he has a familiar under his tongue; he
speaks **not** o' God's name. Go, take him away, I
say, and strike off his head presently; and then
break into his son-in-law's house, Sir James
Cromer, and strike off his head, and bring them
both upon two poles hither.
  All. It shall be done.   120
  Say. Ah, countrymen! if when you make
      your prayers,
God should be so obdurate as yourselves,
How would it fare with your departed souls?
And therefore yet relent, and save my life.
  Cade. Away with him! and do as I command
ye.   [*Exeunt some with Lord Say*.
The proudest peer in the realm shall not wear a
head on his shoulders, unless he pay me tribute;
there shall not a maid be married, but she shall
pay to me her maidenhead ere they have it:
men shall hold of me in capite; and we charge
and command that their wives be as free as
heart can wish or tongue can tell.
  Dick. My lord, when shall we go to Cheapside and take up commodities upon our bills?
  Cade. Marry, presently.
  All. O, brave!

    Re-enter one with the heads.

  Cade. But is not this braver? Let them kiss
one another, for they loved well when they were
alive. Now part them again, lest they consult
about the giving up of some more towns in
France. Soldiers, defer the spoil of the city

95 *caudle*. Warm gruel.

114 *familiar*. Witch's assistant.

131 *in capite*. By direct grant from the king.

135 *bills*. i.e. on credit.

1–2 *Fish Street.* On the north bank of the Thames opposite Southwark. *Saint Magnus' Corner.* End of Fish Street near London Bridge.

Fish Street and Saint Magnus. Detail from plan of London (*c.*1560–1570) by Ralph Agas

43 *at jar.* Quarrelling amongst themselves.

45 *start.* Sudden attack.

48 *'Villiago!'* Villain.

until night: for with these borne before us, instead of maces, will we ride through the streets; and at every corner have them kiss. Away!

[*Exeunt.*

SCENE VIII. *Southwark.*

Alarum and retreat. Enter CADE *and all his rabblement.*

Cade. Up Fish Street! down Saint Magnus' Corner! kill and knock down! throw them into Thames! [*Sound a parley.*] What noise is this I hear? Dare any be so bold to sound retreat or parley, when I command them kill?

Enter BUCKINGHAM *and old* CLIFFORD, *attended.*

Buck. Ay, here they be that dare and will disturb thee:
Know, Cade, we come ambassadors from the king
Unto the commons whom thou hast misled;
And here pronounce free pardon to them all
That will forsake thee and go home in peace. 10
Clif. What say ye, countrymen? will ye relent,
And yield to mercy whilst 'tis offer'd you;
Or let a rebel lead you to your deaths?
Who loves the king and will embrace his pardon,
Fling up his cap, and say 'God save his majesty!'
Who hateth him and honours not his father,
Henry the Fifth, that made all France to quake,
Shake he his weapon at us and pass by.
All. God save the king! God save the king!
Cade. What, Buckingham and Clifford, are ye so brave? And you, base peasants, do ye believe him? will you needs be hanged with your pardons about your necks? Hath my sword therefore broke through London gates, that you should leave me at the White Hart in Southwark? I thought ye would never have given out these arms till you had recovered your ancient freedom: but you are all recreants and dastards, and delight to live in slavery to the nobility. Let them break your backs with burthens, take your houses over your heads, ravish your wives and daughters before your faces: for me, I will make shift for one; and so, God's curse light upon you all!
All. We'll follow Cade, we'll follow Cade!
Clif. Is Cade the son of Henry the Fifth,
That thus you do exclaim you'll go with him?
Will he conduct you through the heart of France,
And make the meanest of you earls and dukes?
Alas, he hath no home, no place to fly to; 40
Nor knows he how to live but by the spoil,
Unless by robbing of your friends and us.
Were't not a shame, that whilst you live at jar,
The fearful French, whom you late vanquished,
Should make a start o'er seas and vanquish you?
Methinks already in this civil broil
I see them lording it in London streets,
Crying 'Villiago!' unto all they meet.
Better ten thousand base-born Cades miscarry 49
Than you should stoop unto a Frenchman's mercy.
To France, to France, and get what you have lost;
Spare England, for it is your native coast:
Henry hath money, you are strong and manly;
God on our side, doubt not of victory.

All. A Clifford! a Clifford! we'll follow the
king and Clifford.
Cade. Was ever feather so lightly blown to
and fro as this multitude? The name of Henry
the Fifth hales them to an hundred mischiefs and
makes them leave me desolate. I see them lay
their heads together to surprise me. My sword
make way for me, for here is no staying. In
despite of the devils and hell, have through the
very middest of you! and heavens and honour be
witness that no want of resolution in me, but only
my followers' base and ignominious treasons,
makes me betake me to my heels. [*Exit.*
Buck. What, is he fled? Go some, and follow him;
And he that brings his head unto the king
Shall have a thousand crowns for his reward. 70
[*Exeunt some of them.*
Follow me, soldiers: we'll devise a mean
To reconcile you all unto the king. [*Exeunt.*

SCENE IX. *Kenilworth Castle.*

Sound trumpets. Enter KING, QUEEN, *and*
SOMERSET, *on the terrace.*

King. Was ever king that joy'd an earthly
throne,
And could command no more content than I?
No sooner was I crept out of my cradle
But I was made a king, at nine months old.
Was never subject long'd to be a king
As I do long and wish to be a subject.

Enter BUCKINGHAM *and old* CLIFFORD.

Buck. Health and glad tidings to your majesty!
King. Why, Buckingham, is the traitor Cade
surprised?
Or is he but retired to make him strong?

*Enter, below, multitudes, with halters about
their necks.*

Clif. He is fled, my lord, and all his powers
do yield; 10
And humbly thus, with halters on their necks,
Expect your highness' doom, of life or death.
King. Then, heaven, set ope thy everlasting
gates,
To entertain my vows of thanks and praise!
Soldiers, this day have you redeem'd your lives
And show'd how well you love your prince and
country:
Continue still in this so good a mind,
And Henry, though he be infortunate,
Assure yourselves, will never be unkind:
And so, with thanks and pardon to you all, 20
I do dismiss you to your several countries.
All. God save the king! God save the king!

Enter a Messenger.

Mess. Please it your grace to be advertised
The Duke of York is newly come from Ireland,
And with a puissant and a mighty power
• Of gallowglasses and stout kerns
Is marching hitherward in proud array,
And still proclaimeth, as he comes along,
His arms are only to remove from thee
The Duke of Somerset, whom he terms a traitor.

Cade's followers with halters around their necks.
Engraving by Kenny Meadows from Barry Cornwall's
Works of Shakspere, 1846

26 *gallowglasses.* Heavily armed Irish foot-soldiers.

4–5 *laid for me.* On the look out for me.

9 *sallet.* Salad.

12 *sallet.* Helmet.

13 *brown bill.* Pike.

27 *fee simple.* i.e. land of which he is the outright owner.

30–31 *eat iron . . . ostrich.* A popular misconception in Elizabethan England – that ostriches could eat nails and other iron objects.

Ostrich eating nails. Illustration from a 15th century manuscript

King. Thus stands my state, 'twixt Cade and York distress'd; 31
Like to a ship that, having 'scaped a tempest,
Is straightway calm'd and boarded with a pirate:
But now is Cade driven back, his men dispersed;
And now is York in arms to second him.
I pray thee, Buckingham, go and meet him,
And ask him what's the reason of these arms.
Tell him I'll send Duke Edmund to the Tower;
And, Somerset, we will commit thee thither,
Until his army be dismiss'd from him. 40
Som. My lord,
I'll yield myself to prison willingly,
Or unto death, to do my country good.
King. In any case, be not too rough in terms;
For he is fierce and cannot brook hard language.
Buck. I will, my lord; and doubt not so to deal
As all things shall redound unto your good.
King. Come, wife, let's in, and learn to govern better;
For yet may England curse my wretched reign.
[*Flourish. Exeunt.*

SCENE X. *Kent. Iden's garden.*

Enter CADE.

Cade. Fie on ambition! fie on myself, that have a sword, and yet am ready to famish! These five days have I hid me in these woods
• and durst not peep out, for all the country is laid for me; but now am I so hungry that if I might have a lease of my life for a thousand years I could stay no longer. Wherefore, on a brick wall have I climbed into this garden, to see if I can
• eat grass, or pick a sallet another while, which is not amiss to cool a man's stomach this hot weather. And I think this word 'sallet' was born to
• do me good: for many a time, but for a sallet,
• my brain-pan had been cleft with a brown bill; and many a time, when I have been dry and bravely marching, it hath served me instead of a quart pot to drink in; and now the word 'sallet' must serve me to feed on.

Enter IDEN.

Iden. Lord, who would live turmoiled in the court,
And may enjoy such quiet walks as these?
This small inheritance my father left me 20
Contenteth me, and worth a monarchy.
I seek not to wax great by others' waning,
Or gather wealth, I care not, with what envy:
Sufficeth that I have maintains my state
And sends the poor well pleased from my gate.
Cade. Here's the lord of the soil come to
• seize me for a stray, for entering his fee-simple without leave. Ah, villain, thou wilt betray me, and get a thousand crowns of the king by carry-
• ing my head to him: but I'll make thee eat iron like an ostrich, and swallow my sword like a great pin, ere thou and I part.
Iden. Why, rude companion, whatsoe'er thou be,
I know thee not; why, then, should I betray thee?
Is't not enough to break into my garden,
And, like a thief, to come to rob my grounds,
Climbing my walls in spite of me the owner,
But thou wilt brave me with these saucy terms?

Cade. Brave thee! ay, by the best blood that ever was broached, and beard thee too. Look on me well: I have eat no meat these five days; yet, come thou and thy five men, and if I do not leave you all as dead as a door-nail, I pray God I may never eat grass more.

Iden. Nay, it shall ne'er be said, while England stands,
That Alexander Iden, an esquire of Kent,
Took odds to combat a poor famish'd man.
Oppose thy steadfast-gazing eyes to mine,
See if thou canst outface me with thy looks:
Set limb to limb, and thou art far the lesser; 50
Thy hand is but a finger to my fist,
Thy leg a stick compared with this truncheon;
My foot shall fight with all the strength thou hast;
And if mine arm be heaved in the air,
Thy grave is digg'd already in the earth.
As for words, whose greatness answers words,
Let this my sword report what speech forbears.

Cade. By my valour, the most complete champion that ever I heard! Steel, if thou turn the edge, or cut not out the burly-boned clown in chines of beef ere thou sleep in thy sheath, I beseech God on my knees thou mayst be turned to hobnails. [*Here they fight. Cade falls.*

O, I am slain! famine and no other hath slain me: let ten thousand devils come against me, and give me but the ten meals I have lost, and I'ld defy them all. Wither, garden; and be henceforth a burying-place to all that do dwell in this house, because the unconquered soul of Cade is fled. 70

Iden. Is't Cade that I have slain, that monstrous traitor?
Sword, I will hallow thee for this thy deed,
And hang thee o'er my tomb when I am dead:
Ne'er shall this blood be wiped from thy point;
But thou shalt wear it as a herald's coat,
To emblaze the honour that thy master got.

Cade. Iden, farewell, and be proud of thy victory. Tell Kent from me, she hath lost her best man, and exhort all the world to be cowards; for I, that never feared any, am vanquished by famine, not by valour. [*Dies.* 81

Iden. How much thou wrong'st me, heaven be my judge.
Die, damned wretch, the curse of her that bare thee;
And as I thrust thy body in with my sword,
So wish I, I might thrust thy soul to hell.
Hence will I drag thee headlong by the heels
Unto a dunghill which shall be thy grave,
And there cut off thy most ungracious head;
Which I will bear in triumph to the king, 89
Leaving thy trunk for crows to feed upon. [*Exit.*

ACT V.

SCENE I. *Fields between Dartford and Blackheath.*

Enter YORK, *and his army of Irish, with drum and colours.*

York. From Ireland thus comes York to claim his right,
And pluck the crown from feeble Henry's head:
Ring, bells, aloud; burn, bonfires, clear and bright,

40 *beard.* Insult.

Iden: 'Let this my sword report what speech forbears'. Drawing of Cade and Iden by John Thurston (1744–1822)

5 *sancta majestas.* Sacred Majesty.

11 *flower-de-luce.* Fleur-de-lis, the heraldic emblem of France.

26 *Ajax Telamonius.* On the death of Achilles both Ulysses and Ajax claimed his armour. When the armour was awarded to Ulysses, Ajax lost his reason and in a frenzy killed a flock of sheep believing them to be his enemies who were insulting him.

46 *Saint George's field.* An open space on the south bank of the Thames between Southwark and Lambeth.

St. George's Field. From Fairthovnes map of London, 1658

To entertain great England's lawful king.
● Ah! sancta majestas, who would not buy thee dear?
Let them obey that know not how to rule;
This hand was made to handle nought but gold.
I cannot give due action to my words,
Except a sword or sceptre balance it:
A sceptre shall it have, have I a soul,   10
● On which I'll toss the flower-de-luce of France.

Enter BUCKINGHAM.

Whom have we here? Buckingham, to disturb me?
The king hath sent him, sure: I must dissemble.
 Buck. York, if thou meanest well, I greet thee well.
 York. Humphrey of Buckingham, I accept thy greeting.
Art thou a messenger, or come of pleasure?
 Buck. A messenger from Henry, our dread liege,
To know the reason of these arms in peace;
Or why thou, being a subject as I am,
Against thy oath and true allegiance sworn,   20
Should raise so great a power without his leave,
Or dare to bring thy force so near the court.
 York. [*Aside*] Scarce can I speak, my choler is so great:
O, I could hew up rocks and fight with flint,
I am so angry at these abject terms;
● And now, like Ajax Telamonius,
On sheep or oxen could I spend my fury.
I am far better born than is the king,
More like a king, more kingly in my thoughts:
But I must make fair weather yet a while,   30
Till Henry be more weak and I more strong.—
Buckingham, I prithee, pardon me,
That I have given no answer all this while;
My mind was troubled with deep melancholy.
The cause why I have brought this army hither
Is to remove proud Somerset from the king,
Seditious to his grace and to the state.
 Buck. That is too much presumption on thy part:
But if thy arms be to no other end,
The king hath yielded unto thy demand: 40
The Duke of Somerset is in the Tower.
 York. Upon thine honour, is he prisoner?
 Buck. Upon mine honour, he is prisoner.
 York. Then, Buckingham, I do dismiss my powers.
Soldiers, I thank you all; disperse yourselves;
● Meet me to-morrow in Saint George's field,
You shall have pay and every thing you wish.
And let my sovereign, virtuous Henry,
Command my eldest son, nay, all my sons,
As pledges of my fealty and love;   50
I'll send them all as willing as I live:
Lands, goods, horse, armour, any thing I have,
Is his to use, so Somerset may die.
 Buck. York, I commend this kind submission:
We twain will go into his highness' tent.

Enter KING *and* Attendants.

 King. Buckingham, doth York intend no harm to us,
That thus he marcheth with thee arm in arm?
 York. In all submission and humility
York doth present himself unto your highness.

King. Then what intends these forces thou
    dost bring? 60
York. To heave the traitor Somerset from
    hence,
And fight against that monstrous rebel Cade,
Who since I heard to be discomfited.

Enter IDEN, *with* CADE's *head.*

Iden. If one so rude and of so mean condition
May pass into the presence of a king,
Lo, I present your grace a traitor's head,
The head of Cade, whom I in combat slew.
King. The head of Cade! Great God, how
    just art Thou!
O, let me view his visage, being dead,
That living wrought me such exceeding trouble.
Tell me, my friend, art thou the man that slew
    him? 71
Iden. I was, an't like your majesty.
King. How art thou call'd? and what is thy
    degree?
Iden. Alexander Iden, that's my name;
A poor esquire of Kent, that loves his king.
Buck. So please it you, my lord, 'twere not
    amiss
He were created knight for his good service.
King. Iden, kneel down. [*He kneels.*] Rise
    up a knight.
We give thee for reward a thousand marks,
And will that thou henceforth attend on us. 80
Iden. May Iden live to merit such a bounty,
And never live but true unto his liege! [*Rises.*

Enter QUEEN *and* SOMERSET.

King. See, Buckingham, Somerset comes
    with the queen:
Go, bid her hide him quickly from the duke.
Queen. For thousand Yorks he shall not hide
    his head,
But boldly stand and front him to his face.
York. How now! is Somerset at liberty?
Then, York, unloose thy long-imprison'd thoughts,
And let thy tongue be equal with thy heart.
Shall I endure the sight of Somerset? 90
False king! why hast thou broken faith with me,
Knowing how hardly I can brook abuse?
King did I call thee? no, thou art not king,
Not fit to govern and rule multitudes,
Which darest not, no, nor canst not rule a traitor.
That head of thine doth not become a crown;
● Thy hand is made to grasp a palmer's staff,
And not to grace an awful princely sceptre.
That gold must round engirt these brows of mine,
● Whose smile and frown, like to Achilles' spear, 100
Is able with the change to kill and cure.
Here is a hand to hold a sceptre up
And with the same to act controlling laws.
Give place: by heaven, thou shalt rule no more
O'er him whom heaven created for thy ruler.
Som. O monstrous traitor! I arrest thee,
    York,
Of capital treason 'gainst the king and crown:
Obey, audacious traitor; kneel for grace.
York. Wouldst have me kneel? first let me
    ask of these,
If they can brook I bow a knee to man. 110
Sirrah, call in my sons to be my bail:
                 [*Exit Attendant.*
I know, ere they will have me go to ward,

Knighting of Iden. Engraving by Kenny Meadows from
Barry Cornwall's *Works of Shakspere*, 1846

97 *palmer's staff.* Pilgrim's staff.

100 *Achilles' spear.* Telephus who had been wounded
by Achilles' spear could not be cured till rust from the
same spear had been put on his wound.

They'll pawn their swords for my enfranchise-
ment.
  Queen. Call hither Clifford; bid him come
amain,
To say if that the bastard boys of York
Shall be the surety for their traitor father.
                      [*Exit Buckingham.*
• *York.* O blood-bespotted Neapolitan,
Outcast of Naples, England's bloody scourge!
The sons of York, thy betters in their birth,
• Shall be their father's bail; and bane to those 120
That for my surety will refuse the boys!

      Enter EDWARD *and* RICHARD.

See where they come: I'll warrant they'll make
it good.

      Enter old CLIFFORD *and his* Son.

  Queen. And here comes Clifford to deny their
bail.
  Clif. Health and all happiness to my lord the
king!   [*Kneels.*
  York. I thank thee, Clifford: say, what news
with thee?
Nay, do not fright us with an angry look:
We are thy sovereign, Clifford, kneel again;
For thy mistaking so, we pardon thee.
  Clif. This is my king, York, I do not mis-
take;
But thou mistakest me much to think I do: 130
To Bedlam with him! is the man grown mad?
  King. Ay, Clifford; a bedlam and ambitious
humour
Makes him oppose himself against his king.
  Clif. He is a traitor; let him to the Tower,
And chop away that factious pate of his.
  Queen. He is arrested, but will not obey;
His sons, he says, shall give their words for him.
  York. Will you not, sons?
  Edw. Ay, noble father, if our words will
serve.
  Rich. And if words will not, then our weapons
shall.   140
  Clif. Why, what a brood of traitors have we
here!
  York. Look in a glass, and call thy image so:
I am thy king, and thou a false-heart traitor.
• Call hither to the stake my two brave bears,
That with the very shaking of their chains
• They may astonish these fell-lurking curs:
Bid Salisbury and Warwick come to me.

     Enter the EARLS OF WARWICK *and* SALISBURY.

  Clif. Are these thy bears? we'll bait thy bears
to death,
• And manacle the bear-ward in their chains,
If thou darest bring them to the baiting place. 150
  Rich. Oft have I seen a hot o'erweening cur
Run back and bite, because he was withheld;
Who, being suffer'd with the bear's fell paw,
Hath clapp'd his tail between his legs and cried:
And such a piece of service will you do,
If you oppose yourselves to match Lord Warwick.
  Clif. Hence, heap of wrath, foul indigested
lump,
As crooked in thy manners as thy shape!
  York. Nay, we shall heat you thoroughly
anon.

117 *Neapolitan.* Margaret's father claimed the title of
King of Naples.

120 *bane.* Destruction.

144–146 *stake, bears, chains, curs.* Image is that of
bear-baiting. Warwick's badge was a bear and a ragged
staff.

Badge of the Warwick family. Engraving by F.W. Fairholt from J.O. Halliwell's edition of Shakespeare's
works, 1853–65

146 *fell-lurking.* Lying in wait to attack someone.

149 *bear-ward.* Bear-keeper.

Opposite : Iden is created a knight. Engraving from Bell's
edition of *Shakespeare,* 1773–74

167 *frosty head.* Silver haired.

174 *mickle.* Great.

187 *reave.* Bereave.

191 *sophister.* One skilled in rhetoric.

200 *burgonet.* Helmet.

A burgonet. Engraving by F.W. Fairholt from J.O. Halliwell's edition of Shakespeare's works, 1853–65

215 *stigmatic.* i.e. a 'deformed person' and a 'criminal who has been branded'.

Clif. Take heed, lest by your heat you burn
yourselves. 160
King. Why, Warwick, hath thy knee forgot
to bow?
Old Salisbury, shame to thy silver hair,
Thou mad misleader of thy brain-sick son!
What, wilt thou on thy death-bed play the
ruffian,
And seek for sorrow with thy spectacles?
O, where is faith? O, where is loyalty?
• If it be banish'd from the frosty head,
Where shall it find a harbour in the earth?
Wilt thou go dig a grave to find out war,
And shame thine honourable age with blood? 170
Why art thou old, and want'st experience?
Or wherefore dost abuse it, if thou hast it?
For shame! in duty bend thy knee to me
• That bows unto the grave with mickle age.
Sal. My lord, I have consider'd with myself
The title of this most renowned duke;
And in my conscience do repute his grace
The rightful heir to England's royal seat.
King. Hast thou not sworn allegiance unto
me?
Sal. I have. 180
King. Canst thou dispense with heaven for
such an oath?
Sal. It is great sin to swear unto a sin,
But greater sin to keep a sinful oath.
Who can be bound by any solemn vow
To do a murderous deed, to rob a man,
To force a spotless virgin's chastity,
• To reave the orphan of his patrimony,
To wring the widow from her custom'd right,
And have no other reason for this wrong
But that he was bound by a solemn oath? 190
• *Queen.* A subtle traitor needs no sophister.
King. Call Buckingham, and bid him arm
himself.
York. Call Buckingham, and all the friends
thou hast,
I am resolved for death or dignity.
Clif. The first I warrant thee, if dreams prove
true.
War. You were best to go to bed and dream
again,
To keep thee from the tempest of the field.
Clif. I am resolved to bear a greater storm
Than any thou canst conjure up to-day;
• And that I'll write upon thy burgonet, 200
Might I but know thee by thy household badge.
War. Now, by my father's badge, old Nevil's
crest,
The rampant bear chain'd to the ragged staff,
This day I'll wear aloft my burgonet,
As on a mountain top the cedar shows
That keeps his leaves in spite of any storm,
Even to affright thee with the view thereof.
Clif. And from thy burgonet I'll rend thy
bear
And tread it under foot with all contempt,
Despite the bear-ward that protects the bear. 210
Y. Clif. And so to arms, victorious father,
To quell the rebels and their complices.
Rich. Fie! charity, for shame! speak not in
spite,
For you shall sup with Jesu Christ to-night.
• *Y. Clif.* Foul stigmatic, that's more than thou
canst tell.

Rich. If not in heaven, you'll surely sup in hell.   [*Exeunt severally.*

SCENE II. *Saint Alban's.*

Alarums to the battle. Enter WARWICK.

War. Clifford of Cumberland, 'tis Warwick calls:
And if thou dost not hide thee from the bear,
Now, when the angry trumpet sounds alarum
And dead men's cries do fill the empty air,
Clifford, I say, come forth and fight with me:
Proud northern lord, Clifford of Cumberland,
Warwick is hoarse with calling thee to arms.

Enter YORK.

How now, my noble lord! what, all afoot?
York. The deadly-handed Clifford slew my steed,
But match to match I have encounter'd him   10
And made a prey for carrion kites and crows
Even of the bonny beast he loved so well.

Enter old CLIFFORD.

War. Of one or both of us the time is come.
York. Hold, Warwick, seek thee out some other chase,
For I myself must hunt this deer to death.
War. Then, nobly, York; 'tis for a crown thou fight'st.
As I intend, Clifford, to thrive to-day,
It grieves my soul to leave thee unassail'd.   [*Exit.*
Clif. What seest thou in me, York? why dost thou pause?
York. With thy brave bearing should I be in love,   20
But that thou art so fast mine enemy.
Clif. Nor should thy prowess want praise and esteem,
But that 'tis shown ignobly and in treason.
York. So let it help me now against thy sword
As I in justice and true right express it.
Clif. My soul and body on the action both!
York. A dreadful lay! Address thee instantly.
     [*They fight, and Clifford falls.*
Clif. La fin couronne les œuvres.   [*Dies.*
York. Thus war hath given thee peace, for thou art still.
Peace with his soul, heaven, if it be thy will!   30
     [*Exit.*

Enter young CLIFFORD.

Y. Clif. Shame and confusion! all is on the rout;
Fear frames disorder, and disorder wounds
Where it should guard. O war, thou son of hell,
Whom angry heavens do make their minister,
Throw in the frozen bosoms of our part
Hot coals of vengeance! Let no soldier fly.
He that is truly dedicate to war
Hath no self-love, nor he that loves himself
Hath not essentially but by circumstance
The name of valour. [*Seeing his dead father*]
   O, let the vile world end,   40
And the premised flames of the last day
Knit earth and heaven together!
Now let the general trumpet blow his blast,

21 *fast.* i.e. so entrenched an enemy.

27 *lay.* Wager, stake.

28 *La fin . . . œuvres.* The end crowns every work.

35 *part.* Party.

41 *premised flames.* The conflagration that was foretold.

48 *chair-days.* Reference to the more sedentary life of the elderly.

59 *wild Medea.* Medea fled with Jason after she had helped him win the Golden Fleece. She killed her brother, Absyrtus, and threw the pieces of his body into the sea so that her father's pursuit of the fugitives would be delayed whilst he stopped to pick up the pieces.

Jason with Medea. Detail from a painting by Jean-Francois Detroy (1679–1752)

62 *Aeneas . . . bear.* After the fall of Troy Aeneas carried his father, Anchises, on his shoulders to safety.

69 *the wizard famous.* In I. iv. 38 the spirit had warned that Somerset should 'shun castles'.

73 *outrun the heavens.* Escape our destiny.

Particularities and petty sounds
To cease! Wast thou ordain'd, dear father,
To lose thy youth in peace, and to achieve
The silver livery of advised age,
● And, in thy reverence and thy chair-days, thus
To die in ruffian battle? Even at this sight   49
My heart is turn'd to stone: and while 'tis mine,
It shall be stony. York not our old men spares;
No more will I their babes: tears virginal
Shall be to me even as the dew to fire,
And beauty that the tyrant oft reclaims
Shall to my flaming wrath be oil and flax.
Henceforth I will not have to do with pity:
Meet I an infant of the house of York,
Into as many gobbets will I cut it
● As wild Medea young Absyrtus did:
In cruelty will I seek out my fame.   60
Come, thou new ruin of old Clifford's house:
● As did Æneas old Anchises bear,
So bear I thee upon my manly shoulders;
But then Æneas bare a living load,
Nothing so heavy as these woes of mine.
    [*Exit, bearing off his father.*

Enter RICHARD *and* SOMERSET *to fight.*
    SOMERSET *is killed.*

  Rich. So, lie thou there;
For underneath an alehouse' paltry sign,
The Castle in Saint Alban's, Somerset
● Hath made the wizard famous in his death.   69
Sword, hold thy temper; heart, be wrathful still:
Priests pray for enemies, but princes kill. [*Exit.*

Fight: excursions. Enter KING, QUEEN, *and others.*

  Queen. Away, my lord! you are slow; for shame, away!
●   *King.* Can we outrun the heavens? good Margaret, stay.
  Queen. What are you made of? you'll nor fight nor fly:
Now is it manhood, wisdom and defence,
To give the enemy way, and to secure us
By what we can, which can no more but fly.
    [*Alarum afar off.*
If you be ta'en, we then should see the bottom
Of all our fortunes: but if we haply scape,
As well we may, if not through your neglect,   80
We shall to London get, where you are loved
And where this breach now in our fortunes made
May readily be stopp'd.

Re-enter young CLIFFORD.

  Y. Clif. But that my heart's on future mischief set,
I would speak blasphemy ere bid you fly:
But fly you must; uncurable discomfit
Reigns in the hearts of all our present parts.
Away, for your relief! and we will live
To see their day and them our fortune give:
Away, my lord, away!   [*Exeunt.*

    SCENE III. *Fields near St Alban's.*

Alarum. Retreat. Enter YORK, RICHARD,
WARWICK, *and* Soldiers, *with drum and colours.*

  York. Of Salisbury, who can report of him,

That winter lion, who in rage forgets
Aged contusions and all brush of time,
And, like a gallant in the brow of youth,
● Repairs him with occasion? This happy day
Is not itself, nor have we won one foot,
If Salisbury be lost.
   Rich.   My noble father,
Three times to-day I holp him to his horse,
Three times bestrid him; thrice I led him off,
Persuaded him from any further act: 10
But still, where danger was, still there I met him;
And like rich hangings in a homely house,
So was his will in his old feeble body.
But, noble as he is, look where he comes.

     Enter SALISBURY.

   Sal. Now, by my sword, well hast thou fought
     to-day;
By the mass, so did we all. I thank you, Richard:
God knows how long it is I have to live;
And it hath pleased him that three times to-day
You have defended me from imminent death.
Well, lords, we have not got that which we have:
'Tis not enough our foes are this time fled,   21
● Being opposites of such repairing nature.
   York. I know our safety is to follow them;
For, as I hear, the king is fled to London,
To call a present court of parliament.
Let us pursue him ere the writs go forth.
What says Lord Warwick? shall we after them?
   War. After them! nay, before them, if we can.
Now, by my faith, lords, 'twas a glorious day:
Saint Alban's battle won by famous York   30
Shall be eternized in all age to come.
Sound drums and trumpets, and to London all:
And more such days as these to us befall!
                        [*Exeunt.*

5 *Repairs . . . occasion.* Rises to the occasion.

22 *opposites . . . nature.* Opponents possessing great powers of recuperation.

Fields near St Albans. Engraving from *Old England,* 1854

King Henry VI

1591

THE THIRD PART of this trilogy is less varied and interesting than the Second; it had such refractory and (to us) more monotonous material to deal with in the ding-dong feuds, slanging-matches and battles of the Wars of the Roses. The dramatist did a most competent job in licking this elongated Chronicle material into shape, foreshortening periods of time for dramatic effect, etc. Nor did this mean that the Third Part was any the less effective with the Elizabethans – it may even have been more so.

For Shakespeare gave them a somewhat different mixture and turned out a revenge-play, a kind that was highly popular at the time, with Kyd's *The Spanish Tragedy* and his lost 'Hamlet'. At this same time the practical actor, with his eye on box-office appeal, was turning out another revenge-play, *Titus Andronicus* (going one better than Kyd in horrors), which has many analogies with *3 Henry VI*.

Here revenge is a *leit-motiv*: Clifford specifically declares his motive for killing York's boy, Rutland, in that York killed Clifford's father; the sons of York declare revenge upon Queen Margaret, for York's death; so that here we have the murder of Henry VI in the Tower, while we can look forward to his son's murder at Tewkesbury in *Richard III*. Richard's character is being carefully prepared here and headed for the next play Shakespeare has in mind. The trilogy is to become a quartet, or tetralogy.

At the same time as we find this play less likable than contemporaries did, we note further improvement in the verse. This is not simply due to a better text, it is that the actor is developing rapidly as a dramatist. Fine, and very long, speeches are charac-teristic of this play – the most famous being poor Henry VI's soliloquy reflecting on the misery of his position, the horror of the war and how much better it would be to be a simple country swain. (He would have done better as such – still better as a cleric, for he was quite well educated and no fool: debilitated, and suffering from breakdowns, he was just not up to his job.)

These speeches are developed in accordance with the proper rules of school rhetoric; *inventio*, *vituperatio*, and all that. Henry's is a refreshing contrast in its kindly preference for rustic simplicity: he is the only person who disclaims and opposes such motives as revenge, but is ineffective and therefore falls victim. His very weakness is pointed out as a prime cause of the troubles, as it was. But the effective power-seekers are – or are to

Henry VI who reigned 1422–61 and 1470–71

be – no better off. The most malign among them, Richard, will receive his due in the next play: meanwhile, he says to Warwick:

> Thy brother's blood the thirsty earth hath drunk,
> Broached with the steely point of Clifford's lance;
> And in the very pangs of death he cried,
> Like to a dismal clangor heard from far,
> 'Warwick! Revenge! Brother, revenge my death!'

This recalls Lodge's reminiscence of Kyd's original 'Hamlet': 'the ghost which cried so miserably at the Theatre [i.e. in Shoreditch], like an oyster-wife, "Hamlet, revenge!"' The most popular play of 1591 and 1592 was *The Spanish Tragedy*, and in the third part of *Henry VI* we find the actor-dramatist competing with Kyd's revenge-play. The word itself occurs more frequently than in any other of his plays, far more than in *Hamlet*. But what an almighty development was to take place between this and that!

Themes. Thus the dominant theme of *3 Henry VI* is clearly revenge. Nemesis followed for the perpetrators of these crimes. The House of Lancaster paid for Henry IV's murder of Richard II in the Yorkist murders of Henry VI and his son. The Yorkists paid for theirs in the killing of Richard, Duke of York, and later on Clarence at the hands of his brother Edward IV. Then Richard III outdid them all with his murders not only of Henry VI but of his brother's great friend Hastings and his brother's children in the Tower. The concept 'Machiavellian' is first applied to him in this play, in a splendid long speech which develops his character and foretells the future:

> I can add colours to the chameleon,
> Change shapes with Proteus for advantages,

(cf. *The Two Gentlemen of Verona* shortly to come)

> And set the murderous Machiavel to school.
> Can I do this, and cannot get a crown?
> Tut! were it further off, I'll pluck it down.

And he did! – a remarkable achievement in its malign way, aided by the chance of his brother's early death.

The play is full of the sudden turns and changes of fortune, the ups and downs of each side in turn – and indeed the wheel of Fortune is a recurring image. This was the dominant theme with Kyd, and witnesses again to his early influence, to which Ben Jonson testified; Kyd, Marlowe and the actor were writing in some proximity. The play again has notable reflections, virtual quotations from Marlowe. Here is one from *Tamburlaine*:

> How sweet a thing it is to wear a crown,
> Within whose circuit is Elysium
> And all that poets feign of bliss and joy.

Another line –

> And we are graced with wreaths of victory –

comes from *The Massacre at Paris*, which is also of this very time, for it ends with the murder of Henri III in 1589.

A theme which everyone has commented upon is that very close to Shakespeare's mind and heart: the breakdown of social order and the release of man's inherent aggressiveness and cruelty with the collapse of authority and the impotence of sovereign rule. For all the sympathy with which he is drawn as a man, Henry VI is not let off the imputation and the responsibility that is laid at his door – by both sides, most bitterly by Queen Margaret, who is driven to fury by his incapacity. We watch her becoming the virago she is destined to be in *Richard III*.

With the anarchy that ensues comes the degeneration of morality, the prevalence of perjury, the breaking of oaths and unscrupulous shifts from side to side. It is the young Richard who proclaims openly,

> An oath is of no moment, being not took
> Before a true and lawful magistrate
> That hath authority over him that swears.
> Henry had none, but did usurp the place.

So the Yorkists break their oath to Henry, and the compromise he sought to arrange by making York Regent, while retaining the title merely of king for his own life. But neither did this arrangement appeal to Queen Margaret and her son. Both sides were eager to fight and kill: it is a bloody play, and there is much stabbing and killing on stage.

At one point we have the horror: 'Enter a Son that hath killed his Father, with the body in his arms', followed shortly by: 'Enter a Father that hath killed his Son, with the body in his arms.' It is like *The Spanish Tragedy*, or the horrors of *Titus Andronicus* with which the actor-dramatist out-did that and won success by it.

In short, when authority goes politics becomes an open, ruthless power-struggle, which it is the whole purpose of politics to direct in a civilised manner, to canalise men's aggressiveness into beneficent courses, for the good of society. As the Prince of Wales says:

> If that be right which Warwick says is right,
> There is no wrong, but every thing is right.

(The Prince was to be killed at Tewkesbury, Warwick at Barnet within a month of each other in 1471.)

Not that Shakespeare has any illusions about the people, here as anywhere else. King Henry says,

> Look, as I blow this feather from my face,
> And as the air blows it to me again,
> Obeying with my wind when I do blow,
> And yielding to another when it blows,
> Commanded always by the greater gust,
> Such is the lightness of you common men.

He goes on to beseech them:

> But do not break your oaths . . .

In vain, of course. For what is the point of beseeching? Power is what they obey, the better if dressed up in a little brief authority, to mitigate the struggle for survival at the bottom of all life. Of course, there are times in history when nothing *can* be done – perhaps Henry VI's long minority and reign formed one of them; then the naked struggle for survival surfaces in all its reptilian horror.

Scenes. A respite from the struggle is given us in only one or two scenes. Poor Henry takes time off from the battlefield to moralise like the countryman he fain would be:

> What time the shepherd, blowing of his nails,
> Can neither call it perfect day nor night.

This Cotswold image will come to mind in the country song that ends *Love's Labour's Lost*. How much happier the King would be if he were but a country shepherd tending his flock:

> So many days my ewes have been with young:
> So many weeks ere the poor fools will ean;
> So many years ere I shall shear the fleece . . .
> Gives not the hawthorn bush a sweeter shade
> To shepherds looking on their silly sheep,
> Than doth a rich embroidered canopy
> To kings that fear their subjects' treachery?

Or, in modern terms, to politicians, fearing the treachery of colleagues.

> . . . the shepherd's homely curds,

Queen Elizabeth Woodville, wife of Edward IV. Engraving (from an old print, Kerrich Collection) from Pictorial History of England, *Vol II, 1856*

His cold thin drink out of his leather bottle,
His wonted sleep under a fresh tree's shade,
All which secure and sweetly he enjoys,
Is far beyond a prince's delicates.

Here speak the preferences of the countryman, who achieved success in London, but never lost touch with the country and preferred to return to it.

Another scene that is a let-up from the horrors of high politics and the power-struggle at the top – compare the bloodshed through which Hitler and Stalin, and many others, waded to power in recent times – is the scene in which Edward IV seeks to win Elizabeth Woodville, Lady Grey, for mistress and, failing that, woos her for wife. A delightful scene in itself, it is one of the play's quick changes.

Quickest of all, and more important to the action, is that in which Warwick, on embassy to Louis XI to arrange a marriage for Edward IV to a French princess, receives the humiliating news of his marriage (his wife was a Lancastrian widow, by the way). Warwick immediately reverses course and goes over to Queen Margaret and her son: they begin to tread the Calvary that leads to Barnet and Tewkesbury – the Yorkist triumph.

Personal. It is from this play that comes the line addressed to Queen Margaret,

O tiger's heart wrapped in a woman's hide!

which Greene parodied with his 'Tiger's heart wrapped in a player's hide', in his attack on Shakespeare and his profession. We need say no more about the matter, except that it is one more indication of the success these plays achieved, which shortly won for him the notice and then the patronage of Southampton. Shortly, too, we find a line from the play reflected in a Sonnet: Clarence's

I will not ruinate my father's house,

is echoed in the early sonnet:

Seeking that beauteous roof to ruinate
Which to repair should be thy chief desire.

Richard Neville, Earl of Warwick. Engraving from Old England, *Vol I, 1854*

Here is an image,

Like one that stands upon a promontory
And spies a far-off shore where he would tread,
Wishing his foot were equal with his eye,
And chides the sea, that sunders him from thence –

which has an echo in a later sonnet:

Let this sad interim like the ocean be
Which parts the shore, where two contracted new
Come daily to the banks . . .

The thought is different, the image similar. The rare word 'promontory' is contemporaneously repeated in *Titus Andronicus*. One would like to know where he had been touring recently: Dover?, as we know the Chamberlain's men did later.

Warwickshire is to the fore in the last Act, and places named which would be familiar to him along the route from London. We have Southam, near Banbury, Dunsmore upon Watling Street, and Daventry, given its old pronunciation of Daintry. Sir John Somerville appears, of the Warwickshire Catholic family which had got into trouble in 1583 for conspiracy against the Queen; this had involved the Ardens, also Catholics.

Richard's murder of Henry VI in the Tower brings up familiar associations to Shakespeare's mind:

> So flies the reckless shepherd from the wolf;
> So first the harmless sheep doth yield his fleece,
> And next his throat unto the butcher's knife.

This, significantly enough, suggests acting, for it is immediately followed by –

> What scene of death hath Roscius now to act?

Amid all the metropolitan horrors, as again notably with *Titus*, the countryman speaks – as never with Marlowe – in out-of-door sports: several references to hawking and falconry; we have a brace of greyhounds

> Having the fearful-flying hare in sight –

shortly to be given extended treatment in the description of hare-coursing inserted into *Venus and Adonis*. Park-keepers in a chase in the North discover the poor wandering King, who has crossed the Border from Scotland:

1st Keeper: Under this thick-grown brake we'll shroud ourselves,
              For through this laund [glade] anon the deer will come;
              And in this covert will we make our stand,
              Culling the principal of all the deer.

2nd Keeper: I'll stay above the hill, so both may shoot.

1st Keeper: That cannot be: the noise of thy cross-bow
              Will scare the herd, and so my shoot is lost.

The reading, the classical quotations are more than ever from Ovid, a chief favourite with Marlowe too, and from the Bible, less in favour with Marlowe. And we have glimpses of subjects in mind that were later to form plays, especially *Julius Caesar*.

Text. An actors' version of the play, suitably cut, was printed in 1595 as the Quarto, *The True Tragedy of Richard Duke of York, and the Death of good King Henry the Sixth*, etc. This, with the Company's transcript from the author's manuscript, formed the basis of the fuller Folio text. Each supplied omissions and emendations from the other, and added dubious readings and errors to the author's natural inconsistencies over such a large canvas. The author seems to have added actors' names he had in mind: in this play, Gabriel, presumably Gabriel Spencer, whom Ben Jonson killed in a duel; also 'Humfrey' and 'Sinklo' or Sinkler, who is named also as appearing in *The Taming of the Shrew*.

THE THIRD PART OF
KING HENRY VI.

DRAMATIS PERSONÆ.

KING HENRY the Sixth.
EDWARD, PRINCE OF WALES, his son.
LEWIS XI. KING OF FRANCE.
DUKE OF SOMERSET.
DUKE OF EXETER.
EARL OF OXFORD.
EARL OF NORTHUMBERLAND.
EARL OF WESTMORELAND.
LORD CLIFFORD.
RICHARD PLANTAGENET, Duke of York.
EDWARD, Earl of March, afterwards
   King Edward IV.,
EDMUND, Earl of Rutland,   his
GEORGE, afterwards Duke of Clarence,   sons.
RICHARD, afterwards Duke of Glou-
   cester,
DUKE OF NORFOLK.
MARQUESS OF MONTAGUE.
EARL OF WARWICK.
EARL OF PEMBROKE.
LORD HASTINGS.

LORD STAFFORD.
SIR JOHN MORTIMER,   } uncles to the Duke of
SIR HUGH MORTIMER,   }   York.
HENRY, Earl of Richmond, a youth.
LORD RIVERS, brother to Lady Grey.
SIR WILLIAM STANLEY.
SIR JOHN MONTGOMERY.
SIR JOHN SOMERVILLE.
Tutor to Rutland.   Mayor of York.
Lieutenant of the Tower.   A Nobleman.
Two Keepers.   A Huntsman.
A Son that has killed his father.
A Father that has killed his son.

QUEEN MARGARET.
LADY GREY, afterwards Queen to Edward IV.
BONA, sister to the French Queen.

Soldiers, Attendants, Messengers, Watchmen, &c.

SCENE: *England and France.*

● *A bullet beside a text line indicates an annotation in the
opposite column*

ACT I.

SCENE I.   *London.   The Parliament-house.*

Alarum. Enter the DUKE OF YORK, EDWARD,
   RICHARD, NORFOLK, MONTAGUE, WARWICK,
   and Soldiers.

   War. I wonder how the king escaped our
      hands.
   York. While we pursued the horsemen of the
      north,
He slily stole away and left his men:
Whereat the great Lord of Northumberland,
Whose warlike ears could never brook retreat,
Cheer'd up the drooping army; and himself,
● Lord Clifford and Lord Stafford, all abreast,
Charged our main battle's front, and breaking in
Were by the swords of common soldiers slain.
   Edw. Lord Stafford's father, Duke of Buck-
      ingham,   10
Is either slain or wounded dangerously;
● I cleft his beaver with a downright blow:
That this is true, father, behold his blood.
   Mont. And, brother, here's the Earl of Wilt-
      shire's blood,
Whom I encounter'd as the battles join'd.
   Rich. Speak thou for me and tell them what
      I did.
   [*Throwing down the Duke of Somerset's head.*
   York. Richard hath best deserved of all my
      sons.
But is your grace dead, my Lord of Somerset?
   Norf. Such hope have all the line of John of
      Gaunt!

7–9 *Lord Clifford . . . slain.* This account of the death of
Clifford conflicts with that in 2 *Henry VI.* II.ii, where he
was killed by York.

12 *beaver.* Face-guard of a helmet.

Opposite: Death of Warwick. Engraving from Bell's
edition of *Shakespeare,* 1773–4

SD *They go up.* To the chair of state or throne where York seats himself.

47 *Warwick . . . bells.* Bells were fastened to the legs of hawks in the belief that this made them more fierce.

61 *gentle.* Noble.

62 *poltroons.* Cowards.

Rich. Thus do I hope to shake King Henry's
    head.   20
War. And so do I. Victorious Prince of York,
Before I see thee seated in that throne
Which now the house of Lancaster usurps,
I vow by heaven these eyes shall never close.
This is the palace of the fearful king,
And this the regal seat: possess it, York;
For this is thine and not King Henry's heirs'.
    York. Assist me, then, sweet Warwick, and
    I will;
For hither we have broken in by force.
    Norf. We'll all assist you; he that flies shall
    die.   30
    York. Thanks, gentle Norfolk: stay by me,
    my lords;
And, soldiers, stay and lodge by me this night.
                   [*They go up.*
    War. And when the king comes, offer him
    no violence,
Unless he seek to thrust you out perforce.
    York. The queen this day here holds her
    parliament,
But little thinks we shall be of her council:
By words or blows here let us win our right.
    Rich. Arm'd as we are, let's stay within this
    house.
    War. The bloody parliament shall this be
    call'd,
Unless Plantagenet, Duke of York, be king, 40
And bashful Henry deposed, whose cowardice
Hath made us by-words to our enemies.
    York. Then leave me not, my lords; be
    resolute;
I mean to take possession of my right.
    War. Neither the king, nor he that loves him
    best,
The proudest he that holds up Lancaster,
 ● Dares stir a wing, if Warwick shake his bells.
I'll plant Plantagenet, root him up who dares:
Resolve thee, Richard; claim the English crown.

Flourish. Enter KING HENRY, CLIFFORD,
NORTHUMBERLAND, WESTMORELAND, EXE-
TER, *and the rest.*

    K. Hen. My lords, look where the sturdy
    rebel sits,   50
Even in the chair of state: belike he means,
Back'd by the power of Warwick, that false peer,
To aspire unto the crown and reign as king.
Earl of Northumberland, he slew thy father,
And thine, Lord Clifford; and you both have
    vow'd revenge
On him, his sons, his favourites and his friends.
    North. If I be not, heavens be revenged on me!
    Clif. The hope thereof makes Clifford mourn
    in steel.
    West. What, shall we suffer this? let's pluck
    him down:
My heart for anger burns; I cannot brook it. 60
 ●   *K. Hen.* Be patient, gentle Earl of West-
    moreland.
 ●   *Clif.* Patience is for poltroons, such as he:
He durst not sit there, had your father lived.
My gracious lord, here in the parliament
Let us assail the family of York.
    North. Well hast thou spoken, cousin: be
    it so.
    K. Hen. Ah, know you not the city favours
    them,

King Henry: 'My lords, look where the sturdy rebel sits . . .' King (David Warner), York (Donald Sinden) and Warwick (Brewster Mason), Royal Shakespeare Co, 1964

And they have troops of soldiers at their beck?
    Exe. But when the duke is slain, they'll quickly fly.
    K. Hen. Far be the thought of this from Henry's heart, 70
● To make a shambles of the parliament-house!
Cousin of Exeter, frowns, words and threats
Shall be the war that Henry means to use.
Thou factious Duke of York, descend my throne,
And kneel for grace and mercy at my feet;
I am thy sovereign.
    York.   I am thine.
    Exe. For shame, come down: he made thee Duke of York.
● *York.* 'Twas my inheritance, as the earldom was.
● *Exe.* Thy father was a traitor to the crown.
    War. Exeter, thou art a traitor to the crown
In following this usurping Henry. 81
    Clif. Whom should he follow but his natural king?
    War. True, Clifford; and that's Richard Duke of York.
    K. Hen. And shall I stand, and thou sit in my throne?
    York. It must and shall be so: content thyself.
    War. Be Duke of Lancaster; let him be king.
    West. He is both king and Duke of Lancaster;
And that the Lord of Westmoreland shall maintain.
    War. And Warwick shall disprove it. You forget 89
That we are those which chased you from the field

71 *shambles.* Slaughter-house.

78 *earldom.* York inherited the earldom of March through his mother, and through this laid claim to the throne.

79 *Thy father . . . crown.* Richard Earl of Cambridge executed for conspiracy; see *Henry V*, II.ii.

105 *Duke of York.* York inherited the title from Edward, elder brother of the Earl of Cambridge.

110 *sith.* Since.

111 *lord protector.* i.e. Humphrey, Duke of Gloucester.

And slew your fathers, and with colours spread
March'd through the city to the palace gates.
   North. Yes, Warwick, I remember it to my grief;
And, by his soul, thou and thy house shall rue it.
   West. Plantagenet, of thee and these thy sons,
Thy kinsmen and thy friends, I'll have more lives
Than drops of blood were in my father's veins.
   Clif. Urge it no more; lest that, instead of words,
I send thee, Warwick, such a messenger
As shall revenge his death before I stir.   100
   War. Poor Clifford! how I scorn his worthless threats!
   York. Will you we show our title to the crown?
If not, our swords shall plead it in the field.
   K. Hen. What title hast thou, traitor, to the crown?
● Thy father was, as thou art, Duke of York;
Thy grandfather, Roger Mortimer, Earl of March:
I am the son of Henry the Fifth,
Who made the Dauphin and the French to stoop
And seized upon their towns and provinces.
●   *War.* Talk not of France, sith thou hast lost it all.   110
●   *K. Hen.* The lord protector lost it, and not I:
When I was crown'd I was but nine months old.
   Rich. You are old enough now, and yet, methinks, you lose.
Father, tear the crown from the usurper's head.
   Edw. Sweet father, do so; set it on your head.
   Mont. Good brother, as thou lovest and honourest arms,
Let's fight it out and not stand cavilling thus.
   Rich. Sound drums and trumpets, and the king will fly.
   York. Sons, peace!
   K. Hen. Peace, thou! and give King Henry leave to speak.   120
   War. Plantagenet shall speak first: hear him, lords;
And be you silent and attentive too,
For he that interrupts him shall not live.
   K. Hen. Think'st thou that I will leave my kingly throne,
Wherein my grandsire and my father sat?
No: first shall war unpeople this my realm;
Ay, and their colours, often borne in France,
And now in England to our heart's great sorrow,
Shall be my winding-sheet. Why faint you, lords?
My title's good, and better far than his.   130
   War. Prove it, Henry, and thou shalt be king.
   K. Hen. Henry the Fourth by conquest got the crown.
   York. 'Twas by rebellion against his king.
   K. Hen. [*Aside*] I know not what to say; my title's weak.—
Tell me, may not a king adopt an heir?
   York. What then?
   K. Hen. An if he may, then am I lawful king;
For Richard, in the view of many lords,
Resign'd the crown to Henry the Fourth,
Whose heir my father was, and I am his.   140
   York. He rose against him, being his sovereign,
And made him to resign his crown perforce.
   War. Suppose, my lords, he did it unconstrain'd,

Think you 'twere prejudicial to his crown?

Exe. No; for he could not so resign his crown
But that the next heir should succeed and reign.

K. Hen. Art thou against us, Duke of Exeter?

Exe. His is the right, and therefore pardon me.

York. Why whisper you, my lords, and answer not?

Exe. My conscience tells me he is lawful king.

K. Hen. [*Aside*] All will revolt from me, and turn to him.   151

North. Plantagenet, for all the claim thou lay'st,
Think not that Henry shall be so deposed.

War. Deposed he shall be, in despite of all.

North. Thou art deceived: 'tis not thy southern power,
Of Essex, Norfolk, Suffolk, nor of Kent,
Which makes thee thus presumptuous and proud,
Can set the duke up in despite of me.

Clif. King Henry, be thy title right or wrong,
Lord Clifford vows to fight in thy defence: 160
May that ground gape and swallow me alive,
Where I shall kneel to him that slew my father!

K. Hen. O Clifford, how thy words revive my heart!

York. Henry of Lancaster, resign thy crown.
What mutter you, or what conspire you, lords?

War. Do right unto this princely Duke of York,
Or I will fill the house with armed men,
And over the chair of state, where now he sits,
Write up his title with usurping blood.

[*He stamps with his foot, and the Soldiers show themselves.*

K. Hen. My Lord of Warwick, hear me but one word: 170
Let me for this my life-time reign as king.

York. Confirm the crown to me and to mine heirs,
And thou shalt reign in quiet while thou livest.

King. I am content: Richard Plantagenet,
Enjoy the kingdom after my decease.

Clif. What wrong is this unto the prince your son!

War. What good is this to England and himself!

West. Base, fearful and despairing Henry!

Clif. How hast thou injured both thyself and us!

West. I cannot stay to hear these articles.

North. Nor I.   181

Clif. Come, cousin, let us tell the queen these news.

West. Farewell, faint-hearted and degenerate king,
In whose cold blood no spark of honour bides.

North. Be thou a prey unto the house of York,
And die in bands for this unmanly deed!

Clif. In dreadful war mayst thou be overcome,
Or live in peace abandon'd and despised!

[*Exeunt North., Cliff., and West.*

War. Turn this way, Henry, and regard them not.

Exe. They seek revenge and therefore will not yield.   190

K. Hen. Ah, Exeter!

War.   Why should you sigh, my lord?

K. Hen. Not for myself, Lord Warwick, but my son,

155 *southern power.* Northumberland, a Percy, came from the north.

Westminster Hall: treaty between Henry VI and Richard, Duke of York. Engraving from *Old England*, 1854

186 *bands.* In bondage.

233 *such head.* Such power.

239 *narrow seas.* Straits of Dover.

Peggy Ashcroft as Queen Margaret, Royal Shakespeare Co, 1964

Vhom I unnaturally shall disinherit.
But be it as it may: I here entail
The crown to thee and to thine heirs for ever;
Conditionally, that here thou take an oath
To cease this civil war, and, whilst I live,
To honour me as thy king and sovereign,
And neither by treason nor hostility
To seek to put me down and reign thyself.　200
　　York.　This oath I willingly take and will
　　perform.
　　War.　Long live King Henry! Plantagenet,
　　embrace him.
　　K. Hen.　And long live thou and these thy
　　forward sons!
　　York.　Now York and Lancaster are reconciled.
　　Exe.　Accursed be he that seeks to make them
　　foes!　　[*Sennet. Here they come down.*
　　York.　Farewell, my gracious lord; I'll to my
　　castle.
　　War.　And I'll keep London with my soldiers.
　　Norf.　And I to Norfolk with my followers.
　　Mont.　And I unto the sea from whence I came.
　　[*Exeunt York and his Sons, Warwick, Norfolk, Montague, their Soldiers, and Attendants.*
　　K. Hen.　And I, with grief and sorrow, to the
　　court.　　210

Enter QUEEN MARGARET *and the* PRINCE OF
WALES.

　　Exe.　Here comes the queen, whose looks
　　bewray her anger:
I'll steal away.
　　K. Hen.　　Exeter, so will I.
　　Q. Mar.　Nay, go not from me; I will follow
　　thee.
　　K. Hen.　Be patient, gentle queen, and I will
　　stay.
　　Q. Mar.　Who can be patient in such extremes?
Ah, wretched man! would I had died a maid,
And never seen thee, never borne thee son,
Seeing thou hast proved so unnatural a father!
Hath he deserved to lose his birthright thus?
Hadst thou but loved him half so well as I,　220
Or felt that pain which I did for him once,
Or nourish'd him as I did with my blood,
Thou wouldst have left thy dearest heart-blood
　　there,
Rather than have made that savage duke thine
　　heir
And disinherited thine only son.
　　Prince.　Father, you cannot disinherit me:
If you be king, why should not I succeed?
　　K. Hen.　Pardon me, Margaret; pardon me,
　　sweet son:
The Earl of Warwick and the duke enforced me.
　　Q. Mar.　Enforced thee! art thou king, and
　　wilt be forced?　230
I shame to hear thee speak. Ah, timorous wretch!
Thou hast undone thyself, thy son and me;
● And given unto the house of York such head
As thou shalt reign but by their sufferance.
To entail him and his heirs unto the crown,
What is it, but to make thy sepulchre
And creep into it far before thy time?
Warwick is chancellor and the lord of Calais;
● Stern Falconbridge commands the narrow seas;
The duke is made protector of the realm;　240

And yet shalt thou be safe? such safety finds
The trembling lamb environed with wolves.
● Had I been there, which am a silly woman,
The soldiers should have toss'd me on their pikes
Before I would have granted to that act.
But thou preferr'st thy life before thine honour:
And seeing thou dost, I here divorce myself
Both from thy table, Henry, and thy bed,
Until that act of parliament be repeal'd
Whereby my son is disinherited.   250
The northern lords that have forsworn thy colours
Will follow mine, if once they see them spread;
And spread they shall be, to thy foul disgrace
And utter ruin of the house of York.
Thus do I leave thee.   Come, son, let's away;
Our army is ready; come, we'll after them.
   K. Hen.   Stay, gentle Margaret, and hear me
    speak.
   Q. Mar.   Thou hast spoke too much already:
    get thee gone.
   K. Hen.   Gentle son Edward, thou wilt stay
    with me?
   Q. Mar.   Ay, to be murder'd by his enemies.
   Prince.   When I return with victory from the
    field   261
I'll see your grace: till then I'll follow her.
   Q. Mar. Come, son, away; we may not linger
    thus.
    [*Exeunt Queen Margaret and the Prince.*
   K. Hen.   Poor queen! how love to me and to
    her son
Hath made her break out into terms of rage!
Revenged may she be on that hateful duke,
Whose haughty spirit, winged with desire,
● Will cost my crown, and like an empty eagle
● Tire on the flesh of me and of my son!
The loss of those three lords torments my heart:
I'll write unto them and entreat them fair.   271
Come, cousin, you shall be the messenger.
   Exe.   And I, I hope, shall reconcile them all.
                  [*Exeunt.*

SCENE II. *Sandal Castle.*

Enter RICHARD, EDWARD, *and* MONTAGUE.

   Rich.   Brother, though I be youngest, give
    me leave.
   Edw.   No, I can better play the orator.
   Mont.   But I have reasons strong and forcible.

   Enter the DUKE OF YORK.

   York.   Why, how now, sons and brother! at
    a strife?
What is your quarrel? how began it first?
   Edw.   No quarrel, but a slight contention.
   York.   About what?
   Rich.   About that which concerns your grace
    and us;
The crown of England, father, which is yours.   9
   York.   Mine, boy? not till King Henry be dead.
   Rich.   Your right depends not on his life or
    death.
   Edw.   Now you are heir, therefore enjoy it now:
By giving the house of Lancaster leave to breathe,
It will outrun you, father, in the end.
   York.   I took an oath that he should quietly
    reign.
   Edw.   But for a kingdom any oath may be
    broken:

243 *silly.* Helpless, feeble.

268 *cost.* Accost, attack.

269 *Tire.* Devour.

Sandal Castle near Wakefield, Yorkshire. Engraving
from *Old England*, 1854

26 *depose.* Testify.

43 *Witty.* Intelligent.

52 *hold.* Stronghold.

I would break a thousand oaths to reign one year.
 Rich. No; God forbid your grace should be
  forsworn.
 York. I shall be, if I claim by open war.
 Rich. I'll prove the contrary, if you'll hear
  me speak.   20
 York. Thou canst not, son; it is impossible.
 Rich. An oath is of no moment, being not took
Before a true and lawful magistrate,
That hath authority over him that swears:
Henry had none, but did usurp the place;
●Then, seeing 'twas he that made you to depose,
Your oath, my lord, is vain and frivolous.
Therefore, to arms! And, father, do but think
How sweet a thing it is to wear a crown;
Within whose circuit is Elysium   30
And all that poets feign of bliss and joy.
Why do we linger thus? I cannot rest
Until the white rose that I wear be dyed
Even in the lukewarm blood of Henry's heart.
 York. Richard, enough; I will be king, or die.
Brother, thou shalt to London presently,
And whet on Warwick to this enterprise.
Thou, Richard, shalt to the Duke of Norfolk,
And tell him privily of our intent.
You, Edward, shall unto my Lord Cobham, 40
With whom the Kentishmen will willingly rise:
In them I trust; for they are soldiers,
● Witty, courteous, liberal, full of spirit.
While you are thus employ'd, what resteth more,
But that I seek occasion how to rise,
And yet the king not privy to my drift,
Nor any of the house of Lancaster?

    Enter a Messenger.

But, stay: what news? Why comest thou in such
  post?
 Mess. The queen with all the northern earls
  and lords
Intend here to besiege you in your castle: 50
She is hard by with twenty thousand men;
● And therefore fortify your hold, my lord.
 York. Ay, with my sword. What! think'st
  thou that we fear them?
Edward and Richard, you shall stay with me;
My brother Montague shall post to London:
Let noble Warwick, Cobham, and the rest,
Whom we have left protectors of the king,
With powerful policy strengthen themselves,
And trust not simple Henry nor his oaths.
 Mont. Brother, I go; I'll win them, fear it
  not: 60
And thus most humbly I do take my leave. [*Exit.*

 Enter Sir John Mortimer *and* Sir Hugh
    Mortimer.

 York. Sir John and Sir Hugh Mortimer,
  mine uncles,
You are come to Sandal in a happy hour;
The army of the queen mean to besiege us.
 Sir John. She shall not need; we'll meet her
  in the field.
 York. What, with five thousand men?
 Rich. Ay, with five hundred, father, for a need:
A woman's general; what should we fear?
         [*A march afar off.*
 Edw. I hear their drums: let's set our men
  in order,   70
And issue forth and bid them battle straight.

York. Five men to twenty! though the odds be great,
I doubt not, uncle, of our victory.
Many a battle have I won in France,
When as the enemy hath been ten to one:
Why should I not now have the like success?
                    [*Alarum. Exeunt.*

SCENE III. *Field of battle betwixt Sandal
        Castle and Wakefield.*

Alarums. Enter RUTLAND *and his* Tutor.

Rut. Ah, whither shall I fly to 'scape their hands?
Ah, tutor, look where bloody Clifford comes!

Enter CLIFFORD *and* Soldiers.

Clif. Chaplain, away! thy priesthood saves thy life.
As for the brat of this accursed duke,
● Whose father slew my father, he shall die.
  Tut. And I, my lord, will bear him company.
  Clif. Soldiers, away with him!
  Tut. Ah, Clifford, murder not this innocent child,
Lest thou be hated both of God and man!
            [*Exit, dragged off by Soldiers.*
  Clif. How now! is he dead already? or is it fear   10
That makes him close his eyes? I'll open them.
  Rut. So looks the pent-up lion o'er the wretch
That trembles under his devouring paws;
And so he walks, insulting o'er his prey,
And so he comes, to rend his limbs asunder.
● Ah, gentle Clifford, kill me with thy sword,
And not with such a cruel threatening look.
Sweet Clifford, hear me speak before I die.
I am too mean a subject for thy wrath:
Be thou revenged on men, and let me live.   20
  Clif. In vain thou speak'st, poor boy; my father's blood
Hath stopp'd the passage where thy words should enter.
  Rut. Then let my father's blood open it again:
He is a man, and, Clifford, cope with him.
  Clif. Had I thy brethren here, their lives and thine
Were not revenge sufficient for me;
No, if I digg'd up thy forefathers' graves
And hung their rotten coffins up in chains,
It could not slake mine ire, nor ease my heart.
The sight of any of the house of York   30
Is as a fury to torment my soul;
And till I root out their accursed line
And leave not one alive, I live in hell.
Therefore—   [*Lifting his hand.*
  Rut. O, let me pray before I take my death!
To thee I pray; sweet Clifford, pity me!
  Clif. Such pity as my rapier's point affords.
  Rut. I never did thee harm: why wilt thou slay me?
  Clif. Thy father hath.
  Rut.   But 'twas ere I was born.
Thou hast one son; for his sake pity me,   40
Lest in revenge thereof, sith God is just,
He be as miserably slain as I.
Ah, let me live in prison all my days;
And when I give occasion of offence,
Then let me die, for now thou hast no cause.

Clifford: 'Chaplain, away! thy priesthood saves thy life'. Murder of Rutland. Engraving from a painting by James Northcote (1746–1831)

5 *Whose father slew my father.* See 2 *Henry VI*, v, ii.

14 *insulting . . . prey.* Triumphing over his enemy.

48 *Di . . . tuæ.* The gods grant that this be the height of your glory.

7 *demean'd.* Behaved.

12 *falchion.* Curved broad sword.

19 *bodged.* Botched.

Battle scene at Wakefield. Woodcut from Holinshed's *Chronicles,* 1577

33 *Phaëthon.* Son of Apollo, the sun god, who tried to drive his father's chariot but was thrown out and killed. The sun was a Yorkist emblem.

34 *noontide prick.* Midday mark on the face of the sundial.

35 *phœnix.* Mythical Arabian bird that resurrected itself from its own funeral pyre.

36 *bird.* i.e. his son Edward who later became Edward IV.

Clif. No cause!
Thy father slew my father; therefore, die.
[*Stabs him.*

Rut. Di faciant laudis summa sit ista tuæ!
[*Dies.*

Clif. Plantagenet! I come, Plantagenet!
And this thy son's blood cleaving to my blade 50
Shall rust upon my weapon, till thy blood,
Congeal'd with this, do make me wipe off both.
[*Exit.*

SCENE IV. *Another part of the field.*

Alarum. Enter RICHARD, Duke of York.

York. The army of the queen hath got the field:
My uncles both are slain in rescuing me;
And all my followers to the eager foe
Turn back and fly, like ships before the wind
Or lambs pursued by hunger-starved wolves.
My sons, God knows what hath bechanced them:
But this I know, they have demean'd themselves
Like men born to renown by life or death.
Three times did Richard make a lane to me,
And thrice cried 'Courage, father! fight it out!'
And full as oft came Edward to my side,   11
With purple falchion, painted to the hilt
In blood of those that had encounter'd him:
And when the hardiest warriors did retire,
Richard cried 'Charge! and give no foot of
    ground!'
And cried 'A crown, or else a glorious tomb!
A sceptre, or an earthly sepulchre!'
With this, we charged again: but, out, alas!
We bodged again; as I have seen a swan
With bootless labour swim against the tide   20
And spend her strength with over-matching
    waves.   [*A short alarum within.*
Ah, hark! the fatal followers do pursue;
And I am faint and cannot fly their fury:
And were I strong, I would not shun their fury:
The sands are number'd that make up my life;
Here must I stay, and here my life must end.

Enter QUEEN MARGARET, CLIFFORD, NORTH-
UMBERLAND, *the* young Prince, *and* Soldiers.

Come, bloody Clifford, rough Northumberland,
I dare your quenchless fury to more rage:
I am your butt, and I abide your shot.   29
North. Yield to our mercy, proud Plantagenet.
Clif. Ay, to such mercy as his ruthless arm,
With downright payment, show'd unto my father.
Now Phaëthon hath tumbled from his car,
And made an evening at the noontide prick.
York. My ashes, as the phœnix, may bring
    forth
A bird that will revenge upon you all:
And in that hope I throw mine eyes to heaven,
Scorning whate'er you can afflict me with.
Why come you not? what! multitudes, and fear?
Clif. So cowards fight when they can fly no
    further;   40
So doves do peck the falcon's piercing talons;
So desperate thieves, all hopeless of their lives,
Breathe out invectives 'gainst the officers.
York. O Clifford, but bethink thee once again,
And in thy thought o'er-run my former time;
And, if thou canst for blushing, view this face,

And bite thy tongue, that slanders him with
    cowardice
Whose frown hath made thee faint and fly ere
    this!
    Clif. I will not bandy with thee word for word,
But buckle with thee blows, twice two for one. 50
    Q. Mar. Hold, valiant Clifford! for a thous-
    and causes
I would prolong awhile the traitor's life.
Wrath makes him deaf: speak thou, Northum-
    berland.
    North. Hold, Clifford! do not honour him so
    much
To prick thy finger, though to wound his heart:
What valour were it, when a cur doth grin,
For one to thrust his hand between his teeth,
When he might spurn him with his foot away?
It is war's prize to take all vantages;
- And ten to one is no impeach of valour.   60
    [*They lay hands on York, who struggles.*
    Clif. Ay, ay, so strives the woodcock with
    the gin.
-    *North.* So doth the cony struggle in the net.
    York. So triumph thieves upon their con-
    quer'd booty;
So true men yield, with robbers so o'ermatch'd.
    North. What would your grace have done
    unto him now?
    Q. Mar. Brave warriors, Clifford and North-
    umberland,
Come, make him stand upon this molehill here,
- That raught at mountains with outstretched arms,
Yet parted but the shadow with his hand.
What! was it you that would be England's king?
Was't you that revell'd in our parliament,   71
And made a preachment of your high descent?
- Where are your mess of sons to back you now?
The wanton Edward, and the lusty George?
- And where's that valiant crook-back prodigy,
Dicky your boy, that with his grumbling voice
Was wont to cheer his dad in mutinies?
Or, with the rest, where is your darling Rutland?
Look, York: I stain'd this napkin with the blood
That valiant Clifford, with his rapier's point,   80
Made issue from the bosom of the boy;
And if thine eyes can water for his death,
I give thee this to dry thy cheeks withal.
Alas, poor York! but that I hate thee deadly,
I should lament thy miserable state.
I prithee, grieve, to make me merry, York.
What, hath thy fiery heart so parch'd thine
    entrails
That not a tear can fall for Rutland's death?
Why art thou patient, man? thou shouldst be
    mad;
And I, to make thee mad, do mock thee thus. 90
Stamp, rave, and fret, that I may sing and dance.
Thou wouldst be fee'd, I see, to make me sport:
York cannot speak, unless he wear a crown.
A crown for York! and, lords, bow low to him:
Hold you his hands, whilst I do set it on.
         [*Putting a paper crown on his head.*
Ay, marry, sir, now looks he like a king!
Ay, this is he that took King Henry's chair,
And this is he was his adopted heir.
But how is it that great Plantagenet
Is crown'd so soon, and broke his solemn oath?
As I bethink me, you should not be king   101
Till our King Henry had shook hands with death.

60 *impeach*. Disparagement.

62 *cony*. Rabbit.

68 *raught*. Reached.

73 *mess*. A group of four.

75 *prodigy*. i.e. monster.

Queen Margaret (Rosalind Boxall) puts a paper crown on the head of York (John Arnatt), Old Vic Theatre, London, 1953

103 *pale*. Enclose.

110 *orisons*. Prayers.

116 *visard-like*. Mask-like.

118 *assay*. Attempt.

121 *type*. Title.

125 *boots*. Avails.

126 *adage*. Maxim.

136 *septentrion*. North.

150 *Beshrew*. Curse it.

155 *Hyrcania*. Caspian Sea area, in tradition the home of the tiger.

Costume design for York by Ann Curtis, Royal Shakespeare Co, 1964

● And will you pale your head in Henry's glory,
And rob his temples of the diadem,
Now in his life, against your holy oath?
O, 'tis a fault too too unpardonable!
Off with the crown; and, with the crown, his head;
And, whilst we breathe, take time to do him dead.
   Clif. That is my office, for my father's sake.
●   *Q. Mar.* Nay, stay; let's hear the orisons he makes.   110
   York. She-wolf of France, but worse than wolves of France,
Whose tongue more poisons than the adder's tooth!
How ill-beseeming is it in thy sex
To triumph, like an Amazonian trull,
Upon their woes whom fortune captivates!
● But that thy face is, visard-like, unchanging,
Made impudent with use of evil deeds,
● I would assay, proud queen, to make thee blush.
To tell thee whence thou camest, of whom derived,
Were shame enough to shame thee, wert thou not shameless.   120
● Thy father bears the type of King of Naples,
Of both the Sicils and Jerusalem,
Yet not so wealthy as an English yeoman.
Hath that poor monarch taught thee to insult?
● It needs not, nor it boots thee not, proud queen,
● Unless the adage must be verified,
That beggars mounted run their horse to death.
'Tis beauty that doth oft make women proud;
But, God he knows, thy share thereof is small:
'Tis virtue that doth make them most admired;
The contrary doth make thee wonder'd at: 131
'Tis government that makes them seem divine;
The want thereof makes thee abominable:
Thou art as opposite to every good
As the Antipodes are unto us,
● Or as the south to the septentrion.
O tiger's heart wrapt in a woman's hide!
How couldst thou drain the life-blood of the child,
To bid the father wipe his eyes withal,
And yet be seen to bear a woman's face?   140
Women are soft, mild, pitiful and flexible;
Thou stern, obdurate, flinty, rough, remorseless.
Bid'st thou me rage? why, now thou hast thy wish:
Wouldst have me weep? why, now thou hast thy will:
For raging wind blows up incessant showers,
And when the rage allays, the rain begins.
These tears are my sweet Rutland's obsequies:
And every drop cries vengeance for his death,
'Gainst thee, fell Clifford, and thee, false French-woman.
●   *North.* Beshrew me, but his passion moves me so   150
That hardly can I check my eyes from tears.
   York. That face of his the hungry cannibals
Would not have touch'd, would not have stain'd with blood:
But you are more inhuman, more inexorable,
● O, ten times more, than tigers of Hyrcania.
See, ruthless queen, a hapless father's tears:
This cloth thou dip'dst in blood of my sweet boy,
And I with tears do wash the blood away.
Keep thou the napkin, and go boast of this:
And if thou tell'st the heavy story right,   160
Upon my soul, the hearers will shed tears;

Yea even my foes will shed fast-falling tears,
And say 'Alas, it was a piteous deed!'
There, take the crown, and, with the crown, my
    curse;
And in thy need such comfort come to thee
As now I reap at thy too cruel hand!
Hard-hearted Clifford, take me from the world:
My soul to heaven, my blood upon your heads!
    North. Had he been slaughter-man to all my
    kin,
I should not for my life but weep with him,   170
To see how inly sorrow gripes his soul.
  • *Q. Mar.* What, weeping-ripe, my Lord North-
    umberland?
Think but upon the wrong he did us all,
And that will quickly dry thy melting tears.
    Clif. Here's for my oath, here's for my father's
    death.   [*Stabbing him.*
    Q. Mar. And here's to right our gentle-hearted
    king.   [*Stabbing him.*
    York. Open Thy gate of mercy, gracious God!
My soul flies through these wounds to seek out
    Thee.   [*Dies.*
    Q. Mar. Off with his head, and set it on York
    gates;
So York may overlook the town of York.   180
                  [*Flourish. Exeunt.*

ACT II.

SCENE I. *A plain near Mortimer's Cross in Herefordshire.*

A march. Enter EDWARD, RICHARD, *and their power.*

    Edw. I wonder how our princely father 'scaped,
Or whether he be 'scaped away or no
From Clifford's and Northumberland's pursuit:
Had he been ta'en, we should have heard the news;
Had he been slain, we should have heard the news;
Or had he 'scaped, methinks we should have heard
The happy tidings of his good escape.
How fares my brother? why is he so sad?
    Rich. I cannot joy, until I be resolved
Where our right valiant father is become.   10
I saw him in the battle range about;
And watch'd him how he singled Clifford forth.
Methought he bore him in the thickest troop
  • As doth a lion in a herd of neat;
Or as a bear, encompass'd round with dogs,
Who having pinch'd a few and made them cry,
The rest stand all aloof, and bark at him.
So fared our father with his enemies;
So fled his enemies my warlike father:
Methinks, 'tis prize enough to be his son.   20
See how the morning opes her golden gates,
And takes her farewell of the glorious sun!
How well resembles it the prime of youth,
  • Trimm'd like a younker prancing to his love!
    Edw. Dazzle mine eyes, or do I see three
    suns?
    Rich. Three glorious suns, each one a perfect
    sun;
Not separated with the racking clouds,
But sever'd in a pale clear-shining sky.
See, see! they join, embrace, and seem to kiss,
As if they vow'd some league inviolable: 30
Now are they but one lamp, one light, one sun.
In this the heaven figures some event.

172 *weeping-ripe.* On the verge of tears.

14 *neat.* Cattle.

24 *younker.* Young man.

36 *meeds*. Deserved rewards.

42 *breeder*. Female sex. Edward was a notorious womaniser.

51 *hope of Troy*. Hector.

74 *soul's palace*. Body.

Edw. 'Tis wondrous strange, the like yet
  never heard of.
I think it cites us, brother, to the field,
That we, the sons of brave Plantagenet,
● Each one already blazing by our meeds,
Should notwithstanding join our lights together
And over-shine the earth as this the world.
Whate'er it bodes, henceforward will I bear
Upon my target three fair-shining suns.   40
  Rich. Nay, bear three daughters: by your
    leave I speak it,
● You love the breeder better than the male.

Enter a Messenger.

But what art thou, whose heavy looks foretell
Some dreadful story hanging on thy tongue?
  Mess. Ah, one that was a woful looker-on
When as the noble Duke of York was slain,
Your princely father and my loving lord!
  Edw. O, speak no more, for I have heard too
    much.
  Rich. Say how he died, for I will hear it all.
  Mess. Environed he was with many foes,   50
● And stood against them, as the hope of Troy
Against the Greeks that would have enter'd Troy.
But Hercules himself must yield to odds;
And many strokes, though with a little axe,
Hew down and fell the hardest-timber'd oak.
By many hands your father was subdued;
But only slaughter'd by the ireful arm
Of unrelenting Clifford and the queen,
Who crown'd the gracious duke in high despite,
Laugh'd in his face; and when with grief he wept,
The ruthless queen gave him to dry his cheeks 61
A napkin steeped in the harmless blood
Of sweet young Rutland, by rough Clifford slain:
And after many scorns, many foul taunts,
They took his head, and on the gates of York
They set the same; and there it doth remain,
The saddest spectacle that e'er I view'd.
  Edw. Sweet Duke of York, our prop to lean
    upon,
Now thou art gone, we have no staff, no stay.
O Clifford, boisterous Clifford! thou hast slain 70
The flower of Europe for his chivalry;
And treacherously hast thou vanquish'd him,
For hand to hand he would have vanquish'd thee.
● Now my soul's palace is become a prison:
Ah, would she break from hence, that this my body
Might in the ground be closed up in rest!
For never henceforth shall I joy again,
Never, O never, shall I see more joy!
  Rich. I cannot weep; for all my body's mois-
    ture
Scarce serves to quench my furnace-burning heart:
Nor can my tongue unload my heart's great
    burthen;   81
For selfsame wind that I should speak withal
Is kindling coals that fires all my breast,
And burns me up with flames that tears would
    quench.
To weep is to make less the depth of grief:
Tears then for babes; blows and revenge for me
Richard, I bear thy name; I'll venge thy death,
Or die renowned by attempting it.
  Edw. His name that valiant duke hath left
    with thee;
His dukedom and his chair with me is left.   90
  Rich. Nay, if thou be that princely eagle's bird,

Show thy descent by gazing 'gainst the sun:
For chair and dukedom, throne and kingdom say;
Either that is thine, or else thou wert not his.

March. Enter WARWICK, MARQUESS OF
MONTAGUE, *and their army.*

War. How now, fair lords! What fare? what
    news abroad?
Rich. Great Lord of Warwick, if we should
    recount
Our baleful news, and at each word's deliverance
● Stab poniards in our flesh till all were told,
The words would add more anguish than the
    wounds.
O valiant lord, the Duke of York is slain!   100
Edw. O Warwick, Warwick! that Plantagenet,
Which held thee dearly as his soul's redemption,
Is by the stern Lord Clifford done to death.
    War. Ten days ago I drown'd these news in
    tears;
And now, to add more measure to your woes,
I come to tell you things sith then befall'n.
After the bloody fray at Wakefield fought,
Where your brave father breathed his latest gasp,
Tidings, as swiftly as the posts could run,
Were brought me of your loss and his depart. 110
I, then in London, keeper of the king,
Muster'd my soldiers, gather'd flocks of friends,
And very well appointed, as I thought,
March'd toward Saint Alban's to intercept the
    queen,
Bearing the king in my behalf along;
For by my scouts I was advertised
That she was coming with a full intent
To dash our late decree in parliament
Touching King Henry's oath and your succession.
Short tale to make, we at Saint Alban's met, 120
Our battles join'd, and both sides fiercely fought:
But whether 'twas the coldness of the king,
Who look'd full gently on his warlike queen,
● That robb'd my soldiers of their heated spleen;
Or whether 'twas report of her success;
Or more than common fear of Clifford's rigour,
Who thunders to his captives blood and death,
I cannot judge: but, to conclude with truth,
Their weapons like to lightning came and went;
Our soldiers', like the night-owl's lazy flight, 130
Or like an idle thresher with a flail,
Fell gently down, as if they struck their friends.
I cheer'd them up with justice of our cause,
With promise of high pay and great rewards:
But all in vain; they had no heart to fight,
And we in them no hope to win the day;
So that we fled; the king unto the queen;
Lord George your brother, Norfolk and myself,
In haste, post-haste, are come to join with you:
● For in the marches here we heard you were, 140
● Making another head to fight again.
    Edw. Where is the Duke of Norfolk, gentle
    Warwick?
And when came George from Burgundy to Eng-
    land?
    War. Some six miles off the duke is with the
    soldiers;
And for your brother, he was lately sent
● From your kind aunt, Duchess of Burgundy,
With aid of soldiers to this needful war.
    Rich. 'Twas odds, belike, when valiant War-
    wick fled:

98 *poniards.* Daggers.

124 *heated spleen.* Fierce valour.

140 *marches.* On the borders (here Wales).

141 *Making . . . head.* Assembling a force.

146 *Duchess of Burgundy.* Isabel, Duchess of Burgundy, grandaughter of John of Gaunt and third cousin, not aunt, of Edward.

KING HENRY VI Part III Act II Scene I

162 *Ave-Maries . . . beads.* Saying Hail Marys on our rosaries.

163–164 *helmets . . . arms.* i.e. count our Hail Marys with their helmets as beads.

170 *moe.* More.

182 *Via.* Away. *amain.* With all speed.

John Palmer, 18th century English actor, as Warwick. Engraving from Bell's edition of *Shakespeare, 1776*

Oft have I heard his praises in pursuit,
But ne'er till now his scandal of retire.   150
    War. Nor now my scandal, Richard, dost thou hear;
For thou shalt know this strong right hand of mine
Can pluck the diadem from faint Henry's head,
And wring the awful sceptre from his fist,
Were he as famous and as bold in war
As he is famed for mildness, peace, and prayer.
    Rich. I know it well, Lord Warwick; blame me not:
'Tis love I bear thy glories makes me speak.
But in this troublous time what's to be done?
Shall we go throw away our coats of steel,   160
And wrap our bodies in black mourning gowns,
Numbering our Ave-Maries with our beads?
Or shall we on the helmets of our foes
Tell our devotion with revengeful arms?
If for the last, say ay, and to it, lords.
    War. Why, therefore Warwick came to seek you out;
And therefore comes my brother Montague.
Attend me, lords. The proud insulting queen,
With Clifford and the haught Northumberland,
And of their feather many moe proud birds,   170
Have wrought the easy-melting king like wax.
He swore consent to your succession,
His oath enrolled in the parliament;
And now to London all the crew are gone,
To frustrate both his oath and what beside
May make against the house of Lancaster.
Their power, I think, is thirty thousand strong:
Now, if the help of Norfolk and myself,
With all the friends that thou, brave Earl of March,
Amongst the loving Welshmen canst procure, 180
Will but amount to five and twenty thousand,
Why, Via! to London will we march amain,
And once again bestride our foaming steeds,
And once again cry 'Charge upon our foes!'
But never once again turn back and fly.
    Rich. Ay, now methinks I hear great Warwick speak:
Ne'er may he live to see a sunshine day,
That cries 'Retire,' if Warwick bid him stay.
    Edw. Lord Warwick, on thy shoulder will I lean;   189
And when thou fail'st—as God forbid the hour!—
Must Edward fall, which peril heaven forfend!
    War. No longer Earl of March, but Duke of York:
The next degree is England's royal throne;
For King of England shalt thou be proclaim'd
In every borough as we pass along;
And he that throws not up his cap for joy
Shall for the fault make forfeit of his head.
King Edward, valiant Richard, Montague,
Stay we no longer, dreaming of renown,
But sound the trumpets, and about our task. 200
    Rich. Then, Clifford, were thy heart as hard as steel,
As thou hast shown it flinty by thy deeds,
I come to pierce it, or to give thee mine.
    Edw. Then strike up drums: God and Saint George for us!

Enter a Messenger.

War. How now! what news?

162

Act II Scene II KING HENRY VI Part III

Mess. The Duke of Norfolk sends you word
by me,
The queen is coming with a puissant host;
And craves your company for speedy counsel.
   War. Why then it sorts, brave warriors, let's
away.   [*Exeunt.*

SCENE II. *Before York.*

Flourish. Enter KING HENRY, QUEEN MAR-
GARET, *the* PRINCE OF WALES, CLIFFORD,
and NORTHUMBERLAND, *with drum and
trumpets.*

   Q. Mar. Welcome, my lord, to this brave
town of York.
Yonder's the head of that arch-enemy
That sought to be encompass'd with your crown:
Doth not the object cheer your heart, my lord?
   K. Hen. Ay, as the rocks cheer them that fear
their wreck:
To see this sight, it irks my very soul.
Withhold revenge, dear God! 'tis not my fault,
Nor wittingly have I infringed my vow.
   Clif. My gracious liege, this too much lenity
And harmful pity must be laid aside.   10
To whom do lions cast their gentle looks?
Not to the beast that would usurp their den.
Whose hand is that the forest bear doth lick?
Not his that spoils her young before her face.
Who 'scapes the lurking serpent's mortal sting?
Not he that sets his foot upon her back.
The smallest worm will turn being trodden on,
And doves will peck in safeguard of their brood.
- Ambitious York did level at thy crown,
Thou smiling while he knit his angry brows: 20
He, but a duke, would have his son a king,
And raise his issue, like a loving sire;
Thou, being a king, blest with a goodly son,
Didst yield consent to disinherit him,
Which argued thee a most unloving father.
Unreasonable creatures feed their young;
And though man's face be fearful to their eyes,
Yet, in protection of their tender ones,
Who hath not seen them, even with those wings
Which sometime they have used with fearful
flight,   30
Make war with him that climb'd unto their nest,
Offering their own lives in their young's defence?
For shame, my liege, make them your prece-
dent!
Were it not pity that this goodly boy
Should lose his birthright by his father's fault,
And long hereafter say unto his child,
'What my great-grandfather and grandsire got
- My careless father fondly gave away'?
Ah, what a shame were this! Look on the boy:
And let his manly face, which promiseth   40
Successful fortune, steel thy melting heart
To hold thine own and leave thine own with him.
   K. Hen. Full well hath Clifford play'd the
orator,
Inferring arguments of mighty force.
But, Clifford, tell me, didst thou never hear
- That things ill-got had ever bad success?
And happy always was it for that son
Whose father for his hoarding went to hell?
I'll leave my son my virtuous deeds behind;
And would my father had left me no more!   50
For all the rest is held at such a rate

Queen Margaret: 'Yonder's the head of that arch-
enemy . . .' Woodcut from Holinshed's *Chronicles*, 1577

19 *level at.* Aspire to.

38 *fondly.* Foolishly.

46 *success.* Result.

64 *apparent.* i.e. heir apparent.

66 *toward.* Promising.

72 *Darraign.* Set in order.

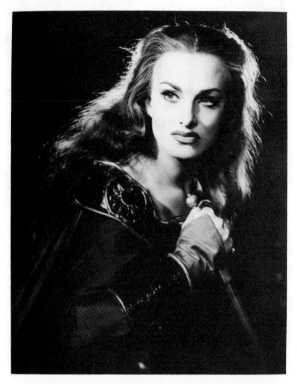

Queen Margaret: 'Go, rate thy minions, proud insulting boy!' Barbara Jefford as Queen Margaret, Old Vic Theatre, London, 1957

As brings a thousand-fold more care to keep
Than in possession any jot of pleasure.
Ah, cousin York! would thy best friends did know
How it doth grieve me that thy head is here!
   Q. Mar. My lord, cheer up your spirits: our foes are nigh,
And this soft courage makes your followers faint.
You promised knighthood to our forward son:
Unsheathe your sword, and dub him presently.
Edward, kneel down.   60
   K. Hen. Edward Plantagenet, arise a knight;
And learn this lesson, draw thy sword in right.
   Prince. My gracious father, by your kingly leave,
• I'll draw it as apparent to the crown,
And in that quarrel use it to the death.
•   *Clif.* Why, that is spoken like a toward prince.

Enter a Messenger.

   Mess. Royal commanders, be in readiness:
For with a band of thirty thousand men
Comes Warwick, backing of the Duke of York;
And in the towns, as they do march along,   70
Proclaims him king, and many fly to him:
• Darraign your battle, for they are at hand.
   Clif. I would your highness would depart the field:
The queen hath best success when you are absent.
   Q. Mar. Ay, good my lord, and leave us to our fortune.
   K. Hen. Why, that's my fortune too; therefore I'll stay.
   North. Be it with resolution then to fight.
   Prince. My royal father, cheer these noble lords
And hearten those that fight in your defence:
Unsheathe your sword, good father; cry 'Saint George!'   80

March. Enter EDWARD, GEORGE, RICHARD, WARWICK, NORFOLK, MONTAGUE, *and* Soldiers.

   Edw. Now, perjured Henry! wilt thou kneel for grace,
And set thy diadem upon my head;
Or bide the mortal fortune of the field?
   Q. Mar. Go, rate thy minions, proud insulting boy!
Becomes it thee to be thus bold in terms
Before thy sovereign and thy lawful king?
   Edw. I am his king, and he should bow his knee;
I was adopted heir by his consent:
Since when, his oath is broke; for, as I hear,
You, that are king, though he do wear the crown,
Have caused him, by new act of parliament,   91
To blot out me, and put his own son in.
   Clif. And reason too:
Who should succeed the father but the son?
   Rich. Are you there, butcher? O, I cannot speak!
   Clif. Ay, crook-back, here I stand to answer thee,
Or any he the proudest of thy sort.
   Rich. 'Twas you that kill'd young Rutland, was it not?

Clif. Ay, and old York, and yet not satisfied.
Rich. For God's sake, lords, give signal to
    the fight.   100
War. What say'st thou, Henry, wilt thou
    yield the crown?
Q. Mar. Why, how now, long-tongued War-
    wick! dare you speak?
When you and I met at Saint Alban's last,
Your legs did better service than your hands.
  War. Then 'twas my turn to fly, and now 'tis
    thine.
  Clif. You said so much before, and yet you
    fled.
  War. 'Twas not your valour, Clifford, drove
    me thence.
  North. No, nor your manhood that durst
    make you stay.
  Rich. Northumberland, I hold thee reverently.
Break off the parley; for scarce I can refrain   110
The execution of my big-swoln heart
Upon that Clifford, that cruel child-killer.
  Clif. I slew thy father, call'st thou him a
    child?
  Rich. Ay, like a dastard and a treacherous
    coward,
As thou didst kill our tender brother Rutland;
But ere sunset I'll make thee curse the deed.
  K. Hen. Have done with words, my lords,
    and hear me speak.
  Q. Mar. Defy them then, or else hold close
    thy lips.
  K. Hen. I prithee, give no limits to my
    tongue:
I am a king, and privileged to speak.   120
  Clif. My liege, the wound that bred this
    meeting here
Cannot be cured by words; therefore be still.
  Rich. Then, executioner, unsheathe thy sword:
By him that made us all, I am resolved
That Clifford's manhood lies upon his tongue.
  Edw. Say, Henry, shall I have my right,
    or no?
A thousand men have broke their fasts to-day,
That ne'er shall dine unless thou yield the crown.
  War. If thou deny, their blood upon thy head;
For York in justice puts his armour on.   130
  Prince. If that be right which Warwick says
    is right,
There is no wrong, but every thing is right.
-   *Rich.* Whoever got thee, there thy mother
    stands;
- For, well I wot, thou hast thy mother's tongue.
  Q. Mar. But thou art neither like thy sire
    nor dam;
- But like a foul mis-shapen stigmatic,
Mark'd by the destinies to be avoided,
As venom toads, or lizards' dreadful stings.
  Rich. Iron of Naples hid with English gilt,
Whose father bears the title of a king,—   140
As if a channel should be call'd the sea,—
- Shamest thou not, knowing whence thou art
    extraught,
To let thy tongue detect thy base-born heart?
  Edw. A wisp of straw were worth a thousand
    crowns,
- To make this shameless callet know herself.
- Helen of Greece was fairer far than thou,
Although thy husband may be Menelaus;
And ne'er was Agamemnon's brother wrong'd

133 *Whoever got thee.* Oblique reference to Margaret's affair with Suffolk.

134 *wot.* Know.

136 *stigmatic.* Deformed.

142 *extraught.* Extracted from.

145 *callet.* Trollop, strumpet.

146–148 *Helen . . . Agamemnon's brother.* Helen, wife of Menelaus king of Sparta, was abducted by Paris of Troy. Agamemnon, king of Mycenae, was brother to Menelaus. The latter was regarded as a typical cuckold.

150 *His father.* Henry V.

155 *graced . . . bridal-day.* Made your impecunious father a present of the wedding expenses.

165 *usurping root.* Reference to the usurpation of the throne by Henry IV from Richard II.

Map showing the locations of Towton and Saxton, Yorkshire. From John Speed's *Theatre of the Empire of Great Britaine*, 1611–12

---

1 *Forspent.* Exhausted.

5 *spite of spite.* In spite of everything.

8 *hap.* Fortune.

12 *Bootless.* Useless.

15 *brother's blood.* The 'bastard of Salisbury'.

By that false woman, as this king by thee.

● His father revell'd in the heart of France,   150
And tamed the king, and made the dauphin stoop;
And had he match'd according to his state,
He might have kept that glory to this day;
But when he took a beggar to his bed,
● And graced thy poor sire with his bridal-day,
Even then that sunshine brew'd a shower for him,
That wash'd his father's fortunes forth of France,
And heap'd sedition on his crown at home.
For what hath broach'd this tumult but thy pride?
Hadst thou been meek, our title still had slept;
And we, in pity of the gentle king,   161
Had slipp'd our claim until another age.

    Geo. But when we saw our sunshine made thy spring,
And that thy summer bred us no increase,
● We set the axe to thy usurping root;
And though the edge hath something hit ourselves,
Yet, know thou, since we have begun to strike,
We'll never leave till we have hewn thee down,
Or bathed thy growing with our heated bloods.

    Edw. And, in this resolution, I defy thee; 170
Not willing any longer conference,
Since thou deniest the gentle king to speak.
Sound trumpets! let our bloody colours wave!
And either victory, or else a grave.

    Q. Mar. Stay, Edward.

    Edw. No, wrangling woman, we'll no longer stay:
These words will cost ten thousand lives this day.   [*Exeunt.*

SCENE III. *A field of battle between Towton and Saxton, in Yorkshire.*

Alarum. Excursions. Enter WARWICK.

●   *War.* Forspent with toil, as runners with a race,
I lay me down a little while to breathe;
For strokes received, and many blows repaid,
Have robb'd my strong-knit sinews of their strength,
● And spite of spite needs must I rest awhile.

Enter EDWARD, *running.*

    Edw. Smile, gentle heaven! or strike, ungentle death!
For this world frowns, and Edward's sun is clouded.
●   *War.* How now, my lord! what hap? what hope of good?

Enter GEORGE.

    Geo. Our hap is loss, our hope but sad despair;
Our ranks are broke, and ruin follows us: 10
What counsel give you? whither shall we fly?
●   *Edw.* Bootless is flight, they follow us with wings;
And weak we are and cannot shun pursuit.

Enter RICHARD.

    Rich. Ah, Warwick, why hast thou withdrawn thyself?
● Thy brother's blood the thirsty earth hath drunk,
Broach'd with the steely point of Clifford's lance:

And in the very pangs of death he cried,
Like to a dismal clangor heard from far,
'Warwick, revenge! brother, revenge my death!'
So, underneath the belly of their steeds,   20
That stain'd their fetlocks in his smoking blood,
The noble gentleman gave up the ghost.
    War.   Then let the earth be drunken with
      our blood:
I'll kill my horse, because I will not fly.
Why stand we like soft-hearted women here,
Wailing our losses, whiles the foe doth rage;
And look upon, as if the tragedy
Were play'd in jest by counterfeiting actors?
Here on my knee I vow to God above,
I'll never pause again, never stand still,   30
Till either death hath closed these eyes of mine
Or fortune given me measure of revenge.
    Edw.   O Warwick, I do bend my knee with
      thine;
And in this vow do chain my soul to thine!
And, ere my knee rise from the earth's cold face,
I throw my hands, mine eyes, my heart to thee,
Thou setter up and plucker down of kings,
Beseeching thee, if with thy will it stands
That to my foes this body must be prey,
Yet that thy brazen gates of heaven may ope,   40
And give sweet passage to my sinful soul!
Now, lords, take leave until we meet again,
Where'er it be, in heaven or in earth.
    Rich.   Brother, give me thy hand; and, gentle
      Warwick,
Let me embrace thee in my weary arms:
I, that did never weep, now melt with woe
That winter should cut off our spring-time so.
    War.   Away, away! Once more, sweet lords,
      farewell.
    Geo.   Yet let us all together to our troops,
And give them leave to fly that will not stay;   50
And call them pillars that will stand to us;
And, if we thrive, promise them such rewards
As victors wear at the Olympian games:
This may plant courage in their quailing breasts;
For yet is hope of life and victory.
● Forslow no longer, make we hence amain.
                         [Exeunt.

SCENE IV.   *Another part of the field.*

Excursions.   Enter RICHARD *and* CLIFFORD.

    Rich.   Now, Clifford, I have singled thee
      alone:
Suppose this arm is for the Duke of York,
And this for Rutland; both bound to revenge,
Wert thou environ'd with a brazen wall.
    Clif.   Now, Richard, I am with thee here
      alone:
This is the hand that stabb'd thy father York;
And this the hand that slew thy brother Rutland;
And here's the heart that triumphs in their death
And cheers these hands that slew thy sire and
      brother
To execute the like upon thyself;   10
And so, have at thee!
    [They fight.   Warwick comes; Clifford flies.
    Rich.   Nay, Warwick, single out some other
      chase;
For I myself will hunt this wolf to death.
                         [Exeunt.

56 *Forslow.* Delay.

13 *fell.* Fierce.

24 *dials quaintly.* i.e. cleverly carve sundials in the turf.

36 *ean.* Give birth.

53 *curious.* Elaborate.

Costume design for King Henry VI by Ann Curtis, Royal Shakespeare Co, 1964

SCENE V. *Another part of the field.*
Alarum. Enter KING HENRY *alone.*

King. This battle fares like to the morning's
  war,
When dying clouds contend with growing light,
What time the shepherd, blowing of his nails,
Can neither call it perfect day nor night.
Now sways it this way, like a mighty sea
Forced by the tide to combat with the wind;
Now sways it that way, like the selfsame sea
Forced to retire by fury of the wind:
Sometime the flood prevails, and then the wind;
Now one the better, then another best;   10
Both tugging to be victors, breast to breast,
Yet neither conqueror nor conquered:
• So is the equal poise of this fell war.
Here on this molehill will I sit me down.
To whom God will, there be the victory!
For Margaret my queen, and Clifford too,
Have chid me from the battle; swearing both
They prosper best of all when I am thence.
Would I were dead! if God's good will were so;
For what is in this world but grief and woe?   20
O God! methinks it were a happy life,
To be no better than a homely swain;
To sit upon a hill, as I do now,
• To carve out dials quaintly, point by point,
Thereby to see the minutes how they run,
How many make the hour full complete;
How many hours bring about the day;
How many days will finish up the year;
How many years a mortal man may live.
When this is known, then to divide the times: 30
So many hours must I tend my flock;
So many hours must I take my rest;
So many hours must I contemplate;
So many hours must I sport myself;
So many days my ewes have been with young;
• So many weeks ere the poor fools will ean;
So many years ere I shall shear the fleece:
So minutes, hours, days, months, and years,
Pass'd over to the end they were created,
Would bring white hairs unto a quiet grave.   40
Ah, what a life were this! how sweet! how lovely!
Gives not the hawthorn-bush a sweeter shade
To shepherds looking on their silly sheep,
Than doth a rich embroider'd canopy
To kings that fear their subjects' treachery?
O, yes, it doth; a thousand-fold it doth.
And to conclude, the shepherd's homely curds,
His cold thin drink out of his leather bottle,
His wonted sleep under a fresh tree's shade,
All which secure and sweetly he enjoys,   50
Is far beyond a prince's delicates,
His viands sparkling in a golden cup,
• His body couched in a curious bed,
When care, mistrust, and treason waits on him.

Alarum. Enter a Son *that has killed his father,*
dragging in the dead body.

Son. Ill blows the wind that profits nobody.
This man, whom hand to hand I slew in fight,
May be possessed with some store of crowns;
And I, that haply take them from him now,
May yet ere night yield both my life and them
To some man else, as this dead man doth me.   60
Who's this? O God! it is my father's face,
Whom in this conflict I unwares have kill'd.

O heavy times, begetting such events!
From London by the king was I press'd forth;
My father, being the Earl of Warwick's man,
Came on the part of York, press'd by his master;
And I, who at his hands received my life,
Have by my hands of life bereaved him.
Pardon me, God, I knew not what I did!
And pardon, father, for I knew not thee!   70
My tears shall wipe away these bloody marks;
And no more words till they have flow'd their fill.
    K. Hen. O piteous spectacle! O bloody times!
Whiles lions war and battle for their dens,
Poor harmless lambs abide their enmity.
Weep, wretched man, I'll aid thee tear for tear;
And let our hearts and eyes, like civil war,
Be blind with tears, and break o'ercharged with
    grief.

Enter a Father *that has killed his son, bringing
in the body.*

    Fath. Thou that so stoutly hast resisted me,
Give me thy gold, if thou hast any gold;   80
For I have bought it with an hundred blows.
But let me see: is this our foeman's face?
Ah, no, no, no, it is mine only son!
Ah, boy, if any life be left in thee,
Throw up thine eye! see, see what showers arise,
Blown with the windy tempest of my heart,
Upon thy wounds, that kill mine eye and heart!
O, pity, God, this miserable age!
What stratagems, how fell, how butcherly,
Erroneous, mutinous and unnatural,   90
This deadly quarrel daily doth beget!
O boy, thy father gave thee life too soon,
And hath bereft thee of thy life too late!
    K. Hen. Woe above woe! grief more than
        common grief!
O that my death would stay these ruthful deeds!
O, pity, pity, gentle heaven, pity!
The red rose and the white are on his face,
The fatal colours of our striving houses:
The one his purple blood right well resembles;
The other his pale cheeks, methinks, presenteth:
Wither one rose, and let the other flourish;   101
If you contend, a thousand lives must wither.
    Son. How will my mother for a father's death
Take on with me and ne'er be satisfied!
    Fath. How will my wife for slaughter of my
        son
Shed seas of tears and ne'er be satisfied!
    K. Hen. How will the country for these woful
        chances
• Misthink the king and not be satisfied!
    Son. Was ever son so rued a father's death?
    Fath. Was ever father so bemoan'd his son?
    K. Hen. Was ever king so grieved for sub-
        jects' woe?   111
Much is your sorrow; mine ten times so much.
    Son. I'll bear thee hence, where I may weep
        my fill.   [*Exit with the body.*
    Fath. These arms of mine shall be thy winding-
        sheet;
My heart, sweet boy, shall be thy sepulchre,
For from my heart thine image ne'er shall go;
My sighing breast shall be thy funeral bell;
• And so obsequious will thy father be,
†Even for the loss of thee, having no more,
• As Priam was for all his valiant sons.   120
I'll bear thee hence; and let them fight that will,

108 *Misthink.* Misjudge.

118 *obsequious.* Scrupulous in funeral rites.

120 *Priam.* King of Troy whose many sons were killed defending the city.

128 *amain.* With great speed.

3 *Lancaster.* House of Lancaster.

Clifford: 'O Phœbus, hadst thou never given consent that Phaëthon should check thy fiery steeds'. Phaëthon's chariot falling to the earth. From a Venetian woodcut, 1553

For I have murdered where I should not kill.
[Exit with the body.
K. Hen. Sad-hearted men, much overgone with care,
Here sits a king more woful than you are.

Alarums: excursions. Enter QUEEN MARGARET, *the* PRINCE, *and* EXETER.

Prince. Fly, father, fly! for all your friends are fled,
And Warwick rages like a chafed bull:
Away! for death doth hold us in pursuit.
Q. Mar. Mount you, my lord; towards Berwick post amain:
Edward and Richard, like a brace of greyhounds
Having the fearful flying hare in sight, 130
With fiery eyes sparkling for very wrath,
And bloody steel grasp'd in their ireful hands,
Are at our backs; and therefore hence amain.
Exe. Away! for vengeance comes along with them:
Nay, stay not to expostulate, make speed;
Or else come after: I'll away before.
K. Hen. Nay, take me with thee, good sweet Exeter:
Not that I fear to stay, but love to go
Whither the queen intends. Forward; away!
[Exeunt.

SCENE VI. *Another part of the field.*

A loud alarum. Enter CLIFFORD, *wounded.*

Clif. Here burns my candle out; ay, here it dies,
Which, whiles it lasted, gave King Henry light.
O Lancaster, I fear thy overthrow
More than my body's parting with my soul!
My love and fear glued many friends to thee;
And, now I fall, thy tough commixture melts.
Impairing Henry, strengthening misproud York,
The common people swarm like summer flies;
And whither fly the gnats but to the sun?
And who shines now but Henry's enemies? 10
O Phœbus, hadst thou never given consent
That Phaëthon should check thy fiery steeds,
Thy burning car never had scorch'd the earth!
And, Henry, hadst thou sway'd as kings should do,
Or as thy father and his father did,
Giving no ground unto the house of York,
They never then had sprung like summer flies;
I and ten thousand in this luckless realm
Had left no mourning widows for our death;
And thou this day hadst kept thy chair in peace.
For what doth cherish weeds but gentle air? 21
And what makes robbers bold but too much lenity?
Bootless are plaints, and cureless are my wounds;
No way to fly, nor strength to hold out flight:
The foe is merciless, and will not pity;
For at their hands I have deserved no pity.
The air hath got into my deadly wounds,
And much effuse of blood doth make me faint.
Come, York and Richard, Warwick and the rest;
I stabb'd your fathers' bosoms, split my breast.
[He faints.

Alarum and retreat. Enter EDWARD, GEORGE, RICHARD, MONTAGUE, WARWICK, *and* Soldiers.

Edw. Now breathe we, lords: good fortune bids us pause, 31

And smooth the frowns of war with peaceful looks.
Some troops pursue the bloody-minded queen,
That led calm Henry, though he were a king,
As doth a sail, fill'd with a fretting gust,
● Command an argosy to stem the waves.
But think you, lords, that Clifford fled with them?
 War. No, 'tis impossible he should escape;
For, though before his face I speak the words,
Your brother Richard mark'd him for the grave:
And wheresoe'er he is, he's surely dead.   41
     [*Clifford groans, and dies.*
 Edw. Whose soul is that which takes her
  heavy leave?
 Rich. A deadly groan, like life and death's
  departing.
 Edw. See who it is: and, now the battle's
  ended,
If friend or foe, let him be gently used.
● *Rich.* Revoke that doom of mercy, for 'tis
  Clifford;
Who not contented that he lopp'd the branch
In hewing Rutland when his leaves put forth,
But set his murdering knife unto the root
From whence that tender spray did sweetly spring,
I mean our princely father, Duke of York. 51
 War. From off the gates of York fetch down
  the head,
Your father's head, which Clifford placed there;
● Instead whereof let this supply the room:
Measure for measure must be answered.
 Edw. Bring forth that fatal screech-owl to our
  house,
That nothing sung but death to us and ours:
Now death shall stop his dismal threatening
  sound,
And his ill-boding tongue no more shall speak.
 War. I think his understanding is bereft. 60
Speak, Clifford, dost thou know who speaks to
  thee?
Dark cloudy death o'ershades his beams of life,
And he nor sees nor hears us what we say.
 Rich. O, would he did! and so perhaps he
  doth:
'Tis but his policy to counterfeit,
Because he would avoid such bitter taunts
Which in the time of death he gave our father.
 Geo. If so thou think'st, vex him with eager
  words.
 Rich. Clifford, ask mercy and obtain no grace.
 Edw. Clifford, repent in bootless penitence.
 War. Clifford, devise excuses for thy faults.
 Geo. While we devise fell tortures for thy
  faults.
 Rich. Thou didst love York, and I am son
  to York.
 Edw. Thou pitied'st Rutland; I will pity thee.
● *Geo.* Where's Captain Margaret, to fence you
  now?
● *War.* They mock thee, Clifford: swear as
  thou wast wont.
 Rich. What, not an oath? nay, then the world
  goes hard
When Clifford cannot spare his friends an oath.
I know by that he's dead; and, by my soul,
If this right hand would buy two hours' life, 80
● That I in all despite might rail at him,
This hand should chop it off, and with the issuing
  blood
● Stifle the villain whose **unstanched** thirst

---

36 *argosy.* Large merchant ship.

46 *doom.* Judgment.

54 *room.* Place.

75 *fence.* Protect.

76 *wont.* Accustomed to.

81 *despite.* Malice.

83 *unstanched.* Insatiable.

95 *buzz.* Spread rumours.

107 *Gloucester's . . . ominous.* The last three Dukes of Gloucester had come to violent ends.

Practising with the cross-bow, 14th century. From Joseph Strutt's *Sports and Pastimes of the People of England*, 1810

---

1 *brake.* Thicket.

2 *laund.* Glade.

4 *Culling.* Choosing.

York and young Rutland could not satisfy.
 War. Ay, but he's dead: off with the traitor's head,
And rear it in the place your father's stands.
And now to London with triumphant march,
There to be crowned England's royal king:
From whence shall Warwick cut the sea to France,
And ask the Lady Bona for thy queen: 90
So shalt thou sinew both these lands together;
And, having France thy friend, thou shalt not dread
The scatter'd foe that hopes to rise again;
For though they cannot greatly sting to hurt,
• Yet look to have them buzz to offend thine ears.
First will I see the coronation;
And then to Brittany I'll cross the sea,
To effect this marriage, so it please my lord.
 Edw. Even as thou wilt, sweet Warwick, let it be;
For in thy shoulder do I build my seat, 100
And never will I undertake the thing
Wherein thy counsel and consent is wanting.
Richard, I will create thee Duke of Gloucester,
And George, of Clarence: Warwick, as ourself,
Shall do and undo as him pleaseth best.
 Rich. Let me be Duke of Clarence, George of Gloucester;
• For Gloucester's dukedom is too ominous.
 War. Tut, that's a foolish observation:
Richard, be Duke of Gloucester. Now to London,
To see these honours in possession. 110
         [*Exeunt.*

ACT III.

SCENE I. *A forest in the north of England.*

Enter two Keepers, *with cross-bows in their hands.*

• *First Keep.* Under this thick-grown brake we'll shroud ourselves;
• For through this laund anon the deer will come;
And in this covert will we make our stand,
• Culling the principal of all the deer.
 Sec. Keep. I'll stay above the hill, so both may shoot.
 First Keep. That cannot be; the noise of thy cross-bow
Will scare the herd, and so my shoot is lost.
Here stand we both, and aim we at the best:
And, for the time shall not seem tedious,
I'll tell thee what befel me on a day 10
In this self-place where now we mean to stand.
 Sec. Keep. Here comes a man; let's stay till he be past.

Enter KING HENRY, *disguised, with a prayer-book.*

 K. Hen. From Scotland am I stol'n, even of pure love,
To greet mine own land with my wishful sight.
No, Harry, Harry, 'tis no land of thine;
Thy place is fill'd, thy sceptre wrung from thee,
Thy balm wash'd off wherewith thou wast anointed:
No bending knee will call thee Cæsar now,
No humble suitors press to speak for right,
No, not a man comes for redress of thee; 20

For how can I help them, and not myself?
  First Keep. Ay, here's a deer whose skin's a
    keeper's fee:
● This is the quondam king; let's seize upon him.
  K. Hen. Let me embrace thee, sour adversity,
For wise men say it is the wisest course.
  Sec. Keep. Why linger we? let us lay hands
    upon him.
  First Keep. Forbear awhile; we'll hear a
    little more.
  K. Hen. My queen and son are gone to France
    for aid;
And, as I hear, the great commanding Warwick
Is thither gone, to crave the French king's sister
To wife for Edward: if this news be true,   31
Poor queen and son, your labour is but lost;
For Warwick is a subtle orator,
And Lewis a prince soon won with moving words.
By this account then Margaret may win him;
For she's a woman to be pitied much:
● Her sighs will make a battery in his breast;
Her tears will pierce into a marble heart;
The tiger will be mild whiles she doth mourn;
● And Nero will be tainted with remorse,   40
To hear and see her plaints, her brinish tears.
Ay, but she's come to beg, Warwick, to give;
She, on his left side, craving aid for Henry,
He, on his right, asking a wife for Edward.
She weeps, and says her Henry is deposed;
He smiles, and says his Edward is install'd;
That she, poor wretch, for grief can speak no
    more;
Whiles Warwick tells his title, smooths the wrong,
Inferreth arguments of mighty strength,
And in conclusion wins the king from her,   50
With promise of his sister, and what else,
To strengthen and support King Edward's place.
O Margaret, thus 'twill be; and thou, poor soul,
Art then forsaken, as thou went'st forlorn!
  Sec. Keep. Say, what art thou that talk'st of
    kings and queens?
  K. Hen. More than I seem, and less than I
    was born to:
A man at least, for less I should not be;
And men may talk of kings, and why not I?
  Sec. Keep. Ay, but thou talk'st as if thou wert
    a king.
  K. Hen. Why, so I am, in mind; and that's
    enough.   60
  Sec. Keep. But, if thou be a king, where is
    thy crown?
  K. Hen. My crown is in my heart, not on my
    head;
● Not deck'd with diamonds and Indian stones,
Nor to be seen: my crown is called content:
A crown it is that seldom kings enjoy.
  Sec. Keep. Well, if you be a king crown'd
    with content,
Your crown content and you must be contented
To go along with us; for, as we think,
You are the king King Edward hath deposed;
And we his subjects sworn in all allegiance   70
Will apprehend you as his enemy.
  K. Hen. But did you never swear, and break
    an oath?
  Sec. Keep. No, never such an oath; nor will
    not now.
  K. Hen. Where did you dwell when I was
    King of England?

23 *quondam.* Former.

37 *battery.* Assault.

40 *Nero.* Roman Emperor whose name has become
synonymous with cruelty.

King Henry VI. Engraving from John Speed's *Theatre
of the Empire of Great Britaine*, 1611–12

63 *Indian stones.* Pearls.

14 *keeps the wind.* Keeps the windward side of the game.

Sec. Keep. Here in this country, where we now remain.

K. Hen. I was anointed king at nine months old;
My father and my grandfather were kings,
And you were sworn true subjects unto me:
And tell me, then, have you not broke your oaths?

First Keep. No; 80
For we were subjects but while you were king.

K. Hen. Why, am I dead? do I not breathe a man?
Ah, simple men, you know not what you swear!
Look, as I blow this feather from my face,
And as the air blows it to me again,
Obeying with my wind when I do blow,
And yielding to another when it blows,
Commanded always by the greater gust;
Such is the lightness of you common men.
But do not break your oaths; for of that sin 90
My mild entreaty shall not make you guilty.
Go where you will, the king shall be commanded:
And be you kings, command, and I 'll obey.

First Keep. We are true subjects to the king, King Edward.

K. Hen. So would you be again to Henry,
If he were seated as King Edward is.

First Keep. We charge you, in God's name, and the king's,
To go with us unto the officers.

K. Hen. In God's name, lead; your king's name be obey'd:
And what God will, that let your king perform:
And what he will, I humbly yield unto. 101

[*Exeunt.*

SCENE II. *London. The palace.*

Enter KING EDWARD, GLOUCESTER, CLARENCE, *and* LADY GREY.

K. Edw. Brother of Gloucester, at Saint Alban's field
This lady's husband, Sir Richard Grey, was slain,
His lands then seized on by the conqueror:
Her suit is now to repossess those lands;
Which we in justice cannot well deny,
Because in quarrel of the house of York
The worthy gentleman did lose his life.

Glou. Your highness shall do well to grant her suit;
It were dishonour to deny it her.

K. Edw. It were no less; but yet I 'll make a pause. 10

Glou. [*Aside to Clar.*] Yea, is it so?
I see the lady hath a thing to grant,
Before the king will grant her humble suit.

Clar. [*Aside to Glou.*] He knows the game: how true he keeps the wind!

Glou. [*Aside to Clar.*] Silence!

K. Edw. Widow, we will consider of your suit;
And come some other time to know our mind.

L. Grey. Right gracious lord, I cannot brook delay:
May it please your highness to resolve me now;
And what your pleasure is, shall satisfy me. 20

Glou. [*Aside to Clar.*] Ay, widow? then I 'll warrant you all your lands,
An if what pleases him shall pleasure you.
Fight closer, or, good faith, you 'll catch a blow.

Clar. [*Aside to Glou.*] I fear her not, unless she chance to fall.

Glou. [*Aside to Clar.*] God forbid that! for he'll take vantages.

K. Edw. How many children hast thou, widow? tell me.

Clar. [*Aside to Glou.*] I think he means to beg a child of her.

Glou. [*Aside to Clar.*] Nay, whip me then: he'll rather give her two.

L. Grey. Three, my most gracious lord.

Glou. [*Aside to Clar.*] You shall have four, if you'll be ruled by him.   30

K. Edw. 'Twere pity they should lose their father's lands.

L. Grey. Be pitiful, dread lord, and grant it then.

K. Edw. Lords, give us leave: I'll try this widow's wit.

Glou. [*Aside to Clar.*] Ay, good leave have you; for you will have leave,
Till youth take leave and leave you to the crutch.
[*Glou. and Clar. retire.*

K. Edw. Now tell me, madam, do you love your children?

L. Grey. Ay, full as dearly as I love myself.

K. Edw. And would you not do much to do them good?

L. Grey. To do them good, I would sustain some harm.

K. Edw. Then get your husband's lands, to do them good.   40

L. Grey. Therefore I came unto your majesty.

K. Edw. I'll tell you how these lands are to be got.

L. Grey. So shall you bind me to your highness' service.

K. Edw. What service wilt thou do me, if I give them?

L. Grey. What you command, that rests in me to do.

K. Edw. But you will take exceptions to my boon.

L. Grey. No, gracious lord, except I cannot do it.

K. Edw. Ay, but thou canst do what I mean to ask.

L. Grey. Why, then I will do what your grace commands.

Glou. [*Aside to Clar.*] He plies her hard; and much rain wears the marble.   50

Clar. [*Aside to Glou.*] As red as fire! nay, then her wax must melt.

L. Grey. Why stops my lord? shall I not hear my task?

K. Edw. An easy task; 'tis but to love a king.

L. Grey. That's soon perform'd, because I am a subject.

K. Edw. Why, then, thy husband's lands I freely give thee.

L. Grey. I take my leave with many thousand thanks.

Glou. [*Aside to Clar.*] The match is made; she seals it with a curtsy.

K. Edw. But stay thee, 'tis the fruits of love I mean.

L. Grey. The fruits of love I mean, my loving liege.

King Edward IV (1461–83).

72 *honesty.* Chastity.

Elizabeth Woodville-Grey, Consort of Edward IV

K. Edw. Ay, but, I fear me, in another
sense. 60
What love, think'st thou, I sue so much to get?
 L. Grey. My love till death, my humble
thanks, my prayers;
That love which virtue begs and virtue grants.
 K. Edw. No, by my troth, I did not mean
such love.
 L. Grey. Why, then you mean not as I
thought you did.
 K. Edw. But now you partly may perceive
my mind.
 L. Grey. My mind will never grant what I
perceive
Your highness aims at, if I aim aright.
 K. Edw. To tell thee plain, I aim to lie
with thee.
 L. Grey. To tell you plain, I had rather lie
in prison. 70
 K. Edw. Why, then thou shalt not have thy
husband's lands.
 L. Grey. Why, then mine honesty shall be
my dower;
For by that loss I will not purchase them.
 K. Edw. Therein thou wrong'st thy children
mightily.
 L. Grey. Herein your highness wrongs both
them and me.
But, mighty lord, this merry inclination
Accords not with the sadness of my suit:
Please you dismiss me, either with 'ay' or 'no.'
 K. Edw. Ay, if thou wilt say 'ay' to my
request;
No, if thou dost say 'no' to my demand. 80
 L. Grey. Then, no, my lord. My suit is at
an end.
 Glou. [*Aside to Clar.*] The widow likes him
not, she knits her brows.
 Clar. [*Aside to Glou.*] He is the bluntest
wooer in Christendom.
 K. Edw. [*Aside*] Her looks do argue her
replete with modesty;
Her words do show her wit incomparable;
All her perfections challenge sovereignty:
One way or other, she is for a king;
And she shall be my love, or else my queen.—
Say that King Edward take thee for his queen?
 L. Grey. 'Tis better said than done, my
gracious lord: 90
I am a subject fit to jest withal,
But far unfit to be a sovereign.
 K. Edw. Sweet widow, by my state I swear
to thee
I speak no more than what my soul intends;
And that is, to enjoy thee for my love.
 L. Grey. And that is more than I will yield
unto:
I know I am too mean to be your queen,
And yet too good to be your concubine.
 K. Edw. You cavil, widow: I did mean,
my queen.
 L. Grey. 'Twill grieve your grace my sons
should call you father. 100
 K. Edw. No more than when my daughters
call thee mother.
Thou art a widow, and thou hast some children;
And, by God's mother, I, being but a bachelor,
Have other some: why, 'tis a happy thing
To be the father unto many sons.

Answer no more, for thou shalt be my queen.
● *Glou.* [*Aside to Clar.*] The ghostly father
    now hath done his shrift.
● *Clar.* [*Aside to Glou.*] When he was made a
    shriver, 'twas for shift.
    K. Edw. Brothers, you muse what chat we
    two have had.
    Glou. The widow likes it not, for she looks
    very sad.   110
    K. Edw. You'ld think it strange if I should
    marry her.
    Clar. To whom, my lord?
    K. Edw.   Why, Clarence, to myself.
    Glou. That would be ten days' wonder at the
    least.
    Clar. That's a day longer than a wonder
    lasts.
    Glou. By so much is the wonder in extremes.
    K. Edw. Well, jest on, brothers: I can tell
    you both
Her suit is granted for her husband's lands.

Enter a Nobleman.

    Nob. My gracious lord, Henry your foe is
    taken,
And brought your prisoner to your palace gate.
    K. Edw. See that he be convey'd unto the
    Tower: 120
And go we, brothers, to the man that took him,
To question of his apprehension.
Widow, go you along. Lords, use her honour-
    ably.   [*Exeunt all but Gloucester.*
    Glou. Ay, Edward will use women honour-
    ably.
Would he were wasted, marrow, bones and all,
That from his loins no hopeful branch may spring,
To cross me from the golden time I look for!
And yet, between my soul's desire and me—
The lustful Edward's title buried—   129
Is Clarence, Henry, and his son young Edward,
And all the unlook'd for issue of their bodies,
To take their rooms, ere I can place myself:
A cold premeditation for my purpose!
Why, then, I do but dream on sovereignty;
Like one that stands upon a promontory,
And spies a far-off shore where he would tread,
Wishing his foot were equal with his eye,
And chides the sea that sunders him from thence,
● Saying, he'll lade it dry to have his way:
So do I wish the crown, being so far off;   140
And so I chide the means that keeps me from it;
And so I say, I'll cut the causes off,
Flattering me with impossibilities.
My eye's too quick, my heart o'erweens too
    much,
Unless my hand and strength could equal them.
Well, say there is no kingdom then for Richard;
What other pleasure can the world afford?
I'll make my heaven in a lady's lap,
And deck my body in gay ornaments,
And witch sweet ladies with my words and
    looks.   150
O miserable thought! and more unlikely
Than to accomplish twenty golden crowns!
Why, love forswore me in my mother's womb:
And, for I should not deal in her soft laws,
She did corrupt frail nature with some bribe,
To shrink mine arm up like a wither'd shrub;
To make an envious mountain on my back,

107 *ghostly father.* Confessor. *done his shrift.* Finished
hearing Confession.

108 *shriver . . . shift.* Popular euphemism for seduction.
shift. Smock, chemise; but also a quibble on the meaning
'trick'.

139 *lade.* Bail out, drain.

Charles Pitt, the Victorian actor, as Gloucester

171 *impaled.* Encircled.

187 *basilisk.* Mythical reptile believed to be able to kill by a mere look.

188 *Nestor.* Wise and venerable old Greek warrior at the siege of Troy.

190 *Sinon.* The Greek who induced the Trojans to allow the wooden horse into the city.

191 *chameleon.* Kind of lizard that can change its colour.

192 *Proteus.* Old man of the sea who could change shape at will.

193 *Machiavel.* Florentine statesman and author whose name has become synonymous with politics devoid of principle.

5 *strike her sail.* Humble herself.

7 *Great Albion's.* England's.

Where sits deformity to mock my body;
To shape my legs of an unequal size;
To disproportion me in every part, 160
Like to a chaos, or an unlick'd bear-whelp
That carries no impression like the dam.
And am I then a man to be beloved?
O monstrous fault, to harbour such a thought!
Then, since this earth affords no joy to me,
But to command, to check, to o'erbear such
As are of better person than myself,
I'll make my heaven to dream upon the crown,
And, whiles I live, to account this world but hell,
Until my mis-shaped trunk that bears this head
• Be round impaled with a glorious crown. 171
And yet I know not how to get the crown,
For many lives stand between me and home:
And I,—like one lost in a thorny wood,
That rends the thorns and is rent with the thorns,
Seeking a way and straying from the way;
Not knowing how to find the open air,
But toiling desperately to find it out,—
Torment myself to catch the English crown:
And from that torment I will free myself, 180
Or hew my way out with a bloody axe.
Why, I can smile, and murder whiles I smile,
And cry 'Content' to that which grieves my heart,
And wet my cheeks with artificial tears,
And frame my face to all occasions.
I'll drown more sailors than the mermaid shall;
• I'll slay more gazers than the basilisk;
• I'll play the orator as well as Nestor,
Deceive more slily than Ulysses could,
• And, like a Sinon, take another Troy. 190
• I can add colours to the chameleon,
• Change shapes with Proteus for advantages,
• And set the murderous Machiavel to school.
Can I do this, and cannot get a crown?
Tut, were it farther off, I'll pluck it down.
[*Exit.*

SCENE III. *France. The* KING'S *palace.*

Flourish. Enter LEWIS *the French King, his sister* BONA, *his Admiral, called* BOURBON: PRINCE EDWARD, QUEEN MARGARET, *and the* EARL OF OXFORD. LEWIS *sits, and riseth up again.*

    K. Lew. Fair Queen of England, worthy Margaret,
Sit down with us: it ill befits thy state
And birth, that thou shouldst stand while Lewis doth sit.
    Q. Mar. No, mighty King of France: now Margaret
• Must strike her sail and learn awhile to serve
Where kings command. I was, I must confess,
• Great Albion's queen in former golden days:
But now mischance hath trod my title down,
And with dishonour laid me on the ground;
Where I must take like seat unto my fortune, 10
And to my humble seat conform myself.
    K. Lew. Why, say, fair queen, whence springs this deep despair?
    Q. Mar. From such a cause as fills mine eyes with tears
And stops my tongue, while heart is drown'd in cares.

K. Lew. Whate'er it be, be thou still like
    thyself,
And sit thee by our side: [*Seats her by him*]
    yield not thy neck
To fortune's yoke, but let thy dauntless mind
Still ride in triumph over all mischance.
Be plain, Queen Margaret, and tell thy grief;
It shall be eased, if France can yield relief.   20
   Q. Mar. Those gracious words revive my
    drooping thoughts
And give my tongue-tied sorrows leave to speak.
Now, therefore, be it known to noble Lewis,
That Henry, sole possessor of my love,
Is of a king become a banish'd man,
And forced to live in Scotland a forlorn;
While proud ambitious Edward Duke of York
Usurps the regal title and the seat
Of England's true-anointed lawful king.
This is the cause that I, poor Margaret,   30
With this my son, Prince Edward, Henry's heir,
Am come to crave thy just and lawful aid;
And if thou fail us, all our hope is done:
Scotland hath will to help, but cannot help;
Our people and our peers are both misled,
Our treasure seized, our soldiers put to flight,
And, as thou seest, ourselves in heavy plight.
   K. Lew. Renowned queen, with patience
    calm the storm,
While we bethink a means to break it off.
   Q. Mar. The more we stay, the stronger
    grows our foe.   40
   K. Lew. The more I stay, the more I'll suc-
    cour thee.
   Q. Mar. O, but impatience waiteth on true
    sorrow.
And see where comes the breeder of my sorrow!

Enter WARWICK.

   K. Lew. What's he approacheth boldly to
    our presence?
   Q. Mar. Our Earl of Warwick, Edward's
    greatest friend.
   K. Lew. Welcome, brave Warwick! What
    brings thee to France?
               [*He descends.   She ariseth.*
   Q. Mar. Ay, now begins a second storm to
    rise;
For this is he that moves both wind and tide.
   War. From worthy Edward, King of Albion,
My lord and sovereign, and thy vowed friend,   50
I come, in kindness and unfeigned love,
First, to do greetings to thy royal person;
And then to crave a league of amity;
And lastly, to confirm that amity
With nuptial knot, if thou vouchsafe to grant
That virtuous Lady Bona, thy fair sister,
To England's king in lawful marriage.
   Q. Mar. [*Aside*] If that go forward, Henry's
    hope is done.
   War. [*To Bona*] And, gracious madam, in
    our king's behalf,
I am commanded, with your leave and favour,   60
Humbly to kiss your hand and with my tongue
To tell the passion of my sovereign's heart;
Where fame, late entering at his heedful ears,
Hath placed thy beauty's image and thy virtue.
   Q. Mar. King Lewis and Lady Bona, hear
    me speak,
Before you answer Warwick. His demand

56 *Lady Bona . . . sister.* i.e. sister-in-law, daughter of the Duke of Savoy and sister to the French queen.

99 *buckler*. Shield, protect.

101 *doom*. Judgment.

Springs not from Edward's well-meant honest
    love,
But from deceit bred by necessity;
For how can tyrants safely govern home,
Unless abroad they purchase great alliance?   70
To prove him tyrant this reason may suffice,
That Henry liveth still; but were he dead,
Yet here Prince Edward stands, King Henry's
    son.
Look, therefore, Lewis, that by this league and
    marriage
Thou draw not on thy danger and dishonour;
For though usurpers sway the rule awhile,
Yet heavens are just, and time suppresseth
    wrongs.
    War. Injurious Margaret!
    Prince.   And why not queen?
    War. Because thy father Henry did usurp;
And thou no more art prince than she is queen. 80
    Oxf. Then Warwick disannuls great John of
    Gaunt,
Which did subdue the greatest part of Spain:
And, after John of Gaunt, Henry the Fourth,
Whose wisdom was a mirror to the wisest;
And, after that wise prince, Henry the Fifth,
Who by his prowess conquered all France:
From these our Henry lineally descends.
    War. Oxford, how haps it, in this smooth
    discourse,
You told not how Henry the Sixth hath lost
All that which Henry the Fifth had gotten?   90
Methinks these peers of France should smile at
    that.
But for the rest, you tell a pedigree
Of threescore and two years; a silly time
To make prescription for a kingdom's worth.
    Oxf. Why, Warwick, canst thou speak against
    thy liege,
Whom thou obeyed'st thirty and six years,
And not bewray thy treason with a blush?
    War. Can Oxford, that did ever fence the
    right,
● Now buckler falsehood with a pedigree?   99
For shame! leave Henry, and call Edward king.
●   *Oxf.* Call him my king by whose injurious
    doom
My elder brother, the Lord Aubrey Vere,
Was done to death? and more than so, my father,
Even in the downfall of his mellow'd years,
When nature brought him to the door of death?
No, Warwick, no; while life upholds this arm,
This arm upholds the house of Lancaster.
    War. And I the house of York.
    K. Lew. Queen Margaret, Prince Edward,
    and Oxford,
Vouchsafe, at our request, to stand aside,   110
While I use further conference with Warwick.
                     [They stand aloof.
    Q. Mar. Heavens grant that Warwick's words
    bewitch him not!
    K. Lew. Now, Warwick, tell me, even upon
    thy conscience,
Is Edward your true king? for I were loath
To link with him that were not lawful chosen.
    War. Thereon I pawn my credit and mine
    honour.
    K. Lew. But is he gracious in the people's
    eye?
    War. The more that Henry was unfortunate.

K. Lew. Then further, all dissembling set aside,
Tell me for truth the measure of his love   120
Unto our sister Bona.
    War.   Such it seems
As may beseem a monarch like himself.
Myself have often heard him say and swear
That this his love was an eternal plant,
Whereof the root was fix'd in virtue's ground,
The leaves and fruit maintain'd with beauty's sun,
Exempt from envy, but not from disdain,
Unless the Lady Bona quit his pain.
    K. Lew. Now, sister, let us hear your firm resolve.
    Bona. Your grant, or your denial, shall be mine: 130
[*To War.*] Yet I confess that often ere this day,
When I have heard your king's desert recounted,
Mine ear hath tempted judgment to desire.
    K. Lew. Then, Warwick, thus: our sister shall be Edward's;
And now forthwith shall articles be drawn
• Touching the jointure that your king must make,
Which with her dowry shall be counterpoised.
Draw near, Queen Margaret, and be a witness
That Bona shall be wife to the English king.
    Prince. To Edward, but not to the English king.   140
    Q. Mar. Deceitful Warwick! it was thy device
By this alliance to make void my suit:
Before thy coming Lewis was Henry's friend.
    K. Lew. And still is friend to him and Margaret:
But if your title to the crown be weak,
As may appear by Edward's good success,
Then 'tis but reason that I be released
From giving aid which late I promised.
Yet shall you have all kindness at my hand
That your estate requires and mine can yield.   150
    War. Henry now lives in Scotland at his ease,
Where having nothing, nothing can he lose.
And as for you yourself, our quondam queen,
You have a father able to maintain you;
And better 'twere you troubled him than France.
    Q. Mar. Peace, impudent and shameless Warwick, peace,
Proud setter up and puller down of kings!
I will not hence, till, with my talk and tears,
Both full of truth, I make King Lewis behold
• Thy sly conveyance and thy lord's false love; 160
For both of you are birds of selfsame feather.
                 [*Post blows a horn within.*
    K. Lew. Warwick, this is some post to us or thee.

            Enter a Post.

    Post. [*To War.*] My lord ambassador, these letters are for you,
Sent from your brother, Marquess Montague:
[*To Lewis*] These from our king unto your majesty:
[*To Margaret*] And, madam, these for you; from whom I know not.
             [*They all read their letters.*
    Oxf. I like it well that our fair queen and mistress

136 *jointure.* Marriage settlement.

160 *conveyance.* Contrivance.

SD *Post.* A messenger.

187 *My father.* Earl of Salisbury executed by the Lancastrians after Wakefield.

188 *abuse . . . niece.* Edward had tried to seduce her.

191 *guerdon'd.* Rewarded.

Costume design for Warwick by Ann Curtis, Royal Shakespeare Co, 1964

Smiles at her news, while Warwick frowns at his.
Prince. Nay, mark how Lewis stamps, as he were nettled:
I hope all's for the best.   170
K. Lew. Warwick, what are thy news? and yours, fair queen?
Q. Mar. Mine, such as fill my heart with unhoped joys.
War. Mine, full of sorrow and heart's discontent.
K. Lew. What! has your king married the Lady Grey?
And now, to soothe your forgery and his,
Sends me a paper to persuade me patience?
Is this the alliance that he seeks with France?
Dare he presume to scorn us in this manner?
Q. Mar. I told your majesty as much before:
This proveth Edward's love and Warwick's honesty.   180
War. King Lewis, I here protest, in sight of heaven,
And by the hope I have of heavenly bliss,
That I am clear from this misdeed of Edward's,
No more my king, for he dishonours me,
But most himself, if he could see his shame.
Did I forget that by the house of York
• My father came untimely to his death?
• Did I let pass the abuse done to my niece?
Did I impale him with the regal crown?
Did I put Henry from his native right?   190
• And am I guerdon'd at the last with shame?
Shame on himself! for my desert is honour:
And to repair my honour lost for him,
I here renounce him and return to Henry.
My noble queen, let former grudges pass,
And henceforth I am thy true servitor:
I will revenge his wrong to Lady Bona
And replant Henry in his former state.
Q. Mar. Warwick, these words have turn'd my hate to love;
And I forgive and quite forget old faults,   200
And joy that thou becomest King Henry's friend.
War. So much his friend, ay, his unfeigned friend,
That, if King Lewis vouchsafe to furnish us
With some few bands of chosen soldiers,
I'll undertake to land them on our coast
And force the tyrant from his seat by war.
'Tis not his new-made bride shall succour him:
And as for Clarence, as my letters tell me,
He's very likely now to fall from him,   209
For matching more for wanton lust than honour,
Or than for strength and safety of our country.
Bona. Dear brother, how shall Bona be revenged
But by thy help to this distressed queen?
Q. Mar. Renowned prince, how shall poor Henry live,
Unless thou rescue him from foul despair?
Bona. My quarrel and this English queen's are one.
War. And mine, fair lady Bona, joins with yours.
K. Lew. And mine with hers, and thine, and Margaret's.
Therefore at last I firmly am resolved
You shall have aid.   220
Q. Mar. Let me give humble thanks for all at once.

K. Lew. Then, England's messenger, return in post,
And tell false Edward, thy supposed king,
● That Lewis of France is sending over masquers
To revel it with him and his new bride :
Thou seest what's past, go fear thy king withal.
    Bona. Tell him, in hope he'll prove a widower shortly,
● I'll wear the willow garland for his sake.
    Q. Mar. Tell him, my mourning weeds are laid aside,
And I am ready to put armour on.   230
    War. Tell him from me that he hath done me wrong,
And therefore I'll uncrown him ere't be long.
There's thy reward : be gone.   [*Exit Post.*
    K. Lew.   But, Warwick,
Thou and Oxford, with five thousand men,
Shall cross the seas, and bid false Edward battle ;
And, as occasion serves, this noble queen
And prince shall follow with a fresh supply.
Yet, ere thou go, but answer me one doubt,
What pledge have we of thy firm loyalty ?   239
    War. This shall assure my constant loyalty,
That if our queen and this young prince agree,
● I'll join mine eldest daughter and my joy
To him forthwith in holy wedlock bands.
    Q. Mar. Yes, I agree, and thank you for your motion.
Son Edward, she is fair and virtuous,
Therefore delay not, give thy hand to Warwick ;
And, with thy hand, thy faith irrevocable,
That only Warwick's daughter shall be thine.
    Prince. Yes, I accept her, for she well deserves it ;
And here, to pledge my vow, I give my hand.   250
        [*He gives his hand to Warwick.*
    K. Lew. Why stay we now? These soldiers shall be levied,
And thou, Lord Bourbon, our high admiral,
Shalt waft them over with our royal fleet.
I long till Edward fall by war's mischance,
For mocking marriage with a dame of France.
        [*Exeunt all but Warwick.*
    War. I came from Edward as ambassador,
But I return his sworn and mortal foe :
Matter of marriage was the charge he gave me,
But dreadful war shall answer his demand.
● Had he none else to make a stale but me ?   260
Then none but I shall turn his jest to sorrow.
I was the chief that raised him to the crown,
And I'll be chief to bring him down again :
Not that I pity Henry's misery,
But seek revenge on Edward's mockery.   [*Exit.*

ACT IV.

Scene I. *London. The palace.*

Enter Gloucester, Clarence, Somerset, *and* Montague.

    Glou. Now tell me, brother Clarence, what think you
Of this new marriage with the Lady Grey?
Hath not our brother made a worthy choice?
    Clar. Alas, you know, 'tis far from hence to France ;
How could he stay till Warwick made return?

224 *masquers.* Actors in a masque.

Masquer at the court of Charles VI of France. Engraving copied from Froissart's *Chronicles*, 15th century

228 *willow garland.* Symbol of spurned love.

242 *eldest daughter.* Younger not elder. The elder daughter, Isabella, was betrothed to Clarence.

260 *stale.* Dupe.

King Edward IV. Initial to Statutes of England c.1500

---

44 *fence.* Defence.

Som. My lords, forbear this talk; here comes the king.
Glou. And his well-chosen bride.
Clar. I mind to tell him plainly what I think.

Flourish. Enter KING EDWARD, *attended;* LADY GREY, *as Queen;* PEMBROKE, STAFFORD, HASTINGS, *and others.*

K. Edw. Now, brother of Clarence, how like you our choice,
That you stand pensive, as half malcontent? 10
Clar. As well as Lewis of France, or the Earl of Warwick,
Which are so weak of courage and in judgement
That they'll take no offence at our abuse.
K. Edw. Suppose they take offence without a cause,
They are but Lewis and Warwick: I am Edward,
Your king and Warwick's, and must have my will.
Glou. And shall have your will, because our king:
Yet hasty marriage seldom proveth well.
K. Edw. Yea, brother Richard, are you offended too?
Glou. Not I: 20
No, God forbid that I should wish them sever'd
Whom God hath join'd together; ay, and 'twere pity
To sunder them that yoke so well together.
K. Edw. Setting your scorns and your mislike aside,
Tell me some reason why the Lady Grey
Should not become my wife and England's queen.
And you too, Somerset and Montague,
Speak freely what you think.
Clar. Then this is mine opinion: that King Lewis
Becomes your enemy, for mocking him 30
About the marriage of the Lady Bona.
Glou. And Warwick, doing what you gave in charge,
Is now dishonoured by this new marriage.
K. Edw. What if both Lewis and Warwick be appeased
By such invention as I can devise?
Mont. Yet, to have join'd with France in such alliance
Would more have strengthen'd this our commonwealth
'Gainst foreign storms than any home-bred marriage.
Hast. Why, knows not Montague that of itself
England is safe, if true within itself? 40
Mont. But the safer when 'tis back'd with France.
Hast. 'Tis better using France than trusting France:
Let us be back'd with God and with the seas
● Which He hath given for fence impregnable,
And with their helps only defend ourselves;
In them and in ourselves our safety lies.
Clar. For this one speech Lord Hastings well deserves
To have the heir of the Lord Hungerford.
K. Edw. Ay, what of that? it was my will and grant;
And for this once my will shall stand for law. 50

Glou. And yet methinks your grace hath not done well,
To give the heir and daughter of Lord Scales
● Unto the brother of your loving bride;
She better would have fitted me or Clarence:
But in your bride you bury brotherhood.
    Clar. Or else you would not have bestow'd the heir
● Of the Lord Bonville on your new wife's son,
And leave your brothers to go speed elsewhere.
    K. Edw. Alas, poor Clarence! is it for a wife
That thou art malcontent? I will provide thee. 60
    Clar. In choosing for yourself, you show'd your judgement,
Which being shallow, you shall give me leave
To play the broker in mine own behalf;
And to that end I shortly mind to leave you.
    K. Edw. Leave me, or tarry, Edward will be king,
And not be tied unto his brother's will.
    Q. Eliz. My lords, before it pleased his majesty
To raise my state to title of a queen,
Do me but right, and you must all confess
That I was not ignoble of descent; 70
And meaner than myself have had like fortune.
But as this title honours me and mine,
So your dislike, to whom I would be pleasing,
Doth cloud my joys with danger and with sorrow.
    K. Edw. My love, forbear to fawn upon their frowns:
What danger or what sorrow can befall thee,
So long as Edward is thy constant friend,
And their true sovereign, whom they must obey?
Nay, whom they shall obey, and love thee too,
Unless they seek for hatred at my hands; 80
Which if they do, yet will I keep thee safe,
And they shall feel the vengeance of my wrath.
    Glou. I hear, yet say not much, but think the more. [*Aside.*

Enter a Post.

    K. Edw. Now, messenger, what letters or what news
From France?
    Post. My sovereign liege, no letters; and few words,
But such as I, without your special pardon,
Dare not relate.
    K. Edw. Go to, we pardon thee: therefore, in brief,
Tell me their words as near as thou canst guess them. 90
What answer makes King Lewis unto our letters?
    Post. At my depart, these were his very words:
'Go tell false Edward, thy supposed king,
That Lewis of France is sending over masquers
To revel it with him and his new bride.'
    K. Edw. Is Lewis so brave? belike he thinks me Henry.
But what said Lady Bona to my marriage?
    Post. These were her words, utter'd with mild disdain:
'Tell him, in hope he'll prove a widower shortly,
I'll wear the willow garland for his sake.' 100
    K. Edw. I blame not her, she could say little less;
She had the wrong. But what said Henry's queen?
For I have heard that she was there in place.

53 *brother . . . bride.* Lord Rivers.

57 *son.* Sir Thomas Grey, Marquess of Dorset.

King, Queen and Court. Engraving from a middle 15th century manuscript

106 *Belike.* Perhaps.

142 *suspect.* Suspicion.

Post. 'Tell him,' quoth she, 'my mourning
    weeds are done,
And I am ready to put armour on.'
  K. Edw. Belike she minds to play the Amazon.
But what said Warwick to these injuries?
  Post. He, more incensed against your majesty
Than all the rest, discharged me with these words:
'Tell him from me that he hath done me wrong,
And therefore I'll uncrown him ere't be long.'
  K. Edw. Ha! durst the traitor breathe out
    so proud words?
Well, I will arm me, being thus forewarn'd:
They shall have wars and pay for their pre-
  sumption.
But say, is Warwick friends with Margaret?
  Post. Ay, gracious sovereign; they are so
    link'd in friendship,
That young Prince Edward marries Warwick's
  daughter.
  Clar. Belike the elder; Clarence will have the
    younger.
Now, brother king, farewell, and sit you fast, 119
For I will hence to Warwick's other daughter;
That, though I want a kingdom, yet in marriage
I may not prove inferior to yourself.
You that love me and Warwick, follow me.
       [*Exit Clarence, and Somerset follows.*
  Glou. [*Aside*] Not I:
My thoughts aim at a further matter: I
Stay not for the love of Edward, but the crown.
  K. Edw. Clarence and Somerset both gone
    to Warwick!
Yet am I arm'd against the worst can happen;
And haste is needful in this desperate case.
Pembroke and Stafford, you in our behalf   130
Go levy men, and make prepare for war;
They are already, or quickly will be landed:
Myself in person will straight follow you.
       [*Exeunt Pembroke and Stafford.*
But, ere I go, Hastings and Montague,
Resolve my doubt. You twain, of all the rest,
Are near to Warwick by blood and by alliance:
Tell me if you love Warwick more than me?
If it be so, then both depart to him;
I rather wish you foes than hollow friends:
But if you mind to hold your true obedience, 140
Give me assurance with some friendly vow,
  That I may never have you in suspect.
  Mont. So God help Montague as he proves
    true!
  Hast. And Hastings as he favours Edward's
    cause!
  K. Edw. Now, brother Richard, will you stand
    by us?
  Glou. Ay, in despite of all that shall withstand
    you.
  K. Edw. Why, so! then am I sure of victory.
Now therefore let us hence; and lose no hour,
Till we meet Warwick with his foreign power.
       [*Exeunt.*

SCENE II. *A plain in Warwickshire.*

Enter WARWICK *and* OXFORD, *with French
soldiers.*

  War. Trust me, my lord, all hitherto goes
    well;
The common people by numbers swarm to us.

Enter CLARENCE *and* SOMERSET.

But see where Somerset and Clarence comes!
Speak suddenly, my lords, are we all friends?
    Clar.   Fear not that, my lord.
    War.   Then, gentle Clarence, welcome unto
    Warwick;
And welcome, Somerset: I hold it cowardice
To rest mistrustful where a noble heart
Hath pawn'd an open hand in sign of love;
Else might I think that Clarence, Edward's bro-
    ther,   10
Were but a feigned friend to our proceedings:
But welcome, sweet Clarence; my daughter shall
    be thine.
● And now what rests but, in night's coverture,
Thy brother being carelessly encamp'd,
His soldiers lurking in the towns about,
And but attended by a simple guard,
We may surprise and take him at our pleasure?
Our scouts have found the adventure very easy:
● That as Ulysses and stout Diomede   19
With sleight and manhood stole to Rhesus' tents,
And brought from thence the Thracian fatal steeds,
So, well cover'd with the night's black mantle,
At unawares may beat down Edward's guard
And seize himself; I say not, slaughter him,
For I intend but only to surprise him.
You that will follow me to this attempt,
Applaud the name of Henry with your leader.
                    [*They all cry,* 'Henry!'
Why, then, let's on our way in silent sort:
For Warwick and his friends, God and Saint
    George!   [*Exeunt.*

SCENE III. *Edward's camp, near Warwick.*

Enter three Watchmen, *to guard the* KING'S
tent.

First Watch. Come on, my masters, each man
    take his stand:
The king by this is set him down to sleep.
    Second Watch. What, will he not to bed?
    First Watch. Why, no; for he hath made a
    solemn vow
Never to lie and take his natural rest
Till Warwick or himself be quite suppress'd.
    Second Watch. To-morrow then belike shall
    be the day,
If Warwick be so near as men report.
    Third Watch. But say, I pray, what noble-
    man is that
That with the king here resteth in his tent?   10
    First Watch. 'Tis the Lord Hastings, the
    king's chiefest friend.
    Third Watch. O, is it so? But why commands
    the king
That his chief followers lodge in towns about him,
While he himself keeps in the cold field?
    Second Watch. 'Tis the more honour, because
    more dangerous.
●   *Third Watch.* Ay, but give me worship and
    quietness;
I like it better than a dangerous honour.
If Warwick knew in what estate he stands,
'Tis to be doubted he would waken him.
●   *First Watch.* Unless our halberds did shut
    up his passage.   20

13 *coverture.* Shelter.

19–21 *Ulysses . . . steeds.* It had been predicted that Troy would not fall if the horses of Rhesus grazed on the Trojan plain. To prevent this Ulysses and Diomede intercepted the Thracian prince, Rhesus, on the night of his arrival, slew him and captured the horses.

Ulysses and Diomede steal the horses of Rhesus. Illustration by John Flaxman from Homer's *Iliad,* translated by Alexander Pope, 1793

16 *worship.* Dignity.

20 *halberd.* Combined spear and battle-axe.

28 *fly*. Flee.

47 *My mind . . . wheel*. My mind can rise above misfortune.

Warwick, the king-maker. Engraving from the Roll of the Earls of Warwick by John Rous (d.1491)

53 *Archbishop of York*. George Neville.

59 *It boots not*. It is useless to.

Second Watch. Ay, wherefore else guard we his royal tent,
But to defend his person from night-foes?

Enter WARWICK, CLARENCE, OXFORD, SOMERSET, *and French soldiers, silent all.*

War. This is his tent; and see where stand his guard.
Courage, my masters! honour now or never!
But follow me, and Edward shall be ours.
First Watch. Who goes there?
Second Watch. Stay, or thou diest!
  [*Warwick and the rest cry all,* 'Warwick! Warwick!' *and set upon the Guard, who fly, crying,* 'Arm! arm!' *Warwick and the rest following them.*

The drum playing and trumpet sounding, re-enter WARWICK, SOMERSET, *and the rest, bringing the* KING *out in his gown, sitting in a chair.* RICHARD *and* HASTINGS *fly over the stage.*

● *Som.* What are they that fly there?
War. Richard and Hastings: let them go; here is
The duke.
 K. Edw. The duke! Why, Warwick, when we parted,   30
Thou call'dst me king.
 War.   Ay, but the case is alter'd:
When you disgraced me in my embassade,
Then I degraded you from being king,
And come now to create you Duke of York.
Alas! how should you govern any kingdom,
That know not how to use ambassadors,
Nor how to be contented with one wife,
Nor how to use your brothers brotherly,
Nor how to study for the people's welfare,
Nor how to shroud yourself from enemies? 40
 K. Edw. Yea, brother of Clarence, art thou here too?
Nay, then I see that Edward needs must down.
Yet, Warwick, in despite of all mischance,
Of thee thyself and all thy complices,
Edward will always bear himself as king:
Though fortune's malice overthrow my state,
● My mind exceeds the compass of her wheel.
 War. Then, for his mind, be Edward England's king: [*Takes off his crown.*
But Henry now shall wear the English crown,
And be true king indeed, thou but the shadow. 50
My Lord of Somerset, at my request,
See that forthwith Duke Edward be convey'd
● Unto my brother, Archbishop of York.
When I have fought with Pembroke and his fellows,
I'll follow you, and tell what answer
Lewis and the Lady Bona send to him.
Now, for a while farewell, good Duke of York.
  [*They lead him out forcibly.*
 K. Edw. What fates impose, that men must needs abide;
● It boots not to resist both wind and tide.
  [*Exit, guarded.*
 Oxf. What now remains, my lords, for us to do 60
But march to London with our soldiers?
 War. Ay, that's the first thing that we have to do;

To free king Henry from imprisonment
And see him seated in the regal throne. [*Exeunt.*

SCENE IV. *London. The palace.*

Enter QUEEN ELIZABETH *and* RIVERS.

Riv. Madam, what makes you in this sudden
    change?
Q. Eliz. Why, brother Rivers, are you yet to
    learn
What late misfortune is befall'n King Edward?
Riv. What! loss of some pitch'd battle against
    Warwick?
Q. Eliz. No, but the loss of his own royal
    person.
Riv. Then is my sovereign slain?
Q. Eliz. Ay, almost slain, for he is taken
    prisoner,
Either betray'd by falsehood of his guard
Or by his foe surprised at unawares:
And, as I further have to understand,   10
Is new committed to the Bishop of York,
Fell Warwick's brother and by that our foe.
  Riv. These news I must confess are full of
    grief;
Yet, gracious madam, bear it as you may:
Warwick may lose, that now hath won the day.
  Q. Eliz. Till then fair hope must hinder life's
    decay.
And I the rather wean me from despair
For love of Edward's offspring in my womb:
This is it that makes me bridle passion
And bear with mildness my misfortune's cross; 20
Ay, ay, for this I draw in many a tear
And stop the rising of blood-sucking sighs,
Lest with my sighs or tears I blast or drown
King Edward's fruit, true heir to the English
    crown.
  Riv. But, madam, where is Warwick then
    become?
Q. Eliz. I am inform'd that he comes towards
    London,
To set the crown once more on Henry's head:
Guess thou the rest: King Edward's friends
    must down,
But, to prevent the tyrant's violence,—
For trust not him that hath once broken faith,— 30
• I'll hence forthwith unto the sanctuary,
To save at least the heir of Edward's right:
There shall I rest secure from force and fraud.
Come, therefore, let us fly while we may fly:
If Warwick take us we are sure to die. [*Exeunt.*

SCENE V. *A park near Middleham Castle in Yorkshire.*

Enter GLOUCESTER, LORD HASTINGS, *and* SIR
WILLIAM STANLEY.

Glou. Now, my Lord Hastings and Sir Wil-
    liam Stanley,
Leave off to wonder why I drew you hither,
Into this chiefest thicket of the park.
Thus stands the case: you know our king, my
    brother,
Is prisoner to the bishop here, at whose hands
He hath good usage and great liberty,
And, often but attended with weak guard,
Comes hunting this way to disport himself.
• I have advertised him by secret means

31 *sanctuary.* Place where fugitives were immune from arrest.

Earl Rivers, Queen Elizabeth's brother, here presenting his book, *Sayings of the Philosophers,* to Edward IV. Engraving from a 15th century manuscript

9 *advertised.* Informed.

11 *colour.* Pretext, disguise.

20 *Lynn.* King's Lynn in Norfolk.

23 *forwardness.* Enterprise.

A stag hunt. Detail from a painting by Johannes Hackaert (*c.*1628–85)

5 *enlargement.* Liberation.

22 *thwarting stars.* Ill-luck.

That if about this hour he make this way   10
Under the colour of his usual game,
He shall here find his friends with horse and men
To set him free from his captivity.

Enter KING EDWARD *and a* Huntsman *with him.*

Hunt. This way, my lord; for this way lies
the game.
K. Edw. Nay, this way, man: see where the
huntsmen stand.
Now, brother of Gloucester, Lord Hastings, and
the rest,
Stand you thus close, to steal the bishop's deer?
Glou. Brother, the time and case requireth
haste:
Your horse stands ready at the park-corner.
K. Edw. But whither shall we then?
Hast.   To Lynn, my lord, 20
And ship from thence to Flanders.
Glou. Well guess'd, believe me; for that was
my meaning.
K. Edw. Stanley, I will requite thy forward-
ness.
Glou. But wherefore stay we? 'tis no time to
talk.
K. Edw. Huntsman, what say'st thou? wilt
thou go along?
Hunt. Better do so than tarry and be hang'd.
Glou. Come then, away; let's ha' no more ado.
K. Edw. Bishop, farewell: shield thee from
Warwick's frown;
And pray that I may repossess the crown.
                              [*Exeunt.*

SCENE VI. *London. The Tower.*

Flourish. Enter KING HENRY, CLARENCE,
WARWICK, SOMERSET, *young* RICHMOND,
OXFORD, MONTAGUE, *and* Lieutenant of the
Tower.

K. Hen. Master lieutenant, now that God
and friends
Have shaken Edward from the regal seat,
And turn'd my captive state to liberty,
My fear to hope, my sorrows unto joys,
At our enlargement what are thy due fees?
Lieu. Subjects may challenge nothing of
their sovereigns;
But if an humble prayer may prevail,
I then crave pardon of your majesty.
K. Hen. For what, lieutenant? for well using
me?   9
Nay, be thou sure I'll well requite thy kindness,
For that it made my imprisonment a pleasure;
Ay, such a pleasure as incaged birds
Conceive when after many moody thoughts
At last by notes of household harmony
They quite forget their loss of liberty.
But, Warwick, after God, thou set'st me free,
And chiefly therefore I thank God and thee;
He was the author, thou the instrument.
Therefore, that I may conquer fortune's spite
By living low, where fortune cannot hurt me, 20
And that the people of this blessed land
May not be punish'd with my thwarting stars,
Warwick, although my head still wear the crown,
I here resign my government to thee,
For thou art fortunate in all thy deeds.

War. Your grace hath still been famed for
    virtuous;
And now may seem as wise as virtuous,
By spying and avoiding fortune's malice,
● For few men rightly temper with the stars:
Yet in this one thing let me blame your grace, 30
● For choosing me when Clarence is in place.
    Clar. No, Warwick, thou art worthy of the
    sway,
To whom the heavens in thy nativity
Adjudged an olive branch and laurel crown,
As likely to be blest in peace and war;
And therefore I yield thee my free consent.
    War. And I choose Clarence only for protector.
    K. Hen. Warwick and Clarence, give me
    both your hands:
Now join your hands, and with your hands your
    hearts,
That no dissension hinder government: 40
I make you both protectors of this land,
While I myself will lead a private life
And in devotion spend my latter days,
To sin's rebuke and my Creator's praise.
    War. What answers Clarence to his sove-
    reign's will?
    Clar. That he consents, if Warwick yield
    consent;
For on thy fortune I repose myself.
    War. Why, then, though loath, yet must I
    be content:
We'll yoke together, like a double shadow
To Henry's body, and supply his place; 50
I mean, in bearing weight of government,
While he enjoys the honour and his ease.
And, Clarence, now then it is more than needful
Forthwith that Edward be pronounced a traitor,
And all his lands and goods be confiscate.
    Clar. What else? and that succession be de-
    termined.
    War. Ay, therein Clarence shall not want
    his part.
    K. Hen. But, with the first of all your chief
    affairs,
Let me entreat, for I command no more, 59
That Margaret your queen and my son Edward
Be sent for, to return from France with speed;
For, till I see them here, by doubtful fear
My joy of liberty is half eclipsed.
    Clar. It shall be done, my sovereign, with all
    speed.
    K. Hen. My Lord of Somerset, what youth
    is that,
Of whom you seem to have so tender care?
●   *Som.* My liege, it is young Henry, earl of
    Richmond.
    K. Hen. Come hither, England's hope. [*Lays
    his hand on his head*] If secret powers
Suggest but truth to my divining thoughts,
This pretty lad will prove our country's bliss. 70
His looks are full of peaceful majesty,
His head by nature framed to wear a crown,
His hand to wield a sceptre, and himself
Likely in time to bless a regal throne.
Make much of him, my lords, for this is he
Must help you more than you are hurt by me.

Enter a Post.

War. What news, my friend?

The Tower of London, with 15th century London in the
background. Engraving from a contemporary manuscript

---

29 *temper . . . stars.* i.e. are reconciled to their fate.

31 *in place.* Here.

67 *Henry . . . Richmond.* Future Henry VII.

79 *he.* i.e. your brother, the Archbishop of York.

81 *convey'd.* Spirited away secretly.

82 *attended.* Waited for.

View of York from the ancient ramparts. Engraving from *Old England*, 1854

---

8 *Ravenspurgh.* At the mouth of the Humber in Yorkshire.

13 *abodements.* Forebodings.

Post. That Edward is escaped from your brother,
And fled, as he hears since, to Burgundy.
  War.   Unsavoury news! but how made he escape? 80
  Post.   He was convey'd by Richard Duke of Gloucester
And the Lord Hastings, who attended him
In secret ambush on the forest side
And from the bishop's huntsmen rescued him;
For hunting was his daily exercise.
  War.   My brother was too careless of his charge.
But let us hence, my sovereign, to provide
A salve for any sore that may betide.
  [*Exeunt all but Somerset, Richmond, and Oxford.*
  Som.   My lord, I like not of this flight of Edward's;
For doubtless Burgundy will yield him help, 90
And we shall have more wars before 't be long.
As Henry's late presaging prophecy
Did glad my heart with hope of this young Richmond,
So doth my heart misgive me, in these conflicts
What may befall him, to his harm and ours:
Therefore, Lord Oxford, to prevent the worst,
Forthwith we'll send him hence to Brittany,
Till storms be past of civil enmity.
  Oxf.   Ay, for if Edward repossess the crown,
'Tis like that Richmond with the rest shall down.
  Som.   It shall be so; he shall to Brittany. 101
Come, therefore, let's about it speedily. [*Exeunt.*

SCENE VII. *Before York.*

Flourish. Enter KING EDWARD, GLOUCESTER, HASTINGS, *and* Soldiers.

  K. Edw.   Now, brother Richard, Lord Hastings, and the rest,
Yet thus far fortune maketh us amends,
And says that once more I shall interchange
My waned state for Henry's regal crown.
Well have we pass'd and now repass'd the seas
And brought desired help from Burgundy:
What then remains, we being thus arrived
From Ravenspurgh haven before the gates of York,
But that we enter, as into our dukedom?
  Glou.   The gates made fast! Brother, I like not this; 10
For many men that stumble at the threshold
Are well foretold that danger lurks within.
  K. Edw.   Tush, man, abodements must not now affright us:
By fair or foul means we must enter in,
For hither will our friends repair to us.
  Hast.   My liege, I'll knock once more to summon them.

Enter, on the walls, the Mayor of York, *and his Brethren.*

  May.   My lords, we were forewarned of your coming,
And shut the gates for safety of ourselves;
For now we owe allegiance unto Henry.
  K. Edw.   But, master mayor, if Henry be your king, 20
Yet Edward at the least is Duke of York.

May. True, my good lord; I know you for no less.

K. Edw. Why, and I challenge nothing but my dukedom,
As being well content with that alone.

Glou. [*Aside*] But when the fox hath once got in his nose,
He'll soon find means to make the body follow.

Hast. Why, master mayor, why stand you in a doubt?
Open the gates; we are King Henry's friends.

May. Ay, say you so? the gates shall then be open'd.   [*They descend.*

Glou. A wise stout captain, and soon persuaded!   30

Hast. The good old man would fain that all were well,
So 'twere not 'long of him; but being enter'd,
I doubt not, I, but we shall soon persuade
Both him and all his brothers unto reason.

Enter the Mayor *and two* Aldermen, *below.*

K. Edw. So, master mayor: these gates must not be shut
But in the night or in the time of war.
What! fear not, man, but yield me up the keys;   [*Takes his keys.*
For Edward will defend the town and thee,
And all those friends that deign to follow me.

March.   *Enter* MONTGOMERY, *with drum and soldiers.*

Glou. Brother, this is Sir John Montgomery,
Our trusty friend, unless I be deceived.   41

K. Edw. Welcome, Sir John! But why come you in arms?

Mont. To help King Edward in his time of storm,
As every loyal subject ought to do.

K. Edw. Thanks, good Montgomery; but we now forget
Our title to the crown and only claim
Our dukedom till God please to send the rest.

Mont. Then fare you well, for I will hence again:
I came to serve a king and not a duke.
Drummer, strike up, and let us march away.   50
    [*The drum begins to march.*

K. Edw. Nay, stay, Sir John, awhile, and we'll debate
By what safe means the crown may be recover'd.

Mont. What talk you of debating? in few words,
If you'll not here proclaim yourself our king,
I'll leave you to your fortune and be gone
To keep them back that come to succour you:
● Why shall we fight, if you pretend no title?

● *Glou.* Why, brother, wherefore stand you on nice points?

K. Edw. When we grow stronger, then we'll make our claim:
Till then, 'tis wisdom to conceal our meaning.   60

Hast. Away with scrupulous wit! now arms must rule.

Glou. And fearless minds climb soonest unto crowns.
● Brother, we will proclaim you out of hand;
● The bruit thereof will bring you many friends.

Costume design for King Edward by Ann Curtis, Royal Shakespeare Co, 1964

---

57 *pretend.* Demand.

58 *stand . . . points.* Be overscrupulous.

63 *out of hand.* At once, on the spot.

64 *bruit.* Rumour.

11 *son Clarence.* Son-in-law.

K. Edw. Then be it as you will; for 'tis my right,
And Henry but usurps the diadem.
  Mont. Ay, now my sovereign speaketh like himself;
And now will I be Edward's champion.
  Hast. Sound trumpet; Edward shall be here proclaim'd:
Come, fellow-soldier, make thou proclamation. 70
                                          [*Flourish.*
  Sold. Edward the Fourth, by the grace of God, king of England and France, and lord of Ireland, &c.
  Mont. And whosoe'er gainsays King Edward's right,
By this I challenge him to single fight.
                        [*Throws down his gauntlet.*
  All. Long live Edward the Fourth!
  K. Edw. Thanks, brave Montgomery; and thanks unto you all:
If fortune serve me, I'll requite this kindness.
Now, for this night, let's harbour here in York;
And when the morning sun shall raise his car   80
Above the border of this horizon,
We'll forward towards Warwick and his mates;
For well I wot that Henry is no soldier.
Ah, froward Clarence! how evil it beseems thee,
To flatter Henry and forsake thy brother!
Yet, as we may, we'll meet both thee and Warwick.
Come on, brave soldiers: doubt not of the day,
And, that once gotten, doubt not of large pay.
                                          [*Exeunt.*

SCENE VIII. *London. The palace.*

Flourish. Enter KING HENRY, WARWICK,
MONTAGUE, CLARENCE, EXETER, *and* OXFORD.

  War. What counsel, lords? Edward from Belgia,
With hasty Germans and blunt Hollanders,
Hath pass'd in safety through the narrow seas,
And with his troops doth march amain to London;
And many giddy people flock to him.
  K. Hen. Let's levy men, and beat him back again.
  Clar. A little fire is quickly trodden out;
Which, being suffer'd, rivers cannot quench.
  War. In Warwickshire I have true-hearted friends,
Not mutinous in peace, yet bold in war;   10
Those will I muster up: and thou, son Clarence,
Shalt stir up in Suffolk, Norfolk and in Kent,
The knights and gentlemen to come with thee:
Thou, brother Montague, in Buckingham,
Northampton and in Leicestershire, shalt find
Men well inclined to hear what thou command'st:
And thou, brave Oxford, wondrous well beloved,
In Oxfordshire shalt muster up thy friends.
My sovereign, with the loving citizens,
Like to his island girt in with the ocean,   20
Or modest Dian circled with her nymphs,
Shall rest in London till we come to him.
Fair lords, take leave and stand not to reply.
Farewell, my sovereign.
  K. Hen. Farewell, my Hector, and my Troy's true hope.
  Clar. In sign of truth, I kiss your highness' hand.

K. Hen. Well-minded Clarence, be thou for-
tunate!
Mont. Comfort, my lord; and so I take my
leave.
Oxf. And thus I seal my truth, and bid adieu.
K. Hen. Sweet Oxford, and my loving
Montague, 30
And all at once, once more a happy farewell.
War. Farewell, sweet lords: let's meet at
Coventry.
    [*Exeunt all but King Henry and Exeter.*
K. Hen. Here at the palace will I rest awhile.
Cousin of Exeter, what thinks your lordship?
Methinks the power that Edward hath in field
Should not be able to encounter mine.
Exe. The doubt is that he will seduce the rest.
 • *K. Hen.* That's not my fear; my meed hath
got me fame:
I have not stopp'd mine ears to their demands,
Nor posted off their suits with slow delays; 40
My pity hath been balm to heal their wounds,
My mildness hath allay'd their swelling griefs,
My mercy dried their water-flowing tears;
I have not been desirous of their wealth,
Nor much oppress'd them with great subsidies,
Nor forward of revenge, though they much err'd:
Then why should they love Edward more than me?
No, Exeter, these graces challenge grace:
And when the lion fawns upon the lamb,
The lamb will never cease to follow him. 50
    [*Shout within,* 'A Lancaster! A Lancaster!'
Exe. Hark, hark, my lord! what shouts are
these?

Enter KING EDWARD, GLOUCESTER, *and
soldiers.*

K. Edw. Seize on the shame-faced Henry,
bear him hence;
And once again proclaim us king of England.
You are the fount that makes small brooks to
flow:
Now stops thy spring; my sea shall suck
them dry,
And swell so much the higher by their ebb.
Hence with him to the Tower; let him not speak.
    [*Exeunt some with King Henry.*
And, lords, towards Coventry bend we our course,
Where peremptory Warwick now remains:
The sun shines hot; and, if we use delay, 60
Cold biting winter mars our hoped-for hay.
Glou. Away betimes, before his forces join,
And take the great-grown traitor unawares:
Brave warriors, march amain towards Coventry.
    [*Exeunt.*

ACT V.

SCENE I. *Coventry.*

Enter WARWICK, *the* Mayor of Coventry, *two*
Messengers, *and others upon the walls.*

War. Where is the post that came from
valiant Oxford?
How far hence is thy lord, mine honest fellow?
 • *First Mess.* By this at Dunsmore, marching
hitherward.
War. How far off is our brother Montague?
Where is the post that came from Montague?
 • *Second Mess.* By this at Daintry, with a
puissant troop.

38 *meed.* Merit.

View of Coventry at the time of Henry VI. Engraving
from *Old England,* 1854

---

3 *Dunsmore.* Dunsmore Heath between Daventry and
Coventry.

6 *Daintry.* The old pronunciation of Daventry.

36 *Thou . . . Atlas.* Atlas in Greek mythology carried the world on his shoulders.

43 *single ten.* A simple ten, not as valuable as a royal card.

Enter SIR JOHN SOMERVILLE.

War. Say, Somerville, what says my loving son?
And, by thy guess, how nigh is Clarence now?
  Som. At Southam I did leave him with his forces,
And do expect him here some two hours hence.
                                 [*Drum heard.*
  War. Then Clarence is at hand; I hear his drum.   11
  Som. It is not his, my lord; here Southam lies:
The drum your honour hears marcheth from Warwick.
  War. Who should that be? belike, unlook'd-for friends.
  Som. They are at hand, and you shall quickly know.

March: flourish. Enter KING EDWARD, GLOUCESTER, *and soldiers.*

  K. Edw. Go, trumpet, to the walls, and sound a parle.
  Glou. See how the surly Warwick mans the wall!
  War. O unbid spite! is sportful Edward come?
Where slept our scouts, or how are they seduced,
That we could hear no news of his repair?   20
  K. Edw. Now, Warwick, wilt thou ope the city gates,
Speak gentle words and humbly bend thy knee,
Call Edward king and at his hands beg mercy?
And he shall pardon thee these outrages.
  War. Nay, rather, wilt thou draw thy forces hence,
Confess who set thee up and pluck'd thee down,
Call Warwick patron and be penitent?
And thou shalt still remain the Duke of York.
  Glou. I thought, at least, he would have said the king;
Or did he make the jest against his will?   30
  War. Is not a dukedom, sir, a goodly gift?
  Glou. Ay, by my faith, for a poor earl to give:
I'll do thee service for so good a gift.
  War. 'Twas I that gave the kingdom to thy brother.
  K. Edw. Why then 'tis mine, if but by Warwick's gift.
  War. Thou art no Atlas for so great a weight:
And, weakling, Warwick takes his gift again;
And Henry is my king, Warwick his subject.
  K. Edw. But Warwick's king is Edward's prisoner:
And, gallant Warwick, do but answer this: 40
What is the body when the head is off?
  Glou. Alas, that Warwick had no more forecast,
But, whiles he thought to steal the single ten,
The king was slily finger'd from the deck!
You left poor Henry at the Bishop's palace,
And, ten to one, you'll meet him in the Tower.
  K. Edw. 'Tis even so; yet you are Warwick still.
  Glou. Come, Warwick, take the time; kneel down, kneel down:

Nay, when? strike now, or else the iron cools.
 War. I had rather chop this hand off at a
  blow,   50
And with the other fling it at thy face,
● Than bear so low a sail, to strike to thee.
 K. Edw. Sail how thou canst, have wind and
  tide thy friend,
This hand, fast wound about thy coal-black hair,
Shall, whiles thy head is warm and new cut off,
Write in the dust this sentence with thy blood,
'Wind-changing Warwick now can change no
  more.'

 Enter OXFORD, *with drum and colours.*

 War. O cheerful colours! see where Oxford
  comes!
 Oxf. Oxford, Oxford, for Lancaster!
    [*He and his forces enter the city.*
 Glou. The gates are open, let us enter too. 60
 K. Edw. So other foes may set upon our
  backs.
Stand we in good array; for they no doubt
Will issue out again and bid us battle:
If not, the city being but of small defence,
We'll quickly rouse the traitors in the same.
 War. O, welcome, Oxford! for we want
  thy help.

 Enter MONTAGUE, *with drum and colours.*

 Mont. Montague, Montague, for Lancaster!
    [*He and his forces enter the city.*
 Glou. Thou and thy brother both shall buy
  this treason
Even with the dearest blood your bodies bear.
 K. Edw. The harder match'd, the greater
  victory: 70
My mind presageth happy gain and conquest.

 Enter SOMERSET, *with drum and colours.*

 Som. Somerset, Somerset, for Lancaster!
    [*He and his forces enter the city.*
● *Glou.* Two of thy name, both Dukes of
  Somerset,
Have sold their lives unto the house of York;
And thou shalt be the third, if this sword hold.

 Enter CLARENCE, *with drum and colours.*

 War. And lo, where George of Clarence
  sweeps along,
Of force enough to bid his brother battle;
With whom an upright zeal to right prevails
More than the nature of a brother's love!
Come, Clarence, come; thou wilt, if Warwick
  call.   80
 Clar. Father of Warwick, know you what
  this means?
    [*Taking his red rose out of his hat.*
Look here, I throw my infamy at thee:
I will not ruinate my father's house,
Who gave his blood to lime the stones together,
● And set up Lancaster. Why, trow'st thou, War-
  wick,
That Clarence is so harsh, so blunt, unnatural,
To bend the fatal instruments of war
Against his brother and his lawful king?
Perhaps thou wilt object my holy oath:
To keep that oath were more impiety 90
● Than Jephthah's, when he sacrificed his daughter.
I am so sorry for my trespass made

52 *bear . . . sail.* So humble or demean myself.

Battle scene before a city. Woodcut from Holinshed's
Chronicles, 1577

73 *Two . . . Somerset.* The second duke, Edward, was
killed at St. Albans in 1455. His son, the third duke, was
executed after the battle of Hexham in 1464.

85 *trow'st thou.* Do you think.

91 *Jephthah's . . . daughter.* From Judges xi.30.

Battle of Barnet. From a contemporary Flemish manuscript

2 *bug.* Bugbear.

14 *Jove's spreading tree.* Oak.

Death of Warwick. *Above:* Drawing by P.J. De Loutherbourg (1740–1812). *Opposite:* Engraving from a painting by J.A. Houston (1812–84)

That, to deserve well at my brother's hands,
I here proclaim myself thy mortal foe,
With resolution, wheresoe'er I meet thee—
As I will meet thee, if thou stir abroad—
To plague thee for thy foul misleading me.
And so, proud-hearted Warwick, I defy thee,
And to my brother turn my blushing cheeks.
Pardon me, Edward, I will make amends: 100
And, Richard, do not frown upon my faults,
For I will henceforth be no more unconstant.
   K. Edw. Now welcome more, and ten times
     more beloved,
Than if thou never hadst deserved our hate.
   Glo. Welcome, good Clarence; this is brother-
     like.
   War. O passing traitor, perjured and unjust!
   K. Edw. What, Warwick, wilt thou leave the
     town and fight?
Or shall we beat the stones about thine ears?
   War. Alas, I am not coop'd here for de-
     fence!
I will away towards Barnet presently,   110
And bid thee battle, Edward, if thou darest.
   K. Edw. Yes, Warwick, Edward dares, and
     leads the way.
Lords, to the field; Saint George and victory!
    [*Exeunt King Edward and his company.*
      March. Warwick and his company
      follow.

SCENE II. *A field of battle near Barnet.*

Alarum and excursions. Enter KING EDWARD,
bringing forth WARWICK *wounded.*

   K. Edw. So, lie thou there: die thou, and
     die our fear;
• For Warwick was a bug that fear'd us all.
Now, Montague, sit fast; I seek for thee,
That Warwick's bones may keep thine company.
        [*Exit.*
   War. Ah, who is nigh? come to me, friend
     or foe,
And tell me who is victor, York or Warwick?
Why ask I that? my mangled body shows,
My blood, my want of strength, my sick heart
     shows,
That I must yield my body to the earth
And, by my fall, the conquest to my foe.   10
Thus yields the cedar to the axe's edge,
Whose arms gave shelter to the princely eagle,
Under whose shade the ramping lion slept,
• Whose top-branch overpeer'd Jove's spreading tree
And kept low shrubs from winter's powerful wind.
These eyes, that now are dimm'd with death's
     black veil,
Have been as piercing as the mid-day sun,
To search the secret treasons of the world:
The wrinkles in my brows, now fill'd with blood,
Were liken'd oft to kingly sepulchres;   20
For who lived king, but I could dig his grave?
And who durst smile when Warwick bent his
     brow?
Lo, now my glory smear'd in dust and blood!
My parks, my walks, my manors that I had,
Even now forsake me, and of all my lands
Is nothing left me but my body's length.
Why, what is pomp, rule, reign, but earth and
     dust?
And, live we how we can, yet die we must.

Field of battle near Barnet. Engraving from *Old England*, 1854

---

5 *sun.* York emblem.

8 *Gallia.* France.

12 *beams.* i.e. from the sun of York.

Enter OXFORD *and* SOMERSET.

Som. Ah, Warwick, Warwick! wert thou as
    we are,
We might recover all our loss again: 30
The queen from France hath brought a puissant
    power:
Even now we heard the news: ah, couldst thou
    fly!
War. Why, then I would not fly. Ah, Mon-
    tague,
If thou be there, sweet brother, take my hand,
And with thy lips keep in my soul awhile!
Thou lovest me not; for, brother, if thou didst,
Thy tears would wash this cold congealed blood
That glues my lips and will not let me speak.
Come quickly, Montague, or I am dead.
Som. Ah, Warwick! Montague hath breathed
    his last;   40
And to the latest gasp cried out for Warwick
And said 'Commend me to my valiant brother.'
And more he would have said, and more he spoke,
Which sounded like a clamour in a vault,
That mought not be distinguish'd; but at last
I well might hear, deliver'd with a groan,
'O, farewell, Warwick!'
War. Sweet rest his soul! Fly, lords, and
    save yourselves;
For Warwick bids you all farewell, to meet in
    heaven.   [*Dies.*
Oxf. Away, away, to meet the queen's great
    power!   [*Here they bear away his body.*
    Exeunt.

SCENE III. *Another part of the field.*

Flourish. Enter KING EDWARD *in triumph;
with* GLOUCESTER, CLARENCE, *and the rest.*

K. Edw. Thus far our fortune keeps an up-
    ward course,
And we are graced with wreaths of victory.
But, in the midst of this bright-shining day,
I spy a black, suspicious, threatening cloud,
That will encounter with our glorious sun,
Ere he attain his easeful western bed:
I mean, my lords, those powers that the queen
Hath raised in Gallia have arrived our coast
And, as we hear, march on to fight with us.
Clar. A little gale will soon disperse that
    cloud   10
And blow it to the source from whence it came:
The very beams will dry those vapours up,
For every cloud engenders not a storm.
Glo. The queen is valued thirty thousand
    strong,
And Somerset, with Oxford, fled to her:
If she have time to breathe, be well assured
Her faction will be full as strong as ours.
K. Edw. We are advertised by our loving
    friends
That they do hold their course toward Tewks-
    bury:
We, having now the best at Barnet field,   20
Will thither straight, for willingness rids way;
And, as we march, our strength will be aug-
    mented
In every county as we go along.
Strike up the drum; cry 'Courage!' and away.
    [*Exeunt.*

SCENE IV. *Plains near Tewksbury.*

March. Enter QUEEN MARGARET, PRINCE
EDWARD, SOMERSET, OXFORD, *and soldiers.*

Q. Mar. Great lords, wise men ne'er sit and
    wail their loss,
But cheerly seek how to redress their harms.
What though the mast be now blown overboard,
The cable broke, the holding-anchor lost,
And half our sailors swallow'd in the flood?
Yet lives our pilot still.   Is't meet that he
Should leave the helm and like a fearful lad
With tearful eyes add water to the sea
And give more strength to that which hath too
    much,   9
Whiles, in his moan, the ship splits on the rock,
Which industry and courage might have saved?
Ah, what a shame! ah, what a fault were this!
Say Warwick was our anchor; what of that?
And Montague our topmast; what of him?
Our slaughter'd friends the tackles; what of
    these?
Why, is not Oxford here another anchor?
And Somerset another goodly mast?
The friends of France our shrouds and tack-
    lings?
And, though unskilful, why not Ned and I
For once allow'd the skilful pilot's charge?   20
We will not from the helm to sit and weep,
But keep our course, though the rough wind say
    no,
From shelves and rocks that threaten us with
    wreck.
As good to chide the waves as speak them fair.
And what is Edward but a ruthless sea?
What Clarence but a quicksand of deceit?
And Richard but a ragged fatal rock?
All these the enemies to our poor bark.
Say you can swim; alas, 'tis but a while!
Tread on the sand; why, there you quickly sink:
Bestride the rock; the tide will wash you off, 31
Or else you famish; that's a threefold death.
This speak I, lords, to let you understand,
If case some one of you would fly from us,
That there's no hoped-for mercy with the brothers
More than with ruthless waves, with sands and
    rocks.
Why, courage then! what cannot be avoided
'Twere childish weakness to lament or fear.
    Prince. Methinks a woman of this valiant
        spirit
Should, if a coward heard her speak these words,
Infuse his breast with magnanimity   41
And make him, naked, foil a man at arms.
I speak not this as doubting any here;
For did I but suspect a fearful man,
He should have leave to go away betimes,
Lest in our need he might infect another
And make him of like spirit to himself.
If any such be here—as God forbid!—
Let him depart before we need his help.
    Oxf. Women and children of so high a cou-
        rage,   50
And warriors faint! why, 'twere perpetual shame.
O brave young prince! thy famous grandfather
Doth live again in thee: long mayst thou live
To bear his image and renew his glories!
    Som. And he that will not fight for such a
        hope,

Battle of Tewksbury. Engraving from John Speed's
Theatre of the Empire of Great Britaine, 1611–12

23 *shelves.* Shoals.

42 *foil . . . arms.* Overcome an armed soldier.

52 *grandfather.* Henry V.

Battle scene at the time of Edward IV. Woodcut from Holinshed's *Chronicles*, 1577

2 *Hames Castle*. Hames Castle near Calais.

Execution of the Duke of Somerset after the Battle of Tewksbury. From a contemporary Flemish manuscript

8 *Jerusalem*. Heaven.

11 *youthful Edward*. Margaret's son.

Go home to bed, and like the owl by day,
If he arise, be mock'd and wonder'd at.
  Q. Mar. Thanks, gentle Somerset; sweet Oxford, thanks.
  Prince. And take his thanks that yet hath nothing else.

Enter a Messenger.

  Mess. Prepare you, lords, for Edward is at hand, 60
Ready to fight; therefore be resolute.
  Oxf. I thought no less: it is his policy
To haste thus fast, to find us unprovided.
  Som. But he's deceived; we are in readiness.
  Q. Mar. This cheers my heart, to see your forwardness.
  Oxf. Here pitch our battle; hence we will not budge.

Flourish and march. Enter KING EDWARD, GLOUCESTER, CLARENCE, *and soldiers.*

  K. Edw. Brave followers, yonder stands the thorny wood,
Which, by the heavens' assistance and your strength,
Must by the roots be hewn up yet ere night.
I need not add more fuel to your fire, 70
For well I wot ye blaze to burn them out:
Give signal to the fight, and to it, lords!
  Q. Mar. Lords, knights, and gentlemen, what I should say
My tears gainsay; for every word I speak,
Ye see, I drink the water of mine eyes.
Therefore, no more but this: Henry, your sovereign,
Is prisoner to the foe; his state usurp'd,
His realm a slaughter-house, his subjects slain,
His statutes cancell'd and his treasure spent;
And yonder is the wolf that makes this spoil. 80
You fight in justice: then, in God's name, lords,
Be valiant and give signal to the fight.
  [*Alarum: Retreat: Excursions. Exeunt.*

SCENE V. *Another part of the field.*

Flourish. Enter KING EDWARD, GLOUCESTER, CLARENCE, *and soldiers; with* QUEEN MARGARET, OXFORD, *and* SOMERSET, *prisoners.*

  K. Edw. Now here a period of tumultuous broils.
Away with Oxford to Hames Castle straight:
For Somerset, off with his guilty head.
Go, bear them hence; I will not hear them speak.
  Oxf. For my part, I'll not trouble thee with words.
  Som. Nor I, but stoop with patience to my fortune.
  [*Exeunt Oxford and Somerset, guarded.*
  Q. Mar. So part we sadly in this troublous world,
To meet with joy in sweet Jerusalem.
  K. Edw. Is proclamation made, that who finds Edward
Shall have a high reward, and he his life? 10
  Glou. It is: and lo, where youthful Edward comes!

Enter soldiers, with PRINCE EDWARD.

K. Edw. Bring forth the gallant, let us hear
him speak.
What! can so young a thorn begin to prick?
Edward, what satisfaction canst thou make
For bearing arms, for stirring up my subjects,
And all the trouble thou hast turn'd me to?
   Prince. Speak like a subject, proud ambitious
York!
Suppose that I am now my father's mouth;
Resign thy chair, and where I stand kneel thou,
Whilst I propose the selfsame words to thee, 20
Which, traitor, thou wouldst have me answer to.
   Q. Mar. Ah, that thy father had been so re-
solved!
   Glou. That you might still have worn the
petticoat,
- And ne'er have stol'n the breech from Lancaster.
-    *Prince.* Let Æsop fable in a winter's night;
His currish riddles sort not with this place.
   Glou. By heaven, brat, I'll plague ye for that
word.
   Q. Mar. Ay, thou wast born to be a plague
to men.
   Glou. For God's sake, take away this captive
scold.
   Prince. Nay, take away this scolding crook-
back rather. 30
   K. Edw. Peace, wilful boy, or I will charm
your tongue.
-    *Clar.* Untutor'd lad, thou art too malapert.
   Prince. I know my duty; you are all un-
dutiful:
Lascivious Edward, and thou perjured George,
And thou mis-shapen Dick, I tell ye all
I am your better, traitors as ye are:
And thou usurp'st my father's right and mine.
   K. Edw. Take that, thou likeness of this
railer here.   [*Stabs him.*
   Glou. Sprawl'st thou? take that, to end thy
agony.   [*Stabs him.*
   Cla. And there's for twitting me with per-
jury.   [*Stabs him.* 40
   Q. Mar. O, kill me too!
   Glou. Marry, and shall.   [*Offers to kill her.*
   K. Edw. Hold, Richard, hold; for we have
done too much.
   Glou. Why should she live, to fill the world
with words?
   K. Edw. What, doth she swoon? use means
for her recovery.
   Glou. Clarence, excuse me to the king my
brother;
I'll hence to London on a serious matter:
Ere ye come there, be sure to hear some news.
   Clar. What? what?
   Glou. The Tower, the Tower.   [*Exit.* 50
   Q. Mar. O Ned, sweet Ned! speak to thy
mother, boy!
Canst thou not speak? O traitors! murderers!
They that stabb'd Cæsar shed no blood at all,
Did not offend, nor were not worthy blame,
If this foul deed were by to equal it:
He was a man; this, in respect, a child:
And men ne'er spend their fury on a child.
What's worse than murderer, that I may name it?
No, no, my heart will burst, an if I speak:
And I will speak, that so my heart may burst. 60

24 *breech.* Breeches.

25–26 *Let Aesop . . . place.* Prince Edward is taking a
jibe at Richard by likening him to Aesop who was
reputed to have been deformed; accusing him of lying,
'fabling', about the relationship between his parents.

32 *malapert.* Pert.

Death of the Prince of Wales. Edward IV (John
Humphrey) Richard of Gloucester (Derek Godfrey),
Queen Margaret (Barbara Jefford), Clarence (David
Dodimead) and the Prince of Wales (John Rye), Old Vic
Theatre, London, 1957

67 *rid.* Murdered.

75 *thou . . . forswear thyself.* You make a practice of going back on your oaths.

80 *put'st back.* Send away.

84 *post.* i.e. post haste.

10 *Roscius.* Renowned Roman actor.

14 *misdoubteth.* Suspects.

Gloucester with King Henry VI. Drawing by J.M. Wright (1777–1866)

Butchers and villains! bloody cannibals!
How sweet a plant have you untimely cropp'd!
You have no children, butchers! if you had,
The thought of them would have stirr'd up re-
   morse:
But if you ever chance to have a child,
Look in his youth to have him so cut off
● As, deathsmen, you have rid this sweet young
   prince!
  K. Edw. Away with her; go, bear her hence
   perforce.
  Q. Mar. Nay, never bear me hence, dispatch
   me here;
Here sheathe thy sword, I'll pardon thee my
   death: 70
What, wilt thou not? then, Clarence, do it thou.
  Clar. By heaven, I will not do thee so much
   ease.
  Q. Mar. Good Clarence, do; sweet Clarence,
   do thou do it.
  Clar. Didst thou not hear me swear I would
   not do it?
● *Q. Mar.* Ay, but thou usest to forswear thy-
   self:
'Twas sin before, but now 'tis charity.
What, wilt thou not? Where is that devil's but-
   cher,
Hard-favour'd Richard? Richard, where art thou?
Thou art not here: murder is thy alms-deed;
● Petitioners for blood thou ne'er put'st back.   80
  K. Edw. Away, I say; I charge ye, bear her
   hence.
  Q. Mar. So come to you and yours, as to this
   prince!   [*Exit, led out forcibly.*
  K. Edw. Where's Richard gone?
  Clar. To London, all in post; and, as I guess,
To make a bloody supper in the Tower.
  K. Edw. He's sudden, if a thing comes in his
   head.
Now march we hence: discharge the common sort
With pay and thanks, and let's away to London
And see our gentle queen how well she fares:
By this, I hope, she hath a son for me.   90
                          [*Exeunt.*

SCENE VI. *London. The Tower.*

Enter KING HENRY *and* GLOUCESTER, *with the*
  Lieutenant, *on the walls.*

  Glou. Good day, my lord. What, at your
   book so hard?
  K. Hen. Ay, my good lord:—my lord, I
   should say rather;
'Tis sin to flatter; 'good' was little better:
'Good Gloucester' and 'good devil' were alike,
And both preposterous; therefore, not 'good
   lord.'
  Glou. Sirrah, leave us to ourselves: we must
   confer.   [*Exit Lieutenant.*
  K. Hen. So flies the reckless shepherd from
   the wolf;
So first the harmless sheep doth yield his fleece
And next his throat unto the butcher's knife.
● What scene of death hath Roscius now to act? 10
  Glou. Suspicion always haunts the guilty mind;
The thief doth fear each bush an officer.
  K. Hen. The bird that hath been limed in a
   bush,
● With trembling wings misdoubteth every bush;

And I, the hapless male to one sweet bird,
Have now the fatal object in my eye
Where my poor young was limed, was caught
    and kill'd.
 Glou. Why, what a peevish fool was that of
    Crete,
That taught his son the office of a fowl! 19
● And yet, for all his wings, the fool was drown'd.
 K. Hen. I, Dædalus; my poor boy, Icarus;
Thy father, Minos, that denied our course;
● The sun that sear'd the wings of my sweet boy
Thy brother Edward, and thyself the sea
Whose envious gulf did swallow up his life.
Ah, kill me with thy weapon, not with words!
My breast can better brook thy dagger's point
Than can my ears that tragic history.
But wherefore dost thou come? is't for my life?
 Glou. Think'st thou I am an executioner? 30
 K. Hen. A persecutor, I am sure, thou art:
If murdering innocents be executing,
Why, then thou art an executioner.
 Glou. Thy son I kill'd for his presumption.
 K. Hen. Hadst thou been kill'd when first
    thou didst presume,
Thou hadst not lived to kill a son of mine.
And thus I prophesy, that many a thousand,
● Which now mistrust no parcel of my fear,
And many an old man's sigh and many a widow's,
● And many an orphan's water-standing eye— 40
Men for their sons, wives for their husbands,
● And orphans for their parents' timeless death—
Shall rue the hour that ever thou wast born.
The owl shriek'd at thy birth,—an evil sign;
● The night-crow cried, aboding luckless time;
Dogs howl'd, and hideous tempest shook down
    trees;
● The raven rook'd her on the chimney's top,
● And chattering pies in dismal discords sung.
Thy mother felt more than a mother's pain,
And yet brought forth less than a mother's hope,
To wit, an indigested and deformed lump, 51
Not like the fruit of such a goodly tree.
Teeth hadst thou in thy head when thou wast
    born,
To signify thou camest to bite the world:
And, if the rest be true which I have heard,
Thou camest—
 Glou. I'll hear no more: die, prophet, in thy
    speech: [*Stabs him.*
For this, amongst the rest, was I ordain'd.
 K. Hen. Ay, and for much more slaughter
    after this.
O, God forgive my sins, and pardon thee! [*Dies.*
 Glou. What, will the aspiring blood of Lan-
    caster 61
Sink in the ground? I thought it would have
    mounted.
See how my sword weeps for the poor king's
    death!
● O, may such purple tears be alway shed
From those that wish the downfall of our house!
If any spark of life be yet remaining,
Down, down to hell; and say I sent thee thither:
    [*Stabs him again.*
I, that have neither pity, love, nor fear.
Indeed, 'tis true that Henry told me of;
For I have often heard my mother say 70
I came into the world with my legs forward:
Had I not reason, think ye, to make haste,

20–23 *wings . . . boy.* Daedalus and his son Icarus tried to escape from King Minos by flying with wings made from wax and feathers. Icarus soared too near the sun, the wax melted and he fell to his death.

Icarus falling to the sea. Dutch engraving, 1733

23 *sun.* Heraldic device of King Edward.

38 *mistrust no parcel.* Have no inkling.

40 *water-standing eye.* Eyes drenched in tears.

42 *timeless.* Untimely.

45 *aboding.* Foreboding.

47 *rook'd her.* Squatted, cowered.

48 *pies.* Magpies.

64 *purple tears.* Drops of blood.

85 *sort . . . day.* Choose a black day.

86 *buz.* Whisper.

King Edward: 'Once more we sit in England's royal throne'. Edward, Elizabeth and the young Prince. Engraving from a painting by James Northcote (1746–1831).

9 *coursers.* War horses, chargers.

10 *bear.* Emblem of the Nevilles.

20–21 *reap . . . laid.* By murdering Edward's son, once the father is dead.

22 *look'd on.* Looked up to, respected.

And seek their ruin that usurp'd our right?
The midwife wonder'd and the women cried
'O, Jesus bless us, he is born with teeth!'
And so I was; which plainly signified
That I should snarl and bite and play the dog.
Then, since the heavens have shaped my body so,
Let hell make crook'd my mind to answer it.
I have no brother, I am like no brother;   80
And this word 'love,' which greybeards call divine,
Be resident in men like one another
And not in me: I am myself alone.
Clarence, beware; thou keep'st me from the light:
• But I will sort a pitchy day for thee;
• For I will buz abroad such prophecies
That Edward shall be fearful of his life,
And then, to purge his fear, I'll be thy death.
King Henry and the prince his son are gone:
Clarence, thy turn is next, and then the rest, 90
Counting myself but bad till I be best.
I'll throw thy body in another room
And triumph, Henry, in thy day of doom.
            [*Exit, with the body.*

SCENE VII. *London.   The palace.*

Flourish. Enter KING EDWARD, QUEEN ELIZA-
BETH, CLARENCE, GLOUCESTER, HASTINGS,
a Nurse *with the young Prince, and* Attendants.

   K. Edw. Once more we sit in England's royal
      throne,
Re-purchased with the blood of enemies.
What valiant foemen, like to autumn's corn,
Have we mow'd down in tops of all their pride!
Three Dukes of Somerset, threefold renown'd
For hardy and undoubted champions;
Two Cliffords, as the father and the son,
And two Northumberlands; two braver men
• Ne'er spurr'd their coursers at the trumpet's
      sound;
• With them, the two brave bears, Warwick and
      Montague,   10
That in their chains fetter'd the kingly lion
And made the forest tremble when they roar'd.
Thus have we swept suspicion from our seat
And made our footstool of security.
Come hither, Bess, and let me kiss my boy.
Young Ned, for thee, thine uncles and myself
Have in our armours watch'd the winter's night,
Went all afoot in summer's scalding heat,
That thou mightst repossess the crown in peace:
• And of our labours thou shalt reap the gain. 20
   Glou. [*Aside*] I'll blast his harvest, if your
      head were laid;
• For yet I am not look'd on in the world.
This shoulder was ordain'd so thick to heave;
And heave it shall some weight, or break my
      back:
Work thou the way,—and thou shalt execute.
   K. Edw. Clarence and Gloucester, love my
      lovely queen;
And kiss your princely nephew, brothers both.
   Clar. The duty that I owe unto your majesty
I seal upon the lips of this sweet babe.
   Q. Eliz. Thanks, noble Clarence; worthy
      brother, thanks.   30
   Glou. And, that I love the tree from whence
      thou sprang'st,
Witness the loving kiss I give the fruit.

[*Aside*] To say the truth, so Judas kiss'd his
    master,
And cried 'all hail!' when as he meant all harm.
    K. Edw. Now am I seated as my soul de-
    lights,
Having my country's peace and brothers' loves.
    Clar. What will your grace have done with
    Margaret?
Reignier, her father, to the king of **France**
- Hath pawn'd the Sicils and Jerusalem,
And hither have they sent it for her ransom.
-   *K. Edw.* Away with her, and waft her hence
    to France.
And now what rests but that we spend the time
With stately triumphs, mirthful comic shows,
Such as befits the pleasure of the court?
Sound drums and trumpets! farewell sour annoy!
For here, I hope, begins our lasting joy.
                        [*Exeunt*

39 *the Sicils.* The kingdoms of the two Sicilies; Naples and Sicily.

41 *waft.* Convey across the sea.

Derek Godfrey as Gloucester, with the young Prince.
Queen Elizabeth (Rosemary Webster), Edward IV
(John Humphrey) and Clarence (David Dodimead),
Old Vic Theatre, London, 1957

King Richard III

1592

RICHARD III is the first of the plays to hold the stage unbrokenly from Shakespeare's day to this. It has always been popular, and it is easy to see why. It offers exciting drama as such, completely integrated as the Chronicle plays of *Henry VI* could not hope to be; though the longest, except for *Hamlet*, one's attention is compelled at every moment. Above all, it has the compulsive fascination of Shakespeare's first fully developed character as a psychological study. Dr. Johnson spotted the psychotic interest of Richard's character – he is not merely a Machiavellian villain: 'the wickedness of Richard proceeded from his deformity, from the envy that rose at the comparison of his own person with others, and which incited him to disturb the pleasures that he could not partake.'

In short, Richard takes his place as first in the remarkable gallery of psychotic characters – Richard II, Othello and perhaps Iago (to whom Richard is closest akin), Macbeth and Lady Macbeth, King Lear and Leontes – who have their special appeal to modern psycho-analysis. The findings of modern psychology – Oedipus complex, paranoia, schizophrenia – Shakespeare astonishingly prefigured. It is perhaps less astonishing in that his knowledge of the human personality was not only that of external observation but understanding of the intuitive and the subconscious.

This had its first full expression in *Richard III*, whose personality lent itself obviously to the treatment. Shakespeare understood Richard as he was historically with his usual penetration; the only thing he added was a certain gaiety, a self-conscious delight in doing evil, which was not present in the historic Richard, who was a morose, unappealing character.

The play is sometimes described, depreciatingly, as a melodrama. But this is only Greek for a musical, and it would make a striking modern musical, as *West Side Story* was made out of *Romeo and Juliet* – such is the undying vitality of Shakespeare's creations.

The Character of Richard. Richard has abounding vitality, a marked character of his own, already adumbrated in *3 Henry VI*; this is in its way a source of attraction. Sixteenth century people were fairly close to Richard – after all, it was Elizabeth I's

*Edmund Kean as
Richard III,
Theatre Royal,
Drury Lane,
London, 1814*

grandfather who had given him his come-uppance – and knew perfectly well what was what about him. Shakespeare's portrait derives, through Holinshed and Hall, mainly from Sir Thomas More. Thomas More was a truth-telling man of great political intelligence and close observation, who had still closer sources of information as to Richard's *coup d'état*, his usurpation of his nephew's throne, and his murders of his brother's boys in the Tower. More was a friend of the Earl of Surrey, afterwards Duke of Norfolk, who was in the room when Richard arrested his brother's great friend, Hastings, and haled him out to summary execution without any pretence at trial. After that there was no turning back, as Richard says in the play – he is so far *in*. More knew Richard Fitz James, Bishop of London and others who were on the spot; his father, Sir John More, was a young lawyer in the city at the time.

Everybody knew what Richard was and what he had done, though the murders were kept a dark secret, and the details were covered up – More as a trained lawyer ferreted them out. In the ghastly Wars of the Roses people had become familiarised with the killing of opponents – after all Richard was known to have been in the Tower the night that Henry VI died there; but it was not done to murder women or children. This was what turned the country's stomach against Richard, and accounted for the defection of his leading supporter, Buckingham. The play itself employs the word 'homicide' for him: the term of the Act of Parliament which condemned him after Bosworth. Actually, at Bosworth, where his army was twice the size of Henry Tudor's, only Richard's cronies fought for him. The Howard 'Jack of Norfolk', whom he had made Duke, was killed with Richard. In Shakespeare's time Norfolk's great-grandson, Lord Henry Howard, in his *Defensative against Supposed Prophecies* (1583), in only the decade before the play, betrays the Howard family tradition as to Richard's 'heinous' crime. Everybody knew. It needs no explaining.

One marked difference is that where More treats Richard with grave and subtle irony, much more searing, Shakespeare treats him with his usual high spirits. There is even a comic aspect in the play. Richard is a conscious hypocrite, over and over, notably in the scene where he displays such reluctance to assume the burden of the crown. In fact, at the time of his *coup d'état*, Richard did a certain amount of ham-acting, which took in nobody; Buckingham had to play up too. This becomes, as the actor-dramatist describes from experience:

> Richard: Come cousin, canst thou quake, and change thy colour,
> Murder thy breath in middle of a word,
> And then again begin, and stop again,
> As if thou wert distraught and mad with terror?
> Buckingham: Tut, I can counterfeit the deep tragedian,
> Speak and look back, and pry on every side,
> Tremble and start at wagging of a straw,
> Intending deep suspicion: ghastly looks
> Are at my service, like enforcèd smiles . . .

Elizabethan acting was oratorical and emphatic – needs must with open-air theatres – very gestural and formal.[1]

Shakespeare took obvious delight in exploring the crevices of his tragic hero – for there is something heroic in Richard's ambition and scheming against such odds, and his eventual arriving where he intended to be, as also his fate was tragic. More subtlety appears in his depiction than in any of Shakespeare's characters so far. One notices that there is an element of neurosis in Richard: in his last interview with Buckingham he is beginning to lose control; on receiving the bad news of Buckingham's revolt, he strikes the messenger and then rewards him 'to cure that blow of thine'. Dr. Johnson noticed a subtlety that few notice. In the very first scene Richard says to Clarence:

1. Cf. B.L. Joseph: *Elizabethan Acting*.

> Whatso'er you will employ me in,
> Were it to call King Edward's *widow* sister,
> I will perform it.

It is a subtle invitation to speed their brother out of this world: his wife is not yet a widow. At Buckingham's revolt Richard is nerve-racked with anxiety – and no wonder, all that effort and scheming had been too much for him. While, in the night before Bosworth, tortured by dreams and the ghosts of his victims – the lights 'burn blue' as in *Julius Caesar* – one can sympathise with him, facing his fearful fate. (The body of an anointed king would never have been so maltreated, as it was after Bosworth, had he not been the criminal he was – led on by the mania for power, like Hitler, who came to a similarly squalid end.)

Characterisation. In spite of this being a one-man play – and so a favourite with great actors, from Burbage onwards – other characters are sufficiently individualised. Queen Margaret appears again in her role of Cassandra; Edward IV's Queen Elizabeth is drawn as the feather-headed light-weight she was, not knowing which way to turn, poor woman. Hastings is the over-confident, lusty extrovert, boon-companion of Edward IV in their womanising. We have no reason to doubt that Richard's disapproval of this was genuine: a wizened, unattractive type physically, unlike his two handsome brothers, he was not very good at sex, and so envious and disapproving (again understandably; life had treated him unfairly: he is getting his own back). Clarence is the 'false, fleeting, perjured' Clarence: wonderfully good-looking, and no good at all. Even his murderers are well-contrasted; the second murderer hasn't the heart to go on with it, and there is a comically realistic passage which is pure Shakespeare on the lower orders:

> 'I'll not meddle with it: it makes a man a coward. A man cannot steal, but it accuseth him; a man cannot swear, but it checks him; a man cannot lie with his neighbour's wife, but it detects him.'

And so on: 'some certain dregs of conscience are yet within me.'
  Richard's answer to that sort of thing is:

> Conscience is but a word that cowards use,
> Devised at first to keep the strong in awe.

His argument is that often advanced at critical junctures – 'the necessity and state of times.' It is in keeping with the casuistry of high politics, and testifies to Shakespeare's growing understanding of their inwardness:

> Look what is done cannot be now amended:
> Men shall deal unadvisedly sometimes,
> Which after-hours gives leisure to repent.

What makes this a tragedy rather than a melodrama is that he had been cruelly tempted and he cruelly fell: if only he had been able to produce the Princes alive from the Tower, he would have been able to answer his enemies. He never could: they were dead precisely two years before Bosworth.
  Of the dreams, omens, prophecies, curses that send a shiver down the spine in these plays, the most justly famous dream – along with Richard's before Bosworth – is

Clarence's in the Tower. He dreams beforehand his death by drowning:

> Methought I saw a thousand fearful wracks,
> A thousand men that fishes gnawed upon;
> Wedges of gold, great ingots, heaps of pearl,
> Inestimable stones, unvalued jewels,
> All scattered in the bottom of the sea.
> Some lay in dead men's skulls; and in the holes
> Where eyes did once inhabit there were crept,
> As 'twere in scorn of eyes, reflecting gems . . .

This would become in the far future, more concisely:

> Those are pearls that were his eyes.

Brackenbury, Constable of the Tower, comments as Clarence falls asleep:

> Princes have but their titles for their glories,
> An outward honour for an inward toil;
> And for unfelt imaginations
> They often feel a world of restless cares,
> So that between their titles and low name
> There's nothing differs but the outward fame.

This would become the dominant theme of the second tetralogy – *Richard II, 1* and *2 Henry IV, Henry V.*

Style. We notice from these speeches, indeed from the word go in the famous first speech of the play, how rapidly the verse has matured from the *Henry VI* plays: the actor is now writing verse with absolute confidence, conviction and precision:

> Now is the winter of our discontent
> Made glorious summer by this sun of York.

Success. In one of the *Parnassus* plays at Cambridge a few years later, in which the triumphs of the London stage and its authors were made fun of, we see how famous these lines had already become. Burbage is trying out a young scholar for the part:

Burbage: I like your face and the proportion of your body [no compliment that!] for Richard III. I pray you, Master Philomusus, let me see you act a little of it.

The young scholar immediately fires off with

> Now is the winter of our discontent
> Made glorious by the sun of York.

The line to become most famous was Richard's cry at Bosworth when unhorsed:

> A horse! a horse! My kingdom for a horse!

This line was repeated and parodied again and again. Burbage was so famous in the role he created that when delightful Bishop Corbet was being shown over the battlefield a generation later, the guide quoted it, but 'when he would have said "King Richard died", he "Burbage" cried.'

Success registered itself, too, in London folklore, the kind of story told about those who penetrate into people's inner consciousness, and which they take absurd delight in retailing. Manningham wrote in his Diary in 1602: 'Upon a time when Burbage played Richard III there was a citizen grew so far in liking with him that, before she went from the play, she appointed him to come that night unto her by the name of Richard III. Shakespeare, overhearing their conclusion, went before, was entertained and at his game ere Burbage came. The message being brought that Richard III was at the door, Shakespeare caused return to be made that William the Conqueror was before Richard III.'

So popular was the play that there was a continual demand for it in print – which, of course, it was not to the interest of Shakespeare or the Company to supply. Somehow, almost certainly through actors, the printers got hold of a shortened, acting version of the play for print as a quarto, which came out in 1597. Between then and 1622 no less than six editions were called for, a number equalled only by the quarto of *1 Henry IV* in which Falstaff figures. It would seem that Richard III and Falstaff were the two favourite Shakespearean characters with the Elizabethan public.

Shakespeare himself was so swept up into his subject that the play does not contain many references to anything extraneous. Everyone has observed that the play is a Marlovian one in the sense of its being dominated by one character and that a Machiavellian villain. I notice a verbal reminiscence of Dr. Faustus' end in Richard's night-thoughts before Bosworth:

> I shall despair. There is no creature loves me;
> And if I die, no soul will pity me.

There is a less obvious echo from Greene's *Farewell to Folly* (1591) in

> My conscience hath a thousand several tongues;

but this may be an Elizabethan commonplace. In the lines –

> Look how my ring encompasseth thy finger,
> Even so thy breast encloseth my poor heart –

I detect the kind of thought running all through the Sonnets contemporaneously. It is thought that the play belongs to the period of the plague years, 1592–3, when Shakespeare was free from playing to write so much. It cannot have come long after the *Third Part of Henry VI*; so 1592 would seem to be about right for its date.

Text. The Folio text in 1623 of this long play was based upon that of the latest quarto, of 1622, which went back to earlier printed versions, compared with one which had served for a prompt book in the theatre. The result was many misprints and dubious readings, which have provided good game for textual editors. These have never stood in the way of the general enjoyment of Shakespeare's first great play.

THE TRAGEDY OF
KING RICHARD THE THIRD.

DRAMATIS PERSONÆ.

KING EDWARD the Fourth.

EDWARD, Prince of Wales, afterwards King Edward V., }
RICHARD, Duke of York, } sons to the King.

GEORGE, Duke of Clarence, }
RICHARD, Duke of Gloucester, afterwards King Richard III., } brothers to the King.

A young son of Clarence.

HENRY, Earl of Richmond, afterwards King Henry VII.

CARDINAL BOURCHIER, Archbishop of Canterbury.

THOMAS ROTHERHAM, Archbishop of York.

JOHN MORTON, Bishop of Ely.

DUKE OF BUCKINGHAM.

DUKE OF NORFOLK.

EARL OF SURREY, his son.

EARL RIVERS, brother to Elizabeth.

MARQUIS OF DORSET and LORD GREY, sons to Elizabeth.

EARL OF OXFORD.

LORD HASTINGS.

LORD STANLEY, called also EARL OF DERBY.

LORD LOVEL.

SIR THOMAS VAUGHAN.

SIR RICHARD RATCLIFF.

SIR WILLIAM CATESBY.

SIR JAMES TYRREL.

SIR JAMES BLOUNT.

SIR WALTER HERBERT.

SIR ROBERT BRAKENBURY, Lieutenant of the Tower.

CHRISTOPHER URSWICK, a priest. Another Priest.

TRESSEL and BERKELEY, gentlemen attending on the Lady Anne.

Lord Mayor of London.   Sheriff of Wiltshire.

ELIZABETH, queen to King Edward IV.

MARGARET, widow of King Henry VI.

DUCHESS OF YORK, mother to King Edward IV.

LADY ANNE, widow of Edward Prince of Wales, son to King Henry VI.; afterwards married to Richard.

A young Daughter of Clarence (MARGARET PLANTAGENET).

Ghosts of those murdered by Richard III., Lords and other Attendants; a Pursuivant, Scrivener, Citizens, Murderers, Messengers, Soldiers, &c.

SCENE: *England.*

● *A bullet beside a text line indicates an annotation in the opposite column*

ACT I.

SCENE I. *London. A street.*

Enter RICHARD, DUKE OF GLOUCESTER, *solus.*

  Glou. Now is the winter of our discontent

● Made glorious summer by this sun of York;
And all the clouds that lour'd upon our house
In the deep bosom of the ocean buried.
Now are our brows bound with victorious wreaths;
Our bruised arms hung up for monuments;
Our stern alarums changed to merry meetings,

● Our dreadful marches to delightful measures.
Grim-visaged war hath smooth'd his wrinkled front;

● And now, instead of mounting barbed steeds 10
To fright the souls of fearful adversaries,
He capers nimbly in a lady's chamber
To the lascivious pleasing of a lute.
But I, that am not shaped for sportive tricks,
Nor made to court an amorous looking-glass;
I, that am rudely stamp'd, and want love's majesty

Richard Burbage, who first played the role of Richard III. Engraving from a painting in Dulwich College

---

2 *sun.* Edward IV was the son of the Duke of York.

8 *measures.* Stately dances.

10 *barbed steeds.* Horses with wild flaring manes; there is also a pun on 'Barbary'.

Opposite: The murder of the Princes in the Tower. Painting by James Northcote (1746–1831)

Two costume designs for Richard. *Above :* A design by Jocelyn Herbert with Sally Jacobs, Stratford-upon-Avon, 1961. *Above right :* A design by Motley, Stratford-upon-Avon, 1953.

32 *inductions.* Preparations.

44 *Tendering.* Concerned.

To strut before a wanton ambling nymph ;
I, that am curtail'd of this fair proportion,
Cheated of feature by dissembling nature,
Deform'd, unfinish'd, sent before my time   20
Into this breathing world, scarce half made up,
And that so lamely and unfashionable
That dogs bark at me as I halt by them ;
Why, I, in this weak piping time of peace,
Have no delight to pass away the time,
Unless to spy my shadow in the sun
And descant on mine own deformity :
And therefore, since I cannot prove a lover,
To entertain these fair well-spoken days,
I am determined to prove a villain   30
And hate the idle pleasures of these days.
• Plots have I laid, inductions dangerous,
By drunken prophecies, libels and dreams,
To set my brother Clarence and the king
In deadly hate the one against the other :
And if King Edward be as true and just
As I am subtle, false and treacherous,
This day should Clarence closely be mew'd up,
About a prophecy, which says that G
Of Edward's heirs the murderer shall be.   40
Dive, thoughts, down to my soul : here Clarence
          comes.

Enter CLARENCE, *guarded, and* BRAKENBURY.

Brother, good day : what means this armed guard
That waits upon your grace ?
    Clar.   His majesty,
• Tendering my person's safety, hath appointed
This conduct to convey me to the Tower.

Glou. Upon what cause?
Clar.　　　　　Because my name is George.
Glou. Alack, my lord, that fault is none of
　　yours;
He should, for that, commit your godfathers:
O, belike his majesty hath some intent
That you shall be new-christen'd in the Tower. 50
But what's the matter, Clarence? may I know?
　　Clar. Yea, Richard, when I know; for I
　　protest
As yet I do not: but, as I can learn,
He hearkens after prophecies and dreams;
● And from the cross-row plucks the letter G,
And says a wizard told him that by G
His issue disinherited should be;
And, for my name of George begins with G,
It follows in his thought that I am he.
These, as I learn, and such like toys as these 60
Have moved his highness to commit me now.
　　Glou. Why, this it is, when men are ruled by
　　women:
'Tis not the king that sends you to the Tower;
● My Lady Grey his wife, Clarence, 'tis she
That tempers him to this extremity.
Was it not she and that good man of worship,
Anthony Woodville, her brother there,
That made him send Lord Hastings to the Tower,
From whence this present day he is deliver'd?
We are not safe, Clarence; we are not safe. 70
　　Clar. By heaven, I think there's no man is
　　secure
But the queen's kindred and night-walking heralds
● That trudge betwixt the king and Mistress Shore.
Heard ye not what an humble suppliant
Lord Hastings was to her for his delivery?
　　Glou. Humbly complaining to her deity
● Got my lord chamberlain his liberty.
I'll tell you what; I think it is our way,
If we will keep in favour with the king,
To be her men and wear her livery: 80
The jealous o'erworn widow and herself,
Since that our brother dubb'd them gentlewomen,
● Are mighty gossips in this monarchy.
　　Brak. I beseech your graces both to pardon
　　me;
His majesty hath straitly given in charge
That no man shall have private conference,
Of what degree soever, with his brother.
　　Glou. Even so; an't please your worship,
　　Brakenbury,
You may partake of any thing we say:
We speak no treason, man: we say the king 90
Is wise and virtuous, and his noble queen
Well struck in years, fair, and not jealous;
We say that Shore's wife hath a pretty foot,
A cherry lip, a bonny eye, a passing pleasing
　　tongue;
And that the queen's kindred are made gentle-
　　folks:
How say you, sir? can you deny all this?
　　Brak. With this, my lord, myself have nought
　　to do.
　　Glou. Naught to do with Mistress Shore! I
　　tell thee, fellow,
He that doth naught with her, excepting one,
Were best he do it secretly, alone. 100
　　Brak. What one, my lord?
　　Glou. Her husband, knave: wouldst thou
　　betray me?

Criminals being escorted to gaol. Engraving from a medieval manuscript

---

55 *cross-row.* Alphabet.

64 *My Lady Grey.* Edward IV's wife, Queen Elizabeth, was the widow of Sir John Grey.

73 *Mistress Shore.* The wife of a goldsmith and the King's mistress.

77 *lord chamberlain.* Lord Hastings.

83 *gossips.* God-mothers.

108–110 *And whatsoever . . . perform it*. See introduction.

115 *lie for*. Either tell lies for or lie in prison for.

139 *evil diet*. Ill mode of life.

153 *Warwick's youngest daughter*. The Lady Anne.

154 *her husband and her father*. Edward, Prince of Wales and her father-in-law, Henry VI.

Richard III, formerly Duke of Gloucester. Drawing by Robert Dighton (1752?–1814)

Brak. I beseech your grace to pardon me, and withal
Forbear your conference with the noble duke.
  Clar. We know thy charge, Brakenbury, and will obey.
  Glou. We are the queen's abjects, and must obey.
Brother, farewell: I will unto the king;
● And whatsoever you will employ me in,
Were it to call King Edward's widow sister,
I will perform it to enfranchise you.   110
Meantime, this deep disgrace in brotherhood
Touches me deeper than you can imagine.
  Clar. I know it pleaseth neither of us well.
  Glou. Well, your imprisonment shall not be long;
● I will deliver you, or else lie for you:
Meantime, have patience.
  Clar.   I must perforce. Farewell.
    [*Exeunt Clarence, Brakenbury, and Guard.*
  Glou. Go, tread the path that thou shalt ne'er return,
Simple, plain Clarence! I do love thee so,
That I will shortly send thy soul to heaven,
If heaven will take the present at our hands. 120
But who comes here? the new-deliver'd Hastings?

Enter LORD HASTINGS.

  Hast. Good time of day unto my gracious lord!
  Glou. As much unto my good lord chamberlain!
Well are you welcome to the open air.
How hath your lordship brook'd imprisonment?
  Hast. With patience, noble lord, as prisoners must:
But I shall live, my lord, to give them thanks
That were the cause of my imprisonment.
  Glou. No doubt, no doubt; and so shall Clarence too;
For they that were your enemies are his, 130
And have prevail'd as much on him as you.
  Hast. More pity that the eagle should be mew'd,
While kites and buzzards prey at liberty.
  Glou. What news abroad?
  Hast. No news so bad abroad as this at home;
The king is sickly, weak and melancholy,
And his physicians fear him mightily.
  Glou. Now, by Saint Paul, this news is bad indeed.
● O, he hath kept an evil diet long,
And overmuch consumed his royal person: 140
'Tis very grievous to be thought upon.
What, is he in his bed?
  Hast. He is.
  Glou. Go you before, and I will follow you.
    [*Exit Hastings.*
He cannot live, I hope; and must not die
Till George be pack'd with post-horse up to heaven.
I'll in, to urge his hatred more to Clarence,
With lies well steel'd with weighty arguments;
And, if I fail not in my deep intent,
Clarence hath not another day to live: 150
Which done, God take King Edward to his mercy,
And leave the world for me to bustle in!
● For then I'll marry Warwick's youngest daughter.
● What though I kill'd her husband and her father?
The readiest way to make the wench amends
Is to become her husband and her father:

The which will I; not all so much for love
As for another secret close intent,
By marrying her which I must reach unto.
● But yet I run before my horse to market: 160
Clarence still breathes; Edward still lives and
    reigns:
When they are gone, then must I count my gains.
                                 [*Exit.*

    SCENE II. *The same. Another street.*

Enter the corpse of KING HENRY *the Sixth,*
    Gentlemen *with halberds to guard it;* LADY
    ANNE *being the mourner.*

    Anne. Set down, set down your honourable
    load,
If honour may be shrouded in a hearse,
● Whilst I awhile obsequiously lament
The untimely fall of virtuous Lancaster.
Poor key-cold figure of a holy king!
Pale ashes of the house of Lancaster!
Thou bloodless remnant of that royal blood!
Be it lawful that I invocate thy ghost,
To hear the lamentations of poor Anne,
Wife to thy Edward, to thy slaughter'd son,   10
Stabb'd by the selfsame hand that made these
    wounds!
Lo, in these windows that let forth thy life,
I pour the helpless balm of my poor eyes.
Cursed be the hand that made these fatal holes!
Cursed be the heart that had the heart to do it!
Cursed the blood that let this blood from hence!
More direful hap betide that hated wretch,
That makes us wretched by the death of thee,
Than I can wish to adders, spiders, toads,
Or any creeping venom'd thing that lives!   20
If ever he have child, abortive be it,
Prodigious, and untimely brought to light,
Whose ugly and unnatural aspect
May fright the hopeful mother at the view;
And that be heir to his unhappiness!
If ever he have wife, let her be made
As miserable by the death of him
As I am made by my poor lord and thee!
Come, now towards Chertsey with your holy load,
Taken from Paul's to be interred there;   30
And still, as you are weary of the weight,
Rest you, whiles I lament King Henry's corse.

        Enter GLOUCESTER.

    Glou. Stay, you that bear the corse, and set
    it down.
    Anne. What black magician conjures up this
    fiend,
To stop devoted charitable deeds?
    Glou. Villains, set down the corse; or, by
    Saint Paul,
I'll make a corse of him that disobeys.
    Gent. My lord, stand back, and let the coffin
    pass.
    Glou. Unmanner'd dog! stand thou, when I
    command:
● Advance thy halberd higher than my breast,   40
Or, by Saint Paul, I'll strike thee to my foot,
And spurn upon thee, beggar, for thy boldness.
    Anne. What, do you tremble? are you all
    afraid?
Alas, I blame you not; for you are mortal,
And mortal eyes cannot endure the devil.

160 *I run before my horse to market.* I count my chickens
before they are hatched.

Halberds and bills. Woodcut from Di Grassi's *True Art
of Defense,* 1594

---

3 *obsequiously.* Mournfully.

40 *halberd.* A combination battle-axe and spear.

49 *curst*. Shrewish.

58 *exhales*. Draws forth. The wounds of a victim were
believed to bleed in the presence of the murderer.

94 *falchion*. A broad curved sword.

Julia Arthur as Lady Anne, Lyceum Theatre, London
1896

Avaunt, thou dreadful minister of hell!
Thou hadst but power over his mortal body,
His soul thou canst not have; therefore, be gone.
•   *Glou.* Sweet saint, for charity, be not so curst.
    Anne. Foul devil, for God's sake, hence, and
      trouble us not;   50
For thou hast made the happy earth thy hell,
Fill'd it with cursing cries and deep exclaims.
If thou delight to view thy heinous deeds,
Behold this pattern of thy butcheries.
O, gentlemen, see, see! dead Henry's wounds
Open their congeal'd mouths and bleed afresh!
Blush, blush, thou lump of foul deformity;
• For 'tis thy presence that exhales this blood
From cold and empty veins, where no blood
    dwells;
Thy deed, inhuman and unnatural,   60
Provokes this deluge most unnatural.
O God, which this blood madest, revenge his
    death!
O earth, which this blood drink'st, revenge his
    death!
Either heaven with lightning strike the murderer
    dead,
Or earth, gape open wide and eat him quick,
As thou dost swallow up this good king's blood,
Which his hell-govern'd arm hath butchered!
    Glou. Lady, you know no rules of charity,
Which renders good for bad, blessings for curses.
    Anne. Villain, thou know'st no law of God
      nor man: 70
No beast so fierce but knows some touch of pity.
    Glou. But I know none, and therefore am no
      beast.
    Anne. O wonderful, when devils tell the truth!
    Glou. More wonderful, when angels are so
      angry.
Vouchsafe, divine perfection of a woman,
Of these supposed evils, to give me leave,
By circumstance, but to acquit myself.
    Anne. Vouchsafe, defused infection of a man,
For these known evils, but to give me leave,
By circumstance, to curse thy cursed self.   80
    Glou. Fairer than tongue can name thee, let
    me have
Some patient leisure to excuse myself.
    Anne. Fouler than heart can think thee, thou
    canst make
No excuse current, but to hang thyself.
    Glou. By such despair, I should accuse myself.
    Anne. And, by despairing, shouldst thou stand
    excused;
For doing worthy vengeance on thyself,
Which didst unworthy slaughter upon others.
    Glou. Say that I slew them not?
    Anne.   Why, then they are not dead:
But dead they are, and, devilish slave, by thee.
    Glou. I did not kill your husband.   91
    Anne.   Why, then he is alive.
    Glou. Nay, he is dead; and slain by Edward's
    hand.
    Anne. In thy foul throat thou liest: Queen
    Margaret saw
• Thy murderous falchion smoking in his blood;
The which thou once didst bend against her breast,
But that thy brothers beat aside the point.
    Glou. I was provoked by her slanderous tongue,
Which laid their guilt upon my guiltless shoulders.
    Anne. Thou wast provoked by thy bloody mind,

Which never dreamt on aught but butcheries: 100
Didst thou not kill this king?
Glou.		I grant ye.
Anne.	Dost grant me, hedgehog? then, God
grant me too
Thou mayst be damned for that wicked deed!
O, he was gentle, mild, and virtuous!
Glou.	The fitter for the King of heaven, that
hath him.
Anne.	He is in heaven, where thou shalt
never come.
Glou.	Let him thank me, that holp to send
him thither;
For he was fitter for that place than earth.
Anne.	And thou unfit for any place but hell.
Glou.	Yes, one place else, if you will hear me
name it.					110
Anne.	Some dungeon.
Glou.			Your bed-chamber.
Anne.	Ill rest betide the chamber where thou
liest!
Glou.	So will it, madam, till I lie with you.
Anne.	I hope so.
Glou.		I know so. But, gentle Lady Anne,
To leave this keen encounter of our wits,
And fall somewhat into a slower method,
● Is not the causer of the timeless deaths
Of these Plantagenets, Henry and Edward,
As blameful as the executioner?
Anne.	Thou art the cause, and most accursed
effect.					120
Glou.	Your beauty was the cause of that effect;
Your beauty, which did haunt me in my sleep
To undertake the death of all the world,
So I might live one hour in your sweet bosom.
Anne.	If I thought that, I tell thee, homicide,
These nails should rend that beauty from my
cheeks.
Glou.	These eyes could never endure sweet
beauty's wreck;
You should not blemish it, if I stood by:
As all the world is cheered by the sun,
So I by that; it is my day, my life.		130
Anne.	Black night o'ershade thy day, and
death thy life!
Glou.	Curse not thyself, fair creature; thou
art both.
Anne.	I would I were, to be revenged on thee.
Glou.	It is a quarrel most unnatural,
To be revenged on him that loveth you.
Anne.	It is a quarrel just and reasonable,
To be revenged on him that slew my husband.
Glou.	He that bereft thee, lady, of thy husband,
Did it to help thee to a better husband.
Anne.	His better doth not breathe upon the
earth.					140
Glou.	He lives that loves thee better than he
could.
Anne.	Name him.
Glou.			Plantagenet.
Anne.				Why, that was he.
Glou.	The selfsame name, but one of better
nature.
Anne.	Where is he?
Glou.			Here. [*She spitteth at him.*]
Why dost thou spit at me?
Anne.	Would it were mortal poison, for thy
sake!
Glou.	Never came poison from so sweet a place.

Hedgehog. Woodcut from *Libellus de Natura Animalium,*
a 15th century bestiary

---

117 *timeless.* Untimely.

151 *basilisks.* Fabled serpents able to kill by a look.

170 *fee.* Reward.

Gloucester: 'I lay it naked to the deadly stroke.'
Drawing by John M. Wright (1777–1866)

Gloucester: 'Was ever woman in this humour woo'd?'
Drawing by H. Fuseli, 1766

Anne. Never hung poison on a fouler toad.
Out of my sight! thou dost infect my eyes.
 Glou. Thine eyes, sweet lady, have infected
  mine.   150
 Anne. Would they were basilisks, to strike
  thee dead!
 Glou. I would they were, that I might die at
  once;
For now they kill me with a living death.
Those eyes of thine from mine have drawn salt
  tears,
Shamed their aspect with store of childish drops:
These eyes, which never shed remorseful tear,
No, when my father York and Edward wept,
To hear the piteous moan that Rutland made
When black-faced Clifford shook his sword at him;
Nor when thy warlike father, like a child, 160
Told the sad story of my father's death,
And twenty times made pause to sob and weep,
That all the standers-by had wet their cheeks,
Like trees bedash'd with rain: in that sad time
My manly eyes did scorn an humble tear;
And what these sorrows could not thence exhale,
Thy beauty hath, and made them blind with weep-
  ing.
I never sued to friend nor enemy;
My tongue could never learn sweet smoothing
  words;
But, now thy beauty is proposed my fee, 170
My proud heart sues and prompts my tongue to
  speak.   [*She looks scornfully at him.*
Teach not thy lips such scorn, for they were made
For kissing, lady, not for such contempt.
If thy revengeful heart cannot forgive,
Lo, here I lend thee this sharp-pointed sword;
Which if thou please to hide in this true bosom,
And let the soul forth that adoreth thee,
I lay it naked to the deadly stroke,
And humbly beg the death upon my knee.
  [*He lays his breast open: she offers at it
         with his sword.*
Nay, do not pause; for I did kill King Henry,
But 'twas thy beauty that provoked me. 181
Nay, now dispatch; 'twas I that stabb'd young
  Edward,
But 'twas thy heavenly face that set me on.
     [*Here she lets fall the sword.*
Take up the sword again, or take up me.
 Anne. Arise, dissembler: though I wish thy
  death,
I will not be the executioner.
 Glou. Then bid me kill myself, and I will do it.
 Anne. I have already.
 Glou.   Tush, that was in thy rage:
Speak it again, and, even with the word,
That hand, which, for thy love, did kill thy love,
Shall, for thy love, kill a far truer love; 191
To both their deaths thou shalt be accessary.
 Anne. I would I knew thy heart.
 Glou. 'Tis figured in my tongue.
 Anne. I fear me both are false.
 Glou. Then never man was true.
 Anne. Well, well, put up your sword.
 Glou. Say, then, my peace is made.
 Anne. That shall you know hereafter.
 Glou. But shall I live in hope?   200
 Anne. All men, I hope, live so.
 Glou. Vouchsafe to wear this ring.
 Anne. To take is not to give.

Glou. Look, how this ring encompasseth thy
finger,
Even so thy breast encloseth my poor heart;
Wear both of them, for both of them are thine.
And if thy poor devoted suppliant may
But beg one favour at thy gracious hand,
Thou dost confirm his happiness for ever.
 Anne. What is it?   210
 Glou. That it would please thee leave these
  sad designs
To him that hath more cause to be a mourner,
• And presently repair to Crosby Place;
Where, after I have solemnly interr'd
At Chertsey monastery this noble king,
And wet his grave with my repentant tears,
I will with all expedient duty see you:
For divers unknown reasons, I beseech you,
Grant me this boon.
 Anne. With all my heart; and much it joys
  me too,   220
To see you are become so penitent.
Tressel and Berkeley, go along with me.
 Glou. Bid me farewell.
 Anne.   'Tis more than you deserve;
But since you teach me how to flatter you,
Imagine I have said farewell already.
  [*Exeunt Lady Anne, Tressel, and Berkeley.*
 Glou. Sirs, take up the corse.
 Gent.   Towards Chertsey, noble lord?
 Glou. No, to White-Friars; there attend my
  coming.   [*Exeunt all but Gloucester.*
Was ever woman in this humour woo'd?
Was ever woman in this humour won?
I'll have her; but I will not keep her long. 230
What! I, that kill'd her husband and his father,
To take her in her heart's extremest hate,
With curses in her mouth, tears in her eyes,
The bleeding witness of her hatred by;
Having God, her conscience, and these bars
  against me,
And I nothing to back my suit at all,
But the plain devil and dissembling looks,
And yet to win her, all the world to nothing!
Ha!
Hath she forgot already that brave prince, 240
Edward, her lord, whom I, some three months since,
Stabb'd in my angry mood at Tewksbury?
A sweeter and a lovelier gentleman,
Framed in the prodigality of nature,
Young, valiant, wise, and, no doubt, right royal,
The spacious world cannot again afford:
And will she yet debase her eyes on me,
That cropp'd the golden prime of this sweet prince,
And made her widow to a woful bed?
• On me, whose all not equals Edward's moiety?
On me, that halt and am unshapen thus? 251
• My dukedom to a beggarly denier,
I do mistake my person all this while:
Upon my life, she finds, although I cannot,
Myself to be a marvellous proper man.
I'll be at charges for a looking-glass,
And entertain some score or two of tailors,
To study fashions to adorn my body:
Since I am crept in favour with myself,
I will maintain it with some little cost. 260
But first I'll turn yon fellow in his grave;
And then return lamenting to my love.
Shine out, fair sun, till I have bought a glass,
That I may see my shadow as I pass. [*Exit.*

213 *Crosby Place.* A residence of Richard's in Bishops-gate, London, now re-erected in Chelsea.

Gloucester: 'Take up the sword again . . .' Engraving from Bell's edition of Shakespeare's works, 1773

250 *moiety.* Half.

252 *denier.* A copper coin worth about one tenth of a penny.

15 *It is . . . concluded yet.* It is decided, but not legalized.

20 *Countess Richmond.* Margaret Beaufort, widow of Edmund Tudor, was married to the Earl of Derby. Henry Tudor, a son by her first marriage, became Henry VII.

Lady Margaret Beaufort

36 *atonement.* Reconciliation.

Scene III. *The palace.*

Enter QUEEN ELIZABETH, LORD RIVERS, *and* LORD GREY.

Riv. Have patience, madam: there's no doubt his majesty
Will soon recover his accustom'd health.
Grey. In that you brook it ill, it makes him worse:
Therefore, for God's sake, entertain good comfort,
And cheer his grace with quick and merry words.
Q. Eliz. If he were dead, what would betide of me?
Riv. No other harm but loss of such a lord.
Q. Eliz. The loss of such a lord includes all harm.
Grey. The heavens have bless'd you with a goodly son,
To be your comforter when he is gone.   10
Q. Eliz. Oh, he is young, and his minority
Is put unto the trust of Richard Gloucester,
A man that loves not me, nor none of you.
Riv. Is it concluded he shall be protector?
• *Q. Eliz.* It is determined, not concluded yet:
But so it must be, if the king miscarry.

Enter BUCKINGHAM *and* DERBY.

Grey. Here come the lords of Buckingham and Derby.
Buck. Good time of day unto your royal grace!
Der. God make your majesty joyful as you have been!
• *Q. Eliz.* The Countess Richmond, good my Lord of Derby,   20
To your good prayers will scarcely say amen.
Yet, Derby, notwithstanding she's your wife,
And loves not me, be you, good lord, assured
I hate not you for her proud arrogance.
Der. I do beseech you, either not believe
The envious slanders of her false accusers;
Or, if she be accused in true report,
Bear with her weakness, which, I think, proceeds
From wayward sickness, and no grounded malice.
Riv. Saw you the king to-day, my Lord of Derby?   30
Der. But now the Duke of Buckingham and I
Are come from visiting his majesty.
Q. Eliz. What likelihood of his amendment, lords?
Buck. Madam, good hope; his grace speaks cheerfully.
Q. Eliz. God grant him health! Did you confer with him?
• *Buck.* Madam, we did: he desires to make atonement
Betwixt the Duke of Gloucester and your brothers,
And betwixt them and my lord chamberlain;
And sent to warn them to his royal presence.
Q. Eliz. Would all were well! but that will never be: 40
I fear our happiness is at the highest.

Enter GLOUCESTER, HASTINGS, *and* DORSET.

Glou. They do me wrong, and I will not endure it:
Who are they that complain unto the king,
That I, forsooth, am stern and love them not?
By holy Paul, they love his grace but lightly

That fill his ears with such dissentious rumours.
Because I cannot flatter and speak fair,
● Smile in men's faces, smooth, deceive and cog,
Duck with French nods and apish courtesy,
I must be held a rancorous enemy.   50
Cannot a plain man live and think no harm,
But thus his simple truth must be abused
● By silken, sly, insinuating Jacks?
  Riv. To whom in all this presence speaks
    your grace?
  Glou. To thee, that hast nor honesty nor grace.
When have I injured thee? when done thee
    wrong?
Or thee? or thee? or any of your faction?
A plague upon you all! His royal person,—
Whom God preserve better than you would
    wish!—
Cannot be quiet scarce a breathing-while,   60
● But you must trouble him with lewd complaints.
  Q. Eliz. Brother of Gloucester, you mistake
    the matter.
The king, of his own royal disposition,
And not provoked by any suitor else;
Aiming, belike, at your interior hatred,
Which in your outward actions shows itself
Against my kindred, brothers, and myself,
Makes him to send; that thereby he may gather
The ground of your ill-will, and so remove it.
  Glou. I cannot tell: the world is grown so
    bad,   70
That wrens make prey where eagles dare not
    perch:
Since every Jack became a gentleman,
There's many a gentle person made a Jack.
  Q. Eliz. Come, come, we know your meaning,
    brother Gloucester;
You envy my advancement and my friends':
God grant we never may have need of you!
  Glou. Meantime, God grants that we have
    need of you:
Our brother is imprison'd by your means,
Myself disgraced, and the nobility
Held in contempt; whilst many fair promotions
Are daily given to ennoble those   81
● That scarce, some two days since, were worth a
    noble.
● *Q. Eliz.* By Him that raised me to this care-
    ful height
From that contented hap which I enjoy'd,
I never did incense his majesty
Against the Duke of Clarence, but have been
An earnest advocate to plead for him.
My lord, you do me shameful injury,
Falsely to draw me in these vile suspects.
  Glou. You may deny that you were not the
    cause   90
Of my Lord Hastings' late imprisonment.
  Riv. She may, my lord, for—
  Glou. She may, Lord Rivers! why, who
    knows not so?
She may do more, sir, than denying that:
She may help you to many fair preferments,
And then deny her aiding hand therein,
And lay those honours on your high deserts.
What may she not? She may, yea, marry, may
    she,—
  Riv. What, marry, may she?
  Glou. What, marry, may she! marry with a
    king,   100

48 *cog.* Cheat.

53 *Jacks.* Common men.

61 *lewd.* Base.

82 *noble.* A gold coin.

83 *careful.* Full of care.

102 *I wis.* Certainly.

130 *battle.* Army.

135 *father.* Father-in-law.

144 *cacodemon.* Evil spirit.

A bachelor, a handsome stripling too:
● I wis your grandam had a worser match.
    Q. Eliz. My Lord of Gloucester, I have too
      long borne
Your blunt upbraidings and your bitter scoffs:
By heaven, I will acquaint his majesty
With those gross taunts I often have endured.
I had rather be a country servant-maid
Than a great queen, with this condition,
To be thus taunted, scorn'd, and baited at:

     Enter QUEEN MARGARET, *behind.*

Small joy have I in being England's queen.   110
    Q. Mar. And lessen'd be that small, God, I
      beseech thee!
Thy honour, state and seat is due to me.
    Glou. What! threat you me with telling of
      the king?
Tell him, and spare not: look, what I have said
I will avouch in presence of the king:
I dare adventure to be sent to the Tower.
'Tis time to speak; my pains are quite forgot.
    Q. Mar. Out, devil! I remember them too
      well:
Thou slewest my husband Henry in the Tower,
And Edward, my poor son, at Tewksbury.   120
    Glou. Ere you were queen, yea, or your hus-
      band king,
I was a pack-horse in his great affairs;
A weeder-out of his proud adversaries,
A liberal rewarder of his friends:
To royalise his blood I spilt mine own.
    Q. Mar. Yea, and much better blood than his
      or thine.
    Glou. In all which time you and your husband
      Grey
Were factious for the house of Lancaster;
And, Rivers, so were you. Was not your husband
● In Margaret's battle at Saint Alban's slain?   130
Let me put in your minds, if you forget,
What you have been ere now, and what you are;
Withal, what I have been, and what I am.
    Q. Mar. A murderous villain, and so still
      thou art.
● *Glou.* Poor Clarence did forsake his father,
      Warwick;
Yea, and forswore himself,—which Jesu par-
    don!—
    Q. Mar. Which God revenge!
    Glou. To fight on Edward's party for the
      crown;
And for his meed, poor lord, he is mew'd up.
I would to God my heart were flint, like Ed-
    ward's;   140
Or Edward's soft and pitiful, like mine:
I am too childish-foolish for this world.
    Q. Mar. Hie thee to hell for shame, and leave
      the world,
● Thou cacodemon! there thy kingdom is.
    Riv. My Lord of Gloucester, in those busy
      days
Which here you urge to prove us enemies,
We follow'd then our lord, our lawful king:
So should we you, if you should be our king.
    Glou. If I should be! I had rather be a pedlar:
Far be it from my heart, the thought of it!   150
    Q. Eliz. As little joy, my lord, as you suppose
You should enjoy, were you this country's king,
As little joy may you suppose in me,

That I enjoy, being the queen thereof.
    Q. Mar. A little joy enjoys the queen thereof;
For I am she, and altogether joyless.
I can no longer hold me patient.   [*Advancing.*
Hear me, you wrangling pirates, that fall out
In sharing that which you have pill'd from me!
Which of you trembles not that looks on me? 160
If not, that, I being queen, you bow like subjects,
Yet that, by you deposed, you quake like rebels?
O gentle villain, do not turn away!
    Glou. Foul wrinkled witch, what makest thou
      in my sight?
    Q. Mar. But repetition of what thou hast
      marr'd;
That will I make before I let thee go.
    Glou. Wert thou not banished on pain of
      death?
    Q. Mar. I was; but I do find more pain in
      banishment
Than death can yield me here by my abode.
A husband and a son thou owest to me;   170
And thou a kingdom; all of you allegiance:
The sorrow that I have, by right is yours,
And all the pleasures you usurp are mine.
    Glou. The curse my noble father laid on
      thee,
● When thou didst crown his warlike brows with
      paper
And with thy scorns drew'st rivers from his eyes,
● And then, to dry them, gavest the duke a clout
Steep'd in the faultless blood of pretty Rut-
      land,—
His curses, then from bitterness of soul   179
Denounced against thee, are all fall'n upon thee;
And God, not we, hath plagued thy bloody deed.
    Q. Eliz. So just is God, to right the inno-
      cent.
    Hast. O, 'twas the foulest deed to slay that
      babe,
And the most merciless that e'er was heard of!
    Riv. Tyrants themselves wept when it was
      reported.
    Dor. No man but prophesied revenge for it.
    Buck. Northumberland, then present, wept
      to see it.
    Q. Mar. What! were you snarling all before I
      came,
Ready to catch each other by the throat,
And turn you all your hatred now on me?   190
Did York's dread curse prevail so much with
      heaven
That Henry's death, my lovely Edward's death,
Their kingdom's loss, my woful banishment,
● Could all but answer for that peevish brat?
Can curses pierce the clouds and enter heaven?
Why, then, give way, dull clouds, to my quick
      curses!
If not by war, by surfeit die your king,
As ours by murder, to make him a king!
Edward thy son, which now is Prince of Wales,
For Edward my son, which was Prince of Wales,
Die in his youth by like untimely violence! 201
Thyself a queen, for me that was a queen,
Outlive thy glory, like my wretched self!
Long mayst thou live to wail thy children's loss;
And see another, as I see thee now,
Deck'd in thy rights, as thou art stall'd in mine!
Long die thy happy days before thy death;
And, after many lengthen'd hours of grief,

Costume design for Queen Margaret by John Bury with
Ann Curtis, Royal Shakespeare Co, 1964

---

175 *When thou . . . paper.* See *3 Henry VI*, I. IV, 95ff.

177 *clout.* Cloth.

194 *but.* Only.

Genevieve Ward, the Edwardian actress, as Queen Margaret. Lyceum Theatre, London, 1897

---

241 *vain flourish.* Hollow show.

242 *bottled.* Swollen.

256 *current.* Genuine.

Die neither mother, wife, nor England's queen!
Rivers and Dorset, you were standers by,   210
And so wast thou, Lord Hastings, when my son
Was stabb'd with bloody daggers: God, I pray him,
That none of you may live your natural age,
But by some unlook'd accident cut off!
  Glou. Have done thy charm, thou hateful wither'd hag!
  Q. Mar. And leave out thee? stay, dog, for thou shalt hear me.
If heaven have any grievous plague in store
Exceeding those that I can wish upon thee,
O, let them keep it till thy sins be ripe,
And then hurl down their indignation   220
On thee, the troubler of the poor world's peace!
The worm of conscience still begnaw thy soul!
Thy friends suspect for traitors while thou livest,
And take deep traitors for thy dearest friends!
No sleep close up that deadly eye of thine,
Unless it be whilst some tormenting dream
Affrights thee with a hell of ugly devils!
Thou elvish-mark'd, abortive, rooting hog!
Thou that wast seal'd in thy nativity
The slave of nature and the son of hell!   230
Thou slander of thy mother's heavy womb!
Thou loathed issue of thy father's loins!
Thou rag of honour! thou detested—
  Glou. Margaret.
  Q. Mar.   Richard!
  Glou.   Ha!
  Q. Mar.   I call thee not.
  Glou. I cry thee mercy then, for I had thought
That thou hadst call'd me all these bitter names.
  Q. Mar. Why, so I did; but look'd for no reply.
O, let me make the period to my curse!
  Glou. 'Tis done by me, and ends in 'Margaret.'
  Q. Eliz. Thus have you breathed your curse against yourself.   240
  Q. Mar. Poor painted queen, vain flourish of my fortune!
Why strew'st thou sugar on that bottled spider,
Whose deadly web ensnareth thee about?
Fool, fool! thou whet'st a knife to kill thyself.
The time will come when thou shalt wish for me
To help thee curse that poisonous bunch-back'd toad.
  Hast. False-boding woman, end thy frantic curse,
Lest to thy harm thou move our patience.
  Q. Mar. Foul shame upon you! you have all moved mine.
  Riv. Were you well served, you would be taught your duty.   250
  Q. Mar. To serve me well, you all should do me duty,
Teach me to be your queen, and you my subjects:
O, serve me well, and teach yourselves that duty!
  Dor. Dispute not with her; she is lunatic.
  Q. Mar. Peace, master marquess, you are malapert:
Your fire-new stamp of honour is scarce current.
O, that your young nobility could judge
What 'twere to lose it, and be miserable!

They that stand high have many blasts to shake
    them; 259
And if they fall, they dash themselves to pieces.
    Glou. Good counsel, marry: learn it, learn it,
    marquess.
    Dor. It toucheth you, my lord, as much as
    me.
    Glou. Yea, and much more: but I was born
    so high,
● Our aery buildeth in the cedar's top,
● And dallies with the wind and scorns the sun.
    Q. Mar. And turns the sun to shade; alas!
    alas!
Witness my son, now in the shade of death;
Whose bright out-shining beams thy cloudy wrath
Hath in eternal darkness folded up.
Your aery buildeth in our aery's nest. 270
O God, that seest it, do not suffer it;
As it was won with blood, lost be it so!
    Buck. Have done! for shame, if not for
    charity.
    Q. Mar. Urge neither charity nor shame to
    me:
Uncharitably with me have you dealt,
And shamefully by you my hopes are butcher'd.
My charity is outrage, life my shame;
And in that shame still live my sorrow's rage!
    Buck. Have done, have done.
    Q. Mar. O princely Buckingham, I'll kiss
    thy hand, 280
In sign of league and amity with thee:
Now fair befal thee and thy noble house!
Thy garments are not spotted with our blood,
Nor thou within the compass of my curse.
    Buck. Nor no one here; for curses never pass
The lips of those that breathe them in the air.
    Q. Mar. I'll not believe but they ascend the
    sky,
And there awake God's gentle-sleeping peace.
O Buckingham, take heed of yonder dog!
Look, when he fawns, he bites; and when he
    bites, 290
His venom tooth will rankle to the death:
Have not to do with him, beware of him;
Sin, death, and hell have set their marks on him,
And all their ministers attend on him.
    Glou. What doth she say, my Lord of Buck-
    ingham?
    Buck. Nothing that I respect, my gracious
    lord.
    Q. Mar. What, dost thou scorn me for my
    gentle counsel?
And soothe the devil that I warn thee from?
O, but remember this another day,
When he shall split thy very heart with sorrow,
And say poor Margaret was a prophetess! 301
Live each of you the subjects to his hate,
And he to yours, and all of you to God's! [*Exit.*
    Hast. My hair doth stand on end to hear her
    curses.
    Riv. And so doth mine: I muse why she's at
    liberty.
    Glou. I cannot blame her: by God's holy
    mother,
She hath had too much wrong; and I repent
My part thereof that I have done to her.
    Q. Eliz. I never did her any, to my knowledge.
    Glou. But you have all the vantage of her
    wrong. 310

264 *aery.* Bird of prey's nest.

265 *scorns the sun.* It was thought that the eagle was the
only bird that could look into the sun without being
blinded.

Queen Margaret: 'Live each of you the subjects to his
hate . . .' Drawing by Henry Singleton (1766–1839)

314 *frank'd up to fatting.* Penned up (like a pig) to be fattened.

317 *scathe.* Harm.

Crosby Place. Engraving from *Old England*, 1854

354 *drop millstones.* Proverbially said of hard-hearted persons.

I was too hot to do somebody good,
That is too cold in thinking of it now.
Marry, as for Clarence, he is well repaid;
● He is frank'd up to fatting for his pains:
God pardon them that are the cause of it!
   Riv. A virtuous and a Christian-like conclusion,
● To pray for them that have done scathe to us.
   Glou. So do I ever: [*Aside*] being well advised.
For had I cursed now, I had cursed myself.

        Enter CATESBY.

   Cates. Madam, his majesty doth call for you;
And for your grace; and you, my noble lords. 321
   Q. Eliz. Catesby, we come. Lords, will you
      go with us?
   Riv. Madam, we will attend your grace.
         [*Exeunt all but Gloucester.*
   Glou. I do the wrong, and first begin to brawl.
The secret mischiefs that I set abroach
I lay unto the grievous charge of others.
Clarence, whom I, indeed, have laid in darkness,
I do beweep to many simple gulls;
Namely, to Hastings, Derby, Buckingham;
And say it is the queen and her allies 330
That stir the king against the duke my brother.
Now, they believe it; and withal whet me
To be revenged on Rivers, Vaughan, Grey:
But then I sigh; and, with a piece of scripture,
Tell them that God bids us do good for evil:
And thus I clothe my naked villany
With old odd ends stolen out of holy writ;
And seem a saint, when most I play the devil.

        Enter two Murderers.

But, soft! here come my executioners.
How now, my hardy, stout resolved mates! 340
Are you now going to dispatch this deed?
   First Murd. We are, my lord; and come to
      have the warrant,
That we may be admitted where he is.
   Glou. Well thought upon; I have it here about
      me.   [*Gives the warrant.*
When you have done, repair to Crosby Place.
But, sirs, be sudden in the execution,
Withal obdurate, do not hear him plead;
For Clarence is well-spoken, and perhaps
May move your hearts to pity, if you mark him.
   First Murd. Tush!   350
Fear not, my lord, we will not stand to prate;
Talkers are no good doers: be assured
We come to use our hands and not our tongues.
● *Glou.* Your eyes drop millstones, when fools'
      eyes drop tears:
I like you, lads; about your business straight;
Go, go, dispatch.
   First Murd. We will, my noble lord. [*Exeunt.*

    SCENE IV. *London. The Tower.*

    Enter CLARENCE *and* BRAKENBURY.

   Brak. Why looks your grace so heavily to-day?
   Clar. O, I have pass'd a miserable night,
So full of ugly sights, of ghastly dreams,
That, as I am a Christian faithful man,
I would not spend another such a night,
Though 'twere to buy a world of happy days,
So full of dismal terror was the time!

Brak. What was your dream? I long to hear
you tell it.
Clar. Methoughts that I had broken from the
Tower,
And was embark'd to cross to Burgundy; 10
And, in my company, my brother Gloucester;
Who from my cabin tempted me to walk
Upon the hatches: thence we look'd toward
England,
And cited up a thousand fearful times,
During the wars of York and Lancaster
That had befall'n us. As we paced along
Upon the giddy footing of the hatches,
Methought that Gloucester stumbled; and, in
falling,
Struck me, that thought to stay him, overboard,
Into the tumbling billows of the main. 20
Lord, Lord! methought, what pain it was to
drown!
What dreadful noise of waters in mine ears!
What ugly sights of death within mine eyes!
● Methought I saw a thousand fearful wrecks;
Ten thousand men that fishes gnaw'd upon;
Wedges of gold, great anchors, heaps of pearl,
Inestimable stones, unvalued jewels,
All scatter'd in the bottom of the sea:
Some lay in dead men's skulls; and, in those holes
Where eyes did once inhabit, there were crept, 30
As 'twere in scorn of eyes, reflecting gems,
Which woo'd the slimy bottom of the deep,
And mock'd the dead bones that lay scatter'd by.
Brak. Had you such leisure in the time of
death
To gaze upon the secrets of the deep?
Clar. Methought I had; and often did I strive
● To yield the ghost: but still the envious flood
Kept in my soul, and would not let it forth
To seek the empty, vast and wandering air;
But smother'd it within my panting bulk, 40
Which almost burst to belch it in the sea.
Brak. Awaked you not with this sore agony?
Clar. O, no, my dream was lengthen'd after
life;
O, then began the tempest to my soul,
● Who pass'd, methought, the melancholy flood,
● With that grim ferryman which poets write of,
Unto the kingdom of perpetual night.
The first that there did greet my stranger soul,
Was my great father-in-law, renowned Warwick;
Who cried aloud, 'What scourge for perjury 50
Can this dark monarchy afford false Clarence?'
And so he vanish'd: then came wandering by
● A shadow like an angel, with bright hair
Dabbled in blood; and he squeak'd out aloud,
● 'Clarence is come; false, fleeting, perjured Cla-
rence,
That stabb'd me in the field by Tewksbury;
Seize on him, Furies, take him to your torments!'
With that, methoughts, a legion of foul fiends
Environ'd me about, and howled in mine ears
Such hideous cries, that with the very noise 60
I trembling waked, and for a season after
Could not believe but that I was in hell,
Such terrible impression made the dream.
Brak. No marvel, my lord, though it affrighted
you;
I promise you, I am afraid to hear you tell it.
Clar. O Brakenbury, I have done those things,
Which now bear evidence against my soul,

Clarence's dream. Watercolour by John M. Wright
(1777–1866)

24–31 *Methought . . . gems.* See introduction.

37 *envious.* Malicious.

45 *flood.* The river Styx in Hades.

46 *ferryman.* Charon who ferried the souls of the dead
across the river Styx.

53 *shadow.* Edward, Prince of Wales.

55 *fleeting.* Inconstant.

78–83 *Princes . . . fame.* See introduction.

For Edward's sake; and see how he requites me!
O God! if my deep prayers cannot appease thee,
But thou wilt be avenged on my misdeeds,   70
Yet execute thy wrath in me alone,
O, spare my guiltless wife and my poor children!
I pray thee, gentle keeper, stay by me;
My soul is heavy, and I fain would sleep.
    Brak. I will, my lord: God give your grace
      good rest!   *[Clarence sleeps.*
Sorrow breaks seasons and reposing hours,
Makes the night morning, and the noon-tide
    night.
● Princes have but their titles for their glories,
An outward honour for an inward toil;
And, for unfelt imagination,   80
They often feel a world of restless cares:
So that, betwixt their titles and low names,
There's nothing differs but the outward fame.

Enter the two Murderers.

    First Murd. Ho! who's here?
    Brak. In God's name what are you, and how
      came you hither?
    First Murd. I would speak with Clarence,
and I came hither on my legs.
    Brak. Yea, are you so brief?
    Sec. Murd. O sir, it is better to be brief than
tedious. Shew him our commission; talk no
more.   *[Brakenbury reads it.*
    Brak. I am, in this, commanded to deliver
The noble Duke of Clarence to your hands:
I will not reason what is meant hereby,
Because I will be guiltless of the meaning.
Here are the keys, there sits the duke asleep:
I'll to the king; and signify to him
That thus I have resign'd my charge to you.
    First Murd. Do so, it is a point of wisdom:
fare you well.   *[Exit Brakenbury.*   100
    Sec. Murd. What, shall we stab him as he
sleeps?
    First Murd. No; then he will say 'twas done
cowardly, when he wakes.
    Sec. Murd. When he wakes! why, fool, he
shall never wake till the judgement-day.
    First Murd. Why, then he will say we
stabbed him sleeping.
    Sec. Murd. The urging of that word 'judge-
ment' hath bred a kind of remorse in me.   110
    First Murd. What, art thou afraid?
    Sec. Murd. Not to kill him, having a war-
rant for it; but to be damned for killing him,
from which no warrant can defend us.
    First Murd. I thought thou hadst been re-
solute.
    Sec. Murd. So I am, to let him live.
    First Murd. Back to the Duke of Gloucester,
tell him so.
    Sec. Murd. I pray thee, stay a while: I hope
my holy humour will change; 'twas wont to hold
me but while one would tell twenty.
    First Murd. How dost thou feel thyself now?
    Sec. Murd. 'Faith, some certain dregs of con-
science are yet within me.
    First Murd. Remember our reward, when
the deed is done.
    Sec. Murd. 'Zounds, he dies: I had forgot the
reward.   129
    First Murd. Where is thy conscience now?

Sec. Murd. In the Duke of Gloucester's purse.

First Murd. So when he opens his purse to give us our reward, thy conscience flies out.

Sec. Murd. Let it go; there's few or none will entertain it.

First Murd. How if it come to thee again?

● *Sec. Murd.* I'll not meddle with it: it is a dangerous thing: it makes a man a coward: a man cannot steal, but it accuseth him; he cannot swear, but it checks him; he cannot lie with his neighbour's wife, but it detects him: 'tis a blushing shamefast spirit that mutinies in a man's bosom; it fills one full of obstacles: it made me once restore a purse of gold that I found; it beggars any man that keeps it: it is turned out of all towns and cities for a dangerous thing; and every man that means to live well endeavours to trust to himself and to live without it.

● *First Murd.* 'Zounds, it is even now at my elbow, persuading me not to kill the duke.   150

Sec. Murd. Take the devil in thy mind, and believe him not: he would insinuate with thee but to make thee sigh.

First Murd. Tut, I am strong-framed, he cannot prevail with me, I warrant thee.

Sec. Murd. Spoke like a tall fellow that respects his reputation. Come, shall we to this gear?

● *First Murd.* Take him over the costard with the hilts of thy sword, and then we will chop
● him in the malmsey-butt in the next room.   161
● *Sec. Murd.* O excellent device! make a sop of him.

First Murd. Hark! he stirs: shall I strike?

Sec. Murd. No, first let's reason with him.

Clar. Where art thou, keeper? give me a cup of wine.

Sec. Murd. You shall have wine enough, my lord, anon.

Clar. In God's name, what art thou?

Sec. Murd. A man, as you are.   170

Clar. But not, as I am, royal.

Sec. Murd. Nor you, as we are, loyal.

Clar. Thy voice is thunder, but thy looks are humble.

Sec. Murd. My voice is now the king's, my looks mine own.

Clar. How darkly and how deadly dost thou speak!
Your eyes do menace me: why look you pale?
Who sent you hither? Wherefore do you come?

Both. To, to, to—

Clar. To murder me?

Both. Ay, ay.

Clar. You scarcely have the hearts to tell me so,   180
And therefore cannot have the hearts to do it.
Wherein, my friends, have I offended you?

First Murd. Offended us you have not, but the king.

Clar. I shall be reconciled to him again.

Sec. Murd. Never, my lord; therefore prepare to die.

Clar. Are you call'd forth from out a world of men
To slay the innocent? What is my offence?
Where are the evidence that do accuse me?
● What lawful quest have given their verdict up
Unto the frowning judge? or who pronounced   190

137–141 *I'll not meddle . . . detects him.* See introduction.

149 *'Zounds.* God's wounds.

159 *costard.* An apple; slang for 'head'.

161 *malmsey-butt.* A cask of sweet wine.

162 *sop.* A cake soaked in wine.

189 *quest.* Inquest.

212 *sovereign's son.* Henry VI's son, Edward, Prince of Wales.

Clarence: 'For Edward, for my brother . . .' Edward IV, brother of Richard, Duke of Gloucester, and of George, Duke of Clarence. Engraving from *Old England*, 1854

224 *indirect.* Unjust.

The bitter sentence of poor Clarence' death?
Before I be convict by course of law,
To threaten me with death is most unlawful.
I charge you, as you hope to have redemption
By Christ's dear blood shed for our grievous sins,
That you depart and lay no hands on me:
The deed you undertake is damnable.
 First Murd. What we will do, we do upon
  command.
 Sec. Murd. And he that hath commanded is
  the king.
 Clar. Erroneous vassal! the great King of
  kings   200
Hath in the tables of his law commanded
That thou shalt do no murder: and wilt thou, then,
Spurn at his edict and fulfil a man's?
Take heed; for he holds vengeance in his hands,
To hurl upon their heads that break his law.
 Sec. Murd. And that same vengeance doth
  he hurl on thee,
For false forswearing and for murder too:
Thou didst receive the holy sacrament,
To fight in quarrel of the house of Lancaster.
 First Murd. And, like a traitor to the name
  of God,   210
Didst break that vow; and with thy treacherous blade
• Unrip'dst the bowels of thy sovereign's son.
 Sec. Murd. Whom thou wert sworn to cherish
  and defend.
 First Murd. How canst thou urge God's
  dreadful law to us,
When thou hast broke it in so dear degree?
 Clar. Alas! for whose sake did I that ill deed?
For Edward, for my brother, for his sake:
Why, sirs,
He sends ye not to murder me for this;
For in this sin he is as deep as I.   220
If God will be revenged for this deed,
O, know you yet, he doth it publicly:
Take not the quarrel from his powerful arm;
• He needs no indirect nor lawless course
To cut off those that have offended him.
 First Murd. Who made thee, then, a bloody
  minister,
When gallant-springing brave Plantagenet,
That princely novice, was struck dead by thee?
 Clar. My brother's love, the devil, and my rage.
 First Murd. Thy brother's love, our duty,
  and thy fault,   230
Provoke us hither now to slaughter thee.
 Clar. Oh, if you love my brother, hate not me;
I am his brother, and I love him well.
If you be hired for meed, go back again,
And I will send you to my brother Gloucester,
Who shall reward you better for my life
Than Edward will for tidings of my death.
 Sec. Murd. You are deceived, your brother
  Gloucester hates you.
 Clar. O, no, he loves me, and he holds me
  dear:
Go you to him from me.
 Both.   Ay, so we will.   240
 Clar. Tell him, when that our princely father
  York
Bless'd his three sons with his victorious arm,
And charged us from his soul to love each other,
He little thought of this divided friendship:
Bid Gloucester think of this, and he will weep.

First Murd. Ay, millstones; as he lesson'd us
    to weep.
Clar. O, do not slander him, for he is kind.
First Murd. Right,
As snow in harvest. Thou deceivest thyself:
'Tis he that sent us hither now to slaughter thee.
  Clar. It cannot be; for when I parted with him,
He hugg'd me in his arms, and swore, with sobs,
That he would labour my delivery.
  Sec. Murd. Why, so he doth, now he delivers
    thee
From this world's thraldom to the joys of heaven.
  First Murd. Make peace with God, for you
    must die, my lord.
  Clar. Hast thou that holy feeling in thy soul,
To counsel me to make my peace with God,
And art thou yet to thy own soul so blind,
That thou wilt war with God by murdering me?
Ah, sirs, consider, he that set you on   261
To do this deed will hate you for the deed.
  Sec. Murd. What shall we do?
  Clar.   Relent, and save your souls.
  First Murd. Relent! 'tis cowardly and wo-
    manish.
  Clar. Not to relent is beastly, savage, devilish.
Which of you, if you were a prince's son,
Being pent from liberty, as I am now,
If two such murderers as yourselves came to you,
Would not entreat for life?
My friend, I spy some pity in thy looks;   270
O, if thine eye be not a flatterer,
Come thou on my side, and entreat for me,
As you would beg, were you in my distress:
A begging prince what beggar pities not?
  Sec. Murd. Look behind you, my lord.
  First Murd. Take that, and that: if all this
    will not do,   [*Stabs him.*
I'll drown you in the malmsey-butt within.
                 [*Exit, with the body.*
  Sec. Murd. A bloody deed, and desperately
    dispatch'd!
How fain, like Pilate, would I wash my hands
Of this most grievous guilty murder done!   280

       Re-enter First Murderer.

  First Murd. How now! what mean'st thou,
    that thou help'st me not?
By heavens, the duke shall know how slack thou
    art!
  Sec. Murd. I would he knew that I had saved
    his brother!
Take thou the fee, and tell him what I say;
For I repent me that the duke is slain.   [*Exit.*
  First Murd. So do not I: go, coward as thou
    art.
Now must I hide his body in some hole,
Until the duke take order for his burial:
And when I have my meed, I must away;
For this will out, and here I must not stay.   290

ACT II.

SCENE I. *London. The palace.*

Flourish. Enter KING EDWARD *sick,* QUEEN
ELIZABETH, DORSET, RIVERS, HASTINGS,
BUCKINGHAM, GREY, *and others.*
  K. Edw. Why, so: now have I done a good
    day's work:

Edward IV holds court. From Laurence Olivier's film
production of *Richard III,* 1955

53 *heap.* Company.

Roy Dotrice as Edward IV and Susan Engel as Queen Elizabeth, Royal Shakespeare Co, 1963

You peers, continue this united league:
I every day expect an embassage
From my Redeemer to redeem me hence;
And now in peace my soul shall part to heaven,
Since I have set my friends at peace on earth.
Rivers and Hastings, take each other's hand;
Dissemble not your hatred, swear your love.
   Riv. By heaven, my heart is purged from
     grudging hate;
And with my hand I seal my true heart's love. 10
   Hast. So thrive I, as I truly swear the like!
   K. Edw. Take heed you dally not before
     your king;
Lest he that is the supreme King of kings
Confound your hidden falsehood, and award
Either of you to be the other's end.
   Hast. So prosper I, as I swear perfect love!
   Riv. And I, as I love Hastings with my heart!
   K. Edw. Madam, yourself are not exempt in
     this,
Nor your son Dorset, Buckingham, nor you;
You have been factious one against the other. 20
Wife, love Lord Hastings, let him kiss your hand;
And what you do, do it unfeignedly.
   Q. Eliz. Here, Hastings; I will never more
     remember
Our former hatred, so thrive I and mine!
   K. Edw. Dorset, embrace him; Hastings,
     love lord marquess.
   Dor. This interchange of love, I here protest,
Upon my part shall be unviolable.
   Hast. And so swear I, my lord.
                        [They embrace.
   K. Edw. Now, princely Buckingham, seal
     thou this league
With thy embracements to my wife's allies, 30
And make me happy in your unity.
   Buck. Whenever Buckingham doth turn his
     hate
On you or yours [*to the Queen*], but with all
     duteous love
Doth cherish you and yours, God punish me
With hate in those where I expect most love!
When I have most need to employ a friend,
And most assured that he is a friend,
Deep, hollow, treacherous, and full of guile,
Be he unto me! this do I beg of God,
When I am cold in zeal to you or yours. 40
                        [They embrace.
   K. Edw. A pleasing cordial, princely Buck-
     ingham,
Is this thy vow unto my sickly heart.
There wanteth now our brother Gloucester here,
To make the perfect period of this peace.
   Buck. And, in good time, here comes the
     noble duke.

        Enter GLOUCESTER.

   Glou. Good morrow to my sovereign king and
     queen;
And, princely peers, a happy time of day!
   K. Edw. Happy, indeed, as we have spent
     the day.
Brother, we have done deeds of charity;
Made peace of enmity, fair love of hate, 50
Between these swelling wrong-incensed peers.
   Glou. A blessed labour, my most sovereign
     liege:
● Amongst this princely heap, if any here,

By false intelligence, or wrong surmise,
Hold me a foe;
If I unwittingly, or in my rage,
● Have aught committed that is hardly borne
By any in this presence, I desire
To reconcile me to his friendly peace:
'Tis death to me to be at enmity; 60
I hate it, and desire all good men's love.
First, madam, I entreat true peace of you,
Which I will purchase with my duteous service;
Of you, my noble cousin Buckingham,
If ever any grudge were lodged between us;
Of you, Lord Rivers, and, Lord Grey, of you;
That all without desert have frown'd on me;
Dukes, earls, lords, gentlemen; indeed, of all.
I do not know that Englishman alive
With whom my soul is any jot at odds 70
More than the infant that is born to-night:
I thank my God for my humility.
   Q. Eliz. A holy day shall this be kept here-
     after:
I would to God all strifes were well compounded.
My sovereign liege, I do beseech your majesty
To take our brother Clarence to your grace.
   Glou. Why, madam, have I offer'd love for
     this,
To be so flouted in this royal presence?
Who knows not that the noble duke is dead?
                   [*They all start.*
You do him injury to scorn his corse. 80
   Riv. Who knows not he is dead! who knows
     he is?
   Q. Eliz. All-seeing heaven, what a world is
     this!
   Buck. Look I so pale, Lord Dorset, as the
     rest?
   Dor. Ay, my good lord; and no one in this
     presence
But his red colour hath forsook his cheeks.
   K. Edw. Is Clarence dead? the order was
     reversed.
   Glou. But he, poor soul, by your first order
     died,
And that a winged Mercury did bear;
Some tardy cripple bore the countermand,
● That came too lag to see him buried. 90
God grant that some, less noble and less loyal,
Nearer in bloody thoughts, but not in blood,
Deserve not worse than wretched Clarence did,
And yet go current from suspicion!

          Enter DERBY.

   Der. A boon, my sovereign, for my service
     done!
   K. Edw. I pray thee, peace: my soul is full
     of sorrow.
   Der. I will not rise, unless your highness grant.
   K. Edw. Then speak at once what is it thou
     demand'st.
●   *Der.* The forfeit, sovereign, of my servant's
     life;
Who slew to-day a riotous gentleman 100
Lately attendant on the Duke of Norfolk.
   K. Edw. Have I a tongue to doom my bro-
     ther's death,
And shall the same give pardon to a slave?
My brother slew no man; his fault was thought,
And yet his punishment was cruel death.
Who sued to me for him? who, in my rage,

57 *hardly borne*. Resented.

Costume design for Queen Elizabeth by John Bury with
Ann Curtis, Royal Shakespeare Co, 1964

---

90 *lag*. Late.

99 *The forfeit . . . life*. Pardon for my servant, whose life
should be forfeit for his crime.

107 *advised.* Careful.

133 *closet.* Private apartment.

137 *still.* Continually.

Sir John Martin-Harvey who played Richard III at the
His Majesty's Theatre, London, 1916. Painting by
Bernard Munns (1870–1942)

8 *cousins.* A term used for a wide variety of family
relationships.

● Kneel'd at my feet, and bade me be advised?
Who spake of brotherhood? who spake of love?
Who told me how the poor soul did forsake
The mighty Warwick, and did fight for me? 110
Who told me, in the field by Tewksbury,
When Oxford had me down, he rescued me,
And said, 'Dear brother, live, and be a king'?
Who told me, when we both lay in the field
Frozen almost to death, how he did lap me
Even in his own garments, and gave himself,
All thin and naked, to the numb cold night?
All this from my remembrance brutish wrath
Sinfully pluck'd, and not a man of you
Had so much grace to put it in my mind. 120
But when your carters or your waiting-vassals
Have done a drunken slaughter, and defaced
The precious image of our dear Redeemer,
You straight are on your knees for pardon, pardon;
And I, unjustly too, must grant it you:
But for my brother not a man would speak,
Nor I, ungracious, speak unto myself
For him, poor soul. The proudest of you all
Have been beholding to him in his life;
Yet none of you would once plead for his life. 130
O God, I fear thy justice will take hold
On me, and you, and mine, and yours for this!
● Come, Hastings, help me to my closet. Oh,
poor Clarence!
   [*Exeunt some with King and Queen.*
 Glou. This is the fruit of rashness! Mark'd
you not
How that the guilty kindred of the queen
Look'd pale when they did hear of Clarence'
death?
● O, they did urge it still unto the king!
God will revenge it. But come, let us in,
To comfort Edward with our company.
 Buck. We wait upon your grace. [*Exeunt.*

SCENE II. *The palace.*

Enter the DUCHESS OF YORK, *with the two
children of* CLARENCE.

 Boy. Tell me, good grandam, is our father
dead?
 Duch. No, boy.
 Boy. Why do you wring your hands, and beat
your breast,
And cry 'O Clarence, my unhappy son!'
 Girl. Why do you look on us, and shake your
head,
And call us wretches, orphans, castaways,
If that our noble father be alive?
● *Duch.* My pretty cousins, you mistake me
much;
I do lament the sickness of the king,
As loath to lose him, not your father's death; 10
It were lost sorrow to wail one that's lost.
 Boy. Then, grandam, you conclude that he is
dead.
The king my uncle is to blame for this:
God will revenge it; whom I will importune
With daily prayers all to that effect.
 Girl. And so will I.
 Duch. Peace, children, peace! the king doth
love you well:
Incapable and shallow innocents,
You cannot guess who caused your father's death.

Boy. Grandam, we can; for my good uncle Gloucester 20
Told me, the king, provoked by the queen,
Devised impeachments to imprison him:
And when my uncle told me so, he wept,
And hugg'd me in his arm, and kindly kiss'd my cheek;
Bade me rely on him as on my father,
And he would love me dearly as his child.
   Duch. Oh, that deceit should steal such gentle shapes,
And with a virtuous vizard hide foul guile!
He is my son; yea, and therein my shame;
● Yet from my dugs he drew not this deceit. 30
   Son. Think you my uncle did dissemble, grandam?
   Duch. Ay, boy.
   Son. I cannot think it. Hark! what noise is this?

Enter QUEEN ELIZABETH, *with her hair about her ears;* RIVERS *and* DORSET *after her.*

   Q. Eliz. Oh, who shall hinder me to wail and weep,
To chide my fortune, and torment myself?
I'll join with black despair against my soul,
And to myself become an enemy.
   Duch. What means this scene of rude impatience?
   Q. Eliz. To make an act of tragic violence:
Edward, my lord, your son, our king, is dead. 40
Why grow the branches now the root is wither'd?
Why wither not the leaves the sap being gone?
If you will live, lament; if die, be brief,
That our swift-winged souls may catch the king's;
Or, like obedient subjects, follow him
To his new kingdom of perpetual rest.
   Duch. Ah, so much interest have I in thy sorrow
As I had title in thy noble husband!
I have bewept a worthy husband's death,
● And lived by looking on his images: 50
But now two mirrors of his princely semblance
Are crack'd in pieces by malignant death,
And I for comfort have but one false glass,
Which grieves me when I see my shame in him.
Thou art a widow; yet thou art a mother,
And hast the comfort of thy children left thee:
But death hath snatch'd my husband from mine arms,
And pluck'd two crutches from my feeble limbs,
Edward and Clarence. O, what cause have I,
Thine being but a moiety of my grief, 60
To overgo thy plaints and drown thy cries!
   Boy. Good aunt, you wept not for our father's death;
How can we aid you with our kindred tears?
   Girl. Our fatherless distress was left unmoan'd;
Your widow-dolour likewise be unwept!
   Q. Eliz. Give me no help in lamentation;
I am not barren to bring forth complaints:
● All springs reduce their currents to mine eyes,
That I, being govern'd by the watery moon,
May send forth plenteous tears to drown the world! 70
Oh for my husband, for my dear lord Edward!
   Chil. Oh for our father, for our dear lord Clarence!
   Duch. Alas for both, both mine, Edward and Clarence!

30 *dugs*. Breasts.

Queen Elizabeth: 'Edward, my lord, your son, our king, is dead.' Woodcut of the death of a king from Holinshed's *Chronicles*, 1577

50 *images*. i.e. children.

68 *reduce*. Bring.

81 *parcell'd.* Particular.

112 *cloudy.* Gloomy.

Costume design for Duke of Buckingham by Jocelyn Herbert with Sally Jacobs, Stratford-upon-Avon, 1961

Q. Eliz. What stay had I but Edward? and he's gone.
Chil. What stay had we but Clarence? and he's gone.
Duch. What stays had I but they? and they are gone.
Q. Eliz. Was never widow had so dear a loss!
Chil. Were never orphans had so dear a loss!
Duch. Was never mother had so dear a loss!
Alas, I am the mother of these moans!   80
● Their woes are parcell'd, mine are general.
She for an Edward weeps, and so do I;
I for a Clarence weep, so doth not she:
These babes for Clarence weep, and so do I;
I for an Edward weep, so do not they:
Alas, you three, on me, threefold distress'd,
Pour all your tears! I am your sorrow's nurse,
And I will pamper it with lamentations.
  Dor. Comfort, dear mother: God is much displeased
That you take with unthankfulness his doing: 90
In common worldly things, 'tis call'd ungrateful,
With dull unwillingness to repay a debt
Which with a bounteous hand was kindly lent;
Much more to be thus opposite with heaven,
For it requires the royal debt it lent you.
  Riv. Madam, bethink you, like a careful mother,
Of the young prince your son: send straight for him;
Let him be crown'd; in him your comfort lives:
Drown desperate sorrow in dead Edward's grave,
And plant your joys in living Edward's throne. 100

Enter GLOUCESTER, BUCKINGHAM, DERBY,
  HASTINGS, *and* RATCLIFF.

  Glou. Madam, have comfort: all of us have cause
To wail the dimming of our shining star;
But none can cure their harms by wailing them.
Madam, my mother, I do cry you mercy;
I did not see your grace: humbly on my knee
I crave your blessing.
  Duch. God bless thee; and put meekness in thy mind,
Love, charity, obedience, and true duty!
  Glou. [*Aside*] Amen; and make me die a good old man!
That is the butt-end of a mother's blessing: 110
I marvel why her grace did leave it out.
● *Buck.* You cloudy princes and heart-sorrowing peers,
That bear this mutual heavy load of moan,
Now cheer each other in each other's love:
Though we have spent our harvest of this king,
We are to reap the harvest of his son.
The broken rancour of your high-swoln hearts,
But lately splinter'd, knit, and join'd together,
Must gently be preserved, cherish'd, and kept:
Me seemeth good, that, with some little train, 120
Forthwith from Ludlow the young prince be fetch'd
Hither to London, to be crown'd our king.
  Riv. Why with some little train, my Lord of Buckingham?
  Buck. Marry, my lord, lest, by a multitude,
The new-heal'd wound of malice should break out;

Which would be so much the more dangerous,
By how much the estate is green and yet un-
govern'd:
● Where every horse bears his commanding rein,
And may direct his course as please himself,
As well the fear of harm, as harm apparent, 130
In my opinion, ought to be prevented.
   Glou. I hope the king made peace with all
of us;
And the compact is firm and true in me.
   Riv. And so in me; and so, I think, in all:
Yet, since it is but green, it should be put
To no apparent likelihood of breach,
Which haply by much company might be urged:
Therefore I say with noble Buckingham,
That it is meet so few should fetch the prince.
   Hast. And so say I. 140
   Glou. Then be it so; and go we to de-
termine
Who they shall be that straight shall post to
Ludlow.
Madam, and you, my mother, will you go
To give your censures in this weighty business?
   Q. Eliz. }
   Duch. } With all our hearts.
   [*Exeunt all but Buckingham and Gloucester.*
   Buck. My Lord, whoever journeys to the
prince,
For God's sake, let not us two be behind;
For, by the way, I'll sort occasion,
● As index to the story we late talk'd of,
To part the queen's proud kindred from the
king. 150
●   *Glou.* My other self, my counsel's consistory,
My oracle, my prophet! My dear cousin,
I, like a child, will go by thy direction,
Towards Ludlow then, for we'll not stay behind.
   [*Exeunt.*

SCENE III. *London. A street.*

Enter two Citizens, *meeting.*

   First Cit. Neighbour, well met: whither away
so fast?
   Sec. Cit. I promise you, I scarcely know
myself:
Hear you the news abroad?
   First Cit.   Ay, that the king is dead.
●   *Sec. Cit.* Bad news, by'r lady; seldom comes
the better:
I fear, I fear 'twill prove a troublous world.

Enter another Citizen.

   Third Cit. Neighbours, God speed!
   First Cit.   Give you good morrow, sir.
   Third Cit. Doth this news hold of good King
Edward's death?
   Sec. Cit. Ay, sir, it is too true; God help
the while!
   Third Cit. Then, masters, look to see a
troublous world.
   First Cit. No, no; by God's good grace his
son shall reign. 10
   Third Cit. Woe to that land that's govern'd
by a child!
   Sec. Cit. In him there is a hope of govern-
ment,
● That in his nonage council under him,
And in his full and ripen'd years himself,

128 *bears . . . rein.* Commands the rein that should control him.

149 *index.* Prologue or table of contents.

151 *consistory.* Council chamber.

Street scene in London. Engraving from *Old England,* 1854

4 *seldom comes the better.* Proverbial; changes are rarely for the better.

13 *nonage.* Minority.

36 *sort*. Order.

Archbishop of York with the young Duke of York and Queen Elizabeth. Engraving from a painting by E.M. Ward (1816–1879)

No doubt, shall then and till then govern well.
   First Cit. So stood the state when Henry the Sixth
Was crown'd in Paris but at nine months old.
   Third Cit. Stood the state so? No, no, good friends, God wot;
For then this land was famously enrich'd
With politic grave counsel; then the king   20
Had virtuous uncles to protect his grace.
   First Cit. Why, so hath this, both by the father and mother.
   Third Cit. Better it were they all came by the father,
Or by the father there were none at all;
For emulation now, who shall be nearest,
Will touch us all too near, if God prevent not.
O, full of danger is the Duke of Gloucester!
And the queen's sons and brothers haught and proud:
And were they to be ruled, and not to rule,
This sickly land might solace as before.   30
   First Cit. Come, come, we fear the worst; all shall be well.
   Third Cit. When clouds appear, wise men put on their cloaks;
When great leaves fall, the winter is at hand;
When the sun sets, who doth not look for night?
Untimely storms make men expect a dearth.
All may be well; but, if God sort it so,
'Tis more than we deserve, or I expect.
   Sec. Cit. Truly, the souls of men are full of dread:
Ye cannot reason almost with a man
That looks not heavily and full of fear.   40
   Third Cit. Before the times of change, still is it so:
By a divine instinct men's minds mistrust
Ensuing dangers; as, by proof, we see
The waters swell before a boisterous storm.
But leave it all to God. Whither away?
   Sec. Cit. Marry, we were sent for to the justices.
   Third Cit. And so was I: I'll bear you company.   [*Exeunt.*

    SCENE IV. *London. The palace.*

Enter the ARCHBISHOP OF YORK, *the young* DUKE OF YORK, QUEEN ELIZABETH, *and the* DUCHESS OF YORK.

   Arch. Last night, I hear, they lay at Northampton;
At Stony-Stratford will they be to-night:
To-morrow, or next day, they will be here.
   Duch. I long with all my heart to see the prince:
I hope he is much grown since last I saw him.
   Q. Eliz. But I hear, no; they say my son of York
Hath almost overta'en him in his growth.
   York. Ay, mother; but I would not have it so.
   Duch. Why, my young cousin, it is good to grow.
   York. Grandam, one night, as we did sit at supper,   10
My uncle Rivers talk'd how I did grow
More than my brother: 'Ay,' quoth my uncle Gloucester,

'Small herbs have grace, great weeds do grow
　　apace:'
And since, methinks, I would not grow so fast,
Because sweet flowers are slow and weeds
　　make haste.
　　Duch. Good faith, good faith, the saying did
　　not hold
In him that did object the same to thee:
He was the wretched'st thing when he was young,
So long a-growing and so leisurely,
That, if this rule were true, he should be gracious.
　　Arch. Why, madam, so, no doubt, he is.　21
　　Duch. I hope he is; but yet let mothers doubt.
　　York. Now, by my troth, if I had been re-
　　member'd,
● I could have given my uncle's grace a flout,
To touch his growth nearer than he touch'd mine.
　　Duch. How, my pretty York? I pray thee,
　　let me hear it.
　　York. Marry, they say my uncle grew so fast
That he could gnaw a crust at two hours old:
'Twas full two years ere I could get a tooth.
Grandam, this would have been a biting jest.　30
　　Duch. I pray thee, pretty York, who told
　　thee this?
　　York. Grandam, his nurse.
　　Duch. His nurse! why, she was dead ere thou
　　wert born.
　　York. If 'twere not she, I cannot tell who
　　told me.
● 　*Q. Eliz.* A parlous boy: go to, you are too
　　shrewd.
　　Arch. Good madam, be not angry with the
　　child.
　　Q. Eliz. Pitchers have ears.

　　　　　Enter a Messenger.

　　Arch. Here comes a messenger. What news?
　　Mess. Such news, my lord, as grieves me to
　　unfold.
　　Q. Eliz. How fares the prince?
　　Mess. 　　　Well, madam, and in health.　40
　　Duch. What is thy news then?
　　Mess. Lord Rivers and Lord Grey are sent to
　　Pomfret,
With them Sir Thomas Vaughan, prisoners.
　　Duch. Who hath committed them?
　　Mess. 　　　　　　The mighty dukes
Gloucester and Buckingham.
　　Q. Eliz. 　　　　　For what offence?
　　Mess. The sum of all I can, I have disclosed;
Why or for what these nobles were committed
Is all unknown to me, my gracious lady.
　　Q. Eliz. Ay me, I see the downfall of our
　　house!
The tiger now hath seized the gentle hind;　50
● Insulting tyranny begins to jet
● Upon the innocent and aweless throne:
Welcome, destruction, death, and massacre!
I see, as in a map, the end of all.
　　Duch. Accursed and unquiet wrangling days,
How many of you have mine eyes beheld!
My husband lost his life to get the crown;
And often up and down my sons were toss'd,
For me to joy and weep their gain and loss:
And being seated, and domestic broils　60
Clean over-blown, themselves, the conquerors,
Make war upon themselves; blood against blood,
Self against self: O, preposterous

24 *flout.* Taunt.

35 *parlous.* Dangerous.

Archbishop: 'Good madam, be not angry with the child'.
Engraving from a 19th century painting by G.B.
Ciprianio (1727–85)

51 *jet.* Strut.

52 *aweless.* Not inspiring awe.

64 *spleen.* Malice.

Archbishop: 'Come, I'll conduct you to the sanctuary.'
Painting by John Opie (1761–1807)

---

1 *chamber.* This title was given to London, or, more particularly, to that part of the royal household concerned with the king's finances.

● And frantic outrage, end thy damned spleen;
Or let me die, to look on death no more!
   Q. Eliz. Come, come, my boy; we will to
     sanctuary.
Madam, farewell.
   Duch.   I'll go along with you.
   Q. Eliz. You have no cause.
   Arch.   My gracious lady, go;
And thither bear your treasure and your goods.
For my part, I'll resign unto your grace   70
The seal I keep: and so betide to me
As well I tender you and all of yours!
Come, I'll conduct you to the sanctuary.
                  [*Exeunt.*

ACT III.

SCENE I. *London. A street.*

The trumpets sound. Enter the young PRINCE,
the Dukes of GLOUCESTER *and* BUCKINGHAM,
CARDINAL BOURCHIER, CATESBY, *and others.*

●   *Buck.* Welcome, sweet prince, to London, to
    your chamber.
   Glou. Welcome, dear cousin, my thoughts'
    sovereign:
The weary way hath made you melancholy.
   Prince. No, uncle; but our crosses on the way
Have made it tedious, wearisome, and heavy:
I want more uncles here to welcome me.
   Glou. Sweet prince, the untainted virtue of
    your years
Hath not yet dived into the world's deceit:
Nor more can you distinguish of a man
Than of his outward show; which, God he knows,
Seldom or never jumpeth with the heart.   11
Those uncles which you want were dangerous;
Your grace attended to their sugar'd words,
But look'd not on the poison of their hearts:
God keep you from them, and from such false
    friends!
   Prince. God keep me from false friends! but
    they were none.
   Glou. My lord, the mayor of London comes
    to greet you.

Enter the Lord Mayor, *and his train.*

   May. God bless your grace with health and
    happy days!
   Prince. I thank you, good my lord; and thank
    you all.
I thought my mother, and my brother York,   20
Would long ere this have met us on the way:
Fie, what a slug is Hastings, that he comes not
To tell us whether they will come or no!

Enter LORD HASTINGS.

   Buck. And, in good time, here comes the
    sweating lord.
   Prince. Welcome, my lord: what, will our
    mother come?
   Hast. On what occasion, God he knows,
    not I,
The queen your mother, and your brother York,
Have taken sanctuary: the tender prince
Would fain have come with me to meet your grace,
But by his mother was perforce withheld.   30
   Buck. Fie, what an indirect and peevish course
Is this of hers! Lord cardinal, will your grace

Persuade the queen to send the Duke of York
Unto his princely brother presently?
If she deny, Lord Hastings, go with him,
And from her jealous arms pluck him perforce.
   Card. My Lord of Buckingham, if my weak
      oratory
Can from his mother win the Duke of York,
Anon expect him here; but if she be obdurate
To mild entreaties, God in heaven forbid   40
We should infringe the holy privilege
Of blessed sanctuary! not for all this land
Would I be guilty of so deep a sin.
   Buck. You are too senseless-obstinate, my lord,
Too ceremonious and traditional:
• Weigh it but with the grossness of this age,
You break not sanctuary in seizing him.
The benefit thereof is always granted
To those whose dealings have deserved the place,
And those who have the wit to claim the place:
This prince hath neither claim'd it nor deserved it;
And therefore, in mine opinion, cannot have it:
Then, taking him from thence that is not there,
You break no privilege nor charter there.
Oft have I heard of sanctuary men;
But sanctuary children ne'er till now.
   Card. My lord, you shall o'er-rule my mind
      for once.
Come on, Lord Hastings, will you go with me?
   Hast. I go, my lord.
   Prince. Good lords, make all the speedy haste
      you may.   60
            [Exeunt Cardinal and Hastings.
Say, uncle Gloucester, if our brother come,
Where shall we sojourn till our coronation?
   Glou. Where it seems best unto your royal
      self.
If I may counsel you, some day or two
Your highness shall repose you at the Tower:
Then where you please, and shall be thought
      most fit
For your best health and recreation.
   Prince. I do not like the Tower, of any place.
Did Julius Cæsar build that place, my lord?
   Buck. He did, my gracious lord, begin that
      place;   70
Which, since, succeeding ages have re-edified.
   Prince. Is it upon record, or else reported
Successively from age to age, he built it?
   Buck. Upon record, my gracious lord.
   Prince. But say, my lord, it were not re-
      gister'd,
Methinks the truth should live from age to age,
As 'twere retail'd to all posterity,
Even to the general all-ending day.
   Glou. [*Aside*] So wise so young, they say, do
      never live long.
   Prince. What say you, uncle?   80
•   *Glou.* I say, without characters, fame lives
      long.
• [*Aside*] Thus, like the formal vice, Iniquity,
I moralize two meanings in one word.
   Prince. That Julius Cæsar was a famous man;
With what his valour did enrich his wit,
His wit set down to make his valour live:
Death makes no conquest of this conqueror;
For now he lives in fame, though not in life.
I'll tell you what, my cousin Buckingham,—
   Buck. What, my gracious lord?   90
   Prince. An if I live until I be a man,

46 *grossness.* Unscrupulousness.

81 *characters.* A pun on the meanings of 'handwriting' and of 'moral quality'.

82 *vice.* The character in the old Morality plays.

94 *lightly.* Usually. *forward.* Early.

The Princes greet each other. Painting by James Northcote (1746–1831)

126 *still be cross.* Always be perverse.

York: 'Because that I am little, like an ape, He thinks that you should bear me on your shoulders.' Woodcut from Joseph Strutt's *The Sports and Pastimes of the People of England*, 1810

I 'll win our ancient right in France again,
Or die a soldier, as I lived a king.
*   *Glou.* [*Aside*] Short summers lightly have a
   forward spring.

     Enter young YORK, HASTINGS, *and the*
             CARDINAL.

   Buck. Now, in good time, here comes the
   Duke of York.
   Prince. Richard of York! how fares our loving
   brother?
   York. Well, my dread lord; so must I call
   you now.
   Prince. Ay, brother, to our grief, as it is
   yours:
Too late he died that might have kept that title,
Which by his death hath lost much majesty. 100
   Glou. How fares our cousin, noble Lord of
   York?
   York. I thank you, gentle uncle. O, my lord,
You said that idle weeds are fast in growth:
The prince my brother hath outgrown me far.
   Glou. He hath, my lord.
   York.   And therefore is he idle?
   Glou. O, my fair cousin, I must not say so.
   York. Then he is more beholding to you
   than I.
   Glou. He may command me as my sovereign;
But you have power in me as in a kinsman.
   York. I pray you, uncle, give me this dagger.
   Glou. My dagger, little cousin? with all my
   heart.   111
   Prince. A beggar, brother?
   York. Of my kind uncle, that I know will give;
And being but a toy, which is no grief to give.
   Glou. A greater gift than that I 'll give my
   cousin.
   York. A greater gift! O, that 's the sword
   to it.
   Glou. Ay, gentle cousin, were it light enough.
   York. O, then, I see, you will part but with
   light gifts;
In weightier things you 'll say a beggar nay.
   Glou. It is too heavy for your grace to wear.
   York. I weigh it lightly, were it heavier. 121
   Glou. What, would you have my weapon,
   little lord?
   York. I would, that I might thank you as you
   call me.
   Glou. How?
   York. Little.
*   *Prince.* My Lord of York will still be cross in
   talk:
Uncle, your grace knows how to bear with him.
   York. You mean, to bear me, not to bear
   with me:
Uncle, my brother mocks both you and me;
Because that I am little, like an ape,   130
He thinks that you should bear me on your
   shoulders.
   Buck. With what a sharp-provided wit he
   reasons!
To mitigate the scorn he gives his uncle,
He prettily and aptly taunts himself:
So cunning and so young is wonderful.
   Glou. My lord, will 't please you pass along?
Myself and my good cousin Buckingham
Will to your mother, to entreat of her
To meet you at the Tower and welcome you.

York. What, will you go unto the Tower, my
 lord?   140
Prince. My lord protector needs will have it so.
York. I shall not sleep in quiet at the Tower.
Glou. Why, what should you fear?
York. Marry, my uncle Clarence' angry ghost:
My grandam told me he was murder'd there.
Prince. I fear no uncles dead.
Glou. Nor none that live, I hope.
Prince. An if they live, I hope I need not fear.
But come, my lord; and with a heavy heart,
Thinking on them, go I unto the Tower.   150
       [*A Sennet. Exeunt all but Gloucester,*
              Buckingham and Catesby.
Buck. Think you, my lord, this little prating
 York
Was not incensed by his subtle mother
To taunt and scorn you thus opprobriously?
Glou. No doubt, no doubt: O, 'tis a parlous
 boy;
Bold, quick, ingenious, forward, capable:
He is all the mother's, from the top to toe.
Buck. Well, let them rest. Come hither,
 Catesby.
Thou art sworn as deeply to effect what we in-
 tend
As closely to conceal what we impart:
Thou know'st our reasons urged upon the way;
What think'st thou? is it not an easy matter 161
To make William Lord Hastings of our mind,
For the instalment of this noble duke
In the seat royal of this famous isle?
Cate. He for his father's sake so loves the
 prince,
That he will not be won to aught against him.
Buck. What think'st thou, then, of Stanley?
 what will he?
Cate. He will do all in all as Hastings doth.
Buck. Well, then, no more but this: go, gentle
 Catesby,
And, as it were far off, sound thou Lord Hastings,
How he doth stand affected to our purpose; 171
And summon him to-morrow to the Tower,
• To sit about the coronation.
If thou dost find him tractable to us,
Encourage him, and show him all our reasons:
If he be leaden, icy-cold, unwilling,
Be thou so too; and so break off your talk,
And give us notice of his inclination:
For we to-morrow hold divided councils,
Wherein thyself shalt highly be employ'd.   180
Glou. Commend me to Lord William: tell
 him, Catesby,
His ancient knot of dangerous adversaries
To-morrow are let blood at Pomfret-castle;
And bid my friend, for joy of this good news,
• Give Mistress Shore one gentle kiss the more.
Buck. Good Catesby, go, effect this business
 soundly.
Cate. My good lords both, with all the heed
 I may.
Glou. Shall we hear from you, Catesby, ere
 we sleep?
Cate. You shall, my lord.
Glou. At Crosby Place, there shall you find us
 both.   [*Exit Catesby.* 190
Buck. Now, my lord, what shall we do, if we
 perceive
Lord Hastings will not yield to our complots?

173 *sit about.* Discuss.

185 *Mistress Shore.* On Edward IV's death, she
became Lord Hastings's mistress.

11 *boar.* Richard III's badge was a boar. *razed his helm.* Plucked off his helmet.

The coat of arms of Richard III with the two boars as supporters.

Glou. Chop off his head, man; somewhat we will do:
And, look, when I am king, claim thou of me
The earldom of Hereford, and the moveables
Whereof the king my brother stood possess'd.
   Buck. I'll claim that promise at your grace's hands.
   Glou. And look to have it yielded with all willingness.
Come, let us sup betimes, that afterwards
We may digest our complots in some form.   200
                    [*Exeunt.*

SCENE II. *Before Lord Hastings' house.*

Enter a Messenger.

Mess. What, ho! my lord!
Hast. [*Within*] Who knocks at the door?
Mess. A messenger from the Lord Stanley.

Enter LORD HASTINGS.

Hast. What is't o'clock?
Mess. Upon the stroke of four.
Hast. Cannot thy master sleep these tedious nights?
Mess. So it should seem by that I have to say.
First, he commends him to your noble lordship.
   Hast. And then?
   Mess. And then he sends you word   10
He dreamt to-night the boar had razed his helm:
Besides, he says there are two councils held;
And that may be determined at the one
Which may make you and him to rue at the other.
Therefore he sends to know your lordship's pleasure,
If presently you will take horse with him,
And with all speed post with him toward the north,
To shun the danger that his soul divines.
   Hast. Go, fellow, go, return unto thy lord;
Bid him not fear the separated councils: 20
His honour and myself are at the one,
And at the other is my servant Catesby;
Where nothing can proceed that toucheth us
Whereof I shall not have intelligence.
Tell him his fears are shallow, wanting instance:
And for his dreams, I wonder he is so fond
To trust the mockery of unquiet slumbers:
To fly the boar before the boar pursues,
Were to incense the boar to follow us
And make pursuit where he did mean no chase.
Go, bid thy master rise and come to me;   31
And we will both together to the Tower,
Where, he shall see, the boar will use us kindly.
   Mess. My gracious lord, I'll tell him what you say.   [*Exit.*

Enter CATESBY.

Cate. Many good morrows to my noble lord!
Hast. Good morrow, Catesby; you are early stirring:
What news, what news, in this our tottering state?
Cate. It is a reeling world, indeed, my lord;
And I believe 'twill never stand upright
Till Richard wear the garland of the realm.   40
   Hast. How! wear the garland! dost thou mean the crown?
   Cate. Ay, my good lord.

Hast. I'll have this crown of mine cut from
    my shoulders
Ere I will see the crown so foul misplaced.
But canst thou guess that he doth aim at it?
    Cate. Ay, on my life; and hopes to find you
    forward
Upon his party for the gain thereof:
And thereupon he sends you this good news,
That this same very day your enemies,   49
The kindred of the queen, must die at Pomfret.
    Hast. Indeed, I am no mourner for that news,
Because they have been still mine enemies:
But, that I'll give my voice on Richard's side,
To bar my master's heirs in true descent,
God knows I will not do it, to the death.
    Cate. God keep your lordship in that gracious
    mind!
    Hast. But I shall laugh at this a twelve-month
    hence,
That they who brought me in my master's hate,
I live to look upon their tragedy.
I tell thee, Catesby,—   60
    Cate. What, my lord?
    Hast. Ere a fortnight make me elder,
I'll send some packing that yet think not on it.
    Cate. 'Tis a vile thing to die, my gracious lord,
When men are unprepared and look not for it.
    Hast. O monstrous, monstrous! and so falls
    it out
With Rivers, Vaughan, Grey: and so 'twill do
With some men else, who think themselves as
    safe
As thou and I; who, as thou know'st, are dear
To princely Richard and to Buckingham.   70
    Cate. The princes both make high account of
    you;
    [*Aside*] For they account his head upon the bridge.
    Hast. I know they do; and I have well de-
    served it.

Enter LORD STANLEY.

Come on, come on; where is your boar-spear,
    man?
Fear you the boar, and go so unprovided?
    Stan. My lord, good morrow; good morrow,
    Catesby:
You may jest on, but, by the holy rood,
I do not like these several councils, I.
    Hast. My lord,
I hold my life as dear as you do yours;   80
And never in my life, I do protest,
Was it more precious to me than 'tis now:
Think you, but that I know our state secure,
I would be so triumphant as I am?
    Stan. The lords at Pomfret, when they rode
    from London,
Were jocund, and supposed their state was sure,
And they indeed had no cause to mistrust;
But yet, you see, how soon the day o'ercast.
This sudden stab of rancour I misdoubt:
Pray God, I say, I prove a needless coward!   90
What, shall we toward the Tower? the day is
    spent.
    Hast. Come, come, have with you. Wot you
    what, my lord?
To-day the lords you talk of are beheaded.
    Stan. They, for their truth, might better wear
    their heads

43 *crown.* i.e. his head.

72 *bridge.* London Bridge where the heads of traitors
were stuck up on poles.

London Bridge. Engraving from *Old England*, 1854

77 *holy rood.* Holy cross.

92 *have with you.* Let's get on.

116 *shriving.* Confession and absolution.

Pomfret Castle. Engraving from *The Pictorial History of England,* 1856

Than some that have accused them wear their
    hats.
But come, my lord, let us away.

Enter a Pursuivant.

Hast. Go on before; I'll talk with this good
    fellow.   *[Exeunt Stanley and Catesby.*
How now, sirrah! how goes the world with thee?
Purs. The better that your lordship please
    to ask.   99
Hast. I tell thee, man, 'tis better with me now
Than when I met thee last where now we meet:
Then was I going prisoner to the Tower,
By the suggestion of the queen's allies;
But now, I tell thee—keep it to thyself—
This day those enemies are put to death,
And I in better state than e'er I was.
Purs. God hold it, to your honour's good
    content!
Hast. Gramercy, fellow: there, drink that for
    me.   *[Throws him his purse.*
Purs. God save your lordship!   *[Exit.*

Enter a Priest.

Priest. Well met, my lord; I am glad to see
    your honour.   110
Hast. I thank thee, good Sir John, with all
    my heart.
I am in your debt for your last exercise;
Come the next Sabbath, and I will content you.
                [He whispers in his ear.

Enter BUCKINGHAM.

Buck. What, talking with a priest, lord cham-
    berlain?
Your friends at Pomfret, they do need the priest;
Your honour hath no shriving work in hand.
Hast. Good faith, and when I met this holy
    man,
Those men you talk of came into my mind.
What, go you toward the Tower?
Buck. I do, my lord; but long I shall not stay:
I shall return before your lordship thence.   121
Hast. 'Tis like enough, for I stay dinner there.
Buck. [*Aside*] And supper too, although thou
    know'st it not.
Come, will you go?
Hast.   I'll wait upon your lordship. [*Exeunt.*

SCENE III. *Pomfret Castle.*

Enter SIR RICHARD RATCLIFF, *with halberds,
carrying* RIVERS, GREY, *and* VAUGHAN *to
death.*

Rat. Come, bring forth the prisoners.
Riv. Sir Richard Ratcliff, let me tell thee this:
To-day shalt thou behold a subject die
For truth, for duty, and for loyalty.
Grey. God keep the prince from all the pack
    of you!
A knot you are of damned blood-suckers.
Vaug. You live that shall cry woe for this
    hereafter.
Rat. Dispatch; the limit of your lives is out.
Riv. O Pomfret, Pomfret! O thou bloody
    prison,
Fatal and ominous to noble peers!   10
Within the guilty closure of thy walls
Richard the second here was hack'd to death;

And, for more slander to thy dismal seat,
We give thee up our guiltless blood to drink.
 Grey. Now Margaret's curse is fall'n upon our
  heads,
For standing by when Richard stabb'd her son.
 Riv. Then cursed she Hastings, then cursed
  she Buckingham,
Then cursed she Richard. O, remember, God,
To hear her prayers for them, as now for us!
And for my sister and her princely sons,   20
Be satisfied, dear God, with our true blood,
Which, as thou know'st, unjustly must be spilt.
 • *Rat.* Make haste; the hour of death is expiate.
 Riv. Come, Grey, come, Vaughan, let us all
  embrace:
And take our leave, until we meet in heaven.
            [Exeunt.

SCENE IV. *The Tower of London.*

Enter BUCKINGHAM, DERBY, HASTINGS, *the*
BISHOP OF ELY, RATCLIFF, LOVEL, *with others,*
and take their seats at a table.

 Hast. My lords, at once: the cause why we
  are met
• Is, to determine of the coronation.
In God's name, speak: when is the royal day?
 Buck. Are all things fitting for that royal time?
 Der. It is, and wants but nomination.
 Ely. To-morrow, then, I judge a happy day.
 Buck. Who knows the lord protector's mind
  herein?
Who is most inward with the noble duke?
 Ely. Your grace, we think, should soonest
  know his mind.
 Buck. Who, I, my lord! we know each other's
  faces,   10
But for our hearts, he knows no more of mine,
Than I of yours;
Nor I no more of his, than you of mine.
Lord Hastings, you and he are near in love.
 Hast. I thank his grace, I know he loves me
  well;
But, for his purpose in the coronation,
I have not sounded him, nor he deliver'd
His gracious pleasure any way therein:
But you, my noble lords, may name the time;
And in the duke's behalf I'll give my voice, 20
Which, I presume, he'll take in gentle part.

Enter GLOUCESTER.

 Ely. Now in good time, here comes the duke
  himself.
 Glou. My noble lords and cousins all, good
  morrow.
I have been long a sleeper; but, I hope,
My absence doth neglect no great designs,
Which by my presence might have been concluded.
 Buck. Had not you come upon your cue, my
  lord,
William Lord Hastings had pronounced your
  part,—
I mean, your voice,—for crowning of the king.
 Glou. Than my Lord Hastings no man might
  be bolder;   30
His lordship knows me well, and loves me well.
 Hast. I thank your grace.
 Glou.   My lord of Ely!
 Ely.   My lord?

Grey: 'Now Margaret's curse is fall'n upon our heads…'
Woodcut from Holinshed's *Chronicles,* 1577

---

23 *expiate.* Fully arrived.

2 *coronation.* Of Edward V.

41 *worshipful.* Respectful.

47 *prolong'd.* Postponed.

51 *conceit.* Idea.

George F. Cooke, 18th century actor, as Richard III.
Engraving from *The Theatrical Inquisitor*, 1813

Glou.   When I was last in Holborn,
I saw good strawberries in your garden there:
I do beseech you send for some of them.
   Ely.   Marry, and will, my lord, with all my
      heart.   [*Exit.*
   Glou.   Cousin of Buckingham, a word with you.
                           [*Drawing him aside.*
Catesby hath sounded Hastings in our business,
And finds the testy gentleman so hot,
As he will lose his head ere give consent   40
● His master's son, as worshipful he terms it,
Shall lose the royalty of England's throne.
   Buck.   Withdraw you hence, my lord, I'll
      follow you.
         [*Exit Gloucester, Buckingham following.*
   Der.   We have not yet set down this day of
      triumph.
To-morrow, in mine opinion, is too sudden;
For I myself am not so well provided
● As else I would be, were the day prolong'd.

Re-enter BISHOP OF ELY.

   Ely.   Where is my lord protector? I have sent
for these strawberries.
   Hast.   His grace looks cheerfully and smooth
      to-day;   50
● There's some conceit or other likes him well,
When he doth bid good morrow with such a spirit.
I think there's never a man in Christendom
That can less hide his love or hate than he;
For by his face straight shall you know his heart.
   Der.   What of his heart perceive you in his face
By any likelihood he show'd to-day?
   Hast.   Marry, that with no man here he is
      offended;
For, were he, he had shown it in his looks.
   Der.   I pray God he be not, I say.   60

Re-enter GLOUCESTER *and* BUCKINGHAM.

   Glou.   I pray you all, tell me what they deserve
That do conspire my death with devilish plots
Of damned witchcraft, and that have prevail'd
Upon my body with their hellish charms?
   Hast.   The tender love I bear your grace, my
      lord,
Makes me most forward in this noble presence
To doom the offenders, whatsoever they be:
I say, my lord, they have deserved death.
   Glou.   Then be your eyes the witness of this ill:
See how I am bewitch'd; behold mine arm   70
Is, like a blasted sapling, wither'd up:
And this is Edward's wife, that monstrous witch,
Consorted with that harlot strumpet Shore,
That by their witchcraft thus have marked me.
   Hast.   If they have done this thing, my gracious
      lord,—
   Glou.   If! thou protector of this damned
      strumpet,
Tellest thou me of 'ifs'? Thou art a traitor:
Off with his head! Now, by Saint Paul I swear,
I will not dine until I see the same.
Lovel and Ratcliff, look that it be done: 80
The rest, that love me, rise and follow me.
   [*Exeunt all but Hastings, Ratcliff, and Lovel.*
   Hast.   Woe, woe for England! not a whit for
      me;
For I, too fond, might have prevented this.
Stanley did dream the boar did raze his helm;
But I disdain'd it, and did scorn to fly:

Three times to-day my foot-cloth horse did stumble,
And startled, when he look'd upon the Tower,
As loath to bear me to the slaughter-house.
O, now I want the priest that spake to me:
I now repent I told the pursuivant,   90
As 'twere triumphing at mine enemies,
How they at Pomfret bloodily were butcher'd,
And I myself secure in grace and favour.
O Margaret, Margaret, now thy heavy curse
Is lighted on poor Hastings' wretched head!

   Rat. Dispatch, my lord; the duke would be at
     dinner:
Make a short shrift; he longs to see your head.

   Hast. O momentary grace of mortal men,
Which we more hunt for than the grace of God!
Who builds his hopes in air of your good looks,
Lives like a drunken sailor on a mast,   101
Ready, with every nod, to tumble down
Into the fatal bowels of the deep.

   Lov. Come, come, dispatch; 'tis bootless to
     exclaim.

   Hast. O bloody Richard! miserable England!
I prophesy the fearfull'st time to thee
That ever wretched age hath look'd upon.
Come, lead me to the block; bear him my head:
They smile at me that shortly shall be dead.

                    [*Exeunt.*

Scene V. *The Tower-walls.*

Enter Gloucester *and* Buckingham, *in rotten
   armour, marvellous ill-favoured.*

   Glou. Come, cousin, canst thou quake, and
     change thy colour,
Murder thy breath in middle of a word,
And then begin again, and stop again,
As if thou wert distraught and mad with terror?

   Buck. Tut, I can counterfeit the deep tragedian;
Speak and look back, and pry on every side,
Tremble and start at wagging of a straw,
Intending deep suspicion: ghastly looks
Are at my service, like enforced smiles;
And both are ready in their offices,   10
At any time, to grace my stratagems.
But what, is Catesby gone?

   Glou. He is; and, see, he brings the mayor
     along.

Enter the Mayor *and* Catesby.

   Buck. Lord mayor,—
   Glou. Look to the drawbridge there!
   Buck. Hark! a drum.
   Glou. Catesby, o'erlook the walls.
   Buck. Lord mayor, the reason we have sent—
   Glou. Look back, defend thee, here are enemies.
   Buck. God and our innocency defend and
     guard us!   20
   Glou. Be patient; they are friends, Ratcliff and
     Lovel.

Enter Lovel *and* Ratcliff, *with* Hastings'
   head.

   Lov. Here is the head of that ignoble traitor,
The dangerous and unsuspected Hastings.

   Glou. So dear I loved the man, that I must
     weep.
I took him for the plainest harmless creature
That breathed upon this earth a Christian;
Made him my book, wherein my soul recorded

---

86 *foot-cloth.* A decorated cloth over the back of a horse.

98 *momentary grace.* Temporary good fortune.

1—9 *Come, cousin . . . enforced smiles.* See introduction.

Jane Shore, wife of a goldsmith and mistress to Edward IV and then Lord Hastings. Engraving from *The Pictorial History of England*, 1856

32 *from . . . suspect*. Free from suspicion.

55 *prevented*. Anticipated.

74 *meet'st . . . time*. At the most advantageous time.

80 *luxury*. Lechery.

The history of all her secret thoughts:
So smooth he daub'd his vice with show of virtue,
That, his apparent open guilt omitted,   30
I mean, his conversation with Shore's wife,
● He lived from all attainder of suspect.
    Buck. Well, well, he was the covert'st shel-
      ter'd traitor
That ever lived.
Would you imagine, or almost believe,
Were't not that, by great preservation,
We live to tell it you, the subtle traitor
This day had plotted, in the council-house
To murder me and my good Lord of Gloucester?
    May. What, had he so?   40
    Glou. What, think you we are Turks or infidels?
Or that we would, against the form of law,
Proceed thus rashly to the villain's death,
But that the extreme peril of the case,
The peace of England and our persons' safety,
Enforced us to this execution?
    May. Now, fair befall you! he deserved his
      death;
And you my good lords, both have well proceeded,
To warn false traitors from the like attempts.
I never look'd for better at his hands,   50
After he once fell in with Mistress Shore.
    Glou. Yet had not we determined he should die,
Until your lordship came to see his death;
Which now the loving haste of these our friends,
● Somewhat against our meaning, have prevented:
Because, my lord, we would have had you heard
The traitor speak, and timorously confess
The manner and the purpose of his treason;
That you might well have signified the same
Unto the citizens, who haply may   60
Misconstrue us in him and wail his death.
    May. But, my good lord, your grace's word
      shall serve,
As well as I had seen and heard him speak:
And doubt you not, right noble princes both,
But I'll acquaint our duteous citizens
With all your just proceedings in this cause.
    Glou. And to that end we wish'd your lord-
      ship here,
To avoid the carping censures of the world.
    Buck. But since you come too late of our
      intents,
Yet witness what you hear we did intend: 70
And so, my good lord mayor, we bid farewell.
                 [*Exit Mayor*.
    Glou. Go, after, after, cousin Buckingham.
The mayor towards Guildhall hies him in all post:
● There, at your meet'st advantage of the time,
Infer the bastardy of Edward's children:
Tell them how Edward put to death a citizen,
Only for saying he would make his son
Heir to the crown; meaning indeed his house,
Which, by the sign thereof, was termed so.
● Moreover, urge his hateful luxury,   80
And bestial appetite in change of lust;
Which stretched to their servants, daughters, wives,
Even where his lustful eye or savage heart,
Without control, listed to make his prey.
Nay, for a need, thus far come near my person:
Tell them, when that my mother went with child
Of that unsatiate Edward, noble York
My princely father then had wars in France;
And, by just computation of the time,

Found that the issue was not his begot; 90
Which well appeared in his lineaments,
Being nothing like the noble duke my father:
But touch this sparingly, as 'twere far off;
Because you know, my lord, my mother lives.
    Buck. Fear not, my lord, I'll play the orator
As if the golden fee for which I plead
Were for myself: and so, my lord, adieu.
    Glou. If you thrive well, bring them to Baynard's Castle;
Where you shall find me well accompanied 99
With reverend fathers and well-learned bishops.
    Buck. I go; and towards three or four o'clock
Look for the news that the Guildhall affords.
                            [Exit.
    Glou. Go, Lovel, with all speed to Doctor Shaw;
[*To Cate.*] Go thou to Friar Penker; bid them both
Meet me within this hour at Baynard's Castle.
              [Exeunt all but Gloucester.
Now will I in, to take some privy order,
To draw the brats of Clarence out of sight;
And to give notice, that no manner of person
At any time have recourse unto the princes. [*Exit.*

SCENE VI. *The same. A street.*

Enter a Scrivener, *with a paper in his hand.*

    Scriv. This is the indictment of the good
      Lord Hastings;
Which in a set hand fairly is engross'd,
That it may be this day read o'er in Paul's.
And mark how well the sequel hangs together:
Eleven hours I spent to write it over,
For yesternight by Catesby was it brought me;
The precedent was full as long a-doing:
And yet within these five hours lived Lord
      Hastings,
Untainted, unexamined, free, at liberty.
Here's a good world the while! Why who's so
      gross, 10
That seeth not this palpable device?
Yet who's so blind, but says he sees it not?
Bad is the world; and all will come to nought,
When such bad dealing must be seen in thought.
                            [Exit.

SCENE VII. *Baynard's Castle.*

Enter GLOUCESTER *and* BUCKINGHAM, *at several doors.*

    Glou. How now, my lord, what say the citizens?
    Buck. Now, by the holy mother of our Lord,
The citizens are mum and speak not a word.
    Glou. Touch'd you the bastardy of Edward's
      children?
    Buck. I did; with his contract with Lady Lucy,
And his contract by deputy in France;
The insatiate greediness of his desires,
And his enforcement of the city wives;
His tyranny for trifles; his own bastardy,
As being got, your father then in France, 10
And his resemblance, being not like the duke:
Withal I did infer your lineaments,
Being the right idea of your father,
Both in your form and nobleness of mind;
Laid open all your victories in Scotland,
Your discipline in war, wisdom in peace,
Your bounty, virtue, fair humility;
Indeed, left nothing fitting for the purpose

98 *Baynard's Castle.* A castle of Richard's on the Thames, close to Blackfriars.

Baynard's Castle. Engraving from *Old England*, 1854

2 *set hand fairly is engross'd.* Beautifully written in the secretary hand (used for legal documents).

7 *precedent.* First draft.

Scrivener at work. Engraving from a medieval manuscript

33 *in warrant from himself*. On his own responsibility.

49 *ground*. Plain song or bass. *descant*. Variation on a plain song.

55 *leads*. Roof.

Lord Mayor of London with sword-bearer and seal-bearer. Engraving from a 17th century German manuscript

Untouch'd, or slightly handled, in discourse:
And when mine oratory grew to an end, 20
I bid them that did love their country's good
Cry 'God save Richard, England's royal king!'
 Glou. Ah! and did they so?
 Buck. No, so God help me, they spake not a word;
But, like dumb statuas or breathing stones,
Gazed each on other, and look'd deadly pale.
Which when I saw, I reprehended them;
And ask'd the mayor what meant this wilful silence:
His answer was, the people were not wont
To be spoke to but by the recorder. 30
Then he was urged to tell my tale again,
'Thus saith the duke, thus hath the duke inferr'd;'
• But nothing spake in warrant from himself.
When he had done, some followers of mine own,
At the lower end of the hall, hurl'd up their caps,
And some ten voices cried 'God save King Richard!'
And thus I took the vantage of those few,
'Thanks, gentle citizens and friends,' quoth I;
'This general applause and loving shout 39
Argues your wisdoms and your love to Richard:'
And even here brake off, and came away.
 Glou. What tongueless blocks were they! would they not speak?
 Buck. No, by my troth, my lord.
 Glou. Will not the mayor then and his brethren come?
 Buck. The mayor is here at hand: intend some fear;
Be not you spoke with, but by mighty suit:
And look you get a prayer-book in your hand,
And stand betwixt two churchmen, good my lord;
• For on that ground I'll build a holy descant:
And be not easily won to our request: 50
Play the maid's part, still answer nay, and take it.
 Glou. I go; and if you plead as well for them
As I can say nay to thee for myself,
No doubt we'll bring it to a happy issue.
• *Buck.* Go, go, up to the leads; the lord mayor knocks.   [*Exit Gloucester.*

   Enter the Mayor *and* Citizens.

Welcome, my lord: I dance attendance here;
I think the duke will not be spoke withal.

   Enter CATESBY.

Here comes his servant: how now, Catesby,
What says he?
 Cate. My lord, he doth entreat your grace
To visit him to-morrow or next day: 60
He is within, with two right reverend fathers,
Divinely bent to meditation;
And in no worldly suit would he be moved,
To draw him from his holy exercise.
 Buck. Return, good Catesby, to thy lord again;
Tell him, myself, the mayor and citizens,
In deep designs and matters of great moment,
No less importing than our general good,
Are come to have some conference with his grace.
 Cate. I'll tell him what you say, my lord. 70
        [*Exit.*
 Buck. Ah, ha, my lord, this prince is not an Edward!
He is not lolling on a lewd day-bed,
But on his knees at meditation;

Not dallying with a brace of courtezans,
But meditating with two deep divines;
● Not sleeping, to engross his idle body,
But praying, to enrich his watchful soul:
Happy were England, would this gracious prince
Take on himself the sovereignty thereof:
But, sure, I fear, we shall ne'er win him to it. 80
  May.   Marry, God forbid his grace should say
    us nay!
  Buck.   I fear he will.

        Re-enter CATESBY.

How now, Catesby, what says your lord?
  Cate.   My lord,
He wonders to what end you have assembled
Such troops of citizens to speak with him,
His grace not being warn'd thereof before:
My lord, he fears you mean no good to him.
  Buck.   Sorry I am my noble cousin should
Suspect me, that I mean no good to him:
By heaven, I come in perfect love to him;   90
And so once more return and tell his grace.
                     [*Exit Catesby.*
When holy and devout religious men
Are at their beads, 'tis hard to draw them thence,
So sweet is zealous contemplation.

Enter GLOUCESTER *aloft, between two* Bishops.
      CATESBY *returns.*

  May.   See, where he stands between two
    clergymen!
  Buck.   Two props of virtue for a Christian
    prince,
To stay him from the fall of vanity:
And, see, a book of prayer in his hand,
True ornaments to know a holy man.
Famous Plantagenet, most gracious prince,   100
Lend favourable ears to our request;
And pardon us the interruption
Of thy devotion and right Christian zeal.
  Glou.   My lord, there needs no such apology:
I rather do beseech you pardon me,
Who, earnest in the service of my God,
Neglect the visitation of my friends.
But, leaving this, what is your grace's pleasure?
  Buck.   Even that, I hope, which pleaseth God
    above,
And all good men of this ungovern'd isle.   110
  Glou.   I do suspect I have done some offence
That seems disgracious in the city's eyes,
And that you come to reprehend my ignorance.
  Buck.   You have, my lord: would it might
    please your grace,
At our entreaties, to amend that fault!
  Glou.   Else wherefore breathe I in a Christian
    land?
  Buck.   Then know, it is your fault that you
    resign
The supreme seat, the throne majestical,
The scepter'd office of your ancestors,
Your state of fortune and your due of birth,   120
The lineal glory of your royal house,
To the corruption of a blemish'd stock:
Whilst, in the mildness of your sleepy thoughts,
Which here we waken to our country's good,
This noble isle doth want her proper limbs;
Her face defaced with scars of infamy,

128 *shoulder'd.* Plunged into.

Buckingham: 'Your gracious self to take on you the charge And kingly government of this your land . . .' The historical Richard III, born in 1452, fought on the Yorkist side in the Wars of the Roses. He usurped the throne from his nephew Edward V in 1483 but was killed at the battle of Bosworth Field by Henry Tudor, afterwards Henry VII

136 *empery.* Empire.

143 *degree.* Rank.

166 *much I need.* I lack the proper ability to help you.

Her royal stock graft with ignoble plants,
● And almost shoulder'd in the swallowing gulf
Of blind forgetfulness and dark oblivion.
Which to recure, we heartily solicit   130
Your gracious self to take on you the charge
And kingly government of this your land,
Not as protector, steward, substitute,
Or lowly factor for another's gain;
But as successively from blood to blood,
● Your right of birth, your empery, your own.
For this, consorted with the citizens,
Your very worshipful and loving friends,
And by their vehement instigation,
In this just suit come I to move your grace.   140
   Glou.   I know not whether to depart in silence,
Or bitterly to speak in your reproof,
● Best fitteth my degree or your condition:
If not to answer, you might haply think
Tongue-tied ambition, not replying, yielded
To bear the golden yoke of sovereignty,
Which fondly you would here impose on me;
If to reprove you for this suit of yours,
So season'd with your faithful love to me,
Then, on the other side, I check'd my friends.
Therefore, to speak, and to avoid the first,   151
And then, in speaking, not to incur the last,
Definitively thus I answer you.
Your love deserves my thanks; but my desert
Unmeritable shuns your high request.
First, if all obstacles were cut away,
And that my path were even to the crown,
As my ripe revenue and due by birth;
Yet so much is my poverty of spirit,
So mighty and so many my defects,   160
As I had rather hide me from my greatness,
Being a bark to brook no mighty sea,
Than in my greatness covet to be hid,
And in the vapour of my glory smother'd.
But, God be thanked, there's no need of me,
● And much I need to help you, if need were;
The royal tree hath left us royal fruit,
Which, mellow'd by the stealing hours of time,
Will well become the seat of majesty,
And make, no doubt, us happy by his reign.   170
On him I lay what you would lay on me,
The right and fortune of his happy stars;
Which God defend that I should wring from him!
   Buck.   My lord, this argues conscience in your
            grace;
But the respects thereof are nice and trivial,
All circumstances well considered.
You say that Edward is your brother's son:
So say we too, but not by Edward's wife;
For first he was contract to Lady Lucy—
Your mother lives a witness to that vow—   180
And afterward by substitute betroth'd
To Bona, sister to the King of France.
These both put by, a poor petitioner,
A care-crazed mother of a many children,
A beauty-waning and distressed widow,
Even in the afternoon of her best days,
Made prize and purchase of his lustful eye,
Seduced the pitch and height of all his thoughts
To base declension and loathed bigamy:
By her, in his unlawful bed, he got   190
This Edward, whom our manners term the prince.
More bitterly could I expostulate,
Save that, for reverence to some alive,
I give a sparing limit to my tongue.

Then, good my lord, take to your royal self
This proffer'd benefit of dignity;
If not to bless us and the land withal,
Yet to draw forth your noble ancestry
From the corruption of abusing times,
Unto a lineal true-derived course. 200
    May. Do, good my lord, your citizens entreat
    you.
    Buck. Refuse not, mighty lord, this proffer'd
    love.
    Cate. O, make them joyful, grant their lawful
    suit!
    Glou. Alas, why would you heap these cares
    on me?
I am unfit for state and majesty:
I do beseech you, take it not amiss;
I cannot nor I will not yield to you.
    Buck. If you refuse it,—as, in love and zeal,
Loath to depose the child, your brother's son;
As well we know your tenderness of heart 210
• And gentle, kind, effeminate remorse,
Which we have noted in you to your kin,
And egally indeed to all estates,—
Yet whether you accept our suit or no,
Your brother's son shall never reign our king;
But we will plant some other in the throne,
To the disgrace and downfall of your house:
And in this resolution here we leave you.—
Come, citizens: 'zounds! I'll entreat no more.
    Glou. O, do not swear, my lord of Buckingham.
           [*Exit Buckingham with the Citizens*.
    Cate. Call them again, my lord, and accept
    their suit. 221
    Another. Do, good my lord, lest all the land
    do rue it.
    Glou. Would you enforce me to a world of
    care?
Well, call them again. I am not made of stones,
But penetrable to your kind entreats,
Albeit against my conscience and my soul.

    Re-enter BUCKINGHAM *and the rest*.

Cousin of Buckingham, and you sage, grave men,
Since you will buckle fortune on my back,
To bear her burthen, whether I will or no,
I must have patience to endure the load: 230
But if black scandal or foul-faced reproach
Attend the sequel of your imposition,
Your mere enforcement shall acquittance me
From all the impure blots and stains thereof;
For God he knows, and you may partly see,
How far I am from the desire thereof.
    May. God bless your grace! we see it, and
    will say it.
    Glou. In saying so, you shall but say the truth.
    Buck. Then I salute you with this kingly
    title:
Long live Richard, England's royal king! 240
    May. and Cit. Amen.
    Buck. To-morrow will it please you to be
    crown'd?
    Glou. Even when you please, since you will
    have it so.
    Buck. To-morrow, then, we will attend your
    grace:
And so most joyfully we take our leave.
    Glou. Come, let us to our holy task again.
Farewell, good cousin; farewell, gentle friends.
           [*Exeunt*.

211 *effeminate remorse*. Womanly pity.

Costume design for Duke of Buckingham by John Bury
with Ann Curtis, Royal Shakespeare Co, 1964

1 *niece.* Granddaughter.

34 *lace.* Cord holding the bodice of her dress together.

Costume design for Lady Anne by Jocelyn Herbert with Sally Jacobs, Stratford-upon-Avon, 1961

ACT IV.

SCENE I. *Before the Tower.*

Enter, on one side, QUEEN ELIZABETH, DUCHESS OF YORK, *and* MARQUESS OF DORSET ; *on the other,* ANNE, DUCHESS OF GLOUCESTER, *leading* LADY MARGARET PLANTAGENET, CLARENCE'S *young Daughter.*

Duch.   Who meets us here ? my niece Plantagenet
Led in the hand of her kind aunt of Gloucester ?
Now, for my life, she's wandering to the Tower,
On pure heart's love to greet the tender princes.
Daughter, well met.
   Anne.   God give your graces both
A happy and a joyful time of day !
   Q. Eliz.   As much to you, good sister ! Whither away ?
   Anne.   No farther than the Tower ; and, as I guess,
Upon the like devotion as yourselves,
To gratulate the gentle princes there.   10
   Q. Eliz.   Kind sister, thanks : we 'll enter all together.

Enter BRAKENBURY.

And, in good time, here the lieutenant comes.
Master lieutenant, pray you, by your leave,
How doth the prince, and my young son of York ?
   Brak.   Right well, dear madam. By your patience,
I may not suffer you to visit them ;
The king hath straitly charged the contrary.
   Q. Eliz.   The king ! why, who's that ?
   Brak.   I cry you mercy : I mean the lord protector.
   Q. Eliz.   The Lord protect him from that kingly title !   20
Hath he set bounds betwixt their love and me ?
I am their mother ; who should keep me from them ?
   Duch.   I am their father's mother ; I will see them.
   Anne.   Their aunt I am in law, in love their mother :
Then bring me to their sights ; I 'll bear thy blame
And take thy office from thee, on my peril.
   Brak.   No, madam, no ; I may not leave it so :
I am bound by oath, and therefore pardon me.
                                  [*Exit.*

Enter LORD STANLEY.

Stan.   Let me but meet you, ladies, one hour hence,
And I 'll salute your grace of York as mother, 30
And reverend looker on, of two fair queens.
[*To Anne*] Come, madam, you must straight to Westminster,
There to be crowned Richard's royal queen.
   Q. Eliz.   O, cut my lace in sunder, that my pent heart
May have some scope to beat, or else I swoon
With this dead-killing news !
   Anne.   Despiteful tidings ! O unpleasing news !
   Dor.   Be of good cheer : mother, how fares your grace ?

Q. Eliz. O Dorset, speak not to me, get thee hence!
Death and destruction dog thee at the heels; 40
Thy mother's name is ominous to children.
If thou wilt outstrip death, go cross the seas,
● And live with Richmond, from the reach of hell:
Go, hie thee, hie thee from this slaughter-house,
Lest thou increase the number of the dead;
And make me die the thrall of Margaret's curse,
Nor mother, wife, nor England's counted queen.
   Stan. Full of wise care is this your counsel, madam.
Take all the swift advantage of the hours;
You shall have letters from me to my son 50
To meet you on the way, and welcome you.
Be not ta'en tardy by unwise delay.
   Duch. O ill-dispersing wind of misery!
O my accursed womb, the bed of death!
● A cockatrice hast thou hatch'd to the world,
Whose unavoided eye is murderous.
   Stan. Come, madam, come; I in all haste was sent.
   Anne. And I in all unwillingness will go.
I would to God that the inclusive verge
Of golden metal that must round my brow 60
Were red-hot steel, to sear me to the brain!
Anointed let me be with deadly venom,
And die, ere men can say, God save the queen!
   Q. Eliz. Go, go, poor soul, I envy not thy glory;
To feed my humour, wish thyself no harm.
   Anne. No! why? When he that is my husband now
Came to me, as I follow'd Henry's corse,
When scarce the blood was well wash'd from his hands
Which issued from my other angel husband
And that dead saint which then I weeping follow'd;
O, when, I say, I look'd on Richard's face, 71
This was my wish: 'Be thou,' quoth I, 'accursed,
For making me, so young, so old a widow!
And, when thou wed'st, let sorrow haunt thy bed;
And be thy wife—if any be so mad—
As miserable by the life of thee
As thou hast made me by my dear lord's death!'
Lo, ere I can repeat this curse again,
Even in so short a space, my woman's heart
Grossly grew captive to his honey words 80
And proved the subject of my own soul's curse,
Which ever since hath kept my eyes from rest;
For never yet one hour in his bed
Have I enjoy'd the golden dew of sleep,
But have been waked by his timorous dreams.
Besides, he hates me for my father Warwick;
And will, no doubt, shortly be rid of me.
   Q. Eliz. Poor heart, adieu! I pity thy complaining.
   Anne. No more than from my soul I mourn for yours.
   Q. Eliz. Farewell, thou woful welcomer of glory! 90
   Anne. Adieu, poor soul, that takest thy leave of it!
   Duch. [*To Dorset*] Go thou to Richmond, and good fortune guide thee!
[*To Anne*] Go thou to Richard, and good angels guard thee!
[*To Queen Eliz.*] Go thou to sanctuary, and good thoughts possess thee!
I to my grave, where peace and rest lie with me!

43 *Richmond.* Henry Tudor, later Henry VII.

Henry VII. From John Speed's *Theatre of the Empire of Great Britaine*, 1611–12

55 *cockatrice.* Like the basilisk, a serpent that could kill by looks.

Cockatrice. Woodcut from Edward Topsell's The *History of Four-footed Beasts*, 1658

97 *teen.* Sorrow.

Laurence Olivier as Richard III, New Theatre, London, 1944

8 *the touch.* Touchstone.

30 *considerate.* Critical.

Richard III. From John Speed's *Theatre of the Empire of Great Britaine*, 1611–12

Eighty odd years of sorrow have I seen,
And each hour's joy wreck'd with a week of teen.
  Q. Eliz. Stay, yet look back with me unto the
    Tower.
Pity, you ancient stones, those tender babes
Whom envy hath immured within your walls! 100
Rough cradle for such little pretty ones!
Rude ragged nurse, old sullen playfellow
For tender princes, use my babies well!
So foolish sorrow bids your stones farewell.
                            [*Exeunt.*

      Scene II. *London. The palace.*

Sennet. Enter Richard, *in pomp, crowned;*
Buckingham, Catesby, *a* Page, *and others.*

  K. Rich. Stand all apart. Cousin of Buck-
    ingham!
  Buck. My gracious sovereign?
  K. Rich. Give me thy hand. [*Here he ascend-
    eth his throne.*] Thus high, by thy advice
And thy assistance, is King Richard seated:
But shall we wear these honours for a day?
Or shall they last, and we rejoice in them?
  Buck. Still live they and for ever may they
    last!
  K. Rich. O Buckingham, now do I play the
    touch,
To try if thou be current gold indeed:
Young Edward lives: think now what I would say.
  Buck. Say on, my loving lord.   11
  K. Rich. Why, Buckingham, I say, I would
    be king.
  Buck. Why, so you are, my thrice renowned
    liege.
  K. Rich. Ha! am I king? 'tis so: but Edward
    lives.
  Buck. True, noble prince.
  K. Rich.   O bitter consequence,
That Edward still should live! 'True, noble
    prince!'
Cousin, thou wert not wont to be so dull:
Shall I be plain? I wish the bastards dead;
And I would have it suddenly perform'd.
What sayest thou? speak suddenly; be brief. 20
  Buck. Your grace may do your pleasure.
  K. Rich. Tut, tut, thou art all ice, thy kind-
    ness freezeth:
Say, have I thy consent that they shall die?
  Buck. Give me some breath, some little pause,
    my lord,
Before I positively speak herein:
I will resolve your grace immediately.   [*Exit.*
  Cate. [*Aside to a stander by*] The king is angry:
    see, he bites the lip.
  K. Rich. I will converse with iron-witted fools
And unrespective boys: none are for me
That look into me with considerate eyes: 30
High-reaching Buckingham grows circumspect.
Boy!
  Page. My lord?
  K. Rich. Know'st thou not any whom cor-
    rupting gold
Would tempt unto a close exploit of death?
  Page. My lord, I know a discontented gen-
    tleman,
Whose humble means match not his haughty
    mind:
Gold were as good as twenty orators,

And will, no doubt, tempt him to any thing.　39
　　K. Rich.　What is his name?
　　Page.　　　　His name, my lord, is Tyrrel.
　　K. Rich.　I partly know the man : go, call him
　　　hither.　　　　　　　　　　[*Exit Page.*
● The deep-revolving witty Buckingham
No more shall be the neighbour to my counsel :
Hath he so long held out with me untired,
And stops he now for breath?

　　　　　Enter STANLEY.

　　　　　　　How now ! what news with you?
　　Stan.　My lord, I hear the Marquis Dorset's
　　　fled
To Richmond, in those parts beyond the sea
Where he abides.　　　　　　[*Stands apart.*
　　K. Rich.　Catesby !
　　Cate.　My lord?　　　　　　　　　50
　　K. Rich.　Rumour it abroad
That Anne, my wife, is sick and like to die :
I will take order for her keeping close.
Inquire me out some mean-born gentleman,
Whom I will marry straight to Clarence' daugh-
　　　ter :
The boy is foolish, and I fear not him.
Look, how thou dream'st ! I say again, give out
That Anne my wife is sick and like to die :
● About it ; for it stands me much upon,　59
To stop all hopes whose growth may damage me.
　　　　　　　　　　　　　　[*Exit Catesby.*
I must be married to my brother's daughter,
Or else my kingdom stands on brittle glass.
Murder her brothers, and then marry her !
Uncertain way of gain ! But I am in
So far in blood that sin will pluck on sin :
Tear-falling pity dwells not in this eye.

　　　　Re-enter Page, *with* TYRREL.

Is thy name Tyrrel?
　　Tyr.　James Tyrrel, and your most obedient
　　　subject.
　　K. Rich.　Art thou, indeed?
　　Tyr. .　　　　Prove me, my gracious sovereign.
　　K. Rich.　Darest thou resolve to kill a friend
　　　of mine?　　　　　　　　　　70
　　Tyr.　Ay, my lord ;
But I had rather kill two enemies.
　　K. Rich.　Why, there thou hast it : two deep
　　　enemies,
Foes to my rest and my sweet sleep's disturbers
Are they that I would have thee deal upon :
Tyrrel, I mean those bastards in the Tower.
　　Tyr.　Let me have open means to come to them,
And soon I 'll rid you from the fear of them.
　　K. Rich.　Thou sing'st sweet music. Hark,
　　　come hither, Tyrrel :
Go, by this token : rise, and lend thine ear :　80
　　　　　　　　　　　　　　[*Whispers.*
There is no more but so : say it is done,
And I will love thee, and prefer thee too.
　　Tyr.　'Tis done, my gracious lord.
　　K. Rich.　Shall we hear from thee, Tyrrel, ere
　　　we sleep?
　　Tyr.　Ye shall, my lord.　　　　　[*Exit.*

　　　　Re-enter BUCKINGHAM.

　　Buck.　My lord, I have consider'd in my mind

42 *deep-revolving.* Deeply considering.

59 *for it stands me much upon.* It is a matter of great importance to me.

Richard ; 'But I am in So far in blood . . .' Drawing by Henry Singleton (1766–1839)

Laurence Olivier as Richard III and Ralph Richardson as the Duke of Buckingham. Scene from the film produced and directed by Laurence Olivier, 1955

117 *Jack.* The figure that struck the hour on clocks.

Opposite : The Princes in the Tower. Painting by Sir John Millais (1829–1896)

The late demand that you did sound me in.
   K. Rich. Well, let that pass. Dorset is fled to Richmond.
   Buck. I hear that news, my lord.
   K. Rich. Stanley, he is your wife's son : well, look to it.   90
   Buck. My lord, I claim your gift, my due by promise,
For which your honour and your faith is pawn'd ;
The earldom of Hereford and the moveables
The which you promised I should possess.
   K. Rich. Stanley, look to your wife : if she convey
Letters to Richmond, you shall answer it.
   Buck. What says your highness to my just demand ?
   K. Rich. As I remember, Henry the Sixth
Did prophesy that Richmond should be king,
When Richmond was a little peevish boy.   100
A king, perhaps, perhaps,—
   Buck. My lord !
   K. Rich. How chance the prophet could not at that time
Have told me, I being by, that I should kill him ?
   Buck. My lord, your promise for the earldom,—
   K. Rich. Richmond ! When last I was at Exeter,
The mayor in courtesy show'd me the castle,
And call'd it Rougemont : at which name I started,
Because a bard of Ireland told me once,
I should not live long after I saw Richmond.   110
   Buck. My lord !
   K. Rich. Ay, what's o'clock ?
   Buck. I am thus bold to put your grace in mind
Of what you promised me.
   K. Rich.   Well, but what's o'clock ?
   Buck. Upon the stroke of ten.
   K. Rich.   Well, let it strike.
   Buck. Why let it strike ?
 • *K. Rich.* Because that, like a Jack, thou keep'st the stroke
Betwixt thy begging and my meditation.
I am not in the giving vein to-day.
   Buck. Why, then resolve me whether you will or no.   120
   K. Rich. Tut, tut,
Thou troublest me ; I am not in the vein.
       [Exeunt all but Buckingham.
   Buck. Is it even so ? rewards he my true service
With such deep contempt ? made I him king for this ?
O, let me think on Hastings, and be gone
To Brecknock, while my fearful head is on !
       [Exit.

SCENE III. *The same.*

Enter TYRREL.

   Tyr. The tyrannous and bloody deed is done,
The most arch act of piteous massacre
That ever yet this land was guilty of.
Dighton and Forrest, whom I did suborn
To do this ruthless piece of butchery,
Although they were flesh'd villains, bloody dogs,
Melting with tenderness and kind compassion
Wept like two children in their deaths' sad stories.

18 *replenished.* Perfect.

Murder of the Princes in the Tower. Painting by James Northcote (1746–1831)

40 *Breton.* Richmond is in Brittany.

42 *looks proudly o'er.* Arrogantly anticipates.

'Lo, thus,' quoth Dighton, 'lay those tender
    babes:'
'Thus, thus,' quoth Forrest, 'girdling one another
Within their innocent alabaster arms: 11
Their lips were four red roses on a stalk,
Which in their summer beauty kiss'd each other.
A book of prayers on their pillow lay;
Which once,' quoth Forrest, 'almost changed my
    mind;
But O! the devil'—there the villain stopp'd;
Whilst Dighton thus told on: 'We smothered
The most replenished sweet work of nature,
That from the prime creation e'er she framed.'
Thus both are gone with conscience and remorse;
They could not speak; and so I left them both,
To bring this tidings to the bloody king.
And here he comes.

        Enter KING RICHARD.

              All hail, my sovereign liege!
K. Rich. Kind Tyrrel, am I happy in thy
    news?
Tyr. If to have done the thing you gave in
    charge
Beget your happiness, be happy then,
For it is done, my lord.
    K. Rich.   But didst thou see them dead?
Tyr. I did, my lord.
K. Rich.   And buried, gentle Tyrrel?
Tyr. The chaplain of the Tower hath buried
    them;
But how or in what place I do not know.   30
    K. Rich. Come to me, Tyrrel, soon at after
    supper,
And thou shalt tell the process of their death.
Meantime, but think how I may do thee good,
And be inheritor of thy desire.
Farewell till soon.   [*Exit Tyrrel.*
The son of Clarence have I pent up close;
His daughter meanly have I match'd in marriage;
The sons of Edward sleep in Abraham's bosom,
And Anne my wife hath bid the world good
    night.
• Now, for I know the Breton Richmond aims 40
At young Elizabeth, my brother's daughter,
• And, by that knot, looks proudly o'er the crown,
To her I go, a jolly thriving wooer.

        Enter CATESBY.

Cate. My lord!
K. Rich. Good news or bad, that thou comest
    in so bluntly?
Cate. Bad news, my lord: Ely is fled to
    Richmond;
And Buckingham, back'd with the hardy Welsh-
    men,
Is in the field, and still his power increaseth.
    K. Rich. Ely with Richmond troubles me
    more near
Than Buckingham and his rash-levied army. 50
Come, I have heard that fearful commenting
Is leaden servitor to dull delay;
Delay leads impotent and snail-paced beggary:
Then fiery expedition be my wing,
Jove's Mercury, and herald for a king!
Come, muster men: my counsel is my shield;
We must be brief when traitors brave the field.
        [*Exeunt.*

SCENE IV. *Before the palace.*

Enter QUEEN MARGARET.

Q. Mar. So, now prosperity begins to mellow
And drop into the rotten mouth of death.
Here in these confines slily have I lurk'd,
To watch the waning of mine adversaries.
A dire induction am I witness to,
And will to France, hoping the consequence
Will prove as bitter, black, and tragical.
Withdraw thee, wretched Margaret: who comes
here?

Enter QUEEN ELIZABETH *and the* DUCHESS
OF YORK.

Q. Eliz. Ah, my young princes! ah, my
tender babes!
My unblown flowers, new-appearing sweets! 10
If yet your gentle souls fly in the air
And be not fix'd in doom perpetual,
Hover about me with your airy wings
And hear your mother's lamentation!
Q. Mar. Hover about her; say, that right
for right
Hath dimm'd your infant morn to aged night.
Duch. So many miseries have crazed my
voice,
That my woe-wearied tongue is mute and dumb,
Edward Plantagenet, why art thou dead?
Q. Mar. Plantagenet doth quit Plantagenet.
• Edward for Edward pays a dying debt. 21
Q. Eliz. Wilt thou, O God, fly from such
gentle lambs,
And throw them in the entrails of the wolf?
When didst thou sleep when such a deed was
done?
Q. Mar. When holy Harry died, and my
sweet son.
Duch. Blind sight, dead life, poor mortal
living ghost,
Woe's scene, world's shame, grave's due by life
usurp'd,
Brief abstract and record of tedious days,
Rest thy unrest on England's lawful earth,
[*Sitting down.*
Unlawfully made drunk with innocents' blood! 30
Q. Eliz. O, that thou wouldst as well afford a
grave
As thou canst yield a melancholy seat!
Then would I hide my bones, not rest them here.
O, who hath any cause to mourn but I?
[*Sitting down by her.*
Q. Mar. If ancient sorrow be most reverend,
Give mine the benefit of seniory,
And let my woes frown on the upper hand.
If sorrow can admit society,
[*Sitting down with them.*
Tell o'er your woes again by viewing mine:
• I had an Edward, till a Richard kill'd him; 40
I had a Harry, till a Richard kill'd him:
• Thou hadst an Edward, till a Richard kill'd him;
Thou hadst a Richard, till a Richard kill'd him.
• *Duch.* I had a Richard too, and thou didst
kill him;
I had a Rutland too, thou holp'st to kill him.
Q. Mar. Thou hadst a Clarence too, and
Richard kill'd him.
From forth the kennel of thy womb hath crept
A hell-hound that doth hunt us all to death:

19 *Edward Plantagenet.* Edward IV.

Edward IV. Engraving from *The Pictorial History of England,* 1856

21 *dying debt.* A debt that could only be paid in death.

40 *Edward.* Her son, Prince Edward.

42–43 *Edward . . . Richard.* The Princes in the Tower.

44 *Richard.* Her husband, the Duke of York and father of Edward IV.

56 *carnal.* Carnivorous.

65 *boot.* Added into the bargain.

The Duchess of York (Esme Church), Queen Margaret (Edith Evans) and Queen Elizabeth (Elizabeth Sellars), Stratford-upon-Avon, 1961

71 *intelligencer.* Agent.

72 *Only . . . souls.* Only alive to work for the devil.

89 *sign.* A symbol, not the reality.

That dog, that had his teeth before his eyes,
To worry lambs and lap their gentle blood,   50
That foul defacer of God's handiwork,
That excellent grand tyrant of the earth,
That reigns in galled eyes of weeping souls,
Thy womb let loose, to chase us to our graves.
O upright, just, and true-disposing God,
● How do I thank thee, that this carnal cur
Preys on the issue of his mother's body,
And makes her pew-fellow with others' moan!
    Duch. O Harry's wife, triumph not in my
      woes!
God witness with me, I have wept for thine.   60
    Q. Mar. Bear with me; I am hungry for
      revenge,
And now I cloy me with beholding it.
Thy Edward he is dead, that stabb'd my Edward;
Thy other Edward dead, to quit my Edward;
● Young York he is but boot, because both they
Match not the high perfection of my loss:
Thy Clarence he is dead that kill'd my Edward;
And the beholders of this tragic play,
The adulterate Hastings, Rivers, Vaughan, Grey,
Untimely smother'd in their dusky graves.   70
● Richard yet lives, hell's black intelligencer,
● Only reserved their factor, to buy souls
And send them thither: but at hand, at hand,
Ensues his piteous and unpitied end:
Earth gapes, hell burns, fiends roar, saints pray,
To have him suddenly convey'd away.
Cancel his bond of life, dear God, I pray,
That I may live to say, The dog is dead!
    Q. Eliz. O, thou didst prophesy the time
      would come
That I should wish for thee to help me curse   80
That bottled spider, that foul bunch-back'd toad!
    Q. Mar. I call'd thee then vain flourish of
      my fortune;
I call'd thee then poor shadow, painted queen;
The presentation of but what I was;
The flattering index of a direful pageant;
One heaved a-high, to be hurl'd down below;
A mother only mock'd with two sweet babes;
A dream of what thou wert, a breath, a bubble,
● A sign of dignity, a garish flag,
To be the aim of every dangerous shot;   90
A queen in jest, only to fill the scene.
Where is thy husband now? where be thy bro-
    thers?
Where are thy children? wherein dost thou joy?
Who sues to thee and cries 'God save the queen'?
Where be the bending peers that flatter'd thee?
Where be the thronging troops that follow'd thee?
Decline all this, and see what now thou art:
For happy wife, a most distressed widow;
For joyful mother, one that wails the name;
For queen, a very caitiff crown'd with care;   100
For one being sued to, one that humbly sues;
For one that scorn'd at me, now scorn'd of me;
For one being fear'd of all, now fearing one;
For one commanding all, obey'd of none.
Thus hath the course of justice wheel'd about,
And left thee but a very prey to time;
Having no more but thought of what thou wert,
To torture thee the more, being what thou art.
Thou didst usurp my place, and dost thou not
Usurp the just proportion of my sorrow?   110
Now thy proud neck bears half my burthen'd
    yoke;

From which even here I slip my weary neck,
And leave the burthen of it all on thee.
Farewell, York's wife, and queen of sad mis-
     chance:
These English woes will make me smile in
     France.
   Q. Eliz. O thou well skill'd in curses, stay
     awhile,
And teach me how to curse mine enemies!
   Q. Mar. Forbear to sleep the nights, and fast
     the days;
Compare dead happiness with living woe;
Think that thy babes were fairer than they were,
And he that slew them fouler than he is: 121
Bettering thy loss makes the bad causer worse:
Revolving this will teach thee how to curse.
   Q. Eliz. My words are dull; O, quicken them
     with thine!
   Q. Mar. Thy woes will make them sharp, and
     pierce like mine.   [*Exit.*
   Duch. Why should calamity be full of words?
   Q. Eliz. Windy attorneys to their client woes,
Airy succeeders of intestate joys,
Poor breathing orators of miseries!
Let them have scope: though what they do im-
     part   130
Help not at all, yet do they ease the heart.
   Duch. If so, then be not tongue-tied: go with
     me,
And in the breath of bitter words let's smother
My damned son, which thy two sweet sons
     smother'd.
I hear his drum: be copious in exclaims.

Enter KING RICHARD, *marching, with drums
and trumpets.*

   K. Rich. Who intercepts my expedition?
   Duch. O, she that might have intercepted
     thee,
By strangling thee in her accursed womb,
From all the slaughters, wretch, that thou hast
     done!
   Q. Eliz. Hidest thou that forehead with a
     golden crown,   140
Where should be graven, if that right were right,
The slaughter of the prince that owed that crown,
And the dire death of my two sons and brothers?
Tell me, thou villain slave, where are my chil-
     dren?
   Duch. Thou toad, thou toad, where is thy
     brother Clarence?
And little Ned Plantagenet, his son?
   Q. Eliz. Where is kind Hastings, Rivers,
     Vaughan, Grey?
   K. Rich. A flourish, trumpets! strike alarum,
     drums!
Let not the heavens hear these tell-tale women
Rail on the Lord's anointed: strike, I say!   150
             [*Flourish. Alarums.*
Either be patient, and entreat me fair,
Or with the clamorous report of war
Thus will I drown your exclamations.
   Duch. Art thou my son?
   K. Rich. Ay, I thank God, my father, and
     yourself.
   Duch. Then patiently hear my impatience.
   K. Rich. Madam, I have a touch of your
     condition,
Which cannot brook the accent of reproof.

Peggy Ashcroft as Queen Margaret, Royal Shakespeare
Co, 1964

---

128 *intestate.* Dead without having made a will.

142 *owed.* Owned.

175 *Humphrey Hour.* 'To dine with Duke Humphrey'
meant to go hungry.

Costume design for Queen Elizabeth by Jocelyn
Herbert with Sally Jacobs, Stratford-upon-Avon, 1961

Duch. O, let me speak!
K. Rich.   Do then; but I'll not hear. 159
Duch. I will be mild and gentle in my speech.
K. Rich. And brief, good mother; for I am
    in haste.
Duch. Art thou so hasty? I have stay'd for
    thee,
God knows, in anguish, pain and agony.
K. Rich. And came I not at last to comfort
    you?
Duch. No, by the holy rood, thou know'st it
    well,
Thou camest on earth to make the earth my hell.
A grievous burthen was thy birth to me;
Tetchy and wayward was thy infancy;
Thy school-days frightful, desperate, wild, and
    furious,
Thy prime of manhood daring, bold, and ven-
    turous,   '170
Thy age confirm'd, proud, subtle, bloody, trea-
    cherous,
More mild, but yet more harmful, kind in hatred:
What comfortable hour canst thou name,
That ever graced me in thy company?
● *K. Rich.* Faith, none, but Humphrey Hour,
    that call'd your grace
To breakfast once forth of my company.
If I be so disgracious in your sight,
Let me march on, and not offend your grace.
Strike up the drum.
Duch.   I prithee, hear me speak.
K. Rich. You speak too bitterly.
Duch.   Hear me a word; 180
For I shall never speak to thee again.
K. Rich. So.
Duch. Either thou wilt die, by God's just
    ordinance,
Ere from this war thou turn a conqueror,
Or I with grief and extreme age shall perish
And never look upon thy face again.
Therefore take with thee my most heavy curse;
Which, in the day of battle, tire thee more
Than all the complete armour that thou wear'st!
My prayers on the adverse party fight;   190
And there the little souls of Edward's children
Whisper the spirits of thine enemies
And promise them success and victory.
Bloody thou art, bloody will be thy end;
Shame serves thy life and doth thy death attend.
                      [*Exit.*
Q. Eliz. Though far more cause, yet much
    less spirit to curse
Abides in me; I say amen to all.
K. Rich. Stay, madam; I must speak a word
    with you.
Q. Eliz. I have no moe sons of the royal
    blood   199
For thee to murder: for my daughters, Richard,
They shall be praying nuns, not weeping queens;
And therefore level not to hit their lives.
K. Rich. You have a daughter call'd Elizabeth,
Virtuous and fair, royal and gracious.
Q. Eliz. And must she die for this? O, let
    her live,
And I'll corrupt her manners, stain her beauty;
Slander myself as false to Edward's bed;
Throw over her the veil of infamy:
So she may live unscarr'd of bleeding slaughter,
I will confess she was not Edward's daughter.

K. Rich. Wrong not her birth, she is of royal
blood.
Q. Eliz. To save her life, I'll say she is not so.
K. Rich. Her life is only safest in her birth.
Q. Eliz. And only in that safety died her
brothers.
K. Rich. Lo, at their births good stars were
opposite.
Q. Eliz. No, to their lives bad friends were
contrary.
K. Rich. All unavoided is the doom of destiny.
• *Q. Eliz.* True, when avoided grace makes
destiny:
My babes were destined to a fairer death,
If grace had bless'd thee with a fairer life.   220
K. Rich. You speak as if that I had slain my
cousins.
Q. Eliz. Cousins, indeed; and by their uncle
cozen'd
Of comfort, kingdom, kindred, freedom, life.
Whose hand soever lanced their tender hearts,
Thy head, all indirectly, gave direction:
No doubt the murderous knife was dull and blunt
Till it was whetted on thy stone-hard heart,
To revel in the entrails of my lambs.
But that still use of grief makes wild grief tame,
My tongue should to thy ears not name my boys
Till that my nails were anchor'd in thine eyes;
And I, in such a desperate bay of death,
Like a poor bark, of sails and tackling reft,
Rush all to pieces on thy rocky bosom.
K. Rich. Madam, so thrive I in my enterprise
And dangerous success of bloody wars,
As I intend more good to you and yours
Than ever you or yours were by me wrong'd!
Q. Eliz. What good is cover'd with the face
of heaven,
To be discover'd, that can do me good?   240
K. Rich. The advancement of your children,
gentle lady.
Q. Eliz. Up to some scaffold, there to lose
their heads?
K. Rich. No, to the dignity and height of
honour,
The high imperial type of this earth's glory.
Q. Eliz. Flatter my sorrows with report of it;
Tell me what state, what dignity, what honour,
• Canst thou demise to any child of mine?
K. Rich. Even all I have; yea, and myself
and all,
Will I withal endow a child of thine;
• So in the Lethe of thy angry soul   250
Thou drown the sad remembrance of those wrongs
Which thou supposest I have done to thee.
Q. Eliz. Be brief, lest that the process of thy
kindness
Last longer telling than thy kindness' date.
K. Rich. Then know, that from my soul I
love thy daughter.
Q. Eliz. My daughter's mother thinks it with
her soul.
K. Rich. What do you think?
Q. Eliz. That thou dost love my daughter
from thy soul:
So from thy soul's love didst thou love her
brothers;   259
And from my heart's love I do thank thee for it.
K. Rich. Be not so hasty to confound my
meaning:

218 *avoided grace.* A man who avoids goodness.

Edmund Kean (1790–1833) as Richard III. Engraving
from the *Theatrical Inquisitor*

247 *demise.* Bequeath.

250 *Lethe.* The river of Forgetfulness in Hades.

ELIZABETHA · VXOR
HENRICI · VII ·

King Richard: 'And mean to make her queen of England.' Elizabeth of York (1465–1503) did, in fact,
become queen by her marriage to Henry Tudor, Earl of
Richmond, later Henry VII

---

283 *conveyance.* Removal.

304 *bid like.* Suffered similarly.

I mean, that with my soul I love thy daughter,
And mean to make her queen of England.
   Q. Eliz. Say then, who dost thou mean shall
    be her king?
   K. Rich. Even he that makes her queen: who
    should be else?
   Q. Eliz. What, thou?
   K. Rich. I, even I: what think you of it,
    madam?
   Q. Eliz. How canst thou woo her?
   K. Rich.   That would I learn of you,
As one that are best acquainted with her humour.
   Q. Eliz. And wilt thou learn of me?
   K. Rich.   Madam, with all my heart. 270
   Q. Eliz. Send to her, by the man that slew
    her brothers,
A pair of bleeding hearts; thereon engrave
Edward and York; then haply she will weep:
Therefore present to her,—as sometime Margaret
Did to thy father, steep'd in Rutland's blood,—
A handkerchief; which, say to her, did drain
The purple sap from her sweet brother's body.
And bid her dry her weeping eyes therewith.
If this inducement force her not to love,
Send her a story of thy noble acts;   280
Tell her thou madest away her uncle Clarence,
Her uncle Rivers; yea, and, for her sake,
 • Madest quick conveyance with her good aunt
    Anne.
   K. Rich. Come, come, you mock me; this is
    not the way
To win your daughter.
   Q. Eliz.   There is no other way;
Unless thou couldst put on some other shape,
And not be Richard that hath done all this.
   K. Rich. Say that I did all this for love of her.
   Q. Eliz. Nay, then indeed she cannot choose
    but hate thee,
Having bought love with such a bloody spoil. 290
   K. Rich. Look, what is done cannot be now
    amended:
Men shall deal unadvisedly sometimes,
Which after hours give leisure to repent.
If I did take the kingdom from your sons,
To make amends, I'll give it to your daughter.
If I have kill'd the issue of your womb,
To quicken your increase, I will beget
Mine issue of your blood upon your daughter:
A grandam's name is little less in love
Than is the doting title of a mother;   300
They are as children but one step below,
Even of your mettle, of your very blood;
Of all one pain, save for a night of groans
 • Endured of her, for whom you bid like sorrow.
Your children were vexation to your youth,
But mine shall be a comfort to your age.
The loss you have is but a son being king,
And by that loss your daughter is made queen.
I cannot make you what amends I would,
Therefore accept such kindness as I can.   310
Dorset your son, that with a fearful soul
Leads discontented steps in foreign soil,
This fair alliance quickly shall call home
To high promotions and great dignity:
The king, that calls your beauteous daughter wife,
Familiarly shall call thy Dorset brother;
Again shall you be mother to a king,
And all the ruins of distressful times
Repair'd with double riches of content.

What ! we have many goodly days to see : 320
The liquid drops of tears that you have shed
Shall come again, transform'd to orient pearl,
Advantaging their loan with interest
Of ten times double gain of happiness.
Go, then, my mother, to thy daughter go ;
Make bold her bashful years with your experience ;
Prepare her ears to hear a wooer's tale ;
Put in her tender heart the aspiring flame
Of golden sovereignty ; acquaint the princess
With the sweet silent hours of marriage joys : 330
And when this arm of mine hath chastised
The petty rebel, dull-brain'd Buckingham,
Bound with triumphant garlands will I come
And lead thy daughter to a conqueror's bed ;
To whom I will retail my conquest won,
And she shall be sole victress, Cæsar's Cæsar.
 Q. Eliz. What were I best to say? her father's
  brother
Would be her lord? or shall I say, her uncle?
Or, he that slew her brothers and her uncles?
Under what title shall I woo for thee, 340
That God, the law, my honour and her love,
Can make seem pleasing to her tender years?
 K. Rich. Infer fair England's peace by this
  alliance.
 Q. Eliz. Which she shall purchase with still
  lasting war.
 K. Rich. Say that the king, which may com-
  mand, entreats.
 Q. Eliz. That at her hands which the king's
  King forbids.
 K. Rich. Say, she shall be a high and mighty
  queen.
 Q. Eliz. To wail the title, as her mother doth.
 K. Rich. Say, I will love her everlastingly.
 Q. Eliz. But how long shall that title 'ever'
  last? 350
 K. Rich. Sweetly in force unto her fair life's
  end.
 Q. Eliz. But how long fairly shall her sweet
  life last?
 K. Rich. So long as heaven and nature
  lengthens it.
 Q. Eliz. So long as hell and Richard likes of it.
 K. Rich. Say, I, her sovereign, am her subject
  love.
 Q. Eliz. But she, your subject, loathes such
  sovereignty.
 K. Rich. Be eloquent in my behalf to her.
 Q. Eliz. An honest tale speeds best being
  plainly told.
 K. Rich. Then in plain terms tell her my
  loving tale.
 Q. Eliz. Plain and not honest is too harsh a
  style. 360
 K. Rich. Your reasons are too shallow and too
  quick.
 Q. Eliz. O no, my reasons are too deep and
  dead ;
Too deep and dead, poor infants, in their grave.
 K. Rich. Harp not on that string, madam ;
  that is past.
 Q. Eliz. Harp on it still shall I till heart-
  strings break.
 K. Rich. Now, by my George, my garter, and
  my crown,—
 Q. Eliz. Profaned, dishonour'd, and the third
  usurp'd.

346 *forbids.* Marriage to a niece was forbidden in canon law.

366 *George.* The figure of St. George on the pendent of the Order of the Garter.

Insignia of the Order of the Garter. From John Speed's *Theatre of the Empire of Great Britaine*, 1611–12

420 *Shall . . . myself?* Shall I forget my present state to become what I used to be: a queen?

424 *nest of spicery.* The phoenix's nest. The phoenix was reborn of its own destruction.

The Phoenix, a mythical Arabian bird. From a 12th century bestiary

K. Rich. I swear—
Q. Eliz. By nothing; for this is no oath:
The George, profaned, hath lost his holy honour;
The garter, blemish'd, pawn'd his knightly virtue;
The crown, usurp'd, disgraced his kingly glory.
If something thou wilt swear to be believed,
Swear then by something that thou hast not
    wrong'd.
K. Rich. Now, by the world—
Q. Eliz. 'Tis full of thy foul wrongs.
K. Rich. My father's death—
Q. Eliz. Thy life hath that dishonour'd.
K. Rich. Then, by myself—
Q. Eliz. Thyself thyself misusest.
K. Rich. Why then, by God—
Q. Eliz. God's wrong is most of all.
If thou hadst fear'd to break an oath by Him,
The unity the king thy brother made
Had not been broken, nor my brother slain: 380
If thou hadst fear'd to break an oath by Him,
The imperial metal, circling now thy brow,
Had graced the tender temples of my child,
And both the princes had been breathing here,
Which now, two tender playfellows for dust,
Thy broken faith hath made a prey for worms.
What canst thou swear by now?
K. Rich. The time to come.
Q. Eliz. That thou hast wronged in the time
    o'erpast;
For I myself have many tears to wash   389
Hereafter time, for time past wrong'd by thee.
The children live, whose parents thou hast
    slaughter'd,
Ungovern'd youth, to wail it in their age;
The parents live, whose children thou hast
    butcher'd,
Old wither'd plants, to wail it with their age.
Swear not by time to come; for that thou hast
Misused ere used, by time misused o'erpast.
K. Rich. As I intend to prosper and repent,
So thrive I in my dangerous attempt
Of hostile arms! myself myself confound!
Heaven and fortune bar me happy hours!   400
Day, yield me not thy light; nor, night, thy rest!
Be opposite all planets of good luck
To my proceedings, if, with pure heart's love,
Immaculate devotion, holy thoughts,
I tender not thy beauteous princely daughter!
In her consists my happiness and thine;
Without her, follows to this land and me,
To thee, herself, and many a Christian soul,
Death, desolation, ruin and decay:
It cannot be avoided but by this;   410
It will not be avoided but by this.
Therefore, good mother,—I must call you so—
Be the attorney of my love to her:
Plead what I will be, not what I have been;
Not my deserts, but what I will deserve:
Urge the necessity and state of times,
And be not peevish-fond in great designs.
Q. Eliz. Shall I be tempted of the devil thus?
K. Rich. Ay, if the devil tempt thee to do good.
Q. Eliz. Shall I forget myself to be myself? 420
K. Rich. Ay, if yourself's remembrance wrong
    yourself.
Q. Eliz. But thou didst kill my children.
K. Rich. But in your daughter's womb I
    bury them:
Where in that nest of spicery they shall breed

Selves of themselves, to your recomforture.
   Q. Eliz. Shall I go win my daughter to thy will?
   K. Rich. And be a happy mother by the deed.
   Q. Eliz. I go. Write to me very shortly,
And you shall understand from me her mind.
   K. Rich. Bear her my true love's kiss; and
   so, farewell.   *[Exit Queen Elizabeth.* 430
Relenting fool, and shallow, changing woman!

     Enter RATCLIFF; CATESBY *following.*

How now! what news?
   Rat. My gracious sovereign, on the western
   coast
Rideth a puissant navy; to the shore
Throng many doubtful hollow-hearted friends,
Unarm'd, and unresolved to beat them back:
'Tis thought that Richmond is their admiral;
● And there they hull, expecting but the aid
Of Buckingham to welcome them ashore.
   K. Rich. Some light-foot friend post to the
   Duke of Norfolk: 440
Ratcliff, thyself, or Catesby; where is he?
   Cate. Here, my lord.
   K. Rich. Fly to the duke: [*To Ratcliff*] Post
   thou to Salisbury:
When thou comest thither,—[*To Catesby*] Dull,
   unmindful villain,
Why stand'st thou still, and go'st not to the duke?
   Cate. First, mighty sovereign, let me know
   your mind,
What from your grace I shall deliver to him.
   K. Rich. O, true, good Catesby: bid him levy
   straight
● The greatest strength and power he can make,
And meet me presently at Salisbury.   450
   Cate. I go.   *[Exit.*
   Rat. What is't your highness' pleasure I shall do
At Salisbury?
   K. Rich. Why, what wouldst thou do there
   before I go?
   Rat. Your highness told me I should post
   before.
   K. Rich. My mind is changed, sir, my mind
   is changed.

     Enter LORD STANLEY.

How now, what news with you?
   Stan. None good, my lord, to please you with
   the hearing;
Nor none so bad, but it may well be told.
   K. Rich. Hoyday, a riddle! neither good nor
   bad!   460
Why dost thou run so many mile about,
When thou mayst tell thy tale a nearer way?
Once more, what news?
   Stan.   Richmond is on the seas.
   K. Rich. There let him sink, and be the seas
   on him!
● White-liver'd runagate, what doth he there?
   Stan. I know not, mighty sovereign, but by
   guess.
   K. Rich. Well, sir, as you guess, as you guess?
   Stan. Stirr'd up by Dorset, Buckingham, and
   Ely,
He makes for England, there to claim the crown.
   K. Rich. Is the chair empty? is the sword
   unsway'd?   470
Is the king dead? the empire unpossess'd?
What heir of York is there alive but we?

438 *hull.* Drift.

449 *power.* Army.

465 *White-liver'd runagate.* Cowardly runaway.

Lord Stanley, Earl of Derby. Engraving from *Old England*, 1854

506 *competitors.* Associates.

Ellen Bateman, the 19th century child actress, as
Richard III, Lyceum Theatre, London, 1877

And who is England's king but great York's heir?
Then, tell me, what doth he upon the sea?
    Stan. Unless for that, my liege, I cannot guess.
    K. Rich. Unless for that he comes to be your
      liege,
You cannot guess wherefore the Welshman comes.
Thou wilt revolt, and fly to him, I fear.
    Stan. No, mighty liege; therefore mistrust
      me not.
    K. Rich. Where is thy power, then, to beat
      him back?   480
Where are thy tenants and thy followers?
Are they not now upon the western shore,
Safe-conducting the rebels from their ships?
    Stan. No, my good lord, my friends are in
      the north.
    K. Rich. Cold friends to Richard: what do
      they in the north,
When they should serve their sovereign in the
      west?
    Stan. They have not been commanded, mighty
      sovereign:
Please it your majesty to give me leave,
I'll muster up my friends, and meet your grace
Where and what time your majesty shall please.
    K. Rich. Ay, ay, thou wouldst be gone to join
      with Richmond:
I will not trust you, sir.
    Stan.   Most mighty sovereign,
You have no cause to hold my friendship doubtful:
I never was nor never will be false.
    K. Rich. Well,
Go muster men; but, hear you, leave behind
Your son, George Stanley: look your faith be
      firm,
Or else his head's assurance is but frail.
    Stan. So deal with him as I prove true to you.
                             [*Exit.*

          Enter a Messenger.

    Mess. My gracious sovereign, now in Devon-
      shire,   500
As I by friends am well advertised,
Sir Edward Courtney, and the haughty prelate
Bishop of Exeter, his brother there,
With many moe confederates, are in arms.

        Enter another Messenger.

    Sec. Mess. My liege, in Kent the Guildfords
      are in arms;
● And every hour more competitors
Flock to their aid, and still their power increaseth.

        Enter another Messenger.

    Third Mess. My lord, the army of the Duke
      of Buckingham—
    K. Rich. Out on you, owls! nothing but songs
      of death?   [*He striketh him.*
Take that, until thou bring me better news. 510
    Third Mess. The news I have to tell your
      majesty
Is, that by sudden floods and fall of waters,
Buckingham's army is dispersed and scatter'd;
And he himself wander'd away alone,
No man knows whither.
    K. Rich.   I cry thee mercy:
There is my purse to cure that blow of thine.
Hath any well-advised friend proclaim'd
Reward to him that brings the traitor in?

Third Mess. Such proclamation hath been made, my liege.

Enter another Messenger.

Fourth Mess. Sir Thomas Lovel and Lord Marquis Dorset, 520
'Tis said, my liege, in Yorkshire are in arms.
Yet this good comfort bring I to your grace,
The Breton navy is dispersed by tempest:
Richmond, in Dorsetshire, sent out a boat
Unto the shore, to ask those on the banks
If they were his assistants, yea or no;
Who answer'd him, they came from Buckingham
Upon his party: he, mistrusting them,
Hoised sail and made away for Brittany.
K. Rich. March on, march on, since we are up in arms; 530
If not to fight with foreign enemies,
Yet to beat down these rebels here at home.

Re-enter CATESBY.

Cate. My liege, the Duke of Buckingham is taken;
That is the best news: that the Earl of Richmond
Is with a mighty power landed at Milford,
Is colder tidings, yet they must be told.
K. Rich. Away towards Salisbury! while we reason here,
A royal battle might be won and lost:
Some one take order Buckingham be brought
To Salisbury; the rest march on with me. 540
[*Flourish. Exeunt.*

SCENE V. *Lord Derby's house.*

Enter DERBY *and* SIR CHRISTOPHER URSWICK.

Der. Sir Christopher, tell Richmond this from me:
That in the sty of this most bloody boar
• My son George Stanley is frank'd up in hold:
If I revolt, off goes young George's head;
The fear of that withholds my present aid.
But, tell me, where is princely Richmond now?
Chris. At Pembroke, or at Ha'rford-west, in Wales.
Der. What men of name resort to him?
Chris. Sir Walter Herbert, a renowned soldier;
Sir Gilbert Talbot, Sir William Stanley; 10
Oxford, redoubted Pembroke, Sir James Blunt,
And Rice ap Thomas, with a valiant crew;
And many moe of noble fame and worth:
And towards London they do bend their course,
If by the way they be not fought withal.
Der. Return unto thy lord; commend me to him:
Tell him the queen hath heartily consented
He shall espouse Elizabeth her daughter.
These letters will resolve him of my mind.
Farewell. [*Exeunt.* 20

ACT V.

SCENE I. *Salisbury. An open place.*

Enter the Sheriff, *and* BUCKINGHAM, *with halberds, led to execution.*

Buck. Will not King Richard let me speak with him?
Sher. No, my good lord; therefore be patient.

3 *hold.* Prison.

Kate Bateman as Richmond. She was the sister of Ellen, and daughter of the American impresario H.L. Bateman who leased the Lyceum Theatre, London, from 1871 to 1877

7 *moody.* Angry.

19 *determined . . . wrongs.* Predetermined end of my crimes.

Buckingham: 'Come, sirs, convey me to the block of shame.' Prisoners being taken to their death. Engraving from a medieval manuscript

Henry, Earl of Richmond and the future Henry VII. Drawing by Henry Singleton (1766–1839)

9 *wash.* Swill.

10 *embowell'd.* Disembowelled.

Buck. Hastings, and Edward's children, Rivers, Grey,
Holy King Henry, and thy fair son Edward,
Vaughan, and all that have miscarried
By underhand corrupted foul injustice,
If that your moody discontented souls
Do through the clouds behold this present hour,
Even for revenge mock my destruction!
This is All-Souls' day, fellows, is it not?   10
    Sher. It is, my lord.
    Buck. Why, then All-Souls' day is my body's doomsday.
This is the day that, in King Edward's time,
I wish'd might fall on me, when I was found
False to his children or his wife's allies;
This is the day wherein I wish'd to fall
By the false faith of him I trusted most;
This, this All-Souls' day to my fearful soul
Is the determined respite of my wrongs:
That high All-Seer that I dallied with   20
Hath turn'd my feigned prayer on my head
And given in earnest what I begg'd in jest.
Thus doth he force the swords of wicked men
To turn their own points on their masters' bosoms:
Now Margaret's curse is fallen upon my head;
'When he,' quoth she, 'shall split thy heart with sorrow,
Remember Margaret was a prophetess.'
Come, sirs, convey me to the block of shame;
Wrong hath but wrong, and blame the due of blame.   [*Exeunt.*

SCENE II.   *The camp near Tamworth.*

Enter RICHMOND, OXFORD, BLUNT, HERBERT, *and others, with drum and colours.*

    Richm. Fellows in arms, and my most loving friends,
Bruised underneath the yoke of tyranny,
Thus far into the bowels of the land
Have we march'd on without impediment;
And here receive we from our father Stanley
Lines of fair comfort and encouragement.
The wretched, bloody, and usurping boar,
That spoil'd your summer fields and fruitful vines,
Swills your warm blood like wash, and makes his trough
In your embowell'd bosoms, this foul swine   10
Lies now even in the centre of this isle,
Near to the town of Leicester, as we learn:
From Tamworth thither is but one day's march.
In God's name, cheerly on, courageous friends,
To reap the harvest of perpetual peace
By this one bloody trial of sharp war.
    Oxf. Every man's conscience is a thousand swords,
To fight against that bloody homicide.
    Herb. I doubt not but his friends will fly to us.
    Blunt. He hath no friends but who are friends for fear,   20
Which in his greatest need will shrink from him.
    Richm. All for our vantage.   Then, in God's name, march:
True hope is swift, and flies with swallow's wings;
Kings it makes gods, and meaner creatures kings.
                    [*Exeunt.*

SCENE III. *Bosworth Field.*

Enter KING RICHARD *in arms, with* NORFOLK, *the* EARL OF SURREY, *and others.*

K. Rich. Here pitch our tents, even here in Bosworth field.
My Lord of Surrey, why look you so sad?
Sur. My heart is ten times lighter than my looks.
K. Rich. My Lord of Norfolk,—
Nor. Here, most gracious liege.
K. Rich. Norfolk, we must have knocks; ha! must we not?
Nor. We must both give and take, my gracious lord.
K. Rich. Up with my tent there! here will I lie to-night;
But where to-morrow? Well, all's one for that.
Who hath descried the number of the foe?
Nor. Six or seven thousand is their utmost power. 10
K. Rich. Why, our battalion trebles that account:
Besides, the king's name is a tower of strength,
Which they upon the adverse party want.
Up with my tent there! Valiant gentlemen,
Let us survey the vantage of the field;
• Call for some men of sound direction:
• Let's want no discipline, make no delay;
For, lords, to-morrow is a busy day. [*Exeunt.*

Enter, on the other side of the field, RICHMOND,
SIR WILLIAM BRANDON, OXFORD, *and others.
Some of the* Soldiers *pitch Richmond's tent.*

Richm. The weary sun hath made a golden set,
And, by the bright track of his fiery car, 20
Gives signal of a goodly day to-morrow.
Sir William Brandon, you shall bear my standard.
Give me some ink and paper in my tent:
I'll draw the form and model of our battle,
• Limit each leader to his several charge,
And part in just proportion our small strength.
My Lord of Oxford, you, Sir William Brandon,
And you, Sir Walter Herbert, stay with me.
The Earl of Pembroke keeps his regiment:
Good Captain Blunt, bear my good-night to him,
And by the second hour in the morning 31
Desire the earl to see me in my tent:
Yet one thing more, good Blunt, before thou go'st,
Where is Lord Stanley quarter'd, dost thou know?
Blunt. Unless I have mista'en his colours much,
Which well I am assured I have not done,
His regiment lies half a mile at least
South from the mighty power of the king.
Richm. If without peril it be possible, 39
Good captain Blunt, bear my good-night to him,
And give him from me this most needful scroll.
Blunt. Upon my life, my lord, I'll undertake it:
And so, God give you quiet rest to-night!
Richm. Good night, good Captain Blunt. Come, gentlemen,
Let us consult upon to-morrow's business:
In to our tent; the air is raw and cold.
[*They withdraw into the tent.*

Stage set from Edmund Kean's *Richard III*, 1854

---

16 *direction.* Judgment of military tactics.

17 *discipline.* Experience.

25 *Limit.* Appoint.

Thomas Howard, Earl of Surrey. Engraving from *Old England*, 1854

50 *beaver*. Faceguard of a helmet; sometimes the helmet itself.

59 *pursuivant at arms*. An officer of the College of Heralds.

65 *staves*. Shafts of lances.

70 *cock-shut*. Twilight.

81 *father-in-law*. Stepfather.

Enter, to his tent, KING RICHARD, NORFOLK, RATCLIFF, CATESBY, *and others*.

K. Rich. What is't o'clock?
Cate. It's supper-time, my lord;
It's nine o'clock.
K. Rich. I will not sup to-night.
Give me some ink and paper.
What, is my beaver easier than it was?　　50
And all my armour laid into my tent?
Cate. It is, my liege; and all things are in readiness.
K. Rich. Good Norfolk, hie thee to thy charge;
Use careful watch, choose trusty sentinels.
Nor. I go, my lord.
K. Rich. Stir with the lark to-morrow, gentle Norfolk.
Nor. I warrant you, my lord.　　[*Exit.*
K. Rich. Catesby!
Cate. My lord?
K. Rich. Send out a pursuivant at arms
To Stanley's regiment; bid him bring his power
Before sunrising, lest his son George fall　　61
Into the blind cave of eternal night.
　　[*Exit Catesby.*
Fill me a bowl of wine. Give me a watch.
Saddle white Surrey for the field to-morrow.
Look that my staves be sound, and not too heavy.
Ratcliff!
Rat. My lord?
K. Rich. Saw'st thou the melancholy Lord Northumberland?
Rat. Thomas the Earl of Surrey, and himself,
Much about cock-shut time, from troop to troop 70
Went through the army, cheering up the soldiers.
K. Rich. So, I am satisfied. Give me a bowl of wine:
I have not that alacrity of spirit,
Nor cheer of mind, that I was wont to have.
Set it down. Is ink and paper ready?
Rat. It is, my lord.
K. Rich. Bid my guard watch; leave me.
Ratcliff, about the mid of night come to my tent
And help to arm me. Leave me, I say.
　　[*Exeunt Ratcliff and the other Attendants.*

Enter DERBY *to* RICHMOND *in his tent, Lords and others attending.*

Der. Fortune and victory sit on thy helm!
Richm. All comfort that the dark night can afford　　80
Be to thy person, noble father-in-law!
Tell me, how fares our loving mother?
Der. I, by attorney, bless thee from thy mother,
Who prays continually for Richmond's good:
So much for that. The silent hours steal on,
And flaky darkness breaks within the east.
In brief,—for so the season bids us be,—
Prepare thy battle early in the morning,
And put thy fortune to the arbitrement
Of bloody strokes and mortal-staring war.　　90
I, as I may—that which I would I cannot,—
With best advantage will deceive the time,
And aid thee in this doubtful shock of arms:
But on thy side I may not be too forward,
Lest, being seen, thy brother, tender George,
Be executed in his father's sight.

105 *peise.* Weigh.

Farewell: the leisure and the fearful time
Cuts off the ceremonious vows of love
And ample interchange of sweet discourse,
Which so long sunder'd friends should dwell upon:
God give us leisure for these rites of love! 101
Once more, adieu: be valiant, and speed well!
  Richm. Good lords, conduct him to his regiment:
I'll strive, with troubled thoughts, to take a nap,
● Lest leaden slumber peise me down to-morrow,
When I should mount with wings of victory:
Once more, good night, kind lords and gentlemen.
                              [*Exeunt all but Richmond.*
O Thou, whose captain I account myself,
Look on my forces with a gracious eye;
Put in their hands thy bruising irons of wrath, 110
That they may crush down with a heavy fall
The usurping helmets of our adversaries!
Make us thy ministers of chastisement,
That we may praise thee in the victory!
To thee I do commend my watchful soul,
Ere I let fall the windows of mine eyes:
Sleeping and waking, O, defend me still!
                              [*Sleeps.*

  Enter the Ghost of PRINCE EDWARD, *son to*
            HENRY *the Sixth.*

  Ghost. [*To Richard*] Let me sit heavy on
    thy soul to-morrow!
Think, how thou stab'dst me in my prime of youth
At Tewksbury: despair, therefore, and die! 120
[*To Richmond*] Be cheerful, Richmond; for
    the wronged souls
Of butcher'd princes fight in thy behalf:
King Henry's issue, Richmond, comforts thee.

  Enter the Ghost of HENRY *the Sixth.*

  Ghost. [*To Richard*] When I was mortal, my
    anointed body
By thee was punched full of deadly holes:
Think on the Tower and me: despair, and die!
Harry the Sixth bids thee despair and die!
[*To Richmond*] Virtuous and holy, be thou
    conqueror!
Harry, that prophesied thou shouldst be king,
Doth comfort thee in thy sleep: live, and flourish!

  Enter the Ghost of CLARENCE.

  Ghost. [*To Richard*] Let me sit heavy on
    thy soul to-morrow!   131
I, that was wash'd to death with fulsome wine,
Poor Clarence, by thy guile betrayed to death!
To-morrow in the battle think on me,
And fall thy edgeless sword: despair, and die!—
[*To Richmond*] Thou offspring of the house of
    Lancaster,
The wronged heirs of York do pray for thee:
Good angels guard thy battle! live, and flourish!

  Enter the Ghosts of RIVERS, GREY, *and*
            VAUGHAN.

  Ghost of R. [*To Richard*] Let me sit heavy
    on thy soul to-morrow,
Rivers, that died at Pomfret! despair, and die!
  Ghost of G. [*To Richard*] Think upon Grey,
    and let thy soul despair!   141
  Ghost of V. [*To Richard*] Think upon
    Vaughan, and, with guilty fear,

David Garrick as Richard III. Painting by William
Hogarth (1697–1764)

173 *for hope.* Hoping to help you.

180 *burns blue.* A sign of the presence of a ghost.

Richard dreams of his victims. Engraving from Rowe's edition of Shakespeare's works, 1709

Let fall thy lance: despair, and die!
  All. [*To Richmond*] Awake, and think our wrongs in Richard's bosom
Will conquer him! awake, and win the day!

Enter the Ghost of HASTINGS.

  Ghost. [*To Richard*] Bloody and guilty, guiltily awake,
And in a bloody battle end thy days!
Think on Lord Hastings: despair, and die!
[*To Richmond*] Quiet untroubled soul, awake, awake!
Arm, fight, and conquer, for fair England's sake!

Enter the Ghosts of the two young Princes.

  Ghosts. [*To Richard*] Dream on thy cousins smother'd in the Tower: 151
Let us be lead within thy bosom, Richard,
And weigh thee down to ruin, shame, and death!
Thy nephews' souls bid thee despair and die!
[*To Richmond*] Sleep, Richmond, sleep in peace, and wake in joy;
Good angels guard thee from the boar's annoy!
Live, and beget a happy race of kings!
Edward's unhappy sons do bid thee flourish.

Enter the Ghost of LADY ANNE.

  Ghost. [*To Richard*] Richard, thy wife, that wretched Anne thy wife,
That never slept a quiet hour with thee,   160
Now fills thy sleep with perturbations:
To-morrow in the battle think on me,
And fall thy edgeless sword: despair, and die!
[*To Richmond*] Thou quiet soul, sleep thou a quiet sleep;
Dream of success and happy victory!
Thy adversary's wife doth pray for thee.

Enter the Ghost of BUCKINGHAM.

  Ghost. [*To Richard*] The first was I that help'd thee to the crown;
The last was I that felt thy tyranny:
O, in the battle think on Buckingham,
And die in terror of thy guiltiness!   170
Dream on, dream on, of bloody deeds and death:
Fainting, despair; despairing, yield thy breath!
• [*To Richmond*] I died for hope ere I could lend thee aid:
But cheer thy heart, and be thou not dismay'd:
God and good angels fight on Richmond's side;
And Richard falls in height of all his pride.
  [*The Ghosts vanish. King Richard starts out of his dream.*

  K. Rich. Give me another horse: bind up my wounds.
Have mercy, Jesu!—Soft! I did but dream.
O coward conscience, how dost thou afflict me!
• The lights burn blue. It is now dead midnight.
Cold fearful drops stand on my trembling flesh.
What do I fear? myself? there's none else by:
Richard loves Richard; that is, I am I.
Is there a murderer here? No. Yes, I am:
Then fly. What, from myself? Great reason why:
Lest I revenge. What, myself upon myself?
Alack, I love myself. Wherefore? for any good
That I myself have done unto myself?
O, no! alas, I rather hate myself
For hateful deeds committed by myself!   190

I am a villain: yet I lie, I am not.
Fool, of thyself speak well: fool, do not flatter.
My conscience hath a thousand several tongues,
And every tongue brings in a several tale,
And every tale condemns me for a villain.
Perjury, perjury, in the high'st degree;
Murder, stern murder, in the direst degree;
● All several sins, all used in each degree,
Throng to the bar, crying all, Guilty! guilty!
● I shall despair. There is no creature loves me;
And if I die, no soul shall pity me: 201
Nay, wherefore should they, since that I myself
Find in myself no pity to myself?
Methought the souls of all that I had murder'd
Came to my tent; and every one did threat
To-morrow's vengeance on the head of Richard.

Enter RATCLIFF.

Rat. My lord!
K. Rich. 'Zounds! who is there?
Rat. Ratcliff, my lord; 'tis I. The early
   village-cock
Hath twice done salutation to the morn;   210
Your friends are up, and buckle on their armour.
  K. Rich. O Ratcliff, I have dream'd a fearful
   dream!
What thinkest thou, will our friends prove all
  true?
  Rat. No doubt, my lord.
  K. Rich.   O Ratcliff, I fear, I fear,—
  Rat. Nay, good my lord, be not afraid of
  shadows.
  K. Rich. By the apostle Paul, shadows to-
  night
Have struck more terror to the soul of Richard
Than can the substance of ten thousand soldiers
● Armed in proof, and led by shallow Richmond.
It is not yet near day. Come, go with me;   220
Under our tents I'll play the eaves-dropper,
To see if any mean to shrink from me. [*Exeunt.*

Enter the Lords *to* RICHMOND, *sitting in his
tent.*

  Lords. Good morrow, Richmond!
  Richm. Cry mercy, lords and watchful gentle-
  men,
That you have ta'en a tardy sluggard here.
  Lords. How have you slept, my lord?
  Richm. The sweetest sleep, and fairest-boding
  dreams
That ever enter'd in a drowsy head,
Have I since your departure had, my lords.
Methought their souls, whose bodies Richard
  murder'd,   230
Came to my tent, and cried on victory:
I promise you, my soul is very jocund
In the remembrance of so fair a dream.
How far into the morning is it, lords?
  Lords. Upon the stroke of four.
  Richm. Why, then 'tis time to arm and give
  direction.

His oration to his soldiers.

More than I have said, loving countrymen,
The leisure and enforcement of the time
Forbids to dwell upon: yet remember this,
God and our good cause fight upon our side;   240
The prayers of holy saints and wronged souls,
Like high-rear'd bulwarks, stand before our faces;

198 *used.* Committed.

200–201 *I shall . . . pity me.* See introduction.

219 *proof.* Tested armour.

John Bannister as Richard III and John Pindar as Sir
Richard Ratcliff, Haymarket Theatre, London, 1794

250 *foil.* Setting for a jewel.

Richard III armed. Costume design by J.R. Planché, the 19th century designer who worked with Charles Kemble

276 *Tell the clock.* Count the strokes.

Duke of Norfolk, father of the Earl of Surrey. Engraving from *Old England*, 1854

Richard except, those whom we fight against
Had rather have us win than him they follow:
For what is he they follow? truly, gentlemen,
A bloody tyrant and a homicide;
One raised in blood, and one in blood establish'd;
One that made means to come by what he hath,
And slaughter'd those that were the means to
　　help him;
● A base foul stone, made precious by the foil　250
Of England's chair, where he is falsely set;
One that hath ever been God's enemy:
Then, if you fight against God's enemy,
God will in justice ward you as his soldiers;
If you do sweat to put a tyrant down,
You sleep in peace, the tyrant being slain;
If you do fight against your country's foes,
Your country's fat shall pay your pains the hire;
If you do fight in safeguard of your wives,
Your wives shall welcome home the conquerors;
If you do free your children from the sword,　261
Your children's children quit it in your age.
Then, in the name of God and all these rights,
Advance your standards, draw your willing
　　swords.
For me, the ransom of my bold attempt
Shall be this cold corpse on the earth's cold face;
But if I thrive, the gain of my attempt
The least of you shall share his part thereof.
Sound drums and trumpets boldly and cheer-
　　fully;
God and Saint George! Richmond and victory!
　　　　　　　　　　　　　　　　[*Exeunt.* 270

Re-enter KING RICHARD, RATCLIFF, *Attend-*
　　ants and Forces.

　K. Rich. What said Northumberland as touch-
　　ing Richmond?
　Rat. That he was never trained up in arms.
　K. Rich. He said the truth: and what said
　　Surrey then?
　Rat. He smiled and said 'The better for our
　　purpose.'
　K. Rich. He was in the right; and so indeed
　　it is. 　　　　　　　　　　[*Clock striketh.*
● Tell the clock there. Give me a calendar.
Who saw the sun to-day?
　Rat.　　　　　　　　　　　　Not I, my lord.
　K. Rich. Then he disdains to shine; for by
　　the book
He should have braved the east an hour ago:
A black day will it be to somebody. 　　　280
Ratcliff!
　Rat. My lord?
　K. Rich.　　　　The sun will not be seen to-day;
The sky doth frown and lour upon our army.
I would these dewy tears were from the ground.
Not shine to-day! Why, what is that to me
More than to Richmond? for the selfsame heaven
That frowns on me looks sadly upon him.

　　　　　　Enter NORFOLK.

　Nor. Arm, arm, my lord; the foe vaunts in
　　the field.
　K. Rich. Come, bustle, bustle; caparison
　　my horse.
Call up Lord Stanley, bid him bring his power:
I will lead forth my soldiers to the plain, 　　291
And thus my battle shall be ordered:

My foreward shall be drawn out all in length,
Consisting equally of horse and foot;
Our archers shall be placed in the midst:
John Duke of Norfolk, Thomas Earl of Surrey,
Shall have the leading of this foot and horse.
They thus directed, we will follow
In the main battle, whose puissance on either
side
Shall be well winged with our chiefest horse. 300
This, and Saint George to boot! What think'st
thou, Norfolk?
Nor. A good direction, warlike sovereign.
This found I on my tent this morning.

[*He sheweth him a paper.*

K. Rich. [*Reads*] 'Jockey of Norfolk, be not
too bold,
For Dickon thy master is bought and sold.'
A thing devised by the enemy.
Go, gentlemen, every man unto his charge:
Let not our babbling dreams affright our souls:
Conscience is but a word that cowards use,
Devised at first to keep the strong in awe: 310
Our strong arms be our conscience, swords our
law.
March on, join bravely, let us to't pell-mell;
If not to heaven, then hand in hand to hell.

His oration to his Army.

What shall I say more than I have inferr'd?
Remember whom you are to cope withal;
A sort of vagabonds, rascals, and runaways,
A scum of Bretons, and base lackey peasants,
Whom their o'er-cloyed country vomits forth
To desperate ventures and assured destruction.
You sleeping safe, they bring to you unrest; 320
You having lands, and blest with beauteous
wives,
They would restrain the one, distain the other.
And who doth lead them but a paltry fellow,
Long kept in Bretagne at our mother's cost?
A milk-sop, one that never in his life
Felt so much cold as over shoes in snow?
Let's whip these stragglers o'er the seas again;
Lash hence these overweening rags of France,
These famish'd beggars, weary of their lives,
Who, but for dreaming on this fond exploit, 330
For want of means, poor rats, had hang'd them-
selves:
If we be conquer'd, let men conquer us,
And not these bastard Bretons; whom our
fathers
Have in their own land beaten, bobb'd, and
thump'd,
And in record, left them the heirs of shame.
Shall these enjoy our lands? lie with our wives?
Ravish our daughters? [*Drum afar off.*] Hark!
I hear their drum.
Fight, gentlemen of England! fight, bold yeomen!
Draw, archers, draw your arrows to the head!
Spur your proud horses hard, and ride in blood;
Amaze the welkin with your broken staves! 341

Enter a Messenger.

What says Lord Stanley? will he bring his
power?
Mess. My lord, he doth deny to come.
K. Rich. Off with his son George's head!
Nor. My lord, the enemy is past the marsh:
After the battle let George Stanley die.

293 *foreward.* Vanguard.

304 *Jockey.* Familiar term for the name Jack. i.e. John Howard.

305 *Dickon.* Dick or Richard.

309–310 *Conscience . . . in awe.* See introduction.

322 *distain.* Defile.

334 *bobb'd.* Cut short.

341 *welkin.* Sky.

William Smith, the 18th century actor, as Richard III. Engraving from Bell's edition of Shakespeare's works, 1775

9 *cast.* Throw of the dice or die.

10 *hazard of the die.* The chance of the dice.

David Garrick as Richard III, 1741

19 *white rose and the red.* The white rose was the symbol of the house of York and the red rose, the house of Lancaster.

K. Rich. A thousand hearts are great within my bosom:
Advance our standards, set upon our foes;
Our ancient word of courage, fair Saint George,
Inspire us with the spleen of fiery dragons! 350
Upon them! Victory sits on our helms.
[*Exeunt.*

SCENE IV. *Another part of the field.*

Alarum: excursions. Enter NORFOLK and forces fighting; to him CATESBY.

Cate. Rescue, my Lord of Norfolk, rescue, rescue!
The king enacts more wonders than a man,
Daring an opposite to every danger:
His horse is slain, and all on foot he fights,
Seeking for Richmond in the throat of death.
Rescue, fair lord, or else the day is lost!

Alarums. Enter KING RICHARD.

K. Rich. A horse! a horse! my kingdom for a horse!
Cate. Withdraw, my lord; I'll help you to a horse.
• *K. Rich.* Slave, I have set my life upon a cast,
• And I will stand the hazard of the die: 10
I think there be six Richmonds in the field;
Five have I slain to-day instead of him.
A horse! a horse! my kingdom for a horse!
[*Exeunt.*

SCENE V. *Another part of the field.*

Alarum. Enter RICHARD and RICHMOND; they fight. RICHARD is slain. Retreat and flourish. Re-enter RICHMOND, DERBY bearing the crown, with divers other Lords.

Richm. God and your arms be praised, victorious friends;
The day is ours, the bloody dog is dead.
Der. Courageous Richmond, well hast thou acquit thee.
Lo, here, this long-usurped royalty
From the dead temples of this bloody wretch
Have I pluck'd off, to grace thy brows withal:
Wear it, enjoy it, and make much of it.
Richm. Great God of heaven, say Amen to all!
But, tell me, is young George Stanley living?
Der. He is, my lord, and safe in Leicester town; 10
Whither, if it please you, we may now withdraw us.
Richm. What men of name are slain on either side?
Der. John Duke of Norfolk, Walter Lord Ferrers,
Sir Robert Brakenbury, and Sir William Brandon.
Richm. Inter their bodies as becomes their births:
Proclaim a pardon to the soldiers fled
That in submission will return to us:
And then, as we have ta'en the sacrament,
• We will unite the white rose and the red:
Smile heaven upon this fair conjunction, 20
That long have frown'd upon their enmity!
What traitor hears me, and says not amen?

England hath long been mad, and scarr'd herself;
The brother blindly shed the brother's blood,
The father rashly slaughter'd his own son,
The son, compell'd, been butcher to the sire:
All this divided York and Lancaster,
Divided in their dire division,
O, now, let Richmond and Elizabeth,
The true succeeders of each royal house,   30
By God's fair ordinance conjoin together!
And let their heirs, God, if thy will be so,
Enrich the time to come with smooth-faced
     peace,
With smiling plenty and fair prosperous days!
Abate the edge of traitors, gracious Lord,
That would reduce these bloody days again,
And make poor England weep in streams of
     blood!
Let them not live to taste this land's increase
That would with treason wound this fair land's
     peace!
Now civil wounds are stopp'd, peace lives again:
That she may long live here, God say amen!
                              [Exeunt.

Edmund Kean as Richard III and John Cooper as
Richmond. Nineteenth century print by W.S. Johnson

King Richard II

1595

The Play. *Richard II* is an utterly different play from *Richard III*; where that was a melodrama, with a distinctly comic aspect in the drawing of the hero-villain, *Richard II* is a lyrical tragedy, highly poetic, with not a joke in it. Exceptionally, it is all verse, with a great deal of rhyme, not only to punctuate the conclusion of speeches and scenes. The verse has a curious feature, which it shares with *King John*, that followed on the heels of this play: both have a number of sestets, rhyming ab ab cc. The whole tone of *Richard II* – except for the patriotic note which it shares with *King John* – is different: it has more in common with the lyrical tragedy of *Romeo and Juliet*, which it followed.

Not much difficulty about date, which is usually assumed to be 1595. Shakespeare drew on Samuel Daniel's *Civil Wars*, of early 1595; they were kindred spirits, drawn together by association with Florio, and there were mutual exchanges in their work – they were not ashamed to be indebted to one another. At the end of 1595 Sir Edward Hoby wrote inviting Sir Robert Cecil to supper in Cannon Row, Westminster, 'where as late as it shall please you a gate for your supper shall be open, and King Richard present himself to your view.' It is probable that this refers to the new play, as it is a more intimate, shorter play, with a smaller cast. Hoby was Lord Chamberlain Hunsdon's son-in-law; the Chamberlain's Men would be available for an evening performance. The busy little politician, doing all the work of Secretary of State, minuted laconically: 'Readily'. Shakespeare drew upon Holinshed as usual for his English history, but he also looked up a French chronicle for the events of Richard's reign. The Plantagenet royal house was French; Richard was pro-French, in favour of peace with France. His speech was French, as was the language of the Court until Henry IV and the Lancastrians. We notice that, though Richard was king of England, he does not make any of the patriotic speeches: they are given to John of Gaunt.

Poetry and Politics. In historic fact Richard II was an aesthete, like Charles I; both were unsuccessful as rulers, and came to tragic ends in consequence. Again and again we find in Shakespeare this confrontation between a ruler who is a failure politically and the real political type – an Antony as against Octavian, poor Henry VI as against York and his sons; here the political type, who has the gift for rule, is Bolingbroke. Richard II is not. In historic fact he was a non-combatant; we may share his preference for peace, but it militated against him in the jungle of medieval politics and war. He was also a neurotic; having been a king since he was a child turned his head. In the last years of his absolutism he would sit in hall wearing his crown, silent, and anyone who caught his gaze had to abase themselves. A line in the play suggests that Shakespeare may have known the tradition. Richard, contemplating himself in the glass, says:

> Was this the face
> That like the sun did make beholders wink?

The strain of rule was too much for him. Most important: he could not be trusted. This was a fatal flaw in a monarch, as again Charles I found. There must be a last court of appeal whose word everybody can trust and therefore accept. Oliver Cromwell decided that he could not trust Charles I's word. Bolingbroke was in a similar position with Richard II: it was simply the sense of self-preservation, in the struggle for survival, that led him forward from claiming his rights as Duke of Lancaster to taking Richard's throne. Had he not, with a turn in the political tide, or in the ups-and-downs of the bucket which are an image in the play – and Richard would have had him by the neck. The Duke of York warns Bolingbroke:

> Take not, good cousin, further than you should,
> Lest you mistake the heavens are over our heads.

Bolingbroke is well aware:

> I know it uncle, and oppose not myself
> Against their will.

The heavens, i.e. the political tide, were with him.

It was a fundamental mistake on Richard's part to have withheld Bolingbroke's inheritance from him: it created a sense of insecurity throughout the whole governing class, sufficiently alienated by Richard's misrule already, and gave them an able leader to overthrow his 'tyranny', i.e. irresponsible rule. Coming to the crown, Bolingbroke shows that he has, what Richard had not, this fundamental quality in a real sovereign (cf. George Washington or Abraham Lincoln): *justice of mind*. He does not allow his resentment as a private person, his sense of injury, to influence the justice he metes out as a sovereign. Henry is willing to restore his former enemy, Mowbray:

> Repealed he shall be
> And, though mine enemy, restored again
> To all his lands and signories.

Aumerle enters into conspiracy against him; as King, Henry judges him:

> Intended, or committed, was this fault?
> If on the first, how heinous e'er it be,
> To win thy after-love I pardon thee.

Such rulers deserve to win: Richard, whatever his good qualities – he was a patron of the arts – was incapable of it: he always acted for personal motives, out of personal resentment, etc. And he would not be advised: historically, so long as his uncle Gaunt was alive to keep things together, Richard kept his throne. After Gaunt's death things went to pieces; Richard surrounded himself with a lot of flatterers. And what a fool he was to go off to Ireland, leaving the coast clear for an injured Bolingbroke to descend upon.

The Tragedy. The tragedy was not so much in Bolingbroke's usurpation: the country (the 'heavens') called him to the throne – but in Richard's murder. Here we are up against one of those inextricable knots in history, which make for true tragedy: neither side could help himself, each was in the clutch of ineluctable forces. Richard *had* to go; Henry *had* to take his place. We must not forget that Henry was Richard's heir in the male line, and Richard had taken no care about the succession. But so long as Richard remained alive, he was a constant threat to the security of the throne. At the first move to restore him – his friends did him no good, as so often in history – he was made away with.

And that was worse than crime, it was sacrilege against the sacred person of an anointed king. Everybody understood that at the time, when we understand it only with the aid of anthropology. It inflicted a terrible sense of guilt upon a medieval person such as Henry IV, and may well have been a factor in the disease that afflicted him. The divinity that shrouds the sacramental person of a monarch is expressed in the famous lines:

> Not all the water in the rough rude sea
> Can wash the balm off from an anointed king.

It is the same anthropological necessity whether among the peoples in what used to be darkest Africa, or in the enlightened and rationalistic United States: the assassination of a President arouses quasi-religious horror.

The sequel was, as Richard's chief supporter, the Bishop of Carlisle, prophesied:

> The blood of English shall manure the ground
> And future ages groan for this foul act . . .
> And in this seat of peace tumultuous wars
> Shall kin with kin and kind with kind confound.

This was given its chance with the next incapable ruler to succeed, Henry's grandson, Henry VI.

Popularity is a weapon in the political game, as all politicians know; some command it, however undeservedly, with effortless ease – compare Baldwin. Others cannot, however well they have deserved of the state: Churchill never could, until the state was in dire peril. Bolingbroke deliberately cultivated popularity, and was rewarded on his entry into London:

> Whilst he, from the one side to the other turning,
> Bareheaded, lower than his proud steed's neck,
> Bespake them thus, 'I thank you, countrymen'.

The common people, whom Richard had never considered, threw 'dust upon his sacred head' – anthropologically, a fallen king becomes a sacrificial victim. One of his followers knows what to think of that, and of them:

> And that's the wavering commons; for their love
> Lies in their purses, and who empties them,
> By so much fills their hearts with deadly hate.

(Shakespeare never lets up in his reflections on them: they do not seem to have minded, or perhaps noticed.) Power is what matters in politics; Richard knew that well enough:

> Yet I well remember
> The favours of these men. Were they not mine?
> Did they not sometime cry 'All hail' to me?

Very well – then he should have kept a more careful grip on the levers of power.

Having lost it, he takes refuge in self-pity – and Shakespeare gives him most of the poetry of the play, and much of the sympathy. It is usual to find the man, under the king, more appealing than he deserves: anyone who loses control in circumstances so favourable to him deserves what he gets. Dr. Johnson, though tender at heart, felt something of this. 'It seems to be the design of the poet to raise Richard to esteem in his fall, and consequently to interest the reader in his favour. He gives him only passive fortitude, the virtue of a confessor rather than of a king. In his prosperity we saw him imperious and oppressive, but in his distress he is wise, patient, and pious.' Even this is an overgenerous judgment: one knows what Richard would have done to Bolingbroke, whom he had treated with conspicuous injustice, if he had had the chance.

Shakespeare did his best for him: he turned the aesthete into a poet. Many beautiful passages occur in which Richard indulges his self-pity.

Patriotism was an element in the appeal of the play. The exuberant jubilation of a small people – only half an island, as Pope Sixtus V said admiringly – who had come through the test of the struggle with the Spanish world-empire, led to a spirit of pride, self-confidence and some boasting that went with youthfulness. Gaunt is given this theme to celebrate, not the King:

> This happy breed of men, this little world,
> This precious stone set in the silver sea,
> Which serves it in the office of a wall,
> Or as a moat defensive to a house,
> Against the envy of less happier lands.

In my time at school we learnt it by heart, and had reason to believe it – no point in reciting it today. Gaunt's splendid apostrophe, developed in accordance with school rhetoric, 'even in American performances', we learn, 'usually evokes a solid round of applause' – but that must have been after the comparably heroic experience of 1940–1945.

> England, bound in with the triumphant sea,
> Whose rocky shore beats back the envious siege
> Of wat'ry Neptune, is now bound in with shame

– as it might be, a supine and work-shy demotic society.

Elizabethan England was apt to be choosy about immigrants, selecting only the best,

Robert Devereux, 2nd Earl of Essex (1566–1601), favourite of Elizabeth I, executed for treason after attempting to raise rebellion. Painting after Marcus Gheeraerts the Younger

and – like all youthful peoples – liable to be anti-foreign. For all that Italy provided such inspiration in the arts, ordinary Protestants looked on her as a school of vice, particularly in its more sophisticated forms – whoring after

> Report of fashions in proud Italy,
> Whose manners still our tardy apish nation
> Limps after in base imitation –

i.e. the English were backward, slow to catch up.

Background. *Richard II* had a topical significance which is hard for us to catch. With Elizabeth I, as with Richard II, the succession was an open question, much in men's minds but dangerous to touch. Essex, darling of the people, pursued popularity; some people thought of him as another Bolingbroke. Richard noted his behaviour much as Elizabeth did Essex's, and

> Observed his courtship to the common people;
> How he did seem to dive into their hearts
> With humble and familiar courtesy . . .
> Wooing poor craftsmen with the craft of smiles . . .
> Off goes his bonnet to an oyster-wench;
> A brace of draymen bid God speed him well . . .
> As were our England in reversion his.

A follower of Essex, Sir John Hayward, dedicated his account of Bolingbroke's assumption of the crown to Essex, rather too obviously, and was sent to the Tower for it. Some joke about Richard II passed between Essex and Sir Robert Cecil, to what effect we do not know. On the eve of Essex's Rebellion in 1601, his agents bribed the Company at the Globe to put on *Richard II*, then an old play, but with its deposition scene to suggest ideas to the audience. The government did not blame the players, but the Queen was furious: 'I am Richard II, know ye not that? This tragedy was played forty times in open streets and houses.'

It was popular, if not as much so as *Richard III*. Three quartos of it appeared in rapid succession in 1597 and 1598; but the deposition scene was censored, until James I had been safely on the throne for some years.

Personal. As in every one of Shakespeare's works, plays, poems, or sonnets, we find revealing references to his profession:

> As in a theatre the eyes of men,
> After a well-graced actor leaves the stage,
> Are idly bent on him that enters next,
> Thinking his prattle to be tedious . . .

That brings him immediately before us: we know that he was well-graced as an actor himself.

It is usual to compare *Richard II* with *Edward II*; actually there is much less of Marlowe's influence in this than there was in *Richard III*, and a world of difference in tone and atmosphere. The one reflection we may detect is where Bolingbroke charges Richard's favourites, Bushy and Green:

292

> You have in manner with your sinful hours
> Made a divorce betwixt his Queen and him,
> Broke the possession of a royal bed,
> And stained the beauty of a fair Queen's cheeks
> With tears drawn from her eyes by your foul wrongs.

There is no warrant for this in historic fact: Richard's Queen was at this time a child of eight. Shakespeare is thinking of Edward II's neglect of *his* Queen for his lover, Gaveston. Nothing of this kind appears in Shakespeare, though in life Richard doted on Robert de Vere, and made him, absurdly, Duke of Ireland. Richard's grand passion is rigorously excluded; this interesting aspect of things did not interest the heterosexual, family man.

We see the subjects of past and future plays teeming in his mind, in 'the sad stories of the deaths of kings':

> How some have been deposed, some slain in war,
> Some haunted by the ghosts they have deposed,
> Some poisoned by their wives, some sleeping killed –

we recognise Kyd's Hamlet waiting to leap out and take shape in the most wonderful play ever written.

Music has a place in *Richard II*: one reference reminds us of the Sonnets:

> Or like a cunning instrument cased up
> Or, being open, put into his hands
> That knows no touch to tune the harmony.

This was not the case with the Lady of the Sonnets –

> How oft, when thou my music, music play'st –

with her fingers touching the jacks of the virginals. Shakespeare's immense sensitiveness to music must have added to her spell over him; and, perhaps significantly, with his unconscious associativeness of mind that betrays him to us, an echo from the Sonnets follows:

> Four lagging winters and four wanton springs.

That experience was not far away in 1595.

Text. The text offers no particular problems. A good text was put out in 1597, subsequently reprinted, but without the deposition scene. This was inserted in a fourth quarto of 1608, but from a faulty copy. This was corrected when it came to the Folio.

THE TRAGEDY OF
KING RICHARD II.

DRAMATIS PERSONÆ.

KING RICHARD the Second.
JOHN OF GAUNT, Duke
  of Lancaster, } uncles to the King.
EDMUND OF LANGLEY,
  Duke of York,
HENRY, surnamed BOLINGBROKE, Duke of
  Hereford, son to John of Gaunt; after-
  wards KING HENRY IV.
DUKE OF AUMERLE, son to the Duke of York.
THOMAS MOWBRAY, Duke of Norfolk.
DUKE OF SURREY.
EARL OF SALISBURY.
LORD BERKELEY.
BUSHY,
BAGOT, } servants to King Richard.
GREEN,
EARL OF NORTHUMBERLAND.
HENRY PERCY, surnamed Hotspur, his son.

LORD ROSS.
LORD WILLOUGHBY.
LORD FITZWATER.
Bishop of Carlisle.
Abbot of Westminster.
Lord Marshal.
SIR STEPHEN SCROOP.
SIR PIERCE of Exton.
Captain of a band of Welshmen.

QUEEN to King Richard.
DUCHESS OF YORK.
DUCHESS OF GLOUCESTER.
Lady attending on the Queen.

Lords, Heralds, Officers, Soldiers, two Gardeners,
Keeper, Messenger, Groom, and other
Attendants.

SCENE : *England and Wales.*

● *A bullet beside a text line indicates an annotation in the
opposite column*

ACT I.

SCENE I. *London.* KING RICHARD'S *palace.*

Enter KING RICHARD, JOHN OF GAUNT, *with
other* Nobles *and* Attendants.

  K. Rich. Old John of Gaunt, time-honour'd

Richard II *c.*1376–1399

Opposite : The abdication of Richard II. Painting by Sir
John Gilbert (1817–1897)

2 *band*. Bond.

4 *appeal*. Accusation of treason.

9 *ancient malice*. Long-lasting personal quarrel.

18 *High-stomach'd*. Haughty and proud.

32 *Tendering*. Holding dear.

34 *appellant*. Accuser.

40 *Too good*. Too noble in birth.

Costume design for Richard II by Tanya Moisewitch, Stratford-upon-Avon, 1951

Lancaster,
- Hast thou, according to thy oath and band,
Brought hither Henry Hereford thy bold son,
- Here to make good the boisterous late appeal,
Which then our leisure would not let us hear,
Against the Duke of Norfolk, Thomas Mowbray?
   Gaunt. I have, my liege.
   K. Rich. Tell me, moreover, hast thou sounded him,
- If he appeal the duke on ancient malice;
Or worthily, as a good subject should,   10
On some known ground of treachery in him?
   Gaunt. As near as I could sift him on that argument,
On some apparent danger seen in him
Aim'd at your highness, no inveterate malice.
   K. Rich. Then call them to our presence; face to face,
And frowning brow to brow, ourselves will hear
The accuser and the accused freely speak:
- High-stomach'd are they both, and full of ire,
In rage deaf as the sea, hasty as fire.

    Enter BOLINGBROKE *and* MOWBRAY.

   Boling. Many years of happy days befal 20
My gracious sovereign, my most loving liege!
   Mow. Each day still better other's happiness;
Until the heavens, envying earth's good hap,
Add an immortal title to your crown!
   K. Rich. We thank you both: yet one but flatters us,
As well appeareth by the cause you come;
Namely, to appeal each other of high treason.
Cousin of Hereford, what dost thou object
Against the Duke of Norfolk, Thomas Mowbray?
   Boling. First, heaven be the record to my speech! 30
In the devotion of a subject's love,
- Tendering the precious safety of my prince,
And free from other misbegotten hate,
- Come I appellant to this princely presence.
Now, Thomas Mowbray, do I turn to thee,
And mark my greeting well; for what I speak
My body shall make good upon this earth,
Or my divine soul answer it in heaven.
Thou art a traitor and a miscreant,
- Too good to be so and too bad to live, 40
Since the more fair and crystal is the sky,
The uglier seem the clouds that in it fly.
Once more, the more to aggravate the note,
With a foul traitor's name stuff I thy throat;
And wish, so please my sovereign, ere I move,
What my tongue speaks my right drawn sword may prove.
   Mow. Let not my cold words here accuse my zeal:
'Tis not the trial of a woman's war,
The bitter clamour of two eager tongues,
Can arbitrate this cause betwixt us twain; 50
The blood is hot that must be cool'd for this:
Yet can I not of such tame patience boast
As to be hush'd and nought at all to say:
First, the fair reverence of your highness curbs me
From giving reins and spurs to my free speech;
Which else would post until it had return'd
These terms of treason doubled down his throat.
Setting aside his high blood's royalty,
And let him be no kinsman to my liege,
I do defy him, and I spit at him; 60

Call him a slanderous coward and a villain:
Which to maintain I would allow him odds,
And meet him, were I tied to run afoot
Even to the frozen ridges of the Alps,
• Or any other ground inhabitable,
Where ever Englishman durst set his foot.
Mean time let this defend my loyalty,
By all my hopes, most falsely doth he lie.
  Boling. Pale trembling coward, there I throw
   my gage,
Disclaiming here the kindred of the king, 70
And lay aside my high blood's royalty,
Which fear, not reverence, makes thee to except.
If guilty dread have left thee so much strength
• As to take up mine honour's pawn, then stoop:
By that and all the rites of knighthood else,
Will I make good against thee, arm to arm,
What I have spoke, or thou canst worse devise.
  Mow. I take it up; and by that sword I swear,
Which gently laid my knighthood on my shoulder,
I'll answer thee in any fair degree, 80
Or chivalrous design of knightly trial:
And when I mount, alive may I not light,
If I be traitor or unjustly fight!
  K. Rich. What doth our cousin lay to Mow-
   bray's charge?
• It must be great that can inherit us
So much as of a thought of ill in him.
  Boling. Look, what I speak, my life shall
   prove it true;
• That Mowbray hath received eight thousand
  nobles
• In name of lendings for your highness' soldiers,
• The which he hath detain'd for lewd employments,
Like a false traitor and injurious villain. 91
Besides I say and will in battle prove,
Or here or elsewhere to the furthest verge
That ever was survey'd by English eye,
That all the treasons for these eighteen years
Complotted and contrived in this land
Fetch from false Mowbray their first head and
  spring.
Further I say and further will maintain
Upon his bad life to make all this good,
• That he did plot the Duke of Gloucester's death,
Suggest his soon-believing adversaries, 101
And consequently, like a traitor coward,
Sluiced out his innocent soul through streams of
  blood:
Which blood, like sacrificing Abel's, cries,
Even from the tongueless caverns of the earth,
To me for justice and rough chastisement;
And, by the glorious worth of my descent,
This arm shall do it, or this life be spent.
  K. Rich. How high a pitch his resolution soars!
Thomas of Norfolk, what say'st thou to this? 110
  Mow. O, let my sovereign turn away his face
And bid his ears a little while be deaf,
Till I have told this slander of his blood,
How God and good men hate so foul a liar.
  K. Rich. Mowbray, impartial are our eyes
   and ears:
Were he my brother, nay, my kingdom's heir,
As he is but my father's brother's son,
Now, by my sceptre's awe, I make a vow,
Such neighbour nearness to our sacred blood
Should nothing privilege him, nor partialize 120
The unstooping firmness of my upright soul:
He is our subject, Mowbray; so art thou:

65 *inhabitable.* Uninhabitable.

74 *pawn.* The glove he has just thrown down.

85 *inherit us.* Make us possess.

88 *nobles.* Gold coins worth six shillings and eight pence.

89 *lendings.* Money to be disbursed among the soldiers.

90 *lewd.* Improper or base.

100 *Duke of Gloucester.* Thomas of Woodstock, uncle of Richard and Bolingbroke, was murdered at Calais.

F. Aiken, 18th century actor, as Bolingbroke. Engraving from Bell's edition of *Shakespeare*, 1776

130 *dear account.* Great debt.

144 *recreant.* Cowardly.

164 *boot.* Alternative.

170 *baffled.* Shamed.

Throwing down the gage. Engraving from a French manuscript of the 15th century

Free speech and fearless I to thee allow.
 Mow.   Then, Bolingbroke, as low as to thy
  heart,
Through the false passage of thy throat, thou liest.
Three parts of that receipt I had for Calais
Disbursed I duly to his highness' soldiers;
The other part reserved I by consent,
For that my sovereign liege was in my debt
Upon remainder of a dear account,   130
Since last I went to France to fetch his queen:
Now swallow down that lie. For Gloucester's
  death,
I slew him not; but to my own disgrace
Neglected my sworn duty in that case.
For you, my noble Lord of Lancaster,
The honourable father to my foe,
Once did I lay an ambush for your life,
A trespass that doth vex my grieved soul;
But ere I last received the sacrament
I did confess it, and exactly begg'd   140
Your grace's pardon, and I hope I had it.
This is my fault: as for the rest appeal'd,
It issues from the rancour of a villain,
A recreant and most degenerate traitor:
Which in myself I boldly will defend;
And interchangeably hurl down my gage
Upon this overweening traitor's foot,
To prove myself a loyal gentleman
Even in the best blood chamber'd in his bosom.
In haste whereof, most heartily I pray   150
Your highness to assign our trial day.
 K. Rich.   Wrath-kindled gentlemen, be ruled
  by me;
Let's purge this choler without letting blood:
This we prescribe, though no physician;
Deep malice makes too deep incision;
Forget, forgive; conclude and be agreed;
Our doctors say this is no month to bleed.
Good uncle, let this end where it begun;
We'll calm the Duke of Norfolk, you your son.
 Gaunt.   To be a make-peace shall become my
  age: 160
Throw down, my son, the Duke of Norfolk's
  gage.
 K. Rich.   And, Norfolk, throw down his.
 Gaunt.   When, Harry, when?
Obedience bids I should not bid again.
 K. Rich. Norfolk, throw down, we bid; there
  is no boot.
 Mow. Myself I throw, dread sovereign, at
  thy foot.
My life thou shalt command, but not my shame:
The one my duty owes; but my fair name,
Despite of death that lives upon my grave,
To dark dishonour's use thou shalt not have.
I am disgraced, impeach'd and baffled here,   170
Pierced to the soul with slander's venom'd spear,
The which no balm can cure but his heart-blood
Which breathed this poison.
 K. Rich.   Rage must be withstood:
Give me his gage: lions make leopards tame.
 Mow. Yea, but not change his spots: take
  but my shame,
And I resign my gage. My dear dear lord,
The purest treasure mortal times afford
Is spotless reputation: that away,
Men are but gilded loam or painted clay.
A jewel in a ten-times-barr'd-up chest   180
Is a bold spirit in a loyal breast.

Mine honour is my life; both grow in one;
Take honour from me, and my life is done:
Then, dear my liege, mine honour let me try;
In that I live and for that will I die.
    K. Rich. Cousin, throw up your gage; do
      you begin.
    Boling. O, God defend my soul from such
      deep sin!
Shall I seem crest-fall'n in my father's sight?
• Or with pale beggar-fear impeach my height 189
Before this out-dared dastard? Ere my tongue
Shall wound my honour with such feeble wrong,
Or sound so base a parle, my teeth shall tear
The slavish motive of recanting fear,
And spit it bleeding in his high disgrace,
Where shame doth harbour, even in Mowbray's
    face.   [*Exit Gaunt.*
    K. Rich. We were not born to sue, but to
      command;
Which since we cannot do to make you friends,
Be ready, as your lives shall answer it,
• At Coventry, upon Saint Lambert's day:
There shall your swords and lances arbitrate 200
The swelling difference of your settled hate:
• Since we can not atone you, we shall see
Justice design the victor's chivalry.
Lord marshal, command our officers at arms
Be ready to direct these home alarms. [*Exeunt.*

SCENE II. *The* DUKE OF LANCASTER'S *palace.*

Enter JOHN OF GAUNT *with the* DUCHESS
OF GLOUCESTER.

Gaunt. Alas, the part I had in Woodstock's
    blood
Doth more solicit me than your exclaims,
To stir against the butchers of his life!
But since correction lieth in those hands
Which made the fault that we cannot correct,
Put we our quarrel to the will of heaven;
Who, when they see the hours ripe on earth,
Will rain hot vengeance on offenders' heads.
    Duch. Finds brotherhood in thee no sharper
      spur?
Hath love in thy old blood no living fire?   10
Edward's seven sons, whereof thyself art one,
Were as seven vials of his sacred blood,
Or seven fair branches springing from one root:
Some of those seven are dried by nature's
    course,
Some of those branches by the Destinies cut;
But Thomas, my dear lord, my life, my Glou-
    cester,
One vial full of Edward's sacred blood,
One flourishing branch of his most royal root,
Is crack'd, and all the precious liquor spilt,
Is hack'd down, and his summer leaves all faded,
By envy's hand and murder's bloody axe.   21
Ah, Gaunt, his blood was thine! that bed, that
    womb,
That metal, that self mould, that fashion'd thee
Made him a man; and though thou livest and
    breathest,
Yet art thou slain in him: thou dost consent
In some large measure to thy father's death,
In that thou seest thy wretched brother die,
Who was the model of thy father's life.
Call it not patience, Gaunt; it is despair:

189 *impeach my height.* Disgrace my noble birth.

199 *Saint Lambert's day.* September 17.

202 *atone.* Reconcile.

Edward III (d.1377) had seven sons. Their attempts to gain the crown decimated the family and plunged England into civil war. From an effigy in Westminster Abbey

46 *cousin.* Generic term of kinship; here, nephew. *fell.* Fierce, cruel.

49 *career.* A gallop at full speed.

A tournament. Woodcut from Holinshed's *Chronicles*, 1577

In suffering thus thy brother to be slaughter'd, 30
Thou showest the naked pathway to thy life,
Teaching stern murder how to butcher thee:
That which in mean men we intitle patience
Is pale cold cowardice in noble breasts.
What shall I say? to safeguard thine own life,
The best way is to venge my Gloucester's death.
    Gaunt. God's is the quarrel; for God's substitute,
His deputy anointed in His sight,
Hath caused his death: the which if wrongfully,
Let heaven revenge; for I may never lift   40
An angry arm against His minister.
    Duch. Where then, alas, may I complain myself?
    Gaunt. To God, the widow's champion and defence.
    Duch. Why, then, I will. Farewell, old Gaunt.
Thou goest to Coventry, there to behold
● Our cousin Hereford and fell Mowbray fight:
O, sit my husband's wrongs on Hereford's spear,
That it may enter butcher Mowbray's breast!
● Or, if misfortune miss the first career,
Be Mowbray's sins so heavy in his bosom,   50
That they may break his foaming courser's back,
And throw the rider headlong in the lists,
A caitiff recreant to my cousin Hereford!
Farewell, old Gaunt: thy sometimes brother's wife
With her companion grief must end her life.
    Gaunt. Sister, farewell; I must to Coventry:
As much good stay with thee as go with me!
    Duch. Yet one word more: grief boundeth where it falls,
Not with the empty hollowness, but weight:
I take my leave before I have begun,   60
For sorrow ends not when it seemeth done.
Commend me to thy brother, Edmund York.
Lo, this is all:—nay, yet depart not so;
Though this be all, do not so quickly go;
I shall remember more. Bid him—ah, what?—
With all good speed at Plashy visit me.
Alack, and what shall good old York there see
But empty lodgings and unfurnish'd walls,
Unpeopled offices, untrodden stones?
And what hear there for welcome but my groans?   70
Therefore commend me; let him not come there,
To seek out sorrow that dwells every where.
Desolate, desolate, will I hence and die:
The last leave of thee takes my weeping eye.
                                    [*Exeunt.*

SCENE III. *The lists at Coventry.*

Enter the Lord Marshal *and the* DUKE OF AUMERLE.

    Mar. My Lord Aumerle, is Harry Hereford arm'd?
    Aum. Yea, at all points; and longs to enter in.
    Mar. The Duke of Norfolk, sprightfully and bold,
Stays but the summons of the appellant's trumpet.
    Aum. Why, then, the champions are prepared, and stay
For nothing but his majesty's approach.

30 *Depose.* Swear under oath.

The trumpets sound, and the KING *enters with his nobles,* GAUNT, BUSHY, BAGOT, GREEN, *and others. When they are set, enter* MOWBRAY *in arms, defendant, with a* Herald.

K. Rich. Marshal, demand of yonder champion
The cause of his arrival here in arms:
Ask him his name and orderly proceed
To swear him in the justice of his cause. 10
Mar. In God's name and the king's, say who thou art
And why thou comest thus knightly clad in arms,
Against what man thou comest, and what thy quarrel:
Speak truly, on thy knighthood and thy oath;
As so defend thee heaven and thy valour!
Mow. My name is Thomas Mowbray, Duke of Norfolk;
Who hither come engaged by my oath—
Which God defend a knight should violate!—
Both to defend my loyalty and truth
To God, my king and my succeeding issue, 20
Against the Duke of Hereford that appeals me;
And, by the grace of God and this mine arm,
To prove him, in defending of myself,
A traitor to my God, my king, and me:
And as I truly fight, defend me heaven!

The trumpets sound. Enter BOLINGBROKE, *appellant, in armour, with a* Herald.

K. Rich. Marshal, ask yonder knight in arms,
Both who he is and why he cometh hither
Thus plated in habiliments of war,
And formaliy, according to our law,
• Depose him in the justice of his cause. 30
Mar. What is thy name? and wherefore comest thou hither,
Before King Richard in his royal lists?
Against whom comest thou? and what's thy quarrel?
Speak like a true knight, so defend thee heaven!
Boling. Harry of Hereford, Lancaster and Derby
Am I; who ready here do stand in arms,
To prove, by God's grace and my body's valour,
In lists, on Thomas Mowbray, Duke of Norfolk,
That he is a traitor, foul and dangerous,
To God of heaven, King Richard and to me; 40
And as I truly fight, defend me heaven!
Mar. On pain of death, no person be so bold
Or daring-hardy as to touch the lists,
Except the marshal and such officers
Appointed to direct these fair designs.
Boling. Lord marshal, let me kiss my sovereign's hand,
And bow my knee before his majesty:
For Mowbray and myself are like two men
That vow a long and weary pilgrimage;
Then let us take a ceremonious leave 50
And loving farewell of our several friends.
Mar. The appellant in all duty greets your highness,
And craves to kiss your hand and take his leave.
K. Rich. We will descend and fold him in our arms.
Cousin of Hereford, as thy cause is right,
So be thy fortune in this royal fight!
Farewell, my blood; which if to-day thou shed,

James Cathcart as Mowbray in Charles Kean's production, Princess's Theatre, London, 1857

67 *regreet.* Salute, greet.

Gaunt: 'God in thy good cause, make thee prosperous!'
Walter Lacy as Gaunt, John Rydel as Bolingbroke in
Charles Kean's production, Princess's Theatre, London, 1857

81 *casque.* Helmet.

Lament we may, but not revenge thee dead.
   Boling. O, let no noble eye profane a tear
For me, if I be gored with Mowbray's spear: 60
As confident as is the falcon's flight
Against a bird, do I with Mowbray fight.
My loving lord, I take my leave of you;
Of you, my noble cousin, Lord Aumerle;
Not sick, although I have to do with death,
But lusty, young, and cheerly drawing breath.
Lo, as at English feasts, so I regreet
The daintiest last, to make the end most sweet:
O thou, the earthly author of my blood,
Whose youthful spirit, in me regenerate, 70
Doth with a twofold vigour lift me up
To reach at victory above my head,
Add proof unto mine armour with thy prayers;
And with thy blessings steel my lance's point,
That it may enter Mowbray's waxen coat,
And furbish new the name of John a Gaunt,
Even in the lusty haviour of his son.
   Gaunt. God in thy good cause make thee
      prosperous!
Be swift like lightning in the execution;
And let thy blows, doubly redoubled, 80
Fall like amazing thunder on the casque
Of thy adverse pernicious enemy:
Rouse up thy youthful blood, be valiant and live.
   Boling. Mine innocency and Saint George to
      thrive!
   Mow. However God or fortune cast my lot,
There lives or dies, true to King Richard's
      throne,
A loyal, just and upright gentleman:
Never did captive with a freer heart
Cast off his chains of bondage and embrace
His golden uncontroll'd enfranchisement, 90
More than my dancing soul doth celebrate
This feast of battle with mine adversary.
Most mighty liege, and my companion peers,
Take from my mouth the wish of happy years:
As gentle and as jocund as to jest
Go I to fight: truth hath a quiet breast.
   K. Rich. Farewell, my lord: securely I espy
Virtue with valour couched in thine eye.
Order the trial, marshal, and begin.
   Mar. Harry of Hereford, Lancaster and
      Derby, 100
Receive thy lance; and God defend the right!
   Boling. Strong as a tower in hope, I cry
      amen.
   Mar. Go bear this lance to Thomas, Duke of
      Norfolk.
   First Her. Harry of Hereford, Lancaster
      and Derby,
Stands here for God, his sovereign and himself,
On pain to be found false and recreant,
To prove the Duke of Norfolk, Thomas Mowbray,
A traitor to his God, his king and him;
And dares him to set forward to the fight.
   Sec. Her. Here standeth Thomas Mowbray,
      Duke of Norfolk, 110
On pain to be found false and recreant,
Both to defend himself and to approve
Henry of Hereford, Lancaster, and Derby,
To God, his sovereign and to him disloyal;
Courageously and with a free desire
Attending but the signal to begin.
   Mar. Sound, trumpets; and set forward, com-
      batants.   [*A charge sounded.*

Stay, the king hath thrown his warder down.
  K. Rich. Let them lay by their helmets and
    their spears,
And both return back to their chairs again: 120
Withdraw with us: and let the trumpets sound
While we return these dukes what we decree.
                           [*A long flourish.*
Draw near,
And list what with our council we have done.
For that our kingdom's earth should not be
    soil'd
With that dear blood which it hath fostered;
And for our eyes do hate the dire aspect
Of civil wounds plough'd up with neighbours'
    sword;
And for we think the eagle-winged pride
Of sky-aspiring and ambitious thoughts, 130
With rival-hating envy, set on you
To wake our peace, which in our country's
    cradle
Draws the sweet infant breath of gentle sleep;
Which so roused up with boisterous untuned
    drums,
With harsh-resounding trumpets' dreadful bray,
And grating shock of wrathful iron arms,
Might from our quiet confines fright fair peace
And make us wade even in our kindred's blood;
Therefore, we banish you our territories:
You, cousin Hereford, upon pain of life, 140
Till twice five summers have enrich'd our fields
Shall not regreet our fair dominions,
But tread the stranger paths of banishment.
  Boling. Your will be done: this must my
    comfort be,
That sun that warms you here shall shine on me;
And those his golden beams to you here lent
Shall point on me and gild my banishment.
  K. Rich. Norfolk, for thee remains a heavier
    doom,
Which I with some unwillingness pronounce:
The sly slow hours shall not determinate 150
The dateless limit of thy dear exile;
The hopeless word of 'never to return'
Breathe I against thee, upon pain of life.
  Mow. A heavy sentence, my most sovereign
    liege,
And all unlook'd for from your highness' mouth:
A dearer merit, not so deep a maim
As to be cast forth in the common air,
Have I deserved at your highness' hands.
The language I have learn'd these forty years,
My native English, now I must forego: 160
And now my tongue's use is to me no more
Than an unstringed viol or a harp,
Or like a cunning instrument cased up,
Or, being open, put into his hands
That knows no touch to tune the harmony:
Within my mouth you have engaol'd my tongue,
Doubly portcullis'd with my teeth and lips;
And dull unfeeling barren ignorance
Is made my gaoler to attend on me.
I am too old to fawn upon a nurse, 170
Too far in years to be a pupil now:
What is thy sentence then but speechless death,
Which robs my tongue from breathing native
    breath?
  K. Rich. It boots thee not to be compas-
    sionate:
After our sentence plaining comes too late.

The start of a tournament. Engraving from a contemporary manuscript

---

118 *warder*. A staff of authority, like a present-day field-marshal's baton.

163–165 *Or like a . . . harmony*. See introduction.

163 *cunning*. Requiring skill, or skilful.

174 *compassionate*. Appealing for pity.

181 *Our part therein.* i.e. as God's deputy.

Richard: 'You never shall, so help you truth and God!
Embrace each other's love in banishment;' Bolingbroke
(Ian Pascoe) Richard (Ian Richardson) and Mowbray
(Denis Holmes), Royal Shakespeare Co, 1973

234 *party-verdict.* Vote with others on the verdict.

Mow. Then thus I turn me from my country's
    light,
To dwell in solemn shades of endless night.
  K. Rich. Return again, and take an oath with
    thee.
Lay on our royal sword your banish'd hands;
Swear by the duty that you owe to God—   180
• Our part therein we banish with yourselves—
To keep the oath that we administer:
You never shall, so help you truth and God!
Embrace each other's love in banishment;
Nor never look upon each other's face;
Nor never write, regreet, nor reconcile
This louring tempest of your home-bred hate;
Nor never by advised purpose meet
To plot, contrive, or complot any ill
'Gainst us, our state, our subjects, or our land. 190
  Boling. I swear.
  Mow. And I, to keep all this.
  Boling. Norfolk, so far as to mine enemy:—
By this time, had the king permitted us,
One of our souls had wander'd in the air,
Banish'd this frail sepulchre of our flesh,
As now our flesh is banish'd from this land:
Confess thy treasons ere thou fly the realm;
Since thou hast far to go, bear not along
The clogging burthen of a guilty soul.   200
  Mow. No, Bolingbroke: if ever I were traitor,
My name be blotted from the book of life,
And I from heaven banish'd as from hence!
But what thou art, God, thou, and I do know;
And all too soon, I fear, the king shall rue.
Farewell, my liege. Now no way can I stray;
Save back to England, all the world's my way.
                        [Exit.
  K. Rich. Uncle, even in the glasses of thine
    eyes
I see thy grieved heart: thy sad aspect
Hath from the number of his banish'd years 210
Pluck'd four away. [*To Boling.*] Six frozen win-
    ters spent,
Return with welcome home from banishment.
  Boling. How long a time lies in one little word!
Four lagging winters and four wanton springs
End in a word: such is the breath of kings.
  Gaunt. I thank my liege, that in regard of me
He shortens four years of my son's exile:
But little vantage shall I reap thereby;
For, ere the six years that he hath to spend
Can change their moons and bring their times
    about,   220
My oil-dried lamp and time-bewasted light
Shall be extinct with age and endless night;
My inch of taper will be burnt and done,
And blindfold death not let me see my son.
  K. Rich. Why, uncle, thou hast many years
    to live.
  Gaunt. But not a minute, king, that thou canst
    give:
Shorten my days thou canst with sullen sorrow,
And pluck nights from me, but not lend a morrow;
Thou canst help time to furrow me with age,
But stop no wrinkle in his pilgrimage;   230
Thy word is current with him for my death,
But dead, thy kingdom cannot buy my breath.
  K. Rich. Thy son is banish'd upon good
    advice,
• Whereto thy tongue a party-verdict gave:
Why at our justice seem'st thou then to lour?

Gaunt. Things sweet to taste prove in digestion sour.
You urged me as a judge; but I had rather
You would have bid me argue like a father.
O, had it been a stranger, not my child,
To smooth his fault I should have been more mild:
● A partial slander sought I to avoid,   241
And in the sentence my own life destroy'd.
Alas, I look'd when some of you should say,
I was too strict to make mine own away;
But you gave leave to my unwilling tongue
Against my will to do myself this wrong.
   K. Rich. Cousin, farewell; and, uncle, bid him so:
Six years we banish him, and he shall go.
   [*Flourish. Exeunt King Richard and train.*
   Aum. Cousin, farewell: what presence must not know,
From where you do remain let paper show.   250
   Mar. My lord, no leave take I; for I will ride,
As far as land will let me, by your side.
   Gaunt. O, to what purpose dost thou hoard thy words,
That thou return'st no greeting to thy friends?
   Boling. I have too few to take my leave of you,
When the tongue's office should be prodigal
To breathe the abundant dolour of the heart.
   Gaunt. Thy grief is but thy absence for a time.
   Boling. Joy absent, grief is present for that time.
   Gaunt. What is six winters? they are quickly gone.   260
   Boling. To men in joy; but grief makes one hour ten.
   Gaunt. Call it a travel that thou takest for pleasure.
   Boling. My heart will sigh when I miscall it so,
Which finds it an inforced pilgrimage.
   Gaunt. The sullen passage of thy weary steps
Esteem as foil wherein thou art to set
The precious jewel of thy home return.
   Boling. Nay, rather, every tedious stride I make
Will but remember me what a deal of world
I wander from the jewels that I love.   270
Must I not serve a long apprenticehood
To foreign passages, and in the end,
Having my freedom, boast of nothing else
But that I was a journeyman to grief?
   Gaunt. All places that the eye of heaven visits
Are to a wise man ports and happy havens.
Teach thy necessity to reason thus;
There is no virtue like necessity.
Think not the king did banish thee,
But thou the king. Woe doth the heavier sit,   280
Where it perceives it is but faintly borne.
Go, say I sent thee forth to purchase honour
And not the king exiled thee; or suppose
Devouring pestilence hangs in our air
And thou art flying to a fresher clime:
Look, what thy soul holds dear, imagine it
To lie that way thou go'st, not whence thou comest:
Suppose the singing birds musicians,
● The grass whereon thou tread'st the presence strew'd,
The flowers fair ladies, and thy steps no more   290
● Than a delightful measure or a dance;
● For gnarling sorrow hath less power to bite
The man that mocks at it and sets it light.
   Boling. O, who can hold a fire in his hand

241 *partial slander.* An accusation of favouritism.

Gaunt: 'O, to what purpose dost thou hoard thy words . . .' Michael Redgrave as Bolingbroke and Leon Quartermaine as Gaunt, Queen's Theatre, London, 1937

289 *the presence strew'd.* The royal presence-chamber which was strewn with rushes.

291 *measure.* Stately dance.

Gaunt: 'Than a delightful measure or a dance.' From a woodcut *c.*1650

292 *gnarling.* Snarling.

6 *for*. By.

24–35 *Observed . . . reversion his*. See introduction.

Ripe Musk Millions *Wood to Cleave* *Tankerd Bearer*

The Night Man *A Bell Man* *nketcher Buttons Mrs*

The 'common people' of different trades. From a 17th century woodcut

30 *affects*. Affections.

39 *Expedient manage*. Swift measures.

By thinking on the frosty Caucasus?
Or cloy the hungry edge of appetite
By bare imagination of a feast?
Or wallow naked in December snow
By thinking on fantastic summer's heat?
O, no! the apprehension of the good   300
Gives but the greater feeling to the worse:
Fell sorrow's tooth doth never rankle more
Than when he bites, but lanceth not the sore.
    Gaunt. Come, come, my son, I'll bring thee
      on thy way:
Had I thy youth and cause, I would not stay.
    Boling. Then, England's ground, farewell;
      sweet soil, adieu;
My mother, and my nurse, that bears me yet!
Where'er I wander, boast of this I can,
Though banish'd, yet a trueborn Englishman.
                    [*Exeunt.*

SCENE IV.   *The court.*

Enter the KING, *with* BAGOT *and* GREEN *at one
door; and the* DUKE OF AUMERLE *at another.*

    K. Rich. We did observe. Cousin Aumerle,
How far brought you high Hereford on his way?
    Aum. I brought high Hereford, if you call
      him so,
But to the next highway, and there I left him.
    K. Rich. And say, what store of parting tears
      were shed?
    Aum. Faith, none for me; except the north-
      east wind,
Which then blew bitterly against our faces,
Awaked the sleeping rheum, and so by chance
Did grace our hollow parting with a tear.
    K. Rich. What said our cousin when you
      parted with him?   10
    Aum. 'Farewell:'
And, for my heart disdained that my tongue
Should so profane the word, that taught me craft
To counterfeit oppression of such grief
That words seem'd buried in my sorrow's grave.
Marry, would the word 'farewell' have lengthen'd
    hours
And added years to his short banishment,
He should have had a volume of farewells;
But since it would not, he had none of me.
    K. Rich. He is our cousin, cousin; but 'tis
      doubt,   20
When time shall call him home from banishment,
Whether our kinsman come to see his friends.
Ourself and Bushy, Bagot here and Green
Observed his courtship to the common people;
How he did seem to dive into their hearts
With humble and familiar courtesy,
What reverence he did throw away on slaves,
Wooing poor craftsmen with the craft of smiles
And patient underbearing of his fortune,
As 'twere to banish their affects with him.   30
Off goes his bonnet to an oyster-wench;
A brace of draymen bid God speed him well
And had the tribute of his supple knee,
With 'Thanks, my countrymen, my loving
    friends;'
As were our England in reversion his,
And he our subjects' next degree in hope.
    Green. Well, he is gone; and with him go
    these thoughts.
Now for the rebels which stand out in Ireland,
Expedient manage must be made, my liege,

Ere further leisure yield them further means   40
For their advantage and your highness' loss.
  K. Rich. We will ourself in person to this war:
And, for our coffers, with too great a court
And liberal largess, are grown somewhat light,
  ● We are inforced to farm our royal realm;
The revenue whereof shall furnish us
For our affairs in hand: if that come short,
  ● Our substitutes at home shall have blank charters;
Whereto, when they shall know what men are rich,
They shall subscribe them for large sums of gold
And send them after to supply our wants;   51
For we will make for Ireland presently.

Enter BUSHY.

Bushy, what news?
  Bushy. Old John of Gaunt is grievous sick, my lord,
Suddenly taken; and hath sent post haste
To entreat your majesty to visit him.
  K. Rich. Where lies he?
  Bushy. At Ely House.
  K. Rich. Now put it, God, in the physician's mind
To help him to his grave immediately!   60
The lining of his coffers shall make coats
To deck our soldiers for these Irish wars.
Come, gentlemen, let's all go visit him:
Pray God we may make haste, and come too late!
  All. Amen.   [*Exeunt.*

ACT II.

SCENE I. *Ely House.*

Enter JOHN OF GAUNT *sick, with the* DUKE OF YORK, *&c.*

  Gaunt. Will the king come, that I may breathe my last
In wholesome counsel to his unstaid youth?
  York. Vex not yourself, nor strive not with your breath;
For all in vain comes counsel to his ear.
  Gaunt. O, but they say the tongues of dying men
Enforce attention like deep harmony:
Where words are scarce, they are seldom spent in vain,
For they breathe truth that breathe their words in pain.
He that no more must say is listen'd more
  ● Than they whom youth and ease have taught to glose;   10
More are men's ends mark'd than their lives before:
The setting sun, and music at the close,
As the last taste of sweets, is sweetest last,
Writ in remembrance more than things long past:
Though Richard my life's counsel would not hear,
My death's sad tale may yet undeaf his ear.
  York. No; it is stopp'd with other flattering sounds,
As praises, of whose taste the wise are fond,
Lascivious metres, to whose venom sound
The open ear of youth doth always listen;   20
  ● Report of fashions in proud Italy,
Whose manners still our tardy apish nation
Limps after in base imitation.

45 *inforced to farm.* Forced to lease out royal lands for revenue.

48 *blank charters.* After they were sealed, any amount could be filled in.

10 *glose.* Flatter.

Male costumes at the time of Richard II. Engraving from a medieval manuscript

21–23 *Report . . . imitation.* See introduction.

The shield of John of Gaunt

45—49 *This happy . . . lands.* See introduction.

55 *Jewry.* Land of the Jews.

60 *pelting.* Paltry.

61—63 *England . . . shame.* See introduction.

Walter Lacy as John of Gaunt in Charles Kean's production, Princess's Theatre, London, 1857

Where doth the world thrust forth a vanity—
So it be new, there's no respect how vile—
That is not quickly buzz'd into his ears?
Then all too late comes counsel to be heard,
Where will doth mutiny with wit's regard.
Direct not him whose way himself will choose:
'Tis breath thou lack'st, and that breath wilt thou
    lose. 30
   Gaunt. Methinks I am a prophet new inspired
And thus expiring do foretell of him:
His rash fierce blaze of riot cannot last,
For violent fires soon burn out themselves;
Small showers last long, but sudden storms are
    short;
He tires betimes that spurs too fast betimes;
With eager feeding food doth choke the feeder:
Light vanity, insatiate cormorant,
Consuming means, soon preys upon itself.
This royal throne of kings, this scepter'd isle, 40
This earth of majesty, this seat of Mars,
This other Eden, demi-paradise,
This fortress built by Nature for herself
Against infection and the hand of war,
- This happy breed of men, this little world,
This precious stone set in the silver sea,
Which serves it in the office of a wall
Or as a moat defensive to a house,
Against the envy of less happier lands,
This blessed plot, this earth, this realm, this
    England, 50
This nurse, this teeming womb of royal kings,
Fear'd by their breed and famous by their birth,
Renowned for their deeds as far from home,
For Christian service and true chivalry,
- As is the sepulchre in stubborn Jewry
Of the world's ransom, blessed Mary's Son,
This land of such dear souls, this dear dear land,
Dear for her reputation through the world,
Is now leased out, I die pronouncing it,
- Like to a tenement or pelting farm: 60
- England, bound in with the triumphant sea,
Whose rocky shore beats back the envious siege
Of watery Neptune, is now bound in with shame,
With inky blots and rotten parchment bonds:
That England, that was wont to conquer others,
Hath made a shameful conquest of itself.
Ah, would the scandal vanish with my life,
How happy then were my ensuing death!

Enter KING RICHARD *and* QUEEN, AUMERLE,
  BUSHY, GREEN, BAGOT, ROSS, *and* WIL-
  LOUGHBY.

   York. The king is come: deal mildly with
    his youth; 69
For young hot colts being raged do rage the more.
   Queen. How fares our noble uncle, Lancaster?
   K. Rich. What comfort, man? how is't with
    aged Gaunt?
   Gaunt. O, how that name befits my compo-
    sition!
Old Gaunt indeed, and gaunt in being old:
Within me grief hath kept a tedious fast;
And who abstains from meat that is not gaunt?
For sleeping England long time have I watch'd;
Watching breeds leanness, leanness is all gaunt:
The pleasure that some fathers feed upon,
Is my strict fast; I mean, my children's looks; 80
And therein fasting, hast thou made me gaunt:
Gaunt am I for the grave, gaunt as a grave,

Whose hollow womb inherits nought but bones.
● *K. Rich.* Can sick men play so nicely with
  their names?
Gaunt. No, misery makes sport to mock itself:
Since thou dost seek to kill my name in me,
I mock my name, great king, to flatter thee.
  K. Rich. Should dying men flatter with those
    that live?
Gaunt. No, no, men living flatter those that die.
  K. Rich. Thou, now a-dying, say'st thou flat-
    terest me.   90
Gaunt. O, no! thou diest, though I the
    sicker be.
  K. Rich. I am in health, I breathe, and see
    thee ill.
Gaunt. Now He that made me knows I see
    thee ill;
Ill in myself to see, and in thee seeing ill.
Thy death-bed is no lesser than thy land
Wherein thou liest in reputation sick;
And thou, too careless patient as thou art,
Commit'st thy anointed body to the cure
Of those physicians that first wounded thee:
A thousand flatterers sit within thy crown,   100
Whose compass is no bigger than thy head;
● And yet, incaged in so small a verge,
The waste is no whit lesser than thy land.
O, had thy grandsire with a prophet's eye
Seen how his son's son should destroy his sons,
From forth thy reach he would have laid thy
    shame,
Deposing thee before thou wert possess'd,
Which art possess'd now to depose thyself.
Why, cousin, wert thou regent of the world,
It were a shame to let this land by lease;   110
But for thy world enjoying but this land,
Is it not more than shame to shame it so?
Landlord of England art thou now, not king:
● Thy state of law is bondslave to the law;
And thou—
  K. Rich. A lunatic lean-witted fool,
Presuming on an ague's privilege,
Darest with thy frozen admonition
Make pale our cheek, chasing the royal blood
With fury from his native residence.
Now, by my seat's right royal majesty,   120
Wert thou not brother to great Edward's son,
This tongue that runs so roundly in thy head
Should run thy head from thy unreverent shoulders.
  Gaunt. O, spare me not, my brother Edward's
    son,
For that I was his father Edward's son;
● That blood already, like the pelican,
Hast thou tapp'd out and drunkenly caroused:
My brother Gloucester, plain well-meaning soul,
Whom fair befal in heaven 'mongst happy souls!
May be a precedent and witness good   130
That thou respect'st not spilling Edward's blood:
Join with the present sickness that I have;
And thy unkindness be like crooked age,
To crop at once a too long wither'd flower.
Live in thy shame, but die not shame with thee!
These words hereafter thy tormentors be!
Convey me to my bed, then to my grave:
Love they to live that love and honour have.
    [*Exit, borne off by his Attendants.*
  K. Rich. And let them die that age and sul-
    lens have;
For both hast thou, and both become the grave.

102 *verge.* Border, margin.

114 *Thy state . . . law.* You, having leased out your land
by bond, are now subject to law.

126 *pelican.* The young of the pelican were believed
to feed upon their mother's blood.

Gaunt: 'Convey me to my bed, then to my grave.'
Drawing by Henry Singleton (1766–1839)

156 *kerns.* Irish foot-soldiers.

Richard: 'We must supplant those rough rug-headed kerns...' Illustration from John Derrick's *The Image of Ireland*, 1581

157 *venom.* Snakes.

167–168 *Nor the . . . marriage.* Richard forbade Bolingbroke to marry the King of France's cousin.

177 *Accomplish'd . . . hours.* At your age.

York. I do beseech your majesty, impute his words 141
To wayward sickliness and age in him:
He loves you, on my life, and holds you dear
As Harry Duke of Hereford, were he here.
 K. Rich. Right, you say true: as Hereford's love, so his;
As theirs, so mine; and all be as it is.

   Enter NORTHUMBERLAND.
 North. My liege, old Gaunt commends him to your majesty.
 K. Rich. What says he?
 North.   Nay, nothing; all is said:
His tongue is now a stringless instrument;
Words, life and all, old Lancaster hath spent. 150
 York. Be York the next that must be bankrupt so!
Though death be poor, it ends a mortal woe.
 K. Rich. The ripest fruit first falls, and so doth he;
His time is spent, our pilgrimage must be.
So much for that. Now for our Irish wars:
• We must supplant those rough rug-headed kerns,
• Which live like venom where no venom else
But only they have privilege to live.
And for these great affairs do ask some charge,
Towards our assistance we do seize to us 160
The plate, coin, revenues and moveables,
Whereof our uncle Gaunt did stand possess'd.
 York. How long shall I be patient? ah, how long
Shall tender duty make me suffer wrong?
Not Gloucester's death, nor Hereford's banishment,
Not Gaunt's rebukes, nor England's private wrongs,
• Nor the prevention of poor Bolingbroke
About his marriage, nor my own disgrace,
Have ever made me sour my patient cheek,
Or bend one wrinkle on my sovereign's face. 170
I am the last of noble Edward's sons,
Of whom thy father, Prince of Wales, was first:
In war was never lion raged more fierce,
In peace was never gentle lamb more mild,
Than was that young and princely gentleman.
His face thou hast, for even so look'd he,
• Accomplish'd with the number of thy hours;
But when he frown'd, it was against the French
And not against his friends; his noble hand
Did win what he did spend and spent not that 180
Which his triumphant father's hand had won;
His hands were guilty of no kindred blood,
But bloody with the enemies of his kin.
O Richard! York is too far gone with grief,
Or else he never would compare between.
 K. Rich. Why, uncle, what's the matter?
 York.   O my liege,
Pardon me, if you please; if not, I, pleased
Not to be pardon'd, am content withal.
Seek you to seize and gripe into your hands 189
The royalties and rights of banish'd Hereford?
Is not Gaunt dead, and doth not Hereford live?
Was not Gaunt just, and is not Harry true?
Did not the one deserve to have an heir?
Is not his heir a well-deserving son?
Take Hereford's rights away, and take from Time
His charters and his customary rights;
Let not to-morrow then ensue to-day;

Be not thyself; for how art thou a king
But by fair sequence and succession?
Now, afore God—God forbid I say true !— 200
If you do wrongfully seize Hereford's rights,
Call in the letters patents that he hath
● By his attorneys-general to sue
His livery, and deny his offer'd homage,
You pluck a thousand dangers on your head,
You lose a thousand well-disposed hearts
And prick my tender patience to those thoughts
Which honour and allegiance cannot think.
   K. Rich. Think what you will, we seize into
    our hands
His plate, his goods, his money and his lands.
   York. I'll not be by the while: my liege,
    farewell: 211
What will ensue hereof, there's none can tell;
But by bad courses may be understood
That their events can never fall out good. [*Exit.*
   K. Rich. Go, Bushy, to the Earl of Wiltshire
    straight:
Bid him repair to us to Ely House
To see this business. To-morrow next
We will for Ireland; and 'tis time, I trow:
And we create, in absence of ourself,
Our uncle York lord governor of England; 220
For he is just and always loved us well.
Come on, our queen: to-morrow must we part;
Be merry, for our time of stay is short.
   [*Flourish. Exeunt King, Queen, Aumerle,*
           Bushy, Green, and Bagot.
   North. Well, lords, the Duke of Lancaster is
    dead.
   Ross. And living too; for now his son is duke.
   Willo. Barely in title, not in revenues.
   North. Richly in both, if justice had her right.
   Ross. My heart is great; but it must break
    with silence,
Ere 't be disburden'd with a liberal tongue.
   North. Nay, speak thy mind; and let him
    ne'er speak more   230
That speaks thy words again to do thee harm !
   Willo. Tends that thou wouldst speak to the
    Duke of Hereford?
If it be so, out with it boldly, man;
Quick is mine ear to hear of good towards him.
   Ross. No good at all that I can do for him;
Unless you call it good to pity him,
Bereft and gelded of his patrimony.
   North. Now, afore God, 'tis shame such
    wrongs are borne
In him, a royal prince, and many moe
Of noble blood in this declining land. 240
The king is not himself, but basely led
By flatterers; and what they will inform,
Merely in hate, 'gainst any of us all,
That will the king severely prosecute
'Gainst us, our lives, our children, and our heirs.
●   *Ross.* The commons hath he pill'd with grievous
    taxes,
†And quite lost their hearts: the nobles hath he
    fined
For ancient quarrels, and quite lost their hearts.
   Willo. And daily new exactions are devised,
● As blanks, benevolences, and I wot not what: 250
But what, o' God's name, doth become of this?
   North. Wars have not wasted it, for warr'd he
    hath not,
But basely yielded upon compromise

203–204 *sue his livery.* Claim his lands and revenues.

Costume design for Richard II by Ann Curtis, Royal
Shakespeare Co, 1964

246 *pill'd.* Plundered.

250 *blanks, benevolences.* Blank charters, and forced
loans.

266 *securely.* Carelessly.

292 *Imp out.* Graft new feathers (a term from falconry).

293 *broking pawn.* The money lenders to the King.

Windsor Castle. Engraving from *Old England,* 1854

That which his noble ancestors achieved with
    blows :
More hath he spent in peace than they in wars.
  Ross. The Earl of Wiltshire hath the realm
    in farm.
  Willo. The king's grown bankrupt, like a
    broken man.
  North. Reproach and dissolution hangeth over
    him.
  Ross. He hath not money for these Irish wars,
His burthenous taxations notwithstanding,   260
But by the robbing of the banish'd duke.
  North. His noble kinsman: most degenerate
    king !
But, lords, we hear this fearful tempest sing,
Yet seek no shelter to avoid the storm ;
We see the wind sit sore upon our sails,
● And yet we strike not, but securely perish.
  Ross. We see the very wreck that we must
    suffer ;
And unavoided is the danger now,
For suffering so the causes of our wreck.
  North. Not so ; even through the hollow eyes
    of death   270
I spy life peering ; but I dare not say
How near the tidings of our comfort is.
  Willo. Nay, let us share thy thoughts, as thou
    dost ours.
  Ross. Be confident to speak, Northumberland :
We three are but thyself ; and, speaking so,
Thy words are but as thoughts ; therefore, be bold.
  North. Then thus : I have from Port le Blanc,
    a bay
In Brittany, received intelligence
That Harry Duke of Hereford, Rainold Lord
    Cobham,
† 280
That late broke from the Duke of Exeter,
His brother, Archbishop late of Canterbury,
Sir Thomas Erpingham, Sir John Ramston,
Sir John Norbery, Sir Robert Waterton and
    Francis Quoint,
All these well furnish'd by the Duke of Bretagne
With eight tall ships, three thousand men of war,
Are making hither with all due expedience
And shortly mean to touch our northern shore :
Perhaps they had ere this, but that they stay
The first departing of the king for Ireland.   290
If then we shall shake off our slavish yoke,
● Imp out our drooping country's broken wing,
● Redeem from broking pawn the blemish'd crown,
Wipe off the dust that hides our sceptre's gilt
And make high majesty look like itself,
Away with me in post to Ravenspurgh ;
But if you faint, as fearing to do so,
Stay and be secret, and myself will go.
  Ross. To horse, to horse ! urge doubts to them
    that fear.
  Willo. Hold out my horse, and I will first be
    there.   [*Exeunt.* 300

SCENE II. *Windsor Castle.*

Enter QUEEN, BUSHY, *and* BAGOT.

  Bushy. Madam, your majesty is too much sad :
You promised, when you parted with the king,
To lay aside life-harming heaviness
And entertain a cheerful disposition.

Queen. To please the king I did; to please myself
I cannot do it; yet I know no cause
Why I should welcome such a guest as grief,
Save bidding farewell to so sweet a guest
As my sweet Richard: yet again, methinks,
Some unborn sorrow, ripe in fortune's womb,
Is coming towards me, and my inward soul   11
With nothing trembles: at some thing it grieves,
More than with parting from my lord the king.
    Bushy. Each substance of a grief hath twenty shadows,
Which shows like grief itself, but is not so;
For sorrow's eye, glazed with blinding tears,
Divides one thing entire to many objects;
Like perspectives, which rightly gazed upon
Show nothing but confusion, eyed awry
Distinguish form: so your sweet majesty,   20
Looking awry upon your lord's departure,
Find shapes of grief, more than himself, to wail;
Which, look'd on as it is, is nought but shadows
Of what it is not. Then, thrice-gracious queen,
More than your lord's departure weep not: more's not seen;
Or if it be, 'tis with false sorrow's eye,
Which for things true weeps things imaginary.
    Queen. It may be so; but yet my inward soul
Persuades me it is otherwise: howe'er it be,
I cannot but be sad; so heavy sad   30
As, though on thinking on no thought I think,
Makes me with heavy nothing faint and shrink.
● *Bushy.* 'Tis nothing but conceit, my gracious lady.
    Queen. 'Tis nothing less: conceit is still derived
From some forefather grief; mine is not so,
For nothing hath begot my something grief;
Or something hath the nothing that I grieve:
'Tis in reversion that I do possess;
But what it is, that is not yet known; what
I cannot name; 'tis nameless woe, I wot.   40

Enter GREEN.

    Green. God save your majesty! and well met, gentlemen:
I hope the king is not yet shipp'd for Ireland.
    Queen. Why hopest thou so? 'tis better hope he is;
For his designs crave haste, his haste good hope:
Then wherefore dost thou hope he is not shipp'd?
● *Green.* That he, our hope, might have retired his power,
And driven into despair an enemy's hope,
Who strongly hath set footing in this land:
The banish'd Bolingbroke repeals himself,
And with uplifted arms is safe arrived   50
At Ravenspurgh.
    Queen.   Now God in heaven forbid!
    Green. Ah, madam, 'tis too true: and that is worse,
The Lord Northumberland, his son young Henry Percy,
The Lords of Ross, Beaumond, and Willoughby,
With all their powerful friends, are fled to him.
    Bushy. Why have you not proclaim'd Northumberland
And all the rest revolted faction traitors?
    Green. We have: whereupon the Earl of Worcester
Hath broke his staff, resign'd his stewardship,

Queen: 'howe'er it be, I cannot but be sad . . .' Drawing by Henry Singleton (1766–1839)

33 *conceit.* Imagination.

46 *retired.* Returned.

64 *prodigy*. Monster.

69 *cozening*. Cheating.

74 *With signs . . . neck*. York wears a piece of neck armour called a gorget.

75 *careful*. Anxious.

101 *untruth*. Disloyalty.

And all the household servants fled with him   60
To Bolingbroke.
  Queen. So, Green, thou art the midwife to my
    woe,
And Bolingbroke my sorrow's dismal heir:
Now hath my soul brought forth her prodigy,
And I, a gasping new-deliver'd mother,
Have woe to woe, sorrow to sorrow join'd.
  Bushy. Despair not, madam.
  Queen.   Who shall hinder me?
I will despair, and be at enmity
With cozening hope: he is a flatterer,
A parasite, a keeper back of death,   70
Who gently would dissolve the bands of life,
Which false hope lingers in extremity.

Enter YORK.

  Green. Here comes the Duke of York.
  Queen. With signs of war about his aged neck:
O, full of careful business are his looks!
Uncle, for God's sake, speak comfortable words.
  York. Should I do so, I should belie my
    thoughts:
Comfort's in heaven; and we are on the earth,
Where nothing lives but crosses, cares and grief.
Your husband, he is gone to save far off,   80
Whilst others come to make him lose at home:
Here am I left to underprop his land,
Who, weak with age, cannot support myself:
Now comes the sick hour that his surfeit made;
Now shall he try his friends that flatter'd him.

Enter a Servant.

  Serv. My lord, your son was gone before
    I came.
  York. He was? Why, so! go all which way
    it will!
The nobles they are fled, the commons they are
    cold,
And will, I fear, revolt on Hereford's side.
Sirrah, get thee to Plashy, to my sister Glou-
    cester;   90
Bid her send me presently a thousand pound:
Hold, take my ring.
  Serv. My lord, I had forgot to tell your lord-
    ship,
To-day, as I came by, I called there;
But I shall grieve you to report the rest.
  York. What is't, knave?
  Serv. An hour before I came, the duchess
    died.
  York. God for his mercy! what a tide of woes
Comes rushing on this woeful land at once!
I know not what to do: I would to God,   100
So my untruth had not provoked him to it,
The king had cut off my head with my brother's.
What, are there no posts dispatch'd for Ireland?
How shall we do for money for these wars?
Come, sister,—cousin, I would say,—pray, par-
    don me.
Go, fellow, get thee home, provide some carts
And bring away the armour that is there.
                       [*Exit Servant*.
Gentlemen, will you go muster men?
If I know how or which way to order these affairs
Thus thrust disorderly into my hands,   110
Never believe me. Both are my kinsmen:
The one is my sovereign, whom both my oath
And duty bids defend; the other again

Is my kinsman, whom the king hath wrong'd,
Whom conscience and my kindred bids to right.
Well, somewhat we must do. Come, cousin, I'll
Dispose of you.
Gentlemen, go, muster up your men,
And meet me presently at Berkeley.
I should to Plashy too;   120
But time will not permit: all is uneven,
And every thing is left at six and seven.
                              [*Exeunt York and Queen.*
    Bushy. The wind sits fair for news to go to
        Ireland,
● But none returns. For us to levy power
Proportionable to the enemy
Is all unpossible.
    Green. Besides, our nearness to the king in
        love
Is near the hate of those love not the king.
    Bagot. And that's the wavering commons:
        for their love
Lies in their purses, and whoso empties them 130
By so much fills their hearts with deadly hate.
    Bushy. Wherein the king stands generally
        condemn'd.
    Bagot. If judgement lie in them, then so do we,
Because we ever have been near the king.
    Green. Well, I will for refuge straight to
        Bristol castle:
The Earl of Wiltshire is already there.
    Bushy. Thither will I with you; for little
        office
The hateful commons will perform for us,
Except like curs to tear us all to pieces.
Will you go along with us?   140
    Bagot. No; I will to Ireland to his majesty.
Farewell: if heart's presages be not vain,
We three here part that ne'er shall meet again.
● *Bushy.* That's as York thrives to beat back
        Bolingbroke.
    Green. Alas, poor duke! the task he under-
        takes
Is numbering sands and drinking oceans dry:
Where one on his side fights, thousands will fly.
Farewell at once, for once, for all, and ever.
    Bushy. Well, we may meet again.
    Bagot.   I fear me, never.
                                    [*Exeunt.*

        SCENE III. *Wilds in Gloucestershire.*

Enter BOLINGBROKE *and* NORTHUMBERLAND,
                with Forces.

    Boling. How far is it, my lord, to Berkeley
        now?
    North. Believe me, noble lord,
I am a stranger here in Gloucestershire:
These high wild hills and rough uneven ways
Draws out our miles, and makes them weari-
        some;
And yet your fair discourse hath been as sugar,
Making the hard way sweet and delectable.
But I bethink me what a weary way
From Ravenspurgh to Cotswold will be found
In Ross and Willoughby, wanting your company,
Which, I protest, hath very much beguiled   11
The tediousness and process of my travel:
But theirs is sweetened with the hope to have
The present benefit which I possess;
And hope to joy is little less in joy

Ships at the time of Richard II. Engraving from a medieval manuscript

144 *That's as.* That depends on.

Map of Gloucestershire. From Michael Drayton's *Polyolbion*, 1613

Berkeley Castle. Engraving from *Old England*, 1854

---

61 *unfelt*. Immaterial.

Than hope enjoy'd: by this the weary lords
Shall make their way seem short, as mine hath
    done
By sight of what I have, your noble company.
  Boling. Of much less value is my company
Than your good words. But who comes here?

Enter HENRY PERCY.

  North. It is my son, young Harry Percy, 21
Sent from my brother Worcester, whencesoever.
Harry, how fares your uncle?
  Percy. I had thought, my lord, to have learn'd
    his health of you.
  North. Why, is he not with the queen?
  Percy. No, my good Lord; he hath forsook
    the court,
Broken his staff of office and dispersed
The household of the king.
  North.   What was his reason?
He was not so resolved when last we spake
    together.
  Percy. Because your lordship was proclaimed
    traitor.   30
But he, my lord, is gone to Ravenspurgh,
To offer service to the Duke of Hereford,
And sent me over by Berkeley, to discover
What power the Duke of York had levied there;
Then with directions to repair to Ravenspurgh.
  North. Have you forgot the Duke of Here-
    ford, boy?
  Percy. No, my good lord, for that is not
    forgot
Which ne'er I did remember: to my knowledge,
I never in my life did look on him.
  North. Then learn to know him now; this is
    the duke.   40
  Percy. My gracious lord, I tender you my
    service,
Such as it is, being tender, raw and young;
Which elder days shall ripen and confirm
To more approved service and desert.
  Boling. I thank thee, gentle Percy; and be
    sure
I count myself in nothing else so happy
As in a soul remembering my good friends;
And, as my fortune ripens with thy love,
It shall be still thy true love's recompense:
My heart this covenant makes, my hand thus
    seals it.   50
  North. How far is it to Berkeley? and what
    stir
Keeps good old York there with his men of war?
  Percy. There stands the castle, by yon tuft
    of trees,
Mann'd with three hundred men, as I have heard;
And in it are the Lords of York, Berkeley, and
    Seymour;
None else of name and noble estimate.

Enter ROSS *and* WILLOUGHBY.

  North. Here come the Lords of Ross and
    Willoughby,
Bloody with spurring, fiery-red with haste.
  Boling. Welcome, my lords. I wot your love
    pursues
A banish'd traitor: all my treasury   60
● Is yet but unfelt thanks, which more enrich'd
Shall be your love and labour's recompense.

Ross. Your presence makes us rich, most noble lord.
Willo. And far surmounts our labour to attain it.
Boling. Evermore thanks, the exchequer of the poor;
Which, till my infant fortune comes to years,
Stands for my bounty. But who comes here?

Enter BERKELEY.

North. It is my Lord of Berkeley, as I guess.
Berk. My Lord of Hereford, my message is to you.   69
● *Boling.* My lord, my answer is—to Lancaster;
And I am come to seek that name in England;
And I must find that title in your tongue,
Before I make reply to aught you say.
Berk. Mistake me not, my lord; 'tis not my meaning
To raze one title of your honour out:
To you, my lord, I come, what lord you will,
From the most gracious regent of this land,
The Duke of York, to know what pricks you on
● To take advantage of the absent time
And fright our native peace with self-born arms.

Enter YORK *attended.*

Boling. I shall not need transport my words by you;   81
Here comes his grace in person.
                                    My noble uncle! [*Kneels.*
York. Show me thy humble heart, and not thy knee,
Whose duty is deceiveable and false.
Boling. My gracious uncle—
York. Tut, tut!
Grace me no grace, nor uncle me no uncle:
I am no traitor's uncle; and that word 'grace'
In an ungracious mouth is but profane.
Why have those banish'd and forbidden legs   90
Dared once to touch a dust of England's ground?
But then more 'why?' why have they dared to march
So many miles upon her peaceful bosom,
Frighting her pale-faced villages with war
● And ostentation of despised arms?
Comest thou because the anointed king is hence?
Why, foolish boy, the king is left behind,
And in my loyal bosom lies his power.
Were I but now the lord of such hot youth
As when brave Gaunt, thy father, and myself 100
● Rescued the Black Prince, that young Mars of men,
From forth the ranks of many thousand French,
O, then how quickly should this arm of mine,
Now prisoner to the palsy, chastise thee
And minister correction to thy fault!
Boling. My gracious uncle, let me know my fault:
On what condition stands it and wherein?
York. Even in condition of the worst degree,
In gross rebellion and detested treason:
Thou art a banish'd man, and here art come 110
Before the expiration of thy time,
In braving arms against thy sovereign.
Boling. As I was banish'd, I was banish'd Hereford;
But as I come, I come for Lancaster.
And, noble uncle, I beseech your grace

70 *Lancaster.* Bolingbroke claims his father's title.

79 *absent time.* Time of the King's absence.

95 *despised.* Despicable.

101 *Black Prince.* Richard's father.

Edward, the Black Prince, was Edward III's heir apparant and a gallant warrior. He died in 1376 before he could come to the throne. Engraving from *Old England,* 1854

116 *indifferent.* Impartial.

131 *distrain'd.* Seized.

156 *attach.* Arrest.

Welsh soldiers of the 13th century. Engraving from a medieval manuscript

● Look on my wrongs with an indifferent eye:
You are my father, for methinks in you
I see old Gaunt alive; O, then, my father,
Will you permit that I shall stand condemn'd
A wandering vagabond; my rights and royalties
Pluck'd from my arms perforce and given away
To upstart unthrifts? Wherefore was I born?
If that my cousin king be King of England,
It must be granted I am Duke of Lancaster.
You have a son, Aumerle, my noble cousin;
Had you first died, and he been thus trod down,
He should have found his uncle Gaunt a father,
To rouse his wrongs and chase them to the bay.
I am denied to sue my livery here,
And yet my letters-patents give me leave: 130
● My father's goods are all distrain'd and sold,
And these and all are all amiss employ'd.
What would you have me do? I am a subject,
And I challenge law: attorneys are denied me;
And therefore personally I lay my claim
To my inheritance of free descent.
   North. The noble duke hath been too much
     abused.
   Ross. It stands your grace upon to do him
     right.
   Willo. Base men by his endowments are
     made great.
   York. My lords of England, let me tell you this:
I have had feeling of my cousin's wrongs   141
And labour'd all I could to do him right;
But in this kind to come, in braving arms,
Be his own carver and cut out his way,
To find out right with wrong, it may not be;
And you that do abet him in this kind
Cherish rebellion and are rebels all.
   North. The noble duke hath sworn his com-
     ing is
But for his own; and for the right of that
We all have strongly sworn to give him aid;   150
And let him ne'er see joy that breaks that oath!
   York. Well, well, I see the issue of these arms:
I cannot mend it, I must needs confess,
Because my power is weak and all ill left:
But if I could, by Him that gave me life,
● I would attach you all and make you stoop
Unto the sovereign mercy of the king;
But since I cannot, be it known to you
I do remain as neuter. So, fare you well;
Unless you please to enter in the castle   160
And there repose you for this night.
   Boling. An offer, uncle, that we will accept:
But we must win your grace to go with us
To Bristol castle, which they say is held
By Bushy, Bagot and their complices,
The caterpillars of the commonwealth,
Which I have sworn to weed and pluck away.
   York. It may be I will go with you: but yet
     I'll pause;
For I am loath to break our country's laws.
Nor friends nor foes, to me welcome you are: 170
Things past redress are now with me past care.
                  [*Exeunt.*

   SCENE IV. *A camp in Wales.*

   Enter SALISBURY *and a* Welsh Captain.

   Cap. My Lord of Salisbury, we have stay'd
     ten days,
And hardly kept our countrymen together,
And yet we hear no tidings from the king;

Therefore we will disperse ourselves: farewell.
 Sal. Stay yet another day, thou trusty Welshman:
The king reposeth all his confidence in thee.
 Cap. 'Tis thought the king is dead; we will not stay.
The bay-trees in our country are all wither'd
And meteors fright the fixed stars of heaven;
The pale-faced moon looks bloody on the earth 10
And lean-look'd prophets whisper fearful change;
Rich men look sad and ruffians dance and leap,
The one in fear to lose what they enjoy,
The other to enjoy by rage and war:
These signs forerun the death or fall of kings.
Farewell: our countrymen are gone and fled,
As well assured Richard their king is dead.
          [*Exit.*
 Sal. Ah, Richard, with the eyes of heavy mind
I see thy glory like a shooting star
Fall to the base earth from the firmament. 20
Thy sun sets weeping in the lowly west,
Witnessing storms to come, woe and unrest:
Thy friends are fled to wait upon thy foes,
● And crossly to thy good all fortune goes. [*Exit.*

ACT III.

Scene I. *Bristol. Before the castle.*

Enter Bolingbroke, York, Northumberland, Ross, Percy, Willoughby, *with* Bushy *and* Green, *prisoners.*

 Boling. Bring forth these men.
Bushy and Green, I will not vex your souls—
Since presently your souls must part your bodies—
With too much urging your pernicious lives,
For 'twere no charity; yet, to wash your blood
From off my hands, here in the view of men
I will unfold some causes of your deaths.
You have misled a prince, a royal king,
A happy gentleman in blood and lineaments,
● By you unhappied and disfigured clean: 10
● You have in manner with your sinful hours
Made a divorce betwixt his queen and him,
Broke the possession of a royal bed
And stain'd the beauty of a fair queen's cheeks
With tears drawn from her eyes by your foul wrongs.
Myself, a prince by fortune of my birth,
Near to the king in blood, and near in love
Till you did make him misinterpret me,
Have stoop'd my neck under your injuries,
And sigh'd my English breath in foreign clouds,
Eating the bitter bread of banishment; 21
● Whilst you have fed upon my signories,
Dispark'd my parks and fell'd my forest woods,
● From my own windows torn my household coat,
● Razed out my imprese, leaving me no sign,
Save men's opinions and my living blood,
To show the world I am a gentleman.
This and much more, much more than twice all this,
Condemns you to the death. See them deliver'd over
To execution and the hand of death. 30
 Bushy. More welcome is the stroke of death to me
Than Bolingbroke to England. Lords, farewell.

24 *crossly.* Adversely.

10 *clean.* Totally.

11–15 *You have . . . wrongs.* See introduction.

22 *signories.* Estates and manors.

24 *household coat.* Coat of arms.

25 *imprese.* Crest with a motto.

Bolingbroke: 'See them deliver'd over To execution and the hand of death.' Woodcut from Holinshed's *Chronicles,* 1577

Arms and crest of Richard II

34 *security.* Careless confidence.

36 *Discomfortable.* Discouraging.

Charles Kean as Richard II, Princess's Theatre, London, 1857

Green. My comfort is that heaven will take our souls
And plague injustice with the pains of hell.
    Boling. My Lord Northumberland, see them dispatch'd.
      [*Exeunt Northumberland and others,
         with the prisoners.*
Uncle, you say the queen is at your house;
For God's sake, fairly let her be entreated:
Tell her I send to her my kind commends;
Take special care my greetings be deliver'd.
    York. A gentleman of mine I have dispatch'd
With letters of your love to her at large.   41
    Boling. Thanks, gentle uncle. Come, lords, away,
To fight with Glendower and his complices:
Awhile to work, and after holiday.   [*Exeunt.*

SCENE II. *The coast of Wales. A castle in view.*

Drums: flourish and colours. Enter KING RICHARD, *the* BISHOP OF CARLISLE, AUMERLE, *and Soldiers.*

    K. Rich. Barkloughly castle call they this at hand?
    Aum. Yea, my lord. How brooks your grace the air,
After your late tossing on the breaking seas?
    K. Rich. Needs must I like it well: I weep for joy
To stand upon my kingdom once again.
Dear earth, I do salute thee with my hand,
Though rebels wound thee with their horses' hoofs:
As a long-parted mother with her child
Plays fondly with her tears and smiles in meeting,
So, weeping, smiling, greet I thee, my earth,   10
And do thee favours with my royal hands.
Feed not thy sovereign's foe, my gentle earth,
Nor with thy sweets comfort his ravenous sense;
But let thy spiders, that suck up thy venom,
And heavy-gaited toads lie in their way,
Doing annoyance to the treacherous feet
Which with usurping steps do trample thee:
Yield stinging nettles to mine enemies;
And when they from thy bosom pluck a flower,
Guard it, I pray thee, with a lurking adder   20
Whose double tongue may with a mortal touch
Throw death upon thy sovereign's enemies.
Mock not my senseless conjuration, lords:
This earth shall have a feeling and these stones
Prove armed soldiers, ere her native king
Shall falter under foul rebellion's arms.
    Car. Fear not, my lord: that Power that made you king
Hath power to keep you king in spite of all.
The means that heaven yields must be embraced,
And not neglected; else, if heaven would,   30
And we will not, heaven's offer we refuse,
The proffer'd means of succour and redress.
    Aum. He means, my lord, that we are too remiss;
 ● Whilst Bolingbroke, through our security,
Grows strong and great in substance and in power.
 ●   *K. Rich.* Discomfortable cousin! know'st thou not

That when the searching eye of heaven is hid,
Behind the globe, that lights the lower world,
Then thieves and robbers range abroad unseen
In murders and in outrage, boldly here;   40
But when from under this terrestrial ball
He fires the proud tops of the eastern pines
And darts his light through every guilty hole,
Then murders, treasons and detested sins,
The cloak of night being pluck'd from off their
    backs,
Stand bare and naked, trembling at themselves?
So when this thief, this traitor, Bolingbroke,
Who all this while hath revell'd in the night
● Whilst we were wandering with the antipodes,
Shall see us rising in our throne, the east,   50
His treasons will sit blushing in his face,
Not able to endure the sight of day,
But self-affrighted tremble at his sin.
● Not all the water in the rough rude sea
Can wash the balm off from an anointed king;
The breath of worldly men cannot depose
The deputy elected by the Lord:
● For every man that Bolingbroke hath press'd
● To lift shrewd steel against our golden crown,
God for his Richard hath in heavenly pay   60
A glorious angel: then, if angels fight,
Weak men must fall, for heaven still guards the
    right.

Enter SALISBURY.

Welcome, my lord: how far off lies your power?
    Sal. Nor near nor farther off, my gracious
        lord,
Than this weak arm: discomfort guides my tongue
And bids me speak of nothing but despair.
One day too late, I fear me, noble lord,
Hath clouded all thy happy days on earth:
O, call back yesterday, bid time return,
And thou shalt have twelve thousand fighting
    men!   70
To-day, to-day, unhappy day, too late,
O'erthrows thy joys, friends, fortune and thy
    state:
For all the Welshmen, hearing thou wert dead,
Are gone to Bolingbroke, dispersed and fled;
    Aum. Comfort, my liege: why looks your
        grace so pale?
    K. Rich. But now the blood of twenty thou-
        sand men
Did triumph in my face, and they are fled;
And, till so much blood thither come again,
Have I not reason to look pale and dead?
All souls that will be safe fly from my side,   80
For time hath set a blot upon my pride.
    Aum. Comfort, my liege; remember who you
        are.
    K. Rich. I had forgot myself: am I not king?
Awake, thou coward majesty! thou sleepest.
Is not the king's name twenty thousand names?
Arm, arm, my name! a puny subject strikes
At thy great glory.   Look not to the ground,
Ye favourites of a king: are we not high?
High be our thoughts: I know my uncle York
Hath power enough to serve our turn.   But who
    comes here?   90

Enter SCROOP.

    Scroop. More health and happiness betide my
        liege

49 *antipodes.* Richard is likening himself to the sun which has been on the other side of the earth.

Ian Richardson as Richard II, Royal Shakespeare Co, 1973

54—55 *Not all . . . king.* See introduction.

58 *press'd.* Conscripted.

59 *shrewd.* Sharp.

116 *beadsmen.* Pensioners, who told their 'beads' or prayers on behalf of those who supported them.

A beadsman. Engraving by F.W. Fairholt from a 15th century manuscript. From J.O. Halliwell's edition of Shakespeare's works, 1853–65

117 *double-fatal.* Because the berries were poisonous, and the wood was used to make bows.

118 *bills.* Weapons like halberds, but with hooks rather than blades.

125 *peaceful.* Unopposed.

Than can my care-tuned tongue deliver him!
   K. Rich. Mine ear is open and my heart prepared:
The worst is worldly loss thou canst unfold.
Say, is my kingdom lost? why, 'twas my care;
And what loss is it to be rid of care?
Strives Bolingbroke to be as great as we?
Greater he shall not be; if he serve God,
We'll serve Him too and be his fellow so:
Revolt our subjects? that we cannot mend; 100
They break their faith to God as well as us:
Cry woe, destruction, ruin and decay;
The worst is death, and death will have his day.
   Scroop. Glad am I that your highness is so arm'd
To bear the tidings of calamity.
Like an unseasonable stormy day,
Which makes the silver rivers drown their shores,
As if the world were all dissolved to tears,
So high above his limits swells the rage
Of Bolingbroke, covering your fearful land 110
With hard bright steel and hearts harder than steel.
White-beards have arm'd their thin and hairless scalps
Against thy majesty; boys, with women's voices,
Strive to speak big and clap their female joints
In stiff unwieldy arms against thy crown:
Thy very beadsmen learn to bend their bows
Of double-fatal yew against thy state;
Yea, distaff-women manage rusty bills
Against thy seat: both young and old rebel,
And all goes worse than I have power to tell. 120
   K. Rich. Too well, too well thou tell'st a tale so ill.
Where is the Earl of Wiltshire? where is Bagot?
What is become of Bushy? where is Green?
That they have let the dangerous enemy
Measure our confines with such peaceful steps?
If we prevail, their heads shall pay for it:
I warrant they have made peace with Bolingbroke.
   Scroop. Peace have they made with him indeed, my lord.
   K. Rich. O villains, vipers, damn'd without redemption!
Dogs, easily won to fawn on any man! 130
Snakes, in my heart-blood warm'd, that sting my heart!
Three Judases, each one thrice worse than Judas!
Would they make peace? terrible hell make war
Upon their spotted souls for this offence!
   Scroop. Sweet love, I see, changing his property,
Turns to the sourest and most deadly hate:
Again uncurse their souls; their peace is made
With heads, and not with hands: those whom you curse
Have felt the worst of death's destroying wound
And lie full low, graved in the hollow ground.
   Aum. Is Bushy, Green, and the Earl of Wiltshire dead? 141
   Scroop. Ay, all of them at Bristol lost their heads.
   Aum. Where is the duke my father with his power?
   K. Rich. No matter where; of comfort no man speak:
Let's talk of graves, of worms and epitaphs;

Make dust our paper and with rainy eyes
Write sorrow on the bosom of the earth,
Let's choose executors and talk of wills:
And yet not so, for what can we bequeath
Save our deposed bodies to the ground?   150
Our lands, our lives and all are Bolingbroke's,
And nothing can we call our own but death
And that small model of the barren earth
Which serves as paste and cover to our bones.
For God's sake, let us sit upon the ground
And tell sad stories of the death of kings:
• How some have been deposed; some slain in
    war;
Some haunted by the ghosts they have deposed;
Some poison'd by their wives; some sleeping
    kill'd;
All murder'd: for within the hollow crown   160
That rounds the mortal temples of a king
• Keeps Death his court and there the antic sits,
Scoffing his state and grinning at his pomp,
Allowing him a breath, a little scene,
To monarchize, be fear'd and kill with looks,
Infusing him with self and vain conceit,
As if this flesh which walls about our life
Were brass impregnable, and humour'd thus
Comes at the last and with a little pin   169
Bores through his castle wall, and farewell king!
Cover your heads and mock not flesh and blood
With solemn reverence: throw away respect,
Tradition, form and ceremonious duty,
For you have but mistook me all this while:
† I live with bread like you, feel want,
Taste grief, need friends: subjected thus,
How can you say to me, I am a king?
    Car. My lord, wise men ne'er sit and wail
    their woes,
• But presently prevent the ways to wail.   179
To fear the foe, since fear oppresseth strength,
Gives in your weakness strength unto your foe,
And so your follies fight against yourself.
Fear, and be slain; no worse can come to fight:
And fight and die is death destroying death;
Where fearing dying pays death servile breath.
    Aum. My father hath a power; inquire of
    him,
And learn to make a body of a limb.
    K. Rich. Thou chidest me well: proud Boling-
    broke, I come
To change blows with thee for our day of doom.
This ague fit of fear is over-blown;   190
An easy task it is to win our own.
Say, Scroop, where lies our uncle with his power?
Speak sweetly, man, although thy looks be sour.
    Scroop. Men judge by the complexion of the
    sky
The state and inclination of the day:
So may you by my dull and heavy eye,
  My tongue hath but a heavier tale to say.
I play the torturer, by small and small
To lengthen out the worst that must be spoken:
Your uncle York is join'd with Bolingbroke,   200
And all your northern castles yielded up,
And all your southern gentlemen in arms
Upon his party.
    K. Rich.   Thou hast said enough.
Beshrew thee, cousin, which didst lead me forth
                       [*To Aumerle.*
Of that sweet way I was in to despair!
What say you now? what comfort have we now?

157–159 *How some . . . kill'd.* See introduction.

King Richard: 'for within the hollow crown . . . Keeps
Death his court . . .' Engraving from *Imagines Mortis*

162 *antic.* Jester.

179 *presently prevent.* Immediately forestall.

323

By heaven, I'll hate him everlastingly
That bids me be of comfort any more.
Go to Flint castle: there I'll pine away;
A king, woe's slave, shall kingly woe obey. 210
That power I have, discharge; and let them go
● To ear the land that hath some hope to grow,
For I have none: let no man speak again
To alter this, for counsel is but vain.
    Aum. My liege, one word.
    K. Rich.   He does me double wrong
That wounds me with the flatteries of his tongue.
Discharge my followers: let them hence away,
From Richard's night to Bolingbroke's fair day.
                         [*Exeunt.*

SCENE III. *Wales. Before Flint castle.*

Enter, with drum and colours, BOLINGBROKE,
YORK, NORTHUMBERLAND, Attendants, *and
forces.*

    Boling. So that by this intelligence we learn
The Welshmen are dispersed, and Salisbury
Is gone to meet the king, who lately landed
With some few private friends upon this coast.
    North. The news is very fair and good, my
        lord:
Richard not far from hence hath hid his head..
    York. It would beseem the Lord Northum-
        berland
To say 'King Richard:' alack the heavy day
When such a sacred king should hide his head.
    North. Your grace mistakes; only to be brief,
Left I his title out.
    York.   The time hath been,   10
Would you have been so brief with him, he would
Have been so brief with you, to shorten you,
For taking so the head, your whole head's length.
    Boling. Mistake not, uncle, further than you
        should.
●   *York.* Take not, good cousin, further than
        you should,
Lest you mistake the heavens are o'er our heads.
    Boling. I know it, uncle, and oppose not my-
        self
Against their will. But who comes here?   19

        Enter PERCY.
Welcome, Harry: what, will not this castle yield?
    Percy. The castle royally is mann'd, my lord,
Against thy entrance.
    Boling. Royally!
Why, it contains no king?
    Percy.   Yes, my good lord,
It doth contain a king; King Richard lies
Within the limits of yon lime and stone:
And with him are the Lord Aumerle, Lord Salis-
        bury,
Sir Stephen Scroop, besides a clergyman
Of holy reverence; who, I cannot learn.
    North. O, belike it is the Bishop of Carlisle.
    Boling. Noble lords,   31
Go to the rude ribs of that ancient castle;
Through brazen trumpet send the breath of parley
Into his ruin'd ears, and thus deliver:
Henry Bolingbroke
On both his knees doth kiss King Richard's hand
And sends allegiance and true faith of heart
To his most royal person, hither come

King Richard: '. . . I'll hate him everlastingly That bids me be of comfort any more.' Drawing by William Hamilton (1751–1801).

212 *ear.* Plough and sow.

15–19 *Take not . . . will.* See introduction.

Even at his feet to lay my arms and power,
Provided that my banishment repeal'd   40
And lands restored again be freely granted:
If not, I'll use the advantage of my power
And lay the summer's dust with showers of blood
Rain'd from the wounds of slaughter'd English-
men:
The which, how far off from the mind of Boling-
broke
It is, such crimson tempest should bedrench
The fresh green lap of fair King Richard's land,
● My stooping duty tenderly shall show.
Go, signify as much, while here we march
Upon the grassy carpet of this plain.   50
Let's march without the noise of threatening
drum,
That from this castle's tatter'd battlements
Our fair appointments may be well perused.
Methinks King Richard and myself should meet
With no less terror than the elements
Of fire and water, when their thundering shock
At meeting tears the cloudy cheeks of heaven.
Be he the fire. I'll be the yielding water:
The rage be his, whilst on the earth I rain
My waters; on the earth, and not on him.   60
March on, and mark King Richard how he looks.

*Parle without, and answer within. Then a
flourish. Enter on the walls*, KING RICHARD,
the BISHOP OF CARLISLE, AUMERLE, SCROOP,
and SALISBURY.

See, see, King Richard doth himself appear,
As doth the blushing discontented sun
From out the fiery portal of the east,
When he perceives the envious clouds are bent
To dim his glory and to stain the track
Of his bright passage to the occident.
    York. Yet looks he like a king: behold,
his eye,
As bright as is the eagle's, lightens forth
Controlling majesty: alack, alack, for woe,   70
That any harm should stain so fair a show!
    K. Rich. We are amazed; and thus long
have we stood
To watch the fearful bending of thy knee,
                              [*To North.*
Because we thought ourself thy lawful king:
And if we be, how dare thy joints forget
To pay their awful duty to our presence?
If we be not, show us the hand of God
That hath dismiss'd us from our stewardship;
For well we know, no hand of blood and bone
Can gripe the sacred handle of our sceptre,   80
Unless he do profane, steal, or usurp.
And though you think that all, as you have done,
Have torn their souls by turning them from us,
And we are barren and bereft of friends;
Yet know, my master, God omnipotent,
Is mustering in his clouds on our behalf
Armies of pestilence; and they shall strike
Your children yet unborn and unbegot,
That lift your vassal hands against my head
And threat the glory of my precious crown.   90
Tell Bolingbroke—for yond methinks he stands—
That every stride he makes upon my land
Is dangerous treason: he is come to open
The purple testament of bleeding war;
But ere the crown he looks for live in peace,
Ten thousand bloody crowns of mothers' sons

48 *My stooping duty.* Kneeling as a loyal subject.

The eagle, king of birds. Woodcut from *Libellus de
Natura Animalium*, a 15th century bestiary

114 *Enfranchisement.* Restoration of his rights.

117 *barbed.* With wild flowing manes.

Richard II consulting with his friends. Engraving from a medieval manuscript

151 *palmer.* Pilgrim.

Shall ill become the flower of England's face,
Change the complexion of her maid-pale peace
To scarlet indignation and bedew
Her pastures' grass with faithful English blood.
   North. The king of heaven forbid our lord
     the king   101
Should so with civil and uncivil arms
Be rush'd upon! Thy thrice noble cousin
Harry Bolingbroke doth humbly kiss thy hand;
And by the honourable tomb he swears,
That stands upon your royal grandsire's bones,
And by the royalties of both your bloods,
Currents that spring from one most gracious head,
And by the buried hand of warlike Gaunt,
And by the worth and honour of himself,   110
Comprising all that may be sworn or said,
His coming hither hath no further scope
Than for his lineal royalties and to beg
• Enfranchisement immediate on his knees:
Which on thy royal party granted once,
His glittering arms he will commend to rust,
• His barbed steeds to stables, and his heart
To faithful service of your majesty.
This swears he, as he is a prince, is just;
And, as I am a gentleman, I credit him.   120
   K. Rich. Northumberland, say thus the king
     returns:
His noble cousin is right welcome hither;
And all the number of his fair demands
Shall be accomplish'd without contradiction:
With all the gracious utterance thou hast
Speak to his gentle hearing kind commends.
We do debase ourselves, cousin, do we not,
                   [To Aumerle.
To look so poorly and to speak so fair?
Shall we call back Northumberland, and send
Defiance to the traitor, and so die?   130
   Aum. No, good my lord; let's fight with
     gentle words
Till time lend friends and friends their helpful
     swords.
   K. Rich. O God, O God! that e'er this tongue
     of mine,
That laid the sentence of dread banishment
On yon proud man, should take it off again
With words of sooth! O that I were as great
As is my grief, or lesser than my name!
Or that I could forget what I have been,
Or not remember what I must be now!
Swell'st thou, proud heart? I'll give thee scope
     to beat,   140
Since foes have scope to beat both thee and me.
   Aum. Northumberland comes back from Bo-
     lingbroke.
   K. Rich. What must the king do now? must
     he submit?
The king shall do it: must he be deposed?
The king shall be contented: must he lose
The name of king? o' God's name, let it go:
I'll give my jewels for a set of beads,
My gorgeous palace for a hermitage,
My gay apparel for an almsman's gown,
My figured goblets for a dish of wood,   150
• My sceptre for a palmer's walking-staff,
My subjects for a pair of carved saints
And my large kingdom for a little grave,
A little little grave, an obscure grave;
Or I'll be buried in the king's highway,
Some way of common trade, where subjects' feet

May hourly trample on their sovereign's head;
For on my heart they tread now whilst I live;
And buried once, why not upon my head?
Aumerle, thou weep'st, my tender-hearted cousin!
We'll make foul weather with despised tears; 161
● Our sighs and they shall lodge the summer corn,
And make a dearth in this revolting land.
Or shall we play the wantons with our woes,
And make some pretty match with shedding
    tears?
As thus, to drop them still upon one place,
● Till they have fretted us a pair of graves
Within the earth; and, therein laid,—there lies
Two kinsmen digg'd their graves with weeping
    eyes.
Would not this ill do well? Well, well, I see 170
I talk but idly, and you laugh at me.
Most mighty prince, my Lord Northumberland,
What says King Bolingbroke? will his majesty
Give Richard leave to live till Richard die?
You make a leg, and Bolingbroke says ay.
    North. My lord, in the base court he doth
        attend
To speak with you; may it please you to come
    down.
● *K. Rich.* Down, down I come; like glistering
    Phaethon,
● Wanting the manage of unruly jades.
In the base court? Base court, where kings
    grow base, 180
To come at traitors' calls and do them grace.
In the base court? Come down? Down, court!
    down, king!
For night-owls shriek where mounting larks
    should sing. [*Exeunt from above.*
    Boling. What says his majesty?
    North.   Sorrow and grief of heart
Makes him speak fondly, like a frantic man:
Yet he is come.

Enter KING RICHARD *and his attendants below.*

    Boling. Stand all apart,
And show fair duty to his majesty.
                    [*He kneels down.*
My gracious lord,—
    K. Rich. Fair cousin, you debase your princely
        knee 190
To make the base earth proud with kissing it:
Me rather had my heart might feel your love
Than my unpleased eye see your courtesy.
Up, cousin, up; your heart is up, I know,
Thus high at least, although your knee be low.
    Boling. My gracious lord, I come but for
        mine own.
    K. Rich. Your own is yours, and I am yours,
        and all.
    Boling. So far be mine, my most redoubted
        lord,
As my true service shall deserve your love.
    K. Rich. Well you deserve: they well deserve
        to have, 200
That know the strong'st and surest way to get.
Uncle, give me your hands: nay, dry your eyes;
Tears show their love, but want their remedies.
Cousin, I am too young to be your father,
Though you are old enough to be my heir.
What you will have, I'll give, and willing too;
For do we must what force will have us do.

Richard: 'Down, down I come; like glistering Phaethon.'
From a 16th century woodcut

162 *lodge.* Beat down.

167 *fretted.* Worn.

178 *Phaethon.* Apollo's son who borrowed his father's chariot, but could not control the horses. To stop the destruction of the earth, Zeus struck him with a thunderbolt.

179 *Wanting . . . of.* Unable to control.

King Richard: 'Fair cousin, you debase your princely knee . . .' John Rydel as Bolingbroke and Charles Kean as Richard, Princess's Theatre, London, 1857

The queen and her ladies. Engraving from a painting by
G.H. Boughton (1833–1905)

---

4 *rubs.* Anything that obstructed the course of the bowl.

5 *bias.* A weight in one side of the bowl which curves
its course.

26 *My wretchedness . . . pins.* I wager my misery against
a trifle . . .

40 *pale.* Enclosure.

46 *knots.* Flower beds.

Set on towards London, cousin, is it so?
  Boling. Yea, my good lord.
  K. Rich.   Then I must not say no.
                  [Flourish. Exeunt.

SCENE IV. *Langley.* The DUKE OF YORK'S
              garden.

Enter the QUEEN *and two* Ladies.

  Queen. What sport shall we devise here in
    this garden,
To drive away the heavy thought of care?
  Lady. Madam, we'll play at bowls.
  Queen. 'Twill make me think the world is full
    of rubs,
And that my fortune runs against the bias.
  Lady. Madam, we'll dance.
  Queen. My legs can keep no measure in delight,
When my poor heart no measure keeps in grief:
Therefore, no dancing, girl; some other sport.
  Lady. Madam, we'll tell tales.   10
  Queen. Of sorrow or of joy?
  Lady.   Of either, madam.
  Queen. Of neither, girl:
For if of joy, being altogether wanting,
It doth remember me the more of sorrow;
Or if of grief, being altogether had,
It adds more sorrow to my want of joy:
For what I have I need not to repeat;
And what I want it boots not to complain.
  Lady. Madam, I'll sing.
  Queen.   'Tis well that thou hast cause;
But thou shouldst please me better, wouldst thou
    weep.   20
  Lady. I could weep, madam, would it do you
    good.
  Queen. And I could sing, would weeping do
    me good,
And never borrow any tear of thee.

Enter a Gardener, *and two* Servants.

But stay, here come the gardeners:
Let's step into the shadow of these trees.
My wretchedness unto a row of pins,
They'll talk of state; for every one doth so
Against a change; woe is forerun with woe.
              [Queen and Ladies retire.
  Gard. Go, bind thou up yon dangling apricocks,
Which, like unruly children, make their sire 30
Stoop with oppression of their prodigal weight:
Give some supportance to the bending twigs.
Go thou, and like an executioner,
Cut off the heads of too fast growing sprays,
That look too lofty in our commonwealth:
All must be even in our government.
You thus employ'd, I will go root away
The noisome weeds, which without profit suck
The soil's fertility from wholesome flowers.
  Serv. Why should we in the compass of a pale
Keep law and form and due proportion, 41
Showing, as in a model, our firm estate,
When our sea-walled garden, the whole land,
Is full of weeds, her fairest flowers choked up,
Her fruit-trees all unpruned, her hedges ruin'd,
Her knots disorder'd and her wholesome herbs
Swarming with caterpillars?
  Gard.   Hold thy peace:

He that hath suffer'd this disorder'd spring
Hath now himself met with the fall of leaf:
The weeds which his broad-spreading leaves did
    shelter,   50
That seem'd in eating him to hold him up,
Are pluck'd up root and all by Bolingbroke,
I mean the Earl of Wiltshire, Bushy, Green.
    Serv. What, are they dead?
    Gard.   They are; and Bolingbroke
Hath seized the wasteful king. O, what pity is it
That he had not so trimm'd and dress'd his land
As we this garden! We at time of year
Do wound the bark, the skin of our fruit-trees,
Lest, being over-proud in sap and blood,
With too much riches it confound itself: 60
Had he done so to great and growing men,
They might have lived to bear and he to taste
Their fruits of duty: superfluous branches
We lop away, that bearing boughs may live:
Had he done so, himself had borne the crown,
Which waste of idle hours hath quite thrown down.
    Serv. What, think you then the king shall be
    deposed?
    Gard. Depress'd he is already, and deposed
'Tis doubt he will be: letters came last night
To a dear friend of the good Duke of York's,   70
That tell black tidings.
    Queen. O, I am press'd to death through want
    of speaking!   [*Coming forward.*
Thou, old Adam's likeness, set to dress this garden,
How dares thy harsh rude tongue sound this
    unpleasing news?
What Eve, what serpent, hath suggested thee
To make a second fall of cursed man?
Why dost thou say King Richard is deposed?
Darest thou, thou little better thing than earth,
Divine his downfal? Say, where, when, and how,
Camest thou by this ill tidings? speak, thou
    wretch.   80
    Gard. Pardon me, madam: little joy have I
To breathe this news; yet what I say is true.
King Richard, he is in the mighty hold
Of Bolingbroke: their fortunes both are weigh'd:
In your lord's scale is nothing but himself,
And some few vanities that make him light;
But in the balance of great Bolingbroke,
Besides himself, are all the English peers,
And with that odds he weighs King Richard down.
Post you to London, and you will find it so;   90
I speak no more than every one doth know.
    Queen. Nimble mischance, that art so light of
    foot,
Doth not thy embassage belong to me,
And am I last that knows it? O, thou think'st
To serve me last, that I may longest keep
Thy sorrow in my breast. Come, ladies, go,
To meet at London London's king in woe.
What, was I born to this, that my sad look
Should grace the triumph of great Bolingbroke?
Gardener, for telling me these news of woe,   100
Pray God the plants thou graft'st may never grow.
            [*Exeunt Queen and Ladies.*
    Gard. Poor queen! so that thy state might
    be no worse,
I would my skill were subject to thy curse.
Here did she fall a tear; here in this place
I'll set a bank of rue, sour herb of grace:
Rue, even for ruth, here shortly shall be seen,
In the remembrance of a weeping queen. [*Exeunt.*

An English garden. Woodcut from Didymus Mountain's *The Gardener's Labyrinth*, 1577

68 *Depress'd.* Brought low.

Queen: 'Thou, old Adam's likeness . . .' Drawing of the Queen and the Gardener by John Thurston (1744–1822)

93 *embassage.* Message.

106 *ruth.* Pity.

Principal entrance to Westminster Hall, Engraving from *Old England,* 1854

4 *wrought it.* Persuaded.

5 *timeless.* Untimely.

21 *fair stars.* Noble birth.

24 *attainder.* Accusation.

33 *sympathy.* Equality in rank.

ACT IV.

Scene I. *Westminster Hall.*

Enter, as to the Parliament, Bolingbroke, Aumerle, Northumberland, Percy, Fitzwater, Surrey, *the* Bishop of Carlisle, *the* Abbot of Westminster, *and another* Lord, Herald, Officers, *and* Bagot.

Boling.   Call forth Bagot.
Now, Bagot, freely speak thy mind;
What thou dost know of noble Gloucester's death,
Who wrought it with the king, and who perform'd
The bloody office of his timeless end.
    Bagot.   Then set before my face the Lord
      Aumerle.
    Boling.   Cousin, stand forth, and look upon
      that man.
    Bagot.   My Lord Aumerle, I know your daring
      tongue
Scorns to unsay what once it hath deliver'd.
In that dead time when Gloucester's death was
    plotted,   10
I heard you say, 'Is not my arm of length,
That reacheth from the restful English court
As far as Calais, to mine uncle's head?'
Amongst much other talk, that very time,
I heard you say that you had rather refuse
The offer of an hundred thousand crowns
Than Bolingbroke's return to England:
Adding withal, how blest this land would be
In this your cousin's death.
    Aum.   Princes and noble lords,
What answer shall I make to this base man? 20
Shall I so much dishonour my fair stars,
On equal terms to give him chastisement?
Either I must, or have mine honour soil'd
With the attainder of his slanderous lips.
There is my gage, the manual seal of death,
That marks thee out for hell: I say, thou liest,
And will maintain what thou hast said is false
In thy heart-blood, though being all too base
To stain the temper of my knightly sword.
    Boling.   Bagot, forbear; thou shalt not take
      it up.   30
    Aum.   Excepting one, I would he were the best
In all this presence that hath moved me so.
    Fitz.   If that thy valour stand on sympathy,
There is my gage, Aumerle, in gage to thine:
By that fair sun which shows me where thou
    stand'st,
I heard thee say, and vauntingly thou spakest it,
That thou wert cause of noble Gloucester's death.
If thou deny'st it twenty times, thou liest;
And I will turn thy falsehood to thy heart,
Where it was forged, with my rapier's point. 40
    Aum.   Thou darest not, coward, live to see
      that day.
    Fitz.   Now, by my soul, I would it were this
      hour.
    Aum.   Fitzwater, thou art damn'd to hell for
      this.
    Percy.   Aumerle, thou liest; his honour is as true
In this appeal as thou art all unjust;
And that thou art so, there I throw my gage,
To prove it on thee to the extremest point
Of mortal breathing: seize it, if thou darest.
    Aum.   An if I do not, may my hands rot off
And never brandish more revengeful steel 50

Over the glittering helmet of my foe!
● *Another Lord.* I task the earth to the like,
    forsworn Aumerle;
And spur thee on with full as many lies
As may be holloa'd in thy treacherous ear
From sun to sun: there is my honour's pawn;
Engage it to the trial, if thou darest.
● *Aum.* Who sets me else? by heaven, I'll throw
    at all:
I have a thousand spirits in one breast,
To answer twenty thousand such as you.
    Surrey. My Lord Fitzwater, I do remember
        well   60
The very time Aumerle and you did talk.
    Fitz. 'Tis very true: you were in presence then;
And you can witness with me this is true.
    Surrey. As false, by heaven, as heaven itself
        is true.
    Fitz. Surrey, thou liest.
    Surrey.   Dishonourable boy!
That lie shall lie so heavy on my sword,
That it shall render vengeance and revenge
Till thou the lie-giver and that lie do lie
In earth as quiet as thy father's skull:
In proof whereof, there is my honour's pawn;   70
Engage it to the trial, if thou darest.
● *Fitz.* How fondly dost thou spur a forward
    horse!
If I dare eat, or drink, or breathe, or live,
I dare meet Surrey in a wilderness,
And spit upon him, whilst I say he lies,
And lies, and lies: there is my bond of faith,
To tie thee to my strong correction.
As I intend to thrive in this new world,
Aumerle is guilty of my true appeal:
Besides, I heard the banish'd Norfolk say   80
That thou, Aumerle, didst send two of thy men
To execute the noble duke at Calais.
    Aum. Some honest Christian trust me with a
        gage,
That Norfolk lies: here do I throw down this,
If he may be repeal'd, to try his honour.
    Boling. These differences shall all rest under
        gage
Till Norfolk be repeal'd: repeal'd he shall be,
And, though mine enemy, restored again
To all his lands and signories: when he's return'd,
Against Aumerle we will enforce his trial.   90
    Car. That honourable day shall ne'er be seen.
Many a time hath banish'd Norfolk fought
For Jesu Christ in glorious Christian field,
Streaming the ensign of the Christian cross
Against black pagans, Turks, and Saracens;
And toil'd with works of war, retired himself
To Italy; and there at Venice gave
His body to that pleasant country's earth,
And his pure soul unto his captain Christ,
Under whose colours he had fought so long.   100
    Boling. Why, bishop, is Norfolk dead?
    Car. As surely as I live, my lord.
    Boling. Sweet peace conduct his sweet soul
        to the bosom
Of good old Abraham! Lords appellants,
Your differences shall all rest under gage
Till we assign you to your days of trial.

Enter YORK, *attended.*

    York. Great Duke of Lancaster, I come to
        thee

The seal of Robert Fitzwater. Engraving from J.R. Green's *Short History of the English People*, 1903

---

52 *I task . . . the like.* I load the earth with a similar burden. i.e. the gage.

57 *sets.* Challenges.

72 *fondly.* Foolishly. *forward.* Eager.

Costume design for Aumerle by Percy Anderson, 1922

115 *Worst.* Lowest in rank.

137–141 *The blood . . . confound.* See introduction.

159 *Procure . . . answer.* Get those men who are prepared to act as guarantors for the day of the trial.

From plume-pluck'd Richard; who with willing
  soul
Adopts thee heir, and his high sceptre yields
To the possession of thy royal hand: 110
Ascend his throne, descending now from him;
And long live Henry, fourth of that name!
    Boling. In God's name, I'll ascend the regal
      throne.
    Car. Marry, God forbid!
• Worst in this royal presence may I speak,
Yet best beseeming me to speak the truth.
Would God that any in this noble presence
Were enough noble to be upright judge
Of noble Richard! then true noblesse would
Learn him forbearance from so foul a wrong. 120
What subject can give sentence on his king?
And who sits here that is not Richard's subject?
Thieves are not judged but they are by to hear,
Although apparent guilt be seen in them;
And shall the figure of God's majesty,
His captain, steward, deputy-elect,
Anointed, crowned, planted many years,
Be judged by subject and inferior breath,
And he himself not present? O, forfend it, God,
That in a Christian climate souls refined   130
Should show so heinous, black, obscene a deed!
I speak to subjects, and a subject speaks,
Stirr'd up by God, thus boldly for his king.
My Lord of Hereford here, whom you call king,
Is a foul traitor to proud Hereford's king:
And if you crown him, let me prophesy:
• The blood of English shall manure the ground,
And future ages groan for this foul act;
Peace shall go sleep with Turks and infidels,
And in this seat of peace tumultuous wars   140
Shall kin with kin and kind with kind confound;
Disorder, horror, fear and mutiny
Shall here inhabit, and this land be call'd
The field of Golgotha and dead men's skulls.
O, if you raise this house against this house,
It will the woefullest division prove
That ever fell upon this cursed earth.
Prevent it, resist it, let it not be so,
Lest child, child's children, cry against you
  'woe!'
    North. Well have you argued, sir; and, for
      your pains,   150
Of capital treason we arrest you here.
My Lord of Westminster, be it your charge
To keep him safely till his day of trial.
May it please you, lords, to grant the commons'
  suit.
    Boling. Fetch hither Richard, that in common view
He may surrender; so we shall proceed
Without suspicion.
    York.   I will be his conduct. [*Exit.*
    Boling. Lords, you that here are under our
      arrest,
• Procure your sureties for your days of answer.
Little are we beholding to your love,   160
And little look'd for at your helping hands.

    Re-enter YORK, *with* RICHARD, *and* Officers
        bearing the regalia.

    K. Rich. Alack, why am I sent for to a king,
Before I have shook off the regal thoughts
Wherewith I reign'd? I hardly yet have learn'd
To insinuate, flatter, bow, and bend my limbs:

167–169 *Yet I . . . to me.* See introduction.

Give sorrow leave awhile to tutor me
To this submission.   Yet I well remember
The favours of these men: were they not mine?
Did they not sometime cry, 'all hail!' to me?
So Judas did to Christ: but he, in twelve,   170
Found truth in all but one; I, in twelve thousand,
none.
God save the king! Will no man say amen?
Am I both priest and clerk? well then, amen.
God save the king! although I be not he;
And yet, amen, if heaven do think him me.
To do what service am I sent for hither?
York. To do that office of thine own good will
Which tired majesty did make thee offer,
The resignation of thy state and crown
To Henry Bolingbroke.   180
K. Rich. Give me the crown. Here, cousin,
seize the crown;
Here cousin;
On this side my hand, and on that side yours.
Now is this golden crown like a deep well
That owes two buckets, filling one another,
The emptier ever dancing in the air,
The other down, unseen and full of water:
That bucket down and full of tears am I,
Drinking my griefs, whilst you mount up on high.
Boling. I thought you had been willing to
resign.   190
K. Rich. My crown I am; but still my griefs
are mine:
You may my glories and my state depose,
But not my griefs; still am I king of those.
Boling. Part of your cares you give me with
your crown.
K. Rich. Your cares set up do not pluck my
cares down.
My care is loss of care, by old care done;
Your care is gain of care, by new care won:
The cares I give I have, though given away:
They tend the crown, yet still with me they
stay.
Boling. Are you contented to resign the
crown?   200
K. Rich. Ay, no; no, ay; for I must
nothing be;
Therefore no no, for I resign to thee.
Now mark me, how I will undo myself:
I give this heavy weight from off my head
And this unwieldy sceptre from my hand,
The pride of kingly sway from out my heart;
With mine own tears I wash away my balm,
With mine own hands I give away my crown,
With mine own tongue deny my sacred state,
With mine own breath release all duty's rites:
All pomp and majesty I do forswear;   211
My manors, rents, revenues I forego;
My acts, decrees, and statutes I deny:
God pardon all oaths that are broke to me!
God keep all vows unbroke that swear to thee!
Make me, that nothing have, with nothing
grieved,
And thou with all pleased, that hast all achieved!
Long mayst thou live in Richard's seat to sit,
And soon lie Richard in an earthy pit!
God save King Harry, unking'd Richard says,
And send him many years of sunshine days! 221
What more remains?
North.   No more, but that you read
These accusations and these grievous crimes

Richard: 'Here, cousin, seize the crown;' Frank Benson
as Richard II, Lyceum Theatre, London, 1900

228 *ravel out*. Unravel.

238 *bait*. Torment.

246 *sort*. Group.

Parliament deposing Richard II and electing Henry IV.
Engraving from a medieval manuscript

Committed by your person and your followers
Against the state and profit of this land;
That, by confessing them, the souls of men
May deem that you are worthily deposed.

●   *K. Rich.* Must I do so? and must I ravel out
My weaved-up folly? Gentle Northumberland,
If thy offences were upon record,   230
Would it not shame thee in so fair a troop
To read a lecture of them? If thou wouldst,
There shouldst thou find one heinous article,
Containing the deposing of a king
And cracking the strong warrant of an oath,
Mark'd with a blot, damn'd in the book of
    heaven:
Nay, all of you that stand and look upon,

● Whilst that my wretchedness doth bait myself,
Though some of you with Pilate wash your hands
Showing an outward pity; yet you Pilates   240
Have here deliver'd me to my sour cross,
And water cannot wash away your sin.
   North. My lord, dispatch; read o'er these
    articles.
   K. Rich. Mine eyes are full of tears, I can-
    not see:
And yet salt water blinds them not so much

● But they can see a sort of traitors here.
Nay, if I turn mine eyes upon myself,
I find myself a traitor with the rest;
For I have given here my soul's consent
To undeck the pompous body of a king;   250
Made glory base and sovereignty a slave,
Proud majesty a subject, state a peasant.
   North. My lord,—
   K. Rich. No lord of thine, thou haught in-
    sulting man,
Nor no man's lord; I have no name, no title,
No, not that name was given me at the font,
But 'tis usurp'd: alack the heavy day,
That I have worn so many winters out,
And know not now what name to call myself!
O that I were a mockery king of snow,   260
Standing before the sun of Bolingbroke,
To melt myself away in water-drops!
Good king, great king, and yet not greatly good,
An if my word be sterling yet in England,
Let it command a mirror hither straight,
That it may show me what a face I have,
Since it is bankrupt of his majesty.
   Boling. Go some of you and fetch a looking-
    glass.   [*Exit an attendant.*
   North. Read o'er this paper while the glass
    doth come.
   K. Rich. Fiend, thou torment'st me ere I
    come to hell!   270
   Boling. Urge it no more, my Lord Northum-
    berland.
   North. The commons will not then be sa-
    tisfied.
   K. Rich. They shall be satisfied: I'll read
    enough,
When I do see the very book indeed
Where all my sins are writ, and that's myself.

     Re-enter Attendant, *with a glass.*

Give me the glass, and therein will I read.
No deeper wrinkles yet? hath sorrow struck
So many blows upon this face of mine,
And made no deeper wounds? O flattering glass,
Like to my followers in prosperity,   280

Thou dost beguile me! Was this face the face
That every day under his household roof
Did keep ten thousand men? was this the face
That, like the sun, did make beholders wink?
Was this the face that faced so many follies,
And was at last out-faced by Bolingbroke?
A brittle glory shineth in this face:
As brittle as the glory is the face;
                [*Dashes the glass against the ground.*
For there it is, crack'd in a hundred shivers.
Mark, silent king, the moral of this sport,   290
How soon my sorrow hath destroy'd my face.
    Boling. The shadow of your sorrow hath
        destroy'd
The shadow of your face.
    K. Rich.   Say that again.
The shadow of my sorrow! ha! let's see:
'Tis very true, my grief lies all within;
And these external manners of laments
Are merely shadows to the unseen grief
That swells with silence in the tortured soul;
There lies the substance: and I thank thee,
        king,
For thy great bounty, that not only givest   300
Me cause to wail but teachest me the way
How to lament the cause. I'll beg one boon,
And then be gone and trouble you no more.
Shall I obtain it?
    Boling.   Name it, fair cousin.
    K. Rich. 'Fair cousin'? I am greater than
        a king:
For when I was a king, my flatterers
Were then but subjects; being now a subject,
I have a king here to my flatterer.
Being so great, I have no need to beg.
    Boling. Yet ask.   310
    K. Rich. And shall I have?
    Boling. You shall.
    K. Rich. Then give me leave to go.
    Boling. Whither?
    K. Rich. Whither you will, so I were from
        your sights.
    Boling. Go, some of you convey him to the
        Tower.
 ● *K. Rich.* O, good! convey? conveyers are
        you all,
That rise thus nimbly by a true king's fall.
            [*Exeunt King Richard, some Lords,
                            and a Guard.*
    Boling. On Wednesday next we solemnly set
        down
Our coronation: lords, prepare yourselves.   320
    [*Exeunt all except the Bishop of Carlisle, the
                Abbot of Westminster, and Aumerle.*
    Abbot. A woeful pageant have we here beheld.
    Car. The woe's to come; the children yet
        unborn
Shall feel this day as sharp to them as thorn.
    Aum. You holy clergymen, is there no plot
To rid the realm of this pernicious blot?
    Abbot. My lord,
Before I freely speak my mind herein,
You shall not only take the sacrament
To bury mine intents, but also to effect
Whatever I shall happen to devise.   330
I see your brows are full of discontent,
Your hearts of sorrow and your eyes of tears:
Come home with me to supper; and I'll lay
A plot shall show us all a merry day. [*Exeunt.*

317 *conveyers.* Slang word for 'thieves'.

Aumerle: 'You holy clergymen, is there no plot To rid the realm of this pernicious blot?' Engraving by Kenny Meadows from Barry Cornwall's *The Works of Shakspere*, 1846

2 *ill-erected.* Built for evil purposes.

11 *Ah, thou, the model . . . stand.* Richard, in his present state, is like the ruins of Troy compared to its former greatness.

The lion, king of beasts. Woodcut from *Libellus de Natura Animalium*, a 15th century bestiary

42 *betid.* Past.

43 *quit.* Top, or cap.

ACT V.

SCENE I. *London. A street leading to the Tower.*

Enter QUEEN *and* Ladies.

Queen. This way the king will come; this is the way
To Julius Cæsar's ill-erected tower,
To whose flint bosom my condemned lord
Is doom'd a prisoner by proud Bolingbroke:
Here let us rest; if this rebellious earth
Have any resting for her true king's queen.

Enter RICHARD *and* Guard.

But soft, but see, or rather do not see,
My fair rose wither: yet look up, behold,
That you in pity may dissolve to dew,   9
And wash him fresh again with true-love tears.
Ah, thou, the model where old Troy did stand.
Thou map of honour, thou King Richard's tomb,
And not King Richard; thou most beauteous inn,
Why should hard-favour'd grief be lodged in thee,
When triumph is become an alehouse guest?
    K. Rich. Join not with grief, fair woman, do not so,
To make my end too sudden: learn, good soul,
To think our former state a happy dream;
From which awaked, the truth of what we are
Shows us but this: I am sworn brother, sweet,   20
To grim Necessity, and he and I
Will keep a league till death. Hie thee to France
And cloister thee in some religious house:
Our holy lives must win a new world's crown,
Which our profane hours here have stricken down.
    Queen. What, is my Richard both in shape and mind
Transform'd and weaken'd? hath Bolingbroke deposed
Thine intellect? hath he been in thy heart?
The lion dying thrusteth forth his paw,
And wounds the earth, if nothing else, with rage
To be o'erpower'd; and wilt thou, pupil-like, 31
Take thy correction mildly, kiss the rod,
And fawn on rage with base humility,
Which art a lion and a king of beasts?
    K. Rich. A king of beasts, indeed; if aught but beasts,
I had been still a happy king of men.
Good sometime queen, prepare thee hence for France:
Think I am dead and that even here thou takest,
As from my death-bed, thy last living leave.
In winter's tedious nights sit by the fire   40
With good old folks and let them tell thee tales
Of woeful ages long ago betid;
And ere thou bid good night, to quit their griefs,
Tell thou the lamentable tale of me
And send the hearers weeping to their beds:
For why the senseless brands will sympathize
The heavy accent of thy moving tongue
And in compassion weep the fire out;
And some will mourn in ashes, some coal-black,
For the deposing of a rightful king.   50

Enter NORTHUMBERLAND *and* others.

North. My lord, the mind of Bolingbroke is changed;
You must to Pomfret, not unto the Tower.

And, madam, there is order ta'en for you;
With all swift speed you must away to France.
   K. Rich. Northumberland, thou ladder where-
       withal
The mounting Bolingbroke ascends my throne,
The time shall not be many hours of age
More than it is ere foul sin gathering head
Shall break into corruption: thou shalt think,
Though he divide the realm and give thee half,
It is too little, helping him to all;   61
And he shall think that thou, which know'st the
       way
To plant unrightful kings, wilt know again,
Being ne'er so little urged, another way
To pluck him headlong from the usurped throne.
The love of wicked men converts to fear;
That fear to hate, and hate turns one or both
To worthy danger and deserved death.
   North. My guilt be on my head, and there an
       end.   69
Take leave and part; for you must part forthwith.
   K. Rich. Doubly divorced! Bad men, you
       violate
A twofold marriage, 'twixt my crown and me,
And then betwixt me and my married wife.
Let me unkiss the oath 'twixt thee and me;
And yet not so, for with a kiss 'twas made.
Part us, Northumberland; I towards the north,
● Where shivering cold and sickness pines the clime;
My wife to France: from whence, set forth in
       pomp,
She came adorned hither like sweet May,
● Sent back like Hallowmas or short'st of day. 80
   Queen. And must we be divided? must we part?
   K. Rich. Ay, hand from hand, my love, and
       heart from heart.
   Queen. Banish us both and send the king
       with me.
   North. That were some love but little policy.
   Queen. Then whither he goes, thither let me go.
   K. Rich. So two, together weeping, make
       one woe.
Weep thou for me in France, I for thee here;
● Better far off than near, be ne'er the near.
Go, count thy way with sighs; I mine with groans.
   Queen. So longest way shall have the longest
       moans.   90
   K. Rich. Twice for one step I'll groan, the
       way being short,
And piece the way out with a heavy heart.
Come, come, in wooing sorrow let's be brief,
Since, wedding it, there is such length in grief:
One kiss shall stop our mouths, and dumbly part;
Thus give I mine, and thus take I thy heart.
   Queen. Give me mine own again; 'twere no
       good part
To take on me to keep and kill thy heart.
So, now I have mine own again, be gone,
That I may strive to kill it with a groan.   100
   K. Rich. We make woe wanton with this fond
       delay:
Once more, adieu; the rest let sorrow say.
                 [*Exeunt.*

SCENE II. *The* DUKE OF YORK'S *palace.*

Enter YORK *and his* DUCHESS.

   Duch. My lord, you told me you would tell
       the rest,

77 *pines.* Afflicts.

80 *Hallowmas.* November 1, All Saints' Day.

88 *Better . . . near.* It is better to be far apart, than near
but unable to see each other.

King Richard: 'Once more, adieu; the rest let sorrow
say.' Scene illustration, Princess's Theatre, London,
1857

9 *Which his . . . know.* Which seemed to know the ambitions of its rider.

18–20 *Whilst he . . . countrymen.* See introduction.

Bolingbroke leading Richard into London. Engraving from a painting by James Northcote (1746–1831)

38 *we bound our calm contents.* We submit our wills calmly.

52 *justs.* Jousts.

When weeping made you break the story off,
Of our two cousins coming into London.
   York. Where did I leave?
   Duch.   At that sad stop, my lord,
Where rude misgovern'd hands from windows' tops
Threw dust and rubbish on King Richard's head.
   York. Then, as I said, the duke, great Bolingbroke,
Mounted upon a hot and fiery steed
Which his aspiring rider seem'd to know,
With slow but stately pace kept on his course, 10
Whilst all tongues cried 'God save thee, Bolingbroke!'
You would have thought the very windows spake,
So many greedy looks of young and old
Through casements darted their desiring eyes
Upon his visage, and that all the walls
With painted imagery had said at once
'Jesu preserve thee! welcome, Bolingbroke!'
Whilst he, from the one side to the other turning,
Bareheaded, lower than his proud steed's neck,
Bespake them thus; 'I thank you, countrymen:'
And thus still doing, thus he pass'd along. 21
   Duch. Alack, poor Richard! where rode he the whilst?
   York. As in a theatre, the eyes of men,
After a well-graced actor leaves the stage,
Are idly bent on him that enters next,
Thinking his prattle to be tedious;
Even so, or with much more contempt, men's eyes
Did scowl on gentle Richard; no man cried 'God save him!'
No joyful tongue gave him his welcome home:
But dust was thrown upon his sacred head; 30
Which with such gentle sorrow he shook off,
His face still combating with tears and smiles,
The badges of his grief and patience,
That had not God, for some strong purpose, steel'd
The hearts of men, they must perforce have melted
And barbarism itself have pitied him.
But heaven hath a hand in these events,
To whose high will we bound our calm contents.
To Bolingbroke are we sworn subjects now,
Whose state and honour I for aye allow. 40
   Duch. Here comes my son Aumerle.
   York.   Aumerle that was;
But that is lost for being Richard's friend,
And, madam, you must call him Rutland now:
I am in parliament pledge for his truth
And lasting fealty to the new made king.

       Enter AUMERLE.

   Duch. Welcome, my son: who are the violets now
That strew the green lap of the new come spring?
   Aum. Madam, I know not, nor I greatly care not:
God knows I had as lief be none as one.
   York. Well, bear you well in this new spring of time, 50
Lest you be cropp'd before you come to prime.
What news from Oxford? hold those justs and triumphs?
   Aum. For aught I know, my lord, they do.
   York. You will be there, I know.
   Aum. If God prevent not, I purpose so.
   York. What seal is that, that hangs without thy bosom?
Yea, look'st thou pale? let me see the writing.

Aum. My lord, 'tis nothing.
York.   No matter, then, who see it:
I will be satisfied; let me see the writing.
Aum. I do beseech your grace to pardon me:
It is a matter of small consequence,   61
Which for some reasons I would not have seen.
York. Which for some reasons, sir, I mean
      to see.
I fear, I fear,—
Duch.   What should you fear?
'Tis nothing but some bond, that he is enter'd
      into
For gay apparel 'gainst the triumph day.
York. Bound to himself! what doth he with
      a bond
That he is bound to? Wife, thou art a fool.
Boy, let me see the writing.
Aum. I do beseech you, pardon me; I may
      not show it.   70
York. I will be satisfied; let me see it, I say.
      [*He plucks it out of his bosom and reads it.*
Treason! foul treason! Villain! traitor! slave!
Duch. What is the matter, my lord?
York. Ho! who is within there?

      Enter a Servant.

                         Saddle my horse.
God for his mercy, what treachery is here!
Duch. Why, what is it, my lord?
York. Give me my boots, I say; saddle my
      horse.   [*Exit Servant.*
Now, by mine honour, by my life, by my troth,
● I will appeach the villain.
Duch.   What is the matter?
York. Peace, foolish woman.   80
Duch. I will not peace. What is the matter,
      Aumerle?
Aum. Good mother, be content; it is no
      more
Than my poor life must answer.
Duch.   Thy life answer!
York. Bring me my boots: I will unto the
      king.

      Re-enter Servant *with boots.*

Duch. Strike him, Aumerle. Poor boy, thou
      art amazed.
Hence, villain! never more come in my sight.
York. Give me my boots, I say.
Duch. Why, York, what wilt thou do?
Wilt thou not hide the trespass of thine own?
Have we more sons? or are we like to have? 90
● Is not my teeming date drunk up with time?
And wilt thou pluck my fair son from mine age,
And rob me of a happy mother's name?
Is he not like thee? is he not thine own?
York. Thou fond mad woman,
Wilt thou conceal this dark conspiracy?
A dozen of them here have ta'en the sacrament,
And interchangeably set down their hands,
To kill the king at Oxford.
Duch.   He shall be none; 99
We'll keep him here: then what is that to him?
York. Away, fond woman! were he twenty
      times my son,
I would appeach him.
Duch.   Hadst thou groan'd for him
As I have done, thou wouldst be more pitiful.
But now I know thy mind; thou dost suspect

79 *appeach.* Accuse.

91 *teeming date.* Child-bearing age.

16 *stews.* Brothels.

Gambling in a brothel. From a contemporary woodcut

That I have been disloyal to thy bed,
And that he is a bastard, not thy son:
Sweet York, sweet husband, be not of that mind:
He is as like thee as a man may be,
Not like to me, or any of my kin,
And yet I love him.
　　York.　　　　　Make way, unruly woman! 110
　　　　　　　　　　　　　　　　　　[Exit.
　　Duch. After, Aumerle! mount thee upon his
　　　　horse;
Spur post, and get before him to the king,
And beg thy pardon ere he do accuse thee.
I'll not be long behind; though I be old,
I doubt not but to ride as fast as York:
And never will I rise up from the ground
Till Bolingbroke have pardon'd thee.　Away, be
　　gone!　　　　　　　　　　　　　*[Exeunt.*

SCENE III.　*A royal palace.*

Enter BOLINGBROKE, PERCY, *and other* Lords.

　　Boling.　Can no man tell me of my unthrifty
　　　　son?
'Tis full three months since I did see him last:
If any plague hang over us, 'tis he.
I would to God, my lords, he might be found:
Inquire at London, 'mongst the taverns there,
For there, they say, he daily doth frequent,
With unrestrained loose companions,
Even such, they say, as stand in narrow lanes,
And beat our watch, and rob our passengers;
Which he, young wanton and effeminate boy, 10
Takes on the point of honour to support
So dissolute a crew.
　　Percy.　My lord, some two days since I saw
　　　　the prince,
And told him of those triumphs held at Oxford.
　　Boling.　And what said the gallant?
　　Percy.　His answer was, he would unto the
　　　　stews,
And from the common'st creature pluck a glove,
And wear it as a favour; and with that
He would unhorse the lustiest challenger.
　　Boling.　As dissolute as desperate; yet through
　　　　both　　　　　　　　　　　　　　　　20
I see some sparks of better hope, which elder
　　years
May happily bring forth.　But who comes here?

Enter AUMERLE.

　　Aum.　Where is the king?
　　Boling.　What means our cousin, that he stares
　　　　and looks
So wildly?
　　Aum.　God save your grace! I do beseech
　　　　your majesty,
To have some conference with your grace alone.
　　Boling.　Withdraw yourselves, and leave us
　　　　here alone.　　[*Exeunt Percy and Lords.*
What is the matter with our cousin now?
　　Aum.　For ever may my knees grow to the
　　　　earth,　　　　　　　　　　　　　　30
My tongue cleave to my roof within my mouth,
Unless a pardon ere I rise or speak.
　　Boling.　Intended or committed was this fault?
If on the first, how heinous e'er it be,
To win thy after-love I pardon thee.
　　Aum.　Then give me leave that I may turn
　　　　the key,

That no man enter till my tale be done.
  Boling. Have thy desire.
  York. [*Within*] My liege, beware: look to thyself;
Thou hast a traitor in thy presence there.   40
  Boling. Villain, I'll make thee safe.
                                    [*Drawing.*
  Aum. Stay, thy revengeful hand; thou hast no cause to fear.
  York. [*Within*] Open the door, secure, foolhardy king:
Shall I for love speak treason to thy face?
Open the door, or I will break it open.

Enter YORK.

  Boling. What is the matter, uncle? speak;
Recover breath; tell us how near is danger,
That we may arm us to encounter it.
  York. Peruse this writing here, and thou shalt know
The treason that my haste forbids me show.   50
  Aum. Remember, as thou read'st, thy promise pass'd:
I do repent me; read not my name there;
My heart is not confederate with my hand.
  York. It was, villain, ere thy hand did set it down.
I tore it from the traitor's bosom, king;
Fear, and not love, begets his penitence:
Forget to pity him, lest thy pity prove
A serpent that will sting thee to the heart.
  Boling. O heinous, strong and bold conspiracy!
O loyal father of a treacherous son!   60
Thou sheer, immaculate and silver fountain,
From whence this stream through muddy passages
Hath held his current and defiled himself!
Thy overflow of good converts to bad,
And thy abundant goodness shall excuse
• This deadly blot in thy digressing son.
  York. So shall my virtue be his vice's bawd;
And he shall spend mine honour with his shame,
As thriftless sons their scraping fathers' gold.
Mine honour lives when his dishonour dies,   70
Or my shamed life in his dishonour lies:
Thou kill'st me in his life; giving him breath,
The traitor lives, the true man 's put to death.
  Duch. [*Within*] What ho, my liege! for God's sake, let me in.
  Boling. What shrill-voiced suppliant makes this eager cry?
  Duch. A woman, and thy aunt, great king; 'tis I.
Speak with me, pity me, open the door:
A beggar begs that never begg'd before.
  Boling. Our scene is alter'd from a serious thing,
• And now changed to 'The Beggar and the King.'
My dangerous cousin, let your mother in: 81
I know she is come to pray for your foul sin.
  York. If thou do pardon, whosoever pray,
More sins for this forgiveness prosper may.
This fester'd joint cut off, the rest rest sound;
This let alone will all the rest confound.

Enter DUCHESS.

  Duch. O king, believe not this hard-hearted man!
• Love loving not itself none other can.

Aumerle: 'Stay thy revengeful hand . . .' Drawing by John M. Wright (1777–1866)

66 *digressing.* Transgressing.

80 '*The Beggar and the King*'. Shakespeare several times refers to the ballad of King Cophetua and a beggar-maid.

88 *loving not itself.* If York cannot even love his own son.

119 *'pardonne moi'*. 'Excuse me' i.e. for not granting pardon.

128 *rehearse*. Pronounce.

Bolingbroke: 'I pardon him, as God shall pardon me.'
Engraving from Bell's edition of *Shakespeare*, 1773

140 *powers*. Bodies of troops.

York. Thou frantic woman, what dost thou make here?
Shall thy old dugs once more a traitor rear? 90
  Duch. Sweet York, be patient. Hear me, gentle liege. [*Kneels.*
  Boling. Rise up, good aunt.
  Duch.   Not yet, I thee beseech:
For ever will I walk upon my knees,
And never see day that the happy sees,
Till thou give joy; until thou bid me joy,
By pardoning Rutland, my transgressing boy.
  Aum. Unto my mother's prayers I bend my knee.
  York. Against them both my true joints bended be.
Ill mayst thou thrive, if thou grant any grace!
  Duch. Pleads he in earnest? look upon his face; 100
His eyes do drop no tears, his prayers are in jest;
His words come from his mouth, ours from our breast:
He prays but faintly and would be denied;
We pray with heart and soul and all beside:
His weary joints would gladly rise, I know;
Our knees shall kneel till to the ground they grow:
His prayers are full of false hypocrisy;
Ours of true zeal and deep integrity.
Our prayers do out-pray his; then let them have
That mercy which true prayer ought to have. 110
  Boling. Good aunt, stand up.
  Duch.   Nay, do not say, 'stand up;'
Say 'pardon' first, and afterwards 'stand up.'
An if I were thy nurse, thy tongue to teach,
'Pardon' should be the first word of thy speech.
I never long'd to hear a word till now;
Say 'pardon,' king; let pity teach thee how:
The word is short, but not so short as sweet;
No word like 'pardon' for kings' mouths so meet.
  York. Speak it in French, king; say, 'pardonne moi.'
  Duch. Dost thou teach pardon pardon to destroy? 120
Ah, my sour husband, my hard-hearted lord,
That set'st the word itself against the word!
Speak 'pardon' as 'tis current in our land;
The chopping French we do not understand.
Thine eye begins to speak; set thy tongue there;
Or in thy piteous heart plant thou thine ear;
That hearing how our plaints and prayers do pierce,
Pity may move thee 'pardon' to rehearse.
  Boling. Good aunt, stand up.
  Duch.   I do not sue to stand;
Pardon is all the suit I have in hand. 130
  Boling. I pardon him, as God shall pardon me.
  Duch. O happy vantage of a kneeling knee!
Yet am I sick for fear: speak it again;
Twice saying 'pardon' doth not pardon twain,
But makes one pardon strong.
  Boling.   With all my heart
I pardon him.
  Duch.   A god on earth thou art.
  Boling. But for our trusty brother-in-law and the abbot,
With all the rest of that consorted crew,
Destruction straight shall dog them at the heels.
Good uncle, help to order several powers 140
To Oxford, or where'er these traitors are:
They shall not live within this world, I swear,

But I will have them, if I once know where.
Uncle, farewell: and, cousin too, adieu:
Your mother well hath pray'd, and prove you true.
 Duch. Come, my old son: I pray God make
 thee new. [*Exeunt.*

SCENE IV. *The same.*

Enter EXTON *and* Servant.

Exton. Didst thou not mark the king, what
 words he spake,
'Have I no friend will rid me of this living fear?'
Was it not so?
 Ser. These were his very words.
 Exton. 'Have I no friend?' quoth he: he
 spake it twice,
And urged it twice together, did he not?
 Serv. He did.
 Exton. And speaking it, he wistly look'd
 on me;
As who should say, 'I would thou wert the man
That would divorce this terror from my heart;'
Meaning the king at Pomfret. Come, let's go: 10
I am the king's friend, and will rid his foe.
 [*Exeunt.*

SCENE V. *Pomfret castle.*

Enter KING RICHARD.

K. Rich. I have been studying how I may
 compare
This prison where I live unto the world:
And for because the world is populous
And here is not a creature but myself,
I cannot do it; yet I'll hammer it out.
My brain I'll prove the female to my soul,
My soul the father; and these two beget
A generation of still-breeding thoughts,
And these same thoughts people this little world,
In humours like the people of this world, 10
For no thought is contented. The better sort,
As thoughts of things divine, are intermix'd
With scruples and do set the word itself
Against the word:
As thus, 'Come, little ones,' and then again,
'It is as hard to come as for a camel
To thread the postern of a small needle's eye.'
Thoughts tending to ambition, they do plot
Unlikely wonders; how these vain weak nails
May tear a passage through the flinty ribs 20
Of this hard world, my ragged prison walls,
And, for they cannot, die in their own pride.
Thoughts tending to content flatter themselves
That they are not the first of fortune's slaves,
Nor shall not be the last; like silly beggars
Who sitting in the stocks refuge their shame,
That many have and others must sit there;
And in this thought they find a kind of ease,
Bearing their own misfortunes on the back
Of such as have before endured the like. 30
Thus play I in one person many people,
And none contented: sometimes am I king;
Then treasons make me wish myself a beggar,
And so I am: then crushing penury
Persuades me I was better when a king;
Then am I king'd again: and by and by
Think that I am unking'd by Bolingbroke,
And straight am nothing: but whate'er I be,
Nor I nor any man that but man is

7 *wistly.* Wistfully.

8 *still-breeding.* Ever-breeding.

13 *the word.* Scriptures.

17 *postern.* Small back gate.

21 *ragged.* Rugged.

26 *refuge.* Take refuge from.

King Richard: 'Then treasons make me wish myself a beggar . . .' Woodcut of a beggar in Elizabethan times

43 *broke.* Out of rhythm. *proportion.* The correct time value of the notes.

46 *check.* Prevent. *disorder'd string.* Out of tune stringed instrument.

51 *jar.* Jerk.

60 *Jack o' the clock.* The figure that strikes the hour.

Jack o' the clock. Engraving by F.W. Fairholt from J.O. Halliwell's edition of Shakespeare's works (1853–65)

67–68 *royal . . . noble . . . ten groats.* The difference in value between the coins; a *royal* and a *noble* were worth ten groats.

94 *jauncing.* A movement from a rider that causes a horse to prance.

With nothing shall be pleased, till he be eased 40
With being nothing. Music do I hear? [*Music.*
Ha, ha! keep time: how sour sweet music is,
● When time is broke and no proportion kept!
So is it in the music of men's lives.
And here have I the daintiness of ear
● To check time broke in a disorder'd string;
But for the concord of my state and time
Had not an ear to hear my true time broke.
I wasted time, and now doth time waste me;
For now hath time made me his numbering
    clock: 50
● My thoughts are minutes; and with sighs they
    jar
Their watches on unto mine eyes, the outward
    watch,
Whereto my finger, like a dial's point,
Is pointing still, in cleansing them from tears.
Now sir, the sound that tells what hour it is
Are clamorous groans, which strike upon my
    heart,
Which is the bell: so sighs and tears and groans
Show minutes, times, and hours: but my time
Runs posting on in Bolingbroke's proud joy,
● While I stand fooling here, his Jack o' the clock.
This music mads me; let it sound no more;   61
For though it have holp madmen to their wits,
In me it seems it will make wise men mad.
Yet blessing on his heart that gives it me!
For 'tis a sign of love; and love to Richard
Is a strange brooch in this all-hating world.

Enter a Groom of the Stable.

● *Groom.* Hail, royal prince!
    K. Rich.   Thanks, noble peer;
The cheapest of us is ten groats too dear.
What art thou? and how comest thou hither,
Where no man never comes but that sad dog 70
That brings me food to make misfortune live?
    Groom. I was a poor groom of thy stable, king,
When thou wert king; who, travelling towards
    York,
With much ado at length have gotten leave
To look upon my sometimes royal master's face.
O, how it yearn'd my heart when I beheld
In London streets, that coronation-day,
When Bolingbroke rode on roan Barbary,
That horse that thou so often hast bestrid,
That horse that I so carefully have dress'd!   80
    K. Rich. Rode he on Barbary? Tell me,
    gentle friend,
How went he under him?
    Groom. So proudly as if he disdain'd the
    ground.
    K. Rich. So proud that Bolingbroke was on
    his back!
That jade hath eat bread from my royal hand;
This hand hath made him proud with clapping
    him.
Would he not stumble? would he not fall down,
Since pride must have a fall, and break the neck
Of that proud man that did usurp his back?
Forgiveness, horse! why do I rail on thee,   90
Since thou, created to be awed by man,
Wast born to bear? I was not made a horse;
And yet I bear a burthen like an ass,
● Spurr'd, gall'd and tired by jauncing Boling-
    broke.

Enter Keeper, *with a dish.*

Keep. Fellow, give place; here is no longer
  stay.
K. Rich. If thou love me, 'tis time thou wert
  away.
Groom. What my tongue dares not, that my
  heart shall say.   [*Exit.*
Keep. My lord, will't please you to fall to?
K. Rich. Taste of it first, as thou art wont
  to do.   99
Keep. My lord, I dare not: Sir Pierce of Ex-
ton, who lately came from the king, commands
the contrary.
K. Rich. The devil take Henry of Lancaster
  and thee!
Patience is stale, and I am weary of it.
                            [*Beats the keeper.*
Keep. Help, help, help!

Enter EXTON *and* Servants, *armed.*

K. Rich. How now! what means death in
  this rude assault?
Villain, thy own hand yields thy death's instru-
  ment.
    [*Snatching an axe from a Servant and kill-
                              ing him.*
Go thou, and fill another room in hell.
    [*He kills another. Then Exton strikes him
                             down.*
That hand shall burn in never-quenching fire
That staggers thus my person. Exton, thy fierce
  hand   110
Hath with the king's blood stain'd the king's own
  land.
Mount, mount, my soul! thy seat is up on high;
Whilst my gross flesh sinks downward, here to
  die.   [*Dies.*
Exton. As full of valour as of royal blood:
Both have I spill'd; O would the deed were
  good!
For now the devil, that told me I did well,
Says that this deed is chronicled in hell.
This dead king to the living king I'll bear:
Take hence the rest, and give them burial here.
                                [*Exeunt.*

SCENE VI. *Windsor castle.*

Flourish. Enter BOLINGBROKE, YORK, *with
  other* Lords, *and* Attendants.

Boling. Kind uncle York, the latest news we
  hear
Is that the rebels have consumed with fire
Our town of Cicester in Gloucestershire;
But whether they be ta'en or slain we hear not.

Enter NORTHUMBERLAND.

Welcome, my lord: what is the news?
North. First, to thy sacred state wish I all
  happiness.
The next news is, I have to London sent
The heads of Oxford, Salisbury, Blunt, and Kent:
The manner of their taking may appear
At large discoursed in this paper here.   10
Boling. We thank thee, gentle Percy, for thy
  pains;
And to thy worth will add right worthy gains.

110 *staggers.* Causes to stagger.

The murder of Richard II. Engraving from a painting by
Francis Wheatley (1749–1801)

Enter FITZWATER.

Fitz. My lord, I have from Oxford sent to London
The heads of Brocas and Sir Bennet Seely,
Two of the dangerous consorted traitors
That sought at Oxford thy dire overthrow.
   Boling. Thy pains, Fitzwater, shall not be forgot;
Right noble is thy merit, well I wot.

Enter PERCY, *and the* BISHOP OF CARLISLE.

Percy. The grand conspirator, Abbot of Westminster,
With clog of conscience and sour melancholy   20
Hath yielded up his body to the grave;
But here is Carlisle living, to abide
Thy kingly doom and sentence of his pride.
   Boling. Carlisle, this is your doom:
Choose out some secret place, some reverend room,
More than thou hast, and with it joy thy life;
So as thou livest in peace, die free from strife:
For though mine enemy thou hast ever been,
High sparks of honour in thee have I seen.

Enter EXTON, *with persons bearing a coffin.*

Exton. Great king, within this coffin I present   30
Thy buried fear: herein all breathless lies
The mightiest of thy greatest enemies,
Richard of Bordeaux, by me hither brought.
   Boling. Exton, I thank thee not; for thou hast wrought
A deed of slander with thy fatal hand
Upon my head and all this famous land.
   Exton. From your own mouth, my lord, did I this deed.
   Boling. They love not poison that do poison need,
Nor do I thee: though I did wish him dead,
I hate the murderer, love him murdered.   40
The guilt of conscience take thou for thy labour,
But neither my good word nor princely favour:
With Cain go wander thorough shades of night,
And never show thy head by day nor light.
Lords, I protest, my soul is full of woe,
That blood should sprinkle me to make me grow:
Come, mourn with me for that I do lament,
● And put on sullen black incontinent:
I'll make a voyage to the Holy Land,
To wash this blood off from my guilty hand: 50
March sadly after; grace my mournings here;
In weeping after this untimely bier.   [*Exeunt.*

48 *incontinent.* At once.

Opposite: Richard II with his patron saints, John the Baptist, Edward the Confessor and Edmund king and martyr. From the Wilton Diptych, French School, *c.*1395

King John

1596

KING JOHN is different again from *Richard II*, though linked to it by the patriotic speeches about England and the sea, given to Richard Coeur-de-Lion's Bastard Faulconbridge, which echo those of Gaunt in the previous play. Where that was a lyrical tragedy, *King John* is a straight chronicle play. It is also coupled with *Richard II* in language, in particular, as we have noticed, by the feature of rhyming sestets which occur in both.

Right: *Frontispiece to* King John, *from Charles Knight's* Pictorial Edition of the Works of Shakspere, *1839–42*

Far right: *This 17th century portrait is thought to be that of King John, who reigned 1199–1216*

King John is a mature play, even more so than its predecessor: in characterisation, with the powerful characters of the Bastard and Constance, young Arthur's mother. And it is mature in language and in thought; the Bastard's famous speech on Commodity, i.e. political convenience or expediency, is of a very mature order, as is his engaging, candid cynicism in general. So also is the convoluted casuistry of Cardinal Pandulph, verging on sophistry. This is not an early play.

Indeed we have an indication of date in the reference –

> So, by a roaring tempest on the flood,
> A whole armado of convicted sail
> Is scattered and disjoined from fellowship.

This is precisely what happened to the second Armada, of the late summer of 1596, which was dispersed by tempest before it reached the English coast.

There had been plays on the subject of King John before, going back to the Protestant rant of the ex-friar John Bale. The subject was an obvious one in the common stock of subjects and themes from the English past, which expressed Elizabethan national pride and Renaissance self-consciousness. Shakespeare took an anonymous play ready to hand, *The Troublesome Reign of John, King of England*, and based himself on that. Holinshed also was drawn upon, with Foxe's *Martyrs* and the Book of Homilies read in church. His real source, as with any creative writer, was his total knowledge and experience, and his genius made a very different thing from his reading.

One thing that is remarkable, and very characteristic of him – we are given none of the Protestant tirades of the time, much to the fore in Foxe. Shakespeare was interested in neither the religious or political propaganda of the age; in that way he was a safe writer, who never got into trouble. This bespoke his nature; not only his courtly tact – he was above the vulgar passions that agitated superficial persons. His passion was human beings in their essence, their characters and conflicts, man as such.

The Bastard. Thus we have an outstanding portrayal of a very manly man in Coeur-de-Lion's Bastard. It is obvious that Shakespeare created him with affection – he is more real to us than anybody in the play, with his downright, rather colloquial language: a no-nonsense fellow, akin to the too masculine Hotspur in *1 Henry IV*. The Bastard, from the fact of his birth, is an Outsider; this gives him the angle from which to observe society, its conventions and pretences. His first long speech is a comment on Elizabethan society much to the point, with its

> dialogue of compliment,
> And talking of the Alps and Appenines,
> The Pyrennean and the River Po –

this was 'worshipful', i.e. upper-class, society. It fitted his 'mounting spirit', his aim to move upwards, very well;

> For he is but a bastard to the time
> That doth not smack of observation.

The precise meaning of this is a little difficult for us to catch; it suggests that to move up in society we must pay attention to what other people are up to.

With regard to them the Bastard has no illusions, as his speech on Commodity, the most famous in the play, makes clear. Commodity means people's self-interest, the sense of their own advantage and convenience, what they can gain, which deflects them from the straight course of justice and virtue, and makes the world run with the bias. (The image is from the gentlemanly game of bowls.) The world's bent this way

> Makes it take head from all indifferency,

i.e. deflects it from impartiality, always in the direction of self-interest. The Bastard has the candour to ask why he himself rails so against Commodity, and answers:

> But for because he hath not wooed me yet.

Such candid self-knowledge is rare and charms us. The importance of his diagnosis for the action is that

> Since kings break faith upon Commodity,
> *Gain*, be my lord – for I will worship thee!

This incorporates Shakespeare's mature thought about society – it hardly differs from Karl Marx or Pareto on the subject. The Bastard's attitude on the humbug bandied about by the great – by the King of France, the Duke of Austria and Cardinal Pandulph, the Legate from Rome – on the political issues, King John's heretical taking of Church lands and his nephew's inheritance, his willingness to patch up a peace at his nephew's expense – is three times expressed thus:

> And hang a calf's-skin on his recreant limbs.

A calf's-skin was the fool's livery, and this is what the Bastard awards those eminent politicians, humbugs all. For, of course, they do not care about the rights and wrongs of poor young Arthur, for all that he was the son and heir of John's older brother: the boy is but a pawn in the world's game of political Commodity.

Constance and Arthur. Constance, Arthur's widowed mother, reacts against the trafficking and bargaining, the *Kuh-handel*, with natural resentment. Her character too is fully developed; it progresses from her forlorn widowed state to apprehension, then anger and resentment at betrayal; lastly, driven crazy by grief, she becomes a virago like Queen Margaret in the earlier plays.

The boy Arthur is charmingly portrayed, if a trifle too knowingly for our taste: that and the sentiment of his appeal to Hubert not to put out his eyes had strong appeal to the emotional Elizabethan audience. There must have been two well-trained boy-actors for these parts.

For us, who realise what was behind the boy's death, it has a more affecting appeal; for this summer saw the death of Shakespeare's own, and only, boy at Stratford at the age of eleven.

> Grief fills the room up of my absent child,
> Lies in his bed, walks up and down with me,
> Puts on his pretty looks, repeats his words,
> Remembers me of all his gracious parts,
> Stuffs out his vacant garments with his form.

Prince Arthur and Hubert. A 19th century engraving from a painting by L.J. Pott (1837–98)

The mother asks the Cardinal, who after all was a priest, whether it is true

> That we shall see and know our friends in heaven.
> If that be true, I shall see my boy again.

This is the father in William Shakespeare speaking; that Stratford was in his mind, or possibly he was writing at Stratford, we can tell – for immediately after talk of young Arthur's death, we have:

> I saw a smith stand with his hammer, thus,
> The whilst his iron did on the anvil cool,
> With open mouth swallowing a tailor's news;
> Who, with his shears and measure in his hand,
> Standing on slippers which his nimble haste
> Had falsely thrust upon contrary feet.

A neighbour in Henley Street was Hornby, the blacksmith; was there a tailor there too? Not improbably.

Personal. Other personal touches bespeak him. We are accustomed to the frequent images from his profession. The men of Angers

> . . . stand securely on their battlements
> As in a theatre, whence they gape and point
> At your industrious scenes and acts of death.

The soldiers on the battlements, so frequently referred to in these warring plays, would be up in the gallery looking down on the stage.

We have often noted his liking for grand, resounding words: 'expedient' march for swift march; 'his marches are expedient to this town'; for words ending in 'ure', ceinture, rondure, expressure. We have comments characteristic of him:

> For new-made honour doth forget men's names.

Again,

> Let not the world see fear and sad distrust
> Govern the motion of a kingly eye;

for 'inferior eyes borrow their behaviours from the great'. The 'lusty English' are described as 'like a jolly troop of huntsmen'. More important is the phrase that expresses Elizabethan thought on the soul:

> . . . his pure brain,
> Which some suppose the soul's frail dwelling-house.

Patriotism is the main argument of the play. The internal division between King John and his barons, plus the King's defiance of Rome, exposed the country to the French invasion. No opportunity is taken to inveigh against Rome, though the Legate Pandulph's statement of the issue is exposed as a tissue of unconvincing sophistry. A little expression is given to anti-French sentiment, notably the inconstancy imputed to the French and their readiness to break oaths. This reflected once more the bad impression made by Henry of Navarre's desertion of the Protestant cause.

Several salutes to England's chief defence in the sea, and the spirit of adventure overseas, are completely in line with the country's mood in the 1580's and early 1590's:

> . . . that pale, that white-faced shore
> Whose foot spurns back the ocean's roaring tides
> And coops from other lands her islanders.

The islanders were adventuring abroad, voyaging, marauding, colonising, joining expeditions to fight on the Continent:

> . . . all the unsettled humours of the land,
> Rash, inconsiderate, fiery, voluntaries . . .
> Have sold their fortunes at their native homes,
> Bearing their birthrights proudly on their backs,
> To make a hazard of new fortunes here.

This was not only a commonplace of the time but common experience.

The moral of the play is that of all the early historical plays and is the expression of the nation's mood in the struggle with Spain: in unity lies strength, internal dissension exposes the country to social disorder and, in *King John*, to foreign invasion. The theme is set out in speeches which are a direct continuation of those of Gaunt in *Richard II*. The concluding lines summing up the play are justly famous:

> This England never did, nor never shall,
> Lie at the proud foot of a conqueror
> But when it first did help to wound itself . . .
> Come the three corners of the world in arms
> And we shall shock them! Naught shall make us rue
> If England to itself do rest but true!

Text. The play was first printed in the First Folio, and offers no problem. The absence of earlier printed versions or records of performance indicate that it was not one of the most popular plays.

THE LIFE AND DEATH OF
KING JOHN.

DRAMATIS PERSONÆ.

KING JOHN.
PRINCE HENRY, son to the king.
ARTHUR, Duke of Bretagne, nephew to the king.
The Earl of PEMBROKE.
The Earl of ESSEX.
The Earl of SALISBURY.
The Lord BIGOT.
HUBERT DE BURGH.
ROBERT FAULCONBRIDGE, son to Sir Robert Faulconbridge.
PHILIP the BASTARD, his half-brother.
JAMES GURNEY, servant to Lady Faulconbridge.
PETER of Pomfret, a prophet.

PHILIP, King of France.

LEWIS, the Dauphin.
LYMOGES, Duke of AUSTRIA.
CARDINAL PANDULPH, the Pope's legate.
MELUN, a French Lord.
CHATILLON, ambassador from France to King John.

QUEEN ELINOR, mother to King John.
CONSTANCE, mother to Arthur.
BLANCH of Spain, niece to King John.
LADY FAULCONBRIDGE.

Lords, Citizens of Angiers, Sheriff, Heralds, Officers, Soldiers, Messengers, and other Attendants.

SCENE: *Partly in England, and partly in France.*

ACT I.

SCENE I. KING JOHN'S *palace.*

Enter KING JOHN, QUEEN ELINOR, PEMBROKE, ESSEX, SALISBURY, *and others, with* CHATILLON.

 K. John. Now, say, Chatillon, what would France with us?
 Chat. Thus, after greeting, speaks the King of France
• In my behaviour to the majesty,
The borrow'd majesty, of England here.
 Eli. A strange beginning: 'borrow'd majesty!'
 K. John. Silence, good mother; hear the embassy.
 Chat. Philip of France, in right and true behalf
Of thy deceased brother Geffrey's son,
Arthur Plantagenet, lays most lawful claim
To this fair island and the territories, 10
To Ireland, Poictiers, Anjou, Touraine, Maine,
Desiring thee to lay aside the sword
Which sways usurpingly these several titles,
And put the same into young Arthur's hand,
Thy nephew and right royal sovereign.
 K. John. What follows if we disallow of this?
• *Chat.* The proud control of fierce and bloody war,
To enforce these rights so forcibly withheld.
 K. John. Here have we war for war and blood for blood,
Controlment for controlment: so answer France.

• *A bullet beside a text line indicates an annotation in the opposite column*

3 *In my behaviour.* Through me.

17 *proud control.* Compulsion.

The coat of arms and supporters of King John

Opposite: Prince Arthur pleads for his life. Painting by George Harlow (1787–1819)

Above: King John out hunting. *Right:* King John receives a cup. Engravings from a medieval manuscript

---

37 *manage.* Government.

Chat. Then take my king's defiance from my
    mouth,   21
The farthest limit of my embassy.
   K. John. Bear mine to him, and so depart in
    peace:
Be thou as lightning in the eyes of France;
For ere thou canst report I will be there,
The thunder of my cannon shall be heard:
So hence! Be thou the trumpet of our wrath
And sullen presage of your own decay.
An honourable conduct let him have:
Pembroke, look to't.   Farewell, Chatillon.   30
     [Exeunt Chatillon and Pembroke.
   Eli. What now, my son! have I not ever said
How that ambitious Constance would not cease
Till she had kindled France and all the world,
Upon the right and party of her son?
This might have been prevented and made whole
With very easy arguments of love,
● Which now the manage of two kingdoms must
With fearful bloody issue arbitrate.
   K. John. Our strong possession and our right
    for us.
   Eli. Your strong possession much more than
    your right,   40
Or else it must go wrong with you and me:
So much my conscience whispers in your ear,
Which none but heaven and you and I shall hear.

      Enter a Sheriff.

   Essex. My liege, here is the strangest con-
    troversy
Come from the country to be judged by you
That e'er I heard: shall I produce the men?
   K. John. Let them approach.
Our abbeys and our priories shall pay
This expedition's charge.

Enter Robert Faulconbridge, *and* Philip *his
    bastard brother.*

           What men are you?
   Bast. Your faithful subject I, a gentleman   50
Born in Northamptonshire and eldest son,

As I suppose, to Robert Faulconbridge,
A soldier, by the honour-giving hand
● Of Cœur-de-lion knighted in the field.
    K. John. What art thou?
    Rob. The son and heir to that same Faulcon-
      bridge.
    K. John. Is that the elder, and art thou the
      heir?
You came not of one mother then, it seems.
    Bast. Most certain of one mother, mighty king;
That is well known; and, as I think, one father:
But for the certain knowledge of that truth   61
I put you o'er to heaven and to my mother:
Of that I doubt, as all men's children may.
    Eli. Out on thee, rude man! thou dost shame
      thy mother
● And wound her honour with this diffidence.
    Bast. I, madam? no, I have no reason for it;
That is my brother's plea and none of mine;
The which if he can prove, a' pops me out
At least from fair five hundred pound a year:
Heaven guard my mother's honour and my land!
    K. John. A good blunt fellow. Why, being
      younger born,   71
Doth he lay claim to thine inheritance?
    Bast. I know not why, except to get the land.
But once he slander'd me with bastardy:
But whether I be as true begot or no,
That still I lay upon my mother's head,
But that I am as well begot, my liege,—
● Fair fall the bones that took the pains for me!—
Compare our faces and be judge yourself.
If old sir Robert did beget us both   80
And were our father and this son like him,
O old sir Robert, father, on my knee
I give heaven thanks I was not like to thee!
    K. John. Why, what a madcap hath heaven
      lent us here!
    Eli. He hath a trick of Cœur-de-lion's face;
The accent of his tongue affecteth him.
Do you not read some tokens of my son
In the large composition of this man?
    K. John. Mine eye hath well examined his
      parts
And finds them perfect Richard. Sirrah, speak, 90
What doth move you to claim your brother's land?
●   *Bast.* Because he hath a half-face, like my
      father.
With half that face would he have all my land:
● A half-faced groat five hundred pound a year!
    Rob. My gracious liege, when that my father
      lived,
Your brother did employ my father much,—
    Bast. Well, sir, by this you cannot get my
      land:
Your tale must be how he employ'd my mother.
    Rob. And once dispatch'd him in an embassy
To Germany, there with the emperor   100
To treat of high affairs touching that time.
The advantage of his absence took the king
And in the mean time sojourn'd at my father's;
Where how he did prevail I shame to speak,
But truth is truth: large lengths of seas and
    shores
Between my father and my mother lay,
As I have heard my father speak himself,
When this same lusty gentleman was got.
Upon his death-bed he by will bequeath'd
His lands to me, and took it on his death   110

Effigy of Richard I. Engraving by F.W. Fairholt from
J.O. Halliwell's edition of Shakespeare's works, 1853–65

54 *Cœur-de-lion.* Richard I, 'the Lionheart', was John's
elder brother.

65 *diffidence.* Distrust.

78 *Fair fall . . . me!* Good fortune befall the man (or his
bones now he's dead) that took the trouble to beget me.

92 *half-face.* Both a 'profile' and a 'thin face'.

94 *half-faced groat.* A coin with the profile of the ruler.

143 *three-farthings*. This coin had a rose behind the queen's head.

147 *Nob*. A familiar form of Robert, but also a sexual pun on 'knob'.

Elinor: 'I like thee well . . .' Kate Crane as Queen Elinor, Her Majesty's Theatre, London, 1899

169 *not by truth*. Not through chastity.

That this my mother's son was none of his;
And if he were, he came into the world
Full fourteen weeks before the course of time.
Then, good my liege, let me have what is mine,
My father's land, as was my father's will.
  K. John. Sirrah, your brother is legitimate;
Your father's wife did after wedlock bear him,
And if she did play false, the fault was hers;
Which fault lies on the hazards of all husbands
That marry wives. Tell me, how if my brother,
Who, as you say, took pains to get this son, 121
Had of your father claim'd this son for his?
In sooth, good friend, your father might have kept
This calf bred from his cow from all the world;
In sooth he might; then, if he were my brother's,
My brother might not claim him; nor your father,
Being none of his, refuse him: this concludes;
My mother's son did get your father's heir;
Your father's heir must have your father's land.
  Rob. Shall then my father's will be of no
    force 130
To dispossess that child which is not his?
  Bast. Of no more force to dispossess me, sir,
Than was his will to get me, as I think.
  Eli. Whether hadst thou rather be a Faul-
    conbridge
And like thy brother, to enjoy thy land,
Or the reputed son of Cœur-de-lion,
Lord of thy presence and no land beside?
  Bast. Madam, an if my brother had my shape,
And I had his, sir Robert's his, like him;
And if my legs were two such riding-rods, 140
My arms such eel-skins stuff'd, my face so thin
That in mine ear I durst not stick a rose
• Lest men should say 'Look, where three-farthings
    goes!'
And, to his shape, were heir to all this land,
Would I might never stir from off this place,
I would give it every foot to have this face;
• I would not be sir Nob in any case.
  Eli. I like thee well: wilt thou forsake thy
    fortune,
Bequeath thy land to him and follow me?
I am a soldier and now bound to France. 150
  Bast. Brother, take you my land, I'll take
    my chance.
Your face hath got five hundred pound a year,
Yet sell your face for five pence and 'tis dear.
Madam, I'll follow you unto the death.
  Eli. Nay, I would have you go before me
    thither.
  Bast. Our country manners give our betters
    way.
  K. John. What is thy name?
  Bast. Philip, my liege, so is my name begun;
Philip, good old sir Robert's wife's eldest son.
  K. John. From henceforth bear his name
    whose form thou bear'st: 160
Kneel thou down Philip, but rise more great,
Arise sir Richard and Plantagenet.
  Bast. Brother by the mother's side, give me
    your hand:
My father gave me honour, yours gave land.
Now blessed be the hour, by night or day,
When I was got, sir Robert was away!
  Eli. The very spirit of Plantagenet!
I am thy grandam, Richard; call me so.
• *Bast.* Madam, by chance but not by truth;
    what though?

Something about, a little from the right, 170
  In at the window, or else o'er the hatch:
Who dares not stir by day must walk by night,
  And have is have, however men do catch:
Near or far off, well won is still well shot,
And I am I, howe'er I was begot.
  K. John. Go, Faulconbridge: now hast thou
    thy desire;
A landless knight makes thee a landed squire.
Come, madam, and come, Richard, we must
    speed
For France, for France, for it is more than need.
  Bast. Brother, adieu: good fortune come to
    thee! 180
For thou wast got i' the way of honesty.
                    [*Exeunt all but Bastard.*
A foot of honour better than I was;
But many a many foot of land the worse.
Well, now can I make any Joan a lady.
'Good den, sir Richard!'—'God-a-mercy, fel-
    low!'—
And if his name be George, I'll call him Peter;
For new-made honour doth forget men's names;
'Tis too respective and too sociable
For your conversion. Now your traveller,
He and his toothpick at my worship's mess, 190
And when my knightly stomach is sufficed,
Why then I suck my teeth and catechize .
My picked man of countries: 'My dear sir,'
Thus, leaning on mine elbow, I begin,
'I shall beseech you'—that is question now;
And then comes answer like an Absey book:
'O sir,' says answer, 'at your best command;
At your employment; at your service, sir:'
'No, sir,' says question, 'I, sweet sir, at yours:'
And so, ere answer knows what question would,
Saving in dialogue of compliment, 201
And talking of the Alps and Apennines,
The Pyrenean and the river Po,
It draws toward supper in conclusion so.
But this is worshipful society
And fits the mounting spirit like myself,
For he is but a bastard to the time
That doth not smack of observation;
And so am I, whether I smack or no;
And not alone in habit and device, 210
Exterior form, outward accoutrement,
But from the inward motion to deliver
Sweet, sweet, sweet poison for the age's tooth:
Which, though I will not practise to deceive,
Yet, to avoid deceit, I mean to learn;
For it shall strew the footsteps of my rising.
But who comes in such haste in riding-robes?
What woman-post is this? hath she no husband
That will take pains to blow a horn before her?

Enter LADY FAULCONBRIDGE *and* JAMES
        GURNEY.

O me! it is my mother. How now, good lady!
What brings you here to court so hastily? 221
  Lady F. Where is that slave, thy brother?
    where is he,
That holds in chase mine honour up and down?
  Bast. My brother Robert? old sir Robert's
    son?
Colbrand the giant, that same mighty man?
Is it sir Robert's son that you seek so?
  Lady F. Sir Robert's son! Ay, thou un-
    reverend boy,

Richard Burton as Philip the Bastard, Old Vic Theatre,
London, 1953

170–175 *Something . . . begot.* A speech full of proverbial sayings and sexual jokes about bastardy.

187–189 *For new-made . . . conversion.* The recently ennobled affect not to remember names, because it is beneath their new-found dignity.

193 *picked.* Affected.

196 *Absey book.* ABC primer.

208 *smack of observation.* Appear rather snobbish.

209 *And so am I.* i.e. a child of the time.

225 *Colbrand the giant.* Killed by Guy of Warwick in the old romances.

231 *Philip! sparrow:* A pet name for sparrows.

Lady Faulconbridge: 'What means this scorn, thou most untoward knave . . .' Drawing by John M. Wright (1777–1866)

244 *Basilisco-like.* A joke in the anonymous play *Solyman and Perseda.*

Richard, Cœur-de-Lion. Engraving from *Old England*, 1854

Sir Robert's son : why scorn'st thou at sir Robert?
He is sir Robert's son, and so art thou.
    Bast. James Gurney, wilt thou give us leave
      awhile? 230
    Gur. Good leave, good Philip.
    Bast.   Philip! sparrow: James,
There's toys abroad : anon I 'll tell thee more.
                  [*Exit Gurney.*
Madam, I was not old sir Robert's son :
Sir Robert might have eat his part in me
Upon Good-Friday and ne'er broke his fast :
Sir Robert could do well : marry, to confess,
Could he get me? Sir Robert could not do it :
We know his handiwork : therefore, good mother,
To whom am I beholding for these limbs?
Sir Robert never holp to make this leg. 240
    Lady F. Hast thou conspired with thy bro-
      ther too,
That for thine own gain shouldst defend mine
      honour?
What means this scorn, thou most untoward
      knave?
    Bast. Knight, knight, good mother, Basilisco-
      like.
What! I am dubb'd! I have it on my shoulder.
But, mother, I am not sir Robert's son;
I have disclaim'd sir Robert and my land;
Legitimation, name and all is gone :
Then, good my mother, let me know my father;
Some proper man, I hope : who was it, mother?
    Lady F. Hast thou denied thyself a Faul-
      conbridge? 251
    Bast. As faithfully as I deny the devil.
    Lady F. King Richard Cœur-de-lion was thy
      father :
By long and vehement suit I was seduced
To make room for him in my husband's bed :
Heaven lay not my transgression to my charge!
Thou art the issue of my dear offence,
Which was so strongly urged past my defence.
    Bast. Now, by this light, were I to get again,
Madam, I would not wish a better father. 260
Some sins do bear their privilege on earth,
And so doth yours; your fault was not your folly:
Needs must you lay your heart at his dispose,
Subjected tribute to commanding love,
Against whose fury and unmatched force
The aweless lion could not wage the fight,
Nor keep his princely heart from Richard's hand.
He that perforce robs lions of their hearts
May easily win a woman's. Ay, my mother,
With all my heart I thank thee for my father! 270
Who lives and dares but say thou didst not well
When I was got, I 'll send his soul to hell.
Come, lady, I will show thee to my kin;
    And they shall say, when Richard me begot,
If thou hadst said him nay, it had been sin :
    Who says it was, he lies; I say 'twas not.
                  [*Exeunt.*

ACT II.

Scene I. *France. Before Angiers.*

Enter Austria *and forces, drums, etc. on one side : on the other* King Philip *of France and his power;* Lewis, Arthur, Constance *and attendants.*

    Lew. Before Angiers well met, brave Austria.
Arthur, that great forerunner of thy blood,

Richard, that robb'd the lion of his heart
And fought the holy wars in Palestine,
By this brave duke came early to his grave:
And for amends to his posterity,
- At our importance hither is he come,
To spread his colours, boy, in thy behalf,
And to rebuke the usurpation
Of thy unnatural uncle, English John: 10
Embrace him, love him, give him welcome hither.

    Arth. God shall forgive you Cœur-de-lion's
     death
The rather that you give his offspring life,
Shadowing their right under your wings of war:
I give you welcome with a powerless hand,
But with a heart full of unstained love:
Welcome before the gates of Angiers, duke.

    Lew. A noble boy! Who would not do thee
     right?

    Aust. Upon thy cheek lay I this zealous kiss,
As seal to this indenture of my love,   20
That to my home I will no more return,
Till Angiers and the right thou hast in France,
Together with that pale, that white-faced shore,
Whose foot spurns back the ocean's roaring tides
And coops from other lands her islanders,
Even till that England, hedged in with the main,
That water-walled bulwark, still secure
And confident from foreign purposes,
Even till that utmost corner of the west
Salute thee for her king: till then, fair boy,   30
Will I not think of home, but follow arms.

    Const. O, take his mother's thanks, a widow's
     thanks,
Till your strong hand shall help to give him
     strength
To make a more requital to your love!

    Aust. The peace of heaven is theirs that lift
     their swords
In such a just and charitable war.

    K. Phi. Well then, to work: our cannon shall
     be bent
Against the brows of this resisting town.
- Call for our chiefest men of discipline,
To cull the plots of best advantages: 40
We'll lay before this town our royal bones,
Wade to the market-place in Frenchmen's blood,
But we will make it subject to this boy.

    Const. Stay for an answer to your embassy,
Lest unadvised you stain your swords with blood:
My Lord Chatillon may from England bring
That right in peace which here we urge in war,
And then we shall repent each drop of blood
That hot rash haste so indirectly shed.

        Enter CHATILLON.

    K. Phi. A wonder, lady! lo, upon thy wish,
Our messenger Chatillon is arrived!   51
What England says, say briefly, gentle lord;
We coldly pause for thee; Chatillon, speak.

    Chat. Then turn your forces from this paltry
     siege
And stir them up against a mightier task.
England, impatient of your just demands,
Hath put himself in arms: the adverse winds,
Whose leisure I have stay'd, have given him time
To land his legions all as soon as I;
- His marches are expedient to this town,   60
His forces strong, his soldiers confident.
With him along is come the mother-queen,

7 *importance.* Importunity.

Constance: 'O, take his mother's thanks, a widow's thanks . . .' Constance (Sheila Allen) and Arthur (Benedict Taylor) Royal Shakespeare Co, 1974

39 *discipline.* Military matters.

60 *expedient.* Speedy.

63 *Ate.* Greek goddess of vengeance and destruction.

A knight in armour. Engraving from a 13th century manuscript

77 *circumstance.* Details.

95 *under-wrought.* Undermined.

111 *articles.* The charges in a formal indictment.

English ships at the time of King John. Engraving from *Old England,* 1854

An Ate, stirring him to blood and strife;
With her her niece, the Lady Blanch of Spain;
With them a bastard of the king's deceased;
And all the unsettled humours of the land,
Rash, inconsiderate, fiery voluntaries,
With ladies' faces and fierce dragons' spleens,
Have sold their fortunes at their native homes,
Bearing their birthrights proudly on their backs,
To make a hazard of new fortunes here: 71
In brief, a braver choice of dauntless spirits
Than now the English bottoms have waft o'er
Did never float upon the swelling tide,
To do offence and scath in Christendom.
                                        [*Drum beats.*
The interruption of their churlish drums
Cuts off more circumstance: they are at hand,
To parley or to fight; therefore prepare.
    K. Phi.   How much unlook'd for is this expe-
        dition!
    Aust.   By how much unexpected, by so much
We must awake endeavour for defence;   81
For courage mounteth with occasion:
Let them be welcome then: we are prepared.

    Enter KING JOHN, ELINOR, BLANCH, *the*
        Bastard, Lords, *and forces.*

    K. John.   Peace be to France, if France in
        peace permit
Our just and lineal entrance to our own;
If not, bleed France, and peace ascend to heaven,
Whiles we, God's wrathful agent, do correct
Their proud contempt that beats His peace to
        heaven.
    K. Phi.   Peace be to England, if that war
        return
From France to England, there to live in peace.
England we love; and for that England's sake 91
With burden of our armour here we sweat.
This toil of ours should be a work of thine;
But thou from loving England art so far,
That thou hast under-wrought his lawful king,
Cut off the sequence of posterity,
Out-faced infant state and done a rape
Upon the maiden virtue of the crown.
Look here upon thy brother Geffrey's face;
These eyes, these brows, were moulded out of his:
This little abstract doth contain that large 101
Which died in Geffrey, and the hand of time
Shall draw this brief into as huge a volume.
That Geffrey was thy elder brother born,
And this his son; England was Geffrey's right
And this is Geffrey's: in the name of God
How comes it then that thou art call'd a king,
When living blood doth in these temples beat,
Which owe the crown that thou o'ermasterest?
    K. John.   From whom hast thou this great
        commission, France,   110
To draw my answer from thy articles?
    K. Phi.   From that supernal judge, that stirs
        good thoughts
In any breast of strong authority,
To look into the blots and stains of right:
That judge hath made me guardian to this boy:
Under whose warrant I impeach thy wrong
And by whose help I mean to chastise it.
    K. John.   Alack, thou dost usurp authority.
    K. Phi.   Excuse; it is to beat usurping down.
    Eli.   Who is it thou dost call usurper, France?
    Const.   Let me make answer; thy usurping son.

Eli. Out, insolent! thy bastard shall be king,
That thou mayst be a queen, and check the
     world!
Const. My bed was ever to thy son as true
As thine was to thy husband; and this boy
Liker in feature to his father Geffrey
Than thou and John in manners; being as like
As rain to water, or devil to his dam.
My boy a bastard! By my soul, I think
His father never was so true begot: 130
It cannot be, an if thou wert his mother.
Eli. There's a good mother, boy, that blots
     thy father.
Const. There's a good grandam, boy, that
     would blot thee.
Aust. Peace!
Bast.   Hear the crier.
Aust.   What the devil art thou?
Bast. One that will play the devil, sir, with you,
An a' may catch your hide and you alone:
You are the hare of whom the proverb goes,
Whose valour plucks dead lions by the beard:
I'll smoke your skin-coat, an I catch you right;
Sirrah, look to't; i' faith, I will, i' faith.   140
Blanch. O, well did he become that lion's robe
That did disrobe the lion of that robe!
Bast. It lies as sightly on the back of him
As great Alcides' shows upon an ass:
But, ass, I'll take that burthen from your back,
Or lay on that shall make your shoulders crack.
Aust. What cracker is this same that deafs
     our ears
With this abundance of superfluous breath?
K. Phi. Lewis, determine what we shall do
     straight.
Lew. Women and fools, break off your con-
     ference.   150
King John, this is the very sum of all;
England and Ireland, Anjou, Touraine, Maine,
In right of Arthur do I claim of thee:
Wilt thou resign them and lay down thy arms?
K. John. My life as soon: I do defy thee,
     France.
Arthur of Bretagne, yield thee to my hand;
And out of my dear love I'll give thee more
Than e'er the coward hand of France can win:
Submit thee, boy.
Eli.   Come to thy grandam, child.
Const. Do, child, go to it grandam, child;   160
Give grandam kingdom, and it grandam will
Give it a plum, a cherry, and a fig:
There's a good grandam.
Arth.   Good my mother, peace!
I would that I were low laid in my grave:
I am not worth this coil that's made for me.
Eli. His mother shames him so, poor boy, he
     weeps.
Const. Now shame upon you, whether she
     does or no!
His grandam's wrongs, and not his mother's
     shames,
Draws those heaven-moving pearls from his poor
     eyes,
Which heaven shall take in nature of a fee;   170
Ay, with these crystal beads heaven shall be
     bribed
To do him justice and revenge on you.
Eli. Thou monstrous slanderer of heaven and
     earth!

Constance: 'There's a good grandam, boy, that would blot thee.' Engraving by Kenny Meadows from Barry Cornwall's *The Works of Shakspere*, 1846

136 *your hide.* Austria is wearing the lion-skin taken from Cœur-de-Lion.

139 *smoke.* Thrash.

144 *Alcides'.* As Hercules's lion-skin would appear on an ass's back.

147 *cracker.* Boaster.

183 *Bedlam*. Lunatic.

185–190 *But God . . . her*. Arthur is punished both for Elinor's sins and by Elinor herself.

188 *beadle*. A parish officer whose duty was to whip offenders.

The seige of a town. Engraving from *Old England*, 1854

215 *winking*. Closed.

Const. Thou monstrous injurer of heaven and earth!
Call not me slanderer; thou and thine usurp
The dominations, royalties and rights
Of this oppressed boy: this is thy eld'st son's son,
Infortunate in nothing but in thee:
Thy sins are visited in this poor child;
The canon of the law is laid on him,   180
Being but the second generation
Removed from thy sin-conceiving womb.
    K. John. Bedlam, have done.
    Const.   I have but this to say,
That he is not only plagued for her sin,
But God hath made her sin and her the plague
On this removed issue, plagued for her
And with her plague; her sin his injury,
Her injury the beadle to her sin,
All punish'd in the person of this child,
And all for her; a plague upon her!   190
    Eli. Thou unadvised scold, I can produce
A will that bars the title of thy son.
    Const. Ay, who doubts that? a will! a wicked will;
A woman's will; a canker'd grandam's will!
    K. Phi. Peace, lady! pause, or be more temperate:
It ill beseems this presence to cry aim
To these ill-tuned repetitions.
Some trumpet summon hither to the walls
These men of Angiers: let us hear them speak
Whose title they admit, Arthur's or John's.   200
    Trumpet sounds.   *Enter certain* Citizens *upon the walls.*
    First Cit. Who is it that hath warn'd us to the walls?
    K. Phi. 'Tis France, for England.
    K. John.   England, for itself.
You men of Angiers, and my loving subjects,—
    K. Phi. You loving men of Angiers, Arthur's subjects,
Our trumpet call'd you to this gentle parle—
    K. John. For our advantage; therefore hear us first.
These flags of France, that are advanced here
Before the eye and prospect of your town,
Have hither march'd to your endamagement:
The cannons have their bowels full of wrath,   210
And ready mounted are they to spit forth
Their iron indignation 'gainst your walls:
All preparation for a bloody siege
And merciless proceeding by these French
Confronts your city's eyes, your winking gates;
And but for our approach those sleeping stones,
That as a waist doth girdle you about,
By the compulsion of their ordinance
By this time from their fixed beds of lime
Had been dishabited, and wide havoc made   220
For bloody power to rush upon your peace.
But on the sight of us your lawful king,
Who painfully with much expedient march
Have brought a countercheck before your gates,
To save unscratch'd your city's threatened cheeks,
Behold, the French amazed vouchsafe a parle;
And now, instead of bullets wrapp'd in fire,
To make a shaking fever in your walls,
They shoot but calm words folded up in smoke,
To make a faithless error in your ears: 230
Which trust accordingly kind citizens,
And let us in, your king, whose labour'd spirits,

Forwearied in this action of swift speed,
Crave harbourage within your city walls.
 K. Phi. When I have said, make answer to us
  both.
Lo, in this right hand, whose protection
Is most divinely vow'd upon the right
Of him it holds, stands young Plantagenet,
Son to the elder brother of this man,
And king o'er him and all that he enjoys: 240
For this down-trodden equity, we tread
In warlike march these greens before your town,
Being no further enemy to you
Than the constraint of hospitable zeal
In the relief of this oppressed child
·Religiously provokes. Be pleased then
To pay that duty which you truly owe
To him that owes it, namely this young prince:
And then our arms, like to a muzzled bear,
Save in aspect, hath all offence seal'd up; 250
Our cannons' malice vainly shall be spent
Against the invulnerable clouds of heaven;
And with a blessed and unvex'd retire,
With unhack'd swords and helmets all unbruised,
We will bear home that lusty blood again
Which here we came to spout against your town,
And leave your children, wives and you in peace.
But if you fondly pass our proffer'd offer,
'Tis not the roundure of your old-faced walls
Can hide you from our messengers of war, 260
Though all these English and their discipline
Were harbour'd in their rude circumference.
Then tell us, shall your city call us lord,
In that behalf which we have challenged it?
Or shall we give the signal to our rage
And stalk in blood to our possession?
 First Cit. In brief, we are the king of
  England's subjects:
For him, and in his right, we hold this town.
 K. John. Acknowledge then the king, and let
  me in.
 First Cit. That can we not; but he that proves
  the king, 270
To him will we prove loyal: till that time
Have we ramm'd up our gates against the world.
 K. John. Doth not the crown of England
  prove the king?
And if not that, I bring you witnesses,
Twice fifteen thousand hearts of England's
  breed,—
 Bast. Bastards, and else.
 K. John. To verify our title with their lives.
 K. Phi. As many and as well-born bloods as
  those,—
 Bast. Some bastards too.
 K. Phi. Stand in his face to contradict his
  claim. 280
 First Cit. Till you compound whose right is
  worthiest,
We for the worthiest hold the right from both.
 K. John. Then God forgive the sin of all those
  souls
That to their everlasting residence,
Before the dew of evening fall, shall fleet,
In dreadful trial of our kingdom's king!
 K. Phi. Amen, amen! Mount, chevaliers!
  to arms!
 Bast. Saint George, that swinged the dragon,
  and e'er since
Sits on his horse back at mine hostess' door,

258 *fondly.* Foolishly.

281 *compound.* Come to an agreement.

Bastard: 'St George, that swinged the dragon . . .' From
a 16th century woodcut

Austria: 'Peace! no more.' Drawing by Anthony Walker (1726–1765)

318 *staff*. Spear.

328 *censured*. Discerned.

Teach us some fence! [*To Aust.*] Sirrah, were I at home,　290
At your den, sirrah, with your lioness,
I would set an ox-head to your lion's hide,
And make a monster of you.
　　Aust.　　　　　　　　Peace! no more.
　　Bast.　O, tremble, for you hear the lion roar.
　　K. John.　Up higher to the plain; where we'll set forth
In best appointment all our regiments.
　　Bast.　Speed then, to take advantage of the field.
　　K. Phi.　It shall be so; and at the other hill
Command the rest to stand.　God and our right!
　　　　　　　　　　　　　　　　　[*Exeunt.*

Here after excursions, enter the Herald of France, *with trumpets, to the gates.*

　　F. Her.　You men of Angiers, open wide your gates,　300
And let young Arthur, Duke of Bretagne, in,
Who by the hand of France this day hath made
Much work for tears in many an English mother,
Whose sons lie scattered on the bleeding ground;
Many a widow's husband grovelling lies,
Coldly embracing the discolour'd earth;
And victory, with little loss, doth play
Upon the dancing banners of the French,
Who are at hand, triumphantly display'd,
To enter conquerors and to proclaim　310
Arthur of Bretagne England's king and yours.

Enter English Herald, *with trumpet.*

　　E. Her.　Rejoice, you men of Angiers, ring your bells;
King John, your king and England's, doth approach,
Commander of this hot malicious day:
Their armours, that march'd hence so silver-bright,
Hither return all gilt with Frenchmen's blood;
There stuck no plume in any English crest
● That is removed by a staff of France;
Our colours do return in those same hands
That did display them when we first march'd forth;
And, like a jolly troop of huntsmen, come　321
Our lusty English, all with purpled hands,
Dyed in the dying slaughter of their foes:
Open your gates and give the victors way.
　　First Cit.　Heralds, from off our towers we might behold,
From first to last, the onset and retire
Of both your armies; whose equality
● By our best eyes cannot be censured:
Blood hath bought blood and blows have answer'd blows;
Strength match'd with strength, and power confronted power:　330
Both are alike; and both alike we like.
One must prove greatest: while they weigh so even,
We hold our town for neither, yet for both.

Re-enter the two KINGS, *with their powers, severally.*

　　K. John.　France, hast thou yet more blood to cast away?
Say, shall the current of our right run on?
Whose passage, vex'd with thy impediment,
Shall leave his native channel and o'erswell

With course disturb'd even thy confining shores,
Unless thou let his silver water keep
A peaceful progress to the ocean.   340
    K. Phi. England, thou hast not saved one
      drop of blood,
In this hot trial, more than we of France;
Rather, lost more.   And by this hand I swear,
• That sways the earth this climate overlooks,
Before we will lay down our just-borne arms,
We'll put thee down, 'gainst whom these arms
      we bear,
Or add a royal number to the dead,
Gracing the scroll that tells of this war's loss
With slaughter coupled to the name of kings.
    Bast. Ha, majesty! how high thy glory towers,
When the rich blood of kings is set on fire!   351
• O, now doth Death line his dead chaps with steel;
The swords of soldiers are his teeth, his fangs;
And now he feasts, mousing the flesh of men,
In undetermined differences of kings.
Why stand these royal fronts amazed thus?
Cry, 'havoc!' kings; back to the stained field,
You equal potents, fiery kindled spirits!
Then let confusion of one part confirm
The other's peace; till then, blows, blood and
      death!   360
    K. John. Whose party do the townsmen yet
      admit?
    K. Phi. Speak, citizens, for England; who's
      your king?
    First Cit. The king of England, when we
      know the king.
    K. Phi. Know him in us, that here hold up
      his right.
    K. John. In us, that are our own great deputy,
And bear possession of our person here,
Lord of our presence, Angiers, and of you.
    First Cit. A greater power than we denies all
      this;
And till it be undoubted, we do lock
Our former scruple in our strong-barr'd gates;
King'd of our fears, until our fears, resolved, 371
Be by some certain king purged and deposed.
•   *Bast.* By heaven, these scroyles of Angiers
      flout you, kings,
And stand securely on their battlements,
As in a theatre, whence they gape and point
At your industrious scenes and acts of death.
Your royal presences be ruled by me:
• Do like the mutines of Jerusalem,
Be friends awhile and both conjointly bend
Your sharpest deeds of malice on this town: 380
By east and west let France and England
      mount
Their battering cannon charged to the mouths,
• Till their soul-fearing clamours have brawl'd down
The flinty ribs of this contemptuous city:
I'ld play incessantly upon these jades,
Even till unfenced desolation
Leave them as naked as the vulgar air.
That done, dissever your united strengths,
And part your mingled colours once again;
Turn face to face and bloody point to point; 390
Then, in a moment, Fortune shall cull forth
Out of one side her happy minion,
To whom in favour she shall give the day,
And kiss him with a glorious victory.
How like you this wild counsel, mighty states?
Smacks it not something of the policy?

Philip: 'England, thou hast not saved one drop of blood.'
William Mollison as King Philip, Her Majesty's
Theatre, London, 1899

---

344 *climate.* Part of the sky.

352 *chaps.* Jaws.

373 *scroyles.* Scoundrels.

378 *mutines of Jerusalem.* In 70 A.D. the opposing
Jewish factions united against the Romans.

383 *soul-fearing.* Frightening.

First Citizen: 'That daughter there of Spain, the Lady Blanche, Is niece to England . . .' Lettice Fairfax as the Lady Blanch, Her Majesty's Theatre, London, 1899

---

448 *spleen.* Passion.

454 *peremptory.* Resolved.

K. John. Now, by the sky that hangs above our heads,
I like it well. France, shall we knit our powers
And lay this Angiers even with the ground;
Then after fight who shall be king of it? 400
Bast. An if thou hast the mettle of a king,
Being wrong'd as we are by this peevish town,
Turn thou the mouth of thy artillery,
As we will ours, against these saucy walls;
And when that we have dash'd them to the ground,
Why then defy each other, and pell-mell
Make work upon ourselves, for heaven or hell.
K. Phi. Let it be so. Say, where will you assault?
K. John. We from the west will send destruction
Into this city's bosom. 410
Aust. I from the north.
K. Phi. Our thunder from the south
Shall rain their drift of bullets on this town.
Bast. O prudent discipline! From north to south:
Austria and France shoot in each other's mouth:
I'll stir them to it. Come, away, away!
First Cit. Hear us, great kings: vouchsafe awhile to stay,
And I shall show you peace and fair-faced league;
Win you this city without stroke or wound;
Rescue those breathing lives to die in beds,
That here come sacrifices for the field: 420
Persever not, but hear me, mighty kings.
K. John. Speak on with favour; we are bent to hear.
First Cit. That daughter there of Spain, the Lady Blanch,
Is niece to England: look upon the years
Of Lewis the Dauphin and that lovely maid:
If lusty love should go in quest of beauty,
Where should he find it fairer than in Blanch?
If zealous love should go in search of virtue,
Where should he find it purer than in Blanch?
If love ambitious sought a match of birth, 430
Whose veins bound richer blood than Lady Blanch?
Such as she is, in beauty, virtue, birth,
Is the young Dauphin every way complete:
If not complete of, say he is not she;
And she again wants nothing, to name want,
If want it be not that she is not he:
He is the half part of a blessed man,
Left to be finished by such as she;
And she a fair divided excellence,
Whose fulness of perfection lies in him. 440
O, two such silver currents, when they join,
Do glorify the banks that bound them in;
And two such shores to two such streams made one,
Two such controlling bounds shall you be, kings,
To these two princes, if you marry them.
This union shall do more than battery can
To our fast-closed gates; for at this match,
• With swifter spleen than powder can enforce,
The mouth of passage shall we fling wide ope,
And give you entrance: but without this match,
The sea enraged is not half so deaf, 451
Lions more confident, mountains and rocks
More free from motion, no, not Death himself
• In mortal fury half so peremptory,
As we to keep this city.

Bast.   Here's a stay
That shakes the rotten carcass of old Death
Out of his rags! Here's a large mouth, indeed,
That spits forth death and mountains, rocks and
          seas,
Talks as familiarly of roaring lions
As maids of thirteen do of puppy-dogs!   460
What cannoneer begot this lusty blood?
• He speaks plain cannon fire, and smoke and
          bounce ;
• He gives the bastinado with his tongue:
Our ears are cudgell'd ; not a word of his
But buffets better than a fist of France:
• Zounds! I was never so bethump'd with words
Since I first call'd my brother's father dad.
     Eli. Son, list to this conjunction, make this
          match ;
Give with our niece a dowry large enough:
For by this knot thou shalt so surely tie   470
Thy now unsured assurance to the crown,
That yon green boy shall have no sun to ripe
The bloom that promiseth a mighty fruit.
I see a yielding in the looks of France ;
Mark, how they whisper: urge them while their
          souls
Are capable of this ambition,
Lest zeal, now melted by the windy breath
Of soft petitions, pity and remorse,
Cool and congeal again to what it was.
     First Cit. Why answer not the double majes-
          ties   480
This friendly treaty of our threaten'd town?
     K. Phi. Speak England first, that hath been
          forward first
To speak unto this city : what say you?
     K. John. If that the Dauphin there, thy
          princely son,
Can in this book of beauty read 'I love,'
Her dowry shall weigh equal with a queen:
For Anjou and fair Touraine, Maine, Poictiers,
And all that we upon this side the sea,
Except this city now by us besieged,
Find liable to our crown and dignity,   490
Shall gild her bridal bed and make her rich
In titles, honours and promotions,
As she in beauty, education, blood,
Holds hand with any princess of the world.
     K. Phi. What say'st thou, boy? look in the
          lady's face.
     Lew. I do, my lord ; and in her eye I find
A wonder, or a wondrous miracle,
• The shadow of myself form'd in her eye ;
Which, being but the shadow of your son,
Becomes a sun and makes your son a shadow : 500
I do protest I never loved myself
Till now infixed I beheld myself
Drawn in the flattering table of her eye.
                    [*Whispers with Blanch.*
Bast. Drawn in the flattering table of her eye!
     Hang'd in the frowning wrinkle of her brow!
And quarter'd in her heart ! he doth espy
     Himself love's traitor: this is pity now,
That, hang'd and drawn and quarter'd, there
          should be
In such a love so vile a lout as he.
     Blanch. My uncle's will in this respect is
          mine: 510
If he see aught in you that makes him like,
That any thing he sees, which moves his liking,

462 *bounce.* Noise or bang.

463 *bastinado.* Thrashing.

466 *Zounds!* A shortened form of the oath 'God's wounds'.

498 *shadow.* Reflection.

Death by quartering. Woodcut from Holinshed's
Chronicles, 1577

522 *still.* Always.

535 *assured.* Betrothed.

King Philip: 'The rites of marriage shall be solemnized.'
Engraving of a royal marriage from a 13th century
manuscript

555 *solemnity.* Marriage ceremony.

561 *composition.* Agreement.

566 *rounded.* Whispered.

I can with ease translate it to my will;
Or if you will, to speak more properly,
I will enforce it easily to my love.
Further I will not flatter you, my lord,
That all I see in you is worthy love,
Than this; that nothing do I see in you,
Though churlish thoughts themselves should be
    your judge,
That I can find should merit any hate.   520
    K. John. What say these young ones? What
      say you, my niece?
    Blanch. That she is bound in honour still to do
What you in wisdom still vouchsafe to say.
    K. John. Speak then, prince Dauphin; can
      you love this lady?
    Lew. Nay, ask me if I can refrain from love;
For I do love her most unfeignedly.
    K. John. Then do I give Volquessen, Tou-
      raine, Maine,
Poictiers and Anjou, these five provinces,
With her to thee; and this addition more,
Full thirty thousand marks of English coin.   530
Philip of France, if thou be pleased withal,
Command thy son and daughter to join hands.
    K. Phi. It likes us well; young princes,
      close your hands.
    Aust. And your lips too; for I am well assured
That I did so when I was first assured.
    K. Phi. Now, citizens of Angiers, ope your
      gates,
Let in that amity which you have made;
For at Saint Mary's chapel presently
The rites of marriage shall be solemnized.
Is not the Lady Constance in this troop?   540
I know she is not, for this match made up
Her presence would have interrupted much:
Where is she and her son? tell me, who knows.
    Lew. She is sad and passionate at your high-
      ness' tent.
    K. Phil. And, by my faith, this league that
      we have made
Will give her sadness very little cure.
Brother of England, how may we content
This widow lady? In her right we came;
Which we, God knows, have turn'd another way,
To our own vantage.
    K. John.   We will heal up all;   550
For we'll create young Arthur Duke of Bretagne
And Earl of Richmond; and this rich fair town
We make him lord of. Call the Lady Constance;
Some speedy messenger bid her repair
To our solemnity: I trust we shall,
If not fill up the measure of her will,
Yet in some measure satisfy her so
That we shall stop her exclamation.
Go we, as well as haste will suffer us,
To this unlook'd for, unprepared pomp.   560
            [Exeunt all but the Bastard.
    Bast. Mad world! mad kings! mad compo-
      sition!
John, to stop Arthur's title in the whole,
Hath willingly departed with a part,
And France, whose armour conscience buckled
    on,
Whom zeal and charity brought to the field
As God's own soldier, rounded in the ear
With that same purpose-changer, that sly devil,
That broker, that still breaks the pate of faith,
That daily break-vow, he that wins of all,

Of kings, of beggars, old men, young men, maids,
Who, having no external thing to lose   571
But the word 'maid,' cheats the poor maid of that,
● That smooth-faced gentleman, tickling Commo-
   dity,
● Commodity, the bias of the world,
● The world, who of itself is peised well,
Made to run even upon even ground,
Till this advantage, this vile-drawing bias,
This sway of motion, this Commodity,
● Makes it take head from all indifferency,
From all direction, purpose, course, intent: 580
And this same bias, this Commodity,
This bawd, this broker, this all-changing word,
Clapp'd on the outward eye of fickle France,
Hath drawn him from his own determined aid,
From a resolved and honourable war,
To a most base and vile-concluded peace.
And why rail I on this Commodity?
But for because he hath not woo'd me yet:
Not that I have the power to clutch my hand,
● When his fair angels would salute my palm;   590
But for my hand, as unattempted yet,
Like a poor beggar, raileth on the rich.
Well, whiles I am a beggar, I will rail
And say there is no sin but to be rich;
And being rich, my virtue then shall be
To say there is no vice but beggary.
Since kings break faith upon commodity,
Gain, be my lord, for I will worship thee. [*Exit.*

ACT III.

SCENE I. *The French* KING'S *pavilion.*

Enter CONSTANCE, ARTHUR, *and* SALISBURY.

Const. Gone to be married! gone to swear a
   peace!
False blood to false blood join'd! gone to be friends!
Shall Lewis have Blanch, and Blanch those pro-
   vinces?
It is not so; thou hast misspoke, misheard;
Be well advised, tell o'er thy tale again:
It cannot be; thou dost but say 'tis so:
I trust I may not trust thee; for thy word
Is but the vain breath of a common man:
Believe me, I do not believe thee, man;
I have a king's oath to the contrary.   10
Thou shalt be punish'd for thus frighting me,
For I am sick and capable of fears,
Oppress'd with wrongs and therefore full of fears,
A widow, husbandless, subject to fears,
A woman, naturally born to fears;
And though thou now confess thou didst but jest,
With my vex'd spirits I cannot take a truce,
But they will quake and tremble all this day.
What dost thou mean by shaking of thy head?
Why dost thou look so sadly on my son?   20
What means that hand upon that breast of thine?
Why holds thine eye that lamentable rheum,
Like a proud river peering o'er his bounds?
Be these sad signs confirmers of thy words?
Then speak again; not all thy former tale,
But this one word, whether thy tale be true.
   Sal. As true as I believe you think them false
That give you cause to prove my saying true.
      Const. O, if thou teach me to believe this sor-
         row,
Teach thou this sorrow how to make me die,   30

573–598 *That smooth-faced . . . thee.* See introduction.

574 *bias.* The lead weight in the side of a bowl that determines its swerve.

Bastard: 'Commodity, the bias of the world . . .' Lewis Waller as the Bastard, Her Majesty's Theatre, London, 1899

575 *peised.* Balanced.

579 *take head . . . indifferency.* Abandon impartiality.

590 *angels.* Gold coins.

46 *prodigious.* Monstrous.

Constance: 'I will not go with thee:' Drawing by John
M. Wright (1777-1866)

And let belief and life encounter so
As doth the fury of two desperate men
Which in the very meeting fall and die.
Lewis marry Blanch! O boy, then where art thou?
France friend with England, what becomes of me?
Fellow, be gone: I cannot brook thy sight:
This news hath made thee a most ugly man.
  Sal. What other harm have I, good lady, done,
But spoke the harm that is by others done?
  Const. Which harm within itself so heinous is
As it makes harmful all that speak of it.   41
  Arth. I do beseech you, madam, be content.
  Const. If thou, that bid'st me be content, wert
     grim,
Ugly and slanderous to thy mother's womb,
Full of unpleasing blots and sightless stains,
Lame, foolish, crooked, swart, prodigious,
Patch'd with foul moles and eye-offending marks,
I would not care, I then would be content,
For then I should not love thee, no, nor thou
Become thy great birth nor deserve a crown.   50
But thou art fair, and at thy birth, dear boy,
Nature and Fortune join'd to make thee great:
Of Nature's gifts thou mayst with lilies boast
And with the half-blown rose. But Fortune, O,
She is corrupted, changed and won from thee;
She adulterates hourly with thine uncle John,
And with her golden hand hath pluck'd on France
To tread down fair respect of sovereignty,
And made his majesty the bawd to theirs.
France is a bawd to Fortune and King John,   60
That strumpet Fortune, that usurping John!
Tell me, thou fellow, is not France forsworn?
Envenom him with words, or get thee gone
And leave those woes alone which I alone
Am bound to under-bear.
  Sal.   Pardon me, madam,
I may not go without you to the kings.
  Const. Thou mayst, thou shalt; I will not go
     with thee:
I will instruct my sorrows to be proud;
For grief is proud and makes his owner stoop.
To me and to the state of my great grief   70
Let kings assemble; for my grief's so great
That no supporter but the huge firm earth
Can hold it up: here I and sorrows sit;
Here is my throne, bid kings come bow to it.
               [*Seats herself on the ground.*

Enter KING JOHN, KING PHILIP, LEWIS, BLANCH,
  ELINOR, *the* BASTARD, AUSTRIA, *and* Attendants.

  K. Phi. 'Tis true, fair daughter; and this
     blessed day
Ever in France shall be kept festival:
To solemnize this day the glorious sun
Stays in his course and plays the alchemist,
Turning with splendour of his precious eye
The meagre cloddy earth to glittering gold: 80
The yearly course that brings this day about
Shall never see it but a holiday.
  Const. A wicked day, and not a holy day!
                      [*Rising.*
What hath this day deserved? what hath it done,
That it in golden letters should be set
Among the high tides in the calendar?
Nay, rather turn this day out of the week,
This day of shame, oppression, perjury.
Or, if it must stand still, let wives with child

Pray that their burthens may not fall this day, 90
Lest that their hopes prodigiously be cross'd:
But on this day let seamen fear no wreck;
No bargains break that are not this day made:
This day, all things begun come to ill end,
Yea, faith itself to hollow falsehood change!
　　K. Phi.　By heaven, lady, you shall have no cause
To curse the fair proceedings of this day:
Have I not pawn'd to you my majesty?
　　Const.　You have beguiled me with a counterfeit
Resembling majesty, which, being touch'd and tried, 100
Proves valueless: you are forsworn, forsworn;
You came in arms to spill mine enemies' blood,
But now in arms you strengthen it with yours:
The grappling vigour and rough frown of war
Is cold in amity and painted peace,
And our oppression hath made up this league.
Arm, arm, you heavens, against these perjured kings!
A widow cries; be husband to me, heavens!
Let not the hours of this ungodly day
Wear out the day in peace; but, ere sunset, 110
Set armed discord 'twixt these perjured kings!
Hear me, O, hear me!
　　Aust.　　　　　　　Lady Constance, peace!
　　Const.　War! war! no peace! peace is to me a war.
O Lymoges! O Austria! thou dost shame
That bloody spoil: thou slave, thou wretch, thou coward!
Thou little valiant, great in villany!
Thou ever strong upon the stronger side!
Thou Fortune's champion that dost never fight
But when her humorous ladyship is by
To teach thee safety! thou art perjured too, 120
And soothest up greatness. What a fool art thou,
A ramping fool, to brag and stamp and swear
Upon my party! Thou cold-blooded slave,
Hast thou not spoke like thunder on my side,
Been sworn my soldier, bidding me depend
Upon thy stars, thy fortune and thy strength,
And dost thou now fall over to my foes?
Thou wear a lion's hide! doff it for shame,
And hang a calf's-skin on those recreant limbs.
　　Aust.　O, that a man should speak those words to me! 130
　　Bast.　And hang a calf's-skin on those recreant limbs.
　　Aust.　Thou darest not say so, villain, for thy life.
　　Bast.　And hang a calf's-skin on those recreant limbs.
　　K. John.　We like not this; thou dost forget thyself.

Enter PANDULPH.

　　K. Phi.　Here comes the holy legate of the pope.
　　Pand.　Hail, you anointed deputies of heaven!
To thee, King John, my holy errand is.
I Pandulph, of fair Milan cardinal,
And from Pope Innocent the legate here,
Do in his name religiously demand 140
Why thou against the church, our holy mother,
So wilfully dost spurn; and force perforce

91 *prodigiously be cross'd.* Give birth to monsters.

100 *touch'd and tried.* Tested by a touchstone.

Constance: 'Hear me, O, hear me!' Drawing by Anthony Walker (1726–1765)

115 *bloody spoil.* Richard I's lion skin.

121 *soothest up.* Flatters.

The seal of Stephen Langton who was Archbishop of Canterbury from 1207–1228. Engraving from J.R. Green's *A Short History of the English People*, 1902

147–148 *What earthy . . . sacred king?* What earthly power has the right to question an anointed king?

165–167 *And by . . . himself.* A reference to those who by selling indulgences damned themselves.

193 *raise the power . . . head.* Raise a French army to attack him.

Keep Stephen Langton, chosen archbishop
Of Canterbury, from that holy see?
This, in our foresaid holy father's name,
Pope Innocent, I do demand of thee.
   K. John. What earthy name to interrogatories
Can task the free breath of a sacred king?
Thou canst not, cardinal, devise a name
So slight, unworthy and ridiculous,   150
To charge me to an answer, as the pope.
Tell him this tale; and from the mouth of England
Add thus much more, that no Italian priest
Shall tithe or toll in our dominions;
But as we, under heaven, are supreme head,
So under Him that great supremacy,
Where we do reign, we will alone uphold,
Without the assistance of a mortal hand:
So tell the pope, all reverence set apart
To him and his usurp'd authority.   160
   K. Phi. Brother of England, you blaspheme
   in this.
   K. John. Though you and all the kings of
   Christendom
Are led so grossly by this meddling priest,
Dreading the curse that money may buy out;
And by the merit of vile gold, dross, dust,
Purchase corrupted pardon of a man,
Who in that sale sells pardon from himself,
Though you and all the rest so grossly led
This juggling witchcraft with revenue cherish,
Yet I alone, alone do me oppose   170
Against the pope and count his friends my foes.
   Pand. Then, by the lawful power that I have,
Thou shalt stand cursed and excommunicate:
And blessed shall he be that doth revolt
From his allegiance to an heretic;
And meritorious shall that hand be call'd,
Canonized and worshipp'd as a saint,
That takes away by any secret course
Thy hateful life.
   Const.   O, lawful let it be
That I have room with Rome to curse awhile! 180
Good father cardinal, cry thou amen
To my keen curses; for without my wrong
There is no tongue hath power to curse him right.
   Pand. There's law and warrant, lady, for
   my curse.
   Const. And for mine too: when law can do
   no right,
Let it be lawful that law bar no wrong:
Law cannot give my child his kingdom here,
For he that holds his kingdom holds the law;
Therefore, since law itself is perfect wrong,
How can the law forbid my tongue to curse? 190
   Pand. Philip of France, on peril of a curse,
Let go the hand of that arch-heretic;
And raise the power of France upon his head,
Unless he do submit himself to Rome.
   Eli. Look'st thou pale, France? do not let go
   thy hand.
   Const. Look to that, devil; lest that France
   repent,
And by disjoining hands, hell lose a soul.
   Aust. King Philip, listen to the cardinal.
   Bast. And hang a calf's-skin on his recreant
   limbs.
   Aust. Well, ruffian, I must pocket up these
   wrongs,   200
Because—
   Bast. Your breeches best may carry them.

K. John. Philip, what say'st thou to the
    cardinal?
Const. What should he say, but as the car-
    dinal?
Lew. Bethink you, father; for the difference
Is purchase of a heavy curse from Rome,
Or the light loss of England for a friend:
Forego the easier.
    Blanch.   That's the curse of Rome.
    Const. O Lewis, stand fast! the devil tempts
    thee here
In likeness of a new untrimmed bride.
    Blanch. The Lady Constance speaks not from
    her faith,   210
But from her need.
    Const.   O, if thou grant my need,
Which only lives but by the death of faith,
That need must needs infer this principle,
That faith would live again by death of need.
O then, tread down my need, and faith
    mounts up;
Keep my need up, and faith is trodden down!
    K. John. The king is moved, and answers
    not to this.
    Const. O, be removed from him, and answer
    well!
    Aust. Do so, King Philip; hang no more
    in doubt.
    Bast. Hang nothing but a calf's-skin, most
    sweet lout.   220
    K. Phi. I am perplex'd, and know not what
    to say.
    Pand. What canst thou say but will perplex
    thee more,
If thou stand excommunicate and cursed?
  • *K. Phi.* Good reverend father, make my per-
    son yours,
And tell me how you would bestow yourself.
This royal hand and mine are newly knit,
And the conjunction of our inward souls
Married in league, coupled and link'd together
With all religious strength of sacred vows;
The latest breath that gave the sound of words 230
Was deep-sworn faith, peace, amity, true love
Between our kingdoms and our royal selves,
And even before this truce, but new before,
No longer than we well could wash our hands
• To clap this royal bargain up of peace,
Heaven knows, they were besmear'd and over-
    stain'd
• With slaughter's pencil, where revenge did paint
The fearful difference of incensed kings:
And shall these hands, so lately purged of blood,
So newly join'd in love, so strong in both,   240
Unyoke this seizure and this kind regreet?
Play fast and loose with faith? so jest with
    heaven,
Make such unconstant children of ourselves,
As now again to snatch our palm from palm,
Unswear faith sworn, and on the marriage-bed
Of smiling peace to march a bloody host,
And make a riot on the gentle brow
Of true sincerity? O, holy sir,
My reverend father, let it not be so!
Out of your grace, devise, ordain, impose   250
Some gentle order; and then we shall be blest
To do your pleasure and continue friends.
    Pand. All form is formless, order orderless,
Save what is opposite to England's love.

Queen Elinor (Hilda Braid) King John (Emrys James)
and Cardinal Pandulph (Jeffrey Dench) Royal Shakespeare Co, 1974

224 *make my person yours.* Put yourself in my place.

235 *clap this royal bargain up.* Seal this bargain by
shaking hands.

237 *pencil.* Brush.

259 *mortal.* Deadly.

270–273 *For that . . . doing it.* If one has promised to do something wrong it is right not to do the wrong thing promised.

274–276 *The better act . . . direct.* If one has taken the wrong path, rather than retrace it, one should try another direction in the hope of returning to the right path more quickly.

Bastard: 'Will not a calf's-skin stop that mouth of thine?' Bastard (Lewis Waller) and Austria (Norman McKinnel), Her Majesty's Theatre, London, 1899

Therefore to arms! be champion of our church,
Or let the church, our mother, breathe her curse,
A mother's curse, on her revolting son.
France, thou mayst hold a serpent by the tongue,
● A chafed lion by the mortal paw,
A fasting tiger safer by the tooth,   260
Than keep in peace that hand which thou dost
  hold.
    K. Phi. I may disjoin my hand, but not
  my faith.
    Pand. So makest thou faith an enemy to faith;
And like a civil war set'st oath to oath,
Thy tongue against thy tongue. O, let thy vow
First made to heaven, first be to heaven perform'd,
That is, to be the champion of our church!
What since thou sworest is sworn against thyself
And may not be performed by thyself,
● For that which thou hast sworn to do amiss   270
Is not amiss when it is truly done,
And being not done, where doing tends to ill,
The truth is then most done not doing it:
● The better act of purposes mistook
Is to mistake again; though indirect,
Yet indirection thereby grows direct,
And falsehood falsehood cures, as fire cools fire
Within the scorched veins of one new-burn'd.
It is religion that doth make vows kept;
But thou hast sworn against religion,   280
By what thou swear'st against the thing thou
  swear'st,
And makest an oath the surety for thy truth
Against an oath: † the truth thou art unsure
To swear, swears only not to be forsworn;
Else what a mockery should it be to swear!
But thou dost swear only to be forsworn;
And most forsworn, to keep what thou dost swear.
Therefore thy later vows against thy first
Is in thyself rebellion to thyself;
And better conquest never canst thou make   290
Than arm thy constant and thy nobler parts
Against these giddy loose suggestions:
Upon which better part our prayers come in,
If thou vouchsafe them. But if not, then know
The peril of our curses light on thee
So heavy as thou shalt not shake them off,
But in despair die under their black weight.
    Aust. Rebellion, flat rebellion!
    Bast.   Will't not be?
Will not a calf's-skin stop that mouth of thine?
    Lew. Father, to arms!
    Blanch.   Upon thy wedding-day?   300
Against the blood that thou hast married?
What, shall our feast be kept with slaughter'd men?
Shall braying trumpets and loud churlish drums,
Clamours of hell, be measures to our pomp?
O husband, hear me! ay, alack, how new
Is husband in my mouth! even for that name,
Which till this time my tongue did ne'er pronounce,
Upon my knee I beg, go not to arms
Against mine uncle.
    Const.   O, upon my knee,
Made hard with kneeling, I do pray to thee,   310
Thou virtuous Dauphin, alter not the doom
Forethought by heaven!
    Blanch. Now shall I see thy love: what mo-
  tive may
Be stronger with thee than the name of wife?
    Const. That which upholdeth him that thee
  upholds,

His honour: O, thine honour, Lewis, thine honour!
 Lew. I muse your majesty doth seem so cold,
When such profound respects do pull you on.
 Pand. I will denounce a curse upon his head.
 K. Phi. Thou shalt not need. England, I
 will fall from thee.   320
 Const. O fair return of banish'd majesty!
 Eli. O foul revolt of French inconstancy!
 K. John. France, thou shalt rue this hour
 within this hour.
 Bast. Old Time the clock-setter, that bald sex-
 ton Time,
Is it as he will? well then, France shall rue.
 Blanch. The sun's o'ercast with blood: fair
 day, adieu!
Which is the side that I must go withal?
I am with both: each army hath a hand;
And in their rage, I having hold of both,
They whirl asunder and dismember me. 330
Husband, I cannot pray that thou mayst win;
Uncle, I needs must pray that thou mayst lose;
Father, I may not wish the fortune thine;
Grandam, I will not wish thy wishes thrive:
Whoever wins, on that side shall I lose;
Assured loss before the match be play'd.
 Lew. Lady, with me, with me thy fortune lies.
 Blanch. There where my fortune lives, there
 my life dies.
 K. John. Cousin, go draw our puissance to-
 gether.   [*Exit Bastard.*
France, I am burn'd up with inflaming wrath; 340
A rage whose heat hath this condition,
That nothing can allay, nothing but blood,
The blood, and dearest-valued blood, of France.
 K. Phi. Thy rage shall burn thee up, and
 thou shalt turn
To ashes, ere our blood shall quench that fire:
Look to thyself, thou art in jeopardy.
 K. John. No more than he that threats. To
 arms let's hie!   [*Exeunt.*

SCENE II. *The same. Plains near Angiers.*

Alarums, excursions. Enter the BASTARD,
with AUSTRIA'S *head.*

 Bast. Now, by my life, this day grows won-
 drous hot;
Some airy devil hovers in the sky
And pours down mischief. Austria's head lie there,
While Philip breathes.

Enter KING JOHN, ARTHUR, *and* HUBERT.

 K. John. Hubert, keep this boy. Philip, make
 up:
My mother is assailed in our tent,
And ta'en, I fear.
 Bast.   My lord, I rescued her;
Her highness is in safety, fear you not:
But on, my liege; for very little pains
Will bring this labour to an happy end. [*Exeunt.*

SCENE III. *The same.*

Alarums, excursions, retreat. Enter KING
JOHN, ELINOR, ARTHUR, *the* BASTARD, HU-
BERT, *and* Lords.

 K. John. [*To Elinor*] So shall it be; your
 grace shall stay behind

324 *sexton.* The bell-ringer and grave-digger of a church.

Bastard: 'Austria's head lie there . . .' Joseph Holman, 18th century English actor, as the Bastard. Engraving from a contemporary portrait

5 *make up.* Hurry.

12 *Bell, book, and candle.* Excommunication.

Bell, book and candle. Engraving by F.W. Fairholt from a 13th century coffin from J.O. Halliwell's edition of Shakespeare's works, 1853–65

36 *gawds.* Trifles, amusements.

50 *conceit.* Thought.

John: 'Hubert, throw thine eye On yon young boy.' Drawing by Anthony Walker (1726–1765)

So strongly guarded.   [*To Arthur*] Cousin, look
   not sad :
Thy grandam loves thee ; and thy uncle will
As dear be to thee as thy father was.
   Arth.   O, this will make my mother die with
   grief !
   K. John. [*To the Bastard*] Cousin, away for
   England ! haste before :
And, ere our coming, see thou shake the bags
Of hoarding abbots ; imprisoned angels
Set at liberty : the fat ribs of peace
Must by the hungry now be fed upon :   10
Use our commission in his utmost force.
 ●   *Bast.*   Bell, book, and candle shall not drive
   me back,
When gold and silver becks me to come on.
I leave your highness.   Grandam, I will pray,
If ever I remember to be holy,
For your fair safety ; so, I kiss your hand.
   Eli.   Farewell, gentle cousin.
   K. John.   Coz, farewell. [*Exit Bastard.*
   Eli. Come hither, little kinsman ; hark, a word.
   K. John. Come hither, Hubert.   O my gentle
   Hubert,
We owe thee much ! within this wall of flesh 20
There is a soul counts thee her creditor
And with advantage means to pay thy love :
And, my good friend, thy voluntary oath
Lives in this bosom, dearly cherished.
Give me thy hand.   I had a thing to say,
But I will fit it with some better time.
By heaven, Hubert, I am almost ashamed
To say what good respect I have of thee.
   Hub.   I am much bounden to your majesty.
   K. John.   Good friend, thou hast no cause to
   say so yet,   30
But thou shalt have ; and creep time ne'er so slow,
Yet it shall come for me to do thee good.
I had a thing to say, but let it go :
The sun is in the heaven, and the proud day,
Attended with the pleasures of the world,
 ● Is all too wanton and too full of gawds
To give me audience : if the midnight bell
Did, with his iron tongue and brazen mouth,
Sound on into the drowsy race of night ;
If this same were a churchyard where we stand,
And thou possessed with a thousand wrongs, 41
Or if that surly spirit, melancholy,
Had baked thy blood and made it heavy-thick,
Which else runs tickling up and down the veins,
Making that idiot, laughter, keep men's eyes
And strain their cheeks to idle merriment,
A passion hateful to my purposes,
Or if that thou couldst see me without eyes,
Hear me without thine ears, and make reply
 ● Without a tongue, using conceit alone,   50
Without eyes, ears and harmful sound of words ;
Then, in despite of brooded watchful day,
I would into thy bosom pour my thoughts :
But, ah, I will not ! yet I love thee well ;
And, by my troth, I think thou lovest me well.
   Hub. So well, that what you bid me undertake,
Though that my death were adjunct to my act,
By heaven, I would do it.
   K. John.   Do not I know thou wouldst?
Good Hubert, Hubert, Hubert, throw thine eye
On yon young boy : I 'll tell thee what, my
   friend,   60
He is a very serpent in my way ;

And wheresoe'er this foot of mine doth tread,
He lies before me: dost thou understand me?
Thou art his keeper.
  Hub.   And I 'll keep him so,
That he shall not offend your majesty.
  K. John.   Death.
  Hub. My lord?
  K. John. A grave.
  Hub.   He shall not live.
  K. John.   Enough.
I could be merry now. Hubert, I love thee;
Well, I 'll not say what I intend for thee:
Remember. Madam, fare you well:
I 'll send those powers o'er to your majesty. 70
  Eli. My blessing go with thee!
  K. John.   For England, cousin, go:
Hubert shall be your man, attend on you
With all true duty. On toward Calais, ho!
            [*Exeunt.*

SCENE IV. *The same. The French* KING'S
tent.

Enter KING PHILIP, LEWIS, PANDULPH, *and*
Attendants.

  K. Phi. So, by a roaring tempest on the flood,
A whole armado of convicted sail
Is scatter'd and disjoin'd from fellowship.
  Pand. Courage and comfort! all shall yet go
   well.
  K. Phi. What can go well, when we have
   run so ill?
Are we not beaten? Is not Angiers lost?
Arthur ta'en prisoner? divers dear friends slain?
And bloody England into England gone,
O'erbearing interruption, spite of France?
  Lew. What he hath won, that hath he for-
   tified: 10
So hot a speed with such advice disposed,
Such temperate order in so fierce a cause,
Doth want example: who hath read or heard
Of any kindred action like to this?
  K. Phi. Well could I bear that England had
   this praise,
So we could find some pattern of our shame.

Enter CONSTANCE.

Look, who comes here! a grave unto a soul;
Holding the eternal spirit, against her will,
In the vile prison of afflicted breath.
I prithee, lady, go away with me. 20
  Const. Lo, now! now see the issue of your
   peace.
  K. Phi. Patience, good lady! comfort, gentle
   Constance!
  Const. No, I defy all counsel, all redress,
But that which ends all counsel, true redress,
Death, death; O amiable lovely death!
Thou odoriferous stench! sound rottenness!
Arise forth from the couch of lasting night,
Thou hate and terror to prosperity,
And I will kiss thy detestable bones
And put my eyeballs in thy vaulty brows 30
And ring these fingers with thy household worms
And stop this gap of breath with fulsome dust
And be a carrion monster like thyself:
Come, grin on me, and I will think thou smilest
And buss thee as thy wife. Misery's love,
O, come to me!

Hubert: 'He shall not live.' Engraving by Kenny
Meadows from Barry Cornwall's *The Works of Shakspere*, 1846

70 *powers.* Armies.

2 *convicted.* Defeated.

King Philip: 'A whole armado . . . Is scattered . . .'
Woodcut from Holinshed's *Chronicles*, 1577

11 *advice.* Determination.

35 *buss.* Kiss.

36 *affliction.* Afflicted one.

40 *fell anatomy.* Cruel skeleton.

42 *modern.* Ordinary.

58 *babe of clouts.* Rag-doll.

Philip: 'Bind up those tresses.' Engraving from a painting by Richard Westall (1765–1836)

80 *suspire.* Breathe.

93–97 *Grief . . . form.* See introduction.

   K. Phi.   O fair affliction, peace!
   Const. No, no, I will not, having breath to
    cry:
O, that my tongue were in the thunder's mouth!
Then with a passion would I shake the world;
And rouse from sleep that fell anatomy   40
Which cannot hear a lady's feeble voice,
Which scorns a modern invocation.
   Pand. Lady, you utter madness, and not
    sorrow.
   Const. Thou art not holy to belie me so;
I am not mad: this hair I tear is mine;
My name is Constance; I was Geffrey's wife;
Young Arthur is my son, and he is lost:
I am not mad: I would to heaven I were!
For then, 'tis like I should forget myself:
O, if I could, what grief should I forget!   50
Preach some philosophy to make me mad,
And thou shalt be canonized, cardinal;
For being not mad but sensible of grief,
My reasonable part produces reason
How I may be deliver'd of these woes,
And teaches me to kill or hang myself:
If I were mad, I should forget my son,
Or madly think a babe of clouts were he:
I am not mad; too well, too well I feel
The different plague of each calamity.   60
   K. Phi. Bind up those tresses. O, what love
    I note
In the fair multitude of those her hairs!
Where but by chance a silver drop hath fallen,
Even to that drop ten thousand wiry friends
Do glue themselves in sociable grief,
Like true, inseparable, faithful loves,
Sticking together in calamity.
   Const. To England, if you will.
   K. Phi.   Bind up your hairs.
   Const. Yes, that I will; and wherefore will I
    do it?
I tore them from their bonds and cried aloud   70
'O that these hands could so redeem my son,
As they have given these hairs their liberty!'
But now I envy at their liberty,
And will again commit them to their bonds,
Because my poor child is a prisoner.
And, father cardinal, I have heard you say
That we shall see and know our friends in
    heaven:
If that be true, I shall see my boy again;
For since the birth of Cain, the first male child,
To him that did but yesterday suspire,   80
There was not such a gracious creature born.
But now will canker sorrow eat my bud
And chase the native beauty from his cheek
And he will look as hollow as a ghost,
As dim and meagre as an ague's fit,
And so he'll die; and, rising so again,
When I shall meet him in the court of heaven
I shall not know him: therefore never, never
Must I behold my pretty Arthur more.
   Pand. You hold too heinous a respect of
    grief.   90
   Const. He talks to me that never had a son.
   K. Phi. You are as fond of grief as of your
    child.
   Const. Grief fills the room up of my absent
    child,
Lies in his bed, walks up and down with me,
Puts on his pretty looks, repeats his words,

Remembers me of all his gracious parts,
Stuffs out his vacant garments with his form;
Then, have I reason to be fond of grief?
Fare you well: had you such a loss as I,
I could give better comfort than you do.   100
I will not keep this form upon my head,
When there is such disorder in my wit.
O Lord! my boy, my Arthur, my fair son!
My life, my joy, my food, my all the world!
My widow-comfort, and my sorrows' cure!   [*Exit.*

    K. Phi.   I fear some outrage, and I'll follow
        her.   [*Exit.*
    Lew.   There's nothing in this world can make
        me joy:
Life is as tedious as a twice-told tale
Vexing the dull ear of a drowsy man;
And bitter shame hath spoil'd the sweet world's
    taste,   110
That it yields nought but shame and bitterness.
    Pand.   Before the curing of a strong disease,
Even in the instant of repair and health,
The fit is strongest; evils that take leave,
On their departure most of all show evil:
What have you lost by losing of this day?
    Lew.   All days of glory, joy and happiness.
    Pand.   If you had won it, certainly you had.
No, no; when Fortune means to men most good,
She looks upon them with a threatening eye.   120
'Tis strange to think how much King John hath
    lost
In this which he accounts so clearly won:
Are not you grieved that Arthur is his prisoner?
    Lew.   As heartily as he is glad he hath him.
    Pand.   Your mind is all as youthful as your
        blood.
Now hear me speak with a prophetic spirit;
For even the breath of what I mean to speak
● Shall blow each dust, each straw, each little rub,
Out of the path which shall directly lead
Thy foot to England's throne; and therefore mark.
John hath seized Arthur; and it cannot be   131
That, whiles warm life plays in that infant's
    veins,
The misplaced John should entertain an hour,
One minute, nay, one quiet breath of rest.
A sceptre snatch'd with an unruly hand
● Must be as boisterously maintain'd as gain'd;
And he that stands upon a slippery place
● Makes nice of no vile hold to stay him up:
That John may stand, then Arthur needs must fall;
So be it, for it cannot be but so.   140
    Lew.   But what shall I gain by young Ar-
        thur's fall?
    Pand.   You, in the right of Lady Blanch your
        wife,
May then make all the claim that Arthur did.
    Lew.   And lose it, life and all, as Arthur did.
    Pand.   How green you are and fresh in this
        old world!
John lays you plots; the times conspire with you;
For he that steeps his safety in true blood
Shall find but bloody safety and untrue.
This act so evilly born shall cool the hearts
Of all his people and freeze up their zeal,   150
That none so small advantage shall step forth
To check his reign, but they will cherish it;
● No natural exhalation in the sky,
No scope of nature, no distemper'd day,

Sarah Siddons as Constance. From a 19th century
engraving

---

128 *rub.* Obstacle.

136 *boisterously.* Violently.

138 *Makes nice of.* Is scrupulous.

153 *exhalation.* Meteor.

173 *charity.* Good will.

175 *train.* Draw.

Louis Calvert as Cardinal Pandulph, Her Majesty's Theatre, London, 1899

2 *arras.* Wall hanging.

16 *wantonness.* Affection.

No common wind, no customed event,
But they will pluck away his natural cause
And call them meteors, prodigies and signs,
Abortives, presages and tongues of heaven,
Plainly denouncing vengeance upon John.
   Lew. May be he will not touch young Arthur's life,   160
But hold himself safe in his prisonment.
   Pand. O, sir, when he shall hear of your approach,
If that young Arthur be not gone already,
Even at that news he dies; and then the hearts
Of all his people shall revolt from him
And kiss the lips of unacquainted change
And pick strong matter of revolt and wrath
Out of the bloody fingers' ends of John.
Methinks I see this hurly all on foot:
And, O, what better matter breeds for you   170
Than I have named! The bastard Faulconbridge
Is now in England, ransacking the church,
Offending charity: if but a dozen French
Were there in arms, they would be as a call
To train ten thousand English to their side,
Or as a little snow, tumbled about,
Anon becomes a mountain. O noble Dauphin,
Go with me to the king: 'tis wonderful
What may be wrought out of their discontent,
Now that their souls are topfull of offence.   180
For England go: I will whet on the king.
   Lew. Strong reasons make strong actions: let us go:
If you say ay, the king will not say no. [*Exeunt.*

ACT IV.

Scene I. *A room in a castle.*

Enter Hubert *and* Executioners.

   Hub. Heat me these irons hot; and look thou stand
Within the arras: when I strike my foot
Upon the bosom of the ground, rush forth,
And bind the boy which you shall find with me
Fast to the chair: be heedful: hence, and watch.
   First Exec. I hope your warrant will bear out the deed.
   Hub. Uncleanly scruples! fear not you: look to't.   [*Exeunt Executioners.*
Young lad, come forth; I have to say with you.

Enter Arthur.

   Arth. Good morrow, Hubert.
   Hub.   Good morrow, little prince.
   Arth. As little prince, having so great a title
To be more prince, as may be. You are sad.   11
   Hub. Indeed, I have been merrier.
   Arth.   Mercy on me!
Methinks no body should be sad but I:
Yet, I remember, when I was in France,
Young gentlemen would be as sad as night,
Only for wantonness. By my christendom,
So I were out of prison and kept sheep,
I should be as merry as the day is long;
And so I would be here, but that I doubt
My uncle practises more harm to me: 20
He is afraid of me and I of him:
Is it my fault that I was Geffrey's son?
No, indeed, is't not; and I would to heaven
I were your son, so you would love me, Hubert.

Hub. [*Aside*] If I talk to him, with his innocent prate
He will awake my mercy which lies dead:
Therefore I will be sudden and dispatch.
 Arth. Are you sick, Hubert? you look pale to-day:
In sooth, I would you were a little sick,
That I might sit all night and watch with you: 30
I warrant I love you more than you do me.
 Hub. [*Aside*] His words do take possession of my bosom.
Read here, young Arthur. [*Showing a paper.*
       [*Aside*] How now, foolish rheum!
● Turning dispiteous torture out of door!
I must be brief, lest resolution drop
Out at mine eyes in tender womanish tears.
Can you not read it? is it not fair writ?
 Arth. Too fairly, Hubert, for so foul effect:
Must you with hot irons burn out both mine eyes?
 Hub. Young boy, I must.
 Arth.   And will you?
 Hub.   And I will. 40
 Arth. Have you the heart? When your head did but ache,
I knit my handkercher about your brows,
The best I had, a princess wrought it me,
And I did never ask it you again;
And with my hand at midnight held your head,
And like the watchful minutes to the hour,
Still and anon cheer'd up the heavy time,
Saying, 'What lack you?' and 'Where lies your grief?'
Or 'What good love may I perform for you?'
● Many a poor man's son would have lien still 50
And ne'er have spoke a loving word to you;
But you at your sick service had a prince.
Nay, you may think my love was crafty love
And call it cunning: do, an if you will:
If heaven be pleased that you must use me ill,
Why then you must. Will you put out mine eyes?
These eyes that never did nor never shall
So much as frown on you.
 Hub.   I have sworn to do it;
And with hot irons must I burn them out.
 Arth. Ah, none but in this iron age would do it!   60
The iron of itself, though heat red-hot,
Approaching near these eyes, would drink my tears
And quench his fiery indignation
Even in the matter of mine innocence;
Nay, after that, consume away in rust,
But for containing fire to harm mine eye.
Are you more stubborn-hard than hammer'd iron?
An if an angel should have come to me
And told me Hubert should put out mine eyes,
I would not have believed him,—no tongue but Hubert's.   70
 Hub. Come forth.   [*Stamps.*

Re-enter Executioners, *with a cord, irons, &c.*

Do as I bid you do.
 Arth. O, save me, Hubert, save me! my eyes are out
Even with the fierce looks of these bloody men.
 Hub. Give me the iron, I say, and bind him here.
 Arth. Alas, what need you be so boisterous-rough?

Hubert: 'Read here, young Arthur.' Drawing by Edward Burney (1760–1848)

34 *dispiteous*. Pitiless.

50 *lien*. Lain.

Arthur: 'O, save me . . .' Painting by James Northcote (1746–1831)

383

Arthur: 'I will not struggle . . .' Engraving from a painting by William Hamilton (1751–1801)

---

117 *tarre.* Urge.

123 *owes.* Owns.

129 *dogged.* Cruel.

I will not struggle, I will stand stone-still.
For heaven sake, Hubert, let me not be bound!
Nay, hear me, Hubert, drive these men away,
And I will sit as quiet as a lamb;   80
I will not stir, nor wince, nor speak a word,
Nor look upon the iron angrily:
Thrust but these men away, and I'll forgive you,
Whatever torment you do put me to.
   Hub. Go, stand within; let me alone with him.
   First Exec. I am best pleased to be from such
     a deed.   [*Exeunt Executioners.*
   Arth. Alas, I then have chid away my friend!
He hath a stern look, but a gentle heart:
Let him come back, that his compassion may
Give life to yours.
   Hub.   Come, boy, prepare yourself. 90
   Arth. Is there no remedy?
   Hub.   None, but to lose your eyes.
   Arth. O heaven, that there were but a mote
     in yours,
A grain, a dust, a gnat, a wandering hair,
Any annoyance in that precious sense!
Then feeling what small things are boisterous there,
Your vile intent must needs seem horrible.
   Hub. Is this your promise? go to, hold your
     tongue.
   Arth. Hubert, the utterance of a brace of
     tongues
Must needs want pleading for a pair of eyes:
Let me not hold my tongue, let me not, Hubert;
Or, Hubert, if you will, cut out my tongue,   101
So I may keep mine eyes: O, spare mine eyes,
Though to no use but still to look on you!
Lo, by my troth, the instrument is cold
And would not harm me.
   Hub.   I can heat it, boy.
   Arth. No, in good sooth; the fire is dead with
     grief,
Being create for comfort, to be used
In undeserved extremes: see else yourself;
There is no malice in this burning coal;
The breath of heaven hath blown his spirit out 110
And strew'd repentant ashes on his head.
   Hub. But with my breath I can revive it, boy.
   Arth. An if you do, you will but make it blush
And glow with shame of your proceedings, Hu-
     bert:
Nay, it perchance will sparkle in your eyes;
And like a dog that is compell'd to fight,
Snatch at his master that doth tarre him on.
All things that you should use to do me wrong
Deny their office: only you do lack
That mercy which fierce fire and iron extends, 120
Creatures of note for mercy-lacking uses.
   Hub. Well, see to live; I will not touch thine
     eye
For all the treasure that thine uncle owes:
Yet am I sworn and I did purpose, boy,
With this same very iron to burn them out.
   Arth. O, now you look like Hubert! all this
     while
You were disguised.
   Hub.   Peace; no more. Adieu.
Your uncle must not know but you are dead;
I'll fill these dogged spies with false reports:
And, pretty child, sleep doubtless and secure, 130
That Hubert, for the wealth of all the world,
Will not offend thee.
   Arth.   O heaven! I thank you, Hubert.

Hub. Silence; no more: go closely in with me:
Much danger do I undergo for thee.   [*Exeunt.*

SCENE II.   KING JOHN's *palace.*

Enter KING JOHN, PEMBROKE, SALISBURY,
and other Lords.

K. John.   Here once again we sit, once again
crown'd,
And look'd upon, I hope, with cheerful eyes.
Pem.   This 'once again,' but that your high-
ness pleased,
Was once superfluous: you were crown'd before,
And that high royalty was ne'er pluck'd off,
The faiths of men ne'er stained with revolt;
Fresh expectation troubled not the land
With any long'd-for change or better state.
Sal.   Therefore, to be possess'd with double
pomp,
● To guard a title that was rich before,   10
To gild refined gold, to paint the lily,
To throw a perfume on the violet,
To smooth the ice, or add another hue
Unto the rainbow, or with taper-light
To seek the beauteous eye of heaven to garnish,
Is wasteful and ridiculous excess.
Pem.   But that your royal pleasure must be
done,
This act is as an ancient tale new told,
And in the last repeating troublesome,
Being urged at a time unseasonable.   20
Sal.   In this the antique and well noted face
Of plain old form is much disfigured;
And, like a shifted wind unto a sail,
● It makes the course of thoughts to fetch about,
Startles and frights consideration,
Makes sound opinion sick and truth suspected,
For putting on so new a fashion'd robe.
Pem.   When workmen strive to do better
than well,
They do confound their skill in covetousness;
And oftentimes excusing of a fault   30
Doth make the fault the worse by the excuse,
As patches set upon a little breach
Discredit more in hiding of the fault
Than did the fault before it was so patch'd.
Sal.   To this effect, before you were new
crown'd,
We breathed our counsel: but it pleased your
highness
To overbear it, and we are all well pleased,
Since all and every part of what we would
● Doth make a stand·at what your highness will.
K. John.   Some reasons of this double coro-
nation   40
I have possess'd you with and think them strong;
And more, more strong, then lesser is my fear,
I shall indue you with: meantime but ask
What you would have reform'd that is not well,
And well shall you perceive how willingly
I will both hear and grant you your requests.
Pem.   Then I, as one that am the tongue
of these
To sound the purposes of all their hearts,
Both for myself and them, but, chief of all,
Your safety, for the which myself and them   50
Bend their best studies, heartily request
The enfranchisement of Arthur; whose restraint
Doth move the murmuring lips of discontent

King John: '. . . once again crown'd . . .' Engraving of
the coronation of a king from a 13th century manuscript

10 *guard.* Ornament.

24 *fetch about.* Alter course.

39 *make a stand.* Conform with.

55 *If what . . . hold.* If what you possess, you hold lawfully.

61 *the time's enemies.* The enemies of the present state.

65 *weal.* Welfare.

William Marshall, Earl of Pembroke, who became protector of John's son, the boy-king Henry III. Engraving from *Old England*, 1854

89 *here or hence.* On earth or in heaven.

93 *apparent.* Obvious.

94 *grossly offer it.* Flagrantly attempt.

To break into this dangerous argument,—
● If what in rest you have in right you hold,
Why then your fears, which, as they say, attend
The steps of wrong, should move you to mew up
Your tender kinsman and to choke his days
With barbarous ignorance and deny his youth
The rich advantage of good exercise?   60
● That the time's enemies may not have this
To grace occasions, let it be our suit
That you have bid us ask his liberty;
Which for our goods we do no further ask
● Than whereupon our weal, on you depending,
Counts it your weal he have his liberty.

Enter HUBERT.

    K. John. Let it be so: I do commit his youth
To your direction. Hubert, what news with you?
                   [*Taking him apart.*
    Pem. This is the man should do the bloody deed;
He show'd his warrant to a friend of mine: 70
The image of a wicked heinous fault
Lives in his eye; that close aspect of his
Does show the mood of a much troubled breast;
And I do fearfully believe 'tis done,
What we so fear'd he had a charge to do.
    Sal. The colour of the king doth come and go
Between his purpose and his conscience,
Like heralds 'twixt two dreadful battles set:
His passion is so ripe, it needs must break.
    Pem. And when it breaks, I fear will issue thence   80
The foul corruption of a sweet child's death.
    K. John. We cannot hold mortality's strong hand:
Good lords, although my will to give is living,
The suit which you demand is gone and dead:
He tells us Arthur is deceased to-night.
    Sal. Indeed we fear'd his sickness was past cure.
    Pem. Indeed we heard how near his death he was
Before the child himself felt he was sick:
● This must be answer'd either here or hence.
    K. John. Why do you bend such solemn brows on me?   90
Think you I bear the shears of destiny?
Have I commandment on the pulse of life?
● *Sal.* It is apparent foul play; and 'tis shame
● That greatness should so grossly offer it:
So thrive it in your game! and so, farewell.
    Pem. Stay yet, Lord Salisbury; I'll go with thee,
And find the inheritance of this poor child,
His little kingdom of a forced grave.
That blood which owed the breadth of all this isle,
Three foot of it doth hold: bad world the while!   100
This must not be thus borne: this will break out
To all our sorrows, and ere long I doubt.
                 [*Exeunt Lords.*
    K. John. They burn in indignation. I repent:
There is no sure foundation set on blood,
No certain life achieved by others' death.

Enter a Messenger.

A fearful eye thou hast: where is that blood
That I have seen inhabit in those cheeks?

So foul a sky clears not without a storm :
Pour down thy weather : how goes all in France?
 Mess. From France to England. Never such
  a power 110
For any foreign preparation
Was levied in the body of a land.
The copy of your speed is learn'd by them ;
For when you should be told they do prepare,
The tidings comes that they are all arrived.
 • *K. John.* O, where hath our intelligence been
  drunk?
Where hath it slept? Where is my mother's care,
That such an army could be drawn in France,
And she not hear of it?
 Mess.   My liege, her ear
Is stopp'd with dust ; the first of April died 120
Your noble mother : and, as I hear, my lord,
The Lady Constance in a frenzy died
Three days before : but this from rumour's tongue
I idly heard ; if true or false I know not.
 K. John. Withhold thy speed, dreadful occa-
  sion !
O, make a league with me, till I have pleased
My discontented peers ! What ! mother dead !
How wildly then walks my estate in France !
Under whose conduct came those powers of France
That thou for truth givest out are landed here?
 Mess. Under the Dauphin.
 K. John.   Thou hast made me giddy 131
With these ill tidings.

  Enter the BASTARD *and* PETER *of Pomfret.*

      Now, what says the world
To your proceedings? do not seek to stuff
My head with more ill news, for it is full.
 Bast. But if you be afeard to hear the worst,
Then let the worst unheard fall on your head.
 K. John. Bear with me, cousin ; for I was
  amazed
Under the tide : but now I breathe again
Aloft the flood, and can give audience
To any tongue, speak it of what it will. 140
 Bast. How I have sped among the clergy-
  men,
The sums I have collected shall express.
But as I travell'd hither through the land,
I find the people strangely fantasied ;
Possess'd with rumours, full of idle dreams,
Not knowing what they fear, but full of fear :
And here's a prophet, that I brought with me
From forth the streets of Pomfret, whom I found
With many hundreds treading on his heels :
To whom he sung, in rude harsh-sounding rhymes,
That, ere the next Ascension-day at noon, 151
Your highness should deliver up your crown.
 K. John. Thou idle dreamer, wherefore didst
  thou so?
 Peter. Foreknowing that the truth will fall
  out so.
 K. John. Hubert, away with him ; imprison
  him ;
And on that day at noon, whereon he says
I shall yield up my crown, let him be hang'd.
• Deliver him to safety ; and return,
For I must use thee. [*Exit Hubert with Peter.*
    O my gentle cousin,
Hear'st thou the news abroad, who are arrived?
 Bast. The French, my lord ; men's mouths
  are full of it : 161

116 *intelligence.* Spies.

Queen Eleanor of Aquitaine was married to Louis VII of France (1137–1152) and then to Henry II of England who imprisoned her for plotting against him. She survived him to become a formidable influence over her sons, Richard I and John. Engraving from *Old England,* 1854

158 *safety.* Safe custody.

165 *to-night.* Last night.

170 *the better foot before.* As quickly as possible.

193–198 *I saw . . . contrary feet.* See introduction.

A smith. Engraving from a 13th century manuscript by F.W. Fairholt from J.O. Halliwell's edition of Shakespeare's works, 1853–65

211–214 *winking of . . . respect.* If a king so much as winks, they think they know his intentions; but his frowns could be just moodiness, yet they act on them.

Besides, I met Lord Bigot and Lord Salisbury,
With eyes as red as new-enkindled fire,
And others more, going to seek the grave
● Of Arthur, whom they say is kill'd to-night
On your suggestion.
  K. John.   Gentle kinsman, go,
And thrust thyself into their companies:
I have a way to win their loves again;
Bring them before me.
  Bast.   I will seek them out.
●   *K. John.* Nay, but make haste; the better
    foot before.   170
O, let me have no subject enemies,
When adverse foreigners affright my towns
With dreadful pomp of stout invasion!
Be Mercury, set feathers to thy heels,
And fly like thought from them to me again.
  Bast. The spirit of the time shall teach me
    speed.   *[Exit.*
  K. John. Spoke like a sprightful noble gentle-
    man.
Go after him; for he perhaps shall need
Some messenger betwixt me and the peers;
And be thou he.
  Mess.   With all my heart, my liege. 180
                             [Exit.

  K. John. My mother dead!

           Re-enter HUBERT.

  Hub. My lord, they say five moons were seen
    to-night;
Four fixed, and the fifth did whirl about
The other four in wondrous motion.
  K. John. Five moons!
  Hub.   Old men and beldams in the streets
Do prophesy upon it dangerously:
Young Arthur's death is common in their mouths:
And when they talk of him, they shake their heads
And whisper one another in the ear;
And he that speaks doth gripe the hearer's wrist,
Whilst he that hears makes fearful action, 191
With wrinkled brows, with nods, with rolling eyes.
● I saw a smith stand with his hammer, thus,
The whilst his iron did on the anvil cool,
With open mouth swallowing a tailor's news;
Who, with his shears and measure in his hand,
Standing on slippers, which his nimble haste
Had falsely thrust upon contrary feet,
Told of a many thousand warlike French
That were embattailed and rank'd in Kent: 200
Another lean unwash'd artificer
Cuts off his tale and talks of Arthur's death.
  K. John. Why seek'st thou to possess me with
    these fears?
Why urgest thou so oft young Arthur's death?
Thy hand hath murder'd him: I had a mighty
    cause
To wish him dead, but thou hadst none to kill
    him.
  Hub. No had, my lord! why, did you not
    provoke me?
  K. John. It is the curse of kings to be attended
By slaves that take their humours for a warrant
To break within the bloody house of life, 210
● And on the winking of authority
To understand a law, to know the meaning
Of dangerous majesty, when perchance it frowns
More upon humour than advised respect.

Opposite: H. Beerbohm Tree as King John. From a drawing by C.A. Buchel (d.1950)

King John (1167–1216) came to the throne in 1199 and after a stormy reign died in 1216. Engraving from *Old England*, 1854

---

222 *Quoted*. Noted.

227 *broke with*. Hinted.

255 *motion*. Impulse.

Hub. Here is your hand and seal for what I did.

K. John. O, when the last account 'twixt heaven and earth
Is to be made, then shall this hand and seal
Witness against us to damnation!
How oft the sight of means to do ill deeds
Make deeds ill done! Hadst not thou been by,
A fellow by the hand of nature mark'd,   221
Quoted and sign'd to do a deed of shame,
This murder had not come into my mind:
But taking note of thy abhorr'd aspect,
Finding thee fit for bloody villany,
Apt, liable to be employ'd in danger,
I faintly broke with thee of Arthur's death;
And thou, to be endeared to a king,
Made it no conscience to destroy a prince.
Hub. My lord,—   230
K. John. Hadst thou but shook thy head or made a pause
When I spake darkly what I purposed,
Or turn'd an eye of doubt upon my face,
As bid me tell my tale in express words,
Deep shame had struck me dumb, made me break off,
And those thy fears might have wrought fears in me:
But thou didst understand me by my signs
And didst in signs again parley with sin;
Yea, without stop, didst let thy heart consent,
And consequently thy rude hand to act   240
The deed, which both our tongues held vile to name.
Out of my sight, and never see me more!
My nobles leave me; and my state is braved,
Even at my gates, with ranks of foreign powers:
Nay, in the body of this fleshly land,
This kingdom, this confine of blood and breath,
Hostility and civil tumult reigns
Between my conscience and my cousin's death.
Hub. Arm you against your other enemies,
I'll make a peace between your soul and you. 250
Young Arthur is alive: this hand of mine
Is yet a maiden and an innocent hand,
Not painted with the crimson spots of blood.
Within this bosom never enter'd yet
The dreadful motion of a murderous thought;
And you have slander'd nature in my form,
Which, howsoever rude exteriorly,
Is yet the cover of a fairer mind
Than to be butcher of an innocent child.
K. John. Doth Arthur live? O, haste thee to the peers,   260
Throw this report on their incensed rage,
And make them tame to their obedience!
Forgive the comment that my passion made
Upon thy feature; for my rage was blind,
And foul imaginary eyes of blood
Presented thee more hideous than thou art
O, answer not, but to my closet bring
The angry lords with all expedient haste.
I conjure thee but slowly; run more fast.
                               [*Exeunt.*

SCENE III. *Before the castle.*

Enter ARTHUR, *on the walls.*

Arth. The wall is high, and yet will I leap down:

Good ground, be pitiful and hurt me not!
There's few or none do know me: if they did,
This ship-boy's semblance hath disguised me
  quite.
I am afraid; and yet I'll venture it.
If I get down, and do not break my limbs,
I'll find a thousand shifts to get away:
As good to die and go, as die and stay.
                              [*Leaps down.*
O me! my uncle's spirit is in these stones:
Heaven take my soul, and England keep my
  bones!   [*Dies.* 10

Enter PEMBROKE, SALISBURY, *and* BIGOT.

Sal. . Lords, I will meet him at Saint Ed-
  mundsbury:
It is our safety, and we must embrace
This gentle offer of the perilous time.
  Pem. Who brought that letter from the card-
  inal?
  Sal. The Count Melun, a noble lord of France;
• Whose private with me of the Dauphin's love
• Is much more general than these lines import.
  Big. To-morrow morning let us meet him then.
  Sal. Or rather then set forward; for 'twill be
Two long days' journey, lords, or ere we meet. 20

Enter the BASTARD.

  Bast. Once more to-day well met, distemp-
  er'd lords!
The king by me requests your presence straight.
  Sal. The king hath dispossess'd himself of us:
We will not line his thin bestained cloak
With our pure honours, nor attend the foot
That leaves the print of blood where'er it walks.
Return and tell him so: we know the worst.
  Bast. Whate'er you think, good words, I
  think, were best.
  Sal. Our griefs, and not our manners, rea-
  ' son now.   29
  Bast. But there is little reason in your grief;
Therefore 'twere reason you had manners now.
  Pem. Sir, sir, impatience hath his privilege.
  Bast. 'Tis true, to hurt his master, no man else.
  Sal. This is the prison. What is he lies here?
                              [*Seeing Arthur.*
  Pem. O death, made proud with pure and
  princely beauty!
The earth had not a hole to hide this deed.
  Sal. Murder, as hating what himself hath
  done,
Doth lay it open to urge on revenge.
  Big. Or, when he doom'd this beauty to a
  grave,
Found it too precious-princely for a grave. 40
  Sal. Sir Richard, what think you? have you
  beheld,
Or have you read or heard? or could you think?
Or do you almost think, although you see,
That you do see? could thought, without this
  object,
Form such another? This is the very top,
• The height, the crest, or crest unto the crest,
Of murder's arms: this is the bloodiest shame,
The wildest savagery, the vilest stroke,
• That ever wall-eyed wrath or staring rage
Presented to the tears of soft remorse. 50

16 *private.* Private communication.

17 *general.* Wide.

Richard Pasco as the Bastard, with the body of Arthur,
Royal Shakespeare Co, 1974

46 *crest.* Device above the shield on a coat of arms.

49 *wall-eyed.* Glaring.

54 *times.* Future times.

83 *forget yourself.* In chivalry it was forbidden for a commoner and a noble to fight.

Pem. All murders past do stand excused in this:
And this, so sole and so unmatchable,
Shall give a holiness, a purity,
• To the yet unbegotten sin of times;
And prove a deadly bloodshed but a jest,
Exampled by this heinous spectacle.
  Bast. It is a damned and a bloody work;
The graceless action of a heavy hand,
If that it be the work of any hand.
  Sal. If that it be the work of any hand!   60
We had a kind of light what would ensue:
It is the shameful work of Hubert's hand;
The practice and the purpose of the king:
From whose obedience I forbid my soul,
Kneeling before this ruin of sweet life,
And breathing to his breathless excellence
The incense of a vow, a holy vow,
Never to taste the pleasures of the world,
Never to be infected with delight,
Nor conversant with ease and idleness,   70
Till I have set a glory to this hand,
By giving it the worship of revenge.
  Pem. ⎱ Our souls religiously confirm thy
  Big. ⎰   words.

Enter HUBERT.

  Hub. Lords, I am hot with haste in seeking you:
Arthur doth live; the king hath sent for you.
  Sal. O, he is bold and blushes not at death.
Avaunt, thou hateful villain, get thee gone!
  Hub. I am no villain.
  Sal.   Must I rob the law?
                    [*Drawing his sword.*
  Bast. Your sword is bright, sir; put it up again.   79
  Sal. Not till I sheathe it in a murderer's skin.
  Hub. Stand back, Lord Salisbury, stand back, I say;
By heaven, I think my sword's as sharp as yours:
• I would not have you, lord, forget yourself,
Nor tempt the danger of my true defence;
Lest I, by marking of your rage, forget
Your worth, your greatness and nobility.
  Big. Out, dunghill! darest thou brave a nobleman?
  Hub. Not for my life: but yet I dare defend
My innocent life against an emperor.
  Sal. Thou art a murderer.
  Hub.   Do not prove me so;   90
Yet I am none: whose tongue soe'er speaks false,
Not truly speaks; who speaks not truly, lies.
  Pem. Cut him to pieces.
  Bast.   Keep the peace, I say.
  Sal. Stand by, or I shall gall you, Faulconbridge.
  Bast. Thou wert better gall the devil, Salisbury:
If thou but frown on me, or stir thy foot,
Or teach thy hasty spleen to do me shame,
I'll strike thee dead. Put up thy sword betime;
Or I'll so maul you and your toasting-iron,
That you shall think the devil is come from hell.   100
  Big. What wilt thou do, renowned Faulconbridge?
Second a villain and a murderer?

Hub. Lord Bigot, I am none.
Big.   Who kill'd this prince?
Hub. 'Tis not an hour since I left him well:
I honour'd him, I loved him, and will weep
My date of life out for his sweet life's loss.
    Sal. Trust not those cunning waters of his
        eyes,
For villany is not without such rheum;
And he, long traded in it, makes it seem
Like rivers of remorse and innocency.   110
Away with me, all you whose souls abhor
The uncleanly savours of a slaughter-house;
For I am stifled with this smell of sin.
    Big. Away toward Bury, to the Dauphin
        there!
    Pem. There tell the king he may inquire
        us out.   [*Exeunt Lords.*
    Bast. Here's a good world! Knew you of
        this fair work?
Beyond the infinite and boundless reach
Of mercy, if thou didst this deed of death,
Art thou damn'd, Hubert.
    Hub.   Do but hear me, sir.
    Bast. Ha! I'll tell thee what;   120
Thou'rt damn'd as black—nay, nothing is so
    black;
Thou art more deep damn'd than Prince Lucifer:
There is not yet so ugly a fiend of hell
As thou shalt be, if thou didst kill this child.
    Hub. Upon my soul—
    Bast.   If thou didst but consent
To this most cruel act, do but despair;
And if thou want'st a cord, the smallest thread
That ever spider twisted from her womb
Will serve to strangle thee; a rush will be a
    beam
To hang thee on; or wouldst thou drown thyself,
Put but a little water in a spoon,   131
And it shall be as all the ocean,
Enough to stifle such a villain up.
I do suspect thee very grievously.
    Hub. If I in act, consent, or sin of thought,
Be guilty of the stealing that sweet breath
Which was embounded in this beauteous clay,
Let hell want pains enough to torture me.
I left him well.
    Bast.   Go, bear him in thine arms.
I am amazed, methinks, and lose my way   140
Among the thorns and dangers of this world.
● How easy dost thou take all England up!
From forth this morsel of dead royalty,
The life, the right and truth of all this realm
Is fled to heaven; and England now is left
To tug and scamble and to part by the teeth
● The unowed interest of proud-swelling state.
Now for the bare-pick'd bone of majesty
Doth dogged war bristle his angry crest
And snarleth in the gentle eyes of peace: 150
Now powers from home and discontents at
    home
Meet in one line; and vast confusion waits,
As doth a raven on a sick-fall'n beast,
The imminent decay of wrested pomp.
Now happy he whose cloak and cincture can
Hold out this tempest. Bear away that child
And follow me with speed: I'll to the king:
● A thousand businesses are brief in hand,
And heaven itself doth frown upon the land.
                              [*Exeunt.*

Hubert de Burgh. Engraving from a drawing by Matthew Paris, 13th century

---

142 *England.* i.e. Arthur.

147 *unowed.* Unowned.

158 *brief in hand.* Needing immediate attention.

John: 'Thus have I yielded up into your hand The circle of my glory.' Engraving from Bell's edition, 1773

13 *Rests by . . . qualified.* Can only be checked by you.

ACT V.

SCENE I. KING JOHN'S *palace.*

Enter KING JOHN, PANDULPH, *and* Attendants.

K. John. Thus have I yielded up into your hand
The circle of my glory.   [*Giving the crown.*
Pand.   Take again
From this my hand, as holding of the pope
Your sovereign greatness and authority.
    K. John. Now keep your holy word: go meet the French,
And from his holiness use all your power
To stop their marches 'fore we are inflamed.
Our discontented counties do revolt;
Our people quarrel with obedience,
Swearing allegiance and the love of soul   10
To stranger blood, to foreign royalty.
This inundation of mistemper'd humour
Rests by you only to be qualified:
Then pause not; for the present time's so sick,
That present medicine must be minister'd,
Or overthrow incurable ensues.
    Pand. It was my breath that blew this tempest up,
Upon your stubborn usage of the pope;
But since you are a gentle convertite,
My tongue shall hush again this storm of war   20
And make fair weather in your blustering land.
On this Ascension-day, remember well,
Upon your oath of service to the pope,
Go I to make the French lay down their arms.
                    [*Exit.*
    K. John. Is this Ascension-day? Did not the prophet
Say that before Ascension-day at noon
My crown I should give off? Even so I have:
I did suppose it should be on constraint;
But, heaven be thank'd, it is but voluntary.

Enter the BASTARD.

    Bast. All Kent hath yielded; nothing there holds out   30
But Dover castle: London hath received,
Like a kind host, the Dauphin and his powers:
Your nobles will not hear you, but are gone
To offer service to your enemy,
And wild amazement hurries up and down
The little number of your doubtful friends.
    K. John. Would not my lords return to me again,
After they heard young Arthur was alive?
    Bast. They found him dead and cast into the streets,
An empty casket, where the jewel of life   40
By some damn'd hand was robb'd and ta'en away.
    K. John. That villain Hubert told me he did live.
    Bast. So, on my soul, he did, for aught he knew.
But wherefore do you droop? why look you sad?
Be great in act, as you have been in thought;
Let not the world see fear and sad distrust
Govern the motion of a kingly eye:
Be stirring as the time; be fire with fire;
Threaten the threatener and outface the brow
Of bragging horror: so shall inferior eyes,   50
That borrow their behaviours from the great,
Grow great by your example and put on
The dauntless spirit of resolution.

Away, and glister like the god of war,
When he intendeth to become the field:
Show boldness and aspiring confidence.
What, shall they seek the lion in his den,
And fright him there? and make him tremble
    there?
O, let it not be said: forage, and run
To meet displeasure farther from the doors,   60
And grapple with him ere he come so nigh.
    K. John. The legate of the pope hath been
    with me,
And I have made a happy peace with him;
And he hath promised to dismiss the powers
Led by the Dauphin.
    Bast.   O inglorious league!
Shall we, upon the footing of our land,
Send fair-play orders and make compromise,
Insinuation, parley and base truce
To arms invasive? shall a beardless boy,
A cocker'd silken wanton, brave our fields,   70
And flesh his spirit in a warlike soil,
Mocking the air with colours idly spread,
And find no check? Let us, my liege, to arms:
Perchance the cardinal cannot make your peace;
Or if he do, let it at least be said
They saw we had a purpose of defence.
    K. John. Have thou the ordering of this pre-
    sent time.
    Bast. Away, then, with good courage! yet, I
    know,
Our party may well meet a prouder foe. [*Exeunt.*

    SCENE II.   *The* DAUPHIN's *camp at St*
          Edmundsbury.

    Enter, in arms, LEWIS, SALISBURY, MELUN,
       PEMBROKE, BIGOT, *and* Soldiers.

    Lew. My Lord Melun, let this be copied out,
And keep it safe for our remembrance:
Return the precedent to these lords again;
That, having our fair order written down,
Both they and we, perusing o'er these notes,
May know wherefore we took the sacrament
And keep our faiths firm and inviolable.
    Sal. Upon our sides it never shall be broken.
And, noble Dauphin, albeit we swear
A voluntary zeal and an unurged faith   10
To your proceedings; yet believe me, prince,
I am not glad that such a sore of time
Should seek a plaster by contemn'd revolt,
And heal the inveterate canker of one wound
By making many. O, it grieves my soul,
That I must draw this metal from my side
To be a widow-maker! O, and there
Where honourable rescue and defence
Cries out upon the name of Salisbury!
But such is the infection of the time,   20
That, for the health and physic of our right,
We cannot deal but with the very hand
Of stern injustice and confused wrong.
And is't not pity, O my grieved friends,
That we, the sons and children of this isle,
Were born to see so sad an hour as this;
Wherein we step after a stranger march
Upon her gentle bosom, and fill up
Her enemies' ranks,—I must withdraw and weep
Upon the spot of this enforced cause,—   30
To grace the gentry of a land remote,
And follow unacquainted colours here?

59 *forage.* Seek out the prey.

70 *cocker'd silken wanton.* Spoiled dandy.

71 *flesh.* Initiate into blood-shed.

Earl of Salisbury. Engraving from *Old England*, 1854

3 *precedent.* First draft.

30 *spot.* Disgrace.

Gerald Lawrence as Lewis the Dauphin, Her Majesty's
Theatre, London, 1899

37 *Where these . . . combine.* If only France and England
could combine in a crusade against the heathen.

64 *angel spake.* Some editors suggest a trumpet sounds,
but others think this refers back to line 61 'the purse of
prosperity' and is a pun on coins.

What, here? O nation, that thou couldst remove!
That Neptune's arms, who clippeth thee about,
Would bear thee from the knowledge of thyself,
And grapple thee unto a pagan shore;
• Where these two Christian armies might combine
The blood of malice in a vein of league,
And not to spend it so unneighbourly!
 Lew. A noble temper dost thou show in this;
And great affections wrestling in thy bosom 41
Doth make an earthquake of nobility.
O, what a noble combat hast thou fought
Between compulsion and a brave respect!
Let me wipe off this honourable dew,
That silverly doth progress on thy cheeks:
My heart hath melted at a lady's tears,
Being an ordinary inundation;
But this effusion of such manly drops,
This shower, blown up by tempest of the soul, 50
Startles mine eyes, and makes me more amazed
Than had I seen the vaulty top of heaven
Figured quite o'er with burning meteors.
Lift up thy brow, renowned Salisbury,
And with a great heart heave away this storm:
Commend these waters to those baby eyes
That never saw the giant world enraged;
Nor met with fortune other than at feasts,
Full of warm blood, of mirth, of gossiping.
Come, come; for thou shalt thrust thy hand as
 deep 60
Into the purse of rich prosperity
As Lewis himself: so, nobles, shall you all,
That knit your sinews to the strength of mine.
• And even there, methinks, an angel spake:

 Enter PANDULPH.

Look, where the holy legate comes apace,
To give us warrant from the hand of heaven,
And on our actions set the name of right
With holy breath.
 Pand.   Hail, noble prince of France!
The next is this, King John hath reconciled
Himself to Rome; his spirit is come in, 70
That so stood out against the holy church,
The great metropolis and see of Rome:
Therefore thy threatening colours now wind up;
And tame the savage spirit of wild war,
That, like a lion foster'd up at hand,
It may lie gently at the foot of peace,
And be no further harmful than in show.
 Lew. Your grace shall pardon me, I will not
  back:
I am too high-born to be propertied,
To be a secondary at control, 80
Or useful serving-man and instrument,
To any sovereign state throughout the world.
Your breath first kindled the dead coal of wars
Between this chastised kingdom and myself,
And brought in matter that should feed this fire;
And now 'tis far too huge to be blown out
With that same weak wind which enkindled it.
You taught me how to know the face of right,
Acquainted me with interest to this land,
Yea, thrust this enterprise into my heart; 90
And come ye now to tell me John hath made
His peace with Rome? What is that peace to me?
I, by the honour of my marriage-bed,
After young Arthur, claim this land for mine;
And, now it is half-conquer'd, must I back
Because that John hath made his peace with Rome?

Am I Rome's slave? What penny hath Rome
    borne,
What men provided, what munition sent,
To underprop this action? Is't not I
That undergo this charge? who else but I,   100
● And such as to my claim are liable,
Sweat in this business and maintain this war?
Have I not heard these islanders shout out
● 'Vive le roi!' as I have bank'd their towns?
Have I not here the best cards for the game,
To win this easy match play'd for a crown?
And shall I now give o'er the yielded set?
No, no, on my soul, it never shall be said.
    Pand. You look but on the outside of this work.
    Lew. Outside or inside, I will not return 110
Till my attempt so much be glorified
As to my ample hope was promised
Before I drew this gallant head of war,
And cull'd these fiery spirits from the world,
To outlook conquest and to win renown
Even in the jaws of danger and of death.
                      [*Trumpet sounds.*
What lusty trumpet thus doth summon us?

    Enter the BASTARD, *attended.*

    Bast. According to the fair play of the world,
Let me have audience; I am sent to speak:
My holy lord of Milan, from the king   120
I come, to learn how you have dealt for him;
And, as you answer, I do know the scope
And warrant limited unto my tongue.
    Pand., The Dauphin is too wilful-opposite,
And will not temporize with my entreaties;
He flatly says he'll not lay down his arms.
    Bast. By all the blood that ever fury breathed,
The youth says well. Now hear our English king;
For thus his royalty doth speak in me.
He is prepared, and reason too he should: 130
This apish and unmannerly approach,
This harness'd masque and unadvised revel,
This unhair'd sauciness and boyish troops,
The king doth smile at; and is well prepared
To whip this dwarfish war, these pigmy arms,
From out the circle of his territories.
That hand which had the strength, even at your
    door,
● To cudgel you and make you take the hatch,
To dive like buckets in concealed wells,
● To crouch in litter of your stable planks, 140
● To lie like pawns lock'd up in chests and trunks,
To hug with swine, to seek sweet safety out
In vaults and prisons, and to thrill and shake
Even at the crying of your nation's crow,
Thinking his voice an armed Englishman;
Shall that victorious hand be feebled here,
That in your chambers gave you chastisement?
No: know the gallant monarch is in arms
And like an eagle o'er his aery towers,
To souse annoyance that comes near his nest. 150
And you degenerate, you ingrate revolts,
You bloody Neroes, ripping up the womb
Of your dear mother England, blush for shame;
For your own ladies and pale-visaged maids
Like Amazons come tripping after drums,
Their thimbles into armed gauntlets change,
Their needles to lances, and their gentle hearts
To fierce and bloody inclination.
    Lew. There end thy brave, and turn thy face
    in peace;

101 *liable.* Subject.

104 *bank'd.* Coasted.

A king of France. Engraving from a late 13th century manuscript

138 *take the hatch.* Jump over the lower half of a divided door.

140 *litter.* Bed straw.

141 *pawns.* Objects in pawn.

169 *braced.* Tightened.

172 *welkin.* Sky.

King John in battle dress. Engraving from *Old England* 1854

King John: '... to my litter straight.' Engraving from an early 14th century manuscript by F.W. Fairholt from J.O. Halliwell's edition of Shakespeare's works, 1853–65

We grant thou canst outscold us: fare thee well;
We hold our time too precious to be spent   161
With such a brabbler.
   Pand.   Give me leave to speak.
   Bast.   No, I will speak.
   Lew.   We will attend to neither.
Strike up the drums; and let the tongue of war
Plead for our interest and our being here.
   Bast.   Indeed, your drums, being beaten, will
   cry out;
And so shall you, being beaten: do but start
An echo with the clamour of thy drum,
And even at hand a drum is ready braced
That shall reverberate all as loud as thine;   170
Sound but another, and another shall
As loud as thine rattle the welkin's ear
And mock the deep-mouth'd thunder: for at hand,
Not trusting to this halting legate here,
Whom he hath used rather for sport than need,
Is warlike John; and in his forehead sits
A bare-ribb'd death, whose office is this day
To feast upon whole thousands of the French.
   Lew.   Strike up our drums, to find this danger
   out.
   Bast.   And thou shalt find it, Dauphin, do not
   doubt.   [*Exeunt.* 180

SCENE III.   *The field of battle.*

Alarums.   *Enter* KING JOHN *and* HUBERT.

   K. John.   How goes the day with us? O, tell
   me, Hubert.
   Hub.   Badly, I fear. How fares your majesty?
   K. John.   This fever, that hath troubled me
   so long,
Lies heavy on me; O, my heart is sick!

Enter a Messenger.

   Mess.   My lord, your valiant kinsman, Faul-
   conbridge,
Desires your majesty to leave the field
And send him word by me which way you go.
   K. John.   Tell him, toward Swinstead, to the
   abbey there.
   Mess.   Be of good comfort; for the great supply
That was expected by the Dauphin here,   10
Are wreck'd three nights ago on Goodwin Sands.
This news was brought to Richard but even now:
The French fight coldly, and retire themselves.
   K. John.   Ay me! this tyrant fever burns me
   up,
And will not let me welcome this good news.
Set on toward Swinstead: to my litter straight;
Weakness possesseth me, and I am faint.
                       [*Exeunt.*

SCENE IV.   *Another part of the field.*

Enter SALISBURY, PEMBROKE, *and* BIGOT.

   Sal.   I did not think the king so stored with
   friends.
   Pem.   Up once again; put spirit in the French:
If they miscarry, we miscarry too.
   Sal.   That misbegotten devil, Faulconbridge,
In spite of spite, alone upholds the day.
   Pem.   They say King John sore sick hath left
   the field.

Enter MELUN, *wounded.*

   Mel.   Lead me to the revolts of England here.

Sal. When we were happy we had other names.
Pem.   It is the Count Melun.
Sal.   Wounded to death.
Mel.   Fly, noble English, you are bought and
  sold;   10
Unthread the rude eye of rebellion
And welcome home again discarded faith.
Seek out King John and fall before his feet;
For if the French be lords of this loud day,
He means to recompense the pains you take
By cutting off your heads: thus hath he sworn
And I with him, and many moe with me,
Upon the altar at Saint Edmundsbury;
Even on that altar where we swore to you
Dear amity and everlasting love.   20
   Sal.   May this be possible? may this be true?
   Mel.   Have I not hideous death within my view,
Retaining but a quantity of life,
Which bleeds away, even as a form of wax
Resolveth from his figure 'gainst the fire?
What in the world should make me now deceive,
Since I must lose the use of all deceit?
Why should I then be false, since it is true
That I must die here and live hence by truth?
I say again, if Lewis do win the day,   30
He is forsworn, if e'er those eyes of yours
Behold another day break in the east:
But even this night, whose black contagious breath
Already smokes about the burning crest
Of the old, feeble and day-wearied sun,
Even this ill night, your breathing shall expire,
● Paying the fine of rated treachery
Even with a treacherous fine of all your lives,
If Lewis by your assistance win the day.
Commend me to one Hubert with your king: 40
The love of him, and this respect besides,
For that my grandsire was an Englishman,
Awakes my conscience to confess all this.
In lieu whereof, I pray you, bear me hence
From forth the noise and rumour of the field,
Where I may think the remnant of my thoughts
In peace, and part this body and my soul
With contemplation and devout desires.
   Sal.   We do believe thee: and beshrew my soul
But I do love the favour and the form   50
Of this most fair occasion, by the which
We will untread the steps of damned flight,
And like a bated and retired flood,
● Leaving our rankness and irregular course,
Stoop low within those bounds we have o'erlook'd
And calmly run on in obedience
Even to our ocean, to our great King John.
My arm shall give thee help to bear thee hence;
For I do see the cruel pangs of death
Right in thine eye. Away, my friends! New
  flight;   60
And happy newness, that intends old right.
                    [*Exeunt, leading off Melun.*

SCENE V.   *The French camp.*

Enter LEWIS *and his train.*

   Lew.   The sun of heaven methought was loath
  to set,
But stay'd and made the western welkin blush,
When English measure backward their own
  ground
In faint retire.   O, bravely came we off,
When with a volley of our needless shot,

37 *rated.* Appraised.

54 *rankness.* Excessiveness.

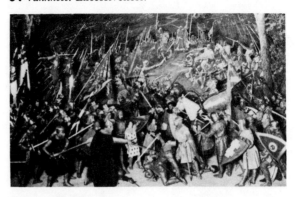

The battle scene from Beerbohm Tree's lavish production at Her Majesty's Theatre, London, 1899

14 *shrewd*. Bitter.

20 *quarter*. Watch.

Franklyn McLeary as Hubert, Her Majesty's Theatre, London, 1899

11 *one way*. One side of my parentage.

28 *taste*. Act as taster.

After such bloody toil, we bid good night;
And wound our tattering colours clearly up,
Last in the field, and almost lords of it!

Enter a Messenger.

Mess. Where is my prince, the Dauphin?
Lew. Here: what news?
Mess. The Count Melun is slain; the English lords 10
By his persuasion are again fall'n off,
And your supply, which you have wish'd so long,
Are cast away and sunk on Goodwin Sands.
• *Lew.* Ah, foul shrewd news! beshrew thy very heart!
I did not think to be so sad to-night
As this hath made me. Who was he that said
King John did fly an hour or two before
The stumbling night did part our weary powers?
Mess. Whoever spoke it, it is true, my lord.
• *Lew.* Well; keep good quarter and good care to-night: 20
The day shall not be up so soon as I,
To try the fair adventure of to-morrow. [*Exeunt.*

Scene VI. *An open place in the neighbourhood of Swinstead Abbey.*

Enter the Bastard *and* Hubert, *severally.*

Hub. Who's there? speak, ho! speak quickly, or I shoot.
Bast. A friend. What art thou?
Hub. Of the part of England.
Bast. Whither dost thou go?
Hub. What's that to thee? why may not I demand
Of thine affairs, as well as thou of mine?
Bast. Hubert, I think?
Hub. Thou hast a perfect thought:
I will upon all hazards well believe
Thou art my friend, that know'st my tongue so well.
Who art thou?
Bast. Who thou wilt: and if thou please,
Thou mayst befriend me so much as to think 10
• I come one way of the Plantagenets.
Hub. Unkind remembrance! thou and eyeless night
Have done me shame: brave soldier, pardon me,
That any accent breaking from thy tongue
Should 'scape the true acquaintance of mine ear.
Bast. Come, come; sans compliment, what news abroad?
Hub. Why, here walk I in the black brow of night,
To find you out.
Bast. Brief, then; and what's the news?
Hub. O, my sweet sir, news fitting to the night,
Black, fearful, comfortless and horrible. 20
Bast. Show me the very wound of this ill news:
I am no woman, I'll not swoon at it.
Hub. The king, I fear, is poison'd by a monk:
I left him almost speechless; and broke out
To acquaint you with this evil, that you might
The better arm you to the sudden time,
Than if you had at leisure known of this.
• *Bast* How did he take it? who did taste to him?

Hub. A monk, I tell you; a resolved villain,
Whose bowels suddenly burst out: the king 30
Yet speaks and peradventure may recover.
  Bast. Who didst thou leave to tend his majesty?
  Hub. Why, know you not? the lords are all come back,
And brought Prince Henry in their company;
At whose request the king hath pardon'd them,
And they are all about his majesty.
  Bast. Withhold thine indignation, mighty heaven,
And tempt us not to bear above our power!
I'll tell thee, Hubert, half my power this night,
Passing these flats, are taken by the tide; 40
These Lincoln Washes have devoured them;
Myself, well mounted, hardly have escaped.
Away before: conduct me to the king;
I doubt he will be dead or ere I come. [*Exeunt.*

SCENE VII. *The orchard in Swinstead Abbey.*

Enter Prince HENRY, SALISBURY, *and* BIGOT.

  P. Hen. It is too late: the life of all his blood
Is touch'd corruptibly, and his pure brain,
Which some suppose the soul's frail dwelling-house,
Doth by the idle comments that it makes
Foretell the ending of mortality.

Enter PEMBROKE.

  Pem. His highness yet doth speak, and holds belief
That, being brought into the open air,
It would allay the burning quality
Of that fell poison which assaileth him.
  P. Hen. Let him be brought into the orchard here. 10
Doth he still rage? [*Exit Bigot.*
  Pem. He is more patient
Than when you left him; even now he sung.
● *P. Hen.* O vanity of sickness! fierce extremes
In their continuance will not feel themselves.
Death, having prey'd upon the outward parts,
Leaves them invisible, and his siege is now
Against the mind, the which he pricks and wounds
With many legions of strange fantasies,
Which, in their throng and press to that last hold,
Confound themselves. 'Tis strange that death should sing. 20
I am the cygnet to this pale faint swan,
Who chants a doleful hymn to his own death,
And from the organ-pipe of frailty sings
His soul and body to their lasting rest.
  Sal. Be of good comfort, prince; for you are born
● To set a form upon that indigest
Which he hath left so shapeless and so rude.

Enter Attendants, *and* BIGOT, *carrying* KING JOHN *in a chair.*

  K. John. Ay, marry, now my soul hath elbow-room;
It would not out at windows nor at doors.
There is so hot a summer in my bosom, 30
That all my bowels crumble up to dust:

Set for King John, Stratford-upon-Avon, 1940

13–14 *fierce extremes . . . themselves.* Sometimes pain is so intense that the sick person is no longer aware of it.

26 *indigest.* Shapeless confusion.

William Marshall, Earl of Pembroke. Engraving from his tomb

42 *strait.* Narrow, mean.

51 *set.* Close.

53 *shrouds.* Sail ropes.

58 *module.* Image.

Death of King John. Drawing by Anthony Walker
(1726–1765)

74 *you stars . . . spheres.* The nobles who are now back in
their proper stations.

I am a scribbled form, drawn with a pen
Upon a parchment, and against this fire
Do I shrink up.
   P. Hen.   How fares your majesty?
   K. John.   Poison'd,—ill fare—dead, forsook,
     cast off:
And none of you will bid the winter come
To thrust his icy fingers in my maw,
Nor let my kingdom's rivers take their course
Through my burn'd bosom, nor entreat the north
To make his bleak winds kiss my parched lips 40
And comfort me with cold. I do not ask you
    much,
• I beg cold comfort; and you are so strait
And so ingrateful, you deny me that.
   P. Hen. O that there were some virtue in
    my tears,
That might relieve you!
   K. John.   The salt in them is hot.
Within me is a hell; and there the poison
Is as a fiend confined to tyrannize
On unreprievable condemned blood.

        Enter the BASTARD.

   Bast. O, I am scalded with my violent motion,
And spleen of speed to see your majesty!   50
• *K. John.* O cousin, thou art come to set mine
    eye:
The tackle of my heart is crack'd and burn'd,
• And all the shrouds wherewith my life should sail
Are turned to one thread, one little hair:
My heart hath one poor string to stay it by,
Which holds but till thy news be uttered;
And then all this thou seest is but a clod
• And module of confounded royalty.
   Bast. The Dauphin is preparing hitherward,
Where heaven He knows how we shall answer
    him;   60
For in a night the best part of my power,
As I upon advantage did remove,
Were in the Washes all unwarily
Devoured by the unexpected flood.
                     [The king dies.
   Sal. You breathe these dead news in as dead
    an ear.
My liege! my lord! but now a king, now thus.
   P. Hen. Even so must I run on, and even so
    stop.
What surety of the world, what hope, what stay,
When this was now a king, and now is clay?
   Bast. Art thou gone so? I do but stay be-
    hind   70
To do the office for thee of revenge,
And then my soul shall wait on thee to heaven,
As it on earth hath been thy servant still.
• Now, now, you stars that move in your right
    spheres,
Where be your powers? show now your mended
    faiths,
And instantly return with me again,
To push destruction and perpetual shame
Out of the weak door of our fainting land.
Straight let us seek, or straight we shall be sought;
The Dauphin rages at our very heels.   80
   Sal. It seems you know not, then, so much
    as we:
The Cardinal Pandulph is within at rest,
Who half an hour since came from the Dauphin,

And brings from him such offers of our peace
As we with honour and respect may take,
With purpose presently to leave this war.
   Bast.   He will the rather do it when he sees
Ourselves well sinewed to our defence.
   Sal.   Nay, it is in a manner done already;
For many carriages he hath dispatch'd   90
To the sea-side, and put his cause and quarrel
To the disposing of the cardinal:
With whom yourself, myself and other lords,
If you think meet, this afternoon will post
To consummate this business happily.
   Bast.   Let it be so: and you, my noble prince,
With other princes that may best be spared,
Shall wait upon your father's funeral.
   P. Hen.   At Worcester must his body be in-
     terr'd;
For so he will'd it.
   Bast.   Thither shall it then: 100
And happily may your sweet self put on
The lineal state and glory of the land!
To whom, with all submission, on my knee
I do bequeath my faithful services
And true subjection everlastingly.
   Sal.   And the like tender of our love we make,
To rest without a spot for evermore.
   P. Hen.   I have a kind soul that would give
     you thanks
And knows not how to do it but with tears.
   Bast.   O, let us pay the time but needful woe,
Since it hath been beforehand with our griefs. 111
• This England never did, nor never shall,
Lie at the proud foot of a conqueror,
But when it first did help to wound itself.
Now these her princes are come home again,
Come the three corners of the world in arms,
And we shall shock them. Nought shall make
     us rue,
If England to itself do rest but true.   [*Exeunt.*

Effigy of John. Engraving from his tomb in Worcester
Cathedral

112–118 *This England . . . true.* See introduction.

King Henry IV

1597

THE TWO PARTS OF HENRY IV are commonly regarded as the apogee of Shakespeare's English history plays; yet they differ from all the others in being almost equally chronicle-plays and comedies. As such, in their mixture of history with fiction they are the effective ancestor of the historical novel; while Falstaff, their grand comic creation, is the progenitor of the humorous types who abound in English literature.

We must note the continuity provided by the dramatist's provident, planning mind. The action of *Henry IV* springs from Richard II's historic deposition; but even before becoming king Bolingbroke laments the 'unthrifty' course of his son and heir Prince Hal. Hal is sowing his wild oats with the old reprobate Falstaff and his boon companions; even so, at his first appearance with them, his regal future is foreshadowed and his dignity saved:

> I know you all, and will awhile uphold
> The unyoked humour of your idleness . . .
> So when this loose behaviour I throw off,
> And pay the debt I never promised,
> By how much better than my word I am . . .
> My reformation, glittering o'er my fault,
> Shall show more goodly, and attract more eyes
> Than that which hath no foil to set it off.

In the event, he will 'redeem the time when men think least I will' – a striking contrast with his successor, the late Duke of Windsor, who showed no capacity for redeeming his time as king. But Hal, underneath his escapades, is not joyous like Falstaff; though engaging in their pranks, he is really detached from them, cool, controlled and contemptuous. He is really a political type like his father and unlike his cousin Richard (whom, in real life, he was fond of as a boy – to add to the tragedy); the Prince is quite consistent with the hero-king he became – he shows his quality already on the battlefield of Shrewsbury.

Though the Prince in his salad days can rival Falstaff in the virtuosity of his abuse –

Falstaff was his butt, as Mark Sykes was Edward VII's butt as Prince of Wales – after
the comic exploit of robbing the King's receivers upon Gadshill, he of course restores
the money, and with interest. There is something deeply touching in the interview
between the troubled father and his disappointing son, between the King with all his
anxieties and cares and the carefree Prince, when one sees it enacted. The Prince
answers his father's searching reproaches:

> Do not think so, you shall not find it so;
> And God forgive them that so much have swayed
> Your Majesty's good thoughts away from me!

He promises:

> I will redeem all this on Percy's head,
> And in the closing of some glorious day
> Be bold to tell you that I am your son.

He kept his word.

Hotspur and Glendower. It is usual to regard Hotspur (Percy) with favour, as a gallant English fellow. His nickname tells us that he is in truth a hot-head, all for action regardless of consequences, ready to risk everything on a single throw. Though not one of the meek, he will inherit six feet of English earth. Nor is he one to take telling or learn from experience:

> By heaven, methinks it were an easy leap
> To pluck bright Honour from the pale-faced moon,
> Or dive into the bottom of the deep,
> Where fathom-line could never touch the ground,
> And pluck up drownèd Honour by the locks,
> So he that doth redeem her thence might wear
> Without co-rival all her dignities.

He is most insensitive and rude to Glendower, as the English are apt to be to Celts – and it is most impolitic of him, for Glendower is his chief ally; he is dependent upon the support of the Welsh in the rebellion against Henry IV. Glendower claims, with the psychic sense of the Celts:

> at my nativity
> The front of heaven was full of fiery shapes,
> Of burning cressets, and at my birth
> The frame and huge foundation of the earth
> Shaked like a coward.

Hotspur replies, with English common sense:

> Why, so it would have done at the same season if your mother's cat had but kittened, though yourself had never been born.

And he goes on at the leader of the Welsh resistance like that. Glendower boasts:

> Three times hath Henry Bolingbroke made head
> Against my power: thrice from the banks of Wye
> And sandy-bottomed Severn have I sent him
> Bootless home, and weather-beaten back.

Hotspur laughs at him:

> Home without boots, and in foul weather too!
> How scapes he agues, in the devil's name?

Now the strange thing is that, in historic fact, Henry IV three times mounted powerful invasions of Wales and each time was thwarted by exceptional bad weather. No wonder Glendower fancied that the elements fought for him – and actually there seem to have been some portents around the time of the birth of this leader with his authentic charisma. Moreover, the Welsh belief in his legend, or aura, was a fighting factor not to be disregarded; Hotspur had not the political sense to see that. The Welsh resistance went on for years, and the English never captured its leader; he died, no-one knows where, as strangely as he had lived.

He is a legend in Wales. He was a Welsh *mage*; Hotspur was a fool.

Falstaff with Hotspur's dead body. Painting by Robert Smirke (1752–1845)

Falstaff is at the Antipodes from Hotspur: he is a coward, but he is certainly no fool. Take the point of Honour, for which Hotspur would throw away his life. On the battle-field Falstaff catechises the concept thus:

> Can honour set to a leg? No. Or an arm? No. Or take away the grief of a wound? No. Honour hath no skill in surgery then? No. What is honour? A word. What is that word honour? Air. A trim reckoning! Who hath it? He that died a-Wednesday. Doth he feel it? No. Doth he hear it? No. 'Tis insensible then? Yea, to the dead. But will it not live with the living? No. . . . Therefore I'll none of it. Honour is a mere scutcheon . . .

Falstaff encounters a dead body:

> Soft! Who are you? Sir Walter Blunt – there's Honour for you.

Falstaff's option is: 'Give me life, which if I can save, so; if not, Honour comes unlooked for, and there's an end.' When he found himself attacked by a 'termagant Scot', he counterfeited death. 'To counterfeit dying, when a man thereby liveth, is to be no counterfeit, but the true and perfect image of life indeed. The better part of valour is discretion, in the which better part I have saved my life.'

Can one doubt that his creation spoke for his creator, that prudent non-combatant? No blame attaches to Henry IV and his sons on that score, for they fought for self-preservation. Falstaff preserved himself by not fighting.

Themes. The main theme is the rebellion against Henry IV by the Percies, who had helped him to the throne and now thought themselves insufficiently regarded. They linked up with the Welsh and the Mortimers to make a dangerous combination, which only Henry's rapid march to Shrewsbury succeeded in forestalling before they could unite their forces. It is not usual to appreciate the politic types in Shakespeare: they have less popular appeal. A more sophisticated judgment can appreciate Henry IV better: he was the right man to occupy the throne. He was an appealing contrast to Richard:

> The skipping King, he ambled up and down,
> With shallow jesters and rash bavin wits . . .
> Mingled his royalty with capering fools,
> Had his great name profanèd with their scorns . . .

While he, when only Bolingbroke, knew how to make himself scarce and the more valued;

> And then I stole all courtesy from heaven,
> And dressed myself in such humility
> That I did pluck allegiance from men's hearts.

It is the subsidiary subject of Falstaff, however, which has captured the world's heart. We do not need to academicise him – ludicrous to add to his weight with 'critical' argy-bargy: far better to let him speak for himself.

Background. True, however, that the contemporary background could do with some elucidation. Falstaff's is that of Elizabethan social life, never more recognisable than in the scenes from low life at the Boar's Head in East Cheap or on the highway, as readers of Simon Forman will know. Shakespeare renders it all with extreme virtuosity and absolute veracity: he must have known it well, not only from observing its humours. Impossible to surpass the depiction of the carriers in the inn-yard at Rochester – quite Dickensian, but Elizabethan: 'An it be not four by the day I'll be hanged – Charles's wain [i.e. the Plough] is over the new chimney, and yet our horse not packed.' That is how they told the time. We hear of criminals packed off to Newgate, two by two.

Hotspur describes, with contempt, a foppish young aristocrat, but of Shakespeare's time, who had plenty of opportunity of observing such fantastics at Court:

> He was perfumed like a milliner,
> And twixt his finger and his thumb he held
> A pouncet-box, which ever and anon
> He gave his nose and took't away again –

in short, a popinjay, like the Earl of Oxford or Sir Edward Hoby.

Personal. We come closer still to Shakespeare with 'any alderman's thumb-ring' – wasn't his father Alderman Shakespeare? We see the son who has gone up in the world in Hotspur's reproof to his wife for saying 'in good sooth':

> Not yours, in good sooth! Heart, you swear like a comfit-maker's wife – 'Not you, in good sooth'!, and 'As true as I live'!, and 'As God shall mend me'!, and 'As sure as day'!

These were all middle-class expressions, not suitable for a Lady Percy.

In addition to the historical reading that went into the play we have a laugh at Euphuism in Falstaff's 'though the camomile, the more it is trodden on the faster it grows, yet youth, the more it is wasted the sooner it wears.' And so on. Falstaff and Prince Hal put on an act of the King examining the Prince on the particulars of his life – greatly to the admiration of the hostess of the Boar's Head:

> O Jesu, he doth it as like one of these harlotry players as ever I see!

More endearing is the phrase 'new reaped showed like a stubble-land at harvest-home' – as one has seen the stubbles on the slopes above Stratford.

Warwickshire is given a good show again – as Cotswold occurred in *Richard II* with no particular necessity. Falstaff, making for Coventry: 'we'll to Sutton Co'fil' tonight', evidently the way Sutton Coldfield was pronounced. But he would not march his mouldy recruits through the city, they would make such a bad impression, with only one shirt among them, and that 'stolen from my host at St. Albans, or the red-nose innkeeper of Daintry' (Daventry).

Sequel. The immense popularity of Falstaff appears in contemporary references, as well as in the demand for printed versions of the play. A quarto of the First Part appeared in 1598, and altogether six printings – equalled only by *Richard III* – before the great Folio of 1623. It is well known that for Falstaff Shakespeare originally used the historic name of Sir John Oldcastle, the famous Lollard who died for his religious faith and had married into the Cobham family. The portrayal of their family precursor as the drunken, thieving old reprobate of the play gave offence to Lord Cobham. Shakespeare changed the names of Oldcastle, Harvey and Russell to Falstaff, Bardolph and Peto. Lord Cobham lived in Blackfriars, so did Lady Russell, Robert Cecil's termagant aunt, who disapproved of players, especially those playing within the precincts.

Jokes about Falstaff circulated in the Essex-Southampton circle – evidently they bore some relevance to the Cobhams that is lost to us. The immense success of the play meant that it was shortly followed by imitations. Shakespeare already had his sequel in mind.

Text and Date offer no problems, since the quartos printed good texts, though a few relics of the original names remained. It is obvious that *The Merry Wives of Windsor* came after the second part of *Henry IV*, since it assumes that the audience is already familiar with Justice Shallow.

THE FIRST PART OF
KING HENRY THE FOURTH.

DRAMATIS PERSONÆ.

KING HENRY the Fourth.
HENRY, Prince of Wales, } sons to the King.
JOHN of Lancaster, }
EARL OF WESTMORELAND.
SIR WALTER BLUNT.
THOMAS PERCY, Earl of Worcester.
HENRY PERCY, Earl of Northumberland.
HENRY PERCY, surnamed HOTSPUR, his son.
EDMUND MORTIMER, Earl of March.
RICHARD SCROOP, Archbishop of York.
ARCHIBALD, Earl of DOUGLAS.
OWEN GLENDOWER.
SIR RICHARD VERNON.
SIR JOHN FALSTAFF.
SIR MICHAEL, a friend to the Archbishop of York.

POINS.
GADSHILL.
PETO.
BARDOLPH.

LADY PERCY, wife to Hotspur, and sister to Mortimer.
LADY MORTIMER, daughter to Glendower, and wife to Mortimer.
MISTRESS QUICKLY, hostess of a tavern in Eastcheap.

Lords, Officers, Sheriff, Vintner, Chamberlain, Drawers, two Carriers, Travellers, and Attendants.

SCENE: *England.*

ACT I.

SCENE I. *London.   The palace.*

Enter KING HENRY, LORD JOHN OF LANCASTER, the EARL OF WESTMORELAND, SIR WALTER BLUNT, *and others.*

King. So shaken as we are, so wan with care,
Find we a time for frighted peace to pant,
And breathe short-winded accents of new broils
To be commenced in strands afar remote.
†No more the thirsty entrance of this soil
Shall daub her lips with her own children's blood;
No more shall trenching war channel her fields,
Nor bruise her flowerets with the armed hoofs
Of hostile paces: those opposed eyes,
Which, like the meteors of a troubled heaven, 10
All of one nature, of one substance bred,
Did lately meet in the intestine shock
And furious close of civil butchery
• Shall now, in mutual well-beseeming ranks,
March all one way and be no more opposed
Against acquaintance, kindred and allies:
The edge of war, like an ill-sheathed knife,
No more shall cut his master. Therefore, friends,
As far as to the sepulchre of Christ,
Whose soldier now, under whose blessed cross 20
We are impressed and engaged to fight,
• Forthwith a power of English shall we levy;
Whose arms were moulded in their mothers' womb
To chase these pagans in those holy fields
Over whose acres walk'd those blessed feet
Which fourteen hundred years ago were nail'd
For our advantage on the bitter cross.
But this our purpose now is twelve month old,
• And bootless 'tis to tell you we will go:
Therefore we meet not now. Then let me hear 30
Of you, my gentle cousin Westmoreland,
What yesternight our council did decree

• *A bullet beside a text line indicates an annotation in the opposite column*

14 *mutual well-beseeming.* Well-ordered.

22 *power.* Army.

29 *bootless.* Useless.

Opposite: Falstaff: 'Let him kill the next'. Drawing by Anthony Walker (1726–65)

Coronation of Henry IV. Engraving from a medieval manuscript

35 *limits of the charge.* Assignments of duty.

40 *irregular and wild.* i.e. engaging in guerrilla tactics.

55 *Holmedon.* Humbleton in Northumberland.

58 *shape of likelihood.* The likely outcome.

66 *smooth.* Soothing.

In forwarding this dear expedience.
   West. My liege, this haste was hot in question,
● And many limits of the charge set down
But yesternight: when all athwart there came
A post from Wales loaden with heavy news;
Whose worst was, that the noble Mortimer,
Leading the men of Herefordshire to fight
● Against the irregular and wild Glendower,   40
Was by the rude hands of that Welshman taken,
A thousand of his people butchered;
Upon whose dead corpse there was such misuse,
Such beastly shameless transformation,
By those Welshwomen done as may not be
Without much shame retold or spoken of.
   King. It seems then that the tidings of this broil
Brake off our business for the Holy Land.
   West. This match'd with other did, my gracious lord;
For more uneven and unwelcome news   50
Came from the north and thus it did import:
On Holy-rood day, the gallant Hotspur there,
Young Harry Percy and brave Archibald,
That ever-valiant and approved Scot,
● At Holmedon met,
Where they did spend a sad and bloody hour:
As by discharge of their artillery,
● And shape of likelihood, the news was told;
For he that brought them, in the very heat
And pride of their contention did take horse,   60
Uncertain of the issue any way.
   King. Here is a dear, a true industrious friend,
Sir Walter Blunt, new lighted from his horse,
Stain'd with the variation of each soil
Betwixt that Holmedon and this seat of ours;
● And he hath brought us smooth and welcome news.
The Earl of Douglas is discomfited:
Ten thousand bold Scots, two and twenty knights,
Balk'd in their own blood did Sir Walter see

On Holmedon's plains. Of prisoners, Hotspur
    took   70
Mordake the Earl of Fife, and eldest son
To beaten Douglas; and the Earl of Athol,
Of Murray, Angus, and Menteith:
And is not this an honourable spoil?
A gallant prize? ha, cousin, is it not?
  West. In faith,
It is a conquest for a prince to boast of.
  King. Yea, there thou makest me sad and
    makest me sin
In envy that my Lord Northumberland
Should be the father to so blest a son,   80
A son who is the theme of honour's tongue;
Amongst a grove, the very straightest plant;
Who is sweet Fortune's minion and her pride:
Whilst I, by looking on the praise of him,
See riot and dishonour stain the brow
Of my young Harry. O that it could be proved
That some night-tripping fairy had exchanged
In cradle-clothes our children where they lay,
And call'd mine Percy, his Plantagenet!
Then would I have his Harry, and he mine. 90
But let him from my thoughts. What think you,
  coz,
Of this young Percy's pride? the prisoners,
Which he in this adventure hath surprised,
To his own use he keeps; and sends me word,
I shall have none but Mordake Earl of Fife.
  West. This is his uncle's teaching: this is
  Worcester,
Malevolent to you in all aspects;
Which makes him prune himself, and bristle up
The crest of youth against your dignity.
  King. But I have sent for him to answer this;
And for this cause awhile we must neglect 101
Our holy purpose to Jerusalem.
Cousin, on Wednesday next our council we
Will hold at Windsor; so inform the lords:
But come yourself with speed to us again;
For more is to be said and to be done
Than out of anger can be uttered.
  West. I will, my liege.   [*Exeunt.*

SCENE II. *London. An apartment of the
Prince's.*

Enter the PRINCE OF WALES *and* FALSTAFF.

Fal. Now, Hal, what time of day is it, lad?
Prince. Thou art so fat-witted, with drinking
of old sack and unbuttoning thee after supper
and sleeping upon benches after noon, that thou
hast forgotten to demand that truly which thou
wouldst truly know. What a devil hast thou to
do with the time of the day? Unless hours were
cups of sack and minutes capons and clocks the
tongues of bawds and dials the signs of leaping-
houses and the blessed sun himself a fair hot
wench in flame-coloured taffeta, I see no reason
why thou shouldst be so superfluous to demand
the time of the day.
Fal. Indeed, you come near me now, Hal;
for we that take purses go by the moon and the
seven stars, and not by Phœbus, he, 'that wandering knight so fair.' And, I prithee, sweet
wag, when thou art king, as, God save thy
grace,—majesty I should say, for grace thou wilt
have none,—   20
Prince. What, none?

94 *To his own use he keeps.* i.e. for ransom.

98 *prune.* As in falconry when a bird trims its feathers; preen.

William Thomas Lewis, the 18th century English actor, as Prince Hal, Covent Garden Theatre, London, 1775

3 *sack.* Spanish white wine.

9–10 *leaping-houses.* Brothels.

16–17 *Phœbus . . . fair.* i.e. not by day like the 'wandering knight' of a popular ballad.

23 *egg and butter.* Friday or Lenten fare, not worthy of much grace.

24 *roundly.* To the point.

29 *Diana.* The goddess of hunting.

40 *'Lay by'.* 'Hands up', 'pull over'.

41 *'Bring in'.* i.e. the fare the inn has to offer.

47–48 *Hybla.* A well-known source of honey in Sicily. *old lad of the castle.* An allusion to Sir John Oldcastle.

51 *quiddities.* Subtleties.

55 *reckoning.* Settlement of the bill.

82 *no lean wardrobe.* The hangman had the right to the clothes of the condemned.

83 *gib cat or a lugged bear.* Tom cat or a baited bear.

88 *Moor-ditch.* The narrow and filthy town ditch of London, associated with misery.

Moorditch and Moorfield. Detail from Ralph Agas's map of London *c.*1560–70

90 *comparative.* Imaginative.

Fal. No, by my troth, not so much as will serve to be prologue to an egg and butter.

Prince. Well, how then? come, roundly, roundly.

Fal. Marry, then, sweet wag, when thou art king, let not us that are squires of the night's body be called thieves of the day's beauty: let us be Diana's foresters, gentlemen of the shade, minions of the moon; and let men say we be men of good government, being governed, as the sea is, by our noble and chaste mistress the moon, under whose countenance we steal.

Prince. Thou sayest well, and it holds well too; for the fortune of us that are the moon's men doth ebb and flow like the sea, being governed, as the sea is, by the moon. As, for proof, now: a purse of gold most resolutely snatched on Monday night and most dissolutely spent on Tuesday morning; got with swearing 'Lay by' and spent with crying 'Bring in;' now in as low an ebb as the foot of the ladder and by and by in as high a flow as the ridge of the gallows.

Fal. By the Lord, thou sayest true, lad. And is not my hostess of the tavern a most sweet wench?

Prince. As the honey of Hybla, my old lad of the castle. And is not a buff jerkin a most sweet robe of durance? 49

Fal. How now, how now, mad wag! what, in thy quips and thy quiddities? what a plague have I to do with a buff jerkin?

Prince. Why, what a pox have I to do with my hostess of the tavern?

Fal. Well, thou hast called her to a reckoning many a time and oft.

Prince. Did I ever call for thee to pay thy part?

Fal. No; I'll give thee thy due, thou hast paid all there. 60

Prince. Yea, and elsewhere, so far as my coin would stretch; and where it would not, I have used my credit.

Fal. Yea, and so used it that, were it not here apparent that thou art heir apparent—But, I prithee, sweet wag, shall there be gallows standing in England when thou art king? and resolution thus fobbed as it is with the rusty curb of old father antic the law? Do not thou, when thou art king, hang a thief. 70

Prince. No; thou shalt.

Fal. Shall I? O rare! By the Lord, I'll be a brave judge.

Prince. Thou judgest false already: I mean, thou shalt have the hanging of the thieves and so become a rare hangman.

Fal. Well, Hal, well; and in some sort it jumps with my humour as well as waiting in the court, I can tell you.

Prince. For obtaining of suits? 80

Fal. Yea, for obtaining of suits, whereof the hangman hath no lean wardrobe. 'Sblood, I am as melancholy as a gib cat or a lugged bear.

Prince. Or an old lion, or a lover's lute.

Fal. Yea, or the drone of a Lincolnshire bagpipe.

Prince. What sayest thou to a hare, or the melancholy of Moor-ditch?

Fal. Thou hast the most unsavoury similes and art indeed the most comparative, rascalliest, sweet young prince. But, Hal, I prithee, trouble me no more with vanity. I would to God thou and I knew where a commodity of good names were to be bought. An old lord of the council rated me the other day in the street about you, sir, but I marked him not; and yet he talked very wisely, but I regarded him not; and yet he talked wisely, and in the street too.

Prince. Thou didst well; for wisdom cries out in the streets, and no man regards it.   100

Fal. O, thou hast damnable iteration and art indeed able to corrupt a saint. Thou hast done much harm upon me, Hal; God forgive thee for it! Before I knew thee, Hal, I knew nothing; and now am I, if a man should speak truly, little better than one of the wicked. I must give over this life, and I will give it over: by the Lord, an I do not, I am a villain: I'll be damned for never a king's son in Christendom.

Prince. Where shall we take a purse to-morrow, Jack?   111

Fal. 'Zounds, where thou wilt, lad; I'll make one; an I do not, call me villain and baffle me.

Prince. I see a good amendment of life in thee; from praying to purse-taking.

Fal. Why, Hal, 'tis my vocation, Hal; 'tis no sin for a man to labour in his vocation.

Enter POINS.

Poins! Now shall we know if Gadshill have set a match. O, if men were to be saved by merit, what hole in hell were hot enough for him? This is the most omnipotent villain that ever cried 'Stand' to a true man.

Prince. Good morrow, Ned.

Poins. Good morrow, sweet Hal. What says Monsieur Remorse? what says Sir John Sack and Sugar? Jack! how agrees the devil and thee 'about thy soul, that thou soldest him on Good-Friday last for a cup of Madeira and a cold capon's leg?   129

Prince. Sir John stands to his word, the devil shall have his bargain; for he was never yet a breaker of proverbs: he will give the devil his due.

Poins. Then art thou damned for keeping thy word with the devil.

Prince. Else he had been damned for cozening the devil.

Poins. But, my lads, my lads, to-morrow morning, by four o'clock, early at Gadshill! there are pilgrims going to Canterbury with rich offerings, and traders riding to London with fat purses: I have vizards for you all; you have horses for yourselves: Gadshill lies to-night in Rochester: I have bespoke supper to-morrow night in Eastcheap: we may do it as secure as sleep. If you will go, I will stuff your purses full of crowns; if you will not, tarry at home and be hanged.

Fal. Hear ye, Yedward; if I tarry at home and go not, I'll hang you for going.   150

Poins. You will, chops?

Fal. Hal, wilt thou make one?

Prince. Who, I rob? I a thief? not I, by my faith.

Fal. There's neither honesty, manhood, nor good fellowship in thee, nor thou camest not of

99–100 *for wisdom . . . regards it.* Biblical allusion (Proverbs i, 20–24).

113 *baffle.* Disgrace, degrade.

119 *set a match.* Planned a robbery.

136 *cozening.* Cheating.

139 *Gadshill.* Hill on the road to Canterbury notorious for its robberies.

142 *vizards.* Masks.

151 *chops.* Fat cheeks.

178 *All-hallown summer.* Fine weather in late autumn.

Prince Henry, Poins and Falstaff. Engraving from a painting by W.Q. Orchardson (1835–1910)

---

201 *cases of buckram.* Rough outer garments.

the blood royal, if thou darest not stand for ten shillings.

Prince. Well then, once in my days I'll be a madcap. 160

Fal. Why, that's well said.

Prince. Well, come what will, I'll tarry at home.

Fal. By the Lord, I'll be a traitor then, when thou art king.

Prince. I care not.

Poins. Sir John, I prithee, leave the prince and me alone: I will lay him down such reasons for this adventure that he shall go. 169

Fal. Well, God give thee the spirit of persuasion and him the ears of profiting, that what thou speakest may move and what he hears may be believed, that the true prince may, for recreation sake, prove a false thief; for the poor abuses of the time want countenance. Farewell: you shall find me in Eastcheap.

Prince. Farewell, thou latter spring! farewell, All-hallown summer! *[Exit Falstaff.*

Poins. Now, my good sweet honey lord, ride with us to-morrow: I have a jest to execute that I cannot manage alone. Falstaff, Bardolph, Peto and Gadshill shall rob those men that we have already waylaid; yourself and I will not be there; and when they have the booty, if you and I do not rob them, cut this head off from my shoulders.

Prince. How shall we part with them in setting forth?

Poins. Why, we will set forth before or after them, and appoint them a place of meeting, wherein it is at our pleasure to fail, and then will they adventure upon the exploit themselves; which they shall have no sooner achieved, but we'll set upon them.

Prince. Yea, but 'tis like that they will know us by our horses, by our habits and by every other appointment, to be ourselves.

Poins. Tut! our horses they shall not see; I'll tie them in the wood; our vizards we will change after we leave them: and, sirrah, I have cases of buckram for the nonce, to immask our noted outward garments.

Prince. Yea, but I doubt they will be too hard for us.

Poins. Well, for two of them, I know them to be as true-bred cowards as ever turned back; and for the third, if he fight longer than he sees reason, I'll forswear arms. The virtue of this jest will be, the incomprehensible lies that this same fat rogue will tell us when we meet at supper: how thirty, at least, he fought with; what wards, what blows, what extremities he endured; and in the reproof of this lies the jest.

Prince. Well, I'll go with thee: provide us all things necessary and meet me to-morrow night in Eastcheap; there I'll sup. Farewell.

Poins. Farewell, my lord. *[Exit.*

Prince. I know you all, and will awhile uphold
The unyoked humour of your idleness:
Yet herein will I imitate the sun, 220
Who doth permit the base contagious clouds
To smother up his beauty from the world,
That, when he please again to be himself,
Being wanted, he may be more wonder'd at,

By breaking through the foul and ugly mists
Of vapours that did seem to strangle him.
If all the year were playing holidays,
To sport would be as tedious as to work;
But when they seldom come, they wish'd for
　　come,
And nothing pleaseth but rare accidents.　230
So, when this loose behaviour I throw off
And pay the debt I never promised,
By how much better than my word I am,
By so much shall I falsify men's hopes;
And like bright metal on a sullen ground,
My reformation, glittering o'er my fault,
Shall show more goodly and attract more eyes
Than that which hath no foil to set it off.
I'll so offend, to make offence a skill;
Redeeming time when men think least I will. 240
　　　　　　　　　　　　　　　　[Exit.

SCENE III. *London. The palace.*

Enter the KING, NORTHUMBERLAND, WORCES-
TER, HOTSPUR, SIR WALTER BLUNT, *with
others.*

　King. My blood hath been too cold and
　　temperate,
Unapt to stir at these indignities,
And you have found me; for accordingly
You tread upon my patience: but be sure
I will from henceforth rather be myself,
Mighty and to be fear'd, than my condition;
Which hath been smooth as oil, soft as young
　　down,
And therefore lost that title of respect
Which the proud soul ne'er pays but to the proud.
　Wor. Our house, my sovereign liege, little
　　deserves　　　　　　　　　　　　　　10
The scourge of greatness to be used on it;
And that same greatness too which our own
　　hands
● Have holp to make so portly.
　North. My lord,—
　King. Worcester, get thee gone; for I do
　　see
Danger and disobedience in thine eye:
O, sir, your presence is too bold and peremptory,
And majesty might never yet endure
The moody frontier of a servant brow.
You have good leave to leave us: when we need
Your use and counsel, we shall send for you.　21
　　　　　　　　　　　　　　　[*Exit Wor.*
You were about to speak.　　　　[*To North.*
　North.　　　　　　Yea, my good lord.
Those prisoners in your highness' name de-
　　manded,
Which Harry Percy here at Holmedon took,
Were, as he says, not with such strength denied
As is deliver'd to your majesty:
● Either envy, therefore, or misprision
Is guilty of this fault and not my son.
　Hot. My liege, I did deny no prisoners.
But I remember, when the fight was done,　30
When I was dry with rage and extreme toil,
Breathless and faint, leaning upon my sword,
Came there a certain lord, neat, and trimly
　　dress'd,
Fresh as a bridegroom; and his chin new reap'd
Show'd like a stubble-land at harvest-home;
He was perfumed like a milliner;

13 *holp.* Helped.

27 *misprision.* Misunderstanding.

38 *pouncet-box.* Scent-box.

58 *parmaceti.* An ointment: spermaceti, a white waxy substance from the head of the sperm whale.

87 *indent.* Make bargains.

94 *fall off.* Break his allegiance.

101 *changing hardiment.* Equal courage.

Hotspur: 'And 'twixt his finger and his thumb he held A pouncet-box . . .' Painting of Hotspur and the Fop by S.J.E. Jones, 1828

And 'twixt his finger and his thumb he held
A pouncet-box, which ever and anon
He gave his nose and took 't away again;   **39**
Who therewith angry, when it next came there,
Took it in snuff; and still he smiled and talk'd,
And as the soldiers bore dead bodies by,
He call'd them untaught knaves, unmannerly,
To bring a slovenly unhandsome corse
Betwixt the wind and his nobility.
With many holiday and lady terms
He question'd me; amongst the rest, demanded
My prisoners in your majesty's behalf.
I then, all smarting with my wounds being cold,
To be so pester'd with a popinjay,   **50**
Out of my grief and my impatience,
Answer'd neglectingly I know not what,
He should, or he should not; for he made me mad
To see him shine so brisk and smell so sweet
And talk so like a waiting-gentlewoman
Of guns and drums and wounds,—God save the mark!—
And telling me the sovereign'st thing on earth
Was parmaceti for an inward bruise;
And that it was great pity, so it was,
This villanous salt-petre should be digg'd   **60**
Out of the bowels of the harmless earth,
Which many a good tall fellow had destroy'd
So cowardly; and but for these vile guns,
He would himself have been a soldier.
This bald unjointed chat of his, my lord,
I answer'd indirectly, as I said;
And I beseech you, let not his report
Come current for an accusation
Betwixt my love and your high majesty.
    Blunt. The circumstance consider'd, good my lord,   **70**
Whate'er Lord Harry Percy then had said
To such a person and in such a place,
At such a time, with all the rest retold,
May reasonably die and never rise
To do him wrong or any way impeach
What then he said, so he unsay it now.
    King. Why, yet he doth deny his prisoners,
But with proviso and exception,
That we at our own charge shall ransom straight
His brother-in-law, the foolish Mortimer;   **80**
Who, on my soul, hath wilfully betray'd
The lives of those that he did lead to fight
Against that great magician, damn'd Glendower,
Whose daughter, as we hear, the Earl of March
Hath lately married. Shall our coffers, then,
Be emptied to redeem a traitor home?
Shall we buy treason? and indent with fears,
When they have lost and forfeited themselves?
No, on the barren mountains let him starve;
For I shall never hold that man my friend   **90**
Whose tongue shall ask me for one penny cost
To ransom home revolted Mortimer.
    Hot. Revolted Mortimer!
He never did fall off, my sovereign liege,
But by the chance of war: to prove that true
Needs no more but one tongue for all those wounds,
Those mouthed wounds, which valiantly he took,
When on the gentle Severn's sedgy bank,
In single opposition, hand to hand,
He did confound the best part of an hour   **100**
In changing hardiment with great Glendower:

108 *policy.* Cunning.

Three times they breathed and three times did
    they drink,
Upon agreement, of swift Severn's flood;
Who then, affrighted with their bloody looks,
Ran fearfully among the trembling reeds,
And hid his crisp head in the hollow bank
Bloodstained with these valiant combatants.
● Never did base and rotten policy
Colour her working with such deadly wounds;
Nor never could the noble Mortimer   110
Receive so many, and all willingly:
Then let not him be slander'd with revolt.
    King. Thou dost belie him, Percy, thou dost
      belie him;
He never did encounter with Glendower:
I tell thee,
He durst as well have met the devil alone
As Owen Glendower for an enemy.
Art thou not ashamed? But, sirrah, henceforth
Let me not hear you speak of Mortimer:
Send me your prisoners with the speediest means,
Or you shall hear in such a kind from me   121
As will displease you. My Lord Northumber-
    land,
We license your departure with your son.
Send us your prisoners, or you will hear of it.
    [*Exeunt King Henry, Blunt, and train.*
    Hot. An if the devil come and roar for them,
I will not send them: I will after straight
And tell him so; for I will ease my heart,
Albeit I make a hazard of my head.
    North. What, drunk with choler? stay and
    pause awhile:
Here comes your uncle.

      Re-enter WORCESTER.

    Hot.   Speak of Mortimer! 130
'Zounds, I will speak of him; and let my soul
Want mercy, if I do not join with him:
Yea, on his part I'll empty all these veins,
And shed my dear blood drop by drop in the dust,
But I will lift the down-trod Mortimer
As high in the air as this unthankful king,
As this ingrate and canker'd Bolingbroke.
    North. Brother, the king hath made your
    nephew mad.
    Wor. Who struck this heat up after I was
    gone?
    Hot. He will, forsooth, have all my pri-
    soners;   140
And when I urged the ransom once again
Of my wife's brother, then his cheek look'd pale,
And on my face he turn'd an eye of death,
Trembling even at the name of Mortimer.
    Wor. I cannot blame him: was not he pro-
    claim'd
By Richard that dead is the next of blood?
    North. He was; I heard the proclamation:
And then it was when the unhappy king,—
Whose wrongs in us God pardon!—did set forth
Upon his Irish expedition;   150
From whence he intercepted did return
To be deposed and shortly murdered.
    Wor. And for whose death we in the world's
    wide mouth
Live scandalized and foully spoken of.
    Hot. But, soft, I pray you; did King Richard
    then
Proclaim my brother Edmund Mortimer

King: 'Thou dost belie him, Percy, thou dost belie him'.
Hotspur with the King. Drawing by Anthony Walker
(1726-65)

168 *predicament*. Category.

207 *corrival*. Associate.

208 *half-faced fellowship*. Sharing of honours.

209 *figures*. Figments of the imagination.

Heir to the crown?
 North.   He did: myself did hear it.
 Hot. Nay, then I cannot blame his cousin
  king,
That wish'd him on the barren mountains starve.
But shall it be, that you, that set the crown 160
Upon the head of this forgetful man
And for his sake wear the detested blot
Of murderous subornation, shall it be,
That you a world of curses undergo,
Being the agents, or base second means,
The cords, the ladder, or the hangman rather?
O, pardon me that I descend so low,
● To show the line and the predicament
Wherein you range under this subtle king;
Shall it for shame be spoken in these days, 170
Or fill up chronicles in time to come,
That men of your nobility and power
Did gage them both in an unjust behalf,
As both of you—God pardon it!—have done,
To put down Richard, that sweet lovely rose,
And plant this thorn, this canker, Bolingbroke?
And shall it in more shame be further spoken,
That you are fool'd, discarded and shook off
By him for whom these shames ye underwent?
No; yet time serves wherein you may redeem 180
Your banish'd honours and restore yourselves
Into the good thoughts of the world again,
Revenge the jeering and disdain'd contempt
Of this proud king, who studies day and night
To answer all the debt he owes to you
Even with the bloody payment of your deaths:
Therefore, I say,—
 Wor.   Peace, cousin, say no more:
And now I will unclasp a secret book,
And to your quick-conceiving discontents
I'll read you matter deep and dangerous, 190
As full of peril and adventurous spirit
As to o'er-walk a current roaring loud
On the unsteadfast footing of a spear.
 Hot. If he fall in, good night! or sink or
  swim:
Send danger from the east unto the west,
So honour cross it from the north to south,
And let them grapple: O, the blood more stirs
To rouse a lion than to start a hare!
 North. Imagination of some great exploit
Drives him beyond the bounds of patience. 200
 Hot. By heaven, methinks it were an easy
  leap,
To pluck bright honour from the pale-faced moon,
Or dive into the bottom of the deep,
Where fathom-line could never touch the ground,
And pluck up drowned honour by the locks;
So he that doth redeem her thence might wear
● Without corrival all her dignities:
● But out upon this half-faced fellowship!
● *Wor.* He apprehends a world of figures here,
But not the form of what he should attend. 210
Good cousin, give me audience for a while.
 Hot. I cry you mercy.
 Wor.   Those same noble Scots
That are your prisoners,—
 Hot.   I'll keep them all;
By God, he shall not have a Scot of them;
No, if a Scot would save his soul, he shall not:
I'll keep them, by this hand.
 Wor.   You start away
And lend no ear unto my purposes.

Those prisoners you shall keep.
    Hot.   Nay, I will; that's flat:
He said he would not ransom Mortimer;
Forbad my tongue to speak of Mortimer;   220
But I will find him when he lies asleep,
And in his ear I'll holla 'Mortimer!'
Nay,
I'll have a starling shall be taught to speak
Nothing but 'Mortimer,' and give it him,
To keep his anger still in motion.
    Wor. Hear you, cousin; a word.
    Hot. All studies here I solemnly defy,
Save how to gall and pinch this Bolingbroke:
• And that same sword-and-buckler Prince of
        Wales,   230
But that I think his father loves him not
And would be glad he met with some mis-
    chance,
I would have him poison'd with a pot of ale.
    Wor. Farewell, kinsman: I'll talk to you
When you are better temper'd to attend.
    North. Why, what a wasp-stung and impa-
    tient fool
Art thou to break into this woman's mood,
Tying thine ear to no tongue but thine own!
    Hot. Why, look you, I am whipp'd and
    scourged with rods,
• Nettled and stung with pismires, when I hear
Of this vile politician, Bolingbroke.   241
In Richard's time,—what do you call the place?—
A plague upon it, it is in Gloucestershire;
• 'Twas where the madcap duke his uncle kept,
His uncle York; where I first bow'd my knee
Unto this king of smiles, this Bolingbroke,—
'Sblood!—
When you and he came back from Ravenspurgh.
    North. At Berkley castle.
    Hot. You say true: 250
Why, what a candy deal of courtesy
This fawning greyhound then did proffer me!
Look, 'when his infant fortune came to age,'
And 'gentle Harry Percy,' and 'kind cousin;'
O, the devil take such cozeners! God forgive me!
Good uncle, tell your tale; I have done.
    Wor. Nay, if you have not, to it again;
We will stay your leisure.
    Hot.   I have done, i' faith.
    Wor. Then once more to your Scottish pri-
    soners.
Deliver them up without their ransom straight,
And make the Douglas' son your only mean   261
For powers in Scotland; which, for divers rea-
    sons
Which I shall send you written, be assured,
Will easily be granted. You, my lord,
               [*To Northumberland.*
Your son in Scotland being thus employ'd,
Shall secretly into the bosom creep
Of that same noble prelate, well beloved,
The archbishop.
    Hot. Of York, is it not?
    Wor. True; who bears hard   270
His brother's death at Bristol, the Lord Scroop.
I speak not this in estimation,
As what I think might be, but what I know
Is ruminated, plotted and set down,
And only stays but to behold the face
Of that occasion that shall bring it on.
    Hot. I smell it: upon my life, it will do well.

230 *sword-and-buckler.* Ruffianly, swashbuckling.

William Creswick, the Victorian actor, as Hotspur,
Sadler's Wells Theatre, London, 1846

240 *pismires.* Ants.

244 *kept.* Resided.

284 *raising of a head.* Raising a force.

285 *even.* Carefully.

288 *pay us home.* Pay us out.

Rochester in Shakespeare's time. Engraving from John Speed's *Theatre of the Empire of Great Britaine,* 1611–12

2 *Charles' wain.* The Great Bear.

6–8 *beat Cut's saddle . . . out of all cess.* Beat the saddle to soften it, put some wool in; the poor nag has a badly galled back.

11 *bots.* Worms.

17 *tench.* A fish with red spots.

22 *jordan.* Chamber pot.

23 *chamber-lie.* Urine.

27 *razes.* Roots.

North. Before the game is afoot, thou still let'st slip.

Hot. Why, it cannot choose but be a noble plot:
And then the power of Scotland and of York, 280
To join with Mortimer, ha?

Wor. And so they shall.

Hot. In faith, it is exceedingly well aim'd.

Wor. And 'tis no little reason bids us speed,
• To save our heads by raising of a head;
• For, bear ourselves as even as we can,
The king will always think him in our debt,
And think we think ourselves unsatisfied,
• Till he hath found a time to pay us home:
And see already how he doth begin
To make us strangers to his looks of love.   290

Hot. He does, he does: we'll be revenged on him.

Wor. Cousin, farewell: no further go in this
Than I by letters shall direct your course.
When time is ripe, which will be suddenly,
I'll steal to Glendower and Lord Mortimer;
Where you and Douglas and our powers at once,
As I will fashion it, shall happily meet,
To bear our fortunes in our own strong arms,
Which now we hold at much uncertainty.

North. Farewell, good brother: we shall thrive, I trust.   300

Hot. Uncle, adieu: O, let the hours be short
Till fields and blows and groans applaud our sport!   [*Exeunt.*

ACT II.

Scene I. *Rochester. An inn yard.*

Enter a Carrier *with a lantern in his hand.*

First Car. Heigh-ho! an it be not four by
• the day, I'll be hanged: Charles' wain is over
the new chimney, and yet our horse not packed.
What, ostler!

Ost. [*Within*] Anon, anon.

First Car. I prithee, Tom, beat Cut's saddle,
put a few flocks in the point; poor jade, is wrung
in the withers out of all cess.

Enter another Carrier.

Sec. Car. Peas and beans are as dank here
as a dog, and that is the next way to give poor
• jades the bots: this house is turned upside down
since Robin Ostler died.

First Car. Poor fellow, never joyed since the
price of oats rose; it was the death of him.

Sec. Car. I think this be the most villanous
house in all London road for fleas: I am stung
• like a tench.

First Car. Like a tench! by the mass, there
is ne'er a king christen could be better bit than I
have been since the first cock.   20

Sec. Car. Why, they will allow us ne'er a
• jordan, and then we leak in your chimney; and
• your chamber-lie breeds fleas like a loach.

First Car. What, ostler! come away and be
hanged! come away.

Sec. Car. I have a gammon of bacon and two
• razes of ginger, to be delivered as far as Charing-
cross.

First Car. God's body! the turkeys in my
pannier are quite starved. What, ostler! A

plague on thee! hast thou never an eye in thy head? canst not hear? An 'twere not as good deed as drink, to break the pate on thee, I am a very villain. Come, and be hanged! hast no faith in thee?

Enter GADSHILL.

Gads. Good morrow, carriers. What's o'clock?
First Car. I think it be two o'clock.
Gads. I prithee, lend me thy lantern, to see my gelding in the stable.
First Car. Nay, by God, soft; I know a trick worth two of that, i' faith. 41
Gads. I pray thee, lend me thine.
Sec. Car. Ay, when? canst tell? Lend me thy lantern, quoth he? marry, I 'll see thee hanged first.
Gads. Sirrah carrier, what time do you mean to come to London?
Sec. Car. Time enough to go to bed with a candle, I warrant thee. Come, neighbour Mugs, we 'll call up the gentlemen: they will along with company, for they have great charge. 51
[*Exeunt Carriers.*
Gads. What, ho! chamberlain!
Cham. [*Within*] At hand, quoth pick-purse.
Gads. That's even as fair as—at hand, quoth the chamberlain; for thou variest no more from picking of purses than giving direction doth from labouring; thou layest the plot how.

Enter Chamberlain.

Cham. Good morrow, Master Gadshill. It holds current that I told you yesternight: there's a franklin in the wild of Kent hath brought three hundred marks with him in gold: I heard him tell it to one of his company last night at supper; a kind of auditor; one that hath abundance of charge too, God knows what. They are up already, and call for eggs and butter: they will away presently.
Gads. Sirrah, if they meet not with Saint Nicholas' clerks, I 'll give thee this neck.
Cham. No, I 'll none of it: I pray thee, keep that for the hangman; for I know thou worshippest Saint Nicholas as truly as a man of falsehood may.
Gads. What talkest thou to me of the hangman? if I hang, I 'll make a fat pair of gallows; for if I hang, old Sir John hangs with me, and thou knowest he is no starveling. Tut! there are other Trojans that thou dreamest not of, the which for sport sake are content to do the profession some grace; that would, if matters should be looked into, for their own credit sake, make all whole. I am joined with no foot land-rakers, no long-staff sixpenny strikers, none of these mad mustachio purple-hued malt-worms; but with nobility and tranquillity, burgomasters and great oneyers, such as can hold in, such as will strike sooner than speak, and speak sooner than drink, and drink sooner than pray: and yet, 'zounds, I lie; for they pray continually to their saint, the commonwealth; or rather, not pray to her, but prey on her, for they ride up and down on her and make her their boots. 91
Cham. What, the commonwealth their boots? will she hold out water in foul way?
Gads. She will, she will; justice hath liquored

The Inn Yard with Gadshill and the Carriers. Painting by Robert Smirke (1752–1845)

50 *will along with.* Wish to go along with.

51 *charge.* Baggage.

60 *franklin.* Freeholder, yeoman.

67—68 *Saint Nicholas' clerks.* Robbers.

81—82 *foot land-rakers . . . long-staff sixpenny strikers.* Foot-pads, robbers.

83 *mustachio . . . worms.* Bewhiskered purple-faced soakers.

85 *oneyers.* Officers.

94 *liquored.* A quibble on 'greased' and 'bribed'.

96 *receipt of fern-seed.* The power of invisibility.

2 *gummed velvet.* Velvet was treated against wear with gum.

13 *squier.* A measuring instrument; a carpenter's square.

39 *colt.* Trick.

Costume design for Falstaff by Tanya Moisewitch, Stratford-upon-Avon, 1951

her. We steal as in a castle, cock-sure; we have the receipt of fern-seed, we walk invisible.

Cham. Nay, by my faith, I think you are more beholding to the night than to fern-seed for your walking invisible.

Gads. Give me thy hand: thou shalt have a share in our purchase, as I am a true man.   101

Cham. Nay, rather let me have it, as you are a false thief.

Gads. Go to; 'homo' is a common name to all men. Bid the ostler bring my gelding out of the stable. Farewell, you muddy knave.

[*Exeunt.*

SCENE II.   *The highway, near Gadshill.*

Enter PRINCE HENRY *and* POINS.

Poins. Come, shelter, shelter: I have removed Falstaff's horse, and he frets like a gummed velvet.

Prince. Stand close.

Enter FALSTAFF.

Fal. Poins! Poins, and be hanged! Poins!

Prince. Peace, ye fat-kidneyed rascal! what a brawling dost thou keep!

Fal. Where's Poins, Hal?

Prince. He is walked up to the top of the hill: I'll go seek him.   9

Fal. I am accursed to rob in that thief's company: the rascal hath removed my horse, and tied him I know not where. If I travel but four foot by the squier further afoot, I shall break my wind. Well, I doubt not but to die a fair death for all this, if I 'scape hanging for killing that rogue. I have forsworn his company hourly any time this two and twenty years, and yet I am bewitched with the rogue's company. If the rascal have not given me medicines to make me love him, I'll be hanged: it could not be else; I have drunk medicines. Poins! Hal! a plague upon you both! Bardolph! Peto! I'll starve ere I'll rob a foot further. An 'twere not as good a deed as drink, to turn true man and to leave these rogues, I am the veriest varlet that ever chewed with a tooth. Eight yards of uneven ground is threescore and ten miles afoot with me; and the stony-hearted villains know it well enough: a plague upon it when thieves cannot be true one to another! [*They whistle.*] Whew! A plague upon you all! Give me my horse, you rogues; give me my horse, and be hanged!

Prince. Peace, ye fat-guts! lie down; lay thine ear close to the ground and list if thou canst hear the tread of travellers.

Fal. Have you any levers to lift me up again, being down? 'Sblood, I'll not bear mine own flesh so far afoot again for all the coin in thy father's exchequer. What a plague mean ye to colt me thus?   40

Prince. Thou liest; thou art not colted, thou art uncolted.

Fal. I prithee, good Prince Hal, help me to my horse, good king's son.

Prince. Out, ye rogue! shall I be your ostler?

Fal. Go hang thyself in thine own heir-apparent garters! If I be ta'en, I'll peach for this. An I have not ballads made on you all and sung to filthy tunes, let a cup of sack be my poison: when a jest is so forward, and afoot too! I hate it.

81 *dole.* Lot.

94 *chuffs.* Misers.

Enter GADSHILL, BARDOLPH *and* PETO *with him.*

Gads. Stand.

Fal. So I do, against my will.

Poins. O, 'tis our setter: I know his voice. Bardolph, what news?

Bard. Case ye, case ye; on with your vizards: there's money of the king's coming down the hill; 'tis going to the king's exchequer.

Fal. You lie, ye rogue; 'tis going to the king's tavern.

Gads. There's enough to make us all.   60

Fal. To be hanged.

Prince. Sirs, you four shall front them in the narrow lane; Ned Poins and I will walk lower: if they 'scape from your encounter, then they light on us.

Peto. How many be there of them?

Gads. Some eight or ten.

Fal. 'Zounds, will they not rob us?

Prince. What, a coward, Sir John Paunch?

Fal. Indeed, I am not John of Gaunt, your grandfather; but yet no coward, Hal.   71

Prince. Well, we leave that to the proof.

Poins. Sirrah Jack, thy horse stands behind the hedge: when thou needest him, there thou shalt find him. Farewell, and stand fast.

Fal. Now cannot I strike him, if I should be hanged.

Prince. Ned, where are our disguises?

Poins. Here, hard by: stand close.

[*Exeunt Prince and Poins.*

Fal. Now, my masters, happy man be his
• dole, say I: every man to his business.

Enter the Travellers.

First Trav. Come, neighbour: the boy shall lead our horses down the hill; we'll walk afoot awhile, and ease our legs.

Thieves. Stand!

Travellers. Jesus bless us!

Fal. Strike; down with them; cut the villains' throats: ah! whoreson caterpillars! bacon-fed knaves! they hate us youth: down with them: fleece them.   90

Travellers. O, we are undone, both we and ours for ever!

Fal. Hang ye, gorbellied knaves, are ye un-
• done? No, ye fat chuffs; I would your store were here! On, bacons, on! What, ye knaves! young men must live. You are grandjurors, are ye? we'll jure ye, 'faith.

[*Here they rob them and bind them. Exeunt.*

Re-enter PRINCE HENRY *and* POINS.

Prince. The thieves have bound the true men. Now could thou and I rob the thieves and go merrily to London, it would be argument for a week, laughter for a month and a good jest for ever.

Poins. Stand close; I hear them coming.

Enter the Thieves again.

Fal. Come, my masters, let us share, and then to horse before day. An the Prince and Poins be not two arrant cowards, there's no equity stirring: there's no more valour in that Poins than in a wild-duck.

Prince. Your money!

Falstaff: 'Come, my masters, let us share . . .' Engraving from a painting by Robert Smirke (1752–1845)

13 *unsorted.* Unsuitable.

16 *hind.* Peasant.

35 *go to buffets.* Fall to blows.

Lewis Waller, the English Edwardian actor, as Hotspur, Haymarket Theatre, London, 1896

44 *stomach.* Appetite.

Poins. Villains!   110
> [*As they are sharing, the Prince and
> Poins set upon them; they all run
> away; and Falstaff, after a blow
> or two, runs away too, leaving the
> booty behind them.*]

Prince. Got with much ease.   Now merrily
   to horse:
The thieves are all scatter'd and possess'd with
   fear
So strongly that they dare not meet each other;
Each takes his fellow for an officer.
Away, good Ned.   Falstaff sweats to death,
And lards the lean earth as he walks along:
Were 't not for laughing, I should pity him.
Poins. How the rogue roar'd!   [*Exeunt.*

Scene III.   *Warkworth castle.*

Enter Hotspur, *solus, reading a letter.*

Hot. ' But, for mine own part, my lord, I could
be well contented to be there, in respect of the
love I bear your house.' He could be contented:
why is he not, then? In respect of the love he
bears our house: he shows in this, he loves his
own barn better than he loves our house. Let me
see some more. 'The purpose you undertake is
dangerous;'—why, that's certain: 'tis dangerous
to take a cold, to sleep, to drink; but I tell you,
my lord fool, out of this nettle, danger, we pluck
this flower, safety. 'The purpose you undertake
is dangerous; the friends you have named uncertain: the time itself unsorted; and your whole
plot too light for the counterpoise of so great an
opposition.' Say you so, say you so? I say unto
you again, you are a shallow cowardly hind, and
you lie. What a lack-brain is this! By the Lord,
our plot is a good plot as ever was laid; our
friends true and constant: a good plot, good
friends, and full of expectation; an excellent plot,
very good friends. What a frosty-spirited rogue
is this! Why, my lord of York commends the
plot and the general course of the action. 'Zounds,
an I were now by this rascal, I could brain him
with his lady's fan. Is there not my father, my
uncle and myself? lord Edmund Mortimer, my
lord of York and Owen Glendower? is there not
besides the Douglas? have I not all their letters
to meet me in arms by the ninth of the next
month? and are they not some of them set forward already? What a pagan rascal is this! an
infidel! Ha! you shall see now in very sincerity
of fear and cold heart, will he to the king and
lay open all our proceedings. O, I could divide
myself and go to buffets, for moving such a dish
of skim milk with so honourable an action! Hang
him! let him tell the king: we are prepared. I
will set forward to-night.

Enter Lady Percy.

How now, Kate! I must leave you within these
   two hours.
Lady. O, my good lord, why are you thus
   alone?   40
For what offence have I this fortnight been
A banish'd woman from my Harry's bed?
Tell me, sweet lord, what is 't that takes from thee
Thy stomach, pleasure and thy golden sleep?
Why dost thou bend thine eyes upon the earth,

And start so often when thou sit'st alone?
Why hast thou lost the fresh blood in thy cheeks;
And given my treasures and my rights of thee
To thick-eyed musing and cursèd melancholy?
In thy faint slumbers I by thee have watch'd, 50
And heard thee murmur tales of iron wars;
• Speak terms of manage to thy bounding steed;
Cry 'Courage! to the field!' And thou hast talk'd
Of sallies and retires, of trenches, tents,
• Of palisadoes, frontiers, parapets,
• Of basilisks, of cannon, culverin,
Of prisoners' ransom and of soldiers slain,
And all the currents of a heady fight.
Thy spirit within thee hath been so at war
And thus hath so bestirr'd thee in thy sleep, 60
That beads of sweat have stood upon thy brow,
Like bubbles in a late-disturbed stream;
And in thy face strange motions have appear'd,
Such as we see when men restrain their breath
On some great sudden hest. O, what portents
   are these?
Some heavy business hath my lord in hand,
And I must know it, else he loves me not.
   Hot. What, ho!

       Enter Servant.
         Is Gilliams with the packet gone?
Serv. He is, my lord, an hour ago.
Hot. Hath Butler brought those horses from
   the sheriff? 70
Serv. One horse, my lord, he brought even
   now.
Hot. What horse? a roan, a crop-ear, is it not?
Serv. It is, my lord.
Hot.   That roan shall be my throne.
• Well, I will back him straight: O esperance!
Bid Butler lead him forth into the park.
                 [*Exit Servant.*
Lady. But hear you, my lord.
Hot. What say'st thou, my lady?
Lady. What is it carries you away?
Hot. Why, my horse, my love, my horse.
Lady. Out, you mad-headed ape! 80
A weasel hath not such a deal of spleen
As you are toss'd with. In faith,
I'll know your business, Harry, that I will.
I fear my brother Mortimer doth stir
About his title, and hath sent for you
To line his enterprize: but if you go,—
   Hot. So far afoot, I shall be weary, love.
• *Lady.* Come, come, you paraquito, answer me
Directly unto this question that I ask:
In faith, I'll break thy little finger, Harry, 90
An if thou wilt not tell me all things true.
   Hot. Away,
Away, you trifler! Love! I love thee not,
I care not for thee, Kate: this is no world
• To play with mammets and to tilt with lips:
We must have bloody noses and crack'd crowns,
• And pass them current too. God's me, my horse!
What say'st thou, Kate? what would'st thou have
   with me?
   Lady. Do you not love me? do you not, indeed?
Well, do not then; for since you love me not, 100
I will not love myself. Do you not love me?
Nay, tell me if you speak in jest or no.
   Hot. Come, wilt thou see me ride?
And when I am o' horseback, I will swear
I love thee infinitely. But hark you, Kate;

52 *manage.* Horsemanship.

55 *palisadoes.* Stakes in the ground to stop a charge.

56 *basilisks . . . culverin.* Small and large cannon.

74 *esperance.* Hope (the Percy battle-cry).

88 *paraquito.* Parrot.

95 *mammets.* Dolls.

97 *pass them current.* i.e. 'deal them out' and 'circulate' (the coins).

Hotspur: 'Come, wilt thou see me ride?' Hotspur and Lady Percy. Drawing by J.M. Wright (1776–1866)

An inn yard, London. Engraving from *Old England*, 1854

---

7 *leash of drawers.* i.e. three waiters.

12 *Jack.* Fellow, knave.

13 *Corinthian.* Splendid fellow.

18 *play.* Toss.

26 *under-skinker.* Tapster's assistant.

30 *bastard in the Half-moon.* Sweet Spanish wine in one of the tavern's rooms.

42 *Pomgarnet.* i.e. Pomegranate, a room in the inn.

I must not have you henceforth question me
Whither I go, nor reason whereabout:
Whither I must, I must; and, to conclude,
This evening must I leave you, gentle Kate.
I know you wise, but yet no farther wise   110
Than Harry Percy's wife: constant you are,
But yet a woman: and for secrecy,
No lady closer; for I well believe
Thou wilt not utter what thou dost not know;
And so far will I trust thee, gentle Kate.
  Lady. How! so far?
  Hot. Not an inch further. But hark you, Kate:
Whither I go, thither shall you go too;
To-day will I set forth, to-morrow you.
Will this content you, Kate?
  Lady.   It must of force. [*Exeunt.* 120

SCENE IV. *The Boar's-Head Tavern, Eastcheap.*

Enter the PRINCE, *and* POINS.

Prince. Ned, prithee, come out of that fat room, and lend me thy hand to laugh a little.
Poins. Where hast been, Hal?
Prince. With three or four loggerheads amongst three or four score hogsheads. I have sounded the very base-string of humility. Sirrah, I am sworn brother to a leash of drawers; and can call them all by their christen names, as Tom, Dick, and Francis. They take it already upon their salvation, that though I be but Prince of Wales, yet I am the king of courtesy; and tell me flatly I am no proud Jack, like Falstaff, but a Corinthian, a lad of mettle, a good boy, by the Lord, so they call me, and when I am king of England, I shall command all the good lads in Eastcheap. They call drinking deep, dyeing scarlet; and when you breathe in your watering, they cry 'hem!' and bid you play it off. To conclude, I am so good a proficient in one quarter of an hour, that I can drink with any tinker in his own language during my life. I tell thee, Ned, thou hast lost much honour, that thou wert not with me in this action. But, sweet Ned,—to sweeten which name of Ned, I give thee this pennyworth of sugar, clapped even now into my hand by an under-skinker, one that never spake other English in his life than 'Eight shillings and sixpence,' and 'You are welcome,' with this shrill addition, 'Anon, anon, sir! Score a pint of bastard in the Half-moon,' or so. But, Ned, to drive away the time till Falstaff come, I prithee, do thou stand in some by-room, while I question my puny drawer to what end he gave me the sugar; and do thou never leave calling 'Francis,' that his tale to me may be nothing but 'Anon.' Step aside, and I'll show thee a precedent.
Poins. Francis!
Prince. Thou art perfect.
Poins. Francis!   [*Exit Poins.* 40

Enter FRANCIS.

Fran. Anon, anon, sir. Look down into the Pomgarnet, Ralph.
Prince. Come hither, Francis.
Fran. My lord?
Prince. How long hast thou to serve, Francis?

Fran. Forsooth, five years, and as much as to—

Poins. [*Within*] Francis!

Fran. Anon, anon, sir.   49

Prince. Five year! by'r lady, a long lease for the clinking of pewter. But, Francis, darest thou be so valiant as to play the coward with thy
● indenture and show it a fair pair of heels and run from it?

Fran. O Lord, sir, I'll be sworn upon all the books in England, I could find in my heart.

Poins. [*Within*] Francis!

Fran. Anon, sir.

Prince. How old art thou, Francis?

Fran. Let me see—about Michaelmas next I shall be—   61

Poins. [*Within*] Francis!

Fran. Anon, sir. Pray stay a little, my lord.

Prince. Nay, but hark you, Francis: for the sugar thou gavest me, 'twas a pennyworth, wast't not?

Fran. O Lord, I would it had been two!

Prince. I will give thee for it a thousand pound: ask me when thou wilt, and thou shalt have it.   70

Poins. [*Within*] Francis!

Fran. Anon, anon.

Prince. Anon, Francis? No, Francis; but to-morrow, Francis; or Francis, o' Thursday; or indeed, Francis, when thou wilt. But, Francis!

Fran. My lord?

Prince. Wilt thou rob this leathern jerkin,
● crystal-button, not-pated, agate-ring, puke-stocking, caddis-garter, smooth-tongue, Spanish-pouch,—   80

Fran. O Lord, sir, who do you mean?

Prince. Why, then, your brown bastard is your only drink; for look you, Francis, your white
● canvas doublet will sully: in Barbary, sir, it cannot come to so much.

Fran. What, sir?

Poins. [*Within*] Francis!

Prince. Away, you rogue! dost thou not hear them call? [*Here they both call him; the drawer stands amazed, not knowing which way to go.*

Enter Vintner.

Vint. What, standest thou still, and hearest such a calling? Look to the guests within. [*Exit Francis.*] My lord, old Sir John, with half-a-dozen more, are at the door: shall I let them in?

Prince. Let them alone awhile, and then open the door. [*Exit Vintner.*] Poins!

Re-enter POINS.

Poins. Anon, anon, sir.

Prince. Sirrah, Falstaff and the rest of the thieves are at the door: shall we be merry?   99

Poins. As merry as crickets, my lad. But hark ye; what cunning match have you made with this jest of the drawer? come, what's the issue?

Prince. I am now of all humours that have showed themselves humours since the old days of goodman Adam to the pupil age of this present twelve o'clock at midnight.

53 *indenture.* Deed of apprenticeship.

78–79 *not-pated.* Short-haired. *puke-stocking.* Woollen stocking. *caddis-garter.* Garter of worsted tape.

84 *it.* i.e. sugar, grown in Barbary.

123–125 *brawn . . . ribs . . . tallow.* Typical products of Eastcheap.

130 *nether stocks.* Stockings.

Roy Byford as Falstaff, Stratford-upon-Avon, 1932

137 *lime.* Added to wine to make it sparkle.

143 *shotten herring.* A thin person; literally, a herring that has shot its roe.

147 *weaver.* Weavers sang at their work; also many were Puritans and given to psalm singing.

Sectarian preachers and weavers. Woodcut from a tract of 1636

Re-enter FRANCIS.

What's o'clock, Francis?

Fran. Anon, anon, sir.   [*Exit.* 109

Prince. That ever this fellow should have fewer words than a parrot, and yet the son of a woman! His industry is up-stairs and down-stairs; his eloquence the parcel of a reckoning. I am not yet of Percy's mind, the Hotspur of the north; he that kills me some six or seven dozen of Scots at a breakfast, washes his hands, and says to his wife 'Fie upon this quiet life! I want work.' 'O my sweet Harry,' says she, 'how many hast thou killed to-day?' 'Give my roan horse a drench,' says he; and answers 'Some fourteen,' an hour after; 'a trifle, a trifle.' I prithee, call in Falstaff: I'll play Percy, and that damned brawn shall play Dame Mortimer his wife. 'Rivo!' says the drunkard. Call in ribs, call in tallow.

Enter FALSTAFF, GADSHILL, BARDOLPH, **and** PETO; FRANCIS *following with wine.*

Poins. Welcome, Jack: where hast thou been?

Fal. A plague of all cowards, I say, and a vengeance too! marry, and amen! Give me a cup of sack, boy. Ere I lead this life long, I'll sew nether stocks and mend them and foot them too. A plague of all cowards! Give me a cup of sack, rogue. Is there no virtue extant?

[*He drinks.*

Prince. Didst thou never see Titan kiss a dish of butter? pitiful-hearted Titan, that melted at the sweet tale of the sun's! if thou didst, then behold that compound.

Fal. You rogue, here's lime in this sack too: there is nothing but roguery to be found in villanous man: yet a coward is worse than a cup of sack with lime in it. A villanous coward! Go thy ways, old Jack; die when thou wilt, if manhood, good manhood, be not forgot upon the face of the earth, then am I a shotten herring. There live not three good men unhanged in England; and one of them is fat and grows old: God help the while! a bad world, I say. I would I were a weaver; I could sing psalms or any thing. A plague of all cowards, I say still.

Prince. How now, wool-sack! what mutter you?   149

Fal. A king's son! If I do not beat thee out of thy kingdom with a dagger of lath, and drive all thy subjects afore thee like a flock of wild-geese, I'll never wear hair on my face more. You Prince of Wales!

Prince. Why, you whoreson round man, what's the matter?

Fal. Are not you a coward? answer me to that: and Poins there?

Poins. 'Zounds, ye fat paunch, an ye call me coward, by the Lord, I'll stab thee.   160

Fal. I call thee coward! I'll see thee damned ere I call thee coward: but I would give a thousand pound I could run as fast as thou canst. You are straight enough in the shoulders, you care not who sees your back: call you that backing of your friends? A plague upon such backing! give me them that will face me. Give me a cup of sack: I am a rogue, if I drunk to-day.

Prince. O villain! thy lips are scarce wiped since thou drunkest last.　171

Fal. All's one for that. [*He drinks.*] A plague of all cowards, still say I.

Prince. What's the matter?

Fal. What's the matter! there be four of us here have ta'en a thousand pound this day morning.

Prince. Where is it, Jack? where is it?

Fal. Where is it! taken from us it is: a hundred upon poor four of us.　180

Prince. What, a hundred, man?

Fal. I am a rogue, if I were not at half-sword with a dozen of them two hours together. I have 'scaped by miracle. I am eight times thrust through the doublet, four through the hose; my buckler cut through and through; my sword hacked like a hand-saw—ecce signum! I never dealt better since I was a man: all would not do. A plague of all cowards! Let them speak: if they speak more or less than truth, they are villains and the sons of darkness.　191

Prince. Speak, sirs; how was it?

Gads. We four set upon some dozen—

Fal. Sixteen at least, my lord.

Gads. And bound them.

Peto. No, no, they were not bound.

Fal. You rogue, they were bound, every man of them; or I am a Jew else, an Ebrew Jew.

Gads. As we were sharing, some six or seven fresh men set upon us—　200

Fal. And unbound the rest, and then come in the other.

Prince. What, fought you with them all?

Fal. All! I know not what you call all; but if I fought not with fifty of them, I am a bunch of radish: if there were not two or three and fifty upon poor old Jack, then am I no two-legged creature.

Prince. Pray God you have not murdered some of them.　210

Fal. Nay, that's past praying for: I have peppered two of them; two I am sure I have paid, two rogues in buckram suits. I tell thee what, Hal, if I tell thee a lie, spit in my face, call me horse. Thou knowest my old ward; here I lay, and thus I bore my point. Four rogues in buckram let drive at me—

Prince. What, four? thou saidst but two even now.

Fal. Four, Hal; I told thee four.　220

Poins. Ay, ay, he said four.

Fal. These four came all a-front, and mainly thrust at me. I made me no more ado but took all their seven points in my target, thus.

Prince. Seven? why, there were but four even now.

Fal. In buckram?

Poins. Ay, four, in buckram suits.

Fal. Seven, by these hilts, or I am a villain else.　230

Prince. Prithee, let him alone; we shall have more anon.

Fal Dost thou hear me, Hal?

Prince. Ay, and mark thee too, Jack.

Fal. Do so, for it is worth the listening to. These nine in buckram that I told thee of—

Prince. So, two more already.

Fal. Their points being broken,—

187 *ecce signum.* Behold the evidence.

213 *paid.* Killed.

215 *ward.* Defensive stand.

Falstaff: '. . . here I lay, and thus I bore my point'. Drawing by Anthony Walker (1726–65)

238 *points.* i.e. of their swords, with a pun on the laces which hold up garments.

252–253 *tallow-catch*. Pan of dripping.

262 *strappado*. Instrument of torture.

268 *sanguine*. Daring.

271–272 *neat's tongue*. Ox tongue. *pizzle*. Penis, sometimes used for flogging. *stock-fish*. Dried cod.

274 *standing-tuck*. Up-ended and useless rapier.

Poins. Down fell their hose.   239

Fal. Began to give me ground: but I followed me close, came in foot and hand; and with a thought seven of the eleven I paid.

Prince. O monstrous! eleven buckram men grown out of two!

Fal. But, as the devil would have it, three misbegotten knaves in Kendal green came at my back and let drive at me; for it was so dark, Hal, that thou couldst not see thy hand.

Prince. These lies are like their father that begets them; gross as a mountain, open, palpable. Why, thou clay-brained guts, thou knotty-pated fool, thou whoreson, obscene, greasy tallow-catch,—

Fal. What, art thou mad? art thou mad? is not the truth the truth?

Prince. Why, how couldst thou know these men in Kendal green, when it was so dark thou couldst not see thy hand? come, tell us your reason: what sayest thou to this?   259

Poins. Come, your reason, Jack, your reason.

Fal. What, upon compulsion? 'Zounds, an I were at the strappado, or all the racks in the world, I would not tell you on compulsion. Give you a reason on compulsion! if reasons were as plentiful as blackberries, I would give no man a reason upon compulsion, I.

Prince. I'll be no longer guilty of this sin; this sanguine coward, this bed-presser, this horseback-breaker, this huge hill of flesh,—   269

Fal. 'Sblood, you starveling, you elf-skin, you dried neat's tongue, you bull's pizzle, you stock-fish! O for breath to utter what is like thee! you tailor's-yard, you sheath, you bow-case, you vile standing-tuck,—

Prince. Well, breathe awhile, and then to it again: and when thou hast tired thyself in base comparisons, hear me speak but this.

Poins. Mark, Jack.

Prince. We two saw you four set on four and bound them, and were masters of their wealth. Mark now, how a plain tale shall put you down. Then did we two set on you four; and, with a word, out-faced you from your prize, and have it; yea, and can show it you here in the house: and, Falstaff, you carried your guts away as nimbly, with as quick dexterity, and roared for mercy and still run and roared, as ever I heard bull-calf. What a slave art thou, to hack thy sword as thou hast done, and then say it was in fight! What trick, what device, what starting-hole, canst thou now find out to hide thee from this open and apparent shame?

Poins. Come, let's hear, Jack; what trick hast thou now?

Fal. By the Lord, I knew ye as well as he that made ye. Why, hear you, my masters: was it for me to kill the heir-apparent? should I turn upon the true prince? why, thou knowest I am as valiant as Hercules: but beware instinct; the lion will not touch the true prince. Instinct is a great matter; I was now a coward on instinct. I shall think the better of myself and thee during my life; I for a valiant lion, and thou for a true prince. But, by the Lord, lads, I am glad you have the money. Hostess, clap to the doors: watch to-night, pray to-morrow. Gallants, lads, boys, hearts of gold, all the titles of good fellowship come to you! What, shall we be merry? shall we have a play extempore?

Prince. Content; and the argument shall be thy running away. 311

Fal. Ah, no more of that, Hal, an thou lovest me!

Enter Hostess.

Host. O Jesu, my lord the prince!

Prince. How now, my lady the hostess! what sayest thou to me?

Host. Marry, my lord, there is a nobleman of the court at door would speak with you: he says he comes from your father. 319

Prince. Give him as much as will make him a royal man, and send him back again to my mother.

Fal. What manner of man is he?

Host. An old man.

Fal. What doth gravity out of his bed at midnight? Shall I give him his answer?

Prince. Prithee, do, Jack.

Fal. 'Faith, and I'll send him packing. [*Exit.*

Prince. Now, sirs: by'r lady, you fought fair; so did you, Peto; so did you, Bardolph: you are lions too, you ran away upon instinct, you will not touch the true prince; no, fie!

Bard. 'Faith, I ran when I saw others run.

Prince. 'Faith, tell me now in earnest, how came Falstaff's sword so hacked?

Peto. Why, he hacked it with his dagger, and said he would swear truth out of England but he would make you believe it was done in fight, and persuaded us to do the like. 339

Bard. Yea, and to tickle our noses with speargrass to make them bleed, and then to beslubber our garments with it and swear it was the blood of true men. I did that I did not this seven year before, I blushed to hear his monstrous devices.

Prince. O villain, thou stolest a cup of sack eighteen years ago, and wert taken with the manner, and ever since thou hast blushed extempore. Thou hadst fire and sword on thy side, and yet thou rannest away: what instinct hadst thou for it? 350

Bard. My lord, do you see these meteors? do you behold these exhalations?

Prince. I do.

Bard. What think you they portend?

Prince. Hot livers and cold purses.

Bard. Choler, my lord, if rightly taken.

Prince. No, if rightly taken, halter.

Re-enter FALSTAFF.

Here comes lean Jack, here comes bare-bone. How now, my sweet creature of bombast! How long is't ago, Jack, since thou sawest thine own knee? 361

Fal. My own knee! when I was about thy years, Hal, I was not an eagle's talon in the waist; I could have crept into any alderman's thumb-ring: a plague of sighing and grief! it blows a man up like a bladder. There's villanous news abroad: here was Sir John Bracy from your father; you must to the court in the morning. That same mad fellow of the north, Percy, and he of Wales, that gave Amamon the bastinado and made Lucifer cuckold and swore the devil

Falstaff and the Prince, with companions, in the Boar's Head. Painting 'The Happiest Land' by Sir John Gilbert, 1862

---

321 *royal.* A pun on Tudor coinage: the royal was worth ten shillings, the noble six shillings and eightpence.

346–347 *taken with the manner.* Caught with the goods.

351 *meteors.* Red blotches on his face.

357 *halter.* A pun on 'choler' and 'collar' (the hangman's noose).

370 *Amamon.* A demon. *bastinado.* Beating (on the soles of the feet).

371 *made Lucifer cuckold.* i.e. gave him his horns.

425 *King Cambyses.* King of Persia and title of a florid verse drama.

427 *leg.* Curtsy.

437 *harlotry.* Scurvy.

Falstaff plays the King. Drawing by Anthony Walker (1726–65)

his true liegeman upon the cross of a Welsh hook—what a plague call you him?

Poins. O, Glendower.

Fal. Owen, Owen, the same; and his son-in-law Mortimer, and old Northumberland, and that sprightly Scot of Scots, Douglas, that runs o' horseback up a hill perpendicular,—

Prince. He that rides at high speed and with his pistol kills a sparrow flying. 380

Fal. You have hit it.

Prince. So did he never the sparrow.

Fal. Well, that rascal hath good mettle in him; he will not run.

Prince. Why, what a rascal art thou then, to praise him so for running!

Fal. O' horseback, ye cuckoo; but afoot he will not budge a foot.

Prince. Yes, Jack, upon instinct. 389

Fal. I grant ye, upon instinct. Well, he is there too, and one Mordake, and a thousand blue-caps more: Worcester is stolen away to-night; thy father's beard is turned white with the news: you may buy land now as cheap as stinking mackerel.

Prince. Why, then, it is like, if there come a hot June and this civil buffeting hold, we shall buy maidenheads as they buy hob-nails, by the hundreds. 399

Fal. By the mass, lad, thou sayest true; it is like we shall have good trading that way. But tell me, Hal, art not thou horrible afeard? thou being heir-apparent, could the world pick thee out three such enemies again as that fiend Douglas, that spirit Percy, and that devil Glendower? Art thou not horribly afraid? doth not thy blood thrill at it?

Prince. Not a whit, i' faith; I lack some of thy instinct. 409

Fal. Well, thou wilt be horribly chid to-morrow when thou comest to thy father: if thou love me, practise an answer.

Prince. Do thou stand for my father, and examine me upon the particulars of my life.

Fal. Shall I? content: this chair shall be my state, this dagger my sceptre, and this cushion my crown.

Prince. Thy state is taken for a joined-stool, thy golden sceptre for a leaden dagger, and thy precious rich crown for a pitiful bald crown! 420

Fal. Well, an the fire of grace be not quite out of thee, now shalt thou be moved. Give me a cup of sack to make my eyes look red, that it may be thought I have wept; for I must speak
• in passion, and I will do it in King Cambyses' vein.
• *Prince.* Well, here is my leg.

Fal. And here is my speech. Stand aside, nobility. 429

Host. O Jesu, this is excellent sport, i' faith!

Fal. Weep not, sweet queen; for trickling tears are vain.

Host. O, the father, how he holds his countenance!

Fal. For God's sake, lords, convey my tristful queen;
For tears do stop the flood-gates of her eyes.

Host. O Jesu, he doth it as like one of these
• harlotry players as ever I see!

Fal. Peace, good pint-pot; peace, good tickle-brain. Harry, I do not only marvel where thou spendest thy time, but also how thou art accompanied: for though the camomile, the more it is trodden on the faster it grows, yet youth, the more it is wasted the sooner it wears. That thou art my son, I have partly thy mother's word, partly my own opinion, but chiefly a villanous trick of thine eye and a foolish hanging of thy nether lip, that doth warrant me. If then thou be son to me, here lies the point; why, being son to me, art thou so pointed at? Shall the blessed sun of heaven prove a micher and eat blackberries? a question not to be asked. Shall the son of England prove a thief and take purses? a question to be asked. There is a thing, Harry, which thou hast often heard of and it is known to many in our land by the name of pitch: this pitch, as ancient writers do report, doth defile; so doth the company thou keepest: for, Harry, now I do not speak to thee in drink but in tears, not in pleasure but in passion, not in words only, but in woes also: and yet there is a virtuous man whom I have often noted in thy company, but I know not his name. 461

Prince. What manner of man, an it like your majesty?

Fal. A goodly portly man, i' faith, and a corpulent; of a cheerful look, a pleasing eye and a most noble carriage; and, as I think, his age some fifty, or, by 'r lady, inclining to three score; and now I remember me, his name is Falstaff: if that man should be lewdly given, he deceiveth me; for, Harry, I see virtue in his looks. If then the tree may be known by the fruit, as the fruit by the tree, then, peremptorily I speak it, there is virtue in that Falstaff: him keep with, the rest banish. And tell me now, thou naughty varlet, tell me, where hast thou been this month?

Prince. Dost thou speak like a king? Do thou stand for me, and I'll play my father.

Fal. Depose me? if thou dost it half so gravely, so majestically, both in word and matter, hang me up by the heels for a rabbit-sucker or a poulter's hare. 481

Prince. Well, here I am set.

Fal. And here I stand: judge, my masters.

Prince. Now, Harry, whence come you?

Fal. My noble lord, from Eastcheap.

Prince. The complaints I hear of thee are grievous.

Fal. 'Sblood, my lord, they are false: nay, I'll tickle ye for a young prince, i' faith. 489

Prince. Swearest thou, ungracious boy? henceforth ne'er look on me. Thou art violently carried away from grace: there is a devil haunts thee in the likeness of an old fat man; a tun of man is thy companion. Why dost thou converse with that trunk of humours, that bolting-hutch of beastliness, that swollen parcel of dropsies, that huge bombard of sack, that stuffed cloak-bag of guts, that roasted Manningtree ox with the pudding in his belly, that reverend vice, that grey iniquity, that father ruffian, that vanity in years? Wherein is he good, but to taste sack and drink it? wherein neat and cleanly, but to carve a capon and eat it? wherein cunning, but in craft? wherein crafty, but in villany? wherein villanous, but in all things? wherein worthy, but in nothing?

Fal. I would your grace would take me with you: whom means your grace?

450 *micher.* Truant.

495 *bolting-hutch.* Sifting-bin.

498 *Manningtree ox.* Famous for its size.

499 *vice.* Chief comic character and villain in Morality plays.

506–507 *take me with you.* Make yourself clear.

544 *major.* Major premise, but quibbling on 'mayor'.

546 *cart.* In which criminals were carried to the gallows.

Cart used to carry criminals. Woodcut from Thomas Harman's *A Caveat on Warening*, 1567

Prince. That villanous abominable misleader of youth, Falstaff, that old white-bearded Satan.

Fal. My lord, the man I know. 510

Prince. I know thou dost.

Fal. But to say I know more harm in him than in myself, were to say more than I know. That he is old, the more the pity, his white hairs do witness it; but that he is, saving your reverence, a whoremaster, that I utterly deny. If sack and sugar be a fault, God help the wicked! if to be old and merry be a sin, then many an old host that I know is damned: if to be fat be to be hated, then Pharaoh's lean kine are to be loved. No, my good lord; banish Peto, banish Bardolph, banish Poins: but for sweet Jack Falstaff, kind Jack Falstaff, true Jack Falstaff, valiant Jack Falstaff, and therefore more valiant, being, as he is, old Jack Falstaff, banish not him thy Harry's company, banish not him thy Harry's company: banish plump Jack, and banish all the world.

Prince. I do, I will. [*A knocking heard.*
[*Exeunt Hostess, Francis, and Bardolph.*

Re-enter BARDOLPH, *running.*

Bard. O, my lord, my lord! the sheriff with a most monstrous watch is at the door. 530

Fal. Out, ye rogue! Play out the play: I have much to say in the behalf of that Falstaff.

Re-enter the Hostess.

Host. O Jesu, my lord, my lord!

Prince. Heigh, heigh! the devil rides upon a fiddlestick: what's the matter?

Host. The sheriff and all the watch are at the door: they are come to search the house. Shall I let them in?

Fal. Dost thou hear, Hal? never call a true piece of gold a counterfeit: thou art essentially mad, without seeming so. 541

Prince. And thou a natural coward, without instinct.

Fal. I deny your major: if you will deny the sheriff, so; if not, let him enter: if I become not a cart as well as another man, a plague on my bringing up! I hope I shall as soon be strangled with a halter as another.

Prince. Go, hide thee behind the arras: the rest walk up above. Now, my masters, for a true face and good conscience. 551

Fal. Both which I have had: but their date is out, and therefore I'll hide me.

Prince. Call in the sheriff.
[*Exeunt all except the Prince and Peto.*

Enter Sheriff *and the* Carrier.

Now, master sheriff, what is your will with me?

Sher. First, pardon me, my lord. A hue and cry
Hath follow'd certain men unto this house.

Prince. What men?

Sher. One of them is well known, my gracious lord,
A gross fat man.

Car.   As fat as butter. 560

Prince. The man, I do assure you, is not here;
For I myself at this time have employ'd him.
And, sheriff, I will engage my word to thee
That I will, by to-morrow dinner-time,
Send him to answer thee, or any man,

For any thing he shall be charged withal:
And so let me entreat you leave the house.
   Sher. I will, my lord.   There are two gentle-
men
Have in this robbery lost three hundred marks.
   Prince. It may be so: if he have robb'd these
men,   570
He shall be answerable; and so farewell.
   Sher. Good night, my noble lord.
   Prince. I think it is good morrow, is it not?
   Sher. Indeed, my lord, I think it be two o'clock.
   [*Exeunt Sheriff and Carrier.*
   Prince. This oily rascal is known as well as
● Paul's.   Go, call him forth.
   Peto. Falstaff!—Fast asleep behind the arras,
and snorting like a horse.
   Prince. Hark, how hard he fetches breath.
Search his pockets. [*He searcheth his pockets,
and findeth certain papers.*] What hast thou
found?
   Peto. Nothing but papers, my lord.
   Prince. Let's see what they be: read them.
   Peto. [*Reads*] Item, A capon, . . 2s. 2d.
             Item, Sauce, . .   4d.
             Item, Sack, two gallons, 5s. 8d.
             Item, Anchovies and sack
                 after supper, . 2s. 6d.
             Item, Bread, . .   ob.
   Prince. O monstrous! but one half-penny-
worth of bread to this intolerable deal of sack!
What there is else, keep close; we'll read it at
more advantage: there let him sleep till day.
I'll to the court in the morning. We must all to
the wars, and thy place shall be honourable. I'll
● procure this fat rogue a charge of foot; and I
● know his death will be a march of twelve-score.
The money shall be paid back again with advantage. Be with me betimes in the morning; and
so, good morrow, Peto.   601
   Peto. Good morrow, good my lord. [*Exeunt.*

ACT III.

Scene I. *Bangor. The Archdeacon's house.*

Enter Hotspur, Worcester, Mortimer, *and*
Glendower.

   Mort. These promises are fair, the parties sure,
And our induction full of prosperous hope.
   Hot. Lord Mortimer, and cousin Glendower,
Will you sit down?
And uncle Worcester: a plague upon it!
I have forgot the map.
   Glend.   No, here it is.
Sit, cousin Percy; sit, good cousin Hotspur,
For by that name as oft as Lancaster
Doth speak of you, his cheek looks pale and with
A rising sigh he wisheth you in heaven.   10
   Hot. And you in hell, as oft as he hears Owen
Glendower spoke of.
   Glend. I cannot blame him: at my nativity
The front of heaven was full of fiery shapes,
● Of burning cressets; and at my birth
The frame and huge foundation of the earth
Shaked like a coward.
   Hot. Why, so it would have done at the same
season, if your mother's cat had but kittened,
though yourself had never been born.   20

576 *Paul's.* St. Paul's Cathedral.

St Paul's Cathedral at the time of Shakespeare. This
building was destroyed in the Great Fire and replaced by
Sir Christopher Wren's St Paul's (completed 1710).
From John Speed's *Theatre of the Empire of Great
Britaine,* 1611–12

597 *charge of foot.* Command of a company of infantry.

598 *twelve-score.* i.e. 240 yards.

15 *cressets.* Stars, burning like fire baskets or beacons.

Owen Glendower. Engraving from his Great Seal in *Old England*, 1854

---

32 *beldam.* Grandmother.

48 *trace me . . . art.* Follow me in the laborious practices of magic.

49 *deep.* Occult.

69 *agues.* Fever.

Glend. I say the earth did shake when I was born.

Hot. And I say the earth was not of my mind,
If you suppose as fearing you it shook.

Glend. The heavens were all on fire, the earth did tremble.

Hot. O, then the earth shook to see the heavens on fire,
And not in fear of your nativity.
Diseased nature oftentimes breaks forth
In strange eruptions; oft the teeming earth
Is with a kind of colic pinch'd and vex'd
By the imprisoning of unruly wind   30
Within her womb; which, for enlargement striving,
• Shakes the old beldam earth and topples down
Steeples and moss-grown towers.   At your birth
Our grandam earth, having this distemperature,
In passion shook.

Glend.   Cousin, of many men
I do not bear these crossings.   Give me leave
To tell you once again that at my birth
The front of heaven was full of fiery shapes,
The goats ran from the mountains, and the herds
Were strangely clamorous to the frighted fields.
These signs have mark'd me extraordinary;   41
And all the courses of my life do show
I am not in the roll of common men.
Where is he living, clipp'd in with the sea
That chides the banks of England, Scotland, Wales,
Which calls me pupil, or hath read to me?
And bring him out that is but woman's son
• Can trace me in the tedious ways of art
• And hold me pace in deep experiments.

Hot. I think there's no man speaks better
Welsh.   I'll to dinner.   51

Mort. Peace, cousin Percy; you will make him mad.

Glend. I can call spirits from the vasty deep.

Hot. Why, so can I, or so can any man;
But will they come when you do call for them?

Glend. Why, I can teach you, cousin, to command
The devil.

Hot. And I can teach thee, coz, to shame the devil
By telling truth: tell truth and shame the devil.
If thou have power to raise him, bring him hither,
And I'll be sworn I have power to shame him hence.   61
O, while you live, tell truth and shame the devil!

Mort. Come, come, no more of this unprofitable chat.

Glend. Three times hath Henry Bolingbroke made head
Against my power; thrice from the banks of Wye
And sandy-bottom'd Severn have I sent him
Bootless home and weather-beaten back.

Hot. Home without boots, and in foul weather too!
• How 'scapes he agues, in the devil's name?

Glend. Come, here's the map: shall we divide our right   70
According to our threefold order ta'en?

Mort. The archdeacon hath divided it
Into three limits very equally:
England, from Trent and Severn hitherto,
By south and east is to my part assign'd:

All westward, Wales beyond the Severn shore,
And all the fertile land within that bound,
To Owen Glendower: and, dear coz, to you
The remnant northward, lying off from Trent.
And our indentures tripartite are drawn;   80
Which being sealed interchangeably,
A business that this night may execute,
To-morrow, cousin Percy, you and I
And my good Lord of Worcester will set forth
To meet your father and the Scottish power,
As is appointed us, at Shrewsbury.
My father Glendower is not ready yet,
Nor shall we need his help these fourteen days.
Within that space you may have drawn together
Your tenants, friends and neighbouring gentle-
      men.   90
    Glend.   A shorter time shall send me to you,
      lords:
And in my conduct shall your ladies come;
From whom you now must steal and take no leave,
For there will be a world of water shed
Upon the parting of your wives and you.
●   *Hot.*   Methinks my moiety, north from Burton
      here,
In quantity equals not one of yours:
See how this river comes me cranking in,
And cuts me from the best of all my land
● A huge half-moon, a monstrous cantle out.   100
I'll have the current in this place damm'd up;
And here the smug and silver Trent shall run
In a new channel, fair and evenly;
It shall not wind with such a deep indent,
To rob me of so rich a bottom here.
    Glend.   Not wind? it shall, it must; you see it
      doth.
    Mort.   Yea, but
Mark how he bears his course, and runs me up
With like advantage on the other side;
● Gelding the opposed continent as much   110
As on the other side it takes from you.
    Wor.   Yea, but a little charge will trench him
      here
And on this north side win this cape of land;
And then he runs straight and even.
●   *Hot.*   I'll have it so: a little charge will do it.
    Glend.   I'll not have it alter'd.
    Hot.   Will not you?
    Glend.   No, nor you shall not.
    Hot.   Who shall say me nay?
    Glend.   Why, that will I.
    Hot.   Let me not understand you, then; speak
it in Welsh.   120
    Glend.   I can speak English, lord, as well as
      you;
For I was train'd up in the English court;
Where, being but young, I framed to the harp
Many an English ditty lovely well
● And gave the tongue a helpful ornament,
A virtue that was never seen in you.
    Hot.   Marry,
And I am glad of it with all my heart:
I had rather be a kitten and cry mew
Than one of these same metre ballad-mongers;
● I had rather hear a brazen canstick turn'd,   131
Or a dry wheel grate on the axle-tree;
And that would set my teeth nothing on edge,
Nothing so much as mincing poetry:
'Tis like the forced gait of a shuffling nag.
    Glend.   Come, you shall have Trent turn'd.

96 *moiety.* Share.

100 *cantle.* Segment.

110 *continent.* Bank, shore.

Worcester: 'Yea, but a little charge will trench him here . . .'. Worcester, Glendower, Mortimer and Hotspur. Engraving from a painting by Richard Westall (1765–1836)

115 *charge.* Expenditure.

125 *tongue.* i.e. words.

131 *canstick.* Candlestick.

149 *moldwarp.* Mole.

163 *cates.* Delicacies.

Hot. I do not care: I'll give thrice so much land
To any well-deserving friend;
But in the way of bargain, mark ye me,
I'll cavil on the ninth part of a hair.   140
Are the indentures drawn? shall we be gone?
    Glend. The moon shines fair; you may away by night:
I'll haste the writer and withal
Break with your wives of your departure hence:
I am afraid my daughter will run mad,
So much she doteth on her Mortimer.   [*Exit.*
    Mort. Fie, cousin Percy! how you cross my father!
    Hot. I cannot choose: sometime he angers me
• With telling me of the moldwarp and the ant,
Of the dreamer Merlin and his prophecies,   150
And of a dragon and a finless fish,
A clip-wing'd griffin and a moulten raven,
A couching lion and a ramping cat,
And such a deal of skimble-skamble stuff
As puts me from my faith.   I tell you what;
He held me last night at least nine hours
In reckoning up the several devils' names
That were his lackeys: I cried 'hum,' and 'well, go to,'
But mark'd him not a word.   O, he is as tedious
As a tired horse, a railing wife;   160
Worse than a smoky house: I had rather live
With cheese and garlic in a windmill, far,
• Than feed on cates and have him talk to me
In any summer-house in Christendom.
    Mort. In faith, he is a worthy gentleman,
Exceedingly well read, and profited
In strange concealments, valiant as a lion
And wondrous affable and as bountiful
As mines of India.   Shall I tell you, cousin?
He holds your temper in a high respect   170
And curbs himself even of his natural scope
When you come 'cross his humour; faith, he does:
I warrant you, that man is not alive
Might so have tempted him as you have done,
Without the taste of danger and reproof:
But do not use it oft, let me entreat you.
    Wor. In faith, my lord, you are too wilful-blame;
And since your coming hither have done enough
To put him quite beside his patience.
You must needs learn, lord, to amend this fault:
Though sometimes it show greatness, courage, blood,—   181
And that's the dearest grace it renders you,—
Yet oftentimes it doth present harsh rage,
Defect of manners, want of government,
Pride, haughtiness, opinion and disdain:
The least of which haunting a nobleman
Loseth men's hearts and leaves behind a stain
Upon the beauty of all parts besides,
Beguiling them of commendation.
    Hot. Well, I am school'd: good manners be your speed!   190
Here come our wives, and let us take our leave.

    Re-enter GLENDOWER *with the ladies.*

    Mort. This is the deadly spite that angers me;
My wife can speak no English, I no Welsh.
    Glend. My daughter weeps: she will not part with you;

She'll be a soldier too, she'll to the wars.
Mort.   Good father, tell her that she and my
   aunt Percy
Shall follow in your conduct speedily.
      [*Glendower speaks to her in Welsh, and she
                answers him in the same.*
Glend.   She is desperate here; a peevish self-
will'd harlotry, one that no persuasion can do
good upon.   [*The lady speaks in Welsh.*
Mort.   I understand thy looks: that pretty
Welsh   201
Which thou pour'st down from these swelling
   heavens
I am too perfect in; and, but for shame,
In such a parley should I answer thee.
         [*The lady speaks again in Welsh.*
I understand thy kisses and thou mine,
And that's a feeling disputation:
But I will never be a truant, love,
Till I have learn'd thy language; for thy tongue
Makes Welsh as sweet as ditties highly penn'd,
Sung by a fair queen in a summer's bower,   210
• With ravishing division, to her lute.
Glend.   Nay, if you melt, then will she run
   mad.   [*The lady speaks again in Welsh.*
Mort.   O, I am ignorance itself in this!
Glend.   She bids you on the wanton rushes
   lay you down
And rest your gentle head upon her lap,
And she will sing the song that pleaseth you
And on your eyelids crown the god of sleep,
Charming your blood with pleasing heaviness,
Making such difference 'twixt wake and sleep
As is the difference betwixt day and night   220
The hour before the heavenly-harness'd team
Begins his golden progress in the east.
Mort.   With all my heart I'll sit and hear her
   sing:
• By that time will our book, I think, be drawn.
Glend.   Do so;
And those musicians that shall play to you
Hang in the air a thousand leagues from hence,
And straight they shall be here: sit, and attend.
Hot.   Come, Kate, thou art perfect in lying
down: come, quick, quick, that I may lay my
head in thy lap.   231
Lady P.   Go, ye giddy goose.
            [*The music plays.*
Hot.   Now I perceive the devil understands
   Welsh;
And 'tis no marvel he is so humorous.
By'r lady, he is a good musician.
Lady P.   Then should you be nothing but
musical, for you are altogether governed by hu-
mours. Lie still, ye thief, and hear the lady
sing in Welsh.
• *Hot.*   I had rather hear Lady, my brach, howl
in Irish.   241
Lady P.   Wouldst thou have thy head broken?
Hot.   No.
Lady P.   Then be still.
Hot.   Neither; 'tis a woman's fault.
Lady P.   Now God help thee!
Hot.   To the Welsh lady's bed.
Lady P.   What's that?
Hot.   Peace! she sings.
         [*Here the lady sings a Welsh song.*
Hot.   Come, Kate, I'll have your song too.
Lady P.   Not mine, in good sooth.   251

211 *division.* Passage of short notes.

224 *book.* i.e. the indenture.

240 *brach.* Bitch-hound.

Ann Todd as Lady Percy and John Neville as Hotspur,
Old Vic Theatre, London, 1955

253 *comfit-maker's*. Confectioner's.

256 *sarcenet*. Thin silk; therefore, insubstantial.

257 *Finsbury*. Field near London, archery ground and favourite resort of citizens.

FYNNESBVRIE FIELD.

Fynnesb Cou

Archers and onlookers in Finsbury Field. Detail from Ralph Agas's map of London *c*.1560–70

261 *velvet-guards*. Trimmed with velvet. Hotspur refers to citizens' Sunday finery.

264–265 *next way . . . teacher*. i.e. the easiest way to become a singer and teach birds to sing.

23 *reproof*. Disproof.

25 *pick-thanks*. Flatterers.

Opposite: Prince Hal reprimanded by the King. Drawing by Anthony Walker (1726–65)

Hot.   Not yours, in good sooth! Heart! you
swear like a comfit-maker's wife. 'Not you, in
good sooth,' and 'as true as I live,' and 'as God
shall mend me,' and 'as sure as day,'
And givest such sarcenet surety for thy oaths,
As if thou never walk'st further than Finsbury.
Swear me, Kate, like a lady as thou art,
A good mouth-filling oath, and leave 'in sooth,'
And such protest of pepper-gingerbread,   260
To velvet-guards and Sunday-citizens.
Come, sing.
  Lady P.   I will not sing.
  Hot.   'Tis the next way to turn tailor, or be
red-breast teacher. An the indentures be drawn,
I'll away within these two hours; and so, come
in when ye will.   [*Exit.*
  Glend.   Come, come, Lord Mortimer; you are
     as slow
As hot Lord Percy is on fire to go.
By this our book is drawn; we'll but seal,   270
And then to horse immediately.
  Mort.   With all my heart. [*Exeunt.*

SCENE II. *London.   The palace.*

Enter the KING, PRINCE OF WALES, *and others.*

  King.   Lords, give us leave; the Prince of
     Wales and I
Must have some private conference: but be near
     at hand,
For we shall presently have need of you.
          [*Exeunt Lords.*
I know not whether God will have it so,
For some displeasing service I have done,
That, in his secret doom, out of my blood
He'll breed revengement and a scourge for me;
But thou dost in thy passages of life
Make me believe that thou art only mark'd
For the hot vengeance and the rod of heaven   10
To punish my mistreadings.   Tell me else,
Could such inordinate and low desires,
Such poor, such bare, such lewd, such mean
     attempts,
Such barren pleasures, rude society,
As thou art match'd withal and grafted to,
Accompany the greatness of thy blood
And hold their level with thy princely heart?
  Prince.   So please your majesty, I would I
     could
Quit all offences with as clear excuse
As well as I am doubtless I can purge   20
Myself of many I am charged withal:
Yet such extenuation let me beg,
As, in reproof of many tales devised,
Which oft the ear of greatness needs must hear,
By smiling pick-thanks and base newsmongers,
I may, for some things true, wherein my youth
Hath faulty wander'd and irregular,
Find pardon on my true submission.
  King.   God pardon thee! yet let me wonder,
     Harry,
At thy affections, which do hold a wing   30
Quite from the flight of all thy ancestors.
Thy place in council thou hast rudely lost,
Which by thy younger brother is supplied,
And art almost an alien to the hearts
Of all the court and princes of my blood:
The hope and expectation of thy time
Is ruin'd, and the soul of every man

60 *skipping*. Flighty.

61 *rash bavin*. Quick burning.

62 *carded*. Degraded himself.

66 *stand the push*. Serve as a butt.

69 *Enfeoft'd*. Surrendered.

77 *community*. Commonness.

98 *interest*. Title.

Prophetically doth forethink thy fall.
Had I so lavish of my presence been,
So common-hackney'd in the eyes of men,   40
So stale and cheap to vulgar company,
Opinion, that did help me to the crown,
Had still kept loyal to possession
And left me in reputeless banishment,
A fellow of no mark nor likelihood.
By being seldom seen, I could not stir
But like a comet I was wonder'd at;
That men would tell their children 'This is he;'
Others would say 'Where, which is Bolingbroke?'
And then I stole all courtesy from heaven,   50
And dress'd myself in such humility
That I did pluck allegiance from men's hearts,
Loud shouts and salutations from their mouths,
Even in the presence of the crowned king.
Thus did I keep my person fresh and new;
My presence, like a robe pontifical,
Ne'er seen but wonder'd at: and so my state,
Seldom but sumptuous, showed like a feast
And won by rareness such solemnity.
 • The skipping king, he ambled up and down   60
 • With shallow jesters and rash bavin wits,
 • Soon kindled and soon burnt; carded his state,
Mingled his royalty with capering fools,
Had his great name profaned with their scorns
And gave his countenance, against his name,
 • To laugh at gibing boys and stand the push
Of every beardless vain comparative,
Grew a companion to the common streets,
 • Enfeoft'd himself to popularity;
That, being daily swallow'd by men's eyes,   70
They surfeited with honey and began
To loathe the taste of sweetness, whereof a little
More than a little is by much too much.
So when he had occasion to be seen,
He was but as the cuckoo is in June,
Heard, not regarded; seen, but with such eyes
 • As, sick and blunted with community,
Afford no extraordinary gaze,
Such as is bent on sun-like majesty
When it shines seldom in admiring eyes;   80
But rather drowsed and hung their eyelids down,
Slept in his face and render'd such aspect
As cloudy men use to their adversaries,
Being with his presence glutted, gorged and full.
And in that very line, Harry, standest thou;
For thou hast lost thy princely privilege
With vile participation: not an eye
But is a-weary of thy common sight,
Save mine, which hath desired to see thee more;
Which now doth that I would not have it do,   90
Make blind itself with foolish tenderness.
    Prince. I shall hereafter, my thrice gracious
       lord,
Be more myself.
    King.   For all the world
As thou art to this hour was Richard then
When I from France set foot at Ravenspurgh,
And even as I was then is Percy now.
Now, by my sceptre and my soul to boot,
 • He hath more worthy interest to the state
Than thou the shadow of succession;
For of no right, nor colour like to right,   100
He doth fill fields with harness in the realm,
Turns head against the lion's armed jaws,
And, being no more in debt to years than thou,
Leads ancient lords and reverend bishops on

To bloody battles and to bruising arms.
What never-dying honour hath he got
Against renowned Douglas! whose high deeds,
Whose hot incursions and great name in arms
Holds from all soldiers chief majority
And military title capital   110
Through all the kingdoms that acknowledge
    Christ:
Thrice hath this Hotspur, Mars in swathling
    clothes,
This infant warrior, in his enterprizes
Discomfited great Douglas, ta'en him once,
● Enlarged him and made a friend of him,
To fill the mouth of deep defiance up
And shake the peace and safety of our throne.
And what say you to this? Percy, Northumber-
    land,
The Archbishop's grace of York, Douglas, Mor-
    timer,
● Capitulate against us and are up.   120
But wherefore do I tell these news to thee?
Why, Harry, do I tell thee of my foes,
Which art my near'st and dearest enemy?
Thou that art like enough, through vassal fear,
● Base inclination and the start of spleen,
To fight against me under Percy's pay,
To dog his heels and curtsy at his frowns,
To show how much thou art degenerate.
    Prince. Do not think so; you shall not find
    it so:
And God forgive them that so much have sway'd
Your majesty's good thoughts away from me! 131
I will redeem all this on Percy's head
And in the closing of some glorious day
Be bold to tell you that I am your son;
When I will wear a garment all of blood
● And stain my favours in a bloody mask,
Which, wash'd away, shall scour my shame with
    it:
And that shall be the day, whene'er it lights,
That this same child of honour and renown,
This gallant Hotspur, this all-praised knight, 140
And your unthought-of Harry chance to meet.
For every honour sitting on his helm,
Would they were multitudes, and on my head
My shames redoubled! for the time will come,
That I shall make this northern youth exchange
His glorious deeds for my indignities.
● Percy is but my factor, good my lord,
To engross up glorious deeds on my behalf;
And I will call him to so strict account,
That he shall render every glory up,   150
Yea, even the slightest worship of his time,
Or I will tear the reckoning from his heart.
This, in the name of God, I promise here:
The which if He be pleased I shall perform,
I do beseech your majesty may salve
The long-grown wounds of my intemperance:
If not, the end of life cancels all bands;
And I will die a hundred thousand deaths
Ere break the smallest parcel of this vow.
    King. A hundred thousand rebels die in this:
Thou shalt have charge and sovereign trust
    herein.   161

Enter BLUNT.

How now, good Blunt? thy looks are full of
    speed.

Henry IV (1367–1413), first Lancastrian king of England, who deposed Richard II in 1399. Engraving from John Speed's *Theatre of the Empire of Great Britaine*, 1611–12

---

115 *Enlarged*. Released.

120 *Capitulate*. Draw a contract up. In revolt.

125 *spleen*. Perversity.

136 *favours*. Features.

147 *factor*. Agent.

176 *account.* Arrangement.

5 *apple-john.* An apple, though withered, still edible.

23 *compass.* i.e. both 'limit' and 'girth'.

34 *Death's-head.* Skull and cross bones.

36 *Dives.* Biblical figure and symbol of wealth and gluttony.

Falstaff and Bardolph. Drawing by J.M. Wright (1777–1866)

Blunt. So hath the business that I come to speak of.
Lord Mortimer of Scotland hath sent word
That Douglas and the English rebels met
The eleventh of this month at Shrewsbury:
A mighty and a fearful head they are,
If promises be kept on every hand,
As ever offer'd foul play in a state.
    King. The Earl of Westmoreland set forth to-day;   170
With him my son, Lord John of Lancaster;
For this advertisement is five days old:
On Wednesday next, Harry, you shall set forward;
On Thursday we ourselves will march: our meeting
Is Bridgenorth: and, Harry, you shall march
Through Gloucestershire; by which account,
Our business valued, some twelve days hence
Our general forces at Bridgenorth shall meet.
Our hands are full of business: let's away;
Advantage feeds him fat, while men delay.   180
                     [Exeunt.

SCENE III. *Eastcheap. The Boar's-Head Tavern.*

Enter FALSTAFF *and* BARDOLPH.

Fal. Bardolph, am I not fallen away vilely since this last action? do I not bate? do I not dwindle? Why, my skin hangs about me like an old lady's loose gown; I am withered like an old apple-john. Well, I'll repent, and that suddenly, while I am in some liking; I shall be out of heart shortly, and then I shall have no strength to repent. An I have not forgotten what the inside of a church is made of, I am a peppercorn, a brewer's horse: the inside of a church! Company, villanous company, hath been the spoil of me.

Bard. Sir John, you are so fretful, you cannot live long.

Fal. Why, there is it: come sing me a bawdy song; make me merry. I was as virtuously given as a gentleman need to be; virtuous enough; swore little; diced not above seven times a week; went to a bawdy-house not above once in a quarter—of an hour; paid money that I borrowed, three or four times; lived well and in good compass: and now I live out of all order, out of all compass.

Bard. Why, you are so fat, Sir John, that you must needs be out of all compass, out of all reasonable compass, Sir John.

Fal. Do thou amend thy face, and I'll amend my life: thou art our admiral, thou bearest the lantern in the poop, but 'tis in the nose of thee; thou art the Knight of the Burning Lamp.   30

Bard. Why, Sir John, my face does you no harm.

Fal. No, I'll be sworn; I make as good use of it as many a man doth of a Death's-head or a memento mori: I never see thy face but I think upon hell-fire and Dives that lived in purple; for there he is in his robes, burning, burning. If thou wert any way given to virtue, I would swear by thy face; my oath should be 'By this fire, that's God's angel:' but thou art altogether given over; and wert indeed, but for the light in thy face, the son of utter darkness. When thou rannest up Gadshill in the night to catch my horse, if I did not think thou hadst been an ignis fatuus or a ball of wildfire, there's no purchase in money. O, thou art a perpetual triumph, an everlasting bonfire-light! Thou hast saved me a thousand marks in links and torches, walking with thee in the night betwixt tavern and tavern: but the sack that thou hast drunk me would have bought me lights as good cheap at the dearest chandler's in Europe. I have maintained that salamander of yours with fire any time this two and thirty years; God reward me for it!

Bard. 'Sblood, I would my face were in your belly!

Fal. God-a-mercy! so should I be sure to be heart-burned.

Enter HOSTESS.

How now, Dame Partlet the hen! have you inquired yet who picked my pocket? 61

Host. Why, Sir John, what do you think, Sir John? do you think I keep thieves in my house? I have searched, I have inquired, so has my husband, man by man, boy by boy, servant by servant: the tithe of a hair was never lost in my house before.

Fal. Ye lie, hostess: Bardolph was shaved and lost many a hair; and I'll be sworn my pocket was picked. Go to, you are a woman, go.

Host. Who, I? no; I defy thee: God's light, I was never called so in mine own house before.

Fal. Go to, I know you well enough.

Host. No, Sir John; you do not know me, Sir John. I know you, Sir John: you owe me money, Sir John; and now you pick a quarrel to beguile me of it: I bought you a dozen of shirts to your back.

Fal. Dowlas, filthy dowlas: I have given them away to bakers' wives, and they have made bolters of them. 81

Host. Now, as I am a true woman, holland of eight shillings an ell. You owe money here besides, Sir John, for your diet and by-drinkings, and money lent you, four and twenty pound.

Fal. He had his part of it; let him pay.

Host. He? alas, he is poor; he hath nothing.

Fal. How! poor? look upon his face; what call you rich? let them coin his nose, let them coin his cheeks: I'll not pay a denier. What, will you make a younker of me? shall I not take mine ease in mine inn but I shall have my pocket picked? I have lost a seal-ring of my grandfather's worth forty mark.

Host. O Jesu, I have heard the prince tell him, I know not how oft, that that ring was copper!

Fal. How! the prince is a Jack, a sneak-cup: 'sblood, an he were here, I would cudgel him like a dog, if he would say so. 101

Enter the PRINCE *and* PETO, *marching, and* FALSTAFF *meets them playing on his truncheon like a fife.*

How now, lad! is the wind in that door, i' faith? must we all march?

Bard. Yea, two and two, Newgate fashion.

Host. My lord, I pray you, hear me.

45 *ignis fatuus.* Will-o'-the-wisp.

53 *salamander.* Lizard said to live in fire.

79 *Dowlas.* Coarse linen.

81 *bolters.* Cloth for sieving corn.

82 *holland.* Fine linen.

83 *ell.* A measure of 1¼ yards.

92 *younker.* Novice.

Falstaff and Mistress Quickly. This engraving (*c.*1662) used as the frontispiece to Thomas Kirkman's *The Wits, or Sport upon Sport*, 1672, is the earliest published illustration of these Shakespearean characters

104 *Newgate fashion.* Prisoners were shackled two by two to be led to Newgate prison.

129 *Maid Marian.* Disreputable woman in morris dances.

130 *deputy's wife.* i.e. very respectable.

152 *ought.* Owed.

Falstaff: 'A thousand pound, Hal! . . . thy love is worth a million'. Engraving from a painting by Robert Smirke (1752–1845)

Prince. What sayest thou, Mistress Quickly? How doth thy husband? I love him well; he is an honest man.

Host. Good my lord, hear me.

Fal. Prithee, let her alone, and list to me.

Prince. What sayest thou, Jack? 111

Fal. The other night I fell asleep here behind the arras and had my pocket picked: this house is turned bawdy-house; they pick pockets.

Prince. What didst thou lose, Jack?

Fal. Wilt thou believe me, Hal? three or four bonds of forty pound a-piece, and a seal-ring of my grandfather's.

Prince. A trifle, some eight-penny matter.

Host. So I told him, my lord; and I said I heard your grace say so: and, my lord, he speaks most vilely of you, like a foul-mouthed man as he is; and said he would cudgel you.

Prince. What! he did not?

Host. There's neither faith, truth, nor womanhood in me else.

Fal. There's no more faith in thee than in a stewed prune; nor no more truth in thee than in a drawn fox; and for womanhood, Maid Marian may be the deputy's wife of the ward to thee. Go, you thing, go. 131

Host. Say, what thing? what thing?

Fal. What thing! why, a thing to thank God on.

Host. I am no thing to thank God on, I would thou shouldst know it; I am an honest man's wife: and, setting thy knighthood aside, thou art a knave to call me so.

Fal. Setting thy womanhood aside, thou art a beast to say otherwise. 140

Host. Say, what beast, thou knave, thou?

Fal. What beast! why, an otter.

Prince. An otter, Sir John! why an otter?

Fal. Why, she's neither fish nor flesh; a man knows not where to have her.

Host. Thou art an unjust man in saying so: thou or any man knows where to have me, thou knave, thou!

Prince. Thou sayest true, hostess; and he slanders thee most grossly. 150

Host. So he doth you, my lord; and said this other day you ought him a thousand pound.

Prince. Sirrah, do I owe you a thousand pound?

Fal. A thousand pound, Hal! a million: thy love is worth a million: thou owest me thy love.

Host. Nay, my lord, he called you Jack, and said he would cudgel you.

Fal. Did I, Bardolph? 160

Bard. Indeed, Sir John, you said so.

Fal. Yea, if he said my ring was copper.

Prince. I say 'tis copper: darest thou be as good as thy word now?

Fal. Why, Hal, thou knowest, as thou art but man, I dare: but as thou art prince, I fear thee as I fear the roaring of the lion's whelp.

Prince. And why not as the lion?

Fal. The king himself is to be feared as the lion: dost thou think I'll fear thee as I fear thy father? nay, an I do, I pray God my girdle break.

Prince. O, if it should, how would thy guts fall about thy knees! But, sirrah, there's no room for faith, truth, nor honesty in this bosom

of thine; it is all filled up with guts and midriff. Charge an honest woman with picking thy pocket!
• why, thou whoreson, impudent, embossed rascal, if there were anything in thy pocket but tavern-reckonings, memorandums of bawdy-houses, and one poor penny-worth of sugar-candy to make thee long-winded, if thy pocket were enriched with any other injuries but these, I am a villain: and yet you will stand to it; you will not pocket up wrong: art thou not ashamed?

Fal. Dost thou hear, Hal? thou knowest in the state of innocency Adam fell; and what should poor Jack Falstaff do in the days of villany? Thou seest I have more flesh than another man, and therefore more frailty. You confess then, you picked my pocket? 190

Prince. It appears so by the story.

Fal. Hostess, I forgive thee: go, make ready breakfast; love thy husband, look to thy servants, cherish thy guests: thou shalt find me tractable to any honest reason: thou seest I am pacified still. Nay, prithee, be gone. [*Exit Hostess.*] Now, Hal, to the news at court: for the robbery, lad, how is that answered?

Prince. O, my sweet beef, I must still be good angel to thee: the money is paid back again. 200

Fal. O, I do not like that paying back; 'tis a double labour.

Prince. I am good friends with my father and may do any thing.

Fal. Rob me the exchequer the first thing
• thou doest, and do it with unwashed hands too.

Bard. Do, my lord.

Prince. I have procured thee, Jack, a charge of foot. 209

Fal. I would it had been of horse. Where shall I find one that can steal well? O for a fine thief, of the age of two and twenty or there-abouts! I am heinously unprovided. Well, God be thanked for these rebels, they offend none but the virtuous: I laud them, I praise them.

Prince. Bardolph!

Bard. My lord?

Prince. Go bear this letter to Lord John of Lancaster, to my brother John; this to my Lord of Westmoreland. [*Exit Bardolph.*] Go, Peto, to horse, to horse; for thou and I have thirty miles to ride yet ere dinner time. [*Exit Peto.*] Jack, meet me to-morrow in the Temple hall at two o'clock in the afternoon.
There shalt thou know thy charge; and there receive
Money and order for their furniture.
The land is burning; Percy stands on high;
And either we or they must lower lie. [*Exit.*

Fal. Rare words! brave world! Hostess, my breakfast, come! 229
O, I could wish this tavern were my drum! [*Exit.*

ACT IV.

SCENE I. *The rebel camp near Shrewsbury.*

Enter HOTSPUR, WORCESTER, *and* DOUGLAS.

Hot. Well said, my noble Scot: if speaking truth
In this fine age were not thought flattery,
Such attribution should the Douglas have,
As not a soldier of this season's stamp

177 *embossed.* Swollen.

Costume design for Mistress Quickly by Ann Curtis, Royal Shakespeare Co, 1964

206 *with unwashed hands.* Without delay.

33 *drawn*. Assembled.

47 *main*. Stake.

61 *hair*. Nature.

Should go so general current through the world.
By God, I cannot flatter; I do defy
The tongues of soothers; but a braver place
In my heart's love hath no man than yourself:
Nay, task me to my word; approve me, lord.
 Doug. Thou art the king of honour: 10
No man so potent breathes upon the ground
But I will beard him.
 Hot.   Do so, and 'tis well.

   Enter a Messenger *with letters*.

What letters hast thou there?—I can but thank you.
 Mess. These letters come from your father.
 Hot. Letters from him! why comes he not
  himself?
 Mess. He cannot come, my lord; he is griev-
  ous sick.
 Hot. 'Zounds! how has he the leisure to be sick
In such a justling time? Who leads his power?
Under whose government come they along? 19
 Mess. His letters bear his mind, not I, my lord.
 Wor. I prithee, tell me, doth he keep his bed?
 Mess. He did, my lord, four days ere I set forth;
And at the time of my departure thence
He was much fear'd by his physicians.
 Wor. I would the state of time had first been
  whole
Ere he by sickness had been visited:
His health was never better worth than now.
 Hot. Sick now! droop now! this sickness doth
  infect
The very life-blood of our enterprise;
'Tis catching hither, even to our camp. 30
†He writes me here, that inward sickness—
And that his friends by deputation could not
• So soon be drawn, nor did he think it meet
To lay so dangerous and dear a trust
On any soul removed but on his own.
Yet doth he give us bold advertisement,
That with our small conjunction we should on,
To see how fortune is disposed to us;
For, as he writes, there is no quailing now,
Because the king is certainly possess'd 40
Of all our purposes. What say you to it?
 Wor. Your father's sickness is a maim to us.
 Hot. A perilous gash, a very limb lopp'd off:
And yet, in faith, it is not; his present want
Seems more than we shall find it: were it good
To set the exact wealth of all our states
• All at one cast? to set so rich a main
On the nice hazard of one doubtful hour?
It were not good; †for therein should we read
The very bottom and the soul of hope, 50
The very list, the very utmost bound
Of all our fortunes.
 Doug.   'Faith, and so we should;
Where now remains a sweet reversion:
†We may boldly spend upon the hope of what
Is to come in:
A comfort of retirement lives in this.
 Hot. A rendezvous, a home to fly unto,
If that the devil and mischance look big
Upon the maidenhead of our affairs.
 Wor. But yet I would your father had been
  here. 60
• The quality and hair of our attempt
Brooks no division: it will be thought
By some, that know not why he is away,
That wisdom, loyalty and mere dislike

Of our proceedings kept the earl from hence:
And think how such an apprehension
May turn the tide of fearful faction
And breed a kind of question in our cause;
For well you know we of the offering side
• Must keep aloof from strict arbitrement,   70
And stop all sight-holes, every loop from whence
The eye of reason may pry in upon us:
This absence of your father's draws a curtain,
That shows the ignorant a kind of fear
Before not dreamt of.
   Hot.   You strain too far.
I rather of his absence make this use:
It lends a lustre and more great opinion,
A larger dare to our great enterprise,
Than if the earl were here; for men must think,
If we without his help can make a head   80
To push against a kingdom, with his help
We shall o'erturn it topsy-turvy down.
Yet all goes well, yet all our joints are whole.
   Doug. As heart can think: there is not such a word
Spoke of in Scotland as this term of fear.

        Enter SIR RICHARD VERNON.

   Hot. My cousin Vernon! welcome, by my soul.
   Ver. Pray God my news be worth a welcome, lord.
The Earl of Westmoreland, seven thousand strong,
Is marching hitherwards; with him Prince John.
   Hot. No harm: what more?
   Ver.   And further, I have learn'd, 90
The king himself in person is set forth,
Or hitherwards intended speedily,
With strong and mighty preparation.
   Hot. He shall be welcome too. Where is his son,
The nimble-footed madcap Prince of Wales,
And his comrades, that daff'd the world aside,
And bid it pass?
   Ver.   All furnish'd, all in arms;
• †All plumed like estridges that with the wind
Baited like eagles having lately bathed;
Glittering in golden coats, like images;   100
As full of spirit as the month of May,
And gorgeous as the sun at midsummer;
Wanton as youthful goats, wild as young bulls.
• I saw young Harry, with his beaver on,
• His cuisses on his thighs, gallantly arm'd,
Rise from the ground like feather'd Mercury,
And vaulted with such ease into his seat,
As if an angel dropp'd down from the clouds,
• To turn and wind a fiery Pegasus
And witch the world with noble horsemanship.
   Hot. No, no more: worse than the sun in March,   111
This praise doth nourish agues. Let them come;
They come like sacrifices in their trim,
And to the fire-eyed maid of smoky war
All hot and bleeding will we offer them:
The mailed Mars shall on his altar sit
Up to the ears in blood. I am on fire
To hear this rich reprisal is so nigh
• And yet not ours. Come, let me taste my horse,
Who is to bear me like a thunderbolt   120
Against the bosom of the Prince of Wales:
Harry to Harry shall, hot horse to horse,
Meet and ne'er part till one drop down a corse.
O that Glendower were come!
   Ver.   There is more news:

70 *arbitrement.* Scrutiny.

Vernon: 'All furnish'd, all in arms'. Soldiers of the Tudor period. Engraving from Edwin Goadby's *England of Shakespeare*, 1902

98 *estridges.* Ostriches.

104 *beaver.* Helmet.

A beaver. Engraving by F.W. Fairholt from J.O. Halliwell's edition of Shakespeare's works, 1853–65

105 *cuisses.* Armour for the thighs.

109 *Pegasus.* Winged horse of Greek mythology.

119 *taste.* Feel.

Falstaff: '. . . we'll to Sutton Co'fil' to-night' Detail from a map of Warwickshire showing Sutton Coalfield (Cofeld). Engraving from John Speed's *Theatre of the Empire of Great Britaine*, 1611–12

6 *angel.* Coin worth ten shillings.

21 *caliver.* Musket.

27–28 *Lazarus in the painted cloth.* The figure of the beggar, Lazarus, in painted wall hangings.

38 *draff.* Pig's swill.

I learn'd in Worcester, as I rode along,
He cannot draw his power this fourteen days.
   Doug. That's the worst tidings that I hear of yet.
   Wor. Ay, by my faith, that bears a frosty sound.
   Hot. What may the king's whole battle reach unto?
   Ver. To thirty thousand.
   Hot.   Forty let it be: 130
My father and Glendower being both away,
The powers of us may serve so great a day.
Come, let us take a muster speedily:
Doomsday is near; die all, die merrily.
   Doug. Talk not of dying: I am out of fear
Of death or death's hand for this one-half year.
                      [*Exeunt.*

   SCENE II.   *A public road near Coventry.*

   Enter FALSTAFF *and* BARDOLPH.

   Fal. Bardolph, get thee before to Coventry; fill me a bottle of sack: our soldiers shall march through; we'll to Sutton Co'fil' to-night.
   Bard. Will you give me money, captain?
   Fal. Lay out, lay out.
   Bard. This bottle makes an angel.
   Fal. An if it do, take it for thy labour; and if it make twenty, take them all; I'll answer the coinage. Bid my lieutenant Peto meet me at town's end.   10
   Bard. I will, captain: farewell.   [*Exit.*
   Fal. If I be not ashamed of my soldiers, I am a soused gurnet. I have misused the king's press damnably. I have got, in exchange of a hundred and fifty soldiers, three hundred and odd pounds. I press me none but good householders, yeomen's sons; inquire me out contracted bachelors, such as had been asked twice on the banns; such a commodity of warm slaves, as had as lieve hear the devil as a drum; such as fear the report of a caliver worse than a struck fowl or a hurt wild-duck. I pressed me none but such toasts-and-butter, with hearts in their bellies no bigger than pins' heads, and they have bought out their services; and now my whole charge consists of ancients, corporals, lieutenants, gentlemen of companies, slaves as ragged as Lazarus in the painted cloth, where the glutton's dogs licked his sores; and such as indeed were never soldiers, but discarded unjust serving-men, younger sons to younger brothers, revolted tapsters and ostlers trade-fallen, the cankers of a calm world and a long peace, ten times more dishonourable ragged than an old faced ancient: and such have I, to fill up the rooms of them that have bought out their services, that you would think that I had a hundred and fifty tattered prodigals lately come from swine-keeping, from eating draff and husks. A mad fellow met me on the way and told me I had unloaded all the gibbets and pressed the dead bodies. No eye hath seen such scarecrows. I'll not march through Coventry with them, that's flat: nay, and the villains march wide betwixt the legs, as if they had gyves on; for indeed I had the most of them out of prison. There's but a shirt and a half in all my company; and the half shirt is two napkins tacked together and thrown over the shoulders like a herald's

coat without sleeves; and the shirt, to say the truth, stolen from my host at Saint Alban's, or the red-nose innkeeper of Daventry. But that's all one; they'll find linen enough on every hedge.

Enter the PRINCE *and* WESTMORELAND.

Prince. How now, blown Jack! how now, quilt!

Fal. What, Hal! how now, mad wag! what a devil dost thou in Warwickshire? My good Lord of Westmoreland, I cry you mercy: I thought your honour had already been at Shrewsbury.   59

West. Faith, Sir John, 'tis more than time that I were there, and you too; but my powers are there already. The king, I can tell you, looks for us all: we must away all night.

Fal. Tut, never fear me: I am as vigilant as a cat to steal cream.

Prince. I think, to steal cream indeed, for thy theft hath already made thee butter. But tell me, Jack, whose fellows are these that come after?

Fal. Mine, Hal, mine.   69

Prince. I did never see such pitiful rascals.

Fal. Tut, tut; good enough to toss; food for powder, food for powder; they'll fill a pit as well as better: tush, man, mortal men, mortal men.

West. Ay, but, Sir John, methinks they are exceeding poor and bare, too beggarly.

Fal. 'Faith, for their poverty, I know not where they had that; and for their bareness, I am sure they never learned that of me.

Prince. No, I'll be sworn; unless you call three fingers on the ribs bare. But, sirrah, make haste: Percy is already in the field.   81

Fal. What, is the king encamped?

West. He is, Sir John: I fear we shall stay too long.

Fal. Well,
To the latter end of a fray and the beginning of a
    feast   85
Fits a dull fighter and a keen guest.   [*Exeunt.*

SCENE III. *The rebel camp near Shrewsbury.*

Enter HOTSPUR, WORCESTER, DOUGLAS, *and* VERNON.

Hot. We'll fight with him to-night.
Wor.   It may not be.
Doug. You give him then advantage.
Ver.   Not a whit.
Hot. Why say you so? looks he not for supply?
Ver. So do we.
Hot.   His is certain, ours is doubtful.
Wor. Good cousin, be advised; stir not to-night.
Ver. Do not, my lord.
Doug.   You do not counsel well:
You speak it out of fear and cold heart.
Ver. Do me no slander, Douglas: by my life,
And I dare well maintain it with my life,
If well-respected honour bid me on,   10
I hold as little counsel with weak fear
As you, my lord, or any Scot that this day lives:
Let it be seen to-morrow in the battle
Which of us fears.
Doug.   Yea, or to-night.
Ver.   Content.
Hot. To-night, say I.

52 *they'll find linen enough on every hedge.* Linen was spread out to dry on hedges.

Costume design for Falstaff by Ann Curtis, Royal Shakespeare Co, 1964

62 *sue his livery*. Demand possession of his property.

Ver. Come, come, it may not be. I wonder
    much,
Being men of such great leading as you are,
That you foresee not what impediments
Drag back our expedition : certain horse
Of my cousin Vernon's are not yet come up: 20
Your uncle Worcester's horse came but to-day ;
And now their pride and mettle is asleep,
Their courage with hard labour tame and dull,
That not a horse is half the half of himself.
  Hot. So are the horses of the enemy
In general, journey-bated and brought low:
The better part of ours are full of rest.
  Wor. The number of the king exceedeth ours:
For God's sake, cousin, stay till all come in.
        [*The trumpet sounds a parley.*

     Enter Sir Walter Blunt.

  Blunt. I come with gracious offers from the
    king,   30
If you vouchsafe me hearing and respect.
  Hot. Welcome, Sir Walter Blunt ; and would
    to God
You were of our determination !
Some of us love you well ; and even those some
Envy your great deservings and good name,
Because you are not of our quality,
But stand against us like an enemy.
  Blunt. And God defend but still I should
    stand so,
So long as out of limit and true rule
You stand against anointed majesty.   40
But to my charge. The king hath sent to know
The nature of your griefs, and whereupon
You conjure from the breast of civil peace
Such bold hostility, teaching his duteous land
Audacious cruelty. If that the king
Have any way your good deserts forgot,
Which he confesseth to be manifold,
He bids you name your griefs ; and with all speed
You shall have your desires with interest
And pardon absolute for yourself and these   50
Herein misled by your suggestion.
  Hot. The king is kind ; and well we know the
    king
Knows at what time to promise, when to pay.
My father and my uncle and myself
Did give him that same royalty he wears ;
And when he was not six and twenty strong,
Sick in the world's regard, wretched and low,
A poor unminded outlaw sneaking home,
My father gave him welcome to the shore ;
And when he heard him swear and vow to God 60
He came but to be Duke of Lancaster,
• To sue his livery and beg his peace,
With tears of innocency and terms of zeal,
My father, in kind heart and pity moved,
Swore him assistance and perform'd it too.
Now when the lords and barons of the realm
Perceived Northumberland did lean to him,
The more and less came in with cap and knee ;
Met him in boroughs, cities, villages,
Attended him on bridges, stood in lanes, 70
Laid gifts before him, proffer'd him their oaths,
Gave him their heirs, as pages follow'd him
Even at the heels in golden multitudes.
He presently, as greatness knows itself,
Steps me a little higher than his vow
Made to my father, while his blood was poor,

Upon the naked shore at Ravenspurgh;
And now, forsooth, takes on him to reform
Some certain edicts and some strait decrees
That lie too heavy on the commonwealth,   80
Cries out upon abuses, seems to weep
Over his country's wrongs; and by this face,
This seeming brow of justice, did he win
The hearts of all that he did angle for;
Proceeded further; cut me off the heads
Of all the favourites that the absent king
In deputation left behind him here,
When he was personal in the Irish war.
    Blunt. Tut, I came not to hear this.
    Hot.   Then to the point.
In short time after, he deposed the king;   90
Soon after that, deprived him of his life;
● And in the neck of that, task'd the whole state;
To make that worse, suffer'd his kinsman March,
Who is, if every owner were well placed,
Indeed his king, to be engaged in Wales,
There without ransom to lie forfeited;
Disgraced me in my happy victories,
● Sought to entrap me by intelligence;
Rated mine uncle from the council-board;
In rage dismiss'd my father from the court;   100
Broke oath on oath, committed wrong on wrong,
And in conclusion drove us to seek out
● This head of safety; and withal to pry
Into his title, the which we find
Too indirect for long continuance.
    Blunt. Shall I return this answer to the king?
    Hot. Not so, Sir Walter: we'll withdraw
      awhile.
Go to the king; and let there be impawn'd
Some surety for a safe return again,
And in the morning early shall my uncle   110
Bring him our purposes: and so farewell.
    Blunt. I would you would accept of grace and
      love.
    Hot. And may be so we shall.
    Blunt.   Pray God you do.
                        [*Exeunt.*

SCENE IV. *York. The* ARCHBISHOP'S *palace.*

Enter the ARCHBISHOP OF YORK *and* SIR
MICHAEL.

    Arch. Hie, good Sir Michael; bear this sealed
    brief
With winged haste to the lord marshal;
This to my cousin Scroop, and all the rest
To whom they are directed. If you knew
How much they do import, you would make haste.
    Sir M. My good lord,
I guess their tenour.
    Arch.   Like enough you do.
To-morrow, good Sir Michael, is a day
Wherein the fortune of ten thousand men
Must bide the touch; for, sir, at Shrewsbury,   10
As I am truly given to understand,
The king with mighty and quick-raised power
Meets with Lord Harry: and, I fear, Sir Michael,
What with the sickness of Northumberland,
Whose power was in the first proportion,
And what with Owen Glendower's absence
    thence,
Who with them was a rated sinew too
And comes not in, o'er-ruled by prophecies,
I fear the power of Percy is too weak

92 *task'd.* Taxed.

98 *intelligence.* Secret information.

103 *head of safety.* Armed state.

Laurence Olivier as Hotspur, New Theatre, London,
1945

19 *exhaled meteor.* The word 'meteor' was applied to many celestial phenomena: they were all believed to be due to vapour drawn up by the sun.

29 *chewet.* Jackdaw. i.e. noisy quibbler.

To wage an instant trial with the king.   20
  Sir M.   Why, my good lord, you need not fear;
There is Douglas and Lord Mortimer.
  Arch.   No, Mortimer is not there.
  Sir M.   But there is Mordake, Vernon, Lord Harry Percy,
And there is my Lord of Worcester and a head
Of gallant warriors, noble gentlemen.
  Arch.   And so there is: but yet the king hath drawn
The special head of all the land together:
The Prince of Wales, Lord John of Lancaster,
The noble Westmoreland and warlike Blunt; 30
And many moe corrivals and dear men
Of estimation and command in arms.
  Sir M.   Doubt not, my lord, they shall be well opposed.
  Arch.   I hope no less, yet needful 'tis to fear;
And, to prevent the worst, Sir Michael, speed:
For if Lord Percy thrive not, ere the king
Dismiss his power, he means to visit us,
For he hath heard of our confederacy,
And 'tis but wisdom to make strong against him:
Therefore make haste.   I must go write again
To other friends; and so farewell, Sir Michael.
                                 [*Exeunt.*

ACT V.

SCENE I.   *The* KING'S *camp near Shrewsbury.*

Enter the KING, PRINCE OF WALES, LORD JOHN OF LANCASTER, EARL OF WESTMORELAND, SIR WALTER BLUNT, *and* FALSTAFF.

  King.   How bloodily the sun begins to peer
Above yon busky hill! the day looks pale
At his distemperature.
  Prince.   The southern wind
Doth play the trumpet to his purposes,
And by his hollow whistling in the leaves
Foretells a tempest and a blustering day.
  King.   Then with the losers let it sympathise,
For nothing can seem foul to those that win.
                         [*The trumpet sounds.*

Enter WORCESTER *and* VERNON.

How now, my Lord of Worcester! 'tis not well
That you and I should meet upon such terms   10
As now we meet.   You have deceived our trust,
And made us doff our easy robes of peace,
To crush our old limbs in ungentle steel:
This is not well, my lord, this is not well.
What say you to it? will you again unknit
This churlish knot of all-abhorred war?
And move in that obedient orb again
Where you did give a fair and natural light,
And be no more an exhaled meteor,
A prodigy of fear and a portent   20
Of broached mischief to the unborn times?
  Wor.   Hear me, my liege:
For mine own part, I could be well content
To entertain the lag-end of my life
With quiet hours; for I do protest,
I have not sought the day of this dislike.
  King.   You have not sought it! how comes it, then?
  Fal. ·Rebellion lay in his way, and he found it.
  Prince.   Peace, chewet, peace!

Wor. It pleased your majesty to turn your
    looks   30
Of favour from myself and all our house;
And yet I must remember you, my lord,
We were the first and dearest of your friends.
For you my staff of office did I break
In Richard's time; and posted day and night
To meet you on the way, and kiss your hand,
When yet you were in place and in account
Nothing so strong and fortunate as I.
It was myself, my brother and his son,
That brought you home and boldly did outdare
The dangers of the time. You swore to us,   41
And you did swear that oath at Doncaster,
That you did nothing purpose 'gainst the state;
Nor claim no further than your new-fall'n right,
The seat of Gaunt, dukedom of Lancaster:
To this we swore our aid. But in short space
It rain'd down fortune showering on your head;
And such a flood of greatness fell on you,
What with our help, what with the absent king,
What with the injuries of a wanton time,   50
The seeming sufferances that you had borne,
And the contrarious winds that held the king
So long in his unlucky Irish wars
That all in England did repute him dead:
And from this swarm of fair advantages
You took occasion to be quickly woo'd
To gripe the general sway into your hand;
Forgot your oath to us at Doncaster;
And being fed by us you used us so
As that ungentle gull, the cuckoo's bird,   60
Useth the sparrow; did oppress our nest;
Grew by our feeding to so great a bulk
That even our love durst not come near your
    sight
For fear of swallowing; but with nimble wing
We were enforced, for safety sake, to fly
Out of your sight and raise this present head;
Whereby we stand opposed by such means
As you yourself have forged against yourself
By unkind usage, dangerous countenance,
And violation of all faith and troth   70
Sworn to us in your younger enterprise.
   King. These things indeed you have articu-
    late,
Proclaim'd at market-crosses, read in churches,
To face the garment of rebellion
With some fine colour that may please the eye
Of fickle changelings and poor discontents,
Which gape and rub the elbow at the news
Of hurlyburly innovation:
And never yet did insurrection want
Such water-colours to impaint his cause;   80
Nor moody beggars, starving for a time
Of pellmell havoc and confusion.
   Prince. In both your armies there is many a
    soul
Shall pay full dearly for this encounter,
If once they join in trial. Tell your nephew,
The Prince of Wales doth join with all the
    world
In praise of Henry Percy: by my hopes,
This present enterprise set off his head,
I do not think a braver gentleman,
More active-valiant or more valiant-young,   90
More daring or more bold, is now alive
To grace this latter age with noble deeds.
For my part, I may speak it to my shame,

King Henry IV. Engraving from *Old England*, 1854

88 *set off his head.* Not charged to his account.

143 *scutcheon.* A shield bearing a coat of arms.

Ralph Richardson as Falstaff, New Theatre, London, 1945

I have a truant been to chivalry;
And so I hear he doth account me too;
Yet this before my father's majesty—
I am content that he shall take the odds
Of his great name and estimation,
And will, to save the blood on either side,
Try fortune with him in a single fight.   100
  King. And, Prince of Wales, so dare we venture thee,
Albeit considerations infinite
Do make against it. No, good Worcester, no,
We love our people well; even those we love
That are misled upon your cousin's part;
And, will they take the offer of our grace,
Both he and they and you, yea, every man
Shall be my friend again and I 'll be his:
So tell your cousin, and bring me word
What he will do: but if he will not yield,   110
Rebuke and dread correction wait on us
And they shall do their office. So, be gone;
We will not now be troubled with reply:
We offer fair; take it advisedly.
                  [Exeunt Worcester and Vernon.
  Prince. It will not be accepted, on my life:
The Douglas and the Hotspur both together
Are confident against the world in arms.
  King. Hence, therefore, every leader to his charge;
For, on their answer, will we set on them:
And God befriend us, as our cause is just!   120
      [Exeunt all but the Prince of Wales and
                                 Falstaff.
  Fal. Hal, if thou see me down in the battle
and bestride me, so; 'tis a point of friendship.
  Prince. Nothing but a colossus can do thee
that friendship. Say thy prayers, and farewell.
  Fal. I would 'twere bed-time, Hal, and all
well.
  Prince. Why, thou owest God a death.
                                  [Exit.
  Fal. 'Tis not due yet; I would be loath to
pay him before his day. What need I be so
forward with him that calls not on me? Well,
'tis no matter; honour pricks me on. Yea, but
how if honour prick me off when I come on?
how then? Can honour set to a leg? no: or an
arm? no: or take away the grief of a wound?
no. Honour hath no skill in surgery, then? no.
What is honour? a word. What is in that word
honour? what is that honour? air. A trim reckoning! Who hath it? he that died o' Wednesday. Doth he feel it? no. Doth he hear it? no.
'Tis insensible, then? Yea, to the dead. But
will it not live with the living? no. Why? detraction will not suffer it. Therefore I 'll none of
it. Honour is a mere scutcheon: and so ends
my catechism.   *[Exit.*

    SCENE II. *The rebel camp.*

    Enter WORCESTER *and* VERNON.

  Wor. O, no, my nephew must not know, Sir
    Richard,
The liberal and kind offer of the king.
  Ver. 'Twere best he did.
  Wor.   Then are we all undone.
It is not possible, it cannot be,
The king should keep his word in loving us;
He will suspect us still and find a time

To punish this offence in other faults:
Suspicion all our lives shall be stuck full of eyes;
For treason is but trusted like the fox,
Who, ne'er so tame, so cherish'd and lock'd up, 10
Will have a wild trick of his ancestors.
Look how we can, or sad or merrily,
Interpretation will misquote our looks,
And we shall feed like oxen at a stall,
The better cherish'd, still the nearer death.
My nephew's trespass may be well forgot;
It hath the excuse of youth and heat of blood,
And an adopted name of privilege,
A hare-brain'd Hotspur, govern'd by a spleen:
All his offences live upon my head   20
And on his father's; we did train him on,
And, his corruption being ta'en from us,
We, as the spring of all, shall pay for all.
Therefore, good cousin, let not Harry know,
In any case, the offer of the king.
    Ver. Deliver what you will; I'll say 'tis so.
Here comes your cousin.

            Enter HOTSPUR *and* DOUGLAS.

    Hot. My uncle is return'd:
Deliver up my Lord of Westmoreland.
Uncle, what news?   30
    Wor. The king will bid you battle presently.
    Doug. Defy him by the Lord of Westmore-
            land.
    Hot. Lord Douglas, go you and tell him so.
    Doug. Marry, and shall, and very willingly.
                                            [*Exit.*
    Wor. There is no seeming mercy in the king.
    Hot. Did you beg any? God forbid!
    Wor. I told him gently of our grievances,
Of his oath-breaking; which he mended thus,
By now forswearing that he is forsworn:
He calls us rebels, traitors; and will scourge   40
With haughty arms this hateful name in us.

            Re-enter DOUGLAS.

    Doug. Arm, gentlemen; to arms! for I have
            thrown
A brave defiance in King Henry's teeth,
And Westmoreland, that was engaged, did
            bear it;
Which cannot choose but bring him quickly on.
    Wor. The Prince of Wales stepp'd forth
            before the king,
And, nephew, challenged you to single fight.
    Hot. O, would the quarrel lay upon our
            heads,
And that no man might draw short breath to-day
But I and Harry Monmouth! Tell me, tell me, 50
How show'd his tasking? seem'd it in contempt?
    Ver. No, by my soul; I never in my life
Did hear a challenge urged more modestly,
Unless a brother should a brother dare
To gentle exercise and proof of arms.
He gave you all the duties of a man;
Trimm'd up your praises with a princely tongue,
Spoke your deservings like a chronicle,
Making you ever better than his praise
By still dispraising praise valued with you;   60
And, which became him like a prince indeed,
He made a blushing cital of himself;
And chid his truant youth with such a grace
As if he master'd there a double spirit
Of teaching and of learning instantly.

---

44 *engaged.* Held as hostage.

51 *tasking.* Challenging.

60 *valued.* Compared.

21 *Semblably furnish'd.* Similarly equipped.

30 *shot-free.* Without paying bills.

46 *Turk Gregory.* Turk (i.e. cruel); Gregory (i.e. Pope Gregory VII, noted for cruelty to Protestants).

61 *carbonado.* Broiled meat.

George Robey as Falstaff, His Majesty's Theatre, London, 1935

Enter HOTSPUR.

Hot. O Douglas, hadst thou fought at Holmedon thus,
I never had triumph'd upon a Scot.
  Doug. All's done, all's won; here breathless lies the king.
  Hot. Where?
  Doug. Here.
  Hot. This, Douglas? no: I know this face full well:
A gallant knight he was, his name was Blunt; 20
Semblably furnish'd like the king himself.
  Doug. A fool go with thy soul, whither it goes!
A borrow'd title hast thou bought too dear:
Why didst thou tell me that thou wert a king?
  Hot. The king hath many marching in his coats.
  Doug. Now, by my sword, I will kill all his coats;
I'll murder all his wardrobe, piece by piece,
Until I meet the king.
  Hot. Up, and away!
Our soldiers stand full fairly for the day. 29
                   [*Exeunt.*

Alarum. Enter FALSTAFF, *solus.*

  Fal. Though I could 'scape shot-free at London, I fear the shot here; here's no scoring but upon the pate. Soft! who are you? Sir Walter Blunt: there's honour for you! here's no vanity! I am as hot as molten lead, and as heavy too: God keep lead out of me! I need no more weight than mine own bowels. I have led my ragamuffins where they are peppered: there's not three of my hundred and fifty left alive; and they are for the town's end, to beg during life. But who comes here? 40

Enter the PRINCE.

  Prince. What, stand'st thou idle here? lend me thy sword:
Many a nobleman lies stark and stiff
Under the hoofs of vaunting enemies,
Whose deaths are yet unrevenged: I prithee, lend me thy sword.
  Fal. O Hal, I prithee, give me leave to breathe awhile. Turk Gregory never did such deeds in arms as I have done this day. I have paid Percy, I have made him sure.
  Prince. He is, indeed; and living to kill thee. I prithee, lend me thy sword. 50
  Fal. Nay, before God, Hal, if Percy be alive, thou get'st not my sword; but take my pistol, if thou wilt.
  Prince. Give it me: what, is it in the case?
  Fal. Ay, Hal; 'tis hot, 'tis hot; there's that will sack a city. [*The Prince draws it out, and finds it to be a bottle of sack.*
  Prince. What, is it a time to jest and dally now? [*He throws the bottle at him. Exit.*
  Fal. Well, if Percy be alive, I'll pierce him. If he do come in my way, so: if he do not, if I come in his willingly, let him make a carbonado of me. I like not such grinning honour as Sir Walter hath: give me life: which if I can save, so; if not, honour comes unlooked for, and there's an end. [*Exit.*

There did he pause: but let me tell the world,
If he outlive the envy of this day,
England did never owe so sweet a hope,
So much misconstrued in his wantonness.
    Hot. Cousin, I think thou art enamoured 70
On his follies: never did I hear
Of any prince so wild a libertine.
But be he as he will, yet once ere night
I will embrace him with a soldier's arm,
That he shall shrink under my courtesy.
Arm, arm with speed: and, fellows, soldiers,
    friends,
Better consider what you have to do
Than I, that have not well the gift of tongue,
Can lift your blood up with persuasion.

        Enter a Messenger.

    Mess. My lord, here are letters for you.   80
    Hot. I cannot read them now.
O gentlemen, the time of life is short!
To spend that shortness basely were too long,
If life did ride upon a dial's point,
Still ending at the arrival of an hour.
An if we live, we live to tread on kings;
If die, brave death, when princes die with us!
Now, for our consciences, the arms are fair,
When the intent of bearing them is just.

      Enter another Messenger.

    Mess. My lord, prepare; the king comes on
    apace.   90
    Hot. I thank him, that he cuts me from my
    tale,
For I profess not talking; only this—
Let each man do his best: and here draw I
A sword, whose temper I intend to stain
With the best blood that I can meet withal
In the adventure of this perilous day.
Now, Esperance! Percy! and set on.
Sound all the lofty instruments of war,
And by that music let us all embrace;
For, heaven to earth, some of us never shall 100
A second time do such a courtesy.
[*The trumpets sound. They embrace, and exeunt.*

    Scene III. *Plain between the camps.*

The King *enters with his power. Alarum to
    the battle. Then enter* Douglas *and* Sir
    Walter Blunt.

    Blunt. What is thy name, that in the battle
    thus
Thou crossest me? what honour dost thou seek
Upon my head?
    Doug.   Know then, my name is Douglas;
And I do haunt thee in the battle thus
Because some tell me that thou art a king.
    Blunt. They tell thee true.
    Doug. The Lord of Stafford dear to-day hath
    bought
Thy likeness, for instead of thee, King Harry,
This sword hath ended him: so shall it thee,
Unless thou yield thee as my prisoner.   10
    Blunt. I was not born a yielder, thou proud
    Scot;
And thou shalt find a king that will revenge
Lord Stafford's death.   [*They fight. Douglas
               kills Blunt.*

A battle scene. Woodcut from Holinshed's *Chronicles,* 1577

---

5 *make up.* Advance.

25 *Hydra's heads.* The Hydra grew two heads for each one cut off.

44 *Cheerly.* Cheer up.

SCENE IV. *Another part of the field.*

Alarum. Excursions. Enter the KING, *the* PRINCE, LORD JOHN OF LANCASTER, *and* EARL OF WESTMORELAND.

King. I prithee,
Harry, withdraw thyself; thou bleed'st too much.
Lord John of Lancaster, go you with him.
    Lan. Not I, my lord, unless I did bleed too.
    Prince. I beseech your majesty, make up,
Lest your retirement do amaze your friends.
    King. I will do so.
My Lord of Westmoreland, lead him to his tent.
    West. Come, my lord, I'll lead you to your tent.
    Prince. Lead me, my lord? I do not need your help: 10
And God forbid a shallow scratch should drive
The Prince of Wales from such a field as this,
Where stain'd nobility lies trodden on,
And rebels' arms triumph in massacres!
    Lan. We breathe too long: come, cousin Westmoreland,
Our duty this way lies; for God's sake, come.
    [*Exeunt Prince John and Westmoreland.*
    Prince. By God, thou hast deceived me, Lancaster;
I did not think thee lord of such a spirit:
Before, I loved thee as a brother, John;
But now, I do respect thee as my soul.   20
    King. I saw him hold Lord Percy at the point
With lustier maintenance than I did look for
Of such an ungrown warrior.
    Prince.   O, this boy
Lends mettle to us all!   [*Exit.*

Enter DOUGLAS.

    Doug. Another king! they grow like Hydra's heads:
I am the Douglas, fatal to all those
That wear those colours on them: what art thou,
That counterfeit'st the person of a king?
    King. The king himself; who, Douglas, grieves at heart
So many of his shadows thou hast met   30
And not the very king. I have two boys
Seek Percy and thyself about the field:
But, seeing thou fall'st on me so luckily,
I will assay thee: so, defend thyself.
    Doug. I fear thou art another counterfeit;
And yet, in faith, thou bear'st thee like a king:
But mine I am sure thou art, whoe'er thou be,
And thus I win thee.   [*They fight; the King being in danger, re-enter Prince of Wales.*
    Prince. Hold up thy head, vile Scot, or thou art like
Never to hold it up again! the spirits   40
Of valiant Shirley, Stafford, Blunt, are in my arms:
It is the Prince of Wales that threatens thee;
Who never promiseth but he means to pay.
    [*They fight: Douglas flies.*
Cheerly, my lord: how fares your grace?
Sir Nicholas Gawsey hath for succour sent,
And so hath Clifton: I'll to Clifton straight.
    King. Stay, and breathe awhile:
Thou hast redeem'd thy lost opinion,
And show'd thou makest some tender of my life,

In this fair rescue thou hast brought to me.   50
Prince. O God! they did me too much injury
That ever said I hearken'd for your death.
If it were so, I might have let alone
The insulting hand of Douglas over you,
Which would have been as speedy in your end
As all the poisonous potions in the world
And saved the treacherous labour of your son.
    King. Make up to Clifton: I'll to Sir Nicholas
        Gawsey.   [*Exit.*

Enter HOTSPUR.

Hot. If I mistake not, thou art Harry Mon-
    mouth.
Prince. Thou speak'st as if I would deny my
    name.   60
Hot. My name is Harry Percy.
Prince.   Why, then I see
A very valiant rebel of the name.
I am the Prince of Wales; and think not, Percy,
To share with me in glory any more:
Two stars keep not their motion in one sphere;
Nor can one England brook a double reign,
Of Harry Percy and the Prince of Wales.
    Hot. Nor shall it, Harry; for the hour is
        come
To end the one of us; and would to God
Thy name in arms were now as great as mine!
    Prince. I'll make it greater ere I part from
        thee;   71
And all the budding honours on thy crest
I'll crop, to make a garland for my head.
    Hot. I can no longer brook thy vanities.
                                   [*They fight.*

Enter FALSTAFF.

Fal. Well said, Hal! to it, Hal! Nay, you
shall find no boy's play here, I can tell you.

Re-enter DOUGLAS; *he fights with* FALSTAFF,
    who falls down as if he were dead, and exit
    DOUGLAS. HOTSPUR *is wounded, and falls.*

    Hot. O, Harry, thou hast robb'd me of my
        youth!
● I better brook the loss of brittle life
Than those proud titles thou hast won of me;
They wound my thoughts worse than thy sword
    my flesh: 80
But thought's the slave of life, and life time's fool;
And time, that takes survey of all the world,
Must have a stop. O, I could prophesy,
But that the earthy and cold hand of death
Lies on my tongue: no, Percy, thou art dust,
And food for—   [*Dies.*
    Prince. For worms, brave Percy: fare thee
        well, great heart!
Ill-weaved ambition, how much art thou shrunk!
When that this body did contain a spirit,
A kingdom for it was too small a bound;   90
But now two paces of the vilest earth
Is room enough: this earth that bears thee dead
Bears not alive so stout a gentleman.
● If thou wert sensible of courtesy,
I should not make so dear a show of zeal:
● But let my favours hide thy mangled face;
And, even in thy behalf, I'll thank myself
For doing these fair rites of tenderness.
Adieu, and take thy praise with thee to heaven!
Thy ignominy sleep with thee in the grave,   100

Hotspur: 'O Harry, thou hast robb'd me of my youth'.
Engraving from a painting by John Francis Rigaud
(1742–1810)

78 *brook.* Endure.

94 *sensible.* Able to feel.

96 *favours.* i.e. the plumes of his helmet.

109 *Embowell'd.* Disembowelled, for embalming.

Falstaff: 'Embowelled! . . .' Drawing by Sir George Romney (1734–1802)

---

112 *powder.* Pickle in saltpetre.

114 *termagant.* Violent.

But not remember'd in thy epitaph!
[*He spieth Falstaff on the ground.*
What, old acquaintance! could not all this flesh
Keep in a little life? Poor Jack, farewell!
I could have better spared a better man:
O, I should have a heavy miss of thee,
If I were much in love with vanity!
Death hath not struck so fat a deer to-day,
Though many dearer, in this bloody fray.
● Embowell'd will I see thee by and by:
Till then in blood by noble Percy lie. [*Exit.* 110
Fal. [*Rising up*] Embowelled! if thou em-
● bowel me to-day, I'll give you leave to powder
me and eat me too to-morrow. 'Sblood, 'twas
● time to counterfeit, or that hot termagant Scot
had paid me scot and lot too. Counterfeit? I lie,
I am no counterfeit: to die, is to be a counterfeit; for he is but the counterfeit of a man who
hath not the life of a man: but to counterfeit
dying, when a man thereby liveth, is to be no
counterfeit, but the true and perfect image of
life indeed. The better part of valour is discretion; in the which better part I have saved my
life. 'Zounds, I am afraid of this gunpowder
Percy, though he be dead: how, if he should
counterfeit too and rise? by my faith, I am
afraid he would prove the better counterfeit.
Therefore I'll make him sure; yea, and I'll swear
I killed him. Why may not he rise as well as I?
Nothing confutes me but eyes, and nobody sees
me. Therefore, sirrah [*stabbing him*], with a
new wound in your thigh, come you along with
me. [*Takes up Hotspur on his back.*

Re-enter the PRINCE OF WALES *and* LORD JOHN
OF LANCASTER.

Prince. Come, brother John; full bravely hast
thou flesh'd
Thy maiden sword.
Lan. But, soft! whom have we here?
Did you not tell me this fat man was dead?
Prince. I did; I saw him dead,
Breathless and bleeding on the ground. Art thou
alive?
Or is it fantasy that plays upon our eyesight?
I prithee, speak; we will not trust our eyes   139
Without our ears: thou art not what thou seem'st.
Fal. No, that's certain; I am not a double
man: but if I be not Jack Falstaff, then am I a
Jack. There is Percy [*throwing the body down*]:
if your father will do me any honour, so; if not,
let him kill the next Percy himself. I look to be
either earl or duke, I can assure you.
Prince. Why, Percy I killed myself and saw
thee dead.
Fal. Didst thou? Lord, Lord, how this world
is given to lying! I grant you I was down and
out of breath; and so was he: but we rose both
at an instant and fought a long hour by Shrewsbury clock. If I may be believed, so; if not, let
them that should reward valour bear the sin upon
their own heads. I'll take it upon my death, I
gave him this wound in the thigh: if the man
were alive and would deny it, 'zounds, I would
make him eat a piece of my sword.
Lan. This is the strangest tale that ever I heard.
Prince. This is the strangest fellow, brother
John.   159
Come, bring your luggage nobly on your back:

For my part, if a lie may do thee grace,
I'll gild it with the happiest terms I have.
　　　　　　　　　　　[*A retreat is sounded.*
The trumpet sounds retreat; the day is ours.
Come, brother, let us to the highest of the field,
To see what friends are living, who are dead.
　　　[*Exeunt Prince of Wales and Lancaster.*
Fal. I'll follow, as they say, for reward. He
that rewards me, God reward him! If I do grow
great, I'll grow less; for I'll purge, and leave
sack, and live cleanly as a nobleman should do.
　　　　　　　　　　　　　　　[*Exit.*

SCENE V. *Another part of the field.*

The trumpets sound. Enter the KING, PRINCE
OF WALES, LORD JOHN OF LANCASTER, EARL
OF WESTMORELAND, *with* WORCESTER *and*
VERNON *prisoners.*

　King. Thus ever did rebellion find rebuke.
Ill-spirited Worcester! did not we send grace,
Pardon and terms of love to all of you?
And wouldst thou turn our offers contrary?
Misuse the tenour of thy kinsman's trust?
Three knights upon our party slain to-day,
A noble earl and many a creature else
Had been alive this hour,
If like a Christian thou hadst truly borne
Betwixt our armies true intelligence.　　10
　Wor. What I have done my safety urged me to;
And I embrace this fortune patiently,
Since not to be avoided it falls on me.
　King. Bear Worcester to the death and Vernon
　　　too:
Other offenders we will pause upon.
　　　[*Exeunt Worcester and Vernon, guarded.*
How goes the field?
　Prince. The noble Scot, Lord Douglas, when
　　　he saw
The fortune of the day quite turn'd from him,
The noble Percy slain, and all his men
Upon the foot of fear, fled with the rest;　　20
And falling from a hill, he was so bruised
That the pursuers took him. At my tent
The Douglas is; and I beseech your grace
I may dispose of him.
　King.　　　　　　With all my heart.
　Prince. Then, brother John of Lancaster, to you
This honourable bounty shall belong:
Go to the Douglas, and deliver him
Up to his pleasure, ransomless and free:
His valour shown upon our crests to-day
Hath taught us how to cherish such high deeds
Even in the bosom of our adversaries.　　31
　Lan. I thank your grace for this high courtesy,
Which I shall give away immediately.
　King. Then this remains, that we divide our
　　　power.
You, son John, and my cousin Westmoreland
Towards York shall bend you with your dearest
　　　speed,
To meet Northumberland and the prelate Scroop,
Who, as we hear, are busily in arms:
Myself and you, son Harry, will towards Wales,
To fight with Glendower and the Earl of March.
Rebellion in this land shall lose his sway,　　41
Meeting the check of such another day:
And since this business so fair is done,
Let us not leave till all our own be won. [*Exeunt.*

Falstaff with Hotspur on his back. Engraving from a
drawing by Henry Bunbury (1750–1811)

King Henry IV

1598

THE SECOND PART OF HENRY IV followed immediately upon the heels of the first. We must always keep in mind what a practical man of the theatre Shakespeare was: he would naturally want to sound again the notes that had been so successful with the first part. Elizabethan usage was flexible and pragmatic in this regard, not rigid. He had it in mind to tell the whole story of Henry V, as Prince and King, since he was such a hero to the Elizabethans. This would mean, in dramatic form, a trilogy, the third – the heroic – part, *Henry V*, varying in character from the two parts of *Henry IV*. These two, though two halves of one story, worked out somewhat differently. The second part did not have the powerful dramatic conflict culminating on the battlefield of Shrewsbury, and it evidently did not grip the audience to the same extent, perhaps because it was the mixture as before.

All the same, it is a mistake to depreciate this part, for it presents brilliant scenes, as effective as and more touching than the first part; if it has less drama in the popular sense, it has more poetry and pathos, more wonderful depictions of contemporary Elizabethan life in town and country, in East Cheap and on the Cotswolds, and – in the absence of the Prince – far more sex and bawdy talk, in which the dramatist was a virtuoso. It is precisely these naughty scenes that give us, as has been well said, 'an irresistible impression of reality, a sense that we are in touch with the living pulse of Shakespeare's England.'[1] That is the point – they exhibit contemporary life as much as anything of Ben Jonson's and are even more living today.

Again, on the historical side, the portrayal of England's past, 'Shakespeare's presentation of history in drama is on the whole far truer to history than that of any of his predecessors.' This is true of Richard II, Henry IV, Henry V, Henry VI and Richard III. This is to be expected, for though Shakespeare did not have the advantages of being a professor of history or an historical researcher, he had a more penetrating understanding of human beings, their characters and conflicts, their agonising temptations and dilemmas. A leading authority on the 15th century,[2] which Shakespeare chiefly dealt with, describes him as after all our greatest historian.

Prince and King. The Elizabethans were fascinated by the compelling and complex personality of Henry V, which to the outer world seemed to fall into two halves: the

1. C.H. Herford, *2 Henry IV*, ix–x. (The Warwick Shakespeare). I should like to pay tribute to this old edition of the play, for this editor was not only a scholar but had a mind on a level with the subject.

2. K.B. McFarlane.

'unthrifty' Prince and the hero-King. And yet he was no schizophrenic: the subtle psychologist saw that there was consistency, in spite of appearances, and the deft dramatist provided for it in his plays.

In this play the Prince is on his way to assuming the burden of kingship and taking upon him the character of a king. (Shakespeare may not have known that on the day of his father's death Henry spent the whole night alone in Westminster Abbey with an anchorite, and underwent something like a religious conversion. But, a medieval man, like his father, he would already have been impregnated by belief and open to such an experience, just as his father longed to die on crusade. It is all very touching.)

Henry IV. His father has never had such an appeal; and yet, to anyone who understands the imperious necessities of rule and the bitter exigencies of politics, Henry IV has great pathos. In the end, he was broken by them, perhaps too by the burden of guilt his conscience carried. But anyone can appreciate the tension in the father-son relationship, especially when the father is a king and the son his heir. It has life's irony in it too, for the Prince was more fond of the dead Richard than he was of his own father. Shakespeare may not have known that, but he intuited, what he makes Falstaff say, that the King's blood was cold and the Prince inherited it.

And yet the son was loyal: he broke Falstaff's head for comparing the King to a singing-man of Windsor. Henry IV suffered from a succession of strokes. But it was not for the heir to put on an outward expression of grief:

> I tell thee, it is not meet that I should be sad now my father is sick. Albeit I could tell to thee . . . I could be sad, and sad indeed too . . . Let the end try the man . . . my heart bleeds inwardly that my father is so sick.

The father's heart also bleeds inwardly that his son is set on such courses: politic as ever, he manages to 'sever' the Prince from Falstaff for a while, sending them off in different directions. What was it that the Prince saw so much in Falstaff? The old rascal tells us: it was his function to keep the Prince in a continual laughter (it should be played as such).

No laughter in the King's care-worn life, and his reproaches to his son are searing:

> Thou has sealed up my expectation.
> Thy life did manifest thou lovedst me not,
> And thou wilt have me die assured of it.

This is when the King is dying and the Prince, thinking him already dead, takes away the crown from his pillow. There follows the wonderful scene in which each is faced with the reality of life and death, understanding and reconciliation at last before the King lays down the cares of this world.

Whether this unexampled episode – so moving on the stage – was historic fact or no, it is certainly symbolic. For during one of Henry's previous illnesses, the Prince had taken hold of the government; the King had recovered, and dismissed him from the Council. The King had already confessed to Warwick, quoting Richard's prophecy what an ill time of care Henry would have as king,

> Though then, God knows, I had no such intent,
> But that necessity so bowed the state
> That I and greatness were compelled to kiss.

This was probably the historic truth. Henry then asks the question that is the kernel of the whole matter:

> . . . Are these things then necessities?

The rejection of Falstaff. From a painting by Robert Smirke (1752–1845)

Warwick, loyal to both, amid all the treacheries of high politics, had defended the Prince to his father and tried to explain – a very human situation we all know:

> My gracious lord, you look beyond him quite:
> The Prince but studies his companions
> Like a strange tongue . . . So, like gross terms,
> The Prince will in the perfectness of time
> Cast off his followers.

Now, facing death, the King lays bare his soul to his son:

> God knows, mv son,
> By what bypaths and indirect crooked ways
> I met this crown. And I myself know well
> How troublesome it sat upon my head.
> To thee it shall descend with better quiet,
> Better opinion, better confirmation,
> For all the soil of the achievement goes
> With me into the earth.

Henry's life of care and toil had laid the foundations for a firmer hold for his son as king; even so, his last counsel, prudent and cautious as ever, was –

> Yet, though thou stand'st more sure than I could do,
> Thou art not firm enough, since griefs are green.

Henry had longed to wipe out the stain of his guilt by going on crusade to the Holy Land. Did Shakespeare know that, as a young man, Henry had already gone on crusade with the Teutonic Knights against the heathen of early Prussia?

The Prince as King. Thus we are led up to the accession of the young Henry as King. The mask drops; the real man, the politic son of his cold, sad father, stands forth and shows his quality as ruler – shows 'indifferency', the Elizabethan word for impartiality, justice of mind. Though the Chief Justice had rebuked him and 'sent to prison the immediate heir of England', the new King confirms him in office and wishes him increase of honour, and that, if a son of his own should offend, the Chief Justice would similarly commit him.

A great deal of fuss has been made by people of no political understanding about the relegation of Falstaff. Of course he had to be relegated; when he stood to 'leer upon' the new-crowned Henry V, he expected to be able to bestow office and favours upon his rascally crew of thieves and rogues. It does not seem to have been noticed that, as King, Henry treats the shameless old ruffian generously:

> For competence of life I will allow you,
> That lack of means enforce you not to evils.
> And, as we hear you do reform yourselves,
> We will, according to your strengths and qualities,
> Give you advancement.

Themes. The main action in this play, the Northern rebellion of Northumberland and

Archbishop Scrope, is far less interesting than the father-son relationship of King and Prince. These together occupy less space than the low life scenes around Falstaff, Justice Shallow and the *habitués* of the Boar's Head. Talk about social realism! – if this is what Marxists want in literature, these scenes are beyond compare. They have too their poetry and pathos, for all their disgrace and bawdiness. They have veracious vividness and intense humanity.

Despite the cursing and swearing, the brawling and bad language of the rogues and their whore, one cannot but be touched when Doll Tearsheet says at length:

> Come, I'll be friends with thee, Jack. Thou art going to the wars, and whether I shall ever see thee again or no, there is nobody cares.

And Falstaff is reduced to confessing,

> I am old, I am old.

> Doll: I love thee better than I love e'er a scurvy young boy of them all.

The pathos is much the same with Justice Shallow in his Gloucestershire home, old age creeping on and he remembering the days of his youth:

> There was I, and little John Doit of Staffordshire, and black George Barnes, and Francis Pickbone, and Will Squele, a Cotswold man: you had not four such swinge-bucklers in all the Inns o'Court again. And I may say to you we knew where the bonarobas were . . . Jesu, Jesu, the mad days that I have spent! And to see how many of my old acquaintance are dead!

Then Falstaff: We have heard the chimes at midnight, Master Shallow.

Personal. Gloucestershire lies in part on the western slopes of the Cotswolds; we notice Shakespeare's kindly remembrance of the familiar places. Shallow's young cousin (Elizabethan for nephew), William, 'is become a good scholar. He is at Oxford still . . . 'a must, then, to the Inns o'Court shortly.' This was the regular course for a young gentleman of expectations. We heard of William Visor of Woncot's case against Clement Perkes of the Hill: Woncot was the regular pronunciation of Woodmancote, the Hill is Stinchcombe Hill. 'Goodman Puff of Barson' – this was how Barcheston was pronounced, where the famous Sheldon tapestries were made. A Gloucestershire place-name, Dumbledon or Dumbleton, is used for a person's surname. Hinckley is a Warwickshire town near Coventry.

At Stratford at this very time Shapespeare was repairing New Place which he had recently bought; so we find:

> When we mean to build
> We first survey the plot, then draw the model.
> And when we see the figure of the house,
> Then must we rate the cost of the erection,
> Which, if we find outweighs ability,
> What do we then but draw anew the model
> In fewer offices, or at least desist
> To build at all?

How like the prudent actor, and unlike his father! The money had been made, not by teaching school –

> like a school broke up,
> Each hurries toward his home and sporting-place –

but by the stage:

> And let this world no longer be a stage
> To feed contention in a lingering act.

Shakespeare's observation-post as an actor and his upward move in society enabled him to spot, and spit, its pretences – such as with

> those that are kin to the king, for they never prick their finger but they say, 'There's some of the king's blood spilt.' 'How comes that?', says he that takes upon him not to conceive. The answer is as ready as a borrower's cap, 'I am the king's poor cousin, sir.'

Fools, that people are, and Shakespeare saw through everybody to be! He gives it to an Archbishop to describe the common people:

> An habitation giddy and unsure
> Hath he that buildeth on the vulgar heart.

They had been all in favour of Bolingbroke; now –

> Thou, beastly feeder, art so full of him
> That thou provok'st thyself to cast him up.

Epilogue. This is important for the explanation it gives. It would seem that originally it was spoken by Shakespeare, for he says 'what I have to say is of my own making, and what indeed I should say will, I doubt, prove mine own marring . . . Be it known unto you, as it is very well, I was lately here in the end of a displeasing play, to pray your patience for it and to promise you a better.' We do not know what play that was; he goes on, 'I meant indeed to pay you with this', and he prays their favour for his new piece with his usual charming courtesy. He promises to continue the story 'with Sir John in it, and make you merry with fair Katherine of France. Where, for anything I know, Falstaff shall die of a sweat, unless already 'a be killed with your hard opinions.' Then came the disclaimer, to meet the objections of the Cobhams: 'for Oldcastle died a martyr, and this is not the man.'

Text. A good text was printed in the quarto of 1600, probably printed from Shakespeare's own manuscript, with the omission of references to Richard II's deposition. These were supplied in the full text of the Folio.

THE SECOND PART OF
KING HENRY IV.

DRAMATIS PERSONÆ.

RUMOUR, the Presenter.
KING HENRY the Fourth.
HENRY, PRINCE OF WALES, afterwards King Henry V.,
THOMAS, DUKE OF CLARENCE, } his sons.
PRINCE JOHN OF LANCASTER,
PRINCE HUMPHREY OF GLOUCESTER,
EARL OF WARWICK.
EARL OF WESTMORELAND.
EARL OF SURREY.
GOWER.
HARCOURT.
BLUNT.
Lord Chief-Justice of the King's Bench
A Servant of the Chief-Justice.
EARL OF NORTHUMBERLAND.
SCROOP, Archbishop of York.
LORD MOWBRAY.
LORD HASTINGS.
LORD BARDOLPH.
SIR JOHN COLEVILE.
TRAVERS and MORTON, retainers of Northumberland.

SIR JOHN FALSTAFF.
His Page.
BARDOLPH.
PISTOL.
POINS.
PETO.
SHALLOW, } country justices.
SILENCE,
DAVY, Servant to Shallow.
MOULDY, SHADOW, WART, FEEBLE, and BULLCALF, recruits.
FANG and SNARE, sheriff's officers.

LADY NORTHUMBERLAND.
LADY PERCY.
MISTRESS QUICKLY, hostess of a tavern in Eastcheap.
DOLL TEARSHEET.

Lords and Attendants; Porter, Drawers, Beadles, Grooms, &c.

A Dancer, speaker of the epilogue.

SCENE: *England.*

● *A bullet beside a text line indicates an annotation in the opposite column*

INDUCTION.

Warkworth. Before the castle.

Enter Rumour, *painted full of tongues.*

Rum. Open your ears; for which of you will stop
The vent of hearing when loud Rumour speaks?
I, from the orient to the drooping west,
Making the wind my post-horse, still unfold
The acts commenced on this ball of earth:
Upon my tongues continual slanders ride,
The which in every language I pronounce,
Stuffing the ears of men with false reports.
I speak of peace, while covert enmity
Under the smile of safety wounds the world: 10
And who but Rumour, who but only I,
Make fearful musters and prepared defence,
Whiles the big year, swoln with some other grief,
Is thought with child by the stern tyrant war,
And no such matter? Rumour is a pipe
Blown by surmises, jealousies, conjectures,
And of so easy and so plain a stop
That the blunt monster with uncounted heads,
The still-discordant wavering multitude,
Can play upon it.   But what need I thus   20
My well-known body to anatomize
Among my household? Why is Rumour here?
I run before King Harry's victory;

Costume design for Rumour by Tanya Moisewitch, Stratford-upon-Avon, 1951

Opposite: Falstaff selecting recruits. Drawing by S.H. Grimm, 1771

Warkworth Castle in Northumberland, the Percys'
principal seat. Engraving from *Old England,* 1854

37 *crafty-sick.* Feigning illness. *tiring on.* Galloping to
exhaustion.

Who in a bloody field by Shrewsbury
Hath beaten down young Hotspur and his troops,
Quenching the flame of bold rebellion
Even with the rebels' blood.   But what mean I
To speak so true at first? my office is
To noise abroad that Harry Monmouth fell
Under the wrath of noble Hotspur's sword,   30
And that the king before the Douglas' rage
Stoop'd his anointed head as low as death.
This have I rumour'd through the peasant towns
Between that royal field of Shrewsbury
And this worm-eaten hold of ragged stone,
Where Hotspur's father, old Northumberland,
Lies crafty-sick: the posts come tiring on,
And not a man of them brings other news
Than they have learn'd of me: from Rumour's
    tongues
They bring smooth comforts false, worse than
    true wrongs.   [*Exit.* 40

ACT I.

Scene I. *The same.*

Enter Lord Bardolph.

L. Bard.   Who keeps the gate here, ho?

The Porter *opens the gate.*

                                    Where is the earl?
Port.   What shall I say you are?
L. Bard.   Tell thou the earl
That the Lord Bardolph doth attend him here.
Port.   His lordship is walk'd forth into the
    orchard:
Please it your honour, knock but at the gate,
And he himself will answer.

46 *rowel-head.* i.e. digging the spur well in.

53 *silken point.* Silk lace to tie up clothes.

Enter NORTHUMBERLAND.

L. Bard.   Here comes the earl.
                              [*Exit Porter.*
North. What news, Lord Bardolph? every
          minute now
Should be the father of some stratagem:
The times are wild; contention, like a horse
Full of high feeding, madly hath broke loose   10
And bears down all before him.
      L. Bard.   Noble earl,
I bring you certain news from Shrewsbury.
      North. Good, an God will!
      L. Bard.   As good as heart can wish:
The king is almost wounded to the death;
And, in the fortune of my lord your son,
Prince Harry slain outright; and both the Blunts
Kill'd by the hand of Douglas; young Prince
          John
And Westmoreland and Stafford fled the field;
And Harry Monmouth's brawn, the hulk Sir John,
Is prisoner to your son: O, such a day,   20
So fought, so follow'd and so fairly won,
Came not till now to dignify the times,
Since Cæsar's fortunes!
      North.   How is this derived?
Saw you the field? came you from Shrewsbury?
      L. Bard. I spake with one, my lord, that
          came from thence,
A gentleman well bred and of good name,
That freely render'd me these news for true.
      North. Here comes my servant Travers,
          whom I sent
On Tuesday last to listen after news.

Enter TRAVERS.

      L. Bard. My lord, I over-rode him on the
          way;   30
And he is furnish'd with no certainties
More than he haply may retail from me.
      North. Now, Travers, what good tidings
          comes with you?
      Tra. My lord, Sir John Umfrevile turn'd me
          back
With joyful tidings; and, being better horsed,
Out-rode me. After him came spurring hard
A gentleman, almost forspent with speed,
That stopp'd by me to breathe his bloodied horse.
He ask'd the way to Chester; and of him
I did demand what news from Shrewsbury: 40
He told me that rebellion had bad luck
And that young Harry Percy's spur was cold.
With that, he gave his able horse the head,
And bending forward struck his armed heels
Against the panting sides of his poor jade
• Up to the rowel-head, and starting so
He seem'd in running to devour the way,
Staying no longer question.
      North.   Ha! Again:
Said he young Harry Percy's spur was cold?
Of Hotspur Coldspur? that rebellion   50
Had met ill luck?
      L. Bard.   My lord, I'll tell you what;
If my young lord your son have not the day,
• Upon mine honour, for a silken point
I'll give my barony: never talk of it.
      North. Why should that gentleman that rode
          by Travers
Give then such instances of loss?

57 *hilding.* Ne'er-do-well.

72 *Priam.* King of Troy.

L. Bard.   Who, he?
● He was some hilding fellow that had stolen
The horse he rode on, and, upon my life,
Spoke at a venture. Look, here comes more news.

Enter MORTON.

North. Yea, this man's brow, like to a title-
leaf,   60
Foretells the nature of a tragic volume:
So looks the strand whereon the imperious flood
Hath left a witness'd usurpation.
Say, Morton, didst thou come from Shrewsbury?
Mor. I ran from Shrewsbury, my noble lord;
Where hateful death put on his ugliest mask
To fright our party.
North.   How doth my son and brother?
Thou tremblest; and the whiteness in thy cheek
Is apter than thy tongue to tell thy errand.
Even such a man, so faint, so spiritless,   70
So dull, so dead in look, so woe-begone,
● Drew Priam's curtain in the dead of night,
And would have told him half his Troy was burnt;
But Priam found the fire ere he his tongue,
And I my Percy's death ere thou report'st it.
This thou wouldst say, 'Your son did thus and
thus;
Your brother thus: so fought the noble Douglas:'
Stopping my greedy ear with their bold deeds:
But in the end, to stop my ear indeed,
Thou hast a sigh to blow away this praise,   80
Ending with 'Brother, son, and all are dead.'
Mor. Douglas is living, and your brother, yet:
But, for my lord your son,—
North.   Why, he is dead.
See what a ready tongue suspicion hath!
He that but fears the thing he would not know
Hath by instinct knowledge from others' eyes
That what he fear'd is chanced. Yet speak,
Morton;
Tell thou an earl his divination lies,
And I will take it as a sweet disgrace
And make thee rich for doing me such wrong. 90
Mor. You are too great to be by me gainsaid:
Your spirit is too true, your fears too certain.
North. Yet, for all this, say not that Percy's
dead.
I see a strange confession in thine eye:
Thou shakest thy head and hold'st it fear or sin
To speak a truth. If he be slain, say so;
The tongue offends not that reports his death:
And he doth sin that doth belie the dead,
Not he which says the dead is not alive.
Yet the first bringer of unwelcome news   100
Hath but a losing office, and his tongue
Sounds ever after as a sullen bell,
Remember'd tolling a departing friend.
L. Bard. I cannot think, my lord, your son
is dead.
Mor. I am sorry I should force you to believe
That which I would to God I had not seen;
But these mine eyes saw him in bloody state,
Rendering faint quittance, wearied and out-
breathed,
To Harry Monmouth; whose swift wrath beat
down
The never-daunted Percy to the earth,   110
From whence with life he never more sprung up.
In few, his death, whose spirit lent a fire
Even to the dullest peasant in his camp,

Being bruited once, took fire and heat away
From the best-temper'd courage in his troops;
For from his metal was his party steel'd;
Which once in him abated, all the rest
Turn'd on themselves, like dull and heavy lead:
And as the thing that's heavy in itself,
Upon enforcement flies with greatest speed, 120
So did our men, heavy in Hotspur's loss,
Lend to this weight such lightness with their fear
That arrows fled not swifter toward their aim
Than did our soldiers, aiming at their safety,
Fly from the field.　Then was that noble Wor-
　　cester
Too soon ta'en prisoner; and that furious Scot,
The bloody Douglas, whose well-labouring sword
Had three times slain the appearance of the king,
'Gan vail his stomach and did grace the shame
Of those that turn'd their backs, and in his
　　flight,　　　　　　　　130
Stumbling in fear, was took.　The sum of all
Is that the king hath won, and hath sent out
A speedy power to encounter you, my lord,
Under the conduct of young Lancaster
And Westmoreland.　This is the news at full.
　　North.　For this I shall have time enough
　　　to mourn.
In poison there is physic; and these news,
Having been well, that would have made me sick,
Being sick, have in some measure made me well:
And as the wretch, whose fever-weaken'd joints,
Like strengthless hinges, buckle under life, 141
Impatient of his fit, breaks like a fire
Out of his keeper's arms, even so my limbs,
Weaken'd with grief, being now enraged with
　　grief,
Are thrice themselves.　Hence, therefore, thou
　　nice crutch!
A scaly gauntlet now with joints of steel
Must glove this hand: and hence, thou sickly
　　quoif!
Thou art a guard too wanton for the head
Which princes, flesh'd with conquest, aim to hit.
Now bind my brows with iron; and approach 150
The ragged'st hour that time and spite dare bring
To frown upon the enraged Northumberland!
Let heaven kiss earth! now let not Nature's
　　hand
Keep the wild flood confined! let order die!
And let this world no longer be a stage
To feed contention in a lingering act;
But let one spirit of the first-born Cain
Reign in all bosoms, that, each heart being set
On bloody courses, the rude scene may end,
And darkness be the burier of the dead!　160
　　Tra.　This strained passion doth you wrong,
　　　my lord.
　　L. Bard.　Sweet earl, divorce not wisdom
　　　from your honour.
　　Mor.　The lives of all your loving complices
Lean on your health; the which, if you give o'er
To stormy passion, must perforce decay.
You cast the event of war, my noble lord,
And summ'd the account of chance, before you
　　said
'Let us make head.'　It was your presurmise,
That, in the dole of blows, your son might drop:
You knew he walk'd o'er perils, on an edge, 170
More likely to fall in than to get o'er;
You were advised his flesh was capable

114 *bruited.* Rumoured.

128–129 *Had . . . stomach.* Killed three knights dressed like the king, before he was discouraged.

147 *quoif.* Night-cap.

157 *Cain.* Son of Adam and Eve who murdered his brother Abel; i.e. the spirit of murder.

168 *make head.* Raise an armed force.

169 *dole.* Giving.

177 *stiff-borne*. Determined.

184 *respect*. Consideration.

189–190 *up With well-appointed powers*. Marching at the head of a large army.

205 *Pomfret*. Pontefract Castle, where Richard II was murdered.

Falstaff and his page. Drawing by J.M. Wright (1776–1866)

2 *water*. Urine.

7 *gird*. Jeer.

Of wounds and scars and that his forward **spirit**
Would lift him where most trade of **danger**
ranged:
Yet did you say 'Go forth;' and none of this,
Though strongly apprehended, could restrain
● The stiff-borne action: what hath then befallen,
Or what hath this bold enterprise brought forth,
More than that being which was like to be?
    L. Bard. We all that are engaged to **this**
loss   **180**
Knew that we ventured on such dangerous seas
That if we wrought out life 'twas ten to one;
● And yet we ventured, for the gain proposed
Choked the respect of likely peril fear'd;
And since we are o'erset, venture again.
Come, we will all put forth, body and goods.
    Mor. 'Tis more than time: and, my **most**
noble lord,
I hear for certain, and do speak the truth,
● The gentle Archbishop of York is up
With well-appointed powers: he is a man   **190**
Who with a double surety binds his followers.
My lord your son had only but the corpse,
But shadows and the shows of men, to **fight**;
For that same word, rebellion, did divide
The action of their bodies from their souls;
And they did fight with queasiness, constrain'd,
As men drink potions, that their weapons only
Seem'd on our side; but, for their spirits **and**
souls,
This word, rebellion, it had froze them up,
As fish are in a pond. But now the bishop   **200**
Turns insurrection to religion:
Supposed sincere and holy in his thoughts,
He's followed both with body and with mind;
And doth enlarge his rising with the blood
● Of fair King Richard, scraped from **Pomfret**
stones;
Derives from heaven his quarrel and his cause;
Tells them he doth bestride a bleeding land,
Gasping for life under great Bolingbroke;
And more and less do flock to follow him.
    North. I knew of this before; but, to **speak**
truth,   **210**
This present grief had wiped it from my mind.
Go in with me; and counsel every man
The aptest way for safety and revenge:
Get posts and letters, and make friends **with**
speed:
Never so few, and never yet more need. [*Exeunt*.

    SCENE II. *London. A street.*

Enter FALSTAFF, *with his* Page *bearing his*
sword and buckler.

    Fal. Sirrah, you giant, what says the **doctor**
● to my water?
    Page. He said, sir, the water itself **was a**
good healthy water; but, for the party **that**
owed it, he might have more diseases than **he**
knew for.
    Fal. Men of all sorts take a pride to **gird at**
● me: the brain of this foolish-compounded clay,
man, is not able to invent any thing that tends **to**
laughter, more than I invent or is invented on
me: I am not only witty in myself, but the **cause**
that wit is in other men. I do here walk before
thee like a sow that hath overwhelmed all **her**
litter but one. If the prince put thee into **my**

service for any other reason than to set me off,
why then I have no **judgement**. Thou whoreson
mandrake, thou art fitter to be worn in my cap
than to wait at my heels. I was never manned
with an agate till now: but I will inset you
neither in gold nor silver, but in vile apparel,
and send you back again to your master, for a
jewel,—the juvenal, the prince your master,
whose chin is not yet fledged. I will sooner
have a beard grow in the palm of my hand than
he shall get one on his cheek; and yet he will
not stick to say his face is a face-royal: God
may finish it when he will, 'tis not a hair amiss
yet: he may keep it still at a face-royal, for a
barber shall never earn sixpence out of it; and
yet he'll be crowing as if he had writ man ever
since his father was a bachelor. He may keep
his own grace, but he's almost out of mine, I
can assure him. What said Master Dombledon
about the satin for my short cloak and my slops?

Page. He said, sir, you should procure him
better assurance than Bardolph: he would not
take his band and yours; he liked not the
security.

Fal. Let him be damned, like the glutton!
pray God his tongue be hotter! A whoreson
Achitophel! a rascally yea-forsooth knave! to
bear a gentleman in hand, and then stand upon
security! The whoreson smooth-pates do now
wear nothing but high shoes, and bunches of
keys at their girdles; and if a man is through
with them in honest taking up, then they must
stand upon security. I had as lief they would
put ratsbane in my mouth as offer to stop it with
security. I looked a' should have sent me two
and twenty yards of satin, as I am a true knight,
and he sends me security. Well, he may sleep
in security; for he hath the horn of abundance,
and the lightness of his wife shines through it:
and yet cannot he see, though he have his own
lanthorn to light him. Where's Bardolph?

Page. He's gone into Smithfield to buy your
worship a horse.

Fal. I bought him in Paul's, and he'll buy
me a horse in Smithfield: an I could get me but
a wife in the stews, I were manned, horsed, and
wived.   61

Enter the Lord Chief-Justice *and* Servant.

Page. Sir, here comes the nobleman that
committed the prince for striking him about
Bardolph.

Fal. Wait close; I will not see him.

Ch. Just. What's he that goes there?

Serv. Falstaff, an't please your lordship.

Ch. Just. He that was in question for the
robbery?   69

Serv. He, my lord: but he hath since done
good service at Shrewsbury; and, as I hear, is
now going with some charge to the Lord John of
Lancaster.

Ch. Just. What, to York? Call him back
again.

Serv. Sir John Falstaff!

Fal. Boy, tell him I am deaf.

Page. You must speak louder; my master is
deaf.   79

Ch. Just. I am sure he is, to the hearing of

16–17 *whoreson mandrake.* Damned midget. The mandrake root was said to resemble a man.

18–19 *manned with an agate.* Served by anyone as small as an agate stone.

22 *juvenal.* Young man.

26 *face-royal.* A pun on the coin, worth ten shillings, and the king's head on the coin.

30 *writ man.* Become an adult.

34 *slops.* Baggy trousers.

37 *band.* Bond.

39 *glutton.* An allusion to Dives (Luke. xvi, 24).

41 *Achitophel.* i.e. who abandoned David for Absalom (2 Samuel xv-xvii).

42 *bear a gentleman in hand.* Encourage.

44–45 *high shoes . . . keys.* Tokens of wealth and position.

47 *as lief.* As soon.

48 *ratsbane.* Rat poison.

52 *horn of abundance.* The cuckold's horn.

56 *Smithfield.* Famous London market.

Smithfield. Detail from Ralph Agas's map of London *c.*1560–70

58 *Paul's.* St. Paul's Cathedral, the nave of which was used as a labour market.

60 *stews.* Brothels.

63 *committed.* i.e. to prison.

102 *counter*. i.e. in the wrong direction with a quibble on Counter, the debtor's prison.

103 *avaunt*. Away.

Falstaff: 'My good lord! God give your lordship good time of day'. Falstaff and the Chief Justice. Engraving by Kenny Meadows from Barry Cornwall's *Works of Shakspere*, 1846

133 *Galen*. Greek physician and writer on medicine of the 2nd century B.C.

148–149 *make some dram of a scruple*. Hesitate to admit, with a quibble on weights: a scruplt weighed one-third of a dram, a dram one-eighth of an apothecaries' ounce.

any thing good. Go, pluck him by the elbow; I must speak with him.

Serv. Sir John!

Fal. What! a young knave, and begging! Is there not wars? is there not employment? doth not the king lack subjects? do not the rebels need soldiers? Though it be a shame to be on any side but one, it is worse shame to beg than to be on the worst side, were it worse than the name of rebellion can tell how to make it.　90

Serv. You mistake me, sir.

Fal. Why, sir, did I say you were an honest man? setting my knighthood and my soldiership aside, I had lied in my throat, if I had said so.

Serv. I pray you, sir, then set your knighthood and your soldiership aside; and give me leave to tell you, you lie in your throat, if you say I am any other than an honest man.

Fal. I give thee leave to tell me so! I lay aside that which grows to me! If thou gettest any leave of me, hang me; if thou takest leave, thou wert better be hanged. You hunt counter: hence! avaunt!

Serv. Sir, my lord would speak with you.

Ch. Just. Sir John Falstaff, a word with you.

Fal. My good lord! God give your lordship good time of day. I am glad to see your lordship abroad: I heard say your lordship was sick: I hope your lordship goes abroad by advice. Your lordship, though not clean past your youth, hath yet some smack of age in you, some relish of the saltness of time; and I most humbly beseech your lordship to have a reverent care of your health.

Ch. Just. Sir John, I sent for you before your expedition to Shrewsbury.

Fal. An't please your lordship, I hear his majesty is returned with some discomfort from Wales.

Ch. Just. I talk not of his majesty: you would not come when I sent for you.　121

Fal. And I hear, moreover, his highness is fallen into this same whoreson apoplexy.

Ch. Just. Well, God mend him! I pray you, let me speak with you.

Fal. This apoplexy is, as I take it, a kind of lethargy, an't please your lordship; a kind of sleeping in the blood, a whoreson tingling.

Ch. Just. What tell you me of it? be it as it is.　130

Fal. It hath it original from much grief, from study and perturbation of the brain: I have read the cause of his effects in Galen: it is a kind of deafness.

Ch. Just. I think you are fallen into the disease; for you hear not what I say to you.

Fal. Very well, my lord, very well: rather, an't please you, it is the disease of not listening, the malady of not marking, that I am troubled withal.　140

Ch. Just. To punish you by the heels would amend the attention of your ears; and I care not if I do become your physician.

Fal. I am as poor as Job, my lord, but not so patient: your lordship may minister the potion of imprisonment to me in respect of poverty; but how I should be your patient to follow your prescriptions, the wise may make some dram of a scruple, or indeed a scruple itself.

Ch. Just. I sent for you, when there were matters against you for your life, to come speak with me.

Fal. As I was then advised by my learned counsel in the laws of this land-service, I did not come.

Ch. Just. Well, the truth is, Sir John, you live in great infamy.

Fal. He that buckles him in my belt cannot live in less.

Ch. Just. Your means are very slender, and your waste is great.   160

Fal. I would it were otherwise; I would my means were greater, and my waist slenderer.

Ch. Just. You have misled the youthful prince.

Fal. The young prince hath misled me: I am the fellow with the great belly, and he my dog.

Ch. Just. Well, I am loath to gall a new-healed wound: your day's service at Shrewsbury hath a little gilded over your night's exploit on Gad's-hill: you may thank the unquiet time for your quiet o'er-posting that action.   171

Fal. My lord?

Ch. Just. But since all is well, keep it so: wake not a sleeping wolf.

Fal. To wake a wolf is as bad as to smell a fox.

Ch. Just. What! you are as a candle, the better part burnt out.

Fal. A wassail candle, my lord, all tallow: if I did say of wax, my growth would approve the truth.   181

Ch. Just. There is not a white hair on your face but should have his effect of gravity.

Fal. His effect of gravy, gravy, gravy.

Ch. Just. You follow the young prince up and down, like his ill angel.

Fal. Not so, my lord; your ill angel is light; but I hope he that looks upon me will take me without weighing: and yet, in some respects, I grant, I cannot go: I cannot tell. Virtue is of so little regard in these costermonger times that true valour is turned bear-herd: pregnancy is made a tapster, and hath his quick wit wasted in giving reckonings: all the other gifts appertinent to man, as the malice of this age shapes them, are not worth a gooseberry. You that are old consider not the capacities of us that are young; you do measure the heat of our livers with the bitterness of your galls: and we that are in the vaward of our youth, I must confess, are wags too.   200

Ch. Just. Do you set down your name in the scroll of youth, that are written down old with all the characters of age? Have you not a moist eye? a dry hand? a yellow cheek? a white beard? a decreasing leg? an increasing belly? is not your voice broken? your wind short? your chin double? your wit single? and every part about you blasted with antiquity? and will you yet call yourself young? Fie, fie, fie, Sir John!

Fal. My lord, I was born about three of the clock in the afternoon, with a white head and something a round belly. For my voice, I have lost it with halloing and singing of anthems. To approve my youth further, I will not: the truth is, I am only old in judgement and understanding; and he that will caper with me for a thousand marks, let him lend me the money, and have at him! For the box of the ear that the prince gave

154 *land-service.* Military service.

169–170 *your night's exploit on Gad's-hill.* The robbery carried out by Falstaff in *1 Henry IV*.

179 *wassail candle.* Large candle used on feast days.

187 *ill angel.* Clipped coin.

191 *costermonger times.* i.e. materialistic times.

192 *pregnancy.* Mental alertness.

199 *vaward.* Vanguard.

J.H. Hackett, the Victorian actor, as Falstaff, 1851

237 *never spit white.* Probably means 'may I never have another drink'.

253 *crosses.* A pun on 'afflictions' and 'coins stamped with crosses'.

255 *fillip me with a three-man beetle.* Hit me with a hammer that needs three men to lift it.

A three-man beetle. Engraving by F.W. Fairholt from J.O. Halliwell's edition of Shakespeare's works, 1853–65

263 *groats.* The groat was worth fourpence.

275 *colour.* Excuse.

you, he gave it like a rude prince, and you took it like a sensible lord. I have checked him for it, and the young lion repents; marry, not in ashes and sackcloth, but in new silk and old sack.

Ch. Just. Well, God send the prince a better companion!

Fal. God send the companion a better prince! I cannot rid my hands of him.

Ch. Just. Well, the king hath severed you and Prince Harry: I hear you are going with Lord John of Lancaster against the Archbishop and the Earl of Northumberland. 230

Fal. Yea; I thank your pretty sweet wit for it. But look you pray, all you that kiss my lady Peace at home, that our armies join not in a hot day; for, by the Lord, I take but two shirts out with me, and I mean not to sweat extraordinarily: if it be a hot day, and I brandish any thing but a bottle, I would I might never spit white again. There is not a dangerous action can peep out his head but I am thrust upon it: well, I cannot last ever: but it was alway yet the trick of our English nation, if they have a good thing, to make it too common. If ye will needs say I am an old man, you should give me rest. I would to God my name were not so terrible to the enemy as it is: I were better to be eaten to death with a rust than to be scoured to nothing with perpetual motion.

Ch. Just. Well, be honest, be honest; and God bless your expedition!

Fal. Will your lordship lend me a thousand pound to furnish me forth? 251

Ch. Just. Not a penny, not a penny; you are too impatient to bear crosses. Fare you well: commend me to my cousin Westmoreland.
    [*Exeunt Chief-Justice and Servant.*

Fal. If I do, fillip me with a three-man beetle. A man can no more separate age and covetousness than a' can part young limbs and lechery: but the gout galls the one, and the pox pinches the other; and so both the degrees prevent my curses. Boy! 260

Page. Sir?

Fal. What money is in my purse?

Page. Seven groats and two pence.

Fal. I can get no remedy against this consumption of the purse: borrowing only lingers and lingers it out, but the disease is incurable. Go bear this letter to my Lord of Lancaster; this to the prince; this to the Earl of Westmoreland; and this to old Mistress Ursula, whom I have weekly sworn to marry since I perceived the first white hair on my chin. About it: you know where to find me. [*Exit Page.*] A pox of this gout! or, a gout of this pox! for the one or the other plays the rogue with my great toe. 'Tis no matter if I do halt; I have the wars for my colour, and my pension shall seem the more reasonable. A good wit will make use of any thing: I will turn diseases to commodity. [*Exit.*

SCENE III. *York. The* ARCHBISHOP'S *palace.*

Enter the ARCHBISHOP, *the* LORDS HASTINGS, MOWBRAY, *and* BARDOLPH.

Arch. Thus have you heard our cause and known our means;
And, my most noble friends, I pray you all,

Speak plainly your opinions of our hopes:
And first, lord marshal, what say you to it?
- *Mowb.* I well allow the occasion of our arms;
  But gladly would be better satisfied
  How in our means we should advance ourselves
  To look with forehead bold and big enough
- Upon the power and puissance of the king.
      Hast. Our present musters grow upon the file   10
  To five and twenty thousand men of choice;
  And our supplies live largely in the hope
  Of great Northumberland, whose bosom burns
  With an incensed fire of injuries.
      L. Bard. The question then, Lord Hastings,
        standeth thus;
  Whether our present five and twenty thousand
  May hold up head without Northumberland?
      Hast. With him, we may.
      L. Bard.   Yea, marry, there's the point:
  But if without him we be thought too feeble,
  My judgement is, we should not step too far   20
  Till we had his assistance by the hand;
  For in a theme so bloody-faced as this
  Conjecture, expectation, and surmise
  Of aids incertain should not be admitted.
      Arch. 'Tis very true, Lord Bardolph; for indeed
  It was young Hotspur's case at Shrewsbury.
      L. Bard. It was, my lord; who lined himself
        with hope,
  Eating the air on promise of supply,
  Flattering himself in project of a power
  Much smaller than the smallest of his thoughts:
  And so, with great imagination   31
  Proper to madmen, led his powers to death
- And winking leap'd into destruction.
      Hast. But, by your leave, it never yet did hurt
  To lay down likelihoods and forms of hope.
- *L. Bard.* †Yes, if this present quality of war,
  Indeed the instant action: a cause on foot
  Lives so in hope as in an early spring
  We see the appearing buds; which to prove fruit,
  Hope gives not so much warrant as despair   40
  That frosts will bite them. When we mean to build,
  We first survey the plot, then draw the model;
  And when we see the figure of the house,
  Then must we rate the cost of the erection;
  Which if we find outweighs ability,
  What do we then but draw anew the model
  In fewer offices, or at last desist
  To build at all? Much more, in this great work,
  Which is almost to pluck a kingdom down
  And set another up, should we survey   50
  The plot of situation and the model,
  Consent upon a sure foundation,
  Question surveyors, know our own estate,
  How able such a work to undergo,
  To weigh against his opposite; or else
- We fortify in paper and in figures,
  Using the names of men instead of men:
  Like one that draws the model of a house
  Beyond his power to build it; who, half through,
  Gives o'er and leaves his part-created cost   60
  A naked subject to the weeping clouds
  And waste for churlish winter's tyranny.
      Hast. Grant that our hopes, yet likely of fair
        birth,
  Should be still-born, and that we now possess'd
  The utmost man of expectation,
  I think we are a body strong enough,
  Even as we are, to equal with the king.

5 *allow the occasion.* Admit the justification.

9 *puissance.* Strength.

33 *winking.* Shutting his eyes.

36—41 *Yes . . . will bite them.* In this instance there is harm in living on hopes, just as it is harmful to be optimistic about the buds of early spring since they are likely to be blighted by frost.

56 *We fortify in paper.* Our strength is all on paper.

70 *as the times do brawl.* As the wars at present waging.

94 *trimm'd.* Dressed.

1–2 *entered the action.* Begun the lawsuit.

4 *yeoman.* Assistant to the sergeant.

L. Bard. What, is the king but five and twenty
    thousand?
Hast. To us no more ; nay, not so much, Lord
    Bardolph.
- For his divisions, as the times do brawl,   70
Are in three heads : one power against the French,
And one against Glendower ; perforce a third
Must take up us : so is the unfirm king
In three divided ; and his coffers sound
With hollow poverty and emptiness.
    Arch. That he should draw his several strengths
    together
And come against us in full puissance,
Need not be dreaded.
    Hast.   If he should do so,
He leaves his back unarm'd, the French and Welsh
Baying him at the heels : never fear that.   80
    L. Bard. Who is it like should lead his forces
    hither?
    Hast. The Duke of Lancaster and Westmore-
    land ;
Against the Welsh, himself and Harry Monmouth :
But who is substituted 'gainst the French,
I have no certain notice.
    Arch.   Let us on,
And publish the occasion of our arms.
The commonwealth is sick of their own choice ;
Their over-greedy love hath surfeited :
An habitation giddy and unsure
Hath he **that** buildeth on the vulgar heart.   90
O thou fond many, with what loud applause
Didst thou beat heaven with blessing Bolingbroke,
Before he was what thou wouldst have him be !
- And being now trimm'd in thine own desires,
Thou, beastly feeder, art so full of him,
That thou provokest thyself to cast him up.
So, so, thou common dog, didst thou disgorge
Thy glutton bosom of the royal Richard ;
And now thou wouldst eat thy dead vomit up,
And howl'st to find it. What trust is in these times?
They that, when Richard lived, would have him
    die,   101
Are now become enamour'd on his grave :
Thou, that threw'st dust upon his goodly head
When through proud London he came sighing on
After the admired heels of Bolingbroke,
Criest now ' O earth, yield us that king again,
And take thou this !' O thoughts of men accursed !
Past and to come seems best ; things present
    worst.
    Mowb. Shall we go draw our numbers and
    set on ?
    Hast. We are time's subjects, and time bids
    be gone.   [*Exeunt.* 110

ACT II.

Scene I. *London. A street.*

Enter Hostess, Fang *and his* Boy *with her,
and* Snare *following.*

- *Host.* Master Fang, have you entered the
action?
    Fang. It is entered.
- *Host.* Where's your yeoman ? Is't a lusty
yeoman ? will a' stand to 't?
    Fang. Sirrah, where's Snare?
    Host. O Lord, ay ! good **Master Snare.**
    Snare. Here, here.

Fang. Snare, we must arrest Sir John Falstaff.

Host. Yea, good **Master Snare**; I have entered him and all.   11

Snare. It may chance cost some of us our lives, for he will stab.

Host. Alas the day! take heed of him; he stabbed me in mine own house, and that most beastly: in good faith, he cares not what mischief he does, if his weapon be out: he will foin like any devil; he will spare neither man, woman, nor child.

Fang. If I can close with him, I care not for his thrust.   21

Host. No, nor I neither: I'll be at your elbow.

Fang. An I but fist him once; an a' come but within my vice,—

Host. I am undone by his going; I warrant you, he's an infinitive thing upon my score. Good Master Fang, hold him sure: good Master Snare, let him not 'scape. A' comes continuantly to Pie-corner—saving your manhoods—to buy a saddle; and he is indited to dinner to the Lubber's-head in Lumbert street, to Master Smooth's the silk-man: I pray ye, since my exion is entered and my case so openly known to the world, let him be brought in to his answer. A hundred mark is a long one for a poor lone woman to bear: and I have borne, and borne, and borne, and have been fubbed off, and fubbed off, and fubbed off, from this day to that day, that it is a shame to be thought on. There is no honesty in such dealing; unless a woman should be made an ass and a beast, to bear every knave's wrong. Yonder he comes; and that arrant malmsey-nose knave, Bardolph, with him. Do your offices, do your offices: Master Fang and Master Snare, do me, do me, do me your offices.

Enter FALSTAFF, Page, *and* BARDOLPH.

Fal. How now! whose mare's dead? what's the matter?

Fang. Sir John, I arrest you at the suit of Mistress Quickly.   49

Fal. Away, varlets! Draw, Bardolph: cut me off the villain's head: throw the quean in the channel.

Host. Throw me in the channel! I'll throw thee in the channel. Wilt thou? wilt thou? thou bastardly rogue! Murder, murder! Ah, thou honey-suckle villain! wilt thou kill God's officers and the king's? Ah, thou honey-seed rogue! thou art a honey-seed, a man-queller, and a woman-queller.

Fal. Keep them off, Bardolph.   60

Fang. A rescue! a rescue!

Host. Good people, bring a rescue or two. Thou wo't, wo't thou? thou wo't, wo't ta? do, do, thou rogue! do, thou hemp-seed!

Fal. Away, you scullion! you rampallian! you fustilarian! I'll tickle your catastrophe.

Enter the LORD CHIEF-JUSTICE, *and his men.*

Ch. Just. What is the matter? keep the peace here, ho!

Host. Good my lord, be good to me. I beseech you, stand to me.   70

Ch. Just. How now, Sir John! what are you brawling here?

17 *foin.* Thrust.

24 *vice.* Grip.

30 *indited.* i.e. invited.

31 *Lumbert street.* Lombard Street.

32 *exion.* Action.

42 *malmsey-nose.* Malmsey was a strong red wine.

51 *quean.* Harlot.

52 *channel.* Gutter.

57 *honey-seed.* i.e. homicide.

58 *man-queller.* Man-killer.

64 *hemp-seed.* Gallows-bird.

65 *rampallian.* Scoundrel.

66 *fustilarian.* A quibble on 'fustylugs', a corpulent person or frowsy woman, and one who speaks fustian, i.e. bombastically. *tickle your catastrophe.* Whip your backside.

83 *mare.* Nightmare.

94 *parcel-gilt.* Partly gilt.

95 *sea-coal.* Mine coal, brought by sea to London from Newcastle.

96 *Wheeson.* Whitsun.

102 *gossip.* Neighbour.

103 *mess.* A small quantity.

106 *green.* Unhealed.

132 *current.* Genuine.

Doth this become your place, your time and business?
You should have been well on your way to York. Stand from him, fellow: wherefore hang'st upon him?

Host. O my most worshipful lord, an't please your grace, I am a poor widow of Eastcheap, and he is arrested at my suit.

Ch. Just. For what sum?

Host. It is more than for some, my lord; it is for all, all I have. He hath eaten me out of house and home; he hath put all my substance into that fat belly of his: but I will have some of it out again, or I will ride thee o' nights like the mare.

Fal. I think I am as like to ride the mare, if I have any vantage of ground to get up.

Ch. Just. How comes this, Sir John? Fie! what man of good temper would endure this tempest of exclamation? Are you not ashamed to enforce a poor widow to so rough a course to come by her own?   90

Fal. What is the gross sum that I owe thee?

Host. Marry, if thou wert an honest man, thyself and the money too. Thou didst swear to me upon a parcel-gilt goblet, sitting in my Dolphin-chamber, at the round table, by a sea-coal fire, upon Wednesday in Wheeson week, when the prince broke thy head for liking his father to a singing-man of Windsor, thou didst swear to me then, as I was washing thy wound, to marry me and make me my lady thy wife. Canst thou deny it? Did not goodwife Keech, the butcher's wife, come in then and call me gossip Quickly? coming in to borrow a mess of vinegar; telling us she had a good dish of prawns; whereby thou didst desire to eat some; whereby I told thee they were ill for a green wound? And didst thou not, when she was gone down stairs, desire me to be no more so familiarity with such poor people; saying that ere long they should call me madam? And didst thou not kiss me and bid me fetch thee thirty shillings? I put thee now to thy bookoath: deny it, if thou canst.

Fal. My lord, this is a poor mad soul; and she says up and down the town that her eldest son is like you: she hath been in good case, and the truth is, poverty hath distracted her. But for these foolish officers, I beseech you I may have redress against them.

Ch. Just. Sir John, Sir John, I am well acquainted with your manner of wrenching the true cause the false way. It is not a confident brow, nor the throng of words that come with such more than impudent sauciness from you, can thrust me from a level consideration: you have, as it appears to me, practised upon the easy-yielding spirit of this woman, and made her serve your uses both in purse and in person.

Host. Yea, in truth, my lord.

Ch. Just. Pray thee, peace. Pay her the debt you owe her, and unpay the villany you have done her: the one you may do with sterling money, and the other with current repentance.

Fal. My lord, I will not undergo this sneap without reply. You call honourable boldness impudent sauciness: if a man will make courtesy and say nothing, he is virtuous: no, my lord, my humble duty remembered, I will not be your suitor. I say to you, I do desire deliverance from

these officers, being upon hasty employment in
the king's affairs.   140
Ch. Just. You speak as having power to do
wrong: but answer in the effect of your reputation, and satisfy the poor woman.
Fal. Come hither, hostess.

Enter GOWER.

Ch. Just. Now, Master Gower, what news?
Gow. The king, my lord, and Harry Prince of
Wales
Are near at hand: the rest the paper tells.
Fal. As I am a gentleman.
Host. Faith, you said so before.
Fal. As I am a gentleman. Come, no more
words of it.   151
Host. By this heavenly ground I tread on, I
must be fain to pawn both my plate and the
tapestry of my dining-chambers.
Fal. Glasses, glasses, is the only drinking:
and for thy walls, a pretty slight drollery, or the
story of the Prodigal, or the German hunting in
water-work, is worth a thousand of these bed-
hangings and these fly-bitten tapestries. Let it
be ten pound, if thou canst. Come, an 'twere not
for thy humours, there's not a better wench in
England. Go, wash thy face, and draw the action.
Come, thou must not be in this humour with me;
dost not know me? come, come, I know thou
wast set on to this.
Host. Pray thee, Sir John, let it be but twenty
nobles: i' faith, I am loath to pawn my plate, so
God save me, la!
Fal. Let it alone; I'll make other shift: you'll
be a fool still.   170
Host. Well, you shall have it, though I pawn
my gown. I hope you'll come to supper. You'll
pay me all together?
Fal. Will I live? [*To Bardolph*] Go, with
her, with her; hook on, hook on.
Host. Will you have Doll Tearsheet meet you
at supper?
Fal. No more words; let's have her.
[*Exeunt Hostess, Bardolph, Officers, and Boy.*
Ch. Just. I have heard better news.
Fal. What's the news, my lord?   180
Ch. Just. Where lay the king last night?
Gow. At Basingstoke, my lord.
Fal. I hope, my lord, all's well: what is the
news, my lord?
Ch. Just. Come all his forces back?
Gow. No; fifteen hundred foot, five hundred
horse,
Are march'd up to my lord of Lancaster,
Against Northumberland and the Archbishop.
Fal. Comes the king back from Wales, my
noble lord?
Ch. Just. You shall have letters of me pre-
sently: 190
Come, go along with me, good Master Gower.
Fal. My lord!
Ch. Just. What's the matter?
Fal. Master Gower, shall I entreat you with
me to dinner?
Gow. I must wait upon my good lord here; I
thank you, good Sir John.
Ch. Just. Sir John, you loiter here too long,
being you are to take soldiers up in counties as
you go.   200

158 *water-work.* Watercolour.

162 *draw.* Withdraw.

175 *hook on.* Stay with her.

206 *right fencing grace.* Correct manner in fencing.

20 *one for superfluity.* An extra one.

21–24 *But that the tennis-court-keeper . . . while.* i.e. a gentleman would change his shirt after playing tennis but Poins's one spare shirt was not enough; so he had not been seen on the tennis courts recently.

25 *low countries.* Brothels frequented by Poins.

26 *holland.* Fine linen.

27 *that bawl out the ruins of thy linen.* i.e. your bastards (who wear your old shirts).

40 *stand the push.* Await the attack.

47 *Very hardly.* With great difficulty.

Prince: '. . . thou thinkest me as far in the devil's book as thou. . . .' Figure of Satan with book from a series of paintings in Carlisle Cathedral. Engraving by F.W. Fairholt from J.O. Halliwell's edition of Shakespeare's works, 1853–65

Fal. Will you sup with me, Master Gower?
Ch. Just. What foolish master taught you these manners, Sir John?
Fal. Master Gower, if they become me not, he was a fool that taught them me. This is the right fencing grace, my lord; tap for tap, and so part fair.
Ch. Just. Now the Lord lighten thee! thou art a great fool. [*Exeunt.*

SCENE II. *London. Another street.*

Enter PRINCE HENRY *and* POINS.

Prince. Before God, I am exceeding weary.
Poins. Is't come to that? I had thought weariness durst not have attached one of so high blood.
Prince. Faith, it does me; though it discolours the complexion of my greatness to acknowledge it. Doth it not show vilely in me to desire small beer?
Poins. Why, a prince should not be so loosely studied as to remember so weak a composition.
Prince. Belike then my appetite was not princely got; for, by my troth, I do now remember the poor creature, small beer. But, indeed, these humble considerations make me out of love with my greatness. What a disgrace is it to me to remember thy name! or to know thy face to-morrow! or to take note how many pair of silk stockings thou hast, viz. these, and those that were thy peach-coloured ones! or to bear the inventory of thy shirts, as, one for superfluity, and another for use! But that the tennis-court-keeper knows better than I; for it is a low ebb of linen with thee when thou keepest not racket there; as thou hast not done a great while, because the rest of thy low countries have made a shift to eat up thy holland: and God knows, whether those that bawl out the ruins of thy linen shall inherit his kingdom: but the midwives say the children are not in the fault; whereupon the world increases, and kindreds are mightily strengthened.
Poins. How ill it follows, after you have laboured so hard, you should talk so idly! Tell me, how many good young princes would do so, their fathers being so sick as yours at this time is?
Prince. Shall I tell thee one thing, Poins?
Poins. Yes, faith; and let it be an excellent good thing.
Prince. It shall serve among wits of no higher breeding than thine.
Poins. Go to; I stand the push of your one thing that you will tell. 41
Prince. Marry, I tell thee, it is not meet that I should be sad, now my father is sick: albeit I could tell to thee, as to one it pleases me, for fault of a better, to call my friend, I could be sad, and sad indeed too.
Poins. Very hardly upon such a subject.
Prince. By this hand, thou thinkest me as far in the devil's book as thou and Falstaff for obduracy and persistency: let the end try the man. But I tell thee, my heart bleeds inwardly that my father is so sick: and keeping such vile company as thou art hath in reason taken from me all ostentation of sorrow.
Poins. The reason?

Prince. What wouldst thou think of me, if I should weep?

Poins. I would think thee a most princely hypocrite. 59

Prince. It would be every man's thought; and thou art a blessed fellow to think as every man thinks: never a man's thought in the world keeps the road-way better than thine: every man would think me an hypocrite indeed. And what accites your most worshipful thought to think so?

Poins. Why, because you have been so lewd and so much engraffed to Falstaff.

Prince. And to thee.

Poins. By this light, I am well spoke on; I can hear it with mine own ears: the worst that they can say of me is that I am a second brother and that I am a proper fellow of my hands; and those two things, I confess, I cannot help. By the mass, here comes Bardolph.

Enter BARDOLPH *and* Page.

Prince. And the boy that I gave Falstaff: a' had him from me Christian; and look, if the fat villain have not transformed him ape.

Bard. God save your grace!

Prince. And yours, most noble Bardolph! 79

Bard. Come, you virtuous ass, you bashful fool, must you be blushing? wherefore blush you now? What a maidenly man-at-arms are you become! Is't such a matter to get a pottle-pot's maidenhead?

Page. A' calls me e'en now, my lord, through a red lattice, and I could discern no part of his face from the window: at last I spied his eyes, and methought he had made two holes in the ale-wife's new petticoat and so peeped through.

Prince. Has not the boy profited? 90

Bard. Away, you whoreson upright rabbit, away!

Page. Away, you rascally Althæa's dream, away!

Prince. Instruct us, boy; what dream, boy?

Page. Marry, my lord, Althæa dreamed she was delivered of a fire-brand; and therefore I call him her dream.

Prince. A crown's worth of good interpretation: there 'tis, boy. 100

Poins. O, that this good blossom could be kept from cankers! Well, there is sixpence to preserve thee.

Bard. An you do not make him hanged among you, the gallows shall have wrong.

Prince. And how doth thy master, Bardolph?

Bard. Well, my lord. He heard of your grace's coming to town: there's a letter for you.

Poins. Delivered with good respect. And how doth the martlemas, your master? 110

Bard. In bodily health, sir.

Poins. Marry, the immortal part needs a physician; but that moves not him: though that be sick, it dies not.

Prince. I do allow this wen to be as familiar with me as my dog; and he holds his place; for look you how he writes.

Poins. [*Reads*] 'John Falstaff, knight,'—every man must know that, as oft as he has occasion to name himself: even like those that are kin to the king; for they never prick their finger but they say, 'There's some of the king's blood spilt.'

64 *accites.* Arouses.

71 *second brother.* Younger son.

75–76 *a' had him from me Christian.* i.e. when he had him from me he was a Christian.

83–84 *to get a pottle-pot's maidenhead.* To knock off a tankard of ale.

86 *red lattice.* Ale houses had red lattice-work windows.

Ale house with lattice-work features. Engraving by F.W. Fairholt from J.O. Halliwell's edition, 1853–65

93 *Althæa's dream.* Althaea is confused with Hecuba, the queen of Troy, who dreamed that she was delivered of a firebrand.

102 *cankers.* Diseased swellings.

110 *martlemas.* Cattle fattened for slaughter on the feast of St. Martin, 11th November.

115 *wen.* Swelling.

128 *Japhet*. i.e. if they cannot claim direct royal kinship they will do so as descendants of Noah's son, Japhet, regarded as the father of all Europeans.

Poins reads Falstaff's letter to the Prince. Engraving by Kenny Meadows from Barry Cornwall's *Works of Shakspere*, 1846

160 *frank*. Sty.

164 *Ephesians*. Boon companions.

168 *pagan*. Strumpet.

183 *road*. Whore.

'How comes that?' says he, that takes upon him not to conceive. The answer is as ready as a borrower's cap, 'I am the king's poor cousin, sir.'

Prince. Nay, they will be kin to us, or they will fetch it from Japhet. But to the letter:

Poins. [*Reads*] 'Sir John Falstaff, knight, to the son of the king, nearest his father, Harry Prince of Wales, greeting.' Why, this is a certificate.

Prince. Peace!

Poins. [*Reads*] 'I will imitate the honourable Romans in brevity:' he sure means brevity in breath, short-winded. 'I commend me to thee, I commend thee, and I leave thee. Be not too familiar with Poins; for he misuses thy favours so much, that he swears thou art to marry his sister Nell. Repent at idle times as thou mayest; and so, farewell. 141

'Thine, by yea and no, which is as much as to say, as thou usest him, JACK FALSTAFF with my familiars, JOHN with my brothers and sisters, and SIR JOHN with all Europe.'

My lord, I'll steep this letter in sack and make him eat it.

Prince. That's to make him eat twenty of his words. But do you use me thus, Ned? must I marry your sister? 151

Poins. God send the wench no worse fortune! But I never said so.

Prince. Well, thus we play the fools with the time, and the spirits of the wise sit in the clouds and mock us. Is your master here in London?

Bard. Yea, my lord.

Prince. Where sups he? doth the old boar feed in the old frank? 160

Bard. At the old place, my lord, in Eastcheap.

Prince. What company?

Page. Ephesians, my lord, of the old church.

Prince. Sup any women with him?

Page. None, my lord, but old Mistress Quickly and Mistress Doll Tearsheet.

Prince. What pagan may that be?

Page. A proper gentlewoman, sir, and a kinswoman of my master's. 170

Prince. Even such kin as the parish heifers are to the town bull. Shall we steal upon them, Ned, at supper?

Poins. I am your shadow, my lord; I'll follow you.

Prince. Sirrah, you boy, and Bardolph, no word to your master that I am yet come to town: there's for your silence.

Bard. I have no tongue, sir.

Page. And for mine, sir, I will govern it. 180

Prince. Fare you well; go. [*Exeunt Bardolph and Page.*] This Doll Tearsheet should be some road.

Poins. I warrant you, as common as the way between Saint Alban's and London.

Prince. How might we see Falstaff bestow himself to-night in his true colours, and not ourselves be seen?

Poins. Put on two leathern jerkins and aprons, and wait upon him at his table as drawers. 191

Prince. From a God to a bull? a heavy
● descension! it was Jove's case. From a prince
to a prentice? a low transformation! that shall
be mine; for in every thing the purpose must
weigh with the folly. Follow me, Ned.

[*Exeunt.*

SCENE III. *Warkworth. Before the castle.*

Enter NORTHUMBERLAND, LADY NORTHUM-
BERLAND, *and* LADY PERCY.

North. I pray thee, loving wife, and gentle
 daughter,
Give even way unto my rough affairs:
Put not you on the visage of the times
And be like them to Percy troublesome.
 Lady N. I have given over, I will speak no
 more:
Do what you will; your wisdom be your guide.
 North. Alas, sweet wife, my honour is at
 pawn;
And, but my going, nothing can redeem it.
 Lady P. O yet, for God's sake, go not to
 these wars!
The time was, father, that you broke your word,
When you were more endear'd to it than now; 11
When your own Percy, when my heart's dear
 Harry,
Threw many a northward look to see his father
Bring up his powers; but he did long in vain.
Who then persuaded you to stay at home?
There were two honours lost, yours and your
 son's.
For yours, the God of heaven brighten it!
For his, it stuck upon him as the sun
In the grey vault of heaven, and by his light
Did all the chivalry of England move   20
To do brave acts: he was indeed the glass
Wherein the noble youth did dress themselves:
He had no legs that practised not his gait;
And speaking thick, which nature made his
 blemish,
Became the accents of the valiant;
For those that could speak low and tardily
Would turn their own perfection to abuse,
To seem like him: so that in speech, in gait,
In diet, in affections of delight,
In military rules, humours of blood,   30
He was the mark and glass, copy and book,
That fashion'd others. And him, O wondrous
 him!
O miracle of men! him did you leave,
Second to none, unseconded by you,
To look upon the hideous god of war
In disadvantage; to abide a field
Where nothing but the sound of Hotspur's name
Did seem defensible: so you left him.
Never, O never, do his ghost the wrong
To hold your honour more precise and nice   40
With others than with him! let them alone:
The marshal and the archbishop are strong:
Had my sweet Harry had but half their numbers,
To-day might I, hanging on Hotspur's neck,
● Have talk'd of Monmouth's grave.
 North.   Beshrew your heart,
Fair daughter, you do draw my spirits from me
With new lamenting ancient oversights.
But I must go and meet with danger there,
Or it will seek me in another place

193 *Jove's case.* For the love of Europa, Jove turned
himself into a bull.

The rape of Europa. Painting after Veronese (d. 1588)

45 *Monmouth's.* Prince Hal's. He was born at Monmouth
in 1387.

61 *recordation.* Memorial.

Tavern scene. Drawer attending at a revel. Woodcut from Martin Parker's *Convivial Ballads*, 17th century

---

2 *apple-johns.* Apples which are shrivelled when ripe.

---

13 *noise.* Band (of musicians).

A band of musicians. Engraving copied from Hanson's *Arches of Triumph*, 1603

21—22 *old Utis.* A noisy row.

25—26 *pulsidge.* Pulse.

---

29 *canaries.* Sweet wine.

And find me worse provided.

Lady N.   O, fly to Scotland,   50
Till that the nobles and the armed commons
Have of their puissance made a little taste.

Lady P.   If they get ground and vantage of
     the king,
Then join you with them, like a rib of steel,
To make strength stronger; but, for all our loves,
First let them try themselves. So did your son;
He was so suffer'd: so came I a widow;
And never shall have length of life enough
To rain upon remembrance with mine eyes,
That it may grow and sprout as high as heaven,
For recordation to my noble husband.   61

North. Come, come, go in with me. 'Tis
     with my mind
As with the tide swell'd up unto his height,
That makes a still-stand, running neither way:
Fain would I go to meet the archbishop,
But many thousand reasons hold me back.
I will resolve for Scotland: there am I,
Till time and vantage crave my company.

                         [*Exeunt.*

SCENE IV.   *London.   The Boar's-head Tavern*
             in Eastcheap.

Enter two Drawers.

First Draw. What the devil hast thou brought
there? apple-johns? thou knowest Sir John cannot endure an apple-john.

Sec. Draw. Mass, thou sayest true. The
prince once set a dish of apple-johns before him,
and told him there were five more Sir Johns,
and, putting off his hat, said 'I will now take my
leave of these six dry, round, old, withered
knights.' It angered him to the heart: but he
hath forgot that.   10

First Draw. Why, then, cover, and set them
down: and see if thou canst find out Sneak's
noise; Mistress Tearsheet would fain hear some
music. Dispatch: the room where they supped
is too hot; they'll come in straight.

Sec. Draw. Sirrah, here will be the prince
and Master Poins anon; and they will put on
two of our jerkins and aprons; and Sir John
must not know of it: Bardolph hath brought
word.   20

First Draw. By the mass, here will be old
Utis: it will be an excellent stratagem.

Sec. Draw. I'll see if I can find out Sneak.

                          [*Exit.*

Enter Hostess *and* DOLL TEARSHEET.

Host. I'faith, sweetheart, methinks now you
are in an excellent good temperality: your pulsidge beats as extraordinarily as heart would
desire; and your colour, I warrant you, is as
red as any rose, in good truth, la! But, i'faith,
you have drunk too much canaries; and that's
a marvellous searching wine, and it perfumes
the blood ere one can say 'What's this?' How
do you now?

Dol. Better than I was: hem!

Host. Why, that's well said; a good heart's
worth gold. Lo, here comes Sir John.

Enter FALSTAFF.

Fal. [*Singing*] 'When Arthur first in court'

—Empty the jordan. [*Exit First Drawer*].— [*Singing*] 'And was a worthy king.' How now, Mistress Doll!

Host. Sick of a calm; yea, good faith.   40

Fal. So is all her sect; an they be once in a calm, they are sick.

Dol. You muddy rascal, is that all the comfort you give me?

Fal. You make fat rascals, Mistress Doll.

Dol. I make them! gluttony and diseases make them; I make them not.

Fal. If the cook help to make the gluttony, you help to make the diseases, Doll: we catch of you, Doll, we catch of you; grant that, my poor virtue, grant that.   51

Dol. Yea, joy, our chains and our jewels.

Fal. 'Your brooches, pearls, and ouches:' for to serve bravely is to come halting off, you know: to come off the breach with his pike bent bravely, and to surgery bravely; to venture upon the charged chambers bravely,—

Dol. Hang yourself, you muddy conger, hang yourself!   59

Host. By my troth, this is the old fashion; you two never meet but you fall to some discord: you are both, i' good truth, as rheumatic as two dry toasts; you cannot one bear with another's confirmities. What the good-year! one must bear, and that must be you: you are the weaker vessel, as they say, the emptier vessel.

Dol. Can a weak empty vessel bear such a huge full hogshead? there's a whole merchant's venture of Bourdeaux stuff in him; you have not seen a hulk better stuffed in the hold. Come, I'll be friends with thee, Jack: thou art going to the wars; and whether I shall ever see thee again or no, there is nobody cares.

Re-enter First Drawer.

First Draw. Sir, Ancient Pistol's below, and would speak with you.

Dol. Hang him, swaggering rascal! let him not come hither: it is the foul-mouthed'st rogue in England.

Host. If he swagger, let him not come here: no, by my faith; I must live among my neighbours; I'll no swaggerers: I am in good name and fame with the very best: shut the door; there comes no swaggerers here: I have not lived all this while, to have swaggering now: shut the door, I pray you.

Fal. Dost thou hear, hostess?

Host. Pray ye, pacify yourself, Sir John: there comes no swaggerers here.

Fal. Dost thou hear? it is mine ancient.   89

Host. Tilly-fally, Sir John, ne'er tell me: your ancient swaggerer comes not in my doors. I was before Master Tisick, the debuty, t'other day; and, as he said to me, 'twas no longer ago than Wednesday last, 'I' good faith, neighbour Quickly,' says he; Master Dumbe, our minister, was by then; 'neighbour Quickly,' says he, 'receive those that are civil; for,' said he, 'you are in an ill name:' now a' said so, I can tell whereupon; 'for,' says he, 'you are an honest woman, and well thought on; therefore take heed what guests you receive: receive,' says he, 'no swaggering companions.' There comes none

37 *jordan.* Chamber-pot.

40 *calm.* Qualm.

41 *sect.* Sex.

53 *ouches.* Gems.

57 *charged chambers.* Small cannon.

64 *confirmities.* i.e. infirmities.

69 *venture of Bourdeaux.* Wine merchant's cargo of Bordeaux wine (claret).

Doll Tearsheet (Vivienne Bennett), Falstaff (George Merritt) and Mistress Quickly (Buena Bent), Old Vic Theatre, London, 1935

74 *Ancient.* Ensign.

108 *Barbary hen.* Guinea fowl.

121–122 *discharge upon mine hostess.* Toast the hostess (bawdy innuendo).

138 *bung.* Pickpocket.

139 *chaps.* Cheeks. *cuttle.* Cut-throat.

141 *basket-hilt stale juggler.* i.e. swashbuckling impostor.

142 *points.* Laces for attaching armour to the shoulders.

161 *'occupy'.* Fornicate.

Costume design for Doll Tearsheet by Tanya Moisewitch, Stratford-upon-Avon, 1951

here: you would bless you to hear what he said: no, I'll no swaggerers.

Fal. He's no swaggerer, hostess; a tame cheater, i' faith; you may stroke him as gently as a puppy greyhound: he'll not swagger with a Barbary hen, if her feathers turn back in any show of resistance. Call him up, drawer.

[Exit First Drawer.

Host. Cheater, call you him? I will bar no honest man my house, nor no cheater: but I do not love swaggering, by my troth; I am the worse, when one says swagger: feel, masters, how I shake; look you, I warrant you.

Dol. So you do, hostess.

Host. Do I? yea, in very truth, do I, an 'twere an aspen leaf: I cannot abide swaggerers.

Enter PISTOL, BARDOLPH, *and* Page.

Pist. God save you, Sir John!   119

Fal. Welcome, Ancient Pistol. Here, Pistol, I charge you with a cup of sack: do you discharge upon mine hostess.

Pist. I will discharge upon her, Sir John, with two bullets.

Fal. She is pistol-proof, sir; you shall hardly offend her.

Host. Come, I'll drink no proofs nor no bullets: I'll drink no more than will do me good, for no man's pleasure, I.

Pist. Then to you, Mistress Dorothy; I will charge you.   131

Dol. Charge me! I scorn you, scurvy companion. What! you poor, base, rascally, cheating, lack-linen mate! Away, you mouldy rogue, away! I am meat for your master.

Pist. I know you, Mistress Dorothy.

Dol. Away, you cut-purse rascal! you filthy bung, away! by this wine, I'll thrust my knife in your mouldy chaps, an you play the saucy cuttle with me. Away, you bottle-ale rascal! you basket-hilt stale juggler, you! Since when, I pray you, sir? God's light, with two points on your shoulder? much!

Pist. God let me not live, but I will murder your ruff for this.

Fal. No more, Pistol; I would not have you go off here: discharge yourself of our company, Pistol.

Host. No, good Captain Pistol; not here, sweet captain.   150

Dol. Captain! thou abominable damned cheater, art thou not ashamed to be called captain? An captains were of my mind, they would truncheon you out, for taking their names upon you before you have earned them. You a captain! you slave, for what? for tearing a poor whore's ruff in a bawdy-house? He a captain! hang him, rogue! he lives upon mouldy stewed prunes and dried cakes. A captain! God's light, these villains will make the word as odious as the word 'occupy;' which was an excellent good word before it was ill sorted: therefore captains had need look to't.

Bard. Pray thee, go down, good ancient.

Fal. Hark thee hither, Mistress Doll.

Pist. Not I: I tell thee what, Corporal Bardolph, I could tear her: I'll be revenged of her.

Page. Pray thee, go down.

Pist. I'll see her damned first; to Pluto's damned lake, by this hand, to the infernal deep, with Erebus and tortures vile also. Hold hook and line, say I. Down, down, dogs! down, faitors! Have we not Hiren here?

Host. Good Captain Peesel, be quiet; 'tis very late, i' faith: I beseek you now, aggravate your choler.

Pist. These be good humours, indeed! Shall pack-horses
And hollow pamper'd jades of Asia,
Which cannot go but thirty mile a-day,
Compare with Cæsars, and with Cannibals, 180
And Trojan Greeks? nay, rather damn them with
King Cerberus; and let the welkin roar.
Shall we fall foul for toys?

Host. By my troth, captain, these are very bitter words.

Bard. Be gone, good ancient: this will grow to a brawl anon.

Pist. Die men like dogs! give crowns like pins! Have we not Hiren here? 189

Host. O' my word, captain, there's none such here. What the good-year! do you think I would deny her? For God's sake, be quiet.

Pist. Then feed, and be fat, my fair Calipolis. Come, give's some sack.
'Si fortune me tormente, sperato me contento.'
Fear we broadsides? no, let the fiend give fire:
Give me some sack: and, sweetheart, lie thou there.   [*Laying down his sword.*
Come we to full points here; and are etceteras nothing?

Fal. Pistol, I would be quiet.

Pist. Sweet knight, I kiss thy neif: what! we have seen the seven stars.   201

Dol. For God's sake, thrust him down stairs: I cannot endure such a fustian rascal.

Pist. Thrust him down stairs! know we not Galloway nags?

Fal. Quoit him down, Bardolph, like a shove-groat shilling: nay, an a' do nothing but speak nothing, a' shall be nothing here.

Bard. Come, get you down stairs.

Pist. What! shall we have incision? shall we imbrue?   [*Snatching up his sword.* 210
Then death rock me asleep, abridge my doleful days!
Why, then, let grievous, ghastly, gaping wounds
Untwine the Sisters Three! Come, Atropos, I say!

Host. Here's goodly stuff toward!

Fal. Give me my rapier, boy.

Dol. I pray thee, Jack, I pray thee, do not draw.

Fal. Get you down stairs.
            [*Drawing, and driving Pistol out.*

Host. Here's a goodly tumult! I'll forswear keeping house, afore I'll be in these tirrits and frights. So; murder, I warrant now. Alas, alas! put up your naked weapons, put up your naked weapons. [*Exeunt Pistol and Bardolph.*

Dol. I pray thee, Jack, be quiet; the rascal's gone. Ah, you whoreson little valiant villain, you!

Host. Are you not hurt i' the groin? methought a' made a shrewd thrust at your belly.

Re-enter BARDOLPH.

Fal. Have you turned him out o' doors?

169–170 *Pluto's damned lake.* Pistol means the river Styx of the underworld.

171 *Erebus.* The darkness of Hades.

173 *faitors.* Rogues. *Have we not Hiren here?* A tag from a play by George Peele.

177–179 *Shall . . . day.* A burlesque of some famous lines in Marlowe's *Tamburlaine* Part II.

180 *Cannibals.* Hannibals.

182 *Cerberus.* The three-headed dog which guarded the the underworld. *welkin.* Sky.

183 *for toys.* Over trifles.

193 *Then . . . Calipolis.* Parody of a line in Peele's *Battle of Alcazar.*

195 *Si . . . contento.* If fortune torments me, hope contents me.

198 *full points.* Full stops.

200 *neif.* Fist.

201 *seven stars.* The Pleiades.

203 *fustian.* Bombastic. Fustian was a cheap cloth.

205 *Galloway nags.* i.e. we know a harlot when we see one. Galloway nags were Irish horses of an inferior breed.

206–207 *shove-groat shilling.* Coin pushed along a shuffle board.

210 *incision.* Bloodshed. *imbrue.* Shed blood.

213 *Sisters Three . . . Atropos.* The Fates, of which Atropos was one.

220 *tirrits.* Fits of temper.

238 *Nine Worthies.* Hector, Alexander, Julius Caesar, Joshua, David, Judas Maccabaeus, Arthur, Charlemagne, Godfrey of Bouillon.

243 *canvass.* i.e. toss between canvas sheets.

250–251 *Bartholomew boar-pig.* Bartholomew Fair, held on 24 August, when pigs were roasted.

Falstaff: 'Peace, good Doll . . .' Engraving from a painting by H. Fuseli (1741–1825)

255 *death's-head.* Skull and cross-bones.

258 *pantler.* Pantryman.

262 *Tewksbury.* From where the best mustard came.

267–268 *drinks . . . flap-dragons.* i.e. performs acts of bravado; flap-dragon was a game in which the players snatched raisins from flaming brandy and ate them. *wild-mare.* See-saw.

271 *sign of the leg.* Sign over a bootmaker's shop.

278 *nave.* Hub.

282 *his poll clawed like a parrot.* Doll is rumpling his hair.

288 *fiery Trigon.* The three fiery signs of the zodiac – Aries, Leo, Sagittarius.

289 *lisping . . . tables.* i.e. making love to his master's old acquaintance (Mistress Quickly).

291 *busses.* Kisses.

Bard. Yea, sir. The rascal's drunk: you have hurt him, sir, i' the shoulder. 231

Fal. A rascal! to brave me!

Dol. Ah, you sweet little rogue, you! Alas, poor ape, how thou sweatest! come, let me wipe thy face; come on, you whoreson chops: ah, rogue! i' faith, I love thee: thou art as valorous as Hector of Troy, worth five of Agamemnon, and ten times better than the Nine Worthies: ah, villain!

Fal. A rascally slave! I will toss the rogue in a blanket. 241

Dol. Do, an thou darest for thy heart: an thou dost, I'll canvass thee between a pair of sheets.

Enter Music.

Page. The music is come, sir.

Fal. Let them play. Play, sirs. Sit on my knee, Doll. A rascal bragging slave! the rogue fled from me like quicksilver.

Dol. I' faith, and thou followedst him like a church. Thou whoreson little tidy Bartholomew boar-pig, when wilt thou leave fighting o' days and foining o' nights, and begin to patch up thine old body for heaven?

Enter, behind, PRINCE HENRY *and* POINS, *disguised.*

Fal. Peace, good Doll! do not speak like a death's-head; do not bid me remember mine end.

Dol. Sirrah, what humour's the prince of?

Fal. A good shallow young fellow: a' would have made a good pantler, a' would ha' chipped bread well.

Dol. They say Poins has a good wit. 260

Fal. He a good wit? hang him, baboon! his wit's as thick as Tewksbury mustard; there's no more conceit in him than is in a mallet.

Dol. Why does the prince love him so, then?

Fal. Because their legs are both of a bigness, and a' plays at quoits well, and eats conger and fennel, and drinks off candles' ends for flap-dragons, and rides the wild-mare with the boys, and jumps upon joined-stools, and swears with a good grace, and wears his boots very smooth, like unto the sign of the leg, and breeds no bate with telling of discreet stories; and such other gambol faculties a' has, that show a weak mind and an able body, for the which the prince admits him: for the prince himself is such another; the weight of a hair will turn the scales between their avoirdupois.

Prince. Would not this nave of a wheel have his ears cut off?

Poins. Let's beat him before his whore. 280

Prince. Look, whether the withered elder hath not his poll clawed like a parrot.

Poins. Is it not strange that desire should so many years outlive performance?

Fal. Kiss me, Doll.

Prince. Saturn and Venus this year in conjunction! what says the almanac to that?

Poins. And, look, whether the fiery Trigon, his man, be not lisping to his master's old tables, his note-book, his counsel-keeper. 290

Fal. Thou dost give me flattering busses.

Dol. By my troth, I kiss thee with a most constant heart.

Fal. I am old, I am old.

Dol. I love thee better than I love e'er a scurvy young boy of them all.

Fal. What stuff wilt have a kirtle of? I shall receive money o' Thursday: shalt have a cap to-morrow. A merry song, come: it grows late; we'll to bed. Thou'lt forget me when I am gone.

Dol. By my troth, thou'lt set me a-weeping, an thou sayest so: prove that ever I dress myself handsome till thy return: well, hearken at the end.

Fal. Some sack, Francis.

Prince. }
Poins. } Anon, anon, sir. [*Coming forward.*

Fal. Ha! a bastard son of the king's? And art not thou Poins his brother?

Prince. Why, thou globe of sinful continents, what a life dost thou lead!   310

Fal. A better than thou: I am a gentleman; thou art a drawer.

Prince. Very true, sir; and I come to draw you out by the ears.

Host. O, the Lord preserve thy good grace! by my troth, welcome to London. Now, the Lord bless that sweet face of thine! O Jesu, are you come from Wales?

Fal. Thou whoreson mad compound of majesty, by this light flesh and corrupt blood, thou art welcome.   321

Dol. How, you fat fool! I scorn you.

Poins. My lord, he will drive you out of your revenge and turn all to a merriment, if you take not the heat.

Prince. You whoreson candle-mine, you, how vilely did you speak of me even now before this honest, virtuous, civil gentlewoman!

Host. God's blessing of your good heart! and so she is, by my troth.   330

Fal. Didst thou hear me?

Prince. Yea, and you knew me, as you did when you ran away by Gad's-hill: you knew I was at your back, and spoke it on purpose to try my patience.

Fal. No, no, no; not so; I did not think thou wast within hearing.

Prince. I shall drive you then to confess the wilful abuse; and then I know how to handle you.

Fal. No abuse, Hal, o' mine honour; no abuse.

Prince. Not to dispraise me, and call me pantler and bread-chipper and I know not what?

Fal. No abuse, Hal.

Poins. No abuse?

Fal. No abuse, Ned, i' the world; honest Ned, none. I dispraised him before the wicked, that the wicked might not fall in love with him; in which doing, I have done the part of a careful friend and a true subject, and thy father is to give me thanks for it. No abuse, Hal: none, Ned, none: no, faith, boys, none.   351

Prince. See now, whether pure fear and entire cowardice doth not make thee wrong this virtuous gentlewoman to close with us. Is she of the wicked? is thine hostess here of the wicked? or is thy boy of the wicked? or honest Bardolph, whose zeal burns in his nose, of the wicked?

Poins. Answer, thou dead elm, answer.

Fal. The fiend hath pricked down Bardolph irrecoverable; and his face is Lucifer's privy-kitchen, where he doth nothing but roast malt-

Doll: 'I love thee better than I love e'er a scurvy young boy of them all.' Engraving by Kenny Meadows from Barry Cornwall's *Works of Shakspere*, 1846

---

297 *kirtle.* Short outer gown.

326 *candle-mine.* Store of tallow.

359 *pricked.* Chosen.

361—362 *malt-worms.* Topers.

392 *south*. i.e. south wind.

413 *peascod-time*. Early summer (when peas are in blossom).

Falstaff takes his leave. Drawing by J.M. Wright (1777–1866)

worms. For the boy, there is a good angel about him; but the devil outbids him too.

Prince. For the women?

Fal. For one of them, she is in hell already, and burns poor souls. For the other, I owe her money; and whether she be damned for that, I know not.

Host. No, I warrant you. 369

Fal. No, I think thou art not; I think thou art quit for that. Marry, there is another indictment upon thee, for suffering flesh to be eaten in thy house, contrary to the law; for the which I think thou wilt howl.

Host. All victuallers do so: what's a joint of mutton or two in a whole Lent?

Prince. You, gentlewoman,—

Dol. What says your grace?

Fal. His grace says that which his flesh rebels against. [*Knocking within.* 380

Host. Who knocks so loud at door? Look to the door there, Francis.

Enter PETO.

Prince. Peto, how now! what news?

Peto. The king your father is at Westminster;
And there are twenty weak and wearied posts
Come from the north: and, as I came along,
I met and overtook a dozen captains,
Bare-headed, sweating, knocking at the taverns,
And asking every one for Sir John Falstaff.

Prince. By heaven, Poins, I feel me much to blame, 390
So idly to profane the precious time,
● When tempest of commotion, like the south
Borne with black vapour, doth begin to melt
And drop upon our bare unarmed heads.
Give me my sword and cloak. Falstaff, good night.
[*Exeunt Prince Henry, Poins, Peto,*
and Bardolph.

Fal. Now comes in the sweetest morsel of the night, and we must hence and leave it unpicked. [*Knocking within.*] More knocking at the door!

Re-enter BARDOLPH.

How now! what's the matter? 400

Bard. You must away to court, sir, presently;
A dozen captains stay at door for you.

Fal. [*To the Page*] Pay the musicians, sirrah. Farewell, hostess; farewell, Doll. You see, my good wenches, how men of merit are sought after: the undeserver may sleep, when the man of action is called on. Farewell, good wenches: if I be not sent away post, I will see you again ere I go.

Dol. I cannot speak; if my heart be not ready to burst,—well, sweet Jack, have a care of thyself.

Fal. Farewell, farewell. [*Exeunt Falstaff*
and Bardolph.

Host. Well, fare thee well: I have known thee
● these twenty nine years, come peascod-time; but an honester and truer-hearted man,—well, fare thee well.

Bard. [*Within*] Mistress Tearsheet!

Host. What's the matter?

Bard. [*Within*] Bid Mistress Tearsheet come to my master. 419

Host. O, run, Doll, run; run, good Doll: come. [*She comes blubbered.*] Yea, will you come, Doll?
[*Exeunt.*

ACT III.

SCENE I. *Westminster. The palace.*

Enter the KING in his nightgown, with a Page.

King. Go call the Earls of Surrey and of
    Warwick;
But, ere they come, bid them o'er-read these
    letters,
And well consider of them: make good speed.
                       [*Exit Page.*
How many thousand of my poorest subjects
Are at this hour asleep! O sleep, O gentle sleep,
Nature's soft nurse, how have I frighted thee,
That thou no more wilt weigh my eyelids down
And steep my senses in forgetfulness?
● Why rather, sleep, liest thou in smoky cribs,
Upon uneasy pallets stretching thee   10
And hush'd with buzzing night-flies to thy slumber,
Than in the perfumed chambers of the great,
Under the canopies of costly state,
And lull'd with sound of sweetest melody?
O thou dull god, why liest thou with the vile
In loathsome beds, and leavest the kingly couch
● A watch-case or a common 'larum-bell?
Wilt thou upon the high and giddy mast
Seal up the ship-boy's eyes, and rock his brains
In cradle of the rude imperious surge   20
And in the visitation of the winds,
Who take the ruffian billows by the top,
Curling their monstrous heads and hanging them
With deafening clamour in the slippery clouds,
That, with the hurly, death itself awakes?
Canst thou, O partial sleep, give thy repose
To the wet sea-boy in an hour so rude,
And in the calmest and most stillest night,
With all appliances and means to boot,
● Deny it to a king? Then happy low, lie down! 30
Uneasy lies the head that wears a crown.

Enter WARWICK and SURREY.

War. Many good morrows to your majesty!
King. Is it good morrow, lords?
War. 'Tis one o'clock, and past.
King. Why, then, good morrow to you all, my
    lords.
Have you read o'er the letters that I sent you?
War. We have, my liege.
King. Then you perceive the body of our
    kingdom
How foul it is; what rank diseases grow,
And with what danger, near the heart of it.   40
War. It is but as a body yet distemper'd;
Which to his former strength may be restored
With good advice and little medicine:
My Lord Northumberland will soon be cool'd.
King. O God! that one might read the book
    of fate,
And see the revolution of the times
● Make mountains level, and the continent,
Weary of solid firmness, melt itself
Into the sea! and, other times, to see
The beachy girdle of the ocean   50
Too wide for Neptune's hips; how chances mock,
And changes fill the cup of alteration
With divers liquors! O, if this were seen,
The happiest youth, viewing his progress through,
What perils past, what crosses to ensue,
Would shut the book, and sit him down and die.

William Charles Macready, the English Victorian actor,
as King Henry IV, Covent Garden Theatre, London,
1847

---

9 *cribs.* Hovels.

17 *watch-case.* Sentry-box.

30 *low.* Lowly people.

47 *continent.* Dry land.

63 *under my foot.* At my disposal.

68 *rated.* Berated.

107 *out of hand.* Over with.

Costume design for Henry IV by Tanya Moisewitch,
Stratford-upon-Avon, 1951

3 *rood.* Cross.

'Tis not ten years gone
Since Richard and Northumberland, great friends,
Did feast together, and in two years after
Were they at wars: it is but eight years since 60
This Percy was the man nearest my soul,
Who like a brother toil'd in my affairs
● And laid his love and life under my foot,
Yea, for my sake, even to the eyes of Richard
Gave him defiance. But which of you was by—
You, cousin Nevil, as I may remember—
        [*To Warwick.*
When Richard, with his eye brimful of tears,
● Then check'd and rated by Northumberland,
Did speak these words, now proved a prophecy?
'Northumberland, thou ladder by the which 70
My cousin Bolingbroke ascends my throne;'
Though then, God knows, I had no such intent,
But that necessity so bow'd the state
That I and greatness were compell'd to kiss:
'The time shall come,' thus did he follow it,
'The time will come, that foul sin, gathering head,
Shall break into corruption:' so went on,
Foretelling this same time's condition
And the division of our amity.
    War. There is a history in all men's lives, 80
Figuring the nature of the times deceased;
The which observed, a man may prophesy,
With a near aim, of the main chance of things
As yet not come to life, which in their seeds
And weak beginnings lie intreasured.
Such things become the hatch and brood of time;
And by the necessary form of this
King Richard might create a perfect guess
That great Northumberland, then false to him,
Would of that seed grow to a greater falseness;
Which should not find a ground to root upon, 91
Unless on you.
    King.   Are these things then necessities?
Then let us meet them like necessities:
And that same word even now cries out on us:
They say the bishop and Northumberland
Are fifty thousand strong.
    War.   It cannot be, my lord;
Rumour doth double, like the voice and echo,
The numbers of the fear'd. Please it your grace
To go to bed. Upon my soul, my lord,
The powers that you already have sent forth 100
Shall bring this prize in very easily.
To comfort you the more, I have received
A certain instance that Glendower is dead.
Your majesty hath been this fortnight ill,
And these unseason'd hours perforce must add
Unto your sickness.
    King.   I will take your counsel:
● And were these inward wars once out of hand,
We would, dear lords, unto the Holy Land.
                    [*Exeunt.*

SCENE II. *Gloucestershire. Before* JUSTICE
            SHALLOW'S *house.*

Enter SHALLOW *and* SILENCE, *meeting;* MOUL-
DY, SHADOW, WART, FEEBLE, BULLCALF, *a
Servant or two with them.*

    Shal. Come on, come on, come on, sir; give
me your hand, sir, give me your hand, sir: an
● early stirrer, by the rood! And how doth my
good cousin Silence?
    Sil. Good morrow, good cousin Shallow.

Shal. And how doth my cousin, your bedfellow? and your fairest daughter and mine, my god-daughter Ellen?

● *Sil.* Alas, a black ousel, cousin Shallow! 9

Shal. By yea and nay, sir, I dare say my cousin William is become a good scholar: he is at Oxford still, is he not?

Sil. Indeed, sir, to my cost.

Shal. A' must, then, to the inns o' court shortly.

● I was once of Clement's Inn, where I think they will talk of mad Shallow yet.

Sil. You were called 'lusty Shallow' then, cousin.

Shal. By the mass, I was called any thing; and I would have done any thing indeed too, and roundly too. There was I, and little John Doit of Staffordshire, and black George Barnes, and Francis Pickbone, and Will Squele, a Cotswold

● man; you had not four such swinge-bucklers in all the inns o' court again: and I may say to you,

● we knew where the bona-robas were and had the

● best of them all at commandment. Then was Jack Falstaff, now Sir John, a boy, and page to Thomas Mowbray, Duke of Norfolk.

Sil. This Sir John, cousin, that comes hither anon about soldiers? 31

Shal. The same Sir John, the very same. I see him break Skogan's head at the court-gate,

● when a' was a crack not thus high: and the very same day did I fight with one Sampson Stockfish,

● a fruiterer, behind Gray's Inn. Jesu, Jesu, the mad days that I have spent! and to see how many of my old acquaintance are dead!

Sil. We shall all follow, cousin. 39

Shal. Certain, 'tis certain; very sure, very sure: death, as the Psalmist saith, is certain to all; all shall die. How a good yoke of bullocks at Stamford fair?

Sil. By my troth, I was not there.

Shal. Death is certain. Is old Double of your town living yet?

Sil. Dead, sir.

Shal. Jesu, Jesu, dead! a' drew a good bow; and dead! a' shot a fine shoot: John a Gaunt loved him well, and betted much money on his

● head. Dead! a' would have clapped i' the clout at twelve score; and carried you a forehand shaft a fourteen and fourteen and a half, that it would have done a man's heart good to see. How a score of ewes now?

Sil. Thereafter as they be: a score of good ewes may be worth ten pounds.

Shal. And is old Double dead?

Sil. Here come two of Sir John Falstaff's men, as I think. 60

Enter BARDOLPH *and one with him.*

Bard. Good morrow, honest gentlemen: I beseech you, which is Justice Shallow?

Shal. I am Robert Shallow, sir; a poor esquire of this county, and one of the king's justices of the peace: what is your good pleasure with me?

Bard. My captain, sir, commends him to you; my captain, Sir John Falstaff, a tall gentleman, by heaven, and a most gallant leader.

Shal. He greets me well, sir. I knew him a

● good backsword man. How doth the good knight? may I ask how my lady his wife doth? 71

Justice Shallow talks with Silence. Engraving by Kenny Meadows from Barry Cornwall's *Works of Shakspere,* 1846

---

9 *ousel.* Blackbird.

15 *Clement's Inn.* One of the Inns of Chancery.

24 *swinge-bucklers.* Swash-bucklers.

26 *bona-robas.* Whores.

27 *commandment.* For the asking.

34 *crack.* Lively boy.

36 *Gray's Inn.* One of the Inns of Court.

51–53 *clapped . . . score.* Hit the target at 240 yards. *carried . . . half.* Shot a heavy arrow point blank which carried 280 or 290 yards.

70 *backsword.* Fencing stock with a basket hilt.

97 *in commission.* i.e. as a Justice of the Peace.

Shadow.

Costume design for Shadow by Tanya Moisewitch,
Stratford-upon-Avon, 1951

Bard. Sir, pardon; a soldier is better accommodated than with a wife.

Shal. It is well said, in faith, sir; and it is well said indeed too. Better accommodated! it is good; yea, indeed, is it: good phrases are surely, and ever were, very commendable. Accommodated! it comes of 'accommodo:' very good; a good phrase. 79

Bard. Pardon me, sir; I have heard the word. Phrase call you it? by this good day, I know not the phrase; but I will maintain the word with my sword to be a soldier-like word, and a word of exceeding good command, by heaven. Accommodated; that is, when a man is, as they say, accommodated; or when a man is, being, whereby a' may be thought to be accommodated; which is an excellent thing.

Shal. It is very just. 89

Enter FALSTAFF.

Look, here comes good Sir John. Give me your good hand, give me your worship's good hand: by my troth, you like well and bear your years very well: welcome, good Sir John.

Fal. I am glad to see you well, good Master Robert Shallow: Master Surecard, as I think?

Shal. No, Sir John; it is my cousin Silence, ● in commission with me.

Fal. Good Master Silence, it well befits you should be of the peace.

Sil. Your good worship is welcome. 100

Fal. Fie! this is hot weather, gentlemen. Have you provided me here half a dozen sufficient men?

Shal. Marry, have we, sir. Will you sit?

Fal. Let me see them, I beseech you.

Shal. Where's the roll? where's the roll? where's the roll? Let me see, let me see, let me see. So, so, so, so, so, so, so: yea, marry, sir: Ralph Mouldy! Let them appear as I call; let them do so, let them do so. Let me see; where is Mouldy? 111

Moul. Here, an't please you.

Shal. What think you, Sir John? a good-limbed fellow; young, strong, and of good friends.

Fal. Is thy name Mouldy?

Moul. Yea, an't please you.

Fal. 'Tis the more time thou wert used.

Shal. Ha, ha, ha! most excellent, i' faith! things that are mouldy lack use: very singular good! in faith, well said, Sir John, very well said.

Fal. Prick him. 121

Moul. I was pricked well enough before, an you could have let me alone: my old dame will be undone now for one to do her husbandry and her drudgery: you need not to have pricked me; there are other men fitter to go out than I.

Fal. Go to: peace, Mouldy; you shall go. Mouldy, it is time you were spent.

Moul. Spent! 129

Shal. Peace, fellow, peace; stand aside: know you where you are? For the other, Sir John: let me see: Simon Shadow!

Fal. Yea, marry, let me have him to sit under: he's like to be a cold soldier.

Shal. Where's Shadow?

Shad. Here, sir.

Fal. Shadow, whose son art thou?

Shad. My mother's son, sir.

Fal. Thy mother's son! like enough, and thy father's shadow: so the son of the female is the shadow of the male: it is often so, indeed; but much of the father's substance!

Shal. Do you like him, Sir John?

Fal. Shadow will serve for summer; prick him, for we have a number of shadows to fill up the muster-book.

Shal. Thomas Wart!

Fal. Where's he?

Wart. Here, sir.

Fal. Is thy name Wart? 150

Wart. Yea, sir.

Fal. Thou art a very ragged wart.

Shal. Shall I prick him down, Sir John?

Fal. It were superfluous; for his apparel is built upon his back and the whole frame stands upon pins: prick him no more.

Shal. Ha, ha, ha! you can do it, sir; you can do it: I commend you well. Francis Feeble!

Fee. Here, sir.

Fal. What trade art thou, Feeble? 160

Fee. A woman's tailor, sir.

Shal. Shall I prick him, sir?

Fal. You may: but if he had been a man's tailor, he 'ld ha' pricked you. Wilt thou make as many holes in an enemy's battle as thou hast done in a woman's petticoat?

Fee. I will do my good will, sir: you can have no more.

Fal. Well said, good woman's tailor! well said, courageous Feeble! thou wilt be as valiant as the wrathful dove or most magnanimous mouse. Prick the woman's tailor: well, Master Shallow; deep, Master Shallow.

Fee. I would Wart might have gone, sir.

Fal. I would thou wert a man's tailor, that thou mightst mend him and make him fit to go. I cannot put him to a private soldier that is the leader of so many thousands: let that suffice, most forcible Feeble.

Fee. It shall suffice, sir. 180

Fal. I am bound to thee, reverend Feeble. Who is next?

Shal. Peter Bullcalf o' the green!

Fal. Yea, marry, let's see Bullcalf.

Bull. Here, sir.

Fal. 'Fore God, a likely fellow! Come, prick me Bullcalf till he roar again.

Bull. O Lord! good my lord captain,—

Fal. What, dost thou roar before thou art pricked? 190

Bull. O Lord, sir! I am a diseased man.

Fal. What disease hast thou?

Bull. A whoreson cold, sir, a cough, sir, which I caught with ringing in the king's affairs upon his coronation-day, sir.

Fal. Come, thou shalt go to the wars in a gown; we will have away thy cold; and I will take such order that thy friends shall ring for thee. Is here all? 199

Shal. Here is two more called than your number; you must have but four here, sir: and so, I pray you, go in with me to dinner.

Fal. Come, I will go drink with you, but I cannot tarry dinner. I am glad to see you, by my troth, Master Shallow.

Shal. O, Sir John, do you remember since we lay all night in the windmill in Saint George's field?

145 *shadows.* Fictitious names on the muster rolls.

Feeble: 'A woman's tailor, sir.' Engraving from a 19th century painting 'The lady's tailor' by H.S. Marks (1829–1898)

178 *thousands.* i.e. of lice.

207 *windmill.* Brothel. *Saint George's field.* Field south of the Thames, between Southwark and Lambeth.

Falstaff: 'We have heard the chimes at midnight . . .' St Clement's Church in the Strand, near to Clement's Inn. Detail from Ralph Agas's map of London *c*.1560–70

236–237 *four . . . crowns.* Worth a pound.

248 *forty.* i.e. shillings.

Fal. No more of that, good Master Shallow, no more of that.

Shal. Ha! 'twas a merry night. And is Jane Nightwork alive? 211

Fal. She lives, Master Shallow.

Shal. She never could away with me.

Fal. Never, never; she would always say she could not abide Master Shallow.

Shal. By the mass, I could anger her to the heart. She was then a bona-roba. Doth she hold her own well?

Fal. Old, old, Master Shallow. 219

Shal. Nay, she must be old; she cannot choose but be old; certain she's old; and had Robin Nightwork by old Nightwork before I came to Clement's Inn.

Sil. That's fifty five year ago.

Shal. Ha, cousin Silence, that thou hadst seen that that this knight and I have seen! Ha, Sir John, said I well?

Fal. We have heard the chimes at midnight, Master Shallow. 229

Shal. That we have, that we have, that we have; in faith, Sir John, we have: our watchword was 'Hem boys!' Come, let's to dinner; come, let's to dinner: Jesus, the days that we have seen! Come, come.

[*Exeunt Falstaff and the Justices.*

Bull. Good Master Corporate Bardolph, stand
● my friend; and here's four Harry ten shillings in French crowns for you. In very truth, sir, I had as lief be hanged, sir, as go: and yet, for mine own part, sir, I do not care; but rather, because I am unwilling, and, for mine own part, have a desire to stay with my friends; else, sir, I did not care, for mine own part, so much.

Bard. Go to; stand aside.

Moul. And, good master corporal captain, for my old dame's sake, stand my friend: she has nobody to do any thing about her when I am gone; and she is old, and cannot help herself:
● you shall have forty, sir.

Bard. Go to; stand aside. 249

Fee. By my troth, I care not; a man can die but once: we owe God a death: I'll ne'er bear a base mind: an't be my destiny, so; an't be not, so: no man is too good to serve's prince; and let it go which way it will, he that dies this year is quit for the next.

Bard. Well said; thou'rt a good fellow.

Fee. Faith, I'll bear no base mind.

Re-enter FALSTAFF *and the* Justices.

Fal. Come, sir, which men shall I have?

Shal. Four of which you please.

Bard. Sir, a word with you: I have three pound to free Mouldy and Bullcalf. 261

Fal. Go to; well.

Shal. Come, Sir John, which four will you have?

Fal. Do you choose for me.

Shal. Marry, then, Mouldy, Bullcalf, Feeble and Shadow.

Fal. Mouldy and Bullcalf: for you, Mouldy, stay at home till you are past service: and for your part, Bullcalf, grow till you come unto it: I will none of you. 271

Shal. Sir John, Sir John, do not yourself

wrong: they are your likeliest men, and I would have you served with the best.

Fal. Will you tell me, Master Shallow, how to choose a man? Care I for the limb, the thewes, the stature, bulk, and big assemblance of a man! Give me the spirit, Master Shallow. Here's Wart; you see what a ragged appearance it is: a' shall charge you and discharge you with the motion of a pewterer's hammer, come off and on swifter than he that gibbets on the brewer's bucket. And this same half-faced fellow, Shadow; give me this man: he presents no mark to the enemy; the foeman may with as great aim level at the edge of a penknife. And for a retreat; how swiftly will this Feeble the woman's tailor run off! O, give me the spare men, and spare me the great ones. Put me a caliver into Wart's hand, Bardolph.   290

Bard. Hold, Wart, traverse; thus, thus, thus.

Fal. Come, manage me your caliver. So: very well: go to: very good, exceeding good. O, give me always a little, lean, old, chapt, bald shot. Well said, i' faith, Wart; thou'rt a good scab: hold, there's a tester for thee.

Shal. He is not his craft's master; he doth not do it right. I remember at Mile-end Green, when I lay at Clement's Inn,—I was then Sir Dagonet in Arthur's show,—there was a little quiver fellow, and a' would manage you his piece thus; and a' would about and about, and come you in and come you in: 'rah, tah, tah,' would a' say; 'bounce' would a' say; and away again would a' go, and again would a' come: I shall ne'er see such a fellow.

Fal. These fellows will do well, Master Shallow. God keep you, Master Silence: I will not use many words with you. Fare you well, gentlemen both: I thank you: I must a dozen mile to-night. Bardolph, give the soldiers coats.   311

Shal. Sir John, the Lord bless you! God prosper your affairs! God send us peace! At your return visit our house; let our old acquaintance be renewed: peradventure I will with ye to the court.

Fal. 'Fore God, I would you would, Master Shallow.

Shal. Go to; I have spoke at a word. God keep you.   320

Fal. Fare you well, gentle gentlemen. [*Exeunt Justices.*] On, Bardolph; lead the men away. [*Exeunt Bardolph, Recruits, &c.*] As I return, I will fetch off these justices: I do see the bottom of Justice Shallow. Lord, Lord, how subject we old men are to this vice of lying! This same starved justice hath done nothing but prate to me of the wildness of his youth, and the feats he hath done about Turnbull Street; and every third word a lie, duer paid to the hearer than the Turk's tribute. I do remember him at Clement's Inn like a man made after supper of a cheeseparing: when a' was naked, he was, for all the world, like a forked radish, with a head fantastically carved upon it with a knife: a' was so forlorn, that his dimensions to any thick sight were invincible: a' was the very genius of famine; yet lecherous as a monkey, and the whores called him mandrake: a' came ever in the rearward of the fashion, and sung those tunes to the overscutched huswives that he heard the carmen

276 *thewes.* Muscles; strength.

282–283 *gibbets on the brewer's bucket.* Hangs the pails of beer on the carrier's yoke.

289 *caliver.* Musket.

296 *tester.* Sixpence.

298 *Mile-end Green.* Training ground for militia.

299–300 *Sir Dagonet in Arthur's show.* King Arthur's fool in an exhibition of archery held annually at Mile-end.

301 *quiver.* Nimble.

Falstaff choosing recruits. Engraving from a drawing by Henry Bunbury (1750–1811)

324 *fetch off.* Get the better of.

329 *Turnbull Street.* Haunt of prostitutes.

330 *duer.* More promptly.

331 *Turk's tribute.* Tribute-money exacted by the Turk.

337 *invincible.* i.e. invisible.

340–341 *over-scutched huswives.* Worn-out hussies. *carmen.* Wagoners.

343 *Vice's dagger.* Wooden dagger carried by Vice, the comic villain in Morality plays.

347 *Tilt-yard.* In Whitehall, used for tournaments.

351 *hautboy.* Oboe.

355 *philosopher's two stones.* For transmuting base metals into gold; and the elixir vitae, a medicine for perpetuating life.

Edward Shuter, 18th century English actor, as Falstaff. Engraving from Bell's edition of *Shakespeare*, 1778

2 *Gaultree Forest.* Royal forest in Yorkshire.

11 *hold sortance.* Accord.

23 *just . . . out.* Exact number we estimated.

whistle, and sware they were his fancies or his good-nights. And now is this Vice's dagger become a squire, and talks as familiarly of John a Gaunt as if he had been sworn brother to him; and I'll be sworn a' ne'er saw him but once in the Tilt-yard; and then he burst his head for crowding among the marshal's men. I saw it, and told John a Gaunt he beat his own name; for you might have thrust him and all his apparel into an eel-skin; the case of a treble hautboy was a mansion for him, a court: and now has he land and beefs. Well, I'll be acquainted with him, if I return; and it shall go hard but I will make him a philosopher's two stones to me: if the young dace be a bait for the old pike, I see no reason in the law of nature but I may snap at him. Let time shape, and there an end.   [*Exit.*

ACT IV.

SCENE I. *Yorkshire. Gaultree Forest.*

Enter the ARCHBISHOP OF YORK, MOWBRAY, HASTINGS, *and others.*

Arch. What is this forest call'd?
Hast. 'Tis Gaultree Forest, an't shall please your grace.
Arch. Here stand, my lords; and send discoverers forth
To know the numbers of our enemies.
Hast. We have sent forth already.
Arch.   'Tis well done.
My friends and brethren in these great affairs,
I must acquaint you that I have received
New-dated letters from Northumberland;
Their cold intent, tenour and substance, thus:
Here doth he wish his person, with such powers
As might hold sortance with his quality,   11
The which he could not levy; whereupon
He is retired, to ripe his growing fortunes,
To Scotland: and concludes in hearty prayers
That your attempts may overlive the hazard
And fearful meeting of their opposite.
Mowb. Thus do the hopes we have in him touch ground
And dash themselves to pieces.

Enter a Messenger.

Hast.   Now, what news?
Mess. West of this forest, scarcely off a mile,
In goodly form comes on the enemy;   20
And, by the ground they hide, I judge their number
Upon or near the rate of thirty thousand.
Mowb. The just proportion that we gave them out.
Let us sway on and face them in the field.
Arch. What well-appointed leader fronts us here?

Enter WESTMORELAND.

Mowb. I think it is my Lord of Westmoreland.
West. Health and fair greeting from our general,
The prince, Lord John and Duke of Lancaster.
Arch. Say on, my Lord of Westmoreland, in peace:
What doth concern your coming?
West.   Then, my lord, 30

Unto your grace do I in chief address
The substance of my speech.   If that rebellion
Came like itself, in base and abject routs,
Led on by bloody youth, guarded with rags,
And countenanced by boys and beggary,
I say, if damn'd commotion so appear'd,
In his true, native and most proper shape,
You, reverend father, and these noble lords
Had not been here, to dress the ugly form
Of base and bloody insurrection   40
With your fair honours.   You, lord archbishop,
Whose see is by a civil peace maintain'd,
Whose beard the silver hand of peace hath touch'd,
Whose learning and good letters peace hath
         tutor'd,
● Whose white investments figure innocence,
The dove and very blessed spirit of peace,
Wherefore do you so ill translate yourself
Out of the speech of peace that bears such grace,
Into the harsh and boisterous tongue of war ;
Turning your books to † graves, your ink to blood,
Your pens to lances and your tongue divine   51
To a loud trumpet and a point of war ?
     Arch.   Wherefore do I this ? so the question
         stands.
Briefly to this end : we are all diseased,
And with our surfeiting and wanton hours
Have brought ourselves into a burning fever,
And we must bleed for it ; of which disease
Our late king, Richard, being infected, died.
But, my most noble Lord of Westmoreland,
I take not on me here as a physician,   60
Nor do I as an enemy to peace
Troop in the throngs of military men ;
But rather show awhile like fearful war,
● To diet rank minds sick of happiness
And purge the obstructions which begin to stop
Our very veins of life.   Hear me more plainly.
I have in equal balance justly weigh'd
What wrongs our arms may do, what wrongs we
         suffer,
And find our griefs heavier than our offences.
We see which way the stream of time doth run,
And are enforced from our most quiet there   71
By the rough torrent of occasion ;
And have the summary of all our griefs,
When time shall serve, to show in articles ;
Which long ere this we offer'd to the king,
And might by no suit gain our audience :
When we are wrong'd and would unfold our griefs,
We are denied access unto his person
Even by those men that most have done us wrong.
The dangers of the days but newly gone,   80
Whose memory is written on the earth
With yet appearing blood, and the examples
Of every minute's instance, present now,
Hath put us in these ill-beseeming arms,
Not to break peace or any branch of it,
But to establish here a peace indeed,
Concurring both in name and quality.
     West.   When ever yet was your appeal denied ?
● Wherein have you been galled by the king ?
● What peer hath been suborn'd to grate on you, 90
That you should seal this lawless bloody book
Of forged rebellion with a seal divine
And consecrate commotion's bitter edge ?
● *Arch.* † My brother general, the commonwealth,
To brother born an household cruelty,
I make my quarrel in particular.

45 *investments.* Vestments.

64 *diet rank minds sick of happiness.* To occupy minds dissatisfied with peace.

89 *galled.* Humiliated.

90 *suborn'd.* Bribed.

94 *brother general.* i.e. my brothers, the common people.

111 *signories.* Lordships.

120 *beavers.* Visors of their helmets.

125 *warder.* Staff.

135 *borne it.* i.e. carried the victor's prize.

138 *Hereford.* i.e. Bolingbroke.

145 *set off.* Removed.

149 *overween.* Are presumptuous.

West. There is no need of any such redress;
Or if there were, it not belongs to you.
Mowb. Why not to him in part, and to us all
That feel the bruises of the days before, 100
And suffer the condition of these times
To lay a heavy and unequal hand
Upon our honours?
West. O, my good Lord Mowbray,
Construe the times to their necessities,
And you shall say indeed, it is the time,
And not the king, that doth you injuries.
Yet for your part, it not appears to me
Either from the king or in the present time
That you should have an inch of any ground
To build a grief on: were you not restored 110
● To all the Duke of Norfolk's signories,
Your noble and right well remember'd father's?
Mowb. What thing, in honour, had my father
lost,
That need to be revived and breathed in me?
The king that loved him, as the state stood then,
Was force perforce compell'd to banish him:
And then that Henry Bolingbroke and he,
Being mounted and both roused in their seats,
Their neighing coursers daring of the spur, 119
● Their armed staves in charge, their beavers down,
Their eyes of fire sparkling through sights of steel
And the loud trumpet blowing them together,
Then, then, when there was nothing could have
stay'd
My father from the breast of Bolingbroke,
● O, when the king did throw his warder down,
His own life hung upon the staff he threw;
Then threw he down himself and all their lives
That by indictment and by dint of sword
Have since miscarried under Bolingbroke.
West. You speak, Lord Mowbray, now you
know not what. 130
The Earl of Hereford was reputed then
In England the most valiant gentleman:
Who knows on whom fortune would then have
smiled?
But if your father had been victor there,
● He ne'er had borne it out of Coventry:
For all the country in a general voice
Cried hate upon him; and all their prayers and
love
Were set on Hereford, whom they doted on
And bless'd and graced indeed, more than the king.
But this is mere digression from my purpose. 140
Here come I from our princely general
To know your griefs; to tell you from his grace
That he will give you audience; and wherein
It shall appear that your demands are just,
● You shall enjoy them, every thing set off
That might so much as think you enemies.
Mowb. But he hath forced us to compel this
offer;
And it proceeds from policy, not love.
● *West.* Mowbray, you overween to take it so;
This offer comes from mercy, not from fear: 150
For, lo! within a ken our army lies,
Upon mine honour, all too confident
To give admittance to a thought of fear.
Our battle is more full of names than yours,
Our men more perfect in the use of arms,
Our armour all as strong, our cause the best;
Then reason will our hearts should be as good:
Say you not then our offer is compell'd.

Mowb. Well, by my will we shall admit no
    parley.

West. That argues but the shame of your
    offence: 160
A rotten case abides no handling.

Hast. Hath the Prince John a full commission,
In very ample virtue of his father,
To hear and absolutely to determine
Of what conditions we shall stand upon?

West. That is intended in the general's name:
● I muse you make so slight a question.

Arch. Then take, my Lord of Westmoreland,
    this schedule,
For this contains our general grievances:
Each several article herein redress'd, 170
All members of our cause, both here and hence,
That are insinew'd to this action,
● Acquitted by a true substantial form
And present execution of our wills
To us and to our purposes confined,
● We come within our awful banks again
And knit our powers to the arm of peace.

West. This will I show the general. Please
    you, lords,
In sight of both our battles we may meet;
● And either end in peace, which God so frame! 180
Or to the place of difference call the swords
Which must decide it.

Arch. My lord, we will do so. [*Exit West.*

Mowb. There is a thing within my bosom tells
    me
That no conditions of our peace can stand.

Hast. Fear you not that: if we can make our
    peace
Upon such large terms and so absolute
As our conditions shall consist upon,
Our peace shall stand as firm as rocky mountains.
● *Mowb.* Yea, but our valuation shall be such
That every slight and false-derived cause, 190
Yea, every idle, nice and wanton reason
Shall to the king taste of this action;
● That, were our royal faiths martyrs in love,
We shall be winnow'd with so rough a wind
That even our corn shall seem as light as chaff
● And good from bad find no partition.

Arch. No, no, my lord. Note this; the king
    is weary
● Of dainty and such picking grievances:
For he hath found to end one doubt by death
Revives two greater in the heirs of life, 200
And therefore will he wipe his tables clean
And keep no tell-tale to his memory
That may repeat and history his loss
To new remembrance; for full well he knows
He cannot so precisely weed this land
As his misdoubts present occasion:
His foes are so enrooted with his friends
That, plucking to unfix an enemy,
He doth unfasten so and shake a friend:
So that this land, like an offensive wife 210
That hath enraged him on to offer strokes,
As he is striking, holds his infant up
● And hangs resolved correction in the arm
That was uprear'd to execution.

Hast. Besides, the king hath wasted all his
    rods
On late offenders, that he now doth lack
The very instruments of chastisement:
So that his power, like to a fangless lion,

167 *muse.* Am astonished.

Archbishop: 'Then take, my Lord of Westmoreland, this schedule . . .' Engraving by Kenny Meadows from Barry Cornwall's *Works of Shakspere*, 1846

173 *substantial form.* Formal agreement.

176 *awful banks.* Lawful bounds.

180 *frame.* Bring to pass.

189 *valuation.* Reputation with the king.

193 *were . . . in love.* Even if we died as martyrs for love of the king.

196 *partition.* Distinction.

198 *dainty.* Small.

213 *hangs resolved correction.* Checks intended punishment.

Lancaster: 'Good day to you, gentle lord archbishop'.
Lancaster (Charles Dance) and Archbishop (Andre van
Gyseghem), Royal Shakespeare Co, 1975

14 *abroach*. Afoot.

20 *opener and intelligencer*. Interpreter and messenger.

33 *in common sense*. In the judgement of the common
people.

38 *Hydra*. Many headed.

May offer, but not hold.
  Arch.   'Tis very true:
And therefore be assured, my good lord marshal,
If we do now make our atonement well,   221
Our peace will, like a broken limb united,
Grow stronger for the breaking.
  Mowb.   Be it so.
Here is return'd my Lord of Westmoreland.

Re-enter WESTMORELAND.

  West. The prince is here at hand: pleaseth
    your lordship
To meet his grace just distance 'tween our armies.
  Mowb. Your grace of York, in God's name,
    then, set forward.
  Arch. Before, and greet his grace: my lord,
    we come.   [*Exeunt.*

SCENE II. *Another part of the forest.*

Enter, from one side, MOWBRAY, *attended;
afterwards the* ARCHBISHOP, HASTINGS, *and
others: from the other side,* PRINCE JOHN OF
LANCASTER, *and* WESTMORELAND; *Officers,
and others with them.*

  Lan. You are well encounter'd here, my cousin
    Mowbray:
Good day to you, gentle lord archbishop;
And so to you, Lord Hastings, and to all.
My Lord of York, it better show'd with you
When that your flock, assembled by the bell,
Encircled you to hear with reverence
Your exposition on the holy text
Than now to see you here an iron man,
Cheering a rout of rebels with your drum,
Turning the word to sword and life to death.   10
That man that sits within a monarch's heart,
And ripens in the sunshine of his favour,
Would he abuse the countenance of the king,
● Alack, what mischiefs might he set abroach
In shadow of such greatness! With you, lord
    bishop,
It is even so. Who hath not heard it spoken
How deep you were within the books of God?
To us the speaker in his parliament;
To us the imagined voice of God himself;
● The very opener and intelligencer   20
Between the grace, the sanctities of heaven
And our dull workings. O, who shall believe
But you misuse the reverence of your place,
Employ the countenance and grace of heaven,
As a false favourite doth his prince's name,
In deeds dishonourable? You have ta'en up,
Under the counterfeited zeal of God,
The subjects of his substitute, my father,
And both against the peace of heaven and him
Have here up-swarm'd them.
  Arch.   Good my Lord of Lancaster, 30
I am not here against your father's peace;
But, as I told my Lord of Westmoreland,
● The time misorder'd doth, in common sense,
Crowd us and crush us to this monstrous form,
To hold our safety up. I sent your grace
The parcels and particulars of our grief,
The which hath been with scorn shoved from the
    court,
● Whereon this Hydra son of war is born;
Whose dangerous eyes may well be charm'd asleep
With grant of our most just and right desires, 40

And true obedience, of this madness cured,
Stoop tamely to the foot of majesty.
    Mowb. If not, we ready are to try our fortunes
To the last man.
    Hast.   And though we here fall down,
We have supplies to second our attempt:
If they miscarry, theirs shall second them;
● And so success of mischief shall be born
And heir from heir shall hold this quarrel up
Whiles England shall have generation.
    Lan. You are too shallow, Hastings, much too
      shallow,   50
To sound the bottom of the after-times.
    West. Pleaseth your grace to answer them
      directly
How far forth you do like their articles.
    Lan. I like them all, and do allow them well,
And swear here, by the honour of my blood,
My father's purposes have been mistook,
And some about him have too lavishly
Wrested his meaning and authority.
My lord, these griefs shall be with speed redress'd;
Upon my soul, they shall. If this may please you,
Discharge your powers unto their several counties,
As we will ours: and here between the armies
Let's drink together friendly and embrace,
That all their eyes may bear those tokens home
Of our restored love and amity.
    Arch. I take your princely word for these re-
      dresses.
    Lan. I give it you, and will maintain my word:
And thereupon I drink unto your grace.
    Hast. Go, captain, and deliver to the army 69
This news of peace: let them have pay, and part:
I know it will well please them. Hie thee, captain.
                        [*Exit Officer.*
    Arch. To you, my noble Lord of Westmore-
      land.
    West. I pledge your grace; and, if you knew
      what pains
I have bestow'd to breed this present peace,
You would drink freely: but my love to ye
Shall show itself more openly hereafter.
    Arch. I do not doubt you.
    West.   I am glad of it.
Health to my lord and gentle cousin, Mowbray.
    Mowb. You wish me health in very happy
      season;
For I am, on the sudden, something ill.   80
    Arch. Against ill chances men are ever merry;
But heaviness foreruns the good event.
    West. Therefore be merry, coz; since sudden
      sorrow
Serves to say thus, 'some good thing comes to-
      morrow.'
    Arch. Believe me, I am passing light in spirit.
    Mowb. So much the worse, if your own rule
      be true.   [*Shouts within.*
    Lan. The word of peace is render'd: hark,
      how they shout!
    Mowb. This had been cheerful after victory.
    Arch. A peace is of the nature of a conquest;
For then both parties nobly are subdued,   90
And neither party loser.
    Lan.   Go, my lord,
And let our army be discharged too.
                 [*Exit Westmoreland.*
● And, good my lord, so please you, let our trains
March by us, that we may peruse the men

47 *success.* Succession.

93 *trains.* Detachments.

95 *coped withal.* Fought with.

120 *stray.* Stragglers.

1–2 *condition.* Rank.

20 *school..* Crowd.

● We should have coped withal.

Arch.　　　　　　Go, good Lord Hastings,
And, ere they be dismiss'd, let them march by.
　　　　　　　　　　　　　　[*Exit Hastings.*
　Lan.　I trust, lords, we shall lie to-night toge-
ther.

　　　　　Re-enter WESTMORELAND.

Now cousin, wherefore stands our army still?
　West.　The leaders, having charge from you to
　　　stand,
Will not go off until they hear you speak.　　100
　Lan.　They know their duties.

　　　　　Re-enter HASTINGS.

　Hast.　My lord, our army is dispersed already:
Like youthful steers unyoked, they take their
　　　courses
East, west, north, south; or, like a school
　　　broke up,
Each hurries toward his home and sporting-place.
　West.　Good tidings, my Lord Hastings; for
　　　the which
I do arrest thee, traitor, of high treason:
And you, lord archbishop, and you, lord Mow-
　　　bray,
Of capital treason I attach you both.
　Mowb.　Is this proceeding just and honourable?
　West.　Is your assembly so?　　　　　　111
　Arch.　Will you thus break your faith?
　Lan.　　　　　　　　　I pawn'd thee none:
I promised you redress of these same grievances
Whereof you did complain; which, by mine
　　　honour,
I will perform with a most Christian care.
But for you, rebels, look to taste the due
Meet for rebellion and such acts as yours.
Most shallowly did you these arms commence,
Fondly brought here and foolishly sent hence.
● Strike up our drums, pursue the scatter'd stray:
God, and not we, hath safely fought to-day.　121
Some guard these traitors to the block of death,
Treason's true bed and yielder up of breath.
　　　　　　　　　　　　　　[*Exeunt.*

　　SCENE III.　*Another part of the forest.*

　　Alarum.　Excursions.　Enter FALSTAFF
　　　　　and COLEVILE, *meeting.*

● *Fal.*　What's your name, sir? of what condi-
tion are you, and of what place, I pray?
　Cole.　I am a knight, sir; and my name is
Colevile of the dale.
　Fal.　Well, then, Colevile is your name, a
knight is your degree, and your place the dale:
Colevile shall be still your name, a traitor your
degree, and the dungeon your place, a place
deep enough; so shall you be still Colevile of
the dale.　　　　　　　　　　　　　　10
　Cole.　Are not you Sir John Falstaff?
　Fal.　As good a man as he, sir, whoe'er I am.
Do ye yield, sir? or shall I sweat for you? If I
do sweat, they are the drops of thy lovers, and
they weep for thy death: therefore rouse up
fear and trembling, and do observance to my
mercy.
　Cole.　I think you are Sir John Falstaff, and
in that thought yield me.　　　　　　　19
● *Fal.*　I have a whole school of tongues in

this belly of mine, and not a tongue of them all speaks any other word but my name. An I had but a belly of any indifferency, I were simply the most active fellow in Europe: my womb, my womb, my womb, undoes me. Here comes our general.

Enter PRINCE JOHN OF LANCASTER, WEST-MORELAND, BLUNT, *and others.*

Lan. The heat is past; follow no further now: Call in the powers, good cousin Westmoreland.
                            [Exit Westmoreland.
Now, Falstaff, where have you been all this
    while?
When every thing is ended, then you come: 30
These tardy tricks of yours will, on my life,
One time or other break some gallows' back.

Fal. I would be sorry, my lord, but it should be thus: I never knew yet but rebuke and check was the reward of valour. Do you think me a swallow, an arrow, or a bullet? have I, in my poor and old motion, the expedition of thought? I have speeded hither with the very extremest inch of possibility; I have foundered nine score and odd posts: and here, travel-tainted as I am, have, in my pure and immaculate valour, taken Sir John Colevile of the dale, a most furious knight and valorous enemy. But what of that? he saw me, and yielded; that I may justly say, with the hook-nosed fellow of Rome, 'I came, saw, and overcame.'

Lan. It was more of his courtesy than your deserving.

Fal. I know not: here he is, and here I yield him: and I beseech your grace, let it be booked with the rest of this day's deeds; or, by the Lord, I will have it in a particular ballad else, with mine own picture on the top on't, Colevile kissing my foot: to the which course if I be enforced, if you do not all show like gilt two-pences to me, and I in the clear sky of fame o'ershine you as much as the full moon doth the cinders of the element, which show like pins' heads to her, believe not the word of the noble: therefore let me have right, and let desert mount.   61

Lan. Thine's too heavy to mount.
Fal. Let it shine, then.
Lan. Thine's too thick to shine.
Fal. Let it do something, my good lord, that may do me good, and call it what you will.

Lan. Is thy name Colevile?
Cole. It is, my lord.
Lan. A famous rebel art thou, Colevile.
Fal. And a famous true subject took him. 70
Cole. I am, my lord, but as my betters are
That led me hither: had they been ruled by me,
You should have won them dearer than you have.

Fal. I know not how they sold themselves: but thou, like a kind fellow, gavest thyself away gratis; and I thank thee for thee.

Re-enter WESTMORELAND.

Lan. Now, have you left pursuit?
West. Retreat is made and execution stay'd.
Lan. Send Colevile with his confederates
To York, to present execution: 80

23 *indifferency.* Moderate size.

39 *foundered.* Lamed.

40 *posts.* i.e. post horses.

52 *particular ballad.* Broadside proclaiming his exploits.

58 *cinders of the element.* Stars.

Falstaff (Brewster Mason) and Lancaster (Charles Dance), Royal Shakespeare Co, 1975

80 *present.* Immediate.

89 *Stand my good lord.* Be my patron.

90 *in my condition.* i.e. as your commanding officer.

100 *green-sickness.* Form of anaemia, usually found in girls.

101 *get.* Beget.

104 *sherris-sack.* Sherry.

Falstaff: 'A good sherris-sack hath a two-fold operation in it'. Tavern drawer with jug and glass of sack. Woodcut from a 17th century ballad

107 *forgetive.* Inventive.

Blunt, lead him hence; and see you guard him sure.
    [Exeunt Blunt and others with Colevile.
And now dispatch we toward the court, my lords:
I hear the king my father is sore sick:
Our news shall go before us to his majesty,
Which, cousin, you shall bear to comfort him,
And we with sober speed will follow you.
    Fal. My lord, I beseech you, give me leave to go
Through Gloucestershire: and, when you come to court,
Stand my good lord, pray, in your good report.
    Lan. Fare you well, Falstaff: I, in my condition,
                        90
Shall better speak of you than you deserve.
    [Exeunt all but Falstaff.
    Fal. I would you had but the wit: 'twere better than your dukedom. Good faith, this same young sober-blooded boy doth not love me; nor a man cannot make him laugh; but that's no marvel, he drinks no wine. There's never none of these demure boys come to any proof; for thin drink doth so over-cool their blood, and making many fish-meals, that they fall into a kind of male green-sickness; and then, when they marry, they get wenches: they are generally fools and cowards; which some of us should be too, but for inflammation. A good sherris-sack hath a two-fold operation in it. It ascends me into the brain; dries me there all the foolish and dull and crudy vapours which environ it; makes it apprehensive, quick, forgetive, full of nimble fiery and delectable shapes; which, delivered o'er to the voice, the tongue, which is the birth, becomes excellent wit. The second property of your excellent sherris is, the warming of the blood; which, before cold and settled, left the liver white and pale, which is the badge of pusillanimity and cowardice; but the sherris warms it and makes it course from the inwards to the parts extreme: it illumineth the face, which as a beacon gives warning to all the rest of this little kingdom, man, to arm; and then the vital commoners and inland petty spirits muster me all to their captain, the heart, who, great and puffed up with this retinue, doth any deed of courage; and this valour comes of sherris. So that skill in the weapon is nothing without sack, for that sets it a-work; and learning a mere hoard of gold kept by a devil, till sack commences it and sets it in act and use. Hereof comes it that Prince Harry is valiant; for the cold blood he did naturally inherit of his father, he hath, like lean, sterile and bare land, manured, husbanded and tilled with excellent endeavour of drinking good and good store of fertile sherris, that he is become very hot and valiant. If I had a thousand sons, the first humane principle I would teach them should be, to forswear thin potations and to addict themselves to sack.

Enter BARDOLPH.

How now, Bardolph?
    Bard. The army is discharged all and gone.
    Fal. Let them go. I'll through Gloucestershire; and there will I visit Master Robert Shallow, esquire: I have him already tempering

between my finger and my thumb, and shortly
will I seal with him.   Come away.   [*Exeunt.*

SCENE IV. *Westminster.   The Jerusalem
Chamber.*

Enter the KING, *the* PRINCES THOMAS OF
CLARENCE *and* HUMPHREY OF GLOUCESTER,
WARWICK, *and others.*

King.   Now, lords, if God doth give success-
ful end
To this debate that bleedeth at our doors,
We will our youth lead on to higher fields
And draw no swords but what are sanctified.
● Our navy is address'd, our power collected,
Our substitutes in absence well invested,
And every thing lies level to our wish:
Only, we want a little personal strength;
And pause us, till these rebels, now afoot,
Come underneath the yoke of government.   10
War.   Both which we doubt not but your
majesty
Shall soon enjoy.
King.   Humphrey, my son of Gloucester,
Where is the prince your brother?
Glou.   I think he's gone to hunt, my lord, at
Windsor.
King.   And how accompanied?
Glou.   I do not know, my lord.
King.   Is not his brother, Thomas of Clarence,
with him?
Glou.   No, my good lord; he is in presence here.
Clar.   What would my lord and father?
King.   Nothing but well to thee, Thomas of
Clarence.
How chance thou art not with the prince thy
brother?   20
He loves thee, and thou dost neglect him, Thomas;
Thou hast a better place in his affection
Than all thy brothers: cherish it, my boy,
And noble offices thou mayst effect
Of mediation, after I am dead,
Between his greatness and thy other brethren:
Therefore omit him not; blunt not his love,
Nor lose the good advantage of his grace
By seeming cold or careless of his will;
For he is gracious, if he be observed: 30
He hath a tear for pity and a hand
Open as day for melting charity:
Yet notwithstanding, being incensed, he's flint,
As humorous as winter and as sudden
● As flaws congealed in the spring of day.
His temper, therefore, must be well observed:
Chide him for faults, and do it reverently,
When you perceive his blood inclined to mirth;
But, being moody, give him line and scope,
Till that his passions, like a whale on ground, 40
Confound themselves with working.   Learn this,
Thomas,
And thou shalt prove a shelter to thy friends,
A hoop of gold to bind thy brothers in,
That the united vessel of their blood,
● Mingled with venom of suggestion—
As, force perforce, the age will pour it in—
Shall never leak, though it do work as strong
● As aconitum or rash gunpowder.
Clar.   I shall observe him with all care and love.
King.   Why art thou not at Windsor with him,
Thomas?   50

Set for the Jerusalem Chamber by Tanya Moisewitch,
Stratford-upon-Avon, 1951

---

5 *address'd.* Ready.

35 *flaws congealed.* Snowflakes.

45 *suggestion.* False insinuation.

48 *aconitum.* Monkshood, a poisonous plant.

66 *opposed decay*. Likely ruin.

77 *mete*. Measure.

79–80 *'Tis seldom . . . dead carrion*. Rarely does the bee leave her honey after building her comb in a carcass.

Costume design for Harcourt by Tanya Moisewitch, Stratford-upon-Avon, 1951

Clar. He is not there to-day; he dines in London.
King. And how accompanied? canst thou tell that?
Clar. With Poins, and other his continual followers.
King. Most subject is the fattest soil to weeds;
And he, the noble image of my youth,
Is overspread with them: therefore my grief
Stretches itself beyond the hour of death:
The blood weeps from my heart when I do shape
In forms imaginary the unguided days
And rotten times that you shall look upon   60
When I am sleeping with my ancestors.
For when his headstrong riot hath no curb,
When rage and hot blood are his counsellors,
When means and lavish manners meet together,
O, with what wings shall his affections fly
• Towards fronting peril and opposed decay!
    War. My gracious lord, you look beyond him quite:
The prince but studies his companions
Like a strange tongue, wherein, to gain the language,
'Tis needful that the most immodest word   70
Be look'd upon and learn'd; which once attain'd,
Your highness knows, comes to no further use
But to be known and hated. So, like gross terms,
The prince will in the perfectness of time
Cast off his followers; and their memory
Shall as a pattern or a measure live,
• By which his grace must mete the lives of others,
Turning past evils to advantages.
•   *King.* 'Tis seldom when the bee doth leave her comb
In the dead carrion.

        Enter WESTMORELAND.

           Who's here? Westmoreland? 80
West.   Health to my sovereign, and new happiness
Added to that that I am to deliver!
Prince John your son doth kiss your grace's hand:
Mowbray, the Bishop Scroop, Hastings and all
Are brought to the correction of your law;
There is not now a rebel's sword unsheathed,
But Peace puts forth her olive every where.
The manner how this action hath been borne
Here at more leisure may your highness read,
With every course in his particular.   90
    King. O Westmoreland, thou art a summer bird,
Which ever in the haunch of winter sings
The lifting up of day.

        Enter HARCOURT.

           Look, here's more news.
Har. From enemies heaven keep your majesty;
And, when they stand against you, may they fall
As those that I am come to tell you of!
The Earl Northumberland and the Lord Bardolph,
With a great power of English and of Scots,
Are by the sheriff of Yorkshire overthrown:
The manner and true order of the fight   100
This packet, please it you, contains at large.
    King. And wherefore should these good news make me sick?
Will Fortune never come with both hands full,
But write her fair words still in foulest letters?

She either gives a stomach and no food;
Such are the poor, in health; or else a feast
And takes away the stomach; such are the rich,
That have abundance and enjoy it not.
I should rejoice now at this happy news;
And now my sight fails, and my brain is giddy:
O me! come near me; now I am much ill.   111
　Glou. Comfort, your majesty!
　Clar.　　　　　　　　　　　O my royal father!
　West. My sovereign lord, cheer up yourself,
　　look up.
　War. Be patient, princes; you do know, these
　　fits
Are with his highness very ordinary.
Stand from him, give him air; he'll straight be
　well.
　Clar. No, no, he cannot long hold out these
　　pangs:
The incessant care and labour of his mind
● Hath wrought the mure that should confine it in
So thin that life looks through and will break out.
　Glou. The people fear me; for they do observe
● Unfather'd heirs and loathly births of nature:
The seasons change their manners, as the year
Had found some months asleep and leap'd them
　over.
　Clar. The river hath thrice flow'd, no ebb
　　between;
And the old folk, time's doting chronicles,
Say it did so a little time before
That our great-grandsire, Edward, sick'd and died.
　War. Speak lower, princes, for the king re-
　　covers.
　Glou. This apoplexy will certain be his end. 130
　King. I pray you, take me up, and bear me
　　hence
Into some other chamber: softly, pray. [*Exeunt.*

SCENE V. *Another chamber.*

The KING *lying on a bed*: CLARENCE, GLOUCES-
TER, WARWICK, *and others in attendance.*

　King. Let there be no noise made, my gentle
　　friends;
Unless some dull and favourable hand
Will whisper music to my weary spirit.
　War. Call for the music in the other room.
　King. Set me the crown upon my pillow here.
　Clar. His eye is hollow, and he changes much.
　War. Less noise, less noise!

Enter PRINCE HENRY

　Prince.　　　　　Who saw the Duke of Clarence?
　Clar. I am here, brother, full of heaviness.
　Prince. How now! rain within doors, and
　　none abroad!
How doth the king?   10
　Glou. Exceeding ill.
　Prince.　　　　　Heard he the good news yet?
Tell it him.
　Glou. He alter'd much upon the hearing it.
　Prince. If he be sick with joy, he'll recover
without physic.
　War. Not so much noise, my lords: sweet
　　prince, speak low;
The king your father is disposed to sleep.
　Clar. Let us withdraw into the other room.

119 *wrought the mure.* Made the wall.

122 *Unfather'd heirs.* Supernatural conceptions. *loathly births of nature.* Monstrous offspring.

Costume design for Gloucester by Tanya Moisewitch,
Stratford-upon-Avon, 1951

27 *biggen.* Nightcap.

36 *rigol.* Circle.

Prince: 'My due from thee is this imperial crown'.
Prince (Robert Donat) and the King (Abraham Sofaer)
Old Vic Theatre, London, 1935

War. Will't please your grace to go along
    with us?
  Prince. No; I will sit and watch here by the
    king.   [*Exeunt all but the Prince.* 20
Why doth the crown lie there upon his pillow,
Being so troublesome a bedfellow?
O polish'd perturbation! golden care!
That keep'st the ports of slumber open wide
To many a watchful night! sleep with it now!
Yet not so sound and half so deeply sweet
● As he whose brow with homely biggen bound
Snores out the watch of night. O majesty!
When thou dost pinch thy bearer, thou dost sit
Like a rich armour worn in heat of day,   30
That scalds with safety. By his gates of breath
There lies a downy feather which stirs not:
Did he suspire, that light and weightless down
Perforce must move. My gracious lord! my
    father!
This sleep is sound indeed; this is a sleep
● That from this golden rigol hath divorced
So many English kings. Thy due from me
Is tears and heavy sorrows of the blood,
Which nature, love, and filial tenderness,
Shall, O dear father, pay thee plenteously: 40
My due from thee is this imperial crown,
Which, as immediate from thy place and blood,
Derives itself to me. Lo, here it sits,
Which God shall guard: and put the world's
    whole strength
Into one giant arm, it shall not force
This lineal honour from me: this from thee
Will I to mine leave, as 'tis left to me.   [*Exit.*
  King. Warwick! Gloucester! Clarence!

Re-enter WARWICK, GLOUCESTER, CLARENCE,
    and the rest.

  Clar. Doth the king call?
  War. What would your majesty? How fares
    your grace?   50
  King. Why did you leave me here alone, my
    lords?
  Clar. We left the prince my brother here, my
    liege,
Who undertook to sit and watch by you.
  King. The Prince of Wales! Where is he?
    let me see him:
He is not here.
  War. This door is open; he is gone this way.
  Glou. He came not through the chamber
    where we stay'd.
  King. Where is the crown? who took it from
    my pillow?
  War. When we withdrew, my liege, we left
    it here.
  King. The prince hath ta'en it hence: go,
    seek him out.   60
Is he so hasty that he doth suppose
My sleep my death?
Find him, my Lord of Warwick; chide him
    hither.   [*Exit Warwick.*
This part of his conjoins with my disease,
And helps to end me. See, sons, what things
    you are!
How quickly nature falls into revolt
When gold becomes her object!
For this the foolish over-careful fathers
Have broke their sleep with thoughts, their
    brains with care,

Opposite: Richard Burton as Prince Hal and Harry
Andrews as Henry IV, Stratford-upon-Avon, 1951

79–80 *This bitter . . . engrossments.* All his labours bring nothing but this bitter taste.

104 *seal'd up.* Confirmed.

King: 'Harry the Fifth is crown'd: up, vanity!' Engraving from Bell's edition of *Shakespeare*, 1773–4

Their bones with industry; 70
For this they have engross'd and piled up
The canker'd heaps of strange-achieved gold;
For this they have been thoughtful to invest
Their sons with arts and martial exercises:
When, like the bee, culling from every flower
The virtuous sweets,
Our thighs pack'd with wax, our mouths with honey,
We bring it to the hive, and, like the bees,
● Are murdered for our pains.   This bitter taste
Yield his engrossments to the ending father. 80

    Re-enter WARWICK.

Now, where is he that will not stay so long
Till his friend sickness hath determined me?
  War.   My lord, I found the prince in the next room,
Washing with kindly tears his gentle cheeks,
With such a deep demeanour in great sorrow
That tyranny, which never quaff'd but blood,
Would, by beholding him, have wash'd his knife
With gentle eye-drops.   He is coming hither.
  King.   But wherefore did he take away the crown?

    Re-enter PRINCE HENRY.

Lo, where he comes.   Come hither to me, Harry.
Depart the chamber, leave us here alone. 91
        [*Exeunt Warwick and the rest.*
  Prince.   I never thought to hear you speak again.
  King.   Thy wish was father, Harry, to that thought:
I stay too long by thee, I weary thee.
Dost thou so hunger for mine empty chair
That thou wilt needs invest thee with my honours
Before thy hour be ripe?   O foolish youth!
Thou seek'st the greatness that will overwhelm thee.
Stay but a little; for my cloud of dignity
Is held from falling with so weak a wind 100
That it will quickly drop: my day is dim.
Thou hast stolen that which after some few hours
Were thine without offence; and at my death
● Thou hast seal'd up my expectation:
Thy life did manifest thou lovedst me not,
And thou wilt have me die assured of it.
Thou hidest a thousand daggers in thy thoughts,
Which thou hast whetted on thy stony heart,
To stab at half an hour of my life. 109
What! canst thou not forbear me half an hour?
Then get thee gone and dig my grave thyself,
And bid the merry bells ring to thine ear
That thou art crowned, not that I am dead.
Let all the tears that should bedew my hearse
Be drops of balm to sanctify thy head:
Only compound me with forgotten dust;
Give that which gave thee life unto the worms.
Pluck down my officers, break my decrees;
For now a time is come to mock at form:
Harry the Fifth is crown'd: up, vanity! 120
Down, royal state! all you sage counsellors, hence!
And to the English court assemble now,
From every region, apes of idleness!
Now, neighbour confines, purge you of your scum:

Have you a ruffian that will swear, drink, dance,
Revel the night, rob, murder, and commit
The oldest sins the newest kind of ways?
Be happy, he will trouble you no more;
England shall double gild his treble guilt, 130
England shall give him office, honour, might;
For the fifth Harry from curb'd license plucks
The muzzle of restraint, and the wild dog
Shall flesh his tooth on every innocent.
O my poor kingdom, sick with civil blows!
When that my care could not withhold thy riots,
What wilt thou do when riot is thy care?
O, thou wilt be a wilderness again,
Peopled with wolves, thy old inhabitants!
   Prince. O, pardon me, my liege! but for my
      tears,
The moist impediments unto my speech, 140
I had forestall'd this dear and deep rebuke
Ere you with grief had spoke and I had heard
The course of it so far. There is your crown;
And He that wears the crown immortally
Long guard it yours! If I affect it more
Than as your honour and as your renown,
Let me no more from this obedience rise,
Which my most inward true and duteous spirit
Teacheth, this prostrate and exterior bending.
God witness with me, when I here came in, 150
And found no course of breath within your ma-
      jesty,
How cold it struck my heart! If I do feign,
O, let me in my present wildness die
And never live to show the incredulous world
The noble change that I have purposed!
Coming to look on you, thinking you dead,
And dead almost, my liege, to think you were,
I spake unto this crown as having sense,
And thus upbraided it: 'The care on thee de-
      pending
Hath fed upon the body of my father; 160
Therefore, thou best of gold art worst of gold:
Other, less fine in carat, is more precious,
Preserving life in medicine potable;
But thou, most fine, most honour'd, most re-
      nown'd,
Hast eat thy bearer up.' Thus, my most royal
      liege,
Accusing it, I put it on my head,
To try with it, as with an enemy
That had before my face murder'd my father,
The quarrel of a true inheritor.
But if it did infect my blood with joy, 170
Or swell my thoughts to any strain of pride;
If any rebel or vain spirit of mine
Did with the least affection of a welcome
Give entertainment to the might of it,
Let God for ever keep it from my head
And make me as the poorest vassal is
That doth with awe and terror kneel to it!
   King. O my son,
God put it in thy mind to take it hence,
That thou mightst win the more thy father's
      love, 180
Pleading so wisely in excuse of it!
Come hither, Harry, sit thou by my bed;
And hear, I think, the very latest counsel
That ever I shall breathe. God knows, my son,
By what by-paths and indirect crook'd ways
I met this crown; and I myself know well
How troublesome it sat upon my head.

Prince: '... There is your crown; And He that wears the crown immortally Long guard it yours!' Drawing by J.M. Wright (1777–1866)

163 *medicine potable.* Gold in solution was often prescribed as medicine.

202 *successively.* By hereditary right.

204 *griefs are green.* Grievances are fresh.

To thee it shall descend with better quiet,
Better opinion, better confirmation;
For all the soil of the achievement goes   196
With me into the earth.   It seem'd in me
But as an honour snatch'd with boisterous hand,
And I had many living to upbraid
My gain of it by their assistances;
Which daily grew to quarrel and to bloodshed,
Wounding supposed peace: all these bold fears
Thou see'st with peril I have answered;
For all my reign hath been but as a scene
Acting that argument: and now my death
Changes the mode; for what in me was pur-
    chased,   200
Falls upon thee in a more fairer sort;
● So thou the garland wear'st successively.
Yet, though thou stand'st more sure than I
    could do,
● Thou art not firm enough, since griefs are green;
And all my friends, which thou must make thy
    friends,
Have but their stings and teeth newly ta'en out;
By whose fell working I was first advanced
And by whose power I well might lodge a fear
To be again displaced: which to avoid,
I cut them off; and had a purpose now   210
To lead out many to the Holy Land,
Lest rest and lying still might make them look
Too near unto my state.   Therefore, my Harry,
Be it thy course to busy giddy minds
With foreign quarrels; that action, hence borne
    out,
May waste the memory of the former days.
More would I, but my lungs are wasted so
That strength of speech is utterly denied me.
How I came by the crown, O God forgive;
And grant it may with thee in true peace live!
    Prince.   My gracious liege,   221
You won it, wore it, kept it, gave it me;
Then plain and right must my possession be:
Which I with more than with a common pain
'Gainst all the world will rightfully maintain.

      Enter LORD JOHN OF LANCASTER.

    King.   Look, look, here comes my John of
    Lancaster.
    Lan.   Health, peace, and happiness to my
    royal father!
    King.   Thou bring'st me happiness and peace,
    son John;
But health, alack, with youthful wings is flown
From this bare wither'd trunk: upon thy sight
My worldly business makes a period.   231
Where is my Lord of Warwick?
    Prince.   My Lord of Warwick!

      Re-enter WARWICK, *and others.*

    King.   Doth any name particular belong
Unto the lodging where I first did swoon?
    War.   'Tis call'd Jerusalem, my noble lord.
    King.   Laud be to God! even there my life
    must end.
It hath been prophesied to me many years,
I should not die but in Jerusalem;
Which vainly I supposed the Holy Land:
But bear me to that chamber; there I'll lie; 240
In that Jerusalem shall Harry die.   [*Exeunt.*

ACT V.

SCENE I. *Gloucestershire.* SHALLOW'S *house.*

Enter SHALLOW, FALSTAFF, BARDOLPH,
and Page.

● *Shal.* By cock and pie, sir, you shall not
away to-night. What, Davy, I say!
Fal. You must excuse me, Master Robert
Shallow.
Shal. I will not excuse you; you shall not be
excused; excuses shall not be admitted; there is
no excuse shall serve; you shall not be excused.
Why, Davy!

Enter DAVY.

Davy. Here, sir.   9
Shal. Davy, Davy, Davy, Davy, let me see,
Davy; let me see, Davy; let me see: yea, marry,
William cook, bid him come hither. Sir John,
you shall not be excused.
Davy. Marry, sir, thus; those precepts cannot be served: and, again, sir, shall we sow the
headland with wheat?
Shal. With red wheat, Davy. But for William
cook: are there no young pigeons?
Davy. Yes, sir. Here is now the smith's note
for shoeing and plough-irons.   20
Shal. Let it be cast and paid. Sir John, you
shall not be excused.
Davy. Now, sir, a new link to the bucket
must needs be had: and, sir, do you mean to stop
any of William's wages, about the sack he lost
the other day at Hinckley fair?
Shal. A' shall answer it. Some pigeons, Davy,
a couple of short-legged hens, a joint of mutton,
● and any pretty little tiny kickshaws, tell William
cook.   30
Davy. Doth the man of war stay all night,
sir?
Shal. Yea, Davy. I will use him well: a
friend i' the court is better than a penny in purse.
Use his men well, Davy; for they are arrant
knaves, and will backbite.
Davy. No worse than they are backbitten,
sir; for they have marvellous foul linen.
Shal. Well conceited, Davy: about thy busi-
ness, Davy.   40
● *Davy.* I beseech you, sir, to countenance
William Visor of Woncot against Clement Perkes
of the hill.
Shal. There is many complaints, Davy, against
that Visor: that Visor is an arrant knave, on my
knowledge.
Davy. I grant your worship that he is a knave,
sir; but yet, God forbid, sir, but a knave should
have some countenance at his friend's request.
An honest man, sir, is able to speak for himself,
when a knave is not. I have served your worship truly, sir, this eight years; and if I cannot
once or twice in a quarter bear out a knave against
an honest man, I have but a very little credit with
your worship. The knave is mine honest friend,
sir; therefore, I beseech your worship, let him be
countenanced.
Shal. Go to; I say he shall have no wrong.
Look about, Davy. [*Exit Davy.*] Where are
you, Sir John? Come, come, come, off with

Costume design for Shallow by Tanya Moisewitch,
Stratford-upon-Avon, 1951

---

1 *By cock and pie.* A mild oath.

29 *kickshaws.* Delicacies; trifles, from the French *quelque
chose.*

41 *countenance.* Favour.

72–73 *semblable coherence.* Similarity.

Falstaff: 'I will devise matter enough out of this Shallow to keep Prince Harry in continual laughter . . .' Hugh Griffith as Falstaff, Royal Shakespeare Co, 1964

90 *four terms.* i.e. a year. *actions.* Suits for recovery of debts.

91 *intervallums.* Interruptions.

95 *ill laid up.* Full of creases.

14 *heavy issue.* Sorrowing sons.

your boots. Give me your hand, Master Bardolph.
 Bard. I am glad to see your worship.
 Shal. I thank thee with all my heart, kind Master Bardolph: and welcome, my tall fellow [*to the Page*]. Come, Sir John.
 Fal. I'll follow you, good Master Robert Shallow. [*Exit Shallow.*] Bardolph, look to our horses. [*Exeunt Bardolph and Page.*] If I were sawed into quantities, I should make four dozen of such bearded hermits' staves as Master
• Shallow. It is a wonderful thing to see the semblable coherence of his men's spirits and his: they, by observing of him, do bear themselves like foolish justices; he, by conversing with them, is turned into a justice-like serving-man: their spirits are so married in conjunction with the participation of society that they flock together in consent, like so many wild-geese. If I had a suit to Master Shallow, I would humour his men with the imputation of being near their master: if to his men, I would curry with Master Shallow that no man could better command his servants. It is certain that either wise bearing or ignorant carriage is caught, as men take diseases, one of another: therefore let men take heed of their company. I will devise matter enough out of this Shallow to keep Prince Harry in continual laughter the wearing out of six fashions, which is
• four terms, or two actions, and a' shall laugh
• without intervallums. O, it is much that a lie with a slight oath and a jest with a sad brow will do with a fellow that never had the ache in his shoulders! O, you shall see him laugh till his
• face be like a wet cloak ill laid up!
 Shal. [*Within*] Sir John!
 Fal. I come, Master Shallow; I come, Master Shallow.   [*Exit.*

SCENE II. *Westminster. The palace.*

Enter WARWICK *and the* LORD CHIEF-JUSTICE, *meeting.*

 War. How now, my lord chief-justice! whither away?
 Ch. Just. How doth the king?
 War. Exceeding well; his cares are now all ended.
 Ch. Just. I hope, not dead.
 War.   He's walk'd the way of nature;
And to our purposes he lives no more.
 Ch. Just. I would his majesty had call'd me with him:
The service that I truly did his life
Hath left me open to all injuries.
 War. Indeed I think the young king loves you not.
 Ch. Just. I know he doth not, and do arm myself   10
To welcome the condition of the time,
Which cannot look more hideously upon me
Than I have drawn it in my fantasy.

Enter LANCASTER, CLARENCE, GLOUCESTER, WESTMORELAND, *and others.*

• *War.* Here come the heavy issue of dead Harry:
O that the living Harry had the temper
Of him, the worst of these three gentlemen!

How many nobles then should hold their places,
● That must strike sail to spirits of vile sort!
   Ch. Just. O God, I fear all will be over-
    turn'd!
   Lan. Good morrow, cousin Warwick, good
    morrow.   20
   Glou.⎱ Good morrow, cousin.
   Clar.⎰
   Lan. We meet like men that had forgot to
    speak.
   War. We do remember; but our argument
Is all too heavy to admit much talk.
   Lan. Well, peace be with him that hath made
    us heavy!
   Ch. Just. Peace be with us, lest we be
    heavier!
   Glou. O, good my lord, you have lost a friend
    indeed;
And I dare swear you borrow not that face
Of seeming sorrow, it is sure your own.
   Lan. Though no man be assured what grace
    to find,   30
You stand in coldest expectation:
I am the sorrier; would 'twere otherwise.
   Clar. Well, you must now speak Sir John
    Falstaff fair;
Which swims against your stream of quality.
   Ch. Just. Sweet princes, what I did, I did in
    honour,
Led by the impartial conduct of my soul:
● And never shall you see that I will beg
A ragged and forestall'd remission.
If truth and upright innocency fail me,
I'll to the king my master that is dead,   40
And tell him who hath sent me after him.
   War. Here comes the prince.

   Enter KING HENRY *the Fifth, attended.*

   Ch. Just. Good morrow; and God save your
    majesty!
   King. This new and gorgeous garment, ma-
    jesty,
Sits not so easy on me as you think.
Brothers, you mix your sadness with some fear:
This is the English, not the Turkish court;
● Not Amurath an Amurath succeeds,
But Harry Harry. Yet be sad, good brothers,
For, by my faith, it very well becomes you: 50
Sorrow so royally in you appears
That I will deeply put the fashion on
And wear it in my heart: why then, be sad;
But entertain no more of it, good brothers,
Than a joint burden laid upon us all.
For me, by heaven, I bid you be assured,
I'll be your father and your brother too;
Let me but bear your love, I'll bear your cares:
Yet weep that Harry's dead; and so will I;
But Harry lives, that shall convert those tears   60
By number into hours of happiness.
   Princes. We hope no other from your majesty.
● *King.* You all look strangely on me: and you
    most;
You are, I think, assured I love you not.
   Ch. Just. I am assured, if I be measured
    rightly,
Your majesty hath no just cause to hate me.
   King. No!
How might a prince of my great hopes forget
So great indignities you laid upon me?

Costume design for Warwick by Tanya Moisewitch,
Stratford-upon-Avon, 1951

18 *strike sail.* Submit themselves.

37–38 *beg . . . remission.* Beg for pardon like a ragged

48 *Amurath.* The Turkish sultan, Murad III, who,
when he succeeded to the throne in 1574, strangled his
five brothers.

63 *strangely.* Suspiciously.

Costume design for the new King Henry V by Tanya Moisewitch, Stratford-upon-Avon, 1951

---

71 *easy*. Insignificant.

72 *Lethe*. In classical mythology, the river of oblivion.

124 *affections*. i.e. his wild behaviour.

128–129 *writ me . . . seeming*. Judged me as they saw me.

What! rate, rebuke, and roughly send to prison
● The immediate heir of England! Was this easy?
● May this be wash'd in Lethe, and forgotten?
 Ch. Just. I then did use the person of your
  father;
The image of his power lay then in me:
And, in the administration of his law,
Whiles I was busy for the commonwealth,
Your highness pleased to forget my place,
The majesty and power of law and justice,
The image of the king whom I presented,
And struck me in my very seat of judgement; 80
Whereon, as an offender to your father,
I gave bold way to my authority
And did commit you. If the deed were ill,
Be you contented, wearing now the garland,
To have a son set your decrees at nought,
To pluck down justice from your awful bench,
To trip the course of law and blunt the sword
That guards the peace and safety of your person;
Nay, more, to spurn at your most royal image
And mock your workings in a second body. 90
Question your royal thoughts, make the case
  yours;
Be now the father and propose a son,
Hear your own dignity so much profaned,
See your most dreadful laws so loosely slighted,
Behold yourself so by a son disdain'd;
And then imagine me taking your part
And in your power soft silencing your son:
After this cold considerance, sentence me;
And, as you are a king, speak in your state
What I have done that misbecame my place, 100
My person, or my liege's sovereignty.
 King. You are right, justice, and you weigh
  this well:
Therefore still bear the balance and the sword:
And I do wish your honours may increase,
Till you do live to see a son of mine
Offend you and obey you, as I did.
So shall I live to speak my father's words:
'Happy am I, that have a man so bold,
That dares do justice on my proper son;
And not less happy, having such a son, 110
That would deliver up his greatness so
Into the hands of justice.' You did commit me:
For which, I do commit into your hand
The unstained sword that you have used to bear;
With this remembrance, that you use the same
With the like bold, just and impartial spirit
As you have done 'gainst me. There is my hand.
You shall be as a father to my youth:
My voice shall sound as you do prompt mine ear,
And I will stoop and humble my intents 120
To your well-practised wise directions.
And, princes all, believe me, I beseech you;
My father is gone wild into his grave,
● For in his tomb lie my affections;
And with his spirit sadly I survive,
To mock the expectation of the world,
To frustrate prophecies and to raze out
● Rotten opinion, who hath writ me down
After my seeming. The tide of blood in me
Hath proudly flow'd in vanity till now: 130
Now doth it turn and ebb back to the sea,
Where it shall mingle with the state of floods
And flow henceforth in formal majesty.
Now call we our high court of parliament:
And let us choose such limbs of noble counsel,

That the great body of our state may go
In equal rank with the best govern'd nation;
That war, or peace, or both at once, may be
As things acquainted and familiar to us;
• In which you, father, shall have foremost hand.
• Our coronation done, we will accite,   141
• As I before remember'd, all our state:
And, God consigning to my good intents,
No prince nor peer shall have just cause to say,
God shorten Harry's happy life one day!

                              [*Exeunt.*

SCENE III. *Gloucestershire.* SHALLOW'S
orchard.

Enter FALSTAFF, SHALLOW, SILENCE, DAVY,
BARDOLPH, *and the* Page.

  Shal. Nay, you shall see my orchard, where,
in an arbour, we will eat a last year's pippin
• of my own graffing, with a dish of caraways,
and so forth: come, cousin Silence: and then
to bed.
  Fal. 'Fore God, you have here a goodly
dwelling and a rich.
  Shal. Barren, barren, barren; beggars all,
• beggars all, Sir John: marry, good air. Spread,
Davy; spread, Davy: well said, Davy.   10
  Fal. This Davy serves you for good uses; he
is your serving-man and your husband.
  Shal. A good varlet, a good varlet, a very
good varlet, Sir John: by the mass, I have
drunk too much sack at supper: a good varlet.
Now sit down, now sit down: come, cousin.
  Sil. Ah, sirrah! quoth-a, we shall
  Do nothing but eat, and make good cheer,
                       [*Singing.*
  And praise God for the merry year;
  When flesh is cheap and females dear,   20
  And lusty lads roam here and there
      So merrily,
  And ever among so merrily.
  Fal. There's a merry heart! Good Master
Silence, I'll give you a health for that anon.
  Shal. Give Master Bardolph some wine,
Davy.
  Davy. Sweet sir, sit; I'll be with you anon;
most sweet sir, sit. Master page, good master
• page, sit. Proface! What you want in meat,
we'll have in drink: but you must bear; the
heart's all.   [*Exit.*
  Shal. Be merry, Master Bardolph; and, my
little soldier there, be merry.
  Sil. Be merry, be merry, my wife has all;
                       [*Singing.*
  For women are shrews, both short and tall:
  'Tis merry in hall when beards wag all,
    And welcome merry Shrove-tide.
  Be merry, be merry.
  Fal. I did not think Master Silence had been
a man of this mettle.   41
  Sil. Who, I? I have been merry twice and
once ere now.

           Re-enter DAVY.

•   *Davy.* There's a dish of leather-coats for you.
                   [*To Bardolph.*
  Shal. Davy!

141 *accite.* Summon.

142 *remember'd.* Mentioned.

Shallow: 'Nay, you shall see my orchard, where, in an arbour, we will eat a last year's pippin . . .' A garden repast. Woodcut from Didymus Mountain's *The Gardener's Labyrinth,* 1577

2 *pippin.* A type of apple.

3 *graffing.* Grafting.

9 *Spread.* Lay the table.

30 *Proface.* Term of welcome to a guest, meaning 'may it do you good'.

44 *leather-coats.* Type of apple.

49 *leman.* Sweetheart.

62 *cavaleros.* Gallants.

68 *pottle-pot.* Two quart tankard.

69 *liggens.* Unexplained. Perhaps 'legiance' for allegiance.

79 *Samingo.* Hero of the song.

Falstaff: 'How now, Pistol!' Scene in Shallow's orchard.
Drawing by J.M. Wright (1776–1866)

103 *foutre.* Coarse term of contempt, from the French.

Davy. Your worship! I'll be with you straight [*to Bardolph*]. A cup of wine, sir?
Sil. A cup of wine that's brisk and fine,
                                          [*Singing.*
          And drink unto the leman mine;
              And a merry heart lives long-a. 50
Fal. Well said, Master Silence.
Sil. An we shall be merry, now comes in the sweet o' the night.
Fal. Health and long life to you, Master Silence.
Sil. Fill the cup, and let it come; [*Singing.*
       I'll pledge you a mile to the bottom.
Shal. Honest Bardolph, welcome: if thou wantest any thing, and wilt not call, beshrew thy heart. Welcome, my little tiny thief [*to the Page*], and welcome indeed too. I'll drink to Master Bardolph, and to all the cavaleros about London.
Davy. I hope to see London once ere I die.
Bard. An I might see you there, Davy,—
Shal. By the mass, you'll crack a quart together, ha! will you not, Master Bardolph?
Bard. Yea, sir, in a pottle-pot.
Shal. By God's liggens, I thank thee: the knave will stick by thee, I can assure thee that. A' will not out; he is true bred. 71
Bard. And I'll stick by him, sir.
Shal. Why, there spoke a king. Lack nothing: be merry. [*Knocking within.*] Look who's at door there, ho! who knocks?
                                          [*Exit Davy.*
Fal. Why, now you have done me right.
       [*To Silence, seeing him take off a bumper.*
Sil.   Do me right,   [*Singing.*
          And dub me knight:
              Samingo.
Is't not so? 80
Fal. 'Tis so.
Sil. Is't so? Why then, say an old man can do somewhat.

Re-enter DAVY.

Davy. An't please your worship, there's one Pistol come from the court with news.
Fal. From the court! let him come in.

Enter PISTOL.

How now, Pistol!
Pist. Sir John, God save you!
Fal. What wind blew you hither, Pistol? 89
Pist. Not the ill wind which blows no man to good. Sweet knight, thou art now one of the greatest men in this realm.
Sil. By'r lady, I think a' be, but goodman Puff of Barson.
Pist. Puff!
Puff in thy teeth, most recreant coward base!
Sir John, I am thy Pistol and thy friend,
And helter-skelter have I rode to thee,
And tidings do I bring and lucky joys
And golden times and happy news of price. 100
Fal. I pray thee now, deliver them like a man of this world.
Pist. A foutre for the world and worldlings base!
I speak of Africa and golden joys.
Fal. O base Assyrian knight, what is thy news?

Let King Cophetua know the truth thereof.
Sil. And Robin Hood, Scarlet, and John.
[*Singing.*
Pist. Shall dunghill curs confront the Helicons?
And shall good news be baffled?
Then, Pistol, lay thy head in Furies' lap. 110
Shal. Honest gentleman, I know not your breeding.
Pist. Why then, lament therefore.
Shal. Give me pardon, sir: if, sir, you come with news from the court, I take it there's but two ways, either to utter them, or to conceal them. I am, sir, under the king, in some authority.
Pist. Under which king, Besonian? speak, or die.
Shal. Under King Harry.
Pist. Harry the Fourth? or Fifth?
Shal. Harry the Fourth.
Pist. A foutre for thine office! 121
Sir John, thy tender lambkin now is king;
Harry the Fifth's the man. I speak the truth:
When Pistol lies, do this; and fig me, like
The bragging Spaniard.
Fal. What, is the old king dead?
Pist. As nail in door: the things I speak are just.
Fal. Away, Bardolph! saddle my horse. Master Robert Shallow, choose what office thou wilt in the land, 'tis thine. Pistol, I will double-charge thee with dignities. 131
Bard. O joyful day!
I would not take a knighthood for my fortune.
Pist. What! I do bring good news.
Fal. Carry Master Silence to bed. Master Shallow, my Lord Shallow,—be what thou wilt; I am fortune's steward—get on thy boots: we'll ride all night. O sweet Pistol! Away, Bardolph! [*Exit Bard.*] Come, Pistol, utter more to me; and withal devise something to do thyself good. Boot, boot, Master Shallow: I know the young king is sick for me. Let us take any man's horses; the laws of England are at my commandment. Blessed are they that have been my friends; and woe to my lord chief-justice!
Pist. Let vultures vile seize on his lungs also!
'Where is the life that late I led?' say they:
Why, here it is; welcome these pleasant days!
[*Exeunt.*

SCENE IV. *London. A street.*

Enter Beadles, *dragging in* HOSTESS QUICKLY *and* DOLL TEARSHEET.

Host. No, thou arrant knave; I would to God that I might die, that I might have thee hanged: thou hast drawn my shoulder out of joint.
First Bead. The constables have delivered her over to me; and she shall have whipping-cheer enough, I warrant her: there hath been a man or two lately killed about her.
Dol. Nut-hook, nut-hook, you lie. Come on; I'll tell thee what, thou damned tripe-visaged rascal, an the child I now go with do miscarry, thou wert better thou hadst struck thy mother, thou paper-faced villain.
Host. O the Lord, that Sir John were come!

106 *King Cophetua*. Allusion to the ballad of King Cophetua and the Beggar Maid.

108 *Helicons*. The nine Muses, whose sacred mountain was Helicon, in Bœotia.

109 *baffled*. Disgraced.

119 *Besonian*. Scoundrel.

124 *fig*. Insult.

5–6 *whipping-cheer*. A whipping for supper.

Manner in which whipping was practised in Henry IV's time. Engraving by F.W. Fairholt from J.O. Halliwell's edition of Shakespeare's works, 1853–65

7 *about her*. On her account.

8 *Nut-hook*. Abusive term for police officer.

17 *cushions.* The beadle accuses Doll Tearsheet of using cushions to simulate pregnancy.

20—21 *thin man in a censer.* Embossed figure on the lid of an incense burner. *swinged.* Beaten.

22 *blue-bottle.* Beadles wore blue coats.

24 *half-kirtles.* Skirts.

Sybil Thorndike as Doll Tearsheet, New Theatre, London, 1946

33 *atomy.* Anatomy, skeleton.

30—31 *'semper idem', for 'obsque hoc nihil est'.* 'Always the same' for 'without this, nothing'.

36 *contagious.* Noxious.

38 *mechanical.* Menial.

he would make this a bloody day to somebody. But I pray God the fruit of her womb miscarry!
First Bead. If it do, you shall have a dozen of cushions again; you have but eleven now. Come, I charge you both go with me; for the man is dead that you and Pistol beat amongst you.
Dol. I'll tell you what, you thin man in a censer, I will have you as soundly swinged for this,—you blue-bottle rogue, you filthy famished correctioner, if you be not swinged, I'll forswear half-kirtles.
First Bead. Come, come, you she knight-errant, come.
Host. O God, that right should thus overcome might! Well, of sufferance comes ease.
Dol. Come, you rogue, come; bring me to a justice.
Host. Ay, come, you starved blood-hound. 30
Dol. Goodman death, goodman bones!
Host. Thou atomy, thou!
Dol. Come, you thin thing; come, you rascal.
First Bead. Very well.   [*Exeunt.*

SCENE V.   *A public place near Westminster Abbey.*

Enter two Grooms, *strewing rushes.*

First Groom. More rushes, more rushes.
Sec. Groom. The trumpets have sounded twice.
First Groom. 'Twill be two o'clock ere they come from the coronation: dispatch, dispatch.
[*Exeunt.*

Enter FALSTAFF, SHALLOW, PISTOL, BAR-
DOLPH, *and* Page.

Fal. Stand here by me, Master Robert Shallow; I will make the king do you grace: I will leer upon him as a' comes by; and do but mark the countenance that he will give me.
Pist. God bless thy lungs, good knight. 9
Fal. Come here, Pistol; stand behind me. O, if I had had time to have made new liveries, I would have bestowed the thousand pound I borrowed of you. But 'tis no matter; this poor show doth better: this doth infer the zeal I had to see him.
Shal. It doth so.
Fal. It shows my earnestness of affection,—
Shal. It doth so.
Fal. My devotion,—
Shal. It doth, it doth, it doth. 20
Fal. As it were, to ride day and night; and not to deliberate, not to remember, not to have patience to shift me,—
Shal. It is best, certain.
Fal. But to stand stained with travel, and sweating with desire to see him; thinking of nothing else, putting all affairs else in oblivion, as if there were nothing else to be done but to see him. 29
Pist. 'Tis 'semper idem,' for 'obsque hoc nihil est:' 'tis all in every part.
Shal. 'Tis so, indeed.
Pist. My knight, I will inflame thy noble liver, And make thee rage.
Thy Doll, and Helen of thy noble thoughts, Is in base durance and contagious prison; Haled thither
By most mechanical and dirty hand:

● Rouse up revenge from ebon den with fell Alecto's
    snake,   39
For Doll is in.   Pistol speaks nought but truth.
    Fal. I will deliver her.
        [*Shouts within, and the trumpets sound.*
    Pist. There roar'd the sea, and trumpet-clangor
    sounds.

Enter the KING *and his train, the* LORD CHIEF-
    JUSTICE *among them.*

    Fal. God save thy grace, King Hal! my royal
Hal!
    Pist.   The heavens thee guard and keep, most
royal imp of fame!
    Fal. God save thee, my sweet boy!
    King. My lord chief-justice, speak to that
vain man.
    Ch. Just. Have you your wits? know you what
    'tis you speak?
    Fal. My king! my Jove! I speak to thee, my
    heart!   50
    King. I know thee not, old man: fall to thy
    prayers;
How ill white hairs become a fool and jester!
I have long dream'd of such a kind of man,
So surfeit-swell'd, so old and so profane;
But, being awaked, I do despise my dream.
Make less thy body hence, and more thy grace;
Leave gormandizing; know the grave doth gape
For thee thrice wider than for other men.
Reply not to me with a fool-born jest:
Presume not that I am the thing I was;   60
For God doth know, so shall the world perceive,
That I have turn'd away my former self;
So will I those that kept me company.
When thou dost hear I am as I have been,
Approach me, and thou shalt be as thou wast,
The tutor and the feeder of my riots:
Till then, I banish thee, on pain of death,
As I have done the rest of my misleaders,
Not to come near our person by ten mile.
● For competence of life I will allow you,   70
That lack of means enforce you not to evil:
And, as we hear you do reform yourselves,
We will, according to your strengths and qualities,
Give you advancement.   Be it your charge, my
    lord,
To see perform'd the tenour of our word.
Set on.   [*Exeunt King, &c.*
    Fal. Master Shallow, I owe you a thousand
pound.
    Shal. Yea, marry, Sir John; which I beseech
you to let me have home with me.   80
    Fal. That can hardly be, Master Shallow.
Do not you grieve at this; I shall be sent for in
private to him: look you, he must seem thus to
the world: fear not your advancements; I will be
the man yet that shall make you great.
    Shal. I cannot well perceive how, unless you
should give me your doublet and stuff me out
with straw. I beseech you, good Sir John, let
me have five hundred of my thousand.
    Fal. Sir, I will be as good as my word: this
● that you heard was but a colour.   91
    Shal. A colour that I fear you will die in, Sir
John.
    Fal. Fear no colours: go with me to dinner:
come, Lieutenant Pistol; come, Bardolph: I shall
be sent for soon at night.

39 *ebon.* Black. *Alecto.* One of the Furies.

70 *competence of life.* Modest allowance.

Rejection of Falstaff. Drawing by J.A. Atkinson
(1775–*c.*1833)

91 *colour.* Pretence.

97 *Fleet.* London prison.

Costume design for Pistol by Tanya Moisewitch, Stratford-upon-Avon, 1951

13 *break.* Am bankrupt.

15–16 *bate me.* Relieve me (of some of my debts).

33 *Oldcastle.* Sir John Oldcastle, executed for treason in 1417. See introduction.

Opposite: Dancer. Engraving by Kenny Meadows from Barry Cornwall's *Works of Shakspere,* 1846

Re-enter PRINCE JOHN, *the* LORD CHIEF-JUSTICE; Officers *with them.*

●   *Ch. Just.*   Go, carry Sir John Falstaff to the Fleet:
Take all his company along with him.
   Fal.   My lord, my lord,—
   Ch. Just.   I cannot now speak: I will hear you soon.   100
Take them away.
   Pist.   Si fortuna me tormenta, spero contenta.
     [*Exeunt all but Prince John and the Chief-Justice.*
   Lan.   I like this fair proceeding of the king's:
He hath intent his wonted followers
Shall all be very well provided for;
But all are banish'd till their conversations
Appear more wise and modest to the world.
   Ch. Just.   And so they are.
   Lan.   The king hath call'd his parliament, my lord.
   Ch. Just.   He hath.   110
   Lan.   I will lay odds that, ere this year expire,
We bear our civil swords and native fire
As far as France: I heard a bird so sing,
Whose music, to my thinking, pleased the king.
Come, will you hence?   [*Exeunt.*

EPILOGUE.

Spoken by a Dancer.

First my fear; then my courtesy; last my speech. My fear is, your displeasure; my courtesy, my duty; and my speech, to beg your pardons. If you look for a good speech now, you undo me: for what I have to say is of mine own making; and what indeed I should say will, I doubt, prove mine own marring. But to the purpose, and so to the venture. Be it known to you, as it is very well, I was lately here in the end of a displeasing play, to pray your patience for it and to promise you a better. I meant indeed to pay you with this; which, if like an ill venture it
● come unluckily home, I break, and you, my gentle creditors, lose. Here I promised you I would be
● and here I commit my body to your mercies: bate me some and I will pay you some and, as most debtors do, promise you infinitely.

If my tongue cannot entreat you to acquit me, will you command me to use my legs? and yet that were but light payment, to dance out of your debt. But a good conscience will make any possible satisfaction, and so would I. All the gentlewomen here have forgiven me: if the gentlemen will not, then the gentlemen do not agree with the gentlewomen, which was never seen before in such an assembly.

One word more, I beseech you. If you be not too much cloyed with fat meat, our humble author will continue the story, with Sir John in it, and make you merry with fair Katharine of France: where, for any thing I know, Falstaff shall die of a sweat, unless already a' be killed with your hard
● opinions; for Oldcastle died a martyr, and this is not the man. My tongue is weary; when my legs are too, I will bid you good night: and so kneel down before you; but, indeed, to pray for the queen.

EPILOGUE,

Spoken by a Dancer.

King Henry V

1599

Henry V, who reigned 1413–22

KING HENRY V is different again from its predecessors, *1* and *2 Henry IV*, as those were from what went before: we see what variety Shakespeare achieved in the rather confined *genre* of the history-play. For in this kind his imagination had to work within a given framework, and accept the limitations of events, whatever liberties he took with chronology to give his material better dramatic shape.

With *Henry V* the dramatist is particularly conscious of the limitations, the difficulty of representing war on the stage, the crossing of the seas, siege and battlefield. He says as much, and introduces a new feature for the purpose: a Chorus, who speaks a Prologue to each act and ends the play with an Epilogue. These sound a particularly personal note, and were no doubt spoken by the actor-author himself. They help to give this play its individual character.

It has not the obvious dramatic issues of Henry IV's mortal struggles to gain and retain the crown, or the tension of his unhappy relationship with his son. Henry V is very much master in his own house, as his father prophesied he would be. Before setting out across the Channel for Agincourt he has the minor affair of the Cambridge-Scrope conspiracy to settle, but that serves mainly to link the action with what has gone before; later, in Henry's meditations, we are given a further link with Richard II. All the same, there *is* dramatic conflict – the war with France; this is given heroic emphasis by the smallness of the English army at Agincourt (the archers who wrought such havoc were Welsh), against the vastly superior forces of outdated, heavy French chivalry.

The subject of the play, then, is heroic valour, the achievement of a king who was a hero to the Elizabethans. Once more it answered to the mood of a small people proud and shrilly confident at the figure they were making in the world. in the conflict with the world-empire and resources of Spain. The year 1596 had seen the capture of Spain's Atlantic fortress of Cadiz – it was a famous victory: would Spaniards not have boasted if they had captured Plymouth?

Professor Dover Wilson says well that '*Henry V* is a play which men of action have been wont silently to admire, and literary men, at any rate during the last hundred and thirty years, volubly to contemn.' So much the worse for the literary men: it condemns them of lack of imagination, which they most stand in need of in their profession. Dover Wilson found that the play spoke for him, when he went abroad to serve his country in the small Expeditionary Force of 1914. Again on 6 June 1944, when the landing craft were nearing the coast of France, to liberate Europe, a Yorkshire captain – who fell in action – repeated to his men the words of Henry V before Agincourt. Those of us who remember D-day in 1944, and have not forgotten what those men died for, think of it still in those terms:

> This day is called the Feast of Crispian:
> He that outlives this day, and comes safe home,
> Will stand a-tiptoe when this day is named,
> And rouse him at the name of Crispian.
> He that shall see this day, and live old age,
> Will yearly on the vigil feast his neighbours,
> And say, 'Tomorrow is Saint Crispian.'

Chorus. The Chorus points the changing scenes of the action for us, but he also describes the theatre and gives us precious indications of what was going on in Shakespeare's own time.

> But pardon, gentles all –

a characteristic note with him –

> The flat unraisèd spirits that hath dared
> On this unworthy scaffold to bring forth
> So great an object. Can this cockpit hold
> The vasty fields of France? Or may we cram
> Within this wooden O the very casques
> That did affright the air at Agincourt?

The wooden O was the Globe Theatre which the Burbages had just erected on the South Bank of the Thames, taking the timbers of the old Theatre in Shoreditch, which had done such good service and given Shakespeare his opportunities earlier. Henceforth the Globe was to be the permanent home of the Company, indisputably the first now in London, the Admiral's taking second place. The audience were bidden to imagine the two monarchies confronting each other 'within the girdle of these walls', and to jump over the years contracted in the play:

> for the which supply,
> Admit me Chorus to this history,
> Who Prologue-like your humble patience pray,
> Gently to hear, kindly to judge, our play.

With that he left the stage.

At each appearance as Chorus he woos the audience – 'We'll not offend one stomach with our play'; next time – 'Still be kind, And eke out our performance with your mind.' Before the fourth Act we have:

> The armourers, accomplishing the knights,

(the very word 'accomplishing' is a Shakespeare signature)

> With busy hammers closing rivets up,
> Give dreadful note of preparation.

This was contemporary; for, in 1599, the largest English army that had ever been sent to Ireland was being prepared, under Essex, to retrieve the disaster of the Yellow Ford in Ulster the year before. The next Chorus describes the historic send-off the ever-popular Essex was given by the city, in similar terms to those of Simon Forman who watched it.

> How London doth pour out her citizens:
> The Mayor and all his brethren in best sort,
> Like to the senators of th'antique Rome,
> With the plebeians swarming at their heels,
> Go forth and fetch their conquering Caesar in.

Julius Caesar, his next play, was already shaping in that teeming mind. Then comes the reference to Essex, whom Southampton was accompanying to Ireland (to be cashiered by the Queen):

> As, by a lower but loving likelihood
> Were now the General of our gracious Empress –
> As in good time he may – from Ireland coming,
> Bringing rebellion broachèd on his sword,
> How many would the peaceful city quit
> To welcome him!

Helmet, shield and saddle of Henry V. Engraving from J.R. Green's A Short History of the English People, *Vol II, 1902*

The hopes placed on Essex were to be falsified: he made a fiasco in Ireland, and returned to ultimate ruin, very nearly bringing Southampton to the scaffold with him. The year is supposed to be that of Agincourt, 1415, but it is also 1599.

It used to be held that Shakespeare so 'transmuted' the events of his time that one could not recognise them in his work. We now know that this was nonsense: but it needs a proper knowledge of the time to be able to recognise them – in the Sonnets, as in the plays. Dr. Johnson was right: it would be quite contrary to a real writer not to incorporate his experience of life in his work.

Henry V as King. Dominant in the play is the development of Henry's character as king. A good critic has noted how much it deepens in the self-revelation before Agincourt, when facing the question of responsibility for the deaths of his fighting men. 'Every subject's duty is the King's, but every subject's soul is his own': Dr. Johnson thought this 'a very just distinction, and the whole argument is well followed and properly concluded.' We do not need to go into the tedious question of the rights and wrongs of the war, particularly in anachronistic terms of academic liberals – quite out of place – but merely point out that it was a renewal of the war, which had been only suspended by Richard II's truce and Henry IV's chronic difficulties; that Henry V, like all the Plantagenets, was more than half-French and his claim to the French throne was about as good as its occupant's. It was six of one side to half-a-dozen of the other. Henry was taking advantage of the divisions within France to advance what he considered his just claims. What is unhistorical is that Archbishop Chichele urged on the war to deflect an attack on the Church and its lands.

The Archbishop does mention Henry's conversion:

> The courses of his youth promised it not.
> The breath no sooner left his father's body
> But that his wildness, mortified in him,
> Seemed to die too.

This was historically true. It prepares us for the most moving passages of the play, the wonderful night-scene before Agincourt, when the King moves among his men disguised as a common soldier, argues the rights and wrongs of it all with another, Michael Williams, and then withdraws to have it out with himself and to pray before battle is joined. Williams is given a very fair argument for the ordinary man's point of view:

> But if the cause be not good, the King himself hath a heavy reckoning to make, when all those legs and arms and heads, chopped off in a battle, shall join together at the latter day and cry all, 'We died at such a place' . . . I am afeared there are few die well that die in a battle, for how can they charitably dispose of anything when blood is their argument? Now, if these men do not die well, it will be a black matter for the King that led them to it.

Henry carefully considers this from every angle in a convincing argument; the simple answer is that everybody is responsible for his own soul. But how about men's lives?

This is the subject of Henry's meditation when left alone by himself, and we are given the famous soliloquy:

> Upon the King! Let us our lives, our souls,
> Our debts, our careful wives,
> Our children, and our sins, lay on the King!
> We must bear all. O hard condition,
> Twin-born with greatness, subject to the breath
> Of every fool, whose sense no more can feel
> But his own wringing!

I fear that this betrays, as usual, Shakespeare's opinion of the average man – not very democratic, no humbug. But Shakespeare has no illusions either about kings (sc. political leaders, Presidents, what not).

> And what have kings that privates have not too,
> Save ceremony, save general ceremony?

This leads to a splendid oration on Ceremony – like that on Commodity in *King John*, or on Rumour in *2 Henry IV*, or Falstaff on Honour. Shakespeare sees through ceremony, as he saw through everything:

> Art thou aught else but place, degree, and form,
> Creating awe and fear in other men?

Not having had the advantage of a course in anthropology, Shakespeare hardly even allows ceremony the plea of social necessity. When, shortly before Charles I's execution,

Cromwellians ceased to kneel to him and kiss his hand, he observed that it was not material, only a matter of custom after all. But, notice, they did not fail to heap upon him as King the responsibility for the Civil War and kill him for it – a sacrificial victim. As, in a way, Richard II had been.

Contrasts. We are given, by the hand of a master, sufficient contrasts to vary and lighten the concentration upon the epic themes of the play. Falstaff's end is charmingly, and affectingly, reported: Mistress Quickly, in character, is able to tell us, 'Nay, sure, he's not in hell: he's in Arthur's bosom, if ever man went to Arthur's bosom', i.e. for Abraham's bosom. And that was well: it would never have done to have had *him* in the play, as Shakespeare had intended but saw to be quite impossible once he got to work on it. Falstaff's cronies go to France as camp-followers, behave as badly as might be expected, filching and stealing, and get their comeuppance. Pistol has quite a part, with his extraordinary, inflated rhodomontade: one wonders, rather, whether he was meant to be quite right in the head.

It is a funny scene where the gallant Welsh captain, Fluellen, makes him eat a leek for his bombastic insults. Fluellen is English for Llewelyn, since the English cannot pronounce the Welsh inflected 'll'. He is well informed about classic military discipline; this is thought to come from Dudley Digges's manual *Stratioticos* – quite likely, since Shakespeare knew the Digges family. The rendering of Welsh, Scotch and Irish accents we are given, with Captain Fluellen, Jamie, and MacMorris, are very effective and bespeak the mimetic observation of the actor, while the dramatist suggests their different national characteristics with skilled economy. Bardolph's trick of saying every now and then, 'And that's the humour of it', is obviously a joke for Ben Jonson, whose *Every Man in his Humour* Shakespeare had played in the year before.

Henry's love-scenes with Katherine of France (ancestress of the Tudors, by the way) have their own charm. They are in French, simple enough, and broken English. We know that Shakespeare could read French; no doubt he wrote these, with their grammatical solecisms, but he may have been helped by the French household in which he lodged in Silver Street, and was on terms of confidence with Madame Montjoie. We note that the French herald, who has a speaking part, is given the name of Montjoy. Henry's marriage with Katherine produced Henry VI, who inherited her father's neurotic imbecility; Henry V's triumph in France led to his early death and the long agony of the English extrusion from France, which ruined his son's reign and helped on the Wars of the Roses.

The wheel came full circle: things were as they were before. Such is political activity.

Background. We have noticed contemporary Elizabethan life showing through the texture of the play. Here are the Irish kerns again: 'you rode like a kern of Ireland, your French hose off, and in your strait strossers', i.e. bare-legged. Pistol is described, like another Parolles: 'a gull, a fool, a rogue, that now and then goes to the wars, to grace himself at his return into London under the form of a soldier. And such fellows are perfect in the great commanders' names, and they will learn you by rote where services were done: at such and such a sconce, at such a breach, at such a convoy; who came off bravely, who was shot, who disgraced, what terms the enemy stood on', etc. 'But you must learn to know such slanders of the age, or else you may be marvellously mistook.' Shakespeare knew such types about London: unlikely to be mistaken, he observed them for his own purpose.

Personal. Personal touches we note in Shakespeare's expert praise of the horse – it takes us back once more to the Sonnets and plodding away wearily from his friend and patron. Still more do we recognise him in the frequently expressed thought:

> There is some soul of goodness in things evil,
> Would men observingly distil it out . . .
> Thus may we gather honey from the weed.

Famous lines have entered into the consciousness of all who speak the language:

> Once more unto the breach, dear friends –

like Henry's father's,

> Uneasy lies the head that wears a crown.

We recognise the characteristic lordly words: crescive for growing, congreeted for met together, rivage for shore, legerity for quickness, etc. The caricature of the French and the anti-French sentiments were for the groundlings: we need not suppose that they speak for William Shakespeare.

The Epilogue takes the form of a sonnet, and we can see him delivering it, for he says, with the usual gentlemanly self-deprecation:

> Thus far, with rough and all-unable pen,
> Our bending author hath pursued the story.

Opportunity should always be taken in the theatre to present the Chorus as the actor-dramatist himself, politely bowing. He then refers to his *Henry VI* plays:

> Which oft our stage hath shown; and, for their sake,
> In your fair minds let this acceptance take.

Sources and Text. The main sources for the play were two: Holinshed, which Shakespeare had open before him for the first Act, since some of it, expounding Henry's claim to the French throne, is chronicle simply versified. The second was the anonymous play, *The Famous Victories of Henry the Fifth*, the form of which the busy actor-dramatist followed for convenience, as he had with *The Troublesome Reign* for *King John*.

The authoritative text in the First Folio is a good one, almost certainly from the author's manuscript. A poor quarto was printed in 1600, a shortened version put together by actors, perhaps for provincial performances. Occasionally a reading in this clarifies a dubious phrase – for example, the most famous emendation in Shakespeare: the Folio misprint, 'a Table of green fields', which the quarto reported as 'talk of flowers' – 'play with flowers' appears a line or two before. In the 18th century Theobald emended this to 'a babbled of green fields' – quite unnecessarily. Anyone familiar with Elizabethan script would recognise the correct reading to be simply, ''a talked of green fields'. As in mathematics, the simplest explanation is always best.

THE LIFE OF
KING HENRY THE FIFTH.

DRAMATIS PERSONÆ.

KING HENRY the Fifth.
DUKE OF GLOUCESTER,} brothers to the King.
DUKE OF BEDFORD,
DUKE OF EXETER, uncle to the King.
DUKE OF YORK, cousin to the King.
EARLS OF SALISBURY, WESTMORELAND, and
   WARWICK.
ARCHBISHOP OF CANTERBURY.
BISHOP OF ELY.
EARL OF CAMBRIDGE.
LORD SCROOP.
SIR THOMAS GREY.
SIR THOMAS ERPINGHAM, GOWER, FLUEL-
   LEN, MACMORRIS, JAMY, officers in King
   Henry's army.
BATES, COURT, WILLIAMS, soldiers in the
   same.
PISTOL, NYM, BARDOLPH.
Boy.
A Herald.

CHARLES the Sixth, King of France.
LEWIS, the Dauphin.
DUKES OF BURGUNDY, ORLEANS, and
   BOURBON.
The Constable of France.
RAMBURES and GRANDPRÉ, French Lords.
Governor of Harfleur.
MONTJOY, a French Herald.
Ambassadors to the King of England.

ISABEL, Queen of France.
KATHARINE, daughter to Charles and Isabel.
ALICE, a lady attending on her.
Hostess of a tavern in Eastcheap, formerly
   Mistress Quickly, and now married to
   Pistol.

Lords, Ladies, Officers, Soldiers, Citizens, Messengers, and Attendants.
          Chorus.

SCENE: *England; afterwards France.*

● *A bullet beside a text line indicates an annotation in the*
opposite column

PROLOGUE.

Enter Chorus.

Chor. O for a Muse of fire, that would ascend
The brightest heaven of invention,
A kingdom for a stage, princes to act
And monarchs to behold the swelling scene!
Then should the warlike Harry, like himself,
Assume the port of Mars; and at his heels,
Leash'd in like hounds, should famine, sword and
    fire
Crouch for employment. But pardon, gentles all,
● The flat unraised spirits that have dared
On this unworthy scaffold to bring forth   10
So great an object: can this cockpit hold
The vasty fields of France? or may we cram
Within this wooden O the very casques
That did affright the air at Agincourt?
O, pardon! since a crooked figure may
Attest in little place a million;
And let us, ciphers to this great accompt,
On your imaginary forces work.
Suppose within the girdle of these walls
Are now confined two mighty monarchies,   20
Whose high upreared and abutting fronts
The perilous narrow ocean parts asunder:
Piece out our imperfections with your thoughts;
Into a thousand parts divide one man,
And make imaginary puissance;
Think, when we talk of horses, that you see them
Printing their proud hoofs i' the receiving earth;
For 'tis your thoughts that now must deck our
    kings,
Carry them here and there; jumping o'er times,
Turning the accomplishment of many years   30

9–14 *The flat . . . Agincourt.* See introduction.

Opposite: The meeting between Henry V and the Queen
of France attended by her daughter Katherine. Painting
by William Kent (1685–1748)

Set design for Henry V by Tanya Moisewitch, Stratford-upon-Avon, 1951

31—34 *for the which . . . our play.* See introduction.

1 *self.* Same.

15 *lazars.* Lepers.

Into an hour-glass: for the which supply,
Admit me Chorus to this history;
Who prologue-like your humble patience pray,
Gently to hear, kindly to judge, our play. [*Exit.*

ACT I.

SCENE I. *London.   An ante-chamber in the*
KING'S palace.

Enter the ARCHBISHOP OF CANTERBURY, *and the*
BISHOP OF ELY.

Cant. My lord, I'll tell you; that self bill is
urged,
Which in the eleventh year of the last king's reign
Was like, and had indeed against us pass'd,
But that the scambling and unquiet time
Did push it out of farther question.
   Ely. But how, my lord, shall we resist it now?
   Cant. It must be thought on. If it pass
against us,
We lose the better half of our possession:
For all the temporal lands which men devout
By testament have given to the church   10
Would they strip from us; being valued thus:
As much as would maintain, to the king's honour,
Full fifteen earls and fifteen hundred knights,
Six thousand and two hundred good esquires;
And, to relief of lazars and weak age,
Of indigent faint souls past corporal toil,
A hundred almshouses right well supplied;
And to the coffers of the king beside,
A thousand pounds by the year: thus runs the bill.
   Ely.   This would drink deep.
   Cant.   'Twould drink the cup and all. 20

Ely. But what prevention?
Cant. The king is full of grace and fair regard.
Ely. And a true lover of the holy church.
● *Cant.* The courses of his youth promised it not.
The breath no sooner left his father's body,
But that his wildness, mortified in him,
Seem'd to die too; yea, at that very moment
Consideration, like an angel, came
● And whipp'd the offending Adam out of him,
Leaving his body as a paradise,   30
To envelope and contain celestial spirits.
Never was such a sudden scholar made;
Never came reformation in a flood,
With such a heady currance, scouring faults;
● Nor never Hydra-headed wilfulness
So soon did lose his seat and all at once
As in this king.   *Ely.* We are blessed in the change.
Cant. Hear him but reason in divinity,
And all-admiring with an inward wish
You would desire the king were made a prelate: 40
Hear him debate of commonwealth affairs,
You would say it hath been all in all his study:
List his discourse of war, and you shall hear
A fearful battle render'd you in music:
Turn him to any cause of policy,
● The Gordian knot of it he will unloose,
Familiar as his garter: that, when he speaks,
The air, a charter'd libertine, is still,
And the mute wonder lurketh in men's ears,
To steal his sweet and honey'd sentences;   50
So that the art and practic part of life
Must be the mistress to this theoric:
Which is a wonder how his grace should glean it,
Since his addiction was to courses vain,
His companies unletter'd, rude and shallow,
His hours fill'd up with riots, banquets, sports,
And never noted in him any study,
Any retirement, any sequestration
From open haunts and popularity.
    Ely. The strawberry grows underneath the
        nettle   60
And wholesome berries thrive and ripen best
Neighbour'd by fruit of baser quality:
And so the prince obscured his contemplation
Under the veil of wildness; which, no doubt,
Grew like the summer grass, fastest by night,
● Unseen, yet crescive in his faculty.
    Cant. It must be so; for miracles are ceased;
And therefore we must needs admit the means
How things are perfected.
    Ely.   But, my good lord,
How now for mitigation of this bill   70
Urged by the commons? Doth his majesty
Incline to it, or no?
    Cant.   He seems indifferent,
Or rather swaying more upon our part
Than cherishing the exhibiters against us;
For I have made an offer to his majesty,
Upon our spiritual convocation
And in regard of causes now in hand,
Which I have open'd to his grace at large,
As touching France, to give a greater sum
Than ever at one time the clergy yet   80
Did to his predecessors part withal.
    Ely. How did this offer seem received, my
        lord?
    Cant. With good acceptance of his majesty;
Save that there was not time enough to hear,

24—27 *The courses . . . die too.* See introduction.

29 *offending Adam.* Original wickedness.

35 *Hydra.* A mythical monster with many heads.

46 *Gordian knot.* A giant knot which, rather than unravel, Alexander cut with his sword; hence a complex problem.

66 *crescive in his faculty.* Growing through natural capacity.

Lewis Waller as Henry V, Lyceum Theatre, London, 1900. Painting by Arthur Hacker (1858–1919)

Costume design for the Duke of Warwick by Tanya Moisewitch, Stratford-upon-Avon, 1951

---

11 *law Salique.* In French law, females were excluded from inheriting the crown. Henry's claim was through his great-great-grandmother.

15 *nicely.* Sophistically.

16 *miscreate.* Illegitimate.

19 *approbation.* Proof.

As I perceived his grace would fain have done,
The severals and unhidden passages
Of his true titles to some certain dukedoms
And generally to the crown and seat of France
Derived from Edward, his great-grandfather.
 Ely. What was the impediment that broke
  this off?   90
 Cant. The French ambassador upon that
  instant
Craved audience; and the hour, I think, is come
To give him hearing: is it four o'clock?
 Ely. It is.
 Cant. Then go we in, to know his embassy;
Which I could with a ready guess declare,
Before the Frenchman speak a word of it.
 Ely. I'll wait upon you, and I long to hear it.
             [*Exeunt.*

SCENE II. *The same.* *The Presence chamber.*

Enter KING HENRY, GLOUCESTER, BEDFORD,
EXETER, WARWICK, WESTMORELAND, *and*
Attendants.

 K. Hen. Where is my gracious Lord of Can-
  terbury?
 Exe. Not here in presence.
 K. Hen.   Send for him, good uncle.
 West. Shall we call in the ambassador, my
  liege?
 K. Hen. Not yet, my cousin: we would be
  resolved,
Before we hear him, of some things of weight
That task our thoughts, concerning us and France.

Enter the ARCHBISHOP OF CANTERBURY, *and*
   the BISHOP OF ELY.

 Cant. God and his angels guard your sacred
  throne
And make you long become it!
 K. Hen.   Sure, we thank you.
My learned lord, we pray you to proceed
And justly and religiously unfold   10
• Why the law Salique that they have in France
Or should, or should not, bar us in our claim:
And God forbid, my dear and faithful lord,
That you should fashion, wrest, or bow your
  reading,
• Or nicely charge your understanding soul
• With opening titles miscreate, whose right
Suits not in native colours with the truth;
For God doth know how many now in health
• Shall drop their blood in approbation
Of what your reverence shall incite us to.   20
Therefore take heed how you impawn our person,
How you awake our sleeping sword of war:
We charge you, in the name of God, take heed;
For never two such kingdoms did contend
Without much fall of blood; whose guiltless drops
Are every one a woe, a sore complaint
'Gainst him whose wrongs give edge unto the
  swords
That make such waste in brief mortality.
Under this conjuration speak, my lord;
For we will hear, note and believe in heart   30
That what you speak is in your conscience wash'd
As pure as sin with baptism.
 Cant. Then hear me, gracious sovereign, and
  you peers,
That owe yourselves, your lives and services

To this imperial throne. There is no bar
To make against your highness' claim to France
● But this, which they produce from Pharamond,
'In terram Salicam mulieres ne succedant:'
'No woman shall succeed in Salique land:'
Which Salique land the French unjustly glose 40
To be the realm of France, and Pharamond
The founder of this law and female bar.
Yet their own authors faithfully affirm
That the land Salique is in Germany,
Between the floods of Sala and of Elbe;
Where Charles the Great, having subdued the
    Saxons,
There left behind and settled certain French;
Who, holding in disdain the German women
● For some dishonest manners of their life,
Establish'd then this law; to wit, no female 50
Should be inheritrix in Salique land:
Which Salique, as I said, 'twixt Elbe and Sala,
Is at this day in Germany call'd Meisen.
Then doth it well appear the Salique law
Was not devised for the realm of France:
Nor did the French possess the Salique land
Until four hundred one and twenty years
After defunction of King Pharamond,
Idly supposed the founder of this law;
Who died within the year of our redemption 60
Four hundred twenty-six; and Charles the Great
Subdued the Saxons, and did seat the French
Beyond the river Sala, in the year
Eight hundred five. Besides, their writers say,
King Pepin, which deposed Childeric,
Did, as heir general, being descended
Of Blithild, which was daughter to King Clothair,
Make claim and title to the crown of France.
Hugh Capet also, who usurp'd the crown 69
Of Charles the duke of Lorraine, sole heir male
Of the true line and stock of Charles the Great,
To find his title with some shows of truth,
Though, in pure truth, it was corrupt and naught,
● Convey'd himself as heir to the Lady Lingare,
● Daughter to Charlemain, who was the son
To Lewis the emperor, and Lewis the son
● Of Charles the Great. Also King Lewis the Tenth,
Who was sole heir to the usurper Capet,
Could not keep quiet in his conscience,
Wearing the crown of France, till satisfied 80
That fair Queen Isabel, his grandmother,
Was lineal of the Lady Ermengare,
Daughter to Charles the foresaid duke of Lorraine:
By the which marriage the line of Charles the
    Great
Was re-united to the crown of France.
So that, as clear as is the summer's sun,
King Pepin's title and Hugh Capet's claim,
King Lewis his satisfaction, all appear
To hold in right and title of the female:
So do the kings of France unto this day; 90
Howbeit they would hold up this Salique law
To bar your highness claiming from the female,
And rather choose to hide them in a net
● Than amply to imbar their crooked titles
Usurp'd from you and your progenitors.
    K. Hen. May I with right and conscience
        make this claim?
    Cant. The sin upon my head, dread sovereign!
For in the book of Numbers is it writ,
When the man dies, let the inheritance
Descend unto the daughter. Gracious lord, 100

37 *Pharamond.* A legendary king of the Franks.

49 *dishonest.* Unchaste.

Henry V. From John Speed's *Theatre of the Empire of Great Britaine,* 1611–12

74 *Convey'd himself.* Passed himself off.

75 *Charlemain.* In historic fact Charles the Bald.

77 *Lewis the Tenth.* Actually Lewis IX.

94 *amply to imbar.* Frankly lay bare.

106–114 *Who on . . . action.* The battle of Crecy, 1346.

The Battle of Crecy, where Edward III defeated the French. Engraving from *Old England*, 1854

137 *lay down our proportions.* Allocate our forces.

140 *marches.* Borders.

148 *unfurnish'd.* Undefended.

155 *fear'd.* Frightened.

161 *King of Scots.* David II, captured at Neville's Cross.

Stand for your own; unwind your bloody flag;
Look back into your mighty ancestors:
Go, my dread lord, to your great-grandsire's tomb,
From whom you claim; invoke his warlike spirit,
And your great-uncle's, Edward the Black Prince,
• Who on the French ground play'd a tragedy,
Making defeat on the full power of France,
Whiles his most mighty father on a hill
Stood smiling to behold his lion's whelp
Forage in blood of French nobility.   110
O noble English, that could entertain
With half their forces the full pride of France
And let another half stand laughing by,
All out of work and cold for action!
 Ely. Awake remembrance of these valiant dead
And with your puissant arm renew their feats:
You are their heir; you sit upon their throne;
The blood and courage that renowned them
Runs in your veins; and my thrice-puissant liege
Is in the very May-morn of his youth,   120
Ripe for exploits and mighty enterprises.
 Exe. Your brother kings and monarchs of the
  earth
Do all expect that you should rouse yourself,
As did the former lions of your blood.
 West. They know your grace hath cause and
  means and might;
So hath your highness; never king of England
Had nobles richer and more loyal subjects,
Whose hearts have left their bodies here in England
And lie pavilion'd in the fields of France.   129
 Cant. O, let their bodies follow, my dear liege,
With blood and sword and fire to win your right;
In aid whereof we of the spiritualty
Will raise your highness such a mighty sum
As never did the clergy at one time
Bring in to any of your ancestors.
 K. Hen. We must not only arm to invade the
  French,
• But lay down our proportions to defend
Against the Scot, who will make road upon us
With all advantages.
• *Cant.* They of those marches, gracious
  sovereign,   140
Shall be a wall sufficient to defend
Our inland from the pilfering borderers.
 K. Hen. We do not mean the coursing snatchers
  only,
But fear the main intendment of the Scot,
Who hath been still a giddy neighbour to us;
For you shall read that my great-grandfather
Never went with his forces into France
• But that the Scot on his unfurnish'd kingdom
Came pouring, like the tide into a breach,
With ample and brim fulness of his force,   150
Galling the gleaned land with hot assays,
Girding with grievous siege castles and towns;
That England, being empty of defence,
Hath shook and trembled at the ill neighbourhood.
• *Cant.* She hath been then more fear'd than
  harm'd, my liege;
For hear her but exampled by herself:
When all her chivalry hath been in France
And she a mourning widow of her nobles,
She hath herself not only well defended
But taken and impounded as a stray   160
• The King of Scots; whom she did send to France,
To fill King Edward's fame with prisoner kings
And make her chronicle as rich with praise

As is the ooze and bottom of the sea
With sunken wreck and sumless treasuries.
   West. But there's a saying very old and true,
     'If that you will France win,
      Then with Scotland first begin:'
For once the eagle England being in prey,
To her unguarded nest the weasel Scot   170
Comes sneaking and so sucks her princely eggs,
Playing the mouse in absence of the cat,
To tear and havoc more than she can eat.
   Exe. It follows then the cat must stay at home:
● Yet that is but a crush'd necessity,
Since we have locks to safeguard necessaries,
And pretty traps to catch the petty thieves.
While that the armed hand doth fight abroad,
● The advised head defends itself at home;
For government, though high and low and lower,
● Put into parts, doth keep in one consent,   181
● Congreeing in a full and natural close,
Like music.
   Cant.   Therefore doth heaven divide
The state of man in divers functions,
Setting endeavour in continual motion;
To which is fixed, as an aim or butt,
Obedience: for so work the honey-bees,
Creatures that by a rule in nature teach
The act of order to a peopled kingdom.
They have a king and officers of sorts;   190
Where some, like magistrates, correct at home,
Others, like merchants, venture trade abroad,
Others, like soldiers, armed in their stings,
● Make boot upon the summer's velvet buds,
Which pillage they with merry march bring
     home
To the tent-royal of their emperor;
Who, busied in his majesty, surveys
The singing masons building roofs of gold,
The civil citizens kneading up the honey,
The poor mechanic porters crowding in   200
Their heavy burdens at his narrow gate,
The sad-eyed justice, with his surly hum,
Delivering o'er to executors pale
The lazy yawning drone.   I this infer,
That many things, having full reference
To one consent, may work contrariously:
As many arrows, loosed several ways,
Come to one mark; as many ways meet in one
     town;
As many fresh streams meet in one salt sea;
As many lines close in the dial's centre;   210
So may a thousand actions, once afoot,
End in one purpose, and be all well borne
Without defeat.   Therefore to France, my liege.
Divide your happy England into four;
Whereof take you one quarter into France,
And you withal shall make all Gallia shake.
If we, with thrice such powers left at home,
Cannot defend our own doors from the dog,
Let us be worried and our nation lose
The name of hardiness and policy.   220
   K. Hen. Call in the messengers sent from the
     Dauphin.   [*Exeunt some Attendants.*
Now are we well resolved; and, by God's help,
And yours, the noble sinews of our power,
France being ours, we'll bend it to our awe,
Or break it all to pieces: or there we'll sit,
● Ruling in large and ample empery
O'er France and all her almost kingly dukedoms,
Or lay these bones in an unworthy urn,

175 *crush'd necessity.* Lessened need.

179 *advised.* Prudent.

181 *consent.* Harmony.

182 *close.* Cadence.

194 *boot.* Booty.

Costume design for the French ambassador, the Duke of Orleans, by Tanya Moisewitch, Stratford-upon-Avon, 1951

226 *empery.* Dominion.

233 *Not worshipp'd ... epitaph.* Without even an epitaph written on wax.

239 *sparingly.* In order not to offend.

252 *galliard.* A lively dance.

Courtiers dancing. Engraving from a painting of the mid-sixteenth century

264 *wrangler.* Opponent.

266 *chaces.* Points in court tennis.

267 *comes o'er.* Taunts.

A game of Tennis. Woodcut from Comenius' *Orbis Sensualium Pictus,* 1659

Tombless, with no remembrance over them:
Either our history shall with full mouth   230
Speak freely of our acts, or else our grave,
Like Turkish mute, shall have a tongueless mouth,
● Not worshipp'd with a waxen epitaph.

Enter Ambassadors *of France.*

Now are we well prepared to know the pleasure
Of our fair cousin Dauphin; for we hear
Your greeting is from him, not from the king.
    First Amb. May't please your majesty to give us leave
Freely to render what we have in charge;
● Or shall we sparingly show you far off
The Dauphin's meaning and our embassy?   240
    K. Hen. We are no tyrant, but a Christian king:
Unto whose grace our passion is as subject
As are our wretches fetter'd in our prisons:
Therefore with frank and with uncurbed plainness
Tell us the Dauphin's mind.
    First Amb.   Thus, then, in few.
Your highness, lately sending into France,
Did claim some certain dukedoms, in the right
Of your great predecessor, King Edward the Third.
In answer of which claim, the prince our master
Says that you savour too much of your youth,   250
And bids you be advised there's nought in France
● That can be with a nimble galliard won;
You cannot revel into dukedoms there.
He therefore sends you, meeter for your spirit,
This tun of treasure; and, in lieu of this,
Desires you let the dukedoms that you claim
Hear no more of you. This the Dauphin speaks.
    K. Hen. What treasure, uncle?
    Exe.   Tennis-balls, my liege.
    K. Hen. We are glad the Dauphin is so pleasant with us;
His present and your pains we thank you for: 260
When we have match'd our rackets to these balls,
We will, in France, by God's grace, play a set
Shall strike his father's crown into the hazard.
● Tell him he hath made a match with such a wrangler
That all the courts of France will be disturb'd
● With chaces. And we understand him well,
● How he comes o'er us with our wilder days,
Not measuring what use we made of them.
We never valued this poor seat of England;
And therefore, living hence, did give ourself   270
To barbarous license; as 'tis ever common
That men are merriest when they are from home.
But tell the Dauphin I will keep my state,
Be like a king and show my sail of greatness
When I do rouse me in my throne of France:
For that I have laid by my majesty
And plodded like a man for working-days,
But I will rise there with so full a glory
That I will dazzle all the eyes of France,
Yea, strike the Dauphin blind to look on us.   280
And tell the pleasant prince this mock of his
Hath turn'd his balls to gun-stones; and his soul
Shall stand sore charged for the wasteful vengeance
That shall fly with them: for many a thousand widows

Shall this his mock mock out of their dear hus-
    bands;
Mock mothers from their sons, mock castles down;
And some are yet ungotten and unborn
That shall have cause to curse the Dauphin's
    scorn.
But this lies all within the will of God,
To whom I do appeal; and in whose name   290
Tell you the Dauphin I am coming on,
To venge me as I may and to put forth
My rightful hand in a well-hallow'd cause.
So get you hence in peace; and tell the Dauphin
His jest will savour but of shallow wit,
When thousands weep more than did laugh at it.
Convey them with safe conduct.   Fare you well.
                    [*Exeunt Ambassadors.*
   Exe.   This was a merry message.
   K. Hen.   We hope to make the sender blush
    at it.
Therefore, my lords, omit no happy hour   300
That may give furtherance to our expedition;
For we have now no thought in us but France,
Save those to God, that run before our business.
Therefore let our proportions for these wars
Be soon collected and all things thought upon
That may with reasonable swiftness add
More feathers to our wings; for, God before,
We'll chide this Dauphin at his father's door.
Therefore let every man now task his thought,
That this fair action may on foot be brought. 310
                      [*Exeunt. Flourish.*

ACT II.

PROLOGUE.

Flourish. Enter Chorus.

   Chor.   Now all the youth of England are on
    fire,
And silken dalliance in the wardrobe lies:
Now thrive the armourers, and honour's thought
Reigns solely in the breast of every man:
They sell the pasture now to buy the horse,
Following the mirror of all Christian kings,
• With winged heels, as English Mercuries.
For now sits Expectation in the air,
And hides a sword from hilts unto the point
With crowns imperial, crowns and coronets,   10
Promised to Harry and his followers.
The French, advised by good intelligence
Of this most dreadful preparation,
Shake in their fear and with pale policy
Seek to divert the English purposes.
O England! model to thy inward greatness,
Like little body with a mighty heart,
• What mightst thou do, that honour would thee do,
Were all thy children kind and natural!
But see thy fault! France hath in thee found out
A nest of hollow bosoms, which he fills   21
With treacherous crowns; and three corrupted
    men,
One, Richard Earl of Cambridge, and the second,
Henry Lord Scroop of Masham, and the third,
Sir Thomas Grey, knight, of Northumberland,
Have, for the gilt of France,—O guilt indeed!—
Confirm'd conspiracy with fearful France;
And by their hands this grace of kings must die,
If hell and treason hold their promises,
Ere he take ship for France, and in Southampton.

Henry V arming for battle with the help of his squires.
Engraving from *Old England*, 1854

7 *Mercuries.* In mythology Mercury was the messenger
of the Gods.

18 *would thee.* Would have thee.

31–32 *we'll digest . . . distance.* Overcome the violation of unity of place.

3 *Ancient.* Ensign; lowest rank of officer.

8 *iron.* Slang for sword.

17 *rest.* Gambling term meaning 'to stake one's all'.

21 *troth-plight.* Betrothed.

31 *tike.* Cur.

44 *Iceland dog.* A curly-haired lap dog.

47 *shog.* Jog.

48 *solus.* Alone.

William Davidge, the Victorian actor, as Pistol, Coburg Theatre, London, 1830

● Linger your patience on; †and we'll digest   31
The abuse of distance; force a play:
The sum is paid; the traitors are agreed;
The king is set from London; and the scene
Is now transported, gentles, to Southampton;
There is the playhouse now, there must you sit:
And thence to France shall we convey you safe,
And bring you back, charming the narrow seas
To give you gentle pass; for, if we may,
We'll not offend one stomach with our play.   40
But, till the king come forth, and not till then,
Unto Southampton do we shift our scene. [*Exit.*

SCENE I. *London. A street.*

Enter Corporal NYM *and* Lieutenant BARDOLPH.

  Bard. Well met, Corporal Nym.
  Nym. Good morrow, Lieutenant Bardolph.
● *Bard.* What, are Ancient Pistol and you friends yet?
  Nym. For my part, I care not: I say little; but when time shall serve, there shall be smiles; but that shall be as it may. I dare not fight; but
● I will wink and hold out mine iron: it is a simple one; but what though? it will toast cheese, and it will endure cold as another man's sword will: and there's an end.   11
  Bard. I will bestow a breakfast to make you friends; and we'll be all three sworn brothers to France: let it be so, good Corporal Nym.
  Nym. Faith, I will live so long as I may, that's the certain of it; and when I cannot live any
● longer, I will do as I may: that is my rest, that is the rendezvous of it.
  Bard. It is certain, corporal, that he is married to Nell Quickly: and certainly she did you
● wrong; for you were troth-plight to her.   21
  Nym. I cannot tell: things must be as they may: men may sleep, and they may have their throats about them at that time; and some say knives have edges. It must be as it may: though patience be a tired mare, yet she will plod. There must be conclusions. Well, I cannot tell.

Enter PISTOL *and* Hostess.

  Bard. Here comes Ancient Pistol and his wife: good corporal, be patient here. How now, mine host Pistol!   30
● *Pist.* Base tike, call'st thou me host?
Now, by this hand, I swear, I scorn the term;
Nor shall my Nell keep lodgers.
  Host. No, by my troth, not long; for we cannot lodge and board a dozen or fourteen gentlewomen that live honestly by the prick of their needles, but it will be thought we keep a bawdy house straight. [*Nym and Pistol draw.*] O well a day, Lady, if he be not drawn now! we shall see wilful adultery and murder committed.   40
  Bard. Good lieutenant! good corporal! offer nothing here.
  Nym. Pish!
● *Pist.* Pish for thee, Iceland dog! thou prick-ear'd cur of Iceland!
  Host. Good Corporal Nym, show thy valour, and put up your sword.
● *Nym.* Will you shog off? I would have you
● solus.
  Pist. 'Solus,' egregious dog? O viper vile!
The 'solus' in thy most mervailous face;   50

The 'solus' in thy teeth, and in thy throat,
● And in thy hateful lungs, yea, in thy maw, perdy,
And, which is worse, within thy nasty mouth!
I do retort the 'solus' in thy bowels;
For I can take, and Pistol's cock is up,
And flashing fire will follow.

● *Nym.* I am not Barbason; you cannot conjure me. I have an humour to knock you indifferently well. If you grow foul with me, Pistol, I will scour you with my rapier, as I may, in fair terms: if you would walk off, I would prick your guts a little, in good terms, as I may: and that's the humour of it.

    Pist. O braggart vile and damned furious wight!
The grave doth gape, and doting death is near;
● Therefore exhale.

    Bard. Hear me, hear me what I say: he that strikes the first stroke, I'll run him up to the hilts, as I am a soldier.   [*Draws.*

●   *Pist.* An oath of mickle might; and fury shall abate.   70
Give me thy fist, thy fore-foot to me give:
Thy spirits are most tall.

    Nym. I will cut thy throat, one time or other, in fair terms: that is the humour of it.

●   *Pist.* 'Couple a gorge!'
That is the word. I thee defy again.
O hound of Crete, think'st thou my spouse to get?
● No; to the spital go,
● And from the powdering-tub of infamy
● Fetch forth the lazar kite of Cressid's kind,   80
Doll Tearsheet she by name, and her espouse:
I have, and I will hold, the quondam Quickly
● For the only she; and—pauca, there's enough.
Go to.

Enter the Boy.

    Boy. Mine host Pistol, you must come to my master, and you, hostess: he is very sick, and would to bed. Good Bardolph, put thy face between his sheets, and do the office of a warming-pan. Faith, he's very ill.
    Bard. Away, you rogue!   90
●   *Host.* By my troth, he'll yield the crow a pudding one of these days. The king has killed his heart. Good husband, come home presently.
[*Exeunt Hostess and Boy.*
    Bard. Come, shall I make you two friends?
We must to France together: why the devil should we keep knives to cut one another's throats?
    Pist. Let floods o'erswell, and fiends for food howl on!
    Nym. You'll pay me the eight shillings I won of you at betting?
    Pist. Base is the slave that pays.   100
    Nym. That now I will have: that's the humour of it.
●   *Pist.* As manhood shall compound: push home.
[*They draw.*
    Bard. By this sword, he that makes the first thrust, I'll kill him; by this sword, I will.
    Pist. Sword is an oath, and oaths must have their course.
    Bard. Corporal Nym, an thou wilt be friends, be friends: an thou wilt not, why, then, be enemies with me too. Prithee, put up.
    Nym. I shall have my eight shillings I won of you at betting?   III

---

52 *maw.* Stomach.

57 *Barbason.* A demon.

66 *exhale.* i.e. draw your sword.

70 *mickle.* Great.

75 *'Couple a gorge!'* Inaccurate French for 'cut the throat'.

78 *spital.* Hospital.

79 *powdering-tub.* Slang for the hot tub treatment of venereal disease.

80 *lazar kite of Cressid's kind.* A leprous whore like Cressid, who, according to Robert Henryson's *Testament of Cressid*, ended her days as leper and beggar.

83 *pauca.* Few, i.e. words.

91—92 *yield the crow a pudding.* Proverbial for 'to be food for crows on the gallows'.

103 *compound.* Decide.

112 *noble*. Coin worth six shillings and eightpence.

116 *sutler*. Seller of provisions.

124 *quotidian tertian*. The Hostess is confusing two different fevers.

130 *fracted*. Broken.

132 *careers*. Gallops at full speed.

8 *bedfellow*. Scroop had been a favourite of Henry.

Pist. A noble shalt thou have, and present pay;
And liquor likewise will I give to thee,
And friendship shall combine, and brotherhood:
I'll live by Nym, and Nym shall live by me;
Is not this just? for I shall sutler be
Unto the camp, and profits will accrue.
Give me thy hand.
   Nym. I shall have my noble?
   Pist. In cash most justly paid.   120
   Nym. Well, then, that's the humour of't.

Re-enter Hostess.

   Host. As ever you came of women, come in
quickly to Sir John. Ah, poor heart! he is so
shaked of a burning quotidian tertian, that it is
most lamentable to behold. Sweet men, come to
him.
   Nym. The king hath run bad humours on the
knight; that's the even of it.
   Pist. Nym, thou hast spoke the right;
His heart is fracted and corroborate.   130
   Nym. The king is a good king: but it must be
as it may; he passes some humours and careers.
   Pist. Let us condole the knight; for, lambkins,
we will live.

SCENE II. *Southampton. A council-chamber.*

Enter EXETER, BEDFORD, *and* WESTMORELAND.

   Bed. 'Fore God, his grace is bold, to trust these
    traitors.
   Exe. They shall be apprehended by and by.
   West. How smooth and even they do bear
    themselves!
As if allegiance in their bosoms sat,
Crowned with faith and constant loyalty.
   Bed. The king hath note of all that they intend,
By interception which they dream not of.
   Exe. Nay, but the man that was his bedfellow,
Whom he hath dull'd and cloy'd with gracious
    favours,
That he should, for a foreign purse, so sell   10
His sovereign's life to death and treachery.

Trumpets sound. Enter KING HENRY, SCROOP,
   CAMBRIDGE, GREY, *and* Attendants.

   K. Hen. Now sits the wind fair, and we will
    aboard.
My Lord of Cambridge, and my kind Lord of
    Masham,
And you, my gentle knight, give me your thoughts:
Think you not that the powers we bear with us
Will cut their passage through the force of France,
Doing the execution and the act
For which we have in head assembled them?
   Scroop. No doubt, my liege, if each man do
    his best.
   K. Hen. I doubt not that; since we are well
    persuaded   20
We carry not a heart with us from hence
That grows not in a fair consent with ours,
Nor leave not one behind that doth not wish
Success and conquest to attend on us.
   Cam. Never was monarch better fear'd and
    loved
Than is your majesty: there's not, I think, a
    subject
That sits in heart-grief and uneasiness
Under the sweet shade of your government.

Grey. True: those that were your father's enemies
Have steep'd their galls in honey and do serve you
With hearts create of duty and of zeal.   31
   K. Hen. We therefore have great cause of thankfulness;
And shall forget the office of our hand,
Sooner than quittance of desert and merit
According to the weight and worthiness.
   Scroop. So service shall with steeled sinews toil,
And labour shall refresh itself with hope,
To do your grace incessant services.
   K. Hen. We judge no less. Uncle of Exeter,
• Enlarge the man committed yesterday,   40
That rail'd against our person: we consider
It was excess of wine that set him on;
• And on his more advice we pardon him.
• *Scroop.* That's mercy, but too much security:
Let him be punish'd, sovereign, lest example
Breed, by his sufferance, more of such a kind.
   K. Hen. O, let us yet be merciful.
   Cam. So may your highness, and yet punish too.
   Grey. Sir,
You show great mercy, if you give him life,   50
After the taste of much correction.
   K. Hen. Alas, your too much love and care of me
• Are heavy orisons 'gainst this poor wretch!
• If little faults, proceeding on distemper,
Shall not be wink'd at, how shall we stretch our eye
When capital crimes, chew'd, swallow'd and digested,
Appear before us? We'll yet enlarge that man,
Though Cambridge, Scroop and Grey, in their dear care
And tender preservation of our person,
Would have him punish'd. And now to our French causes: 60
• Who are the late commissioners?
   Cam. I one, my lord:
Your highness bade me ask for it to-day.
   Scroop. So did you me, my liege.
   Grey. And I, my royal sovereign.
   K. Hen. Then, Richard Earl of Cambridge, there is yours;
There yours, Lord Scroop of Masham; and, sir knight,
Grey of Northumberland, this same is yours:
Read them; and know, I know your worthiness.
My Lord of Westmoreland, and uncle Exeter, 70
We will aboard to night. Why, how now, gentlemen!
What see you in those papers that you lose
So much complexion? Look ye, how they change!
Their cheeks are paper. Why, what read you there,
That hath so cowarded and chased your blood
Out of appearance?
   Cam.   I do confess my fault;
And do submit me to your highness' mercy.
   Grey.
   Scroop. } To which we all appeal.
   K. Hen. The mercy that was quick in us but late,
By your own counsel is suppress'd and kill'd: 80
You must not dare, for shame, to talk of mercy;

40 *Enlarge.* Set free.

43 *on his more advice.* Thinking better of it.

44 *security.* Excessive confidence.

53 *orisons.* Pleas.

54 *distemper.* Drunkenness.

61 *late.* Newly appointed.

Henry: 'What see you in those papers that you lose so much complexion?' Painting by Henry Fuseli (1741–1825)

90 *practices.* Plots.

108 *That admiration . . . them.* That they did not arouse astonishment.

114 *suggest.* Seduce.

116 *fetch'd.* Contrived.

123 *Tartar.* Tartarus, one of the classical names for Hell.

Hell's mouth and interior. Nineteenth century engraving from the chapel at Stratford-upon-Avon

126 *jealousy.* Suspicion.

127 *affiance.* Trust.

134 *complement.* Demeanour.

137 *bolted.* Sifted.

139 *full-fraught.* Fully imbued (with good qualities).

For your own reasons turn into your bosoms,
As dogs upon their masters, worrying you.
See you, my princes and my noble peers,
These English monsters! My Lord of Cambridge here,
You know how apt our love was to accord
To furnish him with all appertinents
Belonging to his honour; and this man
Hath, for a few light crowns, lightly conspired,
● And sworn unto the practices of France,   90
To kill us here in Hampton: to the which
This knight, no less for bounty bound to us
Than Cambridge is, hath likewise sworn. But, O,
What shall I say to thee, Lord Scroop? thou cruel,
Ingrateful, savage and inhuman creature!
Thou that didst bear the key of all my counsels,
That knew'st the very bottom of my soul,
That almost mightst have coin'd me into gold,
Wouldst thou have practised on me for thy use!
May it be possible, that foreign hire   100
Could out of thee extract one spark of evil
That might annoy my finger? 'tis so strange,
That, though the truth of it stands off as gross
As black and white, my eye will scarcely see it.
Treason and murder ever kept together,
As two yoke-devils sworn to either's purpose,
Working so grossly in a natural cause,
● That admiration did not hoop at them:
But thou, 'gainst all proportion, didst bring in
Wonder to wait on treason and on murder: 110
And whatsoever cunning fiend it was
That wrought upon thee so preposterously
Hath got the voice in hell for excellence:
● All other devils that suggest by treasons
Do botch and bungle up damnation
● With patches, colours, and with forms being fetch'd
From glistering semblances of piety;
But he that temper'd thee bade thee stand up,
Gave thee no instance why thou shouldst do treason,
Unless to dub thee with the name of traitor.   120
If that same demon that hath gull'd thee thus
Should with his lion gait walk the whole world,
● He might return to vasty Tartar back,
And tell the legions ' I can never win
A soul so easy as that Englishman's.'
● O, how hast thou with jealousy infected
● The sweetness of affiance!   Show men dutiful?
Why, so didst thou: seem they grave and learned?
Why, so didst thou: come they of noble family?
Why, so didst thou: seem they religious?   130
Why, so didst thou: or are they spare in diet,
Free from gross passion or of mirth or anger,
Constant in spirit, not swerving with the blood,
● Garnish'd and deck'd in modest complement,
Not working with the eye without the ear,
And but in purged judgement trusting neither?
● Such and so finely bolted didst thou seem:
And thus thy fall hath left a kind of blot,
● To mark the full-fraught man and best indued
With some suspicion.   I will weep for thee;   140
For this revolt of thine, methinks, is like
Another fall of man.   Their faults are open:
Arrest them to the answer of the law;
And God acquit them of their practices!
     Exe. I arrest thee of high treason, by the name
of Richard Earl of Cambridge.

I arrest thee of high treason, by the name of
Henry Lord Scroop of Masham.
    I arrest thee of high treason, by the name of
Thomas Grey, knight, of Northumberland.   150
    Scroop. Our purposes God justly hath disco-
        ver'd;
And I repent my fault more than my death;
Which I beseech your highness to forgive,
Although my body pay the price of it.
    Cam. For me, the gold of France did not
        seduce;
Although I did admit it as a motive
The sooner to effect what I intended:
But God be thanked for prevention;
Which I in sufferance heartily will rejoice,
Beseeching God and you to pardon me.   160
    Grey. Never did faithful subject more rejoice
At the discovery of most dangerous treason
Than I do at this hour joy o'er myself,
Prevented from a damned enterprise:
My fault, but not my body, pardon, sovereign.
    K. Hen. God quit you in his mercy! Hear
        your sentence.
You have conspired against our royal person,
Join'd with an enemy proclaim'd and from his
        coffers
● Received the golden earnest of our death;
Wherein you would have sold your king to
        slaughter,   170
His princes and his peers to servitude,
His subjects to oppression and contempt
And his whole kingdom into desolation.
Touching our person seek we no revenge;
But we our kingdom's safety must so tender,
Whose ruin you have sought, that to her laws
We do deliver you.   Get you therefore hence,
Poor miserable wretches, to your death:
The taste whereof, God of his mercy give
You patience to endure, and true repentance   180
● Of all your dear offences!   Bear them hence.
        [*Exeunt Cambridge, Scroop and Grey,*
                        guarded.
Now, lords, for France; the enterprise whereof
Shall be to you, as us, like glorious.
We doubt not of a fair and lucky war,
Since God so graciously hath brought to light
This dangerous treason lurking in our way
To hinder our beginnings.   We doubt not now
● But every rub is smoothed on our way.
Then forth, dear countrymen: let us deliver
Our puissance into the hand of God,   190
Putting it straight in expedition.
Cheerly to sea; the signs of war advance:
No king of England, if not king of France.
                        [*Exeunt.*

        SCENE III.   *London.   Before a tavern.*

Enter PISTOL, Hostess, NYM, BARDOLPH, *and*
        Boy.

    Host. Prithee, honey-sweet husband, let me
bring thee to Staines.
● *Pist.* No; for my manly heart doth yearn.
Bardolph, be blithe: Nym, rouse thy vaunting
        veins:
Boy, bristle thy courage up; for Falstaff he is dead,
And we must yearn therefore.
    Bard. Would I were with him, wheresome'er
he is, either in heaven or in hell!

Costume design for Sir Thomas Grey of Northumberland by Tanya Moisewitch, Stratford-upon-Avon, 1951

169 *golden earnest.* Payment in gold.

181 *dear.* Dire.

188 *rub.* Obstacle.

3 *yearn.* Grieve.

Sir John Falstaff. Engraving from a 19th century painting (detail)

___

12 *christom.* Newly christened.

29 *out of sack.* Against sherry.

51 '*Pitch and Pay*'. No credit; cash only.

55 *Caveto.* Beware.

Pistol (Jeffrey Dench), Boy (Richard Derrington) and the Hostess (Valerie Lush). Royal Shakespeare Co, 1977

Host. Nay, sure, he's not in hell: he's in Arthur's bosom, if ever man went to Arthur's bosom. A' made a finer end and went away an it had been any christom child; a' parted even just between twelve and one, even at the turning o' the tide: for after I saw him fumble with the sheets and play with flowers and smile upon his fingers' ends, I knew there was but one way; for his nose was as sharp as a pen, and a' babbled of green fields. 'How now, Sir John!' quoth I: 'what, man! be o' good cheer.' So a' cried out 'God, God, God!' three or four times. Now I, to comfort him, bid him a' should not think of God; I hoped there was no need to trouble himself with any such thoughts yet. So a' bade me lay more clothes on his feet: I put my hand into the bed and felt them, and they were as cold as any stone; then I felt to his knees, and they were as cold as any stone, and so upward and upward, and all was as cold as any stone.

Nym. They say he cried out of sack.

Host. Ay, that a' did.   30

Bard. And of women.

Host. Nay, that a' did not.

Boy. Yes, that a' did; and said they were devils incarnate.

Host. A' could never abide carnation; 'twas a colour he never liked.

Boy. A' said once, the devil would have him about women.

Host. A' did in some sort, indeed, handle women; but then he was rheumatic, and talked of the whore of Babylon.   41

Boy. Do you not remember, a' saw a flea stick upon Bardolph's nose, and a' said it was a black soul burning in hell-fire?

Bard. Well, the fuel is gone that maintained that fire: that's all the riches I got in his service.

Nym. Shall we shog? the king will be gone from Southampton.

Pist. Come, let's away. My love, give me thy lips.

Look to my chattels and my movables: 50

Let senses rule; the word is 'Pitch and Pay:'

Trust none;

For oaths are straws, men's faiths are wafer-cakes,

And hold-fast is the only dog, my duck:

Therefore, Caveto be thy counsellor.

Go, clear thy crystals. Yoke-fellows in arms,

Let us to France; like horse-leeches, my boys,

To suck, to suck, the very blood to suck!

Boy. And that's but unwholesome food, they say.   60

Pist. Touch her soft mouth, and march.

Bard. Farewell, hostess.   [*Kissing her.*

Nym. I cannot kiss, that is the humour of it; but, adieu.

Pist. Let housewifery appear: keep close, I thee command.

Host. Farewell; adieu.   [*Exeunt.*

SCENE IV. *France. The* KING'S *palace.*

Flourish. Enter the FRENCH KING, *the* DAU-PHIN, *the* DUKES OF BERRI *and* BRETAGNE, *the* CONSTABLE, *and others.*

Fr. King. Thus comes the English with full power upon us;

And more than carefully it us concerns
To answer royally in our defences.
Therefore the Dukes of Berri and of Bretagne,
Of Brabant and of Orleans, shall make forth,
And you, Prince Dauphin, with all swift dispatch,
● To line and new repair our towns of war
With men of courage and with means defendant;
For England his approaches makes as fierce
● As waters to the sucking of a gulf.   10
It fits us then to be as provident
As fear may teach us out of late examples
● Left by the fatal and neglected English
Upon our fields.
              Dau.   My most redoubted father,
It is most meet we arm us 'gainst the foe;
For peace itself should not so dull a kingdom,
Though war nor no known quarrel were in question,
But that defences, musters, preparations,
Should be maintain'd, assembled and collected,
As were a war in expectation.   20
Therefore, I say 'tis meet we all go forth
To view the sick and feeble parts of France:
And let us do it with no show of fear;
No, with no more than if we heard that England
● Were busied with a Whitsun morris-dance:
For, my good liege, she is so idly king'd,
Her sceptre so fantastically borne
By a vain, giddy, shallow, humorous youth,
That fear attends her not.
              Con.   O peace, Prince Dauphin!
You are too much mistaken in this king: 30
Question your grace the late ambassadors,
With what great state he heard their embassy,
How well supplied with noble counsellors,
How modest in exception, and withal
How terrible in constant resolution,
And you shall find his vanities forespent
● Were but the outside of the Roman Brutus,
Covering discretion with a coat of folly;
As gardeners do with ordure hide those roots
That shall first spring and be most delicate.   40
              Dau.   Well, 'tis not so, my lord high constable;
But though we think it so, it is no matter:
In cases of defence 'tis best to weigh
The enemy more mighty than he seems:
So the proportions of defence are fill'd;
Which of a weak and niggardly projection
Doth, like a miser, spoil his coat with scanting
A little cloth.
              Fr. King.   Think we King Harry strong;
And, princes, look you strongly arm to meet him.
● The kindred of him hath been flesh'd upon us; 50
And he is bred out of that bloody strain
That haunted us in our familiar paths:
Witness our too much memorable shame
When Cressy battle fatally was struck,
And all our princes captived by the hand
Of that black name, Edward, Black Prince of
          Wales;
Whiles that his mountain sire, on mountain standing,
Up in the air, crown'd with the golden sun,
Saw his heroical seed, and smiled to see him,
Mangle the work of nature and deface   60
The patterns that by God and by French fathers
Had twenty years been made.   This is a stem

---

7 *line.* Strengthen.

10 *gulf.* Whirlpool.

13 *neglected.* Despised.

25 *Whitsun morris-dance.* Country dances were performed at Whitsuntide.

A morris dance. Engraving by Israel von Mecheln from J.O. Halliwell's edition of Shakespeare's works, 1853–65

37 *Roman Brutus.* Lucius Junius Brutus, who feigned madness to prevent Tarquin, last king of Rome, of suspecting him of conspiracy.

50 *flesh'd.* Initiated to blood-shed.

70 *spend their mouths.* Cry.

Costume design for the Dauphin by John Bury with Ann Curtis, Royal Shakespeare Co, 1964

85 *sinister.* Illegitimate.

91 *evenly.* Truly.

Of that victorious stock; and let us fear
The native mightiness and fate of him.

    Enter a Messenger.

  Mess. Ambassadors from Harry King of England
Do crave admittance to your majesty.
   Fr. King. We'll give them present audience.
    Go, and bring them.
     [*Exeunt Messenger and certain Lords.*
You see this chase is hotly follow'd, friends.
  Dau. Turn head, and stop pursuit; for coward dogs
• Most spend their mouths when what they seem to threaten   70
Runs far before them. Good my sovereign,
Take up the English short, and let them know
Of what a monarchy you are the head:
Self-love, my liege, is not so vile a sin
As self-neglecting.

   Re-enter Lords, *with* EXETER *and train.*

  Fr. King.   From our brother England?
  Exe. From him; and thus he greets your majesty.
He wills you, in the name of God Almighty,
That you divest yourself, and lay apart
The borrow'd glories that by gift of heaven,
By law of nature and of nations, 'long   80
To him and to his heirs; namely, the crown
And all wide-stretched honours that pertain
By custom and the ordinance of times
Unto the crown of France. That you may know
• 'Tis no sinister nor no awkward claim,
Pick'd from the worm-holes of long-vanish'd days,
Nor from the dust of old oblivion raked,
He sends you this most memorable line,
In every branch truly demonstrative;
Willing you overlook this pedigree: 90
• And when you find him evenly derived
From his most famed of famous ancestors,
Edward the Third, he bids you then resign
Your crown and kingdom, indirectly held
From him the native and true challenger.
  Fr. King. Or else what follows?
  Exe. Bloody constraint; for if you hide the crown
Even in your hearts, there will he rake for it:
Therefore in fierce tempest is he coming,
In thunder and in earthquake, like a Jove,   100
That, if requiring fail, he will compel;
And bids you, in the bowels of the Lord,
Deliver up the crown, and to take mercy
On the poor souls for whom this hungry war
Opens his vasty jaws; and on your head
Turning the widows' tears, the orphans' cries,
The dead men's blood, the pining maidens' groans,
For husbands, fathers and betrothed lovers,
That shall be swallow'd in this controversy.
This is his claim, his threatening and my message;   110
Unless the Dauphin be in presence here,
To whom expressly I bring greeting too.
  Fr. King. For us, we will consider of this further:
To-morrow shall you bear our full intent
Back to our brother England.
  Dau.   For the Dauphin,
I stand here for him: what to him from England?

Exe. Scorn and defiance; slight regard, con-
tempt,
And any thing that may not misbecome
The mighty sender, doth he prize you at.
Thus says my king; an if your father's highness
Do not, in grant of all demands at large,   121
Sweeten the bitter mock you sent his majesty,
He'll call you to so hot an answer of it,
● That caves and womby vaultages of France
Shall chide your trespass and return your mock
● In second accent of his ordnance.
    Dau. Say, if my father render fair return,
It is against my will; for I desire
Nothing but odds with England: to that end,
As matching to his youth and vanity,   130
I did present him with the Paris balls.
    Exe. He'll make your Paris Louvre shake
for it,
Were it the mistress-court of mighty Europe:
And, be assured, you'll find a difference,
As we his subjects have in wonder found,
Between the promise of his greener days
And these he masters now: now he weighs time
Even to the utmost grain: that you shall read
In your own losses, if he stay in France.
    Fr. King. To-morrow shall you know our
mind at full.   140
    Exe. Dispatch us with all speed, lest that
our king
Come here himself to question our delay;
For he is footed in this land already.
    Fr. King. You shall be soon dispatch'd with
fair conditions:
A night is but small breath and little pause
To answer matters of this consequence.
                                    [*Flourish. Exeunt.*

ACT III.

PROLOGUE.

Enter Chorus.

● *Chor.* Thus with imagined wing our swift
scene flies
In motion of no less celerity
Than that of thought.   Suppose that you have
seen
The well-appointed king at Hampton pier
Embark his royalty; and his brave fleet
With silken streamers the young Phœbus fanning:
Play with your fancies, and in them behold
Upon the hempen tackle ship-boys climbing;
Hear the shrill whistle which doth order give
To sounds confused; behold the threaden sails,
Borne with the invisible and creeping wind,   11
Draw the huge bottoms through the furrow'd sea,
Breasting the lofty surge: O, do but think
● You stand upon the rivage and behold
A city on the inconstant billows dancing;
For so appears this fleet majestical,
Holding due course to Harfleur. Follow, follow:
Grapple your minds to sternage of this navy,
And leave your England, as dead midnight still,
Guarded with grandsires, babies and old women,
Either past or not arrived to pith and puissance;
For who is he, whose chin is but enrich'd
With one appearing hair, that will not follow
These cull'd and choice-drawn cavaliers to France?

124 *womby vaultages.* Hollow caverns.

126 *second . . . ordnance.* Echoing his artillery.

Henry V, (F.R. Benson) departs for France, Stratford-upon-Avon, 1901.

1 *imagined wing.* The wings of imagination.

14 *rivage.* Shore.

English ships of war. Engraving from a 15th century manuscript

33 *linstock.* The stick which held the gunner's match.

King Henry: 'Once more unto the breach...' Breaching tower, typical of those used at the time of Henry V. Engraving from *Old England*, 1854

10 *portage.* Port holes.

12 *galled.* Worn away.

13 *confounded.* Wasted.

King Henry: 'On, on, you noblest English...' Scene illustration from William Charles Macready's production, Covent Garden Theatre, London, 1839

18 *fet.* Fetched.

31 *slips.* Leashes.

5 *case.* Set.

Work, work your thoughts, and therein see a
    siege;
Behold the ordnance on their carriages,
With fatal mouths gaping on girded Harfleur.
Suppose the ambassador from the French comes
    back;
Tells Harry that the king doth offer him
Katharine his daughter, and with her, to dowry,
Some petty and unprofitable dukedoms.   31
The offer likes not: and the nimble gunner
● With linstock now the devilish cannon touches,
        [*Alarum, and chambers go off.*
And down goes all before them.   Still be kind,
And eke out our performance with your mind.
        [*Exit.*

    SCENE I. *France.* *Before Harfleur.*

Alarum. Enter KING HENRY, EXETER, BED-
FORD, GLOUCESTER, *and* Soldiers, *with scaling-
ladders.*

   K. Hen. Once more unto the breach, dear
    friends, once more;
Or close the wall up with our English dead.
In peace there's nothing so becomes a man
As modest stillness and humility:
But when the blast of war blows in our ears,
Then imitate the action of the tiger;
Stiffen the sinews, summon up the blood,
Disguise fair nature with hard-favour'd rage;
Then lend the eye a terrible aspect;
● Let it pry through the portage of the head   10
Like the brass cannon; let the brow o'erwhelm it
● As fearfully as doth a galled rock
● O'erhang and jutty his confounded base,
Swill'd with the wild and wasteful ocean.
Now set the teeth and stretch the nostril wide,
Hold hard the breath and bend up every spirit
To his full height.   On, on, you noblest English,
● Whose blood is fet from fathers of war-proof!
Fathers that, like so many Alexanders,   19
Have in these parts from morn till even fought
And sheathed their swords for lack of argument:
Dishonour not your mothers; now attest
That those whom you call'd fathers did beget you.
Be copy now to men of grosser blood,
And teach them how to war. And you, good
    yeomen,
Whose limbs were made in England, show us here
The mettle of your pasture; let us swear
That you are worth your breeding; which I
    doubt not;
For there is none of you so mean and base,
That hath not noble lustre in your eyes.   30
● I see you stand like greyhounds in the slips,
Straining upon the start.   The game's afoot:
Follow your spirit, and upon this charge
Cry 'God for Harry, England, and Saint George!'
    [*Exeunt. Alarum, and chambers go off.*

    SCENE II. *The same.*

Enter NYM, BARDOLPH, PISTOL, *and* Boy.

   Bard. On, on, on, on, on! to the breach, to
the breach!
   Nym. Pray thee, corporal, stay: the knocks
are too hot; and, for mine own part, I have not
● a case of lives: the humour of it is too hot, that
is the very plain-song of it.

Pist. The plain-song is most just; for humours
    do abound:
Knocks go and come; God's vassals drop and die;
    And sword and shield,
    In bloody field,   10
    Doth win immortal fame.
Boy. Would I were in an alehouse in London!
I would give all my fame for a pot of ale and
safety.
Pist. And I:
    If wishes would prevail with me,
    My purpose should not fail with me,
    But thither would I hie.
Boy. As duly, but not as truly,
    As bird doth sing on bough.   20

Enter FLUELLEN.

Flu. Up to the breach, you dogs! avaunt,
you cullions!   [*Driving them forward.*
Pist. Be merciful, great duke, to men of
    mould.
Abate thy rage, abate thy manly rage,
Abate thy rage, great duke!
Good bawcock, bate thy rage; use lenity, sweet
    chuck!
Nym. These be good humours! your honour
wins bad humours.   [*Exeunt all but Boy.*
Boy. As young as I am, I have observed these
three swashers. I am boy to them all three: but
all they three, though they would serve me, could
not be man to me; for indeed three such antics
do not amount to a man. For Bardolph, he is
white-livered and red-faced; by the means whereof a' faces it out, but fights not. For Pistol, he
hath a killing tongue and a quiet sword; by the
means whereof a' breaks words, and keeps whole
weapons. For Nym, he hath heard that men of
few words are the best men; and therefore he
scorns to say his prayers, lest a' should be thought
a coward: but his few bad words are matched
with as few good deeds; for a' never broke any
man's head but his own, and that was against a
post when he was drunk. They will steal any
thing, and call it purchase. Bardolph stole a lute-
case, bore it twelve leagues, and sold it for three
half-pence. Nym and Bardolph are sworn brothers in filching, and in Calais they stole a fire-
shovel: I knew by that piece of service the men
would carry coals. They would have me as
familiar with men's pockets as their gloves or
their handkerchers: which makes much against
my manhood, if I should take from another's
pocket to put into mine; for it is plain pocketing
up of wrongs. I must leave them, and seek some
better service: their villany goes against my weak
stomach, and therefore I must cast it up. [*Exit.*

Re-enter FLUELLEN, GOWER *following.*

Gow. Captain Fluellen, you must come presently to the mines; the Duke of Gloucester
would speak with you.   60
Flu. To the mines! tell you the duke, it is not
so good to come to the mines; for, look you, the
mines is not according to the disciplines of the
war: the concavities of it is not sufficient; for,
look you, th' athversary, you may discuss unto
the duke, look you, is digt himself four yard

22 *cullions.* Scoundrels.

23 *mould.* Earth. i.e. mortal men.

26 *bawcock.* Fine fellow; from the French *beau coq.*

Costume design for Boy by John Bury with Ann Curtis,
Royal Shakespeare Co, 1964

30 *swashers.* Blusterers.

32 *antics.* Clowns.

50 *carry coals.* Submit to affronts or perform degrading
work.

68 *plow*. Blow; Fluellen uses 'p' for 'b'.

76 *disciplines*. Tactics.

82 *expedition*. Experience.

92 *pioners*. Sappers and mine diggers.

110 *quit*. Answer you.

Soldiers at the time of Henry V. Nineteenth century engraving from a medieval manuscript.

under the countermines: by Cheshu, I think a'
● will plow up all, if there is not better directions.
 Gow. The Duke of Gloucester, to whom the
order of the siege is given, is altogether directed
by an Irishman, a very valiant gentleman, i' faith.
 Flu. It is Captain Macmorris, is it not?
 Gow. I think it be.
 Flu. By Cheshu, he is an ass, as in the world:
I will verify as much in his beard: he has no
● more directions in the true disciplines of the wars,
look you, of the Roman disciplines, than is a
puppy-dog.

Enter MACMORRIS *and* Captain JAMY.

 Gow. Here a' comes; and the Scots captain,
Captain Jamy, with him.   80
 Flu. Captain Jamy is a marvellous falorous
● gentleman, that is certain; and of great expedition
and knowledge in th' aunchient wars, upon my
particular knowledge of his directions: by Cheshu,
he will maintain his argument as well as any
military man in the world, in the disciplines of
the pristine wars of the Romans.
 Jamy. I say gud-day, Captain Fluellen.
 Flu. God-den to your worship, good Captain
James.   90
 Gow. How now, Captain Macmorris! have
● you quit the mines? have the pioners given o'er?
 Mac. By Chrish, la! tish ill done: the work
ish give over, the trompet sound the retreat. By
my hand, I swear, and my father's soul, the work
ish ill done; it ish give over: I would have blowed
up the town, so Chrish save me, la! in an hour:
O, tish ill done, tish ill done; by my hand, tish
ill done!   99
 Flu. Captain Macmorris, I beseech you now,
will you voutsafe me, look you, a few disputations with you, as partly touching or concerning
the disciplines of the war, the Roman wars, in
the way of argument, look you, and friendly communication; partly to satisfy my opinion, and
partly for the satisfaction, look you, of my mind,
as touching the direction of the military discipline;
that is the point.
 Jamy. It sall be vary gud, gud feith, gud
● captains bath: and I sall quit you with gud leve,
as I may pick occasion; that sall I, marry.   111
 Mac. It is no time to discourse, so Chrish
save me: the day is hot, and the weather, and
the wars, and the king, and the dukes: it is no
time to discourse. The town is beseeched, and
the trumpet call us to the breach; and we talk,
and, be Chrish, do nothing: 'tis shame for us all:
so God sa' me, 'tis shame to stand still; it is shame,
by my hand: and there is throats to be cut, and
works to be done; and there ish nothing done, so
Chrish sa' me, la!   121
 Jamy. By the mess, ere theise eyes of mine
take themselves to slomber, ay'll de gud service,
or ay'll lig i' the grund for it; ay, or go to death:
and ay'll pay 't as valorously as I may, that sall
I suerly do, that is the breff and the long.
Marry, I wad full fain hear some question 'tween
you tway.
 Flu. Captain Macmorris, I think, look you,
under your correction, there is not many of your
nation—   131
 Mac. Of my nation! What ish my nation?
Ish a villain, and a bastard, and a knave, and a

rascal — What ish my nation? Who talks of my nation?

Flu. Look you, if you take the matter otherwise than is meant, Captain Macmorris, peradventure I shall think you do not use me with that affability as in discretion you ought to use me, look you; being as good a man as yourself, both in the disciplines of war, and in the derivation of my birth, and in other particularities.

Mac. I do not know you so good a man as myself: so Chrish save me, I will cut off your head.

Gow. Gentlemen both, you will mistake each other.

Jamy. A! that's a foul fault.

[*A parley sounded.*

Gow. The town sounds a parley. 149

Flu. Captain Macmorris, when there is more better opportunity to be required, look you, I will be so bold as to tell you I know the disciplines of war; and there is an end. [*Exeunt.*

SCENE III. *The same. Before the gates.*

The Governor *and some* Citizens *on the walls; the English forces below. Enter* KING HENRY *and his train.*

K. Hen. How yet resolves the governor of
the town?
This is the latest parle we will admit:
Therefore to our best mercy give yourselves;
Or like to men proud of destruction
Defy us to our worst: for, as I am a soldier,
A name that in my thoughts becomes me best,
If I begin the battery once again,
I will not leave the half-achieved Harfleur
Till in her ashes she lie buried.
The gates of mercy shall be all shut up, 10
And the flesh'd soldier, rough and hard of heart,
In liberty of bloody hand shall range
With conscience wide as hell, mowing like grass
Your fresh-fair virgins and your flowering infants.
What is it then to me, if impious war,
Array'd in flames like to the prince of fiends,
• Do, with his smirch'd complexion, all fell feats
Enlink'd to waste and desolation?
What is't to me, when you yourselves are cause,
If your pure maidens fall into the hand 20
Of hot and forcing violation?
What rein can hold licentious wickedness
When down the hill he holds his fierce career?
We may as bootless spend our vain command
Upon the enraged soldiers in their spoil
As send precepts to the leviathan
To come ashore. Therefore, you men of Harfleur,
Take pity of your town and of your people,
Whiles yet my soldiers are in my command;
Whiles yet the cool and temperate wind of grace
O'erblows the filthy and contagious clouds 31
Of heady murder, spoil and villany.
If not, why, in a moment look to see
• The blind and bloody soldier with foul hand
Defile the locks of your shrill-shrieking daughters;
Your fathers taken by the silver beards,
And their most reverend heads dash'd to the walls,
Your naked infants spitted upon pikes,
Whiles the mad mothers with their howls confused
Do break the clouds, as did the wives of Jewry 40
At Herod's bloody-hunting slaughtermen.

Storming a town. Engraving from *Old England*, 1854

17 *fell.* Cruel.

34 *blind.* Heedless.

A beleaguered city. Engraving from an early 15th century manuscript

What say you? will you yield, and this avoid,
Or, guilty in defence, be thus destroy'd?
 Gov. Our expectation hath this day an end:
The Dauphin, whom of succours we entreated,
Returns us that his powers are yet not ready
To raise so great a siege. Therefore, great king,
We yield our town and lives to thy soft mercy.
Enter our gates; dispose of us and ours;
For we no longer are defensible.   50
 K. Hen. Open your gates. Come, uncle Exeter,
Go you and enter Harfleur; there remain,
And fortify it strongly 'gainst the French:
Use mercy to them all. For us, dear uncle,
The winter coming on and sickness growing
Upon our soldiers, we will retire to Calais.
To-night in Harfleur will we be your guest;
To-morrow for the march are we addrest.
  [*Flourish. The King and his train enter*
            the town.

SCENE IV. *The* FRENCH KING'S *palace.*

Enter KATHARINE *and* ALICE.

 Kath. Alice, tu as été en Angleterre, et tu parles bien le langage.
 Alice. Un peu, madame.
 Kath. Je te prie, m'enseignez; il faut que j'apprenne à parler. Comment appelez-vous la main en Anglois?
 Alice. La main? elle est appelée de hand.
 Kath. De hand. Et les doigts?
 Alice. Les doigts? ma foi, j'oublie les doigts; mais je me souviendrai. Les doigts? je pense qu'ils sont appelés de fingres; oui, de fingres. 11
 Kath. La main, de hand; les doigts, de fingres. Je pense que je suis le bon écolier; j'ai gagné deux mots d'Anglois vîtement. Comment appelez-vous les ongles?
 Alice. Les ongles? nous les appelons de nails.
 Kath. De nails. Écoutez; dites-moi, si je parle bien: de hand, de fingres, et de nails.
 Alice. C'est bien dit, madame; il est fort bon Anglois.   20
 Kath. Dites-moi l'Anglois pour le bras.
 Alice. De arm, madame.
 Kath. Et le coude?
 Alice. De elbow.
 Kath. De elbow. Je m'en fais la répétition de tous les mots que vous m'avez appris dès à présent.
 Alice. Il est trop difficile, madame, comme je pense.
 Kath. Excusez-moi, Alice; écoutez: de hand, de fingres, de nails, de arma, de bilbow. 31
 Alice. De elbow, madame.
 Kath. O Seigneur Dieu, je m'en oublie! de elbow. Comment appelez-vous le col?
 Alice. De neck, madame.
 Kath. De nick. Et le menton?
 Alice. De chin.
 Kath. De sin. Le col, de nick; le menton, de sin.   39
 Alice. Oui. Sauf votre honneur, en vérité, vous prononcez les mots aussi droit que les natifs d'Angleterre.
 Kath. Je ne doute point d'apprendre, par la grace de Dieu, et en peu de temps.

Scene IV. A translation of this 'language lesson' follows:

Katherine. Alice, you've been in England and you speak the language well.

Alice. A little, madam.

Katherine. I pray you, teach me. I must learn to speak it. How do you say *la main* in English?

Alice. La main? It's called de hand.

Katherine. De hand. And *les doigts?*

Alice. Les doigts? My faith, I've forgotten *les doigts,* but I'll remember. *Les doigts?* I think they are called de fingres; yes, de fingres.

Katherine. La main, de hand; *les doigts,* de fingres. I think I'm a good student. I've learned two English words quickly. What do you call *les ongles?*

Alice. Les ongles? We call them de nails.

Katherine. De nails. Listen, tell me if I speak well: de hand, de fingres, and de nails.

Alice. That's well done, madam; it's very good English.

Katherine. What's the English for *le bras?*

Alice. De arm, madam.

Katherine. And *le coude?*

Alice. De elbow.

Katherine. De elbow. I'm going to repeat all the words you have taught me so far.

Alice. I think it's too difficult, madam.

Katherine. Excuse me, Alice; listen: de hand, de fingres, de nails, de arma, de bilbow.

Alice. De elbow, madam.

Katherine. O Lord God, I can't remember! de elbow. How do you say *le col?*

Alice. N'avez vous pas déjà oublié ce que je vous ai enseigné?

Kath. Non, je reciterai à vous promptement: de hand, de fingres, de mails,—

Alice. De nails, madame.

Kath. De nails, de arm, de ilbow.　　50

Alice. Sauf votre honneur, de elbow.

Kath. Ainsi dis-je; de elbow, de nick, et de sin. Comment appelez-vous le pied et la robe?

Alice. De foot, madame; et de coun.

Kath. De foot et de coun! O Seigneur Dieu! ce sont mots de son mauvais, corruptible, gros, et impudique, et non pour les dames d'honneur d'user: je ne voudrais prononcer ces mots devant les seigneurs de France pour tout le monde. Foh! le foot et le coun! Néanmoins, je réciterai une autre fois ma leçon ensemble: de hand, de fingres, de nails, de arm, de elbow, de nick, de sin, de foot, de coun.

Alice. Excellent, madame!

Kath. C'est assez pour une fois: allons-nous à diner.　　　　　　　　　　　　　[*Exeunt.*

SCENE V. *The same.*

Enter the KING OF FRANCE, *the* DAUPHIN, *the* DUKE OF BOURBON, *the* CONSTABLE OF FRANCE, *and others.*

Fr. King. 'Tis certain he hath pass'd the river Somme.

Con. And if he be not fought withal, my lord, Let us not live in France; let us quit all And give our vineyards to a barbarous people.

Dau. O Dieu vivant! shall a few sprays of us,
● The emptying of our fathers' luxury,
Our scions, put in wild and savage stock,
Spirt up so suddenly into the clouds,
● And overlook their grafters?

Bour. Normans, but bastard Normans, Norman bastards!　　　　　　　　　　10
● Mort de ma vie! if they march along
Unfought withal, but I will sell my dukedom,
To buy a slobbery and a dirty farm
● In that nook-shotten isle of Albion.
● *Con.* Dieu de batailles! where have they this mettle?
Is not their climate foggy, raw and dull,
On whom, as in despite, the sun looks pale,
Killing their fruit with frowns? Can sodden water,
● A drench for sur-rein'd jades, their barley-broth,
Decoct their cold blood to such valiant heat?　20
And shall our quick blood, spirited with wine,
Seem frosty? O, for honour of our land,
Let us not hang like roping icicles
Upon our houses' thatch, whiles a more frosty people
Sweat drops of gallant youth in our rich fields!
Poor we may call them in their native lords.

Dau. By faith and honour,
Our madams mock at us, and plainly say
Our mettle is bred out and they will give
Their bodies to the lust of English youth　30
To new-store France with bastard warriors.

Bour. They bid us to the English dancing-schools,
● And teach lavoltas high and swift corantos;
Saying our grace is only in our heels,

Alice. De neck, madam.

Katherine. De nick. And *le menton*?

Alice. De chin.

Katherine. De sin. *Le col*, de nick; *le menton*, de sin.

Alice. Yes. Saving your honour, truly, you pronounce the words as well as a native of England.

Katherine. I've no doubt, with the grace of God, I could learn it quickly.

Alice. You haven't already forgotten what I've taught you?

Katherine. No, I'll recite them for you now: de hand, de fingres, de mails, –

Alice. De nails, madam.

Katherine. De nails, de arm, de ilbow.

Alice. Saving your honour, de elbow.

Katherine. That's what I said; de elbow, de nick, and de sin. What do you call *le pied* and *la robe*?

Alice. De foot, madam; and de coun (gown).

Katherine. De foot and de coun! (Here the Princess associated these words with the indecent French words *foutre* and *con*).

O Lord! These words are bad, wicked, coarse and immodest, and not suitable for well-bred women to use. I wouldn't speak those words in front of the gentlemen of France for all the world. Foh! *le foot* and *le coun*! Nevertheless, I'll recite my entire lesson one more time! de hand, de fingres, de nails, de arm, de elbow, de nick, de sin, de foot, de coun.

Alice. Excellent, madam!

Katherine. That's enough for one time. Let's go to dinner.

6 *luxury.* Lust.

9 *grafters.* The original plant from which a graft (scion) was taken.

11 *Mort de ma vie!* Death of my life!

14 *nook-shotten.* Full of nooks and corners.

15 *Dieu de batailles.* God of battles.

19 *drench for sur-rein'd jades.* A medicinal draft for over-ridden horses.

33 *lavoltas . . . corantos.* Two kinds of energetic dances.

60 *And for achievement.* In place of combat.

Siege of Rouen. Drawing from a series made in 1493

And that we are most lofty runaways.
   Fr. King. Where is Montjoy the herald?
    speed him hence:
Let him greet England with our sharp defiance.
Up, princes! and, with spirit of honour edged
More sharper than your swords, hie to the field:
Charles Delabreth, high constable of France; 40
You Dukes of Orleans, Bourbon, and of Berri,
Alençon, Brabant, Bar, and Burgundy;
Jaques Chatillon, Rambures, Vaudemont,
Beaumont, Grandpré, Roussi, and Fauconberg,
Foix, Lestrale, Bouciqualt, and Charolois;
High dukes, great princes, barons, lords and
    knights,
For your great seats now quit you of great
    shames.
Bar Harry England, that sweeps through our land
With pennons painted in the blood of Harfleur:
Rush on his host, as doth the melted snow 50
Upon the valleys, whose low vassal seat
The Alps doth spit and void his rheum upon:
Go down upon him, you have power enough,
And in a captive chariot into Rouen
Bring him our prisoner.
   Con.   This becomes the great.
Sorry am I his numbers are so few,
His soldiers sick and famish'd in their march,
For I am sure, when he shall see our army,
He'll drop his heart into the sink of fear
And for achievement offer us his ransom.   60
   Fr. King. Therefore, lord constable, haste on
    Montjoy,
And let him say to England that we send
To know what willing ransom he will give.
Prince Dauphin, you shall stay with us in Rouen.
   Dau. Not so, I do beseech your majesty.
   Fr. King. Be patient, for you shall remain
    with us.
Now forth, lord constable and princes all,
And quickly bring us word of England's fall.
                         [*Exeunt.*

SCENE VI. *The English camp in Picardy.*

Enter GOWER *and* FLUELLEN, *meeting.*

   Gow. How now, Captain Fluellen! come you
from the bridge?
   Flu. I assure you, there is very excellent
services committed at the bridge.
   Gow. Is the Duke of Exeter safe?
   Flu. The Duke of Exeter is as magnanimous
as Agamemnon; and a man that I love and
honour with my soul, and my heart, and my
duty, and my life, and my living, and my uttermost power: he is not—God be praised and
blessed!—any hurt in the world; but keeps the
bridge most valiantly, with excellent discipline.
There is an aunchient lieutenant there at the
pridge, I think in my very conscience he is as
valiant a man as Mark Antony; and he is a man
of no estimation in the world; but I did see him
do as gallant service.
   Gow. What do you call him?
   Flu. He is called Aunchient Pistol.
   Gow. I know him not.   20

Enter PISTOL.

   Flu. Here is the man.

Pist. Captain, I thee beseech to do me fa-
  vours:
The Duke of Exeter doth love thee well.
  Flu. Ay, I praise God; and I have merited
some love at his hands.
  Pist. Bardolph, a soldier, firm and sound of
  heart,
And of buxom valour, hath, by cruel fate,
And giddy Fortune's furious fickle wheel,
That goddess blind,
That stands upon the rolling restless stone— 30
  Flu. By your patience, Aunchient Pistol.
Fortune is painted blind, with a muffler afore
her eyes, to signify to you that Fortune is blind;
and she is painted also with a wheel, to signify to
you, which is the moral of it, that she is turning,
and inconstant, and mutability, and variation:
and her foot, look you, is fixed upon a spherical
stone, which rolls, and rolls, and rolls: in good
truth, the poet makes a most excellent descrip-
tion of it: Fortune is an excellent moral. 40
  Pist. Fortune is Bardolph's foe, and frowns
  on him;
● For he hath stolen a pax, and hanged must a' be:
A damned death!
Let gallows gape for dog; let man go free
And let not hemp his wind-pipe suffocate:
But Exeter hath given the doom of death
For pax of little price.
Therefore, go speak: the duke will hear thy voice:
And let not Bardolph's vital thread be cut
With edge of penny cord and vile reproach: 50
Speak, captain, for his life, and I will thee
  requite.
  Flu. Aunchient Pistol, I do partly understand
your meaning.
  Pist. Why then, rejoice therefore.
  Flu. Certainly, aunchient, it is not a thing to
rejoice at: for if, look you, he were my brother,
I would desire the duke to use his good pleasure,
and put him to execution; for discipline ought to
be used.
● *Pist.* Die and be damn'd! and figo for thy
  friendship! 60
  Flu. It is well.
  Pist. The fig of Spain! [*Exit.*
  Flu. Very good.
  Gow. Why, this is an arrant counterfeit rascal;
I remember him now; a bawd, a cutpurse.
  Flu. I'll assure you, a' uttered as prave words
at the pridge as you shall see in a summer's day.
But it is very well; what he has spoke to me, that
is well, I warrant you, when time is serve. 69
  Gow. Why, 'tis a gull, a fool, a rogue, that
now and then goes to the wars, to grace himself
at his return into London under the form of a
soldier. And such fellows are perfect in the great
commanders' names: and they will learn you by
rote where services were done; at such and such
● a sconce, at such a breach, at such a convoy; who
came off bravely, who was shot, who disgraced,
what terms the enemy stood on; and this they
con perfectly in the phrase of war, which they
trick up with new-tuned oaths: and what a beard
of the general's cut and a horrid suit of the camp
will do among foaming bottles and ale-washed
wits, is wonderful to be thought on. But you must
learn to know such slanders of the age, or else you
may be marvellously mistook.

Costume design for Pistol by John Bury with Ann
Curtis, Royal Shakespeare Co, 1964

42 *pax.* A piece of wood or metal with the figure of
Christ on it. Holinshed, however, writes 'pyx' which is
the box containing the consecrated host.

60 *figo.* A gesture of contempt in which the thumb was
thrust between the fingers.

An ornamental figo. Engraving by F.W. Fairholt from
J.O. Halliwell's edition of Shakespeare, 1853–65

76 *sconce.* Round fort.

88—89 *find a hole in his coat.* A chance to expose him.

Henry V. Engraving from the Frontispiece to *History of Henry V,* 1704

---

108 *bubukles, whelks,* Carbuncles, pimples.

121 *habit.* Dress.

129 *bruise an injury.* Squeeze a boil.

Flu. I tell you what, Captain Gower; I do perceive he is not the man that he would gladly make show to the world he is: if I find a hole in his coat, I will tell him my mind. [*Drum heard.*] Hark you, the king is coming, and I must speak with him from the pridge. 91

Drum and colours. **Enter KING HENRY, GLOUCESTER,** *and* Soldiers.

God pless your majesty!

K. Hen. How now, Fluellen! camest thou from the bridge?

Flu. Ay, so please your majesty. The Duke of Exeter has very gallantly maintained the pridge: the French is gone off, look you; and there is gallant and most prave passages; marry, th' athversary was have possession of the pridge: but he is enforced to retire, and the Duke of Exeter is master of the pridge: I can tell your majesty, the duke is a prave man. 101

K. Hen. What men have you lost, Fluellen?

Flu. The perdition of th' athversary hath been very great, reasonable great: marry, for my part, I think the duke hath lost never a man, but one that is like to be executed for robbing a church, one Bardolph, if your majesty know the man: his face is all bubukles, and whelks, and knobs, and flames o' fire: and his lips blows at his nose, and it is like a coal of fire, sometimes plue and sometimes red; but his nose is executed, and his fire's out.

K. Hen. We would have all such offenders so cut off: and we give express charge, that in our marches through the country, there be nothing compelled from the villages, nothing taken but paid for, none of the French upbraided or abused in disdainful language; for when lenity and cruelty play for a kingdom, the gentler gamester is the soonest winner. 120

Tucket. **Enter MONTJOY.**

Mont. You know me by my habit.

K. Hen. Well then I know thee: what shall I know of thee?

Mont. My master's mind.

K. Hen. Unfold it.

Mont. Thus says my king: Say thou to Harry of England: Though we seemed dead, we did but sleep: advantage is a better soldier than rashness. Tell him we could have rebuked him at Harfleur, but that we thought not good to bruise an injury till it were full ripe: now we speak upon our cue, and our voice is imperial: England shall repent his folly, see his weakness, and admire our sufferance. Bid him therefore consider of his ransom; which must proportion the losses we have borne, the subjects we have lost, the disgrace we have digested; which in weight to re-answer, his pettiness would bow under. For our losses, his exchequer is too poor; for the effusion of our blood, the muster of his kingdom too faint a number; and for our disgrace, his own person, kneeling at our feet, but a weak and worthless satisfaction. To this add defiance: and tell him, for conclusion, he hath betrayed his followers, whose condemnation is pronounced. So far my king and master; so much my office.

K. Hen. What is thy name? I know thy quality.

Mont. Montjoy.
K. Hen. Thou dost thy office fairly. Turn thee back,
And tell thy king I do not seek him now;
But could be willing to march on to Calais   150
● Without impeachment: for, to say the sooth,
Though 'tis no wisdom to confess so much
Unto an enemy of craft and vantage,
My people are with sickness much enfeebled,
My numbers lessen'd, and those few I have
Almost no better than so many French;
Who when they were in health, I tell thee, herald,
I thought upon one pair of English legs
Did march three Frenchmen. Yet, forgive me, God,   159
That I do brag thus! This your air of France
Hath blown that vice in me; I must repent.
Go therefore, tell thy master here I am;
My ransom is this frail and worthless trunk,
My army but a weak and sickly guard;
Yet, God before, tell him we will come on,
Though France himself and such another neighbour
Stand in our way. There's for thy labour, Montjoy.
Go, bid thy master well advise himself:
If we may pass, we will; if we be hinder'd,   169
We shall your tawny ground with your red blood
Discolour: and so, Montjoy, fare you well.
The sum of all our answer is but this:
We would not seek a battle, as we are;
Nor, as we are, we say we will not shun it:
So tell your master.
Mont. I shall deliver so. Thanks to your highness.   [*Exit.*
Glou. I hope they will not come upon us now.
K. Hen. We are in God's hand, brother, not in theirs.
March to the bridge; it now draws toward night:
Beyond the river we'll encamp ourselves,   180
And on to-morrow bid them march away.
[*Exeunt.*

SCENE VII. *The French camp, near Agincourt.*

Enter the CONSTABLE OF France, *the* LORD RAMBURES, ORLEANS, DAUPHIN, *with others.*

Con. Tut! I have the best armour of the world. Would it were day!
Orl. You have an excellent armour; but let my horse have his due.
Con. It is the best horse of Europe.
Orl. Will it never be morning?
Dau. My Lord of Orleans, and my lord high constable, you talk of horse and armour?
Orl. You are as well provided of both as any prince in the world.   10
Dau. What a long night is this! I will not change my horse with any that treads but on four pasterns. Ça, ha! he bounds from the earth, as
● if his entrails were hairs; le cheval volant, the
● Pegasus, chez les narines de feu! When I bestride him, I soar, I am a hawk: he trots the air; the earth sings when he touches it; the basest horn of his hoof is more musical than the pipe of Hermes.
Orl. He's of the colour of the nutmeg.   20
Dau. And of the heat of the ginger. It is a

---

151 *impeachment.* Hindrance.

14 *hairs.* i.e. stuffed with hair like a tennis ball.
le cheval volant. The flying horse.

15 *Pegasus.* In classical mythology, the winged horse of Perseus. *chez les narines de feu.* With nostrils of fire.

Pegasus, ridden by Perseus who holds the head of Medusa. A 17th century engraving

34 *lodging.* Lying down.

49 *prescript.* Prescribed.

56–57 *kern.* Irish foot-soldier. *French hose.* Wide breeches. *strait strossers.* Tight trousers.

68–69 '*Le chien . . . au bourbier !*' 'The dog returned to his own vomit, and the sow that was washed, to wallowing in the mire'. 2 Peter 2: xxii.

90 *faced out.* Shamed.

Costume design for Lord Rambures by Tanya Moisewitch, Stratford-upon-Avon, 1951

beast for Perseus : he is pure air and fire ; and the dull elements of earth and water never appear in him, but only in patient stillness while his rider mounts him : he is indeed a horse ; and all other jades you may call beasts.

Con. Indeed, my lord, it is a most absolute and excellent horse.

Dau. It is the prince of palfreys ; his neigh is like the bidding of a monarch and his countenance enforces homage. 31

Orl. No more, cousin.

Dau. Nay, the man hath no wit that cannot, • from the rising of the lark to the lodging of the lamb, vary deserved praise on my palfrey : it is a theme as fluent as the sea : turn the sands into eloquent tongues, and my horse is argument for them all : 'tis a subject for a sovereign to reason on, and for a sovereign's sovereign to ride on ; and for the world, familiar to us and unknown,to lay apart their particular functions and wonder at him. I once writ a sonnet in his praise and began thus : 'Wonder of nature,'—

Orl. I have heard a sonnet begin so to one's mistress.

Dau. Then did they imitate that which I composed to my courser, for my horse is my mistress.

Orl. Your mistress bears well.

• *Dau.* Me well ; which is the prescript praise and perfection of a good and particular mistress.

Con. Nay, for methought yesterday your mistress shrewdly shook your back.

Dau. So perhaps did yours.

Con. Mine was not bridled.

Dau. O then belike she was old and gentle ; • and you rode, like a kern of Ireland, your French hose off, and in your strait strossers.

Con. You have good judgement in horsemanship. 59

Dau. Be warned by me, then : they that ride so and ride not warily, fall into foul bogs. I had rather have my horse to my mistress.

Con. I had as lief have my mistress a jade.

Dau. I tell thee, constable, my mistress wears his own hair.

Con. I could make as true a boast as that, if I had a sow to my mistress.

• *Dau.* 'Le chien est retourné à son propre vomissement, et la truie lavée au bourbier :' thou makest use of any thing. 70

Con. Yet do I not use my horse for my mistress, or any such proverb so little kin to the purpose.

Ram. My lord constable, the armour that I saw in your tent to-night, are those stars or suns upon it?

Con. Stars, my lord.

Dau. Some of them will fall to-morrow, I hope.

Con. And yet my sky shall not want.

Dau. That may be, for you bear a many superfluously, and 'twere more honour some were away. 81

Con. Even as your horse bears your praises ; who would trot as well, were some of your brags dismounted.

Dau. Would I were able to load him with his desert ! Will it never be day ? I will trot to-morrow a mile, and my way shall be paved with English faces.

Con. I will not say so, for fear I should be • faced out of my way : but I would it were morning; for I would fain be about the ears of the English.

Ram. Who will go to hazard with me for twenty prisoners?

Con. You must first go yourself to hazard, ere you have them.

Dau. 'Tis midnight; I'll go arm myself. [*Exit.*

Orl. The Dauphin longs for morning.

Ram. He longs to eat the English.

Con. I think he will eat all he kills. 100

Orl. By the white hand of my lady, he's a gallant prince.

Con. Swear by her foot, that she may tread out the oath.

Orl. He is simply the most active gentleman of France.

Con. Doing is activity; and he will still be doing.

Orl. He never did harm, that I heard of.

Con. Nor will do none to-morrow: he will keep that good name still. 111

Orl. I know him to be valiant.

Con. I was told that by one that knows him better than you.

Orl. What's he?

Con. Marry, he told me so himself; and he said he cared not who knew it.

Orl. He needs not; it is no hidden virtue in him. 119

Con. By my faith, sir, but it is; never any body saw it but his lackey: 'tis a hooded valour; and when it appears, it will bate.

Orl. Ill will never said well.

Con. I will cap that proverb with 'There is flattery in friendship.'

Orl. And I will take up that with 'Give the devil his due.'

Con. Well placed: there stands your friend for the devil: have at the very eye of that proverb with 'A pox of the devil.' 130

Orl. You are the better at proverbs, by how much 'A fool's bolt is soon shot.'

Con. You have shot over.

Orl. 'Tis not the first time you were overshot.

Enter a Messenger.

Mess. My lord high constable, the English lie within fifteen hundred paces of your tents.

Con. Who hath measured the ground?

Mess. The Lord Grandpré.

Con. A valiant and most expert gentleman. Would it were day! Alas, poor Harry of England! he longs not for the dawning as we do. 141

Orl. What a wretched and peevish fellow is this king of England, to mope with his fat-brained followers so far out of his knowledge!

Con. If the English had any apprehension, they would run away.

Orl. That they lack; for if their heads had any intellectual armour, they could never wear such heavy head-pieces. 149

Ram. That island of England breeds very valiant creatures; their mastiffs are of unmatchable courage.

Orl. Foolish curs, that run winking into the mouth of a Russian bear and have their heads crushed like rotten apples! You may as well say, that's a valiant flea that dare eat his breakfast on the lip of a lion.

93 *go to hazard with me.* Wager me.

121 *hooded.* A falcon was hooded until the game was sighted.

122 *bate.* To 'flutter like a hawk', or to 'diminish'.

143 *mope.* Wander.

Rambures: '. . . their mastiffs are of unmatchable courage.' Woodcut of English hunting dogs from George Turberville's *The Noble Art of Venerie or Hunting,* 1611

158 *sympathize.* Resemble.

An army camp. Engraving from Holinshed's *Chronicles,* 1577

2 *poring.* Difficult to see in.

9 *battle.* Army. *umber'd.* Darkened.

12 *accomplishing.* Putting the finishing touches on.

39 *over-bears attaint.* Conquers any signs of exhaustion.

Con. Just, just; and the men do **sympathize** with the mastiffs in robustious and rough **coming on,** leaving their wits with their wives: and then give them great meals of beef and iron and steel, they will eat like wolves and fight like devils.

Orl. Ay, but these English are shrewdly out of beef.

Con. Then shall we find to-morrow they have only stomachs to eat and none to fight. Now is it time to arm: come, shall we about it?

Orl. It is now two o'clock: but, let me see, by ten
We shall have each a hundred Englishmen.

[*Exeunt.*

ACT IV.

PROLOGUE.

Enter Chorus.

Chor. Now entertain conjecture of a time
When creeping murmur and the poring dark
Fills the wide vessel of the universe.
From camp to camp through the foul womb of night
The hum of either army stilly sounds,
That the fix'd sentinels almost receive
The secret whispers of each other's watch:
Fire answers fire, and through their paly flames
Each battle sees the other's umber'd face;   9
Steed threatens steed, in high and boastful neighs
Piercing the night's dull ear; and from the tents
The armourers, accomplishing the knights,
With busy hammers closing rivets up,
Give dreadful note of preparation:
The country cocks do crow, the clocks do toll,
And the third hour of drowsy morning name.
Proud of their numbers and secure in soul,
The confident and over-lusty French
Do the low-rated English play at dice;
And chide the cripple tardy-gaited night   20
Who, like a foul and ugly witch, doth limp
So tediously away. The poor condemned English,
Like sacrifices, by their watchful fires
Sit patiently and inly ruminate
The morning's danger, and their gesture sad
Investing lank-lean cheeks and war-worn coats
Presenteth them unto the gazing moon
So many horrid ghosts. O now, who will behold
The royal captain of this ruin'd band
Walking from watch to watch, from tent to tent,
Let him cry 'Praise and glory on his head!'   31
For forth he goes and visits all his host,
Bids them good morrow with a modest smile
And calls them brothers, friends and countrymen.
Upon his royal face there is no note
How dread an army hath enrounded him;
Nor doth he dedicate one jot of colour
Unto the weary and all-watched night,
But freshly looks and over-bears attaint
With cheerful semblance and sweet majesty;   40
That every wretch, pining and pale before,
Beholding him, plucks comfort from his looks:
A largess universal like the sun
His liberal eye doth give to every one,
Thawing cold fear, that mean and gentle all
Behold, as may unworthiness define,
A little touch of Harry in the night.
And so our scene must to the battle fly;

Where—O for pity!—we shall much disgrace
With four or five most vile and ragged foils,   50
Right ill-disposed in brawl ridiculous,
The name of Agincourt.   Yet sit and see,
• Minding true things by what their mockeries be.
                                              [*Exit.*

SCENE I.   *The English camp at Agincourt.*

Enter KING HENRY, BEDFORD, *and* GLOU-
CESTER.

K. Hen.   Gloucester, 'tis true that we are in
    great danger;
The greater therefore should our courage be.
Good morrow, brother Bedford. God Almighty!
There is some soul of goodness in things evil,
Would men observingly distil it out.
For our bad neighbour makes us early stirrers,
Which is both healthful and good husbandry:
Besides, they are our outward consciences,
And preachers to us all, admonishing
That we should dress us fairly for our end.   10
Thus may we gather honey from the weed,
And make a moral of the devil himself.

Enter ERPINGHAM.

Good morrow, old Sir Thomas Erpingham:
A good soft pillow for that good white head
Were better than a churlish turf of France.
    Erp.   Not so, my liege: this lodging likes me
        better,
Since I may say 'Now lie I like a king.'
    K. Hen.   'Tis good for men to love their pres-
        ent pains
• Upon example; so the spirit is eased:
And when the mind is quicken'd, out of doubt,
The organs, though defunct and dead before,   21
Break up their drowsy grave and newly move,
• With casted slough and fresh legerity.
Lend me thy cloak, Sir Thomas. Brothers both,
Commend me to the princes in our camp;
Do my good morrow to them, and anon
Desire them all to my pavilion.
    Glou.   We shall, my liege.
    Erp.   Shall I attend your grace?
    K. Hen.   No, my good knight;
Go with my brothers to my lords of England: 30
I and my bosom must debate a while,
And then I would no other company.
    Erp.   The Lord in heaven bless thee, noble
        Harry!   [*Exeunt all but King.*
    K. Hen.   God-a-mercy, old heart! thou speak'st
        cheerfully.

Enter PISTOL.

Pist.   Qui va là?
K. Hen.   A friend.
Pist.   Discuss unto me; art thou officer?
Or art thou base, common and popular?
    K. Hen.   I am a gentleman of a company.
    Pist.   Trail'st thou the puissant pike?   40
    K. Hen.   Even so.   What are you?
    Pist.   As good a gentleman as the emperor.
    K. Hen.   Then you are a better than the king.
    Pist.   The king's a bawcock, and a heart of
        gold,
A lad of life, an imp of fame;
Of parents good, of fist most valiant.
I kiss his dirty shoe, and from heart-string

53 *Minding.* Imagining.

Sir Thomas Erpingham. Engraving from *Old England,*
1854

19 *Upon example.* By comparison.

23 *slough.* Cast-off skin of a snake.

54–55 *I'll knock . . . day.* The Welsh celebrated St. David's day by wearing leeks in their caps.

William Mollison as Pistol. Engraving from a painting by George Henry, 1905

I love the lovely bully.   What is thy name?
K. Hen. Harry le Roy.
Pist. Le Roy! a Cornish name: art thou of Cornish crew? 50
K. Hen. No, I am a Welshman.
Pist. Know'st thou Fluellen?
K. Hen. Yes.
Pist. Tell him, I'll knock his leek about his pate
Upon Saint Davy's day.
K. Hen. Do not you wear your dagger in your cap that day, lest he knock that about yours.
Pist. Art thou his friend?
K. Hen. And his kinsman too.
Pist. The figo for thee, then! 60
K. Hen. I thank you: God be with you!
Pist. My name is Pistol call'd. [*Exit.*
K. Hen. It sorts well with your fierceness.

Enter FLUELLEN *and* GOWER.

Gow. Captain Fluellen!
Flu. So! in the name of Jesu Christ, speak lower. It is the greatest admiration in the universal world, when the true and aunchient prerogatifes and laws of the wars is not kept: if you would take the pains but to examine the wars of Pompey the Great, you shall find, I warrant you, that there is no tiddle taddle nor pibble pabble in Pompey's camp; I warrant you, you shall find the ceremonies of the wars, and the cares of it, and the forms of it, and the sobriety of it, and the modesty of it, to be otherwise.
Gow. Why, the enemy is loud; you hear him all night.
Flu. If the enemy is an ass and a fool and a prating coxcomb, is it meet, think you, that we should also, look you, be an ass and a fool and a prating coxcomb? in your own conscience, now?
Gow. I will speak lower.
Flu. I pray you and beseech you that you will. [*Exeunt Gower and Fluellen.*
K. Hen. Though it appear a little out of fashion,
There is much care and valour in this Welshman.

Enter three soldiers, JOHN BATES, ALEXANDER COURT, *and* MICHAEL WILLIAMS.

Court. Brother John Bates, is not that the morning which breaks yonder?
Bates. I think it be: but we have no great cause to desire the approach of day. 90
Will. We see yonder the beginning of the day, but I think we shall never see the end of it. Who goes there?
K. Hen. A friend.
Will. Under what captain serve you?
K. Hen. Under Sir Thomas Erpingham.
Will. A good old commander and a most kind gentleman: I pray you, what thinks he of our estate?
K. Hen. Even as men wrecked upon a sand, that look to be washed off the next tide. 101
Bates. He hath not told his thought to the king?
K. Hen. No; nor it is not meet he should. For, though I speak it to you, I think the king is but a man, as I am: the violet smells to him as it

doth to me; the element shows to him as it doth to me; all his senses have but human conditions: his ceremonies laid by, in his nakedness he appears but a man; and though his affections are higher mounted than ours, yet, when they stoop, they stoop with the like wing. Therefore when he sees reason of fears, as we do, his fears, out of doubt, be of the same relish as ours are: yet, in reason, no man should possess him with any appearance of fear, lest he, by showing it, should dishearten his army.

Bates. He may show what outward courage he will; but I believe, as cold a night as 'tis, he could wish himself in Thames up to the neck; and so I would he were, and I by him, at all adventures, so we were quit here.

K. Hen. By my troth, I will speak my conscience of the king: I think he would not wish himself any where but where he is.

Bates. Then I would he were here alone; so should he be sure to be ransomed, and a many poor men's lives saved.

K. Hen. I dare say you love him not so ill, to wish him here alone, howsoever you speak this to feel other men's minds: methinks I could not die any where so contented as in the king's company; his cause being just and his quarrel honourable.

Will. That's more than we know.

Bates. Ay, or more than we should seek after; for we know enough, if we know we are the king's subjects: if his cause be wrong, our obedience to the king wipes the crime of it out of us.

Will. But if the cause be not good, the king himself hath a heavy reckoning to make, when all those legs and arms and heads, chopped off in a battle, shall join together at the latter day and cry all 'We died at such a place;' some swearing, some crying for a surgeon, some upon their wives left poor behind them, some upon the debts they owe, some upon their children rawly left. I am afeard there are few die well that die in a battle; for how can they charitably dispose of any thing, when blood is their argument? Now, if these men do not die well, it will be a black matter for the king that led them to it; whom to disobey were against all proportion of subjection.

K. Hen. So, if a son that is by his father sent about merchandise do sinfully miscarry upon the sea, the imputation of his wickedness, by your rule, should be imposed upon his father that sent him: or if a servant, under his master's command transporting a sum of money, be assailed by robbers and die in many irreconciled iniquities, you may call the business of the master the author of the servant's damnation: but this is not so: the king is not bound to answer the particular endings of his soldiers, the father of his son, nor the master of his servant; for they purpose not their death, when they purpose their services. Besides, there is no king, be his cause never so spotless, if it come to the arbitrement of swords, can try it out with all unspotted soldiers: some peradventure have on them the guilt of premeditated and contrived murder; some, of beguiling virgins with the broken seals of perjury; some, making the wars their bulwark, that have before gored the gentle bosom of peace with pillage and robbery. Now, if these men have defeated the

107 *element.* Sky.

123–124 *my conscience.* Opinion.

140–152 *But it . . . led them to it.* See introduction.

153 *proportion of subjection.* The proper obligations of a subject to his king.

155 *sinfully miscarry.* Die unabsolved of his sins.

Laurence Olivier as Henry V, Old Vic Theatre, London, 1937

178 *beadle.* A parish officer whose duty was to whip petty offenders.

210 *elder-gun.* A pop-gun made by removing the pith from elder wood.

216 *round.* Frank.

223 *gage.* Pledge.

Henry V: 'Give me any gage of thine . . .' Engraving by Kenny Meadows from Barry Cornwall's *The Works of Shakspere,* 1846

law and outrun native punishment, though they can outstrip men, they have no wings to fly from God : war is his beadle, war is his vengeance ; so that here men are punished for before-breach of the king's laws in now the king's quarrel : where they feared the death, they have borne life away ; and where they would be safe, they perish : then if they die unprovided, no more is the king guilty of their damnation than he was before guilty of those impieties for the which they are now visited. Every subject's duty is the king's ; but every subject's soul is his own. Therefore should every soldier in the wars do as every sick man in his bed, wash every mote out of his conscience : and dying so, death is to him advantage ; or not dying, the time was blessedly lost wherein such preparation was gained : and in him that escapes, it were not sin to think that, making God so free an offer, He let him outlive that day to see His greatness and to teach others how they should prepare.

Will. 'Tis certain, every man that dies ill, the ill upon his own head, the king is not to answer it. 199

Bates. I do not desire he should answer for me ; and yet I determine to fight lustily for him.

K. Hen. I myself heard the king say he would not be ransomed.

Will. Ay, he said so, to make us fight cheerfully : but when our throats are cut, he may be ransomed, and we ne'er the wiser.

K. Hen. If I live to see it, I will never trust his word after.

Will. You pay him then. That's a perilous shot out of an elder-gun, that a poor and a private displeasure can do against a monarch ! you may as well go about to turn the sun to ice with fanning in his face with a peacock's feather. You'll never trust his word after ! come, 'tis a foolish saying.

K. Hen. Your reproof is something too round : I should be angry with you, if the time were convenient.

Will. Let it be a quarrel between us, if you live. 220

K. Hen. I embrace it.

Will. How shall I know thee again ?

K. Hen. Give me any gage of thine, and I will wear it in my bonnet : then, if ever thou darest acknowledge it, I will make it my quarrel.

Will. Here's my glove : give me another of thine.

K. Hen. There.

Will. This will I also wear in my cap : if ever thou come to me and say, after to-morrow, 'This is my glove,' by this hand, I will take thee a box on the ear.

K. Hen. If ever I live to see it, I will challenge it.

Will. Thou darest as well be hanged.

K. Hen. Well, I will do it, though I take thee in the king's company.

Will. Keep thy word : fare thee well.

Bates. Be friends, you English fools, be friends : we have French quarrels enow, if you could tell how to reckon. 241

K. Hen. Indeed, the French may lay twenty French crowns to one, they will beat us ; for they bear them on their shoulders : but it is no

English treason to cut French crowns, and to-
morrow the king himself will be a clipper.
[*Exeunt Soldiers.*
Upon the king! let us our lives, our souls,
Our debts, our careful wives,
Our children and our sins lay on the king!
We must bear all.   O hard condition,   250
Twin-born with greatness, subject to the breath
Of every fool, whose sense no more can feel
But his own wringing!   What infinite heart's-ease
Must kings neglect, that private men enjoy!
And what have kings, that privates have not too,
Save ceremony, save general ceremony?
And what art thou, thou idol ceremony?
What kind of god art thou, that suffer'st more
Of mortal griefs than do thy worshippers?
What are thy rents? what are thy comings in?
O ceremony, show me but thy worth!   261
What is thy soul of adoration?
Art thou aught else but place, degree and form,
Creating awe and fear in other men?
Wherein thou art less happy being fear'd
Than they in fearing.
What drink'st thou oft, instead of homage sweet,
But poison'd flattery?   O, be sick, great greatness,
And bid thy ceremony give thee cure!
Think'st thou the fiery fever will go out   270
With titles blown from adulation?
Will it give place to flexure and low bending?
Canst thou, when thou command'st the beggar's
        knee,
Command the health of it? No, thou proud dream,
That play'st so subtly with a king's repose;
I am a king that find thee, and I know
'Tis not the balm, the sceptre and the ball,
The sword, the mace, the crown imperial,
The intertissued robe of gold and pearl,
The farced title running 'fore the king,   280
The throne he sits on, nor the tide of pomp
That beats upon the high shore of this world,
No, not all these, thrice-gorgeous ceremony,
Not all these, laid in bed majestical,
Can sleep so soundly as the wretched slave,
Who with a body fill'd and vacant mind
Gets him to rest, cramm'd with distressful bread;
Never sees horrid night, the child of hell,
But, like a lackey, from the rise to set
Sweats in the eye of Phœbus and all night   290
Sleeps in Elysium; next day after dawn,
Doth rise and help Hyperion to his horse,
And follows so the ever-running year,
With profitable labour, to his grave:
And, but for ceremony, such a wretch,
Winding up days with toil and nights with sleep,
Had the fore-hand and vantage of a king.
The slave, a member of the country's peace,
Enjoys it; but in gross brain little wots
What watch the king keeps to maintain the peace,
Whose hours the peasant best advantages.   301

Re-enter ERPINGHAM.

Erp. My lord, your nobles, jealous of your
        absence,
Seek through your camp to find you.
  K. Hen.   Good old knight,
Collect them all together at my tent:
I'll be before thee.
  Erp.   I shall do't, my lord. [*Exit.*

245 *treason.* It was treason to clip coins.

246 *clipper.* A pun on *clip*, to 'cut off' and to 'trim the
edges of coins'.

247–253 *Upon the King . . . wringing.* See introduction.

262 *thy . . . adoration.* The nature of the adoration paid
to you.

271 *from adulation.* From flatterers.

277 *balm.* The oil used to anoint the king in the
coronation ceremony.

F.R. Benson as Henry V, Lyceum Theatre, London, 1900

280 *farced.* Stuffed.

290 *Phœbus.* In classical myths, the god of the sun.

291 *Elysium.* The habitation of the virtuous after death.

292 *Hyperion.* Father of the sun-god.

299 *wots.* Knows.

312 *Richard.* Henry IV was responsible for the death of Richard II.

Funeral of Richard II. Engraving from an illumination in Froissart's *Chronicles*, 15th century

2 *Montez à cheval! . . . laquais!* To horse! My horse, lackey!

4 *Via! les eaux et la terre.* Away (over) water and earth.

5 *Rien puis? l'air et le feu.* Orleans jokingly asks if the Dauphin's horse will not soar above the other two elements, air and fire.

6 *Ciel.* To the heavens themselves.

K. Hen. O God of battles! steel my soldiers' hearts;
Possess them not with fear; take from them now
The sense of reckoning, if the opposed numbers
Pluck their hearts from them. Not to-day, O Lord,
O, not to-day, think not upon the fault   310
My father made in compassing the crown!
• I Richard's body have interred new;
And on it have bestow'd more contrite tears
Than from it issued forced drops of blood:
Five hundred poor I have in yearly pay,
Who twice a-day their wither'd hands hold up
Toward heaven, to pardon blood; and I have built
Two chantries, where the sad and solemn priests
Sing still for Richard's soul. More will I do;
Though all that I can do is nothing worth,   320
Since that my penitence comes after all,
Imploring pardon.

Re-enter GLOUCESTER.

Glou. My liege!
K. Hen. My brother Gloucester's voice? Ay;
I know thy errand, I will go with thee:
The day, my friends and all things stay for me.
                               [Exeunt.

SCENE II. *The French camp.*

Enter the DAUPHIN, ORLEANS, RAMBURES, *and others.*

Orl. The sun doth gild our armour; up, my lords!
• *Dau.* Montez à cheval! My horse! varlet! laquais! ha!
Orl. O brave spirit!
• *Dau.* Via! les eaux et la terre.
• *Orl.* Rien puis? l'air et le feu.
• *Dau.* Ciel, cousin Orleans.

Enter CONSTABLE.

Now, my lord constable!
Con. Hark, how our steeds for present service neigh!
Dau. Mount them, and make incision in their hides,
That their hot blood may spin in English eyes,   10
And dout them with superfluous courage, ha!
Ram. What, will you have them weep our horses' blood?
How shall we, then, behold their natural tears?

Enter Messenger.

Mess. The English are embattled, you French peers.
Con. To horse, you gallant princes! straight to horse!
Do but behold yon poor and starved band,
And your fair show shall suck away their souls,
Leaving them but the shales and husks of men.
There is not work enough for all our hands;
Scarce blood enough in all their sickly veins   20
To give each naked curtle-axe a stain,
That our French gallants shall to-day draw out,
And sheathe for lack of sport: let us but blow on them,
The vapour of our valour will o'erturn them.
'Tis positive 'gainst all exceptions, lords,

That our superfluous lackeys and our peasants,
Who in unnecessary action swarm
About our squares of battle, were enow
• To purge this field of such a hilding foe,
Though we upon this mountain's basis by   30
• Took stand for idle speculation:
But that our honours must not.   What's to say?
A very little little let us do,
And all is done.   Then let the trumpets sound
• The tucket sonance and the note to mount;
• For our approach shall so much dare the field
That England shall couch down in fear and yield.

Enter GRANDPRÉ.

Grand.   Why do you stay so long, my lords of
     France?
• Yon island carrions, desperate of their bones,
Ill-favouredly become the morning field: 40
• Their ragged curtains poorly are let loose,
And our air shakes them passing scornfully:
Big Mars seems bankrupt in their beggar'd host
• And faintly through a rusty beaver peeps:
The horsemen sit like fixed candlesticks,
With torch-staves in their hand; and their poor
     jades
• Lob down their heads, dropping the hides and
     hips,
The gum down-roping from their pale-dead eyes,
• And in their pale dull mouths the gimmal bit
Lies foul with chew'd grass, still and motionless;
And their executors, the knavish crows,   51
Fly o'er them, all impatient for their hour.
Description cannot suit itself in words
To demonstrate the life of such a battle
In life so lifeless as it shows itself.
     Con.   They have said their prayers, and they
          stay for death.
     Dau.   Shall we go send them dinners and
          fresh suits
And give their fasting horses provender,
And after fight with them?
• *Con.*   I stay but for my guidon: to the field!   61
I will the banner from a trumpet take,
And use it for my haste.   Come, come, away!
The sun is high, and we outwear the day.
          [*Exeunt.*

SCENE III.   *The English camp.*

Enter GLOUCESTER, BEDFORD, EXETER, ER-
PINGHAM, *with all his host:* SALISBURY *and*
WESTMORELAND.

Glou.   Where is the king?
Bed.   The king himself is rode to view their
     battle.
West.   Of fighting men they have full three
     score thousand.
Exe.   There's five to one; besides, they all
     are fresh.
Sal.   God's arm strike with us! 'tis a fearful
     odds.
God be wi' you, princes all; I'll to my charge:
If we no more meet till we meet in heaven,
Then, joyfully, my noble Lord of Bedford,
My dear Lord Gloucester, and my good Lord
     Exeter,
And my kind kinsman, warriors all, adieu!   10

29 *hilding.* Menial.

31 *speculation.* Looking on.

35 *tucket sonance.* Trumpet sound.

36 *dare.* Challenge.

39 *desperate of.* Desperate to save.

41 *curtains.* Banners, flags.

44 *beaver.* Visor.

47 *Lob.* Hang down.

49 *gimmal.* Jointed.

60 *guidon.* Standard.

Montacute, Earl of Salisbury. Engraving from *Old England*, 1854

579

Earl of Westmoreland. Engraving from *Old England,* 1854

40—46 *This day . . . Crispian.* See introduction.

40 *feast of Crispian.* October 25th. Saints Crispin and Crispinian are the patron saints of shoemakers.

62 *vile.* Of low status.

63 *gentle.* Improve, raise.

Bed. Farewell, good Salisbury; and good
   luck go with thee!
Exe. Farewell, kind lord; fight valiantly to-
   day:
And yet I do thee wrong to mind thee of it,
For thou art framed of the firm truth of valour.
                [*Exit Salisbury.*
Bed. He is as full of valour as of kindness;
Princely in both.

Enter the KING.

West.   O that we now had here
But one ten thousand of those men in England
That do no work to-day!
   K. Hen.   What's he that wishes so?
My cousin Westmoreland? No, my fair cousin:
If we are mark'd to die, we are enow   20
To do our country loss; and if to live,
The fewer men, the greater share of honour.
God's will! I pray thee, wish not one man more.
By Jove, I am not covetous for gold,
Nor care I who doth feed upon my cost;
It yearns me not if men my garments wear;
Such outward things dwell not in my desires:
But if it be a sin to covet honour,
I am the most offending soul alive.   29
No, faith, my coz, wish not a man from England:
God's peace! I would not lose so great an honour
As one man more, methinks, would share from
   me
For the best hope I have. O, do not wish one
   more!
Rather proclaim it, Westmoreland, through my
   host,
That he which hath no stomach to this fight,
Let him depart; his passport shall be made
And crowns for convoy put into his purse:
We would not die in that man's company
That fears his fellowship to die with us.
• This day is call'd the feast of Crispian: 40
He that outlives this day, and comes safe home,
Will stand a tip-toe when this day is named,
And rouse him at the name of Crispian.
He that shall live this day, and see old age,
Will yearly on the vigil feast his neighbours,
And say 'To-morrow is Saint Crispian:'
Then will he strip his sleeve and show his scars,
And say 'These wounds I had on Crispin's day.'
Old men forget; yet all shall be forgot,
But he'll remember with advantages   50
What feats he did that day: then shall our names,
Familiar in his mouth as household words,
Harry the king, Bedford and Exeter,
Warwick and Talbot, Salisbury and Gloucester,
Be in their flowing cups freshly remember'd.
This story shall the good man teach his son;
And Crispin Crispian shall ne'er go by,
From this day to the ending of the world,
But we in it shall be remembered;
We few, we happy few, we band of brothers;   60
For he to-day that sheds his blood with me
• Shall be my brother; be he ne'er so vile,
• This day shall gentle his condition:
And gentlemen in England now a-bed
Shall think themselves accursed they were not
   here,
And hold their manhoods cheap whiles any speaks
That fought with us upon Saint Crispin's day.

Re-enter SALISBURY.

Sal. My sovereign lord, bestow yourself with
 speed :
- The French are bravely in their battles set,
And will with all expedience charge on us. 70
 K. Hen. All things are ready, if our minds
 be so.
 West. Perish the man whose mind is back-
 ward now !
 K. Hen. Thou dost not wish more help from
 England, coz?
 West. God's will ! my liege, would you and
 I alone,
Without more help, could fight this royal battle !
 K. Hen. Why, now thou hast unwish'd five
 thousand men ;
Which likes me better than to wish us one.
You know your places : God be with you all !

Tucket. Enter MONTJOY.

 Mont. Once more I come to know of thee,
 King Harry,
- If for thy ransom thou wilt now compound, 80
Before thy most assured overthrow :
For certainly thou art so near the gulf,
Thou needs must be englutted. Besides, in
 mercy,
The constable desires thee thou wilt mind
Thy followers of repentance ; that their souls
May make a peaceful and a sweet retire
From off these fields, where, wretches, their poor
 bodies
Must lie and fester.
 K. Hen. Who hath sent thee now?
 Mont. The Constable of France.
 K. Hen. I pray thee, bear my former answer
 back : 90
- Bid them achieve me and then sell my bones.
Good God ! why should they mock poor fellows
 thus?
The man that once did sell the lion's skin
While the beast lived, was killed with hunting
 him.
A many of our bodies shall no doubt
Find native graves ; upon the which, I trust,
Shall witness live in brass of this day's work :
And those that leave their valiant bones in France,
Dying like men, though buried in your dunghills,
They shall be famed ; for there the sun shall greet
 them, 100
And draw their honours reeking up to heaven ;
Leaving their earthly parts to choke your clime,
The smell whereof shall breed a plague in
 France.
Mark then abounding valour in our English,
- That being dead, like to the bullet's grazing,
Break out into a second course of mischief,
- Killing in relapse of mortality.
Let me speak proudly : tell the constable
We are but warriors for the working-day ;
Our gayness and our gilt are all besmirch'd 110
With rainy marching in the painful field ;
There's not a piece of feather in our host—
Good argument, I hope, we will not fly—
And time hath worn us into slovenry :
But, by the mass, our hearts are in the trim ;
And my poor soldiers tell me, yet ere night
They'll be in fresher robes, or they will pluck

69 *bravely.* Finely.

80 *compound.* Come to terms.

Costume design for the Earl of Salisbury by Tanya
Moisewitch, Stratford-upon-Avon, 1951

91 *achieve.* Overcome.

105 *grazing.* Glancing off.

107 *relapse of mortality.* A deadly rebound.

130 *vaward*. Vanguard.

2–3 *Je pense . . . qualité*. I think you are a gentleman of good standing.

4 *Qualtitie . . . me*. Pistol does not understand, and replies with the mangled refrain of a popular song.

6 *O Seigneur Dieu*. O Lord God.

Pistol: 'Perpend my words . . .' Drawing by P.J. de Loutherbourg (1740–1812)

9 *fox*. Sword.

12–13 *O, prenez . . . de moi!* O, have mercy! Take pity on me.

14 *Moy*. Pistol thinks this is the name of a coin.

17–18 *Est-il possible . . . ton bras*. Is it possible to escape the strength of your arm?

26 *Écoutez . . . appelé?* Listen, what's your name?

29 *firk*. Beat.

30 *ferret*. Worry.

35 *Que dit-il, monsieur?* What does he say?

The gay new coats o'er the French soldiers'
  heads
And turn them out of service.   If they do this,—
As, if God please, they shall,—my ransom then
Will soon be levied.   Herald, save thou thy
  labour;   121
Come thou no more for ransom, gentle herald:
They shall have none, I swear, but these my
  joints;
Which if they have as I will leave 'em them,
Shall yield them little, tell the constable.
    Mont.   I shall, King Harry.   And so fare
    thee well:
Thou never shalt hear herald any more.   [*Exit.*
    K. Hen.   I fear thou 'lt once more come again
    for ransom.

             Enter YORK.

    York.   My lord, most humbly on my knee
    I beg
The leading of the vaward.   130
    K. Hen.   Take it, brave York.   Now, soldiers,
    march away:
And how thou pleasest, God, dispose the day!
                          [*Exeunt.*

    SCENE IV.   *The field of battle.*

Alarum.   Excursions.   Enter PISTOL, French
      Soldier, *and* Boy.

    Pist.   Yield, cur!
    Fr. Sol.   Je pense que vous êtes gentilhomme
de bonne qualité.
    Pist.   Qualtitie calmie custure me!   Art thou
a gentleman? what is thy name? discuss.
    Fr. Sol.   O Seigneur Dieu!
    Pist.   O, Signieur Dew should be a gentleman:
Perpend my words, O Signieur Dew, and mark;
O Signieur Dew, thou diest on point of fox,
Except, O signieur, thou do give to me   10
Egregious ransom.
    Fr. Sol.   O, prenez miséricorde! ayez pitié
de moi!
    Pist.   Moy shall not serve; I will have forty
    moys;
Or I will fetch thy rim out at thy throat
In drops of crimson blood.
    Fr. Sol.   Est-il impossible d'échapper la force
de ton bras?
    Pist.   Brass, cur!
Thou damned and luxurious mountain goat, 20
Offer'st me brass?
    Fr. Sol.   O pardonnez moi!
    Pist.   Say'st thou me so? is that a ton of
    moys?
Come hither, boy: ask me this slave in French
What is his name.
    Boy.   Écoutez: comment êtes-vous appelé?
    Fr. Sol.   Monsieur le Fer.
    Boy.   He says his name is Master Fer.
    Pist.   Master Fer! I'll fer him, and firk him,
and ferret him: discuss the same in French unto
him.   31
    Boy.   I do not know the French for fer, and
ferret, and firk.
    Pist.   Bid him prepare; for I will cut his
    throat.
    Fr. Sol.   Que dit-il, monsieur?

Boy. Il me commande de vous dire que vous faites vous prêt ; car ce soldat ici est disposé tout à cette heure de couper votre gorge.

Pist. Owy, cuppele gorge, permafoy,
Peasant, unless thou give me crowns, brave
    crowns ;   40
Or mangled shalt thou be by this my sword.

Fr. Sol. O, je vous supplie, pour l'amour de Dieu, me pardonner ! Je suis gentilhomme de bonne maison : gardez ma vie, et je vous donnerai deux cents écus.

Pist. What are his words?

Boy. He prays you to save his life : he is a gentleman of a good house ; and for his ransom he will give you two hundred crowns.

Pist. Tell him my fury shall abate, and I   50
The crowns will take.

Fr. Sol. Petit monsieur, que dit-il?

Boy. Encore qu'il est contre son jurement de pardonner aucun prisonnier, néanmoins, pour les écus que vous l'avez promis, il est content de vous donner la liberté, le franchisement.

Fr. Sol. Sur mes genoux je vous donne mille remercimens ; et je m'estime heureux que je suis tombé entre les mains d'un chevalier, je pense, le plus brave, vaillant, et très distingué seigneur d'Angleterre.   61

Pist. Expound unto me, boy.

Boy. He gives you, upon his knees, a thousand thanks ; and he esteems himself happy that he hath fallen into the hands of one, as he thinks, the most brave, valorous, and thrice-worthy signieur of England.

Pist. As I suck blood, I will some mercy show.
Follow me !   69

Boy. Suivez-vous le grand capitaine. [*Exeunt Pistol, and French Soldier.*] I did never know so full a voice issue from so empty a heart : but the saying is true, 'The empty vessel makes the greatest sound.' Bardolph and Nym had ten times more valour than this roaring devil i' the old play, that every one may pare his nails with a wooden dagger ; and they are both hanged ; and so would this be, if he durst steal any thing adventurously. I must stay with the lackeys, with the luggage of our camp : the French might have a good prey of us, if he knew of it ; for there is none to guard it but boys.   [*Exit.*

SCENE V. *Another part of the field.*

Enter CONSTABLE, ORLEANS, BOURBON, DAUPHIN, *and* RAMBURES.

Con. O diable !

Orl. O seigneur ! le jour est perdu, tout est perdu !

Dau. Mort de ma vie ! all is confounded, all !
Reproach and everlasting shame
Sits mocking in our plumes. O méchante fortune !
Do not run away.   [*A short alarum.*

Con.   Why, all our ranks are broke.

Dau. O perdurable shame ! let's stab ourselves.
Be these the wretches that we play'd at dice for ?

Orl. Is this the king we sent to for his ransom ?

Bour. Shame and eternal shame, nothing but shame !   10
Let us die in honour : once more back again ;

36—38 *Il me commande . . . votre gorge.* He commands me to tell you to prepare yourself, for this soldier has a mind at once to cut your throat.

Pistol: 'What are his words?' Engraving from Bell's *Works . . .* 1773

52 *Petit . . . dit-il?* Little sir, what does he say?

53—56 *Encore qu'il . . . franchisement.* Again, although it is against his oath to pardon any prisoner, nevertheless for the crowns you have promised, he is willing to give you liberty, freedom.

70 *Suivez-vous le grand capitaine.* Follow the great captain.

76 *old play.* The Morality plays in which the Devil was often mocked by the character Vice, who would sometimes belabour him with a wooden sword.

2 *le jour . . . perdu.* The day is lost, all is lost.

5 *O méchante fortune.* O spiteful fortune.

7 *perdurable.* Eternal.

Costume design for the Earl of Exeter by Tanya Moisewitch, Stratford-upon-Avon, 1951

___

8 *Larding*. Enriching.

9 *honour-owing*. Honour-owning.

11 *haggled*. Hacked.

And he that will not follow Bourbon now,
Let him go hence, and with his cap in hand,
Like a base pandar, hold the chamber-door
Whilst by a slave, no gentler than my dog,
His fairest daughter is contaminated.
   Con. Disorder, that hath spoil'd us, friend us now!
Let us on heaps go offer up our lives.
   Orl. We are enow yet living in the field
To smother up the English in our throngs,   20
If any order might be thought upon.
   Bour. The devil take order now! I'll to the throng:
Let life be short; else shame will be too long.
                       [Exeunt.

SCENE VI. *Another part of the field.*

Alarums. Enter KING HENRY *and forces,*
EXETER, *and others.*

   K. Hen. Well have we done, thrice valiant countrymen:
But all's not done; yet keep the French the field.
   Exe. The Duke of York commends him to your majesty.
   K. Hen. Lives he, good uncle? thrice within this hour
I saw him down; thrice up again, and fighting;
From helmet to the spur all blood he was.
   Exe. In which array, brave soldier, doth he lie,
• Larding the plain; and by his bloody side,
• Yoke-fellow to his honour-owing wounds,
The noble Earl of Suffolk also lies.   10
• Suffolk first died: and York, all haggled over,
Comes to him, where in gore he lay insteep'd,
And takes him by the beard; kisses the gashes
That bloodily did yawn upon his face;
And cries aloud 'Tarry, dear cousin Suffolk!
My soul shall thine keep company to heaven;
Tarry, sweet soul, for mine, then fly abreast,
As in this glorious and well-foughten field
We kept together in our chivalry!'
Upon these words I came and cheer'd him up: 20
He smiled me in the face, raught me his hand,
And, with a feeble gripe, says 'Dear my lord,
Commend my service to my sovereign.'
So did he turn and over Suffolk's neck
He threw his wounded arm and kiss'd his lips;
And so espoused to death, with blood he seal'd
A testament of noble-ending love.
The pretty and sweet manner of it forced
Those waters from me which I would have stopp'd;
But I had not so much of man in me,   30
And all my mother came into mine eyes
And gave me up to tears.
   K. Hen.   I blame you not;
For, hearing this, I must perforce compound
With mistful eyes, or they will issue too.
                       [Alarum.
But, hark! what new alarum is this same?
The French have reinforced their scatter'd men:
Then every soldier kill his prisoners;
Give the word through.   *[Exeunt.*

SCENE VII. *Another part of the field.*

Enter FLUELLEN *and* GOWER.

   Flu. Kill the poys and the luggage! 'tis expressly against the law of arms: 'tis as arrant a piece of knavery, mark you now, as can be offer't; in your conscience, now, is it not?

Gow. 'Tis certain there's not a boy left alive; and the cowardly rascals that ran from the battle ha' done this slaughter: besides, they have burned and carried away all that was in the king's tent; wherefore the king, most worthily, hath caused every soldier to cut his prisoner's throat. O, 'tis a gallant king! 11

Flu. Ay, he was porn at Monmouth, Captain Gower. What call you the town's name where Alexander the Pig was born!

Gow. Alexander the Great.

Flu. Why, I pray you, is not pig great? the pig, or the great, or the mighty, or the huge, or the magnanimous, are all one reckonings, save the phrase is a little variations. 19

Gow. I think Alexander the Great was born in Macedon: his father was called Philip of Macedon, as I take it.

Flu. I think it is in Macedon where Alexander is porn. I tell you, captain, if you look in the maps of the 'orld, I warrant you sall find, in the comparisons between Macedon and Monmouth, that the situations, look you, is both alike. There is a river in Macedon; and there is also moreover a river at Monmouth: it is called Wye at Monmouth; but it is out of my prains what is the name of the other river; but 'tis all one, 'tis alike as my fingers is to my fingers, and there is salmons in both. If you mark Alexander's life well,
- Harry of Monmouth's life is come after it indif-
- ferent well; for there is figures in all things. Alexander, God knows, and you know, in his rages, and his furies, and his wraths, and his cholers, and his moods, and his displeasures, and his indignations, and also being a little intoxicates in his prains, did, in his ales and his angers, look
- you, kill his best friend, Cleitus. 41

Gow. Our king is not like him in that: he never killed any of his friends.

Flu. It is not well done, mark you now, to take the tales out of my mouth, ere it is made and finished. I speak but in the figures and comparisons of it: as Alexander killed his friend Cleitus, being in his ales and his cups; so also Harry Monmouth, being in his right wits and his good judgements, turned away the fat knight with the great-belly doublet: he was full of jests, and gipes, and knaveries, and mocks; I have forgot his name.

Gow. Sir John Falstaff.

Flu. That is he: I'll tell you there is good men porn at Monmouth.

Gow. Here comes his majesty.

Alarum. Enter KING HENRY, *and forces;* WARWICK, GLOUCESTER, EXETER, *and others.*

K. Hen. I was not angry since I came to France
Until this instant. Take a trumpet, herald;
Ride thou unto the horsemen on yon hill: 60
If they will fight with us, bid them come down,
Or void the field; they do offend our sight:
If they'll do neither, we will come to them,
- And make them skirr away, as swift as stones
Enforced from the old Assyrian slings:
Besides, we'll cut the throats of those we have,
And not a man of them that we shall take

34 *come after.* Is similar.

35 *figures.* Parallels.

41 *Cleitus.* Alexander killed his best friend in a drunken argument.

64 *skirr.* Scurry.

Costume design for the Earl of Warwick by Tanya Moisewitch, Stratford-upon-Avon, 1951

72 *fined.* Wagered.

83 *Yerk.* Kick.

88 *peer.* Appear.

King Henry: 'For yet a many of your horsemen peer
And gallop o'er the field.' Woodcut of a cavalry charge
from Holinshed's *Chronicles,* 1577

104 *Monmouth caps.* Brimless, circular hats with high
crowns.

Shall taste our mercy.   Go and tell them so.

Enter MONTJOY.

Exe.   Here comes the herald of the French,
my liege.
Glo.   His eyes are humbler than they used
to be.   70
K. Hen.   How now! what means this, herald?
know'st thou not

● That I have fined these bones of mine for ransom?
Comest thou again for ransom?
Mont.   No, great king:
I come to thee for charitable license,
That we may wander o'er this bloody field
To look our dead, and then to bury them;
To sort our nobles from our common men.
For many of our princes—woe the while!—
Lie drown'd and soak'd in mercenary blood;
So do our vulgar drench their peasant limbs   80
In blood of princes; and their wounded steeds
Fret fetlock deep in gore and with wild rage
● Yerk out their armed heels at their dead masters,
Killing them twice.   O, give us leave, great king,
To view the field in safety and dispose
Of their dead bodies!
K. Hen.   I tell thee truly, herald,
I know not if the day be ours or no;
● For yet a many of your horsemen peer
And gallop o'er the field.
Mont.   The day is yours.
K. Hen.   Praised be God, and not our strength,
for it!   90
What is this castle call'd that stands hard by?
Mont.   They call it Agincourt.
K. Hen.   Then call we this the field of Agin-
court,
Fought on the day of Crispin Crispianus.
Flu.   Your grandfather of famous memory,
an't please your majesty, and your great-uncle
Edward the Plack Prince of Wales, as I have
read in the chronicles, fought a most prave pattle
here in France.
K. Hen.   They did, Fluellen.   100
Flu.   Your majesty says very true: if your
majesties is remembered of it, the Welshmen did
good service in a garden where leeks did grow,
● wearing leeks in their Monmouth caps; which,
your majesty know, to this hour is an honourable
badge of the service; and I do believe your majesty takes no scorn to wear the leek upon Saint
Tavy's day.
K. Hen.   I wear it for a memorable honour;
For I am Welsh, you know, good countryman.
Flu.   All the water in Wye cannot wash your
majesty's Welsh plood out of your pody, I can
tell you that: God pless it and preserve it, as long
as it pleases his grace, and his majesty too!
K. Hen.   Thanks, good my countryman.
Flu.   By Jeshu, I am your majesty's countryman, I care not who know it; I will confess it to
all the 'orld: I need not to be ashamed of your
majesty, praised be God, so long as your majesty
is an honest man.   120
K. Hen.   God keep me so!   Our heralds go
with him:
Bring me just notice of the numbers dead
On both our parts.   Call yonder fellow hither.
[*Points to Williams.   Exeunt Heralds
with Montjoy.*

Exe. Soldier, you must come to the king.

K. Hen. Soldier, why wearest thou that glove in thy cap?

Will. An't please your majesty, 'tis the gage of one that I should fight withal, if he be alive.

K. Hen. An Englishman?   129

Will. An't please your majesty, a rascal that swaggered with me last night; who, if alive and ever dare to challenge this glove, I have sworn to take him a box o' th' ear: or if I can see my glove in his cap, which he swore, as he was a soldier, he would wear if alive, I will strike it out soundly.

K. Hen. What think you, Captain Fluellen? is it fit this soldier keep his oath?

Flu. He is a craven and a villain else, an't please your majesty, in my conscience.   140

K. Hen. It may be his enemy is a gentleman
● of great sort, quite from the answer of his degree.

Flu. Though he be as good a gentleman as the devil is, as Lucifer and Belzebub himself, it is necessary, look your grace, that he keep his vow and his oath: if he be perjured, see you now, his
● reputation is as arrant a villain and a Jacksauce, as ever his black shoe trod upon God's ground and his earth, in my conscience, la!   150

K. Hen. Then keep thy vow, sirrah, when thou meetest the fellow.

Will. So I will, my liege, as I live.

K. Hen. Who servest thou under?

Will. Under Captain Gower, my liege.

Flu. Gower is a good captain, and is good knowledge and literatured in the wars.

K. Hen. Call him hither to me, soldier.

Will. I will, my liege.   [*Exit.*

K. Hen. Here, Fluellen; wear thou this favour for me and stick it in thy cap: when Alençon and myself were down together, I plucked this glove from his helm: if any man challenge this, he is a friend to Alençon, and an enemy to our person; if thou encounter any such, apprehend him, an thou dost me love.

Flu. Your grace doo's me as great honours as can be desired in the hearts of his subjects: I would fain see the man, that has but two legs, that shall find himself aggriefed at this glove; that is all; but I would fain see it once, an please God of his grace that I might see.

K. Hen. Knowest thou Gower?

Flu. He is my dear friend, an please you.

K. Hen. Pray thee, go seek him, and bring him to my tent.

Flu. I will fetch him.   [*Exit.*

K. Hen. My Lord of Warwick, and my brother Gloucester,
Follow Fluellen closely at the heels:
The glove which I have given him for a favour
May haply purchase him a box o' th' ear;   181
It is the soldier's; I by bargain should
Wear it myself. Follow, good cousin Warwick:
If that the soldier strike him, as I judge
By his blunt bearing he will keep his word,
Some sudden mischief may arise of it;
For I do know Fluellen valiant
And, touch'd with choler, hot as gunpowder,
And quickly will return an injury;   189
Follow, and see there be no harm between them.
Go you with me, uncle of Exeter.   [*Exeunt.*

Henry V. Engraving from *Old England*, 1854

142–143 *sort.* Status. *quite from . . . degree.* Too much above him in rank to answer a challenge from a mere soldier.

148 *Jacksauce.* Saucy rascal.

Fluellen: 'I will give treason his payment...' Engraving by Kenny Meadows from Barry Cornwall's *The Works of Shakspere*, 1846

38–39 *avouchment.* Acknowledge.

SCENE VIII. *Before* KING HENRY'S *pavilion.*

Enter GOWER *and* WILLIAMS.

Will. I warrant it is to knight you, captain.

Enter FLUELLEN.

Flu. God's will and his pleasure, captain, I beseech you now, come apace to the king: there is more good toward you peradventure than is in your knowledge to dream of.

Will. Sir, know you this glove?

Flu. Know the glove! I know the glove is a glove.

Will. I know this; and thus I challenge it.
[*Strikes him.*

Flu. 'Sblood! an arrant traitor as any is in the universal world, or in France, or in England! 11

Gow. How now, sir! you villain!

Will. Do you think I'll be forsworn?

Flu. Stand away, Captain Gower; I will give treason his payment into plows, I warrant you.

Will. I am no traitor.

Flu. That's a lie in thy throat. I charge you in his majesty's name, apprehend him: he's a friend of the Duke Alençon's. 19

Enter WARWICK *and* GLOUCESTER.

War. How now, how now! what's the matter?

Flu. My Lord of Warwick, here is—praised be God for it!—a most contagious treason come to light, look you, as you shall desire in a summer's day. Here is his majesty.

Enter KING HENRY *and* EXETER.

K. Hen. How now! what's the matter?

Flu. My liege, here is a villain and a traitor, that, look your grace, has struck the glove which your majesty is take out of the helmet of Alençon.

Will. My liege, this was my glove; here is the fellow of it; and he that I gave it to in change promised to wear it in his cap: I promised to strike him, if he did: I met this man with my glove in his cap, and I have been as good as my word.

Flu. Your majesty hear now, saving your majesty's manhood, what an arrant, rascally, beggarly, lousy knave it is: I hope your majesty is pear me testimony and witness, and will avouchment, that this is the glove of Alençon, that your majesty is give me; in your conscience, now. 40

K. Hen. Give me thy glove, soldier: look, here is the fellow of it.
'Twas I, indeed, thou promised'st to strike;
And thou hast given me most bitter terms.

Flu. And please your majesty, let his neck answer for it, if there is any martial law in the world.

K. Hen. How canst thou make me satisfaction?

Will. All offences, my lord, come from the heart: never came any from mine that might offend your majesty. 51

K. Hen. It was ourself thou didst abuse.

Will. Your majesty came not like yourself: you appeared to me but as a common man; witness the night, your garments, your lowliness; and what your highness suffered under that shape, I beseech you take it for your own fault and not mine: for had you been as I took you for, I made

no offence; therefore, I beseech your highness,
pardon me.   60
   K. Hen. Here, uncle Exeter, fill this glove
    with crowns,
And give it to this fellow. Keep it, fellow;
And wear it for an honour in thy cap
Till I do challenge it. Give him the crowns:
And, captain, you must needs be friends with him.
   Flu. By this day and this light, the fellow has
mettle enough in his belly. Hold, there is twelve
pence for you; and I pray you to serve God, and
keep you out of prawls, and prabbles, and quarrels, and dissensions, and, I warrant you, it is the
better for you.   71
   Will. I will none of your money.
   Flu. It is with a good will; I can tell you, it
will serve you to mend your shoes: come, wherefore should you be so pashful? your shoes is not so
good: 'tis a good silling, I warrant you, or I will
change it.

       Enter an English Herald.

   K. Hen. Now, herald, are the dead number'd?
   Her. Here is the number of the slaughter'd
    French.
   K. Hen. What prisoners of good sort are taken,
    uncle?   80
   Exe. Charles Duke of Orleans, nephew to the
    king;
John Duke of Bourbon, and Lord Bouciqualt:
Of other lords and barons, knights and squires,
Full fifteen hundred, besides common men.
   K. Hen. This note doth tell me of ten thou-
    sand French
That in the field lie slain: of princes, in this
    number,
And nobles bearing banners, there lie dead
One hundred twenty six: added to these,
Of knights, esquires, and gallant gentlemen, 89
Eight thousand and four hundred; of the which,
Five hundred were but yesterday dubb'd knights:
So that, in these ten thousand they have lost,
There are but sixteen hundred mercenaries;
The rest are princes, barons, lords, knights, squires,
And gentlemen of blood and quality.
The names of those their nobles that lie dead:
Charles Delabreth, high constable of France;
Jacques of Chatillon, admiral of France;
The master of the cross-bows, Lord Rambures;
Great Master of France, the brave Sir Guichard
    Dolphin,   100
John Duke of Alençon, Anthony Duke of Brabant,
The brother to the Duke of Burgundy,
And Edward Duke of Bar: of lusty earls,
Grandpré and Roussi, Fauconberg and Foix,
Beaumont and Marle, Vaudemont and Lestrale.
Here was a royal fellowship of death!
Where is the number of our English dead?
       [*Herald shews him another paper.*
Edward the Duke of York, the Earl of Suffolk,
Sir Richard Ketly, Davy Gam, esquire:
None else of name; and of all other men 110
But five and twenty. O God, thy arm was here;
And not to us, but to thy arm alone,
Ascribe we all! When, without stratagem,
But in plain shock and even play of battle,
Was ever known so great and little loss
On one part and on the other? Take it, God,
For it is none but thine!

10 *Pales in.* Fences in.

12 *whiffler.* One who carried a staff (whiffle) to clear the way in front of a procession.

21 *signal and ostent.* Signs and displays.

24–28 *How London . . . Cæsar in.* See introduction.

31–34 *As in . . . welcome him.* See introduction.

Henry V's triumphant return to London. Engraving from *Old England*, 1854

38 *emperor's.* Sigismund, Holy Roman Emperor, who visited England in 1416.

Exe.   'Tis wonderful!
K. Hen.   Come, go we in procession to the village:
And be it death proclaimed through our host
To boast of this or take that praise from God   120
Which is his only.
    Flu.   Is it not lawful, an please your majesty,
to tell how many is killed?
    K. Hen.   Yes, captain; but with this acknow-
ledgement,
That God fought for us.
    Flu. Yes, my conscience, he did us great good.
    K. Hen.   Do we all holy rites;
Let there be sung 'Non nobis' and 'Te Deum;'
The dead with charity enclosed in clay:
And then to Calais; and to England then: 130
Where ne'er from France arrived more happy
    men.   [*Exeunt.*

ACT V.

PROLOGUE.

Enter Chorus.

Chor. Vouchsafe to those that have not read
        the story,
That I may prompt them: and of such as have,
I humbly pray them to admit the excuse
Of time, of numbers and due course of things,
Which cannot in their huge and proper life
Be here presented.   Now we bear the king
Toward Calais: grant him there; there seen,
Heave him away upon your winged thoughts
Athwart the sea.   Behold, the English beach   9
• Pales in the flood with men, with wives and
        boys,
Whose shouts and claps out-voice the deep-
        mouth'd sea,
• Which like a mighty whiffler 'fore the king
Seems to prepare his way: so let him land,
And solemnly see him set on to London.
So swift a pace hath thought that even now
You may imagine him upon Blackheath;
Where that his lords desire him to have borne
His bruised helmet and his bended sword
Before him through the city: he forbids it,   19
• Being free from vainness and self-glorious pride;
• Giving full trophy, signal and ostent
Quite from himself to God.   But now behold,
In the quick forge and working-house of thought,
• How London doth pour out her citizens!
The mayor and all his brethren in best sort,
Like to the senators of the antique Rome,
With the plebeians swarming at their heels,
Go forth and fetch their conquering Cæsar in:
As, by a lower but loving likelihood,
Were now the general of our gracious empress,   30
• As in good time he may, from Ireland coming,
Bringing rebellion broached on his sword,
How many would the peaceful city quit,
To welcome him! much more, and much more
        cause,
Did they this Harry.   Now in London place him;
As yet the lamentation of the French
Invites the King of England's stay at home;
• The emperor's coming in behalf of France,
To order peace between them; and omit
All the occurrences, whatever chanced,   40
Till Harry's back-return again to France:

There must we bring him; and myself have
play'd
The interim, by remembering you 'tis past.
Then brook abridgement, and your eyes advance,
After your thoughts, straight back again to
France.   [*Exit.*

SCENE I. *France. The English camp.*

Enter FLUELLEN *and* GOWER.

Gow. Nay, that's right; but why wear you
your leek to-day? Saint Davy's day is past.
Flu. There is occasions and causes why and
wherefore in all things: I will tell you, asse my
friend, Captain Gower: the rascally, scauld, beggarly, lousy, pragging knave, Pistol, which you
and yourself and all the world know to be no petter
than a fellow, look you now, of no merits, he is
come to me and prings me pread and salt yesterday, look you, and bid me eat my leek: it was in
a place where I could not breed no contention
with him; but I will be so bold as to wear it in my
cap till I see him once again, and then I will tell
him a little piece of my desires.

Enter PISTOL.

Gow. Why, here he comes, swelling like a
turkey-cock.
Flu. 'Tis no matter for his swellings nor his
turkey-cocks. God pless you, Aunchient Pistol!
you scurvy, lousy knave, God pless you!
Pist. Ha! art thou bedlam? dost thou thirst,
base Trojan,   20
To have me fold up Parca's fatal web?
Hence! I am qualmish at the smell of leek.
Flu. I peseech you heartily, scurvy, lousy
knave, at my desires, and my requests, and my
petitions, to eat, look you, this leek: because,
look you, you do not love it, nor your affections
and your appetites and your disgestions doo's not
agree with it, I would desire you to eat it.
Pist. Not for Cadwallader and all his goats.
Flu. There is one goat for you. [*Strikes him.*]
Will you be so good, scauld knave, as eat it? 31
Pist. Base Trojan, thou shalt die.
Flu. You say very true, scauld knave, when
God's will is: I will desire you to live in the
mean time, and eat your victuals: come, there is
sauce for it. [*Strikes him.*] You called me yesterday mountain-squire; but I will make you to-
day a squire of low degree. I pray you, fall to:
if you can mock a leek, you can eat a leek.
Gow. Enough, captain: you have astonished
him.   41
Flu. I say, I will make him eat some part of
my leek, or I will peat his pate four days. Bite,
I pray you; it is good for your green wound and
your ploody coxcomb.
Pist. Must I bite?
Flu. Yes, certainly, and out of doubt and out
of question too, and ambiguities.
Pist. By this leek, I will most horribly revenge: I eat and eat, I swear—   50
Flu. Eat, I pray you: will you have some
more sauce to your leek? there is not enough leek
to swear by.
Pist. Quiet thy cudgel; thou dost see I eat.

5 *scauld.* Scabby.

20 *bedlam.* Mad.

21 *Parca.* In classical mythology, the Parcae were the
three Fates.

29 *Cadwallader.* A famous Welsh warrior.

Fluellen: 'Eat, I pray you . . .' Drawing by J. Coghlan,
early 19th century

Pistol eats the leek. Engraving by Henry Bunbury
(1750–1811)

63 *groat*. A coin worth fourpence.

78 *gleeking and galling*. Sneering and jeering.

85 *huswife*. Hussy.

87 *Of malady of France*. i.e. venereal disease.

Flu. Much good do you, scauld knave, heartily.
Nay, pray you, throw none away; the skin is
good for your broken coxcomb. When you take
occasions to see leeks hereafter, I pray you, mock
at 'em; that is all.
   Pist. Good.   60
   Flu. Ay, leeks is good: hold you, there is a
groat to heal your pate.
   Pist. Me a groat!
   Flu. Yes, verily and in truth, you shall take
it; or I have another leek in my pocket, which
you shall eat.
   Pist. I take thy groat in earnest of revenge.
   Flu. If I owe you any thing, I will pay you
in cudgels: you shall be a woodmonger, and buy
nothing of me but cudgels. God b' wi' you, and
keep you, and heal your pate.   [*Exit.* 71
   Pist. All hell shall stir for this.
   Gow. Go, go; you are a counterfeit cowardly
knave. Will you mock at an ancient tradition,
begun upon an honourable respect, and worn as a
memorable trophy of predeceased valour and dare
not avouch in your deeds any of your words? I
have seen you gleeking and galling at this gentleman twice or thrice. You thought, because
he could not speak English in the native garb, he
could not therefore handle an English cudgel:
you find it otherwise; and henceforth let a Welsh
correction teach you a good English condition.
Fare ye well.   [*Exit.*
   Pist. Doth Fortune play the huswife with me
now?
News have I, that my Nell is dead i' the spital
Of malady of France;
And there my rendezvous is quite cut off.
Old I do wax; and from my weary limbs
Honour is cudgelled. Well, bawd I'll turn,   90
And something lean to cutpurse of quick hand.
To England will I steal, and there I'll steal:
And patches will I get unto these cudgell'd scars,
And swear I got them in the Gallia wars. [*Exit.*

SCENE II. *France. A royal palace.*

Enter, at one door, KING HENRY, EXETER,
BEDFORD, GLOUCESTER, WARWICK, WEST-
MORELAND, *and other* Lords; *at another, the*
FRENCH KING, QUEEN ISABEL, *the* PRINCESS
KATHARINE, ALICE *and other* Ladies; *the*
DUKE OF BURGUNDY, *and his train.*

   K. Hen. Peace to this meeting, wherefore we
      are met!
Unto our brother France, and to our sister,
Health and fair time of day; joy and good wishes
To our most fair and princely cousin Katharine;
And, as a branch and member of this royalty,
By whom this great assembly is contrived,
We do salute you, Duke of Burgundy;
And, princes French, and peers, health to you all!
   Fr. King. Right joyous are we to behold
      your face,
Most worthy brother England; fairly met: 10
So are you, princes English, every one.
   Q. Isa. So happy be the issue, brother Eng-
      land,
Of this good day and of this gracious meeting,
As we are now glad to behold your eyes;
Your eyes, which hitherto have borne in them

Against the French, that met them in their bent,
● The fatal balls of murdering basilisks:
The venom of such looks, we fairly hope,
● Have lost their quality, and that this day
Shall change all griefs and quarrels into love. 20
 K. Hen. To cry amen to that, thus we appear.
 Q. Isa. You English princes all, I do salute
  you.
 Bur. My duty to you both, on equal love,
Great Kings of France and England! That I
 have labour'd,
With all my wits, my pains and strong endea-
 vours,
To bring your most imperial majesties
Unto this bar and royal interview,
Your mightiness on both parts best can witness.
Since then my office hath so far prevail'd
That, face to face and royal eye to eye, 30
You have congreeted, let it not disgrace me,
If I demand, before this royal view,
What rub or what impediment there is,
Why that the naked, poor and mangled Peace,
Dear nurse of arts, plenties and joyful births,
Should not in this best garden of the world
Our fertile France, put up her lovely visage?
Alas, she hath from France too long been chased,
And all her husbandry doth lie on heaps,
Corrupting in it own fertility. 40
Her vine, the merry cheerer of the heart,
● Unpruned dies; her hedges even-pleach'd,
Like prisoners wildly overgrown with hair,
● Put forth disorder'd twigs; her fallow leas
● The darnel, hemlock and rank fumitory
● Doth root upon, while that the coulter rusts
That should deracinate such savagery;
The even mead, that erst brought sweetly forth
The freckled cowslip, burnet and green clover,
Wanting the scythe, all uncorrected, rank, 50
Conceives by idleness and nothing teems
● But hateful docks, rough thistles, kecksies, burs,
Losing both beauty and utility.
And as our vineyards, fallows, meads and hedges,
Defective in their natures, grow to wildness,
Even so our houses and ourselves and children
Have lost, or do not learn for want of time,
The sciences that should become our country;
But grow like savages,—as soldiers will
That nothing do but meditate on blood,— 60
● To swearing and stern looks, defused attire
And every thing that seems unnatural.
Which to reduce into our former favour
You are assembled: and my speech entreats
● That I may know the let, why gentle Peace
Should not expel these inconveniences
And bless us with her former qualities.
 K. Hen. If, Duke of Burgundy, you would
  the peace,
Whose want gives growth to the imperfections
Which you have cited, you must buy that peace
With full accord to all our just demands; 71
Whose tenours and particular effects
You have enscheduled briefly in your hands.
 Bur. The king hath heard them; to the which
  as yet
There is no answer made.
 K. Hen.   Well then the peace,
Which you before so urged, lies in his answer.
 Fr. King. I have but with a cursorary eye
O'erglanced the articles: pleaseth your grace

---

17 *fatal balls.* 'Cannonballs' and also 'eyeballs'.
basilisks. 'Large cannons' and 'fabulous serpents whose looks killed'.

19 *quality.* Power.

Burgundy: '. . . this best garden of the world Our fertile France . . .' Agricultural scene in the 16th century. From Flemish engraving

---

42 *even-pleach'd.* Evenly interwined.

44 *leas.* Fields of arable land.

45 *darnel . . . fumitory.* Weeds.

46 *coulter.* Blade in the front part of a share in a plough.

52 *kecksies.* Dry stalks of weeds such as cow parsnip or chervil.

61 *defused.* Wild.

65 *let.* Hindrance.

90 *consign.* Agree.

Henry: 'Do you like me, Kate?' Drawing from William Charles Macready's production, Covent Garden Theatre, London, 1839

112–113 *Que dit-il? . . . anges.* What does he say? That I am like the angels?

114–115 *Oui . . . dit-il.* Yes, truly, save your grace, he says so.

133 *clap hands.* i.e. to seal a bargain.

141 *measure.* Stately dance.

To appoint some of your council presently
To sit with us once more, with better heed　80
To re-survey them, we will suddenly
Pass our accept and peremptory answer.
　K. Hen. Brother, we shall. Go, uncle Exeter,
And brother Clarence, and you, brother Gloucester,
Warwick and Huntingdon, go with the king;
And take with you free power to ratify,
Augment, or alter, as your wisdoms best
Shall see advantageable for our dignity,
Any thing in or out of our demands,
And we'll consign thereto. Will you, fair sister,
Go with the princes, or stay here with us?　91
　Q. Isa. Our gracious brother, I will go with them:
Haply a woman's voice may do some good,
When articles too nicely urged be stood on.
　K. Hen. Yet leave our cousin Katharine here with us:
She is our capital demand, comprised
Within the fore-rank of our articles.
　Q. Isa. She hath good leave.
　　　　[*Exeunt all except Henry, Katharine, and Alice.*
　K. Hen.　　Fair Katharine, and most fair,
Will you vouchsafe to teach a soldier terms
Such as will enter at a lady's ear　100
And plead his love-suit to her gentle heart?
　Kath. Your majesty shall mock at me; I cannot speak your England.
　K. Hen. O fair Katharine, if you will love me soundly with your French heart, I will be glad to hear you confess it brokenly with your English tongue. Do you like me, Kate?
　Kath. Pardonnez-moi, I cannot tell vat is 'like me.'
　K. Hen. An angel is like you, Kate, and you are like an angel.　111
　Kath. Que dit-il? que je suis semblable à les anges?
　Alice. Oui, vraiment, sauf votre grace, ainsi dit-il.
　K. Hen. I said so, dear Katharine; and I must not blush to affirm it.
　Kath. O bon Dieu! les langues des hommes sont pleines de tromperies.
　K. Hen. What says she, fair one? that the tongues of men are full of deceits?　121
　Alice. Oui, dat de tongues of de mans is be full of deceits: dat is de princess.
　K. Hen. The princess is the better Englishwoman. I' faith, Kate, my wooing is fit for thy understanding: I am glad thou canst speak no better English; for, if thou couldst, thou wouldst find me such a plain king that thou wouldst think I had sold my farm to buy my crown. I know no ways to mince it in love, but directly to say 'I love you:' then if you urge me farther than to say 'do you in faith?' I wear out my suit. Give me your answer; i' faith, do: and so clap hands and a bargain: how say you, lady?
　Kath. Sauf votre honneur, me understand vell.
　K. Hen. Marry, if you would put me to verses or to dance for your sake, Kate, why you undid me: for the one, I have neither words nor measure, and for the other, I have no strength in measure, yet a reasonable measure in strength.

If I could win a lady at leap-frog, or by vaulting into my saddle with my armour on my back, under the correction of bragging be it spoken, I should quickly leap into a wife. Or if I might buffet for my love, or bound my horse for her favours, I could lay on like a butcher and sit like a jack-an-apes, never off. But, before God, Kate, I cannot look greenly nor gasp out my eloquence, nor I have no cunning in protestation; only downright oaths, which I never use till urged, nor never break for urging. If thou canst love a fellow of this temper, Kate, whose face is not worth sun-burning, that never looks in his glass for love of any thing he sees there, let thine eye be thy cook. I speak to thee plain soldier: if thou canst love me for this, take me; if not, to say to thee that I shall die, is true; but for thy love, by the Lord, no; yet I love thee too. And while thou livest, dear Kate, take a fellow of plain and uncoined constancy; for he perforce must do thee right, because he hath not the gift to woo in other places: for these fellows of infinite tongue, that can rhyme themselves into ladies' favours, they do always reason themselves out again. What! a speaker is but a prater; a rhyme is but a ballad. A good leg will fall; a straight back will stoop; a black beard will turn white; a curled pate will grow bald; a fair face will wither; a full eye will wax hollow: but a good heart, Kate, is the sun and the moon; or rather the sun and not the moon; for it shines bright and never changes, but keeps his course truly. If thou would have such a one, take me; and take me, take a soldier; take a soldier, take a king. And what sayest thou then to my love? speak, my fair, and fairly, I pray thee.

Kath. Is it possible dat I sould love de enemy of France? 179

K. Hen. No; it is not possible you should love the enemy of France, Kate: but, in loving me, you should love the friend of France; for I love France so well that I will not part with a village of it; I will have it all mine: and, Kate, when France is mine and I am yours, then yours is France and you are mine.

Kath. I cannot tell vat is dat.

K. Hen. No, Kate? I will tell thee in French; which I am sure will hang upon my tongue like a new-married wife about her husband's neck, hardly to be shook off. Je quand sur le possession de France, et quand vous avez le possession de moi,—let me see, what then? Saint Denis be my speed!—donc votre est France et vous êtes mienne. It is as easy for me, Kate, to conquer the kingdom as to speak so much more French: I shall never move thee in French, unless it be to laugh at me.

Kath. Sauf votre honneur, le François que vous parlez, il est meilleur que l'Anglois lequel je parle. 201

K. Hen. No, faith, is't not, Kate: but thy speaking of my tongue, and I thine, most truly-falsely, must needs be granted to be much at one. But, Kate, dost thou understand thus much English, canst thou love me?

Kath. I cannot tell.

K. Hen. Can any of your neighbours tell, Kate? I'll ask them. Come, I know thou lovest me: and at night, when you come into

148 *jack-an-apes.* Monkey.

155–156 *let thine eye be thy cook.* Your imagination must provide me with the charms I lack.

161 *uncoined.* Metal that has never been coined, therefore never passed from hand to hand.

Sarah Siddons as Princess Katherine in John Kemble's production, Theatre Royal, Drury Lane, London, 1789

191–195 *Je quand . . . mienne.* A paraphrase in bad French of his last sentence.

199–201 *Sauf votre . . . je parle.* Save your honour, the French you speak is better than my English.

218 *scambling*. Fighting.

220 *Saint Denis*. The patron saint of France.

224 *flower-de-luce*. Fleur-de-lis, the symbol of France.

Laurence Olivier as Henry V and Jessica Tandy as the Princess Katherine, Old Vic Theatre, London, 1937

230–232 *la plus . . . devin déesse*. The most beautiful Katherine in the world, my dearest divine goddess.

241 *untempering*. Unprepossessing.

273–277 *Laissez, mon seigneur . . . très-puissant seigneur*. Don't, my lord, don't, don't; my faith, I don't want you to lower your dignity by kissing the hand of one of your unworthy servants; Excuse me, I beg you, sovereign lord.

your closet, you'll question this gentlewoman about me; and I know, Kate, you will to her dispraise those parts in me that you love with your heart: but, good Kate, mock me mercifully; the rather, gentle princess, because I love thee cruelly. If ever thou beest mine, Kate, as I have a saving faith within me tells me thou shalt, I get thee with scambling, and thou must therefore needs prove a good soldier-breeder: shall not thou and I, between Saint Denis and Saint George, compound a boy, half French, half English, that shall go to Constantinople and take the Turk by the beard? shall we not? what sayest thou, my fair flower-de-luce?

Kath. I do not know dat.

K. Hen. No; 'tis hereafter to know, but now to promise: do but now promise, Kate, you will endeavour for your French part of such a boy; and for my English moiety take the word of a king and a bachelor. How answer you, la plus belle Katharine du monde, mon très cher et devin déesse?

Kath. Your majestee ave fausse French enough to deceive de most sage demoiselle dat is en France.

K. Hen. Now, fie upon my false French! By mine honour, in true English, I love thee, Kate: by which honour I dare not swear thou lovest me; yet my blood begins to flatter me that thou dost, notwithstanding the poor and untempering effect of my visage. Now, beshrew my father's ambition! he was thinking of civil wars when he got me: therefore was I created with a stubborn outside, with an aspect of iron, that, when I come to woo ladies, I fright them. But, in faith, Kate, the elder I wax, the better I shall appear: my comfort is, that old age, that ill layer up of beauty, can do no more spoil upon my face: thou hast me, if thou hast me, at the worst; and thou shalt wear me, if thou wear me, better and better: and therefore tell me, most fair Katharine, will you have me? Put off your maiden blushes; avouch the thoughts of your heart with the looks of an empress; take me by the hand, and say 'Harry of England, I am thine:' which word thou shalt no sooner bless mine ear withal, but I will tell thee aloud 'England is thine, Ireland is thine, France is thine, and Henry Plantagenet is thine;' who, though I speak it before his face, if he be not fellow with the best king, thou shalt find the best king of good fellows. Come, your answer in broken music; for thy voice is music and thy English broken; therefore, queen of all, Katharine, break thy mind to me in broken English; wilt thou have me?

Kath. Dat is as it sall please de roi mon père.

K. Hen. Nay, it will please him well, Kate; it shall please him, Kate.

Kath. Den it sall also content me.   **270**

K. Hen. Upon that I kiss your hand, and I call you my queen.

Kath. Laissez, mon seigneur, laissez, laissez: ma foi, je ne veux point que vous abaissiez votre grandeur en baisant la main d'une de votre seigneurie indigne serviteur; excusez-moi, je vous supplie, mon très-puissant seigneur.

K. Hen. Then I will kiss your lips, Kate.

Kath. Les dames et demoiselles pour être

baisées devant leur noces, il n'est pas la coutume
de France. 281

K. Hen. Madam my interpreter, what says
she?

Alice. Dat it is not be de fashion pour les
ladies of France,—I cannot tell vat is baiser en
Anglish.

K. Hen. To kiss.

- *Alice.* Your majesty entendre bettre que moi.

K. Hen. It is not a fashion for the maids in
France to kiss before they are married, would
she say?

Alice. Oui, vraiment.

K. Hen. O Kate, nice customs curtsy to
great kings. Dear Kate, you and I cannot be
- confined within the weak list of a country's
fashion: we are the makers of manners, Kate;
and the liberty that follows our places stops the
mouth of all find-faults; as I will do yours, for
upholding the nice fashion of your country in
denying me a kiss: therefore, patiently and
yielding. [*Kissing her.*] You have witchcraft
in your lips, Kate: there is more eloquence in a
sugar touch of them than in the tongues of the
French council; and they should sooner persuade
Harry of England than a general petition of
monarchs. Here comes your father.

Re-enter the FRENCH KING *and his* QUEEN,
BURGUNDY, *and other* Lords.

Bur. God save your majesty! my royal
cousin, teach you our princess English?

K. Hen. I would have her learn, my fair
cousin, how perfectly I love her; and that is
good English.

Bur. Is she not apt?

K. Hen. Our tongue is rough, coz, and my
condition is not smooth; so that, having neither
the voice nor the heart of flattery about me, I
cannot so conjure up the spirit of love in her,
that he will appear in his true likeness.

Bur. Pardon the frankness of my mirth, if I
answer you for that. If you would conjure in
her, you must make a circle; if conjure up love
in her in his true likeness, he must appear naked
and blind. Can you blame her then, being a
maid yet rosed over with the virgin crimson of
modesty, if she deny the appearance of a naked
blind boy in her naked seeing self? It were, my
lord, a hard condition for a maid to consign to.

- *K. Hen.* Yet they do wink and yield, as love
is blind and enforces.

Bur. They are then excused, my lord, when
they see not what they do. 330

K. Hen. Then, good my lord, teach your
cousin to consent winking.

Bur. I will wink on her to consent, my lord,
if you will teach her to know my meaning: for
- maids, well summered and warm kept, are like
flies at Bartholomew-tide, blind, though they
have their eyes; and then they will endure handling, which before would not abide looking on.

K. Hen. This moral ties me over to time and
a hot summer; and so I shall catch the fly, your
cousin, in the latter end and she must be blind too.

Bur. As love is, my lord, before it loves.

K. Hen. It is so: and you may, some of you,
thank love for my blindness, who cannot see

Costume design for Alice by Tanya Moisewitch,
Stratford-upon-Avon, 1951

288 *entendre bettre que moi.* Understands better than I.

295 *list.* Boundary.

327 *wink.* Close both eyes.

335–336 *like flies at Bartholomew-tide.* Like flies in late
August when they become sluggish.

347–348 *perspectively*. Through an optical glass that produces illusions.

367–369 *Notre très . . . France.* Our dear son Henry, King of England and Heir of France.

Henry and Katherine. Drawing from William Charles Macready's production, Covent Garden Theatre, London, 1839

many a fair French city for one fair French maid that stands in my way.

Fr. King. Yes, my lord, you see them perspectively, the cities turned into a maid; for they are all girdled with maiden walls that war hath never entered. 350

K. Hen. Shall Kate be my wife?

Fr. King. So please you.

K. Hen. I am content; so the maiden cities you talk of may wait on her: so the maid that stood in the way for my wish shall show me the way to my will.

Fr. King. We have consented to all terms of reason.

K. Hen. Is't so, my lords of England? 359

West. The king hath granted every article:
His daughter first, and then in sequel all,
According to their firm proposed natures.

Exe. Only he hath not yet subscribed this:
Where your majesty demands, that the King of France, having any occasion to write for matter of grant, shall name your highness in this form and with this addition, in French, *Notre trèscher fils Henri, Roi d'Angleterre, Héritier de France*; and thus in Latin, *Præclarissimus filius noster Henricus, Rex Angliæ, et Hæres Franciæ.*

Fr. King. Nor this I have not, brother, so denied,
But your request shall make me let it pass.

K. Hen. I pray you then, in love and dear alliance,
Let that one article rank with the rest;
And thereupon give me your daughter.

Fr. King. Take her, fair son, and from her blood raise up
Issue to me; that the contending kingdoms
Of France and England, whose very shores look pale
With envy of each other's happiness,
May cease their hatred, and this dear conjunction 380
Plant neighbourhood and Christian-like accord
In their sweet bosoms, that never war advance
His bleeding sword 'twixt England and fair France.

All. Amen!

K. Hen. Now, welcome, Kate: and bear me witness all,
That here I kiss her as my sovereign queen.

[*Flourish.*

Q. Isa. God, the best maker of all marriages,
Combine your hearts in one, your realms in one!
As man and wife, being two, are one in love,
So be there 'twixt your kingdoms such a spousal,
That never may ill office, or fell jealousy,
Which troubles oft the bed of blessed marriage,
Thrust in between the paction of these kingdoms,
To make divorce of their incorporate league;
That English may as French, French Englishmen,
Receive each other. God speak this Amen!

All. Amen!

K. Hen. Prepare we for our marriage: on which day,
My Lord of Burgundy, we'll take your oath,
And all the peers', for surety of our leagues. 400
Then shall I swear to Kate, and you to me;
And may our oaths well kept and prosperous be!

[*Sennet. Exeunt.*

EPILOGUE.

Enter Chorus.

Chor. Thus far, with rough and all-unable pen,
• Our bending author hath pursued the story,
In little room confining mighty men,
• Mangling by starts the full course of their glory.
Small time, but in that small most greatly lived
 This star of England: Fortune made his sword;
By which the world's best garden he achieved,

 And of it left his son imperial lord.
Henry the Sixth, in infant bands crown'd King
 Of France and England, did this king suc-
  ceed;   10
Whose state so many had the managing,
 That they lost France and made his England
  bleed:
Which oft our stage hath shown; and, for their
 sake,
In your fair minds let this acceptance take.
           [Exit.

Henry with Queen Katherine. Drawing by John M. Wright (1777–1866)

----

2 *bending.* Bowing to the audience.

4 *starts.* i.e. in fits and starts.

King Henry VIII

1613

The Play. *Henry VIII* is Shakespeare's last play. There is a certain propriety, typical of the planning mind we have observed all through his work, that he should round off his astonishing production, as he had begun, with a chronicle-play on English history. It gave him the opportunity to pronounce his valediction, his real farewell, to the Elizabethan age – of which, all unknown, he would in time become the brightest jewel in its crown – in Cranmer's famous prophecy in baptising the infant Princess Elizabeth. Thus the play ends: the wheel has come full circle.

That *Henry VIII* is dominantly Shakespeare's, the hand recognisable in the leading characters and famous scenes, we need not doubt. Besides, Heming and Condell would not have included the text, from their theatre scripts, if it had not been his. On the other hand, one has the distinct impression that a subordinate hand had a part in it, and this is likely to have been John Fletcher, the master's successor as dramatist-in-chief to the Company.

Other reasons also account for the idiosyncrasy of this play. One misses the dynamism of Shakespeare's mind, his characteristic attack on his subject. The mood is a more passive one, of observation, sympathy, reflection, almost resignation. That would be natural enough: after his life of constant effort as actor and dramatist, touring, producing, writing, he was a tired man. *Henry VIII* was written in 1612–13; after that, though he lived for another three years, he wrote no more. He was content to enjoy his well-earned retirement, as the gentleman of Stratford, with an occasional visit to London to keep his hand in the Company's affairs

In spite of all reservations we have to admit, with Dr. Johnson, that the play is 'one of those which still keeps possession of the stage, by the splendour of its pageantry . . . Yet pomp is not the only merit of this play. The meek sorrows and virtuous distress of Catherine have furnished some scenes which may be justly numbered among the greatest efforts of tragedy.' This is perhaps too encomiastic; yet Johnson goes further, to say of Catherine's last scene when dying that 'it is, above any other part of Shakespeare's tragedies, and perhaps above any scene of any other poet, tender and pathetic, without gods or furies, or poisons or precipices, without the help of romantic circumstances, without improbable sallies of poetical lamentation, and without any throes of tumultuous misery.'

It is the chaste classicism of the Augustan age that speaks: I suspect that it is precisely the absence of Shakespeare's romantic *fougue* that makes the Doctor so enthusiastic. At the same time actresses have found this a noble part, and artists, notably Blake, have been inspired by the dying Queen's vision of heavenly spirits.

Dr. Johnson failed to observe, what actors have appreciated, that Wolsey's is a fine part too. It has a number of famous passages which have sunk into our communal memory:

> Had I but served my God with half the zeal
> I served my king, he would not in mine age
> Have left me naked to mine enemies.

Or,

> Farewell! A long farewell to all my greatness!

Then there follows an oration, developed in accordance with the rules of rhetoric, such as we have observed again and again, on the stages of man's life; and ending on the wretchedness of him who depends on princes' favour:

> And when he falls, he falls like Lucifer,
> Never to hope again.

Or there is Wolsey's earlier premonition:

> I shall fall
> Like a bright exhalation in the evening,
> And no man see me more.

The Character of the King. A prime trouble with *Henry VIII* is the character of the King: he is hardly worthy of the title-role, and he is not convincing. He posed an insurmountable problem for the dramatist; for he was still a controversial figure – in the way that Richard III was not (everybody knew the truth about him) – and it was hardly possible to tell the whole truth about Henry. After all, he was Queen Elizabeth's father, though he had killed her mother, and was to kill her cousin, Catherine Howard. Nothing of this in the play.

The situation was rather like that with Stalin in Soviet Russia, an overpowering personality, without which the country might not have pulled through its revolution, yet a capricious and cruel monster or, rather, *faux-bonhomme*. Indeed, only a few years before the play, Robert Cecil, James I's chief minister, then Lord Salisbury, in a speech to the Lords openly condemned Henry's cruelty – much as Krushchev spoke up about Stalin's brutality.

Henry VIII inherited his characteristics from his Yorkist stock. He was very like his burly grandfather, Edward IV, who killed his brother, Clarence; his great-uncle was Richard III, who killed his nephews; Henry killed two of his wives, besides various other members of his family – his cousin, Clarence's daughter, the aged Countess of Salisbury, her son, and another cousin, the Marquis of Exeter.

Not much of this appeared in the first half of Henry's life – except for Buckingham's execution, with which the play begins – until the crisis of the Reformation, though

Wolsey and Sir Thomas More (another victim) knew perfectly what was what about Henry. The Reformation was yet another subject that could not be handled in the play – yet it was the backbone of Henry's reign:

> Majestic lord that broke the bonds of Rome.

Thus the play is without a backbone, and wants integration. In place of that, we are given a series of effective scenes, skilfully linked, pulling together disparate events over the years. Shakespeare took advantage of what could be made dramatic use of – for example, Bishop Gardiner's attempt to 'frame' Archbishop Cranmer, which Henry personally frustrated; and then resolved to give the story a ceremonial end with the baptism of Elizabeth.

Shakespeare and Elizabeth I. The tact we have observed all through Shakespeare's career would have prevented him from touching on these controversial issues anyway:

he steered clear of them. It was enough to have to deal with the divorce of Catherine of Aragon, which he does with much sympathy in his portrait of her and managing to save the 'honour' – or, at any rate, dignity – of the King.

The dramatist had paid his meed of tributes to Henry and Anne Bullen's daughter, though with none of the outrageous flattery with which many of the poets treated her: as in everything, he retained his essential independence and dignity – as in his relations with his patron. In the event the Queen had condemned Southampton to death and incarcerated him in the Tower, until her own death freed him. It was observed that her favourite dramatist paid no poetic tribute on her passing. Now, ten years later, at the end of his own career, he could look back over it all and see in the perspective of time – as a prophecy – what her reign had been:

> She shall be loved and feared. Her own shall bless her;
> Her foes shake like a field of beaten corn . . .
> In her days every man shall eat in safety
> Under his own vine what he plants, and sing
> The merry songs of peace to all his neighbours.

The tribute is to the internal peace she kept so successfully during her long reign.

It is not so often noticed that the oration goes on with no less tact to salute her successor. The ashes of the maiden phoenix would create another heir, 'as great in admiration as herself' (forsooth!):

> Wherever the bright sun of heaven shall shine,
> His honour and the greatness of his name
> Shall be, and make new nations . . .

This was already coming to pass: Jamestown had been founded but a few years before, with Southampton a promoter (hence Hampton Roads and Hampton River) to take a leading part later in the colonisation of Virginia.

The existence of the New World is signalled by the old master in an unmistakeable piece of bawdy at the Princess's christening. There is such a crowd that the Porter cries,

> What should you do, but knock 'em down by the dozens? Is this Moorfields to muster in? Or have we some strange Indian with the great tool come to Court, the women so besiege us? Bless me, what a fry of fornication is at door! On my Christian conscience, this one christening will beget a thousand.

His man reports,

> There is a fellow somewhat near the door, he should be a brazier by his face, for, o'my conscience, twenty of the dog-days now reign in's nose.

Isn't that a rather touching tribute to Bardolph, whose red nose was his prominent feature, after all the years? Or perhaps the same actor, whose appurtenance it was, was still with the Company. Then the Porter again:

> These are the youths that thunder at a play-house and fight for bitten apples, that no audience but the tribulation of Tower-Hill, or the limbs of Limehouse, are able to endure.

*Sir Henry Irving
as Wolsey, one of
his greatest
Shakespearean
roles, 1892*

*Sir Henry Irving
as Wolsey, one of
his greatest
Shakespearean
roles, 1892*

Wolsey. Norfolk's description of how Wolsey takes his fall out of favour with the King, reminds us how gestural Elizabethan acting was:

> Some strange commotion
> Is in his brain: he bites his lip, and starts;
> Stops on a sudden, looks upon the ground,
> Then lays his finger on his temple; straight
> Springs out into fast gait; then stops again,
> Strikes his breast hard, and anon he casts
> His eye against the moon.

Traces of fairly recent tradition about Wolsey make a full character of him, more sympathetic too than that generally entertained by either Protestants or Catholics. In the play he is said to have had a 'witchery in's tongue', which exerted a spell over the King. The Cardinal certainly was an eloquent and seductive speaker; but the truth was that, for the first half of the reign, he did Henry's work for him: he administered the country with immense energy and ability. A couple of famous lines describe him:

> Lofty and sour to them that loved him not,
> But to those that sought him, sweet as summer.

Shakespeare gives him historical justice – more so than anyone, except his gentleman-attendant, George Cavendish, who knew him best and wrote his life:

> Though from an humble stock . . .
> Exceeding wise, fair-spoken and persuading.

Richard III. An earlier historic tradition is mentioned that related to Richard III. Buckingham's father had been Richard's chief supporter in taking the throne from his nephew, perhaps understandably; but his stomach had been turned, like everybody else's, by the murder of the Princes, and Buckingham turned against him. When rounded up at Salisbury, if he had been brought before Richard, the Duke had meant to knife him – suspicious Richard was careful not to give him that chance.

With that we go back to Shakespeare's first immense and justified success with an historic character. Richard's great-nephew, who was just as murderous, comes off palely in this last play – only his repeated 'Ha!' has something sinister about it.

The Globe. The Prologue has a similar appeal to that of *Henry V*:

> Think ye see
> The very persons of our noble story
> As they were living . . .

And it assures the audience that they will find truth in what they see and hear:

> I come no more to make you laugh; things now
> That bear a weighty and a serious brow,
> Sad, high, and working, full of state and woe,
> Such noble scenes as draw the eye to flow.

The Epilogue has the regular making up to the audience, especially to the women:

> If they smile,
> And say 'twill do, I know, within a while
> All the best men are ours; for 'tis ill hap
> If they hold when their ladies bid 'em clap.

The play was produced with exceptional pomp and magnificence, 'even to the matting of the stage; the Knights of the Order with their Georges and garters, and Guards with their embroidered coats, and the like: sufficient in truth within a while to make greatness very familiar.' We see how the theatre had gone up in public estimation and prosperity, carrying its creators and leaders upward with it, from those early days when, as Greene said, the players had been glad to carry their playing-fardel a-footback.

At the performance on 29 June 1613, when chambers were shot off to greet the King's entry to Cardinal Wolsey's masquing, the thatch around the Globe caught fire and the theatre was burnt to the ground. Though it rose again, like a phoenix from its ashes, rebuilt more splendidly than before, it marks a term and puts a period to our story.

Text. Many business documents must have been lost, so that we have not those of the Burbages and we have Henslowe's[1]. But, thank heaven, the scripts of the plays, so far as we know, were safe. The text of *Henry VIII*, as it appeared in the Folio, was a tidy one, with many more detailed stage-directions than usual, consistent with the dramatist being retired in the country and giving full instructions for production.

1. Philip Henslowe's dealings as theatrical entrepreneur were mostly with the Lord Admiral's Company.

THE FAMOUS HISTORY OF THE LIFE OF
KING HENRY THE EIGHTH.

DRAMATIS PERSONÆ.

KING HENRY the Eighth.
CARDINAL WOLSEY.
CARDINAL CAMPEIUS.
CAPUCIUS, Ambassador from the Emperor Charles V.
CRANMER, Archbishop of Canterbury.
DUKE OF NORFOLK.
DUKE OF BUCKINGHAM.
DUKE OF SUFFOLK.
EARL OF SURREY.
Lord Chamberlain.
Lord Chancellor.
GARDINER, Bishop of Winchester.
Bishop of Lincoln.
LORD ABERGAVENNY.
LORD SANDS.
SIR HENRY GUILDFORD.
SIR THOMAS LOVELL.
SIR ANTHONY DENNY.
SIR NICHOLAS VAUX.
Secretaries to Wolsey.
CROMWELL, Servant to Wolsey.

GRIFFITH, Gentleman-usher to Queen Katharine.
Three Gentlemen.
DOCTOR BUTTS, Physician to the King.
Garter King-at-Arms.
Surveyor to the Duke of Buckingham.
BRANDON, and a Sergeant-at-Arms.
Door-keeper of the Council-chamber. Porter, and his Man.
Page to Gardiner. A Crier.

QUEEN KATHARINE, wife to King Henry, afterwards divorced.
ANNE BULLEN, her Maid of Honour, afterwards Queen.
An old Lady, friend to Anne Bullen.
PATIENCE, woman to Queen Katharine.

Several Lords and Ladies in the Dumb Shows; Women attending upon the Queen; Scribes, Officers, Guards, and other Attendants. Spirits.

SCENE: *London; Westminster; Kimbolton.*

● *A bullet beside a text line indicates an annotation in the opposite column.*

THE PROLOGUE.

● I COME no more to make you laugh: things now,
That bear a weighty and a serious brow,
● Sad, high, and working, full of state and woe,
Such noble scenes as draw the eye to flow,
We now present. Those that can pity, here
May, if they think it well, let fall a tear;
The subject will deserve it. Such as give
Their money out of hope they may believe,
May here find truth too. Those that come to see
Only a show or two, and so agree   10
The play may pass, if they be still and willing,
I'll undertake may see away their shilling
Richly in two short hours. Only they
That come to hear a merry bawdy play,
● A noise of targets, or to see a fellow
● In a long motley coat guarded with yellow,
Will be deceived; for, gentle hearers, know,
To rank our chosen truth with such a show
As fool and fight is, beside forfeiting
Our own brains, and the opinion that we bring,
To make that only true we now intend,   21
Will leave us never an understanding friend.
Therefore, for goodness' sake, and as you are known
The first and happiest hearers of the town,
Be sad, as we would make ye: think ye see
The very persons of our noble story
As they were living; think you see them great,
And follow'd with the general throng and sweat
Of thousand friends; then in a moment, see
How soon this mightiness meets misery: 30
And, if you can be merry then, I'll say
A man may weep upon his wedding-day.

1—4 *I come no more . . . to flow.* See introduction.

3 *working.* Moving.

15 *targets.* Shields.

16 *motley.* The particoloured dress of the fool. *guarded.* Trimmed.

Opposite : Henry VIII. Painting by Hans Holbein the Younger (1497/8–1543)

The alliance of Henry VIII and Francis I. Engraving from a contemporary woodcut

6 *suns of glory.* Henry VIII and Francis I of France.

7 *Met in the vale of Andren.* Known as the Field of the Cloth of Gold; each king vying with the other in magnificence.

19 *clinquant.* Glittering.

ACT I.

SCENE I. *London.   An ante-chamber in the palace.*

Enter the DUKE OF NORFOLK *at one door; at the other, the* DUKE OF BUCKINGHAM *and the* LORD ABERGAVENNY.

Buck. Good morrow, and well met. How have ye done
Since last we saw in France?
   Nor.   I thank your grace,
Healthful; and ever since a fresh admirer
Of what I saw there.
   Buck.   An untimely ague
Stay'd me a prisoner in my chamber when
• Those suns of glory, those two lights of men,
• Met in the vale of Andren.
   Nor.   'Twixt Guynes and Arde:
I was then present, saw them salute on horseback;
Beheld them, when they lighted, how they clung
In their embracement, as they grew together; 10
Which had they, what four throned ones could have weigh'd
Such a compounded one?
   Buck.   All the whole time
I was my chamber's prisoner.
   Nor.   Then you lost
The view of earthly glory: men might say,
Till this time pomp was single, but now married
To one above itself.   Each following day
Became the next day's master, till the last
Made former wonders its.   To-day the French,
• All clinquant, all in gold, like heathen gods,   19

Shone down the English; and, to-morrow, they
Made Britain India: every man that stood   21
Show'd like a mine. Their dwarfish pages were
As cherubins, all gilt: the madams too,
Not used to toil, did almost sweat to bear
The pride upon them, that their very labour
● Was to them as a painting: now this masque
Was cried incomparable; and the ensuing night
Made it a fool and beggar. The two kings,
Equal in lustre, were now best, now worst,
As presence did present them; him in eye,   30
Still him in praise: and, being present both,
'Twas said they saw but one; and no discerner
Durst wag his tongue in censure. When these
    suns—
For so they phrase 'em—by their heralds chal-
    lenged
The noble spirits to arms, they did perform
Beyond thought's compass; that former fabulous
    story,
Being now seen possible enough, got credit,
● That Bevis was believed.
    Buck.   O, you go far.
●   *Nor.* As I belong to worship and affect
In honour honesty, the tract of every thing   40
Would by a good discourser lose some life,
Which action's self was tongue to. All was royal;
To the disposing of it nought rebell'd,
● Order gave each thing view; the office did
Distinctly his full function.
    Buck.   Who did guide,
I mean, who set the body and the limbs
Of this great sport together, as you guess?
●   *Nor.* One, certes, that promises no element
In such a business.
    Buck.   I pray you, who, my lord?
    Nor. All this was order'd by the good dis-
    cretion   50
Of the right reverend Cardinal of York.
    Buck. The devil speed him! no man's pie is
    freed
From his ambitious finger. What had he
To do in these fierce vanities? I wonder
● That such a keech can with his very bulk
Take up the rays o' the beneficial sun
And keep it from the earth.
    Nor.   Surely, sir,
There's in him stuff that puts him to these ends;
For, being not propp'd by ancestry, whose grace
Chalks successors their way, nor call'd upon   60
For high feats done to the crown; neither allied
To eminent assistants; but, spider-like,
● Out of his self-drawing web, he gives us note,
The force of his own merit makes his way;
A gift that heaven gives for him, which buys
A place next to the king.
    Aber.   I cannot tell
What heaven hath given him,—let some graver
    eye
Pierce into that; but I can see his pride
Peep through each part of him: whence has he
    that,
If not from hell? the devil is a niggard,   70
Or has given all before, and he begins
A new hell in himself.
    Buck.   Why the devil,
Upon this French going out, took he upon him,
● Without the privity o' the king, to appoint
Who should attend on him? He makes up the file

26 *Was to them as a painting.* Gave colour to their cheeks.

38 *Bevis.* Bevis of Hampton was a hero in a favourite medieval romance.

39 *worship.* i.e. the nobility.

44 *office.* Officer.

48 *promises no element.* Seems unlikely to be part of.

55 *keech.* A round lump of animal fat (alluding to the fact that Wolsey was a butcher's son).

63 *self-drawing.* Spun from himself.

74 *privity.* Knowledge.

Sir Johnston Forbes-Robertson as the Duke of Buckingham, Lyceum Theatre, London, 1892

79 *The honourable board of council out.* Without consent of the council.

80 *he papers.* Whomsoever he has put on the list.

84 *Have broke . . . manors on 'em.* Have ruined their estates to pay for the extravagant clothing.

95 *attach'd.* Impounded with due legal process.

97 *silenced.* Confined to his house.

100 *Like it.* If it please.

SD *purse.* Bag containing the great seal.

Cardinal Wolsey and the Duke of Buckingham. Painting by Sir John Gilbert (1817–1897)

115 *surveyor.* Buckingham's cousin. Charles Knyvet, was the overseer of his estates.

116 *examination.* Testimony.

The coat of arms of Cardinal Wolsey

Of all the gentry; for the most part such
To whom as great a charge as little honour
He meant to lay upon: and his own letter,
● The honourable board of council out,
● Must fetch him in he papers.
    Aber.   I do know   80
Kinsmen of mine, three at the least, that have
By this so sicken'd their estates, that never
They shall abound as formerly.
    Buck.   O, many
● Have broke their backs with laying manors on 'em
For this great journey. What did this vanity
But minister communication of
A most poor issue?
    Nor.   Grievingly I think,
The peace between the French and us not values
The cost that did conclude it.
    Buck.   Every man,
After the hideous storm that follow'd, was   90
A thing inspired; and, not consulting, broke
Into a general prophecy; That this tempest,
Dashing the garment of this peace, aboded
The sudden breach on't.
    Nor.   Which is budded out;
● For France hath flaw'd the league, and hath
      attach'd
Our merchants' goods at Bourdeaux.
    Aber.   Is it therefore
● The ambassador is silenced?
    Nor.   Marry, is't.
    Aber. A proper title of a peace; and purchased
At a superfluous rate!
    Buck.   Why, all this business
● Our reverend cardinal carried.
    Nor.   Like it your grace, 100
The state takes notice of the private difference
Betwixt you and the cardinal. I advise you—
And take it from a heart that wishes towards you
Honour and plenteous safety—that you read
The cardinal's malice and his potency
Together; to consider further that
What his high hatred would effect wants not
A minister in his power. You know his nature,
That he's revengeful, and I know his sword
Hath a sharp edge: it's long and, 't may be said,
It reaches far, and where 'twill not extend,   111
Thither he darts it. Bosom up my counsel,
You'll find it wholesome. Lo, where comes that
    rock
That I advise your shunning.

Enter CARDINAL WOLSEY, *the purse borne before
   him, certain of the* Guard, *and two* Secretaries
   with papers. The* CARDINAL *in his passage
   fixeth his eye on* BUCKINGHAM, *and* BUCKING-
   HAM *on him, both full of disdain.*

●   *Wol.* The Duke of Buckingham's surveyor, ha?
● Where's his examination?
    First Secr.   Here, so please you.
    Wol. Is he in person ready?
    First Secr.   Ay, please your grace.
    Wol. Well, we shall then know more; and
      Buckingham
Shall lessen this big look.
         [*Exeunt Wolsey and his Train.*
    Buck. This butcher's cur is venom-mouth'd,
      and I   120
Have not the power to muzzle him; therefore best
Not wake him in his slumber. A beggar's book

Outworths a noble's blood.
    Nor.   What, are you chafed?
Ask God for temperance; that's the appliance
    only
Which your disease requires.
    Buck.   I read in's looks
Matter against me; and his eye reviled
Me, as his abject object: at this instant
He bores me with some trick: he's gone to the
    king;
I'll follow and outstare him.
    Nor.   Stay, my lord,
And let your reason with your choler question
What 'tis you go about: to climb steep hills 131
Requires slow pace at first: anger is like
A full-hot horse, who being allow'd his way,
Self-mettle tires him. Not a man in England
Can advise me like you: be to yourself
As you would to your friend.
    Buck.   I'll to the king;
And from a mouth of honour quite cry down
This Ipswich fellow's insolence; or proclaim
There's difference in no persons.
    Nor.   Be advised;
Heat not a furnace for your foe so hot   140
That it do singe yourself: we may outrun,
By violent swiftness, that which we run at,
And lose by over-running. Know you not,
The fire that mounts the liquor till't run o'er,
In seeming to augment it wastes it? Be advised:
I say again, there is no English soul
More stronger to direct you than yourself,
If with the sap of reason you would quench,
Or but allay, the fire of passion.
    Buck.   Sir,
I am thankful to you; and I'll go along   150
By your prescription: but this top-proud fellow,
Whom from the flow of gall I name not but
From sincere motions, by intelligence,
And proofs as clear as founts in July when
We see each grain of gravel, I do know
To be corrupt and treasonous.
    Nor.   Say not 'treasonous.'
    Buck. To the king I'll say't; and make my
    vouch as strong
As shore of rock. Attend. This holy fox,
Or wolf, or both,—for he is equal ravenous
As he is subtle, and as prone to mischief   160
As able to perform't; his mind and place
Infecting one another, yea, reciprocally—
Only to show his pomp as well in France
As here at home, suggests the king our master
To this last costly treaty, the interview,
That swallow'd so much treasure, and like a glass
Did break i' the rinsing.
    Nor.   Faith, and so it did.
    Buck. Pray, give me favour, sir. This cunning
    cardinal
The articles o' the combination drew
As himself pleased; and they were ratified   170
As he cried 'Thus let be': to as much end
As give a crutch to the dead: but our count-
    cardinal
Has done this, and 'tis well; for worthy Wolsey,
Who cannot err, he did it. Now this follows,—
Which, as I take it, is a kind of puppy
To the old dam, treason,—Charles the emperor,
Under pretence to see the queen his aunt,—
For 'twas indeed his colour, but he came

123 *Outworths.* Is more powerful than.

128 *bores.* Cheats.

139 *difference.* Distinctions in status.

153 *motions.* Motives.

The Emperor Charles V, nephew of Katherine of Aragon. Engraving from a painting by Titian (d. 1576)

178 *colour.* Pretext.

195 *mistaken.* Misjudged.

204 *device and practice.* Intrigues and plots.

217 *attach.* Arrest.

221 *monk o' the Chartreux.* Monk of the Carthusian order.

To whisper Wolsey,—here makes visitation:
His fears were, that the interview betwixt   180
England and France might, through their amity,
Breed him some prejudice; for from this league
Peep'd harms that menaced him: he privily
Deals with our cardinal; and, as I trow,—
Which I do well; for I am sure the emperor
Paid ere he promised; whereby his suit was granted
Ere it was ask'd; but when the way was made,
And paved with gold, the emperor thus desired,
That he would please to alter the king's course,
And break the foresaid peace. Let the king know,
As soon he shall by me, that thus the cardinal 191
Does buy and sell his honour as he pleases,
And for his own advantage.
  Nor.   I am sorry
To hear this of him; and could wish he were
Something mistaken in 't.
  Buck.   No, not a syllable:
I do pronounce him in that very shape
He shall appear in proof.

Enter BRANDON, *a* Sergeant-at-arms *before him,*
and two or three of the Guard.

  Bran.   Your office, sergeant; execute it.
  Serg.   Sir,
My lord the Duke of Buckingham, and Earl
Of Hereford, Stafford, and Northampton, I   200
Arrest thee of high treason, in the name
Of our most sovereign king.
  Buck.   Lo, you, my lord,
The net has fall'n upon me! I shall perish
Under device and practice.
  Bran.   I am sorry
To see you ta'en from liberty, to look on
The business present: 'tis his highness' pleasure
You shall to the Tower.
  Buck.   It will help me nothing
To plead mine innocence; for that dye is on me
Which makes my whitest part black. The will
    of heaven
Be done in this and all things! I obey.   210
O my Lord Abergavenny, fare you well!
  Bran.   Nay, he must bear you company. The
    king   [*To Abergavenny.*
Is pleased you shall to the Tower, till you know
How he determines further.
  Aber.   As the duke said,
The will of heaven be done, and the king's plea-
    sure
By me obey'd!
  Bran.   Here is a warrant from
The king to attach Lord Montacute; and the
    bodies
Of the duke's confessor, John de la Car,
One Gilbert Peck, his chancellor,—
  Buck.   So, so: 219
These are the limbs o' the plot: no more, I hope.
  Bran.   A monk o' the Chartreux.
  Buck.   O, Nicholas Hopkins?
  Bran.   He.
  Buck.   My surveyor is false; the o'er-great
    cardinal
Hath show'd him gold; my life is spann'd
    already:
I am the shadow of poor Buckingham,
Whose figure even this instant cloud puts on,
By darkening my clear sun. My lord, farewell.
                          [*Exeunt.*

SCENE II. *The same. The council-chamber.*

Cornets. Enter the KING, *leaning on the* CARDINAL'S *shoulder, the Nobles, and* SIR THOMAS LOVELL; *the* CARDINAL *places himself under the* KING'S *feet on his right side.*

King. My life itself, and the best heart of it,
● Thanks you for this great care: I stood i' the
    level
Of a full-charged confederacy, and give thanks
To you that choked it. Let be call'd before us
That gentleman of Buckingham's; in person
I'll hear him his confessions justify;
And point by point the treasons of his master
He shall again relate.

A noise within, crying 'Room for the Queen!' *Enter* QUEEN KATHARINE, *ushered by the* DUKE OF NORFOLK, *and the* DUKE OF SUFFOLK: *she kneels. The* KING *riseth from his state, takes her up, kisses and placeth her by him.*

Q. Kath. Nay, we must longer kneel: I am
    a suitor.
King. Arise, and take place by us: half
    your suit   10
Never name to us; you have half our power:
● The other moiety, ere you ask, is given;
Repeat your will and take it.
Q. Kath.   Thank your majesty.
That you would love yourself, and in that love
Not unconsider'd leave your honour, nor
The dignity of your office, is the point
Of my petition.
King.   Lady mine, proceed.
Q. Kath. I am solicited, not by a few,
● And those of true condition, that your subjects
Are in great grievance: there have been com-
    missions   20
Sent down among 'em, which hath flaw'd the
    heart
Of all their loyalties: wherein, although,
My good lord cardinal, they vent reproaches
Most bitterly on you, as putter on
Of these exactions, yet the king our master—
Whose honour heaven shield from soil!—even he
    escapes not
Language unmannerly, yea, such which breaks
The sides of loyalty, and almost appears
In loud rebellion.
Nor.   Not almost appears,
It doth appear; for, upon these taxations,   30
The clothiers all, not able to maintain
● The many to them 'longing, have put off
● The spinsters, carders, fullers, weavers, who,
Unfit for other life, compell'd by hunger
And lack of other means, in desperate manner
Daring the event to the teeth, are all in uproar,
And danger serves among them.
King.   Taxation!
Wherein? and what taxation? My lord cardinal,
You that are blamed for it alike with us,
Know you of this taxation?
Wol.   Please you, sir,   40
● I know but of a single part, in aught
Pertains to the state; and front but in that file
Where others tell steps with me.
Q. Kath.   No, my lord,

2 *level.* Line of fire.

Katherine (Flora Robson), Henry VIII (Charles Laughton) and Cardinal Wolsey (Robert Farquharson) Sadler's Wells Theatre, London, 1933

12 *moiety.* Half.

19 *true condition.* Loyal.

32 *put off.* Dismissed.

33 *spinsters, carders, fullers.* Spinners, combers who prepared the wool for spinning, and those who beat the wool to clean and thicken it.

Carding and spinning. Engraving from a 14th century manuscript

41—43 *I know . . . with me.* I know only that I have my own part in state affairs. It is of the front rank, but no more powerful than others who keep up with me.

45 *alike.* To all.

52 *exclamation.* Reproach.

Ellen Terry as Katherine, Lyceum Theatre, London, 1892

75 *brake.* Thicket.

78 *cope.* Encounter.

81–83 *What we . . . not allow'd.* Our successes incompetents (in a word fools) either do not attribute to us or do not approve.

94 *stick them in our will.* Subject them to our whim.

96 *lop.* Branch.

You know no more than others; but you frame
● Things that are known alike; which are not
wholesome
To those which would not know them, and yet
must
Perforce be their acquaintance. These exactions,
Whereof my sovereign would have note, they are
Most pestilent to the hearing; and, to bear 'em,
The back is sacrifice to the load. They say 50
They are devised by you; or else you suffer
● Too hard an exclamation.
 King.   Still exaction!
The nature of it? in what kind, let's know,
Is this exaction?
 Q. Kath.   I am much too venturous
In tempting of your patience; but am bolden'd
Under your promised pardon. The subjects'
grief
Comes through commissions, which compel from
each
The sixth part of his substance, to be levied
Without delay; and the pretence for this
Is named, your wars in France: this makes bold
mouths: 60
Tongues spit their duties out, and cold hearts
freeze
Allegiance in them; their curses now
Live where their prayers did: and it's come to
pass,
This tractable obedience is a slave
To each incensed will. I would your highness
Would give it quick consideration, for
There is no primer business.
 King.   By my life,
This is against our pleasure.
 Wol.   And for me,
I have no further gone in this than by
A single voice; and that not pass'd me but 70
By learned approbation of the judges. If I am
Traduced by ignorant tongues, which neither
know
My faculties nor person, yet will be
The chronicles of my doing, let me say
● 'Tis but the fate of place, and the rough brake
That virtue must go through. We must not
stint
Our necessary actions, in the fear
● To cope malicious censurers; which ever,
As ravenous fishes, do a vessel follow
That is new-trimm'd, but benefit no further 80
● Than vainly longing. What we oft do best,
By sick interpreters, once weak ones, is
Not ours, or not allow'd; what worst, as oft,
Hitting a grosser quality, is cried up
For our best act. If we shall stand still,
In fear our motion will be mock'd or carp'd at,
We should take root here where we sit, or sit
State-statues only.
 King.   Things done well,
And with a care, exempt themselves from fear;
Things done without example, in their issue 90
Are to be fear'd. Have you a precedent
Of this commission? I believe, not any.
We must not rend our subjects from our laws,
● And stick them in our will. Sixth part of each?
A trembling contribution! Why, we take
● From every tree lop, bark, and part o' the timber;
And, though we leave it with a root, thus hack'd,
The air will drink the sap. To every county

Where this is question'd send our letters, with
Free pardon to each man that has denied   100
The force of this commission: pray, look to't;
I put it to your care.
    Wol.   A word with you.
                  [*To the Secretary.*
Let there be letters writ to every shire,
Of the king's grace and pardon. The grieved
    commons
● Hardly conceive of me; let it be noised
That through our intercession this revokement
And pardon comes: I shall anon advise you
Further in the proceeding. [*Exit Secretary.*

       Enter Surveyor.

    Q. Kath. I am sorry that the Duke of Buck-
    ingham
Is run in your displeasure.
    King.   It grieves many: 110
The gentleman is learn'd, and a most rare
    speaker;
To nature none more bound; his training such,
That he may furnish and instruct great teachers,
And never seek for aid out of himself. Yet see,
When these so noble benefits shall prove
● Not well disposed, the mind growing once
    corrupt,
They turn to vicious forms, ten times more ugly
Than ever they were fair. This man so complete,
Who was enroll'd 'mongst wonders, and when we,
Almost with ravish'd listening, could not find   120
His hour of speech a minute; he, my lady,
Hath into monstrous habits put the graces
That once were his, and is become as black
As if besmear'd in hell. Sit by us; you shall
    hear—
This was his gentleman in trust—of him
Things to strike honour sad. Bid him recount
The fore-recited practices; whereof
We cannot feel too little, hear too much.
    Wol. Stand forth, and with bold spirit relate
    what you,
Most like a careful subject, have collected   130
Out of the Duke of Buckingham.
    King.   Speak freely.
    Surv. First, it was usual with him, every day
It would infect his speech, that if the king
Should without issue die, he'll carry it so
To make the sceptre his: these very words
I've heard him utter to his son-in-law,
Lord Abergavenny; to whom by oath he menaced
Revenge upon the cardinal.
    Wol.   Please your highness, note
This dangerous conception in this point.
● Not friended by his wish, to your high person   140
His will is most malignant; and it stretches
Beyond you, to your friends.
    Q. Kath.   My learn'd lord cardinal,
Deliver all with charity.
    King.   Speak on:
How grounded he his title to the crown,
● Upon our fail? to this point hast thou heard him
At any time speak aught?
    Surv.   He was brought to this
By a vain prophecy of Nicholas Hopkins.
    King. What was that Hopkins?
    Surv.   Sir, a Chartreux friar,
His confessor; who fed him every minute
With words of sovereignty.

Portrait of Thomas Wolsey, Chancellor to Henry VIII
from 1515 to 1529. He was arrested for treason in 1530,
but died before he could stand trial

105 *Hardly conceive.* Think harshly.

116 *disposed.* Applied.

140 *Not friended by his wish.* Unsuccessful in his wish
(that the King die without issue).

145 *fail.* Either 'die' or 'fail to have issue'.

152 *Rose.* The manor of the Rose belonged to the Duke of Buckingham.

The embarkation of Henry VIII at Dover, 1520

167 *demure.* Solemn.

174 *spleen.* Spite; the spleen was regarded as the seat of bitterness and melancholy.

186 *rank.* Corrupt.

198 *made semblance of his duty.* Pretended to kneel dutifully.

King. How know'st thou this? 150
Surv. Not long before your highness sped to France,
The duke being at the Rose, within the parish
Saint Lawrence Poultney, did of me demand
What was the speech among the Londoners
Concerning the French journey: I replied,
Men fear'd the French would prove perfidious,
To the king's danger. Presently the duke
Said, 'twas the fear, indeed; and that he doubted
'Twould prove the verity of certain words
Spoke by a holy monk; 'that oft,' says he, 160
'Hath sent to me, wishing me to permit
John de la Car, my chaplain, a choice hour
To hear from him a matter of some moment:
Whom after under the confession's seal
He solemnly had sworn, that what he spoke
My chaplain to no creature living, but
To me, should utter, with demure confidence
This pausingly ensued: Neither the king nor's heirs,
Tell you the duke, shall prosper: bid him strive
To gain the love o' the commonalty: the duke 170
Shall govern England.'
Q. Kath. If I know you well,
You were the duke's surveyor, and lost your office
On the complaint o' the tenants: take good heed
You charge not in your spleen a noble person
And spoil your nobler soul: I say, take heed;
Yes, heartily beseech you.
King. Let him on.
Go forward.
Surv. On my soul, I'll speak but truth.
I told my lord the duke, by the devil's illusions
The monk might be deceived; and that 'twas dangerous for him
To ruminate on this so far, until 180
It forged him some design, which, being believed,
It was much like to do: he answer'd, 'Tush,
It can do me no damage;' adding further,
That, had the king in his last sickness fail'd,
The cardinal's and Sir Thomas Lovell's heads
Should have gone off.
King. Ha! what, so rank? Ah ha!
There's mischief in this man: canst thou say further?
Surv. I can, my liege.
King. Proceed.
Surv. Being at Greenwich,
After your highness had reproved the duke
About Sir William Blomer,—
King. I remember 190
Of such a time: being my sworn servant,
The duke retain'd him his. But on; what hence?
Surv. 'If,' quoth he, 'I for this had been committed,
As, to the Tower, I thought, I would have play'd
The part my father meant to act upon
The usurper Richard; who, being at Salisbury,
Made suit to come in 's presence; which if granted,
As he made semblance of his duty, would
Have put his knife into him.'
King. A giant traitor!
Wol. Now, madam, may his highness live in freedom, 200
And this man out of prison?

Q. Kath. God mend all!
King. There's something more would out of
thee; what say'st?
Surv. After 'the duke his father,' with 'the
knife,'
• He stretch'd him, and, with one hand on his
dagger,
Another spread on 's breast, mounting his eyes,
He did discharge a horrible oath; whose tenour
Was,—were he evil used, he would outgo
His father by as much as a performance
• Does an irresolute purpose.
King. There's his period,
To sheathe his knife in us. He is attach'd; 210
Call him to present trial: if he may
Find mercy in the law, 'tis his; if none,
Let him not seek 't of us: by day and night,
He's traitor to the height. [*Exeunt.*

SCENE III. *An antechamber in the palace.*

Enter the LORD CHAMBERLAIN *and* LORD
SANDS.

Cham. Is't possible the spells of France
should juggle
• Men into such strange mysteries?
Sands. New customs,
Though they be never so ridiculous,
Nay, let 'em be unmanly, yet are follow'd.
Cham. As far as I see, all the good our
English
Have got by the late voyage is but merely
• A fit or two o' the face; but they are shrewd
ones;
For when they hold 'em, you would swear
directly
Their very noses had been counsellors
• To Pepin or Clotharius, they keep state so. 10
• *Sands.* They have all new legs, and lame
ones: one would take it,
• That never saw 'em pace before, the spavin
Or springhalt reign'd among 'em.
Cham. Death! my lord,
Their clothes are after such a pagan cut too,
That, sure, they've worn out Christendom.

Enter SIR THOMAS LOVELL.

How now!
What news, Sir Thomas Lovell?
Lov. Faith, my lord,
I hear of none, but the new proclamation
• That's clapp'd upon the court-gate.
Cham. What is 't for?
Lov. The reformation of our travell'd gallants,
That fill the court with quarrels, talk, and
tailors. 20
Cham. I'm glad 'tis there: now I would
pray our monsieurs
To think an English courtier may be wise,
And never see the Louvre.
Lov. They must either,
For so run the conditions, leave those remnants
Of fool and feather that they got in France,
With all their honourable points of ignorance
Pertaining thereunto, as fights and fireworks,
Abusing better men than they can be,
Out of a foreign wisdom, renouncing clean
The faith they have in tennis, and tall stockings,

204 *stretch'd him.* Rose to his full height.

209 *period.* Aim.

Costume design for Henry VIII by Tanya Moisewitch,
Stratford-upon-Avon, 1949

2 *mysteries.* Practices.

7 *A fit or two.* A grimace or two.

10 *Pepin or Clotharius.* Early Kings of the Franks.

11 *legs.* Either 'bowing' or 'way of walking'.

12–13 *spavin . . . springhalt.* Two diseases of horses
which affected their gait.

18 *court-gate.* The gate south of the banqueting house
in Whitehall.

31 *blister'd*. Puffed.

34 *'cum privilegio'*. 'With licence'.

38 *trim vanities*. Vain dandies.

40 *speeding*. Successful.

48 *colt's tooth*. Youthful lust.

67 *comptrollers*. Master of ceremonies.

Sir Henry Guildford. Painting by Hans Holbein the Younger (1497/8–1543)

- Short blister'd breeches, and those types of travel,   31
And understand again like honest men;
Or pack to their old playfellows: there, I take it,
- They may, 'cum privilegio,' wear away
The lag end of their lewdness and be laugh'd at.
  Sands. 'Tis time to give 'em physic, their diseases
Are grown so catching.
  Cham.   What a loss our ladies
- Will have of these trim vanities!
  Lov.   Ay, marry,
There will be woe indeed, lords: the sly whore-sons
- Have got a speeding trick to lay down ladies; 40
A French song and a fiddle has no fellow.
  Sands. The devil fiddle 'em! I am glad they are going,
For, sure, there's no converting of 'em: now
An honest country lord, as I am, beaten
A long time out of play, may bring his plain-song
And have an hour of hearing; and, by'r lady,
Held current music too.
  Cham.   Well said, Lord Sands;
- Your colt's tooth is not cast yet.
  Sands.   No, my lord;
Nor shall not, while I have a stump.
  Cham.   Sir Thomas,
Whither were you a-going?
  Lov.   To the cardinal's: 50
Your lordship is a guest too.
  Cham.   O, 'tis true:
This night he makes a supper, and a great one,
To many lords and ladies; there will be
The beauty of this kingdom, I'll assure you.
  Lov. That churchman bears a bounteous mind indeed,
A hand as fruitful as the land that feeds us;
His dews fall every where.
  Cham.   No doubt he's noble;
He had a black mouth that said other of him.
  Sands. He may, my lord; has wherewithal: in him
Sparing would show a worse sin than ill doc-trine: 60
Men of his way should be most liberal;
They are set here for examples.
  Cham.   True, they are so:
But few now give so great ones. My barge stays;
Your lordship shall along. Come, good Sir Thomas,
We shall be late else; which I would not be,
For I was spoke to, with Sir Henry Guildford
- This night to be comptrollers.
  Sands.   I am your lordship's. [*Exeunt.*

SCENE IV. *A Hall in York Place.*

Hautboys. A small table under a state for the CARDINAL, *a longer table for the guests. Then enter* ANNE BULLEN *and divers other* Ladies *and* Gentlemen *as guests, at one door; at another door, enter* SIR HENRY GUILDFORD.

  Guild. Ladies, a general welcome from his grace
Salutes ye all; this night he dedicates
To fair content and you: none here, he hopes,

In all this noble bevy, has brought with her
One care abroad; he would have all as merry
As, first, good company, good wine, good wel-
    come,
Can make good people. O, my lord, **you 're**
    tardy:

Enter LORD CHAMBERLAIN, LORD SANDS, *and*
    SIR THOMAS LOVELL.

The very thought of this fair company
Clapp'd wings to me.
    Cham.   You are young, Sir Harry Guildford.
    Sands. Sir Thomas Lovell, had the cardinal 10
But half my lay thoughts in him, some of these
● Should find a running banquet ere they rested,
I think would better please 'em: by my life,
They are a sweet society of fair ones.
    Lov. O, that your lordship were but now con-
    fessor
To one or two of these!
    Sands.   I would I were;
They should find easy penance.
    Lov.   Faith, how easy?
    Sands. As easy as a down-bed would afford it.
    Cham. Sweet ladies, will it please you sit?
    Sir Harry,   19
● Place you that side; I'll take the charge of this:
His grace is entering. Nay, you must not freeze;
Two women placed together makes cold weather:
My Lord Sands, you are one will keep 'em waking;
Pray, sit between these ladies.
    Sands.   By my faith,
And thank your lordship. By your leave, sweet
    ladies:
If I chance to talk a little wild, forgive me;
I had it from my father.
    Anne.   Was he mad, sir?
    Sands. O, very mad, exceeding mad, in
    love too:
But he would bite none; just as I do now,
He would kiss you twenty with a breath.
                              [*Kisses her.*
    Cham.   Well said, my lord. 30
So, now you're fairly seated. Gentlemen,
The penance lies on you, if these fair ladies
Pass away frowning.
    Sands.   For my little cure,
Let me alone.

    Hautboys. Enter CARDINAL WOLSEY, *and*
        takes his state.

    Wol. You're welcome, my fair guests: that
    noble lady,
Or gentleman, that is not freely merry,
Is not my friend: this, to confirm my welcome;
And to you all, good health.   [*Drinks.*
    Sands.   Your grace is noble:
Let me have such a bowl may hold my thanks,
And save me so much talking.
    Wol.   My Lord Sands, 40
I am beholding to you: cheer your neighbours.
Ladies, you are not merry: gentlemen,
Whose fault is this?
    Sands.   The red wine first must rise
In their fair cheeks, my lord; then we shall have
    'em
Talk us to silence.
    Anne.   You are a merry gamester,
My Lord Sands.

12 *running banquet.* Hurried refreshment.

20 *Place you.* Seat the guests.

A banquet scene. Woodcut from Holinshed's *Chronicles*,
1577

46 *make my play.* Win a trick; usually in a card game.

Dancers from the time of Henry VIII. Illustration by Herbert Norris, 1908

Sands. Yes, if I make my play.
Here's to your ladyship: and pledge it, madam,
For 'tis to such a thing,—
Anne. You cannot show me.
Sands. I told your grace they would talk anon.
  [*Drum and trumpet, chambers discharged.*
Wol. What's that?
Cham. Look out there, some of ye.
  [*Exit Servant.*
Wol. What warlike voice, 50
And to what end, is this? Nay, ladies, fear not;
By all the laws of war you're privileged.

Re-enter Servant.

Cham. How now! what is't?
Serv. A noble troop of strangers;
For so they seem: they 've left their barge and
  landed;
And hither make, as great ambassadors
From foreign princes.
Wol. Good lord chamberlain,
Go, give 'em welcome; you can speak the French
  tongue;
And, pray, receive 'em nobly, and conduct 'em
Into our presence, where this heaven of beauty
Shall shine at full upon them. Some attend him.
  [*Exit Chamberlain, attended. All rise,
    and tables removed.*
You have now a broken banquet; but we'll
  mend it. 61
A good digestion to you all: and once more
I shower a welcome on ye; welcome all.

Hautboys. Enter the KING *and others, as
masquers, habited like shepherds, ushered by
the* LORD CHAMBERLAIN. *They pass directly
before the* CARDINAL, *and gracefully salute
him.*

A noble company! what are their pleasures?
Cham. Because they speak no English, thus
  they pray'd
To tell your grace, that, having heard by fame
Of this so noble and so fair assembly
This night to meet here, they could do no less,
Out of the great respect they bear to beauty,
But leave their flocks; and, under your fair con-
  duct, 70
Crave leave to view these ladies and entreat
An hour of revels with 'em.
Wol. Say, lord chamberlain,
They have done my poor house grace; for which
  I pay 'em
A thousand thanks, and pray 'em take their
  pleasures.
  [*They choose Ladies for the dance. The
    King chooses Anne Bullen.*
King. The fairest hand I ever touch'd! O
  beauty,
Till now I never knew thee! [*Music. Dance.*
Wol. My lord!
Cham. Your grace?
Wol. Pray, tell 'em thus much from me:
There should be one amongst 'em, by his person,
More worthy this place than myself; to whom,
If I but knew him, with my love and duty 80
I would surrender it.
Cham. I will, my lord.
  [*Whispers the Masquers.*
Wol. What say they?

Cham.   Such a one, they all confess,
There is indeed; which they would have your
    grace
Find out, and he will take it.
    Wol.   Let me see, then.
By all your good leaves, gentlemen; here I'll
    make
My royal choice.
    King.   Ye have found him, cardinal:
                        [*Unmasking.*
You hold a fair assembly; you do well, lord:
You are a churchman, or, I'll tell you, cardinal,
I should judge now unhappily.
    Wol.   I am glad
Your grace is grown so pleasant.
    King.   My lord chamberlain, 90
Prithee, come hither: what fair lady's that?
    Cham. An't please your grace, Sir Thomas
    Bullen's daughter,—
The Viscount Rochford,—one of her highness'
    women.
    King. By heaven, she is a dainty one. Sweet-
    heart,
I were unmannerly, to take you out,
And not to kiss you. A health, gentlemen!
Let it go round.
    Wol. Sir Thomas Lovell, is the banquet ready
I' the privy chamber?
    Lov.   Yes, my lord.
    Wol.   Your grace,
I fear, with dancing is a little heated. 100
    King. I fear, too much.
    Wol.   There's fresher air, my lord,
In the next chamber.
    King. Lead in your ladies, every one: sweet
    partner,
I must not yet forsake you: let's be merry,
Good my lord cardinal: I have half a dozen healths
To drink to these fair ladies, and a measure
To lead 'em once again; and then let's dream
Who's best in favour. Let the music knock it.
                  [*Exeunt with trumpets.*

ACT II.

Scene I. *Westminster. A street.*

Enter two Gentlemen, *meeting.*

First Gent. Whither away so fast?
    Sec. Gent.   O, God save ye!
Even to the hall, to hear what shall become
Of the great Duke of Buckingham.
    First Gent.   I'll save you
That labour, sir. All's now done, but the cere-
    mony
Of bringing back the prisoner.
    Sec. Gent.   Were you there?
    First Gent. Yes, indeed, was I.
    Sec. Gent.   Pray, speak what has happen'd.
    First Gent. You may guess quickly what.
    Sec. Gent.   Is he found guilty?
    First Gent. Yes, truly is he, and condemn'd
    upon't.
    Sec. Gent. I am sorry for't.
    First Gent.   So are a number more.
    Sec. Gent. But, pray, how pass'd it? 10
    First Gent. I'll tell you in a little. The great
    duke
Came to the bar; where to his accusations

95 *take you out.* Take you to dance.

106 *measure.* Stately dance.

108 *knock it.* Strike up.

Anne Boleyn and Henry VIII. Engraving after William Hogarth, 1803

29 *Was either . . . or forgotten.* Either produced pity or no effect at all.

41 *Kildare's attainder.* In order to get the Earl of Surrey, Buckingham's son-in-law, out of England, Wolsey appointed him Lord Deputy of Ireland, after Kildare, who had been attainted.

44 *father.* i.e. father-in-law, Buckingham.

45 *envious.* Malicious.

SD *tipstaves.* Law officers whose staves were tipped with metal.

Buckingham: 'I have this day received a traitor's judgement . . .' Traitors' Gate, Tower of London through which passed those accused of treason. They were brought there by boat. Engraving from a drawing by C. Tomkins, 1801

He pleaded still not guilty and alleged
Many sharp reasons to defeat the law.
The king's attorney on the contrary
Urged on the examinations, proofs, confessions
Of divers witnesses; which the duke desired
To have brought vivâ voce to his face:
At which appear'd against him his surveyor;
Sir Gilbert Peck his chancellor; and John Car,
Confessor to him; with that devil-monk,   21
Hopkins, that made this mischief.
   Sec. Gent.   That was he
That fed him with his prophecies?
   First Gent.   The same.
All these accused him strongly; which he fain
Would have flung from him, but, indeed, he
   could not:
And so his peers, upon this evidence,
Have found him guilty of high treason.   Much
He spoke, and learnedly, for life; but all
● Was either pitied in him or forgotten.
   Sec. Gent.   After all this, how did he bear
   himself?   30
   First Gent.   When he was brought again to
   the bar, to hear
His knell rung out, his judgement, he was stirr'd
With such an agony, he sweat extremely,
And something spoke in choler, ill, and hasty:
But he fell to himself again, and sweetly
In all the rest show'd a most noble patience.
   Sec. Gent.   I do not think he fears death.
   First Gent.   Sure, he does not:
He never was so womanish; the cause
He may a little grieve at.
   Sec. Gent.   Certainly
The cardinal is the end of this.
   First Gent.   'Tis likely,   40
● By all conjectures: first, Kildare's attainder,
Then deputy of Ireland; who removed,
● Earl Surrey was sent thither, and in haste too,
● Lest he should help his father.
   Sec. Gent.   That trick of state
● Was a deep envious one.
   First Gent.   At his return
No doubt he will requite it.   This is noted,
And generally, whoever the king favours,
The cardinal instantly will find employment,
And far enough from court too.
   Sec. Gent.   All the commons
Hate him perniciously, and, o' my conscience, 50
Wish him ten fathom deep: this duke as much
They love and dote on; call him bounteous
   Buckingham,
The mirror of all courtesy;—
   First Gent.   Stay there, sir,
And see the noble ruin'd man you speak of.

Enter BUCKINGHAM *from his arraignment; tipstaves before him; the axe with the edge
towards him; halberds on each side: accompanied with* SIR THOMAS LOVELL, SIR NICH-
OLAS VAUX, SIR WILLIAM SANDS, *and common people.*

   Sec. Gent.   Let's stand close, and behold him.
   Buck.   All good people,
You that thus far have come to pity me,
Hear what I say, and then go home and lose me.
I have this day received a traitor's judgement,
And by that name must die: yet, heaven bear
   witness,

And if I have a conscience, let it sink me, 60
Even as the axe falls, if I be not faithful!
The law I bear no malice for my death;
'T has done, upon the premises, but justice:
But those that sought it I could wish more Christians:
Be what they will, I heartily forgive 'em:
Yet let 'em look they glory not in mischief,
Nor build their evils on the graves of great men;
For then my guiltless blood must cry against 'em.
For further life in this world I ne'er hope,
Nor will I sue, although the king have mercies 70
More than I dare make faults.   You few that loved me,
And dare be bold to weep for Buckingham,
His noble friends and fellows, whom to leave
Is only bitter to him, only dying,
Go with me, like good angels, to my end;
And, as the long divorce of steel falls on me,
Make of your prayers one sweet sacrifice,
And lift my soul to heaven.   Lead on, o' God's name.
    Lov. I do beseech your grace, for charity,
If ever any malice in your heart 80
Were hid against me, now to forgive me frankly.
    Buck. Sir Thomas Lovell, I as free forgive you
As I would be forgiven: I forgive all;
There cannot be those numberless offences
'Gainst me, that I cannot take peace with: no black envy
Shall mark my grave.   Commend me to his grace;
And, if he speak of Buckingham, pray, tell him
You met him half in heaven: my vows and prayers
Yet are the king's; and, till my soul forsake,
Shall cry for blessings on him: may he live 90
Longer than I have time to tell his years!
Ever beloved and loving may his rule be!
And when old time shall lead him to his end,
Goodness and he fill up one monument!
    Lov. To the water side I must conduct your grace;
Then give my charge up to Sir Nicholas Vaux,
Who undertakes you to your end.
    Vaux.   Prepare there,
The duke is coming: see the barge be ready;
And fit it with such furniture as suits
The greatness of his person.
    Buck.   Nay, Sir Nicholas, 100
Let it alone; my state now will but mock me.
When I came hither, I was lord high constable
And Duke of Buckingham; now, poor Edward Bohun:
Yet I am richer than my base accusers,
That never knew what truth meant: I now seal it;
And with that blood will make 'em one day groan for't.
My noble father, Henry of Buckingham,
Who first raised head against usurping Richard,
Flying for succour to his servant Banister,
Being distress'd, was by that wretch betray'd, 110
And without trial fell; God's peace be with him!
Henry the Seventh succeeding, truly pitying
My father's loss, like a most royal prince,
Restored me to my honours, and, out of ruins,
Made my name once more noble.   Now his son,
Henry the Eighth, life, honour, name and all
That made me happy at one stroke has taken

71 *More than I dare make faults.* More than I can commit offences.

105 *it.* i.e. the truth.

108 *head.* Army.

Buckingham: 'Henry the Seventh . . . Made my name once more noble.' Henry VII, first Tudor king and restorer of order after the chaos of the Wars of the Roses. Painting by M. Sittow, 1505

124 *end.* Purpose.

127 *loose.* Careless.

129 *rub.* Obstacle.

Henry Ainley as the Duke of Buckingham, Empire Theatre, London, 1925

148 *buzzing.* Rumour.

For ever from the world. I had my trial,
And, must needs say, a noble one; which makes me
A little happier than my wretched father: 120
Yet thus far we are one in fortunes: both
Fell by our servants, by those men we loved most.
A most unnatural and faithless service!
Heaven has an end in all: yet, you that hear me,
This from a dying man receive as certain:
Where you are liberal of your loves and counsels
Be sure you be not loose; for those you make friends
And give your hearts to, when they once perceive
The least rub in your fortunes, fall away
Like water from ye, never found again   130
But where they mean to sink ye. All good people,
Pray for me! I must now forsake ye: the last hour
Of my long weary life is come upon me.
Farewell:
And when you would say something that is sad,
Speak how I fell. I have done; and God forgive me!   [*Exeunt Duke and Train.*
First Gent. O, this is full of pity! Sir, it calls,
I fear, too many curses on their heads
That were the authors.
Sec. Gent.   If the duke be guiltless,
'Tis full of woe: yet I can give you inkling   140
Of an ensuing evil, if it fall,
Greater than this.
First Gent.   Good angels keep it from us!
What may it be? You do not doubt my faith, sir?
Sec. Gent. This secret is so weighty, 'twill require
A strong faith to conceal it.
First Gent.   Let me have it;
I do not talk much.
Sec. Gent.   I am confident;
You shall, sir: did you not of late days hear
A buzzing of a separation
Between the king and Katharine?
First Gent.   Yes, but it held not:
For when the king once heard it, out of anger   150
He sent command to the lord mayor straight
To stop the rumour, and allay those tongues
That durst disperse it.
Sec. Gent.   But that slander, sir,
Is found a truth now: for it grows again
Fresher than e'er it was; and held for certain
The king will venture at it. Either the cardinal,
Or some about him near, have, out of malice
To the good queen, possess'd him with a scruple
That will undo her: to confirm this too,
Cardinal Campeius is arrived, and lately;   160
As all think, for this business.
First Gent.   'Tis the cardinal;
And merely to revenge him on the emperor
For not bestowing on him, at his asking,
The archbishopric of Toledo, this is purposed.
Sec. Gent. I think you have hit the mark: but is't not cruel
That she should feel the smart of this? The cardinal
Will have his will, and she must fall.
First Gent.   'Tis woful.
We are too open here to argue this;
Let's think in private more.   [*Exeunt.*

SCENE II. *An ante-chamber in the palace.*

Enter the LORD CHAMBERLAIN, *reading a letter.*

Cham. 'My lord, the horses your lordship sent for, with all the care I had, I saw well chosen, ridden, and furnished. They were young and handsome, and of the best breed in the north. When they were ready to set out for London, a man of my lord cardinal's, by commission and main power, took 'em from me; with this reason: His master would be served before a subject, if not before the king; which stopped our mouths, sir.'   10
I fear he will indeed: well, let him have them:
He will have all, I think.

Enter, to the LORD CHAMBERLAIN, *the* DUKES OF NORFOLK *and* SUFFOLK.

Nor. Well met, my lord chamberlain.
Cham. Good day to both your graces.
Suf. How is the king employ'd?
Cham.   I left him private,
Full of sad thoughts and troubles.
Nor.   What's the cause?
Cham. It seems the marriage with his brother's wife
Has crept too near his conscience.
Suf.   No, his conscience
Has crept too near another lady.
Nor.   'Tis so:
This is the cardinal's doing, the king-cardinal: 20
• That blind priest, like the eldest son of fortune,
Turns what he list. The king will know him one day.
Suf. Pray God he do! he'll never know himself else.
Nor. How holily he works in all his business!
And with what zeal! for, now he has crack'd the league
Between us and the emperor, the queen's great nephew,
He dives into the king's soul, and there scatters
Dangers, doubts, wringing of the conscience,
Fears, and despairs; and all these for his marriage:
And out of all these to restore the king,   30
He counsels a divorce; a loss of her
That, like a jewel, has hung twenty years
About his neck, yet never lost her lustre;
Of her that loves him with that excellence
That angels love good men with; even of her
That, when the greatest stroke of fortune falls,
Will bless the king: and is not this course pious?
Cham. Heaven keep me from such counsel! 'Tis most true
These news are every where; every tongue speaks 'em,
And every true heart weeps for't: all that dare 40
Look into these affairs see this main end,
The French king's sister. Heaven will one day open
The king's eyes, that so long have slept upon
This bold bad man.
Suf.   And free us from his slavery.
Nor. We had need pray,
And heartily, for our deliverance;
Or this imperious man will work us all

21 *That blind . . . fortune.* Norfolk likens Wolsey to Fortune who is blindfold but controls men's fates.

50 *pitch*. Degree in rank.

'the King . . . sits reading pensively.' Engraving from a contemporary manuscript

70 *estate*. State.

79 *I be not found a talker*. i.e. make sure he's well looked after.

83 *I would not . . . place*. I would not like his high position at the cost of being so sick with pride.

85 *have-at-him*. The cry before one made a thrust in sword-play.

The coat of arms of Cardinal Campeius

From princes into pages: all men's honours
Lie like one lump before him, to be fashion'd
● Into what pitch he please.
   Suf.   For me, my lords, 50
I love him not, nor fear him; there's my creed:
As I am made without him, so I'll stand,
If the king please; his curses and his blessings
Touch me alike, they're breath I not believe in.
I knew him, and I know him; so I leave him
To him that made him proud, the pope.
   Nor.   Let's in;
And with some other business put the king
From these sad thoughts, that work too much
       upon him:
My lord, you'll bear us company?
   Cham.   Excuse me;
The king has sent me otherwhere: besides, 60
You'll find a most unfit time to disturb him:
Health to your lordships.
   Nor.   Thanks, my good lord chamberlain.
        [Exit Lord Chamberlain; and the
           King draws the curtain, and sits
           reading pensively.
   Suf. How sad he looks! sure, he is much
     afflicted.
   King. Who's there, ha?
   Nor.   Pray God he be not angry.
   King. Who's there, I say? How dare you
     thrust yourselves
Into my private meditations?
Who am I? ha?
   Nor. A gracious king that pardons all offences
Malice ne'er meant: our breach of duty this way
● Is business of estate; in which we come 70
To know your royal pleasure.
   King.   Ye are too bold:
Go to; I'll make ye know your times of business:
Is this an hour for temporal affairs, ha?

Enter WOLSEY *and* CAMPEIUS, *with a commission.*

Who's there? my good lord cardinal? O my
     Wolsey,
The quiet of my wounded conscience;
Thou art a cure fit for a king. *[To Camp.]*
     You're welcome,
Most learned reverend sir, into our kingdom:
Use us and it. *[To Wol.]* My good lord, have
     great care
● I be not found a talker.
   Wol.   Sir, you cannot.
I would your grace would give us but an hour 80
Of private conference.
   King. *[To Nor. and Suf.]* We are busy; go.
   Nor. *[Aside to Suf.]* This priest has no pride
     in him?
   Suf. *[Aside to Nor.]* Not to speak of:
● I would not be so sick though for his place:
But this cannot continue.
   Nor. *[Aside to Suf.]* If it do,
● I'll venture one have-at-him.
   Suf.   *[Aside to Nor.]* I another.
             [Exeunt Nor. and Suf.
   Wol. Your grace has given a precedent of
     wisdom
Above all princes, in committing freely
Your scruple to the voice of Christendom:
Who can be angry now? what envy reach you?
The Spaniard, tied by blood and favour to her, 90

100 *conclave.* College of Cardinals.

108 *equal.* Impartial.

Must now confess, if they have any goodness,
The trial just and noble.   All the clerks,
I mean the learned ones, in Christian kingdoms
Have their free voices: Rome, the nurse of
    judgement,
Invited by your noble self, hath sent
One general tongue unto us, this good man,
This just and learned priest, Cardinal Campeius;
Whom once more I present unto your highness.
    King. And once more in mine arms I bid him
        welcome,
● And thank the holy conclave for their loves: 100
They have sent me such a man I would have
    wish'd for.
    Cam. Your grace must needs deserve all
        strangers' loves,
You are so noble.   To your highness' hand
I tender my commission; by whose virtue,
The court of Rome commanding, you, my lord
Cardinal of York, are join'd with me their servant
In the unpartial judging of this business.
●   *King.* Two equal men.   The queen shall be
        acquainted
Forthwith for what you come.   Where's Gardiner?
    Wol. I know your majesty has always loved
        her   110
So dear in heart, not to deny her that
A woman of less place might ask by law:
Scholars allow'd freely to argue for her.
    King. Ay, and the best she shall have; and
        my favour
To him that does best: God forbid else.   Cardinal,
Prithee, call Gardiner to me, my new secretary:
I find him a fit fellow.   [*Exit Wolsey.*

    Re-enter WOLSEY, *with* GARDINER.

    Wol. [*Aside to Gard.*] Give me your hand:
        much joy and favour to you;
You are the king's now.
    Gard. [*Aside to Wol.*] But to be commanded
For ever by your grace, whose hand has raised me.
    King. Come hither, Gardiner.   121
            [*Walks and whispers.*
    Cam. My Lord of York, was not one Doctor
        Pace
In this man's place before him?
    Wol.   Yes, he was.
    Cam. Was he not held a learned man?
    Wol.   Yes, surely.
    Cam. Believe me, there's an ill opinion spread
        then
Even of yourself, lord cardinal.
    Wol.   How! of me?
    Cam. They will not stick to say you envied
        him,
And fearing he would rise, he was so virtuous,
● Kept him a foreign man still; which so grieved
        him,
That he ran mad and died.
    Wol.   Heaven's peace be with him!
That's Christian care enough: for living mur-
        murers   131
There's places of rebuke.   He was a fool;
For he would needs be virtuous: that good fellow,
If I command him, follows my appointment:
I will have none so near else.   Learn this, brother,
● We live not to be griped by meaner persons.
    King. Deliver this with modesty to the queen.
            [*Exit Gardiner.*

Costume design for Gardiner, Bishop of Winchester
by Tanya Moisewitch, Stratford-upon-Avon, 1949

129 *Kept him a foreign man still.* Always kept him
abroad.

136 *griped.* Controlled.

10 *To give her the avaunt.* To give her the order to be gone.

14 *quarrel.* Quarreller.

17 *stranger.* Foreigner.

Anne; 'By my troth and maidenhead, I would not be a queen.' Drawing by Henry Singleton (1766–1839)

31 *Saving your mincing.* In spite of your affectation.

32 *cheveril.* Kid leather, therefore soft and pliable.

The most convenient place that I can think of
For such receipt of learning is Black-Friars;
There ye shall meet about this weighty business.
My Wolsey, see it furnish'd. O, my lord,   141
Would it not grieve an able man to leave
So sweet a bedfellow? But, conscience, conscience!
O, 'tis a tender place; and I must leave her.
[*Exeunt.*

SCENE III. *An ante-chamber of the* Queen's *apartments.*

Enter ANNE BULLEN *and an* Old Lady.

Anne. Not for that neither: here's the pang that pinches:
His highness having lived so long with her, and she
So good a lady that no tongue could ever
Pronounce dishonour of her; by my life,
She never knew harm-doing: O, now, after
So many courses of the sun enthroned,
Still growing in a majesty and pomp, the which
To leave a thousand-fold more bitter than
'Tis sweet at first to acquire,—after this process,
To give her the avaunt! it is a pity   10
Would move a monster.
   Old L.   Hearts of most hard temper
Melt and lament for her.
   Anne.   O, God's will! much better
She ne'er had known pomp: though't be temporal,
Yet, if that quarrel, fortune, do divorce
It from the bearer, 'tis a sufferance panging
As soul and body's severing.
   Old L.   Alas, poor lady!
She's a stranger now again.
   Anne.   So much the more
Must pity drop upon her. Verily,
I swear, 'tis better to be lowly born,
And range with humble livers in content,   20
Than to be perk'd up in a glistering grief,
And wear a golden sorrow.
   Old L.   Our content
Is our best having.
   Anne.   By my troth and maidenhead,
I would not be a queen.
   Old L.   Beshrew me, I would,
And venture maidenhead for't; and so would you,
For all this spice of your hypocrisy:
You, that have so fair parts of woman on you,
Have too a woman's heart; which ever yet
Affected eminence, wealth, sovereignty;
Which, to say sooth, are blessings; and which gifts,   30
Saving your mincing, the capacity
Of your soft cheveril conscience would receive,
If you might please to stretch it.
   Anne.   Nay, good troth.
   Old L. Yes, troth, and troth; you would not be a queen?
   Anne. No, not for all the riches under heaven.
   Old L. 'Tis strange: a three-pence bow'd would hire me,
Old as I am, to queen it: but, I pray you,
What think you of a duchess? have you limbs
To bear that load of title?
   Anne.   No, in truth.

Old L. Then you are weakly made: pluck off
    a little;   40
I would not be a young count in your way,
For more than blushing comes to: if your back
Cannot vouchsafe this burthen, 'tis too weak
Ever to get a boy.
Anne.   How you do talk!
I swear again, I would not be a queen
For all the world.
Old L.   In faith, for little England
You'ld venture an emballing: I myself
Would for Carnarvonshire, although there'long'd
No more to the crown but that. Lo, who comes
    here?

Enter the LORD CHAMBERLAIN.

Cham. Good morrow, ladies. What were't
    worth to know   50
The secret of your conference?
Anne.   My good lord,
Not your demand; it values not your asking:
Our mistress' sorrows we were pitying.
Cham. It was a gentle business, and becoming
The action of good women: there is hope
All will be well.
Anne.   Now, I pray God, amen!
Cham. You bear a gentle mind, and heavenly
    blessings
Follow such creatures. That you may, fair lady,
Perceive I speak sincerely, and high note's   59
Ta'en of your many virtues, the king's majesty
Commends his good opinion of you, and
Does purpose honour to you no less flowing
Than Marchioness of Pembroke; to which title
A thousand pound a year, annual support,
Out of his grace he adds.
Anne.   I do not know
What kind of my obedience I should tender;
More than my all is nothing: nor my prayers
Are not words duly hallow'd, nor my wishes
More worth than empty vanities; yet prayers
    and wishes
Are all I can return. Beseech your lordship,   70
Vouchsafe to speak my thanks and my obedience,
As from a blushing handmaid, to his highness;
Whose health and royalty I pray for.
Cham.   Lady,
I shall not fail to approve the fair conceit
The king hath of you. [*Aside*] I have perused
    her well;
Beauty and honour in her are so mingled
That they have caught the king: and who knows
    yet
But from this lady may proceed a gem
To lighten all this isle? I'll to the king,
And say I spoke with you.
          [*Exit Lord Chamberlain.*
Anne.   My honour'd lord.   80
Old L. Why, this it is; see, see!
I have been begging sixteen years in court,
Am yet a courtier beggarly, nor could
Come pat betwixt too early and too late
For any suit of pounds; and you, O fate!
A very fresh fish here—fie, fie, fie upon
This compell'd fortune!—have your mouth fill'd
    up
Before you open it.
Anne.   This is strange to me.

40 *pluck off a little.* Step down in rank.

47 *emballing.* Investiture with an orb, the symbol of royalty.

78 *gem.* i.e. Elizabeth.

Queen Elizabeth I. Painting by Nicholas Hilliard (*c.*1547–1619)

85 *suit of pounds.* Petition for money.

89 *forty pence.* Proverbial for a small bet.

103 *salute my blood.* Stir my blood.

SD *Sennet. consistory.* Ecclesiastical court.

The Trial of Queen Katherine. Charles Kemble as Henry VIII and his daughter Fanny Kemble as Queen Katherine. Painting by Henry Andrews (d.1868)

● *Old L.* How tastes it? is it bitter? forty
pence, no.
There was a lady once, 'tis an old story, 90
That would not be a queen, that would she not,
For all the mud in Egypt: have you heard it?
Anne. Come, you are pleasant.
Old L. With your theme, I could
O'ermount the lark. The Marchioness of Pem-
broke!
A thousand pounds a year for pure respect!
No other obligation! By my life,
That promises moe thousands: honour's train
Is longer than his foreskirt. By this time
I know your back will bear a duchess: say,
Are you not stronger than you were?
Anne. Good lady, 100
Make yourself mirth with your particular fancy,
And leave me out on 't. Would I had no being,
● If this salute my blood a jot: it faints me,
To think what follows.
The queen is comfortless, and we forgetful
In our long absence: pray, do not deliver
What here you've heard to her.
Old L. What do you think me?
[*Exeunt.*

SCENE IV. *A hall in Black-Friars.*

Trumpets, sennet, and cornets. Enter two
Vergers, *with short silver wands; next them,*
two Scribes, *in the habit of doctors; after*
them, the ARCHBISHOP OF CANTERBURY *alone;*
after him, the BISHOPS OF LINCOLN, ELY, RO-
CHESTER, *and* SAINT ASAPH; *next them, with*
some small distance, follows a Gentleman *bear-*
ing the purse, with the great seal, and a car-
dinal's hat; then two Priests, *bearing each a*
silver cross; then a Gentleman-usher *bare-*
headed, accompanied with a Sergeant-at-arms
bearing a silver mace; then two Gentlemen
bearing two great silver pillars; after them,
side by side, the two CARDINALS; *two* Noblemen *with the sword and mace.* The KING
takes place under the cloth of state; the two
CARDINALS *sit under him as judges.* The
QUEEN *takes place some distance from the*
KING. *The* Bishops *place themselves on each*
side the court, in manner of a consistory;
below them, the Scribes. *The* Lords *sit next*
the Bishops. *The rest of the* Attendants *stand*
in convenient order about the stage.

Wol. Whilst our commission from Rome is
read,
Let silence be commanded.
King. What's the need?
It hath already publicly been read,
And on all sides the authority allow'd;
You may, then, spare that time.
Wol. Be't so. Proceed.
Scribe. Say, Henry King of England, come
into the court.
Crier. Henry King of England, &c.
King. Here.
Scribe. Say, Katharine Queen of England,
come into the court. 11
Crier. Katharine Queen of England, &c.
[*The Queen makes no answer, rises out*
of her chair, goes about the court,

*comes to the King, and kneels at his
feet; then speaks.*

Q. Kath. Sir, I desire you do me right and
justice;
And to bestow your pity on me: for
I am a most poor woman, and a stranger,
Born out of your dominions; having here
● No judge indifferent, nor no more assurance
Of equal friendship and proceeding. Alas, sir,
In what have I offended you? what cause
Hath my behaviour given to your displeasure, 20
That thus you should proceed to put me off,
And take your good grace from me? Heaven
witness,
I have been to you a true and humble wife,
At all times to your will conformable;
Ever in fear to kindle your dislike,
Yea, subject to your countenance, glad or sorry
As I saw it inclined: when was the hour
I ever contradicted your desire,
Or made it not mine too? Or which of your
friends
Have I not strove to love, although I knew 30
He were mine enemy? what friend of mine
● That had to him derived your anger, did I
Continue in my liking? nay, gave notice
He was from thence discharged? Sir, call to
mind
That I have been your wife, in this obedience,
Upward of twenty years, and have been blest
With many children by you: if, in the course
And process of this time, you can report,
And prove it too, against mine honour aught,
My bond to wedlock, or my love and duty, 40
Against your sacred person, in God's name,
Turn me away; and let the foul'st contempt
Shut door upon me, and so give me up
To the sharp'st kind of justice. Please you, sir,
The king, your father, was reputed for
A prince most prudent, of an excellent
And unmatch'd wit and judgement: Ferdinand,
My father, king of Spain, was reckon'd one
The wisest prince that there had reign'd by many
A year before: it is not to be question'd 50
That they had gather'd a wise council to them
Of every realm, that did debate this business,
Who deem'd our marriage lawful: wherefore I
humbly
Beseech you, sir, to spare me, till I may
Be by my friends in Spain advised; whose counsel
I will implore: if not, i' the name of God,
Your pleasure be fulfill'd!
Wol.   You have here, lady,
And of your choice, these reverend fathers; men
Of singular integrity and learning,
Yea, the elect o' the land, who are assembled 60
To plead your cause: it shall be therefore boot-
less
● That longer you desire the court; as well
For your own quiet, as to rectify
What is unsettled in the king.
Cam.   His grace
Hath spoken well and justly: therefore, madam,
It's fit this royal session do proceed;
And that, without delay, their arguments
Be now produced and heard.
Q. Kath.   Lord cardinal,
To you I speak.
Wol.   Your pleasure, madam?

Katherine: 'Sir, I desire you do me right and justice;'
Drawing by Frank Salisbury, 1916

17 *indifferent.* Impartial.

32 *derived.* Drawn.

62 *That longer.* To delay.

Coat of arms of Henry VIII and Katherine of Aragon

79 *blown this coal.* Stir up trouble.

96 *gainsay my deed.* Deny what I have done.

99 *free of your report.* Innocent of your charges.

108 *sign.* Seem.

Katherine: 'I do refuse you for my judge . . .' Sarah Siddons as Katherine, Covent Garden Theatre, London, 1811. Painting by George H. Harlow, 1817

Q. Kath.   Sir,
I am about to weep; but, thinking that   70
We are a queen, or long have dream'd so, certain
The daughter of a king, my drops of tears
I'll turn to sparks of fire.
   Wol.   Be patient yet.
   Q. Kath.   I will, when you are humble; nay,
      before,
Or God will punish me.   I do believe,
Induced by potent circumstances, that
You are mine enemy, and make my challenge
You shall not be my judge: for it is you
• Have blown this coal betwixt my lord and me;
Which God's dew quench! Therefore I say again,
I utterly abhor, yea, from my soul   81
Refuse you for my judge; whom, yet once more,
I hold my most malicious foe, and think not
At all a friend to truth.
   Wol.   I do profess
You speak not like yourself; who ever yet
Have stood to charity, and display'd the effects
Of disposition gentle, and of wisdom
O'ertopping woman's power.   Madam, you do me
      wrong:
I have no spleen against you; nor injustice
For you or any: how far I have proceeded,   90
Or how far further shall, is warranted
By a commission from the consistory,
Yea, the whole consistory of Rome.   You charge
      me
That I have blown this coal: I do deny it:
The king is present: if it be known to him
• That I gainsay my deed, how may he wound,
And worthily, my falsehood! yea, as much
As you have done my truth.   If he know
• That I am free of your report, he knows
I am not of your wrong.   Therefore in him   100
It lies to cure me: and the cure is, to
Remove these thoughts from you: the which be-
      fore
His highness shall speak in, I do beseech
You, gracious madam, to unthink your speaking
And to say so no more.
   Q. Kath.   My lord, my lord,
I am a simple woman, much too weak
To oppose your cunning.   You're meek and
      humble-mouth'd;
• You sign your place and calling, in full seeming,
With meekness and humility; but your heart
Is cramm'd with arrogancy, spleen, and pride. 110
You have, by fortune and his highness' favours,
Gone slightly o'er low steps and now are mounted
Where powers are your retainers, and your words,
Domestics to you, serve your will as't please
Yourself pronounce their office.   I must tell you,
You tender more your person's honour than
Your high profession spiritual: that again
I do refuse you for my judge; and here,
Before you all, appeal unto the pope,
To bring my whole cause 'fore his holiness,   120
And to be judged by him.
   [*She curtsies to the King, and offers to depart.*
   Cam.   The queen is obstinate,
Stubborn to justice, apt to accuse it, and
Disdainful to be tried by't: 'tis not well.
She's going away.
   King.   Call her again.
   Crier.   Katharine Queen of England, come
      into the court.

Grif. Madam, you are call'd back.

Q. Kath. What need you note it? pray you,
    keep your way:
When you are call'd, return. Now, the Lord
    help,
They vex me past my patience! Pray you,
    pass on: 130
I will not tarry; no, nor ever more
Upon this business my appearance make
In any of their courts.

    [Exeunt Queen, and her Attendants.

King.   Go thy ways, Kate:
That man i' the world who shall report he has
A better wife, let him in nought be trusted,
For speaking false in that: thou art, alone,
If thy rare qualities, sweet gentleness,
Thy meekness saint-like, wife-like government,
Obeying in commanding, and thy parts   139
Sovereign and pious else, could speak thee out,
The queen of earthly queens: she's noble born;
And, like her true nobility, she has
Carried herself towards me.

Wol.   Most gracious sir,
In humblest manner I require your highness,
That it shall please you to declare, in hearing
Of all these ears,—for where I am robb'd and
    bound,
There must I be unloosed, although not there
At once and fully satisfied,—whether ever I
Did broach this business to your highness; or
Laid any scruple in your way, which might   150
Induce you to the question on't? or ever
Have to you, but with thanks to God for such
A royal lady, spake one the least word that
    might
Be to the prejudice of her present state,
● Or touch of her good person?

King.   My lord cardinal,
I do excuse you; yea, upon mine honour,
I free you from't. You are not to be taught
That you have many enemies, that know not
Why they are so, but, like to village-curs,
Bark when their fellows do: by some of these   160
The queen is put in anger. You're excused:
But will you be more justified? you ever
Have wish'd the sleeping of this business; never
    desired
It to be stirr'd; but oft have hinder'd, oft,
The passages made toward it: on my honour,
● I speak my good lord cardinal to this point,
And thus far clear him. Now, what moved me
    to't,
I will be bold with time and your attention:
Then mark the inducement. Thus it came; give
    heed to't:
My conscience first received a tenderness,   170
Scruple, and prick, on certain speeches utter'd
By the Bishop of Bayonne, then French am-
    bassador;
Who had been hither sent on the debating
A marriage 'twixt the Duke of Orleans and
Our daughter Mary: i' the progress of this busi-
    ness,
● Ere a determinate resolution, he,
I mean the bishop, did require a respite;
Wherein he might the king his lord advertise
Whether our daughter were legitimate,   179
Respecting this our marriage with the dowager,
● Sometimes our brother's wife. This respite shook

155 *touch of her good person.* Slander her good name.

166 *I speak . . . this point.* I bear witness to the Cardinal's attitude on this matter.

The betrothal of Mary Tudor to the Duke of Orleans. Engraving from a contemporary woodcut

176 *determinate resolution.* Final decision.

181 *Sometimes.* Formerly.

King: 'Sometimes our brother's wife.' Prince Arthur, Henry's elder brother and Katharine's first husband, who died before he could inherit the throne

199 *hulling.* Drifting.

204 *and yet.* And even now.

208 *reek.* Sweat.

King: 'I have spoke long.' Drawing by Henry Singleton (1766–1839)

213–214 *Bearing a state . . . of dread.* Involving state matters of high importance and fearful consequences.

230 *paragon'd.* Regarded as perfect.

The bosom of my conscience, enter'd me,
Yea, with a splitting power, and made to tremble
The region of my breast; which forced such way,
That many mazed considerings did throng
And press'd in with this caution. First, methought
I stood not in the smile of heaven; who had
Commanded nature, that my lady's womb,
If it conceived a male child by me, should
Do no more offices of life to 't than   190
The grave does to the dead; for her male issue
Or died where they were made, or shortly after
This world had air'd them: hence I took a thought,
This was a judgement on me; that my kingdom,
Well worthy the best heir o' the world, should not
Be gladded in 't by me: then follows, that
I weigh'd the danger which my realms stood in
By this my issue's fail; and that gave to me
● Many a groaning throe. Thus hulling in
The wild sea of my conscience, I did steer   200
Toward this remedy, whereupon we are
Now present here together; that's to say,
I meant to rectify my conscience,—which
● I then did feel full sick, and yet not well,—
By all the reverend fathers of the land
And doctors learn'd: first I began in private
With you, my Lord of Lincoln; you remember
● How under my oppression I did reek,
When I first moved you.
    Lin.   Very well, my liege.
    King. I have spoke long: be pleased yourself to say   210
How far you satisfied me.
    Lin.   So please your highness,
The question did at first so stagger me,
● Bearing a state of mighty moment in 't
And consequence of dread, that I committed
The daring'st counsel which I had to doubt;
And did entreat your highness to this course
Which you are running here.
    King.   I then moved you,
My Lord of Canterbury; and got your leave
To make this present summons: unsolicited
I left no reverend person in this court;   220
But by particular consent proceeded
Under your hands and seals: therefore, go on;
For no dislike i' the world against the person
Of the good queen, but the sharp thorny points
Of my alleged reasons, drive this forward:
Prove but our marriage lawful, by my life
And kingly dignity, we are contented
To wear our mortal state to come with her,
Katharine our queen, before the primest creature
● That's paragon'd o' the world.
    Cam.   So please your highness,   230
The queen being absent, 'tis a needful fitness
That we adjourn this court till further day:
Meanwhile must be an earnest motion
Made to the queen, to call back her appeal
She intends unto his holiness.
    King. [*Aside*] I may perceive
These cardinals trifle with me: I abhor
This dilatory sloth and tricks of Rome.
My learn'd and well-beloved servant, Cranmer,
Prithee, return: with thy approach, I know,
My comfort comes along. Break up the court:
I say, set on.   241
    [*Exeunt in manner as they entered.*

ACT III.

SCENE I: *London. The* QUEEN'S *apartments.*

The QUEEN *and her Women, as at work.*

Q. Kath. Take thy lute, wench: my soul
grows sad with troubles;
Sing, and disperse 'em, if thou canst: leave
working.

SONG.

Orpheus with his lute made trees,
And the mountain tops that freeze,
  Bow themselves when he did sing:
To his music plants and flowers
Ever sprung; as sun and showers
  There had made a lasting spring.

Every thing that heard him play,
Even the billows of the sea,   10
  Hung their heads, and then lay by.
In sweet music is such art,
Killing care and grief of heart
  Fall asleep, or hearing, die.

Enter a Gentleman.

Q. Kath. How now!
Gent. An't please your grace, the two great
cardinals
● Wait in the presence.
Q. Kath.   Would they speak with me?
Gent. They will'd me say so, madam.
Q. Kath.   Pray their graces
To come near. [*Exit Gent.*] What can be their
business
With me, a poor weak woman, fall'n from
  favour?   20
I do not like their coming. Now I think on't,
They should be good men; their affairs as right-
eous:
But all hoods make not monks.

Enter the two Cardinals, WOLSEY *and*
CAMPEIUS.

Wol.   Peace to your highness!
Q. Kath. Your graces find me here part of a
housewife,
I would be all, against the worst may happen.
What are your pleasures with me, reverend
lords?
Wol. May it please you, noble madam, to
withdraw
Into your private chamber, we shall give you
The full cause of our coming.
Q. Kath.   Speak it here;
There's nothing I have done yet, o' my con-
science,   30
● Deserves a corner: would all other women
Could speak this with as free a soul as I do!
My lords, I care not, so much I am happy
Above a number, if my actions
Were tried by every tongue, every eye saw 'em,
Envy and base opinion set against 'em,
● I know my life so even. If your business
Seek me out, and that way I am wife in,
Out with it boldly: truth loves open dealing.
● *Wol.* Tanta est erga te mentis integritas,
regina serenissima,—   41
Q. Kath. O, good my lord, no Latin;
I am not such a truant since my coming,

Queen Katherine: 'Take thy lute, wench: my soul
grows sad with troubles;' Ellen Terry as Katherine,
Lyceum Theatre, London, 1892

---

17 *presence.* Presence-chamber.

31 *corner.* Secrecy.

37 *even.* Straight-forward.

40–41 *Tanta est . . . serenissima.* The integrity of our
purpose towards you is so great, most noble queen.

Katherine confronts the Cardinals. Engraving from a painting by Rev. M.W. Peters (d.1814)

---

49 *willing'st*. Most deliberate.

72 *wit*. Intelligence.

86 *desperate*. Reckless.

As not to know the language I have lived in:
A strange tongue makes my cause more strange, suspicious;
Pray, speak in English: here are some will thank you,
If you speak truth, for their poor mistress' sake;
Believe me, she has had much wrong: lord cardinal,
● The willing'st sin I ever yet committed
May be absolved in English.
    Wol.   Noble lady,   50
I am sorry my integrity should breed,
And service to his majesty and you,
So deep suspicion, where all faith was meant.
We come not by the way of accusation,
To taint that honour every good tongue blesses,
Nor to betray you any way to sorrow,
You have too much, good lady; but to know
How you stand minded in the weighty difference
Between the king and you; and to deliver,
Like free and honest men, our just opinions 60
And comforts to your cause.
    Cam.   Most honour'd madam,
My Lord of York, out of his noble nature,
Zeal and obedience he still bore your grace,
Forgetting, like a good man, your late censure
Both of his truth and him, which was too far,
Offers, as I do, in a sign of peace,
His service and his counsel.
    Q. Kath.   [*Aside*] To betray me.—
My lords, I thank you both for your good wills;
Ye speak like honest men; pray God, ye prove so!
But how to make ye suddenly an answer, 70
In such a point of weight, so near mine honour,—
● More near my life, I fear,—with my weak wit,
And to such men of gravity and learning,
In truth, I know not. I was set at work
Among my maids; full little, God knows, looking
Either for such men or such business.
For her sake that I have been,—for I feel
The last fit of my greatness,—good your graces,
Let me have time and counsel for my cause:
Alas, I am a woman, friendless, hopeless! 80
    Wol. Madam, you wrong the king's love with these fears:
Your hopes and friends are infinite.
    Q. Kath.   In England
But little for my profit: can you think, lords,
That any Englishman dare give me counsel?
Or be a known friend, 'gainst his highness' pleasure,
● Though he be grown so desperate to be honest,
And live a subject? Nay, forsooth, my friends,
They that must weigh out my afflictions,
They that my trust must grow to, live not here:
They are, as all my other comforts, far hence 90
In mine own country, lords.
    Cam.   I would your grace
Would leave your griefs, and take my counsel.
    Q. Kath.   How, sir?
    Cam. Put your main cause into the king's protection;
He's loving and most gracious: 'twill be much
Both for your honour better and your cause;
For if the trial of the law o'ertake ye,
You'll part away disgraced.
    Wol.   He tells you rightly.

Q. Kath. Ye tell me what ye wish for both,—
    my ruin:
Is this your Christian counsel? out upon ye!
Heaven is above all yet; there sits a judge   100
That no king can corrupt.
   Cam.   Your rage mistakes us.
   Q. Kath.   The more shame for ye: holy men
    I thought ye,
Upon my soul, two reverend cardinal virtues;
But cardinal sins and hollow hearts I fear ye:
Mend 'em, for shame, my lords. Is this your
    comfort?
The cordial that ye bring a wretched lady,
A woman lost among ye, laugh'd at, scorn'd?
I will not wish ye half my miseries;
I have more charity: but say, I warn'd ye;
● Take heed, for heaven's sake, take heed, lest at
    once   110
The burthen of my sorrows fall upon ye.
   Wol.   Madam, this is a mere distraction;
You turn the good we offer into envy.
   Q. Kath.   Ye turn me into nothing: woe upon
    ye
● And all such false professors! would you have
    me—
If you have any justice, any pity;
If ye be any thing but churchmen's habits—
Put my sick cause into his hands that hates me?
Alas, has banish'd me his bed already,
His love, too long ago! I am old, my lords,   120
And all the fellowship I hold now with him
Is only my obedience. What can happen
● To me above this wretchedness? all your studies
Make me a curse like this.
   Cam.   Your fears are worse.
   Q. Kath.   Have I lived thus long—let me
    speak myself,
Since virtue finds no friends—a wife, a true one?
A woman, I dare say without vain-glory,
Never yet branded with suspicion?
Have I with all my full affections
Still met the king? loved him next heaven?
    obey'd him?   130
● Been, out of fondness, superstitious to him?
Almost forgot my prayers to content him?
And am I thus rewarded? 'tis not well, lords.
Bring me a constant woman to her husband,
One that ne'er dream'd a joy beyond his pleasure;
And to that woman, when she has done most,
Yet will I add an honour, a great patience.
   Wol.   Madam, you wander from the good we
    aim at.
   Q. Kath.   My lord, I dare not make myself so
    guilty,
To give up willingly that noble title   140
Your master wed me to: nothing but death
Shall e'er divorce my dignities.
   Wol.   Pray, hear me.
   Q. Kath.   Would I had never trod this English
    earth,
Or felt the flatteries that grow upon it!
Ye have angels' faces, but heaven knows your
    hearts.
What will become of me now, wretched lady!
I am the most unhappy woman living.
Alas, poor wenches, where are now your fortunes!
Shipwreck'd upon a kingdom, where no pity,
No friends, no hope; no kindred weep for me;
Almost no grave allow'd me: like the lily,   151

110 *at once.* One day.

115 *professors.* i.e. of divinity.

Katherine of Aragon. The Pope's opposition to Henry's divorce from her (1533) caused the secession of the Church in England from papal authority

123–124 *all your . . . like this.* I challenge you to find in your studies a curse like this.

131 *superstitious.* Devoted, idolizing.

Costume design for Katherine by Tanya Moisewitch, Stratford-upon-Avon, 1949

2 *force.* Urge.

10 *uncontemn'd.* Unscorned.

13 *Out of.* Except for.

That once was mistress of the field and flourish'd,
I'll hang my head and perish.
 Wol.   If your grace
Could but be brought to know our ends are honest,
You'ld feel more comfort: why should we, good
    lady,
Upon what cause, wrong you? alas, our places,
The way of our profession is against it:
We are to cure such sorrows, not to sow 'em.
For goodness' sake, consider what you do;
How you may hurt yourself, ay, utterly   160
Grow from the king's acquaintance, by this car-
    riage.
The hearts of princes kiss obedience,
So much they love it; but to stubborn spirits
They swell, and grow as terrible as storms.
I know you have a gentle, noble temper,
A soul as even as a calm: pray, think us
Those we profess, peace-makers, friends, and
    servants.
 Cam. Madam, you'll find it so. You wrong
    your virtues
With these weak women's fears: a noble spirit,
As yours was put into you, ever casts   170
Such doubts, as false coin, from it. The king
    loves you;
Beware you lose it not: for us, if you please
To trust us in your business, we are ready
To use our utmost studies in your service.
 Q. Kath. Do what ye will, my lords; and,
    pray, forgive me,
If I have used myself unmannerly;
You know I am a woman, lacking wit
To make a seemly answer to such persons.
Pray, do my service to his majesty:
He has my heart yet; and shall have my prayers
While I shall have my life. Come, reverend
    fathers,   181
Bestow your counsels on me: she now begs,
That little thought, when she set footing here,
She should have bought her dignities so dear.
              [*Exeunt.*

SCENE II. *Ante-chamber to the* KING'S *apartment.*

Enter the DUKE OF NORFOLK, *the* DUKE OF
  SUFFOLK, *the* EARL OF SURREY, *and the*
  LORD CHAMBERLAIN.

 Nor. If you will now unite in your complaints,
And force them with a constancy, the cardinal
Cannot stand under them: if you omit
The offer of this time, I cannot promise
But that you shall sustain moe new disgraces,
With these you bear already.
 Sur.   I am joyful
To meet the least occasion that may give me
Remembrance of my father-in-law, the duke,
To be revenged on him.
 Suf.   Which of the peers
Have uncontemn'd gone by him, or at least   10
Strangely neglected? when did he regard
The stamp of nobleness in any person
Out of himself?
 Cham.   My lords, you speak your pleasures:
What he deserves of you and me I know;
What we can do to him, though now the time
Gives way to us, I much fear. If you cannot
Bar his access to the king, never attempt

Any thing on him; for he hath a witchcraft
Over the king in's tongue.
    Nor.   O, fear him not;
His spell in that is out: the king hath found   20
Matter against him that for ever mars
The honey of his language.   No, he's settled,
● Not to come off, in his displeasure.
    Sur.   Sir,
I should be glad to hear such news as this
Once every hour.
    Nor.   Believe it, this is true:
In the divorce his contrary proceedings
Are all unfolded; wherein he appears
As I would wish mine enemy.
    Sur.   How came
His practices to light?
    Suf.   Most strangely.
    Sur.   O, how, how?
    Suf.   The cardinal's letters to the pope mis-
      carried,   30
And came to the eye o' the king: wherein was
      read,
How that the cardinal did entreat his holiness
To stay the judgement o' the divorce; for if
It did take place, 'I do,' quoth he, 'perceive
My king is tangled in affection to
A creature of the queen's, Lady Anne Bullen.'
    Sur. Has the king this?
    Suf.   Believe it.
    Sur.   Will this work?
●   *Cham.* The king in this perceives him, how
      he coasts
And hedges his own way. But in this point
All his tricks founder, and he brings his physic
After his patient's death: the king already   41
Hath married the fair lady.
    Sur.   Would he had!
    Suf. May you be happy in your wish, my lord!
For, I profess, you have it.
    Sur.   Now, all my joy
Trace the conjunction!
    Suf.   My amen to't!
    Nor.   All men's!
    Suf.   There's order given for her coronation:
Marry, this is yet but young, and may be left
To some ears unrecounted. But, my lords,
She is a gallant creature, and complete
In mind and feature: I persuade me, from her 50
Will fall some blessing to this land, which shall
● In it be memorized.
    Sur.   But, will the king
● Digest this letter of the cardinal's?
The Lord forbid!
    Nor.   Marry, amen!
    Suf.   No, no;
There be moe wasps that buzz about his nose
Will make this sting the sooner. Cardinal Cam-
      peius
Is stol'n away to Rome; hath ta'en no leave;
Has left the cause o' the king unhandled; and
Is posted, as the agent of our cardinal,
To second all his plot. I do assure you   60
The king cried Ha! at this.
    Cham.   Now, God incense him,
And let him cry Ha! louder!
    Nor.   But, my lord,
When returns Cranmer?
    Suf. He is return'd in his opinions; which
Have satisfied the king for his divorce,

---

23 *come off.* Escape.

38—39 *coasts and hedges.* Follows devious courses and ways.

52 *memorized.* Made memorable.

53 *Digest.* Put up with.

H. Beerbohm Tree as Wolsey, His Majesty's Theatre, London, 1910

99 *spleeny*. Passionate.

101 *hard-ruled*. Difficult to guide.

Together with all famous colleges
Almost in Christendom: shortly, I believe,
His second marriage shall be publish'd, and
Her coronation. Katharine no more
Shall be call'd queen, but princess dowager 70
And widow to Prince Arthur.
Nor.   This same Cranmer's
A worthy fellow, and hath ta'en much pain
In the king's business.
Suf.   He has; and we shall see him
For it an archbishop.
Nor.   So I hear.
Suf.   'Tis so.
The cardinal!

Enter WOLSEY *and* CROMWELL.

Nor.   Observe, observe, he's moody.
Wol. The packet, Cromwell,
Gave't you the king?
Crom.   To his own hand, in's bedchamber.
Wol. Look'd he o' the inside of the paper?
Crom.   Presently
He did unseal them: and the first he view'd,
He did it with a serious mind; a heed 80
Was in his countenance. You he bade
Attend him here this morning.
Wol.   Is he ready
To come abroad?
Crom.   I think, by this he is.
Wol. Leave me awhile.   [*Exit Cromwell.*
[*Aside*] It shall be to the Duchess of Alençon,
The French king's sister: he shall marry her.
Anne Bullen! No; I'll no Anne Bullens for him:
There's more in't than fair visage.   Bullen!
No, we'll no Bullens. Speedily I wish
To hear from Rome. The Marchioness of Pem-
    broke!   90
Nor. He's discontented.
Suf.   May be, he hears the king
Does whet his anger to him.
Sur.   Sharp enough,
Lord, for thy justice!
Wol. [*Aside*] The late queen's gentlewoman,
    a knight's daughter,
To be her mistress' mistress! the queen's queen!
This candle burns not clear: 'tis I must snuff it;
Then out it goes. What though I know her
    virtuous
And well deserving? yet I know her for
● A spleeny Lutheran; and not wholesome to
Our cause, that she should lie i' the bosom of 100
● Our hard-ruled king. Again, there is sprung up
An heretic, an arch one, Cranmer; one
Hath crawl'd into the favour of the king,
And is his oracle.
Nor.   He is vex'd at something.
Sur. I would 'twere something that would
    fret the string,
The master-cord on 's heart!

Enter the KING, *reading of a schedule, and*
                LOVELL.

Suf.   The king, the king!
King. What piles of wealth hath he accumul-
    ated
To his own portion! and what expense by the hour
Seems to flow from him! How, i' the name of
    thrift,
Does he rake this together! Now, my lords, 110

Saw you the cardinal?
Nor.   My lord, we have
● Stood here observing him: some strange com   motion
Is in his brain: he bites his lip, and starts;
Stops on a sudden, looks upon the ground,
Then lays his finger on his temple; straight
Springs out into fast gait; then stops again,
Strikes his breast hard, and anon he casts
His eye against the moon: in most strange pos   tures
We have seen him set himself.
    King.   It may well be;
There is a mutiny in's mind. This morning   120
Papers of state he sent me to peruse,
As I required: and wot you what I found
There,—on my conscience, put unwittingly?
Forsooth, an inventory, thus importing;
The several parcels of his plate, his treasure,
Rich stuffs, and ornaments of household; which
● I find at such proud rate, that it out-speaks
Possession of a subject.
    Nor.   It's heaven's will:
Some spirit put this paper in the packet,
To bless your eye withal.
    King.   If we did think   130
His contemplation were above the earth,
And fix'd on spiritual object, he should still
Dwell in his musings: but I am afraid
His thinkings are below the moon, not worth
His serious considering.
       [*King takes his seat; whispers Lovell, who*
                         goes to the Cardinal.
    Wol.   Heaven forgive me!
Ever God bless your highness!
    King.   Good my lord,
You are full of heavenly stuff, and bear the in   ventory
Of your best graces in your mind; the which
You were now running o'er: you have scarce time
To steal from spiritual leisure a brief span   140
To keep your earthly audit: sure, in that
● I deem you an ill husband, and am glad
To have you therein my companion.
    Wol.   Sir,
For holy offices I have a time; a time
To think upon the part of business which
I bear i' the state; and nature does require
Her times of preservation, which perforce
I, her frail son, amongst my brethren mortal,
Must give my tendance to.
    King.   You have said well.
    Wol. And ever may your highness yoke to   gether,   150
As I will lend you cause, my doing well
With my well saying!
    King.   'Tis well said again;
And 'tis a kind of good deed to say well:
And yet words are no deeds. My father loved
       you:
He said he did; and with his deed did crown
His word upon you. Since I had my office,
I have kept you next my heart; have not alone
Employ'd you where high profits might come home,
But pared my present havings, to bestow
My bounties upon you.
    Wol.   [*Aside*] What should this mean?   160
    Sur.   [*Aside*] The Lord increase this busi   ness!

112–118 *some strange . . . the moon.* See introduction.

127 *rate.* Value.

142 *ill husband.* Bad manager.

Henry VIII in council. Engraving from a contemporary woodcut

171 *filed with*. Matched with.

181–182 *the honour . . . of it*. The reward of loyalty is the honour of being loyal.

197 *chiding*. Scolding.

King: 'Read o'er this;' Engraving from Bell's edition of *Shakespeare*, 1773

King.   Have I not made you
The prime man of the state? I pray you, tell me,
If what I now pronounce you have found true:
And, if you may confess it, say withal,
If you are bound to us or no. What say you?
   Wol. My sovereign, I confess your royal graces,
Shower'd on me daily, have been more than could
My studied purposes requite; which went
Beyond all man's endeavours: my endeavours
Have ever come too short of my desires,   170
● Yet filed with my abilities: mine own ends
Have been mine so that evermore they pointed
To the good of your most sacred person and
The profit of the state. For your great graces
Heap'd upon me, poor undeserver, I
Can nothing render but allegiant thanks,
My prayers to heaven for you, my loyalty,
Which ever has and ever shall be growing,
Till death, that winter, kill it.
   King.   Fairly answer'd;
A loyal and obedient subject is   180
● Therein illustrated: the honour of it
Does pay the act of it; as, i' the contrary,
The foulness is the punishment. I presume
That, as my hand has open'd bounty to you,
My heart dropp'd love, my power rain'd honour, more
On you than any; so your hand and heart,
Your brain, and every function of your power,
Should, notwithstanding that your bond of duty,
As 'twere in love's particular, be more
To me, your friend, than any.
   Wol.   I do profess   190
That for your highness' good I ever labour'd
More than mine own; † that am, have, and will be—
Though all the world should crack their duty to you,
And throw it from their soul; though perils did
Abound, as thick as thought could make 'em, and
Appear in forms more horrid,—yet my duty,
● As doth a rock against the chiding flood,
Should the approach of this wild river break,
And stand unshaken yours.
   King.   'Tis nobly spoken:
Take notice, lords, he has a loyal breast,   200
For you have seen him open't. Read o'er this;
                      [*Giving him papers*.
And after, this: and then to breakfast with
What appetite you have.
           [*Exit King, frowning upon Cardinal
             Wolsey: the Nobles throng after
             him, smiling and whispering.*
   Wol.   What should this mean?
What sudden anger's this? how have I reap'd it?
He parted frowning from me, as if ruin
Leap'd from his eyes: so looks the chafed lion
Upon the daring huntsman that has gall'd him;
Then makes him nothing. I must read this paper;
I fear, the story of his anger. 'Tis so;
This paper has undone me: 'tis the account   210
Of all that world of wealth I have drawn together
For mine own ends; indeed, to gain the pope-dom,
And fee my friends in Rome. O negligence!

- Fit for a fool to fall by: what cross devil
Made me put this main secret in the packet
I sent the king? Is there no way to cure this?
No new device to beat this from his brains?
I know 'twill stir him strongly; yet I know
A way, if it take right, in spite of fortune
Will bring me off again. What's this? 'To the
Pope!' 220
The letter, as I live, with all the business
I writ to's holiness. Nay then, farewell!
I have touch'd the highest point of all my great-
ness;
And, from that full meridian of my glory,
I haste now to my setting: I shall fall
- Like a bright exhalation in the evening,
And no man see me more.

Re-enter to WOLSEY, *the* DUKES OF NORFOLK
and SUFFOLK, *the* EARL OF SURREY, *and the*
LORD CHAMBERLAIN.

Nor. Hear the king's pleasure, cardinal: who
commands you
To render up the great seal presently
Into our hands; and to confine yourself 230
To Asher House, my Lord of Winchester's,
Till you hear further from his highness.
Wol. Stay:
Where's your commission, lords? words cannot
carry
Authority so weighty.
Suf. Who dare cross 'em,
Bearing the king's will from his mouth expressly?
Wol. Till I find more than will or words to
do it,
I mean your malice, know, officious lords,
I dare and must deny it. Now I feel
Of what coarse metal ye are moulded, envy:
How eagerly ye follow my disgraces, 240
- As if it fed ye! and how sleek and wanton
Ye appear in every thing may bring my ruin!
Follow your envious courses, men of malice;
You have Christian warrant for 'em, and, no
doubt,
In time will find their fit rewards. That seal,
You ask with such a violence, the king,
Mine and your master, with his own hand gave
me;
Bade me enjoy it, with the place and honours,
During my life; and, to confirm his goodness,
- Tied it by letters-patents: now, who'll take it?
Sur. The king, that gave it.
Wol. It must be himself, then. 251
Sur. Thou art a proud traitor, priest.
Wol. Proud lord, thou liest:
Within these forty hours Surrey durst better
Have burnt that tongue than said so.
Sur. Thy ambition,
Thou scarlet sin, robb'd this bewailing land
Of noble Buckingham, my father-in-law:
The heads of all thy brother cardinals,
With thee and all thy best parts bound together,
Weigh'd not a hair of his. Plague of your policy!
You sent me deputy for Ireland; 260
Far from his succour, from the king, from all
- That might have mercy on the fault thou gavest
him;
Whilst your great goodness, out of holy pity,
Absolved him with an axe.
Wol. This, and all else

Cardinal Wolsey. Drawing by Seymour Lucas, 1899

---

214 *cross.* Perverse.

226 *exhalation.* Meteor.

241 *wanton.* Relishing.

250 *letters-patents.* Open letters of authorization.

262 *gavest him.* Falsely accused him of.

274 *mate.* Match.

282 *dare us with his cap like larks.* A piece of red cloth and mirrors were used to dazzle larks so that they could be caught.

295 *sacring bell.* Consecration bell.

Surrey: 'Now, if you can blush and cry "guilty," cardinal . . .' Painting by John Pettie (1839–1893)

314 *'Ego et Rex meus'.* 'My King and I'. i.e. Wolsey was the equal of the King ('I and my King' is a literal translation and actually correct Latin for 'My King and I').

This talking lord can lay upon my credit,
I answer is most false.   The duke by law
Found his deserts: how innocent I was
From any private malice in his end,
His noble jury and foul cause can witness.
If I loved many words, lord, I should tell you
You have as little honesty as honour,   271
That in the way of loyalty and truth
Toward the king, my ever royal master,
Dare mate a sounder man than Surrey can be,
And all that love his follies.
      Sur.   By my soul,
Your long coat, priest, protects you; thou shouldst feel
My sword i' the life-blood of thee else.   My lords,
Can ye endure to hear this arrogance?
And from this fellow?   If we live thus tamely,
To be thus jaded by a piece of scarlet,   280
Farewell nobility; let his grace go forward,
And dare us with his cap like larks.
      Wol.   All goodness
Is poison to thy stomach.
      Sur.   Yes, that goodness
Of gleaning all the land's wealth into one,
Into your own hands, cardinal, by extortion;
The goodness of your intercepted packets
You writ to the pope against the king: your goodness,
Since you provoke me, shall be most notorious.
My Lord of Norfolk, as you are truly noble,
As you respect the common good, the state   290
Of our despised nobility, our issues,
Who, if he live, will scarce be gentlemen,
Produce the grand sum of his sins, the articles
Collected from his life.   I'll startle you
Worse than the sacring bell, when the brown wench
Lay kissing in your arms, lord cardinal.
      Wol. How much, methinks, I could despise this man,
But that I am bound in charity against it!
      Nor. Those articles, my lord, are in the king's hand:
But, thus much, they are foul ones.
      Wol.   So much fairer 300
And spotless shall mine innocence arise,
When the king knows my truth.
      Sur.   This cannot save you:
I thank my memory, I yet remember
Some of these articles; and out they shall.
Now, if you can blush and cry 'guilty,' cardinal,
You'll show a little honesty.
      Wol.   Speak on, sir;
I dare your worst objections: if I blush,
It is to see a nobleman want manners.
      Sur.   I had rather want those than my head.
      Have at you!
First, that, without the king's assent or knowledge,   310
You wrought to be a legate; by which power
You maim'd the jurisdiction of all bishops.
      Nor. Then, that in all you writ to Rome, or else
To foreign princes, 'Ego et Rex meus'
Was still inscribed; in which you brought the king
To be your servant.
      Suf.   Then that, without the knowledge
Either of king or council, when you went

Ambassador to the emperor, you made bold
To carry into Flanders the great seal.
    Sur. Item, you sent a large commission   320
To Gregory de Cassado, to conclude,
Without the king's will or the state's allowance,
A league between his highness and Ferrara.
    Suf. That, out of mere ambition, you have
    caused
Your holy hat to be stamp'd on the king's coin.
    Sur. Then that you have sent innumerable
    substance—
By what means got, I leave to your own con-
    science—
To furnish Rome, and to prepare the ways
● You have for dignities; to the mere undoing
Of all the kingdom. Many more there are;   330
Which, since they are of you, and odious,
I will not taint my mouth with.
    Cham.   O my lord,
Press not a falling man too far! 'tis virtue:
His faults lie open to the laws; let them,
Not you, correct him. My heart weeps to see him
So little of his great self.
    Sur.   I forgive him.
    Suf. Lord cardinal, the king's further plea-
    sure is,
Because all those things you have done of late,
By your power legatine, within this kingdom,
● Fall into the compass of a præmunire,   340
That therefore such a writ be sued against you;
To forfeit all your goods, lands, tenements,
Chattels, and whatsoever, and to be
Out of the king's protection. This is my charge.
    Nor. And so we'll leave you to your medi-
    tations
How to live better. For your stubborn answer
About the giving back the great seal to us,
The king shall know it, and, no doubt, shall thank
    you.
So fare you well, my little good lord cardinal. 349
                 [*Exeunt all but Wolsey.*
    Wol. So farewell to the little good you bear me.
Farewell! a long farewell, to all my greatness!
This is the state of man: to-day he puts forth
The tender leaves of hopes; to-morrow blossoms,
And bears his blushing honours thick upon him;
The third day comes a frost, a killing frost,
And, when he thinks, good easy man, full surely
His greatness is a-ripening, nips his root,
And then he falls, as I do. I have ventured,
● Like little wanton boys that swim on bladders,
This many summers in a sea of glory,   360
But far beyond my depth: my high-blown pride
At length broke under me and now has left me,
Weary and old with service, to the mercy
Of a rude stream, that must for ever hide me.
Vain pomp and glory of this world, I hate ye:
I feel my heart new open'd. O, how wretched
Is that poor man that hangs on princes' favours!
There is, betwixt that smile we would aspire to,
● That sweet aspect of princes, and their ruin, 369
More pangs and fears than wars or women have:
And when he falls, he falls like Lucifer,
Never to hope again.

    Enter CROMWELL, *and stands amazed.*
                   Why, how now, Cromwell!
    Crom. I have no power to speak, sir.
    Wol.   What, amazed

329 *mere.* Complete.

340 *præmunire.* A writ against anyone who asserted papal jurisdiction in England. All goods were forfeited for this offence.

359 *wanton.* Sportive.

Wolsey: '. . . my high-blown pride At length broke under me and now has left me . . .' Allegory of Pride. From a contemporary woodcut

369 *their ruin.* i.e. the ruin they can cause.

399 *tomb of orphan's tears.* The chancellor was the guardian of orphans.

420 *make use.* Take the opportunity.

Thomas Cromwell, first Earl of Essex, Chancellor of the Exchequer (1533) and Secretary to Henry VIII (1534). He fell from favour and was executed in 1540. Painting after Hans Holbein

At my misfortunes? can thy spirit wonder
A great man should decline? Nay, an you **weep**,
I am fall'n indeed.
   Crom.   How does your grace?
   Wol.   Why, well;
Never so truly happy, my good Cromwell.
I know myself now; and I feel within me
A peace above all earthly dignities,
A still and quiet conscience. The king has cured me,   380
I humbly thank his grace; and from these shoulders,
These ruin'd pillars, out of pity, **taken**
A load would sink a navy, too much honour:
O, 'tis a burden, Cromwell, 'tis a burden
Too heavy for a man that hopes for heaven!
   Crom. I am glad your grace has made that right use of it.
   Wol. I hope I have: I am able now, methinks,
Out of a fortitude of soul I feel,
To endure more miseries and greater far
Than my weak-hearted enemies dare offer.   390
What news abroad?
   Crom.   The heaviest and the worst
Is your displeasure with the king.
   Wol.   God bless him!
   Crom. The next is, that Sir Thomas More is chosen
Lord chancellor in your place.
   Wol.   That's somewhat sudden:
But he's a learned man. May he continue
Long in his highness' favour, and do justice
For truth's sake and his conscience; that his bones,
When he has run his course and sleeps in blessings,
May have **a** tomb of orphans' tears wept on 'em!
What more?
   Crom. That Cranmer is return'd with welcome,
Install'd lord archbishop of Canterbury.   401
   Wol. That's news indeed.
   Crom.   Last, that the Lady Anne,
Whom the king hath in secrecy long married,
This day was view'd in open as his queen,
Going to chapel; and the voice is now
Only about her coronation.
   Wol. There was the weight that pull'd me down. O Cromwell,
The king has gone beyond me: all my glories
In that one woman I have lost for ever:
No sun shall ever usher forth mine honours,   410
Or gild again the noble troops that waited
Upon my smiles. Go, get thee from me, Cromwell;
I am a poor fall'n man, unworthy now
To be thy lord and master: seek the king;
That sun, I pray, may never set! I have told him
What and how true thou art: he will advance thee;
Some little memory of me will stir him—
I know his noble nature—not to let
Thy hopeful service perish too: good Cromwell,
Neglect him not; make use now, and provide 420
For thine own future safety.
   Crom.   O my lord,
Must I, then, leave you? must I needs forgo
So good, so noble and so true a master?
Bear witness, all that have not hearts of iron,
With what a sorrow Cromwell leaves his lord.
The king shall have my service; but my **prayers**
For **ever** and for **ever** shall be yours.

Wol. Cromwell, I did not think to shed a tear
In all my miseries; but thou hast forced me,
Out of thy honest truth, to play the woman. 430
Let's dry our eyes: and thus far hear me, Crom-
    well;
And, when I am forgotten, as I shall be,
And sleep in dull cold marble, where no mention
Of me more must be heard of, say, I taught thee,
Say, Wolsey, that once trod the ways of glory,
And sounded all the depths and shoals of honour,
Found thee a way, out of his wreck, to rise in;
A sure and safe one, though thy master miss'd it.
Mark but my fall, and that that ruin'd me. 439
Cromwell, I charge thee, fling away ambition:
By that sin fell the angels; how can man, then,
The image of his Maker, hope to win by it?
Love thyself last: cherish those hearts that hate
    thee;
Corruption wins not more than honesty.
Still in thy right hand carry gentle peace,
To silence envious tongues. Be just, and fear not:
Let all the ends thou aim'st at be thy country's,
Thy God's, and truth's; then if thou fall'st, O
    Cromwell,
Thou fall'st a blessed martyr! Serve the king;
And,—prithee, lead me in: 450
There take an inventory of all I have,
To the last penny; 'tis the king's: my robe,
And my integrity to heaven, is all
I dare now call mine own. O Cromwell, Cromwell!
Had I but served my God with half the zeal
I served my king, he would not in mine age
Have left me naked to mine enemies.
    Crom.   Good sir, have patience.
    Wol.   So I have.   Farewell
The hopes of court! my hopes in heaven do
    dwell.   [*Exeunt.*

ACT IV.

SCENE I. *A street in Westminster.*

Enter two Gentlemen, *meeting one another.*

First Gent.   You're well met once again.
Sec. Gent.   So are you.
First Gent.   You come to take your stand here,
    and behold
The Lady Anne pass from her coronation?
Sec. Gent.   'Tis all my business.   At our last
    encounter,
The Duke of Buckingham came from his trial.
    First Gent.   'Tis very true: but that time of-
    fer'd sorrow;
This, general joy.
    Sec. Gent.   'Tis well: the citizens,
● I am sure, have shown at full their royal minds—
● As, let 'em have their rights, they are ever for-
    ward—
In celebration of this day with shows,   10
Pageants and sights of honour.
    First Gent.   Never greater,
Nor, I'll assure you, better taken, sir.
    Sec. Gent.   May I be bold to ask what that
    contains,
That paper in your hand?
    First Gent.   Yes; 'tis the list
Of those that claim their offices this day
By custom of the coronation.
The Duke of Suffolk is the first, and claims

Wolsey: 'Had I but served my God with half the zeal I served my king . . .' Drawing by J. Coghlan (active early 19th century)

8 *royal minds.* Loyal to the King.

9 *let 'em have their rights.* To give them their due.

Lord Mayor and Alderman. Engraving from a contemporary manuscript

---

SD *Garter.* The head of the English College of Heralds. *Collars of SS.* Chains made of S shaped links. *Cinque-ports.* The 'barons' (freemen) of Dover, Hastings, Sandwich, Hythe and Romney. *in her hair.* Her hair hanging loose.

Coat of arms of Henry VIII and Anne Boleyn

To be high-steward; next, the Duke of Norfolk,
He to be earl marshal: you may read the rest.
 Sec. Gent. I thank you, sir: had I not known
  those customs,   20
I should have been beholding to your paper.
But, I beseech you, what's become of Katharine,
The princess dowager? how goes her business?
 First Gent. That I can tell you too. The
  Archbishop
Of Canterbury, accompanied with other
Learned and reverend fathers of his order,
Held a late court at Dunstable, six miles off
From Ampthill where the princess lay; to which
She was often cited by them, but appear'd not:
And, to be short, for not appearance and 30
The king's late scruple, by the main assent
Of all these learned men she was divorced,
And the late marriage made of none effect:
Since which she was removed to Kimbolton,
Where she remains now sick.
 Sec. Gent.   Alas, good lady!
              [*Trumpets.*
The trumpets sound: stand close, the queen is
  coming.   [*Hautboys.*

  THE ORDER OF THE CORONATION.

1. *A lively flourish of Trumpets.*
2. Then, *two Judges.*
3. Lord Chancellor, *with the purse and mace before him.*
4. Choristers, *singing.*   [*Music.*
5. Mayor of London, *bearing the mace. Then Garter, in his coat of arms, and on his head a gilt copper crown.*
6. Marquess DORSET, *bearing a sceptre of gold, on his head a demi-coronal of gold. With him, the* Earl of SURREY, *bearing the rod of silver with the dove, crowned with an earl's coronet. Collars of SS.*
7. Duke of SUFFOLK, *in his robe of estate, his coronet on his head, bearing a long white wand, as high-steward. With him, the* Duke of NORFOLK, *with the rod of marshalship, a coronet on his head. Collars of SS.*
8. *A canopy borne by four of the* Cinque-ports; *under it, the* Queen *in her robe; in her hair richly adorned with pearl, crowned. On each side her, the* Bishops of London *and* Winchester.
9. *The old Duchess of* NORFOLK, *in a coronal of gold, wrought with flowers, bearing the* Queen's *train.*
10. *Certain* Ladies *or* Countesses, *with plain circlets of gold without flowers.*
 They pass over the stage in order and state.

 Sec. Gent. A royal train, believe me. These
  I know:
Who's that that bears the sceptre?
 First Gent.   Marquess Dorset:
And that the Earl of Surrey, with the rod.
 Sec. Gent. A bold brave gentleman. That
  should be   40
The Duke of Suffolk?
 First Gent.   'Tis the same: high-steward.
 Sec. Gent. And that my Lord of Norfolk?
 First Gent.   Yes.
 Sec. Gent.   Heaven bless thee!
          [*Looking on the Queen.*

Thou hast the sweetest face I ever look'd on.
Sir, as I have a soul, she is an angel;
Our king has all the Indies in his arms,
• And more and richer, when he strains that lady:
I cannot blame his conscience.
　　First Gent.　　　　　　　They that bear
The cloth of honour over her, are four barons
Of the Cinque-ports.
　　Sec. Gent.　　Those men are happy; and so are
　　all are near her.　　　　　　　　　　50
I take it, she that carries up the train
Is that old noble lady, Duchess of Norfolk.
　　First Gent.　　It is; and all the rest are count-
　　esses.
　　Sec. Gent.　　Their coronets say so.　These are
　　stars indeed;
And sometimes falling ones.
　　First Gent.　　　　　　　No more of that.
　　　[*Exit procession, and then a great flourish
　　　　　　　　　　　　　　of trumpets.*

　　　　　Enter a third Gentleman.

　　First Gent.　　God save you, sir! where have
　　you been broiling?
　　Third Gent.　　Among the crowd i' the Abbey;
　　where a finger
Could not be wedged in more: I am stifled
With the mere rankness of their joy.
　　Sec. Gent.　　　　　　　　　You saw
The ceremony?
　　Third Gent.　　That I did.
　　First Gent.　　　　　　　How was it?　60
　　Third Gent.　　Well worth the seeing.
　　Sec. Gent.　　　　　　Good sir, speak it to us.
　　Third Gent.　　As well as I am able.　The rich
　　stream
Of lords and ladies, having brought the queen
To a prepared place in the choir, fell off
A distance from her; while her grace sat down
To rest awhile, some half an hour or so,
• In a rich chair of state, opposing freely
The beauty of her person to the people.
Believe me, sir, she is the goodliest woman
That ever lay by man: which when the people 70
Had the full view of, such a noise arose
• As the shrouds make at sea in a stiff tempest,
As loud, and to as many tunes: hats, cloaks,—
Doublets, I think,—flew up; and had their faces
Been loose, this day they had been lost.　Such joy
I never saw before.　Great-bellied women,
• That had not half a week to go, like rams
In the old time of war, would shake the press,
And make 'em reel before 'em.　No man living
Could say 'This is my wife' there; all were woven
So strangely in one piece.
　　Sec. Gent.　　　　　　But, what follow'd?　81
　　Third Gent.　　At length her grace rose, and
　　with modest paces
Came to the altar; where she kneel'd, and saint-
　　like
Cast her fair eyes to heaven and pray'd devoutly.
Then rose again and bow'd her to the people:
When by the Archbishop of Canterbury
She had all the royal makings of a queen;
As holy oil, Edward Confessor's crown,
The rod, and bird of peace, and all such emblems
Laid nobly on her: which perform'd, the choir, 90
• With all the choicest music of the kingdom,

Anne Boleyn. Henry broke away from the Church of Rome in order to marry her, but executed her for adultery in 1536

---

46 *strains.* Embraces.

67 *opposing.* Exposing.

72 *shrouds.* Rigging.

77 *rams.* Battering rams.

91 *music.* Musicians.

14 *tainted*. Disgraced.

19 *covent*. Convent, originally for either sex.

Wolsey is welcomed at Leicester Abbey. Engraving from a painting by Richard Westall (1765–1836)

Together sung 'Te Deum.' So she parted,
And with the same full state paced back again
To York-place, where the feast is held.
 First Gent.   Sir,
You must no more call it York-place, that's past;
For, since the cardinal fell, that title's lost:
'Tis now the king's, and call'd Whitehall.
 Third Gent.   I know it;
But 'tis so lately alter'd, that the old name
Is fresh about me.
 Sec. Gent.   What two reverend bishops
Were those that went on each side of the queen?
 Third Gent.   Stokesly and Gardiner; the one
    of Winchester,   101
Newly preferr'd from the king's secretary,
The other, London.
 Sec. Gent.   He of Winchester
Is held no great good lover of the archbishop's,
The virtuous Cranmer.
 Third Gent.   All the land knows that:
However, yet there is no great breach; when it
  comes,
Cranmer will find a friend will not shrink from him.
 Sec. Gent.   Who may that be, I pray you?
 Third Gent.   Thomas Cromwell;
A man in much esteem with the king, and truly
A worthy friend. The king has made him master
O' the jewel house,   111
And one, already, of the privy council.
 Sec. Gent.   He will deserve more.
 Third Gent.   Yes, without all doubt.
Come, gentlemen, ye shall go my way, which
Is to the court, and there ye shall be my guests:
Something I can command. As I walk thither,
I'll tell ye more.
 Both.   You may command us, sir. [*Exeunt.*

SCENE II.   *Kimbolton.*

Enter KATHARINE, *Dowager, sick; led between*
GRIFFITH, *her gentleman usher, and* PA-
TIENCE, *her woman.*

 Grif.   How does your grace?
 Kath.   O Griffith, sick to death!
My legs, like loaden branches, bow to the earth,
Willing to leave their burthen. Reach a chair:
So; now, methinks, I feel a little ease.
Didst thou not tell me, Griffith, as thou led'st me,
That the great child of honour, Cardinal Wolsey,
Was dead?
 Grif.   Yes, madam; but I think your grace,
Out of the pain you suffer'd, gave no ear to 't.
 Kath.   Prithee, good Griffith, tell me how he
  died:
If well, he stepp'd before me, happily   10
For my example.
 Grif.   Well, the voice goes, madam:
For after the stout Earl Northumberland
Arrested him at York, and brought him forward,
As a man sorely tainted, to his answer,
He fell sick suddenly, and grew so ill
He could not sit his mule.
 Kath.   Alas, poor man!
 Grif.   At last, with easy roads, he came to
  Leicester,
Lodged in the abbey; where the reverend abbot,
With all his covent, honourably received him; 19
To whom he gave these words, 'O, father abbot,

An old man, broken with the storms of state,
Is come to lay his weary bones among ye;
Give him a little earth for charity!'
So went to bed; where eagerly his sickness
Pursued him still: and, three nights after this,
About the hour of eight, which he himself
Foretold should be his last, full of repentance,
Continual meditations, tears, and sorrows,
He gave his honours to the world again,   29
His blessed part to heaven, and slept in peace.
    Kath. So may he rest; his faults lie gently
                    on him!
Yet thus far, Griffith, give me leave to speak him,
And yet with charity.   He was a man
- Of an unbounded stomach, ever ranking
- Himself with princes; one that, by suggestion,
- Tied all the kingdom: simony was fair-play;
- His own opinion was his law: i' the presence
He would say untruths; and be ever double
Both in his words and meaning: he was never,
But where he meant to ruin, pitiful: 40
His promises were, as he then was, mighty;
But his performance, as he is now, nothing:
Of his own body he was ill, and gave
The clergy ill example.
    Grif.   Noble madam,
Men's evil manners live in brass; their virtues
We write in water.   May it please your highness
To hear me speak his good now?
    Kath.   Yes, good Griffith;
I were malicious else.
    Grif.   This cardinal,
Though from an humble stock, undoubtedly   49
Was fashion'd to much honour from his cradle.
He was a scholar, and a ripe and good one;
Exceeding wise, fair-spoken, and persuading:
Lofty and sour to them that loved him not;
But to those men that sought him sweet as
          summer.
And though he were unsatisfied in getting,
Which was a sin, yet in bestowing, madam,
He was most princely: ever witness for him
Those twins of learning that he raised in you,
- Ipswich and Oxford! one of which fell with him,
Unwilling to outlive the good that did it;   60
The other, though unfinish'd, yet so famous,
So excellent in art, and still so rising,
That Christendom shall ever speak his virtue.
His overthrow heap'd happiness upon him;
For then, and not till then, he felt himself,
And found the blessedness of being little:
And, to add greater honours to his age
Than man could give him, he died fearing God.
    Kath. After my death I wish no other herald,
No other speaker of my living actions,   70
To keep mine honour from corruption,
But such an honest chronicler as Griffith.
Whom I most hated living, thou hast made me,
- With thy religious truth and modesty,
Now in his ashes honour: peace be with him!
Patience, be near me still; and set me lower:
I have not long to trouble thee.   Good Griffith,
Cause the musicians play me that sad note
I named my knell, whilst I sit meditating
On that celestial harmony I go to.   80
                    [*Sad and solemn music.*
    Grif. She is asleep: good wench, let's sit
          down quiet,
For fear we wake her: softly, gentle Patience.

34 *stomach.* Pride.

35 *by suggestion.* By devious methods.

36 *simony.* Trafficking in ecclesiastical appointments for money.

37 *i' the presence.* i.e. in the King's presence.

59 *Ipswich and Oxford.* Wolsey founded a college at Ipswich where he was born and another at Oxford, Cardinal College, which became Christchurch.

Christchurch College, Oxford. A facsimile of a drawing by Neele of Oxford, 1566

74 *modesty.* Moderation.

Katherine's dream. Drawing by John M. Wright (1777–1866)

SD *congee.* Curtsy.

SD *changes.* Figures.

The vision. Enter, solemnly tripping one after another, six personages, clad in white robes, wearing on their heads garlands of bays, and golden vizards on their faces; branches of bays or palm in their hands. They first congee unto her, then dance; and, at certain changes, the first two hold a spare garland over her head; at which the other four make reverent curtsies; then the two that held the garland deliver the same to the other next two, who observe the same order in their changes, and holding the garland over her head: which done, they deliver the same garland to the last two, who likewise observe the same order: at which, as it were by inspiration, she makes in her sleep signs of rejoicing, and holdeth up her hands to heaven: and so in their dancing vanish, carrying the garland with them. The music continues.

Kath. Spirits of peace, where are ye? are ye all gone,
And leave me here in wretchedness behind ye?
Grif. Madam, we are here.
Kath. It is not you I call for:
Saw ye none enter since I slept?
Grif. None, madam.
Kath. No? Saw you not, even now, a blessed troop
Invite me to a banquet; whose bright faces
Cast thousand beams upon me, like the sun?
They promised me eternal happiness; 90
And brought me garlands, Griffith, which I feel
I am not worthy yet to wear: I shall, assuredly.
Grif. I am most joyful, madam, such good dreams
Possess your fancy.
Kath. Bid the music leave,
They are harsh and heavy to me. [*Music ceases.*
Pat. Do you note
How much her grace is alter'd on the sudden?
How long her face is drawn? how pale she looks,
And of an earthy cold? Mark her eyes!
Grif. She is going, wench: pray, pray.
Pat. Heaven comfort her!

Enter a Messenger.

Mess. An't like your grace,—
Kath. You are a saucy fellow: 100
Deserve we no more reverence?
Grif. You are to blame,
Knowing she will not lose her wonted greatness,
To use so rude behaviour; go to, kneel.
Mess. I humbly do entreat your highness' pardon;
My haste made me unmannerly. There is staying
A gentleman, sent from the king, to see you.
Kath. Admit him entrance, Griffith: but this fellow
Let me ne'er see again.
[*Exeunt Griffith and Messenger.*

Re-enter GRIFFITH, *with* CAPUCIUS.
If my sight fail not,
You should be lord ambassador from the emperor,
My royal nephew, and your name Capucius. 110
Cap. Madam, the same; your servant.
Kath. O, my lord,
The times and titles now are alter'd strangely

Opposite: The Vision of Queen Katherine. Watercolour by William Blake 1807

134 *breeding*. Schooling.

159 *fashion*. Nature.

With me since first you knew me. But, I pray
    you,
What is your pleasure with me?
  Cap.   Noble lady,
First, mine own service to your grace; the next,
The king's request that I would visit you;
Who grieves much for your weakness, and by me
Sends you his princely commendations,
And heartily entreats you take good comfort.
  Kath. O my good lord, that comfort comes
    too late;   120
'Tis like a pardon after execution:
That gentle physic, given in time, had cured me;
But now I am past all comforts here, but prayers.
How does his highness?
  Cap.   Madam, in good health.
  Kath. So may he ever do! and ever flourish,
When I shall dwell with worms, and my poor
    name
Banish'd the kingdom! Patience, is that letter,
I caused you write, yet sent away?
  Pat.   No, madam.
    [*Giving it to Katharine.*
  Kath. Sir, I most humbly pray you to deliver
This to my lord the king.
  Cap.   Most willing, madam. 130
  Kath. In which I have commended to his
    goodness
The model of our chaste loves, his young daughter;
The dews of heaven fall thick in blessings on her!
● Beseeching him to give her virtuous breeding,—
She is young, and of a noble modest nature,
I hope she will deserve well,—and a little
To love her for her mother's sake, that loved him,
Heaven knows how dearly. My next poor pet-
    ition
Is, that his noble grace would have some pity
Upon my wretched women, that so long   140
Have follow'd both my fortunes faithfully:
Of which there is not one, I dare avow,
And now I should not lie, but will deserve,
For virtue and true beauty of the soul,
For honesty and decent carriage,
A right good husband, let him be a noble:
And, sure, those men are happy that shall have
    'em.
The last is, for my men; they are the poorest,
But poverty could never draw 'em from me; 149
That they may have their wages duly paid 'em,
And something over to remember me by:
If heaven had pleased to have given me longer
    life
And able means, we had not parted thus.
These are the whole contents: and, good my
    lord,
By that you love the dearest in this world,
As you wish Christian peace to souls departed,
Stand these poor people's friend, and urge the
    king
To do me this last right.
  Cap.   By heaven, I will,
● Or let me lose the fashion of a man!
  Kath. I thank you, honest lord. Remember
    me   160
In all humility unto his highness:
Say his long trouble now is passing
Out of this world; tell him, in death I bless'd him,
For so I will. Mine eyes grow dim. Farewell,
My lord. Griffith, farewell. Nay, Patience,

You must not leave me yet: I must to bed;
• Call in more women. When I am dead, good
  wench,
Let me be used with honour: strew me over
With maiden flowers, that all the world may know
I was a chaste wife to my grave: embalm me, 170
Then lay me forth: although unqueen'd, yet like
A queen, and daughter to a king, inter me.
I can no more.   [*Exeunt, leading Katharine.*

ACT V.

SCENE I. *London. A gallery in the palace.*

Enter GARDINER, Bishop of Winchester, *a* Page
  with a torch before him, met by SIR THOMAS
  LOVELL.

   Gar. It's one o'clock, boy, is't not?
   Boy.   It hath struck.
   Gar. These should be hours for necessities,
Not for delights; times to repair our nature
With comforting repose, and not for us
To waste these times. Good hour of night, Sir
  Thomas!
Whither so late?
   Lov.   Came you from the king, my lord?
• *Gar.* I did, Sir Thomas; and left him at
  primero
With the Duke of Suffolk.
   Lov.   I must to him too,
Before he go to bed. I'll take my leave.
   Gar. Not yet, Sir Thomas Lovell. What's
  the matter?   10
It seems you are in haste: an if there be
No great offence belongs to't, give your friend
Some touch of your late business: affairs, that
  walk,
As they say spirits do, at midnight, have
In them a wilder nature than the business
That seeks dispatch by day.
   Lov.   My lord, I love you;
And durst commend a secret to your ear
Much weightier than this work. The queen's in
  labour,
They say, in great extremity; and fear'd
She'll with the labour end.
   Gar.   The fruit she goes with 20
I pray for heartily, that it may find
Good time, and live: but for the stock, Sir
  Thomas,
I wish it grubb'd up now.
   Lov.   Methinks I could
Cry the amen; and yet my conscience says
She's a good creature, and, sweet lady, does
Deserve our better wishes.
   Gar.   But, sir, sir,
Hear me, Sir Thomas: you're a gentleman
• Of mine own way; I know you wise, religious;
And, let me tell you, it will ne'er be well,
'Twill not, Sir Thomas Lovell, take 't of me, 30
Till Cranmer, Cromwell, her two hands, and she,
Sleep in their graves.
   Lov.   Now, sir, you speak of two
The most remark'd i' the kingdom. As for Crom-
  well,
Beside that of the jewel house, is made master
O' the rolls, and the king's secretary; further, sir,
• Stands in the gap and trade of moe preferments,

167 *When I am dead.* See introduction.

Katherine: 'When I am dead, good wench, Let me be
used with honour.' Engraving from a painting by
Richard Westall (1765–1836)

7 *primero.* A card game.

28 *way.* Religious thinking.

36 *gap and trade.* Entrance and open road. *moe.* More.

47 *broken.* Expressed their feelings.

52 *convented.* Summoned.

With which the time will load him. The arch-
        bishop
Is the king's hand and tongue; and who dare
        speak
One syllable against him?
 Gar.   Yes, yes, Sir Thomas,
There are that dare; and I myself have ventured
To speak my mind of him: and indeed this
        day,   41
Sir, I may tell it you, I think I have
Incensed the lords o' the council, that he is,
For so I know he is, they know he is,
A most arch heretic, a pestilence
That does infect the land: with which they
        moved
● Have broken with the king; who hath so far
Given ear to our complaint, of his great grace
And princely care foreseeing those fell mischiefs
Our reasons laid before him, hath commanded 50
To-morrow morning to the council-board
● He be convented. He's a rank weed, Sir
        Thomas,
And we must root him out. From your affairs
I hinder you too long: good night, Sir Thomas.
 Lov. Many good nights, my lord: I rest your
        servant. [*Exeunt Gardiner and Page.*

    Enter the KING *and* SUFFOLK.

 King. Charles, I will play no more to-night;
My mind's not on 't; you are too hard for me.
 Suf. Sir, I did never win of you before.
 King. But little, Charles;
Nor shall not, when my fancy's on my play. 60
Now, Lovell, from the queen what is the news?
 Lov. I could not personally deliver to her
What you commanded me, but by her woman
I sent your message; who return'd her thanks
In the great'st humbleness, and desired your
        highness
Most heartily to pray for her.
 King.   What say'st thou, ha?
To pray for her? what, is she crying out?
 Lov. So said her woman; and that her suf-
        ferance made
Almost each pang a death.
 King.   Alas, good lady!
 Suf. God safely quit her of her burthen, and
With gentle travail, to the gladding of 71
Your highness with an heir!
 King.   'Tis midnight, Charles;
Prithee, to bed; and in thy prayers remember
The estate of my poor queen. Leave me alone;
For I must think of that which company
Would not be friendly to.
 Suf.   I wish your highness
A quiet night; and my good mistress will
Remember in my prayers.
 King. Charles, good night. [*Exit Suffolk.*

    Enter SIR ANTHONY DENNY.

Well, sir, what follows?
 Den. Sir, I have brought my lord the arch-
        bishop,   80
As you commanded me.
 King.   Ha! Canterbury?
 Den. Ay, my good lord.
 King.   'Tis true: where is he, Denny?

Den. He attends your highness' pleasure.
King.   Bring him to us.
                                        [*Exit Denny.*
Lov. [*Aside*] This is about that which the
bishop spake :
I am happily come hither.

                Re-enter DENNY, *with* CRANMER.

● *King.* Avoid the gallery. [*Lovell seems to
       stay.*] Ha! I have said. Be gone.
What!   [*Exeunt Lovell and Denny.*
Cran. [*Aside*] I am fearful : wherefore frowns
       he thus ?
'Tis his aspect of terror. All's not well.
   King. How now, my lord! you do desire to
       know
Wherefore I sent for you.
   Cran. [*Kneeling*] It is my duty
To attend your highness' pleasure.
   King.   Pray you, arise,
My good and gracious Lord of Canterbury.
Come, you and I must walk a turn together ;
I have news to tell you : come, come, give me
       your hand.
Ah, my good lord, I grieve at what I speak,
And am right sorry to repeat what follows :
I have, and most unwillingly, of late
Heard many grievous, I do say, my lord,
Grievous complaints of you ; which, being con-
       sider'd,
Have moved us and our council, that you shall 100
This morning come before us ; where, I know,
You cannot with such freedom purge yourself,
But that, till further trial in those charges
Which will require your answer, you must take
Your patience to you, and be well contented
● To make your house our Tower : you a brother
       of us,
It fits we thus proceed, or else no witness
Would come against you.
   Cran. [*Kneeling*] I humbly thank your
       highness ;
And am right glad to catch this good occasion
Most throughly to be winnow'd, where my chaff
And corn shall fly asunder : for, I know,   111
There's none stands under more calumnious
       tongues
Than I myself, poor man.
   King.   Stand up, good Canterbury :
Thy truth and thy integrity is rooted
In us, thy friend : give me thy hand, stand up :
● Prithee, let's walk. Now, by my holidame,
What manner of man are you? My lord, I look'd
You would have given me your petition, that
I should have ta'en some pains to bring together
Yourself and your accusers ; and to have heard
       you,   120
● Without indurance, further.
   Cran.   Most dread liege,
The good I stand on is my truth and honesty :
If they shall fail, I, with mine enemies,
Will triumph o'er my person ; which I weigh not,
Being of those virtues vacant. I fear nothing
What can be said against me.
   King.   Know you not
How your state stands i' the world, with the
       whole world ?
Your enemies are many, and not small ; their
       practices

86 *Avoid.* Leave.

106 *you a brother of us.* A member of the Council.

King : 'Stand up, good Canterbury :' Drawing by
John M. Wright (1777–1866)

116 *holidame.* Halidom or holiness.

121 *indurance.* Imprisonment.

129 *ever.* Always.

131 *due o' the verdict.* The just verdict.

135 *Ween.* Suppose.

146 *commit you.* i.e. to the Tower.

King: 'if entreaties Will render you no remedy, this ring Deliver them . . .' Matthew Clarke, 18th century actor, as Henry VIII. Engraving from Bell's Edition of *Shakespeare*, 1776

170 *marks.* Not a coin, but value to two-thirds of a pound.

● Must bear the same proportion; and not ever 129
The justice and the truth o' the question carries
● The due o' the verdict with it: at what ease
Might corrupt minds procure knaves as corrupt
To swear against you? such things have been
done.
You are potently opposed; and with a malice
● Of as great size. Ween you of better luck,
I mean, in perjured witness, than your master,
Whose minister you are, whiles here he lived
Upon this naughty earth? Go to, go to;
You take a precipice for no leap of danger,
And woo your own destruction.
    Cran.   God and your majesty
Protect mine innocence, or I fall into   141
The trap is laid for me!
    King.   Be of good cheer;
They shall no more prevail than we give way to.
Keep comfort to you; and this morning see
You do appear before them: if they shall
chance,
● In charging you with matters, to commit you,
The best persuasions to the contrary
Fail not to use, and with what vehemency
The occasion shall instruct you: if entreaties
Will render you no remedy, this ring   150
Deliver them, and your appeal to us
There make before them. Look, the good man
weeps!
He's honest, on mine honour. God's blest
mother!
I swear he is true-hearted; and a soul
None better in my kingdom. Get you gone,
And do as I have bid you. [*Exit Cranmer.*]
               He has strangled
His language in his tears.

    Enter Old Lady, LOVELL *following.*

    Gent. [*Within*] Come back: what mean
you?
    Old L. I'll not come back; the tidings that
I bring
Will make my boldness manners. Now, good
angels
Fly o'er thy royal head, and shade thy person 160
Under their blessed wings!
    King.   Now, by thy looks
I guess thy message. Is the queen deliver'd?
Say, ay; and of a boy.
    Old L.   Ay, ay, my liege;
And of a lovely boy: the God of heaven
Both now and ever bless her! 'tis a girl,
Promises boys hereafter. Sir, your queen
Desires your visitation, and to be
Acquainted with this stranger: 'tis as like you
As cherry is to cherry.
    King.   Lovell!
    Lov.   Sir?
●   *King.* Give her an hundred marks. I'll to
the queen.   [*Exit.*
    Old L. An hundred marks! By this light,
I'll ha' more.   171
An ordinary groom is for such payment.
I will have more, or scold it out of him.
Said I for this, the girl was like to him?
I will have more, or else unsay 't; and now,
While it is hot, I'll put it to the issue.
               [*Exeunt.*

SCENE II. *Before the council-chamber.*

Pursuivants, Pages, &c. attending.

Enter CRANMER, Archbishop of Canterbury.

Cran. I hope I am not too late; and yet the gentleman,
That was sent to me from the council, pray'd me
To make great haste. All fast? what means this? Ho!
Who waits there? Sure, you know me?

Enter Keeper.

Keep.   Yes, my lord;
But yet I cannot help you.
  Cran. Why?

Enter DOCTOR BUTTS.

Keep. Your grace must wait till you be call'd for.
  Cran.   So.
  Butts. [*Aside*] This is a piece of malice. I am glad
I came this way so happily: the king
● Shall understand it presently.   [*Exit.*
  Cran. [*Aside*] 'Tis Butts,   10
The king's physician: as he pass'd along,
How earnestly he cast his eyes upon me!
● Pray heaven, he sound not my disgrace! For certain,
This is of purpose laid by some that hate me—
God turn their hearts! I never sought their malice—
To quench mine honour: they would shame to make me
Wait else at door, a fellow-counsellor,
'Mong boys, grooms, and lackeys. But their pleasures
Must be fulfill'd, and I attend with patience.

Enter the KING *and* BUTTS *at a window above.*

Butts. I'll show your grace the strangest sight—
  King.   What's that, Butts? 20
  Butts. I think your highness saw this many a day.
  King. Body o' me, where is it?
  Butts.   There, my lord:
The high promotion of his grace of Canterbury;
● Who holds his state at door, 'mongst pursuivants,
Pages, and footboys.
  King.   Ha! 'tis he, indeed:
Is this the honour they do one another?
'Tis well there's one above 'em yet. I had thought
● They had parted so much honesty among 'em,
At least, good manners, as not thus to suffer
A man of his place, and so near our favour,   30
To dance attendance on their lordships' pleasures,
And at the door too, like a post with packets.
By holy Mary, Butts, there's knavery:
Let 'em alone, and draw the curtain close:
We shall hear more anon.   [*Exeunt.*

Thomas Cranmer, the first Protestant archbishop of Canterbury, who annulled Katherine of Aragon's marriage to Henry VIII. Under Mary I, he was burnt as a heretic. Painting by G. Fucke, 1546

10 *presently.* Immediately.

13 *sound.* Make known.

24 *pursuivants.* Heralds' officers, messengers.

28 *parted.* Shared.

Costume design for Cranmer by Tanya Moisewitch,
Stratford-upon-Avon, 1949

---

11 *capable.* Susceptible.

22 *Pace 'em not in their hands.* Do not school them by
leading them.

24 *manage.* An equestrian term meaning discipline.

39 *stirs against.* Is more active.

SCENE III. *The Council-Chamber.*

Enter LORD CHANCELLOR; *places himself at
the upper end of the table on the left hand; a
seat being left void above him, as for* CANTER-
BURY'S *seat.* DUKE OF SUFFOLK, DUKE OF
NORFOLK, SURREY, LORD CHAMBERLAIN, GAR-
DINER, *seat themselves in order on each side.*
CROMWELL *at lower end, as secretary.* Keeper
at the door.

Chan. Speak to the business, master secre-
tary:
Why are we met in council?
Crom. Please your honours,
The chief cause concerns his grace of Canter-
bury.
Gar. Has he had knowledge of it?
Crom. Yes.
Nor. Who waits there?
Keep. Without, my noble lords?
Gar. Yes.
Keep. My lord archbishop;
And has done half an hour, to know your plea-
sures.
Chan. Let him come in.
Keep. Your grace may enter now.
[*Cranmer enters and approaches
the council-table.*
Chan. My good lord archbishop, I'm very
sorry
To sit here at this present, and behold
That chair stand empty: but we all are men, 10
In our own natures frail, and capable
Of our flesh; few are angels: out of which frailty
And want of wisdom, you, that best should teach
us,
Have misdemean'd yourself, and not a little,
Toward the king first, then his laws, in filling
The whole realm, by your teaching and your
chaplains,
For so we are inform'd, with new opinions,
Divers and dangerous; which are heresies,
And, not reform'd, may prove pernicious. 19
Gar. Which reformation must be sudden too,
My noble lords; for those that tame wild horses
Pace 'em not in their hands to make 'em gentle,
But stop their mouths with stubborn bits, and
spur 'em,
Till they obey the manage. If we suffer,
Out of our easiness and childish pity
To one man's honour, this contagious sickness,
Farewell all physic: and what follows then?
Commotions, uproars, with a general taint
Of the whole state: as, of late days, our neigh-
bours,
The upper Germany, can dearly witness, 30
Yet freshly pitied in our memories.
Cran. My good lords, hitherto, in all the
progress
Both of my life and office, I have labour'd,
And with no little study, that my teaching
And the strong course of my authority
Might go one way, and safely; and the end
Was ever, to do well: nor is there living,
I speak it with a single heart, my lords,
A man that more detests, more stirs against,
Both in his private conscience and his place, 40
Defacers of a public peace, than I do.

Pray heaven, the king may never find a heart
With less allegiance in it!   Men that make
Envy and crooked malice nourishment
Dare bite the best.   I do beseech your lordships,
That, in this case of justice, my accusers,
Be what they will, may stand forth face to face,
And freely urge against me.
    Suf.   Nay, my lord,
That cannot be: you are a counsellor,
And, by that virtue, no man dare accuse you. 50
    Gar.   My lord, because we have business of
         more moment,
We will be short with you.   'Tis his highness'
         pleasure,
And our consent, for better trial of you,
From hence you be committed to the Tower;
Where, being but a private man again,
You shall know many dare accuse you boldly,
More than, I fear, you are provided for.
    Cran.   Ah, my good Lord of Winchester, I
         thank you;
You are always my good friend; if your will pass,
I shall both find your lordship judge and juror, 60
You are so merciful: I see your end;
'Tis my undoing: love and meekness, lord,
Become a churchman better than ambition:
Win straying souls with modesty again,
Cast none away.   That I shall clear myself,
Lay all the weight ye can upon my patience,
• I make as little doubt, as you do conscience
In doing daily wrongs.   I could say more,
But reverence to your calling makes me modest.
•   *Gar.*   My lord, my lord, you are a sectary, 70
That's the plain truth: your painted gloss dis-
         covers,
To men that understand you, words and weak-
         ness.
    Crom.   My Lord of Winchester, you are a
         little,
By your good favour, too sharp; men so noble,
However faulty, yet should find respect
For what they have been: 'tis a cruelty
To load a falling man.
    Gar.   Good master secretary,
I cry your honour mercy; you may, worst
Of all this table, say so.
    Crom.   Why, my lord?
    Gar.   Do not I know you for a favourer   80
• Of this new sect? ye are not sound.
    Crom.   Not sound?
    Gar.   Not sound, I say.
    Crom.   Would you were half so honest!
Men's prayers then would seek you, not their
         fears.
    Gar.   I shall remember this bold language.
    Crom.   Do.
Remember your bold life too.
    Chan.   This is too much;
Forbear, for shame, my lords.
    Gar.   I have done.
    Crom.   And I.
    Chan.   Then thus for you, my lord: it stands
         agreed,
I take it, by all voices, that forthwith
You be convey'd to the Tower a prisoner;
There to remain till the king's further pleasure
Be known unto us: are you all agreed, lords? 91
    All.   We are.
    Cran.   Is there no other way of mercy,

67 *I make as little doubt, as you do conscience.* I have as little doubt as you have conscience.

70 *sectary.* A member of a sect, a schismatic.

81 *sound.* True.

94 *strangely.* Exceedingly.

Cranmer: 'By virtue of that ring, I take my cause Out of the gripes of cruel men . . .' Drawing by Henry Singleton (1766–1839)

But I must needs to the Tower, my lords?
   Gar.   What other
• Would you expect? you are strangely trouble-
    some.
Let some o' the guard be ready there.

              Enter Guard.

   Cran.   For me?
Must I go like a traitor thither?
   Gar.   Receive him,
And see him safe i' the Tower.
   Cran.   Stay, good my lords,
I have a little yet to say. Look there, my lords;
By virtue of that ring, I take my cause
Out of the gripes of cruel men, and give it   100
To a most noble judge, the king my master.
   Cham.   This is the king's ring.
   Sur.   'Tis no counterfeit.
   Suf. 'Tis the right ring, by heaven: I told
    ye all,
When we first put this dangerous stone a-rolling,
'Twould fall upon ourselves.
   Nor.   Do you think, my lords,
The king will suffer but the little finger
Of this man to be vex'd?
   Chan.   'Tis now too certain:
How much more is his life in value with him?
Would I were fairly out on't!
   Crom.   My mind gave me,
In seeking tales and informations   110
Against this man, whose honesty the devil
And his disciples only envy at,
Ye blew the fire that burns ye: now have at ye!

Enter KING, *frowning on them; takes his seat.*

   Gar. Dread sovereign, how much are we
    bound to heaven
In daily thanks, that gave us such a prince;
Not only good and wise, but most religious:
One that, in all obedience, makes the church
The chief aim of his honour; and, to strengthen
That holy duty, out of dear respect,
His royal self in judgement comes to hear   120
The cause betwixt her and this great offender.
   King. You were ever good at sudden com-
    mendations,
Bishop of Winchester. But know, I come not
To hear such flattery now, and in my presence;
They are too thin and bare to hide offences.
To me you cannot reach, you play the spaniel,
And think with wagging of your tongue to win
    me;
But, whatsoe'er thou takest me for, I'm sure
Thou hast a cruel nature and a bloody.
[*To Cranmer*] Good man, sit down. Now let me
    see the proudest   130
He, that dares most, but wag his finger at thee:
By all that's holy, he had better starve
Than but once think this place becomes thee not.
   Sur. May it please your grace,—
   King.   No, sir, it does not please me.
I had thought I had had men of some under-
    standing
And wisdom of my council; but I find none.
Was it discretion, lords, to let this man,
This good man,—few of you deserve that title,—
This honest man, wait like a lousy footboy   139
At chamber-door? and one as great as you are?

Why, what a shame was this! Did my commission
Bid ye so far forget yourselves? I gave ye
Power as he was a counsellor to try him,
Not as a groom: there's some of ye, I see,
More out of malice than integrity,
Would try him to the utmost, had ye mean;
Which ye shall never have while I live.
    Chan.   Thus far,
My most dread sovereign, may it like your grace
To let my tongue excuse all. What was purposed
Concerning his imprisonment, was rather,   150
If there be faith in men, meant for his trial,
And fair purgation to the world, than malice,
I'm sure, in me.
    King. Well, well, my lords, respect him;
Take him, and use him well, he's worthy of it.
I will say thus much for him, if a prince
May be beholding to a subject, I
Am, for his love and service, so to him.
Make me no more ado, but all embrace him:
Be friends, for shame, my lords! My Lord of
    Canterbury,   160
I have a suit which you must not deny me;
That is, a fair young maid that yet wants baptism,
You must be godfather, and answer for her.
    Cran. The greatest monarch now alive may
    glory
In such an honour: how may I deserve it,
That am a poor and humble subject to you?
    King. Come, come, my lord, you'ld spare
your spoons: you shall have two noble partners
with you; the old Duchess of Norfolk, and Lady
Marquess Dorset: will these please you?   170
Once more, my Lord of Winchester, I charge
    you,
Embrace and love this man.
    Gar.   With a true heart
And brother-love I do it.
    Cran.   And let heaven
Witness, how dear I hold this confirmation.
    King. Good man, those joyful tears show thy
    true heart:
The common voice, I see, is verified
Of thee, which says thus, 'Do my Lord of Canterbury
A shrewd turn, and he is your friend for ever.'
Come, lords, we trifle time away; I long
To have this young one made a Christian.   180
As I have made ye one, lords, one remain;
So I grow stronger, you more honour gain.
                        [*Exeunt.*

SCENE IV. *The palace yard.*

Noise and tumult within. Enter Porter *and
his* Man.

    Port. You'll leave your noise anon, ye rascals:
do you take the court for Paris-garden? ye rude
slaves, leave your gaping.
    [*Within*] Good master porter, I belong to the
larder.
    Port. Belong to the gallows, and be hanged,
ye rogue! is this a place to roar in? Fetch me a
dozen crab-tree staves, and strong ones: these
are but switches to 'em. I'll scratch your heads:

152 *purgation.* Clearing of a name in court.

167–168 *spare your spoons.* Spare yourself the expense
of giving christening spoons.

178 *shrewd turn.* A favour.

2 *Paris-garden.* The centre of bear-and-bull baiting
near the Globe Theatre.

Bear baiting arena on the south bank of the Thames. A
detail from Hollar's Panorama *c.*1647

3 *gaping.* Bawling.

11 *ale and cakes*. Traditionally served on religious festive days.

15 *May-day*. A holiday on which people went to gather garlands early in the morning.

16 *Powle's*. St. Paul's Cathedral.

22 *Samson . . . Sir Guy . . . Colbrand*. Legendary heroes of great strength.

26 *chine*. Backbone (of meat).

27 *not for a cow, God save her*. Not for anything.

32–38 *What should you . . . a thousand*. See introduction.

33 *Moorfields*. Fields in London used by holidayers.

42 *brazier*. Brass-worker. See introduction.

43 *dog-days*. The forty hottest days of the summer.

44 *line*. Equator.

45 *fire-drake*. Meteor.

48 *mortar-piece*. Piece of artillery.

50 *pinked porringer*. A round cap resembling an up-turned dish.

53 *'Clubs'*. The rallying cry of London apprentices to join a fight.

57–58 *broom-staff*. Close quarters.

61 *work*. Fort.

63–67 *These are . . . to endure*. See introduction.

65 *tribulation of Tower-hill*. i.e. executions took place at Tower Hill.

66 *Limehouse*. A rough dock area.

67 *Limbo Patrum*. Slang for prison.

69 *running banquet*. Slang for a public whipping.

you must be seeing christenings? do you look for ale and cakes here, you rude rascals? 11

Man. Pray, sir, be patient: 'tis as much impossible—
Unless we sweep 'em from the door with cannons—
To scatter 'em, as 'tis to make 'em sleep
On May-day morning; which will never be:
We may as well push against Powle's, as stir 'em.

Port. How got they in, and be hang'd?

Man. Alas, I know not; how gets the tide in?
As much as one sound cudgel of four foot—
You see the poor remainder—could distribute, 20
I made no spare, sir.

Port.   You did nothing, sir.

Man. I am not Samson, nor Sir Guy, nor Colbrand,
To mow 'em down before me: but if I spared any
That had a head to hit, either young or old,
He or she, cuckold or cuckold-maker,
Let me ne'er hope to see a chine again;
And that I would not for a cow, God save her!

[*Within*] Do you hear, master porter?

Port. I shall be with you presently, good master puppy. Keep the door close, sirrah. 30

Man. What would you have me do?

Port. What should you do, but knock 'em down by the dozens? Is this Moorfields to muster in? or have we some strange Indian with the great tool come to court, the women so besiege us? Bless me, what a fry of fornication is at door! On my Christian conscience, this one christening will beget a thousand; here will be father, godfather, and all together. 39

Man. The spoons will be the bigger, sir. There is a fellow somewhat near the door, he should be a brazier by his face, for, o' my conscience, twenty of the dog-days now reign in's nose; all that stand about him are under the line, they need no other penance: that fire-drake did I hit three times on the head, and three times was his nose discharged against me; he stands there, like a mortar-piece, to blow us. There was a haberdasher's wife of small wit near him, that railed upon me till her pinked porringer fell off her head, for kindling such a combustion in the state. I missed the meteor once, and hit that woman; who cried out 'Clubs!' when I might see from far some forty truncheoners draw to her succour, which were the hope o' the Strand, where she was quartered. They fell on; I made good my place: at length they came to the broom-staff to me; I defied 'em still: when suddenly a file of boys behind 'em, loose shot, delivered such a shower of pebbles, that I was fain to draw mine honour in, and let 'em win the work: the devil was amongst 'em, I think, surely.

Port. These are the youths that thunder at a playhouse, and fight for bitten apples; that no audience, but the tribulation of Tower-hill, or the limbs of Limehouse, their dear brothers, are able to endure. I have some of 'em in Limbo Patrum, and there they are like to dance these three days; besides the running banquet of two beadles that is to come. 70

Enter LORD CHAMBERLAIN.

Cham. Mercy o' me, what a multitude are here!

They grow still too; from all parts they are com-
    ing,
As if we kept a fair here! Where are these
    porters,
These lazy knaves? Ye have made a fine hand,
    fellows:
There's a trim rabble let in: are all these
Your faithful friends o' the suburbs? We shall
    have
Great store of room, no doubt, left for the ladies,
When they pass back from the christening.
    Port.   An't please your honour,
We are but men; and what so many may do,
Not being torn a-pieces, we have done: 80
An army cannot rule 'em.
    Cham.   As I live,
If the king blame me for't, I'll lay ye all
By the heels, and suddenly; and on your heads
Clap round fines for neglect: ye are lazy knaves;
● And here ye lie baiting of bombards, when
Ye should do service. Hark! the trumpets
    sound;
They're come already from the christening:
Go, break among the press, and find a way out
To let the troop pass fairly; or I'll find
● A Marshalsea shall hold ye play these two
    months.   90
    Port. Make way there for the princess.
    Man.   You great fellow,
Stand close up, or I'll make your head ache.
● *Port.* You i' the camlet, get up o' the rail;
● I'll peck you o'er the pales else.   [*Exeunt.*

SCENE V. *The palace.*

Enter trumpets, sounding; then two Aldermen,
Lord Mayor, Garter, Cranmer, Duke of
Norfolk *with his marshal's staff,* Duke of
Suffolk, *two* Noblemen *bearing great stand-
ing-bowls for the christening-gifts; then four*
Noblemen *bearing a canopy, under which the*
Duchess of Norfolk, *godmother, bearing
the child richly habited in a mantle, &c.,
train borne by a* Lady; *then follows the*
Marchioness Dorset, *the other godmother,
and Ladies. The troop pass once about the
stage, and* Garter *speaks.*

Gart. Heaven, from thy endless goodness,
send prosperous life, long, and ever happy, to
the high and mighty princess of England,
Elizabeth!

Flourish. Enter King *and Guard.*

Cran. [*Kneeling*] And to your royal grace,
    and the good queen,
My noble partners, and myself, thus pray:
All comfort, joy, in this most gracious lady,
Heaven ever laid up to make parents happy,
May hourly fall upon ye!
    King.   Thank you, good lord archbishop:
What is her name?
    Cran.   Elizabeth.
    King.   Stand up, lord.   10
                [*The King kisses the child.*
With this kiss take my blessing: God protect thee!
Into whose hand I give thy life.
    Cran.   Amen.
● *King.* My noble gossips, ye have been too
    prodigal:

Costume design for the Porter by Tanya Moisewitch,
Stratford-upon-Avon, 1949

85 *baiting of bombards.* Drinking from leather bottles.

90 *Marshalsea.* A London prison.

93 *camlet.* A cloth of angora goat's hair and silk.

94 *peck you o'er the pales.* Pitch you over the railings.

13 *gossips.* God-parents.

Cranmer: 'Let me speak, sir,' Engraving from a painting by Rev. M.W. Peters (d.1814)

24 *Saba.* Queen of Sheba.

31–36 *She shall be . . . neighbours.* See introduction.

44 *one.* i.e. James I.

I thank ye heartily; so shall this lady,
When she has so much English.
   Cran.   Let me speak, sir,
For heaven now bids me; and the words I utter
Let none think flattery, for they'll find 'em truth.
This royal infant—heaven still move about her!—
Though in her cradle, yet now promises
Upon this land a thousand thousand blessings, 20
Which time shall bring to ripeness: she shall be—
But few now living can behold that goodness—
A pattern to all princes living with her,
● And all that shall succeed: Saba was never
More covetous of wisdom and fair virtue
Than this pure soul shall be: all princely graces,
That mould up such a mighty piece as this is,
With all the virtues that attend the good,
Shall still be doubled on her: truth shall nurse
   her,
Holy and heavenly thoughts still counsel her: 30
● She shall be loved and fear'd: her own shall
   bless her;
Her foes shake like a field of beaten corn,
And hang their heads with sorrow: good grows
   with her:
In her days every man shall eat in safety,
Under his own vine, what he plants; and sing
The merry songs of peace to all his neighbours:
God shall be truly known; and those about her
From her shall read the perfect ways of honour,
And by those claim their greatness, not by blood.
Nor shall this peace sleep with her: but as when
The bird of wonder dies, the maiden phœnix, 41
Her ashes new create another heir,
As great in admiration as herself;
● So shall she leave her blessedness to one,
When heaven shall call her from this cloud of
   darkness,
Who from the sacred ashes of her honour
Shall star-like rise, as great in fame as she was,
And so stand fix'd: peace, plenty, love, truth,
   terror,
That were the servants to this chosen infant,
Shall then be his, and like a vine grow to him: 50
Wherever the bright sun of heaven shall shine,
His honour and the greatness of his name
Shall be, and make new nations: he shall flourish,
And, like a mountain cedar, reach his branches
To all the plains about him: our children's child-
   ren
Shall see this, and bless heaven.
   King.   Thou speakest wonders.
   Cran. She shall be, to the happiness of Eng-
   land,
An aged princess; many days shall see her,
And yet no day without a deed to crown it. 59
Would I had known no more! but she must die,
She must, the saints must have her; yet a virgin,
A most unspotted lily shall she pass
To the ground, and all the world shall mourn her.
   King. O lord archbishop,
Thou hast made me now a man! never, before
This happy child, did I get any thing:
This oracle of comfort has so pleased me,
That when I am in heaven I shall desire
To see what this child does, and praise my
   Maker.
I thank ye all. To you, my good lord mayor, 70
And your good brethren, I am much beholding;
I have received much honour by your presence,

And ye shall find me thankful.   Lead the way,
    lords:
Ye must all see the queen, and she must thank
    ye,
She will be sick else.   This day, no man think
Has business at his house; for all shall stay:
This little one shall make it holiday.   [*Exeunt.*

EPILOGUE.

'Tis ten to one this play can never please
All that are here: some come to take their ease,
And sleep an act or two; but those, we fear,
We have frighted with our trumpets; so, 'tis
    clear,
They'll say 'tis naught: others, to hear the city
Abused extremely, and to cry 'That's witty!'
Which we have not done neither: that, I fear,
All the expected good we're like to hear
For this play at this time, is only in
The merciful construction of good women;   10
For such a one we show'd 'em: if they smile,
And say 'twill do, I know, within a while
All the best men are ours; for 'tis ill hap,
If they hold when their ladies bid 'em clap.

Elizabeth I. Painting by M. Gheeraerts the Younger,
*c.*1592

Shakespeare's Poems

SHAKESPEARE'S FINEST POETRY is (along with the Sonnets) in his plays: the tensions, the emotional heights, the excitement therein inspired him to his highest reaches of the imagination, screwed him up to verbal flights beyond which nothing in the language has ever gone. Some passages reach unexampled limits:

> The odds is gone, and there is nothing left
> Remarkable beneath the visiting moon.

> Burn the great sphere thou mov'st in, darkling stand
> The varying shore of the world.

> Not poppy nor mandragora,
> Nor all the drowsy syrups of the world,
> Shall ever medicine thee to that sweet sleep
> Which thou owedst yesterday.

To anyone intimately acquainted with the language, especially if it was the language of his childhood, these invocations have the haunting power to turn the heart over, like nothing else in our literature.

On the whole, the language of the poems is gentler, mellifluous and pleasing, altogether less knotty and elliptical, less concentrated and easier to understand. It is also much earlier than those passages from *Antony and Cleopatra* and *Othello*. There are fine, and even powerful, passages in the poems, particularly in the Sonnets, when the poet is strongly moved by personal feelings. Thus it is that, as a poet, he was hailed by contemporaries as 'honey-tongued', his verse described as 'sugared', an epithet stronger than 'sweet' with Elizabethans.

Francis Meres saw in him another Ovid, the Ovid of the *Amores*, and he was Shakespeare's favourite poet as he was Marlowe's. 'So the sweet, witty [i.e. clever, intellectual] soul of Ovid lives in mellifluous and honey-tongued Shakespeare – witness his *Venus and Adonis*, his *Lucrece*, his sugared sonnets among his private friends, etc.' In the same

Illustration from
The Complete
Works of
Shakespeare,
edited by
J.O. Halliwell
1853

year, 1598, a young poet, Richard Barnfield, paid tribute to him,

> whose honey-flowing vein,
> Pleasing the world, thy praises doth obtain;
> Whose *Venus* and whose *Lucrece* sweet and chaste
> Thy name in fame's immortal book have placed.

Next year John Weever addressed a long epigram to 'honey-tongued Shakespeare', while his fellow-Warwickshireman, Drayton, confined himself to Shakespeare's writing for the stage – his comic vein, his powerful conceptions, and the clarity of his tragic rage.

In his earlier verse one sees that he is a child of the new poetry of the 1580's – none of the antique jogtrot of most of the Elizabethan versifiers before the Renaissance flowering in Sidney and Spenser. These set his standards for him, though, surprisingly, he read Chaucer too. In the early work he comes closest in style and spirit to the admirable poet Daniel, Florio's brother-in-law, though he is more spirited and vivacious, always ready for a joke, often a bawdy one, full of naughty, suggestive ideas. Indeed his early verse fulfils his own delineation of himself as Berowne: 'conceit's expositor', always ready with images, puns, notions, jokes, and

> A merrier man I never met withal.

A Lover's
Complaint

1591

His EARLIEST POEM already embodies these recognisable qualities, though it is only prentice-work. It was published by Thomas Thorpe in 1609 at the end of the Sonnets, so it evidently came from the Southampton *cache* for which Thorpe was so profusely grateful to his Mr. W.H., who had got the manuscript – so he too belonged to the connexion of Shakespeare's one and only patron.

The prime Shakespearean quality we observe in this piece is the joking manner – how to describe it? – the serio-comic way of telling the tale, the smile hovering over it, which later becomes the raillery of *Troilus and Cressida* or the enigmatic treatment of Antony and Cleopatra's love. A very clever man once observed that he loved 'the duplicity of things'. This could be said of William Shakespeare. At the same time, he was open and honest, as Ben Jonson tells us, so that beneath the smile we can often recognise the realities.

There is not much difficulty in recognising his youthful patron in *A Lover's Com-*

Right: *Opening page of* A Lover's Complaint *from the Quarto 1609*
Far right: *Southampton at twenty. Miniature by Nicholas Hilliard c.1593*

A Louers complaint.

BY

WILLIAM SHAKE-SPEARE.

FRom off a hill whofe concaue wombe reworded,
A plaintfull ftory from a fiftring vale
My fpirrits t'attend this doble voyce accorded,
And downe I laid to lift the fad tun'd tale,
Ere long efpied a fickle maid full pale
Tearing of papers breaking rings a twaine,
Storming her world with forrowes, wind and raine.

plaint, and it may have been a kind of diploma-piece for his favour. The youth in the poem is obviously the young lord of the Sonnets:

> His qualities were beauteous as his form,
> For maiden-tongued he was, and thereof free.

And like the youth of the Sonnets, who would not get married when it was his duty or respond to women:

> He preached pure maid, and praised cold chastity.

The youths in poem and Sonnets are identical; in the first.

> That he did in the general bosom reign
> Of young, of old, and sexes both enchanted;

in the second,

> A man in hue, all hues in his controlling,
> Which steals men's eyes and women's souls amazeth.

The youth was little more than a boy, whose long locks, like Southampton's, 'did hang in crooked curls', blown about by the wind; and

> Small show of man was yet upon his chin;
> His phoenix down began but to appear
> Like unshorn velvet on that termless skin . . .

just as in the Hilliard miniature of the young peer. The tale is of a country girl, whose plaintful story echoed from 'the concave womb' of 'a sistering vale', as it might be in the Cotswolds, for upon her head she wore 'a platted hive of straw'. She fell for the charms of the chaste-seeming youth:

> So many have, that never touched his hand,
> Sweetly supposed them mistress of his heart . . .
> What with his art in youth and youth in art,

she of course surrendered herself to his charm,

> Reserved the stalk and gave him all my flower.

Such was the joke, the *dénouement* to be expected; but it was a double-joke, for one does not know whether the poet was not egging the youth on to do just that. After all, the strongly sexed, heterosexual poet was all in favour of it himself. It must have given them both a good laugh; and at any rate the poet was received into favour.

The poem was openly entitled to Shakespeare by the publisher; so to what point all the fuss made by imperceptive critics as to its authorship? It already provides examples of Shakespeare's love of rare impressive words – those ending in 'ure', for example, acture; or annexions, for another. We may date it to 1591, when the poet was taken into Southampton's patronage.

A LOVER'S COMPLAINT.

FROM off a hill whose concave womb re-worded
A plaintful story from a sistering vale,
My spirits to attend this double voice accorded,
● And down I laid to list the sad-tuned tale;
Ere long espied a fickle maid full pale,
Tearing of papers, breaking rings a-twain,
Storming her world with sorrow's wind and rain.

Upon her head a platted hive of straw,
Which fortified her visage from the sun,
Whereon the thought might think sometime it saw
The carcass of a beauty spent and done: 11
Time had not scythed all that youth begun,
Nor youth all quit; but, spite of heaven's fell rage,
● Some beauty peep'd through lattice of sear'd age.

Oft did she heave her napkin to her eyne,
Which on it had conceited characters,
Laundering the silken figures in the brine
That season'd woe had pelleted in tears,
And often reading what contents it bears;
As often shrieking undistinguish'd woe,   20
In clamours of all size, both high and low.

Sometimes her levell'd eyes their carriage ride,
As they did battery to the spheres intend;
● Sometime diverted their poor balls are tied
To the orbed earth; sometimes they do extend
Their view right on; anon their gazes lend
To every place at once, and, nowhere fix'd,
The mind and sight distractedly commix'd.

Her hair, nor loose nor tied in formal plat,
Proclaim'd in her a careless hand of pride   30
For some, untuck'd, descended her sheaved hat,
Hanging her pale and pined cheek beside;
● Some in her threaden fillet still did bide,
And true to bondage would not break from
    thence,
Though slackly braided in loose negligence.

● A thousand favours from a maund she drew
Of amber, crystal, and of beaded jet,
Which one by one she in a river threw,
● Upon whose weeping margent she was set;
Like usury, applying wet to wet,   40
Or monarch's hands that let not bounty fall
Where want cries some, but where excess begs all.

● Of folded schedules had she many a one,
Which she perused, sigh'd, tore, and gave the
    flood;
Crack'd many a ring of posied gold and bone,
Bidding them find their sepulchres in mud;
Found yet moe letters sadly penn'd in blood,
● With sleided silk feat and affectedly
Enswathed, and seal'd to curious secrecy.

● These often bathed she in her fluxive eyes, 50

4 *list.* Listen to.

14 *sear'd.* Withered.

24 *diverted.* Turned away.

33 *fillet.* Headband.

36 *favours.* Love-tokens. *maund.* Basket.

39 *margent.* River-bank.

43 *schedules.* Scrolls, papers.

48 *sleided silk.* Combed silk. *feat.* Aptly.

50 *fluxive.* Flowing with tears.

Opposite: The disappointed lover tells her tale. Engraving from Bell's edition of *Shakespeare*, 1773–74

And often kiss'd, and often 'gan to tear :
Cried 'O false blood, thou register of lies,
What unapproved witness dost thou bear !
Ink would have seem'd more black and damned
    here !'

This said, in top of rage the lines she rents,
Big discontent so breaking their contents.

A reverend man that grazed his cattle nigh—
Sometime a blusterer, that the ruffle knew
Of court, of city, and had let go by
The swiftest hours, observed as they flew—   60
Towards this afflicted fancy fastly drew,
And, privileged by age, desires to know
In brief the grounds and motives of her woe.

● So slides he down upon his grained bat,
● And comely-distant sits he by her side ;
When he again desires her, being sat,
Her grievance with his hearing to divide :
If that from him there may be aught applied
Which may her suffering ecstasy assuage,
'Tis promised in the charity of age.   70

'Father,' she says, 'though in me you behold
The injury of many a blasting hour,
Let it not tell your judgement I am old ;
Not age, but sorrow, over me hath power :
I might as yet have been a spreading flower,
Fresh to myself, if I had self-applied
Love to myself and to no love beside.

● 'But, woe is me ! too early I attended
A youthful suit—it was to gain my grace—
Of one by nature's outwards so commended,   80
That maidens' eyes stuck over all his face :
Love lack'd a dwelling, and made him her
    place ;
And when in his fair parts she did abide,
She was new lodged and newly deified.

'His browny locks did hang in crooked curls ;
And every light occasion of the wind
Upon his lips their silken parcels hurls.
What's sweet to do, to do will aptly find :
Each eye that saw him did enchant the mind,
● For on his visage was in little drawn   90
What largeness thinks in Paradise was sawn.

● 'Small show of man was yet upon his chin ;
His phœnix down began but to appear
Like unshorn velvet on that termless skin
Whose bare out-bragg'd the web it seem'd to
    wear :
Yet show'd his visage by that cost more dear ;
And nice affections wavering stood in doubt
If best were as it was, or best without.

'His qualities were beauteous as his form,
For maiden-tongued he was, and thereof free ;   100
Yet, if men moved him, was he such a storm
As oft 'twixt May and April is to see,
When winds breathe sweet, unruly though they
    be.
● His rudeness so with his authorized youth
Did livery falseness in a pride of truth.

'Well could he ride, and often men would say
"That horse his mettle from his rider takes :

64 *bat.* Stick.

65 *comely-distant.* At a seemly distance.

78–79 *I attended A youthful suit.* I received a young
man's attentions.

90–91 *For . . . sawn.* i.e. for in his face was, in miniature,
what most people would imagine can be seen in Paradise.

92 *Small show of man.* Hardly any beard.

104–105 *His . . . truth.* i.e. his rough behaviour belied
his youthful exterior.

Opposite : 'His browny locks did hang in crooked curls'.
Miniature of a young elegant by Nicholas Hilliard
(*c.*1547–1619)

115 *appertainings*. Belongings.

116 *case*. Surroundings.

119 *Pieced*. Made up, composed.

125 *different*. Varied.

139 *moe*. More (in number).

140 *owe*. Own.

144 *fee-simple*. Property.

Proud of subjection, noble by the sway,
What rounds, what bounds, what course, what
    stop he makes!"
And controversy hence a question takes,   110
Whether the horse by him became his deed,
Or he his manage by the well-doing steed.

'But quickly on this side the verdict went:
His real habitude gave life and grace
• To appertainings and to ornament,
• Accomplish'd in himself, not in his case:
All aids, themselves made fairer by their place,
Came for additions; yet their purposed trim
• Pieced not his grace, but were all graced by him.

'So on the tip of his subduing tongue   120
All kind of arguments and question deep,
All replication prompt, and reason strong,
For his advantage still did wake and sleep:
To make the weeper laugh, the laugher weep,
• He had the dialect and different skill,
Catching all passions in his craft of will:

'That he did in the general bosom reign
Of young, of old; and sexes both enchanted,
To dwell with him in thoughts, or to remain
In personal duty, following where he haunted: 130
Consents bewitch'd, ere he desire, have granted;
And dialogued for him what he would say,
Ask'd their own wills, and made their wills obey.

'Many there were that did his picture get,
To serve their eyes, and in it put their mind;
Like fools that in th' imagination set
The goodly objects which abroad they find
Of lands and mansions, theirs in thought assign'd;
• And labouring in moe pleasures to bestow them
• Than the true gouty landlord which doth owe
    them: 140

'So many have, that never touch'd his hand,
Sweetly supposed them mistress of his heart.
My woeful self, that did in freedom stand,
• And was my own fee-simple, not in part,
What with his art in youth, and youth in art,
Threw my affections in his charmed power,
Reserved the stalk and gave him all my flower.

'Yet did I not, as some my equals did,
Demand of him, nor being desired yielded;
Finding myself in honour so forbid,   150
With safest distance I mine honour shielded:
Experience for me many bulwarks builded
Of proofs new-bleeding, which remain'd the foil
Of this false jewel, and his amorous spoil.

'But, ah, who ever shunn'd by precedent
The destined ill she must herself assay?
Or forced examples, 'gainst her own content,
To put the by-past perils in her way?
Counsel may stop awhile what will not stay;
For when we rage, advice is often seen   160
By blunting us to make our wits more keen.

'Nor gives it satisfaction to our blood,
That we must curb it upon others' proof;
To be forbod the sweets that seem so good,
For fear of harms that preach in our behoof.
O appetite, from judgement stand aloof!

The one a palate hath that needs will taste,
Though Reason weep, and cry " It is thy last."

' For further I could say "This man's untrue,"
And knew the patterns of his foul beguiling; 170
Heard where his plants in others' orchards grew,
Saw how deceits were gilded in his smiling;
Knew vows were ever brokers to defiling;
Thought characters and words merely but art,
And bastards of his foul adulterate heart.

' And long upon these terms I held my city,
Till thus he gan besiege me: "Gentle maid,
Have of my suffering youth some feeling pity,
And be not of my holy vows afraid:
That's to ye sworn to none was ever said; 180
For feasts of love I have been call'd unto,
Till now did ne'er invite, nor never woo.

' " All my offences that abroad you see
Are errors of the blood, none of the mind;
● Love made them not: with acture they may be,
Where neither party is nor true nor kind:
They sought their shame that so their shame did
        find;
And so much less of shame in me remains,
By how much of me their reproach contains.

' " Among the many that mine eyes have seen, 190
Not one whose flame my heart so much as
        warm'd,
● Or my affection put to the smallest teen,
Or any of my leisures ever charm'd:
Harm have I done to them, but ne'er was
        harm'd;
Kept hearts in liveries, but mine own was free,
And reign'd, commanding in his monarchy.

' " Look here, what tributes wounded fancies
        sent me,
Of paled pearls and rubies red as blood;
Figuring that they their passions likewise
        lent me
Of grief and blushes, aptly understood   200
In bloodless white and the encrimson'd mood;
Effects of terror and dear modesty,
Encamp'd in hearts, but fighting outwardly.

' " And, lo, behold these talents of their hair,
● With twisted metal amorously impleach'd,
I have received from many a several fair,
Their kind acceptance weepingly beseech'd,
With the annexions of fair gems enrich'd,
And deep-brain'd sonnets that did amplify
Each stone's dear nature, worth, and quality. 210

' " The diamond,—why, 'twas beautiful and hard,
● Whereto his invised properties did tend;
The deep-green emerald, in whose fresh regard
Weak sights their sickly radiance do amend;
The heaven-hued sapphire and the opal blend
With objects manifold: each several stone,
With wit well blazon'd, smiled or made some moan.

' " Lo, all these trophies of affections hot,
Of pensived and subdued desires the tender,
Nature hath charged me that I hoard them not, 220
But yield them up where I myself must render,
That is, to you, my origin and ender;

Gentleman wooing a maiden. Woodcut from *The
Roxburghe Ballads*, 17th century

185 *acture*. Action.

192 *teen*. Regret.

205 *impleach'd*. Intertwined.

212 *invised*. Unseen.

223 *oblations*. Offerings.

242 *gyves*. Fetters, shackles

264 *potential*. Potent.

273 *aloes*. Bitternesses.

● For these, of force, must your oblations be,
Since I their altar, you enpatron me.

' " O, then, advance of yours that phraseless hand,
Whose white weighs down the airy scale of praise ;
Take all these similes to your own command,
Hallow'd with sighs that burning lungs did raise ;
What me your minister, for you obeys,
Works under you ; and to your audit comes   230
Their distract parcels in combined sums.

' " Lo, this device was sent me from a nun,
Or sister sanctified, of holiest note ;
Which late her noble suit in court did shun,
Whose rarest havings made the blossoms dote ;
For she was sought by spirits of richest coat,
But kept cold distance, and did thence remove,
To spend her living in eternal love.

' " But, O my sweet, what labour is't to leave
The thing we have not, mastering what not strives,
† Playing the place which did no form receive, 241
● Playing patient sports in unconstrained gyves ?
She that her fame so to herself contrives,
The scars of battle 'scapeth by the flight,
And makes her absence valiant, not her might.

' " O, pardon me, in that my boast is true :
The accident which brought me to her eye
Upon the moment did her force subdue,
And now she would the caged cloister fly :
Religious love put out Religion's eye :   250
Not to be tempted, would she be immured,
And now, to tempt, all liberty procured.

' " How mighty then you are, O, hear me tell !
The broken bosoms that to me belong
Have emptied all their fountains in my well,
And mine I pour your ocean all among :
I strong o'er them, and you o'er me being strong,
Must for your victory us all congest,
As compound love to physic your cold breast.

' " My parts had power to charm a sacred nun,
Who, disciplined, ay, dieted in grace,   261
Believed her eyes when they to assail begun,
All vows and consecrations giving place :
● O most potential love ! vow, bond, nor space,
In thee hath neither sting, knot, nor confine,
For thou art all, and all things else are thine.

' " When thou impressest, what are precepts worth
Of stale example ? When thou wilt inflame,
How coldly those impediments stand forth
Of wealth, of filial fear, law, kindred, fame ! 270
† Love's arms are peace, 'gainst rule, 'gainst sense, 'gainst shame,
And sweetens, in the suffering pangs it bears,
● The aloes of all forces, shocks, and fears.

' " Now all these hearts that do on mine depend,
Feeling it break, with bleeding groans they pine ;
And supplicant their sighs to you extend,
To leave the battery that you make 'gainst mine,
Lending soft audience to my sweet design,
And credent soul to that strong-bonded oath

That shall prefer and undertake my troth."   280

' This said, his watery eyes he did dismount,
Whose sights till then were levell'd on my face ;
Each cheek a river running from a fount
With brinish current downward flow'd apace :
O, how the channel to the stream gave grace !
• Who glazed with crystal gate the glowing roses
That flame through water which their hue en-
    closes.

' O father, what a hell of witchcraft lies
In the small orb of one particular tear !
But with the inundation of the eyes   290
What rocky heart to water will not wear ?
What breast so cold that is not warmed here ?
• O cleft effect ! cold modesty, hot wrath,
Both fire from hence and chill extincture hath.

' For, lo, his passion, but an art of craft,
Even there resolved my reason into tears ;
• There my white stole of chastity I daff'd,
Shook off my sober guards and civil fears ;
Appear to him, as he to me appears,
All melting ; though our drops this difference
    bore,   300
His poison'd me, and mine did him restore.

' In him a plenitude of subtle matter,
• Applied to cautels, all strange forms receives,
Of burning blushes, or of weeping water,
Or swooning paleness ; and he takes and leaves,
In either's aptness, as it best deceives,
To blush at speeches rank, to weep at woes,
Or to turn white and swoon at tragic shows :

' That not a heart which in his level came
Could 'scape the hail of his all-hurting aim,   310
Showing fair nature is both kind and tame ;
And, veil'd in them, did win whom he would
    maim :
Against the thing he sought he would exclaim ;
When he most burn'd in heart-wish'd luxury,
He preach'd pure maid, and praised cold chastity.

' Thus merely with the garment of a Grace
The naked and concealed fiend he cover'd ;
That th' unexperient gave the tempter place,
Which like a cherubin above them hover'd.
Who, young and simple, would not be so
    lover'd ?   320
Ay me ! I fell ; and yet do question make
What I should do again for such a sake.

' O, that infected moisture of his eye,
O, that false fire which in his cheek so glow'd,
O, that forced thunder from his heart did fly,
O, that sad breath his spongy lungs bestow'd,
O, all that borrow'd motion seeming owed,
Would yet again betray the fore-betray'd,
• And new pervert a reconciled maid !'   329

286 *crystal gate.* Crystal channel, i.e. eyes.

293 *cleft effect !* Twofold effect.

297 *daff'd.* Doffed, put away.

303 *cautels.* Insidious purposes.

329 *reconciled.* Regained.

A lover's complaint. Engraving from a painting by
Thomas Kirk, 1797

Venus
and Adonis

1593

A LOVER'S COMPLAINT remained in manuscript with the Sonnets, until Thorpe got them from the holder for publication years later. But, after the success of Shakespeare's early plays and encouraged by Southampton's patronage, he challenged public recognition as a poet by publishing *Venus and Adonis* in 1593. The challenge was underlined by the self-confident motto from Ovid, 'Vilia miretur vulgus' – let the populace admire what is base; Ben Jonson translated it:

> Kneel hinds to trash: me let bright Phoebus swell,
> With cups flowing from the Muses' well.

That showed very well what Shakespeare thought of himself – and of popular taste, himself more capable of commanding it than any. For the poem was immensely popular, and went into a dozen editions before his death.

It was printed in Blackfriars, that was to become so familiar, by Richard Field, the Stratford lad who had come up to London, married the widow of Vautrollier the printer and carried on the business. The poem was dedicated to the patron with courteous but independent-minded deference, vowing 'to take advantage of all idle hours till I have honoured you with some graver labour.' So he had a companion-piece already in mind in 1593.

The subject reflects what we have already seen to be the patron's situation – the beautiful young Adonis who will not respond to the love of women, even the goddess of love, Venus herself who tries to seduce him. The poem is very much what we know the actor to have been, sensuous and sexy, spirited and stimulating, naughty (and disapproved of by Victorians, who thereby disqualified themselves from judging it). It is far too long; it already has his abundance – everything is brought in: it was characteristic of him to extract the utmost out of everything. It is full of fresh country images and passages; a whole section describes coursing the hare, a favourite sport up on Cotswolds; a stallion scents a mare and gallops off to cover her – though not even this arouses the handsome youth to do likewise by Venus.

The poem is in marked contrast to Marlowe's *Hero and Leander*, which he was

writing in competition with Shakespeare for the favour of the youthful patron. Each knew what the other was writing, for there are several parallel phrases and passages, including the episode of the horse, and even of the youth. (Marlowe's Leander is no dark-haired Greek, but a fair-haired youth with long tresses.) The young man's virgin lips are described as they were in *A Lover's Complaint*;

> The tender spring upon thy tempting lip
> Shows thee unripe, yet mayst thou well be tasted:
> Make use of time, let not advantage slip,
> Beauty within itself should not be wasted.

This is precisely what he was urging contemporaneously in the Sonnets:

> Unthrifty loveliness, why dost thou spend
> Upon thyself thy beauty's legacy? . . .
> Look in thy glass and tell the face thou viewest
> Now is the time that face should form another.

Adonis will not, any more than Southampton would (as yet):

> Upon the earth's increase why shouldst thou feed,
> Unless the earth with thy increase be fed?
> By law of nature thou art bound to breed,
> That thine may live when thou thyself art dead.

It is the Southampton theme, which is reflected in this poem as in the Sonnets, and again contemporaneously in *Love's Labours' Lost*.

We must not go in for critical detail, merely place the poem in proper perspective. The chief literary influence is that of Spenser, though the spirit is very different from that chaste, religious soul. Daniel was closer, but where he is more tasteful and controlled, Shakespeare is abounding, vastly more various and vivacious. We note already his characteristic combination of clever word-play with perfectly natural country images, the dive-dapper, falcon, hare, milch-doe and fawn, stormy country days 'now wind, now rain', along with the Shakespearean message:

> Affection is a coal that must be cooled . . .

and yet,

> They that love best their loves shall not enjoy.

(Did this express recent experience?)

Shakespeare's poem did not have the artistic perfection and control of Marlowe's rival poem; but that went unfinished, for he was killed in the tavern-brawl – so like him – at Deptford at the end of May this year. All the same, one may legitimately read greater capacity for development, wider potentialities, in the actor-dramatist's work; for one thing, he was a strongly sexed heterosexual, very keen on women (he shares Venus' point of view about sex), not limited as Marlowe was by his homosexuality. For another, he had greater variousness and much more sense of comedy. *Venus and Adonis* is amusing all through: there is a broad smile all over it, nothing enigmatic here.

And how much the youth of the time enjoyed it! – as, we may expect, the young patron did. Gabriel Harvey tells us that it was a favourite with 'the younger sort'; and at Cambridge the young men's *Parnassus* plays testify, 'I'll worship sweet Master Shakespeare, and to honour him will lay his *Venus and Adonis* under my pillow.'

Shakespeare had as much reason to be proud of his claim to be a poet – he had read the proofs in Blackfriars with much care – as he had of his success as a playwright. The poem sold edition after edition; his name was now one to conjure with, and publishers were ready to take advantage of it, bringing out other people's work under his name.

VENVS
AND ADONIS

Vilia miretur vulgus: mihi flauus Apollo
Pocula Castalia plena ministret aqua.

LONDON

Imprinted by Richard Field, and are to be sold at the signe of the white Greyhound in Paules Church-yard.
1593.

Title page of
Venus and Adonis
from the Quarto
of 1593

VENUS AND ADONIS.

'Vilia miretur vulgus; mihi flavus Apollo
Pocula Castalia plena ministret aqua.'

TO THE

RIGHT HONOURABLE HENRY WRIOTHESLY,

EARL OF SOUTHAMPTON, AND BARON OF TICHFIELD.

RIGHT HONOURABLE,

I KNOW not how I shall offend in dedicating my unpolished lines to your lordship, nor how the world will censure me for choosing so strong a prop to support so weak a burden: only, if your honour seem but pleased, I account myself highly praised, and vow to take advantage of all idle hours, till I have honoured you with some graver labour. But if the first heir of my invention prove deformed, I shall be sorry it had so noble a god-father, and never after ear so barren a land, for fear it yield me still so bad a harvest. I leave it to your honourable survey, and your honour to your heart's content; which I wish may always answer your own wish and the world's hopeful expectation.

Your honour's in all duty,

WILLIAM SHAKESPEARE.

● *A bullet beside a text line indicates an annotation in the opposite column*

EVEN as the sun with purple-colour'd face
Had ta'en his last leave of the weeping morn,
● Rose-cheek'd Adonis hied him to the chase;
Hunting he loved, but love he laugh'd to scorn;
● Sick-thoughted Venus makes amain unto him,
And like a bold-faced suitor 'gins to woo him.

'Thrice-fairer than myself,' thus she began,
'The field's chief flower, sweet above compare,
● Stain to all nymphs, more lovely than a man,
More white and red than doves or roses are: 10
Nature that made thee, with herself at strife,
Saith that the world hath ending with thy life.

● 'Vouchsafe, thou wonder, to alight thy steed,
● And rein his proud head to the saddle-bow;
● If thou wilt deign this favour, for thy meed
A thousand honey secrets shalt thou know:
Here come and sit, where never serpent hisses,
And being set, I'll smother thee with kisses;

'And yet not cloy thy lips with loathed satiety,
But rather famish them amid their plenty,   20
Making them red and pale with fresh variety,
Ten kisses short as one, one long as twenty:
A summer's day will seem an hour but short,
Being wasted in such time-beguiling sport.'

With this she seizeth on his sweating palm,
● The precedent of pith and livelihood,
And trembling in her passion, calls it balm,
Earth's sovereign salve to do a goddess good:
● Being so enraged, desire doth lend her force
Courageously to pluck him from his horse.   30

Over one arm the lusty courser's rein,
Under her other was the tender boy,

'*Vilia . . . aqua!* 'Let the unworthy dazzle the masses; for me, may golden Apollo furnish full cups from the Castalian spring.'

To . . . Henry Wriothesly. Third Earl of Southampton (1573–1624), Shakespeare's patron.

first . . . invention. This was the first work other than a play.

ear. i.e. cultivate.

3 *hied him.* Hastened.

5 *Sick-thoughted.* Love-sick. *makes amain.* Hurries.

9 *Stain . . . nymphs.* Making all nymphs seem inferior in beauty.

13 *Vouchsafe.* Consent.

14 *rein . . . the saddle-bow.* Curb the horse.

15 *meed.* Wages, reward.

26 *precedent.* Sign. *pith and livelihood.* Strength and energy.

29 *enraged.* Aroused.

Opposite: Venus and Adonis. Painting by Pierre Paul Prud'hon (1758–1823)

VENUS AND ADONIS

34 *to toy.* To dally, make love.

37 *ragged.* Rugged.

53 *'miss.* Amiss, wrongly.

55 *sharp by fast.* Hungry from fasting.

56 *Tires.* Tears ravenously.

Who blush'd and pouted in a dull disdain,
● With leaden appetite, unapt to toy;
    She red and hot as coals of glowing fire,
    He red for shame, but frosty in desire.

● The studded bridle on a ragged bough
Nimbly she fastens:—O, how quick is love!—
The steed is stalled up, and even now
To tie the rider she begins to prove: 40
    Backward she push'd him, as she would be
       thrust,
    And govern'd him in strength, though not in lust.

So soon was she along as he was down,
Each leaning on their elbows and their hips:
Now doth she stroke his cheek, now doth he frown,
And 'gins to chide, but soon she stops his lips;
    And kissing speaks, with lustful language
      broken,
    'If thou wilt chide, thy lips shall never open.'

He burns with bashful shame: she with her tears
Doth quench the maiden burning of his cheeks:
Then with her windy sighs and golden hairs   51
To fan and blow them dry again she seeks:
●   He saith she is immodest, blames her 'miss;
    What follows more she murders with a kiss.

● Even as an empty eagle, sharp by fast,
● Tires with her beak on feathers, flesh and bone,
Shaking her wings, devouring all in haste,
Till either gorge be stuff'd or prey be gone;
    Even so she kissed his brow, his cheek, his chin,
    And where she ends she doth anew begin.   60

Forced to content, but never to obey,
Panting he lies and breatheth in her face;

She feedeth on the steam as on a prey,
And calls it heavenly moisture, air of grace;
   Wishing her cheeks were gardens full of flowers,
   So they were dew'd with such distilling showers.

Look, how a bird lies tangled in a net,
So fasten'd in her arms Adonis lies;
Pure shame and awed resistance made him fret,
Which bred more beauty in his angry eyes: 70
   Rain added to a river that is rank
   Perforce will force it overflow the bank.

Still she entreats, and prettily entreats,
For to a pretty ear she tunes her tale;
Still is he sullen, still he lours and frets,
'Twixt crimson shame and anger ashy-pale:
   Being red, she loves him best; and being white,
   Her best is better'd with a more delight.

Look how he can, she cannot choose but love;
And by her fair immortal hand she swears,   80
From his soft bosom never to remove,
Till he take truce with her contending tears,
   Which long have rain'd, making her cheeks all
      wet;
   And one sweet kiss shall pay this countless
      debt.

Upon this promise did he raise his chin,
Like a dive-dapper peering through a wave,
Who, being look'd on, ducks as quickly in;
So offers he to give what she did crave;
   But when her lips were ready for his pay,
   He winks, and turns his lips another way.   90

Never did passenger in summer's heat
More thirst for drink than she for this good turn.
Her help she sees, but help she cannot get;
She bathes in water, yet her fire must burn:
   'O, pity,' 'gan she cry, 'flint-hearted boy!
   'Tis but a kiss I beg; why art thou coy?

'I have been woo'd, as I entreat thee now,
Even by the stern and direful god of war,
Whose sinewy neck in battle ne'er did bow,
Who conquers where he comes in every jar: 100
   Yet hath he been my captive and my slave,
   And begg'd for that which thou unask'd shalt
      have.

'Over my altars hath he hung his lance,
His batter'd shield, his uncontrolled crest,
And for my sake hath learn'd to sport and dance,
To toy, to wanton, dally, smile and jest,
   Scorning his churlish drum and ensign red,
   Making my arms his field, his tent my bed.

'Thus he that overruled I oversway'd,
Leading him prisoner in a red-rose chain: 110
Strong-tempered steel his stronger strength
      obey'd,
Yet was he servile to my coy disdain.
   O, be not proud, nor brag not of thy might,
   For mastering her that foil'd the god of fight!

'Touch but my lips with those fair lips of thine,—
Though mine be not so fair, yet are they red—
The kiss shall be thine own as well as mine.
What seest thou in the ground? hold up thy head:

71 *rank*. Full.

86 *dive-dapper*. Dabchick.

90 *winks*. Shuts his eyes.

100 *jar*. Fight.

104 *uncontrolled crest*. Helmet which has never bowed in submission.

'Making my arms his field, his tent my bed'. Venus with Mars, the god of war, surprised by Vulcan. Painting by François Boucher (1703–1770)

127 *tender spring.* Incipient beard.

133 *hard-favour'd.* Hard-featured.

135 *O'erworn.* Worn out.

140 *gray.* i.e. blue or grey.

154 *list.* Wish.

157 *to . . . affected.* In love with.

161 *Narcissus.* In classical mythology a youth who was in love with his own image.

Narcissus. Painting by Follower of Giovanni Antonio Boltraffio (*c.*1466/7–1516)

Look in mine eye-balls, there thy beauty lies;
Then why not lips on lips, since eyes in eyes?

'Art thou ashamed to kiss? then wink again, 121
And I will wink: so shall the day seem night;
Love keeps his revels where there are but twain;
Be bold to play, our sport is not in sight:
    These blue-vein'd violets whereon we lean
    Never can blab, nor know not what we mean.

• 'The tender spring upon thy tempting lip
Shows thee unripe; yet mayst thou well be tasted:
Make use of time, let not advantage slip;
Beauty within itself should not be wasted: 130
    Fair flowers that are not gather'd in their prime
    Rot and consume themselves in little time.

• 'Were I hard-favour'd, foul, or wrinkled-old,
Ill-nurtured, crooked, churlish, harsh in voice,
• O'erworn, despised, rheumatic and cold,
Thick-sighted, barren, lean and lacking juice,
    Then mightst thou pause, for then I were not for
      thee;
    But having no defects, why dost abhor me?

'Thou canst not see one wrinkle in my brow;
• Mine eyes are gray and bright and quick in
    turning;   140
My beauty as the spring doth yearly grow,
My flesh is soft and plump, my marrow burning;
    My smooth moist hand, were it with thy hand
      felt,
    Would in thy palm dissolve, or seem to melt.

'Bid me discourse, I will enchant thine ear,
Or, like a fairy, trip upon the green,
Or, like a nymph, with long dishevell'd hair,
Dance on the sands, and yet no footing seen:
    Love is a spirit all compact of fire,
    Not gross to sink, but light, and will aspire. 150

'Witness this primrose bank whereon I lie;
These forceless flowers like sturdy trees support
    me;
Two strengthless doves will draw me through the
    sky,
• From morn till night, even where I list to sport me:
    Is love so light, sweet boy, and may it be
    That thou shouldst think it heavy unto thee?

• 'Is thine own heart to thine own face affected?
Can thy right hand seize love upon thy left?
Then woo thyself, be of thyself rejected,
Steal thine own freedom and complain on theft.
•   Narcissus so himself himself forsook,   161
    And died to kiss his shadow in the brook.

'Torches are made to light, jewels to wear,
Dainties to taste, fresh beauty for the use,
Herbs for their smell, and sappy plants to bear:
Things growing to themselves are growth's abuse:
    Seeds spring from seeds and beauty breedeth
      beauty;
    Thou wast begot; to get it is thy duty.

'Upon the earth's increase why shouldst thou feed,
Unless the earth with thy increase be fed?   170
By law of nature thou art bound to breed,
That thine may live when thou thyself art dead;

And so, in spite of death, thou dost survive,
In that thy likeness still is left alive.'

By this the love-sick queen began to sweat,
For where they lay the shadow had forsook them,
● And Titan, tired in the mid-day heat,
With burning eye did hotly overlook them;
   Wishing Adonis had his team to guide,
   So he were like him and by Venus' side.   180

● And now Adonis, with a lazy spright,
And with a heavy, dark, disliking eye,
His louring brows o'erwhelming his fair sight,
Like misty vapours when they blot the sky,
   Souring his cheeks cries 'Fie, no more of love!
   The sun doth burn my face; I must remove.'

'Ay me,' quoth Venus, 'young, and so unkind?
What bare excuses makest thou to be gone!
I'll sigh celestial breath, whose gentle wind
Shall cool the heat of this descending sun: 190
   I'll make a shadow for thee of my hairs;
   If they burn too, I'll quench them with my tears.

'The sun that shines from heaven shines but warm,
And, lo, I lie between that sun and thee:
The heat I have from thence doth little harm,
Thine eye darts forth the fire that burneth me;
   And were I not immortal, life were done
   Between this heavenly and earthly sun.

'Art thou obdurate, flinty, hard as steel,
Nay, more than flint, for stone at rain relenteth?
Art thou a woman's son, and canst not feel   201
What 'tis to love? how want of love tormenteth?
   O, had thy mother borne so hard a mind,
   She had not brought forth thee, but died unkind.

● 'What am I, that thou shouldst contemn me this?
Or what great danger dwells upon my suit?
What were thy lips the worse for one poor kiss?
Speak, fair; but speak fair words, or else be mute:
   Give me one kiss, I'll give it thee again,   209
   And one for interest, if thou wilt have twain.

'Fie, lifeless picture, cold and senseless stone,
Well-painted idol, image dull and dead,
Statue contenting but the eye alone,
Thing like a man, but of no woman bred!
●   Thou art no man, though of a man's complexion,
●   For men will kiss even by their own direction.'

This said, impatience chokes her pleading tongue,
And swelling passion doth provoke a pause;
Red cheeks and fiery eyes blaze forth her wrong;
● Being judge in love, she cannot right her cause:
   And now she weeps, and now she fain would
      speak,   221
   And now her sobs do her intendments break.

Sometimes she shakes her head and then his hand,
Now gazeth she on him, now on the ground;
Sometimes her arms infold him like a band:
She would, he will not in her arms be bound;
   And when from thence he struggles to be gone,
   She locks her lily fingers one in one.

'Fondling,' she saith, 'since I have hemm'd thee here
● Within the circuit of this ivory pale,   230

177 *Titan.* Sun-god. *tired.* Attired.

'And Titan, tired in the mid-day heat, With burning eye did hotly overlook them'. Drawing of Venus and Adonis by Peter Rudland, 1948

---

181 *lazy spright.* Dull spirit.

205 *this.* Thus.

215 *complexion.* Appearance.

216 *by . . . direction.* Without prompting.

220 *Being . . . cause.* i.e. Venus was the arbiter in all other love-disputes, but is herself unable to win this one.

230 *ivory pale.* Venus's arm.

235 *relief*. Pasture, feeding.

237 *brakes*. Thickets.

243 *if . . . slain*. So that if he himself were slain.

249 *how . . . wits*. How sane is she now?

251 *in thine . . . forlorn*. Wretched under your own rule (i.e. love).

257 *remorse*. Mercy.

260 *jennet*. A small Spanish horse.

272 *compass'd*. Arched.

275 *glisters*. Glitters.

276 *courage*. Spirit.

277 *told*. Counted.

I'll be a park, and thou shalt be my deer;
Feed where thou wilt, on mountain or in dale:
  Graze on my lips; and if those hills be dry,
  Stray lower, where the pleasant fountains lie.

'Within this limit is relief enough,
Sweet bottom-grass and high delightful plain,
Round rising hillocks, brakes obscure and rough,
To shelter thee from tempest and from rain:
  Then be my deer, since I am such a park; 239
  No dog shall rouse thee, though a thousand bark.'

At this Adonis smiles as in disdain,
That in each cheek appears a pretty dimple:
Love made those hollows, if himself were slain,
He might be buried in a tomb so simple;
  Foreknowing well, if there he came to lie,
  Why, there Love lived and there he could not die.

These lovely caves, these round enchanting pits,
Open'd their mouths to swallow Venus' liking.
Being mad before, how doth she now for wits?
Struck dead at first, what needs a second striking?
  Poor queen of love, in thine own law forlorn,
  To love a cheek that smiles at thee in scorn!

Now which way shall she turn? what shall she say?
Her words are done, her woes the more increasing;
The time is spent, her object will away,
And from her twining arms doth urge releasing.
  'Pity,' she cries, 'some favour, some remorse!'
  Away he springs and hasteth to his horse.

But, lo, from forth a copse that neighbours by,
A breeding jennet, lusty, young and proud, 260
Adonis' trampling courser doth espy,
And forth she rushes, snorts and neighs aloud:
  The strong-neck'd steed, being tied unto a tree,
  Breaketh his rein, and to her straight goes he.

Imperiously he leaps, he neighs, he bounds,
And now his woven girths he breaks asunder;
The bearing earth with his hard hoof he wounds,
Whose hollow womb resounds like heaven's thunder;
  The iron bit he crusheth 'tween his teeth,
  Controlling what he was controlled with. 270

His ears up-prick'd; his braided hanging mane
Upon his compass'd crest now stand on end;
His nostrils drink the air, and forth again,
As from a furnace, vapours doth he send:
  His eye, which scornfully glisters like fire,
  Shows his hot courage and his high desire.

Sometime he trots, as if he told the steps,
With gentle majesty and modest pride;
Anon he rears upright, curvets and leaps,
As who should say 'Lo, thus my strength is tried,
  And this I do to captivate the eye 281
  Of the fair breeder that is standing by.'

What recketh he his rider's angry stir,
His flattering 'Holla,' or his 'Stand, I say'?
What cares he now for curb or pricking spur?
For rich caparisons or trapping gay?
  He sees his love, and nothing else he sees,
  For nothing else with his proud sight agrees.

Look, when a painter would surpass the life,
In limning out a well-proportion'd steed,   290
His art with nature's workmanship at strife,
As if the dead the living should exceed;
    So did this horse excel a common one
    In shape, in courage, colour, pace and bone.

Round-hoof'd, short-jointed, fetlocks shag and
        long,
Broad breast, full eye, small head and nostril wide,
High crest, short ears, straight legs and passing
        strong,
Thin mane, thick tail, broad buttock, tender hide:
    Look, what a horse should have he did not lack,
    Save a proud rider on so proud a back.   300

Sometime he scuds far off and there he stares;
Anon he starts at stirring of a feather;
To bid the wind a base he now prepares,
And whether he run or fly they know not whether;
    For through his mane and tail the high wind
        sings,
    Fanning the hairs, who wave like feather'd
        wings.

He looks upon his love and neighs unto her;
She answers him as if she knew his mind:
Being proud, as females are, to see him woo her,
She puts on outward strangeness, seems unkind,
    Spurns at his love and scorns the heat he feels,
    Beating his kind embracements with her heels.

Then, like a melancholy malcontent,
He vails his tail that, like a falling plume,
Cool shadow to his melting buttock lent:
He stamps and bites the poor flies in his fume.
    His love, perceiving how he is enraged,
    Grew kinder, and his fury was assuaged.

His testy master goeth about to take him;
When, lo, the unback'd breeder, full of fear,   320
Jealous of catching, swiftly doth forsake him,
With her the horse, and left Adonis there:
    As they were mad, unto the wood they hie them,
    Out-stripping crows that strive to over-fly them.

All swoln with chafing, down Adonis sits,
Banning his boisterous and unruly beast:
And now the happy season once more fits,
That love-sick Love by pleading may be blest;
    For lovers say, the heart hath treble wrong
    When it is barr'd the aidance of the tongue.   330

An oven that is stopp'd, or river stay'd,
Burneth more hotly, swelleth with more rage:
So of concealed sorrow may be said;
Free vent of words love's fire doth assuage;
    But when the heart's attorney once is mute,
    The client breaks, as desperate in his suit.

He sees her coming, and begins to glow,
Even as a dying coal revives with wind,
And with his bonnet hides his angry brow;
Looks on the dull earth with disturbed mind,   340
    Taking no notice that she is so nigh,
    For all askance he holds her in his eye.

O, what a sight it was, wistly to view
How she came stealing to the wayward boy!

290 *limning out.* Drawing, painting.

292 *dead.* Lifeless image.

'So did this horse excel a common one . . .' Painting of
The Horses of Achilles, style of van Dyck (1599–1641)

295 *shag.* Shaggy.

301 *scuds.* Runs smoothly and fast.

303 *To bid . . . base.* Challenge the wind to a chase.

304 *whether.* Where.

310 *outward strangeness.* A show of indifference.

314 *vails.* Lowers.

320 *unback'd.* Not broken in.

321 *Jealous of catching.* Afraid of being caught.

326 *Banning.* Cursing.

328 *Love.* i.e. Venus.

334 *vent.* Utterance.

335 *heart's attorney.* Tongue.

343 *wistly.* Intently.

359 *his.* Its.

360 *chorus-like.* As a commentary.

363 *band.* Bond.

364 *engirts.* Encloses.

367 *the engine of her thoughts.* i.e. her tongue.

368 *mover . . . round.* Living creature on earth.

372 *bane.* Death by poison.

376 *grave.* Engrave.

"'For shame', he cries, 'let go, and let me go'". Drawing by Peter Rudland, 1948.

381 *bereft.* Deprived of him.

391 *jade.* Inferior horse.

393 *fair fee.* Due reward.

400 *agents.* Senses, organs.

To note the fighting conflict of her hue,
How white and red each other did destroy!
 But now her cheek was pale, and by and by
 It flash'd forth fire, as lightning from the sky.

Now was she just before him as he sat,
And like a lowly lover down she kneels; 350
With one fair hand she heaveth up his hat,
Her other tender hand his fair cheek feels:
 His tenderer cheek receives her soft hand's print,
 As apt as new-fall'n snow takes any dint.

O, what a war of looks was then between them!
Her eyes petitioners to his eyes suing;
His eyes saw her eyes as they had not seen them;
Her eyes woo'd still, his eyes disdain'd the wooing:
 And all this dumb play had his acts made plain
 With tears, which, chorus-like, her eyes did
  rain.

Full gently now she takes him by the hand, 361
A lily prison'd in a gaol of snow,
Or ivory in an alabaster band;
So white a friend engirts so white a foe:
 This beauteous combat, wilful and unwilling,
 Show'd like two silver doves that sit a-billing,

Once more the engine of her thoughts began:
'O fairest mover on this mortal round,
Would thou wert as I am, and I a man, 369
My heart all whole as thine, thy heart my wound;
 For one sweet look thy help I would assure thee,
 Though nothing but my body's bane would cure
  thee.'

'Give me my hand,' saith he, 'why dost thou feel
 it?'
'Give me my heart,' saith she, 'and thou shalt have
 it;
O, give it me, lest thy hard heart do steel it,
And being steel'd, soft sighs can never grave it:
 Then love's deep groans I never shall regard,
 Because Adonis' heart hath made mine hard.'

'For shame,' he cries, 'let go, and let me go;
My day's delight is past, my horse is gone, 380
And 'tis your fault I am bereft him so:
I pray you hence, and leave me here alone:
 For all my mind, my thought, my busy care,
 Is how to get my palfrey from the mare.'

Thus she replies: 'Thy palfrey, as he should,
Welcomes the warm approach of sweet desire:
Affection is a coal that must be cool'd;
Else, suffer'd, it will set the heart on fire:
 The sea hath bounds, but deep desire hath none;
 Therefore no marvel though thy horse be gone.

'How like a jade he stood, tied to the tree, 391
Servilely master'd with a leathern rein!
But when he saw his love, his youth's fair fee,
He held such petty bondage in disdain;
 Throwing the base thong from his bending crest,
 Enfranchising his mouth, his back, his breast.

'Who sees his true-love in her naked bed,
Teaching the sheets a whiter hue than white,
But, when his glutton eye so full hath fed,
His other agents aim at like delight? 400

Who is so faint, that dares not be so bold
To touch the fire, the weather being cold?

'Let me excuse thy courser, gentle boy;
And learn of him, I heartily beseech thee,
To take advantage on presented joy;
Though I were dumb, yet his proceedings teach
   thee:
  O, learn to love; the lesson is but plain,
  And once made perfect, never lost again.'

'I know not love,' quoth he, 'nor will not know it,
Unless it be a boar, and then I chase it;   410
● 'Tis much to borrow, and I will not owe it;
● My love to love is love but to disgrace it;
  For I have heard it is a life in death,
  That laughs and weeps, and all but with a breath.

'Who wears a garment shapeless and unfinish'd
Who plucks the bud before one leaf put forth?
If springing things be any jot diminish'd,
They wither in their prime, prove nothing worth:
● The colt that's back'd and burden'd being young
  Loseth his pride and never waxeth strong. 420

'You hurt my hand with wringing; let us part,
● And leave this idle theme, this bootless chat:
Remove your siege from my unyielding heart;
● To love's alarms it will not ope the gate:
  Dismiss your vows, your feigned tears, your
    flattery;
● For where a heart is hard they make no battery.'

'What! canst thou talk?' quoth she, 'hast thou a
   tongue?
O, would thou hadst not, or I had no hearing!
Thy mermaid's voice hath done me double wrong;
I had my load before, now press'd with bearing:
  Melodious discord, heavenly tune harsh-sound-
    ing,   431
  Ear's deep-sweet music, and heart's deep-sore
    wounding.

'Had I no eyes but ears, my ears would love
That inward beauty and invisible;
Or were I deaf, thy outward parts would move
● Each part in me that were but sensible:
  Though neither eyes nor ears, to hear nor see,
  Yet should I be in love by touching thee.

'Say, that the sense of feeling were bereft me,
And that I could not see, nor hear, nor touch, 440
And nothing but the very smell were left me,
Yet would my love to thee be still as much;
● For from the stillitory of thy face excelling
  Comes breath perfumed that breedeth love by
    smelling.

'But, O, what banquet wert thou to the taste,
Being nurse and feeder of the other four!
Would they not wish the feast might ever last,
And bid Suspicion double-lock the door,
  Lest Jealousy, that sour unwelcome guest, 449
  Should, by his stealing in, disturb the feast?'

Once more the ruby-colour'd portal open'd,
Which to his speech did honey passage yield;
Like a red morn, that ever yet betoken'd
Wreck to the seaman, tempest to the field,

Spearing a boar, 14th century. Illustration from Joseph Strutt's *Sports and Pastimes of the People of England*, 1810

---

411 *owe.* Undertake.

412 *My love . . . disgrace it.* i.e. what I feel about love is but to disgrace it.

419 *back'd.* Broken in.

422 *bootless.* Profitless.

424 *alarms.* Attacks.

426 *battery.* Forced entrance.

436 *sensible.* Sensitive (to impressions).

443 *stillitory.* A still.

456 *flaws*. Squalls.

457 *advisedly*. Attentively.

467 *silly*. Simple.

471 *wittily*. Cleverly.

472 *Fair fall*. Good luck to.

490 *repine*. Vexation.

497 *annoy*. Torment.

500 *shrewd*. Sharp.

506 *crimson liveries wear*. Red colours fade.

509 *writ on death*. Prophesied an epidemic.

Sorrow to shepherds, woe unto the birds,
● Gusts and foul flaws to herdmen and to herds.

● This ill presage advisedly she marketh:
Even as the wind is hush'd before it raineth,
Or as the wolf doth grin before he barketh,
Or as the berry breaks before it staineth,   460
  Or like the deadly bullet of a gun,
  His meaning struck her ere his words begun.

And at his look she flatly falleth down,
For looks kill love and love by looks reviveth;
A smile recures the wounding of a frown;
But blessed bankrupt, that by love so thriveth!
● The silly boy, believing she is dead,
  Claps her pale cheek, till clapping makes it red;

And all amazed brake off his late intent,
For sharply he did think to reprehend her,   470
● Which cunning love did wittily prevent:
● Fair fall the wit that can so well defend her!
  For on the grass she lies as she were slain,
  Till his breath breatheth life in her again.

He wrings her nose, he strikes her on the cheeks,
He bends her fingers, holds her pulses hard,
He chafes her lips; a thousand ways he seeks
To mend the hurt that his unkindness marr'd:
  He kisses her; and she, by her good will,
  Will never rise, so he will kiss her still.   480

The night of sorrow now is turn'd to day:
Her two blue windows faintly she up-heaveth,
Like the fair sun, when in his fresh array
He cheers the morn and all the earth relieveth;
  And as the bright sun glorifies the sky,
  So is her face illumined with her eye;

Whose beams upon his hairless face are fix'd,
As if from thence they borrow'd all their shine.
Were never four such lamps together mix'd,
● Had not his clouded with his brow's repine;   490
  But hers, which through the crystal tears gave
    light,
  Shone like the moon in water seen by night.

'O, where am I?' quoth she, 'in earth or heaven,
Or in the ocean drench'd, or in the fire?
What hour is this? or morn or weary even?
Do I delight to die, or life desire?
● But now I lived, and life was death's annoy;
  But now I died, and death was lively joy.

'O, thou didst kill me: kill me once again: 499
● Thy eyes' shrewd tutor, that hard heart of thine,
Hath taught them scornful tricks and such disdain
That they have murder'd this poor heart of mine;
  And these mine eyes, true leaders to their queen,
  But for thy piteous lips no more had seen.

'Long may they kiss each other, for this cure!
● O, never let their crimson liveries wear!
And as they last, their verdure still endure,
To drive infection from the dangerous year!
● That the star-gazers, having writ on death,   509
  May say, the plague is banish'd by thy breath.

'Pure lips, sweet seals in my soft lips imprinted,
What bargains may I make, still to be sealing?

To sell myself I can be well contented,
So thou wilt buy and pay and use good dealing;
●   Which purchase if thou make, for fear of slips
    Set thy seal-manual on my wax-red lips.

'A thousand kisses buys my heart from me;
And pay them at thy leisure, one by one.
● What is ten hundred touches unto thee?
    Are they not quickly told and quickly gone? 520
     Say, for non-payment that the debt should
      double,
    Is twenty hundred kisses such a trouble?'

'Fair queen,' quoth he, 'if any love you owe me,
Measure my strangeness with my unripe years:
Before I know myself, seek not to know me;
● No fisher but the ungrown fry forbears:
     The mellow plum doth fall, the green sticks fast,
     Or being early pluck'd is sour to taste.

● 'Look, the world's comforter, with weary gait,
    His day's hot task hath ended in the west;   530
    The owl, night's herald, shrieks, "'Tis very late;"
    The sheep are gone to fold, birds to their nest,
     And coal-black clouds that shadow heaven's light
     Do summon us to part and bid good night.

'Now let me say "Good night," and so say you;
If you will say so, you shall have a kiss.'
'Good night,' quoth she, and, ere he says 'Adieu,'
The honey fee of parting tender'd is:
     Her arms do lend his neck a sweet embrace;
     Incorporate then they seem; face grows to
      face.   540

Till, breathless, he disjoin'd, and backward drew
The heavenly moisture, that sweet coral mouth,
Whose precious taste her thirsty lips well knew,
Whereon they surfeit, yet complain on drouth:
     He with her plenty press'd, she faint with
      dearth,
     Their lips together glued, fall to the earth.

Now quick desire hath caught the yielding prey,
And glutton-like she feeds, yet never filleth;
Her lips are conquerors, his lips obey,
Paying what ransom the insulter willeth;   550
●   Whose vulture thought doth pitch the price so
     high,
    That she will draw his lips' rich treasure dry:

And having felt the sweetness of the spoil,
With blindfold fury she begins to forage;
Her face doth reek and smoke, her blood doth boil,
And careless lust stirs up a desperate courage;
     Planting oblivion, beating reason back,
●   Forgetting shame's pure blush and honour's
     wrack.

Hot, faint, and weary, with her hard embracing,
Like a wild bird being tamed with too much
    handling,   560
Or as the fleet-foot roe that's tired with chasing,
Or like the froward infant still'd with dandling,
     He now obeys, and now no more resisteth,
●   While she takes all she can, not all she listeth.

● What wax so frozen but dissolves with tempering,
  And yields at last to every light impression?

515 *slips.* Errors.

519 *touches.* Kisses.

526 *fry.* Young fish.

529 *world's comforter.* i.e. the sun.

'Now let me say "Goodnight", and so say you'. Engraving from a painting by Thomas Kirk, 1797

551 *vulture thought.* Ravenous imagination.

558 *wrack.* Wreck.

564 *listeth.* Wishes.

565 *tempering.* Warming.

568 *leave . . . commission.* i.e. liberties exceed permission.

'To hunt the boar with certain of his friends'. Painting of a huntsman, from the studio of Bonifazio (1487–1553)

590 *lawn.* A kind of fine linen.

595 *lists.* Tournament, jousting.

599 *Tantalus.* Classically, he was punished by sight of unobtainable food and drink. *annoy.* Torment.

600 *clip.* Embrace. *Elysium.* Paradise (classical).

602 *pine the maw.* Starve the stomach.

604 *helpless.* Affording no help.

617 *tushes.* Tusks.

Things out of hope are compass'd oft with venturing,
• Chiefly in love, whose leave exceeds commission:
    Affection faints not like a pale-faced coward,
    But then woos best when most his choice is
        froward.   570

When he did frown, O, had she then gave over,
Such nectar from his lips she had not suck'd.
Foul words and frowns must not repel a lover;
What though the rose have prickles, yet 'tis
        pluck'd:
    Were beauty under twenty locks kept fast,
    Yet love breaks through and picks them all at
        last.

For pity now she can no more detain him;
The poor fool prays her that he may depart:
She is resolved no longer to restrain him;
Bids him farewell, and look well to her heart,   580
    The which, by Cupid's bow she doth protest,
    He carries thence incaged in his breast.

'Sweet boy,' she says, 'this night I'll waste in
        sorrow,
For my sick heart commands mine eyes to watch.
Tell me, Love's master, shall we meet to-morrow?
Say, shall we? shall we? wilt thou make the match?'
    He tells her, no; to-morrow he intends
    To hunt the boar with certain of his friends.

'The boar!' quoth she; whereat a sudden pale,
• Like lawn being spread upon the blushing rose,
Usurps her cheek; she trembles at his tale,   591
And on his neck her yoking arms she throws:
    She sinketh down, still hanging by his neck,
    He on her belly falls, she on her back.

• Now is she in the very lists of love,
Her champion mounted for the hot encounter:
All is imaginary she doth prove,
He will not manage her, although he mount her;
•   That worse than Tantalus' is her annoy,
•   To clip Elysium and to lack her joy.   600

Even as poor birds, deceived with painted grapes,
• Do surfeit by the eye and pine the maw,
Even so she languisheth in her mishaps,
• As those poor birds that helpless berries saw.
    The warm effects which she in him finds missing
    She seeks to kindle with continual kissing.

But all in vain; good queen, it will not be:
She hath assay'd as much as may be proved;
Her pleading hath deserved a greater fee;   609
She's Love, she loves, and yet she is not loved.
    'Fie, fie,' he says, 'you crush me; let me go;
    You have no reason to withhold me so.'

'Thou hadst been gone,' quoth she, 'sweet boy, ere
        this,
But that thou told'st me thou wouldst hunt the boar.
O, be advised! thou know'st not what it is
With javelin's point a churlish swine to gore,
•   Whose tushes never sheathed he whetteth still,
    Like to a mortal butcher bent to kill.

'On his bow-back he hath a battle set
Of bristly pikes, that ever threat his foes;   620

His eyes, like glow-worms, shine when he doth
    fret;
His snout digs sepulchres where'er he goes;
    Being moved, he strikes whate'er is in his way,
    And whom he strikes his crooked tushes slay.

'His brawny sides, with hairy bristles arm'd,
● Are better proof than thy spear's point can enter;
His short thick neck cannot be easily harm'd;
Being ireful, on the lion he will venture:
    The thorny brambles and embracing bushes,
    As fearful of him, part, through whom he rushes.

'Alas, he nought esteems that face of thine, 631
To which Love's eyes pay tributary gazes;
● Nor thy soft hands, sweet lips and crystal eyne,
Whose full perfection all the world amazes;
    But having thee at vantage,—wondrous dread!—
●   Would root these beauties as he roots the mead.

'O, let him keep his loathsome cabin still;
Beauty hath nought to do with such foul fiends:
Come not within his danger by thy will; 639
They that thrive well take counsel of their friends.
    When thou didst name the boar, not to dissemble,
    I fear'd thy fortune, and my joints did tremble.

'Didst thou not mark my face? was it not white?
Saw'st thou not signs of fear lurk in mine eye?
Grew I not faint? and fell I not downright?
Within my bosom, whereon thou dost lie,
    My boding heart pants, beats, and takes no rest,
    But, like an earthquake, shakes thee on my
      breast.

● 'For where Love reigns, disturbing Jealousy
Doth call himself Affection's sentinel; 650
Gives false alarms, suggesteth mutiny,
And in a peaceful hour doth cry "Kill, kill!"
●   Distempering gentle Love in his desire,
    As air and water do abate the fire.

'This sour informer, this bate-breeding spy,
● This canker that eats up Love's tender spring,
This carry-tale, dissentious Jealousy,
That sometime true news, sometime false doth
    bring,
    Knocks at my heart and whispers in mine ear
    That if I love thee, I thy death should fear: 660

'And more than so, presenteth to mine eye
The picture of an angry-chafing boar,
Under whose sharp fangs on his back doth lie
An image like thyself, all stain'd with gore;
    Whose blood upon the fresh flowers being shed
    Doth make them droop with grief and hang the
      head.

'What should I do, seeing thee so indeed,
That tremble at the imagination?
The thought of it doth make my faint heart bleed,
And fear doth teach it divination: 670
    I prophesy thy death, my living sorrow,
    If thou encounter with the boar to-morrow.

'But if thou needs wilt hunt, be ruled by me;
● Uncouple at the timorous flying hare,
Or at the fox which lives by subtlety,
Or at the roe which no encounter dare:

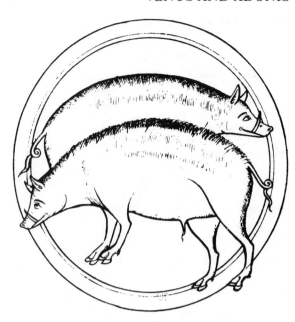

'His brawny sides, with hairy bristles arm'd'. Illustration of wild boars from a 12th century Latin bestiary

---

626 *better proof.* Stronger armour.

633 *eyne.* Eyes.

636 *root.* Root up.

649 *Jealousy.* Anxiety.

653 *Distempering* Diluting

656 *canker.* Disease of roses. *spring.* Bud.

674 *Uncouple.* Loose your hounds.

679 *purblind*. Weak-sighted.

682 *cranks*. Twists.

683 *musets*. Gaps in a hedge.

687 *conies*. Rabbits.

689 *sorteth*. Mingles.

690 *shifts*. Tricks.

694 *cold fault*. Lost scent.

695 *spend their mouths*. Give tongue.

697 *Wat*. Hare.

702 *passing-bell*. Rung for the dying man.

704 *indenting*. Zigzagging.

705 *envious*. Spiteful.

Coursing the hare. From a 17th century woodcut

725 *Dian*. Diana (chaste goddess of the moon).

726 *forsworn*. Having broken her vow of chastity.

728 *Cynthia*. i.e. Diana.

732 *her*. i.e. the moon.

Pursue these fearful creatures o'er the downs,
And on thy well-breath'd horse keep with thy
    hounds.

'And when thou hast on foot the purblind hare,
Mark the poor wretch, to overshoot his troubles
How he outruns the wind and with what care   681
He cranks and crosses with a thousand doubles:
    The many musets through the which he goes
    Are like a labyrinth to amaze his foes.

'Sometime he runs among a flock of sheep,
To make the cunning hounds mistake their smell,
And sometime where earth-delving conies keep,
To stop the loud pursuers in their yell,
    And sometime sorteth with a herd of deer:
    Danger deviseth shifts; wit waits on fear: 690

'For there his smell with others being mingled,
The hot scent-snuffing hounds are driven to
    doubt,
Ceasing their clamorous cry till they have singled
With much ado the cold fault cleanly out;
    Then do they spend their mouths: Echo replies,
    As if another chase were in the skies.

'By this, poor Wat, far off upon a hill,
Stands on his hinder legs with listening ear,
To hearken if his foes pursue him still:
Anon their loud alarums he doth hear;   700
    And now his grief may be compared well
    To one sore sick that hears the passing-bell.

'Then shalt thou see the dew-bedabbled wretch
Turn, and return, indenting with the way;
Each envious brier his weary legs doth scratch,
Each shadow makes him stop, each murmur stay:
    For misery is trodden on by many,
    And being low never relieved by any.

'Lie quietly, and hear a little more;
Nay, do not struggle, for thou shalt not rise: 710
To make thee hate the hunting of the boar,
Unlike myself thou hear'st me moralize,
    Applying this to that, and so to so;
    For love can comment upon every woe.

'Where did I leave?' 'No matter where;' quoth he,
'Leave me, and then the story aptly ends:
The night is spent.' 'Why, what of that?' quoth
    she.
'I am,' quoth he, 'expected of my friends;
    And now 'tis dark, and going I shall fall.'
    'In night,' quoth she, 'desire sees best of all. 720

'But if thou fall, O, then imagine this,
The earth, in love with thee, thy footing trips,
And all is but to rob thee of a kiss.
Rich preys make true men thieves; so do thy lips
    Make modest Dian cloudy and forlorn,
    Lest she should steal a kiss and die forsworn.

'Now of this dark night I perceive the reason:
Cynthia for shame obscures her silver shine,
Till forging Nature be condemn'd of treason, 729
For stealing moulds from heaven that were divine;
    Wherein she framed thee in high heaven's
      despite,
    To shame the sun by day and her by night.

'And therefore hath she bribed the Destinies
- To cross the curious workmanship of nature,
To mingle beauty with infirmities,
- And pure perfection with impure defeature,
Making it subject to the tyranny
Of mad mischances and much misery;

'As burning fevers, agues pale and faint,
- Life-poisoning pestilence and frenzies wood, 740
- The marrow-eating sickness, whose attaint
Disorder breeds by heating of the blood:
- Surfeits, imposthumes, grief, and damn'd despair,
Swear Nature's death for framing thee so fair.

- 'And not the least of all these maladies
But in one minute's fight brings beauty under:
- Both favour, savour, hue and qualities,
Whereat the impartial gazer late did wonder,
Are on the sudden wasted, thaw'd and done,
As mountain-snow melts with the midday sun.

'Therefore, despite of fruitless chastity, 751
Love-lacking vestals and self-loving nuns,
That on the earth would breed a scarcity
And barren dearth of daughters and of sons,
Be prodigal: the lamp that burns by night
Dries up his oil to lend the world his light.

'What is thy body but a swallowing grave,
Seeming to bury that posterity
Which by the rights of time thou needs must have,
If thou destroy them not in dark obscurity? 760
If so, the world will hold thee in disdain,
- Sith in thy pride so fair a hope is slain.

'So in thyself thyself art made away;
A mischief worse than civil home-bred strife,
Or theirs whose desperate hands themselves do slay,
- Or butcher-sire that reaves his son of life.
- Foul-cankering rust the hidden treasure frets,
But gold that's put to use more gold begets.'

'Nay, then,' quoth Adon, 'you will fall again
- Into your idle over-handled theme: 770
The kiss I gave you is bestow'd in vain,
And all in vain you strive against the stream;
For, by this black-faced night, desire's foul nurse,
- Your treatise makes me like you worse and worse.

'If love have lent you twenty thousand tongues,
And every tongue more moving than your own,
Bewitching like the wanton mermaid's songs,
Yet from mine ear the tempting tune is blown;
For know, my heart stands armed in mine ear,
And will not let a false sound enter there; 780

'Lest the deceiving harmony should run
Into the quiet closure of my breast;
And then my little heart were quite undone,
In his bedchamber to be barr'd of rest.
No, lady, no; my heart longs not to groan,
But soundly sleeps, while now it sleeps alone.

- 'What have you urged that I cannot reprove?
The path is smooth that leadeth on to danger:
I hate not love, but your device in love, 789
That lends embracements unto every stranger.

734 *curious.* Ingenious.

736 *defeature.* Disfigurement.

740 *wood.* Mad.

741 *attaint.* Infection.

743 *imposthumes.* Abscesses.

745–746 *And . . . under.* i.e. even the least of these ailments subdues beauty in a minute.

747 *favour.* Countenance.

762 *Sith.* Since.

766 *reaves.* Deprives.

767 *frets.* Eats away.

770 *over-handled.* Worn out.

774 *treatise.* Discourse.

787 *reprove.* Refute.

795 *simple semblance.* Innocent appearance.

808 *teen.* Grief.

813 *laund.* Glade.

848 *parasites.* Attendants.

You do it for increase: O strange excuse,
When reason is the bawd to lust's abuse!

'Call it not love, for Love to heaven is fled,
Since sweating Lust on earth usurp'd his name;
● Under whose simple semblance he hath fed
Upon fresh beauty, blotting it with blame;
   Which the hot tyrant stains and soon bereaves,
   As caterpillars do the tender leaves.

'Love comforteth like sunshine after rain,
But Lust's effect is tempest after sun;   800
Love's gentle spring doth always fresh remain,
Lust's winter comes ere summer half be done;
   Love surfeits not, Lust like a glutton dies;
   Love is all truth, Lust full of forged lies.

'More I could tell, but more I dare not say;
The text is old, the orator too green.
Therefore, in sadness, now I will away;
● My face is full of shame, my heart of teen:
   Mine ears, that to your wanton talk attended,
   Do burn themselves for having so offended.' 810

With this, he breaketh from the sweet embrace,
Of those fair arms which bound him to her breast,
● And homeward through the dark laund runs apace;
Leaves Love upon her back deeply distress'd.
   Look, how a bright star shooteth from the sky,
   So glides he in the night from Venus' eye;

Which after him she darts, as one on shore
Gazing upon a late-embarked friend,
Till the wild waves will have him seen no more,
Whose ridges with the meeting clouds contend:
   So did the merciless and pitchy night   821
   Fold in the object that did feed her sight.

Whereat amazed, as one that unaware
Hath dropp'd a precious jewel in the flood,
Or stonish'd as night-wanderers often are,
Their light blown out in some mistrustful wood,
   Even so confounded in the dark she lay,
   Having lost the fair discovery of her way.

And now she beats her heart, whereat it groans,
That all the neighbour caves, as seeming troubled,
Make verbal repetition of her moans;   831
Passion on passion deeply is redoubled:
   'Ay me!' she cries, and twenty times 'Woe, woe!'
   And twenty echoes twenty times cry so.

She marking them begins a wailing note
And sings extemporally a woeful ditty;
How love makes young men thrall and old men
       dote;
How love is wise in folly, foolish-witty:
   Her heavy anthem still concludes in woe,
   And still the choir of echoes answer so.   840

Her song was tedious and outwore the night,
For lovers' hours are long, though seeming short:
If pleased themselves, others, they think, delight
In such-like circumstance, with such-like sport:
   Their copious stories oftentimes begun
   End without audience and are never done.

For who hath she to spend the night withal
● But idle sounds resembling parasites,

Like shrill-tongued tapsters answering every call,
Soothing the humour of fantastic wits?   850
   She says ''Tis so:' they answer all ''Tis so;'
   And would say after her, if she said 'No.'

Lo, here the gentle lark, weary of rest,
• From his moist cabinet mounts up on high,
And wakes the morning, from whose silver breast
The sun ariseth in his majesty;
   Who doth the world so gloriously behold
   That cedar-tops and hills seem burnish'd gold.

Venus salutes him with this fair good-morrow:
'O thou clear god, and patron of all light,   860
From whom each lamp and shining star doth borrow
The beauteous influence that makes him bright,
   There lives a son that suck'd an earthly mother,
   May lend thee light, as thou dost lend to other.'

This said, she hasteth to a myrtle grove,
Musing the morning is so much o'erworn,
And yet she hears no tidings of her love:
She hearkens for his hounds and for his horn:
   Anon she hears them chant it lustily,
•   And all in haste she coasteth to the cry.   870

And as she runs, the bushes in the way
Some catch her by the neck, some kiss her face,
Some twine about her thigh to make her stay:
She wildly breaketh from their strict embrace,
   Like a milch doe, whose swelling dugs do ache,
   Hasting to feed her fawn hid in some brake.

By this, she hears the hounds are at a bay;
Whereat she starts, like one that spies an adder
Wreathed up in fatal folds just in his way,
The fear whereof doth make him shake and shud-
      der;   880
   Even so the timorous yelping of the hounds
   Appals her senses and her spirit confounds.

For now she knows it is no gentle chase,
But the blunt boar, rough bear, or lion proud,
Because the cry remaineth in one place,
Where fearfully the dogs exclaim aloud:
   Finding their enemy to be so curst,
•   They all strain courtesy who shall cope him first.

This dismal cry rings sadly in her ear,
Through which it enters to surprise her heart; 890
Who, overcome by doubt and bloodless fear,
With cold-pale weakness numbs each feeling part:
   Like soldiers, when their captain once doth yield,
   They basely fly and dare not stay the field.

Thus stands she in a trembling ecstasy;
Till, cheering up her senses all dismay'd,
She tells them 'tis a causeless fantasy,
And childish error, that they are afraid;
   Bids them leave quaking, bids them fear no
      more:—   899
   And with that word she spied the hunted boar,

Whose frothy mouth, bepainted all with red,
Like milk and blood being mingled both together,
A second fear through all her sinews spread,
Which madly hurries her she knows not whither:
   This way she runs, and now she will no further,
•   But back retires to rate the boar for murther.

854 *cabinet.* Nest.

870 *coasteth.* Approaches.

888 *cope.* Attack.

906 *rate.* Berate.

907 *spleens.* Fears.

909 *mated with.* Checked.

911 *respects.* Matters to consider.

914 *caitiff.* Wretch.

921 *welkin.* Sky.

948 *ebon.* Black.

953 *mortal vigour.* Deadly power.

956 *vail'd.* Lowered.

961 *lend and borrow.* i.e. reflect each other.

• A thousand spleens bear her a thousand ways;
She treads the path that she untreads again;
• Her more than haste is mated with delays,
Like the proceedings of a drunken brain,   910
•   Full of respects, yet nought at all respecting;
  In hand with all things, nought at all effecting.

Here kennell'd in a brake she finds a hound,
• And asks the weary caitiff for his master,
And there another licking of his wound,
'Gainst venom'd sores the only sovereign plaster;
  And here she meets another sadly scowling,
  To whom she speaks, and he replies with howl-
    ing.

When he hath ceased his ill-resounding noise,
Another flap-mouth'd mourner, black and grim,
• Against the welkin volleys out his voice;   921
Another and another answer him,
  Clapping their proud tails to the ground below,
  Shaking their scratch'd ears, bleeding as they go.

Look, how the world's poor people are amazed
At apparitions, signs and prodigies,
Whereon with fearful eyes they long have gazed,
Infusing them with dreadful prophecies;
  So she at these sad signs draws up her breath
  And sighing it again, exclaims on Death.   930

'Hard-favour'd tyrant, ugly, meagre, lean,
Hateful divorce of love,'—thus chides she Death,—
'Grim-grinning ghost, earth's worm, what dost
    thou mean
To stifle beauty and to steal his breath,
  Who when he lived, his breath and beauty set
  Gloss on the rose, smell to the violet?

'If he be dead,—O no, it cannot be,
Seeing his beauty, thou shouldst strike at it:—
O yes, it may; thou hast no eyes to see,
But hatefully at random dost thou hit.   940
  Thy mark is feeble age, but thy false dart
  Mistakes that aim and cleaves an infant's heart.

'Hadst thou but bid beware, then he had spoke,
And, hearing him, thy power had lost his power.
The Destinies will curse thee for this stroke;
They bid thee crop a weed, thou pluck'st a flower:
  Love's golden arrow at him should have fled,
•   And not Death's ebon dart, to strike him dead.

'Dost thou drink tears, that thou provokest such
    weeping?
What may a heavy groan advantage thee?   950
Why hast thou cast into eternal sleeping
Those eyes that taught all other eyes to see?
•   Now Nature cares not for thy mortal vigour,
  Since her best work is ruin'd with thy rigour.'

Here overcome, as one full of despair,
• She vail'd her eyelids, who, like sluices, stopt
The crystal tide that from her two cheeks fair
In the sweet channel of her bosom dropt;
  But through the flood-gates breaks the silver
    rain,   959
  And with his strong course opens them again.

• O, how her eyes and tears did lend and borrow!
Her eyes seen in the tears, tears in her eye;

Both crystals, where they view'd each other's
 sorrow,
Sorrow that friendly sighs sought still to dry;
 But like a stormy day, now wind, now rain,
 Sighs dry her cheeks, tears make them wet again.

Variable passions throng her constant woe,
As striving who should best become her grief;
• All entertain'd, each passion labours so,
That every present sorrow seemeth chief, 970
 But none is best: then join they all together,
 Like many clouds consulting for foul weather.

By this, far off she hears some huntsman hollo;
A nurse's song ne'er pleased her babe so well:
The dire imagination she did follow
This sound of hope doth labour to expel;
 For now reviving joy bids her rejoice,
 And flatters her it is Adonis' voice.

Whereat her tears began to turn their tide,
Being prison'd in her eye like pearls in glass; 980
Yet sometimes falls an orient drop beside,
Which her cheek melts, as scorning it should pass,
 To wash the foul face of the sluttish ground,
 Who is but drunken when she seemeth drown'd.

O hard-believing love, how strange it seems
Not to believe, and yet too credulous!
• Thy weal and woe are both of them extremes;
Despair and hope makes thee ridiculous:
 The one doth flatter thee in thoughts unlikely,
 In likely thoughts the other kills thee quickly.

Now she unweaves the web that she hath wrought;
Adonis lives, and Death is not to blame;
It was not she that call'd him all-to naught:
Now she adds honours to his hateful name;
• She clepes him king of graves and grave for
  kings,
 Imperious supreme of all mortal things.

'No, no,' quoth she, 'sweet Death, I did but jest;
Yet pardon me I felt a kind of fear
When as I met the boar, that bloody beast,
Which knows no pity, but is still severe; 1000
 Then, gentle shadow,—truth I must confess,—
 I rail'd on thee, fearing my love's decease.

''Tis not my fault: the boar provoked my tongue;
• Be wreak'd on him, invisible commander;
'Tis he, foul creature, that hath done thee wrong;
I did but act, he's author of thy slander:
 Grief hath two tongues, and never woman yet
 Could rule them both without ten women's wit.'

Thus hoping that Adonis is alive,
• Her rash suspect she doth extenuate; 1010
And that his beauty may the better thrive,
With Death she humbly doth insinuate;
 Tells him of trophies, statues, tombs, and stories
 His victories, his triumphs and his glories.

'O Jove,' quoth she, 'how much a fool was I
To be of such a weak and silly mind
To wail his death who lives and must not die
Till mutual overthrow of mortal kind!
 For he being dead, with him is beauty slain,
 And, beauty dead, black chaos comes again.

969 *entertain'd.* Admitted.

987 *weal.* Well-being.

995 *clepes.* Names.

1004 *wreak'd.* Revenged.

1010 *suspect.* Suspicion.

1032 *ashamed of*. Put to shame by.

Death of Adonis. Engraving from a painting by Thomas Kirk

'Fie, fie, fond love, thou art so full of fear   1021
As one with treasure laden, hemm'd with thieves;
Trifles, unwitnessed with eye or ear,
Thy coward heart with false bethinking grieves.'
  Even at this word she hears a merry horn,
  Whereat she leaps that was but late forlorn.

As falcon to the lure, away she flies;
The grass stoops not, she treads on it so light;
And in her haste unfortunately spies
The foul boar's conquest on her fair delight;   1030
  Which seen, her eyes, as murder'd with the
    view,
  Like stars ashamed of day, themselves withdrew;

Or, as the snail, whose tender horns being hit,
Shrinks backward in his shelly cave with pain,
And there, all smother'd up, in shade doth sit,
Long after fearing to creep forth again;
  So, at his bloody view, her eyes are fled
  Into the deep dark cabins of her head:

Where they resign their office and their light
To the disposing of her troubled brain;   1040
Who bids them still consort with ugly night,
And never wound the heart with looks again;
  Who, like a king perplexed in his throne,
  By their suggestion gives a deadly groan,

Whereat each tributary subject quakes;
As when the wind, imprison'd in the ground,
Struggling for passage, earth's foundation shakes,
Which with cold terror doth men's minds confound.
  This mutiny each part doth so surprise
  That from their dark beds once more leap her
    eyes;   1050

And, being open'd, threw unwilling light
Upon the wide wound that the boar had trench'd
In his soft flank; whose wonted lily white
With purple tears, that his wound wept, was
    drench'd:
  No flower was nigh, no grass, herb, leaf, or weed,
  But stole his blood and seem'd with him to bleed.

This solemn sympathy poor Venus noteth;
Over one shoulder doth she hang her head;
Dumbly she passions, franticly she doteth;
She thinks he could not die, he is not dead: 1060
  Her voice is stopt, her joints forget to bow;
  Her eyes are mad that they have wept till now.

Upon his hurt she looks so steadfastly,
That her sight dazzling makes the wound seem
    three;
And then she reprehends her mangling eye,
That makes more gashes where no breach should
    be:
  His face seems twain, each several limb is
    doubled;
  For oft the eye mistakes, the brain being
    troubled.

'My tongue cannot express my grief for one,
And yet,' quoth she, 'behold two Adons dead!
My sighs are blown away, my salt tears gone,
Mine eyes are turn'd to fire, my heart to lead:
  Heavy heart's lead, melt at mine eyes' red fire!
  So shall I die by drops of hot desire.

'Alas, poor world, what treasure hast thou lost!
What face remains alive that's worth the viewing?
Whose tongue is music now? what canst thou boast
Of things long since, or any thing ensuing?
   The flowers are sweet, their colours fresh and
      trim;   1079
   But true-sweet beauty lived and died with him.

'Bonnet nor veil henceforth no creature wear!
Nor sun nor wind will ever strive to kiss you:
Having no fair to lose, you need not fear;
The sun doth scorn you and the wind doth hiss
   you:
   But when Adonis lived, sun and sharp air
   Lurk'd like two thieves, to rob him of his fair:

'And therefore would he put his bonnet on,
Under whose brim the gaudy sun would peep;
The wind would blow it off and, being gone,
Play with his locks: then would Adonis weep;
   And straight, in pity of his tender years,   1091
   They both would strive who first should dry his
      tears.

'To see his face the lion walk'd along
Behind some hedge, because he would not fear him;
To recreate himself when he hath sung,
The tiger would be tame and gently hear him;
   If he had spoke, the wolf would leave his prey
   And never fright the silly lamb that day.

'When he beheld his shadow in the brook,
The fishes spread on it their golden gills;   1100
When he was by, the birds such pleasure took,
That some would sing, some other in their bills
   Would bring him mulberries and ripe-red cher-
      ries;
   He fed them with his sight, they him with berries.

'But this foul, grim, and urchin-snouted boar,
Whose downward eye still looketh for a grave,
Ne'er saw the beauteous livery that he wore;
Witness the entertainment that he gave:
   If he did see his face, why then I know
   He thought to kiss him, and hath kill'd him so.

''Tis true, 'tis true; thus was Adonis slain: 1111
He ran upon the boar with his sharp spear,
Who did not whet his teeth at him again,
But by a kiss thought to persuade him there;
   And nuzzling in his flank, the loving swine
   Sheathed unaware the tusk in his soft groin.

'Had I been tooth'd like him, I must confess,
With kissing him I should have kill'd him first;
But he is dead, and never did he bless
My youth with his; the more am I accurst.'   1120
   With this, she falleth in the place she stood,
   And stains her face with his congealed blood.

She looks upon his lips, and they are pale;
She takes him by the hand, and that is cold;
She whispers in his ears a heavy tale,
As if they heard the woeful words she told;
   She lifts the coffer-lids that close his eyes,
   Where, lo, two lamps, burnt out, in darkness lies;

Two glasses, where herself herself beheld
A thousand times, and now no more reflect;   1130

'. . . true-sweet beauty lived and died with him'. Detail from a painting of Venus and Adonis by Titian (d. 1576)

1094 *fear*. Frighten.

1105 *urchin-snouted*. Hedgehog-snouted (i.e. rooting).

1108 *entertainment*. Reception.

1114 *persuade him there*. i.e. to stay there.

Venus with the dead Adonis. Engraving from N. Rowe's edition of Shakespeare's works, 1709

1133 *spite*. Grief.

1137 *jealousy*. Mistrust.

1143 *o'erstraw'd*. Strewn.

1147 *sparing . . . riot*. Niggardly and prodigal.

1148 *tread the measures*. Dance.

1149 *staring*. Threatening.

1157 *toward*. Tractable.

1168 *A purple flower*. i.e. the anemone.

1177 *guise*. Habit.

Their virtue lost, wherein they late excell'd,
And every beauty robb'd of his effect:
● 'Wonder of time,' quoth she, 'this is my spite,
That, thou being dead, the day should yet be
light.

'Since thou art dead, lo, here I prophesy:
Sorrow on love hereafter shall attend:
● It shall be waited on with jealousy,
Find sweet beginning, but unsavoury end,
Ne'er settled equally, but high or low, 1139
That all love's pleasure shall not match his woe.

'It shall be fickle, false and full of fraud,
Bud and be blasted in a breathing-while;
● The bottom poison, and the top o'erstraw'd
With sweets that shall the truest sight beguile:
The strongest body shall it make most weak,
Strike the wise dumb and teach the fool to speak.

● 'It shall be sparing and too full of riot,
● Teaching decrepit age to tread the measures;
● The staring ruffian shall it keep in quiet,
Pluck down the rich, enrich the poor with trea-
sures; 1150
It shall be raging-mad and silly-mild,
Make the young old, the old become a child.

'It shall suspect where is no cause of fear;
It shall not fear where it should most mistrust;
It shall be merciful and too severe,
And most deceiving when it seems most just;
● Perverse it shall be where it shows most toward,
Put fear to valour, courage to the coward.

'It shall be cause of war and dire events,
And set dissension 'twixt the son and sire; 1160
Subject and servile to all discontents,
As dry combustious matter is to fire:
Sith in his prime Death doth my love destroy,
They that love best their loves shall not enjoy.'

By this, the boy that by her side lay kill'd
Was melted like a vapour from her sight,
And in his blood that on the ground lay spill'd,
● A purple flower sprung up, chequer'd with white,
Resembling well his pale cheeks and the blood
Which in round drops upon their whiteness stood.

She bows her head, the new-sprung flower to
smell, 1171
Comparing it to her Adonis' breath,
And says, within her bosom it shall dwell,
Since he himself is reft from her by death:
She crops the stalk, and in the breach appears
Green dropping sap, which she compares to tears.

● 'Poor flower,' quoth she, 'this was thy father's
guise—
Sweet issue of a more sweet-smelling sire—
For every little grief to wet his eyes:
To grow unto himself was his desire, 1180
And so 'tis thine; but know, it is as good
To wither in my breast as in his blood.

'Here was thy father's bed, here in my breast;
Thou art the next of blood, and 'tis thy right:
Lo, in this hollow cradle take thy rest,
My throbbing heart shall rock thee day and night:

There shall not be one minute in an hour
Wherein I will not kiss my sweet love's flower.'

Thus weary of the world, away she hies,   1189
And yokes her silver doves; by whose swift aid
Their mistress mounted through the empty skies
In her light chariot quickly is convey'd;
●   Holding their course to Paphos, where their
        queen
Means to immure herself and not be seen.

1193 *Paphos*. The abode of Venus in Cyprus.

Venus and Cupid with doves. Painting by François
Boucher (1703–1770)

The Rape
of Lucrece

1594

SHAKESPEARE fulfilled his promise to his young patron of 'some graver labour' next year, with *The Rape of Lucrece*, again printed by his Stratford schoolfellow (their fathers had business dealings with each other in their home-town, for Field's father was a tanner). Again the proofs were read in Blackfriars with proud care.

Once more the dedication was to Southampton, but with marked warmth of affection: 'the love I dedicate to your lordship is without end . . . What I have done is yours, what I have to do is yours; being part in all I have, devoted yours . . . Your lordship's in all duty, William Shakespeare.' One knows of no other Elizabethan dedication to a peer expressing such warmth of affection. At the same time one must observe the essential self-confidence and independence of spirit under the gentlemanly courtesy. When John Florio dedicated his Italian dictionary to his pupil, Southampton, he did so obsequiously, for he was not an independent gentleman but a household servant.

With typical abundance Shakespeare had intended a companion-piece. Both poems are intimate sex-pieces; in *Venus and Adonis* the youth was impossible to arouse, though Venus tried ever so hard; now the adult male, Tarquin, was all too much aroused, Lucrece his victim. She attached so much importance to her (married) chastity that she killed herself. It seems a bit excessive, and it is hard to take the tragedy seriously. Indeed, it is doubtful if Shakespeare did: the whole episode is depicted as if at a distance, with immense elaboration of every detail, relevant or not, so that one is never moved. One is even amused as the crisis approaches:

> What could he see but mightily he noted?
> What did he note but strongly he desired?
> What he beheld, on that he firmly doted,
> And in his will his wilful eye he tired.

At the crisis one is impelled to laugh:

> Her pity-pleading eyes are sadly fixed
> In the remorseless wrinkles of his face . . .

*Tarquin and
Lucrece.
Frontispiece to
Pope's edition of
the* Works . . . ,
1714

Everything is delineated in the elaborate detail of the Mannerist fashion, of the School of Fontainebleau, or, rather, the overloading of contemporary Netherlandish painting. Indeed, there is an improbable long digression on painting itself, which witnesses to – and was perhaps intended to impress with – the culture the actor-poet was acquiring through his entry into the aristocratic ambience of his patron. One has the feeling that the poem is, as it were, written in inverted commas; one is not moved by the plight of either lady, in the undignified situations in which they are placed – perhaps one can sympathise more with Venus: more fun in that poem. There is not much fun in *Lucrece*; it is a 'graver' labour, and Shakespeare's original bent was for comedy.

The poem has the enclosed atmosphere of a hothouse, with its Elizabethan bed with curtains drawn – no open Roman couch. Country images, however, creep in: we are given a deer-hunt, as in all his early work (what a fixation his 'sportive blood' had!); we have the falcon with its bells, and 'lagging fowls before the northern blast'; a charming description of a snail withdrawing its horns; the 'winter meads when sun doth melt their snow.' The violent tide roaring through an arch reminds us of the tide-race under London bridge.

Nevertheless there is an increased maturity in the reflections in this poem, with accumulating experience, some of them characteristic:

> So that in venturing ill we leave to be
> The things we are for that which we expect.

We cannot but note the fruits of his own experience in,

> The sweets we wish for turn to loathèd sours
> Even in the moment that we call them ours;

for these are precisely the terms in which, remarkably open-eyed and candid, he describes his experience with his dark mistress in the Sonnets:

> The expense of spirit in a waste of shame
> Is lust in action . . .
> Enjoyed no sooner but despisèd straight.

It has often been observed that *The Rape of Lucrece* parallels the Dark Lady sonnets, as *Venus and Adonis* does the earlier Southampton ones. Of course: writers' work reflects their experience. We observe his sympathy with the woman's point of view in,

> Though men can cover crimes with bold stern looks,
> Poor women's faces are their own faults' books –

even if this betrays the naiveté of the genuinely masculine type. One of the few moving lines in the poem describes the woman bearing her grief,

> And he the burden of a guilty mind.

Many classical references appear, the ghastly story of Tereus, for instance, which had gone into *Titus Andronicus*, and a whole passage about the fall of Troy which haunted his mind and would go into *Troilus and Cressida*. There is indeed too much in the poem, too much of everything, as in much of Elizabethan art (the *Faerie Queene*, for example): classic restraint was not yet to be achieved, though Marlowe was on the way to it, and Shakespeare was to achieve it with *Julius Caesar* and *Coriolanus*. It was, however, not natural to him.

The Rape of Lucrece had a measured success: five editions up to Shakespeare's death – not half those of the merrier poem. Gabriel Harvey said that it appealed to 'the wiser sort'. The poem was far, far too long. Shakespeare's instinct told him rightly to concentrate on play-writing and dramatic poetry, after these two noteworthy works to stake his superior claim to be considered a poet.

TO THE RIGHT
HONOVRABLE, HENRY
VVriothesley, Earle of Southhampton,
and Baron of Titchfield.

THE loue I dedicate to your Lordship is without end: wherof this Pamphlet without beginning is but a superfluous Moity. The warrant I haue of your Honourable disposition, not the worth of my vntutord Lines makes it assured of acceptance. VVhat I haue done is yours, what I haue to doe is yours, being part in all I haue, deuoted yours. VVere my worth greater, my duety would shew greater, meane time, as it is, it is bound to your Lordship; To whom I wish long life still lengthned with all happinesse.

Your Lordships in all duety.

William Shakespeare.

A 2

Dedication to the Earl of Southampton, The Rape of Lucrece, Quarto of 1594

THE RAPE OF LUCRECE.

TO THE
RIGHT HONOURABLE HENRY WRIOTHESLY,

EARL OF SOUTHAMPTON, AND BARON OF TICHFIELD.

THE love I dedicate to your lordship is without end; whereof this pamphlet, without beginning, is but a superfluous moiety. The warrant I have of your honourable disposition, not the worth of my untutored lines, makes it assured of acceptance. What I have done is yours; what I have to do is yours; being part in all I have, devoted yours. Were my worth greater, my duty would show greater; meantime, as it is, it is bound to your lordship, to whom I wish long life, still lengthened with all happiness.

Your lordship's in all duty,

WILLIAM SHAKESPEARE.

THE ARGUMENT.

LUCIUS TARQUINIUS, for his excessive pride surnamed Superbus, after he had caused his own father-in-law Servius Tullius to be cruelly murdered, and, contrary to the Roman laws and customs, not requiring or staying for the people's suffrages, had possessed himself of the kingdom, went, accompanied with his sons and other noblemen of Rome, to besiege Ardea. During which siege the principal men of the army meeting one evening at the tent of Sextus Tarquinius, the king's son, in their discourses after supper every one commended the virtues of his own wife: among whom Collatinus extolled the incomparable chastity of his wife Lucretia. In that pleasant humour they all posted to Rome; and intending, by their secret and sudden arrival, to make trial of that which every one had before avouched, only Collatinus finds his wife, though it were late in the night, spinning amongst her maids: the other ladies were all found dancing and revelling, or in several disports. Whereupon the noblemen yielded Collatinus the victory, and his wife the fame. At that time Sextus Tarquinius being inflamed with Lucrece' beauty, yet smothering his passions for the present, departed with the rest back to the camp; from whence he shortly after privily withdrew himself, and was, according to his estate, royally entertained and lodged by Lucrece at Collatium. The same night he treacherously stealeth into her chamber, violently ravished her, and early in the morning speedeth away. Lucrece, in this lamentable plight, hastily dispatcheth messengers, one to Rome for her father, another to the camp for Collatine. They came, the one accompanied with Junius Brutus, the other with Publius Valerius; and finding Lucrece attired in mourning habit, demanded the cause of her sorrow. She, first taking an oath of them for her revenge, revealed the actor, and whole manner of his dealing, and withal suddenly stabbed herself. Which done, with one consent they all vowed to root out the whole hated family of the Tarquins; and bearing the dead body to Rome, Brutus acquainted the people with the doer and manner of the vile deed, with a bitter invective against the tyranny of the king: wherewith the people were so moved, that with one consent and a general acclamation the Tarquins were all exiled, and the state government changed from kings to consuls.

● FROM the besieged Ardea all in post,
Borne by the trustless wings of false desire,
● Lust-breathed Tarquin leaves the Roman host,
And to Collatium bears the lightless fire
Which, in pale embers hid, lurks to aspire
  And girdle with embracing flames the waist
  Of Collatine's fair love, Lucrece the chaste.

Haply that name of 'chaste' unhappily set
● This bateless edge on his keen appetite;
● When Collatine unwisely did not let   10
To praise the clear unmatched red and white
● Which triumph'd in that sky of his delight,
●   Where mortal stars, as bright as heaven's beauties
●   With pure aspects did him peculiar duties.

1 *Ardea.* The capital of the Rutuli, twenty-four miles south of Rome. *all in post.* In great haste.

3 *Lust-breathed.* Inspired by lust.

9 *bateless.* Not to be blunted. *appetite.* Lust.

10 *let.* Forbear.

12 *sky of his delight.* Lucrece's face.

13 *mortal stars.* Eyes.

14 *aspects.* Glances. *peculiar.* Particular.

Opposite : A lady as Lucretia. Detail from a painting by Lorenzo Lotto (b.c.1480)

26 *date*. Bond, lease.

37 *Suggested*. Prompted.

40 *Braving compare*. Challenging comparison.

42 *hap*. Luck.

47 *liver*. The seat of sexual desire.

'When at Collatium this false lord arrived, Well was he welcomed by the Roman dame'. Lucrece and Tarquin. Illustration by J. Yunge-Bateman, 1948

63 *the red . . . white*. Red (the colour of beauty) should defend white (the colour of virtue); that is, by blushing.

For he the night before, in Tarquin's tent,
Unlock'd the treasure of his happy state;
What priceless wealth the heavens had him lent
In the possession of his beauteous mate;
Reckoning his fortune at such high-proud rate,
   That kings might be espoused to more fame, 20
   But king nor peer to such a peerless dame.

O happiness enjoy'd but of a few!
And, if possess'd, as soon decay'd and done
As is the morning's silver-melting dew
Against the golden splendour of the sun!
 ● An expired date, cancell'd ere well begun:
   Honour and beauty, in the owner's arms,
   Are weakly fortress'd from a world of harms.

Beauty itself doth of itself persuade
The eyes of men without an orator; 30
What needeth then apologies be made,
To set forth that which is so singular?
Or why is Collatine the publisher
   Of that rich jewel he should keep unknown
   From thievish ears, because it is his own?

Perchance his boast of Lucrece' sovereignty
 ● Suggested this proud issue of a king;
For by our ears our hearts oft tainted be:
Perchance that envy of so rich a thing,
 ● Braving compare, disdainfully did sting 40
   His high-pitch'd thoughts, that meaner men
     should vaunt
 ● That golden hap which their superiors want.

But some untimely thought did instigate
His all-too-timeless speed, if none of those:
His honour, his affairs, his friends, his state,
Neglected all, with swift intent he goes
 ● To quench the coal which in his liver glows.
   O rash false heat, wrapp'd in repentant cold,
   Thy hasty spring still blasts, and ne'er grows old!

When at Collatium this false lord arrived, 50
Well was he welcomed by the Roman dame,
Within whose face beauty and virtue strived
Which of them both should underprop her fame:
When virtue bragg'd, beauty would blush for
    shame;
   When beauty boasted blushes, in despite
   Virtue would stain that o'er with silver white.

But beauty, in that white intituled,
From Venus' doves doth challenge that fair field:
Then virtue claims from beauty beauty's red,
Which virtue gave the golden age to gild 60
Their silver cheeks, and call'd it then their shield;
   Teaching them thus to use it in the fight,
 ● When shame assail'd, the red should fence the
    white.

This heraldry in Lucrece' face was seen,
Argued by beauty's red and virtue's white:
Of either's colour was the other queen,
Proving from world's minority their right:
Yet their ambition makes them still to fight;
   The sovereignty of either being so great,
   That oft they interchange each other's seat. 70

Their silent war of lilies and of roses,
Which Tarquin view'd in her fair face's field,

In their pure ranks his traitor eye encloses;
Where, lest between them both it should be kill'd,
The coward captive vanquished doth yield
  To those two armies that would let him go,
  Rather than triumph in so false a foe.

Now thinks he that her husband's shallow tongue,—
The niggard prodigal that praised her so,—
In that high task hath done her beauty wrong, 80
Which far exceeds his barren skill to show:
Therefore that praise which Collatine doth owe
  Enchanted Tarquin answers with surmise,
  In silent wonder of still-gazing eyes.

This earthly saint, adored by this devil,
Little suspecteth the false worshipper;
For unstain'd thoughts do seldom dream on evil;
Birds never limed no secret bushes fear:
So guiltless she securely gives good cheer
  And reverend welcome to her princely guest, 90
  Whose inward ill no outward harm express'd:

• For that he colour'd with his high estate,
Hiding base sin in plaits of majesty;
That nothing in him seem'd inordinate,
Save sometime too much wonder of his eye,
Which, having all, all could not satisfy;
  But, poorly rich, so wanteth in his store,
  That, cloy'd with much, he pineth still for more.

But she, that never coped with stranger eyes,
• Could pick no meaning from their parling looks,
Nor read the subtle-shining secrecies   101
Writ in the glassy margents of such books:
She touch'd no unknown baits, nor fear'd no hooks;
• Nor could she moralize his wanton sight,
  More than his eyes were open'd to the light.

He stories to her ears her husband's fame,
Won in the fields of fruitful Italy;
And decks with praises Collatine's high name,
Made glorious by his manly chivalry
• With bruised arms and wreaths of victory: 110
  Her joy with heaved-up hand she doth express,
  And, wordless, so greets heaven for his success.

Far from the purpose of his coming hither,
He makes excuses for his being there:
No cloudy show of stormy blustering weather
Doth yet in his fair welkin once appear;
Till sable Night, mother of Dread and Fear,
  Upon the world dim darkness doth display,
  And in her vaulty prison stows the Day.

For then is Tarquin brought unto his bed,   120
• Intending weariness with heavy spright;
For, after supper, long he questioned
With modest Lucrece, and wore out the night:
Now leaden slumber with life's strength doth fight;
  And every one to rest themselves betake,
  Save thieves, and cares, and troubled minds,
      that wake.

As one of which doth Tarquin lie revolving
The sundry dangers of his will's obtaining;
Yet ever to obtain his will resolving,
Though weak-built hopes persuade him to ab-
      staining: 130
Despair to gain doth traffic oft for gaining;

92 *colour'd.* Cloaked.

100 *parling.* Speaking.

104 *moralize.* Interpret.

110 *bruised arms.* Battered armour.

121 *Intending.* Pretending.

132 *meed*. Reward.

176 *falchion*. A curved sword.

180 *advisedly*. Determinedly.

● And when great treasure is the meed proposed,
Though death be adjunct, there's no death sup-
    posed.

Those that much covet are with gain so fond,
For what they have not, that which they possess
They scatter and unloose it from their bond,
And so, by hoping more, they have but less;
Or, gaining more, the profit of excess
    Is but to surfeit, and such griefs sustain,
    That they prove bankrupt in this poor-rich
      gain.   140

The aim of all is but to nurse the life
With honour, wealth, and ease, in waning age;
And in this aim there is such thwarting strife,
That one for all, or all for one we gage;
As life for honour in fell battle's rage;
    Honour for wealth; and oft that wealth doth
      cost
    The death of all, and all together lost.

So that in venturing ill we leave to be
The things we are for that which we expect;
And this ambitious foul infirmity,   150
In having much, torments us with defect
Of that we have: so then we do neglect
    The thing we have; and, all for want of wit,
    Make something nothing by augmenting it.

Such hazard now must doting Tarquin make,
Pawning his honour to obtain his lust;
And for himself himself he must forsake:
Then where is truth, if there be no self-trust?
When shall he think to find a stranger just,   159
    When he himself himself confounds, betrays
    To slanderous tongues and wretched hateful
      days?

Now stole upon the time the dead of night,
When heavy sleep had closed up mortal eyes:
No comfortable star did lend his light,
No noise but owls' and wolves' death-boding cries;
Now serves the season that they may surprise
    The silly lambs: pure thoughts are dead and
      still,
    While lust and murder wake to stain and kill.

And now this lustful lord leap'd from his bed,
Throwing his mantle rudely o'er his arm;   170
Is madly toss'd between desire and dread;
Th' one sweetly flatters, th' other feareth harm;
But honest fear, bewitch'd with lust's foul charm,
    Doth too too oft betake him to retire,
    Beaten away by brain-sick rude desire.

● His falchion on a flint he softly smiteth,
That from the cold stone sparks of fire do fly;
Whereat a waxen torch forthwith he lighteth,
Which must be lode-star to his lustful eye;
● And to the flame thus speaks advisedly,   180
    'As from this cold flint I enforced this fire,
    So Lucrece must I force to my desire.'

Here pale with fear he doth premeditate
The dangers of his loathsome enterprise,
And in his inward mind he doth debate
What following sorrow may on this arise:
Then looking scornfully, he doth despise

His naked armour of still-slaughter'd lust,
And justly thus controls his thoughts unjust:

'Fair torch, burn out thy light, and lend it not
To darken her whose light excelleth thine:　191
And die, unhallow'd thoughts, before you blot
With your uncleanness that which is divine;
Offer pure incense to so pure a shrine:
　　Let fair humanity abhor the deed
●　　That spots and stains love's modest snow-white
　　　　weed.

'O shame to knighthood and to shining arms!
●O foul dishonour to my household's grave!
O impious act, including all foul harms!
A martial man to be soft fancy's slave!　200
True valour still a true respect should have;
　　Then my digression is so vile, so base,
　　That it will live engraven in my face.

'Yea, though I die, the scandal will survive,
And be an eye-sore in my golden coat;
Some loathsome dash the herald will contrive,
To cipher me how fondly I did dote;
That my posterity, shamed with the note,
　　Shall curse my bones, and hold it for no sin
　　To wish that I their father had not been.　210

'What win I, if I gain the thing I seek?
A dream, a breath, a froth of fleeting joy.
Who buys a minute's mirth to wail a week?
Or sells eternity to get a toy?
For one sweet grape who will the vine destroy?
　　Or what fond beggar, but to touch the crown,
　　Would with the sceptre straight be strucken
　　　　down?

'If Collatinus dream of my intent,
Will he not wake, and in a desperate rage
Post hither, this vile purpose to prevent?　220
This siege that hath engirt his marriage,
This blur to youth, this sorrow to the sage,
　　This dying virtue, this surviving shame,
　　Whose crime will bear an ever-during blame?

'O, what excuse can my invention make,
When thou shalt charge me with so black a deed?
Will not my tongue be mute, my frail joints
　　shake,
Mine eyes forego their light, my false heart bleed?
The guilt being great, the fear doth still exceed;
　　And extreme fear can neither fight nor fly, 230
　　But coward-like with trembling terror die.

'Had Collatinus kill'd my son or sire,
Or lain in ambush to betray my life,
Or were he not my dear friend, this desire
Might have excuse to work upon his wife,
●As in revenge or quittal of such strife:
　　But as he is my kinsman, my dear friend,
　　The shame and fault finds no excuse nor end.

'Shameful it is; ay, if the fact be known:
Hateful it is; there is no hate in loving:　240
I'll beg her love; but she is not her own:
The worst is but denial and reproving:
My will is strong, past reason's weak removing.
　　Who fears a sentence or an old man's saw
　　Shall by a painted cloth be kept in awe.'

196 *love's . . . weed.* i.e. chastity.

198 *household's grave.* Family tomb.

236 *quittal.* Payment.

251 *effects.* Desires.

264 *cheer.* Countenance.

267 *colour.* Pretext.

'Within his thoughts her heavenly image sits, And in the self-same seat sits Collatine'. Illustration by J. Yunge-Bateman, 1948

---

293 *seeks to.* Seeks aid from.

295 *servile powers.* i.e. bodily appetites.

296–298 *leader's . . . captain.* i.e. the heart.

303 *retires his ward.* Draws back the lock.

Thus, graceless, holds he disputation
'Tween frozen conscience and hot-burning will,
And with good thoughts makes dispensation,
Urging the worser sense for vantage still;
Which in a moment doth confound and kill   250
　　All pure effects, and doth so far proceed,
　　That what is vile shows like a virtuous deed.

Quoth he, ' She took me kindly by the hand,
And gazed for tidings in my eager eyes,
Fearing some hard news from the warlike band,
Where her beloved Collatinus lies.
O, how her fear did make her colour rise !
　　First red as roses that on lawn we lay,
　　Then white as lawn, the roses took away.

' And how her hand, in my hand being lock'd,   260
Forced it to tremble with her loyal fear !
Which struck her sad, and then it faster rock'd,
Until her husband's welfare she did hear;
　　Whereat she smiled with so sweet a cheer,
　　That had Narcissus seen her as she stood,
　　Self-love had never drown'd him in the flood.

' Why hunt I then for colour or excuses?
All orators are dumb when beauty pleadeth;
Poor wretches have remorse in poor abuses;
Love thrives not in the heart that shadows
　　　　dreadeth :   270
Affection is my captain, and he leadeth;
　　And when his gaudy banner is display'd,
　　The coward fights and will not be dismay'd.

' Then, childish fear, avaunt ! debating, die !
Respect and reason, wait on wrinkled age !
My heart shall never countermand mine eye :
Sad pause and deep regard beseem the sage;
My part is youth, and beats these from the
　　　　stage :
　　Desire my pilot is, beauty my prize;
　　Then who fears sinking where such treasure
　　　　lies?'   280

As corn o'ergrown by weeds, so heedful fear
Is almost choked by unresisted lust.
Away he steals with open listening ear,
Full of foul hope and full of fond mistrust;
Both which, as servitors to the unjust,
　　So cross him with their opposite persuasion,
　　That now he vows a league, and now invasion.

Within his thought her heavenly image sits,
And in the self-same seat sits Collatine :
That eye which looks on her confounds his wits;
That eye which him beholds, as more divine,   291
Unto a view so false will not incline;
　　But with a pure appeal seeks to the heart,
　　Which once corrupted takes the worser part;

And therein heartens up his servile powers,
Who, flatter'd by their leader's jocund show,
Stuff up his lust, as minutes fill up hours;
And as their captain, so their pride doth grow,
Paying more slavish tribute than they owe.
　　By reprobate desire thus madly led,   300
　　The Roman lord marcheth to Lucrece' bed.

The locks between her chamber and his will,
Each one by him enforced retires his ward;

But, as they open, they all rate his ill,
Which drives the creeping thief to some regard:
The threshold grates the door to have him heard;
   Night-wandering weasels shriek to see him
     there;
   They fright him, yet he still pursues his fear.

As each unwilling portal yields him way,
Through little vents and crannies of the place 310
The wind wars with his torch to make him stay,
And blows the smoke of it into his face,
   Extinguishing his conduct in this case;
   But his hot heart, which fond desire doth scorch,
   Puffs forth another wind that fires the torch:

And being lighted, by the light he spies
Lucretia's glove, wherein her needle sticks:
He takes it from the rushes where it lies,
And griping it, the needle his finger pricks;
As who should say 'This glove to wanton tricks
   Is not inured; return again in haste;   321
   Thou see'st our mistress' ornaments are chaste.'

But all these poor forbiddings could not stay him;
He in the worst sense construes their denial:
The doors, the wind, the glove, that did delay him,
He takes for accidental things of trial;
   Or as those bars which stop the hourly dial,
   Who with a lingering stay his course doth let,
   Till every minute pays the hour his debt.

'So, so,' quoth he, 'these lets attend the time, 330
Like little frosts that sometime threat the spring,
To add a more rejoicing to the prime,
And give the sneaped birds more cause to sing.
Pain pays the income of each precious thing;
   Huge rocks, high winds, strong pirates, shelves
     and sands,
   The merchant fears, ere rich at home he lands.'

Now is he come unto the chamber door,
That shuts him from the heaven of his thought,
Which with a yielding latch, and with no more,
Hath barr'd him from the blessed thing he sought.
So from himself impiety hath wrought,   341
   That for his prey to pray he doth begin,
   As if the heavens should countenance his sin.

But in the midst of his unfruitful prayer,
Having solicited th' eternal power
That his foul thoughts might compass his fair fair,
And they would stand auspicious to the hour,
Even there he starts: quoth he, 'I must deflower:
   The powers to whom I pray abhor this fact,
   How can they then assist me in the act?   350

'Then Love and Fortune be my gods, my guide!
My will is back'd with resolution:
Thoughts are but dreams till their effects be tried;
The blackest sin is clear'd with absolution;
Against love's fire fear's frost hath dissolution.
   The eye of heaven is out, and misty night
   Covers the shame that follows sweet delight.'

This said, his guilty hand pluck'd up the latch,
And with his knee the door he opens wide.
The dove sleeps fast that this night-owl will catch:
Thus treason works ere traitors be espied.   361
Who sees the lurking serpent steps aside;

304 *rate.* Berate, reproach.

313 *conduct.* Guide.

318 *rushes.* Rooms in Shakespeare's time were strewn with rushes.

327 *those bars . . . dial.* Divisions marked on a clock-face.

328 *let.* Hinder.

330 *attend.* Accompany.

332 *prime.* Spring.

333 *sneaped.* Nipped.

334 *income.* Enjoyment.

383 *this blessed league.* i.e. the union between Lucrece and Collatine.

387 *Cozening.* Cheating.

'Where, like a virtuous monument, she lies, To be admired of lewd unhallow'd eyes'. Illustration by J. Yunge-Bateman, 1948

But she, sound sleeping, fearing no such thing,
Lies at the mercy of his mortal sting.

Into the chamber wickedly he stalks,
And gazeth on her yet unstained bed.
The curtains being close, about he walks,
Rolling his greedy eyeballs in his head:
By their high treason is his heart misled;
    Which gives the watch-word to his hand full
      soon   370
    To draw the cloud that hides the silver moon.

Look, as the fair and fiery-pointed sun,
Rushing from forth a cloud, bereaves our sight;
Even so, the curtain drawn, his eyes begun
To wink, being blinded with a greater light:
Whether it is that she reflects so bright,
    That dazzleth them, or else some shame sup-
      posed;
    But blind they are, and keep themselves en-
      closed.

O, had they in that darksome prison died!
Then had they seen the period of their ill;   380
Then Collatine again, by Lucrece' side,
In his clear bed might have reposed still:
● But they must ope, this blessed league to kill:
    And holy-thoughted Lucrece to their sight
    Must sell her joy, her life, her world's delight.

Her lily hand her rosy cheek lies under,
● Cozening the pillow of a lawful kiss:
Who, therefore angry, seems to part in sunder,
Swelling on either side to want his bliss;
Between whose hills her head entombed is: 390
    Where, like a virtuous monument, she lies,
    To be admired of lewd unhallow'd eyes.

Without the bed her other fair hand was,
On the green coverlet; whose perfect white
Show'd like an April daisy on the grass,
With pearly sweat, resembling dew of night.
Her eyes, like marigolds, had sheathed their
    light,
    And canopied in darkness sweetly lay,
    Till they might open to adorn the day.

Her hair, like golden threads, play'd with her
    breath;   400
O modest wantons! wanton modesty!
Showing life's triumph in the map of death,
And death's dim look in life's mortality:
Each in her sleep themselves so beautify,
    As if between them twain there were no strife,
    But that life lived in death, and death in life.

Her breasts, like ivory globes circled with blue,
A pair of maiden worlds unconquered,
Save of their lord no bearing yoke they knew,
And him by oath they truly honoured.   410
These worlds in Tarquin new ambition bred;
    Who, like a foul usurper, went about
    From this fair throne to heave the owner out.

What could he see but mightily he noted?
What did he note but strongly he desired?
What he beheld, on that he firmly doted,
And in his will his wilful eye he tired.
With more than admiration he admired

Her azure veins, her alabaster skin,
Her coral lips, her snow-white dimpled chin.

As the grim lion fawneth o'er his prey,   421
Sharp hunger by the conquest satisfied,
So o'er this sleeping soul doth Tarquin stay,
His rage of lust by gazing qualified;
Slack'd, not suppress'd; for standing by her side,
    His eye, which late this mutiny restrains,
    Unto a greater uproar tempts his veins:

And they, like straggling slaves for pillage fighting,
Obdurate vassals fell exploits effecting,
In bloody death and ravishment delighting,   430
Nor children's tears nor mothers' groans respect-
        ing,
Swell in their pride, the onset still expecting:
    Anon his beating heart, alarum striking,
    Gives the hot charge and bids them do their
        liking.

His drumming heart cheers up his burning eye,
His eye commends the leading to his hand;
His hand, as proud of such a dignity,
Smoking with pride, march'd on to make his stand
On her bare breast, the heart of all her land;
    Whose ranks of blue veins, as his hand did
        scale,   440
    Left their round turrets destitute and pale.

They, mustering to the quiet cabinet
Where their dear governess and lady lies,
Do tell her she is dreadfully beset,
And fright her with confusion of their cries:
She, much amazed, breaks ope her lock'd-up eyes,
    Who, peeping forth this tumult to behold,
    Are by his flaming torch dimm'd and con-
        troll'd.

Imagine her as one in dead of night   449
From forth dull sleep by dreadful fancy waking,
That thinks she hath beheld some ghastly sprite,
Whose grim aspect sets every joint a-shaking;
What terror 'tis! but she, in worser taking,
    From sleep disturbed, heedfully doth view
    The sight which makes supposed terror true.

Wrapp'd and confounded in a thousand fears,
Like to a new-kill'd bird she trembling lies;
She dares not look; yet, winking, there appears
Quick-shifting antics, ugly in her eyes:
Such shadows are the weak brain's forgeries; 460
    Who, angry that the eyes fly from their lights,
    In darkness daunts them with more dreadful
        sights.

His hand, that yet remains upon her breast,—
Rude ram, to batter such an ivory wall!—
May feel her heart—poor citizen!—distress'd,
Wounding itself to death, rise up and fall,
Beating her bulk, that his hand shakes withal.
    This moves in him more rage and lesser pity,
    To make the breach and enter this sweet city.

First, like a trumpet, doth his tongue begin   470
To sound a parley to his heartless foe;
Who o'er the white sheet peers her whiter chin,
The reason of this rash alarm to know,
Which he by dumb demeanour seeks to show;

436 *commends.* Commits.

459 *antics.* Grotesque figures.

476 *colour*. Pretext.

486 *will*. Desire, lust.

507 *Coucheth*. Makes cower.

'If thou deny, then force must work my way . . .'
Tarquinius and Lucretia. Painting after Giovanni
Bilivert (1576–1644)

530 *simple*. Herb.

But she with vehement prayers urgeth still
Under what colour he commits this ill.

● Thus he replies: 'The colour in thy face,
That even for anger makes the lily pale,
And the red rose blush at her own disgrace,
Shall plead for me and tell my loving tale: 480
Under that colour am I come to scale
   Thy never-conquer'd fort: the fault is thine,
   For those thine eyes betray thee unto mine.

'Thus I forestall thee, if thou mean to chide:
Thy beauty hath ensnared thee to this night,
● Where thou with patience must my will abide;
My will that marks thee for my earth's delight,
Which I to conquer sought with all my might;
   But as reproof and reason beat it dead,
   By thy bright beauty was it newly bred.   490

'I see what crosses my attempt will bring;
I know what thorns the growing rose defends;
I think the honey guarded with a sting;
All this beforehand counsel comprehends:
But will is deaf and hears no heedful friends;
   Only he hath an eye to gaze on beauty,
   And dotes on what he looks, 'gainst law or duty.

'I have debated, even in my soul,
What wrong, what shame, what sorrow I shall
      breed;
But nothing can affection's course control,   500
Or stop the headlong fury of his speed.
I know repentant tears ensue the deed,
   Reproach, disdain, and deadly enmity;
   Yet strive I to embrace mine infamy.'

This said, he shakes aloft his Roman blade,
Which, like a falcon towering in the skies,
● Coucheth the fowl below with his wings' shade,
Whose crooked beak threats if he mount he dies:
So under his insulting falchion lies
   Harmless Lucretia, marking what he tells   510
   With trembling fear, as fowl hear falcon's
      bells.

'Lucrece,' quoth he, 'this night I must enjoy
      thee:
If thou deny, then force must work my way,
For in thy bed I purpose to destroy thee:
That done, some worthless slave of thine I'll slay,
To kill thine honour with thy life's decay;
   And in thy dead arms do I mean to place him,
   Swearing I slew him, seeing thee embrace him.

'So thy surviving husband shall remain
The scornful mark of every open eye;   520
Thy kinsmen hang their heads at this disdain,
Thy issue blurr'd with nameless bastardy:
And thou, the author of their obloquy,
   Shalt have thy trespass cited up in rhymes,
   And sung by children in succeeding times.

'But if thou yield, I rest thy secret friend:
The fault unknown is as a thought unacted;
A little harm done to a great good end
For lawful policy remains enacted.
● The poisonous simple sometimes is compacted
   In a pure compound; being so applied,   531
   His venom in effect is purified.

'Then, for thy husband and thy children's sake,
● Tender my suit: bequeath not to their lot
The shame that from them no device can take,
The blemish that will never be forgot;
● Worse than a slavish wipe or birth-hour's blot:
For marks descried in men's nativity
Are nature's faults, not their own infamy.'

● Here with a cockatrice' dead-killing eye   540
He rouseth up himself and makes a pause;
While she, the picture of pure piety,
● Like a white hind under the gripe's sharp claws,
Pleads, in a wilderness where are no laws,
To the rough beast that knows no gentle
right,
Nor aught obeys but his foul appetite.

But when a black-faced cloud the world doth
threat,
In his dim mist the aspiring mountains hiding,
From earth's dark womb some gentle gust doth get,
Which blows these pitchy vapours from their bid-
ing,   550
● Hindering their present fall by this dividing;
So his unhallow'd haste her words delays,
And moody Pluto winks while Orpheus plays.

Yet, foul night-waking cat, he doth but dally,
While in his hold-fast foot the weak mouse panteth:
● Her sad behaviour feeds his vulture folly,
A swallowing gulf that even in plenty wanteth:
His ear her prayers admits, but his heart granteth
No penetrable entrance to her plaining:
Tears harden lust, though marble wear with rain-
ing.   560

Her pity-pleading eyes are sadly fixed
In the remorseless wrinkles of his face;
Her modest eloquence with sighs is mixed,
Which to her oratory adds more grace.
She puts the period often from his place;
And midst the sentence so her accent breaks,
That twice she doth begin ere once she speaks.

She conjures him by high almighty Jove,
By knighthood, gentry, and sweet friendship's
oath,
By her untimely tears, her husband's love,   570
By holy human law, and common troth,
By heaven and earth, and all the power of both,
That to his borrow'd bed he make retire,
And stoop to honour, not to foul desire.

Quoth she, 'Reward not hospitality
● With such black payment as thou hast pretended;
Mud not the fountain that gave drink to thee;
Mar not the thing that cannot be amended;
End thy ill aim before thy shoot be ended;
● He is no woodman that doth bend his bow   580
To strike a poor unseasonable doe.

'My husband is thy friend; for his sake spare me:
Thyself art mighty; for thine own sake leave me:
Myself a weakling; do not then ensnare me:
Thou look'st not like deceit; do not deceive me.
My sighs, like whirlwinds, labour hence to heave
thee:
If ever man were moved with woman's moans,
Be moved with my tears, my sighs, my groans:

534 *Tender*. Regard.

537 *slavish wipe*. Slave's brand. *birth-hour's blot*. Birth mark upon bastards.

540 *cockatrice*. Mythical beast that would kill with a look.

543 *gripe*. Vulture or eagle.

551 *present*. Immediate.

553 *Pluto*. Roman god of the underworld. *Orpheus*. Mythical musician who could move objects with the music of his lyre.

Orpheus in the underworld, before Pluto and Proserpine. From a German woodcut, 1503

556 *vulture folly*. Devouring madness.

576 *pretended*. Proposed.

580 *woodman*. Sportsman.

603 *seeded.* Matured.

605 *in thy hope.* As heir to the throne.

608 *vassal actors.* Those who do the deed, even if subjects.

622 *laud.* Praise.

640 *repeal.* Recall from exile.

'All which together, like a troubled ocean,
Beat at thy rocky and wreck-threatening heart,
To soften it with their continual motion; 591
For stones dissolved to water do convert.
O, if no harder than a stone thou art,
　Melt at my tears, and be compassionate!
　Soft pity enters at an iron gate.

'In Tarquin's likeness I did entertain thee:
Hast thou put on his shape to do him shame?
To all the host of heaven I complain me,
Thou wrong'st his honour, wound'st his princely
　　name.　599
Thou art not what thou seem'st; and if the same,
　Thou seem'st not what thou art, a god, a king;
　For kings like gods should govern every thing.

● 'How will thy shame be seeded in thine age,
When thus thy vices bud before thy spring!
● If in thy hope thou darest do such outrage,
What darest thou not when once thou art a king?
O, be remember'd, no outrageous thing
●　From vassal actors can be wiped away;
　Then kings' misdeeds cannot be hid in clay.

'This deed will make thee only loved for fear; 610
But happy monarchs still are fear'd for love:
With foul offenders thou perforce must bear,
When they in thee the like offences prove:
If but for fear of this, thy will remove;
　For princes are the glass, the school, the book,
　Where subjects' eyes do learn, do read, do look.

'And wilt thou be the school where Lust shall
　　learn?
Must he in thee read lectures of such shame?
Wilt thou be glass wherein it shall discern
Authority for sin, warrant for blame, 620
To privilege dishonour in thy name?
●　Thou back'st reproach against long-living laud,
　And makest fair reputation but a bawd.

'Hast thou command? by him that gave it thee,
From a pure heart command thy rebel will:
Draw not thy sword to guard iniquity,
For it was lent thee all that brood to kill.
Thy princely office how canst thou fulfil,
　When, pattern'd by thy fault, foul sin may say,
　He learn'd to sin, and thou didst teach the way?

'Think but how vile a spectacle it were, 631
To view thy present trespass in another.
Men's faults do seldom to themselves appear;
Their own transgressions partially they smother:
This guilt would seem death-worthy in thy brother.
　O, how are they wrapp'd in with infamies
　That from their own misdeeds askance their
　　eyes!

'To thee, to thee, my heaved-up hands appeal,
Not to seducing lust, thy rash relier:
● I sue for exiled majesty's repeal; 640
Let him return, and flattering thoughts retire:
His true respect will prison false desire,
　And wipe the dim mist from thy doting eyne,
　That thou shalt see thy state and pity mine.'

'Have done,' quoth he: 'my uncontrolled tide
Turns not, but swells the higher by this let.

Small lights are soon blown out, huge fires abide,
And with the wind in greater fury fret:
The petty streams that pay a daily debt
   To their salt sovereign, with their fresh falls'
      haste   650
   Add to his flow, but alter not his taste.'

'Thou art,' quoth she, 'a sea, a sovereign king;
And, lo, there falls into thy boundless flood
Black lust, dishonour, shame, misgoverning,
Who seek to stain the ocean of thy blood.
If all these petty ills shall change thy good,
   Thy sea within a puddle's womb is hearsed,
   And not the puddle in thy sea dispersed.

'So shall these slaves be king, and thou their slave;
Thou nobly base, they basely dignified;   660
Thou their fair life, and they thy fouler grave:
Thou loathed in their shame, they in thy pride:
The lesser thing should not the greater hide;
   The cedar stoops not to the base shrub's foot,
   But low shrubs wither at the cedar's root.

'So let thy thoughts, low vassals to thy state'—
'No more,' quoth he; 'by heaven, I will not hear
      thee:
Yield to my love; if not, enforced hate,
Instead of love's coy touch, shall rudely tear thee:
That done, despitefully I mean to bear thee 670
   Unto the base bed of some rascal groom,
   To be thy partner in this shameful doom.'

This said, he sets his foot upon the light,
For light and lust are deadly enemies:
Shame folded up in blind concealing night,
When most unseen, then most doth tyrannize.
The wolf hath seized his prey, the poor lamb cries;
   Till with her own white fleece her voice controll'd
   Entombs her outcry in her lips' sweet fold:

For with the nightly linen that she wears   680
He pens her piteous clamours in her head;
Cooling his hot face in the chastest tears
That ever modest eyes with sorrow shed.
O, that prone lust should stain so pure a bed!
   The spots whereof could weeping purify,
   Her tears should drop on them perpetually.

But she hath lost a dearer thing than life,
And he hath won what he would lose again:
This forced league doth force a further strife;
This momentary joy breeds months of pain; 690
This hot desire converts to cold disdain:
   Pure Chastity is rifled of her store,
   And Lust, the thief, far poorer than before.

Look, as the full-fed hound or gorged hawk,
Unapt for tender smell or speedy flight,
Make slow pursuit, or altogether balk
The prey wherein by nature they delight;
So surfeit-taking Tarquin fares this night:
   His taste delicious, in digestion souring, 699
   Devours his will, that lived by foul devouring.

O, deeper sin than bottomless conceit
Can comprehend in still imagination!
Drunken Desire must vomit his receipt,
Ere he can see his own abomination.
While Lust is in his pride, no exclamation

678 *controll'd.* Overpowered.

695 *tender smell.* Weak scent, as in hunting.

701 *conceit.* Imagination.

710 *recreant.* False, cowardly.

721 *spotted princess.* i.e. the soul.

722 *subjects.* Senses, passions.

'She bears the load of lust he left behind, And he the burthen of a guilty mind'. Illustration by J. Yunge-Bateman, 1948

---

743 *heavy convertite.* Sad penitent.

755 *water that doth eat in steel,* i.e. aqua fortis (nitric acid).

Can curb his heat or rein his rash desire,
Till like a jade Self-will himself doth tire.

And then with lank and lean discolour'd cheek,
With heavy eye, knit brow, and strengthless
pace,
Feeble Desire, all recreant, poor, and meek, 710
Like to a bankrupt beggar wails his case:
The flesh being proud, Desire doth fight with
Grace,
For there it revels; and when that decays,
The guilty rebel for remission prays.

So fares it with this faultful lord of Rome,
Who this accomplishment so hotly chased;
For now against himself he sounds this doom,
That through the length of times he stands dis-
graced:
Besides, his soul's fair temple is defaced;
To whose weak ruins muster troops of cares, 720
To ask the spotted princess how she fares.

She says, her subjects with foul insurrection
Have batter'd down her consecrated wall,
And by their mortal fault brought in subjection
Her immortality, and made her thrall
To living death and pain perpetual:
Which in her prescience she controlled still,
But her foresight could not forestall their will.

Even in this thought through the dark night he
stealeth,
A captive victor that hath lost in gain; 730
Bearing away the wound that nothing healeth,
The scar that will, despite of cure, remain;
Leaving his spoil perplex'd in greater pain.
She bears the load of lust he left behind,
And he the burthen of a guilty mind.

He like a thievish dog creeps sadly thence;
She like a wearied lamb lies panting there;
He scowls and hates himself for his offence;
She, desperate, with her nails her flesh doth tear;
He faintly flies, sweating with guilty fear; 740
She stays, exclaiming on the direful night;
He runs, and chides his vanish'd, loathed de-
light.

He thence departs a heavy convertite;
She there remains a hopeless castaway;
He in his speed looks for the morning light;
She prays she never may behold the day,
'For day,' quoth she, 'night's scapes doth open lay,
And my true eyes have never practised how
To cloak offences with a cunning brow.

'They think not but that every eye can see 750
The same disgrace which they themselves behold;
And therefore would they still in darkness be,
To have their unseen sin remain untold;
For they their guilt with weeping will unfold,
And grave, like water that doth eat in steel,
Upon my cheeks what helpless shame I feel.'

Here she exclaims against repose and rest,
And bids her eyes hereafter still be blind.
She wakes her heart by beating on her breast,
And bids it leap from thence, where it may find
Some purer chest to close so pure a mind. 761

Frantic with grief thus breathes she forth her
    spite
Against the unseen secrecy of night:

'O comfort-killing Night, image of hell!
Dim register and notary of shame!
Black stage for tragedies and murders fell!
Vast sin-concealing chaos! nurse of blame!
Blind muffled bawd! dark harbour for defame!
    Grim cave of death! whispering conspirator
    With close-tongued treason and the ravisher!

'O hateful, vaporous, and foggy Night!   771
Since thou art guilty of my cureless crime,
Muster thy mists to meet the eastern light,
● Make war against proportion'd course of time;
Or if thou wilt permit the sun to climb
    His wonted height, yet ere he go to bed,
    Knit poisonous clouds about his golden head.

'With rotten damps ravish the morning air;
Let their exhaled unwholesome breaths make sick
The life of purity, the supreme fair,   780
● Ere he arrive his weary noon-tide prick;
And let thy misty vapours march so thick,
    That in their smoky ranks his smother'd light
    May set at noon and make perpetual night.

'Were Tarquin Night, as he is but Night's child,
● The silver-shining queen he would distain;
● Her twinkling handmaids too, by him defiled,
Through Night's black bosom should not peep
    again:
So should I have co-partners in my pain;
    And fellowship in woe doth woe assuage,   790
●   As palmers' chat makes short their pilgrimage.

'Where now I have no one to blush with me,
To cross their arms and hang their heads with mine,
To mask their brows and hide their infamy;
But I alone alone must sit and pine,
Seasoning the earth with showers of silver brine,
    Mingling my talk with tears, my grief with
        groans,
    Poor wasting monuments of lasting moans.

'O Night, thou furnace of foul-reeking smoke,
Let not the jealous Day behold that face   800
Which underneath thy black all-hiding cloak
Immodestly lies martyr'd with disgrace!
Keep still possession of thy gloomy place,
    That all the faults which in thy reign are made
    May likewise be sepulchred in thy shade!

'Make me not object to the tell-tale Day!
The light will show, character'd in my brow,
The story of sweet chastity's decay,
The impious breach of holy wedlock vow:
Yea, the illiterate, that know not how   810
    To cipher what is writ in learned books,
    Will quote my loathsome trespass in my looks.

'The nurse, to still her child, will tell my story,
And fright her crying babe with Tarquin's name:
The orator, to deck his oratory,
Will couple my reproach to Tarquin's shame;
Feast-finding minstrels, tuning my defame,
    Will tie the hearers to attend each line,
    How Tarquin wronged me, I Collatine.

774 *proportion'd.* Regular.

781 *noon-tide prick.* The point of noon.

786 *distain.* Defile.

787 *handmaids.* i.e. stars.

791 *palmers.* Pilgrims.

820 *senseless reputation.* i.e. for being free from sensuality.

825 *attaint.* Disgrace.

828 *crest-wounding.* Striking at family honour.

830 *mot.* Motto (word).

851 *folly.* Sensuality.

859 *barns.* Stores in a barn.

" 'The aged man that coffers-up his gold is plagued with cramps and gouts . . .' " Detail from a painting by Marinus van Reymerswaele (*c.*1509–67)

874 *ill-annexed Opportunity.* Wickedly taken opportunity.

• ' Let my good name, that senseless reputation,
  For Collatine's dear love be kept unspotted : 821
  If that be made a theme for disputation,
  The branches of another root are rotted,
  And undeserved reproach to him allotted
•   That is as clear from this attaint of mine
    As I, ere this, was pure to Collatine.

'O unseen shame! invisible disgrace!
• O unfelt sore! crest-wounding, private scar!
  Reproach is stamp'd in Collatinus' face,
• And Tarquin's eye may read the mot afar, 830
  How he in peace is wounded, not in war.
    Alas, how many bear such shameful blows,
    Which not themselves, but he that gives them
      knows!

'If, Collatine, thine honour lay in me,
From me by strong assault it is bereft.
My honey lost, and I, a drone-like bee,
Have no perfection of my summer left,
But robb'd and ransack'd by injurious theft :
  In thy weak hive a wandering wasp hath crept,
  And suck'd the honey which thy chaste bee kept.

'Yet am I guilty of thy honour's wrack ; 841
Yet for thy honour did I entertain him ;
Coming from thee, I could not put him back,
For it had been dishonour to disdain him :
Besides, of weariness he did complain him,
  And talk'd of virtue : O unlook'd-for evil,
  When virtue is profaned in such a devil!

'Why should the worm intrude the maiden bud?
Or hateful cuckoos hatch in sparrows' nests?
Or toads infect fair founts with venom mud? 850
• Or tyrant folly lurk in gentle breasts?
  Or kings be breakers of their own behests?
    But no perfection is so absolute,
    That some impurity doth not pollute.

'The aged man that coffers-up his gold
Is plagued with cramps and gouts and painful
    fits ;
And scarce hath eyes his treasure to behold,
But like still-pining Tantalus he sits,
• And useless barns the harvest of his wits ;
    Having no other pleasure of his gain 860
    But torment that it cannot cure his pain.

'So then he hath it when he cannot use it,
And leaves it to be master'd by his young ;
Who in their pride do presently abuse it :
Their father was too weak, and they too strong,
To hold their cursed-blessed fortune long.
  The sweets we wish for turn to loathed sours
  Even in the moment that we call them ours.

'Unruly blasts wait on the tender spring ;
Unwholesome weeds take root with precious
    flowers ; 870
The adder hisses where the sweet birds sing ;
What virtue breeds iniquity devours :
We have no good that we can say is ours,
•   But ill-annexed Opportunity
    Or kills his life or else his quality.

'O Opportunity, thy guilt is great!
'Tis thou that executest the traitor's treason :

Thou set'st the wolf where he the lamb may get;
Whoever plots the sin, thou 'point'st the season;
'Tis thou that spurn'st at right, at law, at reason;
    And in thy shady cell, where none may spy him,
    Sits Sin, to seize the souls that wander by him.

'Thou makest the vestal violate her oath;
Thou blow'st the fire when temperance is thaw'd;
Thou smother'st honesty, thou murder'st troth;
Thou foul abettor! thou notorious bawd!
Thou plantest scandal and displacest laud:
    Thou ravisher, thou traitor, thou false thief,
    Thy honey turns to gall, thy joy to grief!

'Thy secret pleasure turns to open shame,   890
Thy private feasting to a public fast,
Thy smoothing titles to a ragged name,
Thy sugar'd tongue to bitter wormwood taste:
Thy violent vanities can never last.
    How comes it then, vile Opportunity,
    Being so bad, such numbers seek for thee?

'When wilt thou be the humble suppliant's friend,
And bring him where his suit may be obtain'd?
When wilt thou sort an hour great strifes to end?
Or free that soul which wretchedness hath chain'd?
Give physic to the sick, ease to the pain'd?   901
    The poor, lame, blind, halt, creep, cry out for
      thee;
    But they ne'er meet with Opportunity.

'The patient dies while the physician sleeps;
The orphan pines while the oppressor feeds;
Justice is feasting while the widow weeps;
Advice is sporting while infection breeds:
Thou grant'st no time for charitable deeds:
    Wrath, envy, treason, rape, and murder's rages,
    Thy heinous hours wait on them as their pages.

'When Truth and Virtue have to do with thee,
A thousand crosses keep them from thy aid:
They buy thy help; but Sin ne'er gives a fee,
He gratis comes; and thou art well appaid
As well to hear as grant what he hath said.
    My Collatine would else have come to me
    When Tarquin did, but he was stay'd by thee.

'Guilty thou art of murder and of theft,
Guilty of perjury and subornation,
Guilty of treason, forgery, and shift,   920
Guilty of incest, that abomination;
An accessary by thine inclination
    To all sins past, and all that are to come,
    From the creation to the general doom.

'Mis-shapen Time, copesmate of ugly Night,
Swift subtle post, carrier of grisly care,
Eater of youth, false slave to false delight,
Base watch of woes, sin's pack-horse, virtue's
      snare;
Thou nursest all and murder'st all that are:
    O, hear me then, injurious, shifting Time! 930
    Be guilty of my death, since of my crime.

'Why hath thy servant, Opportunity,
Betray'd the hours thou gavest me to repose,
Cancell'd my fortunes, and enchained me
To endless date of never-ending woes?
Time's office is to fine the hate of foes;

899 *sort.* Fit.

907 *Advice.* Medical advice.

910 *heinous.* Hateful.

919 *subornation.* Bribing someone to commit perjury.

920 *shift.* Trickery.

924 *general doom.* Last Judgement.

925 *copesmate.* Familiar companion.

926 *post.* Post-rider.

928 *watch of woes.* Watchman counting woes like the passing hours.

930 *shifting.* Cheating.

935 *date.* Lease.

936 *fine.* Bring to an end

'Time's glory is to calm contending kings . . .' Time
rescuing Truth from a cave. From a Venetian engraving,
1552

---

950 *springs*. Saplings.

953 *beldam*. Old woman.

964 *wit*. i.e. wisdom.

985 *orts*. Scraps of food.

To eat up errors by opinion bred,
Not spend the dowry of a lawful bed.

'Time's glory is to calm contending kings,
To unmask falsehood and bring truth to light, 940
To stamp the seal of time in aged things,
To wake the morn and sentinel the night,
To wrong the wronger till he render right,
    To ruinate proud buildings with thy hours,
    And smear with dust their glittering golden
        towers;

'To fill with worm-holes stately monuments,
To feed oblivion with decay of things,
To blot old books and alter their contents,
To pluck the quills from ancient ravens' wings,
● To dry the old oak's sap and cherish springs, 950
    To spoil antiquities of hammer'd steel,
    And turn the giddy round of Fortune's wheel;

● 'To show the beldam daughters of her daughter,
To make the child a man, the man a child,
To slay the tiger that doth live by slaughter,
To tame the unicorn and lion wild,
To mock the subtle in themselves beguiled,
    To cheer the ploughman with increaseful
        crops,
    And waste huge stones with little water-drops.

'Why work'st thou mischief in thy pilgrimage,
Unless thou couldst return to make amends? 961
One poor retiring minute in an age
Would purchase thee a thousand thousand friends,
● Lending him wit that to bad debtors lends:
    O, this dread night, wouldst thou one hour
        come back,
    I could prevent this storm and shun thy wrack!

'Thou ceaseless lackey to eternity,
With some mischance cross Tarquin in his flight:
Devise extremes beyond extremity,
To make him curse this cursed crimeful night:
Let ghastly shadows his lewd eyes affright; 971
    And the dire thought of his committed evil
    Shape every bush a hideous shapeless devil.

'Disturb his hours of rest with restless trances,
Afflict him in his bed with bedrid groans;
Let there bechance him pitiful mischances,
To make him moan; but pity not his moans:
Stone him with harden'd hearts, harder than stones;
    And let mild women to him lose their mildness,
    Wilder to him than tigers in their wildness. 980

'Let him have time to tear his curled hair,
Let him have time against himself to rave,
Let him have time of Time's help to despair,
Let him have time to live a loathed slave,
● Let him have time a beggar's orts to crave,
    And time to see one that by alms doth live
    Disdain to him disdained scraps to give.

'Let him have time to see his friends his foes,
And merry fools to mock at him resort;
Let him have time to mark how slow time goes
In time of sorrow, and how swift and short 991
His time of folly and his time of sport;
    And ever let his unrecalling crime
    Have time to wail th' abusing of his time.

'O Time, thou tutor both to good and bad,
Teach me to curse him that thou taught'st this ill!
At his own shadow let the thief run mad,
Himself himself seek every hour to kill!
Such wretched hands such wretched blood should
    spill;
    For who so base would such an office have   1000
    As slanderous deathsman to so base a slave?

'The baser is he, coming from a king,
● To shame his hope with deeds degenerate:
The mightier man, the mightier is the thing
That makes him honour'd, or begets him hate;
For greatest scandal waits on greatest state.
    The moon being clouded presently is miss'd,
    But little stars may hide them when they list.

'The crow may bathe his coal-black wings in mire,
And unperceived fly with the filth away;   1010
But if the like the snow-white swan desire,
The stain upon his silver down will stay.
● Poor grooms are sightless night, kings glorious
    day:
    Gnats are unnoted wheresoe'er they fly,
    But eagles gazed upon with every eye.

'Out, idle words, servants to shallow fools!
Unprofitable sounds, weak arbitrators!
● Busy yourselves in skill-contending schools;
Debate where leisure serves with dull debaters:
To trembling clients be you mediators: 1020
    For me, I force not argument a straw,
    Since that my case is past the help of law.

'In vain I rail at Opportunity,
At Time, at Tarquin, and uncheerful Night;
In vain I cavil with mine infamy,
● In vain I spurn at my confirm'd despite:
● This helpless smoke of words doth me no right.
    The remedy indeed to do me good
    Is to let forth my foul-defiled blood.

'Poor hand, why quiver'st thou at this decree?
Honour thyself to rid me of this shame;   1031
For if I die, my honour lives in thee;
But if I live, thou livest in my defame:
Since thou couldst not defend thy loyal dame,
    And wast afeard to scratch her wicked foe,
    Kill both thyself and her for yielding so.'

This said, from her be-tumbled couch she starteth,
To find some desperate instrument of death:
But this no slaughterhouse no tool imparteth
To make more vent for passage of her breath; 1040
Which, thronging through her lips, so vanisheth
    As smoke from Ætna, that in air consumes,
    Or that which from discharged cannon fumes.

'In vain,' quoth she, 'I live, and seek in vain
Some happy mean to end a hapless life.
I fear'd by Tarquin's falchion to be slain,
Yet for the self-same purpose seek a knife:
But when I fear'd I was a loyal wife:
    So am I now: O no, that cannot be;
    Of that true type hath Tarquin rifled me. 1050

'O, that is gone for which I sought to live,
And therefore now I need not fear to die.
To clear this spot by death, at least I give

1003 *hope.* Expectation as heir.

1013 *grooms.* Servants, labourers.

1018 *skill-contending schools.* i.e. universities where disputations were regular.

1026 *despite.* Wrong.

1027 *helpless . . . words.* Useless talk.

1062 *graff*. Graft.

'Nor shall he smile at thee in secret thought, Nor laugh with his companions at thy state'. Illustration by J. Yunge-Bateman, 1948

1067 *interest*. Share.

1070 *will dispense*. Pardon.

1074 *sable ground*. Black background.

1079 *Philomel*. The nightingale.

1084 *cloudy*. Sorrowful.

1095 *wayward once*. Having once become angry.

1096 *bear them mild*. Behave mildly.

A badge of fame to slander's livery;
A dying life to living infamy:
  Poor helpless help, the treasure stol'n away,
  To burn the guiltless casket where it lay!

'Well, well, dear Collatine, thou shalt not know
The stained taste of violated troth;
I will not wrong thy true affection so,   1060
To flatter thee with an infringed oath;
● 'This bastard graff shall never come to growth:
  He shall not boast who did thy stock pollute
  That thou art doting father of his fruit.

'Nor shall he smile at thee in secret thought,
Nor laugh with his companions at thy state:
● But thou shalt know thy interest was not bought
Basely with gold, but stol'n from forth thy gate.
For me, I am the mistress of my fate,
● And with my trespass never will dispense, 1070
  Till life to death acquit my forced offence.

'I will not poison thee with my attaint,
Nor fold my fault in cleanly-coin'd excuses;
● My sable ground of sin I will not paint,
To hide the truth of this false night's abuses:
My tongue shall utter all; mine eyes, like sluices,
  As from a mountain-spring that feeds a dale,
  Shall gush pure streams to purge my impure tale.'

● By this, lamenting Philomel had ended
The well-tuned warble of her nightly sorrow, 1080
And solemn night with slow sad gait descended
To ugly hell; when, lo, the blushing morrow
Lends light to all fair eyes that light will borrow:
● But cloudy Lucrece shames herself to see,
  And therefore still in night would cloister'd be.

Revealing day through every cranny spies,
And seems to point her out where she sits weeping;
To whom she sobbing speaks: 'O eye of eyes,
Why pry'st thou through my window? leave thy peeping:
Mock with thy tickling beams eyes that are sleeping: 1090
  Brand not my forehead with thy piercing light,
  For day hath nought to do what's done by night.'

Thus cavils she with every thing she sees:
True grief is fond and testy as a child,
● Who wayward once, his mood with nought agrees:
● Old woes, not infant sorrows, bear them mild;
Continuance tames the one; the other wild,
  Like an unpractised swimmer plunging still,
  With too much labour drowns for want of skill.

So she, deep-drenched in a sea of care,   1100
Holds disputation with each thing she views,
And to herself all sorrow doth compare;
No object but her passion's strength renews;
And as one shifts, another straight ensues:
  Sometime her grief is dumb and hath no words;
  Sometime 'tis mad and too much talk affords.

The little birds that tune their morning's joy
Make her moans mad with their sweet melody:
For mirth doth search the bottom of annoy;
Sad souls are slain in merry company;   1110
Grief best is pleased with grief's society:

True sorrow then is feelingly sufficed
● When with like semblance it is sympathized,

'Tis double death to drown in ken of shore;
He ten times pines that pines beholding food;
To see the salve doth make the wound ache more;
Great grief grieves most at that would do it good;
Deep woes roll forward like a gentle flood,
   Who, being stopp'd, the bounding banks o'er-
     flows;
   Grief dallied with nor law nor limit knows. 1120

'You mocking birds,' quoth she, 'your tunes
    entomb
Within your hollow-swelling feather'd breasts,
And in my hearing be you mute and dumb:
My restless discord loves no stops nor rests;
A woeful hostess brooks not merry guests:
●   Relish your nimble notes to pleasing ears;
●   Distress likes dumps when time is kept with
    tears.

'Come, Philomel, that sing'st of ravishment,
Make thy sad grove in my dishevell'd hair:
As the dank earth weeps at thy languishment,
So I at each sad strain will strain a tear,   1131
● And with deep groans the diapason bear;
●   For burden-wise I'll hum on Tarquin still,
●   While thou on Tereus descant'st better skill.

'And whiles against a thorn thou bear'st thy part,
To keep thy sharp woes waking, wretched I,
To imitate thee well, against my heart
Will fix a sharp knife to affright mine eye;
Who, if it wink, shall thereon fall and die.
●   These means, as frets upon an instrument, 1140
    Shall tune our heart-strings to true languish-
    ment.

'And for, poor bird, thou sing'st not in the day,
As shaming any eye should thee behold,
Some dark deep desert, seated from the way,
That knows not parching heat nor freezing cold,
Will we find out; and there we will unfold
   To creatures stern sad tunes, to change their
    kinds:
   Since men prove beasts, let beasts bear gentle
    minds.'

As the poor frighted deer, that stands at gaze,
Wildly determining which way to fly,   1150
Or one encompass'd with a winding maze,
That cannot tread the way out readily;
So with herself is she in mutiny,
   To live or die which of the twain were better,
   When life is shamed, and death reproach's
    debtor.

'To kill myself,' quoth she, 'alack, what were it,
But with my body my poor soul's pollution?
They that lose half with greater patience bear it
Than they whose whole is swallow'd in confusion.
● That mother tries a merciless conclusion   1160
   Who, having two sweet babes, when death
    takes one,
   Will slay the other and be nurse to none.

'My body or my soul, which was the dearer,
When the one pure, the other made divine?

1113 *When with . . . sympathized.* When it receives sympathy from similar behaviour.

1126 *Relish.* Address.

1127 *dumps.* Slow, sad songs.

1132 *diapason.* The compass of a musical instrument.

1133 *burden-wise.* The 'burden' was the bass part, or under-song.

1134 *Tereus.* The king of Thrace, who violated his sister-in-law, Philomela. His wife rescued her, and was later turned into a swallow, Philomela into a nightingale and Tereus into a hoopoe.

1140 *frets.* The gradations on the fingerboard of a stringed instrument.

'Or one encompass'd with a winding maze . . .' Engraving of a coin of Knossos representing the Cretan labyrinth by F.W. Fairholt, in J.O. Halliwell's edition of Shakespeare's works, 1853–65

1160 *conclusion.* Experiment.

1206 *overseen.* Deceived.

Whose love of either to myself was nearer,
When both were kept for heaven and Collatine?
Ay me! the bark peel'd from the lofty pine,
  His leaves will wither and his sap decay;
  So must my soul, her bark being peel'd away.

'Her house is sack'd, her quiet interrupted, 1170
Her mansion batter'd by the enemy;
Her sacred temple spotted, spoil'd, corrupted,
Grossly engirt with daring infamy:
Then let it not be call'd impiety,
  If in this blemish'd fort I make some hole
  Through which I may convey this troubled soul.

'Yet die I will not till my Collatine
Have heard the cause of my untimely death;
That he may vow, in that sad hour of mine,
Revenge on him that made me stop my breath.
My stained blood to Tarquin I'll bequeath, 1181
  Which by him tainted shall for him be spent,
  And as his due writ in my testament.

'My honour I'll bequeath unto the knife
That wounds my body so dishonoured.
'Tis honour to deprive dishonour'd life;
The one will live, the other being dead:
So of shame's ashes shall my fame be bred,
  For in my death I murder shameful scorn:
  My shame so dead, mine honour is new-born.

'Dear lord of that dear jewel I have lost,   1191
What legacy shall I bequeath to thee?
My resolution, love, shall be thy boast,
By whose example thou revenged mayst be.
How Tarquin must be used, read it in me:
  Myself, thy friend, will kill myself, thy foe,
  And for my sake serve thou false Tarquin so.

'This brief abridgement of my will I make:
My soul and body to the skies and ground;
My resolution, husband, do thou take;   1200
Mine honour be the knife's that makes my wound;
My shame be his that did my fame confound;
  And all my fame that lives disbursed be
  To those that live, and think no shame of me.

'Thou, Collatine, shalt oversee this will;
How was I overseen that thou shalt see it!
My blood shall wash the slander of mine ill;
My life's foul deed, my life's fair end shall free it.
Faint not, faint heart, but stoutly say "So be it:"
  Yield to my hand; my hand shall conquer thee:
  Thou dead, both die, and both shall victors be.'

This plot of death when sadly she had laid,
And wiped the brinish pearl from her bright eyes,
With untuned tongue she hoarsely calls her maid,
Whose swift obedience to her mistress hies;
For fleet-wing'd duty with thought's feathers flies.
  Poor Lucrece' cheeks unto her maid seem so
  As winter meads when sun doth melt their snow.

Her mistress she doth give demure good-morrow,
With soft-slow tongue, true mark of modesty,
And sorts a sad look to her lady's sorrow,   1221
For why her face wore sorrow's livery;
But durst not ask of her audaciously
  Why her two suns were cloud-eclipsed so,
  Nor why her fair cheeks over-wash'd with woe.

But as the earth doth weep, the sun being set,
Each flower moisten'd like a melting eye;
Even so the maid with swelling drops gan wet
Her circled eyne, enforced by sympathy
Of those fair suns set in her mistress' sky,   1230
   Who in a salt-waved ocean quench their light,
   Which makes the maid weep like the dewy
     night.

A pretty while these pretty creatures stand,
● Like ivory conduits coral cisterns filling:
One justly weeps; the other takes in hand
No cause, but company, of her drops spilling:
Their gentle sex to weep are often willing;
   Grieving themselves to guess at others' smarts,
   And then they drown their eyes or break their
     hearts.

For men have marble, women waxen, minds,   1240
And therefore are they form'd as marble will;
● The weak oppress'd, the impression of strange
    kinds
Is form'd in them by force, by fraud, or skill:
Then call them not the authors of their ill,
   No more than wax shall be accounted evil
   Wherein is stamp'd the semblance of a devil.

● Their smoothness, like a goodly champaign plain,
Lays open all the little worms that creep;
In men, as in a rough-grown grove, remain
Cave-keeping evils that obscurely sleep: 1250
Through crystal walls each little mote will peep:
   Though men can cover crimes with bold stern
     looks,
   Poor women's faces are their own faults' books.

No man inveigh against the wither'd flower,
But chide rough winter that the flower hath kill'd:
Not that devour'd, but that which doth devour,
● Is worthy blame.   O, let it not be hild
● Poor women's faults, that they are so fulfill'd
   With men's abuses: those proud lords, to blame,
   Make weak-made women tenants to their shame.

● The precedent whereof in Lucrece view,   1261
Assail'd by night with circumstances strong
Of present death, and shame that might ensue
By that her death, to do her husband wrong:
Such danger to resistance did belong,
   That dying fear through all her body spread;
   And who cannot abuse a body dead?

By this, mild patience bid fair Lucrece speak
● To the poor counterfeit of her complaining:
'My girl,' quoth she, 'on what occasion break
Those tears from thee, that down thy cheeks are
    raining?   1271
If thou dost weep for grief of my sustaining,
   Know, gentle wench, it small avails my mood:
   If tears could help, mine own would do me good.

'But tell me, girl, when went'—and there she
    stay'd
Till after a deep groan—'Tarquin from hence?'
'Madam, ere I was up,' replied the maid,
'The more to blame my sluggard negligence:
Yet with the fault I thus far can dispense;
   Myself was stirring ere the break of day,   1280
   And, ere I rose, was Tarquin gone away.

1234 *conduits.* Fountains. *coral cisterns.* i.e. eyes which are red from weeping.

1242 *strange kinds.* i.e. dispositions other than their own.

1247 *champaign plain.* Flat countryside.

1257 *hild.* Held.

1258 *fulfill'd.* Filled up.

1261 *precedent.* Proof.

1269 *counterfeit.* Image, picture.

1298 *Conceit*. Thought.

1300 *curious-good*. Too well expressed.

1310 *tenour*. Statement.

1316 *stain'd excuse*. Account of her shame.

1319 *fashion*. Manner.

' But, lady, if your maid may be so bold,
She would request to know your heaviness.'
' O, peace !' quoth Lucrece : 'if it should be told,
The repetition cannot make it less ;
For more it is than I can well express :
    And that deep torture may be call'd a hell
    When more is felt than one hath power to tell.

' Go, get me hither paper, ink, and pen :
Yet save that labour, for I have them here. 1290
What should I say ? One of my husband's men
Bid thou be ready, by and by, to bear
A letter to my lord, my love, my dear :
    Bid him with speed prepare to carry it ;
    The cause craves haste, and it will soon be writ.'

Her maid is gone, and she prepares to write,
First hovering o'er the paper with her quill :
● Conceit and grief an eager combat fight ;
What wit sets down is blotted straight with will ;
● This is too curious-good, this blunt and ill : 1300
    Much like a press of people at a door,
    Throng her inventions, which shall go before.

At last she thus begins : ' Thou worthy lord
Of that unworthy wife that greeteth thee,
Health to thy person ! next vouchsafe t' afford—
If ever, love, thy Lucrece thou wilt see—
Some present speed to come and visit me.
    So, I commend me from our house in grief :
    My woes are tedious, though my words are
        brief.'

● Here folds she up the tenour of her woe,   1310
Her certain sorrow writ uncertainly.
By this short schedule Collatine may know
Her grief, but not her grief's true quality :
She dares not thereof make discovery,
    Lest he should hold it her own gross abuse,
●   Ere she with blood had stain'd her stain'd
        excuse.

Besides, the life and feeling of her passion
She hoards, to spend when he is by to hear her :
● When sighs and groans and tears may grace the
        fashion
Of her disgrace, the better so to clear her   1320
From that suspicion which the world might bear
        her.
    To shun this blot, she would not blot the letter
    With words, till action might become them better.

To see sad sights moves more than hear them told ;
For then the eye interprets to the ear
The heavy motion that it doth behold,
When every part a part of woe doth bear.
'Tis but a part of sorrow that we hear :
    Deep sounds make lesser noise than shallow fords,
    And sorrow ebbs, being blown with wind of
        words.   1330

Her letter now is seal'd, and on it writ
' At Ardea to my lord with more than haste.'
The post attends, and she delivers it,
Charging the sour-faced groom to hie as fast
As lagging fowls before the northern blast :
    Speed more than speed but dull and slow she
        deems :
    Extremity still urgeth such extremes.

- The homely villain court'sies to her low;
And, blushing on her, with a steadfast eye
Receives the scroll without or yea or no,   1340
And forth with bashful innocence doth hie.
But they whose guilt within their bosoms lie
  Imagine every eye beholds their blame;
  For Lucrece thought he blush'd to see her
    shame

When, silly groom! God wot, it was defect
Of spirit, life, and bold audacity.
Such harmless creatures have a true respect
To talk in deeds, while others saucily
Promise more speed, but do it leisurely:
  Even so this pattern of the worn-out age   1350
- Pawn'd honest looks, but laid no words to gage.

His kindled duty kindled her mistrust,
That two red fires in both their faces blazed;
She thought he blush'd, as knowing Tarquin's lust,
- And, blushing with him, wistly on him gazed;
Her earnest eye did make him more amazed:
  The more she saw the blood his cheeks replenish,
  The more she thought he spied in her some
    blemish.

But long she thinks till he return again,
And yet the duteous vassal scarce is gone.   1360
The weary time she cannot entertain,
For now 'tis stale to sigh, to weep, and groan:
So woe hath wearied woe, moan tired moan,
  That she her plaints a little while doth stay,
  Pausing for means to mourn some newer way.

At last she calls to mind where hangs a piece
Of skilful painting, made for Priam's Troy:
Before the which is drawn the power of Greece,
For Helen's rape the city to destroy,
- Threatening cloud-kissing Ilion with annoy; 1370
  Which the conceited painter drew so proud,
  As heaven, it seem'd, to kiss the turrets bow'd.

A thousand lamentable objects there,
In scorn of nature, art gave lifeless life:
Many a dry drop seem'd a weeping tear,
Shed for the slaughter'd husband by the wife:
The red blood reek'd, to show the painter's strife;
  And dying eyes gleam'd forth their ashy lights,
  Like dying coals burnt out in tedious nights.

There might you see the labouring pioner   1380
Begrimed with sweat, and smeared all with dust:
And from the towers of Troy there would appear
The very eyes of men through loop-holes thrust,
- Gazing upon the Greeks with little lust:
  Such sweet observance in this work was had,
  That one might see those far-off eyes look sad.

In great commanders grace and majesty
You might behold, triumphing in their faces;
In youth, quick bearing and dexterity;
And here and there the painter interlaces   1390
Pale cowards, marching on with trembling paces;
  Which heartless peasants did so well resemble,
  That one would swear he saw them quake and
    tremble.

In Ajax and Ulysses, O, what art
Of physiognomy might one behold!

1338 *villain.* Servant.

1351 *Pawn'd.* Pledged.

1355 *wistly.* Earnestly.

1370 *annoy.* Injury.

1384 *lust.* Liking.

'In Ajax and Ulysses, O, what art . . .' Ajax with
Ulysses. From a French woodcut, 1557

1401 *Nestor.* The elder statesman on the Greek side in the Trojan war.

Nestor tells the story of the Trojan War.

1407 *purl'd.* Curled.

1412 *nice.* Precise.

1417 *boll'n.* Swollen.

1436 *strand of Dardan.* Shore of Dardania (another name for Troas, the country of which Troy was the capital).

1437 *Simois.* A tributary of the River Scamander in Troy.

1440 *than.* Then.

1444 *stell'd.* Portrayed.

1447–1448 *Hecuba . . . Priam.* The queen and king of Troy.

1449 *Pyrrhus.* The slayer of Priam.

1450 *anatomized.* Dissected.

The face of either cipher'd either's heart;
Their face their manners most expressly told:
In Ajax' eyes blunt rage and rigour roll'd;
   But the mild glance that sly Ulysses lent 1399
   Show'd deep regard and smiling government.

● There pleading might you see grave Nestor stand,
As 'twere encouraging the Greeks to fight;
Making such sober action with his hand,
That it beguiled attention, charm'd the sight:
In speech, it seem'd, his beard, all silver white,
   Wagg'd up and down, and from his lips did fly
●   Thin winding breath, which purl'd up to the sky.

About him were a press of gaping faces,
Which seem'd to swallow up his sound advice;
All jointly listening, but with several graces, 1410
As if some mermaid did their ears entice,
● Some high, some low, the painter was so nice;
   The scalps of many, almost hid behind,
   To jump up higher seem'd, to mock the mind.

Here one man's hand lean'd on another's head,
His nose being shadow'd by his neighbour's ear;
● Here one being throng'd bears back, all boll'n
     and red;
Another smother'd seems to pelt and swear;
And in their rage such signs of rage they bear,
   As, but for loss of Nestor's golden words, 1420
   It seem'd they would debate with angry swords.

For much imaginary work was there;
Conceit deceitful, so compact, so kind,
That for Achilles' image stood his spear,
Griped in an armed hand; himself, behind,
Was left unseen, save to the eye of mind:
   A hand, a foot, a face, a leg, a head,
   Stood for the whole to be imagined.

And from the walls of strong-besieged Troy
When their brave hope, bold Hector, march'd to
    field,   1430
Stood many Trojan mothers, sharing joy
To see their youthful sons bright weapons wield;
And to their hope they such odd action yield,
   That through their light joy seemed to appear,
   Like bright things stain'd, a kind of heavy fear.

● And from the strand of Dardan, where they
    fought,
● To Simois' reedy banks the red blood ran,
Whose waves to imitate the battle sought
With swelling ridges; and their ranks began
● To break upon the galled shore, and than   1440
   Retire again, till, meeting greater ranks,
   They join and shoot their foam at Simois' banks.

To this well-painted piece is Lucrece come,
● To find a face where all distress is stell'd.
Many she sees where cares have carved some,
But none where all distress and dolour dwell'd,
● Till she despairing Hecuba beheld,
   Staring on Priam's wounds with her old eyes,
●   Which bleeding under Pyrrhus' proud foot lies.

● In her the painter had anatomized   1450
   Time's ruin, beauty's wreck, and grim care's reign:
   Her cheeks with chaps and wrinkles were disguised;

Of what she was no semblance did remain:
Her blue blood changed to black in every vein,
  Wanting the spring that those shrunk pipes had
      fed,
  Show'd life imprison'd in a body dead.

On this sad shadow Lucrece spends her eyes,
And shapes her sorrow to the beldam's woes,
Who nothing wants to answer her but cries,
And bitter words to ban her cruel foes: 1460
The painter was no god to lend her those;
  And therefore Lucrece swears he did her wrong,
  To give her so much grief and not a tongue.

'Poor instrument,' quoth she, 'without a sound,
I'll tune thy woes with my lamenting tongue;
And drop sweet balm in Priam's painted wound,
And rail on Pyrrhus that hath done him wrong;
And with my tears quench Troy that burns so long;
  And with my knife scratch out the angry eyes
  Of all the Greeks that are thine enemies.   1470

'Show me the strumpet that began this stir,
That with my nails her beauty I may tear.
Thy heat of lust, fond Paris, did incur
This load of wrath that burning Troy doth bear:
Thy eye kindled the fire that burneth here;
  And here in Troy, for trespass of thine eye,
  The sire, the son, the dame, and daughter die.

'Why should the private pleasure of some one
Become the public plague of many moe?
Let sin, alone committed, light alone   1480
Upon his head that hath trangressed so;
Let guiltless souls be freed from guilty woe:
  For one's offence why should so many fall,
  To plague a private sin in general?

'Lo, here weeps Hecuba, here Priam dies,
Here manly Hector faints, here Troilus swounds,
Here friend by friend in bloody channel lies,
And friend to friend gives unadvised wounds,
And one man's lust these many lives confounds:
  Had doting Priam check'd his son's desire,   1490
  Troy had been bright with fame and not with
      fire.'

Here feelingly she weeps Troy's painted woes:
For sorrow, like a heavy-hanging bell,
Once set on ringing, with his own weight goes;
Then little strength rings out the doleful knell:
So Lucrece, set a-work, sad tales doth tell
  To pencill'd pensiveness and colour'd sorrow;
  She lends them words, and she their looks doth
      borrow.

She throws her eyes about the painting round,
And whom she finds forlorn she doth lament.
At last she sees a wretched image bound,   1501
That piteous looks to Phrygian shepherds lent:
His face, though full of cares, yet show'd content;
  Onward to Troy with the blunt swains he goes,
  So mild, that Patience seem'd to scorn his woes.

In him the painter labour'd with his skill
To hide deceit, and give the harmless show
An humble gait, calm looks, eyes wailing still,
A brow unbent, that seem'd to welcome woe;
Cheeks neither red nor pale, but mingled so   1510

1460 *ban.* Curse.

1471 *the strumpet.* i.e. Helen, wife of the Greek Menelaus.

Venus presenting Helen to Paris. Illustration by John Flaxman from Homer's *Iliad*, translated by Alexander Pope, 1793

1484 *To plague . . . general.* To make the whole public suffer, for the punishment of an individual.

1486 *Hector . . . Troilus.* Trojan princes.

1502 *Phrygian.* i.e. from Phrygia, in Asia minor.

1516 *jealousy*. Suspicion.

1521 *Sinon*. The Greek who persuaded the Trojans to take in the wooden horse.

Sinon with Thersites, a misanthropic Greek in Homer's *Iliad*. Woodcut from Thomas Heywood's *The Iron Age*, 1632

1524 *Ilion*. Alternative name for Troy.

That blushing red no guilty instance gave,
Nor ashy pale the fear that false hearts have.

But, like a constant and confirmed devil,
He entertain'd a show so seeming just,
And therein so ensconced his secret evil,
● That jealousy itself could not mistrust
False-creeping craft and perjury should thrust
　　Into so bright a day such black-faced storms,
　　Or blot with hell-born sin such saint-like forms.

The well-skill'd workman this mild image drew
● For perjured Sinon, whose enchanting story 1521
The credulous old Priam after slew;
Whose words like wildfire burnt the shining glory
● Of rich-built Ilion, that the skies were sorry,
　　And little stars shot from their fixed places,
　　When their glass fell wherein they view'd their
　　　　faces.

This picture she advisedly perused,
And chid the painter for his wondrous skill,
Saying, some shape in Sinon's was abused;
So fair a form lodged not a mind so ill:　　1530
And still on him she gazed; and gazing still,
　　Such signs of truth in his plain face she spied,
　　That she concludes the picture was belied.

'It cannot be,' quoth she, 'that so much guile'—
She would have said 'can lurk in such a look;'
But Tarquin's shape came in her mind the while,
And from her tongue 'can lurk' from 'cannot' took:
'It cannot be' she in that sense forsook,
　　And turn'd it thus, 'It cannot be, I find,
　　But such a face should bear a wicked mind:

'For even as subtle Sinon here is painted,
So sober-sad, so weary, and so mild,
As if with grief or travail he had fainted,
To me came Tarquin armed; so beguiled
With outward honesty, but yet defiled
　　With inward vice: as Priam him did cherish,
　　So did I Tarquin; so my Troy did perish.

'Look, look, how listening Priam wets his eyes,
To see those borrow'd tears that Sinon sheds!
Priam, why art thou old and yet not wise?　　1550
For every tear he falls a Trojan bleeds:
His eye drops fire, no water thence proceeds;
　　Those round clear pearls of his, that move thy
　　　　pity,
　　Are balls of quenchless fire to burn thy city.

'Such devils steal effects from lightless hell;
For Sinon in his fire doth quake with cold,
And in that cold hot-burning fire doth dwell;
These contraries such unity do hold,
Only to flatter fools and make them bold:
　　So Priam's trust false Sinon's tears doth flatter,
　　That he finds means to burn his Troy with water.'

Here, all enraged, such passion her assails,
That patience is quite beaten from her breast.
She tears the senseless Sinon with her nails,
Comparing him to that unhappy guest
Whose deed hath made herself herself detest:
　　At last she smilingly with this gives o'er;
　　'Fool, fool!' quoth she, 'his wounds will not
　　　　be sore.'

Thus ebbs and flows the current of her sorrow,
And time doth weary time with her complaining.
She looks for night, and then she longs for morrow,
And both she thinks too long with her remaining:
Short time seems long in sorrow's sharp sus-
taining:
   Though woe be heavy, yet it seldom sleeps;
   And they that watch see time how slow it creeps.

Which all this time hath overslipp'd her thought,
That she with painted images hath spent;
Being from the feeling of her own grief brought
By deep surmise of others' detriment;
Losing her woes in shows of discontent.   1580
   It easeth some, though none it ever cured,
   To think their dolour others have endured.

But now the mindful messenger, come back,
Brings home his lord and other company;
Who finds his Lucrece clad in mourning black:
And round about her tear-distained eye
Blue circles stream'd, like rainbows in the sky:
   These water-galls in her dim element
   Foretell new storms to those already spent.

Which when her sad-beholding husband saw,
Amazedly in her sad face he stares: 1591
Her eyes, though sod in tears, look'd red and
raw,
Her lively colour kill'd with deadly cares.
He hath no power to ask her how she fares:
   Both stood, like old acquaintance in a trance,
   Met far from home, wondering each other's
   chance.

At last he takes her by the bloodless hand,
And thus begins: 'What uncouth ill event
Hath thee befall'n, that thou dost trembling stand?
Sweet love, what spite hath thy fair colour spent?
Why art thou thus attired in discontent?   1601
   Unmask, dear dear, this moody heaviness,
   And tell thy grief, that we may give redress.'

Three times with sighs she gives her sorrow fire,
Ere once she can discharge one word of woe:
At length address'd to answer his desire,
She modestly prepares to let them know
Her honour is ta'en prisoner by the foe;
   While Collatine and his consorted lords
   With sad attention long to hear her words. 1610

And now this pale swan in her watery nest
Begins the sad dirge of her certain ending;
'Few words,' quoth she, 'shall fit the trespass best,
Where no excuse can give the fault amending:
In me moe woes than words are now depending;
   And my laments would be drawn out too long,
   To tell them all with one poor tired tongue.

'Then be this all the task it hath to say:
Dear husband, in the interest of thy bed
A stranger came, and on that pillow lay   1620
Where thou wast wont to rest thy weary head;
And what wrong else may be imagined
   By foul enforcement might be done to me,
   From that, alas, thy Lucrece is not free.

'For in the dreadful dead of dark midnight,
With shining falchion in my chamber came

1588 *water-galls.* Small haloes in the clouds.

1606 *address'd.* Prepared.

1619 *interest.* Possession.

A creeping creature, with a flaming light,
And softly cried "Awake, thou Roman dame,
And entertain my love; else lasting shame
   On thee and thine this night I will inflict, 1630
   If thou my love's desire do contradict.

'"For some hard-favour'd groom of thine," quoth
     he,
"Unless thou yoke thy liking to my will,
I'll murder straight, and then I'll slaughter thee
And swear I found you where you did fulfil
The loathsome act of lust, and so did kill
   The lechers in their deed: this act will be
   My fame and thy perpetual infamy."

'With this, I did begin to start and cry;
And then against my heart he sets his sword, 1640
Swearing, unless I took all patiently,
I should not live to speak another word;
So should my shame still rest upon record,
   And never be forgot in mighty Rome
   Th' adulterate death of Lucrece and her groom.

'Mine enemy was strong, my poor self weak,
And far the weaker with so strong a fear:
My bloody judge forbade my tongue to speak;
No rightful plea might plead for justice there:
His scarlet lust came evidence to swear   1650
   That my poor beauty had purloin'd his eyes;
   And when the judge is robb'd the prisoner
     dies.

'O, teach me how to make mine own excuse!
Or at the least this refuge let me find;
Though my gross blood be stain'd with this abuse,
Immaculate and spotless is my mind;
That was not forced; that never was inclined
   To accessary yieldings, but still pure
   Doth in her poison'd closet yet endure.'

Lo, here, the hopeless merchant of this loss, 1660
With head declined, and voice damm'd up with
     woe,
With sad set eyes, and wretched arms across,
From lips new-waxen pale begins to blow
The grief away that stops his answer so:
   But, wretched as he is, he strives in vain;
   What he breathes out his breath drinks up
     again.

As through an arch the violent roaring tide
Outruns the eye that doth behold his haste,
Yet in the eddy boundeth in his pride
Back to the strait that forced him on so fast; 1670
In rage sent out, recall'd in rage, being past:
   Even so his sighs, his sorrows, make a saw,
   To push grief on, and back the same grief draw.

Which speechless woe of his poor she attendeth,
And his untimely frenzy thus awaketh:
'Dear lord, thy sorrow to my sorrow lendeth
Another power; no flood by raining slaketh.
My woe too sensible thy passion maketh
   More feeling-painful: let it then suffice   1679
   To drown one woe, one pair of weeping eyes.

  And for my sake, when I might charm thee so
For she that was thy Lucrece, now attend me:
Be suddenly revenged on my foe,

Opposite: 'For she that was thy Lucrece, now attend me...' Early 19th century French engraving of Lucretia

Thine, mine, his own : suppose thou dost defend me
From what is past : the help that thou shalt lend me
  Comes all too late, yet let the traitor die ;
  For sparing justice feeds iniquity.

'But ere I name him, you fair lords,' quoth she,
Speaking to those that came with Collatine,
'Shall plight your honourable faiths to me, 1690
With swift pursuit to venge this wrong of mine ;
For 'tis a meritorious fair design
  To chase injustice with revengeful arms :
  Knights, by their oaths, should right poor
      ladies' harms.'

At this request, with noble disposition
Each present lord began to promise aid,
As bound in knighthood to her imposition,
Longing to hear the hateful foe bewray'd.
But she, that yet her sad task hath not said, 1699
  The protestation stops. 'O, speak,' quoth she,
  'How may this forced stain be wiped from me?

'What is the quality of mine offence,
Being constrain'd with dreadful circumstance?
May my pure mind with the foul act dispense,
My low-declined honour to advance?
May any terms acquit me from this chance?
  The poison'd fountain clears itself again ;
  And why not I from this compelled stain?'

With this, they all at once began to say,
Her body's stain her mind untainted clears ; 1710
While with a joyless smile she turns away
The face, that map which deep impression bears
Of hard misfortune, carved in it with tears.
  'No, no,' quoth she, 'no dame, hereafter living,
  By my excuse shall claim excuse's giving.'

Here with a sigh, as if her heart would break,
She throws forth Tarquin's name: 'He, he,' she says,
But more than 'he' her poor tongue could not
    speak ;
Till after many accents and delays,
Untimely breathings, sick and short assays, 1720
  She utters this, 'He, he, fair lords, 'tis he,
  That guides this hand to give this wound to me.'

Even here she sheathed in her harmless breast
A harmful knife, that thence her soul unsheathed :
That blow did bail it from the deep unrest
Of that polluted prison where it breathed:
Her contrite sighs unto the clouds bequeathed
  Her winged sprite, and through her wounds
    doth fly
  Life's lasting date from cancell'd destiny.

Stone-still, astonish'd with this deadly deed, 1730
Stood Collatine and all his lordly crew ;
Till Lucrece' father, that beholds her bleed,
Himself on her self-slaughter'd body threw ;
And from the purple fountain Brutus drew
  The murderous knife, and, as it left the place,
  Her blood, in poor revenge, held it in chase ;

And bubbling from her breast, it doth divide
In two slow rivers, that the crimson blood
Circles her body in on every side,
Who, like a late-sack'd island, vastly stood 1740
Bare and unpeopled in this fearful flood.

1684 *his own.* Tarquin is enemy to his own salvation.

1698 *bewray'd.* Revealed.

'She throws forth Tarquin's name . . .' Illustration by J. Yunge-Bateman, 1948

1734 *Brutus.* Lucius Junius Brutus, forbear of Marcus Brutus (one of the conspirators against Julius Caesar).

1736 *held it in chase.* i.e. the blood pursued the knife out of her body.

Opposite : Death of Lucrece. Painting by Lucas Cranach the Elder (1472–1553)

1745 *rigol*. Circlet.

1761 *death*. Skull.

1797 *sorrow's interest*. Right to sorrow.

Some of her blood still pure and red remain'd,
And some look'd black, and that false Tarquin
    stain'd.

About the mourning and congealed face
● Of that black blood a watery rigol goes,
Which seems to weep upon the tainted place:
And ever since, as pitying Lucrece' woes,
Corrupted blood some watery token shows;
    And blood untainted still doth red abide,
    Blushing at that which is so putrified.   1750

'Daughter, dear daughter,' old Lucretius cries,
'That life was mine which thou hast here de-
    prived.
If in the child the father's image lies,
Where shall I live now Lucrece is unlived?
Thou wast not to this end from me derived.
    If children pre-decease progenitors,
    We are their offspring, and they none of ours.

'Poor broken glass, I often did behold
In thy sweet semblance my old age new born;
But now that fair fresh mirror, dim and old, 1760
● Shows me a bare-boned death by time outworn:
    O, from thy cheeks my image thou hast torn,
    And shiver'd all the beauty of my glass,
    That I no more can see what once I was!

'O time, cease thou thy course and last no longer,
If they surcease to be that should survive.
Shall rotten death make conquest of the stronger
And leave the faltering feeble souls alive?
The old bees die, the young possess their hive:
    Then live, sweet Lucrece, live again and see
    Thy father die, and not thy father thee!' 1771

By this, starts Collatine as from a dream,
And bids Lucretius give his sorrow place;
And then in key-cold Lucrece' bleeding stream
He falls, and bathes the pale fear in his face,
And counterfeits to die with her a space;
    Till manly shame bids him possess his breath
    And live to be revenged on her death.

The deep vexation of his inward soul
Hath served a dumb arrest upon his tongue; 1780
Who, mad that sorrow should his use control,
Or keep him from heart-easing words so long,
Begins to talk; but through his lips do throng
    Weak words, so thick come in his poor heart's
      aid,
    That no man could distinguish what he said.

Yet sometime 'Tarquin' was pronounced plain,
But through his teeth, as if the name he tore.
This windy tempest, till it blow up rain,
Held back his sorrow's tide, to make it more;
At last it rains, and busy winds give o'er: 1790
    Then son and father weep with equal strife
    Who should weep most, for daughter or for wife.

The one doth call her his, the other his,
Yet neither may possess the claim they lay.
The father says 'She's mine.' 'O, mine she is,'
Replies her husband: 'do not take away
● My sorrow's interest; let no mourner say
    He weeps for her, for she was only mine,
    And only must be wail'd by Collatine.'

'O,' quoth Lucretius, 'I did give that life   1800
Which she too early and too late hath spill'd.'
'Woe, woe,' quoth Collatine, 'she was my wife,
I owed her, and 'tis mine that she hath kill'd.'
'My daughter' and 'my wife' with clamours fill'd
    The dispersed air, who, holding Lucrece' life,
    Answer'd their cries, 'my daughter' and 'my
        wife.'

Brutus, who pluck'd the knife from Lucrece' side,
Seeing such emulation in their woe,
Began to clothe his wit in state and pride,
Burying in Lucrece' wound his folly's show.   1810
He with the Romans was esteemed so
    As silly-jeering idiots are with kings,
    For sportive words and uttering foolish things:

But now he throws that shallow habit by,
Wherein deep policy did him disguise;
And arm'd his long-hid wits advisedly,
To check the tears in Collatinus' eyes.
'Thou wronged lord of Rome,' quoth he, 'arise:
    Let my unsounded self, supposed a fool,
    Now set thy long-experienced wit to school.

'Why, Collatine, is woe the cure for woe?   1821
Do wounds help wounds, or grief help grievous
        deeds?
Is it revenge to give thyself a blow
For his foul act by whom thy fair wife bleeds?
Such childish humour from weak minds pro-
        ceeds:
    Thy wretched wife mistook the matter so,
    To slay herself, that should have slain her foe.

'Courageous Roman, do not steep thy heart
In such relenting dew of lamentations;
But kneel with me and help to bear thy part,
To rouse our Roman gods with invocations,   1831
That they will suffer these abominations,
    Since Rome herself in them doth stand dis-
        graced,
    By our strong arms from forth her fair streets
        chased.

'Now, by the Capitol that we adore,
And by this chaste blood so unjustly stain'd,
By heaven's fair sun that breeds the fat earth's
        store,
By all our country rights in Rome maintain'd,
And by chaste Lucrece' soul that late complain'd
    Her wrongs to us, and by this bloody knife,
    We will revenge the death of this true wife.'

This said, he struck his hand upon his breast,
And kiss'd the fatal knife, to end his vow;
And to his protestation urged the rest,
Who, wondering at him, did his words allow:
Then jointly to the ground their knees they bow;
    And that deep vow, which Brutus made before,
    He doth again repeat, and that they swore.

When they had sworn to this advised doom,
They did conclude to bear dead Lucrece thence;
To show her bleeding body thorough Rome,   1851
And so to publish Tarquin's foul offence:
Which being done with speedy diligence,
    The Romans plausibly did give consent
    To Tarquin's everlasting banishment.

1803 *owed.* Owned.

1829 *relenting.* Melting.

'Now, by the Capitol that we adore . . .' The temple of Jupiter on the Capitoline hill in Rome. Engraving from a coin at the time of Vespasian

1854 *plausibly.* With applause, plausively.

The Sonnets

1592-1594/5

THE SONNETS were written *pari passu* with *Venus and Adonis* and *The Rape of Lucrece*, and like them for the patron, during the three years or so from 1592 to the winter of 1594/5, but not published until years after, in 1609, and then not by Shakespeare. For many of them were far too private, too near the bone; only a few of those more appropriate to the public eye were circulated and very few found their way into print. This was natural, for they were the patron's property, sonnets of duty from the poet, as he makes perfectly clear at the end of the first section, Sonnet 26, in language closely similar to the dedication of *Lucrece*. The poet's duty to his young Lord is three times emphasised:

> Lord of my love, to whom in vassalage
> Thy merit hath my duty strongly knit,
> To thee I send this written ambassage
> To witness duty, not to show my wit:
> Duty so great . . .

The poet had reason to be eternally grateful to his young Lord, for coming to his rescue in 1592-3, two plague years in which the theatres were mostly shut and which wreaked havoc in the profession. The young Lord's patronage enabled Shakespeare to write his poems and sonnets during this period, as well as the two plays produced for the circle, *Love's Labour's Lost* and *A Midsummer Night's Dream*. In the early 1590's sonneteering was all the vogue, set in motion by Sidney's *Astrophil and Stella*. Several sonnet-sequences were published, celebrating various Delias and Celias, but not Shakespeare's. His was much too idiosyncratic and exceptional. In the first place, it was written for his young patron and friend, in terms of affection, gratitude and love, though Shakespeare makes it perfectly clear that he had no sexual interest in the youth: all that went into his infatuation for his mistress, the musical dark lady. For another thing, the relations of the three became too acutely entangled, and Shakespeare, with his open candid nature, laid bare his soul, the anguish he suffered.

It is really necessary to read the Sonnets as a whole to understand the story – quite a

SHAKE-SPEARES

SONNETS.

Neuer before Imprinted.

_____

_____

AT LONDON
By *G. Eld* for *T. T.* and are
to be folde by *Iohn Wright,* dwelling
at Chrift Church gate.
1 6 0 9.

TO.THE.ONLIE.BEGETTER.OF.
THESE.INSVING.SONNETS.
Mʳ. W. H. ALL.HAPPINESSE.
AND.THAT.ETERNITIE.
PROMISED.

BY.

OVR.EVER-LIVING.POET.

WISHETH.

THE.WELL-WISHING.
ADVENTVRER.IN.
SETTING.
FORTH.

T. T.

drama in itself. Shakespeare felt a quasi-parental responsibility for the chaste youth, who would not, in spite of his urging, do his duty by the family, marry, and carry on the line. When the actor-playwright met the fascinating half-Italian Emilia Lanier (née Bassano), the discarded mistress of the Lord Chamberlain – shortly to become patron of Shakespeare's Company – he fell completely under her spell, partly out of pity for her unhappiness; for, when pregnant, she was married off to another of the Queen's musicians whom she disliked. (It was a comedown anyway.) In the usual Elizabethan manner the actor-poet got his grand friend to write to the equivocal lady on his behalf. She, being the kind of woman she was, tried to entangle the young Lord, driving the poet – who was a good deal older than the young people – to distraction as to their relations.

The situation was that commonly, and vulgarly, known as a triangle; but there were several things to complicate it and make it very uncommon. Shakespeare's love for his friend was all the stronger for being platonic, and he felt responsible for this first sordid introduction to sex with women, when the youth had been innocent and chaste, moreover an orphan: he was the head of a noble family with a duty to maintain it. Emilia Lanier was a bad lot – no doubt about that; Shakespeare had no doubt of it, but, a strongly sexed heterosexual, he could not help himself. He was infatuated, under her

Above left: Title page of the Sonnets *from the* Quarto *of 1609*

Above: Dedication of the Sonnets to Mr. W.H. inserted by the publisher Thomas Thorpe and addressed to Sir William Harvey 3rd husband of Southampton's mother, from whom he got the poems. From the Quarto *of 1609*

spell, with his eyes open; and she led him a fearful dance.

Meanwhile, another complication entered briefly into his relations with the golden youth: Marlowe began to compete for Southampton's favour. Marlowe was gallantly, aggressively homosexual; young Southampton was ambivalent, not yet sexually settled: here was another cause for anxiety. To that date Marlowe was the superior artist – as Shakespeare, candid as ever, recognised; he was the better poet and the senior in success from the time of *Tamburlaine*. With the plague still reigning, and with a family to support at Stratford, what would happen to the actor –

> Then if he thrive and I be cast away?

Marlowe, as we know, shortly died; but these strains left a rift within the ideal, paradisial relationship with which the Sonnets began. Shakespeare assured his young patron, and we must believe him, so candid and open he is:

> And life no longer than thy love will stay,
> For it depends upon that love of thine.

The tensions within this complex and subtle relationship, the strains upon it from difference of age, rank and character, the importance it had for Shakespeare, the inspiration he received and the anguish he endured – all led to far finer poetry than the unmoving expertness of *Venus and Adonis* or *Lucrece*. Some of the sonnets are among the most moving things he ever wrote.

Southampton, much less vulnerable to women, disentangled himself from the lady; we know, independently, that he knew her husband and entertained a better opinion of him than she did (she maligned him, as she did Shakespeare). In the end she gave the older man his dismissal; the tempestuous affair broke off, with Shakespeare going to Bath for cure from love's distemper – a contingency which had alarmed him too for young Southampton.

Such is the bare outline of the story, which has to be grasped before the full meaning of the Sonnets can be reached. In 1594 the Lord Chamberlain's Company was formed, with Shakespeare in a key position as both actor and playwright: the patron enabled him to buy a share, and henceforth he was independent.

It is ironical, yet appropriate, that the actor should have fallen for the discarded mistress of the randy old nobleman, first cousin of the Queen, who became patron of his Company. Yet the association could hardly be closer: the Lord Chamberlain had a residence in Blackfriars, James Burbage had always been his man. Southampton's mother married, as her second husband, Vice-Chamberlain Heneage.

The Sonnets silted up in the Southampton household, where they remained for years, except for those few that circulated and became public. In 1609 the publisher Thorpe got hold of them and published them, with a flowery dedication to the person who had got them, the only person to have them: a Mr. W.H. Remember that in Elizabethan social usage it was regular to refer to a knight as Master – one could never refer to a lord as such. In 1607 Southampton's mother left all the household goods and chattels to her young third husband, Sir William Harvey; in 1608 he married a young wife; this is why in 1609 Thorpe wishes him 'all happiness and that eternity promised by our ever-living poet,' i.e. what Shakespeare had promised his young patron years before, if only he would marry and carry on the family to posterity.

The Elizabethan historian can confirm the date of the Sonnets from the topical references: from the fall of the Queen's favourite, Sir Walter Ralegh, in the summer of

1592 ('Great princes' favourites', etc. Sonnet 25), to the series dealing with the rival poet in the present tense (Sonnet 78 following), until suddenly he disappears (in the valedictory Sonnet 86, and is mentioned no more), ending with the death of Marlowe, 30 May 1593. Thence to Sonnet 107, which has *two* topical references converging on one point to give us certainty:

> The mortal moon hath her eclipse endured . . .
> And peace proclaims olives of endless age.

The surrender of Paris to Henri IV in May 1594 gave hope of an end to the religious wars in France, which had been going on all through Shakespeare's life-time so far; at the very same time, the Queen – always 'the mortal moon' – emerged from the shadow of the Lopez threat to her life, with his condemnation and execution. Sonnet 124 concludes with,

> To this I witness call the fools of time,
> Which die for goodness who have lived for crime.

This refers to the persecution of the Jesuits and seminary priests, which rose to a height in the winter of 1594/5. They claimed that they were martyrs for their religion, the government that they were a fifth column, operating against the security and laws of the realm in war-time. Shakespeare, as usual, aligned himself with his countrymen's point of view; i.e. he was not a Catholic. Southampton was a Catholic, but not a political one, and conformed on James I's accession.

The last two Sonnets in the Southampton sequence (124, 125) refer to him as 'the child of state', and to Shakespeare's relationship with him:

> Were't aught to me I bore the canopy,
> With my extern the outward honouring . . .

a clear depiction of the young patron's status as a peer of the realm. But Shakespeare's last words are a dignified, but grand, statement of essential independence: 'no art

> But mutual render, only me for thee.'

For the benefit of the reader it should be pointed out that Sonnets 1 to 125 are in recognisable chronological order. After that, Sonnets 127 to the end deal mainly with Shakespeare's relationship with the Dark Lady – though these sonnets too would be the property of the patron, and ultimately fetched up with the rest in the Southampton *cache*. In dating, however, these sonnets later in numbering come *within* the Southampton sequence, and belong to 1592–3, the plague-years. No point in trying to insert them where they belong. The whole reads intelligibly like a drama, with a dramatic *dénouement*, and should be read as a whole.

Thorpe, not Shakespeare, had got hold of the Sonnets and published them, with their derogatory portrait of the Dark Lady, not meant for her eyes. We now know that two years later she inserted into her own book – a long religious poem, *Salve Deus Rex Judaeorum*, for she had undergone a religious conversion – a scathing prose *riposte* to men for defaming women, a strong feminist manifesto, full of temperament and temper, while her poem reveals her as a remarkably well-educated woman and a good, if long-winded, poet.[1]

1. See my edition, *The Poems of Shakespeare's Dark Lady*, 1978.

SONNETS.

TO THE ONLIE BEGETTER OF
THESE INSUING SONNETS
MR. W. H. ALL HAPPINESSE
AND THAT ETERNITIE
PROMISED BY
OUR EVER-LIVING POET
WISHETH
THE WELL-WISHING
ADVENTURER IN
SETTING
FORTH
                    T. T.

● *A bullet beside a text line indicates an annotation in the opposite column*

I.

FROM fairest creatures we desire increase,
That thereby beauty's rose might never die,
But as the riper should by time decease,
His tender heir might bear his memory:
But thou, contracted to thine own bright eyes,
Feed'st thy light's flame with self-substantial fuel,
Making a famine where abundance lies,
Thyself thy foe, to thy sweet self too cruel.
Thou that art now the world's fresh ornament
● And only herald to the gaudy spring,
Within thine own bud buriest thy content
● And, tender churl, makest waste in niggarding.

Dedication. See introduction.

I
10 *only.* Sole.

12 *niggarding.* Hoarding.

Opposite : Henry Wriothesley, third Earl of Southampton and Shakespeare's patron, for whom the Sonnets were written

753

II

4 *weed.* Garment.

9 *use.* Investment.

11 *sum . . . excuse.* Balance my account.

III

III: 'Look in thy glass, and tell the face thou viewst . . .'
Painting 'The Toilet of Venus' by Diego Velazquez
(1599–1660)

---

4 *unbless some mother.* Deny some woman the blessing of
motherhood.

5 *unear'd.* Uncultivated.

13 *remember'd not to be.* To be forgotten.

IV

4 *frank.* Generous. *free.* Generous.

5 *niggard.* Miser.

8 *live.* 'Make a living', and 'survive through posterity'.

V

2 *gaze.* Spectacle.

4 *unfair.* Deface. *fairly.* In beauty.

9 *summer's distillation.* (Flowers') perfumes.

14 *Leese.* Lose.

Pity the world, or else this glutton be,
To eat the world's due, by the grave and thee

II.

When forty winters shall besiege thy brow,
And dig deep trenches in thy beauty's field,
Thy youth's proud livery, so gazed on now,
● Will be a tatter'd weed, of small worth held:
Then being ask'd where all thy beauty lies,
Where all the treasure of thy lusty days,
To say, within thine own deep-sunken eyes,
Were an all-eating shame and thriftless praise.
● How much more praise deserved thy beauty's use,
If thou couldst answer 'This fair child of mine
● Shall sum my count and make my old excuse,'
Proving his beauty by succession thine!
    This were to be new made when thou art old,
    And see thy blood warm when thou feel'st it cold.

III.

Look in thy glass, and tell the face thou viewest
Now is the time that face should form another;
Whose fresh repair if now thou not renewest,
● Thou dost beguile the world, unbless some mother.
● For where is she so fair whose unear'd womb
Disdains the tillage of thy husbandry?
Or who is he so fond will be the tomb
Of his self-love, to stop posterity?
Thou art thy mother's glass, and she in thee
Calls back the lovely April of her prime:
So thou through windows of thine age shalt see
Despite of wrinkles this thy golden time.
● But if thou live, remember'd not to be,
    Die single, and thine image dies with thee.

IV.

Unthrifty loveliness, why dost thou spend
Upon thyself thy beauty's legacy?
Nature's bequest gives nothing but doth lend,
● And being frank she lends to those are free.
● Then, beauteous niggard, why dost thou abuse
The bounteous largess given thee to give?
Profitless usurer, why dost thou use
● So great a sum of sums, yet canst not live?
For having traffic with thyself alone,
Thou of thyself thy sweet self dost deceive.
Then how, when nature calls thee to be gone,
What acceptable audit canst thou leave?
    Thy unused beauty must be tomb'd with thee,
    Which, used, lives th' executor to be.

V.

Those hours, that with gentle work did frame
● The lovely gaze where every eye doth dwell,
Will play the tyrants to the very same
● And that unfair which fairly doth excel;
For never-resting time leads summer on
To hideous winter and confounds him there;
Sap check'd with frost and lusty leaves quite
    gone,
Beauty o'ersnow'd and bareness every where:
● Then, were not summer's distillation left,
A liquid prisoner pent in walls of glass,
Beauty's effect with beauty were bereft,
Nor it nor no remembrance what it was:
    But flowers distill'd, though they with **winter**
    meet,
● Leese but their show; their substance still lives
    sweet.

VI.

Then let not winter's ragged hand deface
In thee thy summer, ere thou be distill'd:
● Make sweet some vial; treasure thou some place
With beauty's treasure, ere it be self-kill'd.
That use is not forbidden usury
Which happies those that pay the willing loan;
That's for thyself to breed another thee,
Or ten times happier, be it ten for one;
Ten times thyself were happier than thou art,
If ten of thine ten times refigured thee:
Then what could death do, if thou shouldst depart,
Leaving thee living in posterity?
    Be not self-will'd, for thou art much too fair
      To be death's conquest and make worms thine
      heir.

VII.

Lo! in the orient when the gracious light
Lifts up his burning head, each under eye
Doth homage to his new-appearing sight,
Serving with looks his sacred majesty;
And having climb'd the steep-up heavenly hill,
Resembling strong youth in his middle age,
Yet mortal looks adore his beauty still,
Attending on his golden pilgrimage;
● But when from highmost pitch, with weary car,
Like feeble age, he reeleth from the day,
The eyes, 'fore duteous, now converted are
From his low tract and look another way:
    So thou, thyself out-going in thy noon,
    Unlook'd on diest, unless thou get a son.

VIII.

● Music to hear, why hear'st thou music sadly?
Sweets with sweets war not, joy delights in joy.
Why lovest thou that which thou receivest not
    gladly,
● Or else receivest with pleasure thine annoy?
If the true concord of well-tuned sounds,
By unions married, do offend thine ear,
● They do but sweetly chide thee, who confounds
In singleness the parts that thou shouldst bear.
Mark how one string, sweet husband to another,
Strikes each in each by mutual ordering,
Resembling sire and child and happy mother
Who all in one, one pleasing note do sing:
    Whose speechless song, being many, seeming
      one,
●   Sings this to thee: 'thou single wilt prove none.'

IX.

Is it for fear to wet a widow's eye
That thou consumest thyself in single life?
Ah! if thou issueless shalt hap to die,
● The world will wail thee, like a makeless wife;
The world will be thy widow and still weep
That thou no form of thee hast left behind,
● When every private widow well may keep
By children's eyes her husband's shape in mind.
Look, what an unthrift in the world doth spend
Shifts but his place, for still the world enjoys it;
But beauty's waste hath in the world an end,
And kept unused, the user so destroys it.
    No love toward others in that bosom sits
    That on himself such murderous shame com-
    mits.

VI

3 *treasure.* Enrich.

VII

9 *car.* Phoebus' chariot.

VIII

1 *Music to hear.* You whom it is music to hear.

4 *annoy.* i.e. what annoys you.

7–8 *confounds . . . bear.* i.e. destroys harmony by performing alone rather than in concert.

14 *none.* Nothing.

A man playing a lute. Painting by Hendrick ter Brugghen, 1624

IX

4 *makeless.* Mateless.

7 *private.* Separate.

X

6 *stick'st not.* Don't hesitate.

XI

1–2 *thou growest . . . departest.* i.e. you become, in your children, what you cease to be in yourself.

XII

6 *erst.* Formerly.

7 *summer's green.* Wheat.

8 *bier.* i.e. the harvest cart.

XII: 'And nothing 'gainst Time's scythe can make defence . . .' Painting 'Time orders Old Age to destroy Beauty' by Pompeo Girolamo Batoni (1708–87)

14 *breed.* Offspring. *brave.* Defy.

XIII

1 *O, that you were yourself!* O, that you could always be as you are now.

10 *husbandry.* Good management (pun: 'marriage').

X.

For shame! deny that thou bear'st love to any,
Who for thyself art so unprovident.
Grant, if thou wilt, thou art beloved of many,
But that thou none lovest is most evident;
For thou art so possess'd with murderous hate
● That 'gainst thyself thou stick'st not to conspire,
Seeking that beauteous roof to ruinate
Which to repair should be thy chief desire.
O, change thy thought, that I may change my
    mind!
Shall hate be fairer lodged than gentle love?
Be, as thy presence is, gracious and kind,
Or to thyself at least kind-hearted prove:
    Make thee another self, for love of me,
    That beauty still may live in thine or thee.

XI.

● As fast as thou shalt wane, so fast thou growest
In one of thine, from that which thou departest;
And that fresh blood which youngly thou bestowest
Thou mayst call thine when thou from youth con-
    vertest.
Herein lives wisdom, beauty and increase;
Without this, folly, age and cold decay:
If all were minded so, the times should cease
And threescore year would make the world away.
Let those whom Nature hath not made for store,
Harsh featureless and rude, barrenly perish:
Look, whom she best endow'd she gave the more;
Which bounteous gift thou shouldst in bounty
    cherish:
    She carved thee for her seal, and meant thereby
    Thou shouldst print more, not let that copy die.

XII.

When I do count the clock that tells the time,
And see the brave day sunk in hideous night;
When I behold the violet past prime,
And sable curls all silver'd o'er with white;
When lofty trees I see barren of leaves
● Which erst from heat did canopy the herd,
● And summer's green all girded up in sheaves
● Borne on the bier with white and bristly beard,
Then of thy beauty do I question make,
That thou among the wastes of time must go,
Since sweets and beauties do themselves forsake
And die as fast as they see others grow;
    And nothing 'gainst Time's scythe can make
        defence
● Save breed, to brave him when he takes thee
    hence.

XIII.

● O, that you were yourself! but, love, you are
No longer yours than you yourself here live:
Against this coming end you should prepare,
And your sweet semblance to some other give.
So should that beauty which you hold in lease
Find no determination; then you were
Yourself again after yourself's decease,
When your sweet issue your sweet form should
    bear.
Who lets so fair a house fall to decay,
● Which husbandry in honour might uphold
Against the stormy gusts of winter's day
And barren rage of death's eternal cold?
    O, none but unthrifts! Dear my love, you know
    You had a father: let your son say so.

XIV.

Not from the stars do I my judgement pluck;
● And yet methinks I have astronomy,
But not to tell of good or evil luck,
Of plagues, of dearths, or seasons' quality;
● Nor can I fortune to brief minutes tell,
Pointing to each his thunder, rain and wind,
Or say with princes if it shall go well,
By oft predict that I in heaven find:
But from thine eyes my knowledge I derive,
● And, constant stars, in them I read such art
As truth and beauty shall together thrive,
If from thyself to store thou wouldst convert;
   Or else of thee this I prognosticate:
● Thy end is truth's and beauty's doom and date.

XV.

When I consider every thing that grows
Holds in perfection but a little moment,
That this huge stage presenteth nought but shows
Whereon the stars in secret influence comment;
When I perceive that men as plants increase,
Cheered and check'd even by the self-same sky,
Vaunt in their youthful sap, at height decrease,
And wear their brave state out of memory;
Then the conceit of this inconstant stay
Sets you most rich in youth before my sight,
Where wasteful Time debateth with Decay,
To change your day of youth to sullied night;
   And all in war with Time for love of you,
● As he takes from you, I engraft you new.

XVI.

But wherefore do not you a mightier way
Make war upon this bloody tyrant, Time?
And fortify yourself in your decay
With means more blessed than my barren rhyme?
Now stand you on the top of happy hours,
And many maiden gardens yet unset
With virtuous wish would bear your living flowers,
Much liker than your painted counterfeit:
● So should the lines of life that life repair,
Which this, Time's pencil, or my pupil pen,
Neither in inward worth nor outward fair,
Can make you live yourself in eyes of men.
   To give away yourself keeps yourself still,
   And you must live, drawn by your own sweet
      skill.

XVII.

Who will believe my verse in time to come,
If it were fill'd with your most high deserts?
Though yet, heaven knows, it is but as a tomb
Which hides your life and shows not half your parts.
If I could write the beauty of your eyes
And in fresh numbers number all your graces,
The age to come would say 'This poet lies;
Such heavenly touches ne'er touch'd earthly faces.'
So should my papers yellow'd with their age
Be scorn'd like old men of less truth than tongue,
And your true rights be term'd a poet's rage
● And stretched metre of an antique song:
   But were some child of yours alive that time,
   You should live twice; in it and in my rhyme.

XVIII.

Shall I compare thee to a summer's day?
Thou art more lovely and more temperate:

XIV

2 *astronomy.* Astrology.

5 *fortune . . . tell.* i.e. foretell the events of every moment.

10 *read such art.* Learn such information.

14 *doom and date.* Prescribed end.

XV

14 *engraft you new.* Infuse new life into you.

XVI

9 *lines of life.* Living features (i.e. of children).

13 *give away yourself.* i.e. transfer yourself into children.

XVII

12 *stretched metre.* Hyperbole.

XVII: 'You should live twice; in it and in my rhyme'.
Illustration from an Hungarian edition of the *Sonnets*, 1964

XVIII

9 *thou owest.* You own.

XX

1 *with . . . painted.* i.e. without cosmetics.

5 *rolling.* Straying.

11 *defeated.* Cheated.

12 *one thing.* i.e. a penis.

XXI

1 *Muse.* Poet.

4 *rehearse.* Compare.

8 *rondure.* Sphere.

13 *that like . . . well.* i.e. that like rumour.

XXII

4 *expiate.* Wind up.

Rough winds do shake the darling buds of May,
And summer's lease hath all too short a date:
Sometime too hot the eye of heaven shines,
And often is his gold complexion dimm'd;
And every fair from fair sometime declines,
By chance or nature's changing course untrimm'd;
But thy eternal summer shall not fade
● Nor lose possession of that fair thou owest;
Nor shall Death brag thou wander'st in his shade,
When in eternal lines to time thou growest:
  So long as men can breathe or eyes can see,
  So long lives this and this gives life to thee.

XIX.

Devouring Time, blunt thou the lion's paws,
And make the earth devour her own sweet brood;
Pluck the keen teeth from the fierce tiger's jaws,
And burn the long-lived phœnix in her blood;
Make glad and sorry seasons as thou fleets,
And do whate'er thou wilt, swift-footed Time,
To the wide world and all her fading sweets;
But I forbid thee one most heinous crime:
O, carve not with thy hours my love's fair brow,
Nor draw no lines there with thine antique pen;
Him in thy course untainted do allow
For beauty's pattern to succeeding men.
  Yet, do thy worst, old Time: despite thy wrong,
  My love shall in my verse ever live young.

XX.

● A woman's face with Nature's own hand painted
Hast thou, the master-mistress of my passion;
A woman's gentle heart, but not acquainted
With shifting change, as is false women's fashion;
● An eye more bright than theirs, less false in rolling,
Gilding the object whereupon it gazeth;
A man in hue, all 'hues' in his controlling,
Which steals men's eyes and women's souls
    amazeth.
And for a woman wert thou first created;
Till Nature, as she wrought thee, fell a-doting,
● And by addition me of thee defeated,
● By adding one thing to my purpose nothing.
  But since she prick'd thee out for women's
    pleasure,
  Mine be thy love and thy love's use their treasure.

XXI.

● So is it not with me as with that Muse
Stirr'd by a painted beauty to his verse,
Who heaven itself for ornament doth use
● And every fair with his fair doth rehearse;
Making a couplement of proud compare,
With sun and moon, with earth and sea's rich gems,
With April's first-born flowers, and all things rare
● That heaven's air in this huge rondure hems.
O, let me, true in love, but truly write,
And then believe me, my love is as fair
As any mother's child, though not so bright
As those gold candles fix'd in heaven's air:
●   Let them say more that like of hearsay well;
  I will not praise that purpose not to sell.

XXII.

My glass shall not persuade me I am old,
So long as youth and thou are of one date;
But when in thee time's furrows I behold,
● Then look I death my days should expiate.

For all that beauty that doth cover thee
Is but the seemly raiment of my heart,
Which in thy breast doth live, as thine in me :
How can I then be elder than thou art?
O, therefore, love, be of thyself so wary
As I, not for myself, but for thee will;
Bearing thy heart, which I will keep so chary
As tender nurse her babe from faring ill.
●   Presume not on thy heart when mine is slain ;
  Thou gavest me thine, not to give back again.

XXIII.

As an unperfect actor on the stage
Who with his fear is put besides his part,
Or some fierce thing replete with too much rage,
Whose strength's abundance weakens his own
    heart,
● So I, for fear of trust, forget to say
The perfect ceremony of love's rite,
And in mine own love's strength seem to decay,
O'ercharged with burden of mine own love's might.
O, let my books be then the eloquence
● And dumb presagers of my speaking breast,
Who plead for love and look for recompense
More than that tongue that more hath more ex-
    press'd.
  O, learn to read what silent love hath writ :
  To hear with eyes belongs to love's fine wit.

XXIV.

● Mine eye hath play'd the painter and hath stell'd
Thy beauty's form in table of my heart ;
My body is the frame wherein 'tis held,
● And perspective it is best painter's art.
For through the painter must you see his skill,
To find where your true image pictured lies ;
Which in my bosom's shop is hanging still,
That hath his windows glazed with thine eyes.
Now see what good turns eyes for eyes have done :
Mine eyes have drawn thy shape, and thine for me
Are windows to my breast, where-through the sun
Delights to peep, to gaze therein on thee ;
  Yet eyes this cunning want to grace their art ;
  They draw but what they see, know not the
    heart.

XXV.

Let those who are in favour with their stars
Of public honour and proud titles boast,
Whilst I, whom fortune of such triumph bars,
Unlook'd for joy in that I honour most.
Great princes' favourites their fair leaves spread
But as the marigold at the sun's eye,
And in themselves their pride lies buried,
For at a frown they in their glory die.
● The painful warrior famoused for fight,
After a thousand victories once foil'd,
● Is from the book of honour razed quite,
And all the rest forgot for which he toil'd :
  Then happy I, that love and am beloved
  Where I may not remove nor be removed.

XXVI.

Lord of my love, to whom in vassalage
Thy merit hath my duty strongly knit,
To thee I send this written embassage,
To witness duty, not to show my wit :
Duty so great, which wit so poor as mine
May make seem bare, in wanting words to show it,

13 *Presume not on.* Do not expect to regain.

XXIII

5–6 *forget . . . rite.* i.e. am no longer word-perfect in love's ritual.

10 *dumb presagers.* Silent messengers.

XXIV

1 *stell'd.* Portrayed.

4 *perspective it is.* i.e. given perspective, which is.

XXV See introduction.

9 *painful.* Striving.

11 *razed.* Erased.

XXV: 'The painful warrior famoused for fight . . . Is from the book of honour razed quite'. An allusion to the fall of the Queen's favourite, Sir Walter Ralegh, in the summer of 1592. Miniature of Ralegh by Nicholas Hilliard *c.*1585

XXVI See introduction.

7 *conceit.* Concept.

8 *all naked, will bestow it;* even though simple, will store it.

10 *aspect.* The astrological sense.

XXVII

9 *imaginary.* Imagining.

XXVIII

1 *plight.* Mood.

6 *shake hands.* Unite.

7 *the other to complain.* i.e. night making me complain.

12 *twire.* Peer.

XXIX

1 *disgrace.* Disfavour.

10 *state.* State of mind.

XXX

1 *sessions.* Court sittings.

● But that I hope some good conceit of thine
● In thy soul's thought, all naked, will bestow it;
   Till whatsoever star that guides my moving
● Points on me graciously with fair aspect
   And puts apparel on my tatter'd loving,
   To show me worthy of thy sweet respect:
      Then may I dare to boast how I do love thee;
      Till then not show my head where thou mayst
         prove me.

XXVII.

Weary with toil, I haste me to my bed,
The dear repose for limbs with travel tired;
But then begins a journey in my head,
To work my mind, when body's work's expired:
For then my thoughts, from far where I abide,
Intend a zealous pilgrimage to thee,
And keep my drooping eyelids open wide,
Looking on darkness which the blind do see:
● Save that my soul's imaginary sight
Presents thy shadow to my sightless view,
Which, like a jewel hung in ghastly night,
Makes black night beauteous and her old face new.
    Lo! thus, by day my limbs, by night my mind,
    For thee and for myself no quiet find.

XXVIII.

● How can I then return in happy plight,
That am debarr'd the benefit of rest?
When day's oppression is not eased by night,
But day by night, and night by day, oppress'd?
And each, though enemies to either's reign,
● Do in consent shake hands to torture me;
● The one by toil, the other to complain
How far I toil, still farther off from thee.
I tell the day, to please him thou art bright
And dost him grace when clouds do blot the heaven:
So flatter I the swart-complexion'd night,
● When sparkling stars twire not thou gild'st the
      even.
    But day doth daily draw my sorrows longer
    And night doth nightly make grief's strength
      seem stronger.

XXIX.

● When, in disgrace with fortune and men's eyes,
I all alone beweep my outcast state
And trouble deaf heaven with my bootless cries
And look upon myself and curse my fate,
Wishing me like to one more rich in hope,
Featured like him, like him with friends possess'd,
Desiring this man's art and that man's scope,
With what I most enjoy contented least;
Yet in these thoughts myself almost despising,
● Haply I think on thee, and then my state,
Like to the lark at break of day arising
From sullen earth, sings hymns at heaven's gate;
    For thy sweet love remember'd such wealth
      brings
    That then I scorn to change my state with kings.

XXX.

● When to the sessions of sweet silent thought
I summon up remembrance of things past,
I sigh the lack of many a thing I sought,
And with old woes new wail my dear time's waste:
Then can I drown an eye, unused to flow,
For precious friends hid in death's dateless night,

And weep afresh love's long since cancell'd woe,
● And moan the expense of many a vanish'd sight:
Then can I grieve at grievances foregone,
And heavily from woe to woe tell o'er
The sad account of fore-bemoaned moan,
Which I new pay as if not paid before.
   But if the while I think on thee, dear friend,
   All losses are restored and sorrows end.

XXXI.

Thy bosom is endeared with all hearts,
Which I by lacking have supposed dead,
And there reigns love and all love's loving parts,
And all those friends which I thought buried.
● How many a holy and obsequious tear
Hath dear religious love stol'n from mine eye
● As interest of the dead, which now appear
But things removed that hidden in thee lie!
Thou art the grave where buried love doth live,
Hung with the trophies of my lovers gone,
Who all their parts of me to thee did give;
That due of many now is thine alone:
   Their images I loved I view in thee,
   And thou, all they, hast all the all of me.

XXXII.

● If thou survive my well-contented day,
When that churl Death my bones with dust shall
    cover,
And shalt by fortune once more re-survey
These poor rude lines of thy deceased lover,
Compare them with the bettering of the time,
And though they be outstripp'd by every pen,
Reserve them for my love, not for their rhyme,
Exceeded by the height of happier men.
O, then vouchsafe me but this loving thought:
'Had my friend's Muse grown with this growing
    age,
A dearer birth than this his love had brought,
To march in ranks of better equipage:
   But since he died and poets better prove,
   Theirs for their style I'll read, his for his love.'

XXXIII.

Full many a glorious morning have I seen
Flatter the mountain-tops with sovereign eye,
Kissing with golden face the meadows green,
Gilding pale streams with heavenly alchemy;
Anon permit the basest clouds to ride
With ugly rack on his celestial face,
And from the forlorn world his visage hide,
Stealing unseen to west with this disgrace:
Even so my sun one early morn did shine
With all-triumphant splendour on my brow;
But out, alack! he was but one hour mine;
● The region cloud hath mask'd him from me now.
   Yet him for this my love no whit disdaineth;
   Suns of the world may stain when heaven's sun
    staineth.

XXXIV.

Why didst thou promise such a beauteous day
And make me travel forth without my cloak,
To let base clouds o'ertake me in my way,
Hiding thy bravery in their rotten smoke?
'Tis not enough that through the cloud thou break,
To dry the rain on my storm-beaten face,
For no man well of such a salve can speak
That heals the wound and cures not the disgrace:

8 *expense.* Loss.

XXXI

5 *obsequious.* Mourning.

7 *interest.* Rightful due.

XXXII

1 *my well-contented day.* i.e. the fulfilled day of my death.

XXXIII

12 *region cloud.* Clouds of the upper air.

XXXIV

XXIV: 'Though thou repent, yet I have still the loss:'
Illustration by Byam Shaw, *The Chiswick Shakespeare*,
1902

---

14 *ransom*. Atone for.

XXXV

6 *Authorizing*. Justifying.

7 *salving thy amiss*. Excusing your offence.

9 *to thy . . . sense*. To your physical fault I bring in an
argument.

XXXVI

5 *but one respect*. A singleness of regard.

6 *separable spite*. Spiteful separation.

14 *report*. Reputation.

XXXVII

3 *made lame*. Handicapped. *dearest*. Uttermost.

8 *engrafted to this store*. i.e. joined to this abundance.

10 *shadow*. Idea. *substance*. Reality.

XXXVIII

3 *argument*. Theme.

4 *vulgar paper*. Common writing.

Nor can thy shame give physic to my grief;
Though thou repent, yet I have still the loss:
The offender's sorrow lends but weak relief
To him that bears the strong offence's cross.
⠀⠀Ah! but those tears are pearl which thy love
⠀⠀⠀⠀sheds,
● ⠀⠀And they are rich and ransom all ill deeds.

XXXV.

No more be grieved at that which thou hast done:
Roses have thorns, and silver fountains mud;
Clouds and eclipses stain both moon and sun,
And loathsome canker lives in sweetest bud.
All men make faults, and even I in this,
● Authorizing thy trespass with compare,
● Myself corrupting, salving thy amiss,
Excusing thy sins more than thy sins are;
● For to thy sensual fault I bring in sense—
Thy adverse party is thy advocate—
And 'gainst myself a lawful plea commence:
Such civil war is in my love and hate
⠀⠀That I an accessary needs must be
⠀⠀To that sweet thief which sourly robs from me.

XXXVI.

Let me confess that we two must be twain,
Although our undivided loves are one:
So shall those blots that do with me remain
Without thy help by me be borne alone.
● In our two loves there is but one respect,
● Though in our lives a separable spite,
Which though it alter not love's sole effect,
Yet doth it steal sweet hours from love's delight.
I may not evermore acknowledge thee,
Lest my bewailed guilt should do thee shame,
Nor thou with public kindness honour me,
Unless thou take that honour from thy name:
⠀⠀But do not so; I love thee in such sort
● ⠀⠀As, thou being mine, mine is thy good report.

XXXVII.

As a decrepit father takes delight
To see his active child do deeds of youth,
● So I, made lame by fortune's dearest spite,
Take all my comfort of thy worth and truth.
For whether beauty, birth, or wealth, or wit,
Or any of these all, or all, or more,
Entitled in thy parts do crowned sit,
● I make my love engrafted to this store:
So then I am not lame, poor, nor despised,
● Whilst that this shadow doth such substance give
That I in thy abundance am sufficed
And by a part of all thy glory live.
⠀⠀Look, what is best, that best I wish in thee:
⠀⠀This wish I have; then ten times happy me!

XXXVIII.

How can my Muse want subject to invent,
While thou dost breathe, that pour'st into my verse
● Thine own sweet argument, too excellent
● For every vulgar paper to rehearse?
O, give thyself the thanks, if aught in me
Worthy perusal stand against thy sight;
For who's so dumb that cannot write to thee,
When thou thyself dost give invention light?
Be thou the tenth Muse, ten times more in worth
Than those old nine which rhymers invocate;
And he that calls on thee, let him bring forth
Eternal numbers to outlive long date.

● If my slight Muse do please these curious days,
● The pain be mine, but thine shall be the praise.

XXXIX.

O, how thy worth with manners may I sing,
When thou art all the better part of me?
What can mine own praise to mine own self bring?
And what is't but mine own when I praise thee?
Even for this let us divided live,
And our dear love lose name of single one,
That by this separation I may give
That due to thee which thou deservest alone.
O absence, what a torment wouldst thou prove,
Were it not thy sour leisure gave sweet leave
To entertain the time with thoughts of love,
● Which time and thoughts so sweetly doth deceive,
    And that thou teachest how to make one twain,
    By praising him here who doth hence remain!

XL.

Take all my loves, my love, yea, take them all;
What hast thou then more than thou hadst before?
No love, my love, that thou mayst true love call;
All mine was thine before thou hadst this more.
Then if for my love thou my love receivest,
● I cannot blame thee for my love thou usest;
But yet be blamed, if thou thyself deceivest
● By wilful taste of what thyself refusest.
I do forgive thy robbery, gentle thief,
Although thou steal thee all my poverty;
And yet, love knows, it is a greater grief
● To bear love's wrong than hate's known injury.
● Lascivious grace, in whom all ill well shows,
    Kill me with spites; yet we must not be foes.

XLI.

● Those pretty wrongs that liberty commits,
When I am sometime absent from thy heart,
Thy beauty and thy years full well befits,
For still temptation follows where thou art.
Gentle thou art and therefore to be won,
Beauteous thou art, therefore to be assailed;
And when a woman woos, what woman's son
Will sourly leave her till she have prevailed?
● Ay me! but yet thou mightst my seat forbear,
And chide thy beauty and thy straying youth,
● Who lead thee in their riot even there
Where thou art forced to break a twofold truth,
    Hers, by thy beauty tempting her to thee,
    Thine, by thy beauty being false to me.

XLII.

That thou hast her, it is not all my grief,
And yet it may be said I loved her dearly;
That she hath thee, is of my wailing chief,
A loss in love that touches me more nearly.
Loving offenders, thus I will excuse ye:
Thou dost love her, because thou know'st I love her;
● And for my sake even so doth she abuse me,
● Suffering my friend for my sake to approve her.
If I lose thee, my loss is my love's gain,
And losing her, my friend hath found that loss;
Both find each other, and I lose both twain,
And both for my sake lay on me this cross:
    But here's the joy; my friend and I are one;
    Sweet flattery! then she loves but me alone.

13 *curious.* Discriminating.

14 *pain.* Taking of pains.

XXXIX

12 *deceive.* Beguile.

XL

6 *thou usest.* You enjoy.

8 *wilful.* Deliberate.

12 *known.* Open.

13 *Lascivious grace.* You who are gracious even in infidelity.

XLI

1 *pretty wrongs.* Peccadilloes.

9 *my seat forbear.* Forgo the place belonging to me.

11 *riot.* Revels.

XLII

7 *abuse.* Betray.

8 *approve.* Prove, try.

XLII: 'And losing her, my friend hath found that loss:' Painting 'Allegory of Love: I' (Unfaithfulness) by Paulo Veronese (d.1588)

XLIII

1 *wink.* Shut my eyes in sleep.

2 *unrespected.* Unnoticed.

5 *shadow.* Image.

XLIV

2 *Injurious.* Spiteful.

13 *elements so slow.* The elements that make up the body: earth and water – both dull and slow compared with fire and air.

14 *badges . . . woe.* i.e. heaviness (for earth) and tears (for water).

Water, one of the four elements of the universe. Engraving from John Speed's *A Prospect of the Most Famous Parts of the World,* 1631

XLV

8 *melancholy.* Induced by an excess of particular elements, here water and earth.

10 *messengers.* i.e. fire and water.

XLVI

9 *'cide.* Decide. *impanneled.* i.e. drawn up for a jury.

10 *quest.* Inquiry.

12 *moiety.* Share.

XLVII

1 *a league is took.* A pact is drawn up.

XLIII.

- When most I wink, then do mine eyes best see,
- For all the day they view things unrespected;
  But when I sleep, in dreams they look on thee,
  And darkly bright are bright in dark directed.
- Then thou, whose shadow shadows doth make bright,
  How would thy shadow's form form happy show
  To the clear day with thy much clearer light,
  When to unseeing eyes thy shade shines so!
  How would, I say, mine eyes be blessed made
  By looking on thee in the living day,
  When in dead night thy fair imperfect shade
  Through heavy sleep on sightless eyes doth stay!
     All days are nights to see till I see thee,
      And nights bright days when dreams do show thee me.

XLIV.

If the dull substance of my flesh were thought,
- Injurious distance should not stop my way;
  For then despite of space I would be brought,
  From limits far remote, where thou dost stay.
  No matter then although my foot did stand
  Upon the farthest earth removed from thee;
  For nimble thought can jump both sea and land
  As soon as think the place where he would be.
  But, ah! thought kills me that I am not thought,
  To leap large lengths of miles when thou art gone,
  But that so much of earth and water wrought
  I must attend time's leisure with my moan,
-    Receiving nought by elements so slow
-    But heavy tears, badges of either's woe.

XLV.

The other two, slight air and purging fire,
Are both with thee, wherever I abide;
The first my thought, the other my desire,
These present-absent with swift motion slide.
For when these quicker elements are gone
In tender embassy of love to thee,
My life, being made of four, with two alone
- Sinks down to death, oppress'd with melancholy;
  Until life's composition be recured
- By those swift messengers return'd from thee,
  Who even but now come back again, assured
  Of thy fair health, recounting it to me:
     This told, I joy; but then no longer glad,
     I send them back again and straight grow sad.

XLVI.

Mine eye and heart are at a mortal war
How to divide the conquest of thy sight;
Mine eye my heart thy picture's sight would bar,
My heart mine eye the freedom of that right.
My heart doth plead that thou in him dost lie,—
A closet never pierced with crystal eyes—
But the defendant doth that plea deny
And says in him thy fair appearance lies.
- To 'cide this title is impanneled
- A quest of thoughts, all tenants to the heart,
  And by their verdict is determined
- The clear eye's moiety and the dear heart's part:
     As thus; mine eye's due is thy outward part,
     And my heart's right thy inward love of heart.

XLVII.

- Betwixt mine eye and heart a league is took,
  And each doth good turns now unto the other:

When that mine eye is famish'd for a look,
Or heart in love with sighs himself doth smother,
With my love's picture then my eye doth feast
● And to the painted banquet bids my heart;
Another time mine eye is my heart's guest
And in his thoughts of love doth share a part:
So, either by thy picture or my love,
Thyself away art present still with me;
For thou not farther than my thoughts canst move,
● And I am still with them and they with thee;
    Or, if they sleep, thy picture in my sight
    Awakes my heart to heart's and eye's delight.

XLVIII.

How careful was I, when I took my way,
Each trifle under truest bars to thrust,
That to my use it might unused stay
From hands of falsehood, in sure wards of trust!
But thou, to whom my jewels trifles are,
Most worthy comfort, now my greatest grief,
Thou, best of dearest and mine only care,
Art left the prey of every vulgar thief.
Thee have I not lock'd up in any chest,
Save where thou art not, though I feel thou art,
Within the gentle closure of my breast,
From whence at pleasure thou mayst come and
        part;
    And even thence thou wilt be stol'n, I fear,
    For truth proves thievish for a prize so dear.

XLIX.

Against that time, if ever that time come,
When I shall see thee frown on my defects,
● When as thy love hath cast his utmost sum,
● Call'd to that audit by advised respects;
Against that time when thou shalt strangely pass
And scarcely greet me with that sun, thine eye,
When love, converted from the thing it was,
● Shall reasons find of settled gravity,—
Against that time do I ensconce me here
Within the knowledge of mine own desert,
● And this my hand against myself uprear,
To guard the lawful reasons on thy part:
    To leave poor me thou hast the strength of laws,
●   Since why to love I can allege no cause.

L.

How heavy do I journey on the way,
When what I seek, my weary travel's end,
Doth teach that ease and that repose to say
'Thus far the miles are measured from thy friend!'
The beast that bears me, tired with my woe,
Plods dully on, to bear that weight in me,
As if by some instinct the wretch did know
His rider loved not speed, being made from thee:
The bloody spur cannot provoke him on
That sometimes anger thrusts into his hide;
Which heavily he answers with a groan,
More sharp to me than spurring to his side;
    For that same groan doth put this in my mind;
    My grief lies onward and my joy behind.

LI.

● Thus can my love excuse the slow offence
Of my dull bearer when from thee I speed:
From where thou art why should I haste me thence?
● Till I return, of posting is no need.
O, what excuse will my poor beast then find,
● When swift extremity can seem but slow?

6 *painted banquet.* Visual feast.

12 *still.* Always.

XLIX

3 *cast his utmost sum.* Made its final reckoning.

4 *advised respects.* Considered reasons.

8 *of settled gravity.* Of decided weight.

11–12 *And this . . . part.* i.e. to swear, against myself,
that your actions are just.

14 *cause.* Obligation.

LI

1 *slow offence.* Offending delay.

4 *posting.* Riding in haste.

6 *swift extremity.* Extreme swiftness.

14 *go.* Walk.

LII

8 *captain.* Chief. *carcanet.* Jewelled collar.

LIII

2 *strange shadows.* Unknown persons. *tend.* Attend.

4 *And . . . lend.* i.e. each can reflect only one of your excellences.

8 *tires.* Clothes.

9 *foison.* Harvest.

LIV

5 *canker-blooms.* Diseased hedge-roses.

LV

4 *stone.* Memorial tablet.

6 *broils.* Battles.

Then should I spur, though mounted on the wind;
In winged speed no motion shall I know:
Then can no horse with my desire keep pace;
Therefore desire, of perfect'st love being made,
Shall neigh—no dull flesh—in his fiery race;
But love, for love, thus shall excuse my jade;
  Since from thee going he went wilful-slow,
  Towards thee I'll run, and give him leave to go.

LII.

So am I as the rich, whose blessed key
Can bring him to his sweet up-locked treasure,
The which he will not every hour survey,
For blunting the fine point of seldom pleasure.
Therefore are feasts so solemn and so rare,
Since, seldom coming, in the long year set,
Like stones of worth they thinly placed are,
Or captain jewels in the carcanet.
So is the time that keeps you as my chest,
Or as the wardrobe which the robe doth hide,
To make some special instant special blest,
By new unfolding his imprison'd pride.
  Blessed are you, whose worthiness gives scope,
  Being had, to triumph, being lack'd, to hope.

LIII.

What is your substance, whereof are you made,
That millions of strange shadows on you tend?
Since every one hath, every one, one shade,
And you, but one, can every shadow lend.
Describe Adonis, and the counterfeit
Is poorly imitated after you;
On Helen's cheek all art of beauty set,
And you in Grecian tires are painted new:
Speak of the spring and foison of the year;
The one doth shadow of your beauty show,
The other as your bounty doth appear;
And you in every blessed shape we know.
  In all external grace you have some part,
  But you like none, none you, for constant heart.

LIV.

O, how much more doth beauty beauteous seem
By that sweet ornament which truth doth give!
The rose looks fair, but fairer we it deem
For that sweet odour which doth in it live.
The canker-blooms have full as deep a dye
As the perfumed tincture of the roses,
Hang on such thorns and play as wantonly
When summer's breath their masked buds dis-
    closes:
But, for their virtue only is their show,
They live unwoo'd and unrespected fade,
Die to themselves. Sweet roses do not so;
Of their sweet deaths are sweetest odours made:
  And so of you, beauteous and lovely youth,
  When that shall fade, my verse distills your
    truth.

LV.

Not marble, nor the gilded monuments
Of princes, shall outlive this powerful rhyme;
But you shall shine more bright in these contents
Than unswept stone besmear'd with sluttish time.
When wasteful war shall statues overturn,
And broils root out the work of masonry,
Nor Mars his sword nor war's quick fire shall burn
The living record of your memory.

- 'Gainst death and all-oblivious enmity
  Shall you pace forth; your praise shall still find
        room
  Even in the eyes of all posterity
- That wear this world out to the ending doom.
-     So, till the judgement that yourself arise,
    You live in this, and dwell in lovers' eyes.

LVI.

Sweet love, renew thy force; be it not said
Thy edge should blunter be than appetite,
Which but to-day by feeding is allay'd,
To-morrow sharpen'd in his former might:
So, love, be thou; although to-day thou fill
Thy hungry eyes even till they wink with fullness,
To-morrow see again, and do not kill
The spirit of love with a perpetual dullness.
Let this sad interim like the ocean be
- Which parts the shore, where two contracted new
  Come daily to the banks, that, when they see
- Return of love, more blest may be the view;
      Else call it winter, which being full of care
      Makes summer's welcome thrice more wish'd,
          more rare.

LVII.

Being your slave, what should I do but tend
Upon the hours and times of your desire?
I have no precious time at all to spend,
Nor services to do, till you require.
Nor dare I chide the world-without-end hour
Whilst I, my sovereign, watch the clock for you,
Nor think the bitterness of absence sour
When you have bid your servant once adieu;
Nor dare I question with my jealous thought
- Where you may be, or your affairs suppose,
  But, like a sad slave, stay and think of nought
  Save, where you are how happy you make those.
      So true a fool is love that in your will,
      Though you do any thing, he thinks no ill.

LVIII.

That god forbid that made me first your slave,
I should in thought control your times of pleasure,
Or at your hand the account of hours to crave,
Being your vassal, bound to stay your leisure!
O, let me suffer, being at your beck,
- The imprison'd absence of your liberty;
- And patience, tame to sufferance, bide each check,
  Without accusing you of injury.
- Be where you list, your charter is so strong
- That you yourself may privilege your time
  To what you will; to you it doth belong
  Yourself to pardon of self-doing crime.
      I am to wait, though waiting so be hell;
      Not blame your pleasure, be it ill or well.

LIX.

If there be nothing new, but that which is
Hath been before, how are our brains beguiled,
- Which, labouring for invention, bear amiss
  The second burthen of a former child!
  O, that record could with a backward look,
  Even of five hundred courses of the sun,
  Show me your image in some antique book,
- Since mind at first in character was done!
  That I might see what the old world could say
  To this composed wonder of your frame;

9 *all-oblivious enmity.* Oblivion, the enemy of all.

12 *wear.* Last.

13 *judgement that.* Judgement day when.

LVI

10 *parts the shore.* Divides the shores. *contracted new.* Newly betrothed.

12 *love.* The loved one.

LVII

10 *suppose.* Speculate about.

LVIII

6 *The imprison'd . . . liberty.* The imprisonment that your freedom to be absent brings.

7 *tame to sufferance.* Trained to suffering. *bide each check.* Put up with each rebuke.

9 *list.* Wish. *charter.* Privilege.

10 *privilege.* Dispose of.

LIX

3 *invention.* Novelty. *bear amiss.* Miscarry.

8 *Since . . . done!* Since thought was first expressed in writing.

12 *revolution be the same.* One cycle repeats the other.

LX

5 *Nativity.* The new-born. *the main of light.* Light of day.

7 *Crooked.* Malignant.

8 *confound.* Destroy.

13 *times in hope.* Hoped-for times.

LXI

8 *scope and tenour.* Aim and purport.

LXII

10 *chopp'd.* Seamed. *tann'd antiquity.* Leathery old age.

13 *'Tis . . . praise.* I am praising you whom I identify with myself.

LXIII

1 *Against.* In time when.

LXIII: 'Against my love shall be, as I am now, With Time's injurious hand crush'd and o'erworn:' Painting 'An Allegory' (Cupid, Venus and Time) by Bronzino (1503–72)

Whether we are mended, or whether better **they,**
● Or whether revolution be the same.
　　O, sure I am, the wits of former days
　　To subjects worse have given admiring praise.

LX.

Like as the waves make towards the pebbled shore,
So do our minutes hasten to their end;
Each changing place with that which goes before,
In sequent toil all forwards do contend.
● Nativity, once in the main of light,
　Crawls to maturity, wherewith being crown'd,
● Crooked eclipses 'gainst his glory fight,
● And Time that gave doth now his gift confound.
Time doth transfix the flourish set on youth
And delves the parallels in beauty's brow,
Feeds on the rarities of nature's truth,
And nothing stands but for his scythe to mow:
● †And yet to times in hope my verse shall stand,
　Praising thy worth, despite his cruel hand.

LXI.

Is it thy will thy image should keep open
My heavy eyelids to the weary night?
Dost thou desire my slumbers should be broken,
While shadows like to thee do mock my sight?
Is it thy spirit that thou send'st from thee
So far from home into my deeds to pry,
To find out shames and idle hours in me,
● The scope and tenour of thy jealousy?
O, no! thy love, though much, is not so great:
It is my love that keeps mine eye awake;
Mine own true love that doth my rest defeat,
To play the watchman ever for thy sake:
　　For thee watch I whilst thou dost wake elsewhere,
　　From me far off, with others all too near.

LXII.

Sin of self-love possesseth all mine eye
And all my soul and all my every part;
And for this sin there is no remedy,
It is so grounded inward in my heart.
Methinks no face so gracious is as mine,
No shape so true, no truth of such account;
And for myself mine own worth do define,
As I all other in all worths surmount.
But when my glass shows me myself indeed,
● Beated and chopp'd with tann'd antiquity,
Mine own self-love quite contrary I read;
Self so self-loving were iniquity.
● 'Tis thee, myself, that for myself I praise,
　Painting my age with beauty of thy days.

LXIII.

● Against my love shall be, as I am now,
With Time's injurious hand crush'd and o'erworn;
When hours have drain'd his blood and fill'd **his**
　　brow
With lines and wrinkles; when his youthful **morn**
Hath travell'd on to age's steepy night,
And all those beauties whereof now he's king
Are vanishing or vanish'd out of sight,
Stealing away the treasure of his spring;
For such a time do I now fortify
Against confounding age's cruel knife,
That he shall never cut from memory
My sweet love's beauty, though my lover's life:

His beauty shall in these black lines be seen,
And they shall live, and he in them still green.

LXIV.

When I have seen by Time's fell hand defaced
The rich proud cost of outworn buried age;
When sometime lofty towers I see down-razed
● And brass eternal slave to mortal rage;
When I have seen the hungry ocean gain
Advantage on the kingdom of the shore,
And the firm soil win of the watery main,
● Increasing store with loss and loss with store;
When I have seen such interchange of state,
Or state itself confounded to decay;
Ruin hath taught me thus to ruminate,
That Time will come and take my love away.
　　This thought is as a death, which cannot choose
　　But weep to have that which it fears to lose.

LXV.

Since brass, nor stone, nor earth, nor boundless sea,
But sad mortality o'er-sways their power,
● How with this rage shall beauty hold a plea,
● Whose action is no stronger than a flower?
O, how shall summer's honey breath hold out
Against the wreckful siege of battering days,
When rocks impregnable are not so stout,
Nor gates of steel so strong, but Time decays?
O fearful meditation! where, alack,
● Shall Time's best jewel from Time's chest lie hid?
Or what strong hand can hold his swift foot back?
Or who his spoil of beauty can forbid?
　　O, none, unless this miracle have might,
　　That in black ink my love may still shine bright.

LXVI.

Tired with all these, for restful death I cry,
As, to behold desert a beggar born,
● And needy nothing trimm'd in jollity,
And purest faith unhappily forsworn,
And gilded honour shamefully misplaced,
And maiden virtue rudely strumpeted,
And right perfection wrongfully disgraced,
● And strength by limping sway disabled,
And art made tongue-tied by authority,
● And folly doctor-like controlling skill,
● And simple truth miscall'd simplicity,
And captive good attending captain ill:
　　Tired with all these, from these would I be gone,
　　Save that, to die, I leave my love alone.

LXVII.

Ah! wherefore with infection should he live,
And with his presence grace impiety,
That sin by him advantage should achieve
● And lace itself with his society?
Why should false painting imitate his cheek
● And steal dead seeing of his living hue?
● Why should poor beauty indirectly seek
Roses of shadow, since his rose is true?
Why should he live, now Nature bankrupt is,
● Beggar'd of blood to blush through lively veins?
● For she hath no exchequer now but his,
And, proud of many, lives upon his gains.
　　O, him she stores, to show what wealth she had
　　In days long since, before these last so bad.

LXIV

4 *brass eternal.* Everlasting brass. *mortal rage.* Ravages of men.

8 *Increasing store with loss and loss with store.* i.e. one gaining by the other's loss and one losing with the other's gain.

LXV

3 *rage.* Destructive power.

4 *action.* Case.

10 *Time's best jewel.* i.e. beauty.

LXVI

3 *needy . . . jollity.* i.e. empty nobody gaily bedecked.

8 *by . . . disabled.* i.e. weakened by incompetent leadership.

10 *doctor-like.* i.e. pedantically.

11 *simplicity.* Stupidity.

Death with a victim. From a medieval woodcut

LXVII

4 *lace.* Ornament.

6 *dead seeing.* The lifeless appearance.

7 *poor.* Inferior. *indirectly.* By imitation.

10 *Beggar'd . . . veins.* i.e. lacking the blood to blush naturally.

11 *exchequer.* i.e. treasury.

LXVIII

3 *bastard signs.* Cosmetics.

LXIX

4 *commend.* Admit.

LXX

3 *suspect.* Suspicion.

10 *charged.* Attacked.

12 *tie up envy.* i.e. silence malice.

14 *owe.* Own.

LXVIII.

Thus is his cheek the map of days outworn,
When beauty lived and died as flowers do now,
● Before these bastard signs of fair were born,
Or durst inhabit on a living brow;
Before the golden tresses of the dead,
The right of sepulchres, were shorn away,
To live a second life on second head;
Ere beauty's dead fleece made another gay:
In him those holy antique hours are seen,
Without all ornament, itself and true,
Making no summer of another's green,
Robbing no old to dress his beauty new;
   And him as for a map doth Nature store,
   To show false Art what beauty was of yore.

LXIX.

Those parts of thee that the world's eye doth view
Want nothing that the thought of hearts can mend;
All tongues, the voice of souls, give thee that due,
● Uttering bare truth, even so as foes commend.
Thy outward thus with outward praise is crown'd;
But those same tongues that give thee so thine own
In other accents do this praise confound
By seeing farther than the eye hath shown.
They look into the beauty of thy mind,
And that, in guess, they measure by thy deeds;
Then, churls, their thoughts, although their eyes
    were kind,
To thy fair flower add the rank smell of weeds:
   But why thy odour matcheth not thy show,
   The solve is this, that thou dost common grow.

LXX.

That thou art blamed shall not be thy defect,
For slander's mark was ever yet the fair;
● The ornament of beauty is suspect,
A crow that flies in heaven's sweetest air.
So thou be good, slander doth but approve
Thy worth the greater, being woo'd of time;
For canker vice the sweetest buds doth love,
And thou present'st a pure unstained prime.
Thou hast pass'd by the ambush of young days,
● Either not assail'd or victor being charged;
Yet this thy praise cannot be so thy praise,
● To tie up envy evermore enlarged:
   If some suspect of ill mask'd not thy show,
●   Then thou alone kingdoms of hearts shouldst
    owe.

LXXI.

No longer mourn for me when I am dead
Than you shall hear the surly sullen bell
Give warning to the world that I am fled
From this vile world, with vilest worms to dwell:
Nay, if you read this line, remember not
The hand that writ it; for I love you so
That I in your sweet thoughts would be forgot
If thinking on me then should make you woe.
O, if, I say, you look upon this verse
When I perhaps compounded am with clay,
Do not so much as my poor name rehearse,
But let your love even with my life decay,
   Lest the wise world should look into your moan
   And mock you with me after I am gone.

LXXII.

O, lest the world should task you to recite
What merit lived in me, that you should love

After my death, dear love, forget me quite,
For you in me can nothing worthy prove;
Unless you would devise some virtuous lie,
To do more for me than mine own desert,
And hang more praise upon deceased I
Than niggard truth would willingly impart:
O, lest your true love may seem false in this,
That you for love speak well of me untrue,
My name be buried where my body is,
And live no more to shame nor me nor you.
　　For I am shamed by that which I bring forth,
　　And so should you, to love things nothing worth.

LXXIII.

That time of year thou mayst in me behold
When yellow leaves, or none, or few, do hang
Upon those boughs which shake against the cold,
Bare ruin'd choirs, where late the sweet birds
　　　　sang.
In me thou see'st the twilight of such day
As after sunset fadeth in the west,
Which by and by black night doth take away,
● Death's second self, that seals up all in rest.
In me thou see'st the glowing of such fire
That on the ashes of his youth doth lie,
As the death-bed whereon it must expire
● Consumed with that which it was nourish'd by.
　　This thou perceivest, which makes thy love
　　　　more strong,
　　To love that well which thou must leave ere long.

LXXIV.

But be contented: when that fell arrest
● Without all bail shall carry me away,
● My life hath in this line some interest,
Which for memorial still with thee shall stay.
When thou reviewest this, thou dost review
The very part was consecrate to thee:
The earth can have but earth, which is his due;
My spirit is thine, the better part of me:
So then thou hast but lost the dregs of life,
The prey of worms, my body being dead,
The coward conquest of a wretch's knife,
Too base of thee to be remembered.
● 　The worth of that is that which it contains,
● 　And that is this, and this with thee remains.

LXXV.

So are you to my thoughts as food to life,
Or as sweet-season'd showers are to the ground;
● And for the peace of you I hold such strife
As 'twixt a miser and his wealth is found;
Now proud as an enjoyer and anon
● Doubting the filching age will steal his treasure,
Now counting best to be with you alone,
● Then better'd that the world may see my pleasure;
Sometime all full with feasting on your sight
And by and by clean starved for a look;
Possessing or pursuing no delight,
Save what is had or must from you be took.
　　Thus do I pine and surfeit day by day,
● 　Or gluttoning on all, or all away.

LXXVI.

Why is my verse so barren of new pride,
● So far from variation or quick change?
Why with the time do I not glance aside
To new-found methods and to compounds strange?

LXXIII

8 *Death's second self.* i.e. sleep.

12 *with that . . . by.* i.e. the fire of life.

LXXIV

2 *Without all bail.* Without reprieve.

3 *line.* Poem.

13 *worth of that.* Only value of (the body). *is that which it contains.* i.e. the soul.

14 *this.* i.e. his spirit.

LXXV

3 *peace of you.* i.e. the peace you bring me. *hold such strife.* Struggle.

6 *Doubting.* Fearing.

8 *better'd.* Better pleased.

14 *Or . . . away.* Either wholly given up to you or wholly deprived.

LXXVI

2 *quick change.* New fashion.

6 *noted weed*. Familiar garb.

LXXVII

3 *vacant leaves*. Blank pages.

6 *mouthed*. Devouring.

13 *offices*. Regular duties. *look*. i.e. at the mirror, the sundial and the book.

LXXVIII See introduction.

3 *got my use*. Followed my practice.

5 *on high*. Aloud.

LXXIX

4 *give another place*. Give up place to another.

11 *afford*. Offer.

LXXX

2 *better spirit*. More gifted poet.

8 *wilfully*. Boldly.

Why write I still all one, ever the same,
● And keep invention in a noted weed,
That every word doth almost tell my name,
Showing their birth and where they did proceed?
O, know, sweet love, I always write of you,
And you and love are still my argument;
So all my best is dressing old words new,
Spending again what is already spent:
   For as the sun is daily new and old,
   So is my love still telling what is told.

LXXVII.

Thy glass will show thee how thy beauties wear,
Thy dial how thy precious minutes waste;
● The vacant leaves thy mind's imprint will bear,
And of this book this learning mayst thou taste.
The wrinkles which thy glass will truly show
● Of mouthed graves will give thee memory;
Thou by thy dial's shady stealth mayst know
Time's thievish progress to eternity.
Look, what thy memory can not contain
Commit to these waste blanks, and thou shalt find
Those children nursed, deliver'd from thy brain,
To take a new acquaintance of thy mind.
●   These offices, so oft as thou wilt look,
   Shall profit thee and much enrich thy book.

LXXVIII.

So oft have I invoked thee for my Muse
And found such fair assistance in my verse
● As every alien pen hath got my use
And under thee their poesy disperse.
● Thine eyes that taught the dumb on high to sing
And heavy ignorance aloft to fly
Have added feathers to the learned's wing
And given grace a double majesty.
Yet be most proud of that which I compile,
Whose influence is thine and born of thee:
In others' works thou dost but mend the style,
And arts with thy sweet graces graced be;
   But thou art all my art and dost advance
   As high as learning my rude ignorance.

LXXIX.

Whilst I alone did call upon thy aid,
My verse alone had all thy gentle grace,
But now my gracious numbers are decay'd
● And my sick Muse doth give another place.
I grant, sweet love, thy lovely argument
Deserves the travail of a worthier pen,
Yet what of thee thy poet doth invent
He robs thee of and pays it thee again.
He lends thee virtue and he stole that word
From thy behaviour; beauty doth he give
● And found it in thy cheek; he can afford
No praise to thee but what in thee doth live.
   Then thank him not for that which he doth say
   Since what he owes thee thou thyself dost pay

LXXX.

O, how I faint when I of you do write,
● Knowing a better spirit doth use your name,
And in the praise thereof spends all his might,
To make me tongue-tied, speaking of your fame!
But since your worth, wide as the ocean is,
The humble as the proudest sail doth bear,
My saucy bark inferior far to his
● On your broad main doth wilfully appear.

Your shallowest help will hold me up afloat,
Whilst he upon your soundless deep doth ride;
Or, being wreck'd, I am a worthless boat,
He of tall building and of goodly pride:
    Then if he thrive and I be cast away,
    The worst was this; my love was my decay.

LXXXI.

Or I shall live your epitaph to make,
Or you survive when I in earth am rotten;
● From hence your memory death cannot take,
Although in me each part will be forgotten.
Your name from hence immortal life shall have,
Though I, once gone, to all the world must die:
The earth can yield me but a common grave,
When you entombed in men's eyes shall lie.
Your monument shall be my gentle verse,
Which eyes not yet created shall o'er-read,
And tongues to be your being shall rehearse
When all the breathers of this world are dead;
    You still shall live—such virtue hath my pen—
    Where breath most breathes, even in the mouths
        of men.

LXXXII.

I grant thou wert not married to my Muse
● And therefore mayst without attaint o'erlook
The dedicated words which writers use
Of their fair subject, blessing every book.
Thou art as fair in knowledge as in hue,
● Finding thy worth a limit past my praise,
And therefore art enforced to seek anew
Some fresher stamp of the time-bettering days.
And do so, love; yet when they have devised
What strained touches rhetoric can lend,
● Thou truly fair wert truly sympathized
In true plain words by thy true-telling friend;
    And their gross painting might be better used
    Where cheeks need blood; in thee it is abused.

LXXXIII.

I never saw that you did painting need
And therefore to your fair no painting set;
I found, or thought I found, you did exceed
● The barren tender of a poet's debt;
● And therefore have I slept in your report,
That you yourself being extant well might show
How far a modern quill doth come too short,
Speaking of worth, what worth in you doth grow.
This silence for my sin you did impute,
Which shall be most my glory, being dumb;
For I impair not beauty being mute,
● When others would give life and bring a tomb.
    There lives more life in one of your fair eyes
    Than both your poets can in praise devise.

LXXXIV.

Who is it that says most? which can say more
Than this rich praise, that you alone are you?
● In whose confine immured is the store
Which should example where your equal grew.
Lean penury within that pen doth dwell
That to his subject lends not some small glory;
But he that writes of you, if he can tell
That you are you, so dignifies his story,
Let him but copy what in you is writ,
Not making worse what nature made so clear,
And such a counterpart shall fame his wit,
Making his style admired every where.

LXXXI

3 *hence.* This verse.

LXXXII

2 *attaint.* Dishonour.

6 *Finding . . . past.* Knowing your worth is beyond measure.

11 *sympathized.* Represented.

LXXXIII

4 *tender.* Offering.

5 *slept . . . report.* Been inactive in writing of you.

12 *bring a tomb.* Reduce you to a dead image.

LXXXIV

3–4 *In . . . grew.* In whom are locked up all the qualities needed to provide an equal.

LXXXV

1 *her.* Herself.

3 *Reserve.* Preserve. *character.* Writing.

4 *filed.* Polished.

6–7 *cry . . . affords.* i.e. give approval to every poem offered by that able poet.

13 *the breath of words.* Actual words.

LXXXVI See introduction.

6 *dead.* i.e. dead silent.

10 *gulls . . . intelligence.* Cheats him with information.

13 *countenance.* Approval.

LXXXVII

3 *charter.* Privilege. *releasing.* Release from obligation.

7 *cause.* Justification.

11 *upon misprision growing.* Based on error.

LXXXVIII

1 *set me light.* Make light of me.

LXXXVIII: 'When thou shalt be disposed to set me light And place my merit in the eye of scorn'. Painting 'Allegory of Love: II' (Scorn) by Paolo Veronese (d.1588)

You to your beauteous blessings add a curse,
Being fond on praise, which makes your praises
worse.

LXXXV.

● My tongue-tied Muse in manners holds her still,
While comments of your praise, richly compiled,
● Reserve their character with golden quill
● And precious phrase by all the Muses filed.
I think good thoughts whilst other write good
words,
● And like unletter'd clerk still cry 'Amen'
To every hymn that able spirit affords
In polish'd form of well-refined pen.
Hearing you praised, I say ''Tis so, 'tis true,'
And to the most of praise add something more;
But that is in my thought, whose love to you,
Though words come hindmost, holds his rank
before.
● Then others for the breath of words respect,
Me for my dumb thoughts, speaking in effect.

LXXXVI.

Was it the proud full sail of his great verse,
Bound for the prize of all too precious you,
That did my ripe thoughts in my brain inhearse,
Making their tomb the womb wherein they grew?
Was it his spirit, by spirits taught to write
● Above a mortal pitch, that struck me dead?
No, neither he, nor his compeers by night
Giving him aid, my verse astonished.
He, nor that affable familiar ghost
● Which nightly gulls him with intelligence,
As victors of my silence cannot boast;
I was not sick of any fear from thence:
● But when your countenance fill'd up his line,
Then lack'd I matter; that enfeebled mine.

LXXXVII.

Farewell! thou art too dear for my possessing,
And like enough thou know'st thy estimate:
● The charter of thy worth gives thee releasing;
My bonds in thee are all determinate.
For how do I hold thee but by thy granting?
And for that riches where is my deserving?
● The cause of this fair gift in me is wanting,
And so my patent back again is swerving.
Thyself thou gavest, thy own worth then not
knowing,
Or me, to whom thou gavest it, else mistaking;
● So thy great gift, upon misprision growing,
Comes home again, on better judgement making.
Thus have I had thee, as a dream doth flatter,
In sleep a king, but waking no such matter.

LXXXVIII.

● When thou shalt be disposed to set me light
And place my merit in the eye of scorn,
Upon my side against myself I'll fight
And prove thee virtuous, though thou art forsworn.
With mine own weakness being best acquainted,
Upon thy part I can set down a story
Of faults conceal'd, wherein I am attainted,
That thou in losing me shalt win much glory:
And I by this will be a gainer too;
For bending all my loving thoughts on thee,
The injuries that to myself I do,
Doing thee vantage, double-vantage me.

Such is my love, to thee I so belong,
That for thy right myself will bear all wrong.

LXXXIX.

Say that thou didst forsake me for some fault,
And I will comment upon that offence;
● Speak of my lameness, and I straight will halt,
Against thy reasons making no defence.
● Thou canst not, love, disgrace me half so ill,
● To set a form upon desired change,
As I'll myself disgrace: knowing thy will,
I will acquaintance strangle and look strange,
Be absent from thy walks, and in my tongue
Thy sweet beloved name no more shall dwell,
Lest I, too much profane, should do it wrong
And haply of our old acquaintance tell.
● For thee against myself I'll vow debate,
For I must ne'er love him whom thou dost hate.

XC.

Then hate me when thou wilt; if ever, now;
Now, while the world is bent my deeds to cross,
Join with the spite of fortune, make me bow,
● And do not drop in for an after-loss:
Ah, do not, when my heart hath 'scaped this sorrow,
● Come in the rearward of a conquer'd woe;
Give not a windy night a rainy morrow,
To linger out a purposed overthrow.
If thou wilt leave me, do not leave me last,
When other petty griefs have done their spite,
But in the onset come; so shall I taste
At first the very worst of fortune's might,
  And other strains of woe, which now seem woe,
  Compared with loss of thee will not seem so.

XCI.

Some glory in their birth, some in their skill,
Some in their wealth, some in their bodies' force,
Some in their garments, though new-fangled ill,
Some in their hawks and hounds, some in their
      horse;
● And every humour hath his adjunct pleasure,
Wherein it finds a joy above the rest:
But these particulars are not my measure;
All these I better in one general best.
Thy love is better than high birth to me,
Richer than wealth, prouder than garments' cost,
Of more delight than hawks or horses be;
And having thee, of all men's pride I boast:
  Wretched in this alone, that thou mayst take
  All this away and me most wretched make.

XCII.

But do thy worst to steal thyself away,
For term of life thou art assured mine,
And life no longer than thy love will stay,
For it depends upon that love of thine.
Then need I not to fear the worst of wrongs,
When in the least of them my life hath end.
I see a better state to me belongs
● Than that which on thy humour doth depend;
Thou canst not vex me with inconstant mind,
● Since that my life on thy revolt doth lie.
● O, what a happy title do I find,
Happy to have thy love, happy to die!
  But what's so blessed-fair that fears no blot?
  Thou mayst be false, and yet I know it not.

LXXXIX

3 *halt*. Limp.

5 *disgrace*. Disparage.

6 *To . . . change*. To conform to the change that you desire.

13 *vow debate*. Take issue.

XC

4 *drop . . . after-loss*. Casually add to my grief.

6 *Come . . . woe*. Act after I have overcome my grief.

XCI

XCI: 'Some in their garments, though new-fangled ill.'
Illustration by Byam Shaw, *The Chiswick Shakespeare*,
1902

5 *humour*. Disposition. *adjunct*. Corresponding.

XCII

8 *humour*. Whim.

10 *on thy . . . lie*. i.e. ends with your turning away from me.

11 *happy title*. Title to happiness.

XCIII

6 *in that.* i.e. in your eye. *I . . . change.* I cannot know your changes of mood.

8 *strange.* Unfriendly.

XCIV

6 *expense.* Expenditure.

7 *owners . . . faces.* Possessors of the qualities that show in them.

8 *stewards.* Caretakers.

XCV

3 *name.* Reputation.

6 *sport.* Love affairs.

XCVI

3 *of more and less.* By great and small.

8 *translated.* Transformed.

12 *state.* Power.

XCIII.

So shall I live, supposing thou art true,
Like a deceived husband; so love's face
May still seem love to me, though alter'd new;
Thy looks with me, thy heart in other place:
For there can live no hatred in thine eye,
● Therefore in that I cannot know thy change.
In many's looks the false heart's history
● Is writ in moods and frowns and wrinkles strange,
But heaven in thy creation did decree
That in thy face sweet love should ever dwell;
Whate'er thy thoughts or thy heart's workings be,
Thy looks should nothing thence but sweetness
    tell.
  How like Eve's apple doth thy beauty grow,
  If thy sweet virtue answer not thy show!

XCIV.

They that have power to hurt and will do none,
That do not do the thing they most do show,
Who, moving others, are themselves as stone,
Unmoved, cold, and to temptation slow,·
They rightly do inherit heaven's graces
● And husband nature's riches from expense;
● They are the lords and owners of their faces,
● Others but stewards of their excellence.
The summer's flower is to the summer sweet,
Though to itself it only live and die,
But if that flower with base infection meet,
The basest weed outbraves his dignity:
  For sweetest things turn sourest by their deeds;
  Lilies that fester smell far worse than weeds.

XCV.

How sweet and lovely dost thou make the shame
Which, like a canker in the fragrant rose,
● Doth spot the beauty of thy budding name!
O, in what sweets dost thou thy sins enclose!
That tongue that tells the story of thy days,
● Making lascivious comments on thy sport,
Cannot dispraise but in a kind of praise;
Naming thy name blesses an ill report.
O, what a mansion have those vices got
Which for their habitation chose out thee,
Where beauty's veil doth cover every blot,
And all things turn to fair that eyes can see!
  Take heed, dear heart, of this large privilege;
  The hardest knife ill-used doth lose his edge.

XCVI.

Some say thy fault is youth, some wantonness;
Some say thy grace is youth and gentle sport;
● Both grace and faults are loved of more and less;
Thou makest faults graces that to thee resort.
As on the finger of a throned queen
The basest jewel will be well esteem'd,
So are those errors that in thee are seen
● To truths translated and for true things deem'd.
How many lambs might the stern wolf betray,
If like a lamb he could his looks translate!
How many gazers mightst thou lead away,
● If thou wouldst use the strength of all thy state!
  But do not so; I love thee in such sort
  As, thou being mine, mine is thy good report.

XCVII.

How like a winter hath my absence been
From thee, the pleasure of the fleeting year!

What freezings have I felt, what dark days seen!
What old December's bareness every where!
● And yet this time removed was summer's time,
● The teeming autumn, big with rich increase,
● Bearing the wanton burthen of the prime,
Like widow'd wombs after their lords' decease:
Yet this abundant issue seem'd to me
● But hope of orphans and unfather'd fruit;
For summer and his pleasures wait on thee,
And, thou away, the very birds are mute;
Or, if they sing, 'tis with so dull a cheer
   That leaves look pale, dreading the winter's
      near.

XCVIII.

From you have I been absent in the spring,
When proud-pied April dress'd in all his trim
Hath put a spirit of youth in every thing,
● That heavy Saturn laugh'd and leap'd with him.
Yet nor the lays of birds nor the sweet smell
Of different flowers in odour and in hue
Could make me any summer's story tell,
Or from their proud lap pluck them where they
     grew;
Nor did I wonder at the lily's white,
Nor praise the deep vermilion in the rose;
● They were but sweet, but figures of delight,
● Drawn after you, you pattern of all those.
   Yet seem'd it winter still, and, you away,
   As with your shadow I with these did play:

XCIX.

The forward violet thus did I chide:
Sweet thief, whence didst thou steal thy sweet
    that smells,
● If not from my love's breath? The purple pride
Which on thy soft cheek for complexion dwells
● In my love's veins thou hast too grossly dyed.
● The lily I condemned for thy hand,
And buds of marjoram had stol'n thy hair:
The roses fearfully on thorns did stand,
One blushing shame, another white despair;
A third, nor red nor white, had stol'n of both
And to his robbery had annex'd thy breath;
But, for his theft, in pride of all his growth
A vengeful canker eat him up to death.
   More flowers I noted, yet I none could see
   But sweet or colour it had stol'n from thee.

C.

Where art thou, Muse, that thou forget'st so long
To speak of that which gives thee all thy might?
● Spend'st thou thy fury on some worthless song,
Darkening thy power to lend base subjects light?
Return, forgetful Muse, and straight redeem
● In gentle numbers time so idly spent;
Sing to the ear that doth thy lays esteem
And gives thy pen both skill and argument.
● Rise, resty Muse, my love's sweet face survey,
If Time have any wrinkle graven there;
● If any, be a satire to decay,
And make Time's spoils despised every where.
   Give my love fame faster than Time wastes life;
   So thou prevent'st his scythe and crooked knife.

CI.

O truant Muse, what shall be thy amends
For thy neglect of truth in beauty dyed?

XCVII

5 *removed.* When I was absent.

6 *teeming.* Fertile.

7 *wanton burthen.* Rich fruits. *prime.* Spring.

10 *hope of orphans.* Orphaned hope.

XCVIII

4 *heavy Saturn.* i.e. even melancholy Saturn.

11 *figures.* Emblems.

12 *pattern.* Original.

XCIX

3 *purple pride.* Rich colour.

5 *grossly.* Obviously.

6 *condemned for.* Reproached for.

C

3 *fury.* Poetic frenzy.

6 *gentle numbers.* Noble verses.

9 *resty.* Lazy.

11 *be a satire to.* Satirize.

CI

4 *dignified.* i.e. you are respected.

6 *no colour.* No artificial colouring.

7 *lay.* Lay on.

8 *intermix'd.* i.e. with true and false intermingled.

CII

3 *merchandized.* Put on sale. *esteeming.* Valuation.

7 *Philomel.* The nightingale. *summer's front.* The beginning of summer.

14 *dull.* Bore.

CIII

3 *argument all bare.* Plain subject of my verse.

11 *pass.* Purpose.

CIV

10 *his figure.* i.e. 'the dial's numeral', and 'his friend's form'. *and . . . perceived.* Unmarked.

11 *still.* 'Motionless', and 'always'.

13 *unbred.* Unborn.

Both truth and beauty on my love depends;
● So dost thou too, and therein dignified.
Make answer, Muse: wilt thou not haply say
● 'Truth needs no colour, with his colour fix'd;
● Beauty no pencil, beauty's truth to lay;
● But best is best, if never intermix'd?'
Because he needs no praise, wilt thou be dumb?
Excuse not silence so; for't lies in thee
To make him much outlive a gilded tomb,
And to be praised of ages yet to be.
　　Then do thy office, Muse; I teach thee how
　　To make him seem long hence as he shows now.

CII.

My love is strengthen'd, though more weak in
　　seeming;
I love not less, though less the show appear:
● That love is merchandized whose rich esteeming
The owner's tongue doth publish every where.
Our love was new and then but in the spring
When I was wont to greet it with my lays,
● As Philomel in summer's front doth sing
And stops her pipe in growth of riper days:
Not that the summer is less pleasant now
Than when her mournful hymns did hush the night,
But that wild music burthens every bough
And sweets grown common lose their dear delight.
　　Therefore like her I sometime hold my tongue,
●　　Because I would not dull you with my song.

CIII.

Alack, what poverty my Muse brings forth,
That having such a scope to show her pride,
● The argument all bare is of more worth
Than when it hath my added praise beside!
O, blame me not, if I no more can write!
Look in your glass, and there appears a face
That over-goes my blunt invention quite,
Dulling my lines and doing me disgrace.
Were it not sinful then, striving to mend,
To mar the subject that before was well?
● For to no other pass my verses tend
Than of your graces and your gifts to tell;
　　And more, much more, than in my verse can sit
　　Your own glass shows you when you look in it.

CIV.

To me, fair friend, you never can be old,
For as you were when first your eye I eyed,
Such seems your beauty still. Three winters cold
Have from the forests shook three summers' pride,
Three beauteous springs to yellow autumn turn'd
In process of the seasons have I seen,
Three April perfumes in three hot Junes burn'd,
Since first I saw you fresh, which yet are green.
Ah! yet doth beauty, like a dial-hand,
● Steal from his figure and no pace perceived;
● So your sweet hue, which methinks still doth
　　stand,
Hath motion and mine eye may be deceived:
●　　For fear of which, hear this, thou age unbred;
　　Ere you were born was beauty's summer dead.

CV.

Let not my love be call'd idolatry,
Nor my beloved as an idol show,
Since all alike my songs and praises be
To one, of one, still such, and ever so.

Kind is my love to-day, to-morrow kind,
Still constant in a wondrous excellence;
Therefore my verse to constancy confined,
● One thing expressing, leaves out difference.
'Fair, kind, and true' is all my argument,
'Fair, kind, and true' varying to other words;
● And in this change is my invention spent,
Three themes in one, which wondrous scope
    affords.
  'Fair, kind, and true,' have often lived alone,
  Which three till now never kept seat in one.

CVI.

● When in the chronicle of wasted time
● I see descriptions of the fairest wights,
And beauty making beautiful old rhyme
In praise of ladies dead and lovely knights,
● Then, in the blazon of sweet beauty's best,
Of hand, of foot, of lip, of eye, of brow,
I see their antique pen would have express'd
Even such a beauty as you master now.
So all their praises are but prophecies
Of this our time, all you prefiguring;
And, for they look'd but with divining eyes,
They had not skill enough your worth to sing:
  For we, which now behold these present days,
  Have eyes to wonder, but lack tongues to praise.

CVII.

Not mine own fears, nor the prophetic soul
Of the wide world dreaming on things to come,
● Can yet the lease of my true love control,
● Supposed as forfeit to a confined doom.
● The mortal moon hath her eclipse endured
● And the sad augurs mock their own presage;
● Incertainties now crown themselves assured
● And peace proclaims olives of endless age.
Now with the drops of this most balmy time
● My love looks fresh, and Death to me subscribes,
Since, spite of him, I'll live in this poor rhyme,
● While he insults o'er dull and speechless tribes:
  And thou in this shalt find thy monument,
  When tyrants' crests and tombs of brass are
    spent.

CVIII.

● What's in the brain that ink may character
Which hath not figured to thee my true spirit?
What's new to speak, what new to register,
That may express my love or thy dear merit?
Nothing, sweet boy; but yet, like prayers divine,
I must each day say o'er the very same,
Counting no old thing old, thou mine, I thine,
Even as when first I hallow'd thy fair name.
● So that eternal love in love's fresh case
Weighs not the dust and injury of age,
Nor gives to necessary wrinkles place,
But makes antiquity for aye his page,
●   Finding the first conceit of love there bred
  Where time and outward form would show it
    dead.

CIX.

O, never say that I was false of heart,
● Though absence seem'd my flame to qualify.
As easy might I from myself depart
As from my soul, which in thy breast doth lie:
That is my home of love: if I have ranged,
Like him that travels I return again,

CV

8 *difference.* Variety.

11 *change.* Sequence of musical notes used as a theme for variation.

CVI

1 *wasted.* Past.

2 *wights.* Worthies.

5 *blazon.* Show.

CVII See introduction.

3 *lease.* Term.

4 *Supposed . . . doom.* i.e. presumed to be limited.

5 *mortal . . . endured.* The Queen has come through the shadow (eclipse) upon her.

Queen Elizabeth I, who survived the threat to poison her, for which her physician, Roderigo Lopez, was executed in 1594

6 *presage.* Predictions.

7 *Incertainties . . . assured.* Uncertainty is now resolved.

8 *olives . . . age.* Peace promises to be lasting.

10 *subscribes.* Surrenders.

12 *insults.* Triumphs.

CVIII

1 *character.* Inscribe.

9 *fresh case.* Youthful exterior.

13 *conceit.* Conception.

CIX

2 *qualify.* Abate, cool.

779

7 *Just.* Punctual.

10 *blood.* i.e. flesh.

CX

2 *motley.* Jester.

3 *Gored.* Wounded.

6 *strangely.* At a distance.

7 *blenches.* Turnings aside.

8 *essays.* Experiences.

10 *grind.* Whet.

CXI See introduction.

1 *chide.* Quarrel.

3 *life.* Livelihood.

5 *brand.* Mark of infamy.

10 *eisel.* Vinegar (against the plague).

12 *Nor . . . correction.* Nor a cure that is worse than the disease.

A 16th century apothecary. Potions of vinegar and other remedies had little effect on victims of the plague, which raged in London in 1592–3

CXII

2 *vulgar scandal.* i.e. notoriety.

4 *o'er-green.* Cover.

7–8 *None . . . wrong.* i.e. no other relationship affects his fixed sense of right and wrong.

10 *adder's sense.* i.e. deaf ears.

12 *neglect.* i.e. unfriendly opinion

CXIII

6 *latch.* Catch sight of.

7 *quick.* Fleeting.

Just to the time, not with the time exchanged,
So that myself bring water for my stain.
Never believe, though in my nature reign'd
All frailties that besiege all kinds of blood,
That it could so preposterously be stain'd,
To leave for nothing all thy sum of good;
  For nothing this wide universe I call,
  Save thou, my rose; in it thou art my all.

CX.

Alas, 'tis true I have gone here and there
And made myself a motley to the view,
Gored mine own thoughts, sold cheap what is
    most dear,
Made old offences of affections new;
Most true it is that I have look'd on truth
Askance and strangely: but, by all above,
These blenches gave my heart another youth,
And worse essays proved thee my best of love.
Now all is done, have what shall have no end:
Mine appetite I never more will grind
On newer proof, to try an older friend,
A god in love, to whom I am confined.
  Then give me welcome, next my heaven the
      best,
  Even to thy pure and most most loving breast.

CXI.

O, for my sake do you with Fortune chide,
The guilty goddess of my harmful deeds,
That did not better for my life provide
Than public means which public manners breeds.
Thence comes it that my name receives a brand,
And almost thence my nature is subdued
To what it works in, like the dyer's hand:
Pity me then and wish I were renew'd;
Whilst, like a willing patient, I will drink
Potions of eisel 'gainst my strong infection;
No bitterness that I will bitter think,
Nor double penance, to correct correction.
  Pity me then, dear friend, and I assure ye
  Even that your pity is enough to cure me.

CXII.

Your love and pity doth the impression fill
Which vulgar scandal stamp'd upon my brow;
For what care I who calls me well or ill,
So you o'er-green my bad, my good allow?
You are my all the world, and I must strive
To know my shames and praises from your tongue;
None else to me, nor I to none alive,
That my steel'd sense or changes right or wrong.
In so profound abysm I throw all care
Of others' voices, that my adder's sense
To critic and to flatterer stopped are.
Mark how with my neglect I do dispense:
  You are so strongly in my purpose bred
  That all the world besides methinks are dead.

CXIII.

Since I left you, mine eye is in my mind;
And that which governs me to go about
Doth part his function and is partly blind,
Seems seeing, but effectually is out;
For it no form delivers to the heart
Of bird, of flower, or shape, which it doth latch:
Of his quick objects hath the mind no part,
Nor his own vision holds what it doth catch;

For if it see the rudest or gentlest sight,
● The most sweet favour or deformed'st creature,
The mountain or the sea, the day or night,
The crow or dove, it shapes them to your feature:
 Incapable of more, replete with you,
 My most true mind thus makes mine eye untrue.

CXIV.

Or whether doth my mind, being crown'd with
    you,
Drink up the monarch's plague, this flattery?
Or whether shall I say, mine eye saith true,
And that your love taught it this alchemy,
● To make of monsters and things indigest
Such cherubins as your sweet self resemble,
Creating every bad a perfect best,
● As fast as objects to his beams assemble?
O, 'tis the first; 'tis flattery in my seeing,
And my great mind most kingly drinks it up:
● Mine eye well knows what with his gust is 'greeing,
And to his palate doth prepare the cup:
 If it be poison'd, 'tis the lesser sin
 That mine eye loves it and doth first begin.

CXV.

Those lines that I before have writ do lie,
Even those that said I could not love you dearer:
Yet then my judgement knew no reason why
My most full flame should afterwards burn clearer.
● But reckoning time, whose million'd accidents
Creep in 'twixt vows and change decrees of kings,
● Tan sacred beauty, blunt the sharp'st intents,
● Divert strong minds to the course of altering things;
Alas, why, fearing of time's tyranny,
Might I not then say 'Now I love you best,'
When I was certain o'er incertainty,
Crowning the present, doubting of the rest?
 Love is a babe; then might I not say so,
 To give full growth to that which still doth grow?

CXVI.

Let me not to the marriage of true minds
● Admit impediments. Love is not love
Which alters when it alteration finds,
● Or bends with the remover to remove:
O, no! it is an ever-fixed mark
That looks on tempests and is never shaken;
It is the star to every wandering bark,
● Whose worth's unknown, although his height be
    taken.
● Love's not Time's fool, though rosy lips and
    cheeks
Within his bending sickle's compass come;
Love alters not with his brief hours and weeks,
But bears it out even to the edge of doom.
 If this be error and upon me proved,
 I never writ, nor no man ever loved.

CXVII.

● Accuse me thus: that I have scanted all
Wherein I should your great deserts repay,
Forgot upon your dearest love to call,
● Whereto all bonds do tie me day by day;
That I have frequent been with unknown minds
● And given to time your own dear-purchased right;
That I have hoisted sail to all the winds
Which should transport me farthest from your
    sight.

10 *favour.* Face.

CXIV

5 *indigest.* Shapeless.

8 *to . . . assemble.* Are presented to the eye's gaze.

11 *gust.* Taste.

CXV

5 *reckoning . . . accidents.* i.e. time, whose casual events are reckoned in millions.

7 *Tan.* Darken and coarsen.

8 *Divert.* Turn. *altering things.* Altered course.

CXVI

2 *impediments.* A reminder of the marriage service.

4 *bends . . . remove.* Agrees with the withdrawer to withdraw.

8 *his height be taken.* The star's altitude be estimated.

9 *fool.* Plaything.

CXVII

1 *scanted.* Neglected.

4 *bonds.* Obligations.

6 *given to time.* Wasted.

10 *on just . . . accumulate.* Add surmises to what is known.

CXVIII

2 *eager compounds.* Sharp mixtures.

6 *bitter sauces.* Bitter experiences. *frame.* Direct.

7 *meetness.* Appropriateness.

10 *faults assured.* Actual faults.

11 *medicine.* Medical treatment.

12 *rank.* Too full.

CXIX

1 *Siren tears.* i.e. appeals of the temptress.

2 *limbecks.* Alembics, stills.

3 *Applying.* i.e. as a salve.

4 *saw myself.* Expected.

7 *spheres.* Sockets. *fitted.* Forced.

CXX

14 *ransoms.* Redeems, excuses.

CXXI

2 *not to be.* i.e. not to be vile. *being.* i.e. being vile.

3 *just.* Right, proper. *so.* i.e. vile.

5 *false adulterate.* Prurient.

6 *Give salutation to.* Point at.

8 *in their wills count.* Determine.

Book both my wilfulness and errors down
● And on just proof surmise accumulate;
Bring me within the level of your frown,
But shoot not at me in your waken'd hate;
   Since my appeal says I did strive to prove
   The constancy and virtue of your love.

CXVIII.

Like as, to make our appetites more keen,
● With eager compounds we our palate urge,
As, to prevent our maladies unseen,
We sicken to shun sickness when we purge,
Even so, being full of your ne'er-cloying sweet-
       ness,
● To bitter sauces did I frame my feeding
● And, sick of welfare, found a kind of meetness
To be diseased ere that there was true needing.
Thus policy in love, to anticipate
● The ills that were not, grew to faults assured
● And brought to medicine a healthful state
● Which, rank of goodness, would by ill be cured:
   But thence I learn, and find the lesson true,
   Drugs poison him that so fell sick of you.

CXIX.

● What potions have I drunk of Siren tears,
● Distill'd from limbecks foul as hell within,
● Applying fears to hopes and hopes to fears,
● Still losing when I saw myself to win!
What wretched errors hath my heart committed,
Whilst it hath thought itself so blessed never!
● How have mine eyes out of their spheres been
   fitted
In the distraction of this madding fever!
O benefit of ill! now I find true
That better is by evil still made better;
And ruin'd love, when it is built anew,
Grows fairer than at first, more strong, far greater.
   So I return rebuked to my content
   And gain by ill thrice more than I have spent.

CXX.

That you were once unkind befriends me now,
And for that sorrow which I then did feel
Needs must I under my transgression bow,
Unless my nerves were brass or hammer'd steel.
For if you were by my unkindness shaken
As I by yours, you've pass'd a hell of time,
And I, a tyrant, have no leisure taken
To weigh how once I suffer'd in your crime.
O, that our night of woe might have remember'd
My deepest sense, how hard true sorrow hits,
And soon to you, as you to me, then tender'd
The humble salve which wounded bosoms fits!
   But that your trespass now becomes a fee;
●   Mine ransoms yours, and yours must ransom me.

CXXI.

'Tis better to be vile than vile esteem'd,
● When not to be receives reproach of being,
● And the just pleasure lost which is so deem'd
Not by our feeling but by others' seeing:
● For why should others' false adulterate eyes
● Give salutation to my sportive blood?
  Or on my frailties why are frailer spies,
● Which in their wills count bad what I think good?
No, I am that I am, and they that level
At my abuses reckon up their own:

- I may be straight, though they themselves be
    bevel ;
By their rank thoughts my deeds must not be
    shown ;
  Unless this general evil they maintain,
  All men are bad, and in their badness reign.

CXXII.

- Thy gift, thy tables, are within my brain
- Full character'd with lasting memory,
- Which shall above that idle rank remain
Beyond all date, even to eternity ;
Or at the least, so long as brain and heart
Have faculty by nature to subsist ;
Till each to razed oblivion yield his part
Of thee, thy record never can be miss'd.
- That poor retention could not so much hold,
- Nor need I tallies thy dear love to score ;
Therefore to give them from me was I bold,
- To trust those tables that receive thee more :
  To keep an adjunct to remember thee
- Were to import forgetfulness in me.

CXXIII.

No, Time, thou shalt not boast that I do change :
- Thy pyramids built up with newer might
To me are nothing novel, nothing strange ;
- They are but dressings of a former sight.
- Our dates are brief, and therefore we admire
What thou dost foist upon us that is old,
And rather make them born to our desire
Than think that we before have heard them told.
Thy registers and thee I both defy,
Not wondering at the present nor the past,
- For thy records and what we see doth lie,
Made more or less by thy continual haste.
  This I do vow and this shall ever be ;
  I will be true, despite thy scythe and thee.

CXXIV.

- If my dear love were but the child of state,
- It might for Fortune's bastard be unfather'd,
As subject to Time's love or to Time's hate,
Weeds among weeds, or flowers with flowers
    gather'd.
No, it was builded far from accident ;
It suffers not in smiling pomp, nor falls
- Under the blow of thralled discontent,
- Whereto the inviting time our fashion calls :
- It fears not policy, that heretic,
- Which works on leases of short-number'd hours,
- But all alone stands hugely politic,
That it nor grows with heat nor drowns with
    showers.
  To this I witness call the fools of time,
- Which die for goodness, who have lived for
    crime.

CXXV.

- Were 't aught to me I bore the canopy,
- With my extern the outward honouring,
Or laid great bases for eternity,
Which prove more short than waste or ruining ?
- Have I not seen dwellers on form and favour
Lose all, and more, by paying too much rent,
For compound sweet forgoing simple savour,
- Pitiful thrivers, in their gazing spent ?
- No, let me be obsequious in thy heart,
And take thou my oblation, poor but free,

11 *bevel.* Crooked.

CXXII

1 *tables.* Writing-tablet.

2 *character'd.* Inscribed.

3 *idle rank.* Empty leaves.

9 *retention.* Retainer (the tablet).

10 *tallies.* On which scores are kept.

12 *those tables.* i.e. the tablet of the memory.

14 *import.* Impute.

CXXIII

2 *Thy pyramids.* Time's marvels.

4 *dressings.* Imitations.

5 *dates.* Lifespans.

11 *records . . . see.* i.e. both past and present.

CXXIV See introduction.

1 *the child of state.* A person of state. i.e. of high rank.

2 *be unfather'd.* Be disclaimed.

7 *thralled.* Oppressed.

8 *Whereto . . . calls.* To which condition our times invite us.

9 *policy. that heretic.* False practices.

10 *on . . . hours.* On short term leases.

11 *all . . . politic.* i.e. only love is true practice.

14 *Which . . . crime.* Who die as martyrs though convicted of crime.

CXXV See introduction.

1 *Were't aught.* Were it anything. *canopy.* i.e. for a person of high rank.

2 *extern the outward.* Merely honouring exterior appearance.

5 *dwellers on.* i.e. those who depend upon favour.

8 *Pitiful thrivers.* i.e. those who live pitifully, since they gain nothing.

9 *be obsequious.* Be a devotee.

10 *oblation.* Offering.

11 *seconds*. i.e. second-best. *art*. Artifice.

13 *suborn'd informer*. False witness.

CXXVI

2 *glass*. Hourglass.

3 *by waning grown*. i.e. increased in beauty with the passing of time. *show'st*. i.e. shows up.

5 *wrack*. Wreck.

11 *audit*. Final reckoning. *answer'd*. Paid.

12 *quietus*. Settlement. *render*. Surrender.

CXXVII See introduction.

1 *black*. Very dark (not admired in the Elizabethan age).

6 *art's false borrow'd face*. i.e. by cosmetics.

8 *if . . . disgrace*. i.e. since natural beauty is simulated so often it is now discredited.

12 *Slandering . . . esteem*. i.e. slandering nature by a false view.

CXXVIII

2 *wood*. Keys of a virginal.

4 *wiry concord*. Harmony of strings. *confounds*. Confuses.

5 *jacks*. On a virginal.

10 *chips*. Keys.

Lady playing the virginal, with other musicians. From an engraving by Crispin van de Passe in *Hortus Voluptatum*, late 16th century

CXXIX

1 *a waste of shame*. Shameful waste.

● Which is not mix'd with seconds, knows no art,
But mutual render, only me for thee.
●   Hence, thou suborn'd informer! a true soul
When most impeach'd stands least in thy control.

CXXVI.

O thou, my lovely boy, who in thy power
● Dost hold Time's fickle glass, his sickle, hour;
● Who hast by waning grown, and therein show'st
Thy lovers withering as thy sweet self grow'st;
● If Nature, sovereign mistress over wrack,
As thou goest onwards, still will pluck thee back,
She keeps thee to this purpose, that her skill
May time disgrace and wretched minutes kill.
Yet fear her, O thou minion of her pleasure!
She may detain, but not still keep, her treasure:
● Her audit, though delay'd, answer'd must be,
● And her quietus is to render thee.

CXXVII.

● In the old age black was not counted fair,
Or if it were, it bore not beauty's name;
But now is black beauty's successive heir,
And beauty slander'd with a bastard shame:
For since each hand hath put on nature's power,
● Fairing the foul with art's false borrow'd face,
Sweet beauty hath no name, no holy bower,
● But is profaned, if not lives in disgrace.
Therefore my mistress' brows are raven black,
Her eyes so suited, and they mourners seem
At such who, not born fair, no beauty lack,
● Slandering creation with a false esteem:
  Yet so they mourn, becoming of their woe,
  That every tongue says beauty should look so.

CXXVIII.

How oft, when thou, my music, music play'st,
● Upon that blessed wood whose motion sounds
With thy sweet fingers, when thou gently sway'st
● The wiry concord that mine ear confounds,
● Do I envy those jacks that nimble leap
To kiss the tender inward of thy hand,
Whilst my poor lips, which should that harvest reap,
At the wood's boldness by thee blushing stand!
To be so tickled, they would change their state
● And situation with those dancing chips,
O'er whom thy fingers walk with gentle gait,
Making dead wood more blest than living lips.
  Since saucy jacks so happy are in this,
  Give them thy fingers, me thy lips to kiss.

CXXIX.

● The expense of spirit in a waste of shame
Is lust in action; and till action, lust
Is perjured, murderous, bloody, full of blame,
Savage, extreme, rude, cruel, not to trust,
Enjoy'd no sooner but despised straight,
Past reason hunted, and no sooner had
Past reason hated, as a swallow'd bait
On purpose laid to make the taker mad;
Mad in pursuit and in possession so;
Had, having, and in quest to have, extreme;
A bliss in proof, and proved, a very woe;
Before, a joy proposed; behind, a dream.

All this the world well knows; yet none knows
well
To shun the heaven that leads men to this hell.

CXXX.

My mistress' eyes are nothing like the sun;
Coral is far more red than her lips' red;
If snow be white, why then her breasts are dun;
If hairs be wires, black wires grow on her head.
● I have seen roses damask'd, red and white,
But no such roses see I in her cheeks;
And in some perfumes is there more delight
Than in the breath that from my mistress reeks.
I love to hear her speak, yet well I know
That music hath a far more pleasing sound;
I grant I never saw a goddess go;
My mistress, when she walks, treads on the
ground:
And yet, by heaven, I think my love as rare
As any she belied with false compare.

CXXXI.

Thou art as tyrannous, so as thou art,
As those whose beauties proudly make them cruel;
For well thou know'st to my dear doting heart
Thou art the fairest and most precious jewel.
Yet, in good faith, some say that thee behold
Thy face hath not the power to make love groan:
To say they err I dare not be so bold,
Although I swear it to myself alone.
● And, to be sure that is not false I swear,
A thousand groans, but thinking on thy face,
● One on another's neck, do witness bear
Thy black is fairest in my judgement's place.
In nothing art thou black save in thy deeds,
And thence this slander, as I think, proceeds.

CXXXII.

Thine eyes I love, and they, as pitying me,
Knowing thy heart torments me with disdain,
Have put on black and loving mourners be,
● Looking with pretty ruth upon my pain.
And truly not the morning sun of heaven
Better becomes the grey cheeks of the east,
Nor that full star that ushers in the even
Doth half that glory to the sober west,
As those two mourning eyes become thy face:
O, let it then as well beseem thy heart
To mourn for me, since mourning doth thee grace,
● And suit thy pity like in every part.
Then will I swear beauty herself is black
And all they foul that thy complexion lack.

CXXXIII.

Beshrew that heart that makes my heart to groan
For that deep wound it gives my friend and me!
Is't not enough to torture me alone,
● But slave to slavery my sweet'st friend must be?
● Me from myself thy cruel eye hath taken,
● And my next self thou harder hast engross'd:
Of him, myself, and thee, I am forsaken;
A torment thrice threefold thus to be cross'd.
● Prison my heart in thy steel bosom's ward,
● But then my friend's heart let my poor heart bail;
● Whoe'er keeps me, let my heart be his guard;
● Thou canst not then use rigour in my gaol:
And yet thou wilt; for I, being pent in thee,
Perforce am thine, and all that is in me.

5 *damask'd.* Coloured liked the damask (Damascus)
rose.

Dark-haired beauty, as exemplified in this portrait of
Mary Fitton, Maid of Honour to Queen Elizabeth, was
unfashionable in Shakespeare's time. Painting attributed
to John Betts the Younger

CXXXI

9 *to be sure.* i.e. for proof.

11 *One . . . neck.* i.e. in quick succession.

CXXXII

4 *ruth.* Pity.

12 *suit thy pity like.* Dress your pity alike.

CXXXIII

4 *slave to slavery.* i.e. sharer of my enslavement.

5 *myself.* i.e. my true self.

6 *my . . . engross'd.* i.e. you have placed my friend under
harder bondage.

9 *ward.* Lock.

10 *bail.* i.e. free by serving as a substitute.

11 *his guard.* i.e. my friend's guard.

12 *gaol.* i.e. heart which holds the friend.

CXXXIV

3 *other mine.* i.e. my friend.

6 *kind.* Compliant.

7 *surety-like.* i.e. as if to answer for me.

9 *take.* Invoke.

10 *use.* Usury.

11 *came.* Who became.

12 *my unkind abuse.* i.e. your deceiving me.

CXXXV

1 *'Will'.* i.e. sex at her desire; also her husband (or friend), and Will Shakespeare.

William Shakespeare: the 'Tonson' portrait, 1735

2 *to boot.* As well.

4 *will.* Desire (with sexual implication).

6 *hide.* Shelter.

8 *acceptance.* Acceptability.

13 *no unkind.* i.e. no unkind words. *no fair beseechers.* i.e. no applicants for your favours.

CXXXVII

6 *Be . . . ride.* i.e. have brought me to anchor in a common roadway (pun on 'ride').

9 *that a several plot.* i.e. that plot a private one.

14 *false plague.* i.e. plague of falseness, and plaguey mistress.

CXXXIV.
So, now I have confess'd that he is thine,
And I myself am mortgaged to thy will,
● Myself I'll forfeit, so that other mine
Thou wilt restore, to be my comfort still:
But thou wilt not, nor he will not be free,
● For thou art covetous and he is kind;
● He learn'd but surety-like to write for me
Under that bond that him as fast doth bind.
● The statute of thy beauty thou wilt take,
● Thou usurer, that put'st forth all to use,
● And sue a friend came debtor for my sake;
● So him I lose through my unkind abuse.
    Him have I lost; thou hast both him and me
    He pays the whole, and yet am I not free.

CXXXV.
● Whoever hath her wish, thou hast thy 'Will,'
● And 'Will' to boot, and 'Will' in overplus;
More than enough am I that vex thee still,
● To thy sweet will making addition thus.
Wilt thou, whose will is large and spacious,
● Not once vouchsafe to hide my will in thine?
Shall will in others seem right gracious,
● And in my will no fair acceptance shine?
The sea, all water, yet receives rain still
And in abundance addeth to his store;
So thou, being rich in 'Will,' add to thy 'Will'
One will of mine, to make thy large 'Will' more.
●   Let no unkind, no fair beseechers kill;
    Think all but one, and me in that one 'Will.'

CXXXVI.
If thy soul check thee that I come so near,
Swear to thy blind soul that I was thy 'Will,'
And will, thy soul knows, is admitted there;
Thus far for love my love-suit, sweet, fulfil.
'Will' will fulfil the treasure of thy love,
Ay, fill it full with wills, and my will one.
In things of great receipt with ease we prove
Among a number one is reckon'd none:
Then in the number let me pass untold,
Though in thy stores' account I one must be;
For nothing hold me, so it please thee hold
That nothing me, a something sweet to thee:
    Make but my name thy love, and love that still,
    And then thou lovest me, for my name is 'Will.'

CXXXVII.
Thou blind fool, Love, what dost thou to mine eyes,
That they behold, and see not what they see?
They know what beauty is, see where it lies,
Yet what the best is take the worst to be.
If eyes corrupt by over-partial looks
● Be anchor'd in the bay where all men ride,
Why of eyes' falsehood hast thou forged hooks,
Whereto the judgement of my heart is tied?
● Why should my heart think that a several plot
Which my heart knows the wide world's common place?
Or mine eyes seeing this, say this is not,
To put fair truth upon so foul a face?
    In things right true my heart and eyes have err'd,
●   And to this false plague are they now transferr'd.

CXXXVIII.
When my love swears that she is made of truth
I do believe her, though I know she lies,

That she might think me some untutor'd youth,
Unlearned in the world's false subtleties.
Thus vainly thinking that she thinks me young,
Although she knows my days are past the best,
● Simply I credit her false-speaking tongue:
On both sides thus is simple truth suppress'd.
But wherefore says she not she is unjust?
And wherefore say not I that I am old?
● O, love's best habit is in seeming trust,
And age in love loves not to have years told:
● Therefore I lie with her and she with me,
And in our faults by lies we flatter'd be.

CXXXIX.

O, call not me to justify the wrong
● That thy unkindness lays upon my heart;
Wound me not with thine eye but with thy tongue;
Use power with power and slay me not by art.
Tell me thou lovest elsewhere, but in my sight,
Dear heart, forbear to glance thine eye aside:
What need'st thou wound with cunning when
thy might
Is more than my o'er-press'd defence can bide?
Let me excuse thee: ah! my love well knows
Her pretty looks have been mine enemies,
● And therefore from my face she turns my foes,
That they elsewhere might dart their injuries:
Yet do not so; but since I am near slain,
Kill me outright with looks and rid my pain.

CXL.

Be wise as thou art cruel; do not press
My tongue-tied patience with too much disdain;
Lest sorrow lend me words and words express
The manner of my pity-wanting pain.
If I might teach thee wit, better it were,
● Though not to love, yet, love, to tell me so;
As testy sick men, when their deaths be near,
No news but health from their physicians know;
For if I should despair, I should grow mad,
And in my madness might speak ill of thee:
● Now this ill-wresting world is grown so bad,
Mad slanderers by mad ears believed be.
● That I may not be so, nor thou belied,
Bear thine eyes straight, though thy proud
heart go wide.

CXLI.

In faith, I do not love thee with mine eyes,
For they in thee a thousand errors note;
But 'tis my heart that loves what they despise,
Who in despite of view is pleased to dote;
Nor are mine ears with thy tongue's tune delighted,
Nor tender feeling, to base touches prone,
Nor taste, nor smell, desire to be invited
To any sensual feast with thee alone:
But my five wits nor my five senses can
Dissuade one foolish heart from serving thee,
● Who leaves unsway'd the likeness of a man,
Thy proud heart's slave and vassal wretch to be:
Only my plague thus far I count my gain,
That she that makes me sin awards me pain.

CXLII.

Love is my sin and thy dear virtue hate,
Hate of my sin, grounded on sinful loving:
O, but with mine compare thou thine own state,
● And thou shalt find it merits not reproving;

CXXXVIII

7 *Simply.* Pretending to be simple.

11 *habit.* Guise.

13 *lie.* With double meaning.

CXXXIX

2 *unkindness.* Infidelity.

11 *foes.* i.e. pretty looks.

CXL
6 *so.* i.e. that you do love me.

11 *ill-wresting world.* i.e. this world that twists good to
seem evil.

13 *so.* i.e. slandered.

CXLI

11 *Who . . . man.* i.e. which leaves ungoverned the
empty shell of a man.

CXLII

4 *it.* i.e. my state.

6 *scarlet ornaments.* Lips.

8 *Robb'd . . . rents.* i.e. stolen from others the due of the marriage-bed.

13 *hide.* Withhold.

CXLIII

5 *holds . . . chase.* i.e. chases her in turn.

CXLIV

2 *suggest me still.* Always prompt me.

11 *each.* i.e. each other.

14 *fire my good one out.* i.e. infect with venereal disease.

CXLVI

1 *earth.* i.e. the body.

2 (the opening words have been variously guessed at: 'Fooled by' and a repeat of 'My sinful earth'). *rebel powers.* Rebellious flesh.

8 *charge.* i.e. the body.

Or, if it do, not from those lips of thine,
● That have profaned their scarlet ornaments
And seal'd false bonds of love as oft as mine,
● Robb'd others' beds' revenues of their rents.
Be it lawful I love thee, as thou lovest those
Whom thine eyes woo as mine importune thee:
Root pity in thy heart, that when it grows
Thy pity may deserve to pitied be.
● If thou dost seek to have what thou dost hide,
By self-example mayst thou be denied!

CXLIII.

Lo! as a careful housewife runs to catch
One of her feather'd creatures broke away,
Sets down her babe and makes all swift dispatch
In pursuit of the thing she would have stay,
● Whilst her neglected child holds her in chase,
Cries to catch her whose busy care is bent
To follow that which flies before her face,
Not prizing her poor infant's discontent;
So runn'st thou after that which flies from thee,
Whilst I thy babe chase thee afar behind;
But if thou catch thy hope, turn back to me,
And play the mother's part, kiss me, be kind:
   So will I pray that thou mayst have thy 'Will,'
   If thou turn back, and my loud crying still.

CXLIV.

Two loves I have of comfort and despair,
● Which like two spirits do suggest me still:
The better angel is a man right fair,
The worser spirit a woman colour'd ill.
To win me soon to hell, my female evil
Tempteth my better angel from my side,
And would corrupt my saint to be a devil,
Wooing his purity with her foul pride.
And whether that my angel be turn'd fiend
Suspect I may, yet not directly tell;
● But being both from me, both to each friend,
I guess one angel in another's hell:
   Yet this shall I ne'er know, but live in doubt,
● Till my bad angel fire my good one out.

CXLV.

Those lips that Love's own hand did make
Breathed forth the sound that said 'I hate'
To me that languish'd for her sake;
But when she saw my woeful state,
Straight in her heart did mercy come,
Chiding that tongue that ever sweet
Was used in giving gentle doom,
And taught it thus anew to greet;
'I hate' she alter'd with an end,
That follow'd it as gentle day
Doth follow night, who like a fiend
From heaven to hell is flown away;
   'I hate' from hate away she threw,
   And saved my life, saying 'not you.'

CXLVI.

● Poor soul, the centre of my sinful earth,
● †.......... these rebel powers that thee array,
Why dost thou pine within and suffer dearth,
Painting thy outward walls so costly gay?
Why so large cost, having so short a lease,
Dost thou upon thy fading mansion spend?
Shall worms, inheritors of this excess,
● Eat up thy charge? is this thy body's end?

Then, soul, live thou upon thy servant's loss,
● And let that pine to aggravate thy store:
● Buy terms divine in selling hours of dross;
Within be fed, without be rich no more:
   So shalt thou feed on Death, that feeds on men,
   And Death once dead, there's no more dying
      then.

CXLVII.

My love is as a fever, longing still
● For that which longer nurseth the disease,
Feeding on that which doth preserve the ill,
● The uncertain sickly appetite to please.
My reason, the physician to my love,
Angry that his prescriptions are not kept,
Hath left me, and I desperate now approve
● Desire is death, which physic did except.
Past cure I am, now reason is past care,
And frantic-mad with evermore unrest;
My thoughts and my discourse as madmen's are,
At random from the truth vainly express'd;
   For I have sworn thee fair and thought thee
     bright,
   Who art as black as hell, as dark as night.

CXLVIII.

O me, what eyes hath Love put in my head,
Which have no correspondence with true sight!
Or, if they have, where is my judgement fled,
● That censures falsely what they see aright?
If that be fair whereon my false eyes dote,
What means the world to say it is not so?
If it be not, then love doth well denote
● Love's eye is not so true as all men's 'No.'
How can it? O, how can Love's eye be true,
● That is so vex'd with watching and with tears?
No marvel then, though I mistake my view;
The sun itself sees not till heaven clears.
   O cunning Love! with tears thou keep'st me
     blind,
   Lest eyes well-seeing thy foul faults should find.

CXLIX.

Canst thou, O cruel! say I love thee not,
When I against myself with thee partake?
Do I not think on thee, when I forgot
Am of myself, all tyrant, for thy sake?
Who hateth thee that I do call my friend?
On whom frown'st thou that I do fawn upon?
● Nay, if thou lour'st on me, do I not spend
● Revenge upon myself with present moan?
What merit do I in myself respect,
That is so proud thy service to despise,
● When all my best doth worship thy defect,
Commanded by the motion of thine eyes?
   But, love, hate on, for now I know thy mind;
   Those that can see thou lovest, and I am blind.

CL.

O, from what power hast thou this powerful might
With insufficiency my heart to sway?
To make me give the lie to my true sight,
And swear that brightness doth not grace the day?
● Whence hast thou this becoming of things ill,
● That in the very refuse of thy deeds
● There is such strength and warrantise of skill
That, in my mind, thy worst all best exceeds?
Who taught thee how to make me love thee more
The more I hear and see just cause of hate?

10 *aggravate.* Increase.

11 *terms divine.* Immortality in heaven.

CXLVII

2 *longer nurseth.* Prolongs.

4 *uncertain.* Fickle.

8 *Desire . . . except.* i.e. desire, which rejected reason's medicine, proves fatal.

CXLVIII

4 *censures.* Judges.

8 *Love's eye.* i.e. love's 'ay' (pun: 'men's no').

10 *watching.* Lying awake.

CXLIX

7 *thou lour'st.* You frown.

8 *moan.* Suffering.

11 *worship thy defect.* Worship your very faults.

CL

5 *becoming . . . ill.* i.e. power to lend grace to evil things.

6 *very . . . deeds.* Most worthless of your actions.

7 *warrantise.* Evidence.

CLI: 'Love is too young to know what conscience is.' Illustration by Byam Shaw, *The Chiswick Shakespeare*, 1902

O, though I love what others do abhor,
With others thou shouldst not abhor my state:
   If thy unworthiness raised love in me,
   More worthy I to be beloved of thee.

CLI.

● Love is too young to know what conscience is;
   Yet who knows not conscience is born of love?
● Then, gentle cheater, urge not my amiss,
   Lest guilty of my faults thy sweet self prove:
   For, thou betraying me, I do betray
   My nobler part to my gross body's treason;
   My soul doth tell my body that he may
● Triumph in love; flesh stays no farther reason;
● But, rising at thy name, doth point out thee
● As his triumphant prize.   Proud of this pride,
   He is contented thy poor drudge to be,
   To stand in thy affairs, fall by thy side.
●   No want of conscience hold it that I call
   Her 'love' for whose dear love I rise and fall.

CLII.

In loving thee thou know'st I am forsworn,
But thou art twice forsworn, to me love swearing,
● In act thy bed-vow broke and new faith torn
● In vowing new hate after new love bearing.
   But why of two oaths' breach do I accuse thee,
   When I break twenty? I am perjured most;
● For all my vows are oaths but to misuse thee
   And all my honest faith in thee is lost,
   For I have sworn deep oaths of thy deep kindness,
   Oaths of thy love, thy truth, thy constancy,
● And, to enlighten thee, gave eyes to blindness,
   Or made them swear against the thing they see;
     For I have sworn thee fair; more perjured I,
     To swear against the truth so foul a lie!

CLIII.

Cupid laid by his brand, and fell asleep:
● A maid of Dian's this advantage found,
   And his love-kindling fire did quickly steep
● In a cold valley-fountain of that ground;
   Which borrow'd from this holy fire of Love
● A dateless lively heat, still to endure,
   And grew a seething bath, which yet men prove
   Against strange maladies a sovereign cure.
   But at my mistress' eye Love's brand new-fired,
● The boy for trial needs would touch my breast;
   I, sick withal, the help of bath desired,
● And thither hied, a sad distemper'd guest,
     But found no cure: the bath for my help lies
     Where Cupid got new fire—my mistress' eyes.

CLIV.

The little Love-god lying once asleep
Laid by his side his heart-inflaming brand,
Whilst many nymphs that vow'd chaste life to keep
Came tripping by; but in her maiden hand
● The fairest votary took up that fire
   Which many legions of true hearts had warm'd;
● And so the general of hot desire
   Was sleeping by a virgin hand disarm'd
   This brand she quenched in a cool well by,
   Which from Love's fire took heat perpetual,
   Growing a bath and healthful remedy
   For men diseased; but I, my mistress' thrall,
     Came there for cure, and this by that I prove,
     Love's fire heats water, water cools not love.

CLI

1 *conscience.* Awareness.

3 *urge not my amiss.* Do not accuse me for my wants.

8 *reason.* Reasoning.

9 *rising.* Aroused (sexually).

10 *pride.* Sexual heat.

13 *want of conscience.* Lack of awareness.

CLII

3 *bed-vow.* Marriage-vows. *new faith torn.* i.e. a new pledge of fidelity broken.

4 *bearing.* Professing.

7 *but to misuse.* Merely to misrepresent.

11 *gave eyes to blindness.* i.e. made the eyes swear to things they did not see.

CLIII

2 *Dian.* Diana, goddess of chastity. *advantage.* opportunity.

4 *of that ground.* Nearby.

6 *dateless.* External.

10 *for . . . would.* As an experiment had to.

12 *And thither hied.* Would suggest a visit to Bath for treatment.

CLIV

5 *votary.* A nymph to Diana.

7 *general.* i.e. Cupid.

The disarming of Cupid. Engraving from a painting by W.E. Frost (1810–1877)

The Phoenix
and the Turtle

1601

IN 1601 Shakespeare contributed along with other dramatists – Jonson, Chapman, Marston – to a book, *Love's Martyr*, produced by Robert Chester, in honour of the married happiness of Sir John Salusbury and his wife, Ursula Stanley, of the Derby family. Sir John was an Esquire of the Body to the Queen, a remote cousin, and naturally these writers would come in contact with him in presenting plays at Court.

Shakespeare contributed a strange poem, which all poets recognise for the magical work it is: emblematic, touched by the vogue among younger poets for the metaphysical, and today reading like an incursion into surrealism. It has upon it the enigmatic smile, behind which he could always withdraw from the too great exposure of the theatre into the privacy of the poet's life.

It carried his signature in the rare words he liked to use, 'precurrer' for precursor, and his fondness for impressive words ending in 'ive' – 'defunctive', for example. The man of the theatre speaks in,

> Co-supremes and stars of love,
> As chorus to their tragic scene.

But the poem is more an epitaph on dead love than a celebration of a living one.

> So they loved, as love in twain
> Had the essence but in one;
> Two distincts, division none:
> Number there in love was slain.

Where have we read this before but in the Sonnets:

> Let me confess that we two must be twain,
> Although our undivided loves are one.

At this moment, after the Essex rebellion, Southampton had been condemned to death, and was under suspense in the Tower.

'Death is not the
Phoenix' nest.'
From Geoffrey
Whitney, A
Choice of
Emblems, *1586*

THE PHŒNIX AND THE TURTLE.

● *A bullet beside a text line indicates an annotation in the opposite column*

A phœnix. Illustration from a Latin bestiary of the 12th century

---

5 *shrieking harbinger*. i.e. the screech-owl.

7 *Augur*. Prophet or soothsayer.

14 *defunctive*. Funeral.

17 *treble-dated crow*. The crow was noted for its longevity.

27 *distincts*. Separate, distinct things or persons.

34 *his right*. What was due to him.

36 *Either . . . mine*. i.e. lovers were identified with each other.

LET the bird of loudest lay,
On the sole Arabian tree,
Herald sad and trumpet be,
To whose sound chaste wings obey.

● But thou shrieking harbinger,
Foul precurrer of the fiend,
● Augur of the fever's end,
To this troop come thou not near!

From this session interdict
Every fowl of tyrant wing,　　　　　10
Save the eagle, feather'd king:
Keep the obsequy so strict.

Let the priest in surplice white,
● That defunctive music can,
Be the death-divining swan,
Lest the requiem lack his right.

● And thou treble-dated crow,
That thy sable gender makest
With the breath thou givest and takest,
'Mongst our mourners shalt thou go.　　20

Here the anthem doth commence:
Love and constancy is dead;
Phœnix and the turtle fled
In a mutual flame from hence.

So they loved, as love in twain
Had the essence but in one;
● Two distincts, division none:
Number there in love was slain.

Hearts remote, yet not asunder;
Distance, and no space was seen　　　　30
'Twixt the turtle and his queen:
But in them it were a wonder.

So between them love did shine,
● That the turtle saw his right
Flaming in the phœnix' sight;
● Either was the other's mine.

794

The turtle-dove. Illustration from a Latin bestiary of the 12th century

Property was thus appalled,
That the self was not the same:
Single nature's double name
Neither two nor one was called   40

Reason, in itself confounded,
Saw division grow together,
To themselves yet either neither,
Simple were so well compounded,

That it cried, How true a twain
Seemeth this concordant one!
Love hath reason, reason none,
If what parts can so remain.

● Whereupon it made this threne
To the phœnix and the dove,   50
● Co-supremes and stars of love,
As chorus to their tragic scene.

---

49 *threne*. Funeral song.

51 *Co-supremes*. Joint rulers.

THRENOS.

Beauty, truth, and rarity,
Grace in all simplicity,
Here enclosed in cinders lie.

Death is now the phœnix' nest:
And the turtle's loyal breast
To eternity doth rest,

Leaving no posterity:
'Twas not their infirmity,   60
It was married chastity.

Truth may seem, but cannot be:
Beauty brag, but 'tis not she;
Truth and beauty buried be.

To this urn let those repair
That are either true or fair;
For these dead birds sigh a prayer.

Further Reading

The following bibliography has been selected from an enormous literature on the subject, and is intended as a guide for the general reader.

EDITIONS

Recommended editions of Shakespeare in one volume are: The Complete Works edited by Peter Alexander, 1951; the Riverside Shakespeare edited by G. Blakemore Evans; and the Complete Works edited by Charles J. Sisson, 1954.
The most useful editions of the plays in separate volumes are the New Arden Shakespeare (general editors, Harold F. Brooks and Harold Jenkins), which cover textual problems and include commentary on the text; the New Penguin Shakespeare (general editor T. J. B. Spencer); and the Pelican Shakespeare (general editor Alfred Harbage). The New Cambridge Shakespeare edited by Arthur Quiller-Couch and John Dover Wilson is stimulating for its introductions and (not always reliable) suggestions. The most detailed textual commentary including stage history up to its date of publication (1888) is in the New Variorum Shakespeare edited by Horace H. Furness. (Paperback edition by Dover Publications, New York.)

GENERAL REFERENCE

Abbott, E. A. *A Shakespeare Grammar*, 1870
Bartlett, John *A New and Complete Concordance . . . to . . . Shakespeare*, 1962
Bullough, Geoffrey *Narrative and Dramatic Sources of Shakespeare*, 1957–73
Greg, W. W. *The Editorial Problem in Shakespeare*, 1942
Greg, W. W. *The Shakespeare First Folio*, 1955
Hinman, Charlton *The Printing and Proof-Reading of the First Folio of Shakespeare*, 1963
Kökeritz, Helge *Shakespeare's Pronunciation*, 1953
Muir, Kenneth *Shakespeare's Sources*, 1961
Munro, J. (ed.) *The Shakespeare Allusion-Book*, 1932
Onions, Charles T. *A Shakespeare Glossary* (revised ed.), 1953
Partridge, Eric *Shakespeare's Bawdy*, 1948
Sisson, C. J. *New Readings in Shakespeare*, 1956
Thomson, J. A. K. *Shakespeare and the Classics*, 1952
Whitaker, V. K. *Shakespeare's Use of Learning*, 1953

SHAKESPEARE'S LIFE

Alexander, Peter *Shakespeare's Life and Art*, 1964
Bentley, G. E. *Shakespeare. A Biographical Handbook*, 1961
Brinkworth, E. R. C. *Shakespeare and the Bawdy Court of Stratford*, 1972
Chambers, E. K. *Shakespeare: A Survey*, 1925
Chambers, E. K. *Sources for a Biography of Shakespeare*, 1946
Chambers, E. K. *William Shakespeare. A Study of Facts and Problems*, 2 vols. 1930
Eccles, Mark *Shakespeare in Warwickshire*, 1961
Fripp, E. I. *Shakespeare, Man and Artist*, 2 vols. 1938
Fripp, E. I. *Shakespeare Studies, Biographical and Literary*, 1930
Fripp, E. I. *Shakespeare's Haunts near Stratford*, 1929
Joseph, Harriet *John Hall, Man and Physician*, 1964
Rowse, A. L. *Shakespeare the Man*, 1973
Rowse, A. L. *Shakespeare's Southampton, Patron of Virginia*, 1965
Rowse, A. L. *Simon Forman. Sex and Society in Shakespeare's Age*, 1974
Rowse, A. L. *William Shakespeare: A Biography*, 1963
Schoenbaum, S. *William Shakespeare: A Documentary Life* (2nd ed. revised with corrections), 1977
Speaight, Robert *Shakespeare. The Man and his Achievement*, 1977

SHAKESPEARE'S CONTEMPORARIES

Aubrey, J. *Brief Lives* edited by Andrew Clark, 2 vols. 1898
Bald, R. C. *John Donne: A Life*, 1970
Barker, Richard H. *Thomas Middleton*, 1958
Beaumont, F. and Fletcher, J. *Dramatic Works* edited by Fredson Bowers, 1966–76
Boas, F. S. *Christopher Marlowe: A Biographical and Critical Study*, 1940
Chambers, E. K. *Sir Henry Lee*, 1936
Chapman, George *Plays and Poems* edited by T. Parrott, 1910–1914
Dekker, Thomas *The Dramatic Works* edited by Fredson Bowers, 1953–61
Gerrard, Earnest A. *Elizabethan Drama and Dramatists, 1583–1603*, 1928
Greene, Robert *Life and Complete Works* edited by A. B. Grosart, 1881–86
Harrison, G. B. *The Life and Death of Robert Devereux, Earl of Essex*, 1937
Harvey, Gabriel *Complete Works* edited by A. B. Grosart, 1884
Gabriel Harvey's Marginalia edited by G. C. Moore Smith, 1913
Heywood, John *Works* edited by B. A. Milligan, 1956
Heywood, Thomas *Dramatic Works* edited by R. H. Shepherd, 1874
Horne, D. H. *The Life and Minor Works of George Peele*, 1952
Hosking, G. L. *The Life and Times of Edward Alleyn*, 1952
Hunter, G. K. *John Lyly. The Humanist as Courtier*, 1962
Jenkins, Elizabeth *Elizabeth and Leicester*, 1961
Jones, H. S. V. *A Spenser Handbook*, 1930
Jonson, Ben *Works* edited by C. H. Herford, Percy and Evelyn Simpson, 1925–50
Judson, A. C. *The Life of Edmund Spenser*, 1945
Kyd, Thomas *Works* edited by F. S. Boas, 1901
Leishman, J. B. (ed.) *The Three Parnassus Plays, 1598–1601*, 1949
Lyly, John *Complete Works* edited by R. W. Bond, 1902
Marlowe, Christopher *Complete Works* edited by Fredson Bowers, 2 vols. 1973
Marston, John *Works* edited by H. Harvey Wood, 3 vols. 1934
Maurier, Daphne du *Golden Lads. A Study of Anthony Bacon, Francis and their Friends*, 1975
Middleton, Thomas *Works* edited by A. H. Bullen, 1885–86
Mirror for Magistrates edited by Lily B. Campbell, 1938
Nashe, Thomas *Works* edited by R. B. McKerrow and F. P. Wilson, 1958

Prouty, C. T. *George Gascoigne*, 1942
Rees, Joan *Samuel Daniel : A Critical and Biographical Study*, 1964
Rees, Joan *Fulke Greville, Lord Brooke, 1554–1628*, 1971
Rowse, A. L. *Christopher Marlowe : A Biography*, 1964
Sidney, Sir Philip *Arcadia* edited by Maurice Evans, 1977
Sidney, Sir Philip *The Poems* edited by William A. Ringler, 1962
Sisson, C. J. (ed.) *Thomas Lodge and other Elizabethans*, 1933
Stopes, Charlotte C. *The Life of Henry, Third Earl of Southampton, Shakespeare's Patron*, 1922
Stopes, Charlotte C. *Shakespeare's Warwickshire Contemporaries*, 1907
Strachey, Lytton *Elizabeth and Essex*, 1928
Ward, B. M. *The Seventeenth Earl of Oxford, 1550–1604*, 1928
Webster, John *Complete Works* edited by F. L. Lucas, 1927
Yates, Francis A. *John Florio*, 1934

SHAKESPEARE'S ENGLAND

Black, J. B. *The Reign of Elizabeth, 1558–1603*, 1936
Byrne, M. St Clare *Elizabethan Life in Town and Country* (revised ed.), 1961
Byrne, M. St Clare *The Elizabethan Home*, 1930
Davies, Godfrey *The Early Stuarts, 1603–1660*, 1938
Elton, G. R. *England under the Tudors*, 1956
Harrison, G. B. *England in Shakespeare's Day*, 1928
Harrison, G. B. *The Elizabethan Journals, 1591–1603*, 1938
Harrison, G. B. *A Jacobean Journal, 1603–1606*, 1941
Harrison, G. B. *A Second Jacobean Journal, 1607–1610*, 1958
Jones, Richard F. *Ancients and Moderns*, 1965
Judges, A. V. (ed.) *The Elizabethan Underworld*, 1930
Neale, J. E. *Queen Elizabeth*, 1934
Nicoll, Allardyce *The Elizabethans*, 1957
Rowse, A. L. *The Elizabethans and America*, 1959
Rowse, A. L. *The Elizabethan Renaissance :* vol 1, The Life of the Society, 1971; vol 2, The Cultural Achievement, 1972
Rowse, A. L. *The England of Elizabeth*, 1950
Rowse, A. L. *The Expansion of Elizabethan England*, 1955
Shakespeare's England : An Account of the Life and Manners of his Age, 2 vols. 1916–17
Stow's Survey of London edited by C. L. Kingsford, 2 vols. 1908
Strong, Roy *The English Icon : Elizabethan and Jacobean Portraiture*, 1969
Strong, Roy *The Portraits of Queen Elizabeth I*, 1963
Tillyard, E. M. W. *The Elizabethan World Picture*, 1943
Wilson, F. P. *The Plague in Shakespeare's London*, 1927
Wilson, John Dover *Life in Shakespeare's England*, 1911

SHAKESPEARE CRITICISM

Bamborough, J. B. *The Little World of Man*, 1952
Bradby, Anne (ed.) *Shakespearean Criticism, 1919–1935*, 1936
Bush, Douglas *English Literature in the Earlier Seventeenth Century*, 1945
Buxton, John *Elizabethan Taste*, 1965
Clemens, W. H. *The Development of Shakespeare's Imagery*, 1951
Coleridge, S. T. *Notes and Lectures upon Shakespeare*, 1849
Coleridge, S. T. *Shakespearean Criticism* edited by T. M. Raysor, 2 vols. 1930
Eastman, Arthur M. *A Short History of Shakespeare Criticism*, 1968
Eliot, T. S. *Selected Essays*, 1932
Granville-Barker, H. and Harrison, G. B. (eds.) *A Companion to Shakespeare Studies*, 1934
Hazlitt, William *The Characters of Shakespeare's Plays*, 1805
Johnson on Shakespeare edited by Sir Walter Raleigh, 1925
Knights, L. C. *Some Shakespearean Themes*, 1959
Lewis, C. S. *English Literature in the Sixteenth Century*, 1954
Mahood, M. M. *Shakespeare's Wordplay*, 1957
Muir, K. and Schoenbaum, S. *A New Companion to Shakespeare Studies*, 1971
Murry, John Middleton *Shakespeare*, 1936
Ralli, Augustus *A History of Shakespearian Criticism*, 2 vols. 1932
Shakespeare Quarterly edited by J. G. McManaway (periodical)
Shakespeare Survey edited by Kenneth Muir (annual periodical)
Smith, David Nichol (ed.) *Shakespeare Criticism*, 1949
Smith, Gregory *Elizabethan Critical Essays*, 2 vols. 1904
Smith, Logan P. *On Reading Shakespeare*, 1933
Spencer, Theodore *Shakespeare and the Nature of Man*, 1943
Spurgeon, Caroline *Shakespeare's Imagery and What It Tells Us*, 1935
Stewart, J. I. M. *Character and Motive in Shakespeare*, 1951
Wilson, F. P. *Elizabethan and Jacobean*, 1945
Wilson, F. P. *Marlowe and the Early Shakespeare*, 1953

SHAKESPEARE AND THE STAGE

Adams, Joseph Q. *Shakespearean Playhouses*, 1917
Baldwin, T. W. *Organization and Personnel of the Shakespearean Company*, 1927
Banke, C. de *Shakespeare Stage Productions, Then and Now*, 1953
Beckerman, Bernard *Shakespeare at the Globe*, 1962
Bentley, G. E. *The Jacobean and Caroline Stage*, 4 vols. 1941
Bentley, G. E. *The Profession of Dramatist in Shakespeare's Time, 1590–1642*, 1971
Bentley, G. E. *Shakespeare and his Theatre*, 1964
Bethell, S. L. *Shakespeare and the Popular Dramatic Tradition*, 1944
Bradbrook, M. C. *Elizabethan Stage Conditions*, 1932
Bradbrook, M. C. *The Rise of the Common Player*, 1962
Brown, Ivor *Shakespeare and the Actors*, 1970
Chambers, E. K. *The Elizabethan Stage*, 4 vols. 1924
Coghill, Neville *Shakespeare's Professional Skills*, 1964
Gildersleeve, V. C. *Government Regulation of the Elizabethan Drama*, 1908
Greg, W. W. *Henslowe's Papers*, 3 vols. 1904–1908
Greg, W. W. *Dramatic Documents from the Elizabethan Playhouses*, 2 vols. 1931
Harbage, Alfred *As They Liked It*, 1947
Harbage, Alfred *Shakespeare and the Rival Traditions*, 1952
Harbage, Alfred *Shakespeare's Audience*, 1941
Harbage, Alfred *Theatre for Shakespeare*, 1955
Harrison, G. B. *Elizabethan Plays and Players*, 1940
Henslowe's Diary, edited by R. A. Foakes and R. T. Rickert, 1961
Hodges, C. W. *The Globe Restored*, 1953
Holmes, M. *Shakespeare and his Players*, 1973
Holmes, M. *Shakespeare's Public*, 1960
Joseph, Bertram *Acting Shakespeare*, 1960
Knights, L. C. *Drama and Society in the Age of Jonson*, 1937
Lawrence, W. J. *The Physical Conditions of the Elizabethan Public Playhouses*, 1927
Leech, Clifford *The John Fletcher Plays*, 1962
Mehl, Dieter *The Elizabethan Dumb Show*, 1964
Nagler, A. M. *Shakespeare's Stage*, 1958
Poel, William *Shakespeare in the Theatre*, 1913
Purdom, C. B. *Producing Shakespeare*, 1950
Smith, D. Nichol *Shakespeare in the Eighteenth Century*, 1928
Smith, Irwin *Shakespeare's Blackfriars Playhouse*, 1964
Smith, Irwin *Shakespeare's Globe Playhouse*, 1956

Speaight, Robert *Shakespeare on the Stage*, 1973
Speaight, Robert *William Poel and the Elizabethan Revival*, 1954
Sprague, A. C. *Shakespeare and the Actors*, 1945
Sprague, A. C. *Shakespearian Players and Performances*, 1954
Sprague, A. C. and Trewin, J. C. *Shakespeare's Plays Today*, 1970
Stopes, Charlotte C. *Burbage and Shakespeare's Stage*, 1913
Thorndike, Ashley H. *Shakespeare's Theatre*, 1916
Trewin, J. C. *Shakespeare on the English Stage, 1900–1964*, 1964
Welsford, Enid *The Court Masque*, 1927
Wickham, Glynne *Early English Stages, 1300–1660*, 2 vols. 1959–63
Wickham, Glynne *Shakespeare's Dramatic Heritage*, 1969
Wood, Roger and Clarke, Mary *Shakespeare at the Old Vic*, 5 vols. 1955–59

SHAKESPEARE'S HISTORIES & POEMS

Baldwin, T. W. *On the Literary Genetics of Shakespeare's Poems and Sonnets*, 1950
Campbell, L. B. *Shakespeare's 'Histories', Mirrors of Elizabethan Policy*, 1947
Cavendish, G. *Negotiations of Thomas Wolsey*, 1641
Clemens, W. H. *A Commentary on Shakespeare's Richard III*, 1968
Daniel, *The First Fowre Bookes of the Civile Wars*, 1595
Elizabethan History Plays edited by W. A. Armstrong, 1965

The Famous Victories of Henry V, 1598
Foxe, John *Acts and Monuments* (reprinted 1843–49)
Gupta, S. C. Sen *Shakespeare's Historical Plays*, 1964
Hall, Edward *The Union of the Two Noble and Illustre Families of Lancastre and Yorke*, 1809 edition
Holinshed, Raphael *Chronicles of England, Scotland and Ireland* 6 vols. Reprinted 1807–8
Holinshed's Chronicles as Used in Shakespeare's Plays, edited by A. and J. Nicoll, 1927
Jenkins, Harold *The Structural Problem in Shakespeare's Henry the Fourth*, 1956
Ornstein, Robert *A Kingdom for a Stage*, 1972
Partridge, A. C. *The Problem of 'Henry VIII' Reopened*, 1947
Ribner, Irving *The English History Play in the Age of Shakespeare*, 1965
Reese, M. M. *The Cease of Majesty: A Study of Shakespeare's History Plays*, 1961
Scott-Giles, C. W. *Shakespeare's Heraldry*, 1950
Shakespeare's Sonnets, edited with Introduction and Commentary by A. L. Rowse, 1964
Sprague, A. C. *Shakespeare's Histories: Plays for the Stage*, 1964
Stow, John *Chronicles of England*, 1580
Stow, John *Annales of England*, 1592
Tillyard, E. M. W. *Shakespeare's History Plays*, 1944
The Troublesome Raigne of John King of England, edited by C. Praetorius 2 vols, 1888
Wilson, John Dover and Worsley, T. C. *Shakespeare's Histories at Stratford*, 1952

TO THE READER

An obelisk (†) indicates a probable corruption of the original text for which there is no satisfactory or generally acceptable emendation.

Index

This index is limited to proper names excluding Shakespeare and the characters in his plays and poems. Page numbers in *italics* refer to illustrations.

Agas, Ralph *128, 414, 442, 479, 504*
Aickin, J. *111*
Aiken, F. *297*
Ainley, Henry *624*
Allen, Sheila *361*
Anderson, Percy *331*
Andrews, Harry *518*
Andrews, Henry *630*
Arnatt, John *157*
Arthur, Julia *220*
Arthur, Prince of Wales *632*
Ashcroft, Peggy *152, 269*
Atkinson, J.A. *531*
Aubrey, John 73

Bale, John *349*
Bannister, John *283*
Barnfield, Richard 669
Bateman family *276, 277*
Batoni, Pompeo G. *756*

Beaufort, Henry, Cardinal 15
Beaufort, Lady Margaret *224*
Bedford, John, Duke of *21*
Bennett, Vivienne *493*
Benson, Frank R. *333, 577*
Bent, Buena *493*
Bettes, John *785*
Bilivert, Giovanni *722*
Blake, William *601, 652*
Boleyn, Anne *603, 621, 648, 649*
Bolingbroke, Henry *see* Henry IV
Boltraffio, Giovanni A. *688*
Bonifazio *696*
Boucher, Francois *687, 707*
Boughton, G.H. *328*
Boxall, Rosalind *80, 157*
Boydell, Josiah *36*
Braid, Hilda *375*
Bretchgirdle, Vicar John 13
Bronzini *768*
Bronzino, Angelo *67*
Brugghen, Hendrick ter *755*
Buchel, C.A. *388*
Buckingham, Humphrey Stafford, 1st Duke of *210*
Bunbury, Henry *435, 465, 505, 592*

Burbage, Richard *212, 213, 215, 535, 605, 750*
Burgess, John 94
Burgh, Hubert de *393*
Burke, Alfred *41*
Burney, Edward *383*
Burton, Richard *359, 518*
Bury, John *227, 237, 259, 558, 561, 567*
Byford, Roy *430*

Cairncross, Dr. A. S. 17
Calvert, Louis *382*
Campeius, Cardinal *626*
Cathcart, James *301*
Cavendish, George 604
Cecil, Sir Robert, Earl of Salisbury *228*, 228, 232, 409, 601
Chapman, George 792
Charles I, King of England 9, 228, 229, 537, 538
Charles V, King of Spain *611*
Charles VI, King of France 13
Chaucer, Geoffrey 669
Chester, Robert 792
Church, Esme *268*

Cicero, Marcus Tullius 119
Ciprianio, G.B. *243*
Clarke, Matthew *658*
Clarence, Lionel, Duke of 74, *96*
Cobham, Henry Brooke, Lord 409, 471
Coghlan, John *591, 647*
Condell, Henry 600
Cooke, George F. *252*
Cooper, Mr. 287
Corbet, Bishop 213
Courtney, Margaret *89*
Cranach, Lucas the Elder *745*
Crane, Mrs. Kate *358*
Cranmer, Thomas 602, *659*
Creswick, William *421*
Cromwell, Oliver 229
Cromwell, Thomas *646*
Curtis, Ann *158, 168, 182, 193, 227, 237, 259, 311, 449, 453, 558, 561, 567*

Dance, Charles *510, 513*
Daniel, Samuel 11, 228, 669, 682
Dark Lady (Shakespeare's) 233, *710, 748, 751*

Davidge, William 550
Davies, John, of Hereford
  10, 11
Delaroche, Paul 66
Dench, Jeffrey 375
Derby, Lord Stanley, Earl
  of 270
Detroy, Jean-Francois 138
Digges, Dudley 538
Dighton, Robert 218
Dodimead, David 107,
  203, 207
Donat, Robert 518
Dotrice, Roy 236
Drake, Sir Francis 8
Drayton, Michael 11, 315,
  669
Dyck, Antony van 691

Edward II, King of England
  233
Edward III, King of
  England 74, 96, 299,
  317, 546
Edward IV, King of England
  144, 175, 176, 184, 189,
  234, 267, 601
Edward V, King of England
  258
Edward, the Black Prince
  74, 317
Eleanor of Aquitaine 387
Elizabeth I, Queen of
  England 9, 23, 145, 208,
  232, 232, 536, 601, 603,
  629, 667, 750, 759, 779
Elizabeth of York 8, 13, 272
Engel, Susan 236
Erpingham, Sir Thomas 573
Essex, Robert Devereux, 2nd
  Earl of 232, 232, 409,
  536, 792
Evans, Edith 268
Fairfax, Lettice 368
Farquharson, Robert 613
Field, Richard 680, 708
Fitton, Mary 785
Fitz James, Richard,
  Bishop of London 210
Fitzwater, Robert 331
Flaxman, John 187, 739
Fletcher, John 600
Florio, John 228, 669, 708
Forbes-Robertson, J. 609
Froissart, Jean 13, 24,
  183, 378, 578
Frost, W.E. 791
Ford-Davis, Oliver 103
Forman, Simon 408, 536
Foxe, John 349
Fra Angelico 71
Francis I, King of France
  608
Fraser, Ronald 126
Fucke, G. 659
Fuseli, H. 223, 496, 553

Gardiner, Stephen, Bishop
  of Winchester 602
Garrick, David 281, 286
Gaveston, Piers 233
Gheeraerts, Marcus, the

Younger 232, 667
Gilbert, Sir John 295,
  433, 610
Glendower, Owen 97, 406,
  438
Gloucester, Humphrey,
  Duke of 43, 82, 85
Godfrey, Derek 107, 203,
  207
Greene, Robert 8, 11, 12,
  74, 77, 144, 213, 605
Gregory VII, Pope 460
Griffiths, Hugh 524
Grimm, S.H. 473
Guildford, Sir Henry 618
Gwilliam, Jack 107
Gyseghem, Andre van 510

Hackaert, Johannes 190
Hacker, Arthur 543
Hackett, J.H. 481
Hall, Edward 8, 13, 209
Hamilton, William 115,
  324, 384
Harlow, George H. 355,
  633
Harvey, Gabriel 683, 711
Harvey, William 749, 750
Hayward, Sir John 232
Heming, John 600
Heneage, Sir Thomas 750
Henry II, King of England
  387
Henry III, King of France
  142
Henry IV, (Bolingbroke),
  King of England 8, 13,
  74, 228, 229, 232, 334,
  405, 406, 412, 445, 457,
  467, 536, 578
Henry IV, King of France
  (Henry of Navarre) 353,
  751
Henry V, King of England
  13, 466, 467, 534, 536, 538,
  545, 549, 568, 587, 590
Henry VI, King of England
  8, 12, 13, 14, 72, 73, 74, 79,
  141, 210, 228, 230, 538
Henry VII, King of
  England 8, 13, 210, 258,
  261, 273, 623
Henry VIII, King of
  England 601, 602, 602,
  603, 607, 608, 615, 616,
  621, 631, 646, 648
Henry, George 574
Henryson, Robert 551
Henslowe, Philip 605
Herbert, Jocelyn 216, 240,
  260, 270
Heywood, Thomas 740
Hilliard, Nicholas 629, 670,
  671, 675, 759
Hoby, Sir Edward 228, 409
Hogarth, William 281, 621
Holbein, Hans 210, 602,
  607, 618, 646
Holinshed, Raphael 8, 9,
  13, 54, 56, 156, 163, 197,
  202, 209, 228, 239, 251,
  349, 539, 300, 319, 369,

379, 462, 567, 572, 580,
  619
Hollar, Wenceslaus 663
Holman, Mr. 377
Holmes, Denis 304
Homer 38, 187, 739, 740
Houston, J.A. 198
Howard, Alan 103
Howard, Lord Henry 210
Humphrey, John 203, 207
Hunsdon, George Carey,
  Lord Chamberlain 228

Ingres, J. A. D. 19
Innocent, Harold 126
Irving, Henry 604
Isabel, Duchess of Burgundy
  161
Jacobs, Sally 216, 240, 260,
  270
James I, King of England
  232, 601, 666, 751
James, Emrys 375
Jefford, Barbara 89, 107,
  164, 203
John, King of England 348,
  349, 355, 356, 390, 398, 403
John of Gaunt 74, 75, 97,
  308
Johnson, Dr. S. 12, 72,
  208, 210, 231, 536, 600,
  601
Johnson, W.S. 287
Jones, Inigo 120
Jones, S.J.E. 418
Jonson, Ben 142, 145, 466,
  538, 670, 680, 792

Katherine of Aragon 603,
  611, 631, 632, 637, 659
Kay, Charles 47
Kean, Charles 301, 302,
  308, 320, 327
Kean, Edmund 209, 271,
  279, 287
Kemble, Charles 284, 320,
  630
Kemble, Fanny 630
Kemble, John 595, 633
Kent, William 541
Kingsley, Mary 25
Kirk, Thomas 679, 695, 704
Kirkman, Thomas 447
Knyet, Charles 610
Kyd, Thomas 8, 140, 141,
  142, 233
Lacy, Walter 302, 308
Langton, Stephen 374
Lanier, Emilia 749
Laughton, Charles 613
Lawrence, Gerald 396
Leslie, C.R. 654
Lewis, W. T. 413
Lodge, Thomas 141
Lopez, Dr. Roderigo 751,
  779
Lotto, Lorenzo 713
Louis VII, King of France
  387
Loutherbourg, P.J. de
  198, 582
Lucas, Seymour 643

Lucy, Sir William 17
Lyly, John 8

Macready, William Charles
  499, 560, 594, 598
Machiavelli, Niccolo 67,
  67, 141, 178, 208, 213
Manningham, John 213
Margaret of Anjou 14, 15,
  72, 73, 79
Marks, H.S. 503
Marlowe, Christopher 8,
  11, 13, 14, 15, 17, 72, 74,
  142, 145, 232, 495, 668,
  680, 682, 711, 750, 751
Marshall, William, Earl of
  Pembroke 386, 401
Marston, John 792
Marinus, Reymerswaele van
  728
Martin-Harvey, John 238
Mary I, Queen of England
  (Mary Tudor) 633, 659
Mason, Brewster 149, 513
May, Jack 41, 80
McEnery, Peter 64
McKinnel, Norman 376
McLeary, Franklyn 400
Meadows, Kenny 45, 51,
  59, 95, 100, 117, 121,
  129, 133, 335, 363, 379,
  444, 480, 490, 497, 501,
  509, 532, 576, 588
Meres, Francis 668
Merritt, George 493
Millais, John 264
Mirren, Helen 64
Moisewitch, Tanya 296,
  424, 473, 494, 500, 515,
  516, 517, 522, 523, 525,
  526, 532, 542, 544, 547,
  555, 558, 570, 581, 584,
  585, 597, 617, 627, 638,
  660, 665
Mollison, William 367, 574
Montjoie, Madame 538
More, Sir Thomas 209,
  210, 602
Mortimer, Sir Edmund 97
Motley 216
Munday, Anthony 11
Munns, Bernard 238
Murad III 525

Nashe, Thomas 14, 72
Neville, John 441
Norfolk, John Howard,
  Duke of 210, 284
Norris, Herbert 620
Northcote, James 40, 144,
  155, 206, 215, 246, 266,
  338, 383

Oldcastle, Sir John 409,
  414, 471, 532
Olivier, Laurence 235, 262,
  264, 455, 575, 596
Opie, John 35, 90, 244
Orchardson, W.Q. 34, 416
Orleans, Henry, Duke of 633
Ovid 21, 54, 72, 145, 668,
  680

INDEX

Passe, Crispin van de *784*
Parker, Martin *492*
Palmer, Mr. *162*
Pascoe, Ian *304*
Pascoe, Richard *391*
Peele, George *495*
Peters, Rev. W.M. *636*, *666*
Pettie, John *37*, *644*
Philip II, King of Spain 7
Picasso, Pablo *738*
Pindar, John *283*
Pitt, Charles *177*
Planché, J.R. *284*, *594*
Pott, L.J. *351*
Pownall, Gilbert A. *25*
Prud'hon, Pierre Paul *685*

Quartermaine, Leon *305*

Ralegh, Sir Walter *750*, *759*
Randall, J. *228*
Redgrave, Michael *305*
Reynolds, Joshua *116*
Richard I, King of England *357*, *357*, *387*
Richard II, King of England 8, *13*, *74*, *228*, *228*, *229*, *232*, *295*, *307*, *320*, *326*, *334*, *347*, *404*, *467*, *536*, *578*
Richard III, King of England *208*, *210*, *258*, *262*, *601*, *605*
Richardson, Ian *304*, *321*
Richardson, Ralph *264*, *458*
Rigaud, John F. *463*
Rivers, Anthony Woodville,

2nd Earl *189*
Robey, George *460*
Robson, Flora *613*
Romney, Sir George *464*
Rudland, Peter *689*, *692*
Russell, Lady *409*
Rydel, John *302*, *327*
Rye, John *203*

Salisbury, Frank *631*
Salisbury, Thomas de
    Montacute, 4th Earl of *579*
Salisbury, William de
    Longespeé, Earl of *395*
Sellars, Elizabeth *268*
Shakespeare, Hamnet *350*
Shaw, Glen Byam *762*, *775*, *791*
Shore, Mistress Jane *247*, *254*
Shuter, Edward *506*
Siddons, Sarah *381*, *595*, *633*
Sidney, Sir Philip 8, *9*, *669*, *748*
Sigismund, Emperor *590*
Sinden, Donald *149*
Singleton, Henry *229*, *263*, *278*, *309*, *313*, *628*, *634*, *662*
Sinckler, John *145*
Sittow, M. *623*
Sixtus V, Pope *231*
Smirke, Robert *407*, *468*, *423*, *425*, *448*
Smith, Mr. *285*
Sofaer, Abraham *518*
Somerville, Sir John *145*
Southampton, Henry

Wriothesly, 3rd Earl of
    144, *409*, *536*, *603*, *670*, *670*, *671*, *680*, *682*, *685*, *708*, *711*, *711*, *748*, *749*, *749*, *750*, *751*, *753*, *792*
Spenser, Edmund 8, *9*, *13*, *669*, *682*
Spencer, Gabriel *145*
Stanley, Ursula *792*
Surrey, Thomas Howard,
    Earl of *279*
Suzman, Janet *47*

Talbot, John, Earl of
    Shrewsbury *14*, *14*, *29*, *50*
Tandy, Jessica *596*
Taylor, Benedict *361*
Terry, Ellen *614*, *635*
Thorndike, Sybil *530*
Thorpe, Thomas *670*, *680*, *749*, *750*, *751*
Thurston, John *131*, *329*
Titian *611*, *705*
Todd, Ann *441*
Tomkins, C. *622*
Tree, H. Beerbohm *388*, *399*, *640*

Vautrollier, Thomas *680*
Velasquez, Diego *754*
Vere, Robert de *233*
Veronese, Paolo *26*, *491*, *763*, *774*
Vroom, Cornelius 7

Walker, Anthony *366*, *373*, *378*, *402*, *411*, *419*, *431*,

434. *442*
Waller, Lewis *371*, *376*, *426*, *543*
Ward, E.M. *242*
Ward, Genevieve *228*
Ward, Robert *32*
Warner, David *149*
Warwick, (the King-maker)
    Richard Neville, Earl of
    143, *144*, *188*
Watts, A.E. *738*
Webster, John 73
Webster, Rosemary *207*
Weever, John *669*
West, Charles *126*
Westall, Richard *380*, *439*, *650*, *655*
Westmoreland, Ralph
    Neville, 1st Earl of *580*
Wheatley, Francis *345*
Wilson, John Dover *534*, *535*
Witt, Johannes de *16*
Wolsey, Cardinal Thomas
    602, *604*, *609*, *610*, *615*, *622*, *651*
Woodstock, Thomas, Duke
    of Gloucester *297*
Woodville, Elizabeth *144*, *176*, *189*
Wreford, Edgar *41*
Wren, Christopher *437*
Wright, J.M. *63*, *204*, *222*, *231*, *341*, *360*, *372*, *427*, *446*, *478*, *498*, *521*, *528*, *599*, *652*, *657*

Yunge-Bateman, J. *714*, *718*, *720*, *726*, *732*, *745*

ACKNOWLEDGEMENTS

With special thanks to:
Ben and John Freeman
Geoff Goode Photographics
Dermot Hayes
Maire Nic Suibhne

Ashmolean Museum, Oxford
William Barnard
Marquis of Bath, Longleat
Birmingham Public Libraries
The Bodleian Library,
    Oxford
British Film Institute
The British Library
The British Museum
The Duke of Buccleuch and
    Queensberry
Joe Cocks Studio
A. C. Cooper Ltd.
Corpus Christi College,
    Cambridge
County Archives, Essex
    Records Office
Courtauld Institute of Art
Crawford Films Ltd
The Governors of Dulwich
    College Picture Gallery
Mary Evans Picture Library
John R. Freeman Ltd.

John Napier
Charlotte Parry-Crooke
Marian Pringle and the staff
    at the Shakespeare
    Birthplace Trust

The Fine Arts Society Ltd.,
    London
Fitzwilliam Museum,
    Cambridge
Gilling Castle
Goodwood House
Guildhall Library
Harvard Theatre Collection
William Heinemann Ltd.
Holte Photographics Ltd.
Henry E. Huntington
    Library
By Gracious Permission of
    Her Majesty the Queen
Alix Jeffry
George E. Joseph
Kunthaus, Zurich
The Museum of London
Liverpool Art Gallery
Magdalene College,
    Cambridge
Manchester Art Gallery

Sally Rousham
Patrick Rudd
Tantraline Ltd
Robert R. Wark, Huntington
    Library, California

Mander and Mitchenson
Mansell Collection
Mappin Art Gallery
Maudsley Hospital, London
National Galleries of
    Scotland
National Gallery, London
National Portrait Gallery,
    London
National Maritime Museum,
    London
Newport Museum of Art
    Gallery
National Trust
University College of North
    Wales
Queen's College, Cambridge
Preston Art Gallery
Duchess of Portland
Earl of Pembroke
Oliver Robinson (Estate of
    W. Heath Robinson)
Royal Academy of Art

Rita Wuethrich
Sarah Woodcock, Theatre
    Collection, Victoria and
    Albert Museum
Beno Zeiner

Royal Holloway College
Royal Shakespeare Theatre
St. Faith's Church, King's
    Lynn
The Shakespeare Birthplace
    Trust
Sheffield City Art Galleries
Mr Simon Wingfield Digby,
    Sherborne Castle
V. Siviter Smith & Co. Ltd.
The Tate Gallery
Arthur Tooth & Sons
United Artists
Victoria and Albert Museum
Wadsworth Atheneum,
    Hartford
Walker Art Gallery,
    Liverpool
Warburg Institute,
    University of London
Weidenfeld and Nicolson
Wolverhampton Art
    Galleries and Museums

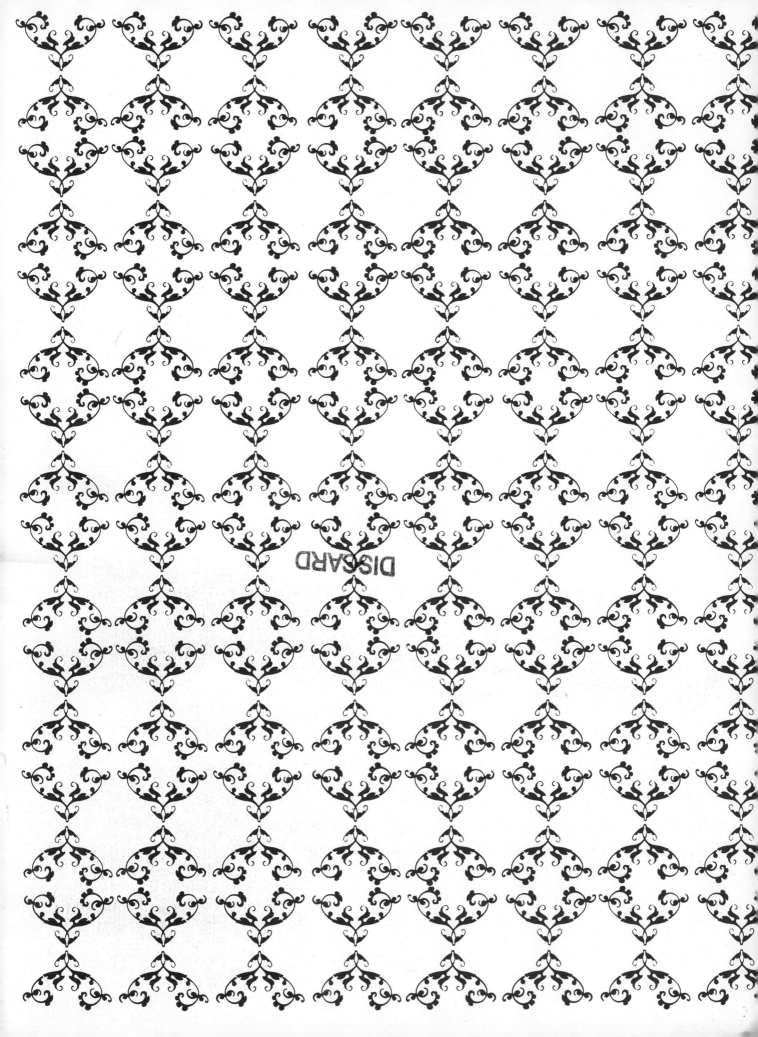